MW01014366

Problems in Professional Responsibility for a Changing Profession

Problems in Professional Responsibility for a Changing Profession

SIXTH EDITION

Andrew L. Kaufman

CHARLES STEBBINS FAIRCHILD PROFESSOR OF LAW
HARVARD LAW SCHOOL

David B. Wilkins

LESTER KISSEL PROFESSOR OF LAW
DIRECTOR, PROGRAM ON THE LEGAL PROFESSION
HARVARD LAW SCHOOL

Eli Wald

CHARLES W. DELANEY JR. PROFESSOR OF LAW
STURM COLLEGE OF LAW
UNIVERSITY OF DENVER

Keith Swisher

PROFESSOR OF LEGAL ETHICS
DIRECTOR, BACHELOR IN LAW AND MASTER OF LEGAL STUDIES PROGRAMS
JAMES E. ROGERS COLLEGE OF LAW
UNIVERSITY OF ARIZONA

CAROLINA ACADEMIC PRESS
Durham, North Carolina

Copyright © 2017
Carolina Academic Press, LLC
All Rights Reserved

ISBN 978-1-61163-893-6
eISBN 978-1-53100-461-3
LCCN 2017947252

Carolina Academic Press, LLC
700 Kent Street
Durham, North Carolina 27701
Telephone (919) 489-7486
Fax (919) 493-5668
www.cap-press.com

Printed in the United States of America

For Linda; Anne and Rob; David and Carol; Daniel and Stefanie; and Sophie, Maya, Nathan, Miriam, and Drew.
—ALK

For Ann Marie and Brian. And for Jim Vorenberg, who taught me ethics, hired me to teach it, and exemplified what it means to lead an ethical life in the law.
—DBW

For Ashley.
—EW

For my inspirations, especially Jen, Stone, Kingston, Larry, Mark, Cathy, and my ethics students.
—KS

Contents

Table of Cases

Principal cases are in bold type.

Table of Authorities

Principal authorities are in bold type.

ABA Special Committee on Professional Responsibility, Comments and Recommendations on the Lawyer's Duties in Representing Husband and Wife (1994), 341–42

ABA Special Committee to Survey Legal Needs, *Final Report*, 729

ABA Standing Committee on Ethics and Professional Responsibility, *Majority Report to the House of Delegates* (Feb. 2009), **318**

ABA Standing Committee on Ethics and Professional Responsibility, *Minority Report to the House of Delegates* (Feb. 2009), **322**

ABA/BNA Lawyers Manual on Judicial Conduct, 505

ABA/BNA Manual on Professional Conduct, 505

Abel, Richard L., *American Lawyers* (1989), xxxv, 959, 968

Abel, *Lawyers: A Critical Reader* (1997), 1041

Abel, *Lawyers in the Dock: Learning from Attorney Disciplinary Proceedings* (2008), xxxv, **809**

Abel, *Lawyers on Trial* (2010), xxxv

Abel, "Practicing Immigration Law in Filene's Basement," 84 N.C. L. Rev. 1449 (2006), **1053**

Abel, "Why Does the ABA Promulgate Ethical Rules?," 59 Tex. L. Rev. 639 (1981), 124, 164

Abel & P. Lewis, *Lawyers in Society* (1988–1995), 968

Abrams, Floyd, "Why Lawyers Lie," N.Y. Times Magazine (Oct. 9, 1994), 561

Adams, Edward, "Rethinking the Law Firm Organizational Form and Capitalization Structure," 78 Mo. L. Rev. 777 (2013), 723

Agnew, Spiro, "What's Wrong With the Legal Services Program," 58 A.B.A. J. 930 (1972), 745

Ainsworth, "Impact of the Code of Judicial Conduct on Federal Judges," 1972 Utah L. Rev. 369 (1972), 858

Alibrandi (with Armani), *Privileged Information* (1984), 115

Allegretti, Joseph, "Lawyers, Clients, and Covenant: A Religious Perspective on Legal Practice and Ethics," 66 Fordham L. Rev. 1101 (1998), **1083**

Allen, Carleton, "R. v. Dean," 225 L.Q. Rev. 85 (1941), 107

Alschuler, Albert W., "The Preservation of a Client's Confidences," 52 U. Colo. L. Rev. 349 (1981), 163

American College of Trust and Estate Counsel, *ACTEC Commentaries on the Model Rules of Professional Conduct* (2d ed. 1995), 342

American Law Institute, *Restatement Third of The Law Governing Lawyers* (2000), xxxvi

Amon, Elizabeth, "Raising the Bar," Nat'l L.J. (Feb. 14, 2003), 707

Applbaum, Arthur Isak, *Ethics for Adversaries: The Morality of Roles in Public and Professional Life* (1998), 153

Ariens, Michael, "The Agony of Modern Legal Ethics, 1970 to 1985," 5 St. Mary's J. Legal Mal. & Ethics 134 (2014), 5

Ariens, "Know the Law: A History of Legal Specialization," 45 S.C. L. Rev. 1003 (1994), 812

Ashley, Louise & Laura Empson, "Differentiation and Discrimination: Understanding Social and Class Exclusion in the UK's Leading Law Firms," 66 Human Relations 219 (2013), 1006

Ashley & Empson, "Explaining Social Exclusion and the 'War for Talent' in the UK's Elite Professional Service

Goldhaber, Michael, "Boies Schiller's Big Year," Nat'l L.J. (Feb. 12, 2001), 1063

Goldman, Alan, *The Moral Foundations of Professional Ethics* (1980), 152

Goldsmith, Jack, *The Terror Presidency* (2007), 15, 444

Goldstein, Tom, "Review: The American Lawyer," 83 Colum. L. Rev. 1351 (1983), 657

Gomes-Casseres, Benjamin, *The Alliance Revolution: The New Shape of Business Rivalry* (1996), 395

Gordon, Robert W., "The Ethical World of Large Law Firm Litigators," 67 Fordham L. Rev. 709 (1999), 577

Gordon, "A New Role for Lawyers? The Corporate Counselor after Enron," 35 Conn. L. Rev. 1185 (2003), 396

Goshko, John, "Police Killing Sparks Debate on Death Penalty in New York," Wash. Post (March 24, 1996), 1068

Gottlieb, Henry, "Looser Rein Given to Lawyers Who May Be Witnesses," N.J.L.J. (Sept. 25, 2002), 238

Graham, Sandy, "Clearing Kobe: Pamela Mackey Reflects on Court Victory that Riveted Millions," ColoradoBiz (May 2005), 1082

Granfield, Robert, *Making Elite Lawyers: Visions of Law at Harvard and Beyond* (1992), 1116

Green, Bruce A., "Conflicts of Interest in Litigation: The Judicial Role," 65 Fordham L. Rev. 71 (1996), 29, 198–199, 213

Green, "Criminal Neglect: Indigent Defense from a Legal Ethics Perspective," 52 Emory L.J. 1169 (2003), 419

Green, "Fear of the Unknown: Judicial Ethics after *Caperton*," 60 Syracuse L. Rev. 229 (2010), 898

Green, "Foreword: Rational Lawyers: Ethical and Professional Issues in the Delivery of Legal Services to Low-Income Clients," 67 Fordham L. Rev. 1713 (1999), 309

Green, "Prosecutors and Professional Regulation," 25 Geo. J. Legal Ethics 873 (2012), 494

Green, "Reply—The Market for Bad Legal Scholarship," 60 Stan. L. Rev. 1605 (2008), 550

Green & Fred C. Zacharias, "Permissive Rules of Professional Conduct," 91 Minn. L. Rev. 265 (2006), 62

Green & Zacharias, "Prosecutorial Neutrality," 2004 Wis. L. Rev. 837, 419

Greenbaum, Arthur, "The Attorney's Duty to Report Professional Misconduct," 16 Geo. J. Legal Ethics 259 (2003), 833

Greenberg, Karen J. & Joshua L. Dratel, eds., *The Torture Papers: The Road to Abu Ghraib* (2005), 443

Gruenbaum & Oppenheimer, "Special Investigative Counsel: Conflicts and Roles," 33 Rutgers L. Rev. 865 (1981), 362

Guinier, L., M. Fine & J. Balin, *Becoming Gentlemen: Women, Law School and Institutional Change* (1997), 1117

Gulati, M., R. Sander & R. Sockloskie, "The Happy Charade: An Empirical Examination of the Third Year of Law School," 52 J. Legal Educ. 235 (2002), 1112

Gutmann, Amy, "Responding to Racial Injustice," in Gutman & Appiah, eds., *Color Conscious: The Political Morality of Race* (1996), 1071

Hacker, Andrew, *Two Nations: Black and White, Separate, Hostile, Unequal* (1992), 1001

lxx

Preface to the Sixth Edition

Much has happened in the eight years since the last edition was published. The profession has changed greatly, bringing new problems for the profession and new developments with respect to long-standing issues of professional responsibility. These are discussed in the Introduction that follows and throughout the book. The purpose of this Preface is only to explain a few matters of form and to express a few words of thanks.

Omission of textual material in excerpted cases, articles, books, or other works is always indicated by ellipses. Footnotes, references to case records, and portions of citations, however, have been omitted freely in cases and in other written material without notation. We have also corrected without notation a variety of minor typographical errors in the quoted materials.

We are grateful to the many authors and publishers who gave us permission to reprint copyrighted material. They are acknowledged in the following pages. Prefaces to earlier editions have recognized the contribution of many friends and colleagues to this work. A number of people, chiefly David Herwitz, Dan Coquillette, Ann Southworth, Detlev Vagts, and James Vorenberg, used earlier versions of this edition and made many useful comments. Our research assistants, Christopher M. Assise, Matthew Bobys, Trevor Farrow, Dan Markel, Darrell Miller, Sava Savov, and David Shelton were invaluable in their assistance. For many years, Melinda Eakin has prepared and read and reread version after version of each new edition, providing an endless number of fabulous editorial services in preparing the manuscript for publication. We are more than grateful for the skill and good cheer with which this unsung hero performed all the major and minor tasks of finding and correcting numerous errors and turning a pile of pages into a book.

Acknowledgments

Richard Wasserstrom, "Lawyers as Professionals: Some Moral Issues," 5 Human Rights 1 (1975). Permission to reprint granted by Richard Wasserstrom, the ABA Section of Individual Rights and Responsibilities, and the Southern Methodist University School of Law.

David Wilkins, "Everyday Practice *is* the Troubling Case," from *Everyday Practices and Trouble Cases*, edited by Austin Sarat, Marianne Constable, David Engel, Valier Hans, and Susan Lawrence. Evanston: Northwestern University Press, 1998, pp. 68, 70–75. Copyright © 1998 by Northwestern University and the American Bar Association. Published 1998. All rights reserved. Reprinted with permission of the author, the editor and Northwestern University Press.

Monroe Freedman and Abbe Smith, *Understanding Lawyers' Ethics.* Copyright 2004 Matthew Bender & Company, Inc. Reprinted with the permission of Matthew Bender & Company, Inc., a member of the LexisNexis Group and with the permission of the authors.

Monroe Freedman, "Professional Responsibility of the Criminal Defense Lawyer: The Three Hardest Questions," 64 Mich. L. Rev. 1469 (1966). Copyright © 1966 and reprinted with permission of Professor Freedman and the Michigan Law Review.

Bryce Nelson, "Ethical Dilemma: Should Lawyers Turn in Clients?" Los Angeles Times, July 2, 1974, p. 1, col. 1, Copyright © 1974, Los Angeles Times. Reprinted by permission.

Stephen Pepper, "The Lawyer's Amoral Ethical Role," 1986 Am. B. Found. Res. J. 613–635. Reprinted with permission of the author and the American Bar Foundation.

David Luban, "The Lysistratian Prerogative: A Response to Stephen Pepper," 1986 Am. B. Found. Res. J. 637–651. Reprinted with permission of the author and the American Bar Foundation.

Andrew L. Kaufman, "A Commentary on Pepper," 1986 Am. B. Found. Res. J. 651. Reprinted with permission of the author and the American Bar Foundation.

Marvin E. Frankel, "The Search for Truth: An Umpireal View," 123 Pa. L. Rev. (1975). Copyright © by the author and reprinted with permission. This article also appears, in slightly different form, in 30 The Record of the Association of the Bar of the City of New York 14 (1975).

William Simon, "Should Lawyers Obey the Law?," 38 Wm. & Mary L. Rev. 217 (1996). © Copyright © 1996 by the *William and Mary Law Review.* Reprinted with permission of the author and the William and Mary Law Review.

David Wilkins, "In Defense of Law and Morality: Why Lawyers Should Have a Prima Facie Duty To Obey the Law," 38 Wm. & Mary L. Rev. 269 (1996). Copyright © 1996 by the *William and Mary Law Review.* Reprinted with permission of the author and the William and Mary Law Review.

Stephen Gillers, "Can a Good Lawyer Be a Bad Person?," 2 J. Inst. Stud. Leg. Eth. 131 (1999). Reprinted with permission of the author and the Monroe H. Freedman Institute for the Study of Legal Ethics, Maurice A. Deane School of Law at Hofstra University.

Susan Koniak, "Feasting While the Widow Weeps," 80 Cornell L. Rev. 1045 (1995). Reprinted with permission of the author and the Cornell Law Review.

William Simon, "The Kaye Scholer Affair: The Lawyer's Duty of Candor and the Bar's Temptations of Evasion and Apology," © 1998 William Simon and John Wiley and Sons. This article originally appeared in 23 Law and Social Inquiry 243 (1998). Reprinted with permission of the author and John Wiley and Sons.

John C. Coffee, *Gatekeepers: The Professions and Corporate Governance* (2006). Reprinted with permission of the author and Oxford University Press.

David B. Wilkins, "Team of Rivals? Toward a New Model of the Corporate Attorney/Client Relationship," 78 Fordham L. Rev. 2067 (2010). Reprinted with the permission of Fordham Law Review.

H. Richard Uviller, "The Neutral Prosecutor," 68 Fordham L. Rev. 1695 (2000). Reprinted with permission of the author and the Fordham Law Review.

Abbe Smith, "Can You Be a Good Person and a Good Prosecutor," 14 Geo. J. Legal Ethics 355 (2001). Reprinted with permission of the publisher, Georgetown Journal of Legal Ethics © 2001, and of the author.

MacLean, Berles and Lamparello, "Stop Blaming the Prosecutors," 44 Hofstra L. Rev. 151 (2015). Reprinted with the permission of the Hofstra Law Review Association and of Professors MacLean and Lamparello.

Norman W. Spaulding, "Professional Independence in the Office of the Attorney General," 60 Stanford Law Review 1931 (2008). Reprinted with the permission of the School of Law, Stanford University (in the format Republish in a book via Copyright Clearance Center), Stanford Law Review and Professor Spaulding.

Neil Mickenberg, "The Silent Clients: Legal and Ethical Considerations in Representing Profoundly Retarded Individuals," 31 Stanford Law Rev. 625 (1979). Copyright © 1979 by the Board of Trustees, Leland Stanford Junior University and reprinted with the permission of the Stanford Law Review and Mr. Mickenberg.

Alan A. Stone, M.D., "The Myth of Advocacy," 30 Hospital and Community Psychiatry 819–822 (December 1979). Reprinted with permission of Dr. Stone and Hospital and Community Psychiatry.

Carr, Alan Z. "Is Business Bluffing Legal?" Adapted and reprinted by permission of *Harvard Business Review*. From "Is Business Bluffing Legal" by Alan Z. Carr, 46 Harv. Business Rev. 143 (1968). Copyright © 1968 by the Harvard Business School Publishing Corporation; all rights reserved.

Alvin B. Rubin, "A Causerie on Lawyers' Ethics in Negotiation," 35 La. L. Rev. 578 (1975). Reprinted with permission of the author and the Louisiana Law Review.

James J. White, "Machiavelli and the Bar," 1980 Am. B. Found Res. J. 926. Reprinted with permission of the author and the American Bar Foundation.

David Wilkins, "Race, Ethics and the First Amendment." This article originally appeared in 63 George Washington Law Review (1995). Reprinted with permission of the author.

Deborah Rhode, "Lawyers as Citizens," 50 Wm. & Mary L. Rev. 1323 (2009). Reprinted with permission of the William & Mary Law Review and of the author.

Eli Wald, "Serfdom Without Overlords," 54 U. Louisville L. Rev. 259 (2016). Reprinted with permission of the University of Louisville Law Review.

David Wilkins & Eli Wald, "The Fourth Responsibility," reprinted with permission of the authors.

Louise Trubek and Jennifer Farnham, "Social Justice Collaboratives: Multidisciplinary Practices for People," 7 Clinical Law Review 227 (2000). This article originally appeared in the Clinical Law Review. It is reproduced here with permission of the Clinical Law Review and of the authors.

John Flood, "Will There Be Fallout From Clementi?," 2012 Mich. St. L. Rev. 537. Reprinted with permission of the author.

Brian Heid and Eitan Misulovin, "Note, The Group Legal Plan Revolution: Bright Horizon or Dark Future?" 18 Hofstra Lab. & Emp. L.J. 335 (2000). Reprinted with the permission of the Hofstra Labor & Employment Law Journal and of the authors.

Roger Cramton, "Crisis in Legal Services for the Poor." Reprinted with permission from the author and Villanova Law Review Volume 26 #3–4 pp. 521–556. © Copyright 1981 by Villanova University.

Kenney Hegland, "Beyond Enthusiasm and Commitment," 13 Ariz. L. Rev. 805 (1971). Copyright © by the Arizona Board of Regents. Reprinted by their permission and that of Professor Hegland.

Scott L. Cummings, "The Politics of Pro Bono." Originally published in 52 UCLA L. Rev. 1 (2004). Reprinted with the permission of the author.

Jeanne Charn & Richard Zorza, "Civil Legal Assistance for All Americans," Bellow-Sacks Access to Civil Legal Services Project. Reprinted with permission of the authors, the WilmerHale Legal Services Center, and Clinical and Pro Bono Programs of Harvard Law School.

Ted Schneyer, "Professional Discipline for Law Firms?," 77 Cornell Law Review 1 (1992). Reprinted with the permission of the author and the Cornell Law Review.

Richard L. Abel, *Lawyers in the Dock: Learning from Attorney Disciplinary Proceedings* (2008). Reprinted with permission of the author and Oxford University Press.

Massachusetts Committee on Professional Ethics, Opinion 99-2. Reprinted with permission of the Massachusetts Bar Association.

Howard T. Markey, "The Delicate Dichotomies of Judicial Ethics," 101 F.R.D. 373 (1984). Reprinted with permission of Thomson Reuters.

Andrew L. Kaufman, "Judicial Ethics: The Less-Often Asked Questions," 64 Wash. L. Rev. 851 (1989). Reprinted with the permission of The Washington Law Review.

Alex Kozinski, "The Real Issues of Judicial Ethics," 32 Hofstra L. Rev. 1095 (2004). Reprinted with the permission of the Hofstra Law Review Association and of the author.

Robert C. Clark, "Why So Many Lawyers? Are They Good or Bad?," 275 Fordham Law Review 1992. Reprinted with permission of the author and the Fordham Law Review.

Ronit Dinovitzer and the AJD Project, *After the JD III*. Reprinted with permission of the NALP Foundation and the American Bar Foundation.

John P. Heinz and Edward O. Laumann, *Chicago Lawyers: The Social Structure of the Bar* (1982). © 1982 Russell Sage Foundation, New York, New York. Reprinted with permission of the Russell Sage Foundation and of Mr. Heinz and Mr. Laumann.

John P. Heinz, Edward O. Laumann, Robert L. Nelson & Ethan Michelson, "The Changing Character of Lawyers' Work: Chicago in 1975 and 1995," 32 Law & Soc'y Rev. 751 (1998). Reprinted by permission of Blackwell Publishing Ltd. and of Mr. Heinz, Mr. Laumann, Mr. Nelson, and Mr. Michelson.

David Wilkins, "Some Realism about Legal Realism," in Levin & Mather, eds. *Lawyers in Practice*, University of Chicago Press. © 2012 by the University of Chicago. Reprinted with permission of the University of Chicago Press.

Gillian Hadfield, "The Price of Law: How the Market for Lawyers Distorts the Justice System," 90 Mich. L. Rev. 953 (2000). This article originally appeared in the Michigan Law Review. Reprinted with the permission of the Michigan Law Review and of the author.

Marc Galanter "'Old and in the Way': The Coming Demographic Transformation of the Legal Profession and its Implications for the Provision of Legal Services," 1999 Wis. L. Rev. 1081. Copyright © 1999 by The Board of Regents of the University of Wisconsin System; reprinted by permission of the Wisconsin Law Review and of the author.

Marc Galanter & Thomas M. Palay, "Why the Big Get Bigger: The Promotion-to-Partner Tournament and the Growth of Large Law Firms," 76 Va. L. Rev. 747 (1990). Reprinted with permission of the Virginia Law Review and of the authors.

David Wilkins and Mitu Gulati, "Reconceiving the Tournament of Lawyers: Tracking, Seeding, and Information Control in the Internal Labor Markets of Elite Law Firms," 84 Va. L. Rev. 1581 (1998). Reprinted with permission of the Virginia Law Review, and of the authors.

Marc Galanter & William Henderson, "The Elastic Tournament: A Second Transformation of the Big Law Firm," 60 Stanford Law Review 1867 (2008). Reprinted with the permission of the School of Law, Stanford University (in the format Republish in a book via Copyright Clearance Center), Stanford Law Review, and Mr. Galanter.

David Wilkins and Mitu Gulati, "Why Are There So Few Black Lawyers in Corporate Law Firms? An Institutional Analysis," 84 Cal. L. Rev. 493 (1996). © 1996 by the California Law Review, Reprinted from California Law Review, Vol. 84, No. 3, pp. 496–625 by permission of the University of California, Berkeley, and by permission of the authors.

Cynthia Fuchs Epstein, et al., "Glass Ceilings and Open Doors," 64 Fordham L. Rev. 291 (1995). Reprinted by permission of Prof. Epstein and the Fordham Law Review.

Deborah Rhode, "Gender and Professional Roles," 63 Fordham L. Rev. 39 (1994). Reprinted by permission of the author and the Fordham Law Review.

Eli Wald, "Glass Ceilings and Dead Ends," 78 Fordham L. Rev. 2245 (2010). Reprinted by permission of the author and Fordham Law Review.

Pearce, Wald & Ballakrishnen, "Difference Blindness vs. Bias Awareness," 83 Fordham L. Rev. 2407 (2015). Reprinted with permission of the Fordham Law Review.

David Wilkins, "Is the In-House Counsel Movement Going Global?," 2012 Wis. L. Rev. 251. Copyright 2016 by The Board of Regents of the University of Wisconsin System; Reprinted by permission of the *Wisconsin Law Review*.

Heineman, Lee & Wilkins, "Lawyers as Professionals and as Citizens," reprinted by permission of the Harvard Law School Center on the Legal Profession and of the authors.

Carol Seron, "The Business of Practicing Law: The Work Lives of Solo and Small-Firm Attorneys" in *Lawyers, A Critical Reader* (1996). This article reprinted with permission from Temple University Press and the author.

Leslie Levin, "The Ethical World of Solo and Small Law Firm...," 41 Hous. L. Rev. 309 (2004). Reprinted with permission of the author and the Houston Law Review.

Richard Abel, "Practicing Immigration Law," 84 N.C. L. Rev. 1449 (2006). Reprinted by permission of the author and the North Carolina Law Review.

Lisa Pruitt, J. Cliff McKinney II & Bart Calhoun, "Justice in the Hinterlands," 37 U. Ark. Little Rock L. Rev. 573 (2015). Reprinted with the permission of the University of Arkansas Little Rock Law Review and of Professor Pruitt.

Stephen Daniels & Joanne Martin, "The Impact That It Has Had is Between People's Ears: Tort Reform, Mass Culture, and Plaintiffs' Lawyers," 50 DePaul L. Rev. 453 (2000). Reprinted with permission of the DePaul Law Review, and of the authors.

David Wilkins, "Beyond 'Bleached-Out' Professionalism: Defining Professional Responsibility for Real Professionals," from Ethics in Practice: Lawyers' Roles, Responsibilities, and Regulation, edited by Deborah Rhode, copyright © (2000) by Oxford University Press, Inc. Reprinted with permission of the Oxford University Press, Inc. and the author.

Eli Wald, "Lawyers' Identity Capital." Reprinted with permission of the author.

Joseph Allegretti, "Lawyers, Clients and Covenant: A Religious Perspective on Legal Practice and Ethics," 66 Fordham Law Review 1101 (1998). Reprinted with permission of the Fordham Law Review and of the author.

Catherine A. Rogers, Ethics in International Arbitration (Oxford University Press 2014). Reprinted with permission of Oxford University Press.

Andrew L. Kaufman, "Who Should Make the Rules Governing Professional Conduct of Lawyers in Federal Matters," originally published in 75 Tul. L. Rev. 149–164 (2000). Reprinted with the permission of the Tulane Law Review Association, which holds the copyright.

N. K. Llewellyn, The Bramble Bush, 1930. Reprinted with permission of Oxford University Press.

N. K. Llewellyn, "On What is Wrong with So-Called Legal Education," 35 Colum. L. Rev. 651 (1935). Reprinted with permission of the Columbia Law Review Association, Inc.

David Wilkins, "Professional Ethics for Lawyers and Law Schools: Interdisciplinary Education and the Law School's Ethical Obligation to Study and Teach about the Profession." Originally published in 12 Legal Education Review 47 (2001). Reprinted with permission of the Legal Education Review and of the author.

Brian Tamahana, Failing Law Schools, © 2012 by The University of Chicago. Reprinted with permission of the University of Chicago Press.

Introduction

A commonplace remark of students, teachers, and practitioners of law is that the practice of professional responsibility is very different from the precepts of the profession in that practice includes a great deal of "unethical" conduct condemned by the precepts. Our view is that whatever the magnitude of "unethical" conduct in the profession—and it is difficult to define and measure—there is widespread insensitivity to issues of professional responsibility. A great deal of the insensitivity derives, we believe, from the fact that the typical lawyer has not devoted enough thought to those issues before they arise in practice. The problems are then often ignored because they are not recognized as such. Or, if they are recognized, they are dealt with inadequately because the lawyer has not developed a philosophy of, or at least a general attitude toward, practice and a sense of the kind of lawyer he or she wants to be. How and why the profession is in that situation is an interesting question. There are many institutions that can share the blame, for there is more than enough to go around.

One impetus for the development of these materials was the desire to expose students to issues of professional responsibility by discussion of the difficult problems that lawyers actually face in their daily practice and the context in which these problems have arisen in the past and are likely to arise in the future. While students are in law school, they are able to examine difficult professional issues without the heavy weight that self-interest exerts on the practitioner to reach a particular result that is expedient or financially rewarding. If students see the issues and competing considerations involved in typical problem situations and begin to develop their own reactions and philosophies before the issues arise in their own professional lives, then they will be better equipped to recognize and respond to them in practice. Obviously, subsequent experience may modify views, but students will have some background with which to face their experiences.

A second impetus to development of these materials was the desire to familiarize students with issues of professional responsibility that are facing the profession as a whole—questions of the quantity and quality of the provision of legal services to the public, admission and discipline, specialization, and the like. The textual materials presented in these particular chapters are somewhat more adapted to discussion in themselves, but even here many of the issues are developed in the problem form that characterizes much of the book.

A third impetus is the desire to present issues relating to the structure, organization, and demographics of the profession. Chapter 12, presenting these materials, reflects recent research on these issues. The profession is changing at a rapid pace—both with respect to its composition and the units in which its members are practicing—and these changes have thrown up new issues that need to be faced by students, by practitioners, and by those who study and those who regulate the profession. Chapter 12 has been placed near the end of the book, but it could well be assigned first or assigned as essential material to be read during the first month of the course because it informs every issue considered in the course. Throughout the book, we note places where the material in Chapter 12 is especially relevant.

Professional responsibility is a course in which students can and should be engaged deeply in the materials. We think it the most important course in the curriculum not only because the material will apply to all soon-to-be lawyers, whatever their chosen or assigned practice area, but because it is the one course that forces students to confront their own futures and the decisions that they will have to make every day in their professional lives. In addition to providing exposure to pervasive ethical issues, the problem method has proved to be an excellent method for achieving student involvement. It also makes classes a good deal more fun. Either we discuss what the lawyer should do, or we take the role of client, and the student-lawyer conducts an interview with us based on the fact situation set out in the Problem. Other students then try their hand as lawyer or evaluate the first lawyer's performance, or sometimes we just discuss the issues. Occasionally, we will take the lawyer's role. We also occasionally invite guests, whom we have scripted in advance to act out the role of a client with a new or otherwise difficult problem, to give the students a sense of how problems are conveyed and how to approach clients and ethical issues in a more experiential setting.

Students sometimes ask whether the Problems around which most Chapters are structured are "real." They are. They have either happened to one of us, or been related by a lawyer or judge to one of us, or adapted by one of us from a reported case or ethics opinion. The Problems have been designed to force students to think through some difficult areas in the practice of law. None is easy or has a noncontroversial solution. The Problems therefore cannot be answered by following the old bar examination cliché of advising the lawyer to do what is "most ethical" or the more cynical version currently in circulation about the Model Professional Responsibility Exam, which cautions students that when in doubt always choose "the second most ethical answer." Where the Problems are concerned, usually a clash of values is involved.

While the Problems are the heart of the course and can be used in a variety of ways, we have provided supporting materials to present background information and insight. We have tried to provide enough materials to illuminate the issues in the Problems without overwhelming the reader. One can focus on either the Problems or the supporting materials. Usually we do one or the other, but sometimes we do both.

One characteristic of this approach to the teaching of professional responsibility is that it is essentially inductive. The idea is for students to face situations, to see what guidelines the law of professional responsibility offers or fails to offer, and to decide for themselves what the appropriate solution or solutions should be. After developing "solutions" to a number of Problems, which is perhaps analogous to developing practical experience, the student should then consider whether these "solutions" fit together into a coherent professional attitude or challenge a preexisting attitude. Obviously, since the materials are designed to provide exposure to professional responsibility problems encountered in actual practice, they presume a legal system that resembles our present one. However, their purpose is not to invite automatic acceptance of our system's premises. The premises should first be understood and then evaluated. A number of places in the book, beginning most explicitly with selections in Chapters 1, 2, and 3, provide some insight into the present system and stimulate consideration of specific and general alternatives to it.

A word about bibliography. Selected materials are referred to at various places. A comprehensive historical treatment would be useful, but we are not able to recommend any one work that does the whole job. The best are James Willard Hurst, *The Growth of American Law* (1950) for pre-1950 coverage and Richard Abel, *American Lawyers* (1989). Recent books that take an overall look at the profession, often in a more apocalyptic vein, are Anthony Kronman, *The Lost Lawyer* (1993); Mary Ann Glendon, *A Nation Under Lawyers* (1994); and Sol Linowitz with Martin Mayer, *The Betrayed Profession: Lawyering at the End of the Twentieth Century* (1994). The best historical work dealing with a bar association is the well-written book by lawyer, opera critic, and public-minded citizen George Martin, entitled *Causes and Conflicts—The Centennial History of the Association of the Bar of the City of New York, 1870–1970* (1970). A useful collection of excerpted materials that complements the coverage of this course is Hazard and Rhode, *The Legal Profession* (3d ed. 1994). A work that also complements this book is Philip Heymann and Lance Liebman, *The Social Responsibilities of Lawyers—Case Studies* (1988). This is a soft-cover collection of quite lengthy case studies of specific problems of professional responsibility that enables students to analyze the issues in the real-world setting of facts and documents that they will work in when they practice law. For more recent case studies of some well-known legal ethics debacles, see Michael L. Seigel and James L. Kelley, *Lawyers Crossing Lines* (2d ed. 2009); see also Richard L. Abel, *Lawyers in the Dock* (2008) and *Lawyers on Trial* (2010) for a comprehensive look into several notable disciplinary cases in New York and California, respectively. Three collections of essays on the lawyer's role that contain essays by academics in fields other than law are *Foundations of the Law and Ethics of Lawyering* (George Cohen and Susan Koniak eds. 2004); *Ethics in Practice: Lawyers' Roles, Responsibilities, and Regulation* (Deborah Rhode ed. 2000); and *The Good Lawyer* (David Luban ed. 1984). For books featuring contrasting attitudes toward the practice of law and the lawyer's role, see David Luban, *Legal Ethics and Human Dignity* (2007) and *Lawyers and Justice* (1988); Daniel Markovits, *A Modern Legal Ethics* (2008); Monroe Freedman and Abbe Smith, *Understanding Lawyers' Ethics* (5th ed. 2016); William Simon, *The Practice of Justice* (1998); and Deborah L. Rhode, *In the Interest of Justice: Reforming the Legal Profession* (2000). A detailed sociological analysis of the structure of the legal profession in one city is Heinz and Laumann, *Chicago Lawyers* (1982), while Michael J. Kelly, *Lives of Lawyers* (1994) looks at the ways lawyers practice in different kinds of organizations. Both studies have been updated: Heinz, Nelson, Sandefur, and Laumann, *Urban Lawyers: The New Social Structure of the Bar* (2005); Michael J. Kelly, *Lives of Lawyers Revisited: Transformation and Resilience in the Organizations of Practice* (2007).

There are some useful books dealing with the substantive law of professional responsibility. The most comprehensive is Charles Wolfram's hornbook, *Modern Legal Ethics* (1986), but although still much-cited, it is getting somewhat out of date. Another, focusing on the Model Rules of Professional Conduct, is Hazard, Hodes, and Jarvis, *The Law of Lawyering* (4th ed. 2015; looseleaf volumes supplemented at regular intervals). A helpful book that discusses lawyers' problems in litigation is Fortune, Underwood and Imwinkelried, *Modern Litigation and Professional Responsibility Handbook* (1996). The standard work on legal malpractice is Ronald Mallen, *Legal Malpractice* (2015 ed. as supplemented). A comprehensive compilation of statistical information about lawyers in the United States is contained in Clara N. Carson, *The Lawyer Statistical Report: The U.S. Legal Profession in 2000* (2004), and the American Bar Association (ABA) maintains a webpage collecting various lawyer-related statistics, <http://www.americanbar.org/resources_for_lawyers/profession_statistics.html>. Finally, the American Law Institute's Restatement Third of The Law Governing Lawyers (2000 as supplemented) is a helpful descriptive and normative guide to resolution of law practice problems, and courts regularly turn to it when addressing professional responsibility issues.

Problems in Professional Responsibility for a Changing Profession

Chapter 1

The Profession — An Introduction

This Chapter introduces issues of professional responsibility with an excerpt from an article by Richard Wasserstrom, a lawyer-philosopher, who opened the modern debate about the professional role of lawyers. His serious and disturbing questions about the lawyer's role should be of concern to every lawyer and should be in every student's mind right from the beginning of the course. Other perspectives on these issues are presented throughout the book. The remaining materials of this Chapter discuss the nature of the substantive law of professional responsibility.

The following article helped to spark a decades-long discussion about whether and to what extent lawyers are morally responsible for their clients' acts and (to a lesser but related extent) whether lawyers appropriately identify and honor their clients' interests.

Richard Wasserstrom
Lawyers as Professionals: Some Moral Issues
5 Human Rights 1 (Fall 1975)

In this paper I examine two moral criticisms of lawyers which, if well-founded, are fundamental. Neither is new but each appears to apply with particular force today. Both tend to be made by those not in the mainstream of the legal profession and to be rejected by those who are in it. Both in some sense concern the lawyer-client relationship.

The first criticism centers around the lawyer's stance toward the world at large. The accusation is that the lawyer-client relationship renders the lawyer at best systematically amoral and at worst more than occasionally immoral in his or her dealings with the rest of mankind.

The second criticism focuses upon the relationship between the lawyer and the client. Here the charge is that it is the lawyer-client relationship which is morally objectionable because it is a relationship in which the lawyer dominates and in which the lawyer typically, and perhaps inevitably, treats the client in both an impersonal and a paternalistic fashion.

To a considerable degree these two criticisms of lawyers derive, I believe, from the fact that the lawyer is a professional. And to the extent to which this is the case, the more generic problems I will be exploring are those of professionalism generally. But in some respects, the lawyer's situation is different from that of other professionals.

The lawyer is vulnerable to some moral criticism that does not as readily or as easily attach to any other professional. And this, too, is an issue that I shall be examining.[1] . . .

I.

As I have indicated, the first issue I propose to examine concerns the ways the professional-client relationship affects the professional's stance toward the world at large. The primary question that is presented is whether there is adequate justification for the kind of moral universe that comes to be inhabited by the lawyer as he or she goes through professional life. For at best the lawyer's world is a simplified moral world; often it is an amoral one; and more than occasionally, perhaps, an overtly immoral one.

To many persons, Watergate[*] was simply a recent and dramatic illustration of this fact. When John Dean testified before the Select Senate Committee inquiring

---

1. Because of the significance for my analysis of the closely related concepts of a profession and a professional, it will be helpful to indicate at the outset what I take to be the central features of a profession.

But first there is an ambiguity that must be noted so that it can be dismissed. There is one sense of "professional" and hence of "profession" with which I am not concerned. That is the sense in which there are in our culture, professional athletes, professional actors, and professional beauticians. In this sense, a person who possesses sufficient skill to engage in an activity for money and who elects to do so is a professional rather than, say, an amateur or a volunteer. This is, as I have said, not the sense of "profession" in which I am interested.

I am interested, instead, in the characteristics of professions such as law, or medicine. There are, I think, at least six that are worth noting.

(1) The professions require a substantial period of formal education — at least as much if not more than that required by any other occupation.

(2) The professions require the comprehension of a substantial amount of theoretical knowledge and the utilization of a substantial amount of intellectual ability. Neither manual nor creative ability is typically demanded. This is one thing that distinguishes the professions both from highly skilled crafts — like glass-blowing — and from the arts.

(3) The professions are both an economic monopoly and largely self-regulating. Not only is the practice of the profession restricted to those who are certified as possessing the requisite competencies, but the questions of what competencies are required and who possesses them are questions that are left to the members of the profession to decide for themselves.

(4) The professions are clearly among the occupations that possess the greatest social prestige in the society. They also typically provide a degree of material affluence substantially greater than that enjoyed by most working persons.

(5) The professions are almost always involved with matters which from time to time are among the greatest personal concerns that humans have: physical health, psychic well-being, liberty, and the like. As a result, persons who seek the services of a professional are often in a state of appreciable concern, if not vulnerability, when they do so.

(6) The professions almost always involve at their core a significant inter-personal relationship between the professional, on the one hand, and the person who is thought to require the professional's services: the patient or the client.

[*] [In the early 1970s, President Nixon's men (and they were almost all men back then) attempted to break into and wiretap the Democratic National Committee's headquarters at the Watergate office complex. Many executive-branch lawyers were involved in these misdeeds and (especially) the resulting cover-ups. Most of these lawyers were eventually disciplined, and this

into the Watergate affair in the Spring of 1973, he was asked about one of the documents that he had provided to the Committee. The document was a piece of paper which contained a list of a number of the persons who had been involved in the cover-up. Next to a number of the names an asterisk appeared. What, Dean was asked, was the meaning of the asterisk? Did it signify membership in some further conspiracy? Did it mark off those who were decision-makers from those who were not? There did not seem to be any obvious pattern: Ehrlichman was starred, but Haldeman was not; Mitchell was starred, but Magruder was not. Oh, Dean answered, the asterisk really didn't mean anything. One day when he had been looking at the list of participants, he had been struck by the fact that so many of them were lawyers. So, he marked the name of each lawyer with an asterisk to see just how many there were. He had wondered, he told the Committee, when he saw that so many were attorneys, whether that had had anything to do with it; whether there was some reason why lawyers might have been more inclined than other persons to have been so willing to do the things that were done in respect to Watergate and the cover-up. But he had not pursued the matter; he had merely mused about it one afternoon.

It is, I think, at least a plausible hypothesis that the predominance of lawyers was not accidental—that the fact that they were lawyers made it easier rather than harder for them both to look at things the way they did and to do the things that were done. The theory that I want to examine in support of this hypothesis connects this activity with a feature of the lawyer's professionalism.

As I have already noted, one central feature of the professions in general and of law in particular is that there is a special, complicated relationship between the professional and the client or patient. For each of the parties in this relationship, but especially for the professional, the behavior that is involved is, to a very significant degree, what I call role-differentiated behavior. And this is significant because it is the nature of role-differentiated behavior that it often makes it both appropriate and desirable for the person in a particular role to put to one side considerations of various sorts—and especially various moral considerations—that would otherwise be relevant if not decisive. Some illustrations will help to make clear what I mean by role-differentiated behavior and by the way role-differentiated behavior often alters, if not eliminates, the significance of those moral considerations that would obtain, were it not for the presence of the role.

Being a parent is, in probably every human culture, to be involved in role-differentiated behavior. In our own culture, and once again in most, if not all, human

---

scandal caused or at least contributed to the ABA's decision to require mandatory legal ethics instruction in law school and to revisit the Model Code of Professional Responsibility (and eventually to adopt the Model Rules of Professional Conduct). See, e.g., Michael S. Ariens, "The Agony of Modern Legal Ethics, 1970 to 1985," 5 St. Mary's J. Legal Mal. & Ethics 134 (2014); Kathleen Clark, "The Legacy of Watergate for Legal Ethics Instruction," 51 Hastings L.J. 673 (1999). Thus, both your legal ethics course and a significant portion of your reading can likely be traced to the Watergate scandal.—Eds.]

cultures, as a parent one is entitled, if not obligated, to prefer the interests of one's own children over those of children generally. That is to say, it is regarded as appropriate for a parent to allocate excessive goods to his or her own children, even though other children may have substantially more pressing and genuine needs for these same items. If one were trying to decide what the right way was to distribute assets among a group of children all of whom were strangers to oneself, the relevant moral considerations would be very different from those that would be thought to obtain once one's own children were in the picture. In the role of a parent, the claims of other children vis-à-vis one's own are, if not rendered morally irrelevant, certainly rendered less morally significant. In short, the role-differentiated character of the situation alters the relevant moral point of view enormously.

A similar situation is presented by the case of the scientist. For a number of years, there has been debate and controversy within the scientific community over the question of whether scientists should participate in the development and elaboration of atomic theory, especially as those theoretical advances could then be translated into development of atomic weapons that would become a part of the arsenal of existing nation states. The dominant view, although it was not the unanimous one, in the scientific community was that the role of the scientist was to expand the limits of human knowledge. Atomic power was a force which had previously not been utilizable by human beings. The job of the scientist was, among other things, to develop ways and means by which that could now be done. And it was simply no part of one's role as a scientist to forego inquiry, or divert one's scientific explorations because of the fact that the fruits of the investigation could be or would be put to improper, immoral, or even catastrophic uses. The moral issues concerning whether and when to develop and use nuclear weapons were to be decided by others; by citizens and statesmen; they were not the concern of the scientist qua scientist.

In both of these cases it is, of course, conceivable that plausible and even thoroughly convincing arguments exist for the desirability of the role-differentiated behavior and its attendant neglect of what would otherwise be morally relevant considerations. Nonetheless, it is, I believe, also the case that the burden of proof, so to speak, is always upon the proponent of the desirability of this kind of role-differentiated behavior. For in the absence of special reasons why parents ought to prefer the interests of their children over those of children in general, the moral point of view surely requires that the claims and needs of all children receive equal consideration. But we take the rightness of parental preference so for granted that we often neglect, I think, the fact that it is anything but self-evidently morally appropriate. My own view, for example, is that careful reflection shows that the *degree* of parental preference systematically encouraged in our own culture is far too extensive to be morally justified.

All of this is significant just because to be a professional is to be enmeshed in role-differentiated behavior of precisely this sort. One's role as a doctor, psychiatrist, or lawyer alters one's moral universe in a fashion analogous to that described above. Of special significance here is the fact that the professional qua professional has a client or patient whose interests must be represented, attended to, or looked after by the professional. And that means that the role of the professional (like that of the parent) is to prefer in a variety of ways the interests of the client or patient over those of individuals generally.

Consider, more specifically, the role-differentiated behavior of the lawyer. Conventional wisdom has it that where the attorney-client relationship exists, the point of view of the attorney is properly different—and appreciably so—from that which would be appropriate in the absence of the attorney-client relationship. For where the attorney-client relationship exists, it is often appropriate and many times even obligatory for the attorney to do things that, all other things being equal, an ordinary person need not, and should not do. What is characteristic of this role of a lawyer is the lawyer's required indifference to a wide variety of ends and consequences that in other contexts would be of undeniable moral significance. Once a lawyer represents a client, the lawyer has a duty to make his or her expertise fully available in the realization of the end sought by the client, irrespective, for the most part, of the moral worth to which the end will be put or the character of the client who seeks to utilize it. Provided that the end sought is not illegal, the lawyer is, in essence, an amoral technician whose particular skills and knowledge in respect to the law are available to those with whom the relationship of client is established. The question, as I have indicated, is whether this particular and pervasive feature of professionalism is itself justifiable. At a minimum, I do not think any of the typical, simple answers will suffice.

One such answer focuses upon and generalizes from the criminal defense lawyer. For what is probably the most familiar aspect of this role-differentiated character of the lawyer's activity is that of the defense of a client charged with a crime. The received view within the profession (and to a lesser degree within the society at large) is that having once agreed to represent the client, the lawyer is under an obligation to do his or her best to defend that person at trial, irrespective, for instance, even of the lawyer's belief in the client's innocence. There are limits, of course, to what constitutes a defense: a lawyer cannot bribe or intimidate witnesses to increase the likelihood of securing an acquittal. And there are legitimate questions, in close cases, about how those limits are to be delineated. But, however these matters get resolved, it is at least clear that it is thought both appropriate and obligatory for the attorney to put on as vigorous and persuasive a defense of a client believed to be guilty as would have been mounted by the lawyer thoroughly convinced of the client's innocence. I suspect that many persons find this an attractive and admirable feature of the life of a legal professional. I know that often I do. The justifications are varied and, as I shall argue below, probably convincing.

But part of the difficulty is that the irrelevance of the guilt or innocence of an accused client by no means exhausts the altered perspective of the lawyer's conscience, even in criminal cases. For in the course of defending an accused, an attorney may have, as a part of his or her duty of representation, the obligation to invoke procedures and practices which are themselves morally objectionable and of which the lawyer in other contexts might thoroughly disapprove. And these situations, I think, are somewhat less comfortable to confront. For example, in California, the case law permits a defendant in a rape case to secure in some circumstances an order from the court requiring the complaining witness, that is the rape victim, to submit to a psychiatric examination before trial.[2] For no other crime is such a pretrial remedy available. In no other case can the victim of a crime be required to undergo psychiatric examination at the request of the defendant on the ground that the results of the examination may help the defendant prove that the offense did not take place. I think such a rule is wrong and is reflective of the sexist bias of the law in respect to rape. I certainly do not think it right that rape victims should be singled out by the law for this kind of special pretrial treatment, and I am skeptical about the morality of any involuntary psychiatric examination of witnesses. Nonetheless, it appears to be part of the role-differentiated obligation of a lawyer for a defendant charged with rape to seek to take advantage of this particular rule of law—irrespective of the independent moral view he or she may have of the rightness or wrongness of such a rule.

Nor, it is important to point out, is this peculiar, strikingly amoral behavior limited to the lawyer involved with the workings of the criminal law. Most clients come to lawyers to get the lawyers to help them do things that they could not easily do without the assistance provided by the lawyer's special competence. They wish, for instance, to dispose of their property in a certain way at death. They wish to contract for the purchase or sale of a house or a business. They wish to set up a corporation which will manufacture and market a new product. They wish to minimize their income taxes. And so on. In each case, they need the assistance of the professional, the lawyer, for he or she alone has the special skill which will make it possible for the client to achieve the desired result.

And in each case, the role-differentiated character of the lawyer's way of being tends to render irrelevant what would otherwise be morally relevant considerations. Suppose that a client desires to make a will disinheriting her children because they oppose the war in Vietnam. Should the lawyer refuse to draft the will because the lawyer thinks this is a bad reason to disinherit one's children? Suppose a client can avoid the payment of taxes through a loophole only available to a few wealthy taxpayers. Should the lawyer refuse to tell the client of a loophole because the lawyer thinks it an unfair advantage for the rich? Suppose a client wants to start a corporation that will manufacture, distribute, and promote a harmful but not illegal substance, e.g., cigarettes. Should the lawyer refuse to prepare the articles of incorporation for the corporation? In each case, the accepted view within the profession is that these matters are just of no concern to the lawyer qua lawyer. The lawyer need not of course agree to represent the client (and that is equally true for the unpopular client accused of a heinous crime), but there is nothing wrong with representing a client whose aims and purposes are quite immoral. And having agreed to do so, the lawyer is required

---

2. Ballard v. Superior Court, 64 Cal. 2d 159 (1966). [Such orders are now prohibited by California Penal Code § 1112, but criminal and civil defendants elsewhere still occasionally succeed in securing psychiatric examinations of their alleged victims.—Eds.]

to provide the best possible assistance, without regard to his or her disapproval of the objective that is sought.

The lesson, on this view, is clear. The job of the lawyer, so the argument typically concludes, is not to approve or disapprove of the character of his or her client, the cause for which the client seeks the lawyer's assistance, or the avenues provided by the law to achieve that which the client wants to accomplish. The lawyer's task is, instead, to provide that competence which the client lacks and the lawyer, as professional, possesses. In this way, the lawyer as professional comes to inhabit a simplified universe which is strikingly amoral—which regards as morally irrelevant any number of factors which nonprofessional citizens might take to be important, if not decisive, in their everyday lives. And the difficulty I have with all of this is that the arguments for such a way of life seem to be not quite so convincing to me as they do to many lawyers. I am, that is, at best uncertain that it is a good thing for lawyers to be so professional—for them to embrace so completely this role-differentiated way of approaching matters.

More specifically, if it is correct that this is the perspective of lawyers in particular and professionals in general, is it right that this should be their perspective? Is it right that the lawyer should be able so easily to put to one side otherwise difficult problems with the answer: but these are not and cannot be my concern as a lawyer? What do we gain and what do we lose from having a social universe in which there are professionals such as lawyers, who, as such, inhabit a universe of the sort I have been trying to describe?

One difficulty in even thinking about all of this is that lawyers may not be very objective or detached in their attempts to work the problem through. For one feature of this simplified, intellectual world is that it is often a very comfortable one to inhabit.

To be sure, on occasion, a lawyer may find it uncomfortable to represent an extremely unpopular client. On occasion, too, a lawyer may feel ill at ease invoking a rule of law or practice which he or she thinks to be an unfair or undesirable one. Nonetheless, for most lawyers, most of the time, pursuing the interests of one's clients is an attractive and satisfying way to live in part just because the moral world of the lawyer is a simpler, less complicated, and less ambiguous world than the moral world of ordinary life. There is, I think, something quite seductive about being able to turn aside so many ostensibly difficult moral dilemmas and decisions with the reply: but that is not my concern; my job as a lawyer is not to judge the rights and wrongs of the client or the cause; it is to defend as best I can my client's interests. For the ethical problems that can arise within this constricted point of view are, to say the least, typically neither momentous nor terribly vexing. Role-differentiated behavior is enticing and reassuring precisely because it does constrain and delimit an otherwise often intractable and confusing moral world.

But there is, of course, also an argument which seeks to demonstrate that it is good and not merely comfortable for lawyers to behave this way.

It is good, so the argument goes, that the lawyer's behavior and concomitant point of view are role-differentiated because the lawyer qua lawyer participates in a complex institution which functions well only if the individuals adhere to their institutional roles.

For example, when there is a conflict between individuals, or between the state and an individual, there is a well-established institutional mechanism by which to get that dispute resolved. That mechanism is the trial in which each side is represented by a lawyer whose job it is both to present his or her client's case in the most attractive, forceful light and to seek to expose the weaknesses and defects in the case of the opponents.

When an individual is charged with having committed a crime, the trial is the mechanism by which we determine in our society whether or not the person is in fact guilty. Just imagine what would happen if lawyers were to refuse, for instance, to represent persons whom they thought to be guilty. In a case where the guilt of a person seemed clear, it might turn out that some individuals would be deprived completely of the opportunity to have the system determine whether or not they are in fact guilty. The private judgment of individual lawyers would in effect be substituted for the public, institutional judgment of the judge and jury. The amorality of lawyers helps to guarantee that every criminal defendant will have his or her day in court.

In addition, of course, appearances can be deceiving. Persons who appear before trial to be clearly guilty do sometimes turn out to be innocent. Even persons who confess their guilt to their attorney occasionally turn out to have lied or to have been mistaken. The adversary system, so this argument continues, is simply a better method than any other that has been established by which to determine the legally relevant facts in any given case. It is certainly a better method than the exercise of private judgment by any particular individual. And the adversary system only works if each party to the controversy has a lawyer, a person whose institutional role it is to argue, plead and present the merits of his or her case and the demerits of the opponent's. Thus if the adversary system is to work, it is necessary that there be lawyers who will play their appropriate, professional, institutional role of representative of the client's cause.

Nor is the amorality of the institutional role of the lawyer restricted to the defense of those accused of crimes. As was indicated earlier, when the lawyer functions in his most usual role, he or she functions as a counselor, as a professional whose task it is to help people realize those objectives and ends that the law permits them to obtain and which cannot be obtained without the attorney's special competence in the law. The attorney may think it wrong to disinherit one's children because of their views about the Vietnam war, but here the attorney's complaint is really with the laws of inheritance and not with his or her client. The attorney may think the tax provision an unfair, unjustifiable loophole, but once more the complaint is really with the Internal Revenue Code and not with the client who seeks to take advantage of it. And these matters, too, lie beyond the ambit of the lawyer's moral point of view as institutional counselor and facilitator. If lawyers were to substitute their own private views of what ought to be legally permissible and impermissible for those of the legislature, this would constitute a surreptitious and undesirable shift from a democracy to an oligarchy of lawyers. For given the fact that lawyers are needed to effectuate the wishes of clients, the lawyer ought to make his or her skills available to those who seek them without regard for the particular objectives of the client.

Now, all of this certainly makes some sense. These arguments are neither specious nor without force. Nonetheless, it seems to me that one dilemma which emerges is that if this line of argument is sound, it also appears to follow that the behavior of the lawyers involved in Watergate was simply another less happy illustration of lawyers playing their accustomed institutional role. If we are to approve on institutional grounds of the lawyer's zealous defense of the apparently guilty client and the lawyer's effective assistance of the immoral cheat, does it not follow that we must also approve of the Watergate lawyer's zealous defense of the interests of Richard Nixon?

As I have indicated, I do not think there is any easy answer to this question. For I am not, let me hasten to make clear, talking about the easy cases—about the behavior of the lawyers that was manifestly illegal. For someone quite properly might reply that it was no more appropriate for the lawyer who worked in the White House to obstruct justice or otherwise violate the criminal law than it would be for a criminal defense lawyer to shoot the prosecution witness to prevent adverse testimony or bribe a defense witness in order to procure favorable testimony. What I am interested in is all of the Watergate behavior engaged in by the Watergate lawyers that was not illegal, but that was, nonetheless, behavior of which we quite properly disapprove. I mean lying to the public; dissembling; stonewalling; tape-recording conversations; playing dirty tricks. Were not these just effective lawyer-like activities pursued by lawyers who viewed Richard Nixon as they would a client and who sought, therefore, the advancement and protection of his interests—personal and political?

It might immediately be responded that the analogy is not apt. For the lawyers who were involved in Watergate were hardly participants in an adversary proceeding. They were certainly not participants in that institutional setting, litigation, in which the amorality of the lawyer makes the most sense. It might even be objected that the amorality of the lawyer qua counselor is clearly distinguishable from the behavior of the Watergate lawyers. Nixon as President was not a client; they, as officials in the executive branch, were functioning as governmental officials and not as lawyers at all.

While not wholly convinced by a response such as the above, I am prepared to accept it because the issue at hand seems to me to be a deeper one. Even if the involvement of so many lawyers in Watergate was adventitious (or, if not adventitious, explicable in terms of some more benign explanation) there still seems to me to be costs, if not problems, with the amorality of the lawyer that derives from his or her role-differentiated professionalism.

As I indicated earlier, I do believe that the amoral behavior of the *criminal* defense lawyer is justifiable. But I think that [justification] depends at least as much upon the special needs of an accused as upon any more general defense of a lawyer's role-differentiated behavior. As a matter of fact I think it likely that many persons such as myself have been misled by the special features of the criminal case. Because a deprivation of liberty is so serious, because the prosecutorial resources of the state are so vast, and because, perhaps, of a serious skepticism about the rightness of punishment even where wrongdoing has occurred, it is easy to accept the view that it makes sense to charge the defense counsel with the job of making the best possible case for the accused—without regard, so to speak, for the merits. This coupled with the fact that it is an adversarial proceeding succeeds, I think, in justifying the amorality of the criminal defense counsel. But this does not, however, justify a comparable perspective on the part of lawyers generally. Once we leave the peculiar situation of the criminal defense lawyer, I think it quite likely that the role-differentiated amorality of the lawyer is almost certainly excessive and at times inappropriate. That is to say, this special case to one side, I am inclined to think that we might all be better served if lawyers were to see themselves less as subject to role-differentiated behavior and more as subject to the demands of the moral point of view. In this sense it may be that we need a good deal less rather than more professionalism in our society generally and among lawyers in particular.

Moreover, even if I am wrong about all this, four things do seem to me to be true and important.

First, all of the arguments that support the role-differentiated amorality of the lawyer on institutional grounds can succeed only if the enormous degree of trust and confidence in the institutions themselves is itself justified. If the institutions work well and fairly, there may be good sense to deferring important moral concerns and criticisms to another time and place, to the level of institutional criticism and assessment. But the less certain we are entitled to be of either the rightness or the self-corrective nature of the larger institutions of which the professional is a part, the less apparent it is that we should encourage the professional to avoid direct engagement with the moral issues as they arise. And we are, today, I believe, certainly entitled to be quite skeptical both of the fairness and of the capacity for self-correction of our larger institutional mechanisms, including the legal system. To the degree to which the institutional rules and practices are unjust, unwise or undesirable, to that same degree is the case for the role-differentiated behavior of the lawyer weakened if not destroyed.

Second, it is clear that there are definite character traits that the professional such as the lawyer must take on if the system is to work. What is less clear is that they are admirable ones. Even if the role-differentiated amorality of the professional lawyer is justified by the virtues of the adversary system, this also means that the lawyer qua lawyer will be encouraged to be competitive rather than cooperative; aggressive rather than accommodating; ruthless rather than compassionate; and pragmatic rather than principled. This is, I think, part of the logic of the role-differentiated behavior of lawyers in particular, and to a lesser degree of professionals in general. It is surely neither accidental nor unimportant that these are the same character traits that are emphasized and valued by the capitalist ethic—and on precisely analogous grounds. Because the ideals of professionalism and capitalism are the dominant ones within our culture, it is harder than most of us suspect even to take seriously the suggestion that radically different styles of living, kinds of occupational outlooks, and types of social institutions might be possible, let alone preferable.

Third, there is a special feature of the role-differentiated behavior of the lawyer that distinguishes it from the comparable behavior of other professionals. What I have in mind can be brought out through the following question: Why is it that it seems far less plausible to talk critically about the amorality of the doctor, for instance, who treats all patients irrespective of their moral character than it does to talk critically about the comparable amorality of the lawyer? Why is it that it seems so obviously sensible, simple and right for the doctor's behavior to be narrowly and rigidly role-differentiated, i.e., just to try to cure those who are ill? And why is it that at the very least it seems so complicated, uncertain, and troublesome to decide whether it is right for the lawyer's behavior to be similarly role-differentiated?

The answer, I think, is twofold. To begin with (and this I think is the less interesting point) it is, so to speak, intrinsically good to try to cure disease, but in no comparable way is it intrinsically good to try to win every lawsuit or help every client realize his or her objective. In addition (and this I take to be the truly interesting point), the lawyer's behavior is different in kind from the doctor's. The lawyer—and especially the lawyer as advocate—directly says and affirms things. The lawyer makes the case for the client. He or she tries to explain, persuade and convince others that the client's cause should prevail. The lawyer lives with and within a dilemma that is not shared by other professionals. If the lawyer actually believes everything that he or she asserts on behalf of the client, then it appears to be proper to regard the lawyer as in fact embracing and endorsing the points of view that he or she articulates. If the lawyer does not in fact believe what is urged by way of argument, if the lawyer is only playing a role, then it appears to be proper to tax the lawyer with hypocrisy and insincerity. To be sure, actors in a play take on roles and say things that the characters, not the actors, believe. But we know it is a play and that they are actors. The law courts are not, however, theaters, and the lawyers both talk about justice and they genuinely seek to persuade. The fact that the lawyer's words, thoughts, and convictions are, apparently, for sale and at the service of the client helps us, I think, to understand the peculiar hostility which is more than occasionally uniquely directed by lay persons toward lawyers. The verbal, role-differentiated behavior of the lawyer qua advocate puts the lawyer's integrity into question in a way that distinguishes the lawyer from the other professionals.[3]

---

3. I owe this insight, which I think is an important and seldom appreciated one, to my colleague, Leon Letwin.

Fourth, and related closely to the three points just discussed, even if on balance the role-differentiated character of the lawyer's way of thinking and acting is ultimately deemed to be justifiable within the system on systemic instrumental grounds, it still remains the case that we do pay a social price for that way of thought and action. For to become and to be a professional, such as a lawyer, is to incorporate within oneself ways of behaving and ways of thinking that shape the whole person. It is especially hard, if not impossible, because of the nature of the professions for one's professional way of thinking not to dominate one's entire adult life. Thus, even if the lawyers who were involved in Watergate were not, strictly speaking, then and there functioning as lawyers, their behavior was, I believe, the likely if not inevitable consequence of their legal acculturation. Having been taught to embrace and practice the lawyer's institutional role, it was natural, if not unavoidable, that they would continue to play that role even when they were somewhat removed from the specific institutional milieu in which that way of thinking and acting is arguably fitting and appropriate. The nature of the professions—the lengthy educational preparation, the prestige and economic rewards, and the concomitant enhanced sense of self—makes the role of professional a difficult one to shed even in those obvious situations in which that role is neither required nor appropriate. In important respects, one's professional role becomes and is one's dominant role, so that for many persons at least they become their professional being. This is at a minimum a heavy price to pay for the professions as we know them in our culture, and especially so for lawyers. Whether it is an inevitable price is, I think, an open question, largely because the problem has not begun to be fully perceived as such by the professionals in general, the legal profession in particular, or by the educational institutions that train professionals. . . .

[The second part of the article takes a critical look at the personal relationship between the lawyer and client.]

Notes

1. Professor Wasserstrom's piece was deliberately chosen for its critical approach, for it is representative of a whole body of modern literature about the norms of the legal profession. He makes a number of controversial assertions, for example: "for at best the lawyer's world is a simplified moral world; often it is an amoral one; and more often than occasionally, perhaps, an overtly immoral one," and "Provided that the end sought is not illegal, the lawyer is, in essence, an amoral technician whose particular skills and knowledge in respect to the law are available to those with whom the relationship of client is established." As we consider the materials of professional responsibility, we need to decide how much we agree with the various insights in the Wasserstrom article. We should also remember, however, that it is not enough to resolve each professional problem for ourselves, i.e., to answer the question "What would I do in this particular situation?" We must then go on to answer the question, "Would I impose my solution on other professionals or would I give them some discretion?" The question regarding discretion then requires us to consider whether

lawyers with discretion in certain circumstances should attempt to let clients and would-be clients know how they will exercise that discretion. Providing that information to clients might, for example, assist in their lawyer selection process, enable them to provide greater input in their case, and assist in their decision-making about what to tell (and what not to tell) the lawyer. And finally, after addressing these difficult questions, we must face the issue: "Should ethical compliance be enforced and, if so, how? Through the market, through privately initiated enforcement, or through a government bureaucracy?" As we shall see throughout these materials, these questions are consistently troublesome.

2. Professor Wasserstrom used the role of lawyers in the Watergate affair as a major example. A more modern governmental example might well be the role of lawyers in the Office of Legal Counsel and the Justice Department in justifying the use of torture as a means of obtaining information from suspected terrorists. See, e.g., Luban, *Torture, Power, and Law* (2014); Goldsmith, *The Terror Presidency* (2007). We will return to this issue in Chapter 5.

3. Professor Wasserstrom returned to the subject of this excerpt many years later in "Roles and Morality," an essay that appears in David Luban ed., *The Good Lawyer* 25 (1984). He advanced a number of arguments that he reported as going "some appreciable distance in reducing or dissolving the initial worry" about the consequences of role-differentiated behavior. The arguments he mentions are that role-differentiated behavior will yield better overall moral outcomes than ad hoc judgments; that the expectations of those to be benefited by such behavior ought to count in arriving at judgment; and that the benefits conferred by role-differentiated behavior often are the trade-off for certain requirements imposed on the beneficiaries of that behavior. Nevertheless, Professor Wasserstrom concludes that he still has "certain nagging dissatisfactions" about efforts to put his worries to rest. Id. at 34. We will return to these general arguments (which have a flavor of rule utilitarianism) in Chapter 3.

Problem 1–1   In Class

While returning from work as a passenger in his employer's car in rural Minnesota, David Spaulding was badly hurt in an automobile accident that killed two people, one in each car, and injured many others. There was no stop sign at the intersection where the accident occurred, and visibility was impaired by corn that was growing in the neighboring fields. Spaulding, who was twenty years old, was still a minor under Minnesota law as it then existed, and his father brought suit on his behalf against the drivers and owners of both cars. Three doctors who treated Spaulding did not discover that he had an aneurysm in his aorta that could be fatal if left untreated, but a doctor hired by the insurance company handling the litigation for the defendants diagnosed the problem and reported it to one of the defense lawyers. Spaulding's young lawyer did not seek to obtain the insurance doctor's report. The defense lawyer did not disclose the doctor's findings to Spaulding and apparently not to his individual clients either, although he may have done so to the insurance company that hired him. At settlement negotiations, the insurance company lawyer made no comments or representations about Spaulding's injuries. The case was settled for $6500; the parties presented the settlement to the court for approval because Spaulding was a minor, and the court approved the settlement.

Notes covered in class

1. As a layperson having read Richard Wasserstrom's article and knowing that in general lawyers and doctors are supposed to keep confidential what they learn during the professional relationship, consider what the various individuals involved in this real situation ought to do—the insurance company doctor; the individual defendants, assuming that they know about the doctor's report; the insurance company itself; and finally the insurance company's lawyers. Should a different responsibility be placed on lawyers? Is there a difference between "legal" and "moral" responsibility? According to Wasserstrom, should there be?

2. Once you have answered those questions, consider whether you would impose a legal obligation on any of the actors to take (or not to take) any action. The description of this case is taken from Spaulding v. Zimmerman, 116 N.W.2d 704 (Minn. 1962) and from the thorough reexamination of the case in Cramton and Knowles, "Professional Secrecy and its Exceptions: *Spaulding v. Zimmerman* Revisited," 83 Minn. L. Rev. 63 (1998). In Chapter 6, we will consider the ramifications of the court's decision in the actual case. See p. 522, Note 3.

3. You might believe that the defense lawyer should have disclosed to the young plaintiff that he was suffering from a life-threatening aneurism (or that the defense lawyer should have attempted to persuade the defendants or the insurance company to make the disclosure). If so, you would not be alone. See Fred C. Zacharias, "Rethinking Confidentiality," 74 Iowa L. Rev. 351 (1989) (reporting results of a survey, albeit with limited respondents, indicating that the public, and even lawyers, believe that the defense lawyer should disclose this potentially fatal condition). How would you go about making sure that future lawyers make such disclosures (or encourage their clients to make such disclosures)? What would be the most effective method to ensure compliance?

A. The Rules of Professional Conduct

The rules governing lawyers' professional responsibility have been receiving increasing attention since the late 1960s, from the general public and from within the profession. The substantive law of professional responsibility has grown increasingly complex and sophisticated as lawyers, courts, and commentators have begun to analyze the ramifications of the various general principles in the context of the many different situations in which lawyers find themselves. The involvement of lawyers in various well-publicized corporate and public scandals (for example) has brought these matters to the attention of press and public.

The resulting rules and commentary often provide important general guidance for lawyers in conducting themselves ethically and prudently in their daily practices, and malpractice insurance companies often use the rules in persuading lawyers to adopt best practices (especially practices designed to avoid or mitigate legal malpractice claims). Perhaps most importantly, however, the rules matter because a violation of an ethical rule is what leads to discipline, e.g., suspension or even disbarment. According to the drafters of the rules, moreover, the rules are designed primarily for such disciplinary proceedings. See Model Rules of Prof'l Conduct Scope cmt. 19–20 ("Failure to comply with an obligation or prohibition imposed by a Rule is a basis for invoking the disciplinary process. . . . The Rules are designed to provide guidance to lawyers and to provide a structure for regulating conduct through disciplinary agencies"). Both new and seasoned lawyers have lost their license for failing to follow the rules, and as with other areas of the law, ignorance of the ethical rules is generally not a defense to disciplinary charges. The Multistate Professional Responsibility Exam (MPRE) now tests basic knowledge of the ethical rules, and virtually every state requires a minimum score on the MPRE before the state will grant the applicant a license to practice law. Thus, for gaining and retaining a law license and for a host of other reasons discussed throughout this book, the ethical rules are worth careful study.

Historically, before the promulgation in 1887 of the first American code of ethics, principles of professional responsibility had developed as part of the lore of the profession and the common law of particular jurisdictions. They were enforced as such in the courts. In the nineteenth century, there was a moderate amount of literature that was devoted to matters of professional responsibility. See M. H. Hoeflich, "Legal Ethics in the Nineteenth Century: The Other Tradition," 47 Kan. L. Rev. 793 (1999). The best-known discussions of principles of legal ethics were David Hoffman's lecture, "Professional Deportment," published in his book, *A Course of Legal Study* (1817), and George Sharswood's lectures to the Law Class of the University of Pennsylvania published in 1854 under the title *Professional Ethics*. Sharswood was a well-known lawyer and teacher and later a justice of the Pennsylvania Supreme Court. His book was widely regarded as authoritative throughout the nineteenth century.

All jurisdictions now have formal statements of the rules governing the conduct of lawyers. The first widely adopted rules were the Canons of Ethics. These had been promulgated by the American Bar Association in 1908 and were amended several times thereafter. They were based on a code of ethics, the first of its kind in the United States, that had been promulgated by the Alabama State Bar Association in 1887. The Alabama Code of Ethics in turn drew heavily on both the Sharswood and Hoffman works. In many states, the Canons of Ethics were formally adopted as the governing law either by statute or by pronouncement of the highest state court, sometimes with local modifications. In most other states, the Canons were recognized as a source of guidance to practitioners and courts, but were not formally adopted. The controversy within the committee that drafted the 1908 Canons, especially differences regarding lawyers' duty to consider the justice of their clients' position in civil cases, has been resurrected by Susan Carle in "Lawyers' Duty to Do Justice: A New Look at the History of the 1908 Canons," 24 Law and Social Inquiry 1 (1999).

It is interesting to reflect upon the changes in the profession and in the society it serves that engendered the reduction of the general "common law" principles of professional responsibility into written codes—first the very general statement of principles in the Canons of Ethics, and then the much more detailed rules of the Model Code of Professional Responsibility and the Model Rules of Professional Conduct. The old Canons of Ethics were quite brief—47 Canons that could be printed on four and a half pages and could be read, if not completely understood in all their ramifications, in a few minutes. With brevity comes generality, and a constant complaint about the Canons was that they were not much help to the lawyer who needed guidance in a particular case. Some guidance had been given in the form of case law and the written opinions of the Committee on Professional Ethics of the American Bar Association and similar committees at the state and local levels. See the brief discussion of the development of the Canons of Ethics in Henry S. Drinker, *Legal Ethics* 23–26 (1953).

[margin note: Improving the Canons.]

In 1964, at the request of its president, later Supreme Court Justice, Lewis F. Powell, the American Bar Association appointed a committee to undertake the task of improving the Canons. In 1969, the committee produced a new Model Code of Professional Responsibility, which was adopted by the House of Delegates, the decision-making body of the American Bar Association. The ABA thereafter amended the Model Code several times. As of August 1983, every state and the District of Columbia had adopted, at least in part, the Model Code of Professional Responsibility as substantive law to govern the conduct of lawyers. In most states the adoption was by formal act of the highest court of the state. In some states, there was a combination of action by either court or legislature and state bar association. California has had a unique combination of court rules and statutes that govern lawyers' conduct.

[margin note: ① Adoption of RPC by states; or ② Action by bar ass'n & state leg.]

Shortly after the Model Code was promulgated, the involvement of so many lawyers in Watergate focused the attention of the public and the profession on lawyers' conduct. In addition, a number of substantive problems, especially those involving conflicts of interest and confidentiality, became part of the staple of a lawyer's daily routine. Moreover, decisions of the Supreme Court held a number of the profession's rules relating to the provision of legal services unconstitutional. These factors, combined with a variety of particular criticisms, led many people to conclude that the Model Code of Professional Responsibility was inadequate for the needs of the profession. Therefore, in 1977 the ABA appointed a Commission on Evaluation of Professional Standards "to undertake a comprehensive rethinking of the ethical premises and problems" of the legal profession.

This commission, which became known as the Kutak Commission, concluded that a new code was needed. Unlike the effort that produced the Model Code, the Kutak Commission's work was involved in controversy from the start. The controversy reflected the change in thinking in the profession and in the general public about problems of professional responsibility. The drafters of the Model Code had worked largely in secret and their product was adopted by the ABA and in the states largely without controversy. Most lawyers still believed then that "legal ethics" was a matter of knowing right from wrong, and they further believed that the rules of professional conduct didn't affect their practices very much. Watergate, disqualification motions for conflict of interest, the debates over whistleblowing and presentation of perjured testimony, and Supreme Court decisions on advertising, solicitation, minimum fee schedules, and group legal services ended that perception (or at least should have ended it).

The discussion of the Kutak Commission's work was intense, and in response the Commission modified many of its positions, especially those with respect to mandatory pro bono service by lawyers and the confidentiality obligation. Finally, in August 1983, the ABA adopted the Model Rules of Professional Conduct and recommended their adoption by state and federal courts.

As a voluntary bar association, however, action of the ABA by itself has no effect on lawyers' obligations. It is only governmental adoption or at least formal declaration by a court that the provisions of the Model Rules are to be looked to for guidance that gives the proposal any authority. By the end of the twentieth century, most states had adopted the Model Rules, although most of the adopting states amended them, sometimes quite substantially. A few states, notably New York and California, retained their own rules of professional conduct. The ABA then undertook in its "Ethics 2000" project—yet another effort to produce a new code of professional responsibility, this time by amendment of the Model Rules. It adopted an amended version of the Model Rules in 2002, although, as we shall see, it has amended several provisions since then. The most recent amendments occurred just a few years ago, following the "Ethics 20/20" Commission's proposals to amend the ethical rules to account more fully for changes in technology and globalization. The various states have been considering those amendments ever since, and the result has been similar to previous recommendations by the ABA. Some states have adopted the recommendations virtually completely. Others have adopted only some of them. New York in late 2008 adopted a new set of rules based on the format of the Model Rules, with substantial changes. California retains its unique mixture of judicial and legislative prescriptions and thus has the distinction or demerit of being the only state with an ethical code not based in whole or part on the ABA's rules. In addition, some federal and state agencies have adopted rules governing the conduct of lawyers practicing before them, and many specialty professional groups—e.g., practitioners in probate, family law, real estate, and the like—have adopted ethics rules as guides to the particular problems faced by lawyers in those fields.

Special note should be taken of the situation in the federal courts, especially the district courts. There is no standard practice. A Report to the Committee on Rules of Practice and Procedure of the Judicial Conference of the United States in 1995 identified seven different models then being followed by the district courts. The leading choice is the adoption of the rules of the state in which the district court is located,

[handwritten margin note: → follow the state RPC, where the dist. ct. sits]

although some districts have adopted both the state rules and either the ABA Model Code or the ABA Model Rules. The proliferation of different versions of the rules at the state level and of differences between the states and the local district courts[1] has led many federal agencies, most notably the Department of Justice, and some law firms and other organizations with national practices to urge federalization of ethics rules, at least with respect to practice in the federal courts. The Department of Justice has claimed the power to formulate the rules of conduct that will govern its own lawyers. The Conference of Chief Justices has defended the traditional primary role of the states to set standards of conduct for lawyers who practice within their jurisdiction. A hybrid solution, which would federalize only those rules that have caused the most difficulty, has been put forth (but never adopted) as well.

The Judicial Conference has, for many years, been considering a variety of options for resolving this very difficult problem. In the meantime, Congress took a hand. Over the objection of the Justice Department, it passed, and President Clinton signed, the so-called McDade Amendment, which provides that Justice Department attorneys "shall be subject to State laws and rules, and local Federal court rules, governing attorneys in each State where such attorney engages in that attorney's duties, to the same extent and in the same manner as other attorneys in that State." 28 U.S.C. § 530B. That statute became effective in April 1999 and several bills have been introduced in Congress to alter it considerably by requiring the Judicial Conference to produce either a partial or a complete set of uniform rules for all federal government attorneys. After the World Trade Center attack on September 11, 2001, the Justice Department sponsored legislation designed to exempt federal government lawyers from discipline for participating in covert investigations involving misrepresentation or deceit, but that legislation has not been passed.

In sum, except in California, the Model Rules or a revised version thereof govern the professional conduct of lawyers. A word about the format of professional rules is therefore in order. The drafters of the Model Code and the Model Rules sought to modernize the professional rules and to be more helpful to practitioners by providing much greater specificity than the drafters of the former Canons of Ethics had done. In attempting to remedy the perceived defects of the former Model Code, the

---

1. One particular and recent example of the different—even conflicting—rules involves marijuana. Several states have legalized medical marijuana, but at the time of this writing, distribution is still illegal under the federal Controlled Substances Act. In Colorado, for example, the state supreme court amended its rules of professional conduct to permit lawyers to assist clients who are involved in the medical marijuana industry, but the federal district court in essence rejected this amendment. See Eli Wald et al., "Representing Clients in the Marijuana Industry: Navigating State and Federal Rules," Colo. Law., Aug. 2015, at 61. Model Rule 1.2, which forbids lawyers from counseling or assisting criminal or fraudulent conduct, does not explicitly address what lawyers should do when faced with conflicting federal and state laws. Although ethics opinions have offered some limited but often conflicting guidance for lawyers, lawyers (who, say, are contemplating whether to incorporate a marijuana dispensary business on behalf of a client) remain in a state of uncertainty, and clients might face a diminished ability to retain competent counsel to handle such matters. See generally Sam Kamin & Eli Wald, "Marijuana Lawyers: Outlaws or Crusaders?," 91 Or. L. Rev. 869 (2013).

drafters of the Model Rules have produced a small book that cannot be read and understood in a few minutes. In fact, it cannot be read consecutively from beginning to end unless one has extraordinary powers of concentration. The Model Rules are like a textbook that is designed to be used by a lawyer with a problem. The concept is similar to that of a Restatement or of the Uniform Commercial Code—a statement of law followed by interpretive Comments. The Scope Note to the Model Rules, which states that the "Comments are intended as guides to interpretation, but the text of each Rule is authoritative," is somewhat disingenuous because sometimes the Comments strike out on their own beyond the language of the Rule and disciplinary authorities not infrequently use the Comments as at least partial authority to sanction lawyers.

The elaborateness and format of the Model Rules make them look more like statutes. Nevertheless, occasionally the rules will literally cover factual situations where their application will seem problematic. The Scope Note anticipates that problem but gives no specific guidance: "The Rules of Professional Conduct are rules of reason. They should be interpreted with reference to the purposes of legal representation and of the law itself." We will encounter problems in which the "rule of reason" is seemingly implicated.

B. Professional Ideology and the Assumptions Underlying the Rules

If the Scope Note just mentioned is to guide effectively the various bodies charged with the task of regulating the conduct of lawyers, it is vital to understand the assumptions that lawyers might possess with respect to the "purposes of legal representation and of the law itself." The following material is an excerpt from an essay that articulates the various assumptions that appear to undergird the legal profession's sense of self-identity, as reflected through the lens of the various codes governing professional responsibility. As you work with the Model Rules, notice to what extent these assumptions are embodied in the rules and to what extent they remain applicable to particular areas of practice and to the changing nature of law practice generally.

David B. Wilkins
Everyday Practice *is* the Troubling Case: Confronting Context in Legal Ethics
in Sarat et al. eds., *Everyday Practices and Trouble Cases* (1998)
pp. 68, 70–75

Traditional legal ethics discourse rests on a set of connected assumptions about the everyday practice of law. In brief, the codes of professional conduct assume that the typical lawyer/client interaction is between a dedicated and skilled solo practitioner and an unsophisticated individual client. The sole purpose of this relationship, according to this traditional account, is for the lawyer to give the client legal advice about how to achieve the client's predetermined objectives.

These assumptions about everyday practice, in turn, produce a standard conception of what constitutes a "troubling" ethical case. At the core of this conception is the concern that in certain situations—for example, when a lawyer has conflicting loyalties to other clients or is concerned about her own financial interests—a lawyer may be tempted to give her vulnerable client something less than the full measure of devotion to which the client is entitled. The traditional model further assumes, however, that through professional training and socialization, lawyers learn to avoid these potentially troubling situations. As a result, the bar's standard ethics discourse assumes that virtually all lawyers will conform their everyday practices to the high standards of professionalism set out in the ethics codes. Those who do not must be weeded out before they cause trouble for honest members of the bar. . . .

I. THE TRADITIONAL MODEL

Lawyer has a duty to both client & legal systems → zealous.

The duty of a lawyer, both to his client and to the legal system, is to represent his client zealously within the bounds of the law. . . . The professional responsibility of a lawyer derives from his membership in a profession which has the duty of assisting members of the public to secure and protect available legal rights and benefits. In our government of laws and not of men, each member of our society is entitled to have his conduct judged and regulated in accordance with the law, to seek any lawful objective through legally permissible means, and to present for adjudication any lawful claim, issue, or defense. (Model Code 1983, EC 7-1.)

This familiar quotation from the Model Code of Professional Responsibility sets out the traditional understanding of the lawyer's role. The quote also suggests the drafters' view of the context in which this role would be carried out: "a lawyer" helping "his client" to "secure and protect available legal rights and benefits." This way of characterizing the everyday practices of lawyers is not just central to the formal codes of professional conduct. It also dominates the "myths, lores, and narratives" that lawyers tell themselves and the public about the nature of the lawyer's role. Sections A, B, and C briefly elaborate the standard assumptions about lawyers, clients, and legal advice that underlie this traditional understanding. . . .

A. LAWYERS

Factual Assumptions

By framing ethics discourse in terms of the obligations that "a lawyer derives from his membership in a profession," the standard paradigm makes three factual assumptions about the everyday world of legal practice. I will call these assumptions individualism, universalism, and professionalism.

1. Individualism

Lawyers used to practice solo.

The codes of professional conduct concentrate almost exclusively on defining the rights and obligations of individual lawyers. Most seminal legal ethics scholarship also adopts this individualistic perspective. Given the profession's history, this focus is hardly surprising. Until the 1950s, the vast majority of lawyers practiced alone or in small, informal groupings. Moreover, in countless after-dinner speeches and professional journals, lawyers are encouraged to protect vigilantly their status as "independent professionals" regardless of the actual circumstances in which they practice. The implicit claim underlying these exhortations is that even lawyers in organizational settings act essentially as individuals, free from external review or supervision by state officials, peers, or clients.

2. Universalism

The constant reference to "a lawyer" and "his client" throughout the profession's formal rules also implies that differences among lawyers are relatively unimportant in the area of ethical decision making. Two kinds of universalizing assumptions are embedded in this worldview. First, the traditional model pays relatively scant attention to distinctions in the tasks lawyers perform (e.g., litigation versus ex ante counseling), the subject areas in which they practice (e.g., criminal versus civil), the clients they represent (e.g., individuals versus corporations), or, as we have seen, the setting in which they work (solo practice versus firms or other institutions). Instead, the model assumes, in the words of the preamble to the Model Code, that except in certain unusual circumstances, the same ethical rules should be applied to "all lawyers, regardless of the nature of their professional activity." These "universal" rules, however, have been written from a particular vantage point. Although the rules themselves do not specify a particular context, the image underlying them is clearly that of the criminal defense lawyer. As a result, the ethics rules reflect the drafter's understanding of the everyday practices of this particular segment of the bar. Similarly, traditional legal scholars invariably test the normative and practical attractiveness of ethical rules and constructs against the perceived demands of criminal defense practice.

Second, the bar's official story completely disregards race, gender, class, or other personal characteristics of practitioners. Lawyers, in other words, are considered to be generic and interchangeable. All that matters is that the person *is* a lawyer, and therefore has adopted a professional identity that subsumes all other personal characteristics.

3. Professionalism

Moreover, according to the traditional view, those who have adopted a lawyer's professional identity have unique skills and beliefs that separate them from those who pursue other occupations. Two empirical contentions underlie this claim. First, the standard model asserts that lawyers possess specialized knowledge about law and legal institutions. Second, the model assumes that lawyers understand that the economic rewards of law practice are incidental to the primary goal of serving the public interest through law. This latter goal of serving the public, according to the official view, includes two distinct, though ultimately complementary, responsibilities. First, as advocates, lawyers have a fiduciary duty to place their client's interests ahead of their own. Second, as "officers of the court," they owe a special duty of loyalty to the fair and efficient administration of justice. Because they are professionals, the traditional model assumes that lawyers understand that both of these duties are to take precedence over their own monetary interests.

B. CLIENTS

The traditional model makes a parallel set of assumptions about clients. I will call these assumptions autonomy, vulnerability, and legalism.

1. Autonomy

Just as the traditional model portrays all lawyers as solo practitioners (in spirit if not in fact), clients are assumed to be autonomous individuals. This characterization implies two things about the average client. First, the client is assumed to be a single person, as opposed to an organization or a group. On the few occasions where the rules discuss representing groups, "the usual response is to treat the group as an entity, thus restoring the single client theory."

Second, these individuals or entities are assumed to be "autonomous," in that they formulate their interests and objectives independent of the lawyer's intervention. The codes of ethics draw a sharp distinction between the means and ends of legal representation. Whereas the former are considered at least partially within the domain of the lawyer-professional, the latter are supposed to be supplied exclusively by the client. The lawyer's role is simply to pursue these objectives within the bounds of the law. [See, e.g., Model Rules of Prof'l Conduct R. 1.2.—Eds.]

In addition, the traditional model privileges client autonomy in an even more fundamental sense. Regardless of the client's specific goals in any given representation, the formal rules assume that making an autonomous decision about these ends remains his or her most important priority. Clients hire lawyers, therefore, to protect or enhance their ability to exercise this fundamental right.

2. Vulnerability

The bar tells a related story about client vulnerability. According to this account, the reason clients are required to hire lawyers to further their autonomy is that "in a highly legalized society such as ours, autonomy is often dependent upon access to the law." And, because the law is often complex and difficult to understand, "meaningful access to law requires the assistance of a lawyer." By the same token, because clients do not understand the law, they cannot accurately assess either their need for legal services or the quality of the services they receive.

The traditional model therefore portrays clients as triply vulnerable. First and foremost, they are vulnerable to the state, which, in the bar's standard lore, constantly stands ready to impose some unjustified punishment or to withhold a deserved benefit. Clients are also vulnerable to themselves, in the sense that they frequently underestimate their need for legal services. Finally, they are vulnerable to their attorneys, whose services they both need and cannot understand.

3. Legalism

The traditional model assumes that clients are primarily interested in maximizing their legal rights. Both the "maximizing" and the "legal" parts of this assumption are significant. The formal rules implicitly assume that clients want to press their interests to the full extent permitted by law. Moreover, what clients want to "win" are legal rights in *legal* fora. Clients come to lawyers in order to gain access to the complex and powerful machinery of the law. What they want in return is for lawyers to use that machinery to bestow upon them all of the legal rights and opportunities that our democratic system has to offer.

C. LEGAL ADVICE

Finally, the traditional model makes three important assumptions about the "advice" that clients seek from their lawyers: the autonomy of legal knowledge, the primacy of formal rules, and the boundary claim.

1. The Autonomy of Legal Knowledge

Not surprisingly, the traditional model assumes that what clients want—and what lawyers give—is advice about how to "secure available legal rights and benefits," as opposed to advice about business, morality, or politics. Although the ethics codes acknowledge that lawyers may occasionally consult other disciplines or offer advice about business or morality, these areas are considered peripheral to the central mission of helping clients "to seek any lawful objective through legally permissible means." The underlying assumption is that law is an "autonomous discipline," distinct from other forms of knowledge or reasoning. As a result, the standard view is that legal advice can be taught, provided, and regulated free from the contested domains of economics, morality, or politics.

2. Formalism

Moreover, the traditional model implies that the advice of a legal expert consists largely of an understanding of the legal system's formal rules and practices. Law, according to this perspective, "is a rule system" and "individual legal actors are highly constrained by a regime of clearly articulated rules." Traditional legal education reinforces this view by concentrating almost exclusively on teaching students to read and interpret authoritative legal texts such as judicial and administrative opinions, statutes, and procedural rules. The message is that conveying this complex and often confusing body of rules to clients and other interested parties constitutes the core of a lawyer's work.

3. The Boundary Claim

Finally, the codes of conduct explicitly suggest that these formal rules and procedures constrain lawyers as well as clients. By instructing lawyers to "zealously represent their clients within the bounds of the law," the traditional model suggests that the typical lawyer/client relationship takes place within objective, universal, and legitimate boundaries. The reassuring message is that democratically accountable decision makers, as opposed to Platonic lawyers exercising their own political or moral judgment, set both the content of and the limits on the advice clients receive.

Notes In Class

Professor Wilkins's essay identifies various assumptions underlying the legal profession's self-image and ideology. These assumptions in turn yield principles designed to govern the conduct of lawyers. Consider the following questions as you learn more about the Model Rules and today's legal profession.

1. Is there a "traditional" model? The so-called traditional or dominant model is disputed, but on the extreme end of the spectrum, it is essentially a view of the lawyer as a "hired gun" who may—if not must—use any lawful means to achieve the client's goals. This approach can come with two constitutive principles: "(1) a role obligation ('the principle of partisanship') that identifies professionalism with extreme partisan zeal on behalf of the client and (2) the 'principle of nonaccountability,' which insists that the lawyer bears no moral responsibility for the client's goals or the means used to attain them." David Luban, *Lawyers and Justice: An Ethical Study*, at xx (1988) (quoting in part William H. Simon, "The Ideology of Advocacy: Procedural Justice and Professional Ethics," 1978 Wis. L. Rev. 29); David Luban, *Legal Ethics and Human Dignity* 9 (2007). Not everyone agrees that this model is consistent with the way most lawyers practice, with the way most lawyers see themselves in practice, or with the way that clients see most lawyers, but the model (in one form or another) has been used by academics a great many times, thus prompting the question: is it ethically defensible? Or are the differences among the governing rules and the practice of law in the various relevant jurisdictions sufficiently great that we should recognize variant traditional models?

2. Do everyday lawyer/client interactions conform to the "traditional" model's assumptions about lawyers, clients, and legal advice? If so, how? If not, how do they differ? What interests and experiences do lawyers have that may transcend the generic package of "professional" commitments and "personal" objectives posited by the traditional model?

3. Think about the many different ways in which lawyers may be involved in shaping client goals. Don't the ways in which lawyers characterize legal rules and factual contingencies to their clients influence, to a greater or lesser degree, what clients see as their goals and how to achieve them? If so, how does this affect your view about whether, and the extent to which, lawyers bear moral responsibility for the ends and means their clients pursue? Revisit these questions after you read Professor Pepper's argument about the lawyer's "amoral ethical role" in Chapter 3.

4. Taking account of these variegated contexts raises a different kind of problem for legal ethics discourse. Current professional codes of conduct posit a unitary set of normative commitments capable of guiding the practices of all lawyers in all contexts. Once we unpack and contextualize the concepts of "lawyer," "client," and "legal advice," however, is it evident that there is no "typical" lawyer/client relationship

capable of supporting such a universal framework? Constructing a model that accounts for the full diversity of contextual differences among both lawyers and clients, however, poses practical and normative difficulties. For example, should every lawyer develop his or her own account of legal ethics capable of responding to all of the particular complexities of each individual case? Is it either theoretically coherent or practically important to attempt to define an account of professional ethics that is distinct from personal morality, on the one hand, or the demands of the market, on the other? If we are to retain a distinct notion of "professionalism," where and under what circumstances can this concept be taught? Does the range of legal practices and contexts mean that different rules should be applied to different types of lawyers, or does it mean that different institutions or control mechanisms should monitor the conduct of different types of lawyers?

5. In paragraph two of the excerpt, Wilkins speaks to the assumption of standard ethics discourse that lawyers will conform to the ethics codes' "high" standard. What is a "high" standard? A confidentiality rule that is nearly absolute and therefore demands a strong degree of client loyalty? Or one that makes many exceptions so as to protect third parties? One may ask similar questions about virtually every issue of legal ethics. Practically, furthermore, many now disagree that ethical codes uphold a "high" standard; the codes instead supposedly codify merely the "floor" (i.e., the minimum) below which lawyers' conduct cannot sink. Should codes strive to announce and enforce (or at least guide) high, low, or common (or reasonable?) standards? And for whose benefit are these high, medium, or low standards? The client, the public generally, the courts, justice, the legal profession, or all or some of the preceding constituencies? And is the answer different (or should it be) for different subjects addressed by the rules? In interpreting statutes, courts often look to the constituency sought to be protected by the applicable statute or common law. Courts and disciplinary authorities are faced with similar questions when interpreting the ethical rules governing lawyers. Finally, as you will consider in Chapter 2, what should we make of a rule that says that a lawyer "may" reveal a client's confidential information? Is it "high" in the sense that permission is given to disclose the important information but "low" in the sense that revelation is not required? And what do "high" and "low" mean anyhow? From whose perspective are we looking—the lawyer's, the client's, or society's?

C. Regulating the Legal Profession Beyond the Rules: An Overview

Although the Model Rules and case law are the primary sources of the law of professional responsibility, it is important to recognize that these rules, and the accompanying system of professional discipline, are only one of the ways in which lawyers are regulated. For more than a century, bar leaders have argued that disciplinary agencies acting under the supervision of state supreme courts should have primary responsibility for enforcing the rules of professional responsibility. Notwithstanding these claims, however, lawyers have always been subject to a variety of "sanctioning systems" that can, and often do, exert an important influence on a lawyer's understanding of his or her ethical responsibilities. These additional sources of regulatory authority can usefully be grouped into six categories: disciplinary controls, liability controls, institutional controls, legislative controls, market controls, and peer group controls. These systems all share many important attributes and often purport to accomplish the same goals. Nevertheless, as you will see from the following brief summaries, each control mechanism has unique structural features. These differences arguably have important implications for each of the three core questions that lie at the heart of any professional regulatory system: what will be the *content* of professional norms; what measures should society take to ensure that lawyers *comply* with those norms; and how to ensure that whatever enforcement system we choose preserves the bar's status as an *independent* profession. You should keep these larger goals in mind as you consider examples of these alternative regulatory structures in the following Chapters. We will return to the general issue of enforcement in the context of competence, malpractice, and professional discipline in Chapter 10.

1. Disciplinary controls: The reference point for this model is the current disciplinary system, in which independent or quasi-independent agencies acting under the supervision of state supreme courts investigate and prosecute violations of the rules of professional conduct. As their hammer, these agencies threaten or impose discipline, which typically means one (or more) of the following sanctions: private or public reprimand, probation, suspension, or disbarment. The basic structure resembles a criminal prosecution. Every jurisdiction has a body that imposes discipline under the authority of the court system. To avoid the appearance of favoritism or bias, disciplinary enforcement is consciously set apart from the day-to-day performance of legal work. The process is conducted almost exclusively ex post by independent officials who have no prior association with the case. These officials are instructed to reach their judgments solely on the basis of the evidence presented at a formal hearing in which the accused lawyer is accorded a wide (but varied) array of due process protections. In keeping with the criminal justice analogy, disciplinary agencies primarily focus on punishment and deterrence, and they often identify their primary goal as public protection. Compensation, although allowed under limited circumstances, remains a secondary goal.

In part to help lawyers avoid this disciplinary system, every jurisdiction also has one or more ethics committees that give advice to lawyers faced with a problem of professional responsibility. Most of these are affiliated with state or local bar associations and have no governmental authority. As such, the opinions they give and the advice they render have little or no official status. Nevertheless, they often provide a safe harbor for lawyers who follow their advice and are quite frequently relied on by courts when an issue arises. A few state ethics committees are court-appointed; their opinions have official status and are subject to judicial review.

2. Liability Controls: Injured clients, and to a limited extent third parties, have traditionally had the right to sue lawyers under a variety of statutory and common law theories. The most common theories of liability include professional negligence, breach of fiduciary duty, and aiding and abetting whatever tort the lawyers' client allegedly committed. Although bar leaders and others have tried to separate "mal-practice" from "discipline," these efforts have been largely unsuccessful. Recent developments are likely to blur the distinction even further. For example, the Resolution Trust Company filed a number of lawsuits alleging that several prominent law firms committed malpractice when, in conjunction with the managers of various savings and loans, they prevented regulators from discovering massive financial impropri-eties at these federally insured institutions. See p. 371ff. Similarly, as courts and legislatures slowly relax the traditional restrictions against lawsuits brought by non-clients, a growing number of third parties are suing lawyers for breaching ethical duties. As a result, litigation is now a viable alternative to professional discipline. Fur-thermore, although the ethical rules are designed primarily for disciplinary enforce-ment, the rules acknowledge (a bit begrudgingly) that a rule violation may be evidence that the lawyer fell below the applicable standard of care or otherwise breached a fidu-ciary duty. (For example: "Violation of a Rule should not itself give rise to a cause of action against a lawyer nor should it create any presumption in such a case that a legal duty has been breached. . . . Nevertheless, since the Rules do establish standards of conduct by lawyers, a lawyer's violation of a Rule may be evidence of breach of the applicable standard of conduct." Model Rules of Prof'l Conduct Scope cmt. 20.)

Like the disciplinary model, liability controls operate on the basis of ex post com-plaints by injured parties (but the parties, not the disciplinary authorities, bear the costs of investigation and prosecution). A victorious claimant, however, is entitled to full compensatory and occasionally even punitive damages. Restrictions on the lawyer's right to practice law, on the other hand, are generally not available. Finally, claims are subject to the normal rules of practice and procedure that govern litiga-tion in state and federal courts, including, when appropriate, trial by jury.

3. Institutional Controls: Lawyers work either directly in, or in the shadow of, state institutions, especially (but not exclusively) courts. With increasing frequency, these institutions are expressly taking responsibility for uncovering and sanctioning lawyer misconduct. For example, Rule 11 authorizes judges to impose sanctions for certain kinds of litigation-related misconduct. As another prominent example, courts dis-qualify lawyers and law firms from cases if the courts find or suspect that those firms or lawyers have violated the ethical rules. Although cries about courts' overuse of this remedy are arguably overblown, disqualification does indeed impose real costs on the lawyer (who may lose the past, present, and future legal fees associated with the case), the client (who loses the lawyer of choice and now has to find and pay a new lawyer), and the system (through, for example, the delay attendant to the dis-qualification proceedings and the need to give the new lawyer time to learn the case). See, e.g., Bruce A. Green, "Conflicts of Interest in Litigation: The Judicial Role," 65 Fordham L. Rev. 71 (1996); Keith Swisher, "The Practice and Theory of Lawyer

Disqualification," 27 Geo. J. Legal Ethics 71 (2014) (identifying ten types of ethical violations that periodically result in disqualification). Because courts often address lawyers' conflicts of interest in the context of disqualification motions, you will see several examples in Chapter 4, which introduces the rules governing conflicts. Interestingly, a majority of state courts will also consider disqualifying a lawyer if that lawyer has created the "appearance of impropriety," even though the lawyer's conduct may not have violated any specific ethical rule. These courts are concerned with (among other considerations) the public's confidence in the judicial system and therefore disqualify lawyers when the circumstances of the representation might appear improper to the public. The Model Code also permitted a lawyer to be disciplined for creating an appearance of impropriety, but the Model Rules have jettisoned this basis as vague and inconsistent with the lawyer's due process rights. (Judges, however, are still subject to an "appearance of impropriety" standard with respect to their own conduct.) Do you believe that the courts should be concerned with, and take action to prevent, the appearance of impropriety in cases before them?

In addition to Rule 11 sanctions and disqualification in the courts, several federal administrative agencies, including the Securities and Exchange Commission (SEC), the former Office of Thrift Services (OTS), the Patent and Trademark Office (PTO), and the Internal Revenue Service (IRS) have sanctioned lawyers who did not properly advise their clients about their duties under these regulatory regimes. These and similar efforts share a common goal: to locate enforcement authority inside the institutions in which lawyers work. As a result, the structure and operation of any particular system will primarily be a function of the institution within which it is situated. Nevertheless, a few generalizations are useful. First, enforcement authorities are in a position to observe lawyer misconduct directly. A judge, for example, will know if a lawyer has failed to file a pleading or is playing conflicting roles in the case. Second, because the enforcement official and the lawyer to be disciplined are involved in a continuing relationship, sanctions can be imposed either immediately or after a separate hearing. Finally, the substantive jurisdiction of these institutional enforcement officials is likely to be confined to the area in which the institution operates. For example, SEC officials cannot discipline lawyers outside of the securities area and courts cannot typically disqualify lawyers from cases before other courts or tribunals.

4. Legislative Controls: Certain public officials and other commentators have proposed a new administrative agency that would have sole responsibility for investigating and prosecuting lawyer misconduct. Although such an agency might be patterned after the agencies that currently regulate doctors in many states, nothing requires this particular form. Instead, an agency might adopt procedures utilized by other regulatory agencies, such as the Occupational Safety and Health Administration (OSHA) or the Securities and Exchange Commission. All that is required of this form of control is that its authority and operation ultimately rest in the hands of the executive or the legislative branch rather than the courts. At present, however,

legislative controls do not govern most lawyers beyond those laws and regulations generally applicable to everyone (e.g., criminal law, fraud regulations, and so on). In many states, furthermore, the legislature is affirmatively limited or outright prohibited from regulating lawyers qua lawyers (including even certain entrance criteria, such as bar examinations or law school requirements). This is often referred to as the "inherent powers" doctrine, in which courts banish or restrict the legislature from infringing on the courts' inherent powers to regulate the practice of law. See, e.g., Laurel A. Rigertas, "Lobbying and Litigating Against 'Legal Bootleggers' — The Role of the Organized Bar in the Expansion of the Courts' Inherent Powers in the Early Twentieth Century," 46 Cal. W. L. Rev. 65 (2009) (discussing the history of the inherent powers doctrine and the bar's efforts to influence it); Charles W. Wolfram, "Inherent Powers in the Crucible of Lawyer Self-Protection: Reflections on the LLP Campaign," 39 S. Tex. L. Rev. 359 (1998) (discussing "affirmative" and "negative" uses of the doctrine); Keith Swisher, "The Short History of Arizona Legal Ethics," 45 Ariz. St. L.J. 813 (2013) (noting failed legislative attempts to regulate bar examinations or law school requirements). When push comes to shove, however, legislatures can get their way or force a compromise given that they hold the power of the purse over judicial funding. Nevertheless, legislatures do not generally assert control over lawyers' ethics (although we will see some actual and potential exceptions later in this book).

5. Market Controls: Lawyers have always delivered their services through the market. As we will see, however, until recently individual lawyers and the profession as a whole enjoyed both formal and informal protection against market competition, including restrictions on fee competition and advertising and substantial deference from clients and other professionals. Although the profession as a whole retains its monopoly status, many of the barriers to competition among lawyers and between lawyers and other professionals have been substantially reduced or eliminated. Indeed, after decades of being of minor importance, the question of who can provide "legal" advice to individuals or corporations and the attendant problem of defining what constitutes "the unauthorized practice of law" have taken center stage. All of these developments have highlighted the importance of market controls as a form of professional regulation.

More recently, another force has appeared in molding professional behavior: malpractice insurance companies. Prodded by an enormous increase in malpractice judgments and settlements, legal malpractice insurers have been taking an increasingly active role not only in educating their insureds but also in monitoring and supervising their practices. The more aggressive carriers have effected many changes in the standards of law practice and in some ways have become the principal regulators. Furthermore, insurance companies generally, not just malpractice carriers, have had a large influence on lawyers' billing practices and exert additional influence on their retained lawyers.

Finally, state supreme courts and bar associations have begun to regulate with an eye toward, or emphasis on, market pressures. For example, to encourage lawyers to secure malpractice insurance for the possible later benefit of aggrieved clients, certain states now publicly post whether a lawyer is insured. Certain states also post public disciplinary sanctions next to a lawyer's contact information in the bar directories, thus making it more likely that prospective clients will see a lawyer's less-than-stellar disciplinary record.

6. Peer Group Control: One's colleagues in a firm or in the specialized part of the bar in which the lawyer works, or in a small town practice or other like context usually exert strong pressure on the manner in which a lawyer practices and therefore constitute an additional mechanism setting the standard by which lawyers conduct themselves in practice. Large and medium-sized firms have also been increasingly adding in-house or general counsel to provide ethical and risk management guidance to the firm's lawyers. Furthermore, lawyer referral networks—bar-related and informal marketing devices that will be discussed in Chapter 9—also can exert pressures and expectations on the lawyers within them.

Finally, beyond the six controls above, bars and courts have been increasingly imposing administrative or educational requirements, designed to foster professional development and client protection. These include mandatory continuing legal education (including, at least in some states, mandatory ethics credits), mandatory trust account reporting, dues for client protection funds, and as noted above, malpractice insurance requirements (or at least required disclosure as to whether a lawyer has malpractice insurance).

Bar & courts → imposing admin / educational req. to foster pd & cp

———

The concluding Problem in this Chapter provides an introduction to the various pressures that may be brought on a lawyer trying to reconcile her job status with her professional role.

Problem 1–2 *In class*

"The Case of the Shredded Memo"

Anita Charles smiled as she walked back to her office at Taylor & Pierce, one of San Francisco's most prestigious law firms. All her law school classmates told her she was crazy for accepting a job at T & P. While everyone acknowledged the quality of the firm's work, especially in the corporate area where Anita wanted to practice, its track record for hiring and promoting women and minorities was probably the worst of any major firm in the city. Indeed, only eight of T & P's 100 partners were women, and Lysa Peters, a sixth-year black associate, had been the firm's only minority lawyer for over two years. Moreover, the firm had a reputation for being tough and associates who could not "cut the mustard" were quickly shown the door. All in all, T & P did not seem to be the ideal place for a black woman who did not want to spend her life at the office.

Yet despite its reputation Anita had been favorably impressed with T & P in the interview process. Unlike other San Francisco firms, T & P had promised Anita a steady diet of sophisticated corporate work. Moreover, when she pressed the head of the Corporate Department about the firm's dismal record with minorities, she felt his response exhibited genuine concern and a commitment to addressing the problem. Trusting her instincts, Anita accepted T & P's offer.

After three months on the job, Anita was sure she had made the right decision. Not only was her work uniformly interesting, but she had been given significant responsibility on a number of projects. The assignment she had just received from Steve Langford, one of the firm's brightest young corporate partners, was no exception.

The assignment involved Speedway Transport Company, a medium-sized entrant in the competitive package delivery market, that Langford had recently brought into the firm (reputedly to much applause from the partnership). In essence, the facts were as follows. About four months ago, John Hartman, a senior vice president of Speedway, informed Langford that some Speedway salesmen were making cash payments to employees of Speedway customers for the purpose of securing business. The company in turn refunded the payment to the salesmen in the form of increased commissions. According to Hartman, payments were made on approximately ten percent of Speedway's gross sales and currently totaled about $500,000. Concerned about the impact on Speedway if these payments became public, Hartman asked Langford for his advice.

Stunned by the news, Langford told Hartman that the payments undoubtedly violated several civil and criminal statutes and that they must be discontinued immediately. He then asked Hartman how the company had treated the payments in its financial statements and federal income tax returns. After some hesitation, Hartman conceded that the payments had been recorded as legitimate commissions and were deducted as business expenses for both financial and federal income tax purposes. Langford stated that this treatment of the illegal payments was fraudulent and that the company should make full disclosure to both its auditors and the IRS. Hartman said he would relate Langford's advice to the president and other senior executives, and would be back in touch shortly.

A few days later, Hartman called Langford to tell him that the company had decided to discontinue the illegal payments. However, the company refused to disclose its past fraud to its auditors or to the IRS. Moreover, Hartman indicated that the company intended to continue treating the payoffs already made as legitimate commissions on both its current financial statement and corporate income tax return. Despite Langford's urgings, Hartman stated that the company was adamant about not making full disclosure. Langford then informed him that T & P could not participate in the filing of a fraudulent tax return. Hartman said he understood and would not ask the firm to assist in any way in the preparation of the return.

This is where the matter stood until two weeks ago when Langford received a standard audit letter from Peat Ross & Anderson, Speedway's auditors. This letter, which was sent by auditors to counsel for audited companies, asked, inter alia, whether the law firm was aware of any material unasserted claims against Speedway that were probable of assertion in the foreseeable future. Auditors rely on the answers to these letters in certifying a company's financial statements.

Langford asked Anita to prepare a short memorandum addressing how the firm should respond to the auditor's letter. While indicating that Anita should survey the relevant ethical issues, Langford stressed that he needed her memo as soon as possible so that the auditors could be answered without undue delay. As an afterthought, Langford told Anita that since this assignment was primarily for the benefit of the firm and not the client, she should bill her time to the firm's Ethics Committee.

For the next three days, Anita buried herself in the Speedway assignment. After skimming the case file, as she always did when starting a new assignment, Anita read all of the relevant code provisions, ethics opinions and judicial decisions she could find. At the end of this intensive investigation, Anita had no doubt as to what the firm should do. Her only doubt was how best to break the news to Langford.

In Anita's mind the issue was straightforward and capable of but one resolution. Speedway had both made illegal payments in the past and expressed its intention to continue to defraud its auditors and the IRS. While the Model Rules prohibited the firm from disclosing its client's confidences, it also mandated that the firm could not counsel or assist the client in the perpetration of a fraud. Anita believed that answering the auditor's letter without disclosing the potential claim against Speedway by the IRS would amount to assisting the client's fraud.

This conclusion was not based on any specific ethics opinion, policy statement or decision. Indeed, the literal language of the source most directly on point, the Statement of Policy Regarding Lawyers' Responses to Auditors' Requests for Information, jointly issued by the ABA and the American Institute of Certified Public Accountants (AICPA), seemed to allow T & P to tell the auditor that there were no material unasserted claims against Speedway. In pertinent part, the joint statement provides that a lawyer should only inform an auditor about those possible unasserted claims that the client has specifically identified as being probable of assertion, likely to result in unfavorable outcomes, and material to its financial condition. Moreover, although the statement requires that the lawyer consult with the client regarding questions of disclosure, and allows her to resign if her advice on this subject is disregarded by the client, such resignation is not mandatory unless it is clear that (1) the undisclosed matter is of material importance and (2) there can be no reasonable doubt that nondisclosure in the client's financial statement would be a violation of law giving rise to material claims.

Anita was well aware that a good faith argument could be made that the potential claim by the IRS was not "probable of assertion" since there was no indication that anyone had detected the illegal payoffs. Similarly, given the uncertainty about whether the payoffs would ever be detected, it could legitimately be argued that it was not "clear" beyond a "reasonable doubt" that the non-disclosure of the potential IRS claim would give rise to "material claims" against Speedway by those relying on the company's financial statement. Under this view, therefore, T & P was not required to resign because Speedway declined to follow the firm's advice regarding disclosure. Instead, the firm would be free to follow the client's instructions and inform the auditors that it had no knowledge of any material unasserted claims that were probable of assertion in the foreseeable future.

Anita, however, was not satisfied with this line of argument. Prior to going to law school, Anita spent two years at a Big Four accounting firm in their audit department. Based on this experience, she knew that Speedway's auditors would use the company's financial statement as the basis for preparing its tax return. Therefore, even though the firm had refused to assist Speedway directly in the preparation of a fraudulent tax return, by helping the company to deceive its auditors into believing that the financial statement was correct, the firm would indirectly be contributing to that effort. This, Anita believed, would violate the spirit of trust between auditors and lawyers that the joint ABA/AICPA statement intended to create.

Moreover, Anita was also concerned that Speedway might be actively misleading T & P as well as its auditors. While leafing through the case file, Anita discovered a memo written by Langford indicating that one month after Speedway discontinued the payments, it increased the commission paid to those salesmen who had been involved in the prior illegal activity in an amount roughly equivalent to the size of the allegedly discontinued payments. According to Langford's memo, Speedway raised the commissions to compensate the salesmen for the loss of business expected to result from the termination of the payments. To Anita's auditor-trained eyes, however, this action provided a strong indication that the improper payments were still being made.

Given all of these factors, Anita was convinced that the firm should decline to answer the audit letter and should resign from any further representation of Speedway. In her memo to Langford setting forth these conclusions, Anita was careful to state all of the arguments in favor of answering the letter and continuing to represent the client. However, relying on the broad rules allowing, though not requiring, a lawyer to withdraw if the client seeks to pursue an illegal course of conduct, Anita argued strongly that withdrawal was in the firm's best interest. With some trepidation, Anita had her memo delivered to Langford.

By the time Anita came in at 9:30 the next morning there were three messages from Langford instructing her to come see him as soon as she arrived. With a sinking feeling in her stomach, Anita went to Langford's office. As she had feared, he was very upset. In the forty-five minutes that followed, Langford berated Anita for her "law school naivete" and unwillingness to focus on what was in the best interest of the client. He flatly stated that he found the first part of her memo, noting the good faith argument in favor of answering the letter as the client wished, dispositive of the matter. T & P's obligation was to represent Speedway zealously within the bounds of the law. So long as the relevant rules could reasonably be interpreted to allow the firm to honor the client's wishes, it was ethically required to do so. Moreover, Langford sharply remarked, to refuse to answer the letter would effectively reveal information reported to the firm in confidence, since it would undoubtedly alert Peat Ross to the possibility of an error in Speedway's financial statement. Langford let Anita know in no uncertain terms that he found her argument that the firm might be assisting an ongoing fraud totally unpersuasive. The relevant inquiry, Langford asserted, was whether the firm directly assisted in the perpetration of a fraud. The combination of the firm's good faith basis for honoring the client's wishes and T & P's refusal to assist in the preparation of the tax return, made clear that no such direct involvement was present in this case.

Finally, Langford dismissed Anita's suggestion that the illegal payments might be ongoing. The client had personally assured Langford that the payments had stopped. This assurance, Langford maintained, was all that a lawyer required. It was neither his responsibility nor even his right to play judge and jury with respect to his client, and he would not have any first-year associate trying to push him into that position.

The meeting concluded by Langford telling Anita that based on the first part of her memo, he was satisfied that the firm should follow the client's instructions on answering the audit letter. Handing her his copy of the memo, he instructed her to collect all other copies and drafts and to "shred" the whole pile as quickly as possible. "We can't have memos like this in our files," Langford stated. "One day it could prove embarrassing to our client."

Anita was stunned. While she knew her memo was controversial, she was shocked by the way Langford had simply dismissed each of her arguments based on little more than his desire to help the client. Moreover, she was deeply disturbed by his instruction to shred her memo. She had never heard of anything like that ever being done before. Anita decided that she needed to talk to someone else before she decided what to do.

Anita went to see Lysa Peters, the firm's only other black lawyer, and briefly told her the whole story. Peters' response was direct and to the point. She began by reminding Anita that Langford was considered to be a rising star in the corporate department. "At this firm," Peters said, "associates are judged by their ability to work well with partners. My advice to you is simply to do what you are told. After all, Langford has been at this business ten or fifteen years longer than you have. His judgment about ethical issues is bound to be better than yours. In any event, if he is wrong, he will be the one to bear the blame. All you can do by protesting further is to get yourself in trouble."

Anita felt even more troubled as she walked back to her office. She knew much of what Lysa Peters said was correct. Where did she get off thinking that she knew more about the practical workings of the ethics rules than a junior partner in the city's leading corporate department? Anita also knew that to take the matter any further would risk getting herself in even more trouble. Yet she could not shake her belief that something was fundamentally wrong with the course Langford intended to pursue. By the time she reached her office, Anita knew that she would not be able to concentrate on anything else until she resolved this issue in her own mind. So she told her secretary she had errands to run for the rest of the day, got her coat, and left T & P to consider what, if anything, she should do.

a. What would you do if you were Anita Charles? In formulating your answer, consider the differences between Anita's and Langford's conception of the lawyer's role. How do you think the two visions were constructed and what interest does each seek to protect? Which of these different visions most closely approximates your understanding of the prevailing formulation of a lawyer's duties and obligations? Consider the ways in which Anita's personal identity and background play into your assessment: is it important for your analysis that she has a background in accounting? That she is a woman? A person of color? If so, why? If not, why not?

b. If you were creating a legal system from scratch, which vision of the lawyer's role would you choose as your organizing principle? Or would you reject both conceptions as being too narrow and design a system in which lawyers would have an affirmative obligation to ensure that a client's fraud did not go undetected? These issues will be discussed more specifically in Chapter 2 and Chapter 5.

c. Does the story of Anita Charles tend to make you more accepting of multidisciplinary practices (MDP), or more leery of unions between lawyers and accountants? Why? The efforts of lawyers and accountants to reconcile different approaches to their duties toward clients and toward the public at large are discussed in Chapter 5. We take up the MDP debate in Chapter 8.

d. Anita's trusted confidant told her two propositions: (1) "Langford has been at this business ten or fifteen years longer than you have. His judgment about ethical issues is bound to be better than yours," and (2) "In any event, if he is wrong, he will be the one to bear the blame." Although both propositions are understandable and not infrequently muttered by new associates, both propositions are false or at least dubious. On the first proposition, some studies suggest that newcomers to the practice of law (or other area) are better at identifying ethical issues and framing problems in moral terms. See, e.g., Catherine Gage O'Grady, "Behavioral Legal Ethics, Decision Making, and the New Attorney's Unique Professional Perspective," 15 Nev. L.J. 671 (2015) (noting that, although new attorneys are more susceptible to certain pressures, they are generally better at identifying ethical issues). On the second proposition, the ethical rules take an individual approach, as noted above; in other words, each lawyer (whatever the place in the firm's hierarchy) is ethically accountable for the lawyer's own misconduct (and a supervisory lawyer may also be accountable for the ethical misconduct of a subordinate lawyer). See Model Rules of Prof'l Conduct R. 5.1–5.2. In Chapter 4, we consider the true story of an associate who was held liable for legal malpractice, even though the partner-in-charge explicitly pushed the associate to take the ethically problematic actions. Do you think that Model Rule 5.2 strikes the right balance of accountability and fairness for associates in similar positions? For a heated debate on the wisdom of the rule, compare Andrew M. Perlman, "The Silliest Rule of Professional Conduct," The Prof'l Lawyer, Vol. 19, No. 3 (2009), at 14, with Douglas R. Richmond, "Academic Silliness About Model Rule 5.2(b)," The Prof'l Lawyer, Vol. 19, No. 3, at 15.

e. Consider how the conduct of Anita Charles and her law firm would be and should be regulated in this context: should disciplinary controls be applied, or should market controls that govern reputations and insurance liability be applied? Some mix of controls?

Chapter 2

Confidentiality

The lawyer's confidentiality obligation is one of the most distinctive, pervasive, and controversial of all professional obligations. This Chapter discusses the obligation in three stages: (A) the lawyer-client relationship, from which the lawyer's obligation of confidentiality typically stems; (B) the general rule of confidentiality and the related but distinct doctrine of attorney-client privilege; and (C) exceptions to the rule of confidentiality.

A. The Lawyer-Client Relationship and Its Obligations

In most instances, the formation of a lawyer-client relationship is a straightforward application of basic contract law. A would-be client with a problem seeks out a lawyer, explains the problem, asks for help, and after discussion of both the problem and the fee agreement, the lawyer agrees to undertake representation. Sometimes the nature of the relationship is such that the lawyer or law firm ends up making a proposal (or even a bid), and the final act is the agreement by the client to hire the lawyer or law firm. In most of the situations we deal with in these materials, the lawyer-client relationship arises in a similar fashion. As the law in this area has developed, however, explicit contract is not the only way in which a lawyer may acquire a client.[1] The watchword is "the reasonable expectations" of the would-be client, and many lawyers have discovered that for a variety of reasons, including carelessness, they have unexpectedly acquired clients, or obligations to would-be clients and others. Electronic communication has dramatically increased the need for lawyers to be aware of the possibility that casual communication may result in a lawyer-client relationship. See, e.g., Model Rules of Prof'l Conduct R. 1.18 cmt. 2 (A lawyer-client

---

1. As the Restatement of the Law Governing Lawyers generally puts it, the "relationship of client and lawyer" arises when:

> (1) a person manifests to a lawyer the person's intent that the lawyer provide legal services for the person; and either
>> (a) the lawyer manifests to the person consent to do so; or
>> (b) the lawyer fails to manifest lack of consent to do so, and the lawyer knows or reasonably should know that the person reasonably relies on the lawyer to provide the services; or
> (2) a tribunal with power to do so appoints the lawyer to provide the services.

Restatement (Third) of the Law Governing Lawyers § 14 (2000).

[handwritten margin note: How relationship is formed.]

"consultation is likely to have occurred if a lawyer, either in person or through the lawyer's advertising in any medium [such as a website or Facebook page], specifically requests or invites the submission of information about a potential representation without clear and reasonably understandable warnings and cautionary statements that limit the lawyer's obligations, and a person provides information in response"); Martyn, "Accidental Clients," 33 Hofstra L. Rev. 913 (2005). We will encounter the problem at numerous places in these materials. However the relationship arises, the critical point is this: *the client is the person to whom you owe the highest fiduciary and ethical obligations, including the duty of confidentiality explored in this Chapter.*

Lawyers must constantly keep in mind not just whether they *have* a client in a particular matter but who the client *actually is.* By way of example, lawyers frequently represent organizations—the government, corporations, LLCs, or unions. Yet lawyers cannot talk directly to "an organization" because it is a legal fiction. Rather, lawyers must get their direction from individual agents of the organization. Those agents will typically have authority to give information and instructions to the lawyers on behalf of the organization. (When that authority is in question, the lawyer for the organization must tread very carefully, a point to which we will turn in Chapter 5.) The tendency is for lawyers who have regular dealings with those agents to come to see those agents, especially high-level agents, as their clients. But when professional responsibility issues arise, we shall see that lawyers constantly need to keep in mind who "the client" is in any given representation and to whom their ultimate fiduciary duties of loyalty and confidentiality (among other duties) are owed. In many cases, it will not be the person from whom they are receiving instructions or legal fees (e.g., the general counsel or the managing member of an LLC). The same problem may arise in some instances of individual representation. Think of the lawyer representing a child when the parents are paying the fee or the lawyer representing an insured when the insurance company is paying the fee. Often substantive law beyond the rules of professional responsibility will define the loyalty obligations of the lawyer. In sum, identifying—and staying strictly loyal to—the client is not always as simple as it might seem. By failing to keep the actual client in mind and at heart, many lawyers have suffered significantly: facing a disqualification, termination, a legal malpractice suit, or a loss or suspension of their law license.

Many of the obligations of a lawyer to a client, including the obligation of confidentiality discussed below, have been codified in the rules of professional responsibility adopted by the different jurisdictions. By way of example, the ABA's Model Rules 1.1 and 1.3 state the basic obligations of competence and diligence. One constantly recurring issue is control over the means used to achieve the client's objectives. Consider the following Problem.

Problem 2–1

In class

Your law firm has been hired on a contingent-fee basis in a dispute between two branches of a family over ownership of a block of stock that will determine control of the family business. The issue involves an ambiguous provision in the will of a recently deceased family member that left shares to "issue" of the decedent. At the time the will was drafted, the decedent's three children had all died. Your client, Leslie, is the only child of Steven, the eldest child of the decedent. The decedent's other two children, Miranda and Isabella, had left four and five children respectively. If the grandchildren inherited the shares equally, your client would be entitled to one-tenth of the shares. If they inherited through their parent by right of representation, your client would be entitled to one-third of the shares, enough to tip control to her family group. Leslie has instructed you that her objective in the litigation is to obtain enough shares, whether by suit or by settlement, to give her family group control of the family business. The contingent-fee arrangement is based on one-third of the value of the stock obtained in the litigation above the one-tenth that everyone concedes is due to your client.

After a great deal of testimony has been taken about the "intent" of the decedent, and settlement talks have been unsuccessful, an aunt of your client, who is now well into her 90s, mentions to you that it was well known among her family's generation that the decedent was not Isabella's biological parent. If that story can be corroborated, then the claim of Isabella's children is considerably weakened, if not destroyed, and your client's claim would be raised to either one-fifth or one half of the devised shares. One-fifth would be sufficient to shift control of the family business to her family group (and for you to receive a large fee).

You inform your client of the aunt's story and express your intent to take her deposition immediately and to press for DNA testing. To your surprise, your client says that she does not want you to do this, and indeed she does not want you to raise this issue or repeat the aunt's story to anyone. Much as she wishes to prevail in the lawsuit, she believes that raising the issue could make currently difficult family relations impossible. You respond that the relations seem impossible in any event, that you were hired to achieve control of the family business, and that it is your best judgment that Leslie will not prevail in the current state of the testimony. You also mention that while Leslie's wishes control the objectives of the representation, the rules of professional responsibility leave the choice of the means of achievement of those objectives largely to the lawyer. Moreover, you point out that Leslie will have great difficulty inducing any replacement lawyer to take on representation on a contingent fee basis unless she allows the lawyer to pursue the aunt's lead. Finally, you add that you do not understand how she expects you to continue to represent her and undertake a difficult trial with your hands tied. Leslie asks whether she understands you to be saying that you will withdraw from the case if she does not permit you to follow the strategy you have outlined. How do you respond? Most jurisdictions have adopted the text of Model Rule 1.2. Does it resolve the dispute between the client and lawyer? Many jurisdictions have not formally adopted the Comments to the Model Rules. Is Comment 2 consistent with the Rule itself? Does it help the lawyer (and client) resolve the disagreement? How does the fact that the ability of the lawyer to earn any fee at all may well turn on the outcome of the dispute over strategy affect your view of your appropriate action? Why, moreover, should a client get to dictate what a lawyer can and cannot say in litigation or elsewhere?

B. The Obligation of Confidentiality

1. The General Rule

The rules relating to lawyer-client confidentiality are at the heart of the adversary system. The breadth of the confidentiality principle is seen by some to be too much of an obstacle to the truth-seeking function of judge or jury and by others to conflict with the normal rules of morality. The exceptions to the broad rule of confidentiality that have been (or will be) recognized determine to a good degree what we mean when we say that we have an adversary system. These exceptions to the confidentiality obligation will be examined by looking at particular categories in which the common or compelling issues arise. This Chapter discusses the doctrine of confidentiality, while Chapter 3 discusses the various justifications for confidentiality. Whether that material is considered before, with, or after this Chapter, it is highly relevant to the issues presented in this Chapter.

The confidentiality obligation states the duty of the attorney to keep information about a client's affairs private as part of the general duty of loyalty that a lawyer as agent owes to a client as principal. Moreover, according to the policy, confidentiality promotes more information sharing between client and attorney, which in turn promotes more fully formed legal advice.

The rules relating to confidentiality in most jurisdictions begin with the sweeping generalization that they cover all "information relating to the representation of a client," thus making it clear that the rule "applies not only to matters communicated in confidence by the client but also to all information relating to the representation, whatever its source." Comment 3 to Model Rule 1.6. (The attorney-client privilege, in contrast, generally includes only private communications between the attorney and client, or their agents, for the purpose of giving or receiving legal advice, as distinguished in the next subsection.) Whether Model Rule 1.6 should be read literally is another matter. Is legal knowledge acquired in the course of handling a client's matter subject to the confidentiality obligation? What about factual information that is common knowledge? The Model Rules deal with that issue in a curious fashion. Rule 1.9(c)(1) states that a lawyer may not use a *former* client's information to that client's disadvantage unless permitted or required by specific Rules or when the information "has become generally known." With respect to the lawyer's current clients, Model Rule 1.6 places information that is "generally known" within the general category of protected information but then creates an exception for it for information learned from former representations. If information that is "generally known" falls within the confidentiality obligation, why was a special exception thought necessary for this one provision? It is difficult to believe that the drafters meant all commonly known information to be protected under the confidentiality rules, but the language of the Model Rules would seem to imply otherwise.[2]

For example, if attorneys truly have an ethical obligation to keep confidential all "information relating to the representation of a client," consider whether the following communications would breach that obligation: (1) informing your spouse that you will miss dinner because you are taking a deposition in a neighboring town; (2) educating your client about the law governing the client's problem even though you learned that law while conducting research for another client; (3) telling prospective clients that you have argued and won a victory in an appellate court and stating the name of the published opinion; or (4) asking a colleague in another firm, or even the same firm, about how to handle a procedural issue that has arisen in one of your cases. Model Rule 1.6(a) explicitly bars each of these communications. Practically or doctrinally, however, such communications have been excepted from the rule (or the rule has been honored only in the breach).

In answering the four questions above, consider these additional factors. First, the Model Rules are "rules of reason" and "should be interpreted with reference to the purposes of legal representation and of the law itself." Model Rules Scope cmt. 14. To hold lawyers in violation of the ethical rules for telling their spouses where they are (and perhaps not even mentioning the case's name when doing so) would be an unreasonable interpretation of the otherwise broad confidentiality obligation. Such a broad interpretation would not help clients and would hamper lawyers. Second, lawyers are supposed to be competent in the law, and if lawyers could not use the legal research and knowledge gained for one client on behalf of a future client, lawyers would be either less competent or unable to take on new clients.[3] (Moreover, as a practical matter, such a regime would likely limit lawyers' ability to practice law for clients, which the rules elsewhere prohibit to ensure that clients have a robust choice of lawyers. See Model Rule 5.6.) Furthermore, some states (but not nearly a majority) explicitly except from the confidentiality obligation "(i) a lawyer's legal knowledge

---

2. The Restatement's definition of confidentiality specifically excepts "information that is generally known." Restatement (Third) of Law Governing Lawyers § 59 (2000). The comments to the Restatement elaborate on what is, and is not, "generally known" information:

> Whether information is generally known depends on all circumstances relevant in obtaining the information. Information contained in books or records in public libraries, public-record depositories such as government offices, or in publicly accessible electronic-data storage is generally known if the particular information is obtainable through publicly available indexes and similar methods of access. Information is not generally known when a person interested in knowing the information could obtain it only by means of special knowledge or substantial difficulty or expense. Special knowledge includes information about the whereabouts or identity of a person or other source from which information can be acquired, if those facts are not themselves generally known.

Id. cmt. d.

3. The Restatement (unlike the Model Rules) avoids this concern by advising that "[c]onfidential client information does not include what a lawyer learns about the law, legal institutions such as courts and administrative agencies, and similar public matters in the course of representing clients." Id. cmt. e.

or legal research or (ii) information that is generally known in the local community or in the trade, field or profession to which the information relates." N.Y. Rules of Prof'l Conduct R. 1.6(a). Third, in addition to states that permit lawyers to reveal information "generally known in the local community or in the . . . profession," the First Amendment may limit the ability of a state ethical rule to ban lawyers from discussing information in public records.[4] But, for example, is a public record of a criminal conviction in the State of Arkansas twenty years ago "generally known"?

Fourth, and finally (for now), the Model Rules permit several avenues through which lawyers might seek professional guidance for others when working on their matters. Lawyers are permitted to communicate about the client's matter to other lawyers within the same firm, unless the client has forbidden such communication, and even if the lawyers are not within the same firm, lawyers may generally make "use of a hypothetical to discuss issues relating to the representation . . . so long as there is no reasonable likelihood that the listener will be able to ascertain the identity of the client or the situation involved." Model Rule 1.6 cmts. 4–5. On its face, this last exception does not seem to limit the use of such unidentifiable hypotheticals to discussions that might assist the representation (e.g., so that the lawyer may gain advice from a more experienced lawyer about a rule of procedure). If there is no such limitation, may you gossip about clients (as long as you redact names and other possibly identifying circumstances)? Furthermore, the rules also allow lawyers "to secure legal advice" about complying with the ethical rules and to check for conflicts before moving firms.[5] Id. Model Rule 1.6(b)(4) and (7).

Thus, the broad command of confidentiality over all "information relating to the representation of a client" is overbroad. The question then is: what information relating to the representation is covered prima facie by the confidentiality obligation? Some states have attempted to define more precisely the types of information that should be kept confidential as information "(a) protected by the attorney-client privilege, (b) likely to be embarrassing or detrimental to the client if disclosed, or (c) information that the client has requested be kept confidential." N.Y. Rules of

Conf. Info.

---

4. This is a controversial issue. Some authorities conclude that lawyers have First Amendment latitude to speak about public records from completed cases, see Hunter v. Virginia State Bar, 744 S.E.2d 611 (Va. 2013), while other authorities conclude that lawyers' contractual, fiduciary, or officer-of-the-court status should in effect limit their First Amendment right to discuss information otherwise protected by the First Amendment. See Chapter 6.

5. The Model Rules now explicitly permit "lawyers in different firms . . . to disclose limited information to each other to detect and resolve conflicts of interest, such as when a lawyer is considering an association with another firm, two or more firms are considering a merger, or a lawyer is considering the purchase of a law practice." Model Rule 1.6(b)(7) cmt. 13; ABA Ethics Op. 09–455 (2009). But "the disclosure of any information is prohibited if it would compromise the attorney-client privilege or otherwise prejudice the client (e.g., the fact that a corporate client is seeking advice on a corporate takeover that has not been publicly announced; that a person has consulted a lawyer about the possibility of divorce before the person's intentions are known to the person's spouse; or that a person has consulted a lawyer about a criminal investigation that has not led to a public charge)." Model Rule 1.6(b)(7) cmt. 13. We address conflicts of interest in Chapter 4 (and see in particular the *Robert Half* case).

Prof'l Conduct R. 1.6(a); Mass Rules of Prof. Conduct R. 1.6 cmt. 3A. (In the Massachusetts rule, part (c) covers information that the *lawyer has agreed* to keep confidential.)

But such narrower approaches have unintended downsides. Although most courts and commentators would agree that the first category (attorney-client privileged information) should generally be protected, the second and third categories both have problems. With respect to information "likely to be embarrassing or detrimental to the client if disclosed," whose judgment—the client's, the lawyer's, the reasonable person's, the reasonable lawyer's—controls?[6] Information may be "embarrassing" or "detrimental" to the client for reasons unknown or unappreciated by the lawyer— including reasons that develop later in time.[7] The current Model Rule, in contrast, makes everything relating to the representation confidential in the first place and then requires lawyers to ask the client for consent to disclose any information relating to the representation (absent an explicit exception).

With respect to information that the client has requested to be kept confidential (see, e.g., N.Y. Rules of Prof'l Conduct R. 1.6(a)), relying on this category to protect client information might inadvertently create a class system in favor of sophisticated or repeat players. Clients who regularly use lawyers or who have in-house lawyers may request confidentiality for information that would not ordinarily be regarded as "confidential." Poor or one-shot clients will not know how to make this request, and the rules do not require lawyers to inform those clients of their right to make it. The New York definition tries to anticipate the problem of an "overreaching" client demanding too much confidentiality by stating that "confidential information" does not ordinarily include (1) a lawyer's legal knowledge or legal research or (2) information that is generally known in the local community or in the trade, field or profession to which the information relates. But that specification fails to cover all information that would ordinarily not be viewed as confidential, especially since New York's definition of what is confidential includes not only information "relating to" the representation but also information acquired "during" the representation. Massachusetts deals with this issue by having as its third category of what constitutes confidential information not just what "the client requests" but what "the lawyer agrees" to keep confidential. Mass. Rules of Prof. Conduct R. 1.6, cmt 3A. In sum, the scope of the general confidentiality rule remains a live issue, with the Model Rule

---

6. The rules already permit lawyers to disclose information "impliedly authorized" to effectuate the agreed-upon objectives of the representation (in addition to several other disclosure exceptions discussed below). See Model Rule 1.6(a)–(b). Additional exceptions might permit a lawyer to make additional disclosures to suit the lawyer's, not the client's, objectives.

7. Alaska, which follows this narrower approach, resolves any uncertainty in favor of confidentiality (and thus in favor of the client): "In determining whether information relating to representation of a client is protected from disclosure under this rule, the lawyer shall resolve any uncertainty about whether such information can be revealed against revealing the information." Alaska Rules of Prof. Conduct R. 1.6(a).

creating certain problems (e.g., absurdity in its breadth) and the narrower state-specific versions creating other problems.

Courts in particular have considered a number of problems relating to the extent of the lawyer's duty of silence, usually in the context of the attorney-client privilege, but in terms that seem applicable to the confidentiality obligation as well. First, does the privilege (and the general confidentiality obligation) survive the death of the client? A typical, albeit dramatic, case was In re John Doe Grand Jury Investigation, 408 Mass. 480 (1990). A grand jury was investigating the involvement of Charles Stuart and his brother in the murder of Charles' wife and son. The day after he spent two hours with his attorney, Charles Stuart committed suicide. The prosecutor sought to compel the attorney to testify about his conversation with Stuart on the ground that Stuart could not be harmed by the disclosure since he was dead. Therefore society's interest in learning the details of the murder outweighed any value of the attorney-client privilege. Stuart's mother, claiming ownership of the attorney-client privilege as administratrix of her son's estate, refused to waive it. The Supreme Judicial Court upheld the mother's claim. It refused to balance society's interest against the value of the privilege because it feared that a balancing rule might deter clients from "telling all" and thus impair an attorney from functioning effectively. One judge dissented on the ground that the majority's rule was inflexible and that there should be a very narrow interest of justice exception. Was there anything the prosecuting attorney might have done after the decision of the Supreme Judicial Court in order to get the attorney's testimony? See District Attorney v. Magraw, 34 Mass. App. Ct. 713 (1993), for a creative approach in a different case.

A few states have crafted different rules. In HLC Properties, Inc., v. Superior Court, 105 P.3d 560 (2005), the California Supreme Court construed the California Evidence Code to conclude that an individual's attorney-client privilege did not survive the death of the individual and the closing of his estate. In In re Investigation of Death of Miller, 358 N.C. 364 (2004), the North Carolina Supreme Court held that communications between an attorney and a now-deceased client that related solely to a third party are not within the attorney-client privilege at all. It further held that communications that relate to a third party and affect the client's own interests are protected, but disclosure may be compelled on "a clear and convincing showing that their disclosure does not expose the client's estate to civil liability and that such disclosure would not likely result in additional harm to loved ones or reputation." Id. at 367.

The issue also surfaced in the context of the Independent Counsel's investigation of matters involving the administration of then-President Bill Clinton. When the grand jury began investigating the dismissal of employees of the White House Travel Office, White House counsel Vince Foster hired private counsel. When he committed suicide, the grand jury issued a subpoena for the notes taken by Foster's counsel. Reversing the Court of Appeals, the Supreme Court held, 6–3, that the attorney-client privilege survived Foster's death and that the Court would not create an exception to permit a grand jury to obtain notes covered by the privilege even if the information was important to its investigation and unavailable elsewhere. Such an exception would defeat the purpose of the privilege to encourage full and frank conversations between client and lawyer. Swidler & Berlin v. United States, 524 U.S. 399 (1998).

Another issue is control of the privilege after the corporate client has gone into bankruptcy or merged with another entity. While the executor of an estate may become the owner of the decedent's attorney-client privilege after death, the ownership of that privilege and of the lawyer's confidentiality obligation may be more complex in a business setting. In Commodity Futures Trading Corp. v. Weintraub, 471 U.S. 343 (1985), the Supreme Court held that the trustee of a bankrupt corporation succeeded to ownership of the corporation's attorney-client privilege and therefore had the power to waive it. The issue is even more difficult in the context of merger. *ACP & Corp.* The New York Court of Appeals had to deal with ownership of the privilege and the confidentiality obligation when a law firm, which had represented a company for a long time, represented the sole stockholder and the company when it conveyed all its assets and liabilities to a shell corporation and then dissolved. The shell corporation then took the name of the dissolved company and operated the old business. The court held that in practice the old company had not died. Its business continued under new management and therefore control of the duty of confidentiality between the old company and the law firm with respect to the operation of the old company passed to the new corporation. Communications regarding the merger agreement, however, were different. The new corporation did not acquire any rights of the stockholder or his company in that regard. They were adverse to one another in that matter and therefore the stockholder and the old company remained in control of those confidential communications. Tekni-Plex, Inc. v. Meyner & Landis, 89 N.Y.2d 123 (1996). See Moeller v. Superior Court, 16 Cal. 4th 1124 (1997), where the court held that a successor trustee controlled the attorney-client privilege regarding communications between its predecessor trustee and counsel about trust matters. The dissent believed that a California statute superseded the common law attorney-client privilege and vested control of the privilege in the client who consulted counsel. See also Dyntel v. Ebner, 120 F.3d 488 (4th Cir. 1997), where the Court of Appeals held, by a four-to-three vote, that a corporate lawyer who handled some business of a subsidiary had no duty to the purchaser of the subsidiary when a question arose relating to the presale conduct of the subsidiary. Indeed, the court concluded that the purchaser and its lawyers had engaged in "spurious ethical warfare" by raising the issue and remanded the case for imposition of sanctions against both.

Two quite controversial examples of the consequences that may occur when a government body inherits the attorney-client privilege or the confidentiality obligation occurred in the Savings and Loan (S & L) context. The first was the Kaye Scholer matter, "Matter of Fishbein," AP 92-19 (March 1, 1992), reprinted in *The Attorney Client Relationship After Kaye Scholer* (PLI 1992), where the Office of Thrift Supervision (OTS) used information it obtained in this fashion to bring charges against a large New York law firm in connection with its conduct as the failed Savings and

Loan's attorney. See pp. 371–384, where the case is discussed at length. Kaye Scholer disputed the charges, but ended up settling the case and paying an enormous fine. The second instance, O'Melveny & Meyers v. FDIC, 512 U.S. 79 (1994), occurred when the Federal Deposit Insurance Corporation, standing in the shoes of the insolvent client, sued a law firm for not doing more to mitigate public harm when it realized it had a dishonest client.

Finally, in these days of growing international practice, lawyers need to be aware that lawyers in other countries may operate under different rules. For example, the European Court of Justice has reaffirmed prior rulings denying any privileged status for communications between in-house counsel and their company. Akzo Nobel Chemicals Ltd. v. Comm'n of the European Communities, Case C-550/07P (ECJ 2010). In the United States, however, communications with a company's in-house counsel can be, and often are, privileged. See, e.g., Upjohn Co. v. United States, 449 U.S. 383 (1981).

What effect, if any, should cases like these have on lawyers' disclosures to clients about the extent of their confidentiality obligations? In one of the many instances in which the governing ethical rules leave the lawyer significant discretion, the rules say almost nothing about what, if anything, a lawyer should tell the client about the scope of the confidentiality obligation and its exceptions.

2. Confidentiality Compared to the Attorney-Client Privilege

The distinction between the attorney-client privilege and the lawyer's obligation of confidentiality is one that is not well understood by many lawyers. Both concepts share similar purposes (e.g., to encourage full and frank communication so that the lawyer can render better advice to the client), and each concept to some extent informs and supports the other.

The confidentiality obligation is imposed by the ethical rules (and by fiduciary obligations), and absent an exception, it broadly prohibits lawyers from disclosing to anyone "information relating to the representation." Breach of this duty may give rise to professional discipline or a suit based in professional negligence or breach of fiduciary duty. The attorney-client privilege, however, is essentially an evidentiary doctrine. Generally speaking, it keeps privileged information out of legal proceedings. In other words, that the information is privileged generally means that it is inadmissible in the proceeding and a party or lawyer may properly refuse to respond to a subpoena or question in a deposition or trial calling for privileged information. The scope of privileged information is far narrower than the scope of confidential information. As classically stated, information is privileged only if the following elements are met: "1) Where legal advice of [any] kind is sought (2) from a professional legal adviser in his capacity as such, (3) the communications relating to that purpose, (4) made in confidence (5) by the client, (6) are at his insistence permanently protected (7) from disclosure by himself or by his legal adviser, (8) except the protection [may] be waived." Newman v. State, 863 A.2d 321, 331 (Md. 2004) (quoting 8 John H. Wigmore on Evidence § 2292, at 554 (McNaughton rev. ed. 1961)) (footnote and internal quotation marks omitted). Thus, if the information at issue fails to meet one (or more) of these elements, the information is not privileged (but may still be confidential). Common examples of instances in which otherwise privileged information loses its privileged character include: conveying the information to a third party (who is not assisting the lawyer) or putting the communication in issue (often through the "advice-of-counsel" defense).

The following case is an example where the court drew a sharp line between confidentiality and privilege. The case arises in the context of the so-called crime-fraud exception to the attorney-client privilege, which rejects (or waives) the privilege when the client intends to use the lawyer's advice to assist the client in criminal or fraudulent activity.

Purcell v. District Attorney for the Suffolk District
424 Mass. 109 (1997)

WILKINS, Chief Justice

On June 21, 1994, Joseph Tyree, who had received a court order to vacate his apartment in the Allston section of Boston, consulted the plaintiff, Jeffrey W. Purcell, an attorney employed by Greater Boston Legal Services, which provides representation to low income individuals in civil matters. Tyree had recently been discharged as a maintenance man at the apartment building in which his apartment was located. On the day that Tyree consulted Purcell, Purcell decided, after extensive deliberation, that he should advise appropriate authorities that Tyree might engage in conduct harmful to others. He told a Boston police lieutenant that Tyree had made threats to burn the apartment building.

The next day, constables, accompanied by Boston police officers, went to evict Tyree. At the apartment building, they found incendiary materials, containers of gasoline, and several bottles with wicks attached. Smoke detectors had been disconnected, and gasoline had been poured on a hallway floor. Tyree was arrested and later indicted for attempted arson of a building.

In August, 1995, the district attorney for the Suffolk district subpoenaed Purcell to testify concerning the conversation Purcell had had with Tyree on June 21, 1994. A Superior Court judge granted Purcell's motion to quash the subpoena. The trial ended in a mistrial because the jury was unable to reach a verdict.

The Commonwealth decided to try Tyree again and once more sought Purcell's testimony. Another Superior Court judge concluded that Tyree's statements to Purcell were not protected by the attorney-client privilege, denied Purcell's motion to quash an anticipated subpoena, and ordered Purcell to testify. Purcell then commenced this action . . . .

There is no question before this court, directly or indirectly, concerning the ethical propriety of Purcell's disclosure to the police that Tyree might engage in conduct that would be harmful to others. As bar counsel agreed . . . this court's disciplinary rules regulating the practice of law authorized Purcell to reveal to the police "[t]he intention of his client to commit a crime and the information necessary to prevent the crime." S.J.C. Rule 3:07, Canon 4, DR 4-101(C)(3), as appearing in 382 Mass. 778 (1981). The fact that the disciplinary code permitted Purcell to make the disclosure tells us nothing about the admissibility of the information that Purcell disclosed. . . .

The attorney-client privilege is founded on the necessity that a client be free to reveal information to an attorney, without fear of its disclosure, in order to obtain informed legal advice. Matter of a John Doe Grand Jury Investigation, 408 Mass. 480, 481–482 (1990). It is a principle of long standing. See Foster v. Hall, 29 Mass. 89, 93 (1831). The debate here is whether Tyree is entitled to the protection of the attorney-client privilege in the circumstances.

The district attorney announces the issue in his brief to be whether a crime-fraud exception to the testimonial privilege applies in this case. He asserts that, even if Tyree's communication with Purcell was made as part of his consultation concerning the eviction proceeding, Tyree's communication concerning his contemplated criminal conduct is not protected by the privilege. We shall first consider the case on the assumption that Tyree's statements to Purcell are protected by the attorney-client privilege unless the crime-fraud exception applies.

"It is the purpose of the crime-fraud exception to the attorney-client privilege to assure that the 'seal of secrecy' . . . between lawyer and client does not extend to communications 'made for the purpose of getting advice for the commission of a fraud' or crime" (citation omitted). United States v. Zolin, 491 U.S. 554, 563 (1989), quoting O'Rourke v. Darbishire, [1920] App. Cas. 581, 604 (P.C.). There is no public interest in the preservation of the secrecy of that kind of communication. See United States v. Zolin, supra at 562–563; Matter of John Doe Grand Jury Investigation, supra at 486.

Our cases have not defined a crime-fraud exception to the attorney-client privilege with any precision. In Matter of John Doe Grand Jury Investigation, supra at 486, the court stated that there was "no legitimate interest of a client and no public interest would be served by a rule that would preserve the secrecy of" a conversation between attorney and client in a conference related to the possible future defrauding of an insurance company. We cited Commonwealth v. Dyer, 243 Mass. 472, cert. denied, 262 U.S. 751 (1923), in which we said that "[t]here is no privilege between attorney and client where the conferences concern the proposed commission of a crime by the client." Id. at 505–506. The cases cited in our *Dyer* opinion and the facts of that case—the attorney was alleged to be part of the conspiracy—demonstrate that the exception asserted concerned conferences in which the attorney's advice was sought in furtherance of a crime or to obtain advice or assistance with respect to criminal activity.

We, therefore, accept the general principle of a crime-fraud exception. The Proposed Massachusetts Rules of Evidence adequately define the crime-fraud exception to the lawyer-client privilege set forth in rule 502(d)(1) as follows: "If the services of the lawyer were sought or obtained to enable or aid anyone to commit or plan to commit what the client knew or reasonably should have known to be a crime or fraud." . . .

The district attorney rightly grants that he, as the opponent of the application of the testimonial privilege, has the burden of showing that the exception applies. . . . In its *Zolin* opinion, the Supreme Court did not have to decide what level of showing the opponent of the privilege must make to establish that the exception applies. See United States v. Zolin, supra, at 563–564 n.7. We conclude that facts supporting the applicability of the crime-fraud exception must be proved by a preponderance of the evidence. However, on a showing of a factual basis adequate to support a reasonable belief that an *in camera* review of the evidence may establish that the exception applies, the judge has discretion to conduct such an *in camera* review. United States v. Zolin, supra at 572. Once the judge sees the confidential information, the burden of proof normally will be unimportant.

In this case, in deciding whether to conduct a discretionary *in camera* review of the substance of the conversation concerning arson between Tyree and Purcell, the judge would have evidence tending to show that Tyree discussed a future crime with Purcell and that thereafter Tyree actively prepared to commit that crime. Without this evidence, the crime of arson would appear to have no apparent connection with Tyree's eviction proceeding and Purcell's representation of Tyree. With this evidence, however, a request that a judge inquire *in camera* into the circumstances of Tyree's apparent threat to burn the apartment building would not be a call for a "fishing expedition," and a judge might be justified in conducting such an inquiry. The evidence in this case, however, was not sufficient to warrant the judge's finding that Tyree consulted Purcell for the purpose of obtaining advice in furtherance of a crime. Therefore, the order denying the motion to quash because the crime-fraud exception applied cannot be upheld.

There is a consideration in this case that does not appear in other cases that we have seen concerning the attorney-client privilege. The testimony that the prosecution seeks from Purcell is available only because Purcell reflectively made a disclosure, relying on this court's disciplinary rule which permitted him to do so. Purcell was under no ethical duty to disclose Tyree's intention to commit a crime. He did so to protect the lives and property of others, a purpose that underlies a lawyer's discretionary right stated in the disciplinary rule. The limited facts in the record strongly suggest that Purcell's disclosures to the police served the beneficial public purpose on which the disciplinary rule was based.

We must be cautious in permitting the use of client communications that a lawyer has revealed only because of a threat to others. Lawyers will be reluctant to come forward if they know that the information that they disclose may lead to adverse consequences to their clients. A practice of the use of such disclosures might prompt a lawyer to warn a client in advance that the disclosure of certain information may not be held confidential, thereby chilling free discourse between lawyer and client and reducing the prospect that the lawyer will learn of a serious threat to the well-being of others. To best promote the purposes of the attorney-client privilege, the crime-fraud exception should apply only if the communication seeks assistance in or furtherance of future criminal conduct. When the opponent of the privilege argues that the communication itself may show that the exception applies and seeks its disclosure *in camera*, the judge, in the exercise of discretion on the question whether to have an *in camera* proceeding, should consider if the public interest is served by disclosure, even *in camera*, of a communication whose existence is known only because the lawyer acted against his client's interests under the authority of a disciplinary rule. The facts of each situation must be considered.

It might seem that this opinion is in a posture to conclude by stating that the order denying the motion to quash any subpoena to testify is vacated and the matter is to be remanded for further proceedings concerning the application of the crime-fraud exception. However, the district attorney's brief appears to abandon its earlier concession that all communications between Tyree and Purcell should be treated as protected by the attorney-client privilege unless the crime-fraud exception applies. The question whether the attorney-client privilege is involved at all will be open on remand. We, therefore, discuss the issue.

The attorney-client privilege applies only when the client's communication was for the purpose of facilitating the rendition of legal services. . . . The burden of proving that the attorney-client privilege applies to a communication rests on the party asserting the privilege. . . . The motion judge did not pass on the question whether the attorney-client privilege applied to the communication at all but rather went directly to the issue of the crime-fraud exception, although not using that phrase.

A statement of an intention to commit a crime made in the course of seeking legal advice is protected by the privilege, unless the crime-fraud exception applies. That exception applies only if the client or prospective client seeks advice or assistance in furtherance of criminal conduct. It is agreed that Tyree consulted Purcell concerning his impending eviction. Purcell is a member of the bar, and Tyree either was or sought to become Purcell's client. The serious question concerning the application of the privilege is whether Tyree informed Purcell of the fact of his intention to commit arson for the purpose of receiving legal advice or assistance in furtherance of criminal conduct. Purcell's presentation of the circumstances in which Tyree's statements were made is likely to be the only evidence presented.

This is not a case in which our traditional view that testimonial privileges should be construed strictly should be applied. . . . A strict construction of the privilege that would leave a gap between the circumstances in which the crime-fraud exception applies and the circumstances in which a communication is protected by the attorney-client privilege would make no sense. The attorney-client privilege "is founded upon the necessity, in the interest and administration of justice, of the aid of persons having knowledge of the law and skilled in its practice, which assistance can only be safely and readily availed of when free from the consequences or the apprehension of disclosure." Matter of a John Doe Grand Jury Investigation, 408 Mass. 480, 481–482 (1990), quoting Hunt v. Blackburn, 128 U.S. 464, 470 [1888]. Unless the crime-fraud exception applies, the attorney-client privilege should apply to communication concerning possible future, as well as past, criminal conduct, because an informed lawyer may be able to dissuade the client from improper future conduct and, if not, under the ethical rules may elect in the public interest to make a limited disclosure of the client's threatened conduct.

A judgment should be entered in the county court ordering that the order denying the motion to quash any subpoena issued to Purcell to testify at Tyree's trial is vacated and that the matter is remanded for further proceedings consistent with this opinion.

Notes

1. The court concluded that the rule that the attorney-client privilege should be construed narrowly ought not apply in this case because "that would leave a gap between the circumstances in which the crime-fraud exception applies and the circumstances in which a communication is protected by the attorney-client privilege" and that "would make no sense." Whether that statement is accurate or not, the court created its own gap between the exceptions to the attorney-client privilege and the lawyer's confidentiality obligation. If it had held that communications about the intent to commit a future crime fell within the crime-fraud exception, as it held that those communications did fall within the attorney-client privilege, there would have been no gap. The gap was created by the court, and in so doing it created the unusual situation where the attorney-client privilege was broader than the confidentiality obligation. Subsequently, when a lawyer revealed a client's angry threats against the judge hearing the case, the same court reaffirmed Purcell, expressing the view that expressions of frustration and anger against the operation of the legal system in the matter at hand were protected by attorney-client privilege. In re Grand Jury Investigation, 453 Mass. 453 (2009). Maryland, as another example, agreed with the Purcell court's reasoning in a case in which a spouse had disclosed to her lawyer that she might hurt one of her children and the lawyer in turn disclosed this threat to the judge. Newman v. State, 863 A.2d 321, 333 (Md. 2004) ("We agree with the Massachusetts Supreme Court that such disclosure is not sufficient to obviate the attorney-client privilege and admit the statements as evidence against the attorney's client, not only because of the chilling effect of the obverse, but also because it pits the attorney, as advocate and adviser, against the client, when the client is charged with a crime. To permit a Rule 1.6 disclosure to destroy the attorney-client privilege and empower the attorney to essentially waive his client's privilege without the client's consent is repugnant to the entire purpose of the attorney-client privilege in promoting candor between attorney and client."). Both actions (disclosure to police and later admission in court) would cause harm to the client. Yet the court is comfortable with preventing only one harm. To explain this result, might different justifications for attorney-client privilege and confidentiality exist?

2. Notwithstanding the purposes behind the confidentiality obligation and the attorney-client privilege, opponents may later obtain confidential communications if the crime-fraud exception applies. To avail themselves of this exception, they typically "must make a prima facie showing: (1) that the client was engaged in (or was planning) criminal or fraudulent activity when the attorney-client communications took place; and (2) that the communications were intended by the client to facilitate or conceal the criminal or fraudulent activity." United States v. Gorski, 807 F.3d 451 (1st Cir. 2015). In the confidence of their attorneys, many clients have threatened others or inquired how to minimize taxes or avoid regulation. But many attorneys will tell you that clients not infrequently "vent," and many more attorneys will tell you that clients often want advice to conform their conduct to the letter (but not necessarily the spirit) of the law. Provided that the clients ultimately do not act on their threats (presumably pursuant to their attorney's advice) and do conform their conduct to the law, should the crime-fraud exception nevertheless apply? Does this exception allow too much spying into attorney-client communications and thereby infringe on clients' privacy, their ability to confide in lawyers and receive legal advice based on their confidences, and the willingness of future clients to confide in lawyers? Consider also Problem 2–11 below.

3. Do you agree with the court's policy justification that permits the lawyer to reveal the confidential information but protects the client against the judicial consequences of that revelation. Or does it? Didn't the lawyer's revelation lead to the arrest and prosecution of the client? Weren't the chances of his arrest and conviction high once the lawyer went to the police? What does that say about the court's policy justification for creating a gap?

4. Consider the court's observation that the lawyer had no ethical duty to reveal that his client intended to burn down the apartment building. That was true under the ethical rules adopted by that court and it is still true under the ethical rules as revised by that court shortly after its decision in Purcell. After finishing the materials on confidentiality, you should presumably have an opinion whether the court should have an ethics rule that required Purcell to keep quiet ("shall not disclose"), that required him to reveal ("shall disclose"), or that gave him discretion to do either ("may disclose"). All three approaches are represented in the various states' rules.

Attorney-client privilege generally keeps "the whole truth" out of legal proceedings. The following case presents some consequences of this.

State of Arizona v. William Wayne Macumber
544 P.2d 1084 (Ariz. 1976)

HAYS, Justice

William Wayne Macumber was found guilty of two counts of first degree murder. He was sentenced to serve two concurrent terms of life imprisonment, and now appeals. . . .

At trial, it was alleged that another individual had confessed to the crime for which Macumber was being tried. This confession had been made to two attorneys who were willing to testify at the trial of the appellant, the person said to have confessed having died. The court refused the evidence finding, sua sponte, that it was privileged.

ARS § 13-1802 provides that an attorney shall not be examined as to any communication made to him by his client without the consent of his client. The privilege is that of the client and only he or someone authorized by law to do so on his behalf may claim it. State v. Gause, 107 Ariz. 491 (1971), vacated on other grounds, 409 U.S. 815. However, in the absence of the privileged individual, the privilege may be asserted by another including the trial court itself. McCormick's Handbook of the Law of Evidence (Cleary, 2nd ed. 1972), § 92.

The privilege does not terminate with death. . . . It has been commonly suspended only in cases where the communication would be logically thought to further the interests of the deceased such as a will . . . or where a person normally able by statute to invoke the privilege for another does so to exclude evidence in a prosecution for a crime against that person. State v. Gause, supra.

The attorney-client privilege is statutory and an attorney is not allowed to waive the privilege under the circumstances of this case. The legislature has presumably weighed the possibility of hampering justice in originally providing for the privilege. . . .

HOLOHAN, Justice (specially concurring)*

. . . Regretfully, I cannot agree with the decision of the majority to refuse to admit evidence of the confession by a third person that he killed the same individuals that the defendant is charged with murdering.

The nature of the defense evidence was contained in an offer of proof. Essentially, the evidence was expected to show that a third person, now deceased, had admitted in 1968 to two attorneys that he had committed the dual murders with which the defendant was charged. At the time of the admission the third person was being tried in federal court for an unrelated murder which occurred in the same general vicinity as the murders in this case. The two lawyers were involved in the defense of the third party for the unrelated murder. Subsequently the third party died.

When the attorneys learned that the defendant was being charged with the murders which their former client claimed to have committed, they sought and received an informal opinion from the Committee on Ethics of the State Bar which advised the attorneys that the privilege of attorney-client did not apply to prevent them from disclosing the information to the defense, prosecution, and court. The attorneys, upon receiving the advice of the Ethics Committee, disclosed their information to

---

* [Although the following opinion reads like a dissent, it is a concurrence because the court reversed and remanded for other reasons, with which this concurring justice agreed. — Eds.]

the defense and prosecution, but the trial judge ruled the information privileged and not admissible.

The information which the attorneys possess is material and relevant to the defense, and while it was excluded solely on the basis of the attorney-client privilege, it is necessary to examine whether the evidence would have been inadmissible on other grounds. Historically, out-of-court confessions of third persons of crimes tending to exonerate the accused have been excluded from the declaration-against-interest hearsay exception. See, e.g., Donnelly v. United States, 228 U.S. 243 (1913); Davis v. Commonwealth, 23 S.W. 585 (Ky. 1893); People v. Hall, 30 P. 7 (Cal. 1892). However, relying on the dissent in *Donnelly*, a substantial number of states have abandoned this rule in criminal cases. . . .

Although this Court has not specifically ruled on the extent of the hearsay exception, it must be acknowledged that the decisions of our Court of Appeals have declared the rule in Arizona to be that the declaration-against-interest exception includes declarations against penal interest. In addition, and more fundamentally, the United States Supreme Court in Chambers v. Mississippi, 410 U.S. 284 (1973), has ruled that it is a violation of due process for a state rule of evidence to preclude the admission of reliable hearsay declarations against penal interest when such evidence is offered to show the innocence of an accused. Thus, the offered evidence of the declarations against penal interest in this case were admissible under both Arizona and Federal standards.

Although the offered testimony should have been admissible under the hearsay exception, the trial court refused to admit it on the grounds that the subject matter was privileged. As the majority point out, the attorney-client privilege has been held to survive the death of the client. Whether the rule should be followed in a case such as this or an exception created would require an extended discussion not called for in a specially concurring opinion. The real problem is whether the privilege can survive the constitutional test of due process.

It is basic that an accused has the right to present a defense to a criminal charge, and, to accomplish this right, accused has the right to compel the attendance of witnesses and the right to present their testimony. Washington v. Texas, 388 U.S. 14 (1967). Even a claim of privilege may have to give way when faced with the necessity by the accused to present a defense. Roviaro v. United States, 353 U.S. 53 (1957). The problem of balancing competing interests, privilege versus a proper defense, is a difficult one, but the balance always weighs in favor of achieving a fair determination of the cause.

A state's rules of evidence cannot deny an accused's right to present a proper defense. Chambers v. Mississippi, supra. In the case at issue the interest to be protected by the privilege would seem to be at an end because of the client's death.

When the client died there was no chance of prosecution for other crimes, and any privilege is merely a matter of property interest. Opposed to the property interest of the deceased client is the vital interest of the accused in this case in defending himself against the charge of first degree murder. When the interests are weighed, I believe that the constitutional right of the accused to present a defense should prevail over the property interest of a deceased client in keeping his disclosures private. I would allow the defendant to offer the testimony of the attorneys concerning the confession of their deceased client.

Notes

1. Notice that, as in the *Purcell* scenario, the attorneys (to whom their client had confessed that he was the actual murderer) were ethically permitted to disclose this confession to third parties, namely Mr. Macumber and his legal team. The next section of materials addresses specific exceptions to the otherwise broad confidentiality of litigation. As a preview to that section, under what exception to the confidentiality obligation did the Ethics Committee permit the attorneys to disclose this information? As a very general statement, the exceptions to the attorney-client privilege are functionally the same as the exceptions to the confidentiality obligation. As *Purcell* and *Macumber* demonstrate, however, general statements do not always hold true. The subtle differences in the exceptions, and the application of the waiver doctrine to the attorney-client privilege, continue to create confusion for attorneys and judges.

2. Assuming (somewhat dubiously) that the ethics rules permitted (then or now) an attorney to disclose this information to prevent an innocent person from serving years in prison, the court created a sharp distinction between the confidentiality obligation and the attorney-client privilege, which in many states is codified in statutes. In codifying the privilege, do you think that state legislatures considered a situation like this? Even if so, do you think the legislatures would have struck the same balance even for *deceased* murderers (who necessarily cannot be put at any physical or emotional risk from the disclosure and the disclosure could free an innocent person)? The client had also confessed to a psychiatrist. Should the psychiatrist be permitted to disclose the confession, and if so, should the psychiatrist be permitted to testify about the confession before the jury? Or do similar policy concerns justify keeping the psychiatrist's information away from the jury?

3. Do you think that murderers (or others accused of crime) will still be candid with their lawyers if they know about this compromise (i.e., that lawyers might be permitted to disclose the confession outside of court but not in court)?

4. Bill Macumber, the defendant in the case above, spent nearly forty years in prison for a crime he likely did not commit. The state governor rejected his request for a reduced sentence (even though the clemency board had unanimously recommended the reduction in large part because it believed that Mr. Macumber was innocent). See, e.g., Adam Liptak, "Governor Rebuffs Clemency Board in Murder Case," New York Times, June 14, 2010. In 2013, Macumber was finally freed as part of a plea

bargain between the state innocence project and the prosecutorial agency. See, e.g., Barry Siegel, *Manifest Injustice: The True Story of a Convicted Murderer and the Lawyers Who Fought for His Freedom* (2013). Was Macumber simply a sacrificial lamb in service of the greater good of the attorney-client privilege? In terms of the evidentiary rulings, the *Purcell* decision was generally pro-defendant (in that it kept damaging information out of evidence), while the *Macumber* decision was generally pro-prosecution (in that it kept exculpatory information out of evidence). Do you believe that the *Purcell* court would have ruled the same way on the *Macumber* facts? Would it have kept the third-party confession out of evidence? Notice that the privilege runs the risk of excluding all types of relevant information from proceedings. For further discussion of problems with privilege and confidentiality in the context of wrongful convictions — which have been increasingly exposed in recent years — see Section C4 below (in particular Problem 2–19 and the following discussion).

3. The Duty to Protect the Confidentiality Obligation

As noted in many examples above, the confidentiality obligation is very broad — and so prohibits lawyers from disclosing most information relating to the representation. The obligation implies (but did not explicitly state until recently) that a lawyer must act competently to prevent others from accessing or receiving such information. The vast majority of privileged and confidential information is not conveyed in private, in-person, attorney-client meetings. Letters and phone calls, which can be intercepted or overheard, have long played an important part. New technology has changed the way in which lawyers and clients share information and has changed and augmented the risks of the information falling into the wrong hands. Currently, the largest share of information is conveyed electronically, via email, portable storage, cloud storage, and databases. If a third party is able to overhear a lawyer's call to a client, intercept an email message, or access an electronic database, has the lawyer acted unethically?

The answer depends on whether "the lawyer has made reasonable efforts to prevent the access or disclosure." Model Rule 1.6 cmt. 18. The ethical rules were recently amended to address the issue, but only in general terms. The rules now state in a comment that "[t]o maintain the requisite knowledge and skill, a lawyer should keep abreast of changes in the law and its practice, including the benefits and risks associated with relevant technology. . . ." Model Rule 1.1 cmt. 8. Indeed, one of the most recent additions to the ethical rules now specifically commands that "[a] lawyer shall make reasonable efforts to prevent the inadvertent or unauthorized disclosure of, or unauthorized access to, information relating to the representation of a client." Model Rule 1.6(c). In considering whether a lawyer has complied with this duty, "[f]actors to be considered in determining the reasonableness of the lawyer's efforts include, but are not limited to, the sensitivity of the information, the likelihood of disclosure if additional safeguards are not employed, the cost of employing additional safeguards, the difficulty of implementing the safeguards, and the extent to which the safeguards adversely affect the lawyer's ability to represent clients (e.g., by making a device or important piece of software excessively difficult to use)." Model Rule 1.6 cmt. 18. Basic security procedures currently in use (e.g., passwords, firewalls, antivirus software, and possibly even encryption) are arguably implied by the new rule and are required, according to many ethics opinions. See, e.g., ABA Ethics Op. 477 (2017). For examples of data breaches and a discussion of how the rules of professional conduct might more adequately guide lawyers in this area, see Eli Wald, "Legal Ethics' Next Frontier: Lawyers and Cybersecurity," 19 Chapman L. Rev. 501 (2016) (noting, among other examples, the "[p]ublication of the Panama Papers containing confidential client information, following a cybersecurity breach at the law firm of Mossack Fonseca, demonstrated what many have long known, that law firms are particularly vulnerable to cyberattacks").

But often the issue is not unauthorized third-party access (e.g., hackers). Instead, the issue is the care (or the lack of it) of the lawyer or the lawyer's agents. For example, lawyers have not infrequently addressed sensitive emails or letters to opposing parties or even reporters, and as another example, lawyers have inadvertently produced privileged materials in response to discovery requests from the opposing side. These mistakes often occur through basic carelessness (e.g., by not double-checking the recipient list on an email or by not closely reviewing the documents collected in response to a discovery request). Mistakes of course will happen to everyone, and fortunately if the unintended recipient is a lawyer (even the opposing lawyer), the ethical rules provide a bit of a safeguard. Model Rule 4.4(b) requires that "[a] lawyer who receives a document or electronically stored information relating to the representation of the lawyer's client and knows or reasonably should know that the document or electronically stored information was inadvertently sent shall promptly notify the sender." The drafters of the civil rules of procedure have required more than the ethics rule.[8] Do you think that the opposing lawyer should have a duty to notify the sending lawyer, to stop reviewing confidential information, and to await a court ruling when the sending lawyer negligently disclosed the information? Does the receiving lawyer have a duty to review and use the confidential information to represent the opposing party competently and diligently? Is the rule primarily about fairness to the other side, or is it primarily about lawyers protecting themselves from their own mistakes?

A related issue is to what extent do opposing lawyers have an obligation to refrain from obtaining and reviewing what they know or suspect is confidential or

---

8. See Fed.R.Civ.P. 26(b)(5)(B) ("If information produced in discovery is subject to a claim of privilege or of protection as trial-preparation material, the party making the claim may notify any party that received the information of the claim and the basis for it. After being notified, a party must promptly return, sequester, or destroy the specified information and any copies it has; must not use or disclose the information until the claim is resolved; must take reasonable steps to retrieve the information if the party disclosed it before being notified; and may promptly present the information to the court under seal for a determination of the claim.")

privileged information. Metadata and spymail present two examples. In the former, the sending lawyer (presumably inadvertently) sends the receiving lawyer an electronic document with sensitive metadata (i.e., information about the document, its creation, or its modification that typically does not appear on the face of the document). In an egregious instance, the sending lawyer might have failed to remove from the document embedded comments containing privileged attorney-client communications or the sending lawyer's strategic judgment on issues in the document (e.g., a demand letter or a contract). May—and should—the receiving lawyer review those comments or other information and use it to the benefit of the lawyer's client? The spymail example is more extreme. There, the lawyer (or the lawyer's agent) embeds a code in an email or attachment sent to the opposing side. The code will then cause the recipient's computer or program to send the lawyer information about the email: when, where, and for how long the email was opened and to whom the email was forwarded. Is it deceitful or unfair for the lawyer to use this tool to glean information about the opposing side's behavior? See generally Model Rules 4.4 and 8.4(c). Or is it primarily the receiving lawyer's problem for failing to install spymail-blocking software in the first place? As technology continues to evolve and multiply, questions about how to access and protect confidential information ethically will continue to present themselves.

Note: Lawyers and the "Obligation" to Commit Contempt

After the Watergate break-in in 1972 (see p. 4 for context), G. Gordon Liddy, its mastermind, went to discuss the break-in and its consequences with Robert Mardian, who had been an Assistant Attorney General in the Internal Security Division of the Justice Department. Mardian had become campaign coordinator for the Committee for the Re-election of the President but had also undertaken to act as counsel for the Committee with respect to Watergate matters. When Mr. Mardian was called to testify before the Senate's Select Committee on Presidential Campaign Activities headed by Senator Ervin, his attorney, Mr. Bress, related the circumstances under which Mr. Mardian came to testify about that conversation with Mr. Liddy before the grand jury and why he was willing to testify before the Ervin Committee notwithstanding his belief that the conversation was protected by the attorney-client privilege.

> MR. BRESS. . . . Mr. Chairman, Mr. Mardian has conferred on two occasions with the United States Attorney's office in May 1973 before his appearance before the grand jury on May 7th. In those conferences and grand jury appearance, Mr. Mardian at no time asserted any constitutional privilege he might have, and he asserts none today.
>
> He did, however, on my advice, assert the attorney-client privilege insofar as questions related to conversations he had with Mr. Liddy on June 21, 1972. But as to all other attorney-client communications with other persons no privilege was asserted because we were satisfied that such other persons had waived the privilege. Accordingly, by prearrangement with the United

States Attorney's Office, when questions were propounded before the grand jury relating to his communications with Mr. Liddy, all counsel proceeded to Judge Sirica's court on the same day and argued the matter. After taking it under advisement the court ordered the questions to be answered and this was done.

Later, Mr. Mardian spent two days conferring with the staff of this Committee on June 1 and July 14, 1973. All questions were fully answered, and he now stands ready to answer any further questions. . . .

6 Hearings before the Senate Select Committee on Presidential Campaign Activities, 93d Cong., 1st Sess. 2345 (1973).

Notes

1. Mr. Mardian apparently instituted the proceeding before Judge Sirica that resulted in the ruling that the lawyer-client privilege did not apply, and Mr. Liddy seems not to have been a party to that proceeding. Although Judge Sirica's order may not have been appealable, it could have been tested through refusal to testify and a contempt proceeding. Was it Mardian's obligation to proceed in that fashion if his "client" Liddy requested it? Indeed, since Liddy refused to testify, was it not fairly clear that he wished Mardian to proceed in that fashion?

2. If the result of such a proceeding were a jail sentence, and no stay were forthcoming, would Mardian have an obligation to go to jail to allow Liddy's rights to be tested? For an opinion that he has such an obligation, see People v. Kor, 277 P.2d 94, 101 (Cal. Dist. Ct. App. 1954). For an instance where a lawyer, there the Attorney General of the United States, accepted a contempt citation to preserve his client's argument, see In re Attorney General, 596 F.2d 58 (2d Cir. 1979) and In re Klein, 776 F.2d 628, 631 n.1 (7th Cir. 1985).

3. Interestingly, the Model Rules permit — but do not require — lawyers to reveal confidential information "to comply with . . . a court order." Model Rule 1.6(b)(6). Thus, if a judge is threatening to hold you in contempt unless you reveal information about your client (e.g., your client's location or your client's criminal history), you at least in theory have discretion under the ethical rules not to comply. Exercising that discretion, however, might well cost you. It is for this reason that some commentators call such lawyers "heroic," because they face jail time to protect their clients. See, e.g., Monroe Freedman & Abbe Smith, *Understanding Lawyers' Ethics* 156 (3d ed. 2004) (recounting the story of lawyer Linda Bakiel who went to jail for refusing to give a grand jury incriminating information about her client). Even if you are not so heroic, however, the rules (and ethics opinions) require at a minimum that "[a]bsent informed consent of the client to do otherwise, the lawyer should assert on behalf of the client all nonfrivolous claims that the order is not authorized by other law or that the information sought is protected against disclosure by the attorney-client privilege or other applicable law," and "[i]n the event of an adverse ruling, the lawyer must consult with the client about the possibility of appeal to the extent required by Rule 1.4." Model Rule 1.6 cmt. 15. Should the ethical rules require additional

action? In many states, for example, you may be able to take an interlocutory appeal (or a "special action") to challenge promptly a trial court's order requiring you to reveal your client's privileged information. If the trial court will not stay its ruling, should you sit in jail silently until (hopefully) you receive appellate relief?

C. The Exceptions to the General Rule of Confidentiality

The following sections discuss most of the key exceptions to the confidentiality obligation. In other words, notwithstanding the broad confidentiality obligation discussed above, certain situations permit or require the lawyer to reveal otherwise confidential information to third parties. Although most of these exceptions are discretionary under the Model Rules, some are mandatory (in other words, the lawyer must disclose the information). Some states go beyond the Model Rules and make additional exceptions mandatory.[9]

Before we turn to the enumerated exceptions in the Model Rules, however, it is important to note the most common "exceptions:" implied authorization and informed consent.[10] First, the Model Rules (and state rules) permit a lawyer to disclose that which "is impliedly authorized to carry out the representation." Model Rule 1.6(a). Much otherwise confidential information falls within this exception (e.g., the basic information in a complaint or demand letter reveals significant "information relating to the representation" but lawyers commonly disclose such information notwithstanding the confidentiality obligation). Second, and perhaps equally obviously, a lawyer may disclose otherwise confidential information with the client's informed consent (in other words, permission). For example, a lawyer might request a client's informed consent to add that client's name to a list of representative current and former clients used for marketing purposes, or the lawyer might request the client's permission to inform the court that the client has a scheduled medical procedure (and therefore cannot attend the scheduled court date). Many other instances will arise below and throughout this book in which a lawyer might, as one mandatory or at least advisable option, seek a client's informed consent to take a particular course of action.[11]

---

9. See generally Bruce A. Green & Fred C. Zacharias, "Permissive Rules of Professional Conduct," 91 Minn. L. Rev. 265 (2006); Rebecca Aviel, "The Boundary Claim's Caveat: Lawyers and Confidentiality Exceptionalism," 86 Tul. L. Rev. 1055 (2012); Rebecca Aviel, "When the State Demands Disclosure," 33 Cardozo L. Rev. 675 (2011).

10. By labeling these "exceptions" in quotation marks, we mean to avoid any terminological debate on whether these categories are exceptions permitting disclosure of confidential information or whether the information is not confidential information because it falls outside the definition of confidential information.

11. See generally Model Rule 1.0(e) ("'Informed consent' denotes the agreement by a person to a proposed course of conduct after the lawyer has communicated adequate information and explanation

1. Revealing the Intent to Commit a Crime or Fraud and the Approach to Exceptions

The Problems that follow deal with the course of action that the lawyer may or must follow upon learning of the client's intention to commit a crime or fraud, except if the crime involves fraud upon a court (which the law of professional responsibility has always treated separately). There are three major models that have been adopted by various jurisdictions. The first is the one originally adopted in the Model Code. Jurisdictions that have followed its policy leave the whole matter to the discretion of individual lawyers in language providing that a lawyer "may" reveal the intention of a client to commit a crime. The wording does not draw distinctions among crimes. It gives lawyers discretion with respect to the most serious and the most trivial crimes. On the other hand, it gives lawyers no discretion to reveal confidences when a client's action or inaction threatens serious harm if no crime is involved. Moreover, the situation must involve a crime by the client, not a third party, before the lawyer may reveal the information necessary to prevent that crime.

The second model is that of the Model Rules prior to amendments made in 2002 and 2003. It aimed to protect confidentiality as much as possible. It did so by removing most of the discretion that lawyers had been given under the previous Model Code. The only exception concerning future conduct was that lawyers may reveal confidential information "to prevent the client from committing a criminal act that the lawyer believes is likely to result in imminent death or substantial bodily harm."

The third model is a compromise between the two extremes. Most jurisdictions rejected the original Model Rules provision and gave discretion to reveal confidential information to prevent serious physical or (less often) financial harm or both. Sometimes the permissible situations were linked to those where the lawyer's services had been used. The ABA consistently refused to follow the majority of jurisdictions until the passage of the Sarbanes–Oxley Act (discussed in Chapter 5) gave lawyers appearing before the SEC permission to reveal confidential information in a variety of situations. The ABA thereupon amended Rule 1.6 into the form in which it currently appears. See Model Rule 1.6(b)(2). The Rules also now permit a lawyer to reveal information reasonably necessary "to prevent reasonably certain death or substantial bodily harm." Id. R. 1.6(b)(1). The discretion given to lawyers in the Model Rules is generally comparable to that given by most jurisdictions to lawyers to reveal confidential information in a variety of situations. Almost no states give lawyers discretion to reveal a client's threatened tort or civil rights violations (unless the tort or violations amount to a crime or fraud). Should the Rules permit disclosure necessary to prevent such conduct? Or should that rule stick to a client's crimes or frauds

---

about the material risks of and reasonably available alternatives to the proposed course of conduct."). Rule 1.0, labeled Terminology, also contains other definitions of pertinent terms in the Model Rules.

risking significant physical or financial injury? And on that last question, should the only cognizable injuries be physical or financial? Massachusetts recently permitted lawyers to disclose information to prevent "other" injuries, e.g., when "[a] person by crime or fraud . . . deprive[s] someone of the right to vote or some other significant right of participation in the political process." Mass. Rules of Prof. Conduct R. 1.6 cmt. 8A.

As the Massachusetts rule suggests, there is considerable variety in the nature of the particular exceptions to the principle of confidentiality, and one needs to read the particular language carefully in each jurisdiction. One idiosyncratic amendment is that of Florida, whose Rule 1.6 reads as follows:

(a) Consent Required to Reveal Information. A lawyer must not reveal information relating to representation of a client except as stated in subdivisions (b), (c), and (d), unless the client gives informed consent.

(b) When Lawyer Must Reveal Information. A lawyer must reveal confidential information to the extent the lawyer reasonably believes necessary:

(1) to prevent a client from committing a crime; or

(2) to prevent a death or substantial bodily harm to another.

(c) When Lawyer May Reveal Information. A lawyer may reveal confidential information to the extent the lawyer reasonably believes necessary:

(1) to serve the client's interest unless it is information the client specifically requires not to be disclosed;

(2) to establish a claim or defense on behalf of the lawyer in a controversy between the lawyer and client;

(3) to establish a defense to a criminal charge or civil claim against the lawyer based on conduct in which the client was involved;

(4) to respond to allegations in any proceeding concerning the lawyer's representation of the client;

(5) to comply with the Rules Regulating The Florida Bar; or

(6) to detect and resolve conflicts of interest between lawyers in different firms arising from the lawyer's change of employment or from changes in the composition or ownership of a firm, but only if the revealed information would not compromise the attorney-client privilege or otherwise prejudice the client.

(d) Exhaustion of Appellate Remedies. When required by a tribunal to reveal confidential information, a lawyer may first exhaust all appellate remedies.

(e) Inadvertent Disclosure of Information. A lawyer must make reasonable efforts to prevent the inadvertent or unauthorized disclosure of, or unauthorized access to, information relating to the representation of a client.

(f) **Limitation on Amount of Disclosure**. When disclosure is mandated or permitted, the lawyer must disclose no more information than is required to meet the requirements or accomplish the purposes of this rule.

Problems 2–2 through 2–11 examine some of the particulars of the various versions of the confidentiality rules. Later Problems invite discussion focusing more on the theory underlying them. The Problems are designed to help us decide which version of the Rules we support. They depict situations in which the lawyer's advice or work product has *not* been involved in the perpetration of crime or fraud. If the lawyer's advice or work product *had* been involved, a different situation would have been presented and mandatory disclosure might have been involved. See Model Rules 1.2(d), 3.3(b), and 4.1(b). These Problems also do not deal with a lawyer's advance or subsequent knowledge of a client's perjury. Those issues are discussed later. We are simply dealing with the variety of situations in which a lawyer learns, with more or less certainty, that the client is intending to engage in a variety of different kinds of wrongdoing. In discussions about the appropriate Rule and about the appropriate exercise of discretion where a lawyer is given discretion, much of the focus is on a calculation of the costs and benefits of confidentiality as against disclosure. Advocates of more disclosure argue that lawyers are in a position to prevent great harm in specific situations to specific people. Advocates of more confidentiality argue that lawyers prevent harm by dissuading clients from pursuing proposed harmful conduct that they learn of only because the client, who has been reassured by the confidentiality principle, confides in them. They contend that lawyers prevent more harm in that fashion than lawyers would prevent were disclosure required because no one would reveal damaging information if the confidentiality principle were diluted. It is not easy to see how reliable information can be obtained to test this hypothesis and so the argument continues primarily on the basis of the different perceptions of the disputants.

Problem 2–2   *In Class*

While Client is at an appointment in Lawyer's office, he excuses himself for a moment, telling Lawyer that he is about to put a second quarter in the meter at which he is parked. This is a misdemeanor. Lawyer tells him so and with a light touch suggests that he not do it. Client laughs and leaves to feed the meter. Lawyer looks out the window and sees a police officer approaching. Under which of the three rule models would Lawyer have discretion to advise the officer of her client's intention to commit a crime? Should she exercise her discretion to do so?

Problem 2–3   *In Class*

Client leaves Lawyer's office for an important appointment in a city 70 miles away with only an hour to spare. The speed limit on the interstate highway between the two cities is 55 mph but Client says that he will make the appointment on time by driving at 80 mph all the way as he usually does. Client also seems to have been drinking rather heavily. Lawyer tries unsuccessfully to stop Client from undertaking the trip. Under which formulation of the disciplinary rules, would Lawyer have discretion to warn the State Police? Should she exercise her discretion to do so?

Problem 2–4

An anti-discrimination law guaranteeing women equal access to places of public accommodation has recently been passed in Lawyer's city. Client has for the past twenty years operated a "men only" bar in the business district. Fearing a loss of distinctiveness with a consequent loss of business he tells Lawyer that he is going to take active steps to discourage patronage by women. He is going to encourage his regular customers to help him but states that he will not condone violence of any sort. His activities violate the statute and clearly constitute criminal conduct. Client says that he is going to take his chances and disregard Lawyer's advice to obey the law. Under which formulation of the disciplinary rules may Lawyer call the police or the district attorney and report Client's intentions to them? Should he exercise his discretion to do so?

Problem 2–5

In discussing a federal tax return almost ready to be filed Lawyer advises a waiter that it is clear that he must report all tips as income. The client replies that it isn't fair to tax such receipts, that none of his friends report such items, that none has ever been caught, and that he will not report the receipts as income. If the client asks what the audit rate is and what his chances of being caught are, how should Lawyer respond? Information about the percentage of audit returns in various categories is in the public domain. In any event, under which formulation of the disciplinary rules may Lawyer warn the IRS that client is not reporting income? Should Lawyer exercise her discretion to do so?

Problem 2–6

Client has been involved in bitter litigation with a former partner who has wound up not only taking control of the whole business but also marrying Client's ex-wife. Client has said several times that if the law doesn't give justice he will get his own justice. After the judge has rendered his decision against Client, Client and Lawyer have a tense meeting discussing whether to appeal. Client storms out of the office, stating that he has brought his gun and is going looking for his former partner. Lawyer tries to stop him but Client breaks away and rushes out of the building. Under which formulation of the disciplinary rules may Lawyer warn the former partner? Should she do so? Under the Florida example (quoted above), does Lawyer have any discretion at all?

In considering Problem 2–6 one should be aware of the possibility that a lawyer's duty may arise from law other than the law of professional responsibility, specifically tort law in such a situation. See Tarasoff v. Regents of University of California, 17

Cal. 3d 425 (1976) (allegation that failure of psychotherapist, who had learned of danger to victim from patient through patient's confidential communication, to warn victim stated a cause of action for damages as a result of subsequent murder of victim by patient; police who had learned of danger and failed to warn victim would not be liable because of lack of special relation to the murderer). Accord, McIntosh v. Milano, 168 N.J. Super. 466 (L. Div. 1979). At the very end of the drafting process of the original Model Rules, the attempt to defend a "may" instead of a "must" provision in the Model Rules for a case like Problem 2–6 was eliminated from the Comment to Rule 1.6. The Washington Supreme Court has stated in dicta that lawyers have a mandatory duty to break confidentiality when they know beyond a reasonable doubt that clients intend to inflict serious physical injury on a third party. Hawkins v. King County Dept. of Rehabilitation Services, 602 P.2d 361 (Wash. 1979).

Problem 2–6 raises another problem regarding lawyer–client confidentiality. Some states now require anyone with knowledge of spousal and/or child abuse to report this information. These statutes are generally aimed at the medical community, though to be sure, one could imagine a statute of general application being extended to lawyers. See, e.g., Ariz. Ethics Op. 01–02 (2001) (reviewing a state statute specifically requiring lawyers to report elder abuse to authorities and concluding that lawyers are ethically permitted, but not required, to disclose the abuse). Should lawyers be expected to comply? Why not? Relatedly, what if the IRS required disclosure of the names of all sources of lawyers' income? Should lawyers presumptively be exempted from these statutes of general application? Should lawyers ever be permitted to act in ways that are otherwise prohibited by statutes of general application?

Problem 2–7

With respect to the Problems already considered, if Lawyer is about to exercise her discretion to reveal a confidence pursuant to discretion granted under the applicable disciplinary rules, should she tell the client in advance? See generally Model Rule 1.4. What should Lawyer then do if the client at that point says, "If you are going to reveal, I'll follow your advice and not do what upset you." Note the Model Rules' Comment 2 to Rule 1.6: "Based upon experience, lawyers know that almost all clients follow the advice given, and the law is upheld." Without such experience, is it your instinct that, unlike the relationship between children and parents, most clients do follow their lawyers' advice?

Problem 2–8

A new client has just come into your office. At the outset of your conversation what, if anything, should you say about the lawyer-client relationship as it pertains to the confidentiality principle? If you should say something, please formulate the "set speech" or "speeches" that you would include in the opening interview. How do you define the principle? What do you say about the exceptions? Do you say anything about your view of the way you should exercise your discretion? Is it permissible to commit yourself in advance? Would you?

Problem 2–9*

Trireme Aluminum Co., a closely held corporation manufacturing alloys primarily used by the aircraft industry, has developed a new, higher-strength aluminum alloy especially for use in light planes. Largely because of significant demand for this one product, Trireme has turned around a three-year earnings deficit and is well into a second profitable year.

One evening over dinner, the company's chief engineer confided to Trireme's outside counsel, who was an old college friend, that he feared the worst. The engineer said that although the new alloy had met all applicable safety standards and design requirements when officially tested, the company lab's recent tests had convinced him that the alloy would crack at extremely cold temperatures; that the potential danger to the public had increased as Trireme marketed the alloy for use in larger planes flying at higher altitudes; and that he had kept the company president informed of this research but had been told not to discuss it with anyone else. He added that his conscience had bothered him for not telling anyone, but that for a number of reasons he was unwilling to "surface" with this information. Primarily, it appeared, he was afraid of losing his job. He told counsel to use this information as needed, but not to mention his name. He reasoned that his identity would be safe because the entire ten-member engineering staff was aware of the problem and most of them agreed with him; no one would immediately think that he was the source.

Counsel preserved his informant's anonymity, but mentioned what he had heard to the company president the next day. The president insisted that despite a majority view of the engineering staff that there was, in fact, a danger, a substantial minority of the more experienced members of that staff believed that the tests showed no danger or at worst were inconclusive. More important, he said, was the fact that the alloy unquestionably met established minimum design requirements and safety standards. He added, finally, that adjustments in the alloy formula were in the process of being tested, so that in due course any problem—which he believed not to exist anyway—would undoubtedly be resolved.

Counsel raised the possibilities of informing Trireme's customers and of suggesting the recall of planes. He also suggested that Trireme consider repurchase of all inventory in the field. The president sharply rebuked him with references not only to the conflicting opinions about the tests themselves but also to the recent

---

* This hypothetical was created by Judge John Ferren of the District of Columbia Court of Appeals for use at a conference on ethical responsibilities of corporate lawyers. A paper by Judge Ferren discussing this hypothetical, "The Corporate Lawyer's Obligation to the Public Interest," appears in 33 Bus. Law. 1253 (1978). It is followed by further remarks by Judge Ferren and a panel discussion of the underlying issues.

turnaround in company fortunes because of the alloy, the fact that 25 percent of company sales were now dependent on the alloy, and that employment in the local community, which had been depressed for years, would suffer severely if there were any break in production.

Counsel informed the board of directors about these conversations at the next regular meeting, but the board unanimously agreed with the president and informed counsel that the matter should be considered closed.

A month later a medium-range, higher altitude plane made of the alloy, the Roton S-12, crashed during a charter flight, killing everyone aboard. The investigation did not conclusively determine the cause; it stated that pilot error appeared to be the principal factor. A portion of the report, however, referred to unusual fractures in the aileron and elevator spars. One investigator questioned the ductility of the basic metal; another surmised that the particular assembly was defective—essentially human error rather than a deficiency in design.

No investigator had contacted Trireme. Without further evidence, however, the National Transportation Safety Board made a most unusual recommendation with respect to such ambiguous facts: that the FAA summarily issue an "Airworthiness Directive" (AD) suspending use of the new alloy until further investigation could take place, and grounding all Roton S-12s and other aircraft made of the alloy. The FAA did so. Trireme's president asked company counsel to join Roton Corp.'s counsel in a challenge to the suspension by going first to the FAA and, if necessary, to court. Counsel agreed.

Trireme and Roton prevailed in court, which ordered revocation of the AD solely on the basis of the government's scanty, ambiguous documentation. Trireme's counsel had successfully moved to quash government subpoenas of company records and employees on the ground of irrelevance, arguing that the FAA's summary issuance of the AD must be judged solely by reference to its prima facie case. The court held that, given the investigative report's emphasis on human error, the AD had been issued arbitrarily on purely speculative grounds. The government filed a notice of appeal and sought a stay of the trial court's action. Without waiting for completion of the judicial process, a Congressional subcommittee, upset by this rebuff to the FAA's authority when the public safety was involved, immediately announced an investigation, issuing subpoenas to company officials and to the engineering staff. The Trireme board of directors has asked to meet with outside counsel.

At this point in the materials consider only the lawyer's responsibility to make disclosure just before—and just after—the crash of the Roton S-12. Does he have any obligation or discretion to reveal the danger he believes to exist? Does the answer turn on whether a crime or fraudulent act has been committed? Why should disclosure of danger to life be forbidden when the danger arises from reckless or negligent (instead of from fraudulent or criminal) conduct? Note that although the Problem deals with the dramatic danger posed by a "defective" airplane, similar issues would be posed by "defective" drugs or food or unnoticeable but "dangerous" pollution or the like. Besides the lawyer's obligation vis-à-vis the public, the problem also raises the question of the lawyer's responsibility to, and within, the corporation. These issues are the subject of Chapter 5.

Problem 2–10

Housing Project, operated by the City Housing Authority, had become the object of a tenants' rent strike to protest intolerable living conditions in the Project. A tenants' association was formed, and rents withheld from the Housing Authority were turned over to representatives of the Tenants' Association. The Housing Authority filed suit for the rent money and sought a court order that the Association turn the rent money over to a custodial receiver. The Association opposed the application by giving assurances in affidavit form that the funds were intact and secure in a safe deposit box.

After oral argument by counsel for the Housing Authority and the Tenants' Association, the court denied the motion of the Housing Authority. It ordered the Association to account for all monies received, and directed that the funds not be removed from the safe deposit box except by order of the court, pending further determination as to the rights of the Housing Authority and the tenants to the funds. Subsequently, the trial judge determined that the tenants were not entitled to rent-free occupancy in the Project because of the living conditions, and that at the most they would be entitled to an abatement of rent. All tenants who had paid rent money into the fund were ordered to show cause on November 17 why the fund should not be turned over to the Housing Authority, subject to the tenants establishing the basis for any claimed refund.

A meeting of the Executive Committee of the Tenants' Association was held on November 13. Possible refund of the rent money to the individual tenants was discussed. Lawyers for the Association counseled strongly against the disbursement of the funds, stating that it would be a violation of the court order and would subject those responsible to charges of contempt. The Executive Committee then decided to hold a meeting of all the contributing tenants the next day to decide what to do with the money. What should Lawyers do? Suppose that there had been discussion at the November 13 meeting of the possibility of having the rent money available at the November 14 meeting. Should that make any difference with respect to Lawyers' course of action?

The facts in this problem are based on In re Callan, 66 N.J. 401 (1975), which arose on contempt charges and did not pass on the issue whether there was any violation of the disciplinary rules. The local grievance committee later dismissed discipline charges against the three lawyers who were involved. The majority of the Supreme Court of New Jersey stated that if the lawyers in *Callan* knew that the Tenants' Association was going to distribute the escrowed funds "they would have been required to inform the court that its order as to the security of the funds was about to be violated. The attorney-client relationship would not require or justify silence in a situation where the integrity of the rule of law was at stake." 66 N.J. at 407. The court does not say where that rule of law comes from. It did not cite its disciplinary rule that stated that a lawyer "may" reveal the client's intention to commit a crime. Perhaps it was announcing a supplementary common law rule, one that applied only to court orders and not to statutory law because otherwise its disciplinary rule would have no function. Does the relationship of the lawyer to the court justify a different rule? Does the more specific focus of a court order justify a different rule?

Problem 2–11

Your client is a principal in an "SDV" business, which are businesses controlled by service-disabled veterans. SDV businesses are potentially lucrative and otherwise attractive because three percent of federal government contracts are specifically reserved for such businesses. Your client is not a service-disabled veteran and has never claimed to be. But to qualify under the federal regulations, service-disabled veterans must own fifty-one percent or more of the company and be involved in the day-to-day management of the company. Your client knew two service-disabled veterans and asked them to join his business in order to qualify for the government contracts. You formed the LLC, and gave each member a one-third interest. When the federal regulations were later amended (to require that a service-disabled veteran be the managing member), moreover, you restructured the LLC so that it continued to meet the minimum requirements to qualify as an SDV business. Recently, a competing business (which lost a bid for a government contract to your client's business) went to the authorities claiming that your client is committing fraud by in essence owning and running the SDV business (and that the minor participation by your client's veteran friends is simply a sham to avoid detection). The government has since taken the competitor's side and has indicted your client for fraud. The government has now subpoenaed your firm for documents relating to the structuring and restructuring of the corporation. First, do you tell your client about the subpoena? (Would there be any basis on which not to tell the client?) Second, do you object to the subpoena (and if so, on what grounds)? The government contends that to the extent the subpoenaed documents otherwise contain attorney-client privileged information, the crime-fraud exception applies. Should the fraud have to be proven first? Is the government really just prematurely and improperly shifting its burden of proof onto your client (at least with respect to your client's privileged information)?

For your part, you knew that the client was deliberately trying to structure and later restructure the LLC to qualify for SDV status. Does that make your client's conduct criminal or fraudulent? If so, does that mean that you counseled or assisted your client in criminal or fraudulent activity? Lawyers have been directly prosecuted for attempting to counsel clients to comply (perhaps just barely) with evolving areas of law. See generally United States v. Anderson, 85 F. Supp. 2d 1047, 1064–65 (D. Kan. 1999); Joan Burgess Killgore, Comment, "Surgery with a Meat Cleaver: The Criminal Indictment of Health Care Attorneys in United States v. Anderson," 43 St. Louis U. L.J. 1215, 1245 (1999). Such prosecutions are occasionally successful but occasionally fail, either because the attorneys lacked the requisite criminal intent or because countervailing considerations (e.g., a First Amendment right to provide good faith legal advice) prevailed.

2. Perjury, Fraud on the Court, and Mandatory Disclosure of Client Confidences

Do it for feedback

Problem 2–12

(a) Client is a defendant in a murder case. From your very first interview when he blurted out his guilt, he has taken the position that, if necessary, he intends to lie about his whereabouts at the crucial time because he knows that identification of him by one witness for the state will be crucial. As the trial date approaches, it is clear that his chances of acquittal are small if he doesn't take the stand. He wants to take the stand and make the most persuasive statement he can that he was not, and has never been, at the place where the victim was killed. What alternatives are available to you? Which will you select? In the future, would you say anything to the client at the first interview to avoid the problem?

(b) In response to a request for production of documents in a civil matter, Client produced a memorandum documenting a conversation with her adversary that was favorable to her cause. During her deposition Client authenticated the document as having been prepared contemporaneously with the conversation. Lawyer was at Client's office after Client's deposition was completed and overheard a conversation between Client and her secretary. The conversation made it apparent that the document had in fact been prepared only after litigation seemed likely and was not an accurate report of the conversation. What alternatives are available to Lawyer? Which would you select?

(c) You represent a spouse in a child custody dispute. He has been accused of currently using methamphetamines and is therefore unfit to have custody of his daughter. Your client insists that he has not used meth in over five years and that his former spouse has falsely accused him to extract additional alimony payments. You ask your client to submit to a drug test to prove his assertions. The next week, the technician from the drug laboratory calls you to tell you the results. Your client has tested negative for meth (good), but your client has tested positive for cocaine (bad). You ask the technician to send you only the portion of the report that shows the negative results for meth. Is that request unethical? Either way, when the report arrives, you see that the technician simply took scissors and cut off the bottom of the report (which presumably showed the positive result for cocaine). You submit the report to the court (attached to your motion to grant custody to your client) and appear for the custody hearing. At the hearing, the court asks you, "Is this the full report?" How may (or must) you respond? Take a look at Model Rule 3.3; does it answer the question? Could you simply rephrase and narrow the judge's question and respond truthfully to the rephrased question? (Cf. Bronston v. United States, 409 U.S. 352 (1973).) Did you violate Model Rule 3.3 or 3.4 in submitting the partial version of the report in the first place? See Lerman and Schrag, *Ethical Problems in the Practice of Law* (3d ed. 2012) (raising and discussing a substantially similar version of this Problem).

———

One fact situation that has been especially troublesome for lawyers is that of client perjury. What is the lawyer to do when the client, a party, says that he or she is going to lie on the stand? Does it make a difference whether the case is civil or criminal? Although the situation might logically be thought to be simply another illustration of the problem of lawyers' obligations when they know of a client's intention to commit a crime, the particular problem of perjury—lying in court—has always been thought to be special. Resolution of this question and the stance it imposes on lawyers have been at the center of much of the debate about the confidentiality principle and the nature of, and justification for, the adversary system.

The debate is not new. A particularly bitter dispute over the confidentiality principle took place in mid–nineteenth century England (see Mellinkoff, *The Conscience of a Lawyer* (1973)), and there have been sporadic disputes in this country too. One was provoked by a speech and article prepared by Charles Curtis, an eminent Boston attorney, in 1951 ("The Ethics of Advocacy," 4 Stan. L. Rev. 3). The theme of his piece was that the devotion that a lawyer owes to the client is so great that it often requires lawyers to do many things for clients that they would not do for themselves.

> And why not? The relation between a lawyer and his client is one of the intimate relations. You would lie for your wife. You would lie for your child. There are others with whom you are intimate enough, close enough, to lie for them when you would not lie for yourself. At what point do you stop lying for them? I don't know and you are not sure. [Id. at 8.]

Curtis did draw the line at lying to the court since a "lawyer's duty to his client cannot rise higher than its source, which is the court." Id. at 7. He went on to indicate, however, that occasionally a lawyer may have a duty "not to speak" to the court, id. at 9.

Mr. Curtis's article provoked angry replies, the principal one from Mr. Henry Drinker, author of the leading work on professional ethics, *Legal Ethics* (1953), and chairman of the ABA Committee on Professional Ethics from 1944–1953 and 1955–1958. "Mr. Curtis to the contrary notwithstanding, no man can be either too honest, too truthful, or too upright to be a thoroughly good lawyer, and an eminently successful one.... A lawyer need never lie for his client.... Of course no one could say that an occasion might not possibly arise when there was no alternative except the truth or a lie and when the consequences of the truth were such that the lawyer might be tempted to lie. This, however, would not make it right for him to do so." Drinker, "Some Remarks on Mr. Curtis' 'The Ethics of Advocacy,'" 4 Stan. L. Rev. 349, 350 (1952). Mr. Drinker did state, however, that there are occasions when a lawyer's duty to keep his client's confidences may require him to refuse to disclose information.

In 1953, shortly after the appearance of these articles, the ABA Committee on Professional Ethics was forced to deal with a situation rather similar to that envisaged by Mr. Curtis. In the best known and most influential opinion it ever wrote,

Opinion 287, it responded to two inquiries relating to client fraud under the pre-1969 Canons of Ethics. The inquiry relevant to the present discussion involved a convicted client obtaining a sentence of probation only because of misinformation received by the judge at the sentencing hearing. The most difficult part of the inquiry related to the lawyer's duty when he knew from confidential information that the client lied to the judge in response to an inquiry about his prior record. The majority of a divided Committee, in an opinion by Mr. Drinker, concluded that the lawyer should "endeavor to persuade the client to tell the court the truth and if he refuses to do so should sever his relations with the client, but should not violate the client's confidence." The Committee advised that in that case the Canon mandating confidentiality should prevail over the Canon requiring disclosure of fraud on a third party and the Canon requiring lawyers to disclose perjury to the prosecuting authorities. Finding the Canons irreconcilable, the Committee viewed the principle of confidentiality as the strongest.

For the past thirty years, Professor Monroe Freedman was a leading proponent of the view that our adversary system requires lawyers to put a criminal defendant client on the stand, conduct the direct examination, and argue the client's testimony in normal fashion even if they know that the testimony is perjured so long as the lawyers have attempted previously to convince the client not to commit perjury. Freedman's position has been rejected by many courts and by the Model Rules, but the issue has not gone away and the debate continues. After a long and notable career, Freedman passed away in 2016, but his position is set forth in the excerpt that follows.

Monroe Freedman and Abbe Smith
Understanding Lawyers' Ethics
pp. 159–173 (3d ed. 2004)*

Is it ever proper for a criminal defense lawyer to present testimony that she knows is perjurious? Our answer is yes. . . .

Underlying proposed solutions to the problem of client perjury are two sharply different models of the lawyer-client relationship. The traditional model, as we have seen, is one of trust and confidence between lawyer and client. The client is urged to confide in the lawyer and is encouraged to do so by a pledge of confidentiality.

The other model is one referred to in the literature as intentional ignorance (or, sometimes, selective ignorance). That is, the lawyer puts the client on notice that the lawyer would prefer not to know certain kinds of facts, and/or that the lawyer can be expected to pass on to the judge or the other party information that the client would prefer to keep confidential. The burden is then on the uncounseled client to speculate about whether to entrust potentially harmful facts to the lawyer — to decide, that is, what is relevant and what is irrelevant, what is incriminating and what is

---

* [Professors Freedman and Smith published a Fifth Edition in 2016, but the following discussion is substantially similar in both versions. — Eds.]

exculpatory. That kind of decision is, of course, uniquely the lawyer's responsibility by virtue of her special training and skills.

The problem for the client is illustrated by a case related by a lawyer who practiced intentional ignorance. The client was accused of stabbing her husband to death with a kitchen knife. In conferences with her lawyer, she consistently denied committing the crime. The facts, however, were damning. The killing had taken place in the couple's kitchen; only her fingerprints were on the knife; she was in the apartment at the time; and she had no other suspect to offer. An investigator informed the lawyer, however, of reports from neighbors that the husband had had a habit of getting drunk and brutalizing the wife. Confronted with that information by her lawyer, the defendant broke down and "confessed." Her husband had been drunk and was about to attack her again. As she backed away, her hand fell upon the knife and, in her terror, she stabbed him.

Why, expostulated the lawyer, had she not volunteered the information to him in the first place? Because, explained his client—who was unsophisticated about the law of self-defense—"it proved I did it."

Apart from the practical problems of requiring clients to do their own lawyering, we might question whether intentional ignorance is a moral resolution of the lawyer's ethical problem. Certainly, lawyers who practice intentional ignorance have the comfort of saying that they have never knowingly presented a client's perjury. On the other hand, by remaining ignorant, these same lawyers have disabled themselves from being in a position to dissuade their clients from committing the perjury. Lawyers can remain aloof from client perjury, but that does not prevent perjury from happening. Indeed, there is good reason to believe that there would be more perjury, not less, if lawyers did not know about it and were not in a position to discourage it. . . .

The lawyer's ethical difficulty has been called a trilemma, because it derives from three obligations. First, in order to give clients the effective assistance of counsel to which they are entitled, lawyers are required to seek out all relevant facts. Second, in order to encourage clients to entrust their lawyers with embarrassing or possibly harmful information, lawyers are under a duty of confidentiality with regard to information obtained in the professional relationship. Third, lawyers are expected to be candid with the court.

A moment's reflection makes it clear, however, that a lawyer cannot do all three of those things—know everything, keep it in confidence, and reveal it to the court over the client's objections. To resolve this trilemma, therefore, one of the three duties must give way.

If we forgo the first duty (seeking all relevant information), we would be adopting the model of intentional ignorance. If we sacrifice the second duty (maintaining confidentiality), clients would quickly learn that their lawyers could not be trusted and would withhold damaging information; again, the result is intentional ignorance. Only by limiting the third duty—by allowing lawyers to be less than candid with the court when necessary to protect clients' confidences—can we maintain the traditional lawyer-client model.

The critical focus of our concern in resolving the problem of client perjury is the initial interview with the client. That is, depending upon how the lawyer resolves the trilemma, she will act upon that decision at the outset of the relationship. . . .

Under the traditional model, she will impress upon her client how important it is that she know everything, and she will assure the client of confidentiality. On the other hand, under the model of intentional ignorance, she will, in one form or another, give the client a "lawyer-client Miranda warning."

Obviously, such a warning is going to impede, if not wholly frustrate, the already difficult task of establishing a relationship of trust and confidence with the client. This problem is particularly acute for the public defender or court-appointed lawyer, who typically meets her client for the first time in jail. The defendant has not chosen the lawyer. On the contrary, the lawyer has been sent by the judge and is part of the system that is trying to convict and punish him. It is no easy matter to persuade this client that he can talk freely to his lawyer without fear of prejudice. The question in the client's mind is, "Can I really trust you?" And the client will not be reassured by a lawyer who invites full disclosure and at the same time cautions the client about the possible betrayal of his confidences.

However, the reluctance to impart embarrassing or harmful information to one's lawyer is not unique to the indigent client or to the criminal defendant. Randolph Paul observed a similar phenomenon among a wealthier class in a far more congenial atmosphere:

> The tax adviser will sometimes have to dynamite the facts of his case out of the unwilling witnesses on his own side—witnesses who are nervous, witnesses who are confused about their own interest, witnesses who try to be too smart for their own good, and witnesses who subconsciously do not want to understand what has happened despite the fact that they must if they are to testify coherently.[12]

Paul goes on to explain that the truth can be obtained only by persuading the client that it would be a violation of a sacred obligation for the lawyer ever to reveal a client's confidence.

Perhaps, though, we are being unduly sympathetic towards a client who does not want to reveal his guilt to his lawyer. One might argue that if it is the client's knowing and voluntary choice, it is on his own head. . . . The lawyer who gives a Miranda warning is not the client's champion against a hostile world; on the contrary, she presents herself at the outset as an agent of that hostile world. . . .

---

12. Randolph Paul, "The Responsibilities of the Tax Adviser," 63 Harv. L. Rev. 377, 383 (1950).

Nor is it accurate or fair to characterize the client's choice to withhold information from his lawyer as a knowing and voluntary one. Particularly when the client is alone against that hostile world, he may well be frightened and confused—even, as Paul has indicated, unable to comprehend fully what is happening to him. What he needs is the wise counsel of his lawyer based upon the facts as they are, not as he would wish them to be. Until the client has had his lawyer's guidance about the case as it really is, the client is not in a position to make a truly knowing and voluntary choice about what to withhold. Put otherwise, to deprive the client of his right to the "guiding hand of counsel" at the outset of the representation is too heavy a penalty to exact, even against the client who might be trying, without the benefit of counsel, to be "too smart for his own good." . . .

Consider the woman with the kitchen knife, who had been fearful of telling her lawyer facts that she thought incriminating but which were actually exculpatory. In that case, the lawyer discovered the information through other sources, but that is not ordinarily likely or even feasible. Or consider the following case, in which an innocent client proposes to commit perjury.

Your client has been erroneously accused of a robbery committed at 16th and P Streets at 11:00 p.m. He tells you at first that at no time on the evening of the crime was he within six blocks of that location. You are able to persuade him, though, that he must tell you the truth and that doing so will in no way prejudice him. He then reveals to you that he was at 15th and P Streets, one block away from the scene of the crime, at 10:55 that evening; however, he was going east, away from the scene of the crime, and by 11:00 p.m. he was six blocks away.

There are two prosecution witnesses. The first mistakenly, but with some degree of persuasion, identifies your client as the criminal. The second witness is an elderly woman who is somewhat nervous and wears glasses. She testifies truthfully and accurately that she saw your client at 15th and P Streets at 10:55 p.m. She has corroborated the erroneous testimony of the first witness and made conviction seem virtually certain. On cross-examination, however, you are able to show that she is easily confused and has poor eyesight. At that point, the prosecution's case rests, in effect, on the first witness, and your successful cross-examination of the second witness may have cast doubt on the prosecution's entire case.

Your client insists upon testifying, which is his right as a matter of due process. He believes that he is more likely to be found not guilty if he takes the stand to testify, truthfully, that he is innocent of the crime and to tell the jury where he was at 11:00 p.m. However, he is convinced that he cannot afford to admit that the second prosecution witness correctly placed him one block from the scene of the crime at 10:55 p.m., because that would rehabilitate both the elderly witness and the prosecution's case against him. You try to dissuade him from testifying perjuriously, but he is adamant. What should you do?

The most obvious way to avoid the ethical difficulty would appear to be withdrawal from the case, if that can be done without prejudice to the client. The client will then find another lawyer and will probably withhold the incriminating information from her. In systemic terms, withdrawal under such circumstances is difficult to defend, since the new lawyer will be in no position to attempt to dissuade the client from presenting it. Only the original attorney, who knows the truth, has that opportunity, but she loses it in the very act of evading the ethical problem. For that reason, we would not require the lawyer to withdraw as long as there is opportunity to dissuade the client.

Moreover, the lawyer should be forbidden to withdraw if doing so would prejudice the client in any way. Prejudice cannot ordinarily be avoided if the case is near to trial or the trial has begun. Replacing the lawyer in those circumstances will delay the calendar, a major concern of all judges and the overriding concern of too many. The court will therefore require the lawyer to give extraordinary reasons for withdrawal, which would require the lawyer to reveal to the judge that the client intends to commit perjury. In addition, the new lawyer might well face the same problem. Indeed, the client might force disqualification of a series of lawyers in the same way, ultimately forcing the judge to try the case without a defense lawyer. That is likely to be an awkward and unsatisfactory procedure.

In most cases, therefore, the attorney can withdraw only by revealing the client's confidences to the judge — that is, by telling the judge that the client has admitted incriminating evidence to the lawyer but intends to try to lie his way out of it. Since the judge will be imposing sentence on the client in the event of a conviction, the prejudice to the client would be severe. The same kind of prejudice might also affect the defendant's appeal.

Even when the lawyer reveals the client's intended perjury to the judge, the motion to withdraw is likely to be denied. Again, the judge can anticipate a series of such motions. A common judicial response, therefore, is to tell the lawyer, "I understand your problem, but the next lawyer might have the same difficulty. You'll just have to go forward as best you can."

This has led to a sophisticated (or disingenuous) variation on withdrawal that is particularly unsatisfactory. The lawyer, well aware that her motion for leave to withdraw "for ethical reasons" will be denied, makes it anyway. Then, having attempted to protect herself from charges of complicity in her client's perjury, she can elicit the client's perjury and argue it to the jury. She has protected herself, however, by engaging in a charade that betrays the client. Again, when it comes time for sentencing and appeal, the judges will know from the defendant's own lawyer that he has committed perjury. . . .

Another effort to deal with the trilemma first appeared as a proposal in Section 7.7 of the 1971 version of the ABA Standards Relating to the Defense Function. Under this "narrative" solution, the lawyer is required to "confine his examination to identifying the witness as the defendant and permitting him to make his statement." . . . That is, the lawyer has the client present his testimony in narrative form, rather than in the normal question-and-answer format. Then, in closing argument, the lawyer is to make no reference to what the lawyer has learned from the client to be false testimony.

Beyond any question, this procedure divulges the client's confidences. The judge is certain to understand what is going on, and it is generally agreed that the jury usually will as well. Even if the jury does not realize the significance of the unusual manner in which the defendant is testifying, the jury is sure to catch on when the defense lawyer in closing argument makes no reference to the defendant's exculpatory testimony.

Ironically, Freedman originally argued that the narrative solution would never work, because the prosecutors would object to the presentation of the defendant's testimony in narrative form. . . . Freedman was, of course, wrong. Neither of us has ever heard of a case in which the prosecutor objected to a defense lawyer asking a defendant to testify in narrative. Why should the prosecutor object, when the defendant's own lawyer is signaling to everyone in the courtroom that the defendant is guilty and trying to lie his way out of it?

The narrative solution was never approved by the ABA, which deleted it from the Standards in 1979, with reference to the emerging Model Rules. Then, in 1983, the Model Rules rejected it, explaining that it "compromises both contending principles; it exempts the lawyer from the duty to disclose false evidence but subjects the client to an implicit disclosure of information imparted to counsel." Also, Chief Justice Burger, who was the first to promote the idea, repudiated the narrative solution in Nix v. Whiteside.

Nevertheless, the narrative solution still has its advocates, and it has been adopted as a part of Rule 3.3 in Massachusetts and in the District of Columbia. Also, some courts have approved its use in decisions. . . .

If intentionally remaining ignorant precludes effective representation, and knowing the truth presents an insoluble dilemma, why not choose a solution that avoids both evils? Speaking before a bar group, Roy Cohn gave his method for dealing with the guilty client who wants to commit perjury:

> Before a client could get three words out, any lawyer with half a brain would say, "You probably don't know whether you're guilty or not, because you don't know the elements of the crime you're charged with."
>
> [Then, to avoid hearing what I'm not supposed to hear, I ask the client:] "If someone was going to get up on the stand and lie about you, who would it be? And what would they lie about?" And if the client's got any brains, he'll know what I'm talking about.[45]

Under Cohn's solution, therefore, the lawyer has it both ways. For tactical purposes, he knows what he has to know. For purposes of any ethical obligation,

---

45. David Berreby, "The Cohn/Dershowitz Debate," Nat'l L.J., June 7, 1982, at 15.

however, he does not know either that the client is guilty or that the client is going to commit perjury when he denies the "lies" about him. Thus, the lawyer in Cohn's scenario would not attempt to dissuade the client from committing perjury (except perhaps for tactical reasons) because the lawyer does not "know" about it.

. . . You might question, though, whether the Cohn solution—knowing enough for tactical purposes but not enough for ethical purposes—can properly be called an ethical one.

There is only one method of anticipating and dealing with client perjury that will maintain the traditional model of lawyer-client trust and confidence, protect the fundamental rights to which that relationship gives expression, and put lawyers in a position to dissuade the client from committing perjury.

At the initial client interview, the lawyer impresses upon the client that it is essential that the lawyer know everything there is to know about the client's case. The lawyer also explains to the client that she will maintain the client's confidences and secrets in strict confidence.

If the lawyer learns that the client is contemplating perjury, she should make continuing, good faith efforts to dissuade the client from that course. The lawyer is permitted to withdraw, as long as withdrawal would not prejudice the client; it is preferable, however, that the lawyer not withdraw, but that she continue to use her relationship of trust and confidence with the client . . . to dissuade the client from committing the perjury.

The client, faced with the threat of prison, may or may not be impressed with the fact that perjury is immoral and illegal, but may well be persuaded by the fact that the judge has the power to increase the sentence if she concludes that the defendant has given false testimony. In any event, there is a professional consensus that lawyers are frequently successful in dissuading client perjury. Note again, however, that lawyers can serve this function—to the benefit of society as well as their clients— only if their clients are willing to entrust them with their confidences and to accept their advice. That is not going to happen under the model of intentional ignorance.

In the relatively small number of cases in which the client who has contemplated perjury rejects the lawyer's advice and decides to proceed to trial, to take the stand, and to give false testimony, the lawyer should go forward in the ordinary way. That is, the lawyer should examine the client in the normal professional manner and should argue the client's testimony to the jury in summation to the extent that sound tactics justify doing so. . . .

We are not completely comfortable with this position. Indeed, one of the reasons that client perjury has produced such a substantial body of literature since 1966 is that no one has been able to resolve the trilemma in a way that is wholly consistent either with general norms of morality or with professional standards of ethics. . . .

The most troubling objection to presenting client perjury is that it is inconsistent with one's personal standards of morality. We like to think that we would not lie on our own behalf, even if five or ten years of freedom depended upon it. We cannot know, however, what we would do under those circumstances. That is not a reason in itself to help a client to present false testimony, but it does give us a sense of compassion for the person who feels driven to that course.

Beyond that, we cannot find—in terms of personal morality—a more acceptable course. We find deep moral significance in the dignity of the individual and in the way that dignity is respected in the American constitutional adversary system. Also, as we have seen, our analysis must focus on the first interview with the client. A lawyer is in no position at that point to make an informed judgment as to whether a client is guilty or innocent, what defenses he might have, or what his degree of culpability might be. The lawyer must act, therefore, upon a presumption of innocence. The lawyer cannot serve the client as he deserves to be served if she does not know everything there is to know about the client's case. Accordingly, the lawyer must urge him to tell her everything, and the lawyer must pledge confidentiality. Having given that pledge, we would be morally bound to keep it.

Would we never break our pledge? . . . [T]here are moral values that, for us, take precedence over truthfulness. One is human life, for example, the innocent person on death row. In addition to the value at stake, the situation will occur so infrequently as to create no systemic threat; that is, there is no likelihood that the existence of this exception would make clients fearful of confiding in their lawyers.

We would also withdraw, despite prejudice to the client, to avoid having to go to trial before a corrupted judge or jury. Again, the situation is so unlikely that there is no significant systemic threat. With respect to client perjury, the adversary system is designed, through cross-examination and otherwise, to take it into account. By contrast, a corrupted judge or juror subverts the adversary system itself.

Finally, we would violate confidentiality to the minimum extent necessary to defend ourselves against formalized charges of unlawful or unprofessional conduct. Admittedly, the morality of this exception is more difficult to defend than the first two. It is analogous, however, to the privilege against self-incrimination, which recognizes the fundamental unfairness of requiring one to be self-destructive. Also, it seems implicit in the situation that the client, in one way or another, is prepared to betray the lawyer. In addition, although this contingency may not be as extraordinary as a threat to life or the corruption of a judge or juror, it is sufficiently uncommon to permit an exception without significant systemic threat.

We doubt that there is a criminal defense lawyer (or prosecutor, or civil litigator) who has not more than once faced the problem of perjury in some form, but there are few who have ever had occasion to divulge client confidences in the areas in which we would allow exceptions.

Would we, then, give the client a *Miranda* warning about these exceptions? No, we would not. The life-and-death exception is the easy one—we put a higher value on being able to save a life than on warning a client (who is hypothetically going to be responsible for a death) that he should keep that particular truth from us. The other two exceptions are, unquestionably, less morally compelling than life and death, but sufficiently important in our scale of values. Again, the likelihood of these contingencies occurring is so slight that the harm that would be done to the lawyer-client relationship by a *Miranda* warning on these particular issues far outweighs the marginal value of fairness to the exceptional client to whom the warning would be relevant.

The argument is sometimes raised that a lawyer who knowingly presents perjured testimony is suborning perjury. Subornation of perjury consists, however, in the corrupt inducement of perjury. . . . Clearly, that is not what happens when the idea of perjury originates with the client, the lawyer uses her knowledge of the perjury to make ongoing, good faith efforts to dissuade the client from committing it, and the lawyer then proceeds with the perjury only if necessary under the compulsion of her role in our constitutionalized adversary system.

A related objection is that the lawyer who examines the client in the ordinary way will coach the client in making the perjury more effective. That is a *non sequitur*. Because the lawyer elicits the false testimony in the normal question-and-answer format in court does not mean that the lawyer either must or will help the client to improve upon his lies. It would be a violation of the plain meaning of a disciplinary rule (and very likely unlawful) to do so; it would go beyond the necessities of confidentiality; and it would undercut the lawyer's efforts to dissuade the client by giving the client what would be, at best, a mixed message.

Notes

1. Freedman and Smith's views, like those of their predecessor Charles Curtis, have provoked a great deal of controversy. Specific disagreement with the Freedman answers is contained in Bress, "Professional Ethics in Criminal Trials: A View of Defense Counsel's Responsibility," 64 Mich. L. Rev. 1493 (1966). Disagreement with his underlying premises and a focus on counsel's obligation to the search for truth is contained in Judge John T. Noonan, Jr., "Professional Ethics and Personal Responsibility," 29 Stan. L. Rev. 363 (1977), and David Luban, *Lawyers and Justice*, especially 197–201 (1988).

2. Freedman and Smith define the perjury trilemma as deriving from the conflict between three obligations, all of which they define as absolute. But that begs the question. As set forth in all versions of the rules of professional conduct, neither the duty of confidentiality nor the duty of candor toward the court is absolute, and the obligation to seek out all relevant facts is not an obligation to do absolutely everything that might lead to discovery of relevant facts. The real issue is how these three important values or considerations should be reconciled with one another when they are in conflict.

3. All the proposed solutions have their problems. Freedman and Smith make a major contribution by pointing out the problems with those solutions that they reject. But there are problems with their argument too. Marvin Frankel's piece, which follows in Chapter 3, points out some of them. There are others. When Freedman and

Smith contend that "selective ignorance precludes effective representation," an opponent might respond that effective representation ought not require or even permit a lawyer to present and argue testimony known to be perjured. Freedman and Smith depend a great deal on carefully chosen examples to point out the difficulties of their opponents' arguments. Do they prove their argument that it is not "accurate or fair to characterize the client's choice to withhold information from his lawyer as a knowing or voluntary one" by showing that they can give one or two examples when it might not be the client's choice? Note that one of their examples depends on their assertion that the client is innocent. How often will a lawyer know that? As for the client who might have had a self-defense argument, was her withholding of evidence any less voluntary because she guessed wrong about the truth? Isn't the real question whether the gain to the system from curing the mistaken beliefs of clients by assuring them confidentiality is greater or less than the gain from involving lawyers in presenting perjured testimony in other cases? Is a significant factor in answering that question whether you conclude that one scenario is much more likely to occur than the other?

4. Freedman and Smith pass off very quickly the notion that their solution may involve the lawyer in helping the client in making the perjury more effective. What will they do when they do a trial run of the client's testimony and the fact of perjury is apparent? Will they say nothing to the client and simply let the client tell an obvious lie? That does not sound very different from the consequence they condemn regarding the narrative form of testimony, for they know that the fact-finder will draw the appropriate conclusion. Moreover, they are not giving the client full information about his plight—the very thing that assuring confidentiality was supposed to ensure. But the lawyer may conclude that he can persuade the client not to commit perjury if he demonstrates that the client will be caught. What if he fails to convince the client because the client uses the information to improve the story? Would Freedman and Smith not have helped the client improve his story? Perhaps they would argue that they are saved by the fact that that was not their purpose. But is it not likely that a less scrupulous lawyer will follow the same course with a different purpose, safe in the knowledge that the motivation can never be uncovered? In any event, whatever the lawyer's motivation, the client's story has been improved by the lawyer's help.

5. Freedman and Smith urge that a lawyer make "continuing, good faith efforts" to dissuade a client from committing perjury. Suppose that the client asks the lawyer for a frank assessment of her chances and the lawyer concludes that she will almost certainly be convicted and that her only hope would be to perjure herself. Will he tell her that? If so, what will his efforts to dissuade her from committing perjury sound like? In a jurisdiction that has adopted either the Model Rule or the narrative statement position, the lawyer has an argument that may well dissuade the client from committing perjury, but Freedman and Smith may well be right that in most cases the client won't let the lawyer know and the issue will not arise.

6. Whether Freedman and Smith would give a *Miranda* warning or not in those situations where they would break the client's confidence is not essential to their main point. Do you agree that such a warning ought not be given in any situation where you conclude that an exception to the confidentiality should be made?

Notwithstanding the criticism of the so-called "narrative form of testimony" solution of this problem, it has retained some attraction as a compromise solution. See People v. DePallo, 96 N.Y.2d 437 (2001); People v. Andrades, 4 N.Y.3d 355 (2005); and People v. Johnson, 72 Cal. Rptr. 2d 805 (Cal. App. 1998), adopting it in dicta. The Massachusetts Supreme Judicial Court, in promulgating its version of the Model Rules in 1998 (later amended), added to Rule 3.3 the following paragraph (e) to deal with the problem of perjury by a criminal defendant.

(e) In a criminal case, defense counsel who knows that the defendant, the client, intends to testify falsely may not aid the client in constructing false testimony, and has a duty strongly to discourage the client from testifying falsely, advising that such a course is unlawful, will have substantial adverse consequences, and should not be followed.

(1) If a lawyer discovers this intention before accepting the representation of the client, the lawyer shall not accept the representation;

(2) If, in the course of representing a defendant prior to trial, the lawyer discovers this intention and is unable to persuade the client not to testify falsely, the lawyer shall seek to withdraw from the representation, requesting any required permission. Disclosure of privileged or prejudicial information shall be made only to the extent necessary to effect the withdrawal. If disclosure of privileged or prejudicial information is necessary, the lawyer shall make an application to withdraw ex parte to a judge other than the judge who will preside at the trial and shall seek to be heard in camera and have the record of the proceeding, except for an order granting leave to withdraw, impounded. If the lawyer is unable to obtain the required permission to withdraw, the lawyer may not prevent the client from testifying.

(3) If a criminal trial has commenced and the lawyer discovers that the client intends to testify falsely at trial, the lawyer need not file a motion to withdraw from the case if the lawyer reasonably believes that seeking to withdraw will prejudice the client. If, during the client's testimony or after the client has testified, the lawyer knows that the client has testified falsely, the lawyer shall call upon the client to rectify the false testimony and, if the client refuses or is unable to do so, the lawyer shall not reveal the false testimony to the tribunal. In no event may the lawyer examine the client in such a manner as to elicit any testimony from the client the lawyer knows to be false, and the lawyer shall not argue the probative value of the false testimony in closing argument or in any other proceedings, including appeals.

Professor Kaufman, a member of the Committee that recommended the proposal, published a statement explaining it as follows:

> There is no easy resolution to the many conflicting policies that are at stake in this situation, and it may well be that the task is to select the least worst, rather than the best, solution. . . . The narrative statement rule has been attacked as reaching essentially the same result as the ABA Model Rule but disingenuously. But it does have one advantage. The Model Rule puts the trial judge to whom the information about perjury is communicated by defense counsel in a difficult position. The trial judge may be forced to make a number of decisions about communicating the information to the trier of the facts and about the ability of defense counsel to continue with representation. The narrative statement rule, by removing the requirement of communication with the court, avoids this confusion. The responsibility for the predicament in which defendants may find themselves will remain where it belongs, with those defendants who commit perjury, presumably after having been informed of the consequences by their lawyers.

As so justified, what do you think of the Massachusetts proposal?

what to do if client commits perjury? the MR mandate:
① disclosure if can't dissuade;
② can't w/d; or
③ w/d ≠ remedy

A Note on the Model Rules

The Model Rules in Rule 3.3(a)(3) and 3.3(b), as expounded upon in the Comments to that Rule, take a clear stance *mandating* (not merely authorizing) disclosure of perjury if the lawyer cannot get the client to correct the testimony, if the lawyer is unable to withdraw, or if withdrawal will not remedy the situation. A major argument in the analysis supporting the "disclosure when necessary" requirement is avoidance by the lawyer of implication in commission of perjury through arguing "known perjury" to the judge or jury or through preparing the client to give testimony when the lawyer knows that the client is ready to give perjured testimony. As such, the requirement is seen as simply a special application of the general prohibition in Rule 1.2(d) that the lawyer avoid counseling or assisting a client in conduct known to be criminal or fraudulent. See Model Rule 3.3 cmt. 11. Thus, were a lawyer to learn that a client had perjured herself, the rules require remediation, including (if necessary) disclosure to the court. Model Rule 3.3(a)(3), (b). The obligation to correct the court record generally trumps the confidentiality obligation to the client. In an adversary system (in which the other side at least in theory has a trained advocate to put forth that side's best case and to correct the record), should the client's lawyer have to betray the client? In addition, the Rules do not require disclosure to save an innocent person from spending life in prison or to prevent a plaintiff's death from a life-threatening aneurism, yet they require disclosure in order to be candid with the court. Why the differing standards?

The obligation may also arise under circumstances where the lawyer has not knowingly been implicated in creation of the false record. A clear case would be where the lawyer learns of the client's perjury while the jury is considering its verdict, that is, after the testimony has been given and argued to the jury. What if you were the lawyer and the client tells you about his perjury two months after the jury verdict? See Model Rule 3.3 cmt. 13 (imposing "[a] practical time limit on the obligation to rectify false evidence or false statements of law and fact," i.e., "when a final judgment in the proceeding has been affirmed on appeal or the time for review has passed").

Other mandatory disclosure requirements are contained in Model Rule 3.3(a)(3), which requires a lawyer in some circumstances to disclose to a tribunal the falsity of material evidence introduced by the lawyer without knowledge of its falsity, and Model Rule 4.1, which requires a lawyer in some circumstances to disclose information to a third party when necessary to avoid assisting a criminal or fraudulent act by a client.

Finally, Model Rule 3.3(d) requires a lawyer proceeding *ex parte* to inform the tribunal of all relevant facts known to the lawyer, adverse or not, to permit the tribunal to make "an informed decision." This latter mandatory disclosure rule rests on a different conceptual foundation from the other mandatory disclosure rules. As stated by the Comment, "The judge has an affirmative responsibility to accord the absent party just consideration. The lawyer for the represented party has the correlative duty to make disclosures of material facts known to the lawyer and that the lawyer reasonably believes are necessary to an informed decision."

The judge has the same duty to afford the parties "just consideration" in proceedings that are not *ex parte*. The difference is that all parties are "present." But when, because of chance or a breakdown in the process, one lawyer knows that important relevant information has not reached the tribunal, then that lawyer and the tribunal are in the same position vis-à-vis one another as in the situation when the lawyer proceeding *ex parte* possesses important adverse relevant facts. It is possible to draw a line where the Rules have drawn it, but that requires more justification than the Comment gives. It remains to be seen whether Rule 3.3(d) represents a small step away from the prior situation, and its further extension to all cases, as recommended by Judge Frankel (in the next Chapter), represents a large step, or whether Rule 3.3(d) represents a large step that if successfully taken will lead to the further small step of making it applicable in all cases. Resolution of that question will in part turn on the eventual interpretation of Rule 3.3(d). It could be interpreted to cover only situations like In re Greene, 290 Or. 291 (1980), where a lawyer was disciplined for failure to disclose in *ex parte* proceedings designed to permit trust funds held by his wife for the benefit of her minor children to be used for real estate investment and improvements, that what was involved was paying off a mortgage and making improvements on a home owned by her. See also The Florida Bar v. Tobin, 674 So. 2d 127 (1996) (lawyer disciplined for a violation of Rule 3.3(d) when he obtained an *ex parte* order for distribution of funds without informing court of a lien against the funds). The Rule might also be interpreted more broadly, however.

The issue of client perjury finally reached the Supreme Court in the context of a claim of ineffective assistance of counsel in the following case.

Nix v. Whiteside

475 U.S. 157 (1986)

Chief Justice BURGER delivered the opinion of the Court.

We granted certiorari to decide whether the Sixth Amendment right of a criminal defendant to assistance of counsel is violated when an attorney refuses to cooperate with the defendant in presenting perjured testimony at his trial.

I

A

Whiteside was convicted of second degree murder by a jury verdict which was affirmed by the Iowa courts. The killing took place on February 8, 1977 in Cedar Rapids, Iowa. Whiteside and two others went to one Calvin Love's apartment late that night, seeking marihuana. Love was in bed when Whiteside and his companions arrived; an argument between Whiteside and Love over the marihuana ensued. At one point, Love directed his girlfriend to get his "piece," and at another point got up, then returned to his bed. According to Whiteside's testimony, Love then started to reach under his pillow and moved toward Whiteside. Whiteside stabbed Love in the chest, inflicting a fatal wound.

Whiteside was charged with murder . . . . Robinson was . . . appointed and immediately began investigation. Whiteside gave him a statement that he had stabbed Love as the latter "was pulling a pistol from underneath the pillow on the bed." Upon questioning by Robinson, however, Whiteside indicated that he had not actually seen a gun, but that he was convinced that Love had a gun. No pistol was found on the premises; shortly after the police search following the stabbing, which had revealed no weapon, the victim's family had removed all of the victim's possessions from the apartment. Robinson interviewed Whiteside's companions who were present during the stabbing and none had seen a gun during the incident. Robinson advised Whiteside that the existence of a gun was not necessary to establish the claim of self defense, and that only a reasonable belief that the victim had a gun nearby was necessary even though no gun was actually present.

Until shortly before trial, Whiteside consistently stated to Robinson that he had not actually seen a gun, but that he was convinced that Love had a gun in his hand. About a week before trial, during preparation for direct examination, Whiteside for the first time told Robinson and his associate Donna Paulsen that he had seen something "metallic" in Love's hand. When asked about this, Whiteside responded that "[I]n Howard Cook's case there was a gun. If I don't say I saw a gun I'm dead." Robinson told Whiteside that such testimony would be perjury and repeated that it was not necessary to prove that a gun was available but only that Whiteside reasonably believed that he was in danger. On Whiteside's insisting that he would testify that he saw "something metallic" Robinson told him, according to Robinson's testimony, we could not allow him to [testify falsely] because that would be perjury, and as officers of the court we would be suborning perjury if we allowed him to do it; . . . I advised him that if he did do that it would be my duty to advise the Court of what he was doing and that I felt he was committing perjury; also, that I probably would be allowed to attempt to impeach that particular testimony.

Robinson also indicated he would seek to withdraw from the representation if Whiteside insisted on committing perjury.

Whiteside testified in his own defense at trial and stated that he "knew" that Love had a gun and that he believed Love was reaching for a gun and he had acted swiftly in self defense. On cross examination, he admitted that he had not actually seen a gun in Love's hand. Robinson presented evidence that Love had been seen with a sawed-off shotgun on other occasions, that the police search of the apartment may have been careless, and that the victim's family had removed everything from the apartment shortly after the crime. Robinson presented this evidence to show a basis for Whiteside's asserted fear that Love had a gun.

The jury returned a verdict of second-degree murder and Whiteside moved for a new trial, claiming that he had been deprived of a fair trial by Robinson's admonitions not to state that he saw a gun or "something metallic." . . .

The Supreme Court of Iowa affirmed respondent's conviction. State v. Whiteside, 272 N.W.2d 468 (1978). That court held that the right to have counsel present all appropriate defenses does not extend to using perjury, and that an attorney's duty to a client does not extend to assisting a client in committing perjury. Relying on DR 7-102(A)(4) of the Iowa Code of Professional Responsibility for Lawyers, which expressly prohibits an attorney from using perjured testimony, and Iowa Code § 721.2 (now Iowa Code § 720.3 (1985)), which criminalizes subornation of perjury, the Iowa court concluded that not only were Robinson's actions permissible, but were required. The court commended "both Mr. Robinson and Ms. Paulsen for the high ethical manner in which this matter was handled."

B

Whiteside then petitioned for a writ of habeas corpus in the United States District Court for the Southern District of Iowa. In that petition Whiteside alleged that he had been denied effective assistance of counsel and of his right to present a defense by Robinson's refusal to allow him to testify as he had proposed. The District Court denied the writ. Accepting the State trial court's factual finding that Whiteside's intended testimony would have been perjurious, it concluded that there could be no grounds for habeas relief since there is no constitutional right to present a perjured defense.

The United States Court of Appeals for the Eighth Circuit reversed and directed that the writ of habeas corpus be granted. Whiteside v. Scurr, 744 F.2d 1323 (CA8

1984). The Court of Appeals accepted the findings of the trial judge, affirmed by the Iowa Supreme Court, that trial counsel believed with good cause that Whiteside would testify falsely and acknowledged that under Harris v. New York, 401 U.S. 222 (1971), a criminal defendant's privilege to testify in his own behalf does not include a right to commit perjury. Nevertheless, the court reasoned that an intent to commit perjury, communicated to counsel, does not alter a defendant's right to effective assistance of counsel and that Robinson's admonition to Whiteside that he would inform the court of Whiteside's perjury constituted a threat to violate the attorney's duty to preserve client confidences. According to the Court of Appeals, this threatened violation of client confidences breached the standards of effective representation set down in Strickland v. Washington, 466 U.S. 668 (1984). The court also concluded that *Strickland*'s prejudice requirement was satisfied by an implication of prejudice from the conflict between Robinson's duty of loyalty to his client and his ethical duties. . . . We granted certiorari, 471 U.S. 1014 (1985), and we reverse.

II

A

The right of an accused to testify in his defense is of relatively recent origin. Until the latter part of the preceding century, criminal defendants in this country, as at common law, were considered to be disqualified from giving sworn testimony at their own trial by reason of their interest as a party to the case. . . .

By the end of the nineteenth century, however, the disqualification was finally abolished by statute in most states and in the federal courts. . . . Although this Court has never explicitly held that a criminal defendant has a due process right to testify in his own behalf, cases in several Circuits have so held and the right has long been assumed. . . . We have also suggested that such a right exists as a corollary to the Fifth Amendment privilege against compelled testimony . . . .

B

In Strickland v. Washington, we held that to obtain relief by way of federal habeas corpus on a claim of a deprivation of effective assistance of counsel under the Sixth Amendment, the movant must establish both serious attorney error and prejudice. To show such error, it must be established that the assistance rendered by counsel was constitutionally deficient in that "counsel made errors so serious that counsel was not functioning as 'counsel' guaranteed the defendant by the Sixth Amendment." . . . To show prejudice, it must be established that the claimed lapses in counsel's performance rendered the trial unfair so as to "undermine confidence in the outcome" of the trial. [466 U.S.] at 694.

In *Strickland*, we acknowledged that the Sixth Amendment does not require any particular response by counsel to a problem that may arise. Rather, the Sixth Amendment inquiry is into whether the attorney's conduct was "reasonably effective." To counteract the natural tendency to fault an unsuccessful defense, a court reviewing a claim of ineffective assistance must "indulge a strong presumption that counsel's conduct falls within the wide range of reasonable professional assistance." Id., at 689. In giving shape to the perimeters of this range of reasonable professional assistance, *Strickland* mandates that

> [p]revailing norms of practice as reflected in American Bar Association Standards and the like . . . are guides to determining what is reasonable, but they are only guides.

Id., at 688.

Under the *Strickland* standard, breach of an ethical standard does not necessarily make out a denial of the Sixth Amendment guarantee of assistance of counsel. When examining attorney conduct, a court must be careful not to narrow the wide range of conduct acceptable under the Sixth Amendment so restrictively as to constitutionalize particular standards of professional conduct and thereby intrude into the State's proper authority to define and apply the standards of professional conduct applicable to those it admits to practice in its courts. In some future case challenging attorney conduct in the course of a state court trial, we may need to define with greater precision the weight to be given to recognized canons of ethics, the standards established by the State in statutes or professional codes, and the Sixth Amendment, in defining the proper scope and limits on that conduct. Here we need not face that question, since virtually all of the sources speak with one voice.

C

We turn next to the question presented: the definition of the range of "reasonable professional" responses to a criminal defendant client who informs counsel that he will perjure himself on the stand. We must determine whether, in this setting, Robinson's conduct fell within the wide range of professional responses to threatened client perjury acceptable under the Sixth Amendment.

In *Strickland*, we recognized counsel's duty of loyalty and his "over-arching duty to advocate the defendant's cause." Ibid. Plainly, that duty is limited to legitimate, lawful conduct compatible with the very nature of a trial as a search for truth. Although counsel must take all reasonable lawful means to attain the objectives of the client, counsel is precluded from taking steps or in any way assisting the client in presenting false evidence or otherwise violating the law. This principle has consistently been recognized in most unequivocal terms by expositors of the norms of professional conduct since the first Canons of Professional Ethics were adopted by the American Bar Association in 1908. . . . Similarly, Canon 37, adopted in 1928, explicitly acknowledges as an exception to the attorney's duty of confidentiality a client's announced intention to commit a crime:

> The announced intention of a client to commit a crime is not included within the confidences which [the attorney] is bound to respect.

These principles have been carried through to contemporary codifications of an attorney's professional responsibility. . . . Indeed, both the Model Code and the Model Rules do not merely *authorize* disclosure by counsel of client perjury; they *require* such disclosure. See Rule 3.3(a)(4); DR 7-102(B)(1) . . . .

These standards confirm that the legal profession has accepted that an attorney's ethical duty to advance the interests of his client is limited by an equally solemn duty to comply with the law and standards of professional conduct; it specifically ensures that the client may not use false evidence. This special duty of an attorney to prevent and disclose frauds upon the court derives from the recognition that perjury is as much a crime as tampering with witnesses or jurors by way of promises and threats, and undermines the administration of justice. . . .

An attorney who aids false testimony by questioning a witness when perjurious responses can be anticipated risks prosecution for subornation of perjury under Iowa Code § 120.3 (1985).

It is universally agreed that at a minimum the attorney's first duty when confronted with a proposal for perjurious testimony is to attempt to dissuade the client from the unlawful course of conduct. Model Rules of Professional Conduct, Rule 3.3, Comment . . . .

. . . Similarly, the Model Rules and the commentary, as well as the Code of Professional Responsibility adopted in Iowa expressly permit withdrawal from representation as an appropriate response of an attorney when the client threatens to commit perjury. Model Rules of Professional Conduct, Rule 1.16(a)(1), Rule 1.6, Comment (1983); Code of Professional Responsibility, DR 2-110(B), (C) (1980). Withdrawal of counsel when this situation arises at trial gives rise to many difficult questions including possible mistrial and claims of double jeopardy. . . .

D

Considering Robinson's representation of respondent in light of these accepted norms of professional conduct, we discern no failure to adhere to reasonable professional standards that would in any sense make out a deprivation of the Sixth Amendment right to counsel. Whether Robinson's conduct is seen as a successful attempt to dissuade his client from committing the crime of perjury, or whether seen as a "threat" to withdraw from representation and disclose the illegal scheme, Robinson's representation of Whiteside falls well within accepted standards of professional conduct and the range of reasonable professional conduct acceptable under *Strickland*. . . .

The Court of Appeals' holding that Robinson's "action deprived [Whiteside] of due process and effective assistance of counsel" is not supported by the record since Robinson's action, at most, deprived Whiteside of his contemplated perjury. Nothing counsel did in any way undermined Whiteside's claim that he believed the victim was reaching for a gun. Similarly, the record gives no support for holding that Robinson's action "also impermissibly compromised [Whiteside's] right to testify in his own defense by conditioning continued representation . . . and confidentiality upon [Whiteside's] restricted testimony." The record in fact shows the contrary: (a) that Whiteside did testify, and (b) he was "restricted" or restrained only from testifying falsely and was aided by Robinson in developing the basis for the fear that Love was reaching for a gun. Robinson divulged no client communications until he was compelled to do so in response to Whiteside's post-trial challenge to the quality of his performance. We see this as a case in which the attorney successfully dissuaded the client from committing the crime of perjury.

Paradoxically, even while accepting the conclusion of the Iowa trial court that Whiteside's proposed testimony would have been a criminal act, the Court of Appeals held that Robinson's efforts to persuade Whiteside not to commit that crime were improper, *first*, as forcing an impermissible choice between the right to counsel and the right to testify; and *second*, as compromising client confidences because of Robinson's threat to disclose the contemplated perjury.

Whatever the scope of a constitutional right to testify, it is elementary that such a right does not extend to testifying *falsely*. . . .

The paucity of authority on the subject of any such "right" may be explained by the fact that such a notion has never been responsibly advanced; the right to counsel includes no right to have a lawyer who will cooperate with planned perjury. A lawyer who would so cooperate would be at risk of prosecution for suborning perjury, and disciplinary proceedings, including suspension or disbarment.

Robinson's admonitions to his client can in no sense be said to have forced respondent into an *impermissible* choice between his right to counsel and his right to testify as he proposed for there was no *permissible* choice to testify falsely. For defense counsel to take steps to persuade a criminal defendant to testify truthfully, or to withdraw, deprives the defendant of neither his right to counsel nor the right to testify truthfully. . . . When an accused proposes to resort to perjury or to produce false evidence, one consequence is the risk of withdrawal of counsel.

. . . A defendant who informed his counsel that he was arranging to bribe or threaten witnesses or members of the jury would have no "right" to insist on counsel's assistance or silence. Counsel would not be limited to advising against that conduct. An attorney's duty of confidentiality, which totally covers the client's admission of guilt, does not extend to a client's announced plans to engage in future criminal conduct. See Clark v. United States, 289 U.S. 1, 15 (1933). In short, the responsibility of an ethical lawyer, as an officer of the court and a key component of a system of justice, dedicated to a search for truth, is essentially the same whether the client announces an intention to bribe or threaten witnesses or jurors or to commit or procure perjury. No system of justice worthy of the name can tolerate a lesser standard. . . .

Whiteside's attorney treated Whiteside's proposed perjury in accord with professional standards, and since Whiteside's truthful testimony could not have prejudiced the result of his trial, the Court of Appeals was in error to direct the issuance of a writ of habeas corpus and must be reversed.

Justice BRENNAN, concurring in the judgment.

This Court has no constitutional authority to establish rules of ethical conduct for lawyers practicing in the state courts. Nor does the Court enjoy any statutory grant of jurisdiction over legal ethics. . . .

Unfortunately, the Court seems unable to resist the temptation of sharing with the legal community its vision of ethical conduct. But let there be no mistake: the Court's essay regarding what constitutes the correct response to a criminal client's suggestion that he will perjure himself is pure discourse without force of law. As Justice Blackmun observes, *that* issue is a thorny one, but it is not an issue presented by this case. Lawyers, judges, bar associations, students and others should understand that the problem has not now been "decided." . . .

Justice BLACKMUN, with whom Justice BRENNAN, Justice MARSHALL, and Justice STEVENS join, concurring in the judgment.

How a defense attorney ought to act when faced with a client who intends to commit perjury at trial has long been a controversial issue. But I do not believe that a federal habeas corpus case challenging a state criminal conviction is an appropriate vehicle for attempting to resolve this thorny problem. When a defendant argues that he was denied effective assistance of counsel because his lawyer dissuaded him from committing perjury, the only question properly presented to this Court is whether the lawyer's actions deprived the defendant of the fair trial which the Sixth Amendment is meant to guarantee. Since I believe that the respondent in this case suffered no injury justifying federal habeas relief, I concur in the Court's judgment.

. . . In this case, respondent has failed to show any legally cognizable prejudice. Nor, as is discussed below, is this a case in which prejudice should be presumed.

The touchstone of a claim of prejudice is an allegation that counsel's behavior did something "to deprive the defendant of a fair trial, a trial whose result is reliable." Strickland v. Washington, 466 U.S., at 687. The only effect Robinson's threat had on Whiteside's trial is that Whiteside did not testify, falsely, that he saw a gun in Love's hand. Thus, this Court must ask whether its confidence in the outcome of Whiteside's trial is in any way undermined by the knowledge that he refrained from presenting false testimony. . . .

This Court long ago noted: "All perjured relevant testimony is at war with justice, since it may produce a judgment not resting on truth. Therefore it cannot be denied that it tends to defeat the sole ultimate objective of a trial." In re Michael, 326 U.S. 224, 227 (1945). When the Court has been faced with a claim by a defendant concerning prosecutorial use of such evidence, it has "consistently held that a conviction obtained by the knowing use of perjured testimony is fundamentally unfair, and must be set aside if there is any reasonable likelihood that the false testimony could have affected the judgment of the jury" (footnote omitted). United States v. Agurs, 427 U.S. 97, 103 (1976). . . .

. . . To the extent that Whiteside's claim rests on the assertion that he would have been acquitted had he been able to testify falsely, Whiteside claims a right the law simply does not recognize. "A defendant has no entitlement to the luck of a lawless decisionmaker, even if a lawless decision cannot be reviewed." Strickland v. Washington, 466 U.S., at 695. Since Whiteside was deprived of neither a fair trial nor any of the specific constitutional rights designed to guarantee a fair trial, he has suffered no prejudice. . . .

. . . [T]he lawyer's interest in not presenting perjured testimony was entirely consistent with Whiteside's best interest. If Whiteside had lied on the stand, he would have risked a future perjury prosecution. Moreover, his testimony would have been contradicted by the testimony of other eyewitnesses and by the fact that no gun was ever found. In light of that impeachment, the jury might have concluded that Whiteside lied as well about his lack of premeditation and thus might have convicted him of first-degree murder. And if the judge believed that Whiteside had lied, he could have taken Whiteside's perjury into account in setting the sentence. . . . In the face of these dangers, an attorney could reasonably conclude that dissuading his client from committing perjury was in the client's best interest and comported with standards of professional responsibility. In short, Whiteside failed to show the kind of conflict that poses a danger to the values of zealous and loyal representation embodied in the Sixth Amendment. A presumption of prejudice is therefore unwarranted. . . .

Whether an attorney's response to what he sees as a client's plan to commit perjury violates a defendant's Sixth Amendment rights may depend on many factors: how certain the attorney is that the proposed testimony is false, the stage of the proceedings at which the attorney discovers the plan, or the ways in which the attorney may be able to dissuade his client, to name just three. The complex interaction of factors, which is likely to vary from case to case, makes inappropriate a blanket rule that defense attorneys must reveal, or threaten to reveal, a client's anticipated perjury to the court. Except in the rarest of cases, attorneys who adopt "the role of the judge or jury to determine the facts," United States ex rel. Wilcox v. Johnson, 555 F.2d 115, 122 (3d Cir. 1977), pose a danger of depriving their clients of the zealous and loyal advocacy required by the Sixth Amendment.

I therefore am troubled by the Court's implicit adoption of a set of standards of professional responsibility for attorneys in state criminal proceedings. . . . The States, of course, do have a compelling interest in the integrity of their criminal trials that can justify regulating the length to which an attorney may go in seeking his client's acquittal. But the American Bar Association's implicit suggestion in its brief *amicus curiae* that the Court find that the Association's Model Rules of Professional Conduct should govern an attorney's responsibilities is addressed to the wrong audience. It is for the States to decide how attorneys should conduct themselves in state criminal proceedings, and this Court's responsibility extends only to ensuring that the restrictions a State enacts do not infringe a defendant's federal constitutional rights. Thus, I would follow the suggestion made in the joint brief *amicus curiae* filed by 37 States at the certiorari stage that we allow the States to maintain their "differing approaches" to a complex ethical question. . . . The signal merit of asking first whether a defendant has shown any adverse prejudicial effect before inquiring into his attorney's performance is that it avoids unnecessary federal interference in a State's regulation of its bar. Because I conclude that the respondent in this case failed to show such an effect, I join the Court's judgment that he is not entitled to federal habeas relief.

Justice STEVENS, concurring in the judgment.

. . . [B]eneath the surface of this case there are areas of uncertainty that cannot be resolved today. A lawyer's certainty that a change in his client's recollection is a harbinger of intended perjury—as well as judicial review of such apparent certainty—should be tempered by the realization that, after reflection, the most honest witness may recall (or sincerely believe he recalls) details that he previously overlooked. Similarly, the post-trial review of a lawyer's pre-trial threat to expose perjury that had not yet been committed—and, indeed, may have been prevented by the threat—is by no means the same as review of the way in which such a threat may actually have been carried out. Thus, one can be convinced—as I am— that this lawyer's actions were a proper way to provide his client with effective representation without confronting the much more difficult questions of what a lawyer must, should, or may do after his client has given testimony that the lawyer does not believe. The answer to such questions may well be colored by the particular circumstances attending the actual event and its aftermath.

Because Justice Blackmun has preserved such questions for another day, and because I do not understand him to imply any adverse criticism of this lawyer's representation of his client, I join his opinion concurring in the judgment.

Notes

1. The majority opinion in *Nix* does not formally adopt a substantive rule establishing the conditions under which lawyers practicing in federal courts are required to disclose perjury. It is, however, strongly suggestive and it remains to be seen what federal district courts will do. The situation is complicated by the fact that many district courts have local rules adopting the professional responsibility rules of the state in which they sit as their own. There is therefore the potential for diametrically opposite obligations in the state and federal court systems should the client's conduct give rise to lawsuits in both jurisdictions.

2. Model Rule 3.3(a)(3) speaks in terms of evidence that the lawyer "knows" to be false. See generally Model Rule 1.0(f). The Comment does not illuminate that term and many different definitions are possible that would expand or contract

the number of situations when a lawyer is required to make a disclosure. For example, does a lawyer ever "know" about a client's false testimony for purposes of this Rule if the source of the purported knowledge is other than the client—that is, the client has not admitted perjury and has not suddenly changed the story under circumstances when the only realistic explanation is that perjury is involved? Should the standard for the lawyer's knowledge be "reasonable doubt," or something else?

3. What would have happened in *Nix* if Robinson had withdrawn when his client stated that he intended to give false testimony and a new lawyer had been appointed who did not realize that Robinson's testimony was false? Would Robinson be required or even permitted to reveal the perjury? If the answer is no, is there a reason for the dramatically different result in the actual *Nix* factual situation? See Model Rule 1.9(c)(2).

4. Note 3 raises a question discussed by Professors Freedman and Smith. They argued that withdrawal in a situation like *Nix* is ethically "indefensible, since the identical perjured testimony will ultimately be presented," albeit via different attorneys. The commission of perjury will be the same, and it will be criminal. But isn't the ethical question: What is the role of the attorney to be in the presentation of perjury? Or perhaps, to put it another way, do we want to create a system that invites the client to tell the lawyer the truth and then forces the lawyer to continue to represent the client who announces that he or she is going to commit perjury? However one answers the question, can it really be maintained that it is ethically "indefensible" to consider allowing an attorney to withdraw in that situation? What about Model Rule 1.16(b)(1), (3), or (4)?

5. What about the law firm that discovers that a client is engaged in an ongoing course of illegal conduct and is promptly fired when it seeks to have the client change its ways? May it inform successor counsel of the client's wrongdoing without violating Rule 1.6, assuming that the version of Rule 1.6 in force in the jurisdiction does not permit disclosure of such confidential information generally? A well-publicized fraud case involving a computer leasing company known as OPM Leasing Services Inc. involved that issue. The company defrauded banks of more than $210 million by obtaining loans on forged computer leases. At some point, its lawyers learned about the fraudulent loans and realized that its services had been used to obtain them. When the company assured them that those practices had ceased, they continued to represent the company, which accounted for 60% of its billings. It finally withdrew when it learned that loans it had closed following the company's disclosure were also fraudulent. When asked by a lawyer at OPM's new law firm why they had withdrawn, the senior partner at the old firm (a close friend of the inquirer) stated only that the termination was by mutual agreement but that the circumstances could not be discussed because of confidentiality obligations. Before the frauds were discovered, OPM used its new law firm to close $15 million in additional fraudulent loans. See Wall Street Journal, Dec. 31, 1982, p. 1, col. 6; New York Times, Jan. 9, 1983, Magazine

Section, p. 31; and Comment, 34 UCLA L. Rev. 925 (1987). What might the new law firm have done to protect itself when the confidentiality obligation was invoked by its predecessor?

An old ABA Ethics Committee opinion construing the former Canons of Ethics advised that the confidentiality obligation precluded a law firm in the position of the original law firm in the OPM matter from disclosing confidences to its successor. ABA Formal Opinion 268 (1945). Is that a sensible conclusion? Even assuming that a confidentiality obligation existed in the first law firm not to make a public disclosure of OPM's past fraud, would not the same obligation exist in OPM's new lawyers? If that is so, is any purpose served by the result in ABA Opinion 268 other than to allow a client like OPM to deceive its new lawyers into assisting it to commit further frauds?

6. Nix v. Whiteside dealt with one constitutional issue that has been much discussed in dealing with the problem of the perjurious client, but there are others it has not resolved. For example, Professor Freedman argued that the Fifth Amendment problem is serious and still unresolved. "Client Confidences and Client Perjury: Some Unanswered Questions," 136 U. Pa. L. Rev. 1939 (1988).

Problem 2–13

You represent plaintiff, Paul Smith, a 55-year-old grocer who is bringing suit against his insurance company to recover for damage to his store resulting from a fire. The evidence is quite clear that the fire was intentional. Plaintiff's theory is that the store had become a hangout for jobless teenagers who were giving it a bad name, and that plaintiff's recent efforts to bar the teenagers had led one or more of them to set the fire. Defendant's theory is that plaintiff set the fire to salvage something from a failing business. The defendant has conducted lengthy depositions which have developed a modest amount of circumstantial evidence in support of its theory, but you think that, based on the evidence to date, your client is highly likely to prevail.

One problem, however, is that five years ago, a printing business in which plaintiff owned one-quarter of the stock was destroyed by fire. The rest of the stock was owned by plaintiff's father-in-law, who ran the business. The plaintiff was secretary of the corporation, but his role was largely formal and he did no other work for the corporation. There was a grand jury investigation of the fire and plaintiff was called to testify. The grand jury, however, did not return any indictments, and subsequently the corporation's insurance company paid the claim. The corporation was then liquidated, and plaintiff received in excess of $25,000 as his share of the distribution, most of that money coming from the insurance company's proceeds.

You are concerned that defendants may try to make something out of that incident if they find out about it. No relevant questions, however, were asked during discovery. You and Mr. Smith have agreed that if questions are asked at trial, you will try to have them excluded on evidentiary grounds but that if you fail, he will tell the truth. You have also advised that given the strength of Smith's case and the outcome of the grand jury investigation, the early incident should not be very harmful.

Plaintiff's case did not go well at trial. Some of his witnesses did badly and he had not done well on his own examination. On cross-examination, defense counsel suddenly started to refer to earlier events. After argument the judge overruled your objections and agreed to let the testimony in conditionally. The following dialogue then occurred on defense counsel's questioning of your client.

Q: Have you ever made a claim against an insurance company or any third party on account of destruction of property by reason of fire?

A: No.

Q: Have you ever been a partner in a business that made such a claim?

A: No.

What alternatives are available to you? Which will you select?

Should or must you correct your client's answer? See Note, "Ethical Abuse of Technicalities: A Comparison of Prospective and Retrospective Legal Ethics," 112 Harv. L. Rev. 1082 (1999). See also Bronston v. United States, 409 U.S. 352 (1973), for a case in which a defendant artfully evaded an examiner's question by negative implication. Could a lawyer instruct a client to respond in such a fashion? See United States v. DeZarn, 157 F.3d 1042 (6th Cir. 1998); Jones v. Clinton, 36 F. Supp. 2d 1118 (E.D. Ark. 1999).

Monroe Freedman
Professional Responsibility of the Criminal Defense Lawyer: The Three Hardest Questions

64 Mich. L. Rev. 1469 (1966)

. . . The third question is whether it is proper to give your client legal advice when you have reason to believe that the knowledge you give him will tempt him to commit perjury. This may indeed be the most difficult problem of all, because giving such advice creates the appearance that the attorney is encouraging and condoning perjury.

If the lawyer is not certain what the facts are when he gives the advice, the problem is substantially minimized, if not eliminated. It is not the lawyer's function to prejudge his client as a perjurer. He cannot presume that the client will make unlawful use of his advice. Apart from this, there is a natural predisposition in most people to recollect facts, entirely honestly, in a way most favorable to their own interest. As Randolph Paul has observed, some witnesses are nervous, some are confused about their own interests, some try to be too smart for their own good, and some subconsciously do not want to understand what has happened to them. Before he begins to remember essential facts, the client is entitled to know what his own interests are.

The above argument does not apply merely to factual questions such as whether a particular event occurred at 10:15 or at 10:45. One of the most critical problems in a criminal case, as in many others, is intention. A German writer, considering the question of intention as a test of legal consequences, suggests the following situation. A young man and a young woman decide to get married. Each has a thousand dollars. They decide to begin a business with these funds, and the young lady gives her money to the young man for this purpose. Was the intention to form a joint venture or a partnership? Did they intend that the young man be an agent or a trustee? Was the transaction a gift or a loan? If the couple should subsequently visit a tax attorney and discover that it is in their interest that the transaction be viewed as a gift, it is submitted that they could, with complete honesty, so remember it. On the other hand, should their engagement be broken and the young woman consult an attorney for the purpose of recovering her money, she could with equal honesty remember that her intention was to make a loan.

Assume that your client, on trial for his life in a first-degree murder case, has killed another man with a penknife but insists that the killing was in self-defense. You ask him, "Do you customarily carry the penknife in your pocket, do you carry it frequently or infrequently, or did you take it with you only on this occasion?" He replies, "Why do you ask me a question like that?" It is entirely appropriate to inform him that his carrying the knife only on this occasion, or infrequently, supports an inference of premeditation, while if he carried the knife constantly, or frequently, the inference of premeditation would be negated. Thus, your client's life may depend upon his recollection as to whether he carried the knife frequently or infrequently. Despite the possibility that the client or a third party might infer that the lawyer was prompting the client to lie, the lawyer must apprise the defendant of the significance of his answer. There is no conceivable ethical requirement that the lawyer trap his client into a hasty and ill-considered answer before telling him the significance of the question.

A similar problem is created if the client has given the lawyer incriminating information before being fully aware of its significance. For example, assume that a man consults a tax lawyer and says, "I am fifty years old. Nobody in my immediate family has lived past fifty. Therefore, I would like to put my affairs in order. Specifically, I understand that I can avoid substantial estate taxes by setting up a trust. Can I do it?" The lawyer informs the client that he can successfully avoid the estate taxes only if he lives at least three years after establishing the trust or, should he die within three years, if the trust is found not to have been created in contemplation of death. The client then might ask who decides whether the trust is in contemplation of death. After learning that the determination is made by the court, the client might inquire about the factors on which such a decision would be based.

At this point, the lawyer can do one of two things. He can refuse to answer the question, or he can inform the client that the court will consider the wording of the trust instrument and will hear evidence about any conversations which he may have or any letters he may write expressing motives other than avoidance of estate taxes. It is likely that virtually every tax attorney in the country would answer the client's question, and that no one would consider the answer unethical. However, the lawyer might well appear to have prompted his client to deceive the Internal Revenue Service and the courts, and this appearance would remain regardless of the lawyer's explicit disclaimer to the client of any intent so to prompt him. Nevertheless, it should not be unethical for the lawyer to give the advice.

In a criminal case, a lawyer may be representing a client who protests his innocence, and whom the lawyer believes to be innocent. Assume, for example, that the charge is assault with intent to kill, that the prosecution has erroneous but credible eyewitness testimony against the defendant, and that the defendant's truthful alibi witness is impeachable on the basis of several felony convictions. The prosecutor, perhaps having doubts about the case, offers to permit the defendant to plead guilty to simple assault. If the defendant should go to trial and be convicted, he might well be sent to jail for fifteen years; on a plea of simple assault, the maximum penalty would be one year, and sentence might well be suspended.

The common practice of conveying the prosecutor's offer to the defendant should not be considered unethical, even if the defense lawyer is convinced of his client's innocence. Yet the lawyer is clearly in the position of prompting his client to lie, since the defendant cannot make the plea without saying to the judge that he is pleading guilty because he is guilty. Furthermore, if the client does decide to plead guilty, it would be improper for the lawyer to inform the court that his client is innocent, thereby compelling the defendant to stand trial and take the substantial risk of fifteen years' imprisonment.

Essentially no different from the problem discussed above, but apparently more difficult, is the so-called *Anatomy of a Murder* situation. The lawyer, who has received from his client an incriminating story of murder in the first degree, says, "If the facts are as you have stated them so far, you have no defense, and you will probably be electrocuted. On the other hand, if you acted in a blind rage, there is a possibility of saving your life. Think it over, and we will talk about it tomorrow." As in the tax case, and as in the case of the plea of guilty to a lesser offense, the lawyer has given his client a legal opinion that might induce the client to lie. This is information which the lawyer himself would have, without advice, were he in the client's position. It is submitted that the client is entitled to have this information about the law and to make his own decision as to whether to act upon it. To decide otherwise would not only penalize the less well-educated defendant, but would also prejudice the client because of his initial truthfulness in telling his story in confidence to the attorney.

III. CONCLUSION

The lawyer is an officer of the court, participating in a search for truth. Yet no lawyer would consider that he had acted unethically in pleading the statute of frauds or the statute of limitations as a bar to a just claim. Similarly, no lawyer would consider it unethical to prevent the introduction of evidence such as a murder weapon seized in violation of the Fourth Amendment or a truthful but involuntary confession, or to defend a guilty man on grounds of denial of a speedy trial. Such actions are permissible because there are policy considerations that at times justify frustrating the search for truth and the prosecution of a just claim. Similarly, there are policies that justify an affirmative answer to the three questions that have been posed in this article. These policies include the maintenance of an adversary system, the presumption of innocence, the prosecution's burden to prove guilt beyond a reasonable doubt, the right to counsel, and the obligation of confidentiality between lawyer and client.

Notes

1. Both Professor Freedman and Judge Frankel (in the next Chapter) refer to the situation portrayed in the novel *Anatomy of a Murder* as illustrative. There Judge John Voelker of the Michigan Supreme Court (under the pseudonym of Robert Traver) put the following thoughts into the mind of the sympathetically portrayed defense lawyer who was the "hero" of the book at the crucial moment in the interview of his client (Traver, *Anatomy of a Murder* 32, 35 (1958)):

> I paused and lit a cigar. I took my time. I had reached a point where a few wrong answers to a few right questions would leave me with a client — if I took his case — whose cause was legally defenseless. Either I stopped now and begged off and let some other lawyer worry over it or I asked him the few fatal questions and let him hang himself. Or else, like any smart lawyer, I went into the Lecture. . . .

> And what is the Lecture?

> The Lecture is an ancient device that lawyers use to coach their clients so that the client won't quite know he has been coached and his lawyer can still preserve the face-saving illusion that he hasn't done any coaching. For coaching clients, like robbing them, is not only frowned upon, it is downright unethical and bad, very bad. Hence the Lecture, an artful device as old as the law itself, and one used constantly by some of the nicest and most ethical lawyers in the land. "Who, me? I didn't tell him what to say," the lawyer can later comfort himself. "I merely explained the law, see." It is a good practice to scowl and shrug here and add virtuously: "That's my duty, isn't it?"

> Verily, the question, like expert lecturing, is unchallengeable.

Is the question unchallengeable? For an informative discussion of the *Anatomy of a Murder* case and other related situations, see Fred C. Zacharias and Shaun Martin, "Coaching Witnesses," 87 Ky. L.J. 1001 (1998–99).

2. After writing the quoted article, Professor Freedman later reconsidered his response to "the third question." He changed his mind with respect to two of the examples he gave—the tax case, and the *Anatomy of a Murder* case. In both examples, he later came to believe that the lawyer crossed the line into active participation in fraud in the tax case and into active participation, indeed initiation, of a perjurious defense in the *Anatomy of a Murder* situation. However, he did not view the lawyer's role in supplying legal information in the penknife or in the gift/loan situations as crossing that line. Freedman, *Lawyers' Ethics in an Adversary System* 70–72 (1975). In the latest edition of his book, Freedman, convinced by his coauthor, blames Judge Voelker for the lawyer's predicament in *Anatomy of a Murder* for creating a "cynical" lawyer who believed the client's initial story and then set about to change it: "in real life . . . both the client's and the lawyer's state of mind are unclear." Monroe Freedman and Abbe Smith, *Understanding Lawyers' Ethics* 208 (5th ed. 2016). He also appears to have reverted to his original position in the tax case. Id. at 194–95. How do lawyers in these cases avoid treating clients as if they believe the clients are likely to commit perjury and at the same time avoid leaving their clients with the impression that they are suggesting, even though they vociferously deny it, that clients ought to remember facts in a certain way?

3. Past Crime or Fraud

Problem 2–14

a) As house counsel for a corporation, you have recently obtained a final judgment for your company in a civil matter. In connection with other business, an employee shows you a document that was called for in the litigation but, it now turns out, was deliberately concealed from you and therefore not produced. The document makes it quite clear that your client should not have prevailed. The board of directors fires the employee for not following instructions about producing all relevant documents but directs you not to reveal the failure to produce. What are your alternatives and which one would you choose?

b) Suppose that the litigation had been handled exclusively by outside counsel and that you had had nothing to do with it at all. The subsequent disclosure of the document, however, is made to you. What are your alternatives when the board of directors fires the employee but directs you not to tell anyone about the failure to produce, not even outside counsel? Which one would you choose?

Problem 2–15

In the *OPM Leasing* case (see the notes following Nix v. Whiteside above), a company had obtained loans from banks using forged computer leases as collateral. Let us assume that there was only one transaction and that some months after the transaction had been completed, the law firm that had handled the transaction for the borrower discovered that its client had obtained the much needed loan with forged collateral. What should the firm do?

———————

The lawyer's obligation with respect to disclosure of crime or fraud that has been completed also has controversial elements. We should keep in mind that there are two situations — those where the crime or fraud is completed in the sense that although the consequences may be continuing there are no new foreseeable ones, and those where there are new foreseeable consequences. Problems 2–14 and 2–15 are examples of the former situation, which is the subject matter of this subsection. The client who tells you that someone else is to be executed tomorrow for the murder he, the client, committed (Problem 2–19) is an example of the latter and will be dealt with in the next subsection.

A paradigm for observing confidentiality in our adversary system involves a client who has hired or is assigned a lawyer to defend against a charge of crime or fraud and the lawyer comes to "know," as well as a lawyer ever "knows," that the client is in fact guilty. Our adversary system is built on the premise that we want (some?) lawyers to carry on the defense, although much has been written on the difficult situation in which that puts them. See John Kaplan, "Defending Guilty People," 7 U. Bridgeport L. Rev. 223 (1986) for an analysis. This subsection, however, does not address that problem. It addresses the rather different situation in which a lawyer discovers that a client has committed some crime or fraud in connection with a matter the lawyer handled. In the last subsection we talked about a similar situation where the lawyer was in a position to prevent the consequences of the perjury. In this subsection, we address the question of whether the lawyer should break a confidence in order to undo the consequences. The situation may involve either completed litigation (Problem 2–14) or a completed transaction (Problem 2–15).

Problem 2–16

The ABC Co. has been obtaining loans from Bank by using forged computer leases as collateral. The three principals of the company, who comprise the board of directors, have all participated in the fraud. The company has used an outside law firm (LF #1) to do the paperwork on these loans. Believing that its assistant general counsel and its law firm are about to discover its fraud, the company transferred the assistant general counsel to its subsidiary truck leasing division, fired LF # 1, and hired a new firm (LF #2) to do the continuing legal work servicing these loans and obtaining new loans. The company instructs LF #1 to return its papers and instructs LF #1 not to discuss the company's affairs with anyone, including LF #2.

a) Assume that as a consequence of the firing, LF #1's suspicions crystallize and it discovers the fraud from documents in its possession. What conversation or action may it engage in with respect to LF #2, the assistant general counsel, and the Bank to apprise them of ABC's fraudulent activities?

b) Assume that the assistant general counsel, who had not done any work concerning the loan transactions other than to engage LF #1, found out about the fraud just before she was transferred. What conversation or action may she engage in with respect to LF #1, LF #2, and the Bank to apprise them of ABC's fraudulent activities?

c) Assume that LF #2 finds out on its own about ABC's fraudulent activities in its preparatory work before even getting in touch with the Bank. What conversation or action may it engage in with LF #1, the assistant general counsel, or the Bank to apprise them of ABC's fraudulent activities?

Problems 2–15 and 2–16 are based upon the *OPM Case* (p. 96, Note 5). Until the revisions of Rule 1.6 in 2002 and 2003, that Rule did not directly permit a lawyer to disclose confidential information of a client when the lawyer discovered that the client had used its services to perpetrate a fraud. A Comment to the Rule, however, stated that nothing in the Rule prevented a lawyer from giving notice of the withdrawal and disaffirming any opinion, document, affirmation, or the like. When the ABA amended Rule 1.6 in 2002 and 2003 to include 1.6(b)(2) and (3), it moved the so-called "noisy withdrawal" Comment to Comment 10 of Rule 1.2.

4. Past Acts with Future Harmful Consequences: "Continuing" Crime or Fraud

This is yet another area that has posed great difficulties in delineating the boundaries of the confidentiality principle. In recent years, there has been hot debate in both the criminal and civil context. The largest issues in the civil context have involved corporate matters, which are discussed in Chapter 5. We have already encountered the lawyer's dilemma in the special situation of perjury committed by a client that is discovered by the lawyer while the trial is still ongoing. That discussion is relevant to some of the Problems that follow, but the factual situation of other Problems is quite different from that of perjury in an ongoing lawsuit. The issue also arises in other circumstances in the criminal context. Consider the following Problems.

Problem 2–17

(a) You represent Peter Jones, who has been charged with breaking and entering and grand larceny and is being held on $5000 bond. Ten days ago, just before his case was scheduled to be tried, Jones disappeared. You appeared in court and reported the disappearance, stating that you had not seen or heard from him since he was released on bail and had been unable to locate him. Several times since that date, on seeing the prosecutor in court, she has asked you whether you have heard from Jones. You have replied "No."

This evening, you receive a call from Jones, who identifies himself and says that he just needs to talk. How would you conduct the telephone conversation? How will you respond to the prosecutor tomorrow when she asks whether you have heard from Jones? Would your response be different if Jones had never been arrested but the police were searching for him under a fugitive warrant and asked you for information, which you had, concerning his whereabouts?

*(b) You just finished handling a divorce for your client, Julie Linsley, on Friday. You strongly disagree with the judge's decision to grant full physical and legal custody of her three children to their father, Paul Linsley, especially because of the father's history of abusive behavior. There have always been rumors about the Judge's attitude towards women, and you learned halfway through the trial that several former female employees of the court have filed a sexual harassment complaint with the EEOC.

While you were catching up on some paperwork on Saturday morning, Julie Linsley calls and tells you that she has taken the kids from her ex-husband. She tells you that their eight-year-old son called her from her ex-husband's house and told her that Paul came home drunk after celebrating over the judge's decision and beat their five-year-old daughter for spilling Froot Loops™ on the kitchen floor. Julie was extremely distraught and frustrated at the legal system and felt that she had no choice but to take the kids while Paul slept and try to get away.

Your client will not tell you where she is, and refuses to turn herself in. She does want to know if you can tell her how to apply for food stamps and any other federal aid program so that she can feed her children while she tries to rebuild her life. Do you help her?

Problem 2–18

An elderly client has consulted you for years about the continuing harassment he has encountered from children in his neighborhood. There have been discussions with police and social workers, but the harassment has continued sporadically and your client has constantly sought your advice. One day he comes to your office and says, "Well, I finally had my turn at bat. I put a laxative in the Halloween candy I gave some of those kids last night." You know that that is a criminal offense. From another matter, you also know that there are some people who have an allergic reaction to that laxative. You are also aware that it is highly likely that some of the recipients have not yet eaten the candy. Assuming that your client refuses to take any remedial action, what will you do? Does it make any difference whether you are in a Model Code or a Model Rules jurisdiction?

(a) Suppose that your client had instead confessed to putting cyanide in pain-killing tablets in the local drugstore? What would you do?

---

* Problem 2–17(b) was created by Joel Johnson, Harvard Law School '96, in connection with class discussion of Problem 2–17(a).

(b) Suppose that an employee for whom you were handling a discriminatory discharge case told you that upon leaving she had inserted a "virus" into her employer's computer program that would destroy a major part of its files in two months. What would you do?

Problem 2–19

A sensational murder case in your hometown resulted in the conviction of the defendant for murder after a trial that turned solely on a question of identification. The conviction was affirmed and efforts at collateral attack have failed. A client of yours, while seeking legal advice, has told you certain facts that have led you to conclude that he, not the defendant, was the murderer. Your client later confessed to you, and some independent checking has led you to be as positive as you can be that he is telling the truth. Efforts to persuade your client to turn himself in have failed. What do you do next? Are you influenced by any of the following factors:

(a) The nature and length of the defendant's sentence—a short or long term of years, life imprisonment, or death.

(b) The circumstances of the defendant's situation—e.g., whether he has a spouse or children; or whether he has a long criminal record, including crimes of violence.

(c) The circumstances of your client's situation—whether he has a wife and children; whether he has a long criminal record, including crimes of violence; whether he has a possible defense, such as self-defense; or whether mitigating circumstances exist, such as mental health issues.

Would your views be any different if the crime was the negligent commission of bodily harm and the defendant's sentence was 30 days in jail? Would it make a difference if the sentence were suspended?

Problem 2–20

Late one night you receive a telephone call from a friend who tells you that he is calling from his house (which is 40 miles away), that he has just had an argument with, and then killed, a friend, and that he is going to commit suicide. If you do not succeed in talking him out of his asserted intention, what should you do? Will your conversation with your friend (who knew you were an attorney) be protected by the attorney-client privilege? (This situation was presented to an attorney in People v. Fentress, 103 Misc. 2d 179 (N.Y. Cty. Ct. 1980), where the court avoided resolving the confidentiality question by finding waiver. For another case with a different bizarre twist, see Colman v. Heidenreich, 269 Ind. 419 (1978).) Legal conversations with a prospective client are ordinarily both privileged and confidential, even if the attorney or client decides not to enter into a formal attorney-client relationship. See Model Rule 1.18. If, however, the attorney advises the client that she will not be representing the client, later conversations might not be privileged (even if they otherwise meet the elements for privilege, e.g., they are communicated privately to the attorney for the purpose of seeking legal advice). See People v. Gionis, 892 P.2d 1199 (Cal. 1995).

———————

Problems 2–19 and 2–20, which do occur as noted above but fortunately do not occur every day in practice, are designed to test the limits of our belief in the principle of confidentiality. Yet Judge Arthur Powell tells us that he experienced Problem 2–19 in the context of a celebrated case, the trial of Leo Frank. See Frank v. Mangum, 237 U.S. 309 (1915). After the conviction of Frank for killing a young girl had been affirmed, a client informed Powell, then a practicing attorney, that he, not Frank, had committed the murder. Powell reported that his decision not to reveal the confidential communication was eased by the commutation of Frank's sentence to life imprisonment. Shortly thereafter, however, Frank was lynched by a mob. See Powell, *I Can Go Home Again* 287–292 (2d printing 1943) and Powell, "Privilege of Counsel and Confidential Communications," 6 Ga. Bar J. 333 (1944). The case returned to the newspapers years later. An eyewitness to the crime broke 69 years of silence to state he had seen the state's chief witness carrying the unconscious or dead body of the victim. Obeying threats from the "murderer" and the injunction of his mother, he had kept quiet. New York Times, Mar. 8, 1982, p. A12, col. 1. The Georgia Board of Pardons, however, at first denied a posthumous pardon to Mr. Frank because it was not possible "to decide conclusively his guilt or innocence," id., Dec. 10, 1983, p. A10, col. 1, but later reversed itself "because the state failed to protect him and because officials failed to bring his killers to justice." Id., Mar. 12, 1986, p. A16.

A similar incident occurred when a lawyer for a defendant came forward ten years after the death penalty conviction of the codefendant to reveal prosecutorial misconduct with respect to his client's testimony against the codefendant about which of the two defendants had actually fired the gun killing the man they had robbed. In the interim the Virginia state bar reversed the original advice it gave the lawyer to remain silent. In response to the lawyer's testimony, the state court reduced the death penalty to life imprisonment. Liptak, "Lawyer Reveals Secret, Toppling Death Sentence," New York Times, Jan. 19, 2008, p. 1.

For an instance where one lawyer, knowing of his client's guilt, successfully pressed a campaign to obtain a pardon by thrusting blame on the client's wife and her mother, and another lawyer eventually thwarted the scheme by revealing what the first lawyer had told him in confidence, see Carleton Allen, "R. v. Dean," 225 L.Q. Rev. 85 (1941). See also Fred Heather, "Attorney-Client Confidentiality: A New Approach," 4 Hofstra L. Rev. 685 (1976) for an attempt to solve Problem 2–19 by providing use immunity for the information derived from the broken confidence. Will the promise of a grant of use immunity be likely to induce a guilty party to come forward?

Commentators and bar authorities often make an exception to the broad confidentiality obligation by allowing for revelation of confidential information when life is at stake—the innocent person on death row, although apparently not the innocent person sentenced to life imprisonment. It should also be noted that in dealing with a similar confidence provision in Canon 37 of the former Canons of Professional Ethics, Henry Drinker, the leading text writer concerning those Canons, stated: "Although Canon 37 contains no specific exception covering communications where disclosure to the authorities is essential to the public safety, such is necessarily implied." Drinker, *Legal Ethics* 137 (1953). The references are to bar opinions dealing with information from a foreign government with whom the United States was at war and with subversive activities committed by a client. Do you think that the Model Rules should be construed in similar fashion?

Generally speaking, prosecutorial agencies used to deny that any wrongful convictions had occurred. But DNA and other forensic tools have since shown (often conclusively) that there have in fact been wrongful convictions in the United States. At the time of this writing, the National Registry of Exonerations (a project at the University of Michigan Law School) has documented over 1900 cases in which defendants were officially exonerated, and this database covers only the last twenty-five years. In light of these disturbing cases, the ABA has amended the Model Rules, requiring in short that prosecutors take appropriate action when new evidence suggests that they have convicted an innocent person. We will discuss these recent amendments in Chapter 5. Arizona also became the first state to require all lawyers (not just defenders and prosecutors) to disclose information indicating that an innocent person has been convicted. See Ariz. Rules of Prof. Conduct ER 3.10 (2014). The rule, however, is arguably swallowed by its own exception, which forbids lawyers from disclosing information protected by the broad confidentiality obligation. Like Arizona, most other states and the ABA have been unwilling to require (or arguably even permit) disclosure of confidential information even when that information might free an innocent person and even in light of the now proven fact that innocent people have received life (or even death) sentences. If the innocent person is facing the death penalty, however, do you see an exception that might permit disclosure? If, however, the person is facing a life sentence or a term of years, under what exception could you disclose? If you do not see such an exception, should one be added? Massachusetts did decide to add an exception to its confidentiality rule in the hope of helping the wrongfully convicted. See, e.g., Mass. Rules of Prof. Conduct R. 1.6(b) (1) ("A lawyer may reveal, and to the extent required by Rule 3.3, Rule 4.1(b), or Rule 8.3 must reveal, [confidential] information . . . to prevent the wrongful execution or incarceration of another"). The state made the exception discretionary, but should it instead require disclosure? What if you did not tell the client about the exception in advance of the client's disclosure to you? Would the client have told you, "I did it, not him," if the client knew that you might or must disclose that information? Do you think the Massachusetts or the ABA approach is better? (See also the more theoretical discussion in Chapter 3 when considering this issue.)

Although the fact situation in Problem 2–19 certainly will not arise, at least not in as stark a fashion, very often, the answer that professional rules provide for such a situation does help set the public image of those rules. The ABA, after many years of criticism, finally addressed the situation for the innocent person on death row (or situations like Problem 1–1) when it amended Rule 1.6 to add subsection (b)(1). Do you think you could interpret Rule 1.6(b)(1) to find discretion if an innocent person were sentenced to anything less than death? If not, would you violate the disciplinary rule in such a situation? If you were to break the confidences in the cases above, how would you do it? Try to keep the identity of the client secret? Tell the client to confess? Would you tell? Anonymously?

If you believe that most lawyers would also violate the Rule in (for example) a life imprisonment case, what is the justification for presenting the profession with a Model Rule that would prohibit breaking a confidence in that case? We take up the general question whether lawyers have a prima facie duty to obey the law in Chapter 3. For better or worse, one of the interesting aspects of ethics rules is that lawyers generally have a great deal of influence in their drafting (both at the ABA and state levels). Thus, if a rule is problematic, or if a new rule is needed, a concerned group of lawyers might well be able to effectuate change.

Note: The Model Rules and Past Acts with Future Harmful Consequences

We need to pay attention to the difference in wording among the first three subsections of Model Rule 1.6. Rule 1.6(b)(1) gives a lawyer discretion to reveal a client's confidential information "to prevent reasonably certain death or substantial bodily harm." The discretion is quite open-ended. It does not require that it be the client who presents the threat of the harm to be prevented or that the client be engaged in any unlawful activity. The lawyer may reveal the information to prevent the harm resulting from an act committed or to be committed either by the client or by a third party. Moreover, the lawyer has discretion to reveal confidential information even if the client reveals completed criminal activity if that activity will result in "reasonably certain death or substantial bodily harm" of a third party in the future. Rules 1.6(b)(2) and (b)(3), which deal with harm to the financial interests or property of a third person, are rather different. The lawyer has discretion to reveal confidential information to prevent or to mitigate harm but only when the client is about to commit, or has committed, a crime or fraud and only when the client has used or is using the lawyer's services in furtherance of the crime or fraud. If the lawyer's services have not been so used, the lawyer has no discretion under Model Rule 1.6 to reveal confidential information in order to prevent, or mitigate the effect of, the crime or fraud. In special circumstances one might consider whether Rules 1.2, 3.3, or 4.1 offer a possibility for lawyer action. (When we turn to the problems of corporate representation in Chapter 5, Rule 1.13 must also be consulted.)

One issue that has been problematic for some time is the so-called "continuing crime" where in revealing information to the lawyer about future criminal or fraudulent activity, the client also reveals that he or she has engaged in such activity in the past. There is a significant difference between this situation and one where the crime or fraud is wholly in the future. In the continuing crime case, revelation of the confidence is likely to reveal the past wrongdoing as well, a situation not present in the wholly future crime case. If there is discretion, a lawyer may wish to take that into account in an appropriate case. But the first question to be decided is whether there is discretion. Read Rule 1.6(b)(3) carefully and decide whether you think its focus on future harm instead of future crime or fraud answers the question.

A case from Pennsylvania that deals with a Problem 2–17 situation is another illustration of the difference between the attorney-client privilege and the confidentiality obligation. Commonwealth v. Maguigan, 511 Pa. 112 (1986), affirmed the contempt conviction of a lawyer for refusing to reveal the whereabouts of a criminal fugitive who had jumped bail. The court reasoned that the attorney-client privilege did not apply because the fugitive had a continuing duty to the court to notify it of his whereabouts and therefore could not be said to have a legitimate expectation of confidentiality.

The court did not address the question whether the same reasoning would apply to, say, an admission by a client that it had not filed a required tax return or other obligatory report to some state or federal agency if an investigator were to ask the lawyer an open-ended question about the filing of all required returns or reports. This may be another instance, like Problem 2–10, where at least some courts will perceive the lawyer as owing a different obligation to the court's law than to the legislature's law. It is worth noting that *Maguigan* did not involve, and the court did not address, whether the lawyer was obliged, or had discretion, voluntarily to break the obligation of confidentiality under the Disciplinary Rules if she had not been asked the question in open court.

The position of the ABA Committee on Ethics and Professional Responsibility with respect to the fugitive issue is interesting. Long ago it issued Opinions taking differing views at different times on the lawyer's duty to reveal the whereabouts of a fugitive who had jumped bail. Opinion 23 (1930) said that the information should not be disclosed to the authorities, but Opinion 155 (1936) stated that it should. Then in Informal Opinion 1141 (1970), the Committee stated that a lawyer should keep the whereabouts of a military deserter confidential if the fugitive had disclosed the information in the course of seeking information about his rights. However, if the fugitive wanted advice about how to remain a fugitive, then the lawyer should advise that he turn himself in, refuse to represent him further if he did not do so, and advise that the lawyer will reveal his whereabouts if the client brings the matter to him again in those circumstances. After the ABA produced the Model Rules, its Committee on Ethics in a brief opinion withdrew Opinion 155 as being inconsistent with both the Model Code and the Model Rules. But it did no more. It did not explain the inconsistency. It did not replace those Opinions. It did not mention Opinion 23 or Informal Opinion 1141.

With this background in the relationship of past wrongdoing and future harm to the confidentiality principle, consider the following dilemma in which two attorneys found themselves.

Bryce Nelson
Ethical Dilemma: Should Lawyers Turn in Clients?
Los Angeles Times, July 2, 1974, p. 1, col. 1

PAIR FACE DISBARMENT THREAT AFTER KEEPING TWO SLAYINGS SECRET

. . . The issue of client-attorney confidentiality received wide attention in recent days after it was disclosed that two Syracuse, N.Y., lawyers, Frank Armani and Francis Belge, had known for six months the location of the bodies of two young women who had been killed but felt legally obligated to keep silent—because they got the information from their client.

Although many legal authorities say Armani and Belge acted properly in keeping their client's information secret, the two court-appointed lawyers have found themselves battered by protests and investigations that could lead to disbarment or criminal prosecution.

"Very rarely are lawyers put to these kinds of tests," Armani commented in an interview.

The case brings into sharp focus the ethical quandary of lawyers trying to protect the confidences of a client—a problem that faces doctors, psychiatrists, accountants, ministers, social workers and journalists also.

According to legal experts, the case promises to become one of the most studied examples of the confidentiality privilege.

"Any lawyer with any guts who knew what he was doing would have done the same thing," Armani said, "but the law profession is composed of many different kinds of lawyers."

Confidentiality is a privilege more easily defended in the tranquility of a law school than in the outside world. . . .

William Hauck, father of one of the murdered girls, has filed a complaint against the lawyers with the Onondaga County Bar Assn., which has referred it to the appellate division of the State Supreme Court, which has, in turn, asked for an investigation by the State Bar Assn.

The two lawyers may well be in a fight for their professional lives, and not all their fellow lawyers support the stand they have taken.

"It's outrageous," said a leading Minneapolis attorney. "They should both be put in jail. You have to report a crime if you know about it."

But the Syracuse lawyers have their supporters too.

"The only way this New York case is different," said George P. Lynch, a leading Chicago criminal lawyer, "is that the evidence is composed of human bodies. I recognize the unappealing position the lawyers were in, but the lawyer is duty-bound to remain silent about information from his client. If you reveal such information, you should be disbarred."

The client who put Armani and Belge on this spot is Robert Garrow, a 38-year-old Syracuse mechanic who has admitted that he killed four persons in upstate New York last summer.

Garrow was arrested Aug. 9 and indicted on charges of murdering 18-year-old Philip Domblewski. The court appointed Belge and Armani as Garrow's attorneys. In his conversations with the lawyers, Garrow told of the other murders he had committed.

One was that of Alicia Hauck, 16, a Syracuse high school student who had disappeared in July; the lawyers later found her body in a Syracuse cemetery. The other murders were those of Daniel Porter, a 22-year-old Harvard student, whose body had been found on July 20, and of Susan Petz, 21, of Skokie, Ill., a Boston University journalism student who had been Porter's camping companion in the Adirondack Mountains.

Following Garrow's directions, the two lawyers found and photographed the bodies of Miss Petz and Miss Hauck—but they said nothing to authorities.

Miss Hauck's family thought she might have run away from home. The Petz family—knowing that their daughter's companion had been killed—feared the worst.

With the knowledge that the two Syracuse lawyers represented a client charged with a killing in the Adirondacks, Earl Petz, Susan's father, went to Syracuse to talk to Belge. The lawyer has since said he felt obligated not to tell Petz anything—and didn't—adding that his silence caused him "many, many sleepless nights."

The bodies of both girls were found accidentally last winter by students.

When Garrow testified at his trial about the other three killings he said he committed, the lawyers felt they had been released from their obligation of secrecy and disclosed they had known the locations of the bodies.

Garrow was convicted of Domblewski's murder Thursday. He was sentenced Monday to the maximum penalty of 25 years to life.

Roberta Petz, mother of Susan, angrily asked for the prosecution of the two attorneys.

She said, as have several lawyers, that she could not understand why the attorneys could not have given the information to the police anonymously, so that the parents could have been spared their troubled and seemingly interminable wait for information on their daughters.

One answer, say legal scholars, is that even an anonymous disclosure, if given without the client's permission, would be a breach of lawyer-client confidentiality. In addition, evidence obtained from or near the bodies, such as fingernail scrapings or footprints, might incriminate the client.

Armani and Belge understand from personal experience the anxieties caused by a death in a family. Belge suffered the death of a 12-year-old son. And Armani's brother was lost during an Air Force reconnaissance mission over the North Sea. The body was never recovered.

"We feel for these parents," Armani said. "I know what torment my mother went through in never having my brother's body returned. We know what hell these parents were going through.

"We both have daughters the same age as the girls who were killed. . . . We just couldn't figure any other way to do it.

"You have your duty to your state, to your law and order, but my primary duty is to my client—so long as I don't jeopardize anybody's life or property. If the girl had been alive, then we would have had the duty to save her life, because life is primary. A body is a sacred thing but I couldn't give it life, and I figured somebody is going to find it."

After their client had told them about the killing last summer, it took a while for the two attorneys to find the abandoned mineshaft in which Susan Petz's body had been left. . . .

The bodies of Miss Petz and of Miss Hauck, which were back in the woods of the Syracuse cemetery, were found months after they had been located by the lawyers but well before Garrow's disclosures in court.

One aspect of the case that has raised questions is the lawyers' attempt to plea bargain with the Hamilton County district attorney and police investigators of four other upstate New York counties.

In September, after the two lawyers had found Miss Petz's body, they offered to help the district attorney and the police solve the Petz and Hauck murders if their client, Garrow, were placed in a mental institution. The district attorney rejected the offer and went ahead with the prosecution of Garrow for the murder of Domblewski. . . .

Several leading prosecutors interviewed, however, said that the New York lawyers had acted properly both in their refusal to divulge information about the bodies and in their attempt to bargain with the prosecutor.

"I'm in complete agreement with these lawyers," said Samuel Skinner, head of the criminal division of the U.S. attorney's office in Chicago. "They operated in accordance with the highest traditions of the legal profession at a time when the profession is in great trouble." . . . But the lawyer-client confidentiality relationship is not clear-cut, and judges and official investigating bodies sometimes have a different view from that of a defense lawyer. . . .

Notes

1. Was it proper for the lawyers to have gone to the mineshaft where the murder victims were alleged to have been left?

2. Having found the victims, what should they have done next?

3. Did they make the issue any different by taking photographs of the victims and keeping them secret?

4. Suppose as they were leaving the mine, one lawyer noted that they had left distinctive footprints in the mud and had not replaced the boulder that blocked the entrance to the mine. Should they smooth over the footprints and replace the boulder? (See Model Rule 3.4.)

5. Suppose the lawyers learned that the authorities had received a tip that the missing victims were murdered, that their bodies had been left in a mine, and, further, that the authorities were sending a team of spelunkers on a very dangerous descent to examine a different mine. Should they say anything? Suppose they learn from the doctor of Mr. and Mrs. Petz that their lives were seriously threatened by the anxiety of not knowing what had happened? Does that make a difference? What if the anxiety and sleepless nights caused these parents to be unable to return to their place of work?

6. What about the efforts of the lawyers to bargain on the basis of their knowledge? Did they need the consent of their client to do that? If they had questions about his mental capacity, how should they have proceeded? (Model Rule 1.14 generally addresses such a client, but does it offer any concrete answers?) If they had client consent and there was no incapacity, was it proper to use the knowledge of where other victims' bodies were to obtain more favorable treatment? If you were one of those lawyers, how would you attempt to bargain? What would you say? As prosecutor, how would you respond?

7. A grand jury that investigated the conduct of one of the lawyers involved in this matter declined to take any action. Boston Globe, Feb. 9, 1975, at 17. The second lawyer was indicted by the same grand jury, not for obstruction of justice but for violation of two statutes—one requiring a decent burial to be accorded to the dead and the other requiring a report of the death of any person without medical attendance. A motion to dismiss, based on the lawyer-client privilege, was granted. On appeal, the Appellate Division, in a brief opinion, affirmed on the basis that the attorney-client privilege "effectively shielded the defendant-attorney from his actions which would otherwise have violated the Public Health Law." The court, however, went on to observe:

> In view of the fact that the claim of absolute privilege was proffered, we note that the privilege is not all-encompassing and that in a given case there may be conflicting considerations. We believe that an attorney must protect his client's interests, but also must observe basic human standards of decency,

having due regard to the need that the legal system accord justice to the interests of society and its individual members.

We write to emphasize our serious concern regarding the consequences which emanate from a claim of an absolute attorney-client privilege. Because the only question presented, briefed and argued on this appeal was a legal one with respect to the sufficiency of the indictments, we limit our determination to that issue and do not reach the ethical questions underlying this case.

People v. Belge, 50 A.D.2d 1088 (4th Dept. 1975), aff'd, 41 N.Y.2d 60 (1976) (under the relevant jurisdictional statute, the court was confined to decide only whether the dismissal of the indictment was an abuse of discretion as a matter of law; it held that the dismissal was not).

After the Court of Appeals handed down its opinion in this case, the Committee on Professional Ethics of the New York State Bar Association released its Opinion No. 479, which it had prepared in 1974 but withheld until the proceedings had been terminated. Aside from stating that a lawyer ought not to move a corpse even for photographic purposes, the committee upheld the ethical propriety of the lawyers' entire conduct. Indeed, the committee stated that the course of conduct was required. See New York Law Journal, March 7, 1978, p. 1, col. 4 and p. 24, col. 1.

The case is discussed in Chamberlain, "Legal Ethics," 25 Buff. L. Rev. 211 (1975), among other places. The whole story of the case, including the differences between the two lawyers for Mr. Garrow, the pressures brought to bear on them by popular disapproval of their professional conduct, and the effect of those pressures on their health and professional careers is told in Alibrandi (with Armani), *Privileged Information* (1984); see also Lisa G. Lerman et al., "The Buried Bodies Case: Alive and Well After Thirty Years," 2007 Prof'l Law. 19; Mark Hansen, "The Toughest Call," 93 A.B.A.J. 28 (2007) (summarizing this well-known case and offering a few insights from some of the lawyers involved).

While we have been discussing the issue of "continuing" crime in the criminal context, the issue arises in the civil context as well, and we shall meet some of those problems in Chapter 5. For the moment consider the issue in the following context.

Problem 2–21

Ms. Smith is a single-parent mother of three small children; she has been on welfare for several years and lives in public housing. After a judge found her to be "indigent," you have been appointed to represent her in connection with a criminal assault charge arising out of an altercation at the housing project. At the initial interview, you discover that Ms. Smith has been threatened that if convicted, she will be evicted from the housing project. You also discover that she has enough part-time earnings to take her out of the indigency category, to require reduction of her welfare payments, and conceivably even to affect her entitlement to public housing. On the other hand, she seems more moved by simply trying to make ends meet than to cheat and you want to help her. She is willing to talk about straightening things out with the welfare department but not until the criminal charges that threaten her freedom and her housing have been resolved.

May you represent her on the criminal charges? Does it depend upon whether you are being paid with public funds as appointed private counsel? Suppose you instead were an assigned public defender (on a set salary). May you begin to straighten out her housing problems? May you talk with her about her welfare problems? Could you draw a will for her?

5. Disclosure of Confidences to Collect a Fee or in Self-Defense

One final piece in the confidentiality puzzle needs to be put in place: the exception in Rule 1.6(b)(5) of the Model Rules that permits lawyers to reveal confidences in order to collect their fees or defend themselves against accusations based on conduct in the client's cause. Many have characterized the exception as a blatant expression of the self-protective exercise of rule-making authority by the profession. See Levine, "Self-Interest or Self-Defense: Lawyer Disregard of the Attorney-Client Privilege for Profit and Protection," 5 Hofstra L. Rev. 783 (1977), for a lengthy review of the exception and its antecedents. For example, a lawyer technically may not reveal confidential information about the whereabouts of a murdered child (unless of course the client consents to this disclosure) — yet the lawyer may disclose information necessary to collect a fee or to respond to a client's negative online review about the lawyer. The existence of the exception raises both normative and practical questions for the profession and for individual lawyers.

Problem 2–22

You are the house counsel in Problem 2–14, p. 102, once again. Assume that you concluded either that you were absolutely precluded by the rules relating to fraud on a third party from disclosing the information relating to the concealed document or that you had discretion under those rules but ought not to exercise it. You are concerned, however, about your own personal liability in the event that the information should be revealed. You have no evidence that you never knew about the document at the time it should have been disclosed other than your own word and the willingness of the employee who concealed it to tell the truth. That employee is unwilling to execute an affidavit exonerating you. What action, if any, may you take under Model Rule 1.6(b)(5) to protect your own interests? A leading case that presented the issue follows:

Meyerhofer v. Empire Fire & Marine Ins. Co.
497 F.2d 1190 (2d Cir. 1974)

MOORE, Circuit Judge

. . . Empire Fire and Marine Insurance Company on May 31, 1972, made a public offering of 500,000 shares of its stock, pursuant to a registration statement filed with the Securities and Exchange Commission (SEC) on March 28, 1972. The stock was offered at $16 a share. Empire's attorney on the issue was the firm of Sitomer, Sitomer & Porgies. Stuart Charles Goldberg was an attorney in the firm and had done some work on the issue.

Plaintiff Meyerhofer, on or about January 11, 1973, purchased 100 shares of Empire stock at $17 a share. He alleges that as of June 5, 1973, the market price of his stock was only $7 a share—hence, he has sustained an unrealized loss of $1,000. Plaintiff Federman, on or about May 31, 1972, purchased 200 shares at $16 a share, 100 of which he sold for $1,363, sustaining a loss of some $237 on the stock sold and an unrealized loss of $900 on the stock retained.

On May 2, 1973, plaintiffs represented by the firm of Bernson, Hoeniger, Freitag & Abbey (the Bernson firm), on behalf of themselves and all other purchasers of Empire common stock, brought this action alleging that the registration statement and the prospectus under which the Empire stock had been issued were materially false and misleading. Thereafter, an amended complaint, dated June 5, 1973, was served. The legal theories in both were identical, namely, violations of various sections of the Securities Act of 1933, the Securities Exchange Act of 1934, Rule 10b5, and common law negligence, fraud and deceit. Damages for all members of the class or rescission were alternatively sought.

The lawsuit was apparently inspired by a Form 10-K which Empire filed with the SEC on or about April 12, 1973. This Form revealed that "The Registration Statement under the Securities Act of 1933 with respect to the public offering of the 500,000 shares of Common Stock did not disclose the proposed $200,000 payment to the law firm as well as certain other features of the compensation arrangements between the Company [Empire] and such law firm [defendant Sitomer, Sitomer and Porges]." Later that month Empire disseminated to its shareholders a proxy statement and annual report making similar disclosures.

The defendants named were Empire, officers and directors of Empire, the Sitomer firm and its three partners, A. L. Sitomer, S. J. Sitomer and R. E. Porges, Faulkner, Dawkins & Sullivan Securities Corp., the managing underwriter, Stuart Charles Goldberg, originally alleged to have been a partner of the Sitomer firm, and certain selling stockholders of Empire shares.

On May 2, 1973, the complaint was served on the Sitomer defendants and Faulkner. No service was made on Goldberg who was then no longer associated with the Sitomer firm. However, he was advised by telephone that he had been made a defendant. Goldberg inquired of the Bernson firm as to the nature of the charges against him and was informed generally as to the substance of the complaint and in particular the lack of disclosure of the finder's fee arrangement. Thus informed, Goldberg requested an opportunity to prove his non-involvement in any such arrangement and his lack of knowledge thereof. At this stage there was unfolded the series of events which ultimately resulted in the motion and order thereon now before us on appeal.

Goldberg, after his graduation from Law School in 1966, had rather specialized experience in the securities field and had published various books and treatises on related subjects. He became associated with the Sitomer firm in November 1971. While there Goldberg worked on phases of various registration statements including Empire, although another associate was responsible for the Empire registration statement and prospectus. However, Goldberg expressed concern over what he regarded as excessive fees, the nondisclosure or inadequate disclosure thereof, and the extent to which they might include a "finder's fee," both as to Empire and other issues.

The Empire registration became effective on May 31, 1972. The excessive fee question had not been put to rest in Goldberg's mind because in middle January 1973 it arose in connection with another registration (referred to as "Glacier"). Goldberg had worked on Glacier. Little purpose will be served by detailing the events during the critical period January 18 to 22, 1973, in which Goldberg and the Sitomer partners were debating the fee disclosure problem. In summary Goldberg insisted on a full and complete disclosure of fees in the Empire and Glacier offerings. The Sitomer partners apparently disagreed and Goldberg resigned from the firm on January 22, 1973.

On January 22, 1973, Goldberg appeared before the SEC and placed before it information subsequently embodied in his affidavit dated January 26, 1973, which becomes crucial to the issues now to be considered.

Some three months later, upon being informed that he was to be included as a defendant in the impending action, Goldberg asked the Bernson firm for an opportunity to demonstrate that he had been unaware of the finder's fee arrangement which, he said, Empire and the Sitomer firm had concealed from him all along. Goldberg met with members of the Bernson firm on at least two occasions. After consulting his own attorney, as well as William P. Sullivan, Special Counsel with the Securities and Exchange Commission, Division of Enforcement, Goldberg gave plaintiffs' counsel a copy of the January 26th affidavit which he had authored more than three months earlier. He hoped that it would verify his nonparticipation in the finder's fee omission and convince the Bernson firm that he should not be a defendant. The Bernson firm was satisfied with Goldberg's explanations and, upon their motion, granted by the court, he was dropped as a defendant. After receiving Goldberg's affidavit, the Bernson firm amended plaintiffs' complaint. The amendments added more specific facts but did not change the theory or substance of the original complaint.

By motion dated June 7, 1973, the remaining defendants moved "pursuant to Canons 4 and 9 of the Code of Professional Responsibility, the Disciplinary Rules and

Ethical Considerations applicable thereto, and the supervisory power of this Court" for the order of disqualification now on appeal.

By memorandum decision and order, the District Court ordered that the Bernson firm and Goldberg be barred from acting as counsel or participating with counsel for plaintiffs in this or any future action against Empire involving the transactions placed in issue in this lawsuit and from disclosing confidential information to others.

The complaint was dismissed without prejudice. The basis for the Court's decision is the premise that Goldberg had obtained confidential information from his client Empire which, in breach of relevant ethical canons, he revealed to plaintiffs' attorneys in their suit against Empire. The Court said its decision was compelled by "the broader obligations of Canons 4 and 9."

There is no proof—not even a suggestion—that Goldberg had revealed any information, confidential or otherwise, that might have caused the instigation of the suit. To the contrary, it was not until after the suit was commenced that Goldberg learned that he was in jeopardy. The District Court recognized that the complaint had been based on Empire's—not Goldberg's—disclosures, but concluded because of this that Goldberg was under no further obligation "to reveal the information or to discuss the matter with plaintiffs' counsel."

Despite the breadth of paragraphs EC 4-4 and DR 4-101(B), DR 4-101(C) recognizes that a lawyer may reveal confidences or secrets necessary to defend himself against "an accusation of wrongful conduct." This is exactly what Goldberg had to face when, in their original complaint, plaintiffs named him as a defendant who willfully violated the securities laws.

The charge, of knowing participation in the filing of a false and misleading registration statement, was a serious one. The complaint alleged violation of criminal statutes and civil liability computable at over four million dollars. The cost in money of simply defending such an action might be very substantial. The damage to his professional reputation which might be occasioned by the mere pendency of such a charge was an even greater cause for concern.

Under these circumstances Goldberg had the right to make an appropriate disclosure with respect to his role in the public offering. Concomitantly, he had the right to support his version of the facts with suitable evidence.

The problem arises from the fact that the method Goldberg used to accomplish this was to deliver to Mr. Abbey, a member of the Bernson firm, the thirty page affidavit, accompanied by sixteen exhibits, which he had submitted to the SEC. This document not only went into extensive detail concerning Goldberg's efforts to cause the Sitomer firm to rectify the nondisclosure with respect to Empire but even more extensive detail concerning how these efforts had been precipitated by counsel for the underwriters having come upon evidence showing that a similar nondisclosure was contemplated with respect to Glacier and their insistence that full corrective measures should be taken. Although Goldberg's description reflected seriously on his employer, the Sitomer firm and, also, in at least some degree, on Glacier, he was clearly in a situation of some urgency. Moreover, before he turned over the affidavit, he consulted both his own attorney and a distinguished practitioner of securities law, and he and Abbey made a joint telephone call to Mr. Sullivan of the SEC. Moreover, it is not clear that, in the context of this case, Canon 4 applies to anything except information gained from Empire. Finally, because of Goldberg's apparent intimacy with the offering, the most effective way for him to substantiate his story was for him to disclose the SEC affidavit. It was the fact that he had written such an affidavit at an earlier date which demonstrated that his story was not simply fabricated in response to plaintiffs' complaint.

The District Court held: "All that need be shown . . . is that during the attorney-client relationship Goldberg had access to his client's information relevant to the issues here." See Emle Industries, Inc. v. Patentex, Inc., 478 F.2d 562 (2d Cir. 1973). However, the irrebuttable presumption of *Emle* has no application to the instant circumstances because Goldberg never sought to "prosecute litigation," either as a party, compare Richardson v. Hamilton International Corp., 62 F.R.D. 413 (E.D. Pa. 1974), or as counsel for a plaintiff party. Compare T. C. Theatre Corporation v. Warner Brothers Pictures, 113 F. Supp. 265 (S.D.N.Y. 1953). At most the record discloses that Goldberg might be called as a witness for the plaintiffs but that role does not invest him with the intimacy with the prosecution of the litigation which must exist for the *Emle* presumption to attach.

In addition to finding that Goldberg had violated Canon 4, the District Court found that the relationship between Goldberg and the Bernson firm violated Canon 9 of the Code of Professional Responsibility which provides that: "EC 9-6. Every lawyer [must] strive to avoid not only professional impropriety but also the appearance of impropriety." The District Court reasoned that even though there was no evidence of bad faith on the part of either Goldberg or the Bernson firm, a shallow reading of the facts might lead a casual observer to conclude that there was an aura of complicity about their relationship. However, this provision should not be read so broadly as to eviscerate the right of self-defense conferred by DR 4-101(C)(4).

Nevertheless, Emle Industries, Inc. v. Patentex, Inc., supra, requires that a strict prophylactic rule be applied in these cases to ensure that a lawyer avoids representation of a party in a suit against a former client where there may be the appearance of a possible violation of confidence. To the extent that the District Court's order prohibits Goldberg from *representing* the interests of these or any other plaintiffs in this or similar actions, we affirm that order. We also affirm so much of the District Court's order as enjoins Goldberg from disclosing material information except on discovery or at trial.

The burden of the District Court's order did not fall most harshly on Goldberg; rather its greatest impact has been felt by Bernson, Hoeniger, Freitag & Abbey, plaintiffs' counsel, which was disqualified from participation in the case. The District Court based its holding, not on the fact that the Bernson firm showed bad faith when it received Goldberg's affidavit, but rather on the fact that it was involved in a tainted association with Goldberg because his disclosures to them inadvertently violated Canons 4 and 9 of the Code of Professional Responsibility. Because there are no violations of either of these Canons in this case, we can find no basis to hold that the relationship between Goldberg and the Bernson firm was tainted. The District Court was apparently unpersuaded by appellees' salvo of innuendo to the effect that Goldberg "struck a deal" with the Bernson firm or tried to do more than prove his innocence to them. Since its relationship with Goldberg was not tainted by violations of the Code of Professional Responsibility, there appears to be no warrant for its disqualification from participation in either this or similar actions. *A fortiori* there was no sound basis for disqualifying plaintiffs or dismissing the complaint. . . .

Notes

1. Later we shall discuss more specifically the efforts by the SEC to impose rather strict disclosure requirements on attorneys in connection with matters under its jurisdiction. See Chapter 5. At this point, consider whether Goldberg's original disclosure to the SEC would be justified under Model Rule 1.6(b)(5). The court did not decide that issue (because it did not have to) under the predecessor to that Rule. Is the reasonable likelihood of future accusation of wrongful conduct sufficient to permit the revelation of confidential communications by clients? If so, was there any other method of self-protection that would have been sufficiently effective besides disclosure to the SEC? Or should an attorney be permitted to make the form of disclosure that will be most self-protective?

2. *Meyerhofer* involved revelation of confidences because of accusations of wrongful conduct by third parties over whom the client had no control. If part of our concern in Problems 2–2 through 2–11 and the Bodies Case involves the effect of disclosure on free communication between clients and attorneys, how is our response affected by the rather open-ended exception in DR 4-101(C)(4) as interpreted in *Meyerhofer*? How do you assess the necessity for an exception in this case as compared to the necessity in Problems 2–17 through 2–20?

3. What if the disclosure comes about as a result of advice the client received from another law firm? In Goldberg v. Hirschberg, 806 N.Y.S.2d 333 (Sup. Ct. N.Y. 2005), appeal dismissed, 2005 N.Y.App.Div. LEXIS 11738 (1st Dept. 2005), a New York judge ruled that a former client was required to disclose legal advice it had received from its present law firm with respect to the matter for which it was suing its first law firm for malpractice. In so ruling, the judge relied in part on the fact that the client was seeking nearly $2 million in legal fees owed to the current firm as part of the damages owed by the former firm.

This phenomenon is not completely reciprocal, however. If a lawyer in a firm commits a potential ethical or legal misstep when representing a client, the lawyer may consult the firm's general counsel for advice in handling the problem. See generally Elizabeth Chambliss & David B. Wilkins, "The Emerging Role of Ethics Advisors,

General Counsel, and Other Compliance Specialists in Large Law Firms," 44 Ariz. L. Rev. 559 (2002). If that client later sues the firm for malpractice, the trend lately has been for courts to deny the client access to the communications between the lawyer and the firm's general counsel—even communications that occurred while the fiduciary attorney-client relationship was still in effect. See, e.g., Stock v. Schnader Harrison Segal & Lewis LLP, 142 A.D.3d 210, 241 (N.Y. App. Div. 2016) (rejecting former client's motion to compel disclosure of the firm's internal communications about a conflict of interest because the communications were covered by the firm's attorney-client privilege with its general counsel). As some corporate clients have grumbled, is the assertion of the privilege an example of lawyers placing their own interests over their clients' interests? Should a client not be entitled to voluntary disclosure, or at least formal discovery, of a lawyer's communications about the client's case? Should, instead, the attorney-client privilege be used adversely to clients? Is what is good for the goose good for the gander?

4. Recall the discussion of *Miranda*-like warnings regarding a lawyer's potential discretion or obligation to reveal a client's otherwise confidential information. Do you think you should (also) have to give a *Miranda* warning for the exception of revealing confidences when the lawyer's conduct is in question? If so, what kind of warning would you give? Could you word the warning in a way to avoid it sounding like a threat?

———————

As we hope you see, the scope of the lawyer's duty of confidentiality is an important and recurring issue. As you review the Chapters ahead, you will further see in Chapters 3, 5, and 6 the confidentiality obligation in tension with general candor norms, with the truth-finding purpose of tribunals, and with the appearance of integrity.

Chapter 3

The Literature of Confidentiality and the Adversary System

The last forty years have seen a vast outpouring of writing on the confidentiality obligation and the adversary system. Much of the best of this writing is cited in the footnotes of the following excerpt. Not only lawyers but philosophers have become interested in the obligations of lawyers to clients, the profession, and society. One focus of attention has been whether and when, on the one hand, lawyers should be permitted—or indeed required—to perform what they regard as antisocial activities for their clients, and on the other hand, whether and when lawyers should be required to perform pro bono activities of the "whistleblowing" variety on their clients and on other lawyers, when ordinary citizens would not be required to do so.

At this point in the book it seems advisable to put some of the issues we have been discussing into a larger context. Some of the materials of this book—for example, the excerpts from Wasserstrom (Chapter 1) and Freedman (Chapter 2)—have already addressed themselves to various aspects of these issues and should be considered in connection with the materials of this Chapter. The following article by Professor Pepper does not focus specifically on the confidentiality obligation. It attempts to provide a moral justification for an amoral stance by lawyers in all their roles in our system. As such, it is relevant not only to the materials we have been considering up to now but also to those that we shall consider in succeeding Chapters.

Stephen Pepper
The Lawyer's Amoral Ethical Role:
A Defense, A Problem, and Some Possibilities*

1986 Am. B. Found. Res. J. 613

Eleven years ago Richard Wasserstrom published a provocative paper focusing attention on the moral dimension of the lawyer-client relationship.[1] In the intervening decade the topic has received a great deal of attention both in the profession and

---

* This essay was the winning submission in the Association of American Law Schools' 1985 "Call for Scholarly Papers" competition, and was presented at the 1986 annual meeting, where it was commented upon by Professors Andrew Kaufman and David Luban. Those comments follow [but a rejoinder by Professor Pepper is not reprinted here].

1. Wasserstrom, "Lawyers as Professionals: Some Moral Issues," 5 Hum. Rts. 1 (1975) [reprinted in part in Chapter 1].

in the academy.[3] Much of Wasserstrom's exposition concerned the role-differentiated morality of the lawyer-client relationship, what he referred to as the amoral professional role. Wasserstrom was critical, but "undecided," about the value of that role. This essay is a defense of the lawyer's amoral role.

The role of all professionals, observed Wasserstrom, "is to prefer . . . the interests of client or patient" over those of other individuals. "[W]here the attorney-client relationship exists, it is often appropriate and many times even obligatory for the attorney to do things that, all other things being equal, an ordinary person need not, and should not do."[4] This remains the generally accepted understanding within the profession of a lawyer's proper function. Once a lawyer has entered into the professional relationship with a client, the notion is that conduct by the lawyer in service to the client is judged by a different moral standard than the same conduct by a layperson. Through cross-examination, a lawyer may suggest to a jury that a witness is lying when the lawyer knows the witness is telling the truth. A lawyer may draft contracts or create a corporation for a client to enable the distribution and sale of cigarettes, Saturday Night Specials, or pornography. A lawyer may draft a will for a client disinheriting children should they marry outside the faith. The traditional view is that if such conduct by the lawyer is lawful, then it is morally justifiable, even if the same conduct by a layperson is morally unacceptable and even if the client's goals or means are morally unacceptable. As long as what lawyer and client do is lawful, it is the client who is morally accountable, not the lawyer.

Although this amoral role is the accepted standard within the profession, no generally accepted moral justification for it has been articulated.[5] This remains true despite heated academic discourse on the subject during the ten years following Wasserstrom's article, discourse symbolized by the question: Can a good person be a good lawyer?[6] The criticism of the amoral role has been extraordinarily diverse, ranging from economics through jurisprudence to religion.[7] The most common

---

3. E.g., G. Bellow & B. Moulton, *The Lawyering Process—Ethics and Professional Responsibility* (1981); M. Freedman, *Lawyers' Ethics in an Adversary System* (1975); G. Hazard, *Ethics in the Practice of Law* (1978); Schneyer, "Moral Philosophy's Standard Misconception of Legal Ethics," 1984 Wis. L. Rev. 1529; Dauer & Leff, Correspondence, "The Lawyer as Friend," 86 Yale L.J. 573 (1977); Fried, "The Lawyer as Friend: The Moral Foundations of the Lawyer-Client Relation," 85 Yale L.J. 1060 (1976). See also sources cited infra note 7.

4. Wasserstrom, supra note 1, at 5.

5. Prominent descriptions and justifications are found in Curtis, "The Ethics of Advocacy," 4 Stan. L. Rev. 3 (1951); Fried, supra note 3; and Freeman, "Personal Responsibility in a Professional System," 27 Cath. U. L. Rev. 191 (1978). In some respects, the justification provided here is an elaboration and modification of those presented by Freedman and Fried.

6. The question, phrased slightly differently, is the first line of Charles Fried's article, supra note 3, at 1060.

7. See, e.g. Luban, "The Adversary System Excuse," in D. Luban, ed., *The Good Lawyer* 83 (1984) (moral philosophy); M. Frankel, *Partisan Justice* (1980); T. Shaffer, *On Being a Christian and a Lawyer* (1981) (religion); Abel, "Why Does the ABA Promulgate Ethical Rules?" 59 Tex. L. Rev. 639 (1981) (socioeconomic analysis); D'Amato & Eberle, "Three Models of Legal Ethics," 27 St. Louis U.

justification for the role is framed in the language of the "adversary system," focusing on the justifiably different roles of the advocate and the judge.[8] Part I of this essay will suggest a far broader moral justification for the amoral professional role of the lawyer, the "first-class citizenship model." Part II will address two of the most common criticisms of the amoral role. Part III poses the serious difficulty for the model created when the amoral professional role is combined with the dominant legal realist view of the law. Part IV canvasses some possibilities for ameliorating the legal realism difficulty.

I. THE FIRST-CLASS CITIZENSHIP MODEL

As an introduction to the first-class citizenship model, I would like to begin with a brief explanation of the concept of professional obligation. The very idea of a profession connotes the function of service, the notion that to some degree the professional is to subordinate his interests to the interests of those in need of his services.[9] This orientation is suggested by the following seven characteristics that define the concept of a profession.[10]

1. A profession is a means of making a living.

2. A profession is based on specialized knowledge, training, and ability, often requiring intellectual labor and many years of higher education.

3. The services rendered by the professional, based upon this foundation of knowledge and ability, are necessary to individuals at various points in their lives and are frequently of the utmost personal concern (for example, services relating to physical health, liberty, religious salvation, or psychological well-being).

4. Because of the specialized knowledge involved, the quality of the services rendered by the professional is untestable from the perspective of the layman. The individual *needs* the service but is unable to evaluate it, and therefore the individual is *vulnerable* in relation to the professional.

5. The profession holds a monopoly on a service frequently needed by individuals, and as a result wields significant economic power.

L.J. 761 (1983) (moral philosophy); Rhode, "Why the ABA Bothers: A Functional Perspective on Professional Codes," 59 Tex. L. Rev. 689 (1981) (socioeconomic analysis); Schwartz, "The Zeal of the Civil Advocate," 1983 Am. B. Found. Res. J. 543 (legal analysis); Simon, "The Ideology of Advocacy: Procedural Justice and Professional Ethics," 1978 Wis. L. Rev. 30 (jurisprudence); Wasserstrom, supra note 1 (moral philosophy).

8. See, e.g., Freedman, supra note 3; Fuller & Randall, "Professional Responsibility: Report of the Joint Conference," 44 A.B.A. J. 1159 (1958); Curtis, supra note 5.

9. B. Bledstein, *The Culture of Professionalism* 87 (1976); M. S. Larson, *The Rise of Professionalism* 56–63 (1977); W. E. Moore, *The Professions: Roles and Rules* 13–15 (1970).

10. These characteristics are derived from a similar definition provided by Wasserstrom, supra note 1, at 2 n.1. See also Bledstein, supra note 9, at 87; Larson, supra note 9, at x; Moore, supra note 9, at 4–22.

6. The profession is largely self-regulated in determining and administering the qualifications for membership and in policing professional activities.

7. Part of the self-regulation usually includes ethical prescriptions that articulate a service orientation.

The sixth and seventh characteristics are the quid pro quo for the fact that the profession has a monopoly on and is making a living from a service the public needs but cannot evaluate.

The seven characteristics add up to an inherent advantage for the professional over those in need of his services and to a pervasive economic conflict of interest between the professional and those who need (and pay for) his services. As a remedy for this unbalanced conflict, there is a primary underlying professional obligation: When the client's interest and the professional's interest conflict, the professional is to forgo his interest in favor of the client's.

The legal profession's ethical code reflects the factors and the conflict listed above. Much of [it] appears to be designed to enhance the economic well-being of the profession. But much of it also appears designed to put the client's interest above that of the lawyer, to protect the client from the lawyer's self-interest. It is this second aspect of the legal profession's ethics with which this essay is concerned. Leaving aside the "guild" provisions, the role of the professional is to serve the client ahead of himself or herself. If anything justifies the asymmetrical power and opportunity sketched in the seven definitional elements listed above, it is this underlying ethic of professionalism. This ethic alone suggests that if a moral conflict between lawyer and client develops, the lawyer should honor the client's view. But this is not the argument to be presented here. This view of the theoretical service orientation of the professions only sets the stage.

The premise with which we begin is that law is a public good available to all. Society, through its "lawmakers"—legislatures, courts, administrative agencies, and so forth—has created various mechanisms to ease and enable the private attainment of individual or group goals. The corporate form of enterprise, the contract, the trust, the will, and access to civil court to gain the use of public force for the settlement of private grievance are all vehicles of empowerment for the individual or group; all are "law" created by the collectivity to be generally available for private use. In addition to these structuring mechanisms are vast amounts of law, knowledge of which is intended to be generally available and is empowering: landlord/tenant law, labor law, OSHA, Social Security—the list can be vastly extended. Access to both forms of law increases one's ability to successfully attain goals.

The second premise is a societal commitment to the principle of individual autonomy. This premise is founded on the belief that liberty and autonomy are a moral good, that free choice is better than constraint, that each of us wishes, to the extent possible, to make our own choices rather than to have them made for us. This belief is incorporated into our legal system, which accommodates individual autonomy by leaving as much room as possible for liberty and diversity. Leaving regulatory law aside for the moment (and granting that it has grown immensely, contributing to the legalization to be mentioned below), our law is designed (1) to allow the private structuring of affairs (contracts, corporations, wills, trusts, etc.) and (2) to define conduct that is intolerable. The latter sets a floor below which one cannot go, but leaves as much room as possible above that floor for individual decision making. It may be morally wrong to manufacture or distribute cigarettes or alcohol, or to disinherit one's children for marrying outside the faith, but the generality of such decisions are left in the private realm. Diversity and autonomy are preferred over "right" or "good" conduct. The theory of our law is to leave as much room as possible for private, individual actions concerning what is right and wrong, as opposed to public, collective decisions.

Our first premise is that law is intended to be a public good which increases autonomy. The second premise is that increasing individual autonomy is morally good. The third step is that in a highly legalized society such as ours, autonomy is often dependent upon access to the law. Put simply, first-class citizenship is dependent on access to the law. And while access to law—to the creation and use of a corporation, to knowledge of how much overtime one has to pay or is entitled to receive—is fully available to all, in reality it is available only through a lawyer. Our law is usually not simple, usually not self-executing. For most people most of the time, meaningful access to the law requires the assistance of a lawyer. Thus the resulting conclusion: First-class citizenship is frequently dependent upon the assistance of a lawyer. If the conduct which the lawyer facilitates is above the floor of the intolerable—is not unlawful— then this line of thought suggests that what the lawyer does is a social good. The lawyer is the means to first-class citizenship, to meaningful autonomy, for the client.

For the lawyer to have moral responsibility for each act he or she facilitates, for the lawyer to have a moral obligation to refuse to facilitate that which the lawyer believes to be immoral, is to substitute lawyers' beliefs for individual autonomy and diversity. Such a screening submits each to the prior restraint of the judge/facilitator and to rule by an oligarchy of lawyers. (If in the alternative, the suggestion is that the lawyer's screening should be based not on the lawyer's personal morality, but on the lawyer's assessment of society's moral views or on guidelines spelled out in a professional code of ethics, then one has substituted collective moral decision making for individual moral decision making, contrary to the principle of autonomy. Less room has been left for private decision making through a sub rosa form of lawmaking.) If the conduct is sufficiently "bad," it would seem that it ought to be made explicitly unlawful. If it is not that bad, why subject the citizenry to the happenstance of the moral judgment of the particular lawyer to whom each has access? If making the conduct unlawful is too onerous because the law would be too vague, or it is too difficult to identify the conduct in advance, or there is not sufficient social or political concern, do we intend to delegate to the individual lawyer the authority for case-by-case legislation and policing?

An example may help. Professor Wasserstrom implies that a lawyer ought to refuse to draft a will disinheriting a child because of the child's views concerning the war in Nicaragua. "But," asks Professor Freedman, "is the lawyer's paternalism toward the client preferable—morally or otherwise—to the client's paternalism toward her children?" And, he asks further, is there any reason to substitute the diversity of lawyers' opinions on the issue of disinheritance based on political belief for the diversity of clients' opinions? Ought we to have a law on the issue? If not, why screen use of the legal device of testacy either through the diverse consciences of lawyers or through the collective conscience of the profession? And if the law is clear but contrary to the lawyer's moral beliefs, such as a tax loophole for the rich or impeachment-oriented cross-examination of the truthful witness, why allow (let alone require) that the lawyer legislate for this particular person or situation?

It is apparent that a final significant value supporting the first-class citizenship model is that of equality. If law is a public good, access to which increases autonomy, then equality of access is important. For access to the law to be filtered unequally through the disparate moral views of each individual's lawyer does not appear to be justifiable. Even given the current and perhaps permanent fact of unequal access to the law, it does not make sense to compound that inequality with another. If access to a lawyer is achieved (through private allocation of one's means, public provision, or the lawyer's—or profession's—choice to provide it), should the extent of that access depend upon individual lawyer conscience? The values of autonomy and equality suggest that it should not; the client's conscience should be superior to the lawyer's. One of the unpleasant concomitants of the view that a lawyer should be morally responsible for all that she does is the resulting inequality: unfiltered access to the law is then available only to those who are legally sophisticated or to those able to educate themselves sufficiently for access to the law, while those less sophisticated—usually those less educated—are left with no access or with access that subjects their use of the law to the moral judgment and veto of the lawyer.

II. THE CRITIQUE AND A RESPONSE

A. THE ECONOMIC INEQUALITY CRITICISM

The foregoing quickly leads to the observation that law is a public good in theory but not in fact, and that one of the key premises justifying the first-class citizenship model is therefore false. Like almost everything else in our society, access to law is rationed through the market—in this case, the market for lawyers' services. Thus, the rich have disproportionate access over the poor, and this is particularly unacceptable given the public nature of law and its implementing relationship to individual autonomy and first-class citizenship. This is the focus of the first criticism of the amoral role: it would be justified if everyone had access to "first-class citizenship" through a lawyer, but everyone does not. The drastic and fundamental inequality of means in America vitiates the moral justification for an amoral professional ethic for lawyers.

Granting the truth of economic inequality does not, however, mean that the amoral role is a bad role, or that the lawyer currently fulfilling the role cannot be a good person. An analogous criticism might be made of the grocer and the housing contractor. Although food and shelter are (in our system) not public goods, they are more fundamentally enabling to autonomy than is law. Yet there is much less disquiet over the moral role of the grocer, housing contractor, or landlord than that of the lawyer. We live in a primarily market system, not a primarily socialist system, and the contemporary problem in defining lawyers' ethics is likely to have to be answered in this market context. Lawyers cannot magically socialize the economy or legal services.

Another way of saying this, perhaps more to the point, is that there are two issues here: the distribution of legal services and the content of what is distributed. The moral content of what is distributed—the ethical nature of the lawyer-client relationship once established—is the subject of this essay. The distribution of access to the law (legal services) is a different subject. While the effort to make law a more truly public good is under way (or assuming it fails and we are left with the status quo), the other issue remains: what is to be the moral content of the legal services that are available? To suggest that transforming the amoral facilitator role of the lawyer into the judge/facilitator role follows from the insufficient availability of legal services is a non sequitur. Such a transformation would compound inequality upon inequality—first the inequality of access to a lawyer, then the inequality of what law that particular lawyer will allow the client access to.

One can argue that the judge/facilitator role will not compound inequality but, to the contrary, will balance power because the advantage accruing to those with access to the law over those without will be balanced by the restraint of the lawyer's moral screening of access to the law. There are at least two reasons to react with skepticism to this argument. First, the inequality of distribution is neither complete nor uniform. At least some of the "outs" have had significant access to the law through lawyers. Labor unions, criminal defendants, and civil rights organizations are three prominent examples. Lawyers have played key roles in areas where many perceive gains to have been made in social justice. Second, there is little likelihood of a large difference in moral perception between lawyers and their "in" clients. Perhaps we need more (historical? empirical?) data: Looking back, would there have been more social justice, equality, or general welfare if lawyers had altered or withheld services on the basis of their own (largely middle- or upper-class) values? How would a moralistic as opposed to an amoral role for lawyers have affected 20th century American social history? However one is inclined to answer such questions, to the extent that the first-class citizenship argument is otherwise valid, expansion and equalization of access to lawyers is a goal which is both consistent with and suggested by that argument. Transforming lawyers into moral screens for client access to the law, to the contrary, is a project quite problematic in its relation to equality of access to law.

Before moving on, one caveat related to the economic inequality criticism should be entered. The first-class citizenship model suggests that lawyers are a necessary item in a highly legalized society and that they should have an amoral role in relation to facilitating clients' wishes. It does not suggest how access to lawyers should be organized. The nature and extent of the legal profession's monopoly—for example, whether paraprofessionals should be allowed to practice independently, or whether unauthorized practice rules should be enforced against bankers, realtors, or accountants—is a separate question from that examined in this paper.[32] The term "deprofessionalization" can refer to either (1) the market-limiting nature of professional rules or (2) the amoral professional role. The argument up to this point in this essay is that deprofessionalization in the second sense is a bad idea, but no position has been taken on deprofessionalization in the first sense.

B. THE ADVERSARY SYSTEM CRITICISM

Much writing on the amoral role of the lawyer has dealt with the layperson's common conception of what lawyers do: criminal defense. The amoral role is justified by the need of the "man in trouble" for a champion familiar with the law to aid him in facing the vast resources of the State bearing down on him, attempting to seize his most basic liberties and put him in jail. In this context, however, there is another champion, the prosecutor, with greater resources, opposing and balancing the lawyer's amorality. More important, there are a neutral judge and a jury whose roles are significantly less amoral than the advocate's. Critics of the lawyer's role have had a field day distinguishing this situation from civil litigation and from nonlitigation (what most lawyers are working on most of the time). The critics suggest that a role justified by the rather unusual context of the criminal justice system simply is not justified in the far more common lawyer roles. Where there is no judge responsible for applying the law from a neutral stance, where there is no lawyer protecting those who may be victimized or exploited by another person's use of "the law"—in these situations the critics of the amoral role argue that the lawyer must take on the neutral judge's role and screen access to and use of the law. Their point is that a role modeled on Perry Mason does not fit the lawyer working for Sears drafting form consumer contracts.

It is therefore significant that the justification for the lawyer's amoral role sketched above has not once mentioned the adversary system, has not been based on any premise involving an opposing lawyer or a neutral judge or jury. In the usual justification of the lawyer's amoral role, the model is adjudication, and there is a difficult stretch adapting and applying this to the lawyer's office. In this essay, the model is the office lawyer advising about the law and implementing client goals through legally available devices, and one need not stretch to apply that model to litigation. Litigation is simply one of the available devices for implementing goals, like a trust or a corporation. When one focuses on a defendant, either civil or criminal, the moral validity of the autonomy and equality arguments is more apparent because the legal mechanism is being imposed on the individual rather than freely chosen, but the moral

---

32. The literature is vast. See, e.g., Rhode, "Policing the Professional Monopoly: A Constitutional and Empirical Analysis of Unauthorized Practice Prohibitions," 34 Stan. L. Rev. 1 (1981); . . . Ehrlich & Schwartz, "Reducing the Costs of Legal Services: Possible Approaches by the Federal Government," reprinted in A. Kaufman, *Problems in Professional Responsibility* at 582 (1st ed. 1976).

validity is not dependent on the defendant role. Thus, the arguments for the amoral role premised on the adversary system supplement the first-class citizenship model in the litigation setting, and the critique based on the limited scope of the adversary system is largely beside the point under the first-class citizenship model.

Two further observations concerning the relationship between the first-class citizenship model and the adversary system model are apposite. First, as noted above, the criminal defendant is only a special instance of the first-class citizenship model. In the criminal context the moral value of full access to all that the law allows is simply clearer and more dramatic. However, because of what is at stake and the procedural safeguards of the adversary system (an opponent lawyer, neutral decision makers), the law may allow more in the criminal context. For example, the criminal defendant has the right to not incriminate himself and he suffers no legal liability for exercising that right. (The jury is told *not* to base convictions on the exercise of that right.) Outside the context of litigation, however, civil liability may be based on nondisclosure of incriminating facts in certain contexts, such as sales of securities under federal regulatory laws or the sale of a house under the common law tort doctrine of misrepresentation. Similarly, to take an example with which we began, the litigant through her lawyer may mislead the court with a cross-examination that intentionally and incorrectly implies the witness was not telling the truth on direct examination, and there will be no liability under the law for the client or the lawyer. In the nonlitigation context of selling a termite-ridden house, however, utilizing similar implications and half-truths to communicate the absence of termites may generate tort liability on the part of the client for misrepresentation and an ethical violation on the part of the lawyer if she "assisted" the client in "fraudulent conduct."

Second, the lines between criminal and civil litigation and between litigation and nonlitigation are not as clear as the critics suggest. The criminal system pits "the state," with all its power, against an individual. But the very point of civil litigation is to allow the private plaintiff to gain the power of "the state" to enforce her claim against the defendant, thus removing the need for, or utility of, acquiring private police or armies to enforce claims. Civil litigation is a contest over which side is to have the vast power of "the state" on its side in a dispute.

Certainly the distinction between litigation and nonlitigation is clearer, but even that line is not as bright as one might at first assume. When the consumer and Sears differ over the validity of a form contract or the misleading nature of advertising or displays, the disparity in power and means is huge. Moving across the line into litigation does equalize the power in both form and substance. But a good deal of that equalization is due to the presence of a lawyer. "Having a lawyer on your side" is a lot of what litigation implies. (To what extent would the filing of a complaint by a *pro se* consumer plaintiff against Sears change the balance of power?) Thus, the more significant transaction — the brighter line — may be between having and not having a lawyer. For the consumer to have access to the law through a lawyer *prior* to litigation would seem to be a more realistic possibility for equalizing power (or actualizing autonomy) than would an obligation on the part of Sears's in-house lawyer to function as a moral screen and filter for Sears's use of the law. This observation circles us back to both the first-class citizenship justification for the amoral role and to the economic inequality critique.

Before moving on from the adversary system criticism, it is appropriate to note that the adversary system image of the lawyer as the champion against a hostile world — the hired gun — is not the proper image for the general role of the lawyer presented here (although it may be the proper image for the criminal defense lawyer). Rather, the image more concordant with the first-class citizenship model is that of the individual facing and needing to use a very large and very complicated machine (with lots of whirring gears and spinning data tapes) that he can't get to work. This is "the law" that confronts the individual in our society. It is theoretically there for his use, but he can't use it for his purposes without the aid of someone who has the correct wrenches, meters, and more esoteric tools, and knows how and where to use them. Or the image is that of someone who stands frustrated before a photocopier that won't copy (or someone whose car won't go) and needs a technician (or mechanic) to make it go. It is ordinarily not the technician's or mechanic's moral concern whether the content of what is about to be copied is morally good or bad, or for what purpose the customer intends to use the car.

III. THE PROBLEM OF LEGAL REALISM

This paper began with a moral justification for the lawyer's amoral ethical role. It then addressed, and for the most part rejected, two of the most common criticisms of that role. We turn now to a third, rarely articulated problem presented by the first-class citizenship justification for the amoral role. Up to this point in the discussion, access to the law as the primary justification for the amoral professional role has been presented with relatively little focus on what "the law" refers to. Three different facets of law have been recognized: (1) structuring mechanisms (trusts, corporations, civil litigation), (2) definitions of intolerable conduct (criminal law and litigation), and (3) regulatory law. The implication has been that the law is existent and determinable, that there is "something there" for the lawyer to find (or know) and communicate to the client. The "thereness" of the law is also the assumption underlying the commonly understood limit on the amoral role: the lawyer can only assist the client "within the bounds of the law."[41] This accords with the usual understanding of the law from the lay or client point of view, but not from the lawyer's point of view. The dominant view of law inculcated in the law schools, which will be identified here as "legal realism" approaches law without conceiving of it as objectively "out there" to be discovered and applied. A relatively little explored problem is the dynamic between the amoral professional role and a skeptical attitude toward law.

By "legal realism" I mean a view of law which stresses its open-textured, vague nature over its precision; its manipulability over its certainty; and its instrumental

---

41. ABA Code of Professional Responsibility, Ethical Considerations 7-1 and 7-19. . . .

possibilities over its normative content. From "positivism" modern legal education takes the notion of the separation of law and morality: in advising the client, the lawyer is concerned with the law as an "is," a fact of power and limitation, more than as an "ought." From "legal realism" it takes the notion of law as a prediction of what human officials will do, more than as an existent, objective, determinable limit or boundary on client behavior. From "process jurisprudence" it takes an emphasis on client goals and private structuring, an instrumental use of law that deemphasizes the determination of law through adjudication or the prediction of the outcome of adjudication. These three views of "the law" are mutually reinforcing rather than conflicting. To the extent that legal education inculcates these views, "the law" becomes a rather amorphous thing, dependent upon the client's situation, goals, and risk preferences. What is the interaction between this view of the law and the view of the lawyer as an amoral servant of the client whose assistance is limited only by "the law"?

The apt image is that of Holmes's "bad man." The modern lawyer is taught to look at the law as the "bad man" would, "who cares only for the material consequences." The lawyer discovers and conveys "the law" to his client from this perspective and then is told to limit his own assistance to the client based upon this same view of "the law." The modern view of contract law, for example, deemphasizes the normative obligation of promises and views breach of contract as a "right" that is subject to the "cost" of damages. Breach of contract is not criminal and, normally, fulfillment of a contractual obligation is not forced on a party (not "specifically enforced," in contract law terminology). The client who comes in with a more normative view of the obligation of contracts (whether wishing the lawyer to assist in structuring a transaction through a prospective contract or in coping with the unwelcome constraints of a past contract) will be educated by the competent lawyer as to the "breach as cost" view of "the law." Similarly, modern tort law has emphasized allocation of the "costs" of accidents, as opposed to the more normative view of 19th- and early 20th-century negligence law. Thus, negligence law can be characterized as establishing a right to a nonconsensual taking from the injured party on the part of the tortfeasor, subject once again to the "cost" of damages. An industrial concern assessing and planning conduct which poses risks of personal injury or death to third parties will be guided by a lawyer following this view away from perceiving the imposition of unreasonable risk as a "wrong" and toward perceiving it as a potential cost.

There are, of course, variations in the extent to which legal realism will be encountered in a lawyer's office. One is more likely to find the cost-predictive view presented in relation to a contract problem than a tort problem, and it is more likely to come from a lawyer advising a large corporate enterprise than one advising an individual. But it is valid as a general suggestive model that most clients, most of the time, (1) will enter the lawyer's office thinking of law as more normative and more certain than does the lawyer, and (2) will go out having been influenced toward thinking of the law in terms of possible or probable costs more than they would have had they not consulted a lawyer.

From the perspective of fully informed access to the law, this modification of the client's view is good because it accords with the generally accepted understanding of the law among those who are closest to its use and administration—lawyers and judges. It is accurate; it is useful to the client. From the perspective of the ethical relationship between lawyer and client, it is far more problematic. First, the lawyer is to be an amoral technician who serves rather than judges the client. The lawyer is not the repository of moral limits on the client's behavior. Second, the law itself, as presented by the lawyer, also is not a source of moral limits. Rather, it is presented from the lawyer's technical, manipulative stance as a potential constraint, as a problem, or as data to be factored into decisions as to future conduct. Finally, in determining how far he or she can go in helping the client, the lawyer is instructed to look to that same uncertain, manipulable source: "the law." "Within the bounds of the law" sounds like an objective, knowable moral guide. Any second-year law student knows that as to any but the most obvious (and therefore uninteresting) questions, there will probably be no clear line, no boundary, but only a series of possibilities. Thus, if one combines the dominant "legal realism" understanding of law with the traditional amoral role of the lawyer, *there is no moral input or constraint in the present model of the lawyer-client relationship.*

Again, from the premises of the first-class citizenship model, this is as it should be. The client's autonomy should be limited by the law, not by the lawyer's morality. And if "the law" is manipulable and without clear limits on client conduct, that aspect of the law should be available to the client. If moral limits are not provided by the law and are not imposed by the lawyer, their source will be where it ought to be: the client. Morality is not to be inserted in the lawyer's office, its source either the lawyer or the law. Morality comes through the door as part of the client.

This shifts our focus from the lawyer and the law to the client. It should come as no surprise that many clients will come through the door without much internal moral guidance. Common sources of moral guidance are on the decline: religion, community, family. In a secularized society such as ours, religion no longer functions as the authoritative moral guide it once was. Geographic mobility and divorce have robbed many of the multigenerational moral guidance that families can provide. Small, supportive, usually continuous and homogenous moral communities are the experience of fewer and fewer people. The rural town, the ethnic neighborhood, the church attended for several generations, the local business or trade community (the chamber of commerce or the grocers' trade association)—all are the experience of a far smaller segment of the population than before. Even the role of the public school in inculcating values may have declined. For many, law has replaced alternative sources of moral guidance.

Our problem now posits: (1) a client seeking access to the law who frequently has only weak internal or external sources of morality; (2) a lawyer whose professional role mandates that he or she not impose moral restraint on the client's access to the law; (3) a lawyer whose understanding of the law deemphasizes its moral content and certainty, and perceives it instead as instrumental and manipulable; and (4) law designed as (*a*) neutral structuring mechanisms to increase individual power (contracts, the corporate form, civil litigation), (*b*) a floor delineating minimum tolerable behavior rather than moral guidance, and (*c*) morally neutral regulation. From this perspective, access to the law through a lawyer appears to systematically screen out or deemphasize moral considerations and moral limits. The client who consults a lawyer will be guided to maximize his autonomy through the tools of the law—tools designed and used to maximize freedom, not to provide a guide to good behavior. If one cannot rely on the client or an alternative social institution to provide that guide, to suggest a moral restraint on that which is legally available, then what the lawyer does may be evil: lawyers in the aggregate may consistently guide clients away from moral conduct and restraint.

Assume client consults lawyer concerning discharge of polluted water from a rural plant. Client wants to know what the law requires, respects "the law," and intends to comply. Removing ammonia from the plant's effluent is very expensive. The EPA limit is .050 grams of ammonia per liter of effluent, and the EPA has widely publicized this standard to relevant industries. In addition to this information, however, lawyer informs client that inspection in rural areas of the state is rare and that enforcement officials always issue a warning (give a second chance) prior to applying sanctions unless the violation is extreme. Moreover, lawyer also informs client that it is known informally that violations of .075 grams per liter or less are ignored because of a limited enforcement budget. In such a situation, lay ignorance of legal technicalities and the realities of enforcement would seem to lead toward more obedience of "the law" (the .050 gram limit). Access to an amoral, "legal realist" lawyer leans toward violation of "the law." Given the model elaborated above, unless the client comes equipped with strong moral guidance, there will be no pressure to obey the law as written. (Worse, if the client is a corporate manager, she may be bound by her own amoral professional role which perceives shareholder profit as its primary guide.)

IV. POTENTIAL ANSWERS TO THE PROBLEM OF LEGAL REALISM

What follows is a brief canvassing of the major responses that might ameliorate the dilemma sketched above. The first two possibilities are societal responses that do not focus on the ethic of the lawyer-client relation, while the last three explore various approaches to lawyers' ethics.

A. INCREASED SOCIETAL RESOURCES APPLIED TO LAW ENFORCEMENT

The first alternative is to accept the situation described above as either proper or unavoidable. To the extent that the pure "legal realist" view is the basis for conduct, law without enforcement is rendered meaningless. This in turn suggests the need for vast increases in resources devoted to law enforcement. Such a prospect is rather daunting in an era of insufficient government means. More important, the societal atmosphere likely to accompany such an emphasis on law enforcement is not pleasant to contemplate.

B. REBUILDING (OR CREATING ANEW) SOURCES OF MORAL AUTHORITY AND GUIDANCE OTHER THAN LAW

From right-wing fundamentalism through "values clarification" in the public schools to the renaissance in academic moral philosophy, the perceived need to revive or create sources of moral authority and guidance has become a pervasive societal concern. Commencing with the Enlightenment, secularization has progressively and thoroughly removed religion as the central source of moral authority in Western thought. Science and rationalism, whether taking the forms of logical positivism, anthropology, psychology, or scientism, are increasingly perceived as unable to answer moral and ethical questions. It is safe to say that the search for values and alternative methodologies to elucidate, compare, and validate values is and will remain one of the predominant intellectual (and perhaps political) themes of the last third of the 20th century. "Watergate" is often cited as the cause of the current academic interest in lawyers' professional ethics. Both that scandal and our intellectual endeavors, however, are part of a larger and more important historical process. To the extent that values and sources of moral authority are rebuilt external to the law, the moral vacuum of the "amoral lawyer/realism" combination will be ameliorated.

As elaborated above, law itself as it is currently conceived is not a primary source of moral authority or guidance. It is possible that the dominant political philosophy conveyed in the law schools will dominate, and lawyers' understanding of and approach to the law will change also, but this seems less likely than does a change in the understanding of the lawyer-client ethic. We therefore turn now to some of the possible changes in lawyers' professional ethics.

C. THE LAWYER AS POLICEMAN, JUDGE, AND/OR DECEIVER

The lawyer-client ethic analogous to the first possibility above, that of enhanced resources devoted to law enforcement, would alter the traditional balance of lawyer allegiance away from the client and toward society. In the 1970s the SEC took such a position toward the securities bar. In essence it asserted that the lawyer in our hypothetical above would have had to report to the government consistent discharges above .050 grams per liter, regardless of the likelihood or nature of enforcement and regardless of whether his knowledge was based upon client confidences. This is indeed to give policing responsibilities to the lawyer and, depending upon the client's understanding of the confidential nature of communications to a lawyer, perhaps makes the lawyer a deceiver.

If the lawyer does not become a policeman, but instead injects morality by refusing to communicate the legal realism view of law to the client, this is still a significant problem. For the lawyer to communicate to the client a "thereness" and a normative obligation to a written law that is contrary to the lawyer's legal realist view of that particular law is to practice deception, deception in service to obedience of the law. Imagine, for example, a lawyer advising a couple for whom there are significant tax and economic advantages in living together unmarried, in a jurisdiction where fornication remains a crime on the books but is never prosecuted. Is it not deception to fail to inform them of the benefits, or to inform them, but to add that the benefits are not available because the conduct would be criminal, but then to say nothing further?

To replace the amoral role with a moral responsibility role also transmutes the lawyer into an enforcement mechanism, although now it is not the written law but the lawyer's ethics which are being enforced on the client. The lawyer has become the judge of the client. This approach does ameliorate the dilemma by an injection of ethical constraint, but it does so at the expense of the moral values that inhere in the premises of the first-class citizenship justification elaborated above. That elaboration suggests that this would be a considerable price to pay because the values of individual autonomy, diversity, and equality are relatively fundamental to the traditional understanding of our society. Perhaps that expertise is merited if one perceives the synergism of the lawyer's amoral role and the legal realist view of law as sufficiently destructive.

D. THE LAWYER AND CLIENT IN MORAL DIALOGUE

The fourth possibility emphasizes the utility of wide-ranging communication between lawyer and client. Instead of defining the client's goals in narrow material terms and approaching the law solely as means to or constraint on such goals, this view opens the relationship to moral input in two ways.

First, the lawyer's full understanding of the situation, including the lawyer's moral understanding, can be communicated to the client. The professional role remains amoral in that the lawyer is still required to provide full access to the law for the client, but the dilemma sketched above is ameliorated by moral input from the lawyer which supplements access to the law. The autonomy of the client remains in that she is given access to all that the law allows, but the client's decisions are informed by the lawyer's moral judgment. Just as the lawyer/policeman role is the analogue in ethics to the alternative of enhanced resource investment in law enforcement, the dialogue role is one possible source for rebuilding moral authority aside from the law. While the lawyer still may not judge or police the client in the sense of screening access to the law, this view of the professional role does allow the lawyer the moral role of moral educator.

The second way the dialogue model infuses a moral element into the lawyer-client relationship is from the side of the client. The current situation minimizes the client's moral input as well as the lawyer's. The client comes in with a human problem (family, business, corporate, etc.); the lawyer defines it in legal terms, usually including a legal goal and legal means to that goal, all perceived from the amoral legal realist stance. Both goal and means may well be defined by the client's interests as presumed by the lawyer: usually maximization of wealth or avoidance of incarceration. More communication drawn from the client by an open lawyer may substantially qualify those presumed goals as well as limit means. To the extent that the lawyer makes room in the professional relationship for a moral dialogue, the client's moral and ethical perceptions can affect decisions. Part of the dilemma sketched above was based on the limited extent of moral guidance with which many clients now come equipped; the dialogue model aims to draw out and actualize that which is there.

This paper began with the example of the lawyer cross-examining a witness known to be truthful in such a way as to suggest to the jury that the witness might be lying. Dialogue with the client may educate the lawyer to the fact that the client does not want to win that way, that the lawyer is wrong in assuming that winning by all lawfully available means is the task the client intended for the lawyer. To the contrary, the client may want to have "the facts" judged by "the law" and may have no desire to win if the truth does not lead to that decision. Or the client may believe that exposing the truthful witness to the implied accusation of dishonesty is a moral wrong of sufficient import to prevent its use even to gain that to which he believes justice entitles him. The client may simply not want to win by immoral means. Or, looking at the dialogue with the moral input coming from the lawyer, if the lawyer is the one morally troubled by such a cross-examination and the client is not, the lawyer's perception may engage or educate the client, or the client's overall regard for the lawyer may be sufficient for the client to agree that the tactic should not be used.

Two limits on the "moral dialogue" approach must be recognized. First, it is expensive. Such a dialogue requires time, and time is the lawyer's stock in trade. Either the client must be willing and able to pay for the expanded conversation at the lawyer's regular hourly rate, or the lawyer must be willing to accept a lower income. With traditional forms of legal services perceived as too expensive for the middle and lower classes, and a consequent shift occurring toward less expensive, more efficient structures for providing legal services, the dialogue model may be difficult (perhaps impossible) to incorporate as an integral part of the lawyers' professional ethic. It may be more likely to occur at the level of complex corporate practice because more time is devoted to analysis of legal alternatives. But even in this area of practice, efforts to limit the costs of legal services have been rapidly expanding.

Second, client receptivity to the approach will vary with the context. The criminal defendant facing years in prison and represented by a public defender will be less open to the dialogue than will the corporate officer dealing with in-house counsel. Lawyers in some contexts may be simply unable to engage in dialogue with their clients; the larger the cultural and economic gap between lawyer and client, the less likely is meaningful moral dialogue. Thus, both limits suggest there will be a spectrum of the kinds of legal practice for which the moral dialogue ethic is suitable or possible.

E. CONSCIENTIOUS OBJECTION

Part I of this essay suggests a moral justification for the amoral role of the lawyer. That there is such a moral justification does not tell us how that justification will balance with competing moral values which may be present in any given situation. Assuming a lawyer feels bound (either morally or under legally enforced professional ethics) to the amoral ethic, he or she may perceive in a particular situation a higher value that supports conduct contrary to the lawyer role. Conscientious objection always remains an alternative in such a situation: one can recognize the moral and legal validity of the amoral role, but choose not to follow it. This possibility ameliorates the dilemma sketched above by injecting the moral perception of the lawyer into certain cases. In such cases, the lawyer's moral perception will screen the client's access to all that the law allows.

If such conscientious objection is not limited to extreme cases, however, it is little different from the lawyer as policeman, judge, and/or deceiver. To the extent the lawyer allows moral considerations to trump professional obligation, his role is no longer amoral. David Luban appears to have reached this point in his conclusion that the amoral role is supported only by very weak moral values. He argues that in the absence of any countervailing moral value, the lawyer should follow the role. But if there is any valid moral objection to conduct mandated by the amoral role, he concludes that the role provides no justification. Part I above suggests, to the contrary, that the lawyer's amoral professional role has strong justification in several moral values. If this is true, conscientious objection should be rarely exercised by the lawyer.

The well-known "hidden bodies" case provides an example. A criminal defendant revealed to his lawyers the location of the hidden bodies of two murder victims, and the lawyers visited the location to determine the accuracy of the information. The lawyers did not reveal this information for six months, even when it was personally sought from them by the parents of one of the victims. Normal morality would condemn such callous behavior. The amoral role demanded such behavior, for the lawyers were not legally obligated to disclose the information and they perceived it to be in the client's legal interest to delay divulging the information. Professor Luban's approach implies that normal morality should have been applied by the lawyers. The first-class citizenship model suggests the contrary, particularly in the context of criminal defense. Assume for a moment, however, that upon investigation by the lawyers, one of the victims was observed to be alive. Assume further that there was no legal or professional obligation to assist or reveal the existence and location of the live victim to others who would assist (which is quite possibly an accurate statement of the law). Here one has the kind of extreme case for which conscientious objection to the amoral role seems appropriate. Even if the client will be hurt by the lawyers' revealing the plight of the living victim, normal morality in this instance must outweigh the generally strong moral values underlying the amoral role.

V. CONCLUSION: ON THE MORAL AUTONOMY OF THE LAWYER

This paper began by presenting a moral justification for the lawyer's amoral professional role. It then turned briefly to two of the criticisms aimed at the amoral role: the economic one that focuses on the unequal distribution of legal service, and the "adversary system" one that focuses on the usual absence of a judge and the frequent absence of a second, counterbalancing advocate from the situations in which most lawyers function. The difficulty presented by the combination of the amoral professional role and the lawyer's "legal realism" was then elaborated. Last, some possible remedies for this problem were presented.

Where are we left? I would suggest that the moral values of autonomy and equality are imperative in relation to access to the law. Genuine autonomy is so dependent on access to the law, and inequality of access bears so directly on autonomy, that we are indeed dealing with a question of first- and second-class citizenship. This imperative is sufficient, in my view, to outweigh the problems presented by the amoral professional role.

Given this essay's stress on autonomy, it is fair to ask: Where in the amoral role is there a place for the lawyer's moral autonomy? Lawyers are far more intimately involved with and identified with their clients than grocers or landlords are with their customers and tenants. This causes much of the disquiet with the amoral role both within and without the profession. If the client chooses to be the "bad man," to do that which is lawful but morally wrong, does not the lawyer become a bad person, compelled by the immoral role to assist, yet intimately connected to and identified with the client's wrongdoing?

Part of the answer lies in the principle of professionalism sketched at the beginning of part I. Because of the large advantages over the client built into the lawyer's professional role, and because of the disadvantages and vulnerability built into the client's role, the professional must subordinate his interest to the client's when there is a conflict. That the conflict may be a moral one ought not change this precept. The lawyer is a good person in that he provides access to the law; in providing such access without moral screening, he serves the moral values of individual autonomy and equality. This ought to be enough, for the underlying professional ethic cautions that when there is a conflict between lawyer and client, the professional must remember that the raison d'être for his role is service to the client.

The rest of the answer can be found in those limited areas in which the moral autonomy of the lawyer can function compatibly with the amoral professional ethic. Initially, the lawyer has the choice of whether or not to be a lawyer. It should be clear that this choice involves important moral consequences. Second, the lawyer has the choice of whether or not to accept a person as a client. This choice also involves the exercise of moral autonomy. In light of the first-class citizenship model, exercise of the choice of client aspect of the moral autonomy of the lawyer is troubling if it reacts to foreclosure of a person's access to the law. In that situation, the lawyer's autonomy results in second-class citizenship status for the denied individual. Third, a large degree of moral autonomy can be exercised through the lawyer-client moral dialogue. While there is a wide range of financial feasibility and client receptivity which will set limits on the extent of such dialogue, all lawyers have some opportunity in this area; and to a significant extent, each lawyer can take part in determining those limits. Fourth, conscientious objection is an ever present option within the realm of the lawyer's moral autonomy. These four areas combined create a meaningful field for the exercise of the lawyer's autonomy.

More important, if one adds together (1) the conscientious objection possibility, (2) the wide scope for moral dialogue, and (3) the inherent moral value of facilitating access to the law, the result, I believe is that the good lawyer can be a good person; not comfortable, but good.

David Luban
The Lysistratian Prerogative:
A Response to Stephen Pepper

1986 Am. B. Found. Res. J. 637

My overall assessment of Stephen Pepper's interesting and complex argument may be summed up as follows:

I. Regarding his defense of the lawyer's amoral role: I disagree.

II. Regarding his claim that the existence of economic inequality does not vitiate the defense because to abdicate the amoral role "would compound inequality upon inequality—first the inequality of access to a lawyer, then the inequality of what law that particular lawyer will allow the client access to": I disagree.

III. Regarding his argument that the adversary system need not figure large in the justification of the amoral role: I partially agree.

IV. Regarding the "problem of realism": I completely agree, and indeed I view this as the major contribution of Pepper's essay.

V. Regarding his canvassing of possible solutions to the problem: I agree, with a few minor qualifications.

These are the five sections of my response.

I

. . .

The argument for the amoral role goes as follows: *First premise*: "law is intended to be a public good which increases autonomy." *Second premise*: "autonomy [is] preferred over 'right' or 'good' conduct"; "increasing individual autonomy is morally good." *Third premise*: "in a highly legalized society such as ours, . . . access to the law . . . in reality . . . is available only through a lawyer." *Conclusion*: "What the lawyer does is a social good." "The lawyer is a good person in that he provides access to the law."

I deny the second premise that individual autonomy is preferred over right or good conduct: it is the point at which the rabbit gets into the hat. Pepper appears to have blurred the crucial distinction between *the desirability of people acting autonomously* and *the desirability of their autonomous act*. It is good, desirable, for me to make my own decisions about whether to lie to you; it is bad, undesirable, for me to lie to you. It is good that people act autonomously, that they make their own choices about what to do; what they choose to do, however, need not be good.[13] Pepper's second premise

---

13. I'm not sure what force Pepper intends by calling it a "*social*" good. To be a social good is not quite the same as to be a moral good, since social goods—things that are good for a society—can be morally unacceptable. (Example: It was good for Spanish society that the conquistadores

is plausible only when we focus exclusively on the first of each of these pairs of propositions; it loses its plausibility when we turn our attention to the second. *Other things being equal*, Pepper is right that "increasing individual autonomy is morally good," but when the exercise of autonomy results in an immoral action, other things aren't equal. You must remember that some things autonomously done are not morally right.

Pepper's subsequent argument is that since exercising autonomy is good, helping people exercise autonomy is good. Though this is true, it too is only half the story. The other half is that since doing bad things is bad, helping people do bad things is bad. The two factors must be weighed against each other, and this Pepper does not do.

Compare this case: The automobile, by making it easier to get around, increases human autonomy; hence, other things being equal, it is morally good to repair the car of someone who is unable by himself to get it to run. But such considerations can hardly be invoked to defend the morality of fixing the getaway car of an armed robber, assuming that you know in advance what the purpose of the car is. The moral wrong of assisting the robber outweighs the abstract moral goodness of augmenting the robber's autonomy.

Pepper admits that it "may be morally wrong to manufacture or distribute cigarettes or alcohol, or to disinherit one's children for marrying outside the faith, but the generality of such decisions are left in the private realm." That is true, but that doesn't imply that such exercises of autonomy are morally acceptable. On the contrary, it concedes that they are immoral. And this is simply to return to the distinction between the desirability of exercising autonomy and the undesirability of exercising it wrongly.

Pepper sees this. To make his argument work, he distinguishes between (merely) *immoral* conduct and *intolerable* conduct, and says that intolerable conduct "ought to be made explicitly unlawful"; at one point, indeed, he equates "not unlawful" conduct with conduct "above the floor of the intolerable." Using this distinction, he argues in effect that unlawful conduct *is* conduct the immorality of which does not outweigh the value of autonomous decision making. If we didn't want people to make up their own minds about such conduct, we would make it illegal, and thus the fact that we haven't shows that we do not disapprove of it sufficiently to take the decision out of people's own hands.

The conclusion does not follow, however. There are many reasons for not prohibiting conduct besides the reason that we don't think it's bad enough to take it out of people's hands. We should not put into effect prohibitions that are unenforceable, or that are enforceable only at enormous cost, or through unacceptably or

---

plundered the Inca Empire, but it was also immoral. "What the conquistadores did was socially good" is true, but so is "what the conquistadores did was immoral.") I shall assume that Pepper means "moral good," not "social good."

disproportionately invasive means. We should not prohibit immoral conduct if it would be too difficult to specify the conduct, or if the laws would of necessity be vague or either over- or underinclusive, or if enforcement would destroy our liberties.

All these are familiar and good reasons for refraining from prohibiting conduct that have nothing whatever to do with the intensity of our disapprobation of the conduct. It is illegal to smuggle a bottle of non-duty-free Scotch into the country. It is not illegal to seduce someone through honey-tongued romancing, maliciously intending to break the lover's heart afterward (as in Kierkegaard's *Diary of a Seducer*). Surely this discrepancy does not show that we judge the smuggling (but not the seduction) "intolerable," or even that we judge the smuggling to be morally worse than the seduction. On the contrary, we judge the seduction to be worse conduct, perhaps even intolerable conduct, but we realize that prohibiting seductions would have obvious enormous social costs. The distinction between legal and illegal conduct simply does not correspond to the distinction between conduct that we think on moral grounds people should be free to engage in and conduct we find morally intolerable.

Pepper acknowledges this too, but resists its implication by posing this rhetorical question: "If making the conduct unlawful is too onerous because the law would be too vague, or it is too difficult to identify the conduct in advance, or there is not sufficient social or political concern, do we intend to delegate to the individual lawyer the autonomy for case-by-case legislation and policing?"

I do not mean this question as rhetorical; I answer it "yes." The reason goes, I think, to the heart of my disagreement with Pepper. What bothers Pepper the most, I believe, is the idea that lawyers should impose themselves and their moral concerns as "filters" of what legally permissible projects clients should be able to undertake. His concern, in turn, appears to have two aspects to it, one specific to lawyers, the other more general: "Such a screening submits each to . . . rule by oligarchy of lawyers." More generally, it appears to me that Pepper objects to *anyone*, lawyer or not, interposing his or her scruples to filter the legally permissible projects of autonomous agents. He objects, that is, to informal obstacles to autonomy, allowing only the formal obstacles raised by the law itself. (That seems to be the force of his argument that any conduct which is not illegal is up to "individual decision making.") I suspect that part of Pepper's worry here is that to allow informal obstacles to autonomy is to take away people's first-class citizenship as granted by the law and thus to threaten the rule of law itself.

The first of these worries is illusory, for there is no oligarchy of lawyers, actual or potential, to worry about. An oligarchy is a group of people ruling *in concert*, whereas lawyers who refuse to execute projects to which they object on moral grounds will do so as individuals, without deliberating collectively with other lawyers. The worry about a hidden Central Committee of lawyers evaporates when we realize that the committee will never hold a meeting, and that its members don't even know they are on it. An analogy will clarify this. No doubt throughout history people have often been dissuaded from undertaking immoral projects by the anger, threats, and uncooperativeness of their spouses. It would scarcely make sense, however, to worry that this amounts to subjecting autonomous action "to rule by an oligarchy of spouses." There *is* no oligarchy of spouses.

The second worry is more interesting. Unlike Pepper, I am not troubled by the existence of informal filters of people's legally permissible projects. Far from seeing these as a threat to the rule of law, I regard them as essential to its very existence.

We—people, that is—are tempted to a vast array of reprehensible conduct. Some of it can be and is tolerated; some of it we do not engage in because of our scruples; and some of it the law proscribes. But the law cannot proscribe all intolerable conduct, for human society would then be crushed flat by a monstrous, incomprehensible mass of law. And scruples—conscience, morality—will not take up all the slack.

Instead, we rely to a vast extent on informal social pressure to keep this in check. Why do people break into the line at the cafeteria so seldom? Why do they bus their own trays? Why do they keep malicious, gossiping tongues in (relative!) check at the office? Why are they civil to subordinate employees? Why do they keep their word? Why are Kierkegaardian seducers few and far between? For many people the answer is scruples, morality; but for many people it is not. When conscience is too faint, I submit, the answer to all these questions is that people worry about what other people will say, think, and do, and guide their behavior accordingly.

Imagine now what would happen if we could no longer count on this sort of motivation, so that we would have to enforce desirable behavior legally—imprison or fine line-skippers or tray nonbussers, gossips and rude deans and heartbreakers. Imagine policing these offenses! When we begin to reflect on the sheer magnitude of altruistic behavior we take for granted in day-to-day life, we realize that society could not exist without the dense network of informal filters provided by other people.

Among those filters is noncooperation. Many nefarious schemes are aborted because an agent's associates or partners or friends or family or financial backers or employees will have nothing to do with them. My argument is that far from this being an objectionable state of affairs, neither society nor law could survive without such filters.

And, to conclude the argument, I do not see why a lawyer's decision not to assist a client in a scheme that the lawyer finds nefarious is any different from these other instances of social control through private noncooperation. It is no more an affront to the client's autonomy for the lawyer to refuse to assist in the scheme than it is for the client's wife to threaten to move out if he goes ahead with it. Indeed, the lawyer's autonomy allows him to exercise the "Lysistratian prerogative"—to withhold services from those of whose projects he disapproves, to decide not to go to bed with clients who want to "set a whole neighborhood at loggerheads."

Pepper wants to allow the lawyer's autonomy a narrower scope: to refrain from being a lawyer, to engage in moral dialogue with clients, to decline to represent a client, and in extreme cases to engage in conscientious objection against odious professional obligations. The last two of these together add up to the Lysistratian prerogative, except for Pepper's limitation of conscientious objection to extreme cases.

He includes this limitation because he thinks that only extremely objectionable actions outweigh the value of enhancing client autonomy. I believe, however, that in almost every case of significant client immorality the good of helping the client realize his autonomy will be outweighed by the bad of the immoral action the client proposes. The argument for this point will complete my response to Pepper's defense of the amoral role.

Autonomous decision making is valuable for two complementary reasons: metaphysically and axiologically, the exercise of freedom is one of the most important (if not the most important) components of human well-being; and psychologically, the exercise of freedom is developed in tandem with prized traits of character: rationality and prudence, adult commitment, self-actualization, and responsibility.

It is crucial to realize, however, that none of these values require *unlimited* autonomy in order to be satisfactorily realized—if they did, of course, then human autonomy would be incompatible with the very existence of law. This fact in turn implies that occasional or limited impositions pose no threat to the values underlying my autonomy, provided that my life contains plenty of other opportunities for developing, and exercising the capacities associated with autonomous decision making—provided, in other words, that my life is by and large autonomous. A parent's autonomy is not jeopardized because her lawyer refuses to draft a will disinheriting her child because of the child's opposition to the war in Nicaragua: the parent still has plenty of other opportunities for free decision making (indeed, the parent probably even has plenty of other opportunities to make her child miserable). Her life is by and large autonomous.

And, since lawyers' interactions with clients are mostly occasional, lawyers' refusal to execute immoral designs of clients will not threaten the values underlying autonomy if the clients' lives are by and large autonomous in their other interactions. For this reason, in cases of conflict the threat to autonomy posed by Lincoln-like lawyers will typically be outweighed by the immorality of helping the clients.

In effect, Pepper has argued for a strong and a weak thesis. The strong thesis is that helping clients, even when they are doing a bad, is good. The weak thesis is that withholding help from clients is bad. But both arguments fall: the rabbits came out of the hat only because they were waiting there to begin with.

II

What about the "economic inequality criticism"? Pepper puts his reply to it nicely when he distinguishes two issues: "the distribution of legal services and the content of what is distributed." He agrees that our current distribution of legal services is far from desirable but denies that this alters the moral standing of the content of what is distributed. I disagree.

The problem is that the content of what is distributed is *on Pepper's own account of the matter* partly a comparative good: first-class citizenship. It is comparative because its value is partly defined relative to other people's holdings of it—first class is first class only relative to second class. In this respect it is like a number at a "take-a-number" deli counter, the value of which is determined solely by how many people have lower numbers. Moreover, to give first-class citizenship selectively to some people is tantamount to bumping everyone else down one class: those who were first-class citizens are now second-class citizens, those who were second-class citizens — if such there were — are now third-class, and so on.

These facts are relevant because they undercut the case for saying that giving first-class citizenship to some but not all people is good — not as good as giving it to all but better than giving it to none, or to fewer. That case, I take it, is simply that Pareto improvements — distributional moves in which some people are helped and no one is hurt — are good. The comparative character of first-class citizenship, however, means that those who don't have it *are* hurt by others having it, as I am hurt if the deli manager gives his friends tickets with lower numbers than mine.

This becomes apparent when we look at the components of first-class citizenship that Pepper inventories. First-class citizenship makes available, among many other benefits, the "corporate form of enterprise, the contract, the trust, the will, and access to civil court to gain the use of public force for the settlement of private grievance." As he notes, all are "vehicles of empowerment for the individual or group." That is, the components of first-class citizenship allow you to leverage yourself in a better position (economic or otherwise) than those who don't have them. The resulting competitive advantage in turn gives you further leverage to augment your position still more. And, insofar as the socio-economic game is zero-sum — it isn't always, but it is often — the more the rich get richer, the more the poor get poorer. Finally, your augmented position will get you the influence and power to push for rule changes that further enhance the packet of perks accruing to first-class citizens.

In this way, the differential granting of first-class citizenship yields a self-producing vicious spiral of social inequality and outright damage to those who don't have it. The problem is that when first-class citizenship is not universally available, its components are not mere *benefits*, they are *advantages*. Conferring benefits selectively can be a Pareto improvement, but conferring advantages is not, and I don't believe that it is good.

Am I arguing, then, that if everyone can't have first-class citizenship no one should? I believe I am. Lest this seem outrageous, let me present an analogous case. Let our society be as it is now, with second-class citizens — those who, because they can't afford lawyers, have no access to the law — and first-class citizens. Suppose the administration (in a fit of supply-side enthusiasm) proposes a bill to create a new, exclusive, very special kind of citizenship — "executive class citizenship." It contains all the perks of first-class citizenship plus a few others: dandy new tax shelters, first-refusal mineral rights in the national wilderness, no-wait federal courts unavailable to anyone else, diplomatic passports. Executive class citizenship is awarded to all and only those Americans in the top 1% of individual income.

Would you support the bill? Or would you say, as I would, that *if everyone can't have executive-class citizenship no one should*?

III

I agree with Pepper that his first-class citizenship theory of lawyers' ethics, which models the activity of the office lawyer rather well, is better than an adversary-system-based theory, which models the activity of the trial lawyer rather well. This is for the obvious reason that there are many more office lawyers than trial lawyers. I nevertheless believe that the adversary system must still figure prominently in the debate because so many of the morally disturbing behaviors in legal practice grew up in the shadow of the courtroom and thus in the shadow of the adversary system. This affects even office law practice, in at least three ways.

1. Because of the adversary system, American lawyers are socialized into a "hardball culture" that necessarily affects even office practice. Lawyers are accustomed to discount the interests of nonclients to the extent that I believe is inexplicable without referring to the adversary system.

2. Deal making and document drafting, the paradigmatic office lawyering activities, must be done with the worst-case scenario in mind, and these are scenarios of breakdown and litigation. The more adversarial the litigation practices are in a legal culture, the more cautious and complicated and fail-safe their anticipatory moves must be. This is true even of counseling: Consider how much a tax lawyer's advice on recordkeeping and creative accounting is colored by the level of adversariality adopted by the IRS.

3. Ethical rules that are unusual from the point of view of ordinary morality, such as the rules governing disclosures of confidential information to prevent clients from wrongdoing, are fashioned according to arguments based on the adversary systems. It was, after all, the trial lawyers, using arguments of Professor Freedman, who succeeded in weakening the disclosure provisions in the Model Rules of Professional Conduct. The arguments invoked had to do with the exigencies of the adversary system, and thus they apply preeminently to courtroom lawyers, but the disclosure rules finally adopted govern office lawyers as well. The point is that the adversary system shapes the rules, and the rules shape even nonadversarial law practice. . . .

[Section 4 of Professor Luban's response, which deals with "legal realism" has been omitted. Professor Pepper's response to both commentaries, which includes a response to Professor Luban on this point, has also been omitted. They are in substantial agreement on the effects of "legal realism" on lawyers' conceptions of their obligations. They disagree, however, on where Professor Pepper's views fit in this debate.]

V

My comments on section IV of Pepper's essay are quite brief.[38] The responses to the problem he canvasses do seem to me to be the right ones. I myself sympathize

---

38. One small point . . . Pepper says (discussing the hidden bodies case), "Professor Luban's approach implies that normal morality should have been applied by the lawyers" (i.e., they should have revealed where the bodies were hidden). I have it on the best of authority that Luban thinks the opposite. He distinguishes the hidden bodies case from the fact situation of Spaulding v.

most with the "moral dialogue" approach, which can be used in tandem with any of the others and should always constitute a lawyer's first step. That is, before a lawyer should consider conscientious objection, say, by blowing the whistle on a client, the lawyer should engage in moral dialogue with the client in order to change his or her purposes. My main criticism of this section is that I think that the difference between Pepper's section IV.C, the lawyer as judge—which Pepper rejects—and section IV.E, conscientious objection—which Pepper accepts—is more a matter of degree than kind. And, for reasons that I detailed at the end of section I, I see the difference in degree as being much slighter than Pepper does, so that in the end I assimilate C to E. Since (in my view) his reasons for accepting E are good ones, I think he should accept C as well.

<h2 style="text-align:center">Andrew L. Kaufman
A Commentary on Pepper*</h2>

1986 Am. B. Found. Res. J. 651

. . . I would like to make my comments from the perspective of practitioners, for after all it is lawyers who have to make decisions daily with respect to the issues that are the subject of today's essay. Ever since Charles Curtis gave a provocative talk on the topic of the lawyer's ethical role some 35 years ago, the subject has received increasing attention, first from lawyers and more recently from philosophers. With the notable exceptions of the contributions of Monroe Freedman and Charles Fried, however, most of the writings have been critical of the position that argues for an amoral ethical role. Moreover, the more completely argued presentations have tended to be those of the critics. Now, drawing on the insights of Freedman and Fried but advancing beyond them, Professor Pepper has produced a first-rate paper presenting a complete theory that seeks to justify, at least presumptively, an amoral role for lawyers.

As I survey the field of professional responsibility today, I must confess to a feeling of nakedness. Everyone who is anyone has either created or adopted a model. We have "the lawyer as moral force in a non-differentiated or weakly-differentiated role"; "the lawyer as friend"; and now "the lawyer as facilitator of first-class citizenship."

To start with a conclusion, my sense after practicing law for ten years and teaching professional responsibility for nearly twenty years is that both sides of the

---

Zimmerman, 116 N.W.2d 704 (1962) (in which a personal injury defense lawyer kept confidential the fact—known to him through a physician's report but not known to the plaintiff—that the plaintiff had a potentially fatal aortic aneurysm). Luban says that, unlike the hidden bodies case, here there is no strong reason for the lawyer to keep the confidence, thereby implying (if I read him aright) that there *is* strong reason to keep confidential the knowledge of where the bodies are hidden. Luban, "The Adversary System Excuse," in Luban, ed. *The Good Lawyer*, 83, at 114–115 (1983).

* This comment was prepared for delivery in oral form on January 5, 1986, at the special session of the Association of American Law Schools' annual meeting held to honor Professor Pepper's prize-winning essay. The author has not attempted to redraft his remarks into a more formal presentation and they are being published in virtually the exact text that he prepared for the AALS session.

argument over the moral accountability of lawyers have a good deal to teach practitioners—but that neither has the full answer, for there is more paradox in the lawyer's role than either theory provides for. In holding high the importance of autonomy, diversity, and equality, Professor Pepper links those goals with the notion that if proposed conduct has not been made unlawful, then at least generally the lawyer should help the client achieve his or her objective. Note that Professor Pepper does not make the lesser point that it is *permissible* for the lawyer to aid the client. He seems to be making the larger point that it is *wrong* for lawyers, except perhaps in exceptional cases, *to refuse to help their clients to achieve lawful ends.*

The comparison is to the technician fixing a car. Such a person, we are told, is normally held to have no responsibility for the use to which the car is to be put. But that judgment, I suggest, stems from the fact that the technician normally has no dilemma. Suppose that a technician fixes and delivers a car to a husband who tells the technician that he is leaving his wife and taking their jointly owned car with him at the time when the technician knows that the wife is expecting a child and needs the car to get to the hospital. Do we then all agree that the technician has no moral problem? The real difference between the lawyer's situation and that of the technician is simply one of opportunity: the opportunity to learn of other people's troubles creates moral dilemmas.

Professor Pepper's presentation on this point shares the same problem as Professor Fried's piece, since he finds it necessary to argue that it is always, or almost always, morally good to help the client achieve an end that is not unlawful. It is one thing, however, to *play up* the autonomy and equality points in urging an amoral role for lawyers. It is quite another to *play down* the moral aspect of the reality that sometimes—for a variety of reasons having nothing to do with morality—conduct generally agreed to be immoral is not made unlawful.

For example, to take a homely situation, it is not unlawful for a wife to cut her husband out of her will without telling him, even though she knows that his will favors her, but I think that most of us would agree that there are many situations in which it would be immoral for her to do so. As a lawyer drafting the will, I would not be assuaged by the argument that I am facilitating the wife's first-class citizenship in doing so. Moral dialogue may not be enough in that kind of case. And if that example does not grab you, how about doing the legal work that sets the seller of Saturday Night Specials up in business and helps him to continue? Professor Pepper is not bothered by that one, at least not in the abstract. Is it unfair of me to ask how many dead people shot by guns sold by his client would begin to make him worry? Note that I am not even arguing for the proposition that the lawyer ought to refuse to form the corporation for the client. I am only arguing for the proposition that the professional rules ought not to prevent him from declining to do so.

I realize that there is the problem of "the last lawyer in town" and that that situation sometimes does occur, but Professor Pepper is not dealing with that very special problem. His is a much more across-the-board view. Professor Pepper does leave the "out" of conscientious objection for extreme cases — but I don't think he would regard either of the ones I have put as extreme cases. In making that judgment I rely on his use of the "hidden bodies" case to make his point about extreme cases. He would find an extreme case if the lawyer were to discover that the body he had found were still alive. In choosing that example, I assume that he rejected the one that was much closer at hand, namely, that the lawyer is told by the doctor of the parent of the murder victim that the strain for the parent of not knowing whether her child was dead or alive was highly likely to kill her because she had a bad heart. We can change the adjectives describing the certainty of harm as much as we want, but moral dialogue is not going to work in this situation. The killer is not likely to allow the lawyer to let the parent know by any means that her daughter is dead. I believe that the case I have put, which is disturbingly close to the real case, is one that at least ought to be regarded as raising a hard question as to whether the amoral role is justified in that situation.

And so I have two problems with where Professor Pepper comes out on this point. For me and for many lawyers, I suspect that there are enough situations where the moral constraints are such that they outweigh what Professor Pepper calls the first-class citizenship considerations that they cannot be called truly exceptional. Moreover I wonder about a system of law that compels lawyers to be conscientious objectors, that is, that makes the law such that lawyers must break it in order to achieve what are conceded to be highly desirable moral ends. It is an insufficient answer to say that it enables us to put a satisfactory label — "amorality" — on the role of the lawyer. And so I think that the ethic of professional responsibility should and does recognize that it is entirely appropriate for the lawyer to refuse the amoral role in a significant number of situations — not just in the matter of choice of client, but also in the performance of the actual tasks the client wishes the lawyer to do.

However, having said all that, I think I should also say that I part company with Professor Luban on the general thrust of his position as I have understood it. I believe that there is a great deal more scope for role-differentiated behavior than his position allows and that lawyers have to be very careful about overriding clients' wishes in the name of morality.

The issues we like to discuss under the heading of morality often turn out to be considerably less clear-cut in reality than we portray them in the classroom. It may not be so much that, as Professor Pepper suggests, our value sources have disappeared in the 20th century. (Indeed, it seems to me that as to some things — at least, for example, care about have-nots — there is more moral awareness in this century than there was in most recent ones.) But moral issues are often cloudy in the law — because in many, if not most, situations when people come to lawyers, it is very difficult for lawyers to get a strong sense of moral right and wrong because of one-sided, incomplete information about facts and especially about the consequences of particular actions.

And so the occasions on which lawyers may have a real moral choice to make in the advice they give — aside from the important initial choice they make about the kind of practice to which they aspire — may not be so numerous as the protagonists on this issue would have us believe. Likewise, there are other situations where it is perfectly appropriate for a lawyer with a strong moral position to recognize that there are other reasonable solutions to the moral dilemma and thus to defer to the client's differing moral judgment. That kind of deferring has a moral quality to it too. Thus, I believe that in a great many situations it is proper to separate Professor Pepper's view of the lawyer's role as "amoral" into two words. The role should in fact be regarded as "a moral" role.

Finally, there is the relationship stressed by Professor Pepper between legal realism and an amoral ethic for lawyers — the notion that the lawyer's role requires education of clients in the indeterminacy and manipulability of law. As law teachers, we are all realists who recognize the fictional nature of the common view that there is, in Professor Pepper's words, "something there for the lawyer to find (or know) and communicate to the client." He tells us that all second-year students know that where setting forth "the law" is concerned, except for obvious and therefore uninteresting questions, there are no lines, only possibilities. While that is all true, I think most practicing lawyers know that there is a great deal of law — statutes, doctrine — that informs our judgment about possibilities. We teachers are so caught up in the frontier questions that we sometimes see more chaos and manipulability than there really is. The lawyer who tells the client, "Do what you want; it is all indeterminate and manipulable" does the client no favor.

And while I am at it, I might add that I am a little puzzled by Professor Pepper's tendency to make his point that lawyers should not be screeners of moral conduct by treating as equivalent those situations in which lawyers are pictured as concealing the uncertainty of legal doctrine or enforcement of law from clients and those situations in which lawyers decline to undertake certain lawful means or ends for clients. For me, those two types of cases present very different moral issues in that the former involves a lawyer in deceiving a client whereas the latter does not.

Professor Pepper concludes his paper by saying that there is enough latitude for lawyers' exercise of their own moral autonomy in his picture of the generally amoral role he envisages, that "the good lawyer can be a good person, not comfortable, but good." It is a nice, ironic turn of phrase, but I can hear his critics saying that he has got it backwards, that the prescription is one for making lawyers comfortable at a time when they are not being good.

I do not know how Professor Luban comes out on the issue of comfort, but I am fairly certain that he believes that his own formulation comes closer to making the lawyer a good person than does Professor Pepper's. For myself, I hold eclectic views on the theoretical issue that divides Professors Pepper and Luban — and indeed, the whole community of professional commentators.

On those occasions when the issue of the appropriate professional role arises, it seems to me that there is no need to make the choice for all cases, even for all ordinary cases, between the views expressed by Professors Pepper and Luban. Here is where it is a good thing not to have a model that justifies, at least presumptively, an amoral or a moral role. In my opinion, it has been a good thing and not a bad thing that the rules of professional responsibility have recognized that there are strong principles supporting both views and that they have not opted for a mandatory rule one way or the other in a great many situations, and especially not at the metalevel of theory.

I do not think it all bad that the kind of advice clients get depends to some extent on the chance of whom they choose or have chosen for them as lawyers. That kind of chance happens all through life with the chance of whom we wind up with as parents, children, priests, ministers or rabbis, teachers, friends, and leaders. In some cases there are costs of leaving things to chance. But so are there costs in trying to force very different lawyers with very different sensibilities into one attitudinal mold for nearly all situations.

In any event, when the issue of role arises in a particular situation that does not fit into an area where there is a rule, I think that it is good that we lawyers are not always given a prepackaged answer. There is something to be said for our being forced to figure out for ourselves what action is called for by the facts of a particular situation, being, in Professor Pepper's words, as good as we can, or perhaps, to put it another way, doing the least bad that we must — even if it is uncomfortable to have to work it out for ourselves.

Notes

1. Another counterweight to Professor Pepper's views is contained in the chapter on lawyers in Professor Alan Goldman's *The Moral Foundations of Professional Ethics* (1980). The central question posed by Professor Goldman, a philosopher, is whether lawyers (and political officials, judges, doctors, and businesspeople) should be governed in their decision-making by the moral rules that govern decision-making in everyday life or whether their roles require or permit the use of special moral rules justifying conduct that would otherwise be viewed as immoral. The latter role is denominated "strongly differentiated."

Professor Goldman regards the profession's general stance of "full advocacy" as requiring or permitting a lawyer to pursue any objective of the client by any tactic as long as neither the objective nor the tactic is illegal, without any obligation to take account of the moral rights of others who may be affected. He construes the Model Code's explicit limitations on zealous advocacy as unimportant either because they have been watered down or because they merely prohibit what is otherwise illegal. He then considers and rejects the major justifications that have been advanced for the model of full advocacy: advancement of the truth-seeking function of the adversary system, the autonomy of clients, the duty of confidentiality, and the preservation of democratic values by not permitting lawyers to control exercise of legal choice through refusal to fully advocate clients' legal interests. Only in the defense of those accused of crime does Professor Goldman see substantial justification for strong role differentiation and then only in situations of defendants not known to be guilty and in those cases involving important procedural rights where the crime alleged is "not serious."

2. Other philosophers have also looked closely at the morality of the legal profession's rules in recent years. A comprehensive and challenging philosophical account of "adversary ethics" in law and other domains is presented in Arthur Isak Applbaum, *Ethics for Adversaries: The Morality of Roles in Public and Professional Life* (1998). Among other provocative arguments, Applbaum compares the standard account of legal ethics to the ethics of the executioner of Paris during the Reign of Terror, who happily lopped off the heads of revolutionaries and royalty alike depending upon who was in power. Postema, "Moral Responsibility in Professional Ethics," 55 N.Y.U. L. Rev. 63 (1980) is a thoughtful view from a different perspective from that presented by Goldman. Luban, "The Adversary System Excuse," in Luban ed., *The Good Lawyer* (1984) takes a position somewhat similar to the Goldman view, which he elaborates substantially in his later book, *Lawyers and Justice* (1988); see also generally Luban, *Legal Ethics and Human Dignity* (2007). See also Simon, "The Ideology of Advocacy: Procedural Justice and Professional Ethics," 1978 Wis. L. Rev. 29 and his later book, *The Practice of Justice* (1998). For the views of a philosopher who takes a contrary position, see Kipnis, "Professional Responsibility and the Responsibility of Professions," in W. Robison, M. Pritchard, and J. Ellin eds., *Profits and Professions* (1983) and his later small volume, *Legal Ethics* (1986). For a recent argument in favor of the adversary system and of lawyers' fidelity to clients' positions within that system, see Daniel Markovits, *A Modern Legal Ethics* (2011). Finally, but not exhaustively, an interesting attempt by two lawyers at a nonutilitarian, or deontological, view of the duties of lawyers is D'Amato and Eberle, "Three Models of Legal Ethics," 27 St. Louis U. L.J. 761 (1983).

3. Both Pepper above and Wasserstrom (in Chapter 1) rely in part on the premise that law and procedure are known and practiced only by lawyers (i.e., competence and unauthorized-practice-of-law ["UPL"] issues). These premises are of course true to some extent, but they may have been overstated at the time and, more importantly, are certainly overstated in light of recent developments: free and increasingly accessible law on the Internet, free (or inexpensive) and increasingly accessible downloadable forms, and legal software; under-enforcement against those who may arguably be practicing law without a license, and the explicit creation of non-lawyer positions providing legal services (e.g., certified document preparers, limited-practice technicians, and compliance officers). To what extent do these developments call into question Pepper's and Wasserstrom's arguments (or arguments like theirs)? In other words, how, if at all, do — or should — these developments impact lawyers' ethics?

4. Professor Pepper says in his essay that lawyers should "give the law" to their clients as a legal realist would. Consider the following "legal realist" assessment of criminal justice by Alan Dershowitz. At the beginning of his book *The Best Defense*, Professor Dershowitz recounts the following rules as governing "the justice game"

in a world in which all participants—defense lawyers, prosecutors, judges—understand that "almost all defendants are in fact guilty" and that it is sometimes difficult and occasionally impossible, to convict guilty defendants while complying with the Constitution:

> Almost all police lie about whether they violated the Constitution in order to convict guilty defendants. . . .
>
> Most trial judges pretend to believe police officers who they know are lying. . . .
>
> Most judges disbelieve defendants about whether their constitutional rights have been violated, even if they are telling the truth. . . .
>
> Nobody really wants justice.

Alan M. Dershowitz, *The Best Defense* xxi–xxii (1983). How does Professor Dershowitz's claim about the rules of the justice game map onto the arguments suggested by Pepper? Luban? Kaufman? Do you think Dershowitz's assessment is descriptively true? If so, what rules, if any, structuring professional conduct need to be revised?

5. Professor Pepper claims that "realist" accounts of the law such as Professor Dershowitz's support his general claim that lawyers should be amoral facilitators of their clients' objectives. Do you agree? Pepper argues that giving the client access to the lawyer's "realist" interpretation ensures that all clients who can afford a lawyer are treated equally by only being constrained by the manner in which the law is actually enforced. But consider the manner in which a client's resources can affect the generation of "plausible" legal arguments about what the law "really" is:

> Habit and routine are the defining characteristics of virtually every law practice. Lawyers inhabit a world of standardized contracts, pleading files, checklists, form books, computerized discovery requests, received wisdom, and longstanding relationships. In such a world, the possibility of employing innovative approaches is often discarded as unnecessary or disruptive. . . . [R]esource constraints . . . accentuate this tendency. . . . The more time the lawyer invests, the more likely it is that she can generate plausible new arguments. And in a system in which legal services are generally distributed through the market, lawyer time means money.
>
> This reality . . . is the antithesis of the normative vision promised by [the claim that zealous advocacy is constrained by the bounds of the law]. Far from helping to create a world of objective and consistent limitations on the pursuit of client interest, these practical constraints highlight the extent to which the actual effects of legal boundaries are contingent upon the individual characteristics and fee generating potential of particular clients and cases. Lawyers representing poor clients are much more likely to depend on mass-processing techniques that discourage the development of creative legal arguments. Wealthy clients, on the other hand, are likely to receive customized legal services designed to discover and exploit every available

opportunity. In addition, these clients have a greater potential to affect directly the formal content of the boundary itself by playing for the rules, either by lobbying for rule changes or by pressing or defending only those cases most likely to generate favorable outcomes. . . . The existence of economic disparities also undermines the claim that whatever boundaries that do result in practice are legitimate, because these restraints can no longer be viewed as solely the product of democratic decisionmaking. A system in which some clients can buy their way out of legal limitations exemplifies the kind of power-driven regime that the rule of law is supposed to avoid.

David B. Wilkins, "Legal Realism for Lawyers," 104 Harv. L. Rev. 468, 494–496 (1990); cf. generally Stephen L. Pepper, "Three Dichotomies in Lawyers' Ethics (With Particular Attention to the Corporation as Client)," 28 Geo. J. Legal Ethics 1069 (2015) (focusing arguments over the lawyer's role not on vulnerable clients but on powerful corporate clients).

The next piece puts several of the adversary-system criticisms into a more practical perspective and framework. In his Benjamin N. Cardozo Lecture, Judge Marvin Frankel addressed the subject of the lawyer's confidentiality obligation a few years before he resigned from the bench, returned to private practice, and served as a member of the Kutak Commission, which drafted the Model Rules.

Marvin Frankel
The Search for Truth: An Umpireal View
123 U. Pa. L. Rev. 1031 (1975)

. . .

My theme, to be elaborated at some length, is that our adversary system rates truth too low among the values that institutions of justice are meant to serve. Having worked for nine years at judging, and having evolved in that job the doubts and questions to be shared with you, I find it convenient to move into the subject with some initial reminders about our judges: who they are, how they come to be, and how their arena looks to them. . . .

. . . Trials occur because there are questions of fact. In principle, the paramount objective is the truth. Nevertheless, for the advocate turned judge this objective marks a sharp break with settled habits of partisanship. The novelty is quickly accepted because it has been seen for so long from the other side. But the novelty is palpable, and the change of role may be unsettling. Many judges, withdrawn from the fray, watch it with benign and detached affection, chuckling nostalgically now and then as the truth suffers injury or death in the process.[9] The shop talk in judges'

---

9. As in the sentence just ended, this essay will be laced with general statements about matters of fact that are neither quantified nor tightly documented. These rest variously upon introspection,

lunchrooms includes tales, often told with pleasure, of wily advocates who bested the facts and prevailed. For many other judges, however, probably a majority at one time or another, the habit of adversariness tends to be rechanneled, at least in some measure, into a combative yearning for truth. With perhaps a touch of the convert's zeal, they may suffer righteously when the truth is being blocked or mutilated, turn against former comrades in the arena, feel (and sometimes yield to) the urge to spring into the contest with brilliant questions that light the way.

However the trial judge reacts, in general or from time to time, the bench affords a changed and broadened view of the adversary process. . . . In the strictest sense I can speak only for myself, but I believe many other trial judges would affirm that the different perspective helps to arouse doubts about a process that there had been neither time nor impetus to question in the years at the bar. It becomes evident that the search for truth fails too much of the time. The rules and devices accounting for the failures come to seem less agreeable and less clearly worthy than they once did. The skills of the advocate seem less noble, and the place of the judge, which once looked so high, is lowered in consequence. There is, despite the years of professional weathering that went before the assumption of the judicial office, a measure of disillusionment. . . .

THE ADVERSARIAL POSTURE

The preceding comments on the transition from bar to bench have touched explicitly upon the role of the advocate. That role is not, however, a matter of sharp and universally agreed definition. The conception from which this paper proceeds must now be outlined.

. . . Presiding Justice David W. Peck [has] said:

> The object of a lawsuit is to get at the truth and arrive at the right result. That is the sole objective of the judge, and counsel should never lose sight of that objective in thinking that the end purpose is to win for his side. Counsel exclusively bent on winning may find that he and the umpire are not in the same game.[11]

Earlier, stating his theme that court and counsel "complement" each other, Justice Peck said:

> Unfortunately, true understanding of the judicial process is not shared by all lawyers or judges. Instead of regarding themselves as occupying a reciprocal relationship in a common purpose, they are apt to think of themselves as representing opposite poles and exercising divergent functions. The lawyer is active, the judge passive. The lawyer partisan, the judge neutral. The lawyer imaginative, the judge reflective.[12]

---

observation, reading, and conversations with fellow judges. They are believed to be accurate, but they are undoubtedly debatable in many instances.

11. D. Peck, *The Complement of Court and Counsel* 9 (1954) (13th Annual Benjamin N. Cardozo Lecture).

12. Id. at 7.

Perhaps unfortunately, and certainly with deference, I find myself leaning toward the camp the Justice criticized. The plainest thing about the advocate is that he is indeed partisan, and thus exercises a function sharply divergent from that of the judge. Whether or not the judge generally achieves or maintains neutrality, it is his assigned task to be nonpartisan and to promote through the trial an objective search for the truth. The advocate in the trial courtroom is not engaged much more than half the time—and then only coincidentally—in the search for truth. The advocate's prime loyalty is to his client, not to truth as such. All of us remember some stirring and defiant declarations by advocates of their heroic, selfless devotion to The Client—leaving the nation, all other men, and truth to fend for themselves. Recall Lord Brougham's familiar words:

> [A]n advocate, in the discharge of his duty, knows but one person in all the world, and that person is his client. Trying to save that client by all means and expedients, and at all hazards and costs to other persons, and, among them, to himself; is his first and only duty; and in performing this duty he must not regard the alarm, the torments, the destruction which he may bring upon others. Separating the duty of a patriot from that of an advocate, he must go on reckless of consequences, though it should be his unhappy fate to involve his country in confusion.[13]

Neither the sentiment nor even the words sound archaic after a century and a half. . . .

We are unlikely ever to know how effectively the adversary technique would work toward truth if that were the objective of the contestants. Employed by interested parties, the process often achieves truth only as a convenience, a byproduct, or an accidental approximation. The business of the advocate, simply stated, is to win if possible without violating the law. (The phrase "if possible" is meant to modify what precedes it, but the danger of slippage is well known.) His is not the search for truth as such. To put that thought more exactly, the truth and victory are mutually incompatible for some considerable percentage of the attorneys trying cases at any given time. . . .

Whatever doctrine teaches, it is a fact of interest here that most criminal defense counsel are not at all bent upon full disclosure of the truth. To a lesser degree, but stemming from the same ethos, we know how fiercely prosecutors have resisted disclosure, how often they have winked at police lapses, how mixed has been their enthusiasm for the principle that they must seek justice, not merely convictions. While the patterns of civil cases are different, and variable, we may say that it is the rare case in which either side yearns to have the witnesses, or anyone, give *the whole truth*. And our techniques for developing evidence feature devices for blocking and limiting such unqualified revelations.

The devices are too familiar to warrant more than a fleeting reminder. To begin with, we leave most of the investigatory work to paid partisans, which is scarcely a guarantee of thorough and detached exploration. Our courts wait passively for what

---

13. 2 Trial of Queen Caroline 8 (1 Nightingale ed. 1821).

the parties will present, almost never knowing—often not suspecting—what the parties have chosen not to present. The ethical standards governing counsel command loyalty and zeal for the client, but no positive obligation at all to the truth. Counsel must not knowingly break the law or commit or countenance fraud. Within these unconfining limits, advocates freely employ time-honored tricks and stratagems to block or distort the truth.

As a matter of strict logic, in the run of cases where there are flatly contradictory assertions about matters of fact, one side must be correct, the other wrong. Where the question is "Did the defendant pass a red light?" or "Does the plaintiff have a scarred retina?" or "Was the accused warned of the reasons why anyone of sound mind would keep quiet and did he then proceed nevertheless like a suicidal idiot to destroy himself by talking?" the "facts" are, or were, one way or the other. To be sure, honest people may honestly differ, and we mere lawyers cannot—actually, must not—set ourselves up as judges of the facts. That is the great release from effective ethical inhibitions. We are not to pass judgment, but only to marshal our skills to present and test the witnesses and other evidence—the skills being to make the most of these for our side and the least for the opposition. What will out, we sometimes tell ourselves and often tell others, is the truth. And, if worse comes to worst, in the end who really knows what is truth?

There is much in this of cant, hypocrisy, and convenient overlooking. As people, we know or powerfully suspect a good deal more than we are prepared as lawyers to admit or explore further. The clearest cases are those in which the advocate has been informed directly by a competent client, or has learned from evidence too clear to admit of genuine doubt, that the client's position rests upon falsehood. It is not possible to be certain, but I believe from recollection and conversation such cases are far from rare. Much more numerous are the cases in which we manage as counsel to avoid too much knowledge. The sharp eye of the cynical lawyer becomes at strategic moments a demurely averted and filmy gaze. It may be agreeable not to listen to the client's tape recordings of vital conversations that may contain embarrassments for the ultimate goal of vindicating the client. Unfettered by the clear prohibitions actual "knowledge" of the truth might impose, lawyers may be effective and exuberant in employing the familiar skills: techniques that make a witness look unreliable although the look stems only from counsel's artifice, cunning questions that stop short of discomfiting revelations, complaisant experts for whom some shopping may have been necessary. The credo that frees counsel for such arts is not a doctrine of truth-seeking.

The litigator's devices, let us be clear, have utility in testing dishonest witnesses, ferreting out falsehoods, and thus exposing the truth. But to a considerable degree these devices are like other potent weapons, equally lethal for heroes and villains. It is worth stressing, therefore, that the gladiator using the weapons in the courtroom is not primarily crusading after truth, but seeking to win. If this is banal, it is also overlooked too much and, in any event, basic to my thesis. . . .

I am among those who believe the laity have ground to question our service in the quest for truth. The ranks of lawyers and judges joining in this rueful stance are vast. Many have sought over the years to raise our standards and our functioning, not merely our image. There has been success. Liberalized discovery has helped, though the struggles over that, including the well-founded fears of tampering with the evidence, highlight the hardy evils of adversary management. We have, on the whole, seemed to become better over time, occasional lapses notwithstanding. At any rate, the main object of this talk is not merely to bewail, but to participate in the ongoing effort to improve. Modest thoughts on that subject . . . follow. . . .

SOME PROPOSALS

Having argued that we are too much committed to contentiousness as a good in itself and too little devoted to truth, I proceed to some prescriptions of a general nature for remedying these flaws. Simply stated, these prescriptions are that we should:

> (1) modify (not abandon) the adversary ideal,
>
> (2) make truth a paramount objective, and
>
> (3) impose upon the contestants a duty to pursue that objective.

A. MODIFYING THE ADVERSARY IDEAL

We should begin, as a concerted professional task, to question the premise that adversariness is ultimately and invariably good. For most of us trained in American law, the superiority of the adversary process over any other is too plain to doubt or examine. The certainty is shared by people who are in other respects widely separated on the ideological spectrum. The august Code of Professional Responsibility, as has been mentioned, proclaims, in order, the "Duty of the Lawyer to a Client," then the "Duty of the Lawyer to the Adversary System of Justice." There is no announced "Duty to the Truth" or "Duty to the Community." Public interest lawyers, while they otherwise test the law's bounds, profess a basic commitment "to the adversary system itself" as the means of giving "everyone affected by corporate and bureaucratic decisions . . . a voice in those decisions . . . ."[57] We may note similarly the earnest and idealistic scholar who brought the fury of the (not necessarily consistent) establishment upon himself when he wrote, reflecting upon experience as devoted defense counsel for poor people, that as an advocate you must (a) try to destroy a witness "whom you know to be telling the truth," (b) "put a witness on the stand when you know he will commit perjury," and (c) "give your client legal advice when you have reason to believe that the knowledge you give him will tempt him to commit perjury."[58] The "policies" he found to justify these views, included, as the first and most fundamental, the maintenance of "an adversary system based upon the presupposition that the most effective means of determining truth is to present to a judge and jury a clash between proponents of conflicting views."[59]

---

57. Halpern & Cunningham, "Reflections on the New Public Interest Law," 59 Geo. L.J. 1095, 1109 (1971).

58. Freedman, "Professional Responsibility of the Criminal Defense Lawyer: The Three Hardest Questions," 64 Mich. L. Rev. 1469 (1966).

59. Id. 1470. See also id. 1471, 1477–1478, 1482.

Our commitment to the adversary or "accusatorial" mode is buttressed by a corollary certainty that other, alien systems are inferior. We contrast our form of criminal procedure with the "inquisitorial" system, conjuring up visions of torture, secrecy, and dictatorial government. Confident of our superiority, we do not bother to find out how others work. It is not common knowledge among us that purely inquisitorial systems exist scarcely anywhere; that elements of our adversary approach exist probably everywhere; and that the evolving procedures of criminal justice, in Europe and elsewhere, are better described as "mixed" than as strictly accusatorial or strictly inquisitorial.[60]

In considering the possibility of change, we must open our minds to the variants and alternatives employed by other communities that also aspire to civilization. Without voting firmly, I raise the question whether the virginally ignorant judge is always to be preferred to one with an investigative file. We should be prepared to inquire whether our arts of examining and cross-examining, often geared to preventing excessive outpourings of facts, are inescapably preferable to safeguarded interrogation by an informed judicial officer. It is permissible to keep asking, because nobody has satisfactorily answered, why our present system of confessions in the police station versus no confessions at all is better than an open and orderly procedure of having a judicial official question suspects.

If the mention of such a question has not exhausted your tolerance, consider whether our study of foreign alternatives might suggest means for easing the unending tension surrounding the privilege against self-incrimination as it frequently operates in criminal trials. It would be prudent at least to study closely whether our criminal defendant, privileged to stay suspiciously absent from the stand or to testify subject to a perjury prosecution or "impeachment" by prior crimes, is surely better off than the European defendant who cannot escape questioning both before and at trial, though he may refuse to answer, but is free to tell his story without either the oath or the impeachment pretext for using his criminal record against him. Whether or not the defendant is better off, the question remains open whether the balance we have struck is the best possible.

To propose only one other topic for illustration, we need to study whether our elaborate struggles over discovery, especially in criminal cases, may be incurable symptoms of pathology inherent in our rigid insistence that the parties control the evidence until it is all "prepared" and packaged for competitive manipulation at the eventual continuous trial. Central in the debates on discovery is the concern of the ungenerous that the evidence may be tainted or alchemized between the time it is discovered and the time it is produced or countered at the trial. The concern, though the debaters report it in differing degrees, is well founded. It is significant enough to warrant our exploring alternative arrangements abroad where investigation "freezes" the evidence (that is, preserves usable depositions and other forms of relatively

---

60. W. Schaefer, *The Suspect and Society* 71 (1967); Damaska, "Evidentiary Barriers to Conviction and Two Models of Criminal Procedure: A Comparative Study," 121 U. Pa. L. Rev. 506, 557–561, 569–570 (1973).

contemporaneous evidence) for use at trial, thus serving both to inhibit spoilage and to avoid pitfalls and surprises that may defeat justice. . . .

B. MAKING TRUTH THE PARAMOUNT OBJECTIVE

We should consider whether the paramount commitment of counsel concerning matters of fact should be to the discovery of truth rather than to the advancement of the client's interest. This topic heading contains for me the most debatable and the least thoroughly considered of the thoughts offered here. It is a brief suggestion for a revolution, but with no apparatus of doctrine or program.

We should face the fact that the quality of "hired gun" is close to the heart and substance of the litigating lawyer's role. As is true always of the mercenary warrior, the litigator has not won the highest esteem for his scars and his service. Apart from our image, we have had to reckon for ourselves in the dark hours with the knowledge that "selling" our stories rather than striving for the truth cannot always seem, because it is not, such noble work as befits the practitioner of a learned profession. The struggle to win, with its powerful pressures to subordinate the love of truth, is often only incidentally, or coincidentally, if at all, a service to the public interest.

We have been bemused through the ages by the hardy (and somewhat appealing) notion that we are to serve rather than judge the client. Among the implications of this theme is the idea that lawyers are not to place themselves above others and that the client must be equipped to decide for himself whether or not he will follow the path of truth and justice. This means quite specifically, whether in *Anatomy of a Murder*[66] or in Dean Freedman's altruistic sense of commitment, that the client must be armed for effective perjury as well as he would be if he were himself legally trained. To offer anything less is arrogant, elitist, and undemocratic.

It is impossible to guess closely how prevalent this view may be as a practical matter. Nor am I clear to what degree, if any, received canons of legal ethics give it sanction. My submission is in any case that it is a crass and pernicious idea, unworthy of a public profession. It is true that legal training is a source of power, for evil as well as good, and that a wicked lawyer is capable of specially skilled wrongdoing. It is likewise true that a physician or pharmacist knows homicidal devices hidden from the rest of us. Our goals must include means for limiting the numbers of crooked and malevolent people trained in the vital professions. We may be certain, notwithstanding our best efforts, that some lawyers and judges will abuse their trust. But this is no reason to encourage or facilitate wrongdoing by everyone.

Professional standards that placed truth above the client's interests would raise more perplexing questions. The privilege for client's confidences might come in for reexamination and possible modification. We have all been trained to know

---

66. R. Traver, *Anatomy of a Murder* (1958). For those who did not read or have forgotten it, the novel, by a state supreme court justice, involved an eventually successful homicide defense of impaired mental capacity with the defendant supplying the requisite "facts" after having been told in advance by counsel what type of facts would constitute the defense.

without question that the privilege is indispensable for effective representation. The client must know his confidences are safe so that he can tell all and thus have fully knowledgeable advice. We may want to ask, nevertheless, whether it would be an excessive price for the client to be stuck with the truth rather than having counsel allied with him for concealment and distortion. The full development of this thought is beyond my studies to date. Its implications may be unacceptable. I urge only that it is among the premises in need of examination. . . .

C. A DUTY TO PURSUE THE TRUTH

The rules of professional responsibility should compel disclosures of material facts and forbid material omissions rather than merely proscribe positive frauds. This final suggestion is meant to implement the broad and general proposition that precedes it. In an effort to be still more specific, I submit a draft of a new disciplinary rule . . . . The draft says:

> (1) In his representation of a client, unless prevented from doing so by a privilege reasonably believed to apply, a lawyer shall:

> (a) Report to the court and opposing counsel the existence of relevant evidence or witnesses where the lawyer does not intend to offer such evidence or witnesses.

> (b) Prevent, or when prevention has proved unsuccessful, report to the court and opposing counsel the making of any untrue statement by client or witness or any omission to state a material fact necessary in order to make statements made, in the light of the circumstances under which they were made, not misleading.

> (c) Question witnesses with a purpose and design to elicit the whole truth, including particularly supplementary and qualifying matters that render evidence already given more accurate, intelligible, or fair than it otherwise would be.

> (2) In the construction and application of the rules in subdivision (1), a lawyer will be held to possess knowledge he actually has or, in the exercise of reasonable diligence, should have.

Key words in the draft, namely, in (1)(b), have been plagiarized, of course, from the Securities and Exchange Commission's Rule 10b-5. That should serve not only for respectability; it should also answer, at least to some extent, the complaint that the draft would impose impossibly stringent standards. The morals we have evolved for business clients cannot be deemed unattainable by the legal profession. . . .

If we must choose between truth and liberty, the decision is not in doubt. If the choice seemed to me that clear and that stark, this essay would never have reached even the tentative form of its present submission. But I think the picture is quite unclear. I lean to the view that we can hope to preserve the benefits of a free, skeptical, contentious bar while paying a lesser price in trickery and obfuscation.

Predictably, there has been critical response to Judge Frankel's views, which also form a main theme of his book *Partisan Justice*. See Freedman, "Judge Frankel's Search for the Truth," 123 U. Pa. L. Rev. 1060 (1975); Uviller, "The Advocate, The Truth, and Judicial Hackles," 123 U. Pa. L. Rev. 1067 (1975); Alschuler, "The Preservation of a Client's Confidences," 52 U. Colo. L. Rev. 349 (1981); and Pizzi, "Judge Frankel and the Adversary System," 52 U. Colo. L. Rev. 357 (1981). One way to test Judge Frankel's general views about the undervaluation of truth as an objective in our adversary system is by his own specific proposal. Assuming for a moment that the proposal is desirable, is it practicable? Under proposed (1)(a), would a lawyer be obligated to report to court and counsel every relevant and material variation in a story told by a witness in successive interviews? Under proposed (1)(b), what would be the standard to guide a lawyer in deciding whether a witness had made an untrue or a misleading statement? Under (1)(c), would a lawyer be required when a client testified to a particular series of events to cross-examine that client before the court and jury with respect to every relevant and material variation in that story? Is the combined subjective–objective nature of Judge Frankel's "reasonably believed" test in subsection (1) a helpful guide to lawyers? What would be the consequence of the adoption of, and full compliance with, Judge Frankel's proposed rule? In answering this question, assume that the "unless" clause in paragraph 1 is not meant to nullify with respect to "clients" what seems to be required in subparagraphs (a) and (b), and perhaps (c), although in (b) he seems to exclude "clients" from the category of "witnesses." Are any disadvantages that you perceive worth incurring in order to achieve the goal? Could one modify the disadvantages without sacrificing the objectives of the proposal? Assuming that the proposal is practicable, is it desirable, as compared with the present disciplinary rule or some other alternative that you favor?

Some of the earlier drafts of the Model Rules, which would have permitted or required greater breaches in confidentiality and greater openness by lawyers with other persons affected by a client's actions, reflected views similar to those expressed by Judge Frankel in this article, for he was a member of the Kutak Commission. Indeed, his presence on the Commission caused its work to be regarded with much suspicion by many proponents of a rule of strong confidentiality. Even if you disagree with (or are not yet persuaded by Judge Frankel's particular proposals), do you think the adversary system works well? Are there at least parts of the system that seem suboptimal or unfair to you? If so, how if at all might the rules and practice of legal ethics address those issues?

One interesting claim that Pepper and Dershowitz make is that the system under inquiry itself requires role-differentiated behavior in order to satisfy what appears to be a worthy obligation to the goals of the system—in law, justice, and in business, generating wealth. In that vein law and economics scholars have become increasingly interested in questions relating to legal ethics and the legal profession. See, e.g., Kaplow and Shavell, "Legal Advice About Information to Present in

Litigation," 102 Harv. L. Rev. 567 (1989); Macey and Miller, "An Economic Analysis of Conflict of Interest Litigation," 82 Iowa L. Rev. 965 (1997); Bundy and Elhauge, "Do Lawyers Improve the Adversary System," 79 Cal. L. Rev. 315 (1991). Often these scholars, like Daniel Fischel, conclude that ethical rules serve little purpose other than to protect the economic interests of lawyers. See "Lawyers and Confidentiality," 65 U. Chi. L. Rev. 1 (1998). Ironically, these law and economics critics echo an earlier set of criticisms by sociologists and critical scholars who claimed that ethics codes are nothing more than the hypocritical dress that lawyers use to disguise their "professionalism project" designed to maximize the value of their services by restricting supply and increasing demand. See, e.g., Richard Abel, "Why Does the ABA Promulgate Ethical Rules?," 59 Tex. L. Rev. 639 (1981). Fischel assumes that the most important way to evaluate the worth or legitimacy of the duty of confidentiality is to ask: "Who benefits from these communications?" Do you agree? See Lawrence Fox, "Dan's World: A Free Enterprise Dream; An Ethics Nightmare," 55 The Business Lawyer 1533 (2000), for a free-swinging response by a believer in the professional role of the lawyer.

Fischel argues that one of the major reasons to abolish confidentiality is that it would increase compliance with legal rules. But the assumption underlying this goal is that our laws merit full compliance. Even Pepper, when he worries about "the problem of legal realism," seems to assume that lawyers ought to counsel their clients to obey the law even though it may not always be clear what the law is. Although the claim that citizens should obey the law may seem like an incontrovertible truth, finding an acceptable philosophical grounding for such a duty has always been controversial. Whatever the scope for conscientious objection on the part of citizens, however, the traditional view among lawyers and the public alike has always been that lawyers have a special obligation to obey the law. Thus, in the words of the Preamble to the Model Rules, "[a]s advocate, a lawyer zealously asserts the client's position under the rules of the adversary system." And similarly, the Preamble proclaims "the lawyer's obligation zealously to protect and pursue a client's legitimate interests, within the bounds of the law . . . ." As the following exchange between Professors Simon and Wilkins suggests, however, even this standard professional injunction is more problematic than typically thought.

William Simon
Should Lawyers Obey the Law?
38 Wm. & Mary L. Rev. 217 (1996)

At the same time that it denies authority to nonlegal norms, the dominant view of legal ethics (the "Dominant View") insists on deference to legal ones. "Zealous advocacy" stops at the "bounds of the law."

By and large, critics of the Dominant View have not challenged this categorical duty of obedience to law. They typically want to add further public-regarding duties, but they are as insistent on this one as the Dominant View.

Now the idea that lawyers should obey the law seems so obvious that it is rarely examined within the profession. In fact, however, once you start to think about it, the argument for a categorical duty of legal obedience encounters difficulties, and these difficulties have revealing implications for legal ethics generally.

The basic difficulty is that the plausibility of a duty of obedience to law depends on how we define law. If we define law in narrow Positivist terms, then we cannot provide plausible reasons why someone should obey a norm just because it is "law." In order to give substance to the idea that law entails respect and obligation, we have to resort to broader, more substantive notions of law. These broader notions of law are hostile to both the narrowness and the categorical quality of the Dominant View's idea of legal obligation. . . . [T]hese broader notions often require advocacy to stop short of the limits prescribed by the Dominant View. Here I want to consider that they sometimes may warrant the lawyer to go beyond them.

I. Lawyer Obligation in the Dominant View

Suppose we are in a jurisdiction with an old-fashioned divorce statute that conditions divorce upon proof of one of a small number of specified grounds, such as adultery or abuse. A childless husband and wife have agreed that they want a divorce and on reasonable arrangements for separating their financial affairs. The lawyer believes that the proposed divorce and financial arrangements are in the interests of each of them. They cannot honestly prove, however, any of the grounds the statute requires. Suppose further, as was true in some of the jurisdictions that used to have such statutes, that it is possible, at little risk to either lawyer or clients, for the lawyer to help the couple get a divorce by coaching and presenting perjured testimony about, say, adultery.[4] The Dominant View forbids the lawyer to help clients in this way, no matter how strongly she believes that the couple is entitled to a divorce. If the lawyer believes the divorce statute is unjust, it says, she should work to induce the legislature to change it. This view condemns coaching and presenting perjury as a transgression of the "bounds of the law."

The Dominant View, however, is considerably less clear about lawyer activities that encourage or facilitate illegal conduct. Some advice—for example, information about the core terms of a statute—is clearly both a right of the client and a core function of lawyering. Other forms of advice—say, about where to hide from the police or how to build a bomb—clearly represent improper participation in illegal conduct.

However, at least one form of advice that clients often seek is harder to classify. This is advice about the enforcement practices of officials. Suppose I say to a tax client that, while the aggressive position she wants to take is unlikely to survive an audit, less than five percent of returns in her class are in fact audited. Or suppose, knowing

---

4. . . . The risk is small because judges, although aware of the practice, accept such testimony passively, and prosecutors and the police devote no resources to uncovering these practices. (Say there is a substantial probability that, if they were confronted with a flagrant case, the authorities might initiate charges of some sort, though even this is not clear. In any event, only the most careless or unlucky lawyer would create a flagrant case.)

my client's expenses are considerably lower than seventy percent of revenues, I tell her that the IRS's practice is not to question returns for businesses like hers unless they show expenses above seventy percent. Such advice is probably not unlawful, but since its only effect is to impede the enforcement process, it is troubling.

The Dominant View has yet to produce a clear answer to the question of whether such advice is improper. It hesitates between, on the one hand, defining it as legal advice and thus categorically appropriate, and on the other hand, defining it as assisting illegal conduct and thus categorically improper.

In fact, neither answer is plausible. The only satisfactory answer calls for contextual judgment. Most lawyers will readily concede this in the case of enforcement advice, for this is one area where the commitment of the Dominant View to categorical judgment is out of step with mainstream views and practices. The conclusion may be harder to accept in the case of direct participation, such as the Divorce Perjury story, but the same considerations that support contextual judgment in the indirect cases apply here as well.

II. Positivist Versus Substantive Conceptions of Law

Positivism is committed to differentiating legal from nonlegal norms and to doing so by virtue of a norm's "pedigree" rather than its intrinsic content. A pedigree links a legal norm to a sovereign institution through jurisdictional criteria that specify institutional formalities. An example of such a jurisdictional criterion is Article I, section seven, of the United States Constitution, which says that when each house of Congress overrides the President's veto of a bill by a two-thirds vote, the bill "shall become a Law."

When legal norms conflict, the Positivist resolves them in terms of jurisdictional criteria that specify which of the institutions to which the norms are traced should prevail. If the conflicting norms emanate from the same institution, then the Positivist applies further jurisdictional criteria—for example, later over earlier or specific over general—to decide which should have priority. . . .

Moralistic Positivism makes three arguments for a categorical duty of legal obedience. First, obedience to law promotes social order; without it we would have anarchy. Second, obedience promotes fairness; because we get the benefits of other people's obedience, we ought to give them the benefits of our obedience. Third, obedience promotes democracy; the laws are made pursuant to procedures of popular representation and accountability that entitle them to respect.

These arguments might be persuasive against a position asserting that one ought categorically to *disobey* the law, but hardly anyone has ever asserted such a position. Against the various positions of selective disobedience, such as those we shall shortly consider, they are entirely unpersuasive.

The problem with the arguments is that each rests on an appeal to a value that does not consistently track the Positivist's jurisdictional criteria of legality. However the Positivist specifies her criteria, there will always be particular situations in which obedience to what the Positivist's criteria identify as law will not serve social order, fairness, or democracy. . . .

For example, several years ago Raoul Berger decided, on the basis of extensive historical research that the Reconstruction Congress did not expect the Fourteenth Amendment to ban racial segregation. Under his criteria, the expectations of the Congress determined the correct interpretation of the Amendment, so it did not forbid segregation, and Brown v. Board of Education [347 U.S. 483 (1954)] was incorrectly decided. Berger became quite exercised about the Warren Court's Fourteenth Amendment cases and condemned them as betrayals of the rule of law.

Berger's argument was controversial. Some people insisted he was wrong about what the expectations of Congress were. Some people thought that the congressional expectations were not the critical criterion; they argued either that some other set of expectations—say, those of the members of the ratifying conventions—or something beside expectations—say, the current conventional meaning of the Amendment's language—was the critical criterion.

The most vulnerable part of Berger's argument was the assumption that, if he had been right about what the Fourteenth Amendment provided as law, that law would have deserved any respect. Why should we not simply admire the Warren Court for flouting this unappealing law and lending its efforts to the fight against segregation?

The arguments from social order, fairness, and democracy do not seem powerful here. The Warren Court's decisions may have contributed to social disorder, but anarchy did not ensue, and arguably what Berger thought was the legally correct decision would have caused more disorder. Few people today would regard a ruling against the *Brown* plaintiffs as a contribution to fairness. The balance of burden and benefit in the legal order of the day was not fairly struck for African-Americans; the Warren Court's arguably lawless decision inarguably pushed the balance toward greater fairness. Further, although the United States was in some relative sense a democracy, that fact did not cut toward the Berger result, because the country was a highly deficient democracy, and the Warren Court result was plausibly calculated to alleviate those deficiencies.

The Dominant View's arguments for obedience demand that we look at the legal system as a whole, ask if on balance it serves some good, and if the answer is yes, obey its commands categorically. However, unless we have some reason to think our selective disobedience will trigger some generalized lawlessness, we should not consider our disobedience a threat to the desirable aspects of the legal order. The fact that other people are obeying the law is often a fairness reason why we should, but if the law itself is unfair, the fairness concerns supporting disobedience will usually outweigh those supporting obedience. The fact that the law has been enacted or acquiesced in by a generally democratic political process is a reason for obedience, but not one that should prevail over a discovery that the process has not been democratic in this particular case.

Now turn to a conception of law radically opposed to Positivism. We can call this conception "Substantive," though there are many variations of and names for it. Some people prefer the term "natural law," though that term has connotations too exotic and metaphysical for what, I hope to show, is a familiar, mainstream notion.

The Substantive conception rejects Positivism's core premises—that law is strongly separated from nonlaw and that law is distinguished by jurisdictional criteria. It interprets specific legal norms as expressions of more general principles that are indissolubly legal and moral. It acknowledges the jurisdictional rules that Positivism regards as preeminent, but it regards them differently. First, it does not regard them as independent or ultimate social facts, but as expressions of underlying values, such as order, fairness, and democracy, and it insists on interpreting the rules in the light of these values. Second, it denies that these jurisdictional principles are categorically more important than substantive principles that prescribe, not the allocation of authority for dispute resolution, but the just ordering of the social world.

Consider the case of Walker v. Birmingham [388 U.S. 307 (1967)]. At the high tide of civil rights activism in the South, Martin Luther King, Jr. and the Southern Christian Leadership Conference planned a march in Birmingham to protest racial practices they believed were unconstitutional. At the behest of the city's white leadership, the local state court issued an injunction forbidding the march. Believing that the injunction was unconstitutional, they marched in defiance of it. The court held the organizers of the march guilty of contempt and jailed them.

When the Supreme Court reviewed the lower court's contempt judgment, it held that whether the protesters were correct in their belief that the injunction was unconstitutional made no difference. The Court decided that, since the lower court had jurisdiction and the protesters had ignored available procedures for appealing the injunction to higher tribunals, respect for law required affirming the punishment.

The *Walker* conclusion is plausible only under a Positivist conception of legality. On a Substantive conception, a "citizen's allegiance is to the law, not to any particular person's view of what the law is." From this perspective, an officially promulgated norm merits respect only by virtue of its substantive validity, and the *Walker* injunction, as the Supreme Court later recognized, had none. Respect for law required vindication of the protester's conduct. . . .

In contemporary legal culture, the broadest acknowledgment of the more radical manifestations of Substantivism occurs in discussions of nullification. Nullification is a term most readily associated with the power of the jury to disregard the judge's instructions and acquit even in the face of conclusive proof of what the judge has defined as an offense. This power was secured and legitimated in many nineteenth-century state constitutions. These provisions have disappeared over the years in all but two states—Indiana and Maryland—and the practice has been explicitly disapproved in many others.

Nevertheless, nullification has strong defenders, and it continues to lead a "subterranean life" in jury practice. Today, as before, nullification occurs with significant frequency when the jury finds prescribed punishments excessively harsh, especially in cases of victimless crimes. The histories of nullification in the North in Fugitive Slave Law cases and in the South in trials of white killers of blacks and civil rights activists serve as reminders of the noble and ignoble aspects of the dramatic history of the practice.

Nullification also describes two other important and less controversial practices — the judge's power to declare invalid unconstitutional legislation and the prosecutor's power to decline to enforce legislation when enforcement would not serve the public interest. Prosecutorial nullification is widely considered legitimate in circumstances where the application of a statute produces an especially harsh or anomalous result or where an entire statute, usually an old one, seems out of tune with contemporary sentiment — for example, the laws against fornication.

These nullification practices are never defended as forms of lawlessness, but rather as decentralizations of law application. The power to nullify is not a license to impose one's own views, but a duty to interpret what the law requires. . . .

Unlike the Positivist, once the Substantivist has defined the law, she does not need to struggle for a further argument as to why it should be obeyed. The duty to obey follows more or less straightforwardly from the definition. Any argument for disobedience against a particular command would also be an argument that the command was an incorrect interpretation of the law.

The Substantivist may well experience conflict between different values — say, between the values of majoritarian democracy that support deference to the legislature and the values of fairness that cut against enforcement of statutes disadvantaging minority groups. Unlike the Positivist, she understands such conflicts as occurring between competing legal values, not between law and nonlaw.

At best, however, explicit legitimate nullification occupies a marginal and uneasy place in the legal culture. Strong Substantivism threatens anarchy, and lawyers are dispositionally repelled by the prospect of anarchy. No doubt this is partly a matter of occupational self-interest; there is not much work for lawyers in anarchy. Beyond self-interest, it also reflects a plausible belief that anything approaching full-blown anarchy is unlikely to accommodate a high level of justice or welfare.

Thus neither Positivism nor Substantivism, in the uncompromising, full-strength versions, are plausible. Positivism seems incompatible with any sense of legal obligation. It either disavows normative intentions, or it defends them clumsily and over-inclusively. Substantivism, by incorporating the reasons for obedience directly into its description of law, makes a clear case for obedience, but it tends to erode commitments to a stable institutional structure. . . .

VIII. A Prima Facie Obligation?

Theorists who appreciate the implausibility of a categorical duty of obedience sometimes retreat to a "prima facie" or rebuttable duty. You can't say this idea is wrong, but it is not especially useful, and it can be misleading. Abstractly stated, it still begs the question of what we mean by law. If the phrase refers to a Substantivist conception, then it is tautological. If it refers to a Positivist conception, then it is misleading.

Law is prima facie binding if it is prima facie just (subsuming such values as order, fairness, and democracy under this heading). On a Substantive view, law is prima facie just *by definition*. The Substantivist insists that at least some dimensions of justice be incorporated into law and does so precisely in order to make law binding. So the claim of a prima facie duty adds nothing to the Substantivist definition of the legal enterprise.

Under a Positivist view, where law is not just by definition, a prima facie duty might have two different meanings. First, it might mean that the jurisdictional principles that define the law constitute a process that is intrinsically just, for example, democratic, and therefore entitled to presumptive respect. Or it might mean that the law that emerges from this process is usually just, and there is thus a strong empirical likelihood that any particular norms it now produces will be just. . . .

IX. Divorce Perjury and Enforcement Advice Revisited

We should now return to the problems of divorce perjury and enforcement advice discussed above as illustrations of the treatment in the Dominant View of direct and indirect participation in illegality.

Begin with the latter problem, because the inadequacy of categorical approaches is most obvious here. In at least some cases, enforcement advice would be unacceptable to nearly everyone. For example, the client is a serial rapist who wants information about the schedules and routes of police patrols in the area where he plans to strike next. Giving such information might constitute unlawful assistance under the criminal law, but that is far from clear. If it is not itself illegal, then it is not unethical under the Dominant View, and that surely is an objection to the Dominant View.

On the other hand, hardly anyone is going to support a categorical ban on such information either. Many feel strongly that clients are entitled to know the extent to which the laws against fornication, sodomy, misprision of felony (failing to report someone else's criminal activity), small stakes gambling, marijuana possession, and nonpayment of employment taxes for part-time domestic workers are unenforced or underenforced.

Health and safety regulations and environmental regulatory enforcement also resist categorical treatment. Where evasive behavior threatens serious harm the regulatory scheme is designed to protect against, advice that facilitates evasion seems wrong. On the other hand, sometimes evasion seems not only not to threaten major harm, but to be acceptable to the enforcement authorities and perhaps even the legislature. Maybe the agency underenforces because it thinks the statutory standards are too strict. Maybe it underenforces because the legislature, divided on the efficacy of the statute, has cut the agency's enforcement budget, intending to limit enforcement.

Of course, there are objections to this type of administrative and legislative behavior. There is no doubt, however, that it occurs, and given that it occurs, it seems both unfair and inefficient to preclude lawyers from providing relevant information about enforcement practices.

Any plausible assessment of the propriety of enforcement advice requires a willingness to distinguish the relative weights of different substantive norms. This requires an at least moderately Substantive approach and contextual judgment.

Some cases are easy. (Although not everyone will have the same list of easy cases, each person will have some list of cases she finds easy, and some cases will appear on most people's lists.) Advice that facilitates violence and large-scale property crime will usually seem clearly inappropriate. Advice that facilitates moderate speeding, misprision of felony, and consensual fornication will usually seem proper, or at least tolerable.

Other cases are harder. For example, there is playing the "tax lottery" by submitting a weakly grounded tax claim, knowing it is unlikely to be audited. The case is potentially hard because of the possibility that, while the claim may be weak in terms of the narrow positive law, it may be stronger when viewed more broadly and substantively. Playing the "tax lottery" might then be viewed as an appropriate form of nullification of a normatively weak positive law. This may seem unlikely—it does to me—but the point is that a plausible defense of advice that has little function other than to facilitate evasion requires the type of principled Substantive justification associated with nullification.

Although it may seem more radical in the context of direct lawyer illegality, the same analysis applies there. We have already noted the broad variety of circumstances in which the culture accepts, and occasionally exalts, direct violation of the positive law. Many of these examples, however, involve citizens rather than lawyers, and some lawyers believe that their duties differ in this regard. These lawyers feel that they have a stronger obligation to the law than do lay people because they publicly profess commitment to it, have a strong exemplary influence on the lay public, or acquire special privileges through participation in a regulated monopoly. Thus, a categorical prohibition of direct participation in illegality makes more sense for lawyers than for lay people.

Of course, this argument is yet another variation on the jurisprudential mistake we have noted repeatedly. It does not follow from the fact that lawyers have a stronger obligation to the "law" that the type of conduct we are considering is less appropriate for them. For the conceptions of law most compatible with strong obligations are Substantive, and on a Substantive conception, obligation to "law" may require violation of some legal norms in order to vindicate more basic ones.

The argument comes close to making explicit the effect I noted above of the Dominant View's jurisprudential commitments. By adopting a Positivist notion of law, it characterizes the considerations favoring compliance as legal and those weighing against it as nonlegal, perhaps "moral." If we accept the definitional premise, unless we are prepared to reject the appealing proposition that lawyers have an exceptionally strong obligation to law, we will find it very hard to support lawyer noncompliance.

However, there is no reason why we should accept the premise. Many of the most important reasons weighing toward noncompliance can be aptly expressed in legal—especially nullification—terms. For example, perhaps the strongest case for lawyer participation in the Divorce Perjury example would portray it as an instance of Calabresian nullification. First, the statute is an old one. Second, it is out of harmony with more recent legal developments that imply that, where there are no children, the social interest in preserving marriage is much weaker and the individual interests in structuring one's own intimate relations are much stronger than the statute presupposes. Third, there are apparent institutional dysfunctions that provide more likely explanations for the failure to repeal the statute than current popular support. Perhaps the statute is supported by only a small minority. This group would not be able to secure the enactment of the statute today, but it can block repeal because it is well-organized; because most who oppose the statute feel less intensely; and because those who are tangibly harmed by the statute, such as the clients in question here, are not able to organize (because their status is hard to anticipate and episodic) and are relatively poor (because affluent people can avoid its effects by taking advantage of the more accommodating laws of other states).

Of course, we should consider why, if there is a strong case for nullification, it has to be accomplished by the lawyer rather than, as Calabresi proposed, the court. Why not have the lawyer bring an action on the true facts urging the court to nullify and grant the divorce? One answer is that most states reject judicial nullification except on constitutional grounds, which might not be available. Even if judges could nullify, they might refuse to do so because, for example, they are unwilling to take the heat from the small but passionate minority that intensely supports the statute. Or perhaps the judges would think that the existence of such a minority would make nullification illegitimate. It might be, however, that the statute is of largely symbolic importance to this group, and it has no stake in low visibility enforcement decisions. Thus, while public judicial nullification would not be feasible, low visibility ad hoc lawyer nullification would be.

X. Conclusion

The answer to the question whether lawyers should obey the law turns out to depend on what we mean by law. If we define law in terms of the Positivist's jurisdictional criteria, then lawyers have no strong reason to obey it. If we define law Substantively, we make transparent the obligation that attaches to it, but we also erase the line between law and morals. . . .

David Wilkins
In Defense of Law *and* Morality:
Why Lawyers Should Have a Prima Facie Duty
to Obey the Law

38 Wm. & Mary L. Rev. 269 (1996)

In his important essay [excerpted above], William Simon continues and refines his attack on "categorical" legal norms. This latest installment calls into question the categorical norm that has traditionally been the one relatively fixed star in the legal ethics universe: that zealous advocacy stops at "the bounds of the law." He does so by reminding us that the ethical legitimacy of this traditional "boundary claim" depends upon what we mean by "law." ...

II. What is Law?

Narrow Positivism fails as both a descriptive and a normative theory largely for the reasons Simon posits. ...

Substantivism [fails on both levels as well]. Descriptively, Substantivism ignores the fact, mentioned but then dismissed by Simon, that "for whatever reasons, people simply do regard the law as binding." Thus, when people drive in excess of the speed limit, they do not generally consider that they have a "right" to drive faster than fifty-five miles per hour, or that the legal limit is really seventy miles per hour. Instead, most people acknowledge that they are "breaking the law" when they drive seventy miles per hour even though they may also believe that the latter speed is the one better designed to promote the underlying values of safety and efficiency that speed limits are supposed to further.

The fact that most people actually view law as binding also underscores the normative dangers of Substantivism. By pointing to one of the most common and pernicious examples of nullification — the refusal of southern white juries to convict white people accused of crimes against blacks — Simon acknowledges the pernicious side of Substantivism: its tendency to "erode commitments to a stable institutional structure." He argues, however, that these dangers are often exaggerated. As proof, he points to the fact that driving (at least in most places) is not "anarchy" even though many drivers ignore the fifty-five miles per hour speed limit. Nor did the Supreme Court's decision to "nullify" its prior understanding of the Fourteenth Amendment in Brown v. Board of Education [347 U.S. 483 (1954)] plunge the country into chaos. These examples, however, trade on the fact that most people do not operate on the Substantivist view that Simon advocates. The fact that safety improved even though many Americans did not decrease their rate of speed after the speed limit was lowered to fifty-five miles per hour is plausibly the result of the fact that drivers who are exceeding the posted limit are driving more carefully *precisely because they know that they are breaking the law* and therefore run the risk of being sanctioned. Similarly, one reason why the *Brown* decision did not plunge the nation into civil war is because many Americans, including many politicians who vehemently disagreed with the decision (most notably President Eisenhower, who detested *Brown*), "believed that the ruling should be respected because it was the law." To the extent that the motoring public or white Americans who disapproved of *Brown* adopted the kind of Substantivist stand towards law currently being espoused by those in the militia movement, the threat of anarchy would have been much more pronounced.

More important, a functioning legal system should do more than protect against anarchy. Although theorists frequently exaggerate the extent to which legal rules actually produce the kind of objectivity, predictability, consistency, and accountability associated with "the rule of law," these values nevertheless constitute important aspirational goals. Despite the fact that it aims directly at achieving these ends, Substantivism, by removing boundaries between legal and moral decision making, is likely to underproduce important qualities associated with the rule of law.

Simon asserts that legal reasoning, although "loose," is "typically thought [to be] more structured and grounded than popular moral discourse." . . . I am inclined to agree with this assessment. I suspect that this is true, however, because the conventions and practices of legal reasoning relegate the kind of broad, natural-law-based nullification arguments employed by Simon to a few, well-regulated areas of legal discourse. In each of the areas where Simon claims that nullification is considered a part of the law (as opposed to an act of conscientious objection *to* the law), the ground for treating the action as legitimate is plausibly linked to the special circumstances in which the act takes place. Thus, when Congress votes to ignore a specific constitutional provision, a judge nullifies an outdated statute, or a prosecutor refuses to bring charges on the ground that it would not serve justice, each of these decisions has been made in such a manner that the decision maker's interpretive choices are on the record and subject to review. Similarly, jury nullification is tightly constrained both procedurally and substantively. Proposals to liberate it from these constraints — particularly those that arguably seek to accomplish this goal by covert manipulation — are generally greeted with alarm. Even the civil disobedience of the 1950s and 1960s, frequently cited by Simon as a shining example of Substantivism, was subject to the constraints of publicity and accountability. Whether marching without a permit or sitting at a segregated lunch counter, Martin Luther King, Jr. and his compatriots believed in openly defying what they considered to be unjust laws and subjecting themselves to judgment from both the courts and the court of public opinion.

Simon acknowledges the importance of publicity and accountability, but argues that "the Substantivist is open to considering that these institutional values, even where present, might be outweighed by competing values. This, however, conflates the moral weight of law with the definition of law. . . . [T]here certainly will be circumstances in which legal and moral concerns, separate and apart from considerations of publicity and accountability of the interpretive process, will counsel against obeying the law. Nevertheless, in order to decide what law *is*, we must first agree on a set of evaluative criteria. Those criteria, in turn, must be defined in terms of the conventions of the practice — legal reasoning in this case — that give meaning to the enterprise. Legal reasoning confines arguments about nullification to certain spheres of legal decisionmaking. To do otherwise . . . threatens the very integrity of the practice as a whole. . . .

Neither narrow Positivism nor Substantivism, therefore, provides an adequate definitional account of law. Instead, in order to both account for the ordinary understanding of "law" and to facilitate the development of a legal system that promotes the values of order, fairness, and democracy, the definition of law can neither be severed from these underlying values nor subsumed within them. Purposivism aims at providing such an account. Briefly, Purposivism insists that legal rules must be interpreted in light of the purposes or social functions that the law is designed to serve. These purposes, in turn, must be defined against the backdrop of practices and conventions that make legal analysis moderately, as opposed to radically, indeterminate. Central to this practice is "a moral commitment to the rule of law itself, to government according to general laws, impartially and equally administered." This allegiance includes a commitment to regard government commands, enacted according to established legal processes, as presumptively "law." A Purposivist always is open to the possibility that what at first appears to be the law may in fact not be entitled to this designation. Examples of this situation include: when a literal reading of the law would undermine its intended purposes; when the enforcement agency actually wishes to induce something less than perfect compliance; or when changes in social conditions have sapped the command of a law's legitimate authority. A Purposivist, however, is committed to reaching judgments about the authority of law on the basis of interpretive arguments that are appropriate to the time and place where the decision will occur. . . . [I]t is this commitment to using interpretive norms that are appropriate to the circumstances of the particular case that underscores the importance of professional role. . . .

IV. THE IMPORTANCE OF ROLE

Notwithstanding the title to his paper, very little of Simon's argument hinges on claims that are unique to lawyers. Essentially, Simon argues that lawyers do not have a categorical duty to obey the law because no one is under such an obligation. Moreover, to support his argument about legal ethics, Simon makes frequent comparisons to the acceptance of Substantivist principles in the decision-making processes of other legal actors such as judges, jurors, legislators, and public prosecutors. By so doing, he hopes to reduce the distance between the styles of deliberation accepted in these domains and the ethics of lawyers.

I have argued elsewhere at some length that conflating the jurisprudential styles of lawyers and judges is a mistake. Our acceptance of discretionary judgment on the part of judges and other public officials is inextricably intertwined with the institutional checks and balances within which this discretion is exercised. Lawyers, on the other hand, operate in a world of legally and constitutionally sanctioned secrecy. Consequently, in order to establish a meaningful precedent, arguments for extending the discretionary power of judges and other legal actors to lawyers must be accompanied by proposals to replicate some of the legal and institutional checks and balances governing judges to this new context. In the last section of this paper I propose that we ought to do just that.

Before embarking on this task, however, it is important to emphasize two characteristics about the legal profession that, when taken together, suggest that lawyers stand in a different relationship to the duty to obey the law than do either citizens or other legal actors.

First, unlike ordinary citizens, lawyers have expressly promised to obey the law. Virtually every lawyer takes an oath to support and defend the law as a condition of gaining admission to the bar. By expressly undertaking this commitment, lawyers have entered into a voluntary agreement with society that, like any other promise, has independent moral weight.

Simon . . . might contend that there is a simple solution to this problem: either stop requiring that lawyers make this promise, or reinterpret this commitment to require only that lawyers obey the law when doing so furthers the underlying goals of the legal system. Although both these proposals would change the terms of the debate, they would not negate the claim that lawyers have a contractual obligation to obey the law that is higher than that of an ordinary citizen.

Even if no individual lawyer promised to obey the law, the regulatory structure that permits lawyers to exercise rights and privileges unavailable to ordinary citizens rests on an implicit commitment to legality emanating from the profession as a whole. Lawyers are given access to virtually every aspect of the legal framework. In addition, they receive special permission to engage in conduct (for example, keeping client confidences or helping known-to-be-guilty clients avoid punishment) that would subject ordinary citizens to sanction. In return, society has the right to expect that lawyers will not abuse their power "so as to subvert and nullify the purposes of the rules." The common claim that lawyers are officers of the court—whether they want to be or not—is a reflection of this implicit social bargain. To be sure, this obligation to legality should be understood in Purposivist, as opposed to narrowly Positivist terms. As we have seen, however, this construction does not license the full range of interpretive tools contemplated by Simon's strong commitment to Substantivism. . . .

[Moreover,] law breaking by lawyers will often produce different consequences from similar conduct by nonlawyers. . . . [To be sure,] a lawyer's unique skill and training make her well-positioned to contribute to the development of the legal framework by identifying laws that either poorly serve their intended purposes or conflict with other important moral or legal values. It is largely for this reason that the ethics rules encourage lawyers to engage in law reform activity. By the same token, however, noncompliance by lawyers is likely to have larger negative consequences than similar actions by clients. Given their status as knowledgeable insiders, lawyers have a greater ability to avoid the kind of checks and balances that either constrain or legitimate lawbreaking by ordinary citizens. Moreover, the attitudes that lawyers convey about the law are likely to rub off on their clients, thereby multiplying the effects of lawyer noncompliance. Even nonclients are likely to pick up important messages about the appropriate moral standing of law from the conduct of lawyers. . . .

None of this should be taken to imply that the unique position occupied by lawyers places them under an absolute duty to obey every legal command. Lawyers—like citizens—are under only a prima facie obligation to obey the law. The content of that prima facie duty, however, must respond to the distinctive character of the lawyer's role. . . .

V. IN PRAISE OF LAW AND MORALITY

. . . Lawyers who disobey the law on moral grounds have an ethical obligation to replicate, to the extent possible, some of the institutional checks and balances that legitimate conscientious objection in other arenas. Two of the most important of these legitimating principles are candor and publicity. Consider the following scenario, loosely based on a recent incident involving two district attorneys in New York state. True to his campaign promises, the new Governor of New York recently signed into law a statute authorizing capital punishment. Both District Attorneys are morally opposed to the death penalty. One District Attorney publicly declares that he will refuse to seek the death penalty in any case even in cases in which it is clearly called for under the newly mandated criteria—on grounds of both legal merit and morality. The second District Attorney, although also having decided that he will never seek the death penalty for reasons similar to those articulated by the first DA, simply states that he will review each death penalty decision on a case-by-case basis, correctly perceiving that his commitment never to invoke the new statute will be more difficult to detect and sanction than his colleague's open defiance. In my judgment, so long as we assume that we are living in a tolerably just world in which the commands of the legislature are entitled to presumptive weight, the first District Attorney has acted more ethically than the second.

Finally, any plausible account of legal ethics must address lawyers at all points along the "good faith" spectrum. System designers must anticipate the degree to which the combination of broad discretionary norms coupled with inadequate enforcement might encourage lawyers to engage in even more self-interested manipulation of legal rules. Although every system of legal regulation depends substantially on a measure of voluntary compliance, it is only by facing up to the most banal—and undoubtedly the most common examples where lawyers fail to obey the law that we can create an understanding of legal ethics that promotes the goals that Simon . . . and I all seek to achieve.

The oaths of admission in nearly all states require lawyers to uphold the state and federal constitutions. The prevailing ethical rules also seem to limit lawyers' advocacy to the "bounds of the law" and to forbid counseling or assisting in any criminal, fraudulent, or dishonest behavior. See, e.g., Model Rules Pmbl., 1.2, 3.1, and 8.4(c). Yet, a constitution might permit or require repugnant behavior (such as invidious discrimination), or a lawyer's client might be facing an adversary with such evil ends that questionable means might seem justifiable, or at least excusable, to thwart those evil ends. Do the prevailing rules requiring fidelity to the law have any exceptions? See generally Model Rule 3.1: do you see an exception there? If it is an exception, is it broad enough? Is there something special about the role of the lawyer that commands a stronger fidelity to the law than, say, the role of the client?

Turning to a final thought, we shall assume now that the lawyer's proposed course of action is not illegal, being instead within the bounds of the law. But the action is not required by the law or the ethical rules. Indeed, both in general practice and in ethical problems the particular action (or inaction) is often committed to the lawyer's "discretion." (As Wilkins notes above, this is not invariably a good thing because "broad discretionary norms" might lead to lawyers' "self-interested manipulation of legal rules," among other consequences. As Simon has elsewhere noted, for example, lawyers are periodically hired to give opinions immunizing both clients' past misconduct and their law firms' morally and even legally questionable advice. William H. Simon, "The Market for Bad Legal Advice: Academic Professional Responsibility Consulting as an Example," 60 Stan. L. Rev. 1555 (2008).) The final piece below explores whether an act's "discretionary" status might be ethically relevant:

Stephen Gillers
Can A Good Lawyer Be a Bad Person?
2 J. Inst. Stud. Leg. Eth. 131 (1999)

Assume a just legal system in a constitutional democracy. Imagine a person wishing to achieve a lawful goal. Imagine a lawyer who agrees to assist her. If the lawyer uses only legal means consonant with the jurisdiction's legal ethics rules, can a coherent theory of moral philosophy nevertheless label the lawyer's conduct immoral? Can a good lawyer be a bad person? . . .

While we wait to learn what, if any, influence moral philosophy will have on the rules that define acceptable lawyer behavior, I suggest that we can and should busy ourselves with the anterior question that titles this essay. That we can do so, is evident. But why should we? I offer two reasons. First, criticism of "good" lawyers — those who conscientiously obey the rules set down — for being "bad" people (or for doing "bad" things) may, if valid, hasten change in the rules the lawyers cite in defense. If a lawyer can be called "bad" while obeying the rule — ordinarily a "good" thing to do — then the rule will be shown to need adjustment. My second reason is logically antecedent to the first reason. We should decide whether it is ever valid to criticize a lawyer who does nothing "wrong," measured by positive law and the professional responsibility rules that govern the lawyer's behavior. Perhaps we will conclude that we must aim our criticism only (or nearly only) at the rules the lawyer obeys, and not the lawyer who obeys them, especially when disobedience can carry a heavy price. In fact, we may go further. We may decide that preservation of our legal system's values requires us to defend lawyers who obey the rules yet become targets of criticism from others (the public, the press, politicians), even while we challenge the rules they obey.

So then, can a good lawyer be a bad person? Let us distinguish, first, between a client's ends and the means employed to achieve them; second, between the behavior of the bar as an enterprise engaged in rulemaking and the behavior of individual lawyers who are required to obey the bar's rules; and third, between rules that mandate an act and those that commit the decision whether to engage in the act to the lawyer's discretion. I will try to draw these distinctions using the following hypotheticals. I do not expect that they address all cases or resolve all questions, but they should illustrate the utility of the proposed distinctions and advance our effort to answer the question at hand. Readers may disagree with my solutions to the hypothetical facts, yet find the categories they define analytically congenial. . . .

Hypothetical II (a) A man whose lifelong dream has been to open a restaurant persuades a billionaire cousin to lend him $100,000. The man is unsophisticated in business matters while the cousin is not. The man signs a demand note for the loan and opens the restaurant. Food critics give it excellent reviews; great success is predicted. Seeing this, the cousin calls the note, then brings an action on it, intending to acquire the restaurant in a foreclosure sale. The man goes to a lawyer who sees improbable defenses on the merits and who proceeds to make a series of nonfrivolous procedural motions calculated to gain time for her client until either the restaurant's cash flow is great enough to pay the note or a bank loan can be obtained. The motions are either weak, with the lawyer expecting them to fail, or they are highly technical.

(b) While on her way home from her job as a housekeeper, a single mother of three children is hurt by falling debris at a construction site. She suffers permanent injuries that prevent her from resuming gainful employment. She sues the construction company. Its lawyer, recognizing only weak defenses on the merits, makes procedural motions of the kind described in II(a). These will have the effect of increasing pressure on the financially desperate plaintiff to settle for a fifth of what she could reasonably expect to recover at trial.

Hypothetical II posits two situations in which lawyers, with no realistic defense on the merits, make weak or technical procedural motions in order to delay plaintiffs' efforts to vindicate their legal rights. The lawyer in II(a) means to buy time for his client to extinguish a debt. The delay in II(b) aims to force a financially desperate plaintiff to accept a modest settlement. Assume the motions are addressed to the sufficiency of service of process. One motion alleges that service was made by someone a month under eighteen years of age. If true, service was improper, but the motion must be counted as highly technical. Another motion makes a weak assertion that the agent served with process was not one identified in applicable law.

If the Code and the Rules mean to forbid this sort of "indirect" strategy, they certainly say so obscurely. I assume they permit the motions on the posited facts. The rules that identify the minimum age of a process server and the agents eligible to receive service either mean what they say or they do not. If they do, then a defendant must be able to challenge service when there is reason to believe these rules were ignored. The right to challenge, furthermore, does not accrue only to those defendants who can, in good faith, demonstrate a probable defense on the merits.

Nevertheless, even if law and the governing ethical document permit the motions, does the lawyer who makes them act badly by "frustrating an opposing party's attempt to obtain rightful redress or repose"? I believe the answer may be yes. On these facts, a good lawyer may be a bad person.

. . . Hypothetical II addresses the propriety of taking action (making the motions) that neither the Code nor the Rules expressly require. To infer a requirement, one must argue that a lawyer may not reject an effective and permissible strategy if her only reason for doing so is that she finds the strategy morally objectionable. The duty to represent a client loyally or zealously, the argument might go, means at least as much.

I realize that this argument is syllogistically possible. Further, we could certainly create a system of legal ethics in which it is valid. Then, the lawyers in Hypothetical II . . . would have no choice but to exercise the discretionary authority on the client's behalf. If so, they could not be criticized for doing so, although the rules that constrained them could be criticized. However, a proponent of a "mandatory" syllogism in the current rules—i.e., one in which authority plus a duty of loyalty equals a "mandatory" duty—has a serious problem. The texts of the ethics codes don't recognize it. . . . I also know of no judicial decision that has disciplined a lawyer or imposed civil liability on a lawyer for choosing not to take a discretionary action, though it might have benefitted the client to do so, because the lawyer found the strategy morally dubious.

Consequently, a lawyer may refrain from making the motions, even if requested to do so by her client, without violating either document. Because the tactic is discretionary, the lawyer who invokes it by making the motions is as morally accountable as the client on whose behalf she acts. I do not mean to say that the lawyer who makes the motions will necessarily have acted badly, but only that she stands in no better position than her client. Whether the conduct of a lawyer and client may be criticized morally hinges on the entire factual context, including the particular circumstances of the case and the behavior of the adverse client and lawyer. It may be that the conduct in Hypothetical II(a) can be defended, while the conduct in Hypothetical II(b) cannot.

In criminal cases, especially, a lawyer will usually act morally even though he delays trial by contending for nonfrivolous procedural rights. Some such contentions succeed. New rights are recognized, or old rights are applied, to better contain prosecutorial excess or to honor a constitutional value. These rights will evolve or be enforced only if defense lawyers insist. Who else will do it? Furthermore, judges are generally less passive in criminal than in civil contests, and so better able to forestall specious delay strategies.

An objection to the argument here is that it allows a lawyer to subordinate the client's interests to the lawyer's view of what is right without the client's knowledge. That, in turn, disrespects the client's autonomy. Even if the lawyer has the identified discretion—even if the "mandatory" syllogism is not part of our legal ethics codes—doesn't the client have a right to know at the outset, perhaps in the retainer agreement, how the lawyer will exercise the discretion? Maybe the client wanted to hire a "junkyard dog" and is instead getting a "nice guy." This is a valid objection. . . .

––––––––––

As you move on through the materials and eventually on to practice, what principles will guide your discretion? To the extent you come to a fixed (rather than constantly contextual) view of your professional role or how you exercise your discretion, will you tell your clients at the outset of the representation? What if you are the "nice person," but certain clients really want or even need the "junkyard dog"? Should the clients know about the differing approaches to the lawyer's role (several of which have been sketched above) and where you fall on the spectrum? Should they be told which decisions are essentially yours, and not theirs, to make? Should you also tell them that you often have the discretion to give them the discretion to make the final decision?

Chapter 4

Representation of Conflicting Interests

The problem of representation of conflicting interests has dimensions of its own but it is also related to the issue of preserving the confidential information of a client. As we have seen, a reason often given for a broad interpretation of the prohibitions in the conflict of interest rules is the desirability of preserving the already represented client's confidences.

Once a lawyer or law firm has more than one client, it must consider whether its present or past representations preclude it from taking on a new matter. Obviously, lawyers could not serve their function in anything like our present system of justice if they were to represent both the prosecution and the defense in a criminal case, or the buyer and the seller of goods in the trial of a breach of contract matter. But the issues are not so clear when the question is whether different members of a firm may be on opposite sides of the same matter or whether a lawyer may oppose a former client in a matter unrelated to the former representation.

Conflict of interest problems did not used to be regarded as presenting difficult problems for law firms. Now, however, the use of the motion to disqualify opposing counsel in litigation, the growth in size of law firms, and the increasing amount and sophistication of the substantive law of conflicts of interest have made the subject of paramount interest for anyone who practices law. Today conflicts of interest concerns constitute one of the, if not *the*, most frequent legal ethics issues facing practitioners (e.g., for bar associations that offer legal ethics advice to their members, conflict-of-interest–related dilemmas account for a sizeable percentage of the advice). Indeed, most law firms with more than a few lawyers now use complex computer programs to help them keep track of their cases and clients in order to be able to identify conflict problems more readily. Lawyers in major firms report that new business listings that arrive on their computer screens every morning occupy a substantial amount of their time. Just consider for a moment what data you would like to see in such a listing. Is the client's name enough? How about the name of the client's spouse, especially if the last name was different? Anticipated witnesses at trial? If a company, how about the names of major or controlling stockholders? Subsidiaries and affiliated companies? Major creditors? The issues involved in the representation?

The following materials present a variety of situations in which conflict of interest problems occur. All involve to some extent considerations of the fiduciary principle, the loyalty owed to clients and would-be clients. The fiduciary consideration is

[handwritten margin notes:]
Cat Implicates:
① duty of fid:
② Freedom to select lawyer/ client;
③ Freedom to det what → cat; &
④ Jud. eff.

[lower handwritten margin note:]
screening may resolve cat.

often a double-edged sword. Loyalty toward one client may suggest or even require rejection of another. But the rejected client also may have demands of loyalty on the attorney, having spent much time, effort, and money educating the lawyer about the complexities of the client's life or business only to be told to seek a new lawyer because of the law of professional responsibility. Conflict of interest problems also implicate other principles besides the fiduciary principle, such as the freedom of individuals to select their own lawyers, or the freedom of lawyers to make their own assessment of what constitutes a conflict, or the principle of promoting economic efficiency by not increasing the costs of representation through rules that require hiring new, uneducated counsel.

One problem for those charged with formulating the law of professional responsibility has been whether rules relating to conflict of interest should be codified, and if so, whether they should be codified at a fairly abstract level, leaving considerable leeway to lawyers as they decide how to resolve particular problems, or whether they should be stated as specifically as possible to guide and constrain lawyers' decisions.

The organization of the materials of this Chapter presents some difficulties, for it would be useful in discussing the earlier subsections to have some knowledge about the concluding subsections. Nevertheless, experience suggests that it is preferable to examine first the situations when a lawyer or law firm seeks to represent either simultaneously or successively clients with actual or potentially conflicting interests. That is where the substantive law developed first. In the last twenty-five years or so, serious consideration has been given to the possibility that the disqualification of a member of a law firm might not necessarily require the disqualification of the whole firm if the disqualified member is "screened off" from participation in the matter. That argument was first accepted, for policy reasons relating to maintaining the attractiveness of public service, in a number of cases involving former government employees joining private law firms. More recently, the argument has been increasingly made that policy reasons justify a similar result not only in cases of successive representation but also in cases involving simultaneous representation in the totally private law firm context. Consideration of these developments is postponed to the end of the Chapter because the basic problems of conflicts need to be dealt with first. The possibility of a "screening" defense, however, should be kept in mind as we proceed through the materials that develop the justifications for the substantive law of disqualification for conflict of interest.

One final point to keep in mind as you review these materials. Courts and commentators typically discuss conflicts issues in terms of the applicability and interpretation of the relevant disciplinary rules and other precedents. Practicing lawyers, however, often employ another vocabulary. Although practitioners realize that conflicts can sometimes present complex legal questions, they are keenly aware that these issues also strike at the heart of the business of practicing law. Consider the following findings from a comprehensive study of conflicts issues by a sociologist affiliated with the American Bar Foundation in a random sample of 128 Illinois law firms of varying sizes:

Of more than one hundred accounts offered in the interviews [of conflicts cases the respondent found "difficult"] only seven make questions of law or legal interpretation problematic. Four of these problematic accounts describe cases that raised questions about who may be considered a client, two concerned when a client can be considered a former client, and one addressed which of several sets of contradictory conflicts rules applies in a multistate transaction. The other 95% of the cases involved clashing interests that aroused wrenching business or client-relations problems or irate colleagues, not questions of law. [As one respondent from a large law firm explained:]

> The complexity of the law is there and it presents a problem. And we're lawyers; we can deal with those things. You make decisions. Sometimes you're right and sometimes you're wrong, as the cases decide later. But you make decisions. The toughest part of the job is the personal part of the job—either from the client or from your partners—where they absolutely either do not understand or refuse to understand what's going on. In the substantive areas, though, there are areas that are tougher rather than easier because there's no clarity in the law. So it's hard to advise your client or your partner. . . . But that's what lawyers do. Again, my hardest job is not to do that. We can ferret out and make our judgments. My hardest job is to deal with the personalities and the individuals who just don't seem to be willing to regard that as a significant part of the practice of law—either the client or the lawyer.

Susan P. Shapiro, "Everests of the Mundane: Conflict of Interest in Real-World Legal Practice," 69 Fordham L. Rev. 1139, 1142 (2000).

What the quoted excerpt seems to be saying is that most conflict problems arise not because of uncertainty about the governing legal principles but because lawyers or clients do not wish to follow clear mandates forbidding representation in a given circumstance. Lawyers do not wish to send clients elsewhere because of the conflict rules; clients often do not wish to lose their lawyers because of the same rules. As you examine the following materials, you should ask yourself what the implications of Ms. Shapiro's findings are for the manner in which conflicts issues should be regulated. Would any plausible regulatory scheme for "business conflicts" likely do more harm than good? Would greater enforcement of the existing rules help lawyers and clients to see conflicts questions "as a significant part of the practice of law"? We will return to these issues periodically throughout this Chapter. In addition, you may also want to consult the materials in Chapter 12 that address the factors that are shaping the business of legal practice in various parts of the profession. The complete findings of Shapiro's important study are contained in Susan P. Shapiro, *Tangled Loyalties: Conflict of Interest in Legal Practice* (2002). For a general account of the difference between the manner in which legal scholars and social scientists define "hard" cases, see *Everyday Practices and Trouble Cases* (Austin Sarat, et al., eds. 1998). For a comparison between the way that U.S. lawyers and their counterparts in UK law firms handle potential conflicts, see Nancy J. Moore, "Regulating Law Firm

Conflicts in the 21st Century: Implications of the Globalization of Legal Services and the Growth of the 'Mega Firm,'" 18 Geo. J. Legal Ethics 521 (2005) (reporting that U.S. and UK lawyers have substantially identical conflicts rules but that U.S. lawyers are more willing to comply with these restrictions even when adherence is contrary to their business interests, whereas English lawyers are more willing to bypass rules they consider obsolete or counterproductive). We will return to the complex implications of globalization for legal ethics in Chapter 12. We also need to keep in mind the possibility that increasing emphasis on conflict of interest problems since Ms. Shapiro's study may well be changing the results that she found in the direction of more compliance with the ever-increasing body of conflict of interest law. For a study asserting that lawyers' (and others') cognitive biases and heuristics render spotting and assessing one's own conflicts difficult (although not impossible), see Tigran W. Eldred, "The Psychology of Conflicts of Interest," 58 Kan. L. Rev. 43, 47–72 (2009).

Finally, a useful and constantly updated compendium of the developments in conflict of interest law is contained in Freivogel on Conflicts, <www.freivogelonconflicts.com>.

A. Who is My Lawyer?

A constant concern for lawyers is the question "who or what is my client in this matter?" An analogous question for clients is "who is my lawyer in this matter?" The problem arises both in the context of solo or small firm lawyers practicing together with other lawyers in some loose association and in the context of "megafirms" trying to arrange their affairs in such a way as to lessen conflict of interest problems. The following materials illustrate the problem.

In re Certain Laser Abraded Denim Garments
Inv. No. 337-TA-930, ITC Lexis 359
United States International Trade Commission (2015)

On March 11, 2015, Respondent The Gap, Inc. ("Gap") filed a motion seeking to disqualify Dentons US LLP ("Dentons US") as counsel for Complainants. Gap says that Dentons US cannot continue to pursue a complaint against Gap at the ITC because it is a "portal" of the Swiss verein Dentons ("Dentons"), which represents Gap on fourteen open matters elsewhere. According to Gap, for more than two decades, Dentons and its predecessor firm have represented Gap in multiple matters around the world, including a recent engagement involving a Canadian Border Services Agency customs audit. Gap explains that not only does Dentons US have an ethical conflict, but Dentons' relationship with Gap means that Dentons has had ongoing and unfettered access to Gap's confidential and privileged information relevant to the claims and defenses in this Investigation, including Gap's "U.S. importation, exportation, financial, and taxation structure, records, and information" and accused products. Thus, Gap says, any continued representation of Complainants by a Dentons "portal" prejudices Gap's ability to defend against Complainants' claims and to negotiate a settlement.

Gap further points out that Dentons did not inform Gap of the conflict prior to filing suit on behalf of Complainants in the Northern District of Ohio or at the ITC. Instead, it was Gap who discovered the conflict at the end of January, 2015. In addition, Gap says that Dentons never sought to obtain a conflict waiver from Gap. Gap argues that under Dentons' contract with Gap, California law should be applied to this situation and that "California law mandates Dentons' automatic disqualification from this proceeding." Even if California law does not apply, the Gap alternatively argues that the ABA Model Rules of Professional Conduct, which Gap says the ITC has adopted, still require disqualification. Gap says that it engaged in several weeks of negotiation with Dentons in an unsuccessful attempt to get Dentons US to withdraw as counsel. . . .

. . . Commission Investigative Staff . . . relies on Commission precedent and the ABA Model Rules to argue that Gap has demonstrated that Dentons' representation of Complainants presents "a serious risk of taint to this investigation." Staff also argues that Dentons Canada and Dentons US are both part of the Dentons' verein structure, which Staff says is an "association" within the meaning of the Model Rules. Staff concludes that unless there effectively was a pre-existing ethical screen, "the potential prejudice to Gap outweighs the prejudice to Complainants in not having their choice of counsel."

On March 30, Complainants opposed the motion, arguing that Dentons US is separate from Dentons Canada LLP ("Dentons Canada"). As evidence of this separation, Complainants say that Dentons' US and Canada "Legal Practices"

- do not have access to each other's client files;

- do not share client confidential information unless acting "as co-counsel";

- do not share profits and losses; and

- are financially and operationally separate.

As a result, Complainants argue, Dentons US is not counsel for Gap and does not have an ethical conflict. Furthermore, Complainants say that all of the Dentons US attorneys and paralegals who have worked for Complainants confirmed that they have not "accessed any files, or received any documents or information from any lawyer, at Dentons Canada LLP or Dentons Europe LLP relating to Gap." Thus, Complainants say that there is effectively an ethical screen in place between Dentons US and Dentons Canada and that Gap cannot be prejudiced. In contrast, Complainants argue, they will be greatly prejudiced if Dentons is disqualified and the public interest will be affected.

In addition to their separate entity arguments, Complainants argue that the Dentons Canada retainer agreement that Gap signed contains a provision waiving potential future conflicts. Thus, they reason, if there had been a conflict, Gap consented in advance. Complainants also say that they would be prejudiced if they were deprived of counsel mid-way through the Investigation. According to Complainants, Gap only identified the conflict after it was "unsuccessful in obtaining a settlement[,]" "unable to meaningfully contradict [Complainants'] allegations of infringement," and had "acknowledged that it had failed to properly identify suppliers of the infringing accused products." . . .

. . . Gap says the Funding Agreement between Longford Capital Fund I, LP and RevoLaze and its attachments (collectively, the "Funding Agreement") demonstrate that Dentons US disclosed to Complainants (at least as of February 2014) that it has a current conflict with Gap, as well as with Respondents Guess and Diesel. Second, Gap says that Dentons has a partial contingency fee arrangement giving it a heightened interest in the outcome of the Investigation, which Gap says increases the need to disqualify Dentons because Dentons "stands to directly benefit from its own unethical conduct." In addition, Gap questions the probity of Complainants' opposition in light of the specific admission made by Dentons US in the Funding Agreement. Gap also questions why Dentons disclosed the conflict to Complainants but not to Gap. With respect to Complainants' arguments regarding the separation between Dentons US and Dentons Canada, Gap responds that there are deficiencies and inconsistencies in the number and substance of the declarations provided by Dentons. Finally, Gap argues that Complainants' argument regarding prejudice is belied by their awareness and waiver of the conflict prior to bringing their Complaint to the ITC.

On April 8, 2015, Complainants sought an extension of time to respond to Gap's reply motion. The undersigned granted this request.

On April 17, 2015, Complainants' opposed Gap's motion for leave to file a reply, arguing that Gap did not raise new matters for consideration and that "Gap's motion for leave to file a reply is nothing more than a strategic maneuver to get the last word in." Complainants also say that "Gap's proposed reply identifies no specific prejudice, or even any prejudice at all." Complainants also dispute Gap's criticism of the declarations their counsel submitted and dispute the issue regarding disclosure of suppliers. With respect to the disclosure of the conflict in the Funding Agreement, Complainants say that counsel later "received confirmation that no legal conflict existed."

Based on a review of the motion papers and responses thereto, the undersigned finds as follows.

The authority to disqualify counsel derives from presiding officers' inherent power to control their proceedings. Certain Network Interface Cards, etc., Inv. No. 337-TA-455, Order No. 26 at 3 (U.S.I.T.C., August 2, 2001) (reviewed and aff'd) ("Network Interface") (citing 5 U.S.C. § 556(c)(5) and (7); 19 C.F.R. § 201.15(a)). However, this authority has rarely been exercised, as disqualification of counsel is drastic and disfavored. Certain Baseband Processor Chips and Chipsets, etc., Inv. No. 337-TA-543, Order No. 29 at 19 (U.S.I.T.C., March 9, 2006) ("Baseband").

The American Bar Association's Model Rules of Professional Conduct provide guidance in resolving motions to disqualify counsel, as reflected in Commission precedent.

Network Interface, Order No. 26 at 4; Baseband, at 20; Certain Ground Fault Circuit Interrupters, etc., Inv. No. 337-TA-615, Order No. 17 at 4 (U.S.I.T.C., February 29, 2008). The current Model Rules, which "reflect a national consensus," are instructive here:

Client-Lawyer Relationship, Rule 1.0 Terminology

(c) "Firm" or "law firm" denotes a lawyer or lawyers in a law partnership, professional corporation, sole proprietorship or other association authorized to practice law; or lawyers employed in a legal services organization or the legal department of a corporation or other organization. . . .

(e) "Informed consent" denotes the agreement by a person to a proposed course of conduct after the lawyer has communicated "adequate information and explanation about the material risks of and reasonably available alternatives to the proposed course of conduct."

Client-Lawyer Relationship, Rule 1.7 Conflict Of Interest: Current Clients

(a) Except as provided in paragraph (b), a lawyer shall not represent a client if the representation involves a concurrent conflict of interest. A concurrent conflict of interest exists if:

> (1) the representation of one client will be directly adverse to another client; . . .

(b) Notwithstanding the existence of a concurrent conflict of interest under paragraph (a), a lawyer may represent a client if:

> (1) the lawyer reasonably believes that the lawyer will be able to provide competent and diligent representation to each affected client;

> (2) the representation is not prohibited by law;

> (3) the representation does not involve the assertion of a claim by one client against another client represented by the lawyer in the same litigation or other proceeding before a tribunal; and

> (4) each affected client gives informed consent, confirmed in writing.

Model Rules 1.0(c), (e), 1.7 (2013).

In addition, there are other considerations, as "[a] violation of the ethical rules does not result in per se disqualification of the attorney involved. Rather, the crucial issue is whether continued representation will cause prejudice to or adversely impact the rights of another party in the matter and whether such prejudice outweighs the prejudice caused by disqualification of another party's choice of counsel. Thus to warrant the severe sanction of disqualification, there must be a showing that the unethical conduct has somehow 'tainted' the investigation." Certain Unified Communications Systems, etc. No. 337-TA-598, Order No. 14 at 9–10 (U.S.I.T.C., September 25, 2007) ("Unified Communics").

Factors considered in making such a determination include the nature of the ethical violation, the prejudice to the parties, the effectiveness of counsel in light of the violation, the public's perception of the profession, and whether a disqualification motion was used as a means of harassment. . . .

The first issue presented here is whether the Swiss verein "Dentons" is a "firm" or "law firm" as defined by the Model Rules. Staff argues that it is. Complainants argue that Dentons US is sufficiently separate from the other Dentons Legal Practices that its representation of Complainants is tantamount to representation by a separately named law firm. Gap argues that the Swiss verein Dentons is "an incorporated membership association" that does not have an equivalent form in the United States, but should be treated as an association. . . .

Gap also argues that in one of the few instances where a U.S. court has looked at the issue of conflicts with respect to a Swiss verein law firm, the court found that it would not be possible for a law firm that "holds itself out to the world as one firm" to represent, via its two component entities, both a debtor and creditor "without violating ethical standards" (quoting Project Orange, [431 B.R. 363, at 371, n.3 (Bankr. S.D.N.Y. 2010].) Gap says that like the law firm in Project Orange, Dentons holds itself out as a single law firm with a "seamless delivery of services[.]") Thus, Gap argues, all of Dentons' worldwide Legal Practices owe it an undivided duty of loyalty. Gap says that Dentons has breached that duty by taking on representation adverse to Gap, and that this is true "under the rules of professional conduct of any jurisdiction."

The parties dispute the significance of the Dentons US retainer agreement attached to the Funding Agreement, which identifies Gap as a conflict. The undersigned cannot fully credit Mr. Hogge's representations that he only intended to identify Gap "as a potential business conflict" for two reasons. First, Dentons US specifically identified the conflict with Gap in its retainer agreement with Complainant RevoLaze as an "existing conflict." It is textbook contract law that the words in the final written agreement trump Mr. Hogge's subjective intent. The identification of Gap as an existing conflict serves as an admission that Dentons US did not, at the time when it took on representation of Complainants and entered into the Funding Agreement, believe that it was sufficiently separate from the other Legal Practices to be able to represent Complainants against Gap. Second, Complainants' opposition papers show a lack of understanding of the nuances of the ABA Model Rules between current and former clients and when ethical screens may be implemented. This unfamiliarity with the rules undermines the persuasiveness of Mr. Hogge's later determination that Dentons US could proceed without conflict.

The undersigned finds that the definitions of "firm" or "law firm" are broad enough to include a Swiss verein structure. Model Rule 1.0. Dentons holds itself out to the public as a single law finn, but says that it is divided into "Legal Practices." Either way, the verein is an "other association authorized to practice law" or is made up of lawyers "employed in a legal services organization or the legal department of a corporation or other organization." Model Rule 1.0(c); id., Comment 2. The undersigned finds that the ABA guidance here is particularly instructive, as it says that a factual scenario involving a direct conflict may be weighed differently than lesser situations:

Whether two or more lawyers constitute a firm within paragraph (c) can depend on the specific facts. For example, two practitioners who share office space and occasionally consult or assist each other ordinarily would not be regarded as constituting a firm. However, if they present themselves to the public in a way that suggests that they are a firm or conduct themselves as a firm, they should be regarded as a firm for purposes of the Rules. The terms of any formal agreement between associated lawyers are relevant in determining whether they are a firm, as is the fact that they have mutual access to information concerning the clients they serve. Furthermore, it is relevant in doubtful cases to consider the underlying purpose of the Rule that is involved. A group of lawyers could be regarded as a firm for purposes of the Rule that the same lawyer should not represent opposing parties in litigation, while it might not be so regarded for purposes of the Rule that information acquired by one lawyer is attributed to another.

Thus, in the event of a direct conflict such as the one presented here, the ABA would rather regard a group of lawyers as a firm — even if the case is "doubtful." (Id.) The undersigned concludes that the Swiss verein Dentons is a "firm" or "law firm" within the meaning of Model Rule 1.0(c).

Because this definition is met, the two Model Rules regarding conflicts with a current client and imputed conflicts among members of a firm apply here, since no party denies that, at a minimum, Dentons Canada has been representing Gap while Dentons US has been concurrently representing Complainants. See Model Rules 1.7, 1.10. Dentons Canada's representation of Gap is imputed to Dentons US. Model Rule 1.10. Dentons US is therefore banned under the Model Rules from helping Complainants bring claims against Gap in this Investigation. Although the Model Rules permit such representation if the law firm obtains informed consent from both clients, Dentons US did not do so here. Indeed, Dentons US asserts that it does not rely on an advance waiver for establishing that a conflict does not exist. Thus, it is the undersigned's determination that Dentons US has committed an ethical violation in the form of a concurrent conflict of interest.

The second issue presented here is whether ethical violation discussed above has tainted the Investigation. The undersigned has considered the factors set forth in Network Interface Cards and concludes, for the reasons discussed below, that disqualification is warranted. The first factor — the nature of the ethical violation — weighs in favor of disqualification. Dentons owes Gap a duty of loyalty, yet it stands to benefit both in terms of legal fees and a share in certain proceeds by representing other clients who are seeking to bar Gap's imports into the U.S. Additionally, although Dentons apparently realized that there was a conflict, it did not attempt to obtain Gap's informed consent. This inaction shows disregard for the rules of professional conduct.

The undersigned must also consider potential remedies in assessing whether the nature of the conflict weighs in favor of disqualification. Complainants cite cases in which the Commission denied motions for disqualification and instead recommended that an ethical screen be put in place to safeguard against improper disclosure of client information. Notably, these cases all involved prior representations of clients—not current ones. Ethical walls, pre-existing or otherwise, are not considered by the ABA to be a viable remedy in this situation. The Model Rules do not provide for the implementation of an ethical wall unless the situation involves a prohibition based on a disqualified lawyer's association with a prior firm. Model Rule 1.10(2). Thus, even if the undersigned were to recommend that an ethical screen be put in place, Dentons would still be in violation of its ethical rules. Moreover, the ABA commentary repeatedly states that a law firm should withdraw from representation in the event of a direct conflict. See, e.g., Model Rule 1.7, Comment 4.

Next, the undersigned must consider prejudice to both Complainants and Gap. In its briefing, Gap submits that its confidential and attorney-client information are at risk and that Dentons is violating the most basic duties it owes to Gap. Dentons has submitted that its attorneys in this Investigation have not had access to any of Gap's confidential or privileged information. Because there has not been a disclosure of information, the undersigned finds that the prejudice to Gap weighs against disqualification.

The undersigned further finds that the prejudice to Complainants also weighs against disqualification. It is important that parties be able to choose and maintain counsel. Additionally, as Complainants note, they have been working with Dentons US for more than 15 months. During this time, Dentons US "has acquired knowledge about [Complainants'] business, intellectual property, and [litigation] strategies" and has "developed expertise regarding the factual and legal issues present in the current investigation." Complainants also assert that retaining new counsel would impose "significant and unnecessary costs." Accordingly, the prejudice to Dentons at this point in the Investigation would be severe. This prejudice, however, is somewhat mitigated by the fact that the ethical conflict was disclosed to Complainant RevoLaze, who nevertheless proceeded against Gap as a named Respondent.

The next factor, the public's perception of the profession is also significant. Dentons holds itself out to the public as a unified global law firm in order to attract business and Dentons' continued representation in the face of a direct conflict would both contradict this public image and impact negatively on the law profession as a whole. With respect to the last factor, the undersigned finds that the consideration of whether a disqualification motion was used as a means of harassment weighs in favor of Complainants but does not overcome the other factors. There is an undeniable tactical advantage to a respondent in disqualifying lead counsel. However, as with the issue of prejudice, Complainants were fully informed of and assumed this risk when they named Gap as a respondent. Although the undersigned concludes that several of the factors weigh against disqualification, this drastic remedy is appropriate in this case. The undersigned cannot condone the continued violation of an ethical rule and therefore disqualification is necessary. The undersigned concludes, under the circumstances presented here, that Dentons US may not continue to represent Complainants while Gap is a respondent in this Investigation.

Accordingly, Gap's motion to disqualify Dentons as counsel for Complainants is granted. . . .

Notes

1. The ITC eventually vacated the judge's disqualification order as moot. All relevant parties, including movant The Gap, were no longer part of the proceedings. The court also concluded that the current record was insufficient to support Dentons's disqualification. Most notably, the ITC did not have before it the relevant agreements governing Dentons's verein structure, including the treatment of confidential information among the firms belonging to the verein. Although the ITC could have ordered more proceedings to discover the relevant agreements and the actual interactions between the firms, the ITC concluded, in short, that such an exploration would be a waste of its resources, particularly given that The Gap was no longer involved. Because it ultimately did not address the merits, the ITC left very much alive the issue of whether vereins—and similarly structured mega-firms—should be treated as one firm for imputation purposes. (In addition, the issue is still very much alive for the parties because RevoLaze, Dentons's former client, has now sued Dentons in state court in Ohio for breach of fiduciary duty based in part on the imputed conflict with The Gap.)

2. What are the implications of this case for the way in which Dentons practices law? Is it possible to adjust Dentons's verein organization and avoid the conflict of interest problems revealed by the Gap litigation and at the same time retain the advantages of the worldwide service it advertises? Is Dentons any better (or any worse) off than the multibranch worldwide law firm that seeks to protect itself with advance waivers? See generally Model Rule 1.7 cmt. 22 (discussing consent to future conflicts of interest). Dentons argued that the member firms shared neither confidences nor profits. If they also do not share individual members' expertise, what is the basis for holding themselves out as a major international law firm? See Dentons US LLP v. Republic of Guinea, 208 F. Supp. 3d 330 (DDC 2016), for further discussion of the relationship between the Swiss verein and its individual components.

3. At the other end of the size scale, consider the loose association of solo practitioners who seek to obtain the advantages of partnership status without actually being partners. In a malpractice action seeking to hold three lawyers liable for the malpractice of a fourth lawyer who shared their offices but was not in a partnership with them, the court reversed a summary judgment for the three lawyers on the basis of the following facts presented by the plaintiff Gosselin:

> First, O'Dea told the Gosselins he was "with" Field, Hurley. While the term "with" may be ambiguous as the district court found, when viewed in the light most favorable to the Gosselins, it, along with the other evidence of "holding out" may convey to a reasonable factfinder that O'Dea shared equal standing with the other attorneys who make up the "firm" Field, Hurley. Second, there is the lobby directory: "Field, Hurley, Webb, Sullivan Attorneys at Law" with O'Dea's name listed under the individual Appellees' names. Such a listing

implies a "partnership-like arrangement." . . . The directory listing utilized by Appellees contains no disclaimer of partnership, nor does it include any limiting description of O'Dea's actual relationship to the other "Attorneys at Law" listed. Third, O'Dea arranged to meet with Gosselin at the Field, Hurley offices and arranged for the Gosselins to go there to sign bankruptcy papers at a time when he would not be there, all of which may be taken to imply that he had the authority to use the Field, Hurley offices as an equal member of the "firm." Fourth, on at least one occasion, Gosselin called Field, Hurley and spoke with Sullivan, and on several other occasions, Gosselin called Field, Hurley and spoke with a secretary there "[t]o find out what was going on as far as back wages and ADA [Americans With Disabilities Act] claim (sic) and also bankruptcy." Fifth, in January 1993, Sullivan agreed to assist with the execution of the Gosselins' bankruptcy petition and accommodated O'Dea's request that the Gosselins come to the Field, Hurley offices to sign papers. Sullivan later met with Mrs. Gosselin and advised her regarding the bankruptcy filing, and acknowledged that he knew that O'Dea was working on Mr. Gosselin's claims for back wages and damages under the ADA.

Gosselin v. Webb, Sullivan, Hurley and Field, 242 F.3d 412 (1st Cir. 2001).

Analogously, many lawyers are "of counsel" to one or more firms. Generally, such lawyers are considered to be associated with the firm and conflicts of interest are therefore imputed from the firm to the lawyer and from the lawyer to the firm. See, e.g., Ariz. Ethics Op. 16-01 (2016). But not always. See Hempstead v. Valley Stream, discussed at p. 215, Note 9.

B. Simultaneous Representation — Opposing a Current Client

Some people used to complain that the profession's ethics rules were tools of oppression imposed by the bar's elite on their less fortunate colleagues. Whether that complaint was ever accurate, one does not hear it as much today. Compliance is a large issue across the entire spectrum of the profession. The case that follows is intended as an object lesson in how a lax attitude toward compliance with obligations that ought to have been seen as clear led to a well-publicized finding that two lawyers in a prominent firm had committed malpractice.

Murphy & Demory, Ltd., et al.
v.
Admiral Daniel J. Murphy
(Chancery Number 128219, Virginia 1994)

. . . Murphy & Demory alleges a cause of action against the Defendants Pillsbury, Madison & Sutro, [Partner] Deanne Siemer and [Senior Associate] Keith

Mendelson for malpractice. . . . I've considered and carefully reviewed the Rules of Professional Conduct of the District of Columbia . . . as well as the testimony of the Plaintiff's expert witness, Mr. David Epstein.

I find Murphy & Demory has proven by a preponderance of the evidence that the Pillsbury Defendants have committed legal malpractice by violating the standard of care for attorneys practicing in the District of Columbia, by accepting representation of Admiral Murphy in his efforts either to take control of Murphy & Demory or to form, prior to his resignation from Murphy & Demory, a new corporation to compete with Murphy & Demory, and the exercise of their professional judgment on behalf of the corporation would likely be adversely affected by simultaneously representing Admiral Murphy in matters adverse to their client, Murphy & Demory, without disclosing to the corporation or to Admiral Murphy the fact of the dual representation in obtaining the corporation's consent of such representation; by meeting with the director of the corporation, Margot Bester, for the purpose of enlisting her support in Admiral Murphy's plans to take over control of the corporation; by inducing or attempting to induce employees of Murphy & Demory to resign from Murphy & Demory and to join Murphy & Associates and by assisting Murphy & Demory employees in drafting their letters of resignation from the company; by generally assisting Admiral Murphy in his plans to either take control of Murphy & Demory or to divert business from Murphy & Demory in favor of his new competing company, Murphy & Associates while at the same time representing Murphy & Demory without the corporation's consent to the dual representation after full disclosure of all materials facts by drafting the restructuring or takeover proposal for Admiral Murphy; by drafting letters for Murphy & Demory clients to send, terminating their relationship with Murphy & Demory and directing that their files be transferred to Murphy & Associates; by assisting Admiral Murphy while still counsel to Murphy & Demory in preparing his remarks to be delivered to the Murphy Demory employees on August 10, 1992 in which, among other things, Admiral Murphy in effect invited employees to join him in his new company if the board of Murphy & Demory did not accede to his demands for control of the corporation; by calling and/or attending meetings with Mr. Demory and other Murphy & Demory employees in the Pillsbury Defendants' capacity as the corporation's counsel; in using confidential information obtained at such meetings for the benefit of Admiral Murphy; by failing to disclose to Murphy & Demory material information known to the Pillsbury Defendants that might affect how the board of directors of Murphy & Demory might act; by filing on behalf of Murphy & Demory a lawsuit seeking judicial dissolution of their by-then former client, Murphy & Demory, based in part on the confidential information obtained from Murphy & Demory employees during the course of their representation of Murphy & Demory.

The Pillsbury Defendants ignored the warnings of junior associates at the law firm that the dual representation of Admiral Murphy was rife with conflicts of interest and the matters on which they were advising the Admiral entailed possible breaches of fiduciary duty and use of corporate opportunities. I was struck and disturbed by the fact that every inquiry by an associate into the propriety of the firm's actions was referred back to Ms. Siemer for resolution. Clearly, Pillsbury, Madison & Sutro's internal mechanisms for resolution of ethical issues are seriously deficient. The partner in charge of the client relationship affected by the issues, who is least likely to be objective, is the ultimate arbiter of whether the firm has a conflict of interest. I found Ms. Siemer's testimony to lack credibility when she stated that she wrestled with the ethical issues posed by the joint representation of Murphy & Demory and Admiral Murphy and concluded that there was no conflict because both clients had an identical interest—ensuring that Admiral Murphy had the best information possible as to what his options were, even if one option was to divert business from Murphy & Demory and let the company wither. As Mr. Epstein aptly noted in his expert testimony, Murphy & Demory had no interest in Admiral Murphy's knowledge of how to undermine the company. I find that Ms. Siemer willfully ignored the District of Columbia Rules of Professional Conduct with which she was well familiar, having written a treatise on legal ethics. I find that Pillsbury, Madison & Sutro is equally responsible for Ms. Siemer's lapses in this regard, particular because in the face of warning bells from the associates, the firm allowed Ms. Siemer to be the final determiner of whether the firm had a conflict of interest.

Although I'm not unsympathetic to Mr. Mendelson's difficult position at the time of most of the activities complained of, I find that he too was equally responsible for the legal malpractice. Simply put, Mr. Mendelson was senior enough that he should have put a stop to the undisclosed dual representation of Admiral Murphy and Murphy & Demory by disclosing the conflict to Admiral Murphy and Murphy & Demory's board in obtaining their consent or, failing that, by withdrawing from the representation. . . .

In their briefs, counsel debated whether the Court should apply a "but for" standard of causation for Murphy & Demory's damages resulting from the Pillsbury Defendants' legal malpractice, or the more liberal standard suggested by the Second Circuit in the Milbank Tweed case. I find that I do not need to apply the Milbank Tweed standard in order to find Murphy & Demory was damaged as a direct and proximate result of the Pillsbury Defendants' legal malpractice. I find that the Plaintiffs have satisfied the stricter "but for" test. I find that but for the legal malpractice of the Pillsbury Defendants, Murphy & Demory's damages would not have been as severe as they ultimately proved to be.

For example, but for their dual representation of Murphy & Demory, the Pillsbury Defendants would not have had access to confidential information obtained from interviews with Mr. Demory and other Murphy & Demory employees that was later used for the benefit of Admiral Murphy. I find that as a direct and proximate result of the Pillsbury Defendants' legal malpractice, Murphy & Demory suffered compensatory damages in the amount of $500,000.

Accordingly, on count VI of the bill of the complaint, I will enter judgment in favor of Murphy & Demory against the Pillsbury Defendants, Pillsbury, Madison & Sutro,

Ms. Seimer and Mr. Mendelson, jointly and severally in the amount of $500,000, plus interest on that amount from May 2, 1994 at the judgment rate until paid. I do not award any punitive damages against the Pillsbury Defendants. . . .

Notes

1. It is instructive that the trial judge, although "sympathetic" to the difficulty of Mr. Mendelson's situation as a senior associate with consideration of partnership pending, nevertheless concluded that he was senior enough that he ought to have taken steps to resolve the conflict. He was therefore held equally responsible with Ms. Siemer for the malpractice committed by the firm. As a practical matter, once the chair of the firm's ethics committee indicated that he thought the firm's course of action was permissible and that the final decision was up to Ms. Siemer, what should Mr. Mendelson have done next? See Model Rule 5.2. The plaintiff's ethics expert testified that the question of professional duty was not "arguable" and that Ms. Siemer's resolution was not "reasonable." At the time of the trial Ms. Siemer was the president-elect of the National Institute of Trial Advocacy and the author of a text on legal ethics.

2. After the trial judge's order, the parties entered into a settlement agreement and there was therefore no appeal of the judge's findings and conclusions. Mr. Mendelson was made a partner at the Pillsbury firm the following year. Ms. Siemer, who had been General Counsel of the Defense Department prior to joining the Pillsbury firm, left the firm and opened a firm with her husband on Saipan in the Marianas Islands.

Wald 3. Another lawyer in a major law firm encountered even more serious consequences for a conflict of interest violation. John Gellene, a partner at Milbank, Tweed, Hadley & McCloy, a major New York law firm, was convicted and sentenced to prison for violation of federal criminal statutes for failure to make disclosures of various representations of conflicting interests in connection with a bankruptcy reorganization proceeding in Wisconsin (the Bucyrus matter). This was not a lawyer struggling to eke out a living. This was a partner in a big law firm who had earned $2,720,000 between 1992 and 1996. He threw away his professional life by telling lies in order to avoid his firm's disqualification and ended up going to jail. See United States v. Gellene, 182 F.2d 578, rehearing and rehearing en banc denied (7th Cir. 1999).

4. Why would a partner at a Wall Street law firm violate what seems to be a clear rule of disclosure? Is it simply that Gellene was an "unethical person"? He held himself out as a lawyer for almost a decade even though he had not formally been admitted to practice (although he had passed the bar exam), and he made other misstatements and omissions to various courts. Or could there be more to the story? Consider, for example, that in the 1980s a power struggle erupted within Milbank Tweed and other similar firms between older partners who worked for the firm's longstanding clients and who wanted to maintain traditional practices such as "lock-step compensation" (under which all partners of a certain age share equally in

the firm's profits), and younger partners who wanted the firm to move into more aggressive, entrepreneurial fields such as mergers and acquisitions and who demanded to be compensated on the basis of the revenue that they generated for the firm (often called an "eat-what-you-kill" compensation system). By the end of the decade, the "young turks" had seized control of Milbank. See generally Ellen Joan Pollock, *Turks and Brahmins: Upheaval at Milbank Tweed: Wall Street's Gentlemen Take Off Their Gloves* (1990). Shortly thereafter, Lawrence Lederman was lured away from Wachtell Lipton Rosen and Katz, one of the country's leading takeover firms, to run Milbank's small M&A department. Lederman hoped to make Milbank a "player" in the lucrative M&A market by combining his expertise in representing so-called "vulture funds" (which specialized in investing in struggling companies and then siphoning off their assets through leveraged buyouts and other risky strategies) with Milbank's reputation as a leading bankruptcy firm. It was in this capacity that he asked Gellene, then a young partner in the firm, to work with him on the Bucyrus matter. See Paul M. Barrett, "Inside a White Shoe Firm's Conflict Case," Wall St. Journal, Jan. 23, 1998.

5. How might these developments have affected Gellene's actions? To the extent that changes in Milbank's practice and culture may have contributed to Gellene's misconduct, should the firm bear any responsibility? Should Lederman? See Rule 5.1. Although the firm dismissed Gellene (while continuing to pay for his legal fees through the trial), no action was taken against Lederman, who was praised by his partners as being "absolutely ethical at every step." Barrett, supra (quoting Milbank's outside counsel). In the reverse situation in Murphy & Demory, the subordinate lawyer, Mendelson, was held liable for malpractice for failing to go over the head of Deanne Siemer, the partner in charge of the litigation, to take the appropriate "ethical" action.

6. Acting under new management, Bucyrus sued Milbank for the $1.9 million in fees that it had paid the firm and $100 million in other compensatory and punitive damages. Milbank settled the case by agreeing to repay the entire fee and to enter into arbitration to settle the remaining claims. Paul M. Barrett, "Milbank Agrees to Repay Ex-Client $1.9 Million in Fees to End Litigation," Wall St. Journal, Dec. 18, 1997.

7. The Gellene saga is the subject of a book-length study by Milton Regan called, appropriately, *Eat What You Kill* (2004). Professor Regan uses Gellene's fall to illuminate large professional issues that he believes help explain why Gellene did what he did—casting partners as players in an internal "tournament competition"; seeing the bankruptcy context as supplying a different set of norms of professional conduct; and suggesting the operation of a special moral universe for the teams with which Gellene worked. The explanatory strength of these professional forces as applied to the special case of Mr. Gellene has been strongly challenged. See Book Note, 118 Harv. L. Rev. 2422 (2005). For a discussion of the function of the courts in governing lawyers' professional conduct, see Green, "Conflicts of Interest in Litigation:

The Judicial Role," 65 Fordham L. Rev. 71 (1996) and Wilkins, "Who Should Regulate Lawyers?," 105 Harv. L. Rev. 799 (1992).

Problem 4–1 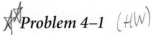 (HW)

Lawyer practices in a small town, which has three active practitioners. She is handling a title closing for Brenda Buyer when Mark Merchant, a regular client who owns a local store, requests Lawyer to take action, including suit if necessary, against Buyer, who has run up a $10,000 bill. Lawyer is currently handling two small matters for Merchant, and the other two lawyers in town are engaged on the opposite side of those matters. The nearest town in which there are other lawyers is 25 miles away, and Merchant states that to his knowledge they are not very good. What response does Lawyer make to Merchant's request for representation?

Problem 4–2

Laura Lund, a partner in Lee, Jackson, Blaine & Lund, is a specialist in oil and gas leases. Petroleum Co. comes to her to work out a complication that has arisen with one of its leases. While she is working on the matter, Oil Co. comes to her partner, Bob Blaine, who has always done its antitrust work, to start an antitrust action against Petroleum Co. The oil leases on which Lund is working have nothing to do with the antitrust action. The assistant to the firm's executive committee, which is responsible for keeping track of new matters, puts the fact of the representation of, and against, Petroleum on the committee's agenda. What course of action should it follow? In the future should Lund be told to tell clients who bring specialized one-shot matters to her that the firm reserves the right to take matters against their interests or even against them on behalf of regular firm clients?

Problem 4–3

Getty and Sinclair have been charged with housebreaking and grand larceny and wish you to represent them. They are partners in a gas station and long-time clients. Both insist that they are innocent, that at the time the crime was committed they were with another person, and that the case must be one of mistaken identity. Would you represent both? If you could obtain separate trials for Getty and Sinclair, what effect would that have on your decision? Is your ability to represent both a proper factor to consider in making a decision whether to seek separate trials? In what capacity would you participate in that decision? Suppose that after you have undertaken the representation, you discover that the prosecution has a modest amount of evidence linking Getty to the crime but very little linking Sinclair to it. Does that change the situation? What do you do?

Do you agree with the statement in Comment 23 to Rule 1.7 that "[t]he potential for conflict of interest in representing multiple defendants in a criminal case is so grave that ordinarily a lawyer should decline to represent more than one codefendant"? Suppose Getty and Sinclair were also brother and sister?

———————

The United States Supreme Court has dealt with the potential that joint representation may interfere with the constitutional guarantee of effective assistance of counsel. Although a trial court has a duty to inquire into possible conflicts of interest when questions are raised, the court has no affirmative duty to initiate an inquiry unless it knows or reasonably should know that a conflict exists. Holloway v. Arkansas, 435 U.S. 475 (1978). Furthermore, a defendant in a multiple representation case who raised no objection at trial "must establish that an actual conflict of interest adversely affected his lawyer's performance." Cuyler v. Sullivan, 446 U.S. 335, 350 (1980). But even if a defendant waives his right to conflict-free representation, a court may refuse to permit the defendant to substitute a co-defendant's counsel for his own. Wheat v. United States, 486 U.S. 153 (1988). But see Commonwealth v. Hodge, 386 Mass. 165 (1982), for a different conclusion from *Cuyler* under state law. If you decide that you should not continue to represent both defendants in Problem 4–3, and Sinclair says that he will get another lawyer, would you represent Getty? In that event, do you need Sinclair's consent to do so?

There have been an enormous number of cases and a great deal of writing on the subject of multiple representation of criminal defendants, especially as prosecutors faced with the difficulty of bargaining with several defendants who have the same lawyer have pushed for more restrictive conflict rules in this situation. See Geer, "Representation of Multiple Criminal Defendants," 62 Minn. L. Rev. 119 (1978); Forsgren, "The Outer Edge of the Envelope: Disqualification of White Collar Criminal Defense Attorneys under the Joint Defense Doctrine," 78 Minn. L. Rev. 1219 (1994); and Swisher, "Disqualifying Defense Counsel: The Curse of the Sixth Amendment," 45 St. Mary's J. on Legal Ethics and Malpractice 374 (2014) (pointing out that more restrictive conflicts rules occasionally work in criminal defendants' favor).

A recent case involving private counsel in which the court disqualified that counsel notwithstanding arguments based on both waiver and the Sixth Amendment was United States v. Bikundi, 80 F.Supp.3d 9 (D.D.C. 2015). Counsel was retained to represent a stepfather under indictment for Medicare fraud after having represented the stepson co-defendant and several related companies for ten weeks during the investigatory phase of the same Medicare fraud proceeding. Counsel had ceased the earlier representation and then undertook representation of the stepfather after his indictment in the same matter. The stepson, also indicted, was then represented by a public defender. The stepson "consented" to counsel's representation of his stepfather but would not waive attorney-client privilege with respect to use of confidential information he had supplied the attorney. The court concluded that given the incompleteness of the consent and the likelihood of serious conflict, the lawyer should be disqualified. Following the Supreme Court's decision in Wheat v. United States, 486 U.S. 153 (1988), appellate courts rarely reverse a trial court's decision to disqualify an arguably conflicted lawyer, notwithstanding the defendant's Sixth Amendment right to counsel of choice.

Problem 4–4

The legislature in your state has passed a statute permitting silent prayer in public school classrooms at the start of each school day. You discover that different branches of your law firm have filed declaratory judgment suits in different county courts, one attacking and another defending the constitutionality of the statute under the federal Constitution. May the firm handle both suits? Assume first that both sides consent and then that they do not. Would it make a difference if the two branches of the firm were located in Denver and Seattle but the Colorado and Washington statutes were identically worded? Is paragraph 24 of the Comment to Model Rule 1.7 sufficiently responsive to this issue? Would it make a difference if the issue on which the branches of the firm were on opposite sides involved an evidentiary matter in otherwise unrelated litigation, such as the reach of the attorney-client privilege to a low-level corporate employee?

Compare ABA Formal Opinion 93-377 (finding a prohibited conflict of interest in many issue conflict situations) with California Standing Committee on Professional Responsibility and Conduct Formal Opinion 1989-108 (advising that issue conflicts never involve a violation of conflict of interest rules). For more on positional conflicts, see John Dzienkowski, "Positional Conflicts of Interest," 71 Tex. L. Rev. 457 (1993) and Williams v. State, 805 A.2d 880 (Del. Sup. Ct. 2002).

1. The General Rule

At war in Problems 4–1 through 4–4 are the notion that effective representation means whole-hearted devotion to the interests of the client (which may not be possible if the interests of two clients are in actual or potential conflict) and the notion that in many situations of potential or even actual conflicts of interest independent representation of each party merely means added legal expense without commensurate benefit to the parties.

Conflict of interest has long been the most frequent professional problem faced by most lawyers. The disciplinary rules have been reformulated many times in the past century, and the Comments have sought to give increasingly specific advice in the most problematic situations. (Indeed, Model Rule 1.8 is a collection of, in essence, specific conflicts-of-interest–related prohibitions.) The current definition in Model Rule 1.7, which has been widely adopted, follows the conceptual framework of its predecessors. The same three conditions for multiple representation, even in the face of a conflict—disclosure, consent, and an objective standard—have been retained. Why shouldn't informed consent be sufficient? Aren't there some clients who are sophisticated enough that they should be able to assess the risks and consent even to severe conflicts? Or is there some public interest at stake that overrides client wishes? What is it? Are Comments 14–17 to Rule 1.7 helpful in this regard?

A major difficulty for lawyers attempting to sort through problems of representation of multiple parties is the abstract quality of the formal rules. The text of Model

Rule 1.7 is not much help in resolving difficult cases. The Comments give some insights but not in any connected way. If anything, they emphasize the essentially ad hoc nature of the resolution of each situation. The concerns of the rules are with the lawyer's obligation not to reveal or misuse confidential information and with the lawyer's obligation of independent judgment and loyalty to clients, looked at from the perspective of the clients' situations and of the needs of clients and the profession more generally. The Model Rules speak directly to confidentiality in Rule 1.6, but take independent judgment and loyalty rather for granted, perhaps assuming familiarity with the general principles of fiduciary duty owed by an agent to a principal. What we mean when we say that a lawyer owes a duty of loyalty to a client is at the core of our notion of what kind of adversary system we have (see Chapter 2 and especially Chapter 3). There is no obvious answer. The British system, from which ours is derived, has a very different view of the issue insofar as client representation is concerned. Resolving these differences over how client information is treated will be especially relevant for global firms like Dentons, with over 7000 lawyers and a special organizational setup (see pp. 186ff.), and Baker & McKenzie and DLA Piper, with 3500–4500 lawyers.

At all events, it is important in resolving questions of conflict of interest to keep in mind what interests are being served by the particular principles being advocated. It is not enough to invoke the biblical injunction from Matthew 6:24, as so many courts are fond of doing, that "No man can serve two masters." Of course a lawyer can serve two masters, i.e., two clients. They do it all the time. The question is to identify the problem with such representation in a particular case with specificity and to make an estimate of the likelihood and seriousness of harm to one or more of the relevant interests from the proposed concurrent representation.

For example, consider the situation when a lawyer (L) is asked to represent a client, C-2, in connection with a matter in which he is already representing C-1, and the proposed representation is adverse. Taking on C-2 would affect L's representation of C-1 in three ways. First, there is the potential that advancing C-2's interests would harm C-1's interests in the very matter in which L was hired by C-1. That would be disloyal. Second, there is the possibility that representing C-2 would cause L to diminish his efforts on behalf of C-1. That would also be disloyal, although one could characterize the action as a threat to L's competence. Third, there is the substantial possibility that confidential information of C-1 would be abused in the service of C-2. That would violate the specific aspect of the duty of loyalty that the professional rules deal with under the heading of confidentiality. However, let us change the example so that there are two completely unrelated matters. L represents only C-1 in matter one and only C-2 in matter two. C-1's interests in matter two, which are adverse to C-2, are represented by someone else. Then the analysis is different. Since the matters are different, there will probably not be any problem of abuse of confidential information. Likewise, there is no problem of disloyalty from harming C-1's interests in matter one. By definition, success for C-2 in matter two has nothing to do with matter one. Diminishment of L's efforts on behalf of C-1 in matter one by reason of being adverse to C-1 in matter two is still a possibility but somewhat less obvious than it was in the first example.

But there is another aspect to the loyalty problem here. L has put himself in a position where he can do real harm to C-1 in matter two. Indeed, if the matter is litigated, he may even personally subject C-1 to unpleasant cross-examination. The effect of such action, especially in litigation, is likely to disrupt the attorney-client relation between L and C-1 in matter one. Hence the action of L in taking on C-2 in matter two in such a case can be analyzed in terms of breach of duty of loyalty, both from the client-oriented perspective ("my lawyer is attacking me") and from the likely effect on the lawyer's independent professional judgment and zealousness on behalf of C-2.*

These examples and analyses of problems of representation of conflicting interests could be multiplied indefinitely. They are offered here as illustrations of the need to analyze each specific fact situation to understand why the prohibitions should or should not be applied in a particular case.

Aside from the duty of loyalty and the issue of confidential communications, courts also occasionally refer to one other factor in deciding conflict of interest questions, what the former Model Code referred to as "the appearance of impropriety." The expression was meant to evoke the potential erosion of confidence in the profession that might occur if its members were seen in situations that carried the potential for improper conduct even if there was no actual misconduct in the particular case. But the term was often used as a substitute for analysis and what was really meant was that a client had reasonable grounds to fear that the lawyer might misuse confidential information or act disloyally. The term was eliminated in the Model Rules, although state courts still employ it when analyzing whether to disqualify a lawyer or law firm on the basis of a conflict of interest (and although it is no longer used in lawyers' ethics codes, it is still used in judicial ethics codes). See Swisher, "The Practice and Theory of Lawyer Disqualification," 27 Geo. J. Legal Ethics 71 (2014). One place where the concept has real meaning is public employment, where courts sometimes use the notion of appearance of impropriety to reflect the importance of the public's impression of government lawyering. We shall examine such issues later.

There has been interaction between increasing interest in the subject of professional responsibility since the early 1970s and the discovery of tactical advantages to be gained by successful motions for disqualification of opposing counsel who are discovered to be involved in a forbidden conflict of interest. Indeed, there has been

---

* The analysis in the last two paragraphs owes a great deal to the work of Donald P. Board, Harvard Law School '83, then Prof. Kaufman's research assistant, as it appears in "Developments in the Law—Conflicts of Interest in the Legal Profession," 94 Harv. L. Rev. 1244, 1292–1303 (1981), of which section he was the principal author, and in "A Unified Analysis of Forbidden Representations" (unpublished manuscript on file in Harvard Law School Library). He will understand, albeit he may not agree with, our failure to accept all the categories he uses in his lengthy analysis.

unfavorable reaction in some courts to the increase in the number of disqualification motions because many are believed to be made for purposes of harassment or delay. The reaction has taken two forms. In the first place, although originally the majority of federal courts of appeals had permitted appeals from denials of motions to disqualify counsel, many reversed themselves and the Supreme Court finally ruled that courts of appeals had no jurisdiction to entertain appeals from such nonfinal orders. Mandamus is still available as a remedy, but only in exceptional circumstances. Firestone Tire & Rubber Co. v. Risjord, 449 U.S. 368 (1981).

Following *Firestone*, the Supreme Court held in Flanagan v. United States, 465 U.S. 259 (1984), and then in Richardson-Merrell, Inc. v. Koller, 472 U.S. 424 (1985), that orders disqualifying counsel in criminal and in civil cases are not immediately appealable. The Court did leave open the possibility of mandamus, certification of the question for interlocutory review under 28 U.S.C. § 1292(b), or even eventual reversal of the judgment on the merits in a particular case as methods of correcting erroneous disqualifications. It seems unlikely that the latter event will occur very often. One state court that does not permit an appeal from an order granting disqualification has suggested that the way around that rule is for the disqualified lawyer to submit to a contempt order for refusal to withdraw and then to appeal the contempt order. See Index Futures Group v. Street, 163 Ill. App. 3d 654 (1st Dist. 1987). Adoption of that suggestion, however, would cut the heart out of the "final judgment" rule and be very risky for the lawyer in contempt.

In addition, some state and federal courts began to clamp down on disqualification motions in other ways. Invoking a doctrine akin to "standing," some courts began to ask whether the party raising the issue was the party harmed or whether a prohibited conflict was likely to disadvantage a party in the proceeding before it. The courts did not reject the traditional notion that they had power, on their own motion, to raise questions of the violation of their own disciplinary rules and hence could act when a party brought the matter to their attention, but rather they asserted that a disciplinary matter ought to be handled as such by the regular disciplinary process unless the representation interfered with the trial itself. A leading case is Board of Education v. Nyquist, 590 F.2d 1241 (2d Cir. 1979). We need to remember that violation of the disciplinary rules on conflicts may not necessarily lead to disqualification in particular litigation. Some courts use language suggesting almost automatic disqualification, see *Stratagem*, infra p. 215, and Oxford Systems, Inc. v. Cellpro, Inc., 45 F. Supp. 2d 1055 (W.D. Wash. 1999), while others state strongly that violation of the rules and disqualification of an offending law firm are different inquiries. SWS Financial Fund A v. Salomon Brothers, Inc., 790 F. Supp. 1392 (N.D. Ill. 1992) (citing cases). When motions to disqualify for a conflict of interest first became frequent in the second half of the twentieth century, a finding of impermissible conflict usually led to disqualification of the offending law firm. The growing frequency of such motions, the suspicion that they were being used strategically, and the consequent effect on judicial resources led many courts to refuse to disqualify a lawyer even if the disciplinary rules were violated unless the conflict somehow "tainted" the trial.

See Carlyle Towers Condominium Ass'n v. Crossland Savings, FSB, 944 F. Supp. 341, 346 (D.N.J. 1996), citing cases illustrating the split with respect to automatic disqualification for violation of the conflict rules. The issue of the appropriate forum for dealing with prohibited regulations of conflicting interests should be considered in the context of the larger framework presented by the Wilkins article on who should regulate lawyers, cited at p. 199, Note 7.

There was also a reaction on the part of many lawyers who were disqualified against this use of the conflict of interest rules. Although an argument has been made that some of the conflict rules represent the profession's effort to make more work for lawyers and spread it around, see Morgan, "The Evolving Concept of Professional Responsibility," 90 Harv. L. Rev. 702, 727–728 (1977), lawyers individually do not like to lose clients and the spate of successful disqualification decisions in the 1970s produced a great deal of discontent throughout the profession, especially in large law firms and in small firms in small communities, both of which have substantial conflict of interest problems. The combination of those views of courts and firms may account for the language in the Scope of the Model Rules that "violation of a Rule does not necessarily warrant any other nondisciplinary remedy, such as disqualification of a lawyer in pending litigation," and "the purpose of the Rules can be subverted when they are invoked by opposing parties as procedural weapons."

There is, however, another side to the issue. The fact that many disqualification motions have been granted suggests that there is a problem of obedience to the disciplinary rules. In addition, these rules are the courts' own rules and they are as appropriate a body to enforce their own rules in the first instance as the regular disciplinary bodies. The disciplinary machinery is so uncertain in many states (see Chapter 10) that the threat of prompt disqualification is likely to be a more effective enforcement mechanism than a disciplinary sanction. Furthermore, courts rarely refer lawyers to the disciplinary authorities to investigate and prosecute alleged conflicts of interest, and anecdotal evidence suggests that lawyers in the past have rarely been disciplined for conflicts of interest (even if a court has found the conflict and disqualified the lawyer). Moreover, many conflict problems do not have obvious solutions and disqualification in such difficult cases will usually be a much more appropriate remedy than disciplinary punishment. If these arguments are sound, one can only hope that courts will not overreact to whatever abuses may have occurred by abdicating the field to the much slower, overworked, and perhaps inappropriate disciplinary process. See Swisher, "The Practice and Theory of Lawyer Disqualification," 27 Geo. J. Legal Ethics 71 (2014) for a thorough analysis of the phenomenon, its costs, and suggestions for improving the process of, and necessity for, disqualification.

2. Simultaneously Representing and Opposing a Client in Litigation

It remains now to consider some typical cases involving simultaneous representation of multiple clients. Most of them involve simultaneous representation in the litigation context. The following leading case, which resembles Problem 4–2, is a good example of how a conflict may arise in the ordinary course of a busy law firm's practice and how failure to pay enough attention to the problem when it arises may lead to difficulties. While the case was decided under the former Model Code, the result is typical under the Model Rules as well. It is a useful case for study because in a few pages it discusses a number of very important principles—what makes a client a "current" client; the application of the imputation principle to simultaneous representations in unrelated matters; and what constitutes consent to adverse representation. The case also illustrates the need to be wary in taking on a new client that one does not jeopardize the relationship with an old client.

International Business Machines Corp. v. Levin
579 F.2d 271 (3d Cir. 1978)

MARIS, Circuit Judge.

This petition for a writ of mandamus and these appeals and cross-appeals seek our review of an interlocutory order of the United States District Court for the District of New Jersey entered in this private antitrust suit directing Carpenter, Bennett & Morrissey (herein "CBM"), counsel for the plaintiffs, Howard S. Levin (herein "Levin") and Levin Computer Corporation (herein "LCC"), to withdraw from the case and allowing CBM to turn over its past work on the case to substitute counsel for the plaintiffs with consultation with such counsel to effect the turnover permitted for a period of sixty days.

The plaintiffs' lawsuit against the International Business Machines Corporation (herein "IBM"), alleging violations of sections 1 and 2 of the Sherman Act, 15 U.S.C.A. §§ 1 and 2, and of the laws of the State of New Jersey, was filed about ten months after Levin caused LCC to be incorporated under the laws of New Jersey for the purpose, stated in the complaint, of engaging in the business of purchasing for lease certain data processing equipment manufactured by IBM, known as the 370 series or IBM fourth generation computer equipment. When IBM refused to extend installment credit to Levin and LCC on other than terms which the latter considered to be unfair and unreasonable, this action was filed . . . .

[Motions and discovery occupied the period from 1973 to 1977, when the disqualification motion was filed.]

We turn then to outline the facts out of which this controversy arose. It appears that CBM had represented both Levin and the corporation with which he was then associated, Levin Townsend Computer Corporation (herein "LTC"), a computer leasing corporation, from 1965 to 1969. From 1966 to 1969 CBM performed considerable work for LTC including representing the corporation in several disputes with IBM in connection with IBM's installment sale to LTC of IBM computer equipment. In January 1970 when Levin terminated his association with LTC, CBM withdrew as attorneys for LTC but continued to represent Levin sporadically in matters unrelated to LTC. In the latter part of 1971 CBM resumed an active attorney-client relationship with Levin. At that time CBM arranged for the incorporation of LCC on behalf of Levin. One of the firm's partners, Stanley Weiss, became a director of LCC and another, David M. McCann, assumed the office of secretary of the corporation.

LCC's effort in late 1971 and 1972 to secure installment credit on terms acceptable to it for the purchase of IBM equipment was handled by McCann dealing with Joseph W. S. Davis, Jr., counsel for IBM's Data Processing Division located in White Plains, New York. As LCC's prospects for a satisfactory credit arrangement with IBM diminished with IBM's successive rejections of LCC's applications for installment credit, Levin's determination to take legal action against IBM grew. In February 1972 McCann advised Davis of the plaintiffs' intention to file suit to enjoin IBM from imposing more stringent credit requirements on LCC than were applied to prospective lessees of the equipment LCC desired to purchase. . . .

. . . On June 23, 1972, CBM filed the present suit on behalf of the plaintiffs and has prosecuted it until the present time.

In April 1970 a member of IBM's legal staff in the general counsel's office at Armonk, Robert Troup, contacted Edward F. Ryan, a CBM partner and one of five members of the firm specializing in labor matters, for the purpose of retaining CBM's services in the preparation of an opinion letter for IBM regarding a jurisdictional dispute with an electrical workers' union. The CBM partners considered and rejected the possibility that acceptance of the IBM assignment in the labor matter might create a conflict of interest in the light of CBM's former representation of LTC. Ryan prepared an opinion on the jurisdictional dispute question and accepted a second assignment from Troup in July 1970 dealing with a union's right to picket IBM in the event IBM canceled a subcontracting arrangement and a third assignment in May 1971 relating to the availability of injunctive relief against certain union picketing.

In April 1972 Ryan accepted Troup's telephoned request for another opinion letter in a labor matter concerning the right of temporary employees to form a separate bargaining unit. At this point Ryan's account of the facts diverges from that of Troup. Ryan's sworn statement is that his acceptance of IBM's fourth assignment caused him some concern since he was aware of CBM's current representation of LCC and LCC's difficulty in procuring credit from IBM. Consequently, a few days after Troup's call, Ryan consulted with McCann and Weiss about a possible conflict of interest in CBM's representation of both IBM and LCC simultaneously. Weiss informed Ryan of the contemplated antitrust suit against IBM and advised him to obtain IBM's consent to the firm's representation of both IBM and the plaintiffs. Ryan stated that shortly thereafter he called Troup at his Armonk office and in a conversation lasting about three minutes brought to Troup's attention the contemplated antitrust suit against IBM by CBM's client, Levin. Troup's response, according to Ryan's testimony, was that the matter was not significant from IBM's point of view and he directed Ryan to proceed with the assignment given him. Various members of the CBM firm testified to their understanding at the time that Ryan had obtained IBM's consent to the dual representation. Troup, however, by affidavit and deposition, denied ever having been informed by Ryan of the proposed Levin lawsuit or that CBM might represent another client in a suit against IBM. CBM obtained Levin's consent to CBM's representation of IBM in labor matters and the antitrust suit was filed by Weiss acting for the firm June 23, 1972, one week after the completion of CBM's fourth opinion letter for IBM.

Weiss testified, also, in connection with IBM's knowledge of CBM's possible conflict of interest involving IBM, that in July 1973 while he and Charles Danzig, a partner of Riker, Danzig, Scherer & Debevoise, IBM's counsel in the antitrust suit, rode together in a train from Philadelphia to Newark, Weiss mentioned that CBM performed occasional work for IBM in labor matters. Danzig denied that such a statement was made to him by Weiss.

It is undisputed that during CBM's prosecution of the antitrust suit, Ryan accepted four additional labor relations assignments from Troup without further discussing with Troup CBM's concurrent representation of Levin and LCC. . . .

Subsequently, at a law school alumni luncheon in New York City on January 28, 1977, John Lynch, a partner of CBM, met Richard McDonough, then a member of IBM's legal staff, and Lynch mentioned to McDonough his role in prosecuting the plaintiffs' antitrust suit against IBM. McDonough indicated surprise in that CBM was, to his knowledge, representing IBM in labor matters. In April 1977, at a dinner attended by McDonough and counsel for IBM in the antitrust suit, McDonough expressed to the latter an interest in knowing how CBM's conflict of interest had been reconciled to permit CBM's representation of Levin and LCC in the suit against IBM. McDonough's remarks caused IBM to investigate the matter further and led to the filing in June 1977 of the motion to disqualify CBM. . . .

We turn then to consider the order under review. . . .

CBM's principal contention . . . is that under a proper interpretation of the disciplinary rules . . . an attorney who has asserted a claim against a client pursuant to his representation of a second client may continue to represent the first client with respect to matters unrelated to the lawsuit without disclosing fully the facts of the dual representation to the client being sued and without obtaining his consent. [The court then quoted the wording of the ABA's then-recommended conflict of interest rule. While the current Model Rule wording is different, the principle set forth in Model Rule 1.7 is the same and a lawyer could make the same arguments about its applicability.]

CBM argues that [the Rule is] not applicable since no effect adverse to IBM resulted from CBM's concurrent representation of both IBM and the plaintiffs and no adverse effect on CBM's exercise of its independent professional judgment on behalf of IBM was likely to result from CBM's representation of these clients in two entirely unrelated areas. . . .

We think, however, that it is likely that some "adverse effect" on an attorney's exercise of his independent judgment on behalf of a client may result from the attorney's adversary posture toward the client in another legal matter. See Cinema 5, Ltd. v. Cinerama, Inc., 528 F.2d 1384, 1386–1387 (2d Cir. 1976); Grievance Committee of the Bar of Hartford County v. Rottner, 152 Conn. 59, 65 (1964) . . . . For example, a possible effect on the quality of the attorney's services on behalf of the client being sued may be a diminution in the vigor of his representation of the client in the other matter. See Cinema 5, Ltd. v. Cinerama, Inc., supra, at 1387. A serious effect on the attorney-client relationship may follow if the client discovers from a source other than the attorney that he is being sued in a different matter by the attorney. The fact that a deleterious result cannot be identified subsequently as having actually occurred does not refute the existence of a likelihood of its occurrence, depending upon the facts and circumstances, at the time the decision was made to represent the client without having obtained his consent. . . .

An attorney must be cautious in this area and, if he is to adhere to the high standards of professional responsibility, he must resolve all doubts in favor of full disclosure to a client of the facts of the attorney's concurrent representation of another client in a lawsuit against him. As the Second Circuit Court of Appeals has stated, "Putting it as mildly as we can, we think it would be questionable conduct for an attorney to participate in any lawsuit against his own client without the knowledge and consent of all concerned." Cinema 5, Ltd. v. Cinerama, Inc., at 1384, 1386 (1976). Indeed, in the present case the record indicates that the members of CBM themselves apparently took the same view of the applicability of the disciplinary rules to their situation both during the course of the dual representation and, it appears, in their arguments and admissions in the district court. . . .

The district court concluded that its rule . . . required that CBM obtain IBM's consent to the firm's representation of it after full disclosure of the facts of CBM's representation of the plaintiffs. In support of this conclusion the court made several findings. The court found as a fact that at all relevant times CBM had an ongoing attorney-client relationship with both IBM and the plaintiffs. This assessment of the relationship seems entirely reasonable to us. Although CBM had no specific assignment from IBM on hand on the day the antitrust complaint was filed and even though CBM performed services for IBM on a fee for service basis rather than pursuant to a retainer arrangement, the pattern of repeated retainers, both before and after the filing of the complaint, supports the finding of a continuous relationship.

The court also found that although the services required of CBM by IBM dealt consistently exclusively with labor matters, this was not the result of any special arrangement between them and that at any time IBM, unaware of CBM's participation in the plaintiffs' action, might have sought CBM's assistance in legal matters more closely related to the lawsuit. Thus, it was perhaps fortuitous that CBM, as the court found, never acquired any confidential information from IBM useful in the prosecution of the antitrust suit.

These findings, with which we agree, support the district court's conclusion, which seems to us reasonable and just, that CBM was obligated in these circumstances at the very least to disclose fully to IBM the facts of its representation of the plaintiffs and obtain its consent.

The district court determined that CBM did not meet its burden of proving that such a full disclosure was made and that consent by IBM to CBM's dual representation was obtained thereafter. CBM asserts that disclosure and consent were not necessary in that IBM had constructive knowledge of the pertinent facts since its labor lawyers knew of CBM's representation of IBM in that area and its lawyers handling the defense of IBM in the antitrust action knew of CBM's participation in that matter. This assertion is without merit. [The Rule] specifically imposes upon an attorney the burden of affirmatively providing disclosure and obtaining consent. Clearly, full and effective disclosure of all the relevant facts must be made and brought home to the prospective client. The facts required to be disclosed are peculiarly within the knowledge of the attorney bearing the burden of making the disclosure. To accept CBM's position would be to engraft an unwarranted exception on the requirement of [the Rule] that disclosure must be sufficient to enable the prospective client himself to make an informed decision as to whether in the circumstances counsel will be retained. . . .

CBM alternatively argues that IBM's consent was in fact obtained. . . .

The district court did not deem it necessary to resolve these issues of credibility between Ryan and Troup and between Weiss and Danzig since it determined that even accepting CBM's version of this disputed testimony a full and adequate disclosure as required by [the Rule] had not been made to IBM and that the IBM antitrust attorneys did not in fact know during the relevant period that CBM was representing IBM in labor matters. We conclude that the district court did not err in so determining and in concluding that since IBM's informed consent to the concurrent representation by CBM of it and the plaintiffs had not been obtained, CBM had violated [the relevant disciplinary Rule]. While we accept the district court's finding that the antitrust lawyers in IBM's legal department did not know that its labor lawyer in the same department was repeatedly retaining the services of CBM in labor matters, we cannot refrain from expressing our belief that such a situation could not have existed for over five years if the activities of the IBM legal department had been properly coordinated and controlled. . . .

CBM and the plaintiffs urge that even if CBM is held to have violated [the Rule], the district court's disqualification of CBM from the case is too harsh a sanction and penalizes the plaintiffs unnecessarily in view of the termination of CBM's relationship with IBM and the district court's finding that, in the course of its representation of IBM, CBM did not obtain any information which would aid it in the prosecution of the antitrust suit against IBM.

In considering this contention, we bear in mind the proposition that the plaintiffs do not have an absolute right to retain particular counsel. . . . The plaintiffs' interest in retaining counsel of its choice and the lack of prejudice to IBM resulting from CBM's violation of professional ethics are not the only factors to be considered in this disqualification proceeding. An attorney who fails to observe his obligation of undivided loyalty to his client injures his profession and demeans it in the eyes of the public. The maintenance of the integrity of the legal profession and its high standing in the community are important additional factors to be considered in determining the appropriate sanction for a Code violation. See Hull v. Celanese Corp., 513 F.2d 568, 572 (2d Cir. 1975). The maintenance of public confidence in the propriety of the conduct of those associated with the administration of justice is so important a consideration that we have held that a court may disqualify an attorney for failing to avoid even the appearance of impropriety. . . . Indeed, the courts have gone so far as to suggest that doubts as to the existence of an asserted conflict of interest should be resolved in favor of disqualification. . . . Mindful of these considerations, we cannot say that the district court erred in ordering the disqualification of CBM.

It is true that plaintiffs will be injured by the disqualification of CBM, their counsel for a number of years. Here the district court ameliorated the harsh effect upon the plaintiffs of its sanction against CBM by permitting the turnover to substitute counsel for the plaintiffs within sixty days of the past work product of CBM on the case. IBM contends that the allowance of a turnover of work product with consultation, particularly work product prepared after the filing of IBM's motion, was an abuse of discretion.

In support of its contention IBM cites First Wisconsin Mortgage Trust v. First Wisconsin Corp., 571 F.2d 390 (7th Cir. 1978), and Fund of Funds, Ltd. v. Arthur Andersen & Co., 567 F.2d 225 (2d Cir. 1977). To the extent that the Seventh Circuit Court of Appeals lays down a legal tenet in *First Wisconsin Mortgage Trust* against permitting the turnover of a disqualified attorney's work product, we disagree, but we note that the court in that case expressly limited its holding to the facts of the case. 571 F.2d 390, 399. . . .

As we have already indicated, disqualification in circumstances such as these where specific injury to the moving party has not been shown is primarily justified as a vindication of the integrity of the bar. We think the turnover provisions of the district court's order of disqualification are sufficient for that purpose and a proper exercise of the court's discretion. . . .

Notes

1. *Levin* arose under DR 5-105 of the former Model Code of Professional Conduct. But the major issues in *Levin* (Who is a current client? Is simultaneous representation of a second client against a first client on a completely unrelated matter "directly adverse" to the first client? Does a finding of adverseness depend on the acquisition of relevant confidential information? What constitutes a valid consent?) are still issues under the language of current Model Rule 1.7. While the language of former DR 5-105

and Model Rule 1.7 differ, the general purpose of the two rules to prevent simultaneous representation of conflicting interests is the same, and the twin conditions for overcoming the prohibition — informed client consent and meeting an objective test — are the same. Courts interpreting Model Rule 1.7 have continued to cite prior precedent like *Levin* as relevant.

For example, in Oxford Systems, Inc. v. Cellpro, Inc., 45 F. Supp. 2d 1055 (W.D. Wash. 1999), a law firm that had advised a client in patent infringement litigation against an alleged infringer of its client's license was disqualified from representing the lawyers for the alleged infringer in related securities fraud litigation even though at the moment the securities litigation began, the law firm was not doing any legal work for the client licensee. The court examined thirteen years of extensive work done by the law firm for the client licensee, including some within a year of the commencement of the securities fraud litigation. The client licensee was not a party to the securities fraud litigation, but it intervened in order to disqualify the law firm because it had a pecuniary interest in the outcome. The court concluded that the licensee had a reasonable belief that the firm was its lawyer at that time and that therefore the conflict was a concurrent conflict. In addition, the Court of Appeals for the Sixth Circuit reversed a summary judgment for a Canadian law firm that represented the City of Windsor, Ontario in opposing the building of a bridge between that city and Detroit at the same time it was representing the bridge builder in obtaining money for the construction. The suit was for damages for breach of contract, breach of fiduciary duty, and malpractice. The court held that there were jury issues as to consent and consentability to cure the conflict. Centra, Inc. v. Estrin, 538 F.3d 402 (2008).

2. The court in IBM v. Levin addressed both general loyalty and the specific confidentiality problems presented by CBM's representation of, and against, IBM. Under the former topic, it discussed the possible effect on the quality of the lawyer's services and also the effect on the lawyer-client relationship. It might also have mentioned the financial aspect of the representation — IBM's financial support of a firm that was suing it without consent. Note that the court viewed the case as one of simultaneous representation because CBM was representing IBM at the same time it was suing IBM, even though it ceased to represent IBM after the disqualification motion was filed. That was an issue in the next principal case.

3. As a simultaneous representation case, what are the disqualifying factors here? Lack of independent judgment in representing Levin because of representing IBM? How is that affected by Levin's consent? Lack of independent judgment in representing IBM in the labor matters because the firm is suing IBM in an antitrust matter? Is that likely? Or is it obvious that CBM could not adequately represent the interests of Levin and IBM in their respective matters? Or is it that in representing Levin against IBM without IBM's consent, the firm has impaired IBM's confidence in its ability to represent IBM zealously? Is that a reasonable reaction by IBM? Is our judgment on this issue clouded by the fact that the client is IBM? If the firm had sued Levin on behalf of IBM while it was representing Levin on another matter, would

we feel differently? Does this explain the need for a prophylactic rule because it is so difficult to measure both the effect on the independent professional judgment of the lawyer and the reasonableness of the client's perception? Indeed, does it matter at all whether the aggrieved client could possibly be harmed at all by the simultaneous representation? In State ex rel. S.G., 175 N.J. 132, 143 (2003), a lawyer for a defendant accused of firing a gun indiscriminately into a crowd and killing a man was disqualified from representing the shooter because the lawyer's partner was the lawyer of record on two unrelated drug cases for the man who was killed. The court, noting that the second client remained alive for two weeks while the lawyer represented the alleged shooter, rejected the contention that his subsequent death mooted the conflict issue. The New Jersey Supreme Court stated that the "pointedly direct and adverse position inherent in defending the accused killer is exactly the sort of conflict that the professional rules of conduct ought not and do not permit."

4. Should the court disqualify lawyers if the effect of that disqualification is detrimental to the client? Wouldn't a fine assessed against the lawyers target the wrongdoers more accurately? See Bruce A. Green, "Conflicts of Interest in Litigation: The Judicial Role," 65 Fordham L. Rev. 71, 85 (1996) (arguing for sanctions to be leveled personally at the lawyers in cases like *Levin*). If the lawyer is nevertheless disqualified, should the lawyer have to pay back (i.e., disgorge) to the client all of the fees earned in the conflicted representation? Some courts have so ordered, particularly for egregious conflicts of interest. See generally Eriks v. Denver, 824 P.2d 1207 (Wash. 1992); Restatement (Third) of the Law Governing Lawyers § 37 (2000). What should constitute an "egregious" conflict of interest?

5. Comment 6 to Model Rule 1.7 rejects the contention that simultaneous representation on a completely unrelated matter is not "directly adverse."

6. The trial court also found a pattern of continuous representation of IBM by CBM that made IBM a current client when the antitrust complaint was filed, even though CBM was not handling any matter for IBM at that precise moment. The court appears to be saying that that would be the case even if no matters had come to CBM from IBM after the antitrust complaint was filed. That decision of the Court not to rely on a mechanical rule of actual current representation is an important one for lawyers, for it adds an element of significant uncertainty to a firm's attempt to keep track of its "current" clients for purposes of the conflict of interest rules.

However, does the court really mean that if CBM had properly sought IBM's consent and been turned down, it could not have severed its connection with IBM at that time and, assuming it had no relevant confidential information, brought the suit by Levin against IBM? That would seem harsh in view of the fact that CBM was not handling any matter for IBM at that moment and was not in any sense its general outside counsel. Note that if CBM would have been permitted to represent Levin in that circumstance, the result of its failure to seek IBM's consent in the actual case was that CBM ended up representing neither party. See GATX/Airlog Co. v. Evergreen Int'l Airlines, Inc., 8 F. Supp. 2d 1182 (N.D. Cal. 1998), where under the unique

California Rules, a court disqualified a law firm for simultaneous adverse representation under far-reaching facts. The law firm was held to have had a conflict from the moment it began to defend a lawsuit on behalf of a defendant because it should have known that another client had the same claim against the defendant that the plaintiff was asserting in this case. The court relied on *Levin* to conclude that the other client was a "current" client at that time and that therefore the arguments being made on behalf of the defendant hurt its other client. This type of conflict will be discussed further in relation to issue conflicts.

7. The court's holding on what constitutes consent after full disclosure should also be noted. The court apparently holds that brief mention to the client's lawyers followed by a direction to continue representation is not enough. The Model Rules use the words "informed consent," as a condition to continued representation in a situation like *Levin*. "Informed consent" is defined in the Terminology section of the Model Rules to mean communication of "adequate information and explanation about the material risks of and reasonably available alternatives to the proposed course of conduct." Would CBM have fared better under that definition in its effort to prove consent of IBM to its representation of Levin?

Neither the district court nor the Court of Appeals wanted to touch the issue of credibility between Ryan and Troup. The Court of Appeals said it didn't matter. Did the court really mean that if Troup had written CBM a letter saying that in IBM's view the Levin matter was insignificant and CBM should continue its representation of IBM, it would still have disqualified CBM? If so, do you agree?

8. In allowing CBM to consult with, and to turn over its work product to, successor counsel, the court was impressed with the harsh consequences for plaintiff of a contrary ruling, especially since the case had progressed so far. The opinion in First Wisconsin Mortgage Trust v. First Wisconsin Corp., which it distinguished and with which it disagreed, was withdrawn after rehearing en banc, the court holding that denial of access to the work product was not warranted in the circumstances of that case. See 584 F.2d 201 (7th Cir. 1978). See Fund of Funds, Ltd. v. Arthur Andersen & Co., 567 F.2d 225 (2d Cir. 1977), for a case where the court refused to grant the even more severe sanction of dismissal of the complaint with prejudice or suppression of all information gathered by the disqualified firms.

9. The Third Circuit in *Levin* relied heavily on the prior opinion of the Second Circuit in Cinema 5, Ltd. v. Cinerama, Inc., 528 F.2d 1384 (2d Cir. 1976). That much-cited case reached the same result as IBM v. Levin in a case in which the firm in the position of CBM was really two firms in different cities linked by one common partner who had participated minimally in one of the lawsuits. Yet the court treated the firms as one for purposes of disqualification. In Ex parte Terminix International Co., 736 So. 2d 1092 (Ala. 1998) (modified on denial of petition for rehearing 1999), the Alabama Supreme Court, citing other cases, refused to expand the *Cinerama* holding to impute confidential information of a defendant to a plaintiff firm from its cocounsel in related litigation in which defendant was

not a party. The court held that an actual sharing of confidential information would have to be shown.

But a Second Circuit opinion suggests that *Cinerama* is at the outer limit of disqualification in an "of counsel" matter and perhaps even beyond it. In Hempstead Video, Inc. v. Valley Stream, 409 F.3d 127 (2d Cir. 2005), Judge Leval concluded that disqualification was not required when a lawyer who was representing a video store in an employment discrimination case became "of counsel" to a firm that was representing a town that was seeking to revoke the store's permit to operate. He emphasized that the lawyer was "of counsel" only with respect to a few matters and permitted rebuttal of the presumption that confidences had been shared even in this situation of concurrent representation. He also indicated that the result would be the same even if a formal screening mechanism was not in place so long as there was a "de facto separation that effectively protects against any sharing of confidential information." Id. at 138. One can easily see that this opinion may well be used to argue against disqualification in other situations where the connection between the lawyers handling adverse matters can be called attenuated. See Bussel, "No Conflict," 25 Geo. J. Legal Ethics 207 (2015) for a strongly worded argument that the prohibition in Rule 1.7 against concurrent representation in unrelated matters is a misguided use of the loyalty and fiduciary concepts in this age of very large law firms, especially because of the use of disqualification motions as strategic weapons.

10. For a case where different branches of a large law firm represented a client in a judicial forum, and opposed the same client on essentially the same subject matter in a legislative forum, see Westinghouse Elec. Corp. v. Kerr-McGee Corp., 580 F.2d 1311 (7th Cir. 1978). The court held that members of a trade association who, on request, transmitted information to Washington counsel for the association reasonably believed they did so in the context of a fiduciary relationship, even though no attorney-client relationship may have been formed. In that situation, it violated confidentiality and conflict of interest principles for counsel's Chicago office to represent a client suing these members with respect to the same matter on which the Washington office was representing the trade association. In framing a remedy, the court presented the client with the choice of either dismissing the law firm as counsel in the lawsuit or dismissing those defendants who had conveyed confidential data to the Washington office.

Stratagem Development Corp. v. Heron Int'l, N.V.
756 F. Supp. 789 (S.D.N.Y. 1991)

KRAM, District Judge.

Defendants in this case, involving claims of breach of a real estate joint venture agreement, have moved for disqualification of Epstein, Becker & Green ("Epstein

Becker" or the "Firm") as plaintiff's counsel, because of alleged dual representation. Epstein Becker has taken certain steps to withdraw as counsel in other legal matters in which it represented a subsidiary of the defendants in this case; but there remains a question about the effectiveness of the Firm's withdrawal as counsel in the other matters.

Epstein Becker represents plaintiff Stratagem Development Corporation in the instant action, involving an alleged breach of a joint venture agreement to develop certain properties . . . in midtown Manhattan known as "Heron Tower I" and "Heron Tower II," and the present dispute involves Heron Tower II. Plaintiff Stratagem's role in the venture was to acquire parcels of land for real estate development. The role of the defendants, Heron International N.V. and Heron Properties, Inc. (hereinafter "Heron entities") was to develop the sites for the joint benefits of the participants in the venture.

During the same time period, plaintiff's counsel, Epstein Becker, also represented a wholly-owned subsidiary of defendant Heron Properties. That representation is in the context of a labor lawsuit and a related labor arbitration involving the security guards at Heron Tower I, and is essentially unrelated to this action. The subsidiary is known as Fidelity Services Corporation ("FSC"), and the labor matters are referred to by the parties as the "*Bevona* matters." The *Bevona* lawsuit is currently on the suspense docket of the United States Court of Appeals for the Second Circuit pending settlement discussions; the related labor arbitration is in the discovery phase, with Epstein Becker, until recently, assisting in the union's audit of FSC's books and with document production.

On November 10, 1989, Jerrold F. Goldberg, a member of Epstein Becker, wrote to Kathleen Panciera, an officer of Heron, to review the status of the *Bevona* matters.

On June 27, 1990, Heron terminated the agreement between it and Stratagem relating to Heron Tower II.

Just over two weeks later, Goldberg again wrote to Panciera. After listing the active matters in which his firm represents FSC "and other Heron Entities," he stated:

> In light of the recent unfortunate developments between Heron and Stratagem Development Corp., of which I am sure you are aware, we must raise the question of our continued representation of Fidelity Services Corporation in connection with this labor matter.

Kenneth J. Kelly, Esq., of Epstein Becker, followed up with a letter, dated August 3, 1990, to Ms. Panciera. The letter pointedly stated:

> We will soon commence an action against Heron Properties and Heron International. Unless we hear otherwise from you, we plan to resign as Heron's counsel in the federal action and arbitration on the day we file Stratagem's complaint.

On August 8, 1990, Peter Kompaniez, the CEO of FSC, wrote back, expressing "surprise[] at your statement that your firm 'will soon commence an action against

Heron Properties and Heron International.'" He stated that it would be a violation of serious provisions of New York's Code of Professional Responsibility for Kelly's firm to sue Heron.

Another Epstein Becker lawyer, Samuel Goldman, replied on August 14, 1990, as follows:

> From the tone and tenor of your letter, it is apparent that you would feel uncomfortable if we were to continue to represent Fidelity Service Corp. in the captioned litigation. Accordingly, we hereby notify you that we are with-drawing as counsel to Fidelity in this lawsuit.
>
> As you are aware, we have represented Stratagem Development Corp. in all of its dealings with Heron since the inception of the relationship between these two companies. There is no conflict in our continued representation of Stratagem.

The parties' attorneys exchanged two further letters in subsequent weeks; by September 4, 1990, Michael Delikat, Esq., of the law firm of Baer Marks & Upham ("Baer Marks") had contacted Epstein Becker to advise that it would take over the representation of FSC in the *Bevona* matters. During that conversation, as related in a confirming letter from Mr. Delikat to Mr. Goldberg, Mr. Delikat indicated that he would "prepare a formal substitution and forward same to you under separate cover. In the meantime, I would appreciate receiving a copy of the entire file at your earli-est convenience."

The contemplated exchange of files and substitution forms did not take place at that time.[6] Less than a month later, on October 2, 1990, Epstein Becker filed the com-plaint in this action.

Defendants point out that coincidentally, also on October 2, 1990, Mr. Goldberg wrote to Stanley Bass, Staff Counsel of the United States Court of Appeals for the Second Circuit to attend to some ministerial matters in the *Bevona* actions. In that letter, he identified Epstein Becker as the attorneys for Fidelity Service Corp. By way of explanation, Mr. Goldberg now submits that he was left no alternative but to describe himself as FSC's counsel because of Baer Marks' failure to forward the signed substitution form.

On October 9, 1990, Heron's counsel in the instant action wrote to this Court, indicating its intention to file the present motion; that same day, Epstein Becker sent the files in the *Bevona* matter to Baer Marks. Two days later, Mr. Goldberg forwarded to Baer Marks a substitution of counsel form. The substitution form has not yet been filed.

---

6. The parties engage in a great deal of finger-pointing on this subject: Delikat, on behalf of FSC, states that he never sent the form because Epstein Becker did not forward the files as prom-ised; Epstein Becker in turn accuses FSC of directing Baer Marks not to send the form in order to better situate Heron to prevail in the instant motion. The Court notes that the letter does not indi-cate that Delikat's sending of the form was contingent upon receipt of the files.

Canon 5 of the New York Code of Professional Responsibility provides that an attorney owes a duty of undivided loyalty to the client. Where an attorney takes part in a suit against an existing client, the propriety of the conduct "... must be measured not so much against the similarities in litigation, as against the duty of undivided loyalty which an attorney owes to each of his clients." Cinema 5, Ltd. v. Cinerama, Inc., 528 F.2d 1384, 1386 (2d Cir. 1976). The duty applies with equal force where the client is a subsidiary of the entity to be sued. See Glueck v. Jonathan Logan, Inc., 512 F. Supp. 223, 227 (S.D.N.Y.), aff'd, 653 F.2d 746 (2d Cir. 1981) (firm representing trade association could not also represent individual client in suit against corporation belonging to association); see also Rosman v. Shapiro, 653 F. Supp. 1441 (S.D.N.Y. 1987) (disqualifying defendant's attorneys because firm represented closely held corporation in which plaintiff and defendant each held 50% of the stock). In the case at bar, the relationship between the two entities represented by Epstein Becker, that of parent and wholly-owned subsidiary, is even closer than that between the parties in *Glueck* and *Shapiro*, because the liabilities of a subsidiary corporation directly affect the bottom line of the corporate parent. *A fortiori*, the duty of undivided loyalty, as set forth in Canon 5, attaches in this case. As the *Glueck* Court noted,

> the Bar has an independent interest in avoiding even the appearance of impropriety, and that interest mandates a clear margin of protection against potentially conflicting arrangements .... [A]ny doubt in the disqualification situation is to be resolved in favor of disqualification.

512 F. Supp. at 228.

The Court must therefore consider whether Epstein Becker's actions in this case should disqualify it from representing plaintiff Stratagem. There are two different standards by which courts evaluate disqualification motions because of alleged dual representation; which standard to apply depends on whether the representation of the two clients is simultaneous or successive. When the firm concurrently represents both parties, Courts are to apply a per se prohibition; but if the case involves former clients of the firm, the Court will inquire into whether there is a "substantial relationship" between the two matters. ...

Defendants in the present case argue that Epstein Becker did not effectively withdraw from its representation of FSC in the *Bevona* matters until at least October 9, when it finally sent the files to Baer Marks, and perhaps later, because the substitution form has not been filed to this day. They therefore advocate the application of the per se rule. Equally predictably, plaintiffs argue for application of the "substantial relationship" test, stating that FSC "has not been Epstein Becker's client since September 4, 1990," approximately one month before the instant complaint was filed.

As the Second Circuit has explained, in order to justify application of the more lenient "substantial relationship" test the firm in question must show that "the representation of a former client has been terminated and the parameters of such relationship have been fixed." *Cinema 5*, supra, 528 F.2d at 1387. In the present case, the parties vigorously dispute the question of precisely when, if ever, Epstein Becker effectively withdrew from representing FSC. However, Epstein Becker does concede that it represented FSC as late as September 4, 1990. Id. Accordingly, the record is undisputed that the Firm was clearly contemplating, if not actively planning, litigation against its client's parent corporation as early as July 13, 1990. The Court must therefore conclude that the Firm was still in FSC's employ when it investigated and was drafting the complaint against FSC's parent company. . . . Because Epstein Becker had not clearly terminated its representation of FSC and fixed the parameters of its representation of FSC by the time preparations for the instant litigation were begun, Epstein Becker is per se ineligible to represent Stratagem in this matter. *Cinema 5*, supra, 528 F.2d at 1387.

Moreover, even if Epstein Becker could have resolved this problem by obtaining both clients' consent, such consent was not forthcoming from FSC. The Court of Appeals has explained that:

> Under the Code, the lawyer who would sue his own client, asserting in justification the lack of "substantial relationship" between the litigation and the work he has undertaken to perform for that client, is leaning on a slender reed indeed. Putting it as mildly as we can, we think it would be questionable conduct for any attorney to participate in any lawsuit against his own client without the knowledge and consent of all concerned.

Id.

Wald

In the present case Epstein Becker did seek, in its letter of July 13, 1990, to "raise the question of our continued representation of Fidelity Services Corporation in connection with this labor matter." However, the letter was phrased, not as a request for FSC's consent to proceed with the Stratagem litigation, but as a request for FSC's consent to continue with the labor representation. The letter stated:

> Should you feel that a conflict, actual or potential, may exist, or should you want us to resign from this case because of our ongoing representation of Stratagem and affiliates, please let us know and we will resign as counsel in the labor matter.

The follow-up letter dated August 3, 1990, reads less like a request for consent and more like a threat: "We will soon commence an action against Heron Properties and Heron International. Unless we hear otherwise from you, we plan to resign as Heron's counsel in the federal action and arbitration on the day we file Stratagem's complaint. Please advise." *threat, not IC* Heron's reply, listing the provisions of the New York Code of Professional Responsibility which it believed Epstein Becker would be violating by suing Heron, is hardly the "knowledge and consent" that the Code requires in such a situation. Epstein Becker's third missive on the subject does not even purport to seek Heron's consent: "From the tone and tenor of your letter, it is apparent that you would feel uncomfortable if we were to continue to represent [FSC] . . . . Accordingly, we hereby notify you that we are withdrawing as counsel to Fidelity in this lawsuit."

As is evident from this series of letters, Epstein Becker was not able to obtain the requisite consent from its client FSC before undertaking representation adverse to FSC's parent company. Absent such prior consent, a firm is to remain with the client in the already-existing litigation and seek new counsel to represent the other, not vice-versa. . . .

Epstein Becker points out that Samuel Goldman has been Stratagem's real estate lawyer since 1983. It thereby attempts to refute Heron's theory that Epstein Becker dropped FSC "like a hot potato" in order to represent a more favored client.

Epstein Becker's obligations to Stratagem do not trump those it owes to FSC, even if they pre-dated them. Once Epstein Becker undertook to represent FSC, it assumed the full panoply of duties that a law firm owes to its client. Epstein Becker may not undertake to represent two potentially adverse clients and then, when the potential conflict becomes actuality, pick and choose between them. Nor may it seek consent for dual representation and, when such is not forthcoming, jettison the uncooperative client. Under these circumstances, Epstein Becker has no choice but to withdraw from representing either client in this case. . . .

Notes

1. The factual situation in this case is very much like *Levin*. A law firm with a major client decides to represent a party with whom its major client is doing business at a time when all is well between the two clients. The problem arises when all ceases to be well and the law firm wants to continue representing its major client. The main legal issue in *Stratagem* was the ability of the law firm to solve an impending conflict of interest problem by dropping Heron. The court refused to allow it to drop Heron like a "hot potato," and the issue has been known by that name ever since. Once it undertook to represent the Heron subsidiary in litigation that was ongoing when trouble developed between Stratagem and Heron, it could not represent Stratagem against Heron without Heron's consent. There was no legal impediment to its continued representation of the Heron subsidiary, but there were doubtless good business reasons relating to its relationship to Stratagem why it might not wish to do so even if it could not represent Stratagem in its lawsuit against Heron.

2. The federal district court relied on New York's rules of professional conduct. New York had at that time an updated version of the Model Code of Professional Responsibility whose general principles on this issue seem quite similar to those contained in the Model Rules, and *Stratagem* is often cited in Model Rules jurisdictions. As already noted, New York has since revised its disciplinary rules using the format of the Model Rules.

3. The *Stratagem* case raises the general issue of business conflicts. Think of situations, as a client, where you might want your lawyer to have a business conflict. One reason clients might wish to have lawyers with business conflicts is that lawyer may be "iced" from any adverse case brought against the client in the future. Another reason is that conflicts may serve as a market signal of the lawyer's desirability. To the

extent this market signal is effective, consider what other sources of regulation might constrain a lawyer's behavior with respect to conflicts. What social norms might affect a lawyer with business conflicts? How will they affect the lawyer? How might the market or the geographical context affect these business conflicts? Cf. Lessig, "The New Chicago School," 27 J. Legal Stud. 661, 662–66 (1998) (examining how laws, norms, markets, and architecture operate as constraints on behavior). These ancillary restraints are important to consider both in the presence and absence of clear legal rules.

4. An earlier, much cited case announcing the "hot potato" principle as a general rule was Unified Sewerage Authority v. Jelco, 646 F.2d 1339 (9th Cir. 1981). But the *Jelco* court permitted a law firm to represent and oppose a client at the same time. A general contractor engaged a law firm to represent it in a dispute against a subcontractor despite the fact that the law firm informed the general contractor that one of its clients was another subcontractor who had a potential dispute with the general contractor arising out of the same project. The general contractor consented several times to the potential conflict, but discharged the firm and sought to have the firm disqualified when the firm brought a suit on behalf of the subcontractor against it. The court concluded that the law firm met both tests that would enable it to continue to represent the subcontractor even though it had represented and sued the general contractor at the same time. The general contractor had consented. Moreover, the firm met the objective test for simultaneous representation. Although the same project was involved, the nature of the disputes was so different that no confidential information was involved and the firm got no advantage in the second suit from its representation of the general contractor in the first suit.

Jelco is not a model for good legal practice. The law firm regarded its subcontractor client as its principal client all along and allowed the general contractor's offer of business to lull it into a sense of ethical security. It should have realized that consent might not save it in the event that the dispute that was on the horizon became a reality. It might have obtained disqualifying confidential information from the general contractor or a court might have regarded the two lawsuits as substantially related so that the objective test for dual representation could not have been met. There is a strong overtone in the opinion that the court believed that the general contractor had tried to take advantage of the law firm, but the law firm could not rely on the court taking such a view. See Ferguson Elec. Co., Inc. v. Suffolk Construction Co., Inc., 1998 Mass. Super. Lexis 289 (Mass. Super. Ct. 1998) for a case where an attorney's claim that a one-shot representation had concluded and that his client was therefore a former client was rejected because the attorney's engagement letter contemplated more work than he had completed. Moreover, he had not indicated that the representation was complete until he sought to drop his client like a "hot potato" in order to bring suit against it.

5. An important technique for avoiding disqualification is illustrated by the early case of Kennecott Copper Corp. v. Curtiss-Wright Corp., 78 Civ. 1295 (S.D.N.Y. 1978)

(unpublished opinion), 449 F. Supp. 951 (1978). A law firm, specializing in corporate takeover matters, was asked by Curtiss-Wright to represent it on a one-shot basis. It sought to protect itself against subsequent disqualification problems by discussing potential conflicts with the lawyer-president and the general counsel of the company and then entering into the following agreement: "Should your corporation or any person affiliated with it seek to acquire or invest in any company which is a client of our office we will be free to represent that client and the same shall not result in a reduction of the retainer." Was that agreement sufficient to accomplish the law firm's purpose? Later, at a time when the takeover attempt had failed but the law firm was still representing Curtiss-Wright in litigation arising out of the takeover, the firm represented Kennecott in a divestiture and an acquisition matter. Curtiss-Wright then attempted to take over Kennecott, and the firm advised the Kennecott management of its rights in the ensuing proxy fight waged by Curtiss-Wright. Litigation developed and regular counsel represented Kennecott. Curtiss-Wright's effort to disqualify regular counsel and the firm from any representation of Kennecott failed because of the quoted waiver provision. See Galderma Laboratories, L.P. v. Actavis Mid-Atlantic LLC, 927 F. Supp. 2d 390 (N.D. Tex. 2013) for another case in which written advance consent to representation of an adversary was sufficient to avoid disqualification. Compare St. Barnabas Hospital v. New York City Health & Hospitals Corp., 775 N.Y.S.2d 9 (N.Y. App. 2004) (court enforced advance waiver in litigation even though it did not mention litigation) with All American Semiconductor, Inc. v. Hynix Semiconductor, Inc., 2008 U.S. Dist. Lexis 106619 (N.D. Cal. 2008). Comment 22 to Model Rule 1.7 discusses various considerations that may govern the effectiveness of advance consent waivers.

6. We will return to the issue of advance waivers and other techniques for avoiding or mitigating actual or potential conflicts later in this Chapter. For present purposes, however, consider how you would draft a consent clause after the *Kennecott* case. Would you make it as broad as possible? Is there anything you would exclude? Future clients? Simultaneous representation? Substantially related matters? Use of confidential information? Use of some confidential information? Would you agree to screen off some employees in any situations? Would you preserve a right to withdraw in a situation of actual conflict? See Worldspan, L.P. v. The Sabre Group Holdings, Inc., 5 F. Supp. 2d 1356 (N.D. Ga. 1998), where the court found an advance conflicts waiver inadequate. Given that it would be "most difficult for a consent that may have been thoroughly informed in 1992 to be informed in 1998" and that the waiver did not specifically mention "directly adverse" litigation, the court refused to give effect to the waiver in this circumstance. Or recently Kirkland & Ellis was disqualified from representing a client in a hostile takeover of another client (represented by a different firm) in part because, although Kirkland had secured an advance waiver from its to-be-taken-over client and the waiver mentioned the possibility of adversity and litigation, the waiver did not specifically mention the possibility of a hostile takeover. Mylan, Inc. v. Kirkland & Ellis (W.D. Pa. 2015) (report and recommendation), case subsequently dismissed as moot. See also City of El Paso v. Soule,

6 F. Supp. 2d 616 (W.D. Tex. 1998), involving invalidity of an advance waiver when the subsequent litigation against the client was in a matter substantially related to the former representation of the client.

What do you think of the following view taken by some law firms? Advance waivers should be thought of in the context of their business ramifications. A client might think it advisable to seek independent legal advice regarding a written advance waiver presented to it by its lawyers. The law firm consulted has every incentive to "nitpick" the written document so that the client appreciates the potential conflict with the firm seeking the advance waiver. The client might then think it wise to use the independent law firm to handle the particular business as to which the advance waiver was sought. Therefore, while advance waivers of the Curtiss-Wright type should sometimes be obtained from clients, they should never be reduced to writing. For a helpful review of cases involving advance waivers and a proposal that the rules should be amended to allow waivers in cases where the client is represented by independent counsel and the waiver is unambiguous, see Richard C. Painter, "Advance Waiver of Conflicts," 13 Geo. J. Legal Ethics 289 (2000).

7. In the very old case of In re Boone, 83 F. 944 (C.C.N.D. Cal. 1897), a lawyer sought to interpret a release from a client as permitting him to be employed by an adversary with respect to the very matter in which he had represented his client. The court refused to interpret the release in that fashion, but went on to state emphatically that a "client may waive a privilege which the relation of attorney and client confers upon him, but he cannot enter into an agreement whereby he consents that the attorney may be released from all the duties, burdens, obligations and privileges pertaining to the duty of attorney and client.... The inevitable result of such a doctrine would be to degrade the profession and bring the courts themselves into disrepute.... Courts owe a duty to themselves, to the public, and to the profession which the temerity or improvidence of clients cannot supersede." Id. at 957.

A later case relying on In re Boone is Westinghouse Elec. Corp. v. Gulf Oil Corp., 588 F.2d 221 (7th Cir. 1978), another piece of the much-cited litigation discussed in Note 10, p. 215. In disqualifying a law firm notwithstanding client A's alleged consent that the firm would not be precluded from representing client B in the event of conflict, the court held that such an agreement would not be read as including consent to possible use of A's confidential information against it.

8. The growing tendency of law firms to merge with one another presents great danger that the merged firm may find itself representing conflicting interests simultaneously. Such a situation occurred in Harte Biltmore Ltd. v. First Penn. Bank, N.A., 655 F. Supp. 419 (S.D. Fla. 1987). The firm sought to resolve the problem of representing and suing a client at the same time by withdrawing from its representation. It was nevertheless disqualified in the second suit. Accord Western Sugar Corp. v. Archer-Daniels-Midland Co., 98 F. Supp.3d 1074 (C.D. Cal. 2015); see also Leigh Jones, "Client Conflicts: The Hidden Cost of Law Firm Mergers," Nat'l L.J., Feb. 15, 2005 (reporting that "checking for . . . conflicts is perhaps the most underestimated

cost of completing a merger" and can impose significant costs on clients who may be denied their counsel of choice). As we will see at the conclusion of this Chapter, these costs—especially the costs to lawyers—contributed to the ABA's decision to propose changes to the rules on imputed disqualification. We will explore consequences of the exploding number of law firm mergers since 2000 in Chapter 12.

9. A fascinating analysis of the charges of unethical conduct made against Louis Brandeis at the time of his appointment by President Wilson to the Supreme Court is contained in John P. Frank, "The Legal Ethics of Louis D. Brandeis," 17 Stan. L. Rev. 683 (1965), reprinted almost in its entirety and followed by author's Notes at pp. 93–109 of the first edition of this book. Most of the charges involved conflict of interest matters. See also Clyde Spillenger, "Elusive Advocate: Reconsidering Brandeis as People's Lawyer," 105 Yale L.J. 1445 (1996) for a persuasive revisionist view of Brandeis the practitioner.

3. Simultaneously Representing and Opposing Affiliated Companies

Problem 4–5

Law Firm has done the labor relations work for Conglomerate for years and is currently handling numerous matters for it out of its New York City office. Its Seattle office represents the Workers Insurance Company, a small carrier that does business only in the state of Washington. The Seattle office of Law Firm has been asked by Workers to handle a relatively modest subrogation claim against Metal Fabricators, Inc., a small specialty steel company whose major client is Boeing. Metal Fabricators, Inc. was recently bought by Metal Corporation of America, which is wholly owned by Conglomerate. The Seattle office of Law Firm has never done any work for Conglomerate. May it take on the Workers' subrogation claim without asking for Conglomerate's permission? Would it make any difference if Metal Fabricators and not Conglomerate was a regular client of the New York office and Law Firm's Seattle office was being asked to take on a claim against Conglomerate? Would it make any difference in that scenario if Metal Fabricators and Conglomerate were both subsidiaries of SuperGiant?

———————

Special problems arise in the application of conflict rules to situations when the lawyer is representing and opposed to affiliated clients, that is, when a lawyer represents a subsidiary and at the same time sues its parent, or vice versa. The problem was discussed in cursory fashion in *Stratagem*. A leading case is Pennwalt v. Plough, 85 F.R.D. 264 (D. Del. 1980), summarized at p. 227, Note 2, and the whole subject matter was canvassed at large under the Model Rules by the ABA's Committee on Ethics and Professional Responsibility in its Opinion 95-390. Prompted by the growth in national and multi-national corporations, the Committee attempted in this Opinion to provide guidance concerning the issue of undertaking representation adverse to a corporate affiliate of a current corporate client in an unrelated matter without obtaining the client's consent. The focus of the Opinion is on circumstances where there is no clear, pre-established understanding between lawyer and client as to which entity or entities in the "corporate family" are to be the clients, or at least treated as such for conflict purposes.

A majority of the Committee agreed that Model Rule 1.7 does "not prohibit a lawyer from representing a party adverse to a particular corporation merely because the lawyer (or another lawyer in the same firm) represents, in an unrelated matter, another corporation that owns the potentially adverse corporation, or is owned by it, or is, together with the adverse corporation, owned by a third entity." The majority went on to suggest that circumstances might indicate that an affiliate of a corporate client should itself be viewed as a client, at least for purposes of avoiding conflicts, as where there was an express understanding to that effect, or a reasonable implication from the relations among the parties, the transmission of confidential information from the affiliate, or the like; in that event, the consent of the affiliate would be required. But where those circumstances did not exist, the question was whether an unrelated suit against an affiliate should be regarded as "directly adverse" to the corporate client, in which case the latter's consent would be required under Rule 1.7(a). The answer of the majority was that adverseness in such a case was indirect, since its immediate impact was on the affiliate and only derivatively upon the client. Accordingly, it was Rule 1.7(b) that applied; hence the lawyer was free to take on the representation adverse to the affiliate unless such representation would be materially limited by the lawyer's responsibility to the corporate client, or, correlatively, the representation of the corporate client would be materially limited by the representation adverse to the affiliate. In either of those cases the lawyer should not proceed unless the lawyer reasonably concluded that the representation would not be adversely affected and the potentially affected client consented.

The majority's conclusion was somewhat tempered by its closing suggestions that (1) "doubts about whether one or another requirement of the Rule applies should be resolved by a presumption that favors the client who will be adversely affected by the prospective representation," and (2) when "it is difficult to ascertain whether a matter will be directly adverse to an existing client, or to judge whether taking on the matter will affect the lawyer's relationship with the client, a lawyer ordinarily would be well advised as a matter of prudence and good practice to discuss the matter with his existing client before undertaking a representation adverse to an affiliate of the client, even though consent may not be ethically required." However, the latter recommendation was immediately qualified by the observation that "the fact that the lawyer has as a matter of prudence and good practice sought consent where consent was not ethically required does not make the lawyer's undertaking the new representation in the absence of consent a disciplinable ethical violation."

There were several sharp dissents to Opinion 95-390. One of them described the situation this way:

The majority view, when reduced to its most simplistic terms, is as follows: XYZ Corporation is represented by the law firm of Roe & Doe. XYZ has a number of subsidiaries which the majority characterizes as "corporate affiliates." One of them is about to be sued by another client of Roe & Doe in an "unrelated matter." In such a case, the majority opines that even if the suit threatens to adversely impact XYZ's economic interest, the conflict is governed not by Model Rule 1.7(a) which would require the consent of XYZ, but by Model Rule 1.7(b) which does not require the consent of XYZ, thus depriving it of a veto power which would prevent Roe & Doe from suing its subsidiary.

It may very well be that in the rarified Fortune 500 world, a suit against a subsidiary might be considered as having only a derivative impact upon the parent, but outside those elevated precincts most parent companies would view such a suit as outrageous and a clear conflict of interest.

The dissent goes on to decry the suggestion that parent corporations can avoid this outcome by having an express understanding with their lawyers, insisting that this amounts to shifting the lawyer's burden of protecting the client to the client. The dissent also observes that if parent corporation XYZ "is maintaining a subsidiary, it does so with the expectancy that the subsidiary's profits will add to the bottom line of XYZ's annual report and that the subsidiary's reputation will add to the luster of XYZ's reputation. From XYZ's point of view, the suit against the subsidiary will always have a direct impact on it and no matter what the majority opines, will be a conflict of interest."

Finally, the dissent contrasts the situation when the adverse claim would be against a directly owned division of the parent company instead of a subsidiary:

The majority's repeated use of the term "corporate affiliate" must be viewed as an elevation of form over substance. Even the majority doesn't go so far as to suggest that if the XYZ Corporation had a number of divisions under its corporate umbrella, a suit brought by its lawyers, Roe & Doe, against one of those divisions would be indirectly adverse. [Rule 1.7(b)]. What they do say is that because XYZ chose to or was by law required to operate via corporate subsidiaries, if a profitable case against XYZ's subsidiary comes to Roe & Doe, it is free to make a business decision to take that case without XYZ's consent and the only recourse XYZ has is to discharge Roe & Doe or move to disqualify it.

Notes

1. The split in the ABA Committee is replicated in the case law. Compare Reuben H. Donnelly Corp. v. Sprint Publishing, 1996 U.S. Dist. LEXIS 2363 (N.D. Ill. 1996) (relying on ABA 95-350 in finding no violation of Rule 1.7(a) in representing affiliated subsidiaries in unrelated matters) with North Star Hotels Corp. v. Mid-City Hotel Associates, 118 F.R.D. 109 (D. Minn. 1987) (precluding a law firm from suing an entity owned in part by an individual who was the sole owner and the major

owner of two other clients of the law firm; success in the lawsuit represented a substantial threat to the financial viability of its other two clients so as to make the representation "directly adverse" within the meaning of Rule 1.7(a)). Since the majority in the ABA Committee sent such a strong message that in doubtful cases prudence suggests that the lawyer seek client consent before undertaking representation adverse to an affiliate, why does it resist so strongly the dissent's interpretation of the words "directly adverse" even when it concedes that there is authority for such a reading? Is it just that the majority doesn't want lawyers who fail to seek such consent to be disciplined? Or are there situations when requiring consent ought not be mandated as a matter of policy? In assessing the policy considerations, we should keep in mind that a question we are addressing is: loyalty to whom? Are obligations owed to the "family" of the specific entity that hired the lawyer? The Model Rules have been revised to accept the position of the majority. See Rule 1.7, Comment 34. There are dozens of cases dealing with the issue. Most are heavily fact dependent. See, e.g., GSI Commerce Solutions, Inc. v. BabyCenter, L.L.C., 618 F.3d 204 (2d Cir. 2010).

2. In the much cited case of Pennwalt v. Plough, 85 F.R.D. 264 (1980), a law firm was representing client one as plaintiff in one litigation and client two as defendant in another. The parent of the defendant in case one acquired the defendant in case two so that the law firm was representing and suing wholly owned subsidiaries of the parent corporations in unrelated lawsuits at the same time. After the law firm was permitted to withdraw from case two, the judge in case one refused to disqualify it. Although one legal office of the parent controlled the legal affairs of both subsidiaries so that the law firm could not have continued its representation in case two, it withdrew from that unrelated litigation without having obtained any confidential information. That was all that was required in these circumstances. The court apparently thought that there were circumstances where it might be possible for a firm to represent and to be adverse to affiliated subsidiaries at the same time. Moreover, the actual case involved a conflict that was caused by action of the client in purchasing its new subsidiary and not by the law firm. In allowing a law firm to drop a client in this situation, courts sometimes refer to a "thrust upon" exception. See Rule 1.7, Comment 5.

3. In In re Cendant Corp. Securities Litigation, 124 F. Supp. 2d 235 (D.N.J. 2000), the court held that the "directly adverse" test of Rule 1.7(a) was met by simultaneous firm representation of a defendant and a key witness who was the former general counsel of the co-defendant/cross claimant.

4. Joint Representation of an Entity and Its Employees

Problem 4–6

Lawyer has been retained to represent Towing Service, Inc. against prospective claims of large property damage brought by businesses whose property was destroyed

in the fire that followed an accident between one of Towing's wreckers and a gasoline truck. Lawyer is about to interview Towing's driver. What, if anything, should
she say to Towing Service about the matter of representing Driver? Should she tell
Driver to get his own lawyer?

The following group of materials presents a common and difficult problem that
a lawyer may face: simultaneous representation by an attorney of an entity and some
of its employees. The question may come up as an evidentiary matter in the context
of litigation against the company. Discovery may be sought of relevant communications between company counsel and company employees. In that setting, attention
is focused on the reach of the attorney-client privilege via the attorney's representation of the company and not on whether the employee has also become a client. The
question asked is: How does the general rule—that communications received by
the attorney from the client during the course of representation are privileged
from inquiry during litigation—apply to employees of a corporation or other
business entity? Obviously, such an entity can act only through agents. Are all
communications between the corporation counsel and corporation employees
covered by the attorney-client privilege? Or are there circumstances in which the
position of the corporate employee is more analogous to that of a witness? Some
divergence of views exists among the courts that have considered the issue. See the
discussion in Note, "Attorney-Client Privilege for Corporate Clients: The Control
Group Test," 84 Harv. L. Rev. 424 (1970), contrasting the "traditional view," allowing the corporation to claim privilege so long as the employees were acting as agents
of the corporation in making the communication; the "dominant" state court view,
allowing the corporation to claim privilege if the communication was made by the
employee at the direction of the employer for the purpose of obtaining legal advice;
the test of Harper & Row Publishers, Inc. v. Decker, 423 F.2d 487, 491–492 (7th Cir.
1970), aff'd by an equally divided Court, 400 U.S. 348 (1971), allowing the corporation
to claim privilege "where the employee makes the communication at the direction
of his superiors in the corporation and where the subject matter upon which the
attorney's advice is sought by the corporation and dealt with in the communication is
the performance by the employee of the duties of his employment"; and the "control
group" test, enunciated first in City of Philadelphia v. Westinghouse Elec. Corp., 210
F. Supp. 483, 485 (E.D. Pa. 1962), which would allow the corporation to claim the
privilege only if the employee "is in a position to control or even to take a substantial part in a decision about any action which the corporation may take upon the
advice of the attorney, or if he is an authorized member of a body or group which
has that authority."

A substantial amount of confusion in the federal courts was cleared away
by the Supreme Court's decision in Upjohn Co. v. United States, 449 U.S. 383
(1981). Although the Court refused to lay down a general rule, it also refused to
adopt the control group test, and its holding protected communication of

information from lower-level employees that was needed to provide a basis for legal advice. While the reach of the attorney-client privilege is now clearer in federal courts, there still exists the possibility of different rules in federal and state courts in a given jurisdiction as well as different rules in different states. Since lawyers are likely to be unable to predict the forum of future litigation when they discuss business with corporate or other entity employees, any conflict in potentially applicable law makes the process of communication with lower-level employees very difficult.

Sometimes, however, the issue is not whether the corporate attorney's relationship with the corporate employee is such that communications between them are privileged, but whether the attorney may undertake representation of one or more entity employees at the same time that he or she is representing the entity with respect to the same subject matter. The issue arose in that context in the following case, which should be read not only from the perspective of passing judgment after the fact but also in terms of the choice that was made by the attorney when asked to act. There is further discussion of related aspects of this issue in Chapter 5.

In re Merrill Lynch, Pierce, Fenner & Smith, Inc.

Securities and Exchange Commission, File No. 3-4329
(Unpublished opinion, December 6, 1973)

SIDNEY ULLMAN, Administrative Law Judge.

These proceedings were instituted by Commission order dated June 22, 1973 (Order) to determine whether respondents have violated certain provisions of the Securities Exchange Act of 1934 (Exchange Act) and of the Securities Act of 1933 (Securities Act), and if so, what remedial action is appropriate. The Order names as respondents Merrill Lynch, Pierce, Fenner and Smith (Merrill Lynch or Registrant), two men employed in its Research Division during the relevant period of approximately 21 months from March 1968 to November 1969, Philip E. Albrecht (Albrecht) and Willard Pierce (Pierce), and 47 persons then employed as registered representatives in Merrill Lynch offices throughout the nation.

The Order asserts charges by the Division of Enforcement (Division) that the Research Division employees . . . violated the anti-fraud provisions of the securities laws[1] by preparing and disseminating to 250 branch offices and to Merrill Lynch registered representatives a series of false and misleading opinions and recommendations with respect to Scientific Control Corporation (Scientific), a company then in the business of manufacturing computers and components thereof. The Order alleges, and the answer of Merrill Lynch admits, that during the relevant period "a

---

1. Section 17(a) of the Securities Act, Section 10(b) of the Exchange Act and Rule 10b-5 thereunder.

minimum of 4,000 public customers of Registrant purchased a minimum of 400,000 shares of the common stock of Scientific." It alleges also that these opinions and recommendations for the purchase and holding of Scientific shares were transmitted in both oral and written form to customers of Merrill Lynch.

Also transmitted to purchasers and prospective purchasers of Scientific, in violation of the anti-fraud provisions by the 47 registered representatives named as respondents, were untrue statements of material facts relating to Scientific, and statements made untrue by omissions of material facts, according to the allegations of the Order.

In addition, Albrecht and Pierce are alleged to have violated and aided and abetted violations of Section 10(b) of the Exchange Act and Rule 10b-5 thereunder in connection with the purchase and sale of securities of Scientific by making "recommendations concerning transactions in the said securities and [inducing] the purchase thereof by said customers and prospective customers . . . in part on the basis of material information . . . received from Scientific and not . . . disclosed or disseminated to the investing public, including those persons on the other side of said securities transactions."

Merrill Lynch is charged with failure to supervise the persons subject to its supervision who committed the violations charged in the Order, and Albrecht, similarly, is charged with failure to supervise "a person who was subject to his supervision and who committed such violations." Merrill Lynch is charged with responsibility for all of the violations allegedly committed by each of the 49 other respondents.

The law firm Brown, Wood, Fuller, Caldwell and Ivey ("Brown Wood") filed answers on behalf of all but two respondents. . . .

Brown Wood's documents . . . included a written opinion dated September 24, 1973 from the law firm Simpson Thatcher & Bartlett ("Simpson Thatcher") to the effect that on the basis of the facts then known to that firm and stated in its opinion letter, Brown Wood's representation of Merrill Lynch and the . . . other respondents in these proceedings presented "no legal or ethical impediments." . . .

The conclusion reached in this order is that if the decisions of the individual respondents to retain Brown Wood as their counsel are *informed* decisions, such representation may be continued. Accordingly, this order is being directed to each individual respondent to assure that he is substantially apprised of the arguments on both sides of the issue, and that his decision with regard to the selection of counsel, whether now re-affirmed or changed, is made with such knowledge. . . .

The basic contentions of the Division are that Brown Wood, having served for years as counsel to Merrill Lynch, and serving at present as its counsel in a host of legal proceedings including class actions deriving from the sale of Scientific shares, is unable to give to the defense of individual respondents its undivided loyalty and to defend their positions with the zeal required in an attorney-client relationship.[2]

Apart from the Division's contentions with regard to professional ethics inherent in requirements and proscriptions of the pertinent codes of ethics applicable to attorneys, it disputes the adequacy of representation by Brown Wood, and maintains that during the proceeding conflicts will arise which will make it impossible for Brown Wood to serve with equal diligence two masters, one of which is a substantial source of business for the firm. Without in any way questioning the integrity of the firm, the Division contends that Brown Wood has an indomitable desire to protect the Registrant, and that it is not sufficiently mindful of the needs of the individuals in anticipating their respective defenses. It seems to suggest, also, that the ability of a competent attorney to develop arguments in his client's favor cannot be minimized, and that the direction and emphasis of the attorney's thinking are important factors in developing such arguments and positions: that wholehearted attention and zeal cannot be given to such effort when presented with divergent positions of two clients. . . .

. . . [T]he Division contends that the exploration of the many charges during the hearing will be extensive and complex, and that differing approaches will be required for the defenses of individual respondents and for that of Merrill Lynch during the examination or cross-examination of witnesses and perhaps of individual respondents, whether account executives or research analysts. It also argues that because of the several pending class actions against Merrill Lynch arising out of the sale of Scientific, Brown Wood would be unable to fairly evaluate and recommend a settlement favorable to an individual respondent in the event Merrill Lynch believed that a settlement or settlements generally might compromise its own defense either in the instant proceedings or in other litigation.

The Division recognizes that a respondent in administrative proceedings normally has the right to be represented by counsel of his choice, and that an unfair denial of that right might constitute a denial of due process under the Constitution. It was pointed out and agreed at the oral argument, for example, that the Commission has no obligation to appoint counsel for a respondent who is unable to pay counsel fees. And in its reply brief the Division seems to concede that where it is not clear that a conflict of interests will occur between two or more clients of an attorney, the informed consent of the client or clients whose interests more likely would suffer in the event a conflict should develop can provide justification for the continuation of multiple representation, as here. This is the position reached in this order.

Brown Wood points out that it has represented each of the individual respondents during and prior to their respective depositions by the Division; that in each of the interviews the individual respondent was advised of Brown Wood's long-standing

---

2. The Division also asserts that potential pressure exists on individual respondents currently serving as account executives because their salaries and bonuses are subject to flexible subjective standards of management. [Footnote moved from omitted portion of opinion.]

representation of Merrill Lynch, and was told that representation of the individual would be feasible "only if he was sure in his own mind that he had done nothing wrong"; that if a conflict of interest appeared to develop, Brown Wood would have to withdraw as his counsel and that, in turn, if a respondent felt that there was divergence of interest "he need only advise us and we would withdraw." Brown Wood points out that each individual respondent whom the firm represents has independently decided to retain it, that at the taking of depositions the Division advised each deposed witness of his right to choose other counsel; that in questionnaires sent by the Division to other registered representatives they were advised of their right to confer with and choose counsel other than Merrill Lynch's counsel; and that each registered representative chose to adhere to his original decision. They point out, further, that a copy of a letter of August 20, 1973 to the undersigned from William D. Moran, Regional Administrator of the Commission's New York Regional Office (representing the Division) was sent by Brown Wood "to each individual respondent whom we represent," and that no negative response was made to the suggestion that "if any respondent wished to engage different counsel he should so advise us."

The conclusion reached here is consistent with the requirements of due process, with the decisions of the courts insofar as the factual situations of related cases approximate those before us, and at this stage of the proceedings it has not been shown to be inconsistent with the applicable codes of ethics. The opinion of Simpson Thatcher reaches a similar conclusion but expresses a caveat clearly recognized by Brown Wood—that it is Brown Wood's continuing duty to be on the alert for new information that may change what now appears to it to be proper representation into representation that is improper for counsel and precarious for the client.

This is a basis for the Division argument that Brown Wood is accepting and crediting assertions of innocence by all of the individual respondents it represents, while failing to recognize, for example, that investor-witnesses may give credible testimony as to false and improper representations regarding Scientific by any or all of such respondents. A Merrill Lynch employee, says the Division, does not tell Merrill Lynch attorneys that he violated the law.

Brown Wood argues that this argument is based on only a slight and a hypothetical possibility of any conflict of interest arising, and it maintains that it can adequately represent all of its clients in this proceeding. The firm recognizes its professional responsibility and values highly its reputation: it is entirely familiar with the ethical considerations involved here, and its decision on this issue has not been made lightly. . . . Of course Brown Wood agrees with the caveat in the Simpson Thatcher opinion, that it must be continually alert for information which might indicate a conflict of interest; and that if such information is received it must apprise its client or clients thereof and re-evaluate its position. This is a part of the risk taken by individual respondents who retain Brown Wood as counsel—that at some stage of the proceedings it is possible that new counsel, unfamiliar with the case, may have to be substituted.

The decision reached here also is consistent with the precept that a litigant's choice of counsel is an extremely important right which should not be denied him, absent considerations compelling a contrary conclusion: and it is consistent with a practical approach of permitting the clients to choose as their counsel, if they wish to do so on an informed basis, the attorneys who are most familiar with the case and with the potential vulnerability of those charged with the offenses. Apparently, it also may obviate problems that could arise with regard to some of the respondents—the matter of the cost of retaining counsel for their defense, even though reasonable efforts will be made to limit the introduction of evidence against individual respondents to particular sessions of hearing. . . .

While the courts have stated that "The obligation to search out and disclose potential conflicts is placed on the attorney in order to put the client in a position to protect himself by retaining substitute counsel if he so desires,"[4] the client is not thereby freed from responsibility for his own informed decision. It is understood that the individual respondents are educated, experienced business-men. . . .

Notes

1. What is the importance of the last sentence of the *Merrill Lynch* case to the holding? How does it relate to footnote 2 and the other arguments of the Division? In other cases, we have seen courts stressing the importance of prophylactic rules. Here we see the "court" engaging in a weighing test measuring the experience of the individual respondents and their desire to choose their own counsel against the pressures to maintain a common front that are inherent in the employer–employee relationship. Would a prophylactic rule barring joint representation be a wiser policy? Even if it meant that some of the individual respondents had no counsel? Why would employers seek joint representation? Why might employees? Why would the SEC oppose them? How does the situation described in this case resemble what game theorists would call a prisoner's dilemma? Does cooperation or defection make sense in this context? How could we know?

In thinking about these questions, consider the following opinion by Judge Carney in a case involving the simultaneous representation of a company and one of its employees:

> In May 2006, Irell & Manella LLP ("Irell") undertook three separate, but inextricably related, representations of Broadcom Corporation ("Broadcom") and its Chief Financial Officer, Defendant William J. Ruehle. More specifically, Irell represented Broadcom in connection with the company's internal investigation of its stock option granting practices. At the same time, Irell also represented Mr. Ruehle in connection with two shareholder lawsuits filed against him regarding those same stock option granting

---

4. E. F. Hutton & Company v. Brown . . . [305 F. Supp. 371 (S.D. Tex. 1969)].

practices. Prior to undertaking these representations of clients with adverse interests, Irell failed to obtain Mr. Ruehle's informed consent.

In June of 2006, Irell lawyers met with Mr. Ruehle at his office to discuss the stock option granting practices at Broadcom. During this meeting, Mr. Ruehle told the Irell lawyers about Broadcom's stock option granting practices and his role in them. Before questioning Mr. Ruehle, however, the Irell lawyers never disclosed to him that they were representing only Broadcom at the meeting, not him individually, and that whatever he said to them could be used against him by Broadcom or disclosed by the company to third parties. Subsequently, Broadcom directed Irell to disclose statements Mr. Reuhle made to the Irell lawyers about Broadcom's stock option granting practices to Broadcom's outside auditors, Ernst & Young, as well as to the Securities and Exchange Commission ("SEC") and the United States Attorney's Office (the "Government"). Prior to making these disclosures Irell never obtained Mr. Ruehle's consent.

United States v. Henry T. Nicholas, III and William J. Ruehle et al., 606 F. Supp. 2d 1109, 1111–1112 (C.D. Cal. 2009). If you find this conduct amazing, see SCIF v. Drobot, 192 F.Supp.3d 1080 (C.D.Cal. 2016), in which an Irell split-off firm was disqualified from representing both the victim and one of the alleged perpetrators of fraud in one or the other of the civil and criminal actions resulting from the fraud. The court held that consent could not cure the conflict because "informed consent" was not possible.

Does this change your mind about the wisdom of allowing joint representation of an entity and its employees? Note that in this case, the firm was representing the company and the employee in cases that were related but technically distinct. Does this raise additional complications for lawyers who perform internal investigations for corporate clients? Finally, would your opinion about this case be any different if the lawyers had obtained an advance conflict waiver of the kind secured by lawyers in the *Merrill Lynch* case?

Should the CFO, as an "educated, experienced business[man]," be deemed to understand such an agreement and therefore waive his right to object to the disclosure of his confidential information to a third party? Even if the company is prohibited from disclosing the CFO's information, is there anything that would prevent it from firing him based on what he told the company's lawyers during the investigation? We will return to the responsibility of lawyers who perform internal investigations for corporate clients in Chapter 5. For the District Court's disposition of the actual case, see id. at 1121 (barring the government from using the CFO's confidential information and referring Irell to the state disciplinary authorities for the firm's "very troubling" ethical breach of its duty of loyalty). The appellate court, however, reversed the district court's decision, for the following stated reason: Ruehle's statements to the Irell attorneys were not 'made in confidence' but rather for the purpose of disclosure to the outside auditors. That he might regret those statements after later learning of the subsequent corporate disclosure to law enforcement officials is not material to the privilege determination as of June 2006." United States v. Ruehle, 583 F.3d 600, 609 (9th Cir. 2009). The court was unwilling to conclude that the firm's conduct could be used to suppress evidence against a criminal defendant: "Irell's allegedly unprofessional conduct in counseling Broadcom to disclose, without obtaining written consent from Ruehle, while troubling, provides no independent basis for suppression of statements he made in June 2006." Id. at 613.

2. What is the difference between an argument by Brown Wood's counsel in *Merrill Lynch* that its conduct was proper and an "expert opinion" from Simpson Thatcher to the same effect? Should the court have permitted the expert testimony of Simpson Thatcher that there was no conflict of interest in the Brown Wood representation of the employees? If so, should courts generally permit expert testimony from law firms and law professors about every legal issue in a case? We will return to the issue of law professors testifying as "ethics experts" in Chapter 6.

3. If a firm hires the same person regularly as an expert in litigation, it runs the risk of waiving confidentiality with respect to prior advice given to it by that expert on related issues. That is what occurred in Herrick v. Vetta Sports, 1998 U.S. Dist. Lexis 14544 (S.D.N.Y. 1998), with respect to advice given by Professor Charles Wolfram to the Skadden, Arps firm. Even though the prior advice would have otherwise been protected by the attorney-client privilege, the court concluded that the firm had waived the privilege by putting Professor Wolfram's expert opinion and credibility in issue in the case.

4. The issue of the *Merrill Lynch* case may come up in contexts other than a corporation and its employees, and the reservation of the right to represent the entity if a conflict develops with its employees is not always successful. Yablonski v. United Mine Workers, 448 F.2d 1175 (D.C. Cir. 1971), is an example of both those propositions. It involved a suit by a dissident member of the UMW against the union, its president, and two other officers under the Labor-Management Reporting and Disclosure Act. The suit alleged misappropriation of union funds by the individual defendants. The court concluded that regular UMW outside counsel, who had appeared on behalf of both the union and the individual defendants and then withdrew from representation of the individual defendants, was disqualified from continuing its representation of the union in this case. The court held that the ability of counsel to advise the union with respect to its true interests was undermined by the fact that counsel was concurrently representing the union's president in many other lawsuits in which his activities as a union official were being examined. Although it noted that any successor union counsel would be chosen by the union president, it stated that at least successor counsel would have only the union as its client.

In view of that result, counsel probably withdrew from representation of the wrong clients. Its past representation of the union would not seem to have precluded it from continuing to represent the individual defendants in this suit if it had withdrawn from representing the union.

After remand, the firm withdrew from representation of the UMW, and the UMW general counsel and all four members of his staff entered appearances for the UMW. The district court refused to disqualify them but a petition for mandamus to compel compliance with its earlier order was granted by the court of appeals on the ground that house counsel were disqualified for the same reasons that had disqualified original counsel. 454 F.2d 1036 (1971), cert. denied, 406 U.S. 906 (1972); cf. United States v. Schwarz, 298 F.3d 76, 81 (2d Cir. 2002) (holding that the defendant's "convictions for the civil rights violations must be vacated and remanded for a new trial because his attorney's unwaivable conflict of interest denied him effective assistance of counsel"; this unwaivable conflict arose in part because the attorney's firm had a multi-million–dollar retainer agreement with a police union that had adverse interests to the defendant.)

5. During a strike against the Washington Post and at a time when a large number of pressmen were in the pressroom, damage estimated to be in excess of one million dollars was inflicted on the machinery at the Post and a foreman was beaten. The pressmen's union hired Mr. Sol Rosen to represent its members in connection with a grand jury investigation arising out of that incident. Recognizing the professional difficulties involved in representing all the potential witnesses, Mr. Rosen advised them as a group and gave them photocopies of instructions regarding the invocation of the privilege against self-incrimination. He did not interview the witnesses personally so that he did not advise with respect to each witness's potential criminal liability or chances for a grant of immunity. He did, however, advert to the possibility of each individual's potential liability as a conspirator regardless of actual participation in the destruction.

The grand jury subpoenaed 21 union members who were working in the pressroom at the critical time. Except for two who testified that they had seen nothing, the remainder invoked the privilege against self-incrimination, many quite indiscriminately. On motion of the government, Judge Jones disqualified Mr. Rosen from representing more than one individual at the grand jury hearing and required pressmen who wanted counsel to hire counsel who did not represent any other subpoenaed pressman. Balancing the interests of the witnesses to counsel of their choice against the harm to the public interest in effective functioning of the grand jury, although not including cost of separate counsel in the balance, he found only slight impairment to the interests of the former but substantial impairment to those of the latter. He noted the inability of Mr. Rosen to advise each client of his best interest because of potential harm to his other clients and the consequent unnecessary and uninformed invocation of the privilege by each pressman. Furthermore, he pointed out that the multiple representation would lead to breach of the secrecy of grand jury proceedings. Finally, he stressed that the consequences of the multiple representation made it impossible for the government to determine to whom immunity should be granted to further the investigation. In re Grand Jury Investigation, 403 F. Supp. 1176 (D.D.C. 1975).

On appeal, the Court of Appeals reversed. 531 F.2d 600, 607 (D.C. Cir. 1976). The court noted that:

> what is strikingly absent from the record is any indication of the views of the individual witnesses with respect to their legal representation. . . . It may well be . . . that the subpoenaed witnesses do not view Mr. Rosen as their personal legal representative, but rather as a legal consultant retained *by the union* both to instruct them with respect to the protection afforded by the Fifth Amendment and to be on hand outside the grand jury room in the event they have any general questions on that matter; and the individual subpoenaed witnesses may also have no intention of retaining personal legal representatives to investigate the particulars of their involvement, to offer qualified legal advice with respect to their assertion of the privilege and their available options, or to negotiate on their behalf with the United States Attorney.

The court also stated that the district court's invocation of grand jury secrecy was erroneous since federal grand jury witnesses could discuss their testimony with anyone. It concluded that the government should proceed in the traditional way to bring each witness before the district court for a ruling with respect to proper assertion of the privilege against self-incrimination and that if the privilege had been properly invoked, the government could then decide whether to grant immunity. Until those procedures had been pursued and demonstrated to be not feasible or not in the public interest, the court held that it was "premature to seek it through disqualification of counsel whose advice to his clients the Government does not like."

6. A common situation in which joint representation of an entity and its employees raises conflict of interest problems involves suits under 42 U.S.C. § 1983 against a municipality and some of its officials and employees, for example, the mayor, the police chief, police officers, and individual police on account of actions taken by the latter. The conflict of interest questions are intertwined with the potential liability of each of the defendants as a matter of federal constitutional and statutory law and state law, including state indemnity law. Courts have divided in their attitude toward allowing joint representation of defendants, although sometimes the result has appeared to depend very much on the particular factual and legal situation. Compare Blakeslee v. Ruffo, 2000 U.S. App. Lexis 11013 (2d Cir. 2000); Dunton v. County of Suffolk, 729 F.2d 903 (2d Cir. 1984); and Shadid v. Jackson, 521 F. Supp. 87 (E.D. Tex. 1983) (holding joint representation improper) with In re Petition for Review of Opinion 552, 102 N.J. 194 (1986) (rejecting an ethics committee opinion adopting a per se rule against joint representation of a governmental entity and its employees in a civil rights action); Rodick v. Schenectady, 1 F.3d 1341 (2d Cir. 1993); and Sherrod v. Barry, 589 F. Supp. 433 (N.D. Ill. 1984) (holding joint representation proper).

7. The danger posed by the disqualification rules to lawyers representing more than one client in litigation was dramatically presented by In re Corn Derivatives Antitrust Litig., 748 F.2d 157 (2d Cir. 1984). A law firm represented three named

plaintiffs, but not the entire class, in class action litigation. When a settlement was negotiated, two of the firm's clients accepted it while one was opposed. After the law firm filed an appeal on behalf of the dissenter from the district court's order approving the settlement, it withdrew from representation of the two clients who had accepted the settlement. One of them moved in the Court of Appeals to disqualify it from representing the dissenter. The court, finding guidance in both the Model Rules and the Model Code, granted the motion, finding that considerations of loyalty, the keeping of confidences relating to strengths and weaknesses of the case, and the maintenance of public confidence in the integrity of the bar warranted application of the general rule forbidding the law firm from taking a position adverse to its clients in the very same case. The majority opinion, and especially the concurring opinion, noted that the situation would have been quite different if counsel had been class counsel. As noted in the *Merrill Lynch* opinion, the situation might also have been different if the law firm had explained at the outset of the litigation that its principal client was the dissenting client and that in the event of a difference of opinion over strategy, it would withdraw from representation of the other two. See generally Model Rule 1.7 cmts. 4–5.

The problems of class counsel in mass tort cases have become a major issue. The Court of Appeals for the Third Circuit reversed a court-approved settlement in the asbestos litigation involving millions of persons occupationally exposed to asbestos on the basis that the class there certified for settlement purposes did not meet the various requirements of Rule 23 of the Federal Rules of Civil Procedure, but the court also noted the conflict of interest problems of class counsel. Georgine v. Amchem, Inc., 83 F.3d 610 (3d Cir. 1996). The Supreme Court affirmed on the class representation issues. Its holdings with respect to the conflicts among the persons represented by the named plaintiffs implicitly indicated that counsel for the named plaintiffs had similar problems. Amchem, Inc. v. Windsor, 521 U.S. 591 (1997). Similar problems of class and counsel conflict also resulted in the upsetting of the global settlements in another massive asbestos litigation. See Ortiz v. Fibreboard Corp., 527 U.S. 815 (1999). We will return to these issues in Chapter 8.

8. Another area of disqualification for lawyers is when they serve as advocate and witness at the same time. The law in this area became moderately complex and was a major problem for law firms when the disqualification resulted, as it did under the Model Code, in the vicarious disqualification of the whole firm. Model Rule 3.7 limits the disqualification to the testifying lawyer and greatly diminishes the difficulty caused by a lawyer's need to testify, except for solo practitioners. For relatively recent cases involving interpretations of the Rule, see Mark Hamblett, "Prosecution Sees Stewart's Lawyer as Potential Witness," N.Y.L.J., Feb. 11, 2004 (reporting that the judge in the Martha Stewart case refused to allow prosecutors to question Stewart's lawyer during the discovery phase of the case simply because the defense might decide to call the lawyer as a witness during the trial to rebut statements by a prosecution witness); Henry Gottlieb, "Looser Rein Given to Lawyers Who May Be Witnesses," N.J.L.J., Sept. 25, 2002 (reporting a New Jersey district court decision allowing a

lawyer who will be called as a witness at trial to continue representing his client during the discovery phase of the case). The advocate-as-witness prohibition is based in part on conflicts of interest but is based as much or more on the risk of jury confusion. Absent a rule along the lines of Model Rule 3.7, it might be difficult for juries to discern when the lawyer was testifying as to facts and when the lawyer was merely serving as an advocate (whose words are not evidence).

5. Simultaneously Representing and Opposing a Client in Transactional Matters

Problem 4-7 — Parts = Marshall (N.Y.) ; Auto = Houston (Wash.)

Parts Corporation and Auto Corporation are both regular clients of X, Y, and Z. They are interested in negotiating a supply contract. It is expected that the negotiations will be lengthy and complicated. For many years Partner Marshall of the New York office has handled contracts work for Parts and Partner Houston of the Washington office has done the same for Auto. Marshall has never worked on an Auto matter and Houston has never worked on a Parts matter. Both Parts and Auto ask Marshall and Houston to represent them in the negotiations. May they do so? Is there any kind of disclosure, other than the fact of representation of the other side by a partner, that they should make?

[handwritten: They may. Disclose CoI; get waiver; keep evolving & if CoI → retain original. Look for hot potatoe doctrine.]

Problem 4-8

Seller and Buyer have agreed on the terms for the sale of Seller's house—the price, the items of personal property that will be sold with the house, and the date of the closing of title—and have signed a memorandum of agreement on a broker's standard form. Lawyer handled Seller's original purchase of the property and is familiar with the chain of title and its problems. Buyer wants to avoid the additional expense required for another attorney to familiarize himself with the title and wishes Lawyer to represent him in closing the title. There are currently no matters in dispute between the parties. May Lawyer undertake to represent Buyer while also representing Seller in the same transaction?

(a) Does it make a difference that it is common practice in the community for the same attorney to represent buyer and seller in this type of transaction?

(b) Does it make a difference that this type of transaction is usually consummated without any major problem?

(c) Suppose Lawyer undertakes the representation and, because of some problem, the closing date must be extended. Buyer, however, wishes to move in and is willing to pay rent. Can Lawyer satisfy his obligation by getting the parties together, explaining the advantages and dangers of this procedure to the parties, and then saying, "You decide what you wish you to do"? *[handwritten: Based on Miller]*

[handwritten: This is CoI, it needs ICW.]

Problem 4–9

Two large corporate banks seek to join forces through a friendly merger and both sides want the same law firm to oversee the merger. Problem? For whom? If so, what should the proper remedy be? See Richard B. Schmitt, "All the Way to the Bank: Wachtell Is an Omnipresent Mergers Firm," Wall St. Journal, April 22, 1998 at B6 (describing Wachtell's presence on both sides of several multibillion-dollar deals).

––––––––––

The issues with respect to simultaneous representation of multiple clients in situations that do not involve litigation are even murkier than those involving litigation. Consider how this point was raised in the excerpt of Professor Wilkins's article, "Everyday Practice . . ." in Chapter 1, p. 21. The same words of Model Rule 1.7 apply to conflict problems whether litigation is involved or not. But the setting is different, as paragraphs 26–28 of the Comment to that Rule suggest. Although the courts have dealt with conflicts much less often in nonlitigation matters, one can perceive a somewhat more lenient attitude toward permitting multiple representation with consent, even in situations where one might have expected a prophylactic prohibition of representation because of the inherently antagonistic positions of the parties. One recurrent, troublesome situation involves purchase and sale of real estate. The Supreme Court of New Jersey has considered the situation involved in Problem 4–8 several times since 1963. It began by laying down the following rule in In re Kamp, 40 N.J. 588, 595–596 (1963):

> A conflict of interest is inherent in the relationship of buyer and seller; and Canon 6 [of the former Canons of Ethics] is applicable to every occasion in which an attorney undertakes to represent both the seller and the buyer under a sales contract. . . .
>
> Full disclosure requires the attorney not only to inform the prospective client of the attorney's relationship to the seller, but also to explain in detail the pitfalls that may arise in the course of the transaction which would make it desirable that the buyer have independent counsel. The full significance of the representation of conflicting interests should be disclosed to the client so that he may make an intelligent decision before giving his consent. If the attorney cannot properly represent the buyer in all aspects of the transaction because of his relationship to the seller, full disclosure requires that he inform the buyer of the limited scope of his intended representation of the buyer's interests and point out the advantages of the buyer's retaining independent counsel. A similar situation may occur, for example, when the buyer of real estate utilizes the services of the attorney who represents a party financing the transaction. To the extent that both parties seek a marketable title, there would appear to be no conflict between their interests. Nevertheless, a possible conflict may arise concerning the terms of the financing, and therefore at the time of the retainer the attorney should make clear to the

buyer the potential area of conflict. In addition, if the buyer's interests are protected only to the extent that they coincide with those of the party financing the transaction, the attorney should explain the limited scope of this protection so that the buyer may act intelligently with full knowledge of the facts.

The New Jersey Supreme Court treated the problem as one of disclosure. It pointed out, however, that a "conflict of interest is inherent in the relationship of buyer and seller." Would it have been preferable for the court to lay down a rule that an attorney may never represent both the buyer and the seller of property? Even if one believed in a prophylactic rule of that sort, are there exceptions that ought to be considered?

The court went on to deal with a situation where it believed that a lawyer might represent two parties (the buyer and the lender) to a transaction to the limited extent that their interests were not in conflict. Is it healthy for a buyer to be relying on an attorney and to enter a confidential relation with him or her with respect to part of a transaction but to be at arm's length for another part of the transaction? Does it make a difference whether the buyer has an independent attorney with regard to the other part of the transaction? Is the reluctance to enforce rigid prohibitions on representation conceivably a reflection of the idea that in some situations it is unsound as a practical matter, and even a poor use of the pool of lawyers' talents, to require multiple lawyers? If that is so, should the prohibition be stated solely in terms of the loss of independence of judgment or representation of differing interests, or should the practical economic and societal interests be introduced frankly into the balance? How should individual lawyers be instructed to strike the balance in particular cases?

The New Jersey Supreme Court reconsidered the *Kamp* decision in In re Dolan, 76 N.J. 1 (1978), and while elaborating on the nature of the disclosure and consent that were required, it essentially retained a rule that required consideration of the facts of each case before deciding whether dual representation was permissible. The majority and a concurring judge debated the propriety of a per se disqualification. The majority stated:

> While tenable arguments have been made in favor of a complete bar to any dual representation of buyer and seller in a real estate transaction . . . on balance we decline to adopt an inflexible per se rule. Confining ourselves to the type of situation before us (assuredly there are others, entirely unrelated to financial pressures), the stark economic realities are such that were an unyielding requirement of individual representation to be declared, many prospective purchasers in marginal financial circumstances would be left without representation. That being so, the legal profession must be frank to recognize any element of economic compulsion attendant upon a client's consent to dual representation in a real estate purchase and to be circumspect in avoiding any penalization or victimization of those who, by force of these economic facts of life, give such consent.

Judge Pashman, however, viewed the matter differently:

The result herein continues the Court's acceptance of dual representation in circumstances where, notwithstanding full disclosure and knowing consent by the derivative client, the intrinsic degree of divided allegiance is so intolerable that the proscribed adverse effect on the exercise of the attorney's independent professional judgment on behalf of that client must ipso facto be conclusively presumed. . . . In so doing, the Court relies on the fiction that a lay client can effectively consent to dual representation and perpetuates the cruel myth that adequate representation can be provided in such cases by an attorney who supposedly can simultaneously protect the inevitably adverse interests of his two masters. The reality, of course, is that it is well-nigh impossible for the derivative client to be so well attuned to the numerous legal nuances of the transaction that his consent can be said to have been truly informed. The propriety of according dispositive effect to consent so obtained is further undermined when it is frankly acknowledged that the consent is induced by the derivative client's reliance on a promise by the attorney which cannot be fulfilled—the promise of adequate representation of each of his two clients.

Surely the Court is not so naive as to the economic realities of such transactions as its utopian stance would indicate. Any conflicting interests which are potentially disruptive of the ultimate goal—the expeditious consummation of the sales transaction—must inevitably be resolved in favor of the primary client and for that same reason will probably not even be brought to the attention of the derivative client. This problem is even more aggravated in circumstances such as those of the instant case where the primary client of the attorney is a developer with whom the attorney has a potentially long-term and profitable relationship. Consequently, the attorney has a substantial economic stake in maintaining the continued goodwill of this primary client.

The New Jersey Supreme Court revisited the topic once again in 1993 in the context of a suit by sellers of real estate against the buyer when both had been represented by the same attorney. Baldasarre v. Butler, 132 N.J. 278, 295–296 (1993). After dealing with the merits of that lawsuit, the court turned to the role of the lawyer:

This case graphically demonstrates the conflicts that arise when an attorney, even with both clients' consent, undertakes the representation of the buyer and the seller in a complex commercial real estate transaction. The disastrous consequences of [the lawyer's] dual representation convinces us that a new bright-line rule prohibiting dual representation is necessary in commercial real estate transactions where large sums of money are at stake, where contracts contain certain complex contingencies, or where options are numerous. The potential for conflict in that type of complex real estate transaction is too great to permit even consensual dual representation of both buyer and seller. . . .

Did the court really create a bright-line rule for identifying when dual representation is prohibited? What is holding the court back from creating a real bright-line rule? Why is the court looking to create such a rule for complex transactions where presumably the consenting clients are sophisticated but not in the ordinary consumer house purchase transaction?

Kamp and *Dolan* were typical cases for testing the propriety of representation of multiple parties to a contract in that they came up in the context of disciplinary action against a lawyer. That context may exert subtle pressure on a court to avoid finding a violation when it wishes to avoid imposing discipline in what it regards as a close case. That impulse was present in *Baldasarre* where the New Jersey Supreme Court did not refer the lawyer for discipline but rather announced a prospective rule. See also Beal v. Mars Larsen Ranch Corp., 586 P.2d 1378 (Idaho 1978) (not misconduct for lawyer to draft contract as "scrivener" for buyer and seller, with their consent, after they have agreed upon its basic terms). A dramatic illustration of the conclusion that the pressure of imposing discipline need not inhibit courts from imposing discipline for violation of the conflict rules, even in nonlitigation circumstances, is afforded by the Oregon experience. The Oregon Supreme Court imposed discipline, at least in part, in the nonlitigation context, in 43 instances of improper simultaneous representation of multiple parties between 1980 and 2015. It may be that in some jurisdictions the courts are less likely to find a violation of the rules in the nonlitigation as opposed to the litigation context, but Oregon demonstrates that the rules are capable of being applied equally strictly in both cases. In a disciplinary matter, the burden is generally on the disciplinary authorities to show, by clear and convincing evidence, that the lawyer violated an ethical rule (here, a conflicts rule). In close cases, or in states like New Jersey that have taken ambivalent approaches to the applicable rule, should a lawyer be disciplined for playing on or near the line? The burden would seem to suggest "no," but is that the best policy for clients?

What difference does it make that the parties may be legally unsophisticated? Should there be additional restrictions on these representations? Consider Problem 4–9, where a law firm wanted to serve as counsel for both sides of a large friendly merger.

Closely related to the problem of simultaneous representation of multiple parties is simultaneous representation of a client and of the lawyer's own interests. Model Rule 1.7(b) deals with that problem in the same way that it deals with the representation of multiple clients under that provision. This is becoming an increasingly important issue as law firms start buying shares in companies they represent, or in some cases, exchanging legal services for stakes in the companies they advise. See Carrick Mollenkamp, "Region's Lawyers Buying Stakes in Tech Firms," Wall Street Journal, Jan. 14, 1998 at S2; ABA Ethics Op. 00-418 (2000) (discussing the ethical implications of this practice in the context of the dot-com bubble).

Model Rule 1.8 goes beyond the more general language of Model Rule 1.7 to pro-hibit or regulate a number of specific transactions between lawyers and clients. Note that client consent after consultation removes some of the prohibitions but not others. Note also that the disqualification enforced by Model Rule 1.8(k) when a specified relative is representing an adverse party is personal and is not imputed to other mem-bers of the firm.

C. Successive Representation — Opposing a Former Client

Problem 4–10

(a) In the situations involved in Problems 4–1 and 4–2, would it make any differ-ence if the second client had come to the office shortly after the work for the first client had been completed?

(b) Now suppose that in the former client scenario in Problem 4–1, Lawyer had been directed to put title to the real estate in the name of Buyer's son, who lived out of state, and had learned that Buyer kept virtually all his unmortgaged assets in Canada. Would that make any difference?

(c) Now suppose that in the former client scenario in Problem 4–2, Lund had learned in casual conversation with the general counsel of Petroleum Co. that the CEO had a pathological fear of testifying and would do almost anything to avoid it. Would that make any difference?

———————

Analysis of problems of conflict of interest with respect to simultaneous repre-sentation requires us to pay attention to both confidential communications and broader aspects of the duty of loyalty to clients. In dealing with problems of succes-sive representation, we deal with duties that, by hypothesis, arise only by reason of a former relationship. In that setting, the focus of analysis has been primarily on the duty to the client that arises out of the past receipt of confidential information. Those are not the only issues, however, for problems may arise if a lawyer's current employment is perceived as involving an attack on a result achieved for a former client.

The following case presents an interesting discussion of successive representation rules. The court did not even pause to state whether it was applying the Model Code, the Model Rules, or simply a common law of professional responsibility. It doubtless regarded them as fungible for purposes of this problem. The case is yet another exam-ple of how a lawyer may be found to have undertaken, by design or inadvertence, a secondary representation that later precludes representation of a regular client. The case also discusses the increasingly important issue of how lawyers may assume at least some of the obligations of an attorney-client relation with a party even though no formal relation has been undertaken.

Analytica, Inc. v. NPD Research, Inc.

708 F.2d 1263 (7th Cir. 1983)

POSNER, Circuit Judge.

Two law firms, Schwartz & Freeman and Pressman and Hartunian, appeal from orders disqualifying them from representing Analytica, Inc. in an antitrust suit against NPD, Inc. . . .

John Malec went to work for NPD, a closely held corporation engaged in market research, in 1972. His employment agreement allowed him to, and he did buy two shares of NPD stock, which made him a 10 percent owner. It also gave him an option to buy two more shares. He allowed the option to expire in 1975, but his two co-owners, in recognition of Malec's substantial contributions to the firm (as executive vice-president and manager of the firm's Chicago office), decided to give him the two additional shares—another 10 percent of the company—anyway and they told Malec to find a lawyer who would structure the transaction the least costly way. He turned to Richard Fine, a partner in Schwartz & Freeman. Fine devised a plan whereby the other co-owners would each transfer one share of stock back to the corporation, which would then issue the stock to Malec together with a cash bonus. Because the stock and the cash bonus were to be deemed compensation for Malec's services to the corporation, the value of the stock, plus the cash, would be taxable income to Malec (the purpose of the cash bonus was to help him pay the income tax that would be due on the value of the stock), and a deductible business expense to the corporation. A value had therefore to be put on the stock. NPD gave Fine the information he needed to estimate that value—information on NPD's financial condition, sales trends, and management—and Fine fixed a value which the corporation adopted. Fine billed NPD for his services and NPD paid the bill, which came to about $850, for 11½ hours of Fine's time plus minor expenses.

While the negotiations over the stock transfer were proceeding, relations between Malec and his co-owners were deteriorating, and in May 1977 he left the company and sold his stock to them. His wife, who also had been working for NPD since 1972, left NPD at the same time and within a month had incorporated Analytica to compete with NPD in the market-research business. She has since left Analytica; Mr. Malec apparently never had a position with it.

In October 1977, several months after the Malecs had left NPD and Analytica had been formed, Analytica retained Schwartz & Freeman as its counsel. Schwartz & Freeman forthwith complained on Analytica's behalf to the Federal Trade Commission, charging that NPD was engaged in anticompetitive behavior that was preventing Analytica from establishing itself in the market. When the FTC would do nothing,

Analytica decided to bring its own suit against NPD, and it authorized Schwartz & Freeman to engage Pressman and Hartunian as trial counsel. The suit was filed in June 1979 and charges NPD with various antitrust offenses, including abuse of a monopoly position that NPD is alleged to have obtained before June 1977.

. . . In June 1981 the judge disqualified both firms and ordered Schwartz & Freeman to pay NPD's fees and expenses. Analytica has not appealed the orders of disqualification, having retained substitute counsel to prosecute its suit against NPD. . . .

For rather obvious reasons a lawyer is prohibited from using confidential information that he has obtained from a client against that client on behalf of another one. But this prohibition has not seemed enough by itself to make clients feel secure about reposing confidences in lawyers, so a further prohibition has evolved: a lawyer may not represent an adversary of his former client if the subject matter of the two representations is "substantially related," which means: if the lawyer could have obtained confidential information in the first representation that would have been relevant in the second. It is irrelevant whether he actually obtained such information and used it against his former client, or whether—if the lawyer is a firm rather than an individual practitioner—different people in the firm handled the two matters and scrupulously avoided discussing them. . . .

There is an exception for the case where a member or associate of a law firm (or government legal department) changes jobs, and later he or his new firm is retained by an adversary of a client of his former firm. In such a case, even if there is a substantial relationship between the two matters, the lawyer can avoid disqualification by showing that effective measures were taken to prevent confidences from being received by whichever lawyers in the new firm are handling the new matter. See Novo Terapeutisk Laboratorium A/S v. Baxter Travenol Laboratories, Inc., 607 F.2d 186, 197 (7th Cir. 1979) (en banc); Freeman v. Chicago Musical Instrument Co., 689 F.2d [715] at 722–23; LaSalle Nat'l Bank v. County of Lake, 703 F.2d 252 (7th Cir. 1983). The exception is inapplicable here; the firm itself changed sides.

Schwartz & Freeman's Mr. Fine not only had access to but received confidential financial and operating data of NPD in 1976 and early 1977 when he was putting together the deal to transfer stock to Mr. Malec. Within a few months, Schwartz & Freeman popped up as counsel to an adversary of NPD's before the FTC, and in that proceeding and later in the antitrust lawsuit advanced contentions to which the data Fine received might have been relevant. Those data concerned NPD's profitability, sales prospects, and general market strength—all matters potentially germane to both the liability and damage phases of an anti-trust suit charging NPD with monopolization. The two representations are thus substantially related, even though we do not know whether any of the information Fine received would be useful in Analytica's lawsuit (it might just duplicate information in Malec's possession, but we do not know his role in Analytica's suit), or if so whether he conveyed any of it to his partners and associates who were actually handling the suit. If the "substantial relationship" test applies, however, "it is not appropriate for the court to inquire into whether actual confidences were dis-closed," Westinghouse Elec. Corp. v. Gulf Oil Corp., 588 F.2d [221] at 224, unless the exception noted above for cases where the law firm itself did not switch sides is applicable, as it is not here. . . .

Schwartz & Freeman argues . . . that Malec rather than NPD retained it to struc-ture the stock transfer, but this is both erroneous and irrelevant. NPD's three co-owners retained Schwartz & Freeman to work out a deal beneficial to all of them. All agreed that Mr. Malec should be given two more shares of the stock; the only ques-tion was the cheapest way of doing it; the right answer would benefit them all. Cf. Coase, "The Problem of Social Cost," 3 J. Law & Econ. 1 (1960). The principals saw no need to be represented by separate lawyers, each pushing for a bigger slice of a fixed pie and a fee for getting it. Not only did NPD rather than Malec pay Schwartz & Freeman's bills (and there is no proof that it had a practice of paying its officers' legal expenses), but neither NPD nor the co-owners were represented by counsel other than Schwartz & Freeman. Though Millman, an accountant for NPD, did have a law degree and did do some work on the stock-transfer plan, he was not acting as the co-owners' or NPD's lawyer in a negotiation in which Fine was acting as Malec's lawyer. As is common in closely held corporations, Fine was counsel to the firm, as well as to all of its principals, for the transaction. If the position taken by Schwartz & Freeman prevailed a corporation that used only one lawyer to counsel it on matters of shareholder compensation would run the risk of the lawyer's later being deemed to have represented a single shareholder rather than the whole firm, and the corpora-tion would lose the protection of the lawyer-client relationship. Schwartz & Free-man's position thus could force up the legal expenses of owners of closely held corporations.

But it does not even matter whether NPD or Malec was the client. In Westing-house's antitrust suit against Kerr-McGee and other uranium producers [see p. 215, Note 10], Kerr-McGee moved to disqualify Westinghouse's counsel, Kirkland & Ellis, because of a project that the law firm had done for the American Petroleum Institute, of which Kerr-McGee was a member, on competition in the energy indus-tries. Kirkland & Ellis's client had been the Institute rather than Kerr-McGee but we held that this did not matter; what mattered was that Kerr-McGee had furnished confidential information to Kirkland & Ellis in connection with the law firm's work for the Institute. As in this case, it was not shown that the information had actually been used in the antitrust litigation. The work for the Institute had been done almost entirely by Kirkland & Ellis's Washington office, the antitrust litigation was being handled in the Chicago office, and Kirkland & Ellis is a big firm. The connection between the representation of a trade association of which Kerr-McGee happened to be a member and the representation of its adversary thus was rather tenuous; one may doubt whether Kerr-McGee really thought its confidences had been abused by Kirkland & Ellis. If there is any aspect of the *Kerr-McGee* decision that is subject to criticism, it is this. The present case is a much stronger one for disqualification. If NPD did not retain Schwartz & Freeman—though we think it did—still it supplied

Schwartz & Freeman with just the kind of confidential data that it would have furnished a lawyer that it had retained; and it had a right not to see Schwartz & Freeman reappear within months on the opposite side of a litigation to which that data might be highly pertinent.

We acknowledge the growing dissatisfaction . . . with the use of disqualification as a remedy for unethical conduct by lawyers. The dissatisfaction is based partly on the effect of disqualification proceedings in delaying the underlying litigation and partly on a sense that current conflict of interest standards, in legal representation as in government employment, are too stringent, particularly as applied to large law firms—though there is no indication that Schwartz & Freeman is a large firm. But we cannot find any authority for withholding the remedy in a case like this, even if we assume contrary to fact that Schwartz & Freeman is as large as Kirkland & Ellis. NPD thought Schwartz & Freeman was its counsel and supplied it without reserve with the sort of data—data about profits and sales and marketing plans—that play a key role in a monopolization suit—and lo and behold, within months Schwartz & Freeman had been hired by a competitor of NPD's to try to get the Federal Trade Commission to sue NPD; and later that competitor, still represented by Schwartz & Freeman, brought its own suit against NPD. We doubt that anyone would argue that Schwartz & Freeman could resist disqualification if it were still representing NPD, even if no confidences were revealed, and we do not think that an interval of a few months ought to make a critical difference.

The "substantial relationship" test has its problems, but conducting a factual inquiry in every case into whether confidences had actually been revealed would not be a satisfactory alternative, particularly in a case such as this where the issue is not just whether they have been revealed but also whether they will be revealed during a pending litigation. Apart from the difficulty of taking evidence on the question without compromising the confidences themselves, the only witnesses would be the very lawyers whose firm was sought to be disqualified (unlike a case where the issue is what confidences a lawyer received while at a former law firm), and their interest not only in retaining a client but in denying a serious breach of professional ethics might outweigh any felt obligation to "come clean." While "appearance of impropriety" as a principle of professional ethics invites and maybe has undergone uncritical expansion because of its vague and open-ended character, in this case it has meaning and weight. For a law firm to represent one client today, and the client's adversary tomorrow in a closely related matter, creates an unsavory appearance of conflict of interest that is difficult to dispel in the eyes of the lay public—or for that matter the bench and bar—by the filing of affidavits, difficult to verify objectively, denying that improper communication has taken place or will take place between the lawyers in the firm handling the two sides. Clients will not repose confidences in lawyers whom they distrust and will not trust firms that switch sides as nimbly as Schwartz & Freeman. . . .

. . . The order assessing fees and expenses against Schwartz & Freeman is affirmed. No costs will be awarded in this court.

[Judge Coffey agreed that the substantial relationship test applied to disqualify Richard Fine, the "ostensible" counsel for NPD because of his access to confidential financial and operating data that would be vital in the monopolization suit. He strongly dissented, however, from the holding that his firm should be automatically disqualified because of an irrebuttable presumption that the confidences were shared with the entire firm. The matter of vicarious disqualification is the subject of the next section of materials.]

Notes

1. We have already seen in the *Westinghouse* case, p. 215, Note 10, how a law firm can find itself in a fiduciary, if not an actual attorney-client, relationship with a party who never formally retained it. Judge Posner relied on that case to find that Schwartz & Freeman, which was hired by Malec, occupied a fiduciary relationship towards NPD by reason of the transmission of confidential information and also occupied an actual attorney status to NPD on the facts of the case. The *Westinghouse* opinion awakened the profession to that issue, and it has now been litigated in a number of cases.

A securities case discussed the problem at length, holding that in the circumstances of that case, counsel for an investment banker became counsel for the corporate client of the investment banker, notwithstanding the fact that that corporation also had its own counsel. Jack Eckerd Corp. v. Dart Group Corp., 621 F. Supp. 725 (D. Del. 1985). The court reached its conclusion both under the *Westinghouse* reasoning and under the more restrictive dictum of Committee on Professional Ethics & Griev. v. Johnson, 447 F.2d 169, 174 (3d Cir. 1971), which stated that "an attorney-client relationship is one of agency and arises only when the parties have given their consent, either express or implied, to its formation." The court distinguished In re John Doe Corp., 675 F.2d 482 (2d Cir. 1982), a case where an underwriter's attorney was held not to be the attorney for a company whose stock was being underwritten by reason of its demand for, and receipt of, an internal report that had been prepared by the company. In that case, however, the company was being investigated by a grand jury and the report had been demanded so that the underwriter could decide whether to go ahead with the offering.

Even a government lawyer has been held to have become an attorney for a private entity by virtue of his responsibilities to the government agency in which he was employed. Production Credit Assn. v. Buckentin, 410 N.W.2d 820 (Minn. 1987), involved the responsibilities of an attorney for one of the 12 Federal Intermediate Credit Banks (FICB), federal agencies set up regionally under the Farm Credit System to lend money to independent cooperative associations called Production Credit Associations (PCAs), which exist to lend money to farmers. The district FICBs have supervisory authority over the local PCAs and can even remove their officers and directors and set officers' salaries. As part of their duties, federal lawyers conducted seminars for the local PCAs that discussed, among other things, the kinds of legal issues likely to arise between the PCAs and their farmer-borrowers. In *Buckentin*, a former general counsel to an FICB was disqualified from representing two farmer-debtors against two different PCAs in proceedings arising out of PCA loans. The trial judges each rejected the former government lawyer's argument that his federal responsibility was adverse to the PCAs and indeed that part of his job was to see that PCAs had their own independent attorneys, finding instead that an attorney-client relationship had been created. The Minnesota Supreme Court, although noting that it might have found differently as an original matter, affirmed the finding as not clearly erroneous.

These cases point out the importance to lawyers of being aware of the possibility that their dealings with other parties may involve the creation of an unexpected, and even undesired, fiduciary relationship. One often given example is the following: a slip and fall victim calls up a lawyer, seeking representation. The lawyer says she cannot do the representation, but will send the case to another lawyer. Meanwhile a year passes and the lawyer never passed on the case, rendering the case untriable because the statute of limitations passed. Should the lawyer be liable for malpractice? Situations like these scare lawyers and they have responded in a variety of ways. See Chapter 10, p. 816ff. One example of avoiding unwanted relationships is the way many firm websites now expressly disclaim the creation of any lawyer–client relation by contact over the internet.

2. Judge Posner argued that if the Schwartz & Freeman position were accepted, there was a risk to the corporation that used only one lawyer to advise it on matters of shareholder compensation, namely, that the lawyer might be held to have represented a shareholder and hence the corporation would lose the attorney-client privilege. Is that argument applicable to these facts? Fine had never been NPD's lawyer and indeed was selected by Malec. His relationship to NPD was ambiguous, especially in view of the deteriorating relations among the stockholders of the close corporation. The *Westinghouse* reasoning helps the court's conclusion considerably. Suppose that NPD had had its own lawyer in the transaction but had supplied the same financial and market information to Fine. Would the result in *Analytica* be the same?

Judge Posner, however, casts some doubt on the correctness of the application of the *Westinghouse* "rule" to the actual facts in that case. He doubts whether Kerr-McGee, which transmitted confidential information to counsel for the trade association of which it was a member, really thought that its confidences "had been" (might be?) abused. But Judge Posner really doesn't know what Kerr-McGee thought, and we may wonder whether he really would want to substitute that subjective test for the objective test of "substantial relationship" that he made the basis for his conclusion that Schwartz & Freeman ought to be disqualified.

3. Judge Posner also argued that acceptance of the Schwartz & Freeman position could force up the legal expenses of owners of closely held corporations. That argument sounds rather strange in the context of the facts of this case. Mr. Fine charged only $850 for the 11½ hours of work that he did. That sounds like something of a

bargain for work done for three individuals and their closely held corporation. Given the deteriorating relationships among the parties, it ought to have been obvious if in fact Schwartz & Freeman had thought it was representing everyone that there was considerable exposure to the firm in that representation. If it was responsible for looking out for everyone's interests in that situation, it was entitled to have its bill reflect that exposure. Indeed, the low charge is some evidence of its contention that it was not representing everyone. Moreover, with respect to Judge Posner's larger argument, it will not always be the case that the charge of one lawyer representing all the parties in a touchy situation will be less than the combined charges of, say, two lawyers where one does the work for one of the parties clearly seen as the only client and the other simply reviews that work. The exposure factor may cause the bill of one lawyer to be higher than the bill of two lawyers.

Another point to note is Judge Posner's use of the fact of NPD's payment of Schwartz & Freeman's bill to support his conclusion that the firm represented NPD. But other courts have quite properly pointed out that that circumstance is not of itself conclusive. See DCA Food Industries, Inc. v. Tasty Foods, Inc., 626 F. Supp. 54 (W.D. Wis. 1985), distinguishing *Analytica* and citing other cases.

4. For a case that on its face appeared to allow a form of side-switching and was described by the court as probably bringing it "as close to the outer limits as we shall want to go," see Mailer v. Mailer, 390 Mass. 371, 375 (1983). Mrs. Mailer consulted a lawyer in 1973 about the possibility of bringing a divorce action against her husband, the author Norman Mailer. After discussing the matter for about an hour with the lawyer Mrs. Mailer left and decided not to file suit. Five years later, represented by another attorney, she filed a suit for divorce. Mr. Mailer was represented by the original lawyer whom she consulted. The trial court refused to disqualify the attorney and eventually the Supreme Judicial Court concluded that the original lawyer's representation of Mr. Mailer "does not require reversal of the judgment of divorce." It relied on the combination of the weakness of the relationship between Mrs. Mailer and the original lawyer, the length of time since her discussions with him, and the evidence, which permitted a finding that most of the information she supplied was known to the defendant and that no confidential information was used by the original attorney against her. It did not mention the rule that confidential information is presumed to have been transmitted in a successive representation case, perhaps because a formal attorney-ciient relationship was never formed.

The problem of the *Mailer* case can arise in the more typical case when a client shops around for a lawyer, thus creating the possibility of intentionally or unintentionally disqualifying many law firms from representing the adverse party. The court noted that problem in Poly Software Int'l., Inc. v. Su, 880 F. Supp. 1487 (D. Utah 1995), in the course of holding that an interviewing lawyer had sufficiently guarded against potential disqualification by offering a cursory or a thorough initial interview. The prospective client was held to have chosen the former and to have revealed insufficient confidential information to disqualify the interviewed law firm from representing his adversary when he chose another law firm to represent him.

5. Similar concerns may arise when a nonlawyer employee of a law firm leaves one firm and joins another that is representing an adverse interest. One court dealt with the problem of a secretary with confidential information switching sides by applying the Seventh Circuit's rebuttable presumption doctrine. It held that the presumption had been rebutted in that case, even in the absence of formal screening mechanisms. Kapco Mfg. Co. v. C. & O. Enterprises, Inc., 637 F. Supp. 1231 (N.D. Ill. 1985). Other courts have applied different tests. The Florida intermediate appellate courts have considered the issues several times and are in conflict. One court has held that when a side-switching secretary has been privy to confidences in her former firm, it nevertheless must be shown that the result of her employment by her new firm was that its client had "obtained an advantage over the other [client] that can only be alleviated by removal of the lawyer." Esquire Care Inc. v. Maguire, 532 So. 2d 740 (2d Dist. 1988). Another court, however, has held that the same rule should be applied to secretaries as to attorneys and that it is enough to disqualify the new firm that the side-switching secretary had been primarily assigned to the case in the original firm and that she was privy to relevant confidential information. Koulisis v. Rivers, 730 So. 2d 289 (4th Dist. 1999). Accord, Ciaffone v. Eighth Judicial District Court, 945 P.2d 950 (Nev. 1997).

6. Summer associates who move from firm to firm in a given summer or who obtain permanent employment in a firm that is different from the one in which they worked during the summer, and spouses who work in different practice settings in the same community also have faced difficult conflict problems, although there is not a great deal of case law dealing with those problems.

D. Conflicting Representation in the Transactional Context

The following case is an important, controversial application of the conflict of interest rules. As you read it, ask yourself whether there was a way that the law firm might have conducted itself so that it could have undertaken the second representation without violating the conflict rules.

Maritrans v. Pepper, Hamilton & Scheetz

529 Pa. 241 (1992)

PAPADAKOS, Justice

This case involves the question of whether the conduct of Appellee-attorneys is actionable independent of any violation of the Code of Professional Responsibility. While we agree that violations of the Code do not per se give rise to legal actions that may be brought by clients or other private parties, we, nevertheless, conclude that the record supports a finding that Appellees' conduct here constituted a breach of common law fiduciary duty owed to Appellant-clients and that, contrary to Appellees' argument that they cannot be prevented from representing a former client's competitors, the injunction issued by the trial court against Appellees should have been sustained by the Superior Court. As a result, we reverse the decision of the Superior Court, as more fully explained below.

Appellants . . . are Maritrans GP Inc., Maritrans Partners L.P. and Maritrans Operating Partners L.P. (hereinafter, collectively, "Maritrans"). Appellees . . . are the Philadelphia law firm of Pepper, Hamilton & Scheetz (hereinafter "Pepper"), and one of Pepper's partners, J. Anthony Messina, Jr. (hereinafter "Messina"). In February, 1988, Maritrans brought an action for preliminary and permanent injunctive relief, as well as for compensatory and punitive damages, against Pepper and Messina, its former attorneys of more than ten years. Maritrans' action arises out of Pepper and Messina's representation of Maritrans' competitors, entities whose interests were found to be adverse to the interests of Maritrans, in matters substantially related to matters in which they had represented Maritrans.

On May 1, 1989, the Court of Common Pleas of Philadelphia County entered an order preliminarily enjoining Pepper and Messina from continuing to act as labor counsel for seven of Maritrans' New York–based competitors, with the exception of one discrete piece of litigation then scheduled to commence on May 8, 1989. The trial court ruled that preliminary injunctive relief was necessary given the existence of a substantial relationship (i.e., a conflict of interest in derogation of Pepper and Messina's fiduciary duties to Maritrans) between Pepper and Messina's current representation of the New York companies, whose interests were adverse to the interests of Maritrans, and their former long-standing representation of Maritrans. . . .

Pepper and Messina then appealed the trial court's preliminary injunction order to the Superior Court which issued a judgment and opinion . . . reversing the preliminary injunction order. . . .

The facts taken in a light most favorable to Maritrans, the winner at the trial court level, are as follows:

Maritrans is a Philadelphia-based public company in the business of transporting petroleum products along the East and Gulf coasts of the United States by tug and barge. Maritrans competes in the marine transportation business with other tug and/or barge companies, including a number of companies based in New York. Pepper is an old and established Philadelphia law firm. Pepper and Messina represented Maritrans or its predecessor companies in the broadest range of labor relations matters for well over a decade. In addition, Pepper represented Maritrans in a complex public offering of securities, a private offering of $115 million in debt, a conveyance of all assets, and a negotiation and implementation of a working capital line of credit. Over the course of the representation, Pepper was paid approximately $1 million for its labor representation of Maritrans and, in the last year of the representation, approximately $1 million for its corporate and securities representation of Maritrans.

During the course of their labor representation of Maritrans, Pepper and Messina became "intimately familiar with Maritrans' operations" and "gained detailed financial and business information, including Maritrans' financial goals and projections, labor cost/savings, crew costs and operating costs." . . . This information was discussed with Pepper's labor attorneys, and particularly with Messina, for the purpose of developing Maritrans' labor goals and strategies. In addition, during the course of preparing Maritrans' public offering, Pepper was furnished with substantial confidential commercial information in Maritrans' possession—financial and otherwise—including projected labor costs, projected debt coverage and projected revenues through the year 1994, and projected rates through the year 1990. Pepper and Messina, during the course of their decade-long representation of Maritrans, came to know the complete inner-workings of the company along with Maritrans' long-term objectives, and competitive strategies in a number of areas including the area of labor costs, a particularly sensitive area in terms of effective competition. In furtherance of its ultimate goal of obtaining more business than does its competition, including the New York–based companies, Maritrans analyzed each of its competitors with Pepper and Messina. These analyses included an evaluation of each competitor's strengths and weaknesses, and of how Maritrans deals with its competitors.

Armed with this information, Pepper and Messina subsequently undertook to represent several of Maritrans' New York–based competitors. Indeed, Pepper and Messina undertook to represent the New York companies in their labor negotiations, albeit with a different union, during which the New York companies sought wage and benefit reductions in order to compete more effectively with, i.e., to win business away from, Maritrans.

In September, 1987, Maritrans learned from sources outside of Pepper that Pepper and Messina were representing four of its New York–based competitors in their labor relations matters. Maritrans objected to these representations, and voiced those objections to many Pepper attorneys, including Mr. Messina. Pepper and Messina took the position that this was a "business conflict," not a "legal conflict," and that they had no fiduciary or ethical duty to Maritrans that would prohibit these representations.

To prevent Pepper and Messina from taking on the representation of any other competitors, especially its largest competitor, Bouchard Transportation Company, Maritrans agreed to an arrangement proposed by Pepper whereby Pepper would continue as Maritrans' counsel but would not represent any more than the four New York companies it was then already representing. In addition, Messina—the Pepper attorney with the most knowledge about Maritrans—was to act not as counsel for Maritrans but, rather, as counsel for the New York companies, while two other Pepper labor attorneys would act as counsel for Maritrans; the attorneys on one side of this "Chinese Wall" would not discuss their respective representations with the attorneys on the other side. Maritrans represented that it agreed to this arrangement because it believed that this was the only way to keep Pepper and Messina from representing yet more of its competitors, especially Bouchard.

Unbeknownst to Maritrans, however, Messina then "parked" Bouchard and another of the competitors, Eklof, with Mr. Vincent Pentima, a labor attorney then at another law firm, at the same time that Messina was negotiating with Pentima for Pentima's admission into the partnership at Pepper. Moreover, notwithstanding Pepper's specific agreement not to represent these other companies, Messina for all intents and purposes was representing Bouchard and Eklof, as he was conducting joint negotiating sessions for those companies and his other four New York clients. On November 5, 1987, Maritrans executives discussed with Pepper attorneys, inter alia, Maritrans' plans and strategies of an aggressive nature in the event of a strike against the New York companies. Less than one month later, on December 2, 1987, Pepper terminated its representation of Maritrans in all matters. Later that month, on December 28, 1987, Pepper undertook the representation of the New York companies. Then, on January 4, 1988, Mr. Pentima joined Pepper as a partner and brought with him, as clients, Bouchard and Eklof. In February, 1988, Maritrans filed a complaint in the trial court against Pepper and Messina.

Discovery procedures produced evidence as follows: (i) testimony by principals of the New York companies to the effect that the type of information that Pepper and Messina possess about Maritrans is of the type considered to be confidential commercial information in the industry and that they would not reveal that information about their companies to their competitors; (ii) testimony by principals of the New York companies that they were desirous of obtaining Maritrans' confidential commercial information; (iii) testimony by principals of the New York companies that labor costs are the one item that make or break a company's competitive posture; (iv) an affidavit from the United States Department of Labor attesting that, contrary to defendant Messina's sworn testimony at the first preliminary hearing in February, 1988, Maritrans' labor contracts are not on file with the Department of Labor and thus not available under the Freedom of Information Act; and other information as well.

After initially denying the preliminary injunction, the trial court delivered a bench opinion in which it was stated that the court had sua sponte reconsidered its decision not to enter injunctive relief against Pepper and Messina. The trial court specifically noted that by denying Maritrans' request for preliminary injunctive relief the week before—even in the face of various breaches of Pepper and Messina's fiduciary duties to Maritrans—it had not "fully account[ed] for the special relationship between attorney and client . . ." but, rather, had inappropriately treated the case as a "commercial dispute involving ordinary business interests." Upon further reflection and after re-reviewing the voluminous record in this case, the trial court determined that preliminary injunctive relief was both justified and appropriate. . . .

In reconsidering sua sponte the initial decision not to enjoin Pepper and Messina, the trial court held that by initially focusing on only the November 5, 1987, meeting between Pepper attorneys and the Maritrans executives—and not on Pepper and Messina's entire representation of Maritrans—the court had taken too restrictive a view of the test to determine whether attorneys have breached their fiduciary duties by engaging in former-client conflicts of interest, i.e., the substantial relationship test. The trial court went on to hold that a substantial relationship exists between Pepper and Messina's former representation of Maritrans and their current representation of the competitors, entities whose interests are materially adverse to the interests of Maritrans in the current representation. The trial court also found that Pepper breached its obligation, which was fortified by a specific promise, to keep from Messina that which was learned after the erection of the "Chinese wall." Concluding that Maritrans was entitled to be able to proceed in its business with confidence that its plans and strategies would not be disclosed or used by Appellees, even inadvertently, the trial court ruled that preliminary injunctive relief was warranted given the existence of material adversity between Maritrans and the New York competitors, of a substantial relationship between the representations, and the fact that Maritrans had carried its burden, in proving the necessity for a preliminary injunction.

The Superior Court reversed stating that the trial court erred by issuing a preliminary injunction based upon Pepper's alleged violation of the [Pennsylvania] Rule of Professional Conduct without making any independent finding that Pepper's conduct was actionable. The Superior Court found that the trial court's use of Pennsylvania Rules of Professional Conduct 1.7 and 1.9 as points of reference for its breach of fiduciary duty analysis improperly augmented the substantive law of our Commonwealth. The Superior Court did not analyze whether the common law principles of fiduciary duty, embodied in those rules nonetheless apply to this case. The Superior Court then held that an attorney's conflict of interest in representing a subsequent client whose interests are materially adverse to a prior client in a substantially related matter is not "actionable" in Pennsylvania. As already noted, we reverse. . . .

Contrary to the arguments used by Pepper and Messina, we conclude that the Superior Court badly confused the relationship between duties under the rules of ethics and legal rules that create actionable liability apart from the rules of ethics. The Superior Court correctly recognized that simply because a lawyer's conduct may violate the rules of ethics does not mean that the conduct is actionable, in damages or for injunctive relief. The court was also correct in saying that the trial court's finding of violation of the ethical rules concerning misuse of a client's confidences is not as such a basis for issuing an injunction. These propositions are correct under either the Code of Professional Responsibility or the Rules of Professional Conduct.

However, the Superior Court then stood this correct analysis on its head. That court held that the trial judge's reference to violations of the rules of ethics somehow negated or precluded the existence of a breach of legal duty by the Pepper firm to its former client. The court also held that the presumption of misuse of a former client's confidences, developed in the law of disqualification, is inapplicable because the present case involves an injunction. Both of these propositions involve serious confusion in the law governing lawyers.

Long before the Code of Professional Responsibility was adopted, and before the Rules of Professional Conduct were adopted, the common law recognized that a lawyer could not undertake a representation adverse to a former client in a matter "substantially related" to that in which the lawyer previously had served the client. . . .

The Superior Court seems to have the idea that because conduct is not a tort simply because it is a disciplinary violation, then conduct ceases to be a tort when it is at the same time a disciplinary violation. This is an inversion of logic and legal policy and misunderstands the history of the disciplinary rules. . . .

Courts throughout the country have ordered the disgorgement of fees paid or the forfeiture of fees owed to attorneys who have breached their fiduciary duties to their clients by engaging in impermissible conflicts of interests. . . .

Courts have also allowed civil actions for damages for an attorney's breach of his fiduciary duties by engaging in conflicts of interest. See, e.g., . . . David Welch Co. v. Erskine & Tulley, [203 Cal. App. 3d 884 (1988)] (where the court affirmed a judgment of $350,000 against a law firm that breached its fiduciary duties toward a former client after being privy to the former client's confidential information by, inter alia, failing to inform the former client that the law firm prepared business proposals designed to undercut the former client's business relationships).

Courts throughout the United States have not hesitated to impose civil sanctions upon attorneys who breach their fiduciary duties to their clients, which sanctions have been imposed separately and apart from professional discipline. What must be decided in this case is whether, under the instant facts, an injunction lies to prohibit a potential conflict of interest from resulting in harm to Appellant Maritrans. Resort to simple equitable principles, as applied to the facts of this case, renders an affirmative answer to this question. . . .

Pepper and Messina argue that a preliminary injunction was an abuse of discretion where it restrains them from representing a former client's competitors, in order to supply the former client with a "sense of security" that they will not reveal confidences to those competitors where there has been no revelation or threat of revelations up to that point. We disagree. Whether a fiduciary can later represent competitors or whether a law firm can later represent competitors of its former client is a matter that must be decided from case to case and depends on a number of factors. One factor is the extent to which the fiduciary was involved in its former client's affairs. The greater the involvement, the greater the danger that confidences (where such exist) will be revealed. Here, Pepper and Messina's involvement was extensive as was their knowledge of sensitive information provided to them by Maritrans. We do *not* wish to establish a blanket rule that a law firm may not later represent the economic competitor of a former client in matters in which the former client is not also a party to a law suit. But situations may well exist where the danger of revelation of the confidences of a former client is so great that injunctive relief is warranted. This is one of those situations. There is a substantial relationship here between Pepper and Messina's former representation of Maritrans and their current representation of Maritrans' competitors such that the injunctive relief granted here was justified. It might be theoretically possible to argue that Pepper and Messina should merely be enjoined from revealing the confidential material they have acquired from Maritrans but such an injunction would be difficult, if not impossible, to administer. . . . As fiduciaries, Pepper and Messina can be fully enjoined from representing Maritrans' competitors as that would create too great a danger that Maritrans' confidential relationship with Pepper and Messina would be breached.

Here, the trial court did not commit an abuse of discretion. On these facts, it was perfectly reasonable to conclude that Maritrans' competitive position could be irreparably injured if Pepper and Messina continued to represent their competitors and that Maritrans' remedy at law, that is their right to later seek damages, would be difficult if not impossible to sustain because of difficult problems of proof, particularly problems related to piercing what would later become a confidential relationship between their competitors and those competitors' attorneys (Pepper and Messina). . . .

In reversing the trial court's preliminary injunction, the Superior Court ignored the fact that there already exists in this Commonwealth a well-entrenched body of substantive law prohibiting fiduciaries from engaging in conflicts of interest, and that there is no law excepting attorneys from that prohibition. The Superior Court therefore erroneously concluded that the trial court had augmented the substantive law of this Commonwealth. . . .

Obviously, there are some disciplinary rules, such as Rule 3.3 of the Pennsylvania Rules of Professional Conduct (Candor Toward the Tribunal), which, if violated, may not give rise to civil liability. But could it be said that an attorney who misappropriates client funds is not civilly liable to his client, and that the client's only recourse upon discovery that his attorney has misappropriated his funds is to report the attorney to the Disciplinary Board? It is obvious that this is not and cannot be the rule. Misappropriating client funds is actionable, and was actionable long before the promulgation of any rule of professional conduct prohibiting such conduct. Just as there would be an independent cause of action available to a client whose attorney has misappropriated his funds, so too there is an independent cause of action available to a client whose attorney engaged in impermissible conflicts of interest vis-à-vis that client. The violator is subject to civil liability as well as injunctive relief. . . .

NIX, Chief Justice, dissenting.

In the instant matter the majority has concluded that appellee, Pepper, Hamilton & Scheetz ("Pepper"), was properly enjoined from representing Maritrans' competitors because of the significant risk of the disclosure of confidential information. The majority finds the creation of the relationship which harbors this risk to be a breach of Pepper's fiduciary duty to Maritrans. I believe that in reaching this result, the majority overlooks the significant body of case law that has developed in this area, as well as a key factor that renders its conclusion unreasonable.

The Chinese wall defense is set forth in the Model Rules of Professional Conduct, Rule 1.11. The procedure established is one whereby a single attorney or group of attorneys who has represented a particular client is isolated from another attorney or attorneys within the same firm who represent a client whose interests are substantially related but materially adverse to those of the initial client. The goal of such a procedure is to minimize the potential for the transmission of confidential information between attorneys representing clients with competing interests.

The Chinese wall defense is asserted in the following manner. First, in attempting to have an attorney disqualified, the former client must show that matters embraced within a pending lawsuit, in which his former attorney appears on behalf of an adversary, are substantially related to matters wherein the attorney had previously represented the former client. . . . Once this burden, called the "substantial relationship test," is met, and the complainant has shown that the former representation exposed the attorney to confidences or secrets arguably pertinent in the present dispute, a rebuttable presumption arises that those confidences were shared. *Freeman v. Chicago Musical Instrument Co.*, 689 F.2d 715, 723 (7th Cir. 1982); *Novo Terapeutisk Laboratories v. Baxter Travenol Labs.*, 607 F.2d 186, 196 (7th Cir. 1979).

To overcome this presumption, the Chinese wall defense is asserted, and the attorney and firm must demonstrate sufficient facts and circumstances of their particular case to establish the probable effectiveness of the wall. . . . The factors to be considered in the acceptance of the Chinese wall defense are the substantiality of the relationship between the attorney and the former client, . . . the time lapse between the matters in dispute, . . . the size of the firm and the number of disqualified attorneys, the nature of the disqualified attorney's involvement, . . . and the timing of the wall. Relevant features of the wall itself include the following:

    a. the prohibition of discussion of sensitive matters

    b. restricted circulation of sensitive documents

    c. restricted access to files

    d. strong firm policy against breach, including sanctions, physical and/ or geographical separation

ABA Opinion 342, 62 ABA J. 517, 521 (1976).

Applying these factors to the instant matter, we would be inclined initially to agree with Maritrans' assertions that the wall in this case was probably defective. Despite the size of the firm and the number of attorneys involved, the timing of the wall was delayed in relation to the existence of the conflict. The relationship between Maritrans and Pepper was substantial, as was Messina's involvement with Maritrans. Of particular significance is the fact that the conflict existed not merely within the firm as a whole but within a single attorney who sought to represent competing clients.

These factors reveal serious concerns which must have been patently obvious at the time the conflict arose. Nevertheless, *Maritrans was informed of this peculiar arrangement and consented to it.* It is well-settled in the field of legal ethics *that a client's consent*, upon full disclosure of a conflict of interest, *is sufficient to permit the attorney to continue the otherwise objectionable representation.* . . . Thus, while Maritrans' concerns may have been legitimate, their initial acquiescence must be construed as a forbearance of any objections based upon the *potential* for breach of confidentiality. Having consented to the arrangement, they are now bound by their consent until such time as an actual breach of confidentiality occurs. As was previously found by this writer, Maritrans G.P., Inc. v. Pepper, Hamilton & Scheetz, 524 Pa. 415 (1990) (Memorandum Opinion), and as Maritrans implicitly concedes, no actual disclosure of confidential information has occurred. Maritrans' prior consent amounts to a waiver of their right to an objection based upon the fear of disclosure. . . .

FLAHERTY, Justice, dissenting.

I join the dissenting opinion authored by Mr. Chief Justice Nix inasmuch as the record discloses consent was given by Maritrans to the arrangement and no actual breach of confidentiality is present, thus the remedy sought in this case is not warranted. The so-called "Chinese wall" defense, however, is fraught with problems, and, I strongly believe, should be scrutinized closely by the courts.

Notes

1. Note that on December 2, 1987, Pepper Hamilton terminated its representation of Maritrans and on December 28, it undertook to represent the New York competitors of Maritrans. Then a week later it brought in as a lateral partner the lawyer with whom other Maritrans competitors had been parked and he brought those clients with him. Given the background discussions between Pepper Hamilton and Maritrans over representation of competitors, does that timetable not suggest that there was a "hot potato" problem in this case? If there was such a problem, did Pepper Hamilton violate Model Rule 1.7(a)? 1.7(b)?

2. On the assumption that this is a former client and not a simultaneous representation case, is there tension between the court's holding and the assumption underlying Rule 1.9 that a lawyer may represent competitors of a former client even in a generally similar matter? Did Pepper Hamilton violate Model Rule 1.9(a)? What was the threat of future violation that warranted the issuance of an injunction? Is the problem here that the nature of the representation threatened disclosure of confidential information of Maritrans? Pennsylvania is a jurisdiction that permits screening off of members of a firm in a situation like this to protect against revelation of confidential information. Is the court telling us that the screen that Pepper Hamilton used didn't work or that no screen would work on the facts of this case? Does the sophistication of the parties seem to matter here? Should it?

3. A decision of the House of Lords that excited a great deal of interest among those concerned with the problem of multidisciplinary law practice was Prince Jefri Bolkiah v. KPMG, 149 NLJ 16 (1998). KPMG, one of the then so-called Big Five accounting firms, provided litigation support services to Prince Jefri individually and also to the Brunei Investment Agency when he was chairman. Subsequently,

after Prince Jefri was removed as chairman, KPMG was asked by the Agency to assist in investigating transfers of funds made at a time when Prince Jefri was chairman. Recognizing that it possessed confidential information, KPMG set up a screen to prevent transfer of information between those working on the new investigation and those with confidential information. The House of Lords enjoined the representation. The leading opinion of Lord Millett stated that the same rules that would apply to a solicitor should be applied to accountants performing litigation support services. It was his opinion that in the case of a former client, there should be no imputation of knowledge of one partner to another. The lawyer's duty was to preserve confidentiality and a court should intervene unless satisfied that there is "no risk" of disclosure. The screen in this case was ad hoc and was established within a single department between teams of employees with rotating memberships who were accustomed to working with one another. On the facts of the case he concluded that KPMG had not met its heavy burden of showing that there was no risk that Prince Jefri's confidential information might be inadvertently leaked. Should we have the same view in America? Does it make a difference if screens are used on an ad hoc basis? We will discuss the feasibility of screening to cure conflict problems in section E of this Chapter, where we address vicarious disqualification.

Note that what would ordinarily be the first issue in an American case was a non-issue in Great Britain. Accountants, and anyone else for that matter, may provide all sorts of legal services to clients except for the so-called "reserved services," which include conveyancing, taking out grants of probate to administer a will, and providing advocacy services, including the conduct of litigation. See testimony of Allison Crawley, Law Society of England and Wales, before the ABA Multidisciplinary Commission, <http://www.americanbar.org/groups/professional_responsibility /commission_multidisciplinary_practice/crawley1198.html>. We will return to the recent developments in the UK regarding multidisciplinary practice and other forms of non-lawyer ownership and practice in Chapter 8.

Maling v. Finnegan, Henderson, Farabow, Garrett & Dunner, LLP

473 Mass. 336 (2015)

Cordy, J.

In this case we consider whether an actionable conflict of interest arises under Mass. R. Prof. C. 1.7 when attorneys in different offices of the same law firm simultaneously represent business competitors in prosecuting patents on similar inventions, without informing them or obtaining their consent to the simultaneous representation. *Issue*

The plaintiff, Chris E. Maling, engaged the defendant law firm Finnegan, Henderson, Farabow, Garrett & Dunner, LLP (Finnegan), including the three individual attorneys named in this suit, to represent him in connection with the prosecution of patents for Maling's inventions for a new screwless eyeglass. After obtaining his patents, Maling learned that Finnegan had been simultaneously representing another client that competed with Maling in the screwless eyeglass market. Maling then commenced this action, alleging harm under various legal theories resulting from Finnegan's failure to disclose the alleged conflict of interest. A judge in the Superior Court dismissed Maling's complaint for failure to state a claim under Mass. R. Civ. P. 12(b)(6). Maling appealed, and we transferred the case to this court on our own motion. We conclude that the simultaneous representation by a law firm in the prosecution of patents for two clients competing in the same technology area for similar inventions is not a per se violation of Mass. R. Prof. C. 1.7. We further conclude that based on the facts alleged in his complaint, Maling failed to state a claim for relief. Accordingly, we affirm the judgment of dismissal.

Holding {

Ruling (

1. *Background.* In 2003, Maling engaged Finnegan to perform legal services in connection with the filing and prosecution of patents for Maling's inventions for a new screwless eyeglass, including a screwless eyeglass hinge block design. Finnegan prepared patent applications for Maling's inventions after ordering "prior art" searches. Over the next several years, Finnegan successfully obtained four separate patents for Maling.

Attorneys in Finnegan's Boston office represented Maling from approximately April, 2003, to May, 2009. During this period of time, attorneys in Finnegan's Washington, D.C., office represented Masunaga Optical Manufacturing Co., Ltd. (Masunaga), a Japanese corporation that also sought patents for its screwless eyeglass technology. Upon learning of Finnegan's representation of Masunaga, Maling brought suit, asserting claims stemming from the alleged conflict of interest that arose from Finnegan's simultaneous representation of both clients. We describe the allegations in Maling's complaint germane to our decision.

Maling alleges that he engaged Finnegan to "file and prosecute a patent for [his] inventions for a new screwless eyeglass, including without limitation, his invention of a 'screwless' eyeglasses hinge block design," and that in September, 2003, Finnegan ordered prior art searches relating to Maling's inventions.[5] Maling alleges that Finnegan "belatedly" commenced preparation of a patent application for his inventions in or about May, 2004, and that it "[inexplicably] took [fourteen] months" to do so. Maling also alleges that Finnegan filed patent applications for Masunaga more quickly than it did for him. At the same time, Maling acknowledges that Finnegan successfully obtained patents for his inventions. Maling further claims that he paid Finnegan in excess of $100,000 for its services, and that he invested "millions of dollars" to develop his product. He claims he would not have made this investment had

---

5. Prior art is "the collection of everything in a particular art of science that pre-dates the patent-in-suit." Princeton Biochemicals, Inc. v. Beckman Coulter, Inc., No. 96-5541, 2004 U.S. Dist. LEXIS 11918 (D.N.J. June 17, 2004), aff'd 411 F.3d 1332 (Fed. Cir. 2005). See 35 U.S.C. § 102 (2012).

Finnegan "disclosed its conflict of interest and/or its work on the competing Masunaga patent." He further alleges that the Masunaga applications are very similar to the Maling applications, and that Finnegan knew it was performing work in the "same patent space" for both clients. Maling also alleges that he was harmed when Finnegan, in 2008, declined to provide him with a legal opinion addressing similarities between the Masunaga patents and the Maling patents. Because Finnegan did not provide the legal opinion Maling claims, he was unable to obtain funding for his invention, and his product was otherwise unmarketable on account of its similarities to the Masunaga device; as a result, his patents and inventions have diminished in value. In sum, Maling contends, Finnegan's simultaneous representation of both clients, as well as its failure to disclose the alleged conflict, resulted in "great harm" and "tremendous financial hardship" for Maling.

Finnegan moved to dismiss Maling's complaint for failure to state a claim under Mass. R. Civ. P. 12(b)(6). The motion was granted in October, 2013, and Maling appealed. We then transferred the case to this court on our own motion.

2. *Discussion.* We review the sufficiency of Maling's complaint de novo, taking as true the factual allegations set forth therein and drawing all inferences in his favor. . . . "[W]e look beyond the conclusory allegations in the complaint and focus on whether the factual allegations plausibly suggest an entitlement to relief." Id., citing Iannacchino v. Ford Motor Co., 451 Mass. 623, 635–636 (2008).

Maling's complaint sets forth four bases for relief: (1) breach of fiduciary duty; (2) legal malpractice; (3) unfair or deceptive practices in violation of G. L. c. 93A; and (4) "inequitable conduct" before the United States Patent and Trademark Office (USPTO). Because each count hinges on the existence of an undisclosed conflict of interest arising from Finnegan's representation of both Maling and Masunaga, we focus our inquiry on whether, under the facts alleged, an actionable conflict arose in violation of the Massachusetts Rules of Professional Conduct.

Rule 1.7 of the Massachusetts Rules of Professional Conduct, which applies to conflicts of interests between current clients, governs the issues in this case. By its terms, rule 1.7, with limited exceptions, provides that a lawyer shall not represent a client if the representation is "directly adverse to another client," Mass. R. Prof. C. 1.7(a)(1), or where "there is a significant risk that the representation of one or more clients will be materially limited by the lawyer's responsibilities to another client, a former client or a third person or by a personal interest of the lawyer," Mass. R. Prof. C. 1.7(a)(2). The purpose of rule 1.7 is twofold. It serves as a "prophylactic [measure] to protect confidences that a client may have shared with his or her attorney . . . [and] safeguard[s] loyalty as a feature of the lawyer-client relationship." SWS Fin. Fund A v. Salomon Bros. Inc., 790 F. Supp. 1392, 1401 (N.D. Ill. 1992).[7]

In the practice of patent law, the simultaneous representation of clients competing for patents in the same technology area is sometimes referred to as a "subject matter conflict." See, e.g., Dolak, "Recognizing and Resolving Conflicts of Interest in Intellectual Property Matters," 42 IDEA 453, 463 (2002); Hricik, "Trouble Waiting to Happen: Malpractice and Ethical Issues in Patent Prosecution," 31 AIPLA Q.J. 385, 412 (2003). Subject matter conflicts do not fit neatly into the traditional conflict analysis. Maling advocates for a broad interpretation of rule 1.7 that would render all subject matter conflicts actionable, per se violations. We disagree. Rather, we conclude that although subject matter conflicts in patent prosecutions often may present a number of potential legal, ethical, and practical problems for lawyers and their clients, they do not, standing alone, constitute an actionable conflict of interest that violates rule 1.7.

a. *Adverse representation under rule 1.7(a)(1)*. Representation is "directly adverse" in violation of rule 1.7(a)(1) when a lawyer "act[s] as an advocate in one matter against a person the lawyer represents in some other matter, even when the matters are wholly unrelated." Mass. R. Prof. C. 1.7 comment 6. In other words, "[a] law firm that represents client A in the defense of an action may not, at the same time, be counsel for

---

7. The USPTO also sets standards of conduct for attorneys who practice before it. In 2013, the USPTO adopted new ethics rules based on the American Bar Association's Model Rules of Professional Conduct. See 78 Fed. Reg. 20,180 (2013). The current regulation on concurrent conflicts of interest, 37 C.F.R. § 11.107 (2013), is virtually identical in language to Mass. R. Prof. C. 1.7.

At the time this action was brought, concurrent conflicts of interest were governed by 37 C.F.R. § 10.66 (2012) (entitled, "Refusing to accept or continue employment if the interests of another client may impair the independent professional judgment of the practitioner"), which provided

(a) A practitioner shall decline proffered employment if the exercise of the practitioner's independent professional judgment in behalf of a client will be or is likely to be adversely affected by the acceptance of the proffered employment, or if it would be likely to involve the practitioner in representing differing interests, except to the extent permitted under paragraph (c) of this section.

(b) A practitioner shall not continue multiple employment if the exercise of the practitioner's independent professional judgment in behalf of a client will be or is likely to be adversely affected by the practitioner's representation of another client, or if it would be likely to involve the practitioner in representing differing interests, except to the extent permitted under paragraph (c) of this section.

(c) In the situations covered by paragraphs (a) and (b) of this section a practitioner may represent multiple clients if it is obvious that the practitioner can adequately represent the interest of each and if each consents to the representation after full disclosure of the possible effect of such representation on the exercise of the practitioner's independent professional judgment on behalf of each.

(d) If a practitioner is required to decline employment or to withdraw from employment under a Disciplinary Rule, no partner, or associate, or any other practitioner affiliated with the practitioner or the practitioner's firm, may accept or continue such employment unless otherwise ordered by the Director or Commissioner.

a plaintiff in an action brought against client A, at least without the consent of both clients." McCourt Co. v. FPC Props., Inc., 386 Mass. 145 (1982).

In the instant case, Maling and Masunaga were not adversaries in the traditional sense, as they did not appear on opposite sides of litigation. Rather, they each appeared before the USPTO in separate proceedings to seek patents for their respective screwless eyeglass devices.

Maling contends, however, that he and Masunaga were directly adverse within the meaning of rule 1.7(a)(1) because they were competing in the "same patent space." We disagree that the meaning of "directly adverse" stretches so far. The rules of professional conduct make clear that "simultaneous representation in unrelated matters of clients whose interests are only economically adverse, such as representation of competing economic enterprises in unrelated litigation, does not ordinarily constitute a conflict of interest and thus may not require consent of the respective clients." Mass. R. Prof. C. 1.7 comment 6. Put differently, "[d]irect adverseness requires a conflict as to the legal rights and duties of the clients, not merely conflicting economic interests." American Bar Association Standing Committee on Ethics and Professional Responsibility, Formal Op. 05–434, at 140 (Dec. 8, 2004). *Wald*

Curtis v. Radio Representatives, Inc., 696 F. Supp. 729 (D.D.C. 1988), a case involving broadcast licenses, offers a useful example. In *Curtis*, the United States District Court for the District of Columbia found that no actionable conflict of interest existed where a law firm simultaneously represented clients in the preparation and prosecution of applications for radio broadcast licenses from the Federal Communications Commission (FCC). Id. at 731–32, 737. The court reasoned that "the fact that an attorney is simultaneously representing two companies that are competitors in the same industry does not itself establish an actionable breach of an attorney's fiduciary duty." Id. at 736, quoting D.J. Horan & G.W. Spellmire, Jr., *Attorney Malpractice: Prevention and Defense* 17-1 (1987). It went on to explain that a conflict of interest could develop between clients seeking broadcast licenses under circumstances where "objectionable electrical interference existed between two stations." *Curtis*, supra. However, because the defendant failed to assert such interference, or even the potential for such interference, the court could not conclude that a conflict of interest existed in violation of the rules of professional conduct adopted by the District of Columbia. Id. at 736–37.

The analysis undertaken by the court in *Curtis* is instructive in our evaluation of Maling's claims. Finnegan's representation of Maling and Masunaga is analogous to that undertaken by the law firm in *Curtis*. Finnegan represented two clients competing in the screwless eyeglass device market in proceedings before the USPTO. As Maling acknowledges, Finnegan was able successfully to obtain patents from the USPTO for both his device and Masunaga's, in the same way that the law firm in *Curtis* was able to obtain radio broadcast licenses for each of its clients from the FCC. Maling and Masunaga were not competing for the same patent, but rather different patents for similar devices.

Like the court in *Curtis*, we acknowledge that an actionable conflict of interest could arise under different factual circumstances. For example, where claims in two patent applications filed prior to March 16, 2013, are identical or obvious variants of each other, the USPTO can institute an "interference proceeding" to determine which inventor would be awarded the claims contained in the patent applications. 35 U.S.C. § 135(a) (2002).[10] If the USPTO had called an interference proceeding to resolve conflicting claims in the Maling and Masunaga patent applications, or if Finnegan, acting as a reasonable patent attorney, believed such a proceeding was likely, the legal rights of the parties would have been in conflict, as only one inventor can prevail in an interference proceeding. In such a case, rule 1.7 would have obliged Finnegan to disclose the conflict and obtain consent from both clients or withdraw from representation. See Mass. R. Prof. C. 1.7 comments 3, 4.

Maling's conclusory allegations as to the high degree of similarity between his device and the Masunaga device are contradicted by his acknowledgment elsewhere in the complaint that patents issued for both his applications and the Masunaga applications. Although Maling alleges that the Masunaga and Maling applications are "similar . . . in many important respects," he does not allege that the claims are identical or obvious variants of each other such that the claims in one application would necessarily preclude claims contained in the other. Additionally, we appreciate that the claims comprising a patent application may be sufficiently distinct so as to permit the issuance of multiple patents for similar inventions, or components of an invention, as was the case here. Accordingly, Maling's allegations do not permit any inference as to whether the similarities between the inventions at the time Finnegan was retained to prepare and prosecute Maling's patent applications were of such a degree that Finnegan should have reasonably foreseen the potential for an interference proceeding.[11] Maling's conclusory statement that the inventions were very similar is precisely the type of legal conclusion that we do not credit. See *Iannacchino*, 451 Mass. at 636. Moreover, Maling makes no allegations that an interference proceeding was instituted, nor has he alleged facts supporting the inference that Finnegan

---

10. Interference proceedings are meant to assist the director of the USPTO in determining priority, that is, which party first invented the commonly claimed invention. See MPEP, supra at § 2301 (rev. Oct. 2015) at <http://www.uspto.gov/web/offices/pac/mpep/mpep-2300.pdf> [<http://perma.cc/T2D9-G62D>]. This first-to-invent system was supplanted by the enactment of the America Invents Act, which updated various provisions of the patent code, and which gives priority to the first party to file an application. See 35 U.S.C. § 135 (2012). Prior to the America Invents Act, 35 U.S.C. § 135(a) (2006) provided, in relevant part:

> Whenever an application is made for a patent which, in the opinion of the Director [of the USPTO], would interfere with any pending application, or with any unexpired patent, an interference may be declared and the Director shall give notice of such declaration to the applicants, or applicant and patentee, as the case may be. The Board of Patent Appeals and Interferences shall determine questions of priority of the inventions and may determine questions of patentability.

11. Maling's allegation that he and Masunaga competed in the "same patent space," without more, fails to demonstrate entitlement to relief. Maling cites no authority, and we have found none, that gives this term special meaning in the context of patent jurisprudence.

took positions adverse to Maling and favorable to Masunaga in the prosecution of their respective patents.

We also recognize that subject matter conflicts can give rise to conflicts of interest under rule 1.7(a)(1) in nonlitigation contexts. . . .

Here, such a conflict likely arose in 2008 when Maling sought a legal opinion from Finnegan regarding the likelihood that he might be exposed to claims by Masunaga for patent infringement. Finnegan declined to provide the opinion, and Maling alleges that he lost financing as a result. Providing the opinion arguably would have rendered the interests of Maling and Masunaga "directly adverse" within the meaning of rule 1.7(a)(1), and either declining representation or disclosing the conflict and obtaining consent would have been the proper course of action.[12] But there is no allegation that Finnegan had agreed to provide such opinions in its engagement to prosecute Maling's patents. Without such a claim, we cannot conclude that a conflict based on direct adversity has been adequately alleged.

b. *Material limitation under rule 1.7(a)(2)*. We turn next to the question whether Finnegan's representation of Masunaga "materially limited" its representation of Maling in contravention of rule 1.7(a)(2), which prohibits representation where "there is no direct adverseness . . . [but] there is a significant risk that a lawyer's ability to consider, recommend or carry out an appropriate course of action for the client will be materially limited as a result of the lawyer's other responsibilities or interests." Mass. R. Prof. C. 1.7 comment 8. The "critical inquiry" in analyzing potential conflicts under rule 1.7(a)(2), "is whether the lawyer has a competing interest or responsibility that 'will materially interfere with the lawyer's independent professional judgment in considering alternatives or foreclose courses of action that reasonably should be pursued on behalf of the client.'" Matter of Driscoll, 447 Mass. 678, 686 (2006) . . . .

In his complaint, Maling alleges in conclusory terms that Finnegan was unable to protect both his interests and Masunaga's and ultimately chose to protect Masunaga at his expense in the patent prosecution process. In Maling's view, Finnegan "pulled its punches" and got more for Masunaga than for Maling before the USPTO. He has failed, however, to allege sufficient facts to support such a proposition. . . .

. . . Maling's complaint provides little more than speculation that Finnegan's judgment was impaired or that he obtained a less robust patent than if he had been represented by other, "conflict-free" counsel. Maling does not allege that the claims contained in his applications were altered or narrowed in light of the Masunaga applications . . . or, importantly, that his client confidences were disclosed or used in any way to Masunaga's advantage. Nor does he allege that Finnegan delayed filing his patent application to ensure the success of Masunaga's application over his own. Ultimately, Maling's bare assertions that Masunaga was given preferential treatment and

---

12. The record does not reflect Finnegan's rationale for declining to provide the opinion.

was "enrich[ed]" to his "detriment" as a consequence do not support an inference that Finnegan was "materially limited" in its ability to obtain patents for Maling's inventions.

Finnegan's subsequent inability or unwillingness to provide a legal opinion regarding the similarities between the Maling and Masunaga inventions also raises a question whether the simultaneous representation "foreclose[d] [a] course[ ] of action" that should have been pursued on Maling's behalf. Mass. R. Prof'l C. 1.7 comment 8. As previously discussed, rendering such an opinion would likely have created a direct conflict between Maling and Masunaga in violation of rule 1.7(a)(1). To the extent that such a conflict was foreseeable, because, as Maling alleges, the Masunaga and Maling inventions were so similar, it is possible that Finnegan should have declined to represent Maling from the outset of his case so as to also avoid a violation of rule 1.7(a)(2). This, however, depends in large measure on the nature of Finnegan's engagement by Maling in 2003.

Before engaging a client, a lawyer must determine whether the potential for conflict counsels against undertaking representation. Comment 8 to rule 1.7 elaborates:

> The mere possibility of subsequent harm does not itself require disclosure and consent. The critical questions are the likelihood that a difference in interests will eventuate and, if it does, whether it will materially interfere with the lawyer's independent professional judgment in considering alternatives or foreclose courses of action that reasonably should be pursued on behalf of the client.

Maling's complaint does not contain any allegations as to the services or scope of representation agreed upon by Maling and Finnegan other than that Finnegan "agreed to file and prosecute a patent for Maling's inventions." Nor is it adequately alleged that Finnegan should have reasonably anticipated that Maling would need a legal opinion that would create a conflict of interest. There are simply too few facts from which to infer that Finnegan reasonably should have foreseen the potential conflict in the first place. See, e.g., Vaxiion Therapeutics, Inc. v. Foley & Lardner LLP, 593 F. Supp. 2d 1153, 1173 (S.D. Cal. 2008) (deciding that expert testimony created question of fact as to likelihood that conflict of interest would develop from firm's simultaneous representation of competitor clients in patent prosecution). Based on these inadequacies, we agree with the motion judge that the complaint does not sufficiently allege that Finnegan violated its duties under rule 1.7(a)(2) by undertaking representation of both Maling and Masunaga.

Because Maling's claims hinge on the existence of a conflict of interest, and because we conclude there was none adequately alleged in this case, he fails to state a claim on each of the counts in his complaint.

c. *Identifying conflicts of interest.* This case also raises important considerations under Mass. R. Prof. C. 1.10, . . . which prohibits lawyers associated in a firm from "knowingly represent[ing] a client when any one of them practicing alone would be prohibited from doing so by Rule[ ] 1.7." Mass R. Prof. C. 1.10(a).[16] To ensure compliance with both rules 1.7 and 1.10, firms must implement procedures to identify and remedy actual and potential conflicts of interest. See Mass. R. Prof. C. 5.1 comment 2 . . . (requiring firms to make "reasonable efforts to establish internal policies . . . designed to detect and resolve conflicts of interest").

What constitutes an adequate conflict check is a complex question. As a member of this court observed, "[a]gainst a backdrop of increasing law firm reorganizations and mergers, lateral transfers, and the rise of large-scale firms that transcend State and national borders, the issue of dual representation is one of multifaceted overtones and novel complexity." Coke v. Equity Residential Props. Trust, 440 Mass. 511, 518 (2003) (Cowin, J., concurring). Nothing we say here today, however, should be construed to absolve law firms from the obligation to implement robust processes that will detect potential conflicts.

This court has not defined a minimum protocol for carrying out a conflict check in the area of patent practice, or in any other area of law. However, no matter how complex such a protocol might be, law firms run significant risks, financial and reputational, if they do not avail themselves of a robust conflict system adequate to the nature of their practice. Although Maling's complaint does not plead an actionable violation of rule 1.7 sufficiently, the misuse of client confidences and the preferential treatment of the interests of one client, to the detriment of nearly identical interests of another, are serious matters that cannot be reconciled with the ethical obligations of our profession.

3. *Conclusion.* As noted throughout this opinion, there are various factual scenarios in the context of patent practice in which a subject matter conflict may give rise to an actionable violation of rule 1.7. On the facts alleged in Maling's complaint, however, we find that no actionable conflict of interest existed. The dismissal of the complaint is affirmed.

Notes

Wald 1. The nationwide interest generated by this case within the patent bar is illustrated by the amicus brief on behalf of the defendants joined by ten major law firms. Presumably the interest was generated by the fear that a contrary decision might have a substantial impact on the way patent firms conduct their business.

2. One way to read the court's opinion is that it desperately sought to avoid deciding a difficult and important professional responsibility problem by imposing a high pleading requirement on plaintiffs' causes of action for breach of professional duty. Underlying the court's opinion, however, appears to be the substantive

---

16. The lawyers working on Masunaga's prosecution worked out of a different office than the lawyers working on the prosecution of Maling's patents. Although the risks of inadvertent confidential client information disclose or misuse may be reduced in such circumstances, this makes little difference from a disciplinary rules standpoint as conflicts are generally imputed to all members of the firm regardless of their geographical location or work assignments.

conclusion that there is no requirement to make disclosure to a potential client of information that might reasonably be thought to be important, even crucial, to the hiring decision unless that information creates, or at least raises a substantial possibility of, a disqualifying conflict of interest. Do you agree with that conclusion?

yes

3. Should the decision whether there was a conflict of interest turn on the likelihood that the Patent Office would institute an interference proceeding or award more than one patent? To put it another way, was the issuance of patents to both Masunaga and Maling conclusive that there was no forbidden conflict of interest?

4. Is competition among screwless eyeglass frame manufacturers like competition for broadcast licenses, especially when the broadcast license competition is not for the same frequency? Is *Maling* more like *Curtis* or like *Maritrans*?

?? 5. Why doesn't the suggestion that a conflict "likely arose" in 2008 when Maling asked for an opinion concerning infringement indicate that a law firm representing two clients seeking patents for screwless eyeglass frames ought to have foreseen the possibility of conflict at the time of taking on the second representation?

6. Does the court's reference to the need for "robust processes" for detecting possible conflict suggest that the real problem here was that Finnegan did not have such a system and was not aware of the potential for conflict when it took on Maling as a client? Which way should that cut in resolving the issue before the court?

typo 7. If you were the Finnegan lawyer representing Masunaga, what would do when you saw on the Finnegan new business database that one of your partners had taken on a new client seeking a patent for a screwless eyeglass frame? What could that partner tell you when you raised the question whether there was a conflict? Whatever the partner replied, what would you communicate, if anything, to your client Masunaga? Would you have taken him on if you had concluded that you would not be violating Rule 1.7 to do so? In such circumstances, how would you have answered Maling if he had asked the direct question whether you were representing anyone seeking a patent for a screwless eyeglass frame? Whatever your answer, what light does that answer throw on your action if Maling does not know enough to ask the question?

If same lawyer rep. both in patent (similar invention) → COI. it under 1.7(a)(2)

8. Under the applicable Rule of Professional Conduct, the result in *Maling* would have been the same if the same lawyer in the Finnegan firm had worked on both patents. In that situation, assuming, as the court held, that it was not a violation of Rule 1.7 for the lawyer to handle both matters, how should that lawyer reply if Maling asks whether the lawyer is representing anyone else seeking a patent for something similar to his invention? How does your answer to that question reflect on the decision in the actual case? Does it suggest that the outcome in the actual case turned on whether Maling was smart enough to ask the right question in the absence of being given any information that he needed to ask such a question?

9. In a subsequent case, a Massachusetts trial court dismissed a complaint by Gillette Co. against a former in-house patent counsel who had gone to work for a

competitor. Gillette sought to use professional responsibility law to take the place of a non-compete clause that had expired. Gillette Co. v. Provost, 201 Mass. Super. LEXIS 40 (Mass. Super. 2016).

The court concluded that "[i]t is perfectly lawful for Gillette's former patent attorney to help a competitor avoid infringing Gillette patents, so long as he does not disclose or use any confidential information obtained from Gillette."

The court went on to say that:

> Gillette's allegations that [former counsel] was hired by [competitor] to help it figure out how to compete with Gillette without infringing on any of Gillette's patent do not plausibly suggest that [former counsel] has breached his fiduciary duty to Gillette. . . . [T]he interests of [the competitor] are not "materially adverse" to those of Gillette within the meaning of Rule 1.9 merely because [the competitor] seeks to compete by selling shaving products that are designed so as not to infringe upon any patent held by Gillette.

> The allegations that [former counsel] developed expertise regarding the scope and meaning of some of Gillette's patents while he worked for Gillette as a patent attorney are beside the point. Patents are public documents that may be read and analyzed by anyone . . . .

> The successful prosecution of a particular patent for a former client "is not substantially related" to a later representation concerning whether a different client has infringed that patent because, "in patent law, '[v]alidity'—and thus patentability—'and infringement are distant issues, bearing different burdens, different presumptions, and different evidence.'" . . . The mere fact that both representations involved the same patent is not enough to establish that the two matters are substantially related within the meaning of Rule 1.9.

The court stated that "[t]he allegations that [former counsel] developed expertise regarding the scope and meaning of some of Gillette's patents while he worked for Gillette as a patent attorney are beside the point." Do you agree with the court's conclusion that it would therefore be futile to permit Gillette to amend its complaint to set forth with specificity the allegation that former counsel is advising competitor with respect to the very patents on which he worked at Gillette because Gillette is only asserting that former counsel was advising with respect to infringement of Gillette patents, not with respect to validity? That conclusion rests heavily on the court's view that former counsel could not have any relevant protected confidential information with respect to the patent coverage because all that information is by law public information. If you were hiring a lawyer to advise on how to avoid infringing Gillette's patents, would it be irrelevant to you that one of the candidates was the very lawyer who had obtained the patents for Gillette?

———————

Handwritten margin notes (top left):
A = Brains
B = Money $
C = Comm & Mktg } ⇒ L

Problem 4–11

A, B, and C, represented by L, form a corporation to develop a new business. A supplies the scientific know-how; B, the necessary capital and financial and management ability; and C, the promotional and sales ability. They are the only stockholders and each owns one-third of the stock. Initially the business is small, the stock is of little value, and the owners do not want to bother with a stockholders' agreement or employment contracts. L becomes the corporation's lawyer, attending board meetings and drafting its minutes, negotiating and drawing contracts, and handling its few small litigation matters. When the business becomes profitable, L suggests that the time has come for the stockholders to "bother" with their personal arrangements with one another. All agree but close investigation by them into operation of the business leads A and C to become very unhappy with B's past management. They decide to sue him for misappropriation of corporate opportunities. A and C ask L to represent them in the lawsuit. B objects. L says that there is no problem in such representation: his representation of A and C is not substantially related to the work he did for B in organizing the corporation; moreover, to the extent that he has any confidential information from B, he learned it in the context of joint representation of A, B, and C and for that reason it is not confidential among them. Therefore, he does not need B's consent and there is no impediment to his representation of A and C and indeed the corporation against B. Is he correct?

Handwritten margin note (left): 1.7(b)(3) hard to meet, B/c its a litigation

Handwritten annotation after "Is he correct?": No. 1.7(a)(1) → directly adverse b/c L knows how B setup & managed $.

Handwritten margin note (left): 1.7(a)(2) comes into play. Even if not directly adverse, there's strg. risk that mat. lim. ability of L. → L has an interest b/c the corp. is making $.

Brennan's, Inc., which follows, is a leading illustration of the problems that may arise for a lawyer who has represented several clients jointly in a common enterprise when the clients' relationship ruptures. It also illustrates the tie between the rules governing conflicts of interest and the rules governing confidential information. There is a general rule of evidence, often called the co-client or joint attorney rule, that no attorney-client privilege exists in litigation between two parties jointly represented by a lawyer in a common enterprise with respect to testimony relating to that enterprise, although the privilege does exist with respect to the outside world. See 8 *Wigmore on Evidence* §2312 (McNaughton rev. ed. 1961). There is less substantive law with respect to whether the same policy considerations that gave rise to the rule of evidence should also produce the same result with respect to the lawyer's obligations as a matter of the rules of ethics. The issue may arise in two contexts: representation of one joint client against another (the subject of the case that follows) and the decision whether to transmit relevant information from one joint client to another over the objection of the confiding client (treated at the end of this Chapter).

What the use of the co-client evidence rule as a rule of ethics means in a case like Problem 4–11 or the following case is that a joint client sued by one of the group that was jointly represented may not be able to use the general rule regarding transmission of confidential information in order to disqualify the common attorney. But, as *Brennan's* indicates, that is not the end of the matter.

Brennan's, Inc. v. Brennan's Restaurants, Inc.

590 F.2d 168 (5th Cir. 1979)

TJOFLAT, Circuit Judge:

This is an action for trademark infringement and unfair competition. This appeal, however, concerns the disqualification of attorneys. The district court barred the appellants' attorneys from further representing them on grounds of conflict of interest. The correctness of this order is the only issue before us.

The underlying dispute in this case arises out of the business affairs of the Brennan family of New Orleans, Louisiana, who have been in the restaurant business for many years. All of the corporate parties are owned and closely held by various members of the Brennan family. Appellee Brennan's, Inc., the plaintiff below, owns and operates Brennan's restaurant at 417 Royal Street in New Orleans. The corporate appellants own and operate other restaurants in Louisiana, Texas, and Georgia. There has been no trial as yet, but a review of the facts leading to the present suit, as disclosed by the pleadings and affidavits, is necessary to a decision of this appeal. For convenience, the parties will be referred to in the capacities in which they appear in the court below.

Prior to 1974, all the members of the Brennan family were stockholders and directors of plaintiff, and some of them were stockholders and directors of the corporate defendants. All the corporations were independent legal entities in the sense that none held any of the stock of another, but they were all owned by members of the Brennan family and had interlocking boards of directors. In 1971, Edward F. Wegmann became general counsel for the family businesses, and his retainer was paid pro rata by all the corporations. He continued this joint representation until November 1973.

As part of his services, Mr. Wegmann, in close cooperation with trademark counsel in Washington, D.C., prosecuted applications for the federal registration of three service marks: "Brennan's," "Breakfast at Brennan's," and a distinctive rooster design. . . . Registrations were subsequently issued in plaintiff's name in March 1973. These registered service marks are the subject of this lawsuit.

Later in 1973 a dispute developed within the Brennan family over the operation and management of the family businesses. This dispute was resolved in November 1974 by dividing the corporations' stock between the two opposing family groups. Plaintiff became 100% owned by one group and the corporate defendants became 100% owned by the second group, composed of the individual defendants. Mr. Wegmann elected to continue to represent defendants and severed his connections with plaintiff and its shareholders.

At no time during the negotiations which culminated in the November 1974 settlement was there any discussion of who would have the right to use the registered service marks. Both sides claimed ownership of the marks and continued to use them after the settlement. Attempts to negotiate a license or concurrent registration were unsuccessful. Plaintiff filed this suit for trademark infringement and unfair competition on May 21, 1976. In their answer and counterclaim defendants alleged that the marks were registered in plaintiff's name for convenience only, and, "in truth and actuality, the applications were filed and the registrations issued for the benefit and ownership of all of the Brennan family restaurants, including the corporate defendants." Defendants also alleged that the marks and registrations are invalid.

Upon the filing of this suit, Mr. Wegmann, on behalf of the defendants, retained the services of Arnold Sprung, a New York patent and trademark attorney, to assist him in the defense of the case. On October 22, 1976, plaintiff moved for the disqualification of both attorneys: Mr. Wegmann on the ground that his present representation was at odds with the interests of plaintiff, his former client, and Mr. Sprung by imputation of Mr. Wegmann's conflict. After a hearing, the district court granted the motion. It found that the subject matter of the present suit is substantially related to matters in which Mr. Wegmann formerly represented plaintiff, and to allow him now to represent an interest adverse to his former client creates the appearance of impropriety. It also found that "the close working relationship which has been shown to exist between Mr. Wegmann and Mr. Sprung creates a significant likelihood that Mr. Sprung would have had access to or been informed of confidential disclosures made to Mr. Wegmann by his former client." . . .

We have not addressed this precise question before. In Wilson P. Abraham Construction Corp. v. Armco Steel Corp., [559 F.2d 250 (5th Cir. 1977)], we reaffirmed the standard that "a former client seeking to disqualify an attorney who appears on behalf of his adversary need only to show that the matters embraced within the pending suit are *substantially related* to the matters or cause of action wherein the attorney previously represented him," 559 F.2d at 252 (emphasis in original), but we acknowledged that "[t]his rule rests upon the presumption that confidences potentially damaging to the client have been disclosed to the attorney during the former period of representation," id. Defendants contend that this presumption cannot apply in this case. This argument, in our view, interprets too narrowly an attorney's duty to "preserve the confidences and secrets of a client." ABA Code of Professional Responsibility, Canon 4 (1970). The fundamental flaw in defendants' position is a confusion of the attorney-client evidentiary privilege with the ethical duty to preserve a client's confidences. Assuming the prior representation was joint, defendants are quite correct that neither of the parties to this suit can assert the attorney-client privilege against the other as to matters comprehended by that joint representation. Garner v. Wolfinbarger, 430 F.2d 1093, 1103 (5th Cir. 1970), cert. denied, 401 U.S. 974 (1971). But the ethical duty is broader than the evidentiary privilege . . . . The obligation of an attorney not to misuse information acquired in the course of representation serves to vindicate the trust and reliance that clients place in their attorneys. A client would feel wronged if an opponent prevailed against him with the aid of an attorney who formerly represented the client in the same matter. As the court recognized in E. F. Hutton & Co. v. Brown, 305 F. Supp. 371, 395 (S.D. Tex. 1969), this would undermine public confidence in the legal system as a means for adjudicating disputes. We recognize that this concern implicates the principle embodied in Canon 9 that attorneys "should avoid even the appearance of professional impropriety." ABA Code of Professional Responsibility, Canon 9 (1970). We have said that under this canon there must be a showing of a reasonable possibility that some specifically identifiable impropriety in fact occurred and that the likelihood of public suspicion must be weighed against the interest in retaining counsel of one's choice. Woods v. Covington County Bank, 537 F.2d 804, 812–813 (5th Cir. 1976). The conflict of interest is readily apparent here, however, and we think that the balance weighs in favor of disqualification. . . . Since the district court's findings of prior representation and substantial relationship are not disputed, we affirm the disqualification of Mr. Wegmann.

Whether Mr. Sprung should be disqualified presents a more difficult case. He has never had an attorney-client relationship with plaintiff; the district court disqualified him by imputation of Mr. Wegmann's conflict. Up to this point we have accepted, for the sake of argument, defendants' assertion that they were formerly joint clients with plaintiff of Mr. Wegmann. There is no dispute that plaintiff and defendants were previously represented by Mr. Wegmann simultaneously, but plaintiff maintains that, at least with respect to the registration of the service marks, Mr. Wegmann was representing plaintiff alone. The district court made no findings on the issue. Because we think that the disqualification of Mr. Sprung may turn on this fact and others not found by the court below, we vacate that part of the court's order relating to Mr. Sprung and remand the cause for further proceedings. For the guidance of the court on remand, we set forth our view of the applicable ethical standards.

If the court finds that Mr. Wegmann previously represented plaintiff and defendants jointly, we can see no reason why Mr. Sprung should be disqualified. As between joint clients there can be no "confidences" or "secrets" unless one client manifests a contrary intent. . . . Thus, Mr. Sprung could not have learned anything from Mr. Wegmann that defendants did not already know or have a right to know. Plaintiff argues that this permits the defendants indirectly to gain the benefit of Mr. Wegmann's services when they could not do so directly. If the representation was joint, however, defendants possess no information as to which plaintiff could have had any expectation of privacy in relation to the defendants. The only remaining ground for disqualification then would be an appearance of impropriety. [Earlier in] this opinion, we decided there is such an appearance when an attorney represents an interest adverse to that of a former client in a matter substantially related to the subject of the prior representation. Mr. Sprung has never been plaintiff's counsel, however; he is only the cocounsel of one who was. We are enjoined not to give Canon 9 an overly broad application and to maintain "a reasonable balance between the need to ensure ethical conduct on the part of lawyers . . . and other social interests, which include the litigant's right to freely chosen counsel." Woods v. Covington County

Bank, at 810. In the case of Mr. Sprung, we think the balance weighs against disqualification. Assuming that Mr. Wegmann's prior retainer was joint, plaintiff has suffered no actual prejudice from communications between Mr. Wegmann and Mr. Sprung. There is a possibility that Mr. Sprung has obtained informally information that he would otherwise have had to seek through discovery.[7] The Second Circuit has indicated that circumvention of the discovery rules is grounds for automatic disqualification. See NCK Organization v. Bregman, 542 F.2d 128, 131–132, 134 (2d Cir. 1976). This seems to us an overly rigid approach. In a disqualification case, it is well to remember that "in deciding questions of professional ethics men of good will often differ in their conclusions." Fund of Funds, Ltd. v. Arthur Andersen & Co., 567 F.2d 225, 227 (2d Cir. 1977). . . . Under the peculiar facts of this case, we do not think there would be such an appearance of impropriety in Mr. Sprung's continued representation of defendants as to warrant his disqualification.

If the district court finds that Mr. Wegmann did not previously represent these parties jointly, it does not necessarily follow that Mr. Sprung should be disqualified. The courts have abjured a per se approach to the disqualification of cocounsel of disqualified counsel. Akerly v. Red Barn System, Inc., 551 F.2d 539 (3d Cir. 1977); American Can Co. v. Citrus Feed Co., 436 F.2d 1125 (5th Cir. 1971). In the absence of an attorney-client relationship between Mr. Sprung and plaintiff, a presumption of disclosure of confidences is inappropriate. Wilson P. Abraham Construction Corp. v. Armco Steel Corp., at 253. Mr. Sprung should not be disqualified unless he has learned from Mr. Wegmann information the plaintiff had intended not be disclosed to the defendants. See id. . . .

Notes

1. The reference in the opinion to "confidences" and "secrets" is to the division in the Model Code of protected confidential information into two categories: "confidences," which included information protected by the attorney-client privilege, and "secrets," which included "other information gained in the professional relationship that the client has requested be held inviolate or the disclosure of which would be embarrassing or would be likely to be detrimental to the client." The drafters of the Model Rules believed that that definition was too narrow and sought broadening language in current Rule 1.6.

2. Rosman v. Shapiro, 653 F. Supp. 1441 (S.D.N.Y. 1987), followed *Brennan's* in the situation of an attorney representing a close corporation with two 50–50

---

7. It is very likely that Mr. Wegmann will be a witness in this case. He handled the registrations for the service marks which are the subject of this suit. Moreover, he prepared and notarized two affidavits that were executed at the time the registrations were issued. Defendants rely on these affidavits in support of their claim of ownership of the marks. The circumstances of their execution and the facts to which these affidavits purport to attest will undoubtedly be a subject of dispute at trial and Mr. Wegmann's knowledge may be relevant. If he represented all the family corporations at the time, however, none of his knowledge is privileged and his testimony could freely be sought by either side.

shareholders who then sought to represent the corporation and one shareholder against the other. The court held that it was reasonable for the shareholders to believe that the attorney was representing them individually. Although the court held that neither shareholder could have had an expectation of confidentiality with respect to the other when there was joint representation, the court held that the loyalty obligation required the lawyer's disqualification in the litigation.

3. There is a line of cases, discussed in Kempner v. Oppenheimer & Co., 662 F. Supp. 1271 (S.D.N.Y. 1987), that reaches a conclusion opposite to *Brennan's* by stopping in the middle of the reasoning used by the *Brennan's* court. *Kempner* and the cases it cites conclude that since there was no confidentiality between the joint clients, a suit brought by the attorney for joint clients against one of them did not threaten any confidentiality interest of the defendant and hence disqualification was not required. *Kempner* and most if not all of the cases it cites may perhaps be explained on the basis that it was understood that one of the joint clients was the primary client of the attorney and that in the event of dispute the attorney was free to continue representing its primary client. See also *Merrill Lynch*, p. 229 supra. The *Kempner* court does refer briefly to that factor. Moreover, it points out that in the particular case it was the joint client, there an employee of the primary client, who switched sides in the midst of the litigation, and not the attorney. However, while the expectations of the joint clients may be important in differentiating these two cases, the differentiation is not so sharp as the court's language makes it appear. In some cases, at least, the joint subsidiary client will have imparted very damaging confidential information to the attorney and the threat that such information will be used to his or her detriment by a former lawyer raises a strong loyalty issue that looks toward disqualification. (On the issue of the advance consent by a client to such adverse representation, see p. 221, Note 5.) See Anchor Packing Co. v. Pro-Seal, Inc., 688 F. Supp. 1215 (E.D. Mich. 1988), comparing the two lines of cases and indicating strong support for the *Brennan's* approach. But see Harris v. Agrivest Limited Partnership, 818 F. Supp. 1035 (E.D. Mich. 1993), from the same district, reaching a somewhat different conclusion.

4. The court notes the instruction to avoid even the appearance of impropriety contained in the ABA's former Model Code of Professional Responsibility. Although that concept was removed from the Model Rules because it was both open-ended and vague, some courts still fall back on it. The *Brennan's* court attempted a definition to cure both faults.

Another situation of successive representation has been a hotly debated issue of professional responsibility: the government lawyer who goes into private practice. But before discussing that issue, we should turn to the matter of vicarious disqualification because that concept relates quite specifically to the former government lawyer problem.

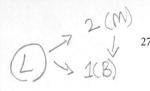

E. Vicarious Disqualification

1. The General Rule

Problem 4–12

(a) In the situation involved in Problem 4–1, may Lawyer's partner, Smith, handle Merchant's suit against Buyer? *Yes*

(b) Suppose that after Lawyer represented Buyer but before Merchant arrived at her office with respect to this particular problem, Smith and Lawyer had dissolved their partnership. When Lawyer declines to represent Merchant in his suit against Buyer, may Smith represent him? *No.*

(c) Suppose that Lawyer had agreed to represent Merchant against Buyer and thereafter Lawyer and Smith dissolved their partnership. Buyer's lawyer filed a disqualification motion against Lawyer, who then withdrew from the case. May Smith *No* represent Merchant against Buyer? Is Rule 1.10(b) dispositive? *23*

(d) Suppose that Lawyer works in a big international law firm in one office and his partner, Smith, works in another office in another country. May Smith represent Merchant in his suit against Buyer? Should it matter that the firm is fully integrated by technology, meaning that all of Smith's files have been accessible by Lawyer?

The common law of vicarious disqualification, codified in Model Rule 1.10(a), imputes disqualification of one member of a firm under particular Rules to the rest of the firm. As the common law of disqualification developed, it worked out a series of presumptions to avoid the necessity for a person seeking to disqualify a present or former lawyer from having to reveal the very confidences that the rules are designed to protect. The first is that a client who consults a lawyer is presumed to have transmitted confidences about the matter. The second is that the lawyer is presumed to have transmitted those confidences to all partners and associates at the firm. The current debate is over the circumstances in which those presumptions ought to be able to be rebutted.

The Model Code provisions were drafted so broadly that they could not be enforced literally. Exceptions to vicarious disqualifications had to be recognized, and therefore common law development continued. When the Model Rules were drafted, the vicarious disqualification principles were enunciated much more carefully and precisely in Rules 1.9(b), 1.10 and 1.11. The specific codification of recognized common law exceptions may work to freeze further development of the principle, and that problem has been an issue for drafters and especially for courts, both in their legislative (i.e., shall this particular Model Rule be adopted?) and in their judicial capacities. There is enough ambiguity in the Rules, however, with respect to specific fact situations that further common law development may be expected.

A major issue with respect to vicarious disqualification relates to the extent to which lawyers vicariously disqualified in Firm A carry that disqualification with them when they move to Firm B so that not only they but all members of Firm B are disqualified. Model Rule 1.9(b) and the following leading case and Notes discuss the issue. (See also Rule 1.10(b), which views the problem from the former firm's perspective.) The principal case also discusses the extent to which a lawyer in Firm A needs to work on a client's affairs to warrant personal, as opposed to vicarious, disqualification.

Steel v. General Motors Corporation
912 F. Supp. 724 (D.N.J. 1995)

KUGLER, Magistrate Judge:

This matter comes before the court upon motion by Defendant General Motors Corporation to disqualify plaintiff's counsel, the firm of Kimmel & Silverman, due to that firm's recent hiring of Jay M. London, Esquire, former counsel for GM. The above-captioned matter involves a single-vehicle breach of warranty action, commonly referred to as a "lemon law" case. In addition to the above-captioned matter, there currently are twenty (20) lemon law cases pending in the District of New Jersey against GM filed by Kimmel & Silverman, and this motion, by agreement of counsel, shall apply to all of them. . . .

FINDINGS OF FACT

1. Jay M. London, Esquire, is an attorney currently employed by the law firm of Kimmel & Silverman, P.C., in Bluebell, Pennsylvania. He is licensed in both Pennsylvania and New Jersey and has been practicing for approximately eight years. From August, 1988 through March, 1993, Mr. London was employed as an associate at the Philadelphia law firm of George J. Lavin, Jr. and Associates . . . (the "Lavin firm"). In March, 1993, he left the Lavin firm and joined the firm of Harvey, Pennington, Herting, & Rennelsen ("Harvey Pennington") as a litigation associate. In April, 1994, he left the Harvey Pennington firm and joined the firm of McBreen, McBreen & Kopko (the "McBreen firm"). Mr. London resigned from the McBreen firm on May 26, 1995 and joined the firm of Kimmel & Silverman on June 2, 1995.

2. Laurie Adams is employed by General Motors Corporation ("GM") as a legal assistant in Farmington Hills, Michigan. Her department is responsible for handling single vehicle breach of warranty cases, otherwise known as "lemon law" cases. She has been involved in lemon law cases since September, 1988, and her jurisdiction currently covers sixteen states, including New Jersey and Pennsylvania. Her responsibilities include supervising local counsel and managing lemon law cases on behalf of GM. Although Ms. Adams reports to a supervisor, she has the primary authority for selecting local counsel and making decisions regarding the progress of individual cases.

3. The employees of GM's field offices, called "zone personnel," actively participate and cooperate with local counsel in the litigation of lemon law cases. These zone personnel are individuals with automotive technical background and experience,

and, as part of their litigation duties, they review repair records, conduct inspections of allegedly defective vehicles, and provide their analysis and recommendations to GM and local counsel.

4. Kimmel & Silverman, P.C., is a law firm of five attorneys with offices in Bluebell, Pennsylvania and Haddonfield, New Jersey. Since 1991, the firm has engaged almost exclusively in lemon law matters. Robert Silverman, Esquire, and Craig Kimmel, Esquire, are the firm's managing partners.

5. GM and Kimmel & Silverman have jointly created an early resolution program in which plaintiff's counsel and GM legal and technical personnel attempt to work out a particular claim prior to a lawsuit being instituted. If a matter cannot be settled, then it is referred to local counsel for litigation. Through this program, approximately half of all claims settle before suit is filed.

6. The Lavin firm was designated as local counsel for GM during the time that Mr. London was employed there. From March, 1990 through his departure from the Lavin firm in March, 1993, Mr. London was assigned to work on approximately 25–30 lemon law cases on behalf of GM, all in Pennsylvania. None of those cases involved Kimmel & Silverman as plaintiffs' counsel.

7. Although none of the lemon law cases that Mr. London handled on behalf of GM went to trial, Mr. London had significant responsibilities with respect to the management of individual cases. He propounded and responded to interrogatories and other discovery requests, conducted depositions of plaintiffs, participated in vehicle inspections along with GM zone personnel, and discussed the technical aspects of a case with zone personnel. He arbitrated one case, contacting Ms. Adams for her consent with respect to the arbitration strategy and tactics.

He provided opinion letters to GM on individual cases which included his analysis of the facts, his legal opinion as to whether the facts of a particular case met the statutory requirements for a claim for damages, and his advice on what types of defenses should be raised and whether to settle or proceed to arbitration and/or trial. He also orally communicated this information to Ms. Adams on a regular basis. In addition, Ms. Adams discussed with Mr. London information that she had received from other local counsel regarding defense of GM lemon law cases.

8. At the time that Mr. London joined the McBreen firm, that firm was not representing GM in any capacity. GM subsequently retained the McBreen firm as local counsel in the Philadelphia area after a meeting was held in August, 1994 at GM headquarters between GM legal staff, including Ms. Adams, and Mr. London and Steven Kantrowitz on behalf of the Philadelphia office of the McBreen firm. One topic of discussion at that meeting was GM's concern over the increasing number of cases being filed by Kimmel & Silverman in the Philadelphia area.

9. While at the McBreen firm, Mr. London worked on approximately 25–30 GM lemon law cases in which the firm of Kimmel & Silverman represented the plaintiffs. On each particular GM lemon law case, he would initially receive an analysis and recommendation from a GM zone representative. He would then conduct a

preliminary evaluation of a particular case, contact Mr. Silverman via telephone or in person to discuss the case, and, if necessary, contact the GM zone representative — usually Mr. Logue — to confirm GM's initial position and/or provide further information that Mr. London had received. He participated in a vehicle inspection on one occasion. He discussed settlement and evaluation of the cases with his supervisor, Steven Kantrowitz, and with Ms. Adams. At Ms. Adams' request, Mr. London coordinated his defense of Kimmel & Silverman's cases with the Lavin firm and attended joint defense committee meetings on behalf of GM in the Philadelphia area.

He designed and prepared case information statements which were analogous to the opinion letters he had prepared for GM while at the Lavin firm and which contained his analysis, comments, suggestions, and legal advice and opinions regarding each case. On the top of each of these statements was stamped "Attorney-Client Privilege." He acknowledges that these statements contained privileged and confidential information. He often transmitted these statements to GM, and otherwise communicated with Ms. Adams, through GM's electronic mailing system, to which he was issued a user password.

10. At some point, GM, through Ms. Adams, provided the McBreen firm with standing settlement authority; Mr. London did not have to contact her to confirm settlement unless the claim for settlement exceeded a certain pre-authorized amount. Under this settlement authority, in many cases Mr. London would settle cases and explain the reasons why to Ms. Adams later. Mr. London acknowledges that the process by which this settlement authority is carried out is privileged and confidential information. The significance of this settlement authority is shown by the fact that of the approximately 50 firms in Ms. Adams' jurisdiction that have been retained as GM's local counsel, such standing settlement authority has only been provided to three.

11. GM'S "Guidelines for Handling Warranty and Lemon Law Litigation" are provided in confidence to all of GM's local counsel. Although Mr. London claims that he does not remember specifically if he ever received and reviewed a copy of these guidelines and procedures while at the Lavin or McBreen firms, he does recognize the cover page, and he does remember a "several page document" which he identified as "single vehicle breach of warranty guidelines for local counsel" provided by GM. These guidelines also were discussed during the August, 1994 meeting in Detroit between Ms. Adams and members of the McBreen firm where copies were distributed. Mr. London does not believe that these guidelines contain any information about handling lemon law cases that is not otherwise publicly available, except for internal information about the divisions and organization of GM. He also received information about preparing pleadings in a GM lemon law case and sample evaluation letters that were to be submitted to GM.

12. Mr. London became dissatisfied with his employment at the McBreen firm, and he resigned on Friday, May 26, 1995. He testified that in order to protect GM's interests, and with the consent of Mr. Kantrowitz, he felt he should contact plaintiff's counsel, Mr. Silverman, to ask for extensions of time in which to file three

answers which were due the week of May 29, 1995. That weekend being the Memorial Day holiday, Mr. London telephoned Mr. Silverman at his beach house on Monday, May 29, 1995, ostensibly to ask for these extensions and to notify plaintiff's counsel of his resignation.

During that telephone call, Mr. Silverman asked Mr. London if he would be interested in coming to work for Kimmel & Silverman. According to Mr. Silverman, the firm needed an experienced litigator to help with the workload of cases against manufacturers other than GM. Mr. Silverman testified that he extended this proposal because he knew Mr. London to be a hard-working attorney from his dealings with him at the McBreen firm.

13. As a result of this inquiry, Mr. London conducted some research into his ethical obligations. He consulted the Pennsylvania Rules of Professional Conduct, researched Pennsylvania cases, and contacted a lawyer on the Philadelphia Bar Association Professional Guidance Committee, who told him that Pennsylvania recognizes the use of ethics screens—or "Chinese walls"—in situations where lawyers effectively "switch sides." He did no research under New Jersey law. Mr. London concluded that he would not violate his ethical obligations to GM as long as there was a proper ethics screen in place at Kimmel & Silverman to prevent the disclosure of GM confidences.[3]

14. On Wednesday, May 31, 1995, Mr. London went to the offices of Kimmel & Silverman to discuss the employment proposal. Earlier that morning, he and his wife had prepared a document that contained the parameters of an ethics screen to be implemented at Kimmel & Silverman. When he arrived at Kimmel & Silverman, he sat down with Mr. Kimmel and discussed the ethics screen and how it would work. Mr. Silverman testified that 99% of the discussion that day centered around the implementation of the ethics screen. The final document containing the operation of the screen was distributed to all of Kimmel & Silverman's employees for endorsement. It is undisputed that no inquiry was made into New Jersey ethics rules.

The record indicates that Mr. London left the offices of Kimmel & Silverman that afternoon with an offer of employment. Although Mr. London had equal or less legal experience than the other two associates who then had been working at Kimmel & Silverman for over one year, he was offered a substantially higher salary and a more prestigious placement of his name on the firm's letterhead. . . .

15. On the morning of June 2, 1995, Mr. London called Ms. Adams at her home and notified her that he had resigned from the McBreen firm and was considering joining Kimmel & Silverman. He attempted to assure her that the interests of GM would be fully protected. Later that day, he sent a disclosure letter to GM via certified mail and faxed a copy to Ms. Adams on June 7, 1995, to which GM did not give its consent or otherwise reply.

---

3. Mr. London testified that even absent an ethics screen, he believes that he is not ethically prohibited from representing plaintiffs against GM in lemon law cases.

16. Mr. London reported for work on Wednesday, June 7, 1995 under the supervision of Mr. Kimmel who, along with Mr. London, would work on all lemon law cases that did not involve GM. Mr. Silverman would work on all GM cases, and the ethics screen would purportedly prevent Mr. London or Mr. Kimmel—as the managing partner with GM clients—from having any intentional or inadvertent contact with GM cases.

Since Mr. London has joined Kimmel & Silverman, he has represented plaintiffs in approximately one hundred lemon law cases against auto manufacturers other than GM. The cases that are the subject of this motion were brought by Mr. Silverman or Michael Power, Esquire, a Kimmel & Silverman associate.

17. The office space of Kimmel & Silverman at Blue Bell, Pennsylvania houses all of the clients' files. The firm leases approximately 10,000 square feet of office space which includes fourteen separate offices and two conference rooms. Each attorney's office locks by a separate key. There are three entrances to the space, each locking with a master key possessed by Mr. Silverman only.

As a result of Mr. London joining the firm, Mr. Silverman spent a "significant amount of money" to knock down a wall in his office to create a "sub-office" where all the GM files are housed. The only access to this room is through Mr. Silverman's office. Each GM file is labelled and marked with blue electrical tape on the front for easy identification. There is a sign-out log for anyone removing a GM file. Neither Mr. London nor Mr. Kimmel is allowed in this sub-office or in any other room containing a file marked with the blue GM tape.

The offices of Mr. Kimmel, Mr. London, and Mr. Silverman are all in separate corners of the office space. Mr. London's office is located approximately forty feet from Mr. Silverman's office, with four offices and several secretary carrels in between. All files which Mr. London handles are kept in his office, and Mr. London does not have a key to anyone's office other than his own. Every attorney in the firm has his or her own computer, but they are not on a network. Mr. London has a secretary assigned to him alone.

All telephone calls to Mr. London are received first by a receptionist and then by Mr. London's secretary who verify that the call does not involve GM matters. When Mr. Kimmel, Mr. Silverman, and the office manager leave the building, all telephone calls are forwarded to an answering service. Mr. Silverman also receives and reviews all incoming mail before Mr. London sees it.

18. Although the operation of this ethics screen seems straightforward, there are inconsistencies in the witness' testimony with respect to certain incidents which lead this court to conclude that the operation may not always run so smoothly and that the contours of the screen may not be so clear. Mr. Silverman testified that under the ethics screen, he receives all incoming faxes. If he is away for a short period of time during the day, all incoming faxes are placed on his chair to await his return. Under no circumstances are Mr. Kimmel or Mr. London to see any faxed correspondence before Mr. Silverman has had a chance to review it. When asked what happens to

the faxes when he goes on vacation, Mr. Silverman responded that there had not been occasion to address that situation as he had not taken a vacation from the time the ethics screen was implemented to the time of the hearing.

Despite this recitation of the fax procedure in place under the ethics screen, the court was presented with a document dated July 11, 1995 which Mr. Kimmel signed on behalf of a plaintiff in a lemon law case. The document accepted a settlement offer in a pre-suit case against GM. When asked how it could have happened that Mr. Kimmel signed his name on a GM matter, Mr. Kimmel responded that it was included in a packet of documents that he had received via telefax, not from GM, but from the Better Business Bureau, that a quick response was required, and that Mr. Silverman was on trial. Mr. Kimmel testified that he neither looked at the file nor consulted with the client.

When Mr. Silverman was asked whether this constituted a violation of the ethics screen, he responded that the letter should not have been written, that it was a violation of the firm's policy, and that if it had been done by one of the firm's employees, that employee would be reprimanded and subject to termination for a second violation. He testified:

> There is no excuse for this. He should not have written this letter. I could look into it to see why he wrote the letter but that still wouldn't give an excuse. He shouldn't have written the letter, and he will be talked to.

During the next day's testimony, however, Mr. Silverman's position changed:

> If I testified that there was a breaching of the wall, I mis-spoke. There was in my opinion a violation of our firm administrative policy with regard to the segregation of cases. But at no time has there ever been a violation of or a breach of the actual screening procedures or of the wall.

According to Mr. Silverman's clarified testimony, the assignment of GM files to Mr. Silverman and non-GM files to Mr. Kimmel is an administrative decision only and is not a component of the ethics screen, despite its incorporation into the screening document prepared by Mr. Kimmel and Mr. London.

Further questions by the court prompted the following dialogue:

> THE COURT: Excuse me, I'm sorry, are you saying you, today, you don't think there is anything wrong with Mr. Kimmel having sent that letter of July 11th . . . is that your testimony?

> THE WITNESS: My testimony yesterday—after I looked into it and looked at the file, I think he had to do that to protect [the client's] interest. The offer would lapse, and I was on trial.

> THE COURT: The question I had, did you think it was wrong for him to have sent that letter marked Exhibit D-3?

> THE WITNESS: I believe that it was—he had to do it, but I wish he hadn't.

THE COURT: Was it wrong or not?

THE WITNESS: No, Sir.

THE COURT: You agree yesterday you testified that it was wrong. It was a violation of policy, didn't you?

THE WITNESS: It was a violation of our policy.

THE COURT: It shouldn't have been done. That's what you testified to yesterday?

THE WITNESS: Yes, Your Honor.

In addition, the court asked Mr. Silverman whether it would be a violation of the ethics screen if Mr. Kimmel had looked at the case file when he signed the July 11, 1995 letter. Mr. Silverman responded that it would not; in contrast, Mr. Kimmel testified that it would violate the ethics screen.

There also were several instances of Mr. Kimmel signing recent letters of representation on GM cases. Neither Mr. Silverman nor Mr. Kimmel believes this to be a violation of the ethics screen.

19. There is no accounting system set up at Kimmel & Silverman that prevents Mr. London from receiving any part of his salary from revenues generated in GM cases. All revenues received by Kimmel & Silverman from all sources are deposited in a general fund from which salaries of all the Kimmel & Silverman employees are drawn. Mr. London would be precluded, however, from sharing in any proceeds that may be received from GM over and above the usual fee.

CONCLUSIONS OF LAW

I. NEW JERSEY LAW GOVERNS

[The court concluded that under the local federal district court rules, New Jersey ethics rules controlled. New Jersey's Rules 1.9 and 1.10 then in force embodied the general principles of Model Rules 1.9 and 1.10, except that they did not contain a screening provision.]

GM, as the petitioner, bears the burden of proving that disqualification is appropriate. . . . GM claims that RPC 1.10 mandates disqualification of an entire firm when a lawyer associated with that firm would be disqualified under RPC 1.9. GM advances three reasons under RPC 1.9 why Mr. London would be disqualified from the cases that are the subject of this motion, resulting in the imputed disqualification of Kimmel & Silverman. First, GM contends that Mr. London would be disqualified from these matters under RPC 1.9(a)(1) because they are "substantially related" to matters in which Mr. London represented GM during his employ with the Lavin and McBreen firms. Second, GM contends that Mr. London would be disqualified under RPC 1.9(a)(2) because he obtained information while representing GM which is not generally known and which could be used to GM's detriment. Third, GM contends that Mr. London's employment with Kimmel & Silverman creates an "appearance of impropriety" under RPC 1.9(b) and 1.7(c). . . .

It is undisputed that Mr. London formerly represented GM within an attorney-client relationship and that GM has not consented to or waived a potential conflict of interest. Analysis of the current motion is therefore confined to: (1) whether any of the cases now being handled by Kimmel & Silverman against GM are matters which are "the same" or "substantially related" to matters previously handled by Mr. London while he was employed at the Lavin and McBreen firms, RPC 1.9(a)(1); (2) whether Kimmel & Silverman is using "information relating to the representation" which was obtained by Mr. London while he was employed at the Lavin and McBreen firms to the disadvantage of GM and which is not generally known, RPC 1.9(a)(2); and (3) whether, in the absence of an actual conflict, an "appearance of impropriety" exists sufficient to warrant disqualification. If any of these three situations exists, the court must determine whether the ethics screen currently operating at Kimmel & Silverman prevents the imputed disqualification of the entire firm.

II. DISQUALIFICATION OF JAY LONDON

A. RPC 1.9(a)(1) — "Same or Substantially Related Matter"

Kimmel & Silverman currently have no cases pending on which Mr. London represented GM while he was employed at the Lavin or McBreen firms; all of the cases in that category were referred away to outside counsel when Mr. London joined Kimmel & Silverman.

Kimmel & Silverman argue that neither are any of the present cases "substantially related" to the cases London worked on as GM counsel because they are factually distinct from one another. . . .

GM conceded that although the legal theories and defenses in all the lemon law cases are virtually identical, the facts giving rise to each lawsuit vary according to the mechanical problems associated with each vehicle. According to the testimony of Ms. Adams and Mr. Logue, there is no actual or logical connection between the mechanical problems of one vehicle and those of another, and the settlement amounts for each vehicle vary with the facts of each case. . . .

GM claims that a factual nexus among cases that are alleged to be "substantially related" is not necessary, arguing that the test to be applied is whether "adversity between the interests of the attorney's former and present clients has created a climate for the disclosure of relevant confidential information." Kaselaan & D'Angelo, 144 F.R.D. [235 (D.N.J. 1992)] at 238 (quoting Reardon v. Marlayne, 83 N.J. 460 (1980) at 472). . . .

. . . Reardon v. Marlayne . . . held that one prong of a three-part test for disqualification of a lawyer who brings an action against a former client was whether "a substantial relationship or a reasonable perception, from the public's perspective, of a substantial relationship" exists "between the subject matter of the present suit and that of cases worked on during the former representation." Id. at 474. Under this prong "a substantial relationship between matters will exist where the adversity between the interests of the attorney's former and present clients has created a climate for disclosure of relevant confidential information." Id. at 472. Disqualification is mandated where "the issues between the former and present suits are practically the same or where there is a 'patently clear' relationship between them." Id. . . .

It is evident from the record that while Mr. London was employed at the Lavin and McBreen firms, he was in a position to obtain information from GM regarding its legal policies and strategies, approaches to settlement, and bargaining positions with respect to individual cases. He formed a close professional relationship with Laurie Adams and dealt with her on lemon law matters over a number of years. He met with Ms. Adams and other GM legal personnel at GM headquarters, and he received a password to log into GM's electronic mail system. He had primary authority to handle most of his lemon law cases and was the primary contact for Ms. Adams. Notwithstanding Mr. London's account that he did not receive a copy of GM's guidelines for handling lemon law cases, and that even if he did there was no confidential information contained therein, the mere fact that he had access to confidential information is enough for this court to presume that he in fact learned of such confidential claims handling and settlement information. He actively participated in the settlement of lemon law cases on behalf of GM, and he learned enough about GM's litigation and settlement strategies to author opinion letters to Ms. Adams in which he analyzed the factual and legal issues of each case and recommended a certain course of action.

He is now employed by a firm who represents plaintiffs with interests that are directly adverse to those of GM. It is undisputed that the legal issues in the lemon law cases handled by Mr. London on behalf of GM and those now being handled by Kimmel & Silverman against GM are virtually identical, the only differences being the mechanical defects and the purchase and repair history associated with each particular vehicle. While it is true that these facts vary with each case, it is also apparent that the universe of automotive mechanical problems is not endless, and it is likely that in litigating dozens of lemon law cases involving one manufacturer, a lawyer encounters many alleged mechanical defects of the same kind. It is illogical to suggest that each new lemon law case is a creature of a different stripe, presenting unfamiliar circumstances to an experienced lemon law attorney. In light of all these relevant factors, the court rejects the respondents' argument that there is no substantial relationship among these lemon law cases. Although the court has no reason to believe that Mr. London would intentionally disclose any relevant confidential information he possesses regarding GM's handling of lemon law cases, actual disclosure is not the test for a substantial relationship. The adversity between the interests of GM and those of the plaintiffs currently being represented by Kimmel & Silverman has created a climate whereby relevant confidential information may be disclosed in the interests of effective representation of the plaintiffs.

B. RPC 1.9(a)(2) — Use of Information to the Disadvantage of the Former Client That is Not "Generally Known"

The court further holds that Mr. London would be disqualified under RPC 1.9(a)(2). Where a substantial relationship exists, the court will assume that confidential information has passed between an attorney and a former client, notwithstanding the attorney's declarations to the contrary. This presumption of access to and knowledge of confidences may not be rebutted.

Moreover, Rule 1.9(a)(2) does not limit its protection to confidential information. The factual record discussed herein reveals that Mr. London possesses "information relating to the representation" of GM, and the direct adversity between the plaintiffs and GM, along with the legal and factual similarity of the cases, indicate that if Mr. London were to represent the plaintiffs, his ethical obligation to fully protect their interests would necessarily require him to use that information to the advantage of the plaintiffs and to the disadvantage of GM. . . .

Respondents make a strong argument that much of the information "relating to the representation" of GM is generally known. Advice and information about how to conduct lemon law litigation against various manufacturers, including GM, along with form pleadings and interrogatories, proliferate in legal periodicals, practice manuals, law review articles, textbooks, and through bar association conferences and publications. However, this is true of just about every type of matter there is to litigate. The information age has not neglected the legal profession, and step-by-step checklists on litigating a particular type of case can be found in every law library and computerized legal database in the country. The fact that this type of information is publicly available does not make "information relating to the representation" of GM "generally known." Rule 1.9(a)(2) also contemplates knowledge of the decision-making processes of GM personnel regarding legal claims, the internal workings of the GM organization, the particular personalities, expectations, negotiating techniques, and management styles of GM personnel, historical and technical information regarding GM vehicles, and GM claims handling processes and procedures. This type of information is protected by the attorney-client relationship whether the matter involves complicated legal issues, such as in antitrust law, or whether it involves the "pro forma" litigation of lemon law claims. It would be available to someone whose extensive experience as local counsel for GM on over fifty lemon law matters has resulted in a close, professional working relationship with GM legal and technical personnel and who was trusted enough for his firm to be one of only a few granted blanket settlement authority by GM, but it is not generally known.

Moreover, the fact that plaintiff's counsel has litigated hundreds of cases against GM, generally considers himself knowledgeable of GM's settlement philosophy, and considers that philosophy to be elementary, does not lead to the conclusion that all is well under Rule 1.9(a)(2). Mr. Silverman points out that approximately half of the claims settle through the early resolution program before being referred to local counsel, and he emphasizes his role in this process and his direct contact with GM legal and technical personnel. However, the fact that half of them do *not* settle belies Mr. Silverman's assertion that GM's settlement process is merely a one-dimensional information exchange. Despite Mr. Silverman's exhaustive coverage of the steps that GM takes to settle each and every case, he has not shed light on the reasons why half of them do not settle through the early resolution program. In the absence of any sort of acknowledgment by GM that Mr. Silverman, through his experience in litigating cases against GM, has gained knowledge of confidential information, counsel's personal opinion that he is privy to his opponent's settlement strategies is not a sufficient showing to demonstrate to the court that information relating to the representation of GM is "generally known." The court is certain that many a litigator, if asked, would be similarly confident of the extent of his or her knowledge of an adversary's legal strategies. For these reasons, the court finds that RPC 1.9(a)(2) would mandate Mr. London's disqualification.

C. RPC 1.9(b) — "Appearance of Impropriety"

Even if there is no actual conflict of interest, disqualification is warranted if the subsequent representation creates an "appearance of impropriety," as that standard is used in [New Jersey's] RPC 1.7. An appearance of impropriety exists where "an ordinary knowledgeable citizen acquainted with the facts would conclude that the multiple representation poses substantial risk of disservice to either the public interest or the interest of one of the clients." RPC 1.7(c). . . .

The "appearance doctrine," as it is often called by the many New Jersey courts that have considered its application, has been heavily litigated and artfully described. It is intended "not to prevent any actual conflicts of interest but to bolster the public's confidence in the integrity of the legal profession." . . . What the application of the appearance doctrine comes down to is a careful consideration of all the relevant facts and circumstances to determine what a reasonable person would perceive as proper or improper. Although the appearance doctrine is not recognized in other jurisdictions, including Pennsylvania, it remains of vital importance to the New Jersey bar. . . .

Mr. London represented GM for approximately five years while at the Lavin and McBreen firms. During that time, he worked on over fifty lemon law cases, gaining extensive knowledge and experience in GM vehicles, the GM organization, the GM decision-making process and hierarchy, and GM's approach to litigating or settling lemon law claims. He worked closely with and formed a close professional relationship with GM legal and technical personnel, and had access to GM's electronic mail system. Ms. Adams trusted Mr. London "implicitly" and provided him with information over the course of their professional relationship with the expectation that any confidences and secrets would be protected by the attorney-client relationship and Mr. London's ethical obligations to GM. He now is employed in a law firm of five attorneys who work almost exclusively on lemon law matters against many manufacturers, including GM. The record indicates that GM is a large source of revenue for Kimmel & Silverman, and all of the revenue generated from GM is deposited into a general fund from which the salaries of the three Kimmel & Silverman associates are paid. It is reasonable to assume that Mr. London derives at least part of his salary from lawsuits filed against his former client.

Despite the fact that Mr. London never represented GM on cases in New Jersey, and even assuming that Mr. London is not going to work on cases against GM, that Mr. Silverman has learned much of GM's settlement and litigation style, and that the fundamentals of lemon law litigation are available within the public domain, the court finds that Mr. London's five years of extensive involvement in the defense of GM lemon law claims would inevitably create a strong perception on the part of the public of knowledge of GM confidences.

Although the court has no reason to believe that Mr. London and the firm of Kimmel & Silverman would intentionally disseminate confidential information learned during the course of Mr. London's representation of GM, the appearance doctrine is in place to protect the public's perception of the legal profession, and the New Jersey bar in particular, not to castigate an individual lawyer's conduct. . . . Accordingly, the court finds that Mr. London's employment with Kimmel & Silverman creates an impermissible appearance of impropriety under RPC 1.9(b).

III. DISQUALIFICATION OF KIMMEL & SILVERMAN

Kimmel & Silverman argue that even if Mr. London would be disqualified from representing the plaintiffs, he has no intention of ever bringing suit against GM in New Jersey, and the ethics screen that currently exists within their firm effectively prevents Mr. London from inadvertently or intentionally spreading GM confidential information and protects the entire firm from disqualification. . . .

Disciplinary rules, however, are particular to each state, and, as stated earlier, this court must look to the interpretation given to the RPC by the courts of New Jersey. Unlike Pennsylvania's version of RPC 1.10, the rule in New Jersey does not specifically provide for the use of ethics screens. After a careful review of the law in New Jersey, this court finds that the type of ethics screen currently in place at Kimmel & Silverman has not been recognized by the New Jersey courts. . . .

Recognition of screening mechanisms is not uniform among the states and is heavily dependent upon each state's public policies with respect to the regulation of attorneys practicing within its borders. The state of New Jersey has demonstrated that its policy is to ensure strict compliance with its RPC, and those RPC provisions dealing with conflicts of interest go beyond those of other states. . . . Many state courts have underscored the general ineffectiveness of ethics screens, and this court notes that temptation is pervasive, policing is difficult, and violations are almost impossible to prove. See, e.g., Henriksen v. Great American Savings and Loan, 11 Cal. App. 4th 109 (Ct. App. 1992); Nebraska v. Buckley, 244 Neb. 36 (1993); Towne Dev. of Chandler, Inc. v. Superior Court, 173 Ariz. 364 (Ct. App. 1992); Lansing-Delaware Water District v. Oak Lane Park, Inc., 248 Kan. 563 (1991). Keeping these considerations in mind, this court will not read into RPC 1.10 the implicit meaning that Kimmel & Silverman seek to give it and recognize the effectiveness of an ethics screen where the New Jersey courts have not.

IV. COMPETING INTERESTS

. . . [T]he court's final task in a disqualification motion is to balance the competing interests, weighing the need to maintain the highest standards of the legal profession against a client's right to freely choose its counsel. [Dewey v. R.J. Reynolds Tobacco Co.,]109 N.J. [201 (1988)] at 218. Kimmel & Silverman assert that it is the only firm prosecuting a significant number of lemon law cases against automobile manufacturers in New Jersey, and is one of two firms doing so in Pennsylvania. They submit the affidavits of several New Jersey plaintiffs who state that they are pleased with the services provided by Kimmel & Silverman, and they do not believe that they could obtain similar representation, if any at all, in such matters if the firm were disqualified. These individuals were prepared to testify at the hearings in accordance with their affidavits. Kimmel & Silverman argue that GM is brandishing its corporate might against the claims of powerless individuals who only seek an honest bargain in the purchase of a GM automobile, and the court should not allow the interests and rights of these individuals to be prejudiced by GM's smear campaign against Kimmel & Silverman.

The court understands the plaintiffs' desire to continue to be represented by Kimmel & Silverman. The firm certainly possesses extensive experience in litigating lemon law claims and has demonstrated its ability to protect its clients' interests while generating substantial revenue for itself. The firm's phenomenal success in the lemon law area in Pennsylvania is apparent from the record . . . . However, amidst the surge of lemon law claims, the increasing workload, the twelve-hour workdays, and the planned expansion of the firm into surrounding geographical areas, all of which spawned the need to hire one or more additional attorneys, Mr. Silverman and Mr. Kimmel, along with Mr. London, may not have stopped to consider their ethical obligations imposed by states other than Pennsylvania. . . .

. . . As has been repeatedly stated by Mr. Silverman, Mr. Kimmel, and Mr. London during the hearings and in all of their motion papers and affidavits, the issues in lemon law litigation are not complex and do not require a significant amount of legal analysis or novel pleading. The cases themselves have a lifespan of approximately six to twelve months. There is no reason why other firms in New Jersey could not just as adequately protect the plaintiffs' interests in lemon law litigation. . . . Under New Jersey law, Mr. London must be disqualified under RPC 1.9 and that disqualification is imputed to the firm of Kimmel & Silverman through RPC 1.10. This is not the "extraordinary case" . . . where a client's right to counsel of his or her choice outweighs the need to maintain the highest standards of the profession. Although disqualification of Kimmel & Silverman may cause inconvenience and some delay to the plaintiffs, the harm to the public interest if Kimmel & Silverman is permitted to remain as counsel for plaintiffs outweighs the prejudice to the plaintiffs.

The court is aware of and must be sensitive to the fact that motions for disqualification are often filed to improperly delay proceedings and to deny a party the counsel of her choice. . . . Many representations were made during the hearing that GM's motivation for filing this motion was to drive Kimmel & Silverman out of business because of their great success in litigating lemon law claims against GM. However, the factual record shows that GM filed this motion on July 3, 1995, very soon after it became known that Kimmel & Silverman hired Mr. London on May 31, 1995. There is no evidence before the court that GM sought to unduly delay these proceedings or harass the respondents by filing this motion. . . .

CONCLUSION

For the reasons discussed above, the court finds that Mr. London would be disqualified from representing the plaintiffs in the matters that are the subject of this motion pursuant to RPC 1.9(a)(1), 1.9(a)(2), and 1.9(b). The firm of Kimmel & Silverman is also disqualified pursuant to RPC 1.10.

Notes

1. The court at one point notes that the ethics screen had been ineffective with respect to the activities of Mr. Kimmel. Was there any necessity under Pennsylvania law to screen off Mr. Kimmel, who had no confidential information from GM?

2. The discussion of the substantial relation test indicates that there are many possible interpretations of those words. A requirement that the cases themselves be substantively related, as suggested by the opinion of the New Jersey Ethics Committee, would narrow the doctrine's applicability substantially. The purpose of the doctrine to protect confidential information of the former client would not be accomplished by such a test. But note how broad the matters were that the court considered under the heading of confidential information: GM's legal strategies, its bargaining positions, and his knowledge of the personality characteristics of key GM employees who handled lemon law matters. Translated into different factual situations, these considerations, if broadly used, could result in widespread disqualification in situations where the factual and legal issues of the former and current litigation were very different. See Velazquez-Velez v. Molina-Rodrigues, 2017 U.S. Dist. LEXIS 13902 (D. P.R. 2017), where the federal district court disqualified a law firm that had represented a municipality for many years from representing fired municipal employees who were claiming political discrimination. The court held that the firm's extensive representation of the municipality over many years put it in a position to have acquired "playbook" information about strategies and policies that might be useful in the current case, especially because the change of municipal administration that led to new municipal counsel did not involve a change of political party or indeed even a complete change in personnel.

3. A leading case on disqualification that involved a junior lawyer at a major New York law firm, Kelly, Drye & Warren, who had worked on a client's matters and then sued that client after he had moved to another firm was Silver Chrysler Plymouth Corp. v. Chrysler Motors Corp., 518 F.2d 751 (2d Cir. 1975). The court concluded that the work that the lawyer had done in his former firm on Chrysler matters did not give him sufficient confidential information relevant to the later suits to bring the later suits within the substantial relationship doctrine. The court rejected Chrysler's argument that the lawyer had confidential information relating to its practices, procedures, methods of operation, and contemplated conduct, perhaps because the charges were not so specific as those made by GM in *Steel*. How much should the law presume that young lawyers know about a given deal or litigation project? Consider that Anita Charles in Problem 1–2 read through the whole file of the client. How

much follow-up should we do to see if junior lawyers do know more than partners might think? Does a categorical rule make sense? A presumption?

4. The fact that the federal district courts in New Jersey and Pennsylvania each followed the professional conduct rules of their respective jurisdictions meant that a "screen" was available to cure the conflict problem in Pennsylvania but not in New Jersey. Is it more desirable that the results in the two federal district courts be uniform or that the results within the two geographic areas be uniform? This is a highly controversial subject at the moment.

5. London seems to have practiced only in Pennsylvania, where screening was allowed. Is the effect of the *Steel* court's decision to require Kimmel & Silverman to follow New Jersey ethics law in their Pennsylvania office simply because they bring suits in federal district court in New Jersey? What is the justification for that? Is the further result of *Steel* that when London left the McBreen office, he should have been shunned by any law firm wanting to sue GM in lemon law matters in any jurisdiction that would not permit any conflict to be cured by screening?

6. *Steel* is one of relatively few cases in which there has been extensive discussion of what it means for information to be "generally known." That phrase appears only in Model Rule 1.9(c)(1). Why? Why isn't information that is "generally known" excluded from the definition of information required to be confidential in Rule 1.6? What is information that is "generally known" anyhow? Is information that is in a public record "generally known"? Even if very few people know about it? Under Rule 1.9(c)(1), may a lawyer use information that is "generally known" to the disadvantage of a former client by revealing the information to someone who does not know it even if the former client has begged the lawyer not to reveal it to that person?

7. The "appearance of impropriety" standard was a feature of the former Model Code of Professional Conduct and was quite controversial because it was so general and amorphous as a standard. Its elimination from the words of the Model Rules was a reflection of the thought that cases of appearance of impropriety were better analyzed under the more precise rules. One situation where the standard has independent content is that of government lawyers, where public perception of their conduct is an important value.

8. *Silver Chrysler Plymouth*, Note 3, involved the effect on the departing associate of the usual rule imputing the firm's knowledge to him and held that the usual rule did not apply once he had left the firm. Novo-Terapeutisk Laboratorium A/S v. Baxter Travenol Laboratories, Inc., 607 F.2d 186, 194 (7th Cir. 1979) (en banc), involved the reverse situation. In that case, the partner who had Baxter's confidential information regarding a potential suit by Novo left the firm and continued representing Baxter. Subsequently the firm undertook to represent Novo against Baxter with respect to that very suit. The court refused to disqualify the law firm from representing Novo against Baxter in the absence of any allegation that the departing partner shared confidences with his firm and in the face of denials from the firm that he had. The result in *Baxter Laboratories* has been codified in Model Rule

1.10(b) and the result in *Silver Chrysler Plymouth* would appear to be codified in Model Rule 1.9(b), especially as explained in the Comment to that Rule.

2. Public Interest Lawyers and the Conflict Rules

Problem 4–13

Law Firm has just about decided that it is going to become general counsel to a cigarette manufacturer when it discovers that on her own time, Associate (with firm knowledge) has been doing pro bono legal work for the Citizens' Lobby Against Smoking and through that connection is assisting in a lawsuit brought by a lung cancer victim against the cigarette manufacturer. Must Law Firm decline the position of general counsel? If Associate ceases to work on the case, may the firm accept the representation? Suppose that instead of doing legal work for the Lobby, Associate was President of the organization? Should the combination of Rule 1.7(b) and Rule 1.10(a) of the Model Rules preclude Law Firm from accepting the position of general counsel?

Problem 4–14*

County Legal Services, Inc. is a nonprofit corporation whose direction is vested in a board of directors. Members of the board control the general policy of the project, including determination of eligibility standards and determination of the type of services to be rendered. Members may, on occasion, determine the eligibility of specific clients by name and may determine the propriety of the project's furnishing specific types of service to named clients.

No member of the board has access to any client's file. In determining the services to be rendered in general, or to particular clients, the board merely sets general policy guidelines. It may not control the actual handling of a case, dictate strategy or otherwise direct the attorney in the handling of a case. Questions of this nature are passed upon by the project administrator.

The project operates on a countywide basis. It does a substantial amount of matrimonial, consumer, and landlord and tenant litigation, which are also fields for specialization by the private bar. It is thus inevitable that from time to time attorneys employed by the project will be called upon to defend actions instituted either by board members, or by associates in firms in which board members are employed.

1. May project attorneys defend an action instituted by a partner in a firm in which one of the board members is a partner or associate?

2. Since membership of the board changes from time to time, how long after a board member resigns may project attorneys defend actions instituted by the board member or by the firm of which he is an associate or partner?

---

* Adapted from an opinion of the New Jersey Advisory Committee on Professional Ethics, 94 N.J.L.J. 801 (1971).

3. Does it make a difference that the particular board member whose firm has brought the action is one of the three board members (out of 15) selected by the local bar association?

4. Does it make a difference that the law firm instituting the suit had reason to know that the defendant would seek representation by County Legal Services, Inc.?

Problem 4–15*

Six months ago a legal assistance office opened in a neighborhood where there already was an active, outspoken community organization comprised almost exclusively of low income black residents. The immediate neighborhood where the office and organization are located is almost 100% black, but it is included within larger political and school districts that are approximately 60% white.

The purposes of the organization, which supports no political party as such, are (1) to awaken interest of the black citizenry in ward politics, in order to promote "reform" candidates for city council and state representatives who will represent the "people" instead of the "bosses"; (2) to inform the school board about incidents of arbitrary and discriminatory treatment of black schoolchildren by white teachers in the local school, which has a 40%–50% black enrollment, and to press for more black teachers and a greater voice in school affairs by the local community; (3) to expose incidents of police brutality against black teenagers and to achieve a more just handling of complaints against juveniles; (4) to establish a local credit union as an alternative to hard-sell, high-interest small loan companies; (5) to inform people about their legal rights under the welfare laws and as tenants; (6) to press the city for more frequent garbage collection and sewer inspections; and (7) to pressure local chain stores and industrial plants into hiring more blacks.

From time to time the legal assistance office has assisted the organization with community education programs about the law. Usually these have been group discussions in the evening, but one lawyer in the office also has written a pamphlet entitled "Tenants' Rights." Its cover carries the names of both the legal assistance office and the organization. A neighborhood aide from the legal assistance office has been going around the community with officers of the organization looking for people who have legal problems. Last week the office agreed to draw up the papers for the organization's proposed credit union.

Today, 15 minutes ago, the chief staff attorney of the office received a telephone call from the president of the organization, who said that he was on his way over to the office with ten families, "each of which has a child who was summarily expelled today from high school for fighting with white students in the school cafeteria." In most cases both the child and at least one parent will be coming. Only two of the

---

* This problem was developed by, and is used with the permission of, Judge John M. Ferren of the District of Columbia Court of Appeals, who used it in legal services courses and professional responsibility courses while teaching at Harvard Law School.

families are members of the organization, but the president said that he hopes his obtaining legal assistance for the other eight will inspire them to join the organization. He added that from the evidence he has gathered "this will be a great way for a lot of people to take a stand together against those high-handed school administrators and their discriminatory expulsion tactics."

The president has just arrived at the office with 25 people—fathers and/or mothers of all ten who were expelled, and nine of the ten students; at the last minute one student refused to come. Three staff attorneys, including the chief, are on hand. What should the chief do?

(a) Who is the client in this case? Would it make any difference if the credit union matter had already been completed, or if the office has never represented the organization before the school board?

(b) May the office represent both the children and the organization? If the office has several branches, may a different branch represent some of the children?

(c) May the office represent more than one child?

(d) How does the office obtain the facts to permit it to decide what to do?

(e) What happens in the event of a difference of opinion about a proposed course of action between a child and his or her parents?

(f) Suppose it looks as if this matter will consume a tremendous amount of the office's time and cause it to turn away other business. May it decide not to take the case? What factors ought it to consider before reaching such a decision?

(g) Should the office have taken on the organization as a client in the first place? What effect might that have on its ability to serve the needs of individuals in the community?

Problem 4–16

Legal Aid Office, not operated with federal funding, instituted a class action suit to force a public Housing Authority to afford tenants their statutory right to safe, decent housing. The court, finding widespread and persistent violations of statute, appointed a receiver of the Housing Authority to run its public housing projects for a temporary period. Subsequently, an agreement was negotiated between class counsel and the receiver and embodied in a court order that permitted the receiver to use expedited eviction procedures whenever a tenant or member of the tenant's household committed or threatened to commit certain specific crimes of violence against other tenants in or near a housing authority project or carried or kept on the premises specified "controlled substances." Another attorney in the Legal Aid Office had for a long time represented an individual tenant on a variety of matters. That tenant sought advice from the attorney about the possibility that she was subject to eviction under the court order. The attorney, seeing the possibility of conflict between his client and the tenant class represented by his office with respect to both the validity of the original order and its current application, sent a memorandum to the Executive

Director of the Legal Aid office advising her that he was about to refer the client to a specified legal aid office. The Executive Director, who was heavily involved in supervising the class action, responded that she wanted to review the file to determine whether there was any conflict and that, if there was, she would make the referral. The attorney asks your legal advice about the propriety of turning over the file. What advice do you give? (The general problem is suggested by Spence v. Reeder, 382 Mass. 398 (1981).)

In re Charlisse C.
45 Cal. 4th 145 (2008)

CHIN, J.—We granted review in this case to determine whether the juvenile court correctly disqualified the Children's Law Center of Los Angeles (CLC) from representing Charlisse C., a minor, in this dependency action. CLC is a publicly funded, nonprofit law office that represents parties in the Los Angeles County Juvenile Dependency Court. It currently comprises three units: a core unit, known as Unit 1, and two conflict units, known as Units 2 and 3. Unit 3 undertook to represent Charlisse in this action, which arose when a juvenile dependency petition was filed under Welfare and Institutions Code section 300 alleging in part that Charlisse was at substantial risk of being abused or neglected due to the emotional and mental health problems of her mother, Shadonna C. Shadonna is a former client of CLC's Unit 1 (or its predecessor). Although finding no actual conflict of interest and no improper disclosure of confidential information, the juvenile court, citing Castro v. Los Angeles County Bd. of Supervisors, 232 Cal.App.3d 1432 (1991), and People v. Christian, 41 Cal.App.4th 986 (1996), found that an erosion of the ethical screens separating CLC's units created a structural conflict of interest warranting CLC's disqualification. In a divided decision, a majority of the Court of Appeal reversed the disqualification order. For reasons set forth below, we conclude the trial court applied the wrong legal standard in ordering CLC's disqualification and therefore abused its discretion. We remand the matter for further consideration in accordance with the standards this opinion sets forth.

Factual Background

On July 26, 2006, the Los Angeles County Department of Children and Family Services (DCFS) filed a petition alleging that six-day-old Charlisse came within the juvenile court's jurisdiction for two reasons: (1) she was at substantial risk of suffering serious physical harm because the "emotional/mental health condition" of her 19-year-old mother, Shadonna, "at times ha[d] interfered with [Shadonna's] ability to provide regular care, supervision and a home"; and (2) Charlisse's sister, Donna, had been abused or neglected by Shadonna and there was substantial risk that Charlisse would also be abused or neglected. Regarding the latter allegation, the petition explained that Donna, who was born when Shadonna was 14 years old, is a former juvenile court dependent and that the dependency ended with Donna's adoption by her grandmother. A simultaneously filed detention report noted that Shadonna is "a former foster youth" with a "history of behavioral problems."

At the detention hearing on July 26, 2006, the juvenile court appointed a CLC attorney to represent Charlisse. CLC is a publicly funded, nonprofit legal services organization that the County of Los Angeles created in 1989 to provide statutorily required legal representation to parents and children in the dependency court. It initially operated under a 1990 agreement with the Los Angeles County Board of Supervisors (Board) requiring CLC to maintain a structure that enabled it to "represent as many as three separate parties in a dependency proceeding, even if they [had] conflicting interests." The 1990 agreement also required CLC to follow specified operating rules and procedures, including the following: (1) CLC's staff attorneys had to "be organized into three separate offices of comparable quality," each with "its own separate administrator" with "full case management authority over all cases assigned to that office"; (2) "[e]ach office [had to] maintain separate case files," and staff attorneys assigned to one office could not "have access to the case files of [another] office"; (3) "[a]ttorneys [could] not be transferred between offices"; and (4) CLC "corporate officers [could] promote, discipline, or dismiss a staff attorney only upon the recommendation of that attorney's office administrator." In *Castro*, the Court of Appeal rejected the claim that CLC's separate offices could not represent separate parties with potentially adverse interests in a single dependency proceeding, reasoning in part that CLC had "been structured so its attorneys and its separate groups [had] no contact with one another," and that its "structures ... reinforce[d]" the ethical duty of CLC's attorneys not to violate their clients' confidences or compromise their legal interests.

In July 2005, CLC began providing legal services under an agreement with California's Administrative Office of the Courts. At about the same time, CLC reorganized its three offices into three litigation units: a "core" unit, known as Unit 1, and two "conflict" units, known as Units 2 and 3. . . .

. . . Shadonna moved to disqualify CLC and Unit 3 from further representation of any party. In her moving papers, she asserted that she became a dependent child in December 2001 after her mother died, that CLC's Unit 1 represented her when she was a dependent child, that Unit 1 later represented her again as a parent when her first child was detained in June 2002, that she received reunification services through December 2003 in connection with her first child, and that her first child was adopted and jurisdiction was terminated in February 2005. She then argued that because CLC's prior representation of her substantially related to CLC's current representation of Charlisse, disqualification was appropriate unless CLC showed that "it complie[d] with the structure set forth in *Castro*." She further argued that CLC's "current structure" did not comply with *Castro*, that "[t]here ha[d] been no attempt to maintain ethical walls among [CLC's] three units," and that the ability of CLC's administration "to dictate policy, hire, fire, set salaries, and interfere with the assignment of cases create[d] a de facto conflict of interest for every client with an adverse interest to another client within the organization."

In support of her motion, Shadonna submitted declarations from Kenneth Sherman, Anne Fragasso, Allen Korenstein, and Angela Pierce di Donato, all former CLC employees. Sherman joined CLC in 1990 as a senior trial attorney and, in September 1997, became director of the office now known as Unit 2. He stated generally that after Miriam Krinsky became CLC's executive director in April 2002, she "repeatedly violated the ethical walls" separating CLC's units. Specifically, he stated:

1. In January 2003, Krinsky tried to convince him, one of his attorneys, and one of his supervisors to "quash" a subpoena for a DCFS employee in a case Sherman's office was handling, because Krinsky was concerned "it would not look good if it appeared that [CLC] was not cooperating with" DCFS.

2. In early 2003, Krinsky asked fact-specific questions of an attorney in Sherman's office who was representing a dependent child. It was clear from the nature of the questions that Krinsky knew many of the facts of the case. Sherman later discovered that the head of Unit 1 represented a sibling with a conflicting interest.

3. In June 2003, "it was discovered" that Krinsky "surreptitiously had [CLC's] computer administrator put her email address on each of the intraoffice confidential emails of the three law firms. These intraoffice email lists were intended to be distribution lists for the staff within each office in order to ensure that there was no breach of confidentiality when information about cases was transmitted within the office. . . . When [Krinsky] was informed of the breach of confidentiality and how this act could endanger the viability of the corporation, she relented and permitted the three firms to maintain intraoffice confidential email address lists."

4. In fall 2003, Krinsky imposed a policy requiring her approval before a Code of Civil Procedure section 170.6 affidavit of prejudice could be used on a "blanket" basis or in a "class of cases" to disqualify a judicial officer. She suspended the policy about a year later when Sherman provided her with an opinion on the policy from an "ethics expert."

5. In spring 2005, when an attorney left Sherman's office, Krinsky transferred one of the former attorney's cases to Unit 1. Krinsky felt it was not necessary to provide the client with notice and an opportunity to be heard, or to obtain a court order permitting the substitution, because CLC was counsel for the children. More generally, Krinsky pursued transferring cases at will among the three firms.

6. Krinsky "indicated" to Sherman "[m]any times . . . that she felt that the interests of the organization as a whole [were] paramount to the interests of the law firms."

Fragasso was a CLC employee from 1999 until the middle of 2005. At some point, she was a director of one of CLC's three firms. Like Sherman, Fragasso discussed (1) the policy Krinsky instituted in 2003 regarding blanket disqualification of judges, (2) Krinsky's addition of herself in 2003 to each firm's intraoffice e-mail address list without informing the firm directors, and (3) Krinsky's view in 2005 that cases could be transferred to Unit 1 without giving clients notice and an opportunity to be heard or obtaining a court order. According to Fragasso, regarding the last issue, Krinsky stated that as executive director, she had authority "to create whatever structure" she deemed appropriate. Fragasso also stated that when she refused to transfer cases without speaking to her clients in confidence and obtaining both their approval and a court order, Krinsky removed her as a law firm director.

Korenstein worked for what is now CLC Unit 2 from May 2004 through March 2006. He stated that he had "witnessed the transfer of a CLC [Unit] 2 secretary to CLC [Unit] 1 without, to [his] knowledge any conflict checks and/or screens." He also stated that once, when he asked the head of his unit to "approve funding for an expert psychologist to review [a] case and possibly testify in court," Unit 2's head told him "to forward [the] request to" the "head of CLC [Unit] 1."

Di Donato was a Unit 2 attorney from December 1996 until January 2005. She stated that Krinsky came into her office one evening after entering Unit 2 through a locked door that was not open to the public. She told Krinsky she "was working on a difficult case that needed more attention." Krinsky asked questions "about the facts of the case," "the client," "what was going on in court," and "what work [di Donato] was doing on" the case. When di Donato decided to leave CLC in November 2004, she wanted to keep 15 cases. Krinsky said the cases belonged to CLC and that she would decide which cases di Donato could take. After di Donato explained the facts of each case to Krinsky, Krinsky permitted di Donato to keep only two child clients.

With these declarations, Shadonna submitted a copy of the revised operating procedures CLC adopted in October 2005 (Revised Operating Procedures), which stated in relevant part:

1. CLC['s] staff will continue to be assigned by CLC's executive leadership to a core unit or such other conflict unit or units as CLC may choose to maintain over time (currently denoted as CLC [Units] 1, 2, and 3). The conflict unit or units will handle cases with siblings where conflicts of interest are present ('conflict cases')—to be denoted on CLC's file and records as conflict cases—as well as any other nonconflict cases that may previously or in the future be assigned to that unit. . . . Any determination that a conflict exists in a given case will be made only after consultation with, and approval by, a supervisor, as set forth in CLC's conflict policy.

2. Each of CLC's units will operate pursuant to the procedures set forth herein to ensure that ethical walls for handling conflict cases within CLC remain in place and are honored at all times. Any questions or concerns that these procedures do not adequately preserve the separateness of conflict cases or that these procedures are not being complied with shall be directed to CLC's Executive Director or the appropriate unit head.

3. Each CLC unit shall have a unit head. The conflict unit head(s) shall ensure that conflict case files and all confidential case information relating to conflict cases assigned to a given unit are maintained by that unit, remain separate from the case files and confidential case information of the core firm and any other conflict unit(s), and cannot be accessed by any staff outside the conflict unit. The conflict unit(s) head(s) and any other conflict unit supervisors shall supervise, direct and coordinate the day-to-day representation and case-related decision making in regard to conflict

cases and conflict clients assigned to that unit and will be the final decision-maker in regard to those case-specific issues.

4. [CLC's] practice for promoting, terminating or disciplining CLC lawyers or staff members is unchanged. The CLC Executive Director or his or her designee will remain the final decision-maker after considering a recommendation from the unit head or supervisor of that staff member, along with the basis for that recommendation. In evaluating that recommendation, the CLC Executive Director will not have access to conflict unit case files, or any conflict unit client confidential information.

5. No attorney shall have access to the case files or confidential client information relating to any clients of other units in conflict with that attorney's clients.

6. Where no conflict of interest or ethical concerns exist, cases may be reassigned within CLC, and in particular from the conflict unit(s) to the core firm.

7. CLC's executive leadership shall be responsible for hiring and training staff attorneys and for assigning them, as appropriate and consistent with the Board's restructuring plan, to the core firm or conflict unit(s). All attorneys and staff shall receive training regarding the necessity of maintaining client confidences.

8. CLC will continue to remain counsel for all clients assigned to CLC. To ensure that the appropriate staff member receives notices, pleadings, and other information relating to clients, individual attorneys within CLC will serve as the responsible attorney—the attorney of record—for cases assigned to that attorney. If those individual attorneys leave CLC's employ or change courtrooms or caseloads, a notice will be filed with the court and sent to all critical persons and entities, designating the new responsible attorney of record within CLC. As noted above, the conflict unit head(s) will maintain ultimate and final responsibility for the supervision, direction and coordination of case-related decision making in regard to conflict cases and conflict clients assigned to that unit and will be the final decision-maker in regard to those case-specific issues.

In opposition to the motion, CLC argued that Shadonna's evidentiary showing was insufficient to warrant disqualification and that CLC's structure and operating procedures closely complied with the standards set forth in *Castro* and several other decisions . . . . CLC submitted declarations from Krinsky explaining that when CLC shifted its focus from representing both parents and children to representing only children, its tripartite structure of three semi-autonomous divisions became outdated and unnecessary. Thus, in early 2005, CLC's board of directors decided to begin "'moving CLC to a unified and more cohesive organizational structure.'" The Revised Operating Procedures were later adopted to "implement" a "gradual shift . . . toward a more unified organizational structure with a 'core firm' and 'conflict units.'"

In her declarations, Krinsky stated that CLC strictly adhered to its Revised Operating Procedures and enforced existing ethical walls, and that she was unaware "of any material breaches" of CLC's Revised Operating Procedures, ethical walls, or conflicts policy. She denied that she or other executive officers, attorneys, or staff from

Unit 1 had access to case files in Units 2 and 3; that Unit 1 leadership and attorneys had access to client confidential information relating to cases of Units 2 and 3; that she had ever used a key to access the office spaces of Units 2 and 3 or any confidential case files; that she had received any confidential information relating to, or exercised any control over, this case; that she had ever "forced any CLC lawyer to discuss a conflict case or reveal client confidential information"; that CLC's "executive leadership" had any involvement in case-specific decisions of Units 2 and 3 or supervision of cases assigned to those units; or that attorneys working in Units 2 and 3 needed approval from her or from Unit 1 before paying ordinary trial expenses, such as the costs of retaining expert witnesses. She also stated that extraordinary expenses for Units 2 and 3 might need her approval in order to ensure that CLC operated within its budgetary limitations, but that in evaluating an extraordinary expense request, neither she nor her staff had inquired into the specific facts of any case or obtained confidential information.

Regarding some of the other specific charges detailed in the declarations Shadonna submitted, Krinsky explained that she added her name to the intraoffice e-mail list of all CLC units in June 2003 "in order to be kept apprised of general office email discussions of events, issues of common concern, or other non-case specific matters." She also stated that when concern was raised "that these email groups might on occasion also include emails relating to case-specific and confidential information, [she] immediately directed that a client confidential email group be created for each unit, without [her] inclusion in those groups, and informed [CLC's] staff that all client confidential and case specific email communication should occur on that email group." Krinsky also stated that she had "no recollection" of a meeting in early 2003 during which, according to Sherman's declaration, she asked fact-specific questions of one of Sherman's lawyers, and that she had "no specific recollection" of the conversation that, according to di Donato, occurred in di Donato's office. She did recall what she described as "a late-night 'rapport-building' conversation" with di Donato. She acknowledged having had conversations with di Donato concerning which cases di Donato could take with her when she left CLC, but denied that any "client confidential information was ever passed to" her during those conversations. Krinsky also acknowledged that CLC had once adopted a policy regarding "the exercise of *blanket* peremptory challenges that were not tethered to a particular case," but stated that the policy (1) "made clear that it in no way constrained the exercise of decision-making in individual cases and that those decisions remained the prerogative of individual attorneys, under the supervision of their unit heads," and (2) "clearly precluded the sharing of any confidential or case specific information with the Executive Director or among unit heads." She also declared that the policy had been put "in abeyance."

Regarding employment practices, Krinsky stated that "[a]s was the case under" the operating procedures *Castro* reviewed, under CLC's Revised Operating Procedures, she, as CLC's executive director, had (1) "final authority, upon the recommendation of the CLC Unit Heads, with regard to promoting, terminating, or disciplining CLC['s] lawyers or staff members," (2) "authority over CLC['s] budget and how funds get allocated in relation to CLC['s] operating costs," and (3) "authority over hiring decisions, and assignment of lawyers to particular CLC units." Krinsky also acknowledged that secretaries were moved between units, but stated that this practice predated her employment as executive director and that she directed that secretaries be advised of the need to preserve client confidences.

CLC also submitted declarations from its unit heads, David Estep, Marc Leftwich, and Ivy Carey. Estep, who headed Unit 1, which formerly represented Shadonna, denied that he, the executive officers, or any Unit 1 attorney had access to files of cases assigned to Units 2 and 3. He also stated that Krinsky had underscored the need to ensure that secretaries were advised of and abided by the rules for preserving client confidences and maintaining ethical walls, and that CLC strictly enforced ethical walls separating Units 1, 2, and 3, and the executive leadership. Finally, he stated that one of his "role[s]" as unit head was to "ensure that no attorneys or staff from" Units 2 and 3 "have access to the case files and client confidential information relating to cases assigned to" Unit 1, and that he neither was "aware" of nor "believe[d]" there had been any "material breaches of CLC Operating Procedures, CLC's ethical walls, or the CLC conflicts policy." Leftwich, who headed Unit 2, and Carey, who headed Unit 3, made similar statements. Leftwich also stated that he had complete autonomy in funding ordinary trial expenses consistent with the limitations of the Unit 2 budget. As to Korenstein's statement that he was once directed to forward a request for expert witness funding to the head of Unit 1, Leftwich noted Korenstein's failure to identify the case or client involved and stated his (Leftwich's) recollection that "the request was for an extraordinary expense and that the decision not to hire this particular expert witness was made independent of cost and based on strategic reasons related to the specifics of the case and discussed *only* with and among [Unit 2] attorneys and supervisors." Carey stated that she opposed the disqualification motion as head of Unit 3, no one had pressured her to do so, and she had "full autonomy with regard to representing" Charlisse.

The juvenile court granted the disqualification motion. In the court's view, the key issue was whether CLC's current structure "either inherently or in practice violates the ethical walls that *Castro* mandated to be in place in order to allow an umbrella organization to represent more than one party in a pending lawsuit." Finding the declarations supporting the disqualification motion to be "more persuasive than the opposition motion," the court explained: "I get the impression that CLC says one thing and does something else. They have established a structure which they claim they strictly adhere to, but the underlying facts suggest otherwise." The court noted that it was basing its decision on "the whole picture, . . . taking all of the declarations together," but that two things in particular "jumped out" of the record: (1) Sherman's "allegations or assertions" that Krinsky "went into their computer system without getting permission or consent in order to get access to confidential communications that were being circulated in each office"; and (2) a "subtle change" since *Castro* in CLC's rules regarding certain employment decisions. Regarding the latter, the court reasoned that whereas the operating rules at issue in *Castro* permitted promotion, discipline, and termination to be initiated *only* by the chief attorney of each CLC unit, the Revised Operating Procedures, although possibly "ambiguous," "seem[ed] to imply that the executive director could initiate" these actions and had "assumed the responsibility or the authority to fire or promote, etcetera." Finally, although acknowledging CLC's point that there had "been no evidence presented of any specific breach of confidentiality in any particular case," the court stated: "The courts seem to be really concerned about, in addition, the appearance of conflict. And it seems to me that in the consolidation of all of the cases into one core unit and the practice that's been presented in the declarations, . . . the ethical walls may have been breached." Summarizing, the court explained that it was disqualifying CLC based on "a violation . . . of the *Castro* and *Christian* safeguards regarding conflict of interest in representing multiple parties in the same action." . . .

Conflicts of interest commonly arise in one of two factual contexts: (1) in cases of successive representation, where an attorney seeks to represent a client with interests that are potentially adverse to a former client of the attorney; and (2) in cases of simultaneous representation, where an attorney seeks to represent in a single action multiple parties with potentially adverse interests. The primary fiduciary value at stake in each of these context differs, and the applicable disqualification standards vary accordingly. In successive representation cases, "the chief fiduciary value jeopardized is that of client *confidentiality*." (Flatt v. Superior Court, 9 Cal.4th 275, 283 (1994).) Therefore, the disqualification standards we have developed for such cases focus on the former client's interest "in ensuring the permanent confidentiality of matters disclosed to the attorney in the course of the prior representation." (Ibid.) In simultaneous representation cases, "[t]he primary value at stake . . . is the attorney's duty—and the client's legitimate expectation—of *loyalty*, rather than confidentiality." (Id. at p. 284.) . . .

In light of these principles, we conclude the juvenile court here applied an incorrect legal standard in disqualifying CLC. As explained above, the juvenile court stated it was ordering disqualification based on CLC's failure to observe the structural safeguards discussed in *Castro* and *Christian*. However, unlike the case now before us, which involves *successive* representation—i.e., CLC's proposed representation of a client, Charlisse, whose interests arguably are adverse to a *former* CLC client, Shadonna—*Castro* and *Christian* involved . . . simultaneous representation, the disqualification standards they applied necessarily were different from—and more stringent than—the standards that govern the *successive* representation case now before us. Accordingly, as the lead opinion here observed, the factors emphasized in *Castro* and *Christian* are not necessarily dispositive in this case, and the juvenile court's finding that CLC did not observe some of the safeguards *Castro* and *Christian* discussed does not automatically warrant disqualification. The juvenile court committed legal error—and thus, abused its discretion—in concluding otherwise. . . .

CLC does not dispute that a substantial relationship exists between the subjects of the former and current representations at issue here. Accordingly, for purposes of analyzing this case, we assume that the Unit 1 attorney who formerly represented Shadonna has a disqualifying conflict of interest. Thus, the only question here is whether, under the vicarious disqualification rule, that disqualifying conflict of interest requires disqualification of all other CLC attorneys, including the Unit 3 attorney the juvenile court appointed to represent Charlisse.

In answering this question, we begin by noting that there are court-created limitations to the vicarious disqualification rule . . . . California courts have generally declined to apply an automatic and inflexible rule of vicarious disqualification in the context of public law offices. Instead, in this context, courts have looked to whether the public law office has adequately protected, and will continue to adequately protect, the former client's confidences through timely, appropriate, and effective screening measures and/or structural safeguards. . . .

Courts have cited several considerations in declining to apply an automatic and inflexible rule of vicarious disqualification in the context of public law offices. Summarizing some of these considerations, the court in [City of] *Santa Barbara* [v. Superior Court, 122 Cal.App.4th 17 (2004)] explained: "Unlike their private sector counterparts, public sector lawyers do not have a financial interest in the matters on which they work. As a result, they may have less, if any, incentive to breach client confidences. Public sector lawyers also do not recruit clients or accept fees. As a result, they have no financial incentive to favor one client over another. . . . [V]icarious disqualification in the public sector context imposes different burdens on the affected public entities, lawyers and clients. Most frequently cited is the difficulty public law offices would have in recruiting competent lawyers. Private sector law firms may hesitate to hire a lawyer from a public law office, to avoid being disqualified in future matters involving that office. Individual lawyers may hesitate to accept public sector jobs, to avoid limiting their future opportunities in the private sector. Clients whose interests are adverse to a public entity could be deprived of their chosen counsel, or find it difficult to retain counsel at all, particularly in highly specialized areas of the law. Public entities may face the same difficulty and be forced to avoid hiring lawyers with relevant private sector experience. Disqualification increases costs for public entities just as it does for private sector litigants. When a public entity is involved, these higher costs raise the possibility that litigation decisions will be driven by financial considerations rather than by the public interest." [*Santa Barbara*, supra at 24–25] . . . As the *Christian* court put it, "in the public sector, in light of the somewhat lessened potential for conflicts of interest and the high public price paid for disqualifying whole offices of government-funded attorneys, use of internal screening procedures or 'ethical walls' to avoid conflicts within government offices . . . have been permitted" (*Christian*, supra, at p. 998).

Courts have also held, however, that where the attorney with the actual conflict has managerial, supervisorial, and/or policymaking responsibilities in a public law office, screening may not be sufficient to avoid vicarious disqualification of the entire office. . . .

. . . "Individuals who head a government law office occupy a unique position because they are ultimately responsible for making policy decisions that determine how the agency's resources and efforts will be used. Moreover, the attorneys who serve directly under them cannot be entirely insulated from those policy decisions, nor can they be freed from real or perceived concerns as to what their boss wants. The power to review, hire, and fire is a potent one. Thus, a former client may legitimately question whether a government law office, now headed by the client's former counsel, has the unfair advantage of knowing the former client's confidential information when it litigates against the client in a matter substantially related to the attorney's prior representation of that client." Finally, "[p]ublic perception that a city attorney and his deputies might be influenced by the city attorney's previous representation of the client, at the expense of the best interests of the city, would insidiously undermine public confidence in the integrity of municipal government and its city attorney's office." ([City and County of San Francisco v. Cobra Solutions, Inc., 38 Cal.4th 839 (2006)] at p. 854.) . . .

The approach the decisions discussed above have taken with respect to public law offices is the approach the juvenile court should have taken here in deciding whether to disqualify CLC. In other words, the juvenile court should have determined whether CLC has adequately protected, and will continue to adequately protect, Shadonna's confidences through timely, appropriate, and effective screening measures and/or structural safeguards. . . .

However, we do not agree . . . that the evidentiary burden on this issue falls on Shadonna as the party seeking disqualification. Instead, the burden is on CLC to show that, through timely, appropriate, and effective screening measures and/or structural safeguards, the confidential information acquired during Unit 1's prior representation of Shadonna has been, and will be, adequately protected during Unit 3's proposed representation of Charlisse. This burden properly falls on CLC because it has unique access to the relevant information. . . .

It is unclear from the record here whether, under the proper standards, the juvenile court would have disqualified CLC. On the one hand, it is significant that the juvenile court found no evidence "of any specific breach of confidentiality in any particular case," "no evidence . . . of an actual factual conflict," and "no specific—to this case—conflict raised in terms of the divulgence of any confidential or privileged communication." On the other hand, potentially significant evidentiary omissions exist in the record that make it inadvisable to make a disqualification determination in the first instance on appeal. For example, the record contains no evidence as to whether Shadonna's former Unit 1 attorney is still with that unit, has transferred to another unit, or has left CLC altogether. Nor is there any evidence as to whether the Unit 3 attorney who proposes to represent Charlisse now either was with CLC when Unit 1 represented Shadonna or was with Unit 1 at some point. Notably, neither attorney submitted a declaration with factual information relevant to Shadonna's disqualification motion. Because the parties and the juvenile court focused on the wrong legal standards, and because the rules we discuss here are new in some respects (e.g., regarding placement of the evidentiary burden), "[w]e cannot foreclose the possibility that further information was available, but not presented, at the time the [juvenile] court ruled upon the motion." (People v. Calderon, 9 Cal.4th 69, 81 (1994).) Accordingly, the prudent course is to remand the matter to the juvenile court for rehearing of the disqualification motion, rather than to decide the matter on the existing state of the evidentiary record. . . .

Notes

1. The public policy arguments that moved courts to relax the vicarious disqualification rules first in "revolving door" situations of lawyers moving in and out of government and then in "public interest" cases like *Charlisse C.* and *Castro* paved the way for the adoption by the ABA of Resolution 109 relaxing the vicarious disqualification rules in purely private lawyer situations. But, as the principal case indicates, even when there are strong public policy considerations for permitting screening to cure a conflict, clients continue to be nervous. And the efficacy of screening can produce tensions even within the lawyering organization itself.

2. If the issue in this case is properly viewed as whether public policy considerations justify screening, with all its dangers, how much of our judgment ought to turn on the facts of how the separate offices operate and how much on the "appearance" to clients and the general public? If the latter consideration is important, did the court deal with it adequately?

3. In People v. Banks, 121 Ill. 2d 36 (1987), reh'g denied (1988), the Illinois Supreme Court held that an assistant public defender appointed to challenge the effectiveness of the assistance rendered by an assistant public defender from the same office was not automatically disqualified. Overruling earlier cases, the court stated that a case-by-case review was required to determine whether there were any peculiar circumstances to indicate the presence of an actual conflict of interest. A powerful dissent by Judge Simon collected cases coming out the other way and argued that the difficulty of arguing the incompetence of one's colleagues justified a per se rule of disqualification.

4. In Fiandaca v. Cunningham, 827 F.2d 825 (1st Cir. 1987), the court held that it was an abuse of discretion for a district court to have denied a motion to disqualify a legal services organization when its representation of a class of patients with intellectual disabilities housed in a building at Laconia State School interfered with its ability to consider an offer of settlement by the state to a class of incarcerated female inmates. The inmates were also represented by the organization, and the state proposed to relocate them to the same facility, displacing members of the legal organization's patient class.

5. A general approach to the fact situation of Problem 4–14 is set forth in Model Rule 6.3, which tends toward a permissive solution for service on the board of directors of a legal service organization notwithstanding the fact that the board member's law firm is representing adverse interests to a client of the organization. In Estep v.

Johnson, 383 F. Supp. 1323 (D. Conn. 1974), Judge (later Chief Judge of the Court of Appeals for the Second Circuit) Jon Newman concluded that the only ethical stumbling block to a legal services organization and a board member being on opposite sides from one another was the economic authority over salary and promotion wielded by the board member. Is there any practical way to overcome that obstacle? Note the discussion in the principal case.

6. Other kinds of professional responsibility problems may also arise in group legal service programs. Conflict of interest problems, for example, may occur in rather unusual ways when a group legal service program does not consider its role carefully enough. One such situation occurred in Board of Education v. Nyquist, 590 F.2d 1241 (2d Cir. 1979). New York State United Teachers, an association of 180,000 school employees, provided legal representation free of charge to members in cases that were job-related and, in the judgment of the staff, meritorious. When the Board of Education of New York City was faced with opposite determinations from state and federal authorities about the use of separate seniority lists for male and female teachers, it brought a declaratory judgment action naming as defendants the various governmental parties and named male and female teachers as class representatives. The United Teachers took no position in the litigation but the male teachers sought and obtained representation under the group legal services program.

On motion of the female teachers, who objected to paying their opponents' legal expenses, the district judge ordered that either program counsel be disqualified or that the United Teachers should pay counsel for the female teachers. The Court of Appeals reversed. The Court rejected the argument that first amendment associational rights recognized in the line of cases from NAACP v. Button through In re Primus (see pp. 640ff., 726–729) protected either the lawyer's rights to make his views known or to represent a client in a particular matter in the circumstances of this case. In addition, the court believed that the ethical question "could be a very close one." Nevertheless, it thought disqualification was inappropriate. After referring to the delay caused by motions for disqualification, the Court noted that there was no question that the program counsel's representation of the men would be vigorous or that he had access to any privileged information about the women. Except "in the rarest of cases," appearance of impropriety is "too slender a reed upon which to rest a disqualification order."

The Court noted briefly that part of the apparent unfairness of what occurred might be traced to the nature of the program, which left so much to its counsel's discretion. This is the sort of issue that ought to have been foreseen and provided for either substantively or procedurally—that is, either a rule should have been written into the program or a procedure should have been provided for resolution of disputes.

7. A thoughtful consideration of professional responsibility problems of lawyers for the poor that concludes by offering a model of a much less adversarial system is Bellow and Kettleson, "From Ethics to Politics: Confronting Scarcity and Fairness

in Public Interest Practice," 58 B.U. L. Rev. 337 (1978); see also generally Bruce A. Green, "Foreword: Rationing Lawyers: Ethical and Professional Issues in the Delivery of Legal Services to Low-Income Clients," 67 Fordham L. Rev. 1713 (1999).

While the conflict of interest rules work somewhat differently in legal services organizations for those unable to afford to hire their own lawyers, they cannot be ignored, as the previous case and especially the case that follows demonstrate.

People v. Watson
26 N.Y.3d 620 (2016)

Stein, J.:

Notwithstanding the general rule that, for the purposes of conflict of interest analysis, knowledge of a large public defense organization's current and former clients is typically not imputed to each attorney employed by the organization, conflicts may nevertheless arise in certain circumstances involving multiple representations within such organizations. In this case, Supreme Court was placed in the difficult position of having to either relieve defense counsel—thereby depriving defendant of the counsel of his choosing—or permit counsel to continue his representation despite a potential conflict of interest, thereby impinging on defendant's right to the effective assistance of counsel. Under the circumstances presented here, the court did not abuse its discretion by relieving defendant's assigned counsel and appointing conflict-free counsel to represent him. Therefore, we reverse.

I.

Defendant showed a friend a gun in his waistband and threatened to use it against another person. He then went to a park, where he was seen near Toi Stephens. When police arrived, defendant and Stephens fled separately. Witnesses saw defendant throw a gun during the chase, and a gun was subsequently found in the identified location. Cocaine and marihuana were also found on the ground, and Stephens admitted that the drugs belonged to him. Defendant was charged with criminal possession of a weapon in the second degree (two counts) and resisting arrest. Stephens was charged with drug possession.

Robert Fisher, an attorney employed by New York County Defender Services (NYCDS), was assigned to represent defendant. Eight months later, the People turned over *Rosario* material that revealed that a different attorney from NYCDS had represented Stephens on his criminal charge arising from the same incident. Fisher immediately brought this to the attention of Supreme Court. Fisher stated that he had been looking for Stephens as a possible witness for defendant before becoming aware of the potential conflict of interest. Even though defendant wanted Fisher to continue as his attorney, Fisher was not sure it would be appropriate to do so. The court granted an adjournment to determine whether the situation could be resolved.

At an appearance a few days later, Fisher advised the court that Stephens had entered a guilty plea shortly after his arraignment, and NYCDS no longer represented him. However, because Stephens had not waived confidentiality, Fisher's supervisors at NYCDS prohibited him from searching for Stephens, calling Stephens as a witness, or conducting any cross-examination if the People called him to testify. Fisher advised defendant that he could not continue to represent defendant unless defendant agreed to waive even the attempt to call Stephens as a witness. Fisher also asked the court to prohibit the People from calling Stephens, because his supervisors had determined that Fisher could represent defendant only under those conditions.

The court stated that it could not prevent the People from calling a relevant witness, and explained to defendant the potential conflict and the difficult position confronting Fisher. Defendant responded that he wanted to keep Fisher as his attorney and waive the conflict, but also that he wanted Stephens to testify. After hearing these statements that were incompatible with an unequivocal waiver, the court relieved Fisher of his assignment and assigned a new attorney, who represented defendant at trial. The jury convicted defendant of all charges.

The Appellate Division, with one Justice dissenting, reversed the judgment on the ground that the trial court had abused its discretion in relieving Fisher (124 A.D.3d 95 [1st Dept. 2014]). The majority concluded that, because Fisher did not represent Stephens and was not privy to any of his confidential information, the relationship between NYCDS and Stephens did not constitute a conflict. The dissent would have held that, at the very least, a potential conflict existed, and the trial court properly acted within its discretion in disqualifying counsel. The dissenting Justice granted the People leave to appeal to this Court.

II.

A determination to substitute or disqualify counsel falls within the trial court's discretion (see People v. Carncross, 14 N.Y.3d 319, 330 [2010]; People v. Tineo, 64 N.Y.2d 531, 536 [1985]). . . . Criminal courts faced with counsel who allegedly suffer from a conflict of interest must balance two conflicting constitutional rights: the defendant's right to effective assistance of counsel; and the defendant's right to be represented by counsel of his or her own choosing (see U.S. Const., 6th Amend; *Carncross*, 14 N.Y.3d at 327; People v. Gomberg, 38 N.Y.2d 307, 312–313 [1975]). . . .

Particularly relevant here, the presumption in favor of a client being represented by counsel of his or her choosing may be overcome by demonstration of an actual conflict or a serious potential for conflict. The court may appropriately place great weight upon counsel's representations regarding the presence or absence of a conflict (see *Gomberg*, 38 N.Y.2d at 314), because the attorney is generally in the best position to determine when a conflict of interest exists or is likely to develop during trial. Depending on when a potential conflict becomes evident, the court may not be aware of the details and ramifications of any conflict, or of the evidence, strategies or defenses that will emerge at trial . . . . However, if the court waits until trial—to ascertain what witnesses testify or what strategy or defenses are employed—it runs a serious risk of a mistrial based on the conflict.

Where there have been successive representations of individuals with different goals or strategies, a concern arises that counsel's loyalties may be divided because a lawyer has continuing professional obligations to former clients. Those obligations include a duty to maintain the former client's confidences and secrets, "'which may potentially create a conflict between the former client and present client'" (People v. Prescott, 21 N.Y.3d 925, 928 [2013], quoting People v. Ortiz, 76 N.Y.2d 652, 656 [1990]. Here, prior to defendant's trial, Fisher's NYCDS supervisors noted the institutional duty of loyalty to its former client, Stephens. Those supervisors—who presumably were familiar with Stephens's file—determined that there was a potential or actual conflict that prevented Fisher from investigating Stephens, attempting to locate him, calling him as a witness, or cross-examining him if he was called by the People. Under these circumstances, the trial court did not err in concluding that defendant's statements were insufficient to waive the conflict.

Our decision in People v. Wilkins (28 N.Y.2d 53 [1971]) does not compel a contrary result. In that case, this Court found that no conflict of interest existed merely because a defendant was represented by the Legal Aid Society and a different staff attorney from that same organization had previously represented—in an unrelated criminal proceeding—the person who was now the complaining witness against Wilkins. There, the purported conflict was not discovered until after Wilkins's trial, and his counsel had no prior knowledge of the separate case involving charges against the complaining witness. Thus, the prior representation could not have affected the representation of Wilkins. We held that, unlike private law firms where knowledge of one member of the firm is imputed to all, large public defense organizations are not subject to such imputation, so there was no inferred or presumed conflict.

The current case is distinguishable from *Wilkins*, and we do not disturb the general rule against imputation of knowledge created there. In both cases, counsel worked for a large public defense organization and was initially unaware of another staff attorney's representation of a potential witness in the client's case, because there was apparently no free flow of information among staff attorneys. However, unlike counsel in *Wilkins*, defense counsel here became aware before defendant's trial of NYCDS's prior representation of Stephens, and the organization's representation of Stephens arose from the same incident that led to defendant's arrest. Additionally, Fisher's supervisors expressly prohibited him from attempting to locate Stephens (apparently even by searching in publicly-available sources) or questioning him. This directly impinged on Fisher's representation of defendant. Not only did the supervisors instruct Fisher to refrain from investigating Stephens, they also directed that he could not cross-examine Stephens if he was called by the People. Therefore, even if the institutional representation of Stephens did not, in and of itself, present a conflict, such a conflict was created by the conditions imposed by Fisher's supervisors, which hampered his ability to zealously and single-mindedly represent defendant. Although the court could have inquired as to why NYCDS took the position of forbidding any investigation into or questioning of Stephens, the court was in a precarious situation because such an inquiry might have intruded into confidential attorney-client information. Thus, the court did not abuse its discretion by relieving counsel once those restrictions were announced.

Defendant's assertion that he was never given the opportunity to waive the conflict is unavailing. Although defendant indicated that he would be willing to waive the conflict, almost immediately thereafter he said that he wanted Stephens to be called as a witness at trial. These competing statements did not clearly demonstrate a knowing waiver, or that defendant would knowingly waive Fisher's conflict. Moreover, had he attempted to do so, it would have been within the court's authority to decline to accept such a waiver. . . .

Further, while defendant might have agreed to allow counsel to refrain from calling Stephens, the People indicated the possibility that they would call him as a witness, depending on the defense that was raised—including the potential assertion that someone other than defendant possessed and dropped the gun—which would not be known until trial. Although a waiver of the conflict by defendant would have permitted counsel to refrain from cross-examining Stephens if he was called, that would be a tactic based on loyalty to Stephens as a former NYCDS client, not a strategy employed in the best interest of defendant. Additionally, if the court had waited until trial and the People had decided to call Stephens, a mistrial could have resulted. Thus, the court could properly decide that it would not accept a waiver in these circumstances, instead choosing to protect defendant's right to the effective assistance of counsel in order to ensure a fair trial.

In sum, the Appellate Division erred in holding that the trial court abused its discretion. Supreme Court appropriately balanced defendant's countervailing rights, based on the information it had at the time, and reasonably concluded that Fisher could not effectively represent defendant due to NYCDS's representation of Stephens and the duty of loyalty Fisher's supervisors were asserting toward that former client. Accordingly, the Appellate Division order should be reversed and the case remitted to that court for consideration of the facts and issues raised, but not determined, on the appeal to that court.

3. Government Lawyers and Vicarious Disqualification

Problem 4–17

George Hall, the Attorney General of a western state, had been elected after a bitter campaign in which he charged that certain large mining companies were polluting the environment in violation of state laws and local ordinances. He immediately opened an investigation and induced Georgia Morisot, a partner from his former law firm, to become an assistant attorney general specifically to conduct the investigation. After two years, Morisot had collected enough evidence to file criminal and civil proceedings against two mining companies. The suits were nearing trial when Morisot decided that, for personal financial reasons, she had to return to private practice, and she accepted a partnership in her former firm. Hall asked if she would continue to handle both the criminal and civil proceedings as special counsel for the state. May she do so?

May she also handle a civil suit against the same defendants arising out of the same alleged acts of the defendant brought by a town whose ordinances are claimed to have been violated? See Model Rule 1.11(a) and (c) and consider especially what makes a client a "private client" for purposes of Rule 1.11(c).

Suppose that with respect to these matters Hall had been the Attorney General of the United States and Morisot an Assistant Attorney General of the United States. Might that make a difference?

Note: Problems of Government Employees and Vicarious Disqualification

In *Silver Chrysler Plymouth*, p. 292, Note 3, the court decided that although the departing attorney had been vicariously disqualified while at Kelly, Drye, he was not personally disqualified because he was not in possession of relevant confidential information. The court refused to pile vicarious disqualification upon vicarious disqualification. When the junior lawyer moved to a new firm, he therefore shed the vicarious disqualification. The more debated question, however, has been the effect on a new firm that hires a lawyer who is personally disqualified from representing interests adverse to a former client. Should the general rule that the whole firm is disqualified when one lawyer is disqualified by reason of conflict of interest be rigorously applied in that circumstance?

The first cases in which the issue was debated involved the former government lawyer who joins a private firm upon leaving government service, although it should be pointed out that the issue of the application of the disqualification rules, especially the vicarious disqualification rules, to former government lawyers went largely unnoticed in the profession for a long time. After a long period of debate, screening to avoid vicarious disqualification of the new firm of the former government lawyer has become the general rule. Model Rule 1.11 permits it in both the situation where the former government lawyer had participated substantially in a matter and also where the former government lawyer has confidential information about a person acquired in government service that could be used in a particular matter adversely to that person. Interestingly, insofar as the personal disqualification of the former government lawyer is concerned, it can be removed by government consent in the former situation, where the government's interests are involved, but not in the latter situation, where they are not. In addition, the screening that avoids vicarious disqualification requires notification to the government, but not its consent, in the former situation. No notification is required to make the screening effective in the latter situation. Various agencies of the federal government also adopted rules that authorize screening devices. See, e.g., 46 C.F.R. § 502.32(c) (1978) (Federal Maritime Commission); 31 C.F.R. § 10.26(c) (IRS); 17 C.F.R. § 200.735-8(e) (SEC); and 16 C.F.R. § 4.1(b)(8) (FTC).

An important issue relating to former government lawyers was raised in General Motors Corp. v. New York, 501 F.2d 639 (2d Cir. 1974). George Reycraft, an attorney in the Department of Justice's Antitrust Division, participated in the investigation of alleged monopolization of the bus business by GM and signed the government's complaint against GM that charged violation of the Sherman Act. Subsequently, after he had left the government and with the consent of the Justice Department, Reycraft agreed to represent New York City in a private antitrust action against GM that the court found sufficiently similar to the United States' action to constitute the "same matter" under the Model Code's DR 9-101(B). The court, noting that "there lurks great potential for lucrative returns in following into private practice the course already charted with the aid of government resources," id. at 650, held that Reycraft should be disqualified because of the appearance of impropriety. It is clear that if Reycraft had moved from one private firm to another and were representing a different, but nonadverse, private interest in the same matter with the consent of the former client, there would be no problem. Government employment, however, is one area where the admonition against an "appearance of impropriety" contained in former Canon 9 supplied independent justification for disqualification. The theory is that since the client of the government is, in some sense, "the public interest," there is more reason to take steps to avert public suspicion, where feasible, than with the ordinary private employment case. Would *General Motors* come out the other way under Model Rule 1.11(a) and (c)? Prior to 2002, the Comments to this Rule indicated that a "public" client may sometimes be a "private" client for purposes of the Rule. Under the current version, would New York City be a public or a private client of George Reycraft? Note also that consent is a feature of Model Rule 1.11(a) but not of Model Rule 1.11(b).

The *General Motors* result has not always been followed, however, to an inexorable conclusion. In Woods v. Covington County Bank, 537 F.2d 804 (5th Cir. 1976), the court refused to disqualify a lawyer from representing an ex-serviceman whom he had first represented in the same matter while he was engaged in his annual two-week tour of duty as a reserve officer in the Judge Advocate General's Corps. The court first held that by statute the lawyer had not been a federal employee while in training. The court distinguished the *General Motors* case because there could be no suspicion of misuse of public position inasmuch as the lawyer acted under orders from his superior when he was in service and also because as a legal assistance officer, his duty had been owed to the individual client and not to the government. There had thus been no exercise of any official governmental authority by the lawyer.

Another issue that must often be faced in cases in which former government lawyers or their firms are sought to be disqualified is whether the "matter" in which the firm is seeking to participate is the same "matter" in which the former government lawyer participated when a government employee.

A good example of the difficulties of defining what is the same matter is Brown v. Dist. of Columbia Board of Zoning Adjustment, 486 A.2d 37 (D.C. Ct. App. 1984) (en banc). A developer was seeking approval for a residential and commercial complex known as the Westbridge. There were negotiations with the Corporation Counsel's office over building height restrictions, the legality of a proposed air rights condominium, and an application for a special exception permitting increased off-street parking spaces. After the first two problems had been disposed of, the Corporation Counsel and his assistant joined the law firm representing the developer with respect to the parking problem.

The Board of Zoning Adjustment made factual findings that the underlying facts and issues of each of the three transactions were not related. The Court of Appeals relied on those findings to hold that the former government employees were not disqualified from representing the developer with respect to the parking problem. The dissenters would have disqualified them and required "screening" partly because parking spaces were necessarily involved in the first two negotiations and partly because the same economic unit was involved. They were also willing, where the majority was not, to rely heavily on the appearance of impropriety where former government lawyers were involved.

Brown presents an important problem for the future and it offers two different approaches: the majority's factually oriented approach focusing on the precise issues and the precise conduct of government lawyers, and the dissent's more broad-ranging view of what constitutes a single piece of litigation or a single project and its perception that a prophylactic rule is better than trying to judge the zealousness of performance by government counsel on a case-by-case basis. The majority does not quite address the argument that its approach looks at the "trees" of particular issues instead of the "forest" of a single project and that side-switching with respect to a project presents such a significant danger of impropriety, or public perception thereof, that actual proof ought not be required where government attorneys are involved.

Former federal government counsel must pay close attention to the federal conflict of interest statute and to similar state statutes, which are common, in connection with subsequent private representation. The federal conflict of interest statutes are contained in 18 U.S.C. § 207. In general, they make criminal (1) representation of a party other than the United States by a former government employee in connection with any matter in which *the employee participated personally and substantially as an employee*; (2) personal appearance by a former employee (or aiding someone else's personal appearance) within two years after cessation of employment before any department, court, or agency of the United States on behalf of anyone other than the United States in a matter in which the United States is interested and *that was under the employee's official responsibility*, at any time within one year prior to the termination of such responsibility; and (3) *personal appearance* within a year after leaving government employment by a former employee, except a special employee serving less than 60 days in a given year, on behalf of a party other than the United States *before a department in which the employee served* in connection with any proceeding before it or in which it has a substantial interest.

The federal Ethics in Government Act of 1978, in addition to revising § 207, also established an Office of Government Ethics, under the supervision of the Office of Personnel Management. One job of the Office of Government Ethics is, in consultation with the Attorney General, to coordinate conflict of interest policies in the executive branch. Its advisory opinions may be found in the Ethics in Government Reporter, and lawyers must be aware that policies may, and do, change when administrations change.

The disqualification issue arises not only when the government lawyer enters private practice but also when the private lawyer enters government service. In Arkansas v. Dean Foods Prods. Inc., 605 F.2d 380 (8th Cir. 1979), when a private practitioner became head of the Arkansas state antitrust division, not only he but the whole division he supervised was disqualified from prosecuting an antitrust action for price-fixing against a former client even though the trial court found that he personally had received no relevant confidences relating to this matter while in private practice. The implications for the state of the vicarious disqualification of staff seem considerable since it removes the making of policy from the responsible department. Those considerations led another court of appeals not to disqualify the entire United States Attorney's Office from prosecuting a defendant when one of his lawyers joined the Office. United States v. Caggiano, 660 F.2d 184 (6th Cir. 1981), cert. denied, 455 U.S. 945 (1982). The Model Rules also adopt the policy of not disqualifying the entire office of a public agency when one lawyer is disqualified by virtue of his former or prospective private practice activities. See Model Rule 1.11(c) and Comment.

A similar kind of problem has arisen with respect to a different kind of government employee, the public defender. In United States v. Judge, 625 F. Supp. 901 (D. Hawaii 1986), the court permitted such an office to represent a defendant when it had also previously represented a crucial government witness against the defendant. The government sought disqualification because of its fear that defendant's counsel would use confidential information to attack the witness's credibility. The court held that the defendant's choice of counsel was entitled to great deference and that the screening procedures adopted were sufficient to prevent such misuse of confidential information.

Not all the problems of vicarious disqualification of government lawyers involve the "former" lawyer. An issue may arise for current government employees as well. For example, in some places in the country it is common for prosecutors to hold those positions part-time and to have a private practice in addition. Indeed, without private income they could not survive. The question will then arise whether members of their law firms may represent criminal defendants. The Georgia Supreme Court has declined to follow a host of ethics opinions from other jurisdictions to hold that so long as the state continued to use part-time prosecutors, necessity required relaxation of the usual rules of vicarious disqualification so that no disqualification would be ordered without a finding of actual conflict of interest. Thompson v. State, 254 Ga. 393 (1985).

4. Vicarious Disqualification — Screening in the Private Context

Once an exception to the vicarious disqualification rules had been made for the former government employee on the basis of public policy considerations, it was natural for parties in other situations to seek like exemptions by urging other kinds of public policy considerations. Lawyers who formerly worked in legal services organizations have urged that the need of those public service organizations to attract lawyers to these relatively low-paying jobs justifies the same kind of exceptions as are enjoyed by former government employees. The specific issue has arisen in only a few cases and the argument has not been accepted. See, for example, Cheng v. GAF Corp., 631 F.2d 1052 (2d Cir. 1980), vacated on jurisdictional grounds, 450 U.S. 903 (1981), where the court disqualified the firm to which a former legal services employee had moved because it doubted the efficacy of the screening procedures that had been adopted and because it viewed the public policy considerations as weaker than in the former government lawyer context. One may assume, however, that former legal services employees moving to private firms will not be worse off than lawyers moving from one private law firm to another, and that to the extent that there is any relaxation of the vicarious disqualification rules in the latter situation, it will apply to the former situation as well. And indeed, there are opinions holding that because of public policy considerations the traditional vicarious disqualification rules themselves will not be applied to large public-defense entities so that they may represent adverse interests even simultaneously as long as there are no actual conflicts of interests through sharing of confidential information or the like. See People v. Chambers, 508 N.Y.S.2d 378 (Sup. Ct. 1986) (citing other cases throughout the country); Matter of Assane D., 23 A.D.3d 654 (N.Y. 2005); and In re Charlisse C., p. 297 supra.

There has been increasing pressure on the vicarious disqualification rules from large law firms as they have grown larger and opened more and more branches throughout the country and the world. They have urged that many instances of vicarious disqualification ought to be dealt with by screening-off procedures. The arguments have produced a great deal of debate within the profession. Until 2009, the Model Rules did not permit a screening process to avoid imputed disqualification when a personally disqualified lawyer moves from one private firm to another. Some states modified their rules to permit screening, at least sometimes, in that situation; and some courts, especially federal courts, have been more receptive to the idea in the context of disqualification as opposed to discipline of counsel. See Nelson v. Green Builders, Inc., 823 F. Supp. 1439 (E.D. Wis. 1993); and NFC, Inc. v. General Nutrition, Inc., 562 F. Supp. 332 (D. Mass. 1983).

One example of a federal court that allowed screening even in a case that did not involve movement of a lawyer from one firm to another was Hughes v. Paine, Webber, Jackson and Curtis, Inc., 565 F. Supp. 663 (N.D. Ill. 1983). A lawyer was representing plaintiffs in a dispute with defendants. An individual defendant consulted another partner in that firm about the possibility of representation in connection with an SEC investigation of the matter, although that defendant eventually found representation elsewhere. When that firm brought suit with respect to plaintiffs' claim, defendants sought to disqualify it. Relying on the *Westinghouse* case, p. 215, Note 10, the court found that an attorney-client relationship had existed between the firm and the individual defendant. Reviewing the somewhat muddled state of the law of successive representation in the Seventh Circuit, the court concluded that it would not permit the presumption that the individual defendant imparted confidential information to the firm about the matter in issue to be rebutted. The court then held that the second presumption, that the information was communicated by the particular lawyer who had it to other members of the firm, should not be irrebuttable in the circumstances of this case. Since the individual defendant did not become a firm client and since a long-established relationship between the firm and plaintiffs would be destroyed by the brief conversation between the partner and the individual defendant, the court permitted the defendant to rebut that presumption. Moreover, it did not regard the fact that the firm did not undertake a screening procedure until the matter was brought to their attention by the defendant as requiring disqualification.

The New York Court of Appeals has also permitted screening to avoid vicarious disqualification of a firm with respect to former clients of a lateral hire even though its disciplinary rules did not then, and still do not, contain a screening provision. Kassis v. TIAA, 93 N.Y.2d 611 (1999).

The ABA's House of Delegates, after several setbacks, finally amended Model Rule 1.10 in 2009 so as to permit screening in lateral hiring cases with respect to former clients. The debate over this screening amendment was very strong, and the arguments pro and con are set forth in the Majority and Minority Reports that accompanied the proposal.

American Bar Association Standing Committee on Ethics and Professional Responsibility Majority Report to the House of Delegates
February 2009

Model Rule of Professional Conduct 1.10(a) imputes the disqualification under Rule 1.7 or 1.9 of one lawyer in a law firm to all other lawyers associated in the firm except when the disqualification is based on a personal interest of the lawyer that will not limit the ability of the other lawyers in the firm to represent the client. The only other exceptions to the broad application of imputation are in Model Rules 1.11 (addressing private firms that hire former government lawyers), 1.12 (addressing private firms that hire a former judge, judicial law clerk, arbitrator, mediator, or other "third-party neutral"), and 1.18 (discussing situation in which material non-public information has been imparted by a prospective client). In each of those situations, the law firm may avoid imputed disqualification by screening the disqualified lawyer from any involvement in the matter.

To date, proposals to amend the Model Rules to allow screening when a lawyer moves from one private firm to another have been unsuccessful. A proposal by the Commission on Evaluation of the Rules of Professional Conduct ("Ethics 2000") was rejected in 2002 by the House of Delegates by a margin of 176 to 130. Since the advent of the Model Rules, however, 23 states have adopted rules of professional conduct generally permitting the movement of a personally disqualified lawyer to a new firm without imputing that lawyer's disqualification to other lawyers in the new firm, if the lawyer is timely screened from participation in the matter. Ten of those states adopted their screening rules since the Ethics 2000 vote. Although twelve of the 23 rules are consistent with this proposal, many of the rules vary in significant details. This variation underscores the need for leadership by the ABA on the topic.

The Standing Committee on Ethics and Professional Responsibility carefully considered the issues relating to imputed disqualification, and concluded that it is time for the American Bar Association to extend the concept of screening, which the Model Rules have long permitted in other contexts, to lawyers who move between private firms. Such a change must be accomplished without diminishing the duties that a lawyer owes to a former client. Screening "denotes isolation of a lawyer" to prohibit both his participation in a matter and his communication or use of information he may have about the matter. Rule 1.0(k). Screening therefore serves to reinforce the lawyer's duties to former clients under Rules 1.6 and 1.9. . . .

. . . The Committee believes that the Rule's stringent screening and notice procedures, if adhered to, resolve legitimate client concerns about a transferring lawyer's conduct. The certification requirement focuses the lawyer and the new firm on their responsibilities for protecting the former client's interest. Consequently, it should rarely be necessary to impute the transferring lawyer's disqualification to all of her new lawyer colleagues in order to meet the former client's concerns. In exceptional cases, disqualification by a tribunal is available when lawyers themselves fail to exercise the necessary restraint.

Lawyer Mobility and Protection of Confidentiality. The Committee believes that framing the issue of imputation as a choice between client protection and lawyer mobility presents a false choice. Clients <u>must</u> be protected, and their confidence (as well as that of the public) in their lawyers' promise to keep their secrets must be preserved. The question is not *whether* but *how* that should be accomplished. No one contends that the lawyer himself may represent others against a former client on substantially related matters after moving to a new firm. Rule 1.9(a) is unequivocal on this subject. In addition, no one disputes that the confidentiality duty continues after termination of the client-lawyer relationship. If a lawyer breaches that duty, she is subject to discipline, whether she has changed firms or not. Screening is a mechanism to give effect to the duty of confidentiality, not a tool to undermine it.

History Reveals No Problems with Ethical Screens. The Committee inquired of states with screening and received responses from disciplinary counsel, state bar association officials, and practicing lawyers in those jurisdictions that properly established screens are effective to protect confidentiality. Moreover, the Committee considered the applicable case law, and found that courts have exhibited no difficulty in reviewing and, where screening was found to have been effective, approving screening mechanisms. . . .

The Requirement of Client Consent. An often heard argument against permitting private lateral screening, articulated in the dissent, is the notion that a lawyer's client should effectively hold veto power over the lawyer's transferring to a new firm. The Committee is very concerned that clients' rights be protected, but we do not think protection of a client's confidentiality interests requires a ban on mobility unless the client consents to the lawyer's move. Clients have no obligation not to withhold consent unreasonably. This change permitting private lateral screening is particularly timely now, when law firms are downsizing and new job opportunities are shrinking, and a substantial number of lateral moves by lawyers may be involuntary. In addition, restrictions on mobility affect the interests of other clients in being represented by the lawyer of their choice. . . .

Even if in a rare case the lead lawyer in a litigation moves to the opposing party's law firm, the court may disqualify that firm rather than authorize it to screen the disqualified lateral lawyer. The same would continue to be true under the proposed amendment. The court can disqualify a firm when it is reasonable in the particular circumstances for the former client to fear that a screen may not be effective.

Screening Protects the Interests of the Clients Both of a New Law Firm and of a Former Law Firm. Although much of the debate over lateral screening has been focused on the concerns of the clients of the lateral's former firm, there is a parallel set of interests: after a transferring lawyer has been hired, every imputed disqualification based on the unavailability of screening results in a client that loses its law firm of choice. The harm to all such clients is real, not theoretical. Often the disqualification of a firm, based upon an imputed conflict of a newly-hired lawyer, occurs after a matter is well under way and the affected client has spent substantial sums in fees. Typically, such clients have played no part in the circumstances that led to the imputed disqualification, yet they suffer the cost, disruption, and delay resulting from it.

If the new firm does represent a client adverse to the former client, in many cases the new firm could, consistent with Rule 1.16, withdraw from representing such a client in order that it can hire the transferring lawyer. That client may be adversely impacted because it has lost the law firm of its choice. If that firm, on the other hand, declines to hire the lawyer because of the conflict, clients of the new firm will be deprived of a lawyer the new firm thinks would serve their interests. Thus, clients have interests on both sides of the screening question. Screening does not solve all such problems, but reduces them to situations where the interests of the former clients cannot adequately be addressed by the screening mechanism. . . .

"Side Switching" Is Not the Issue. Certain opponents of screening contend it permits "side switching," which is a misnomer. A lawyer disqualified by a conflict of interest may never assist the "other side" in a matter by changing firms. The point of screening is to isolate that lawyer from participating in or communicating about the matter, underscoring that the transferring lawyer is disqualified from "switching sides." The purpose of this recommendation is to avoid <u>imputed</u> disqualification of all the other lawyers in the new firm, lawyers who have not changed sides at all.

Screening Employed after Public/Private Moves. Rules 1.11 (private firms hiring former government lawyers) and 1.12 (hiring a former judge, judicial law clerk, arbitrator, mediator, or other "third-party neutral") have provided for screening since 1983 when the Rules were first adopted. The Comment to those rules explains that the government client need not have a veto on lawyer mobility and describes how screening procedures can adequately protect the government client's interest.

The conclusion reflected in the rule was certainly influenced by a desire to promote lawyers' entry into government service by not barring future employment in the private sector, where the former government lawyer will utilize the skills and experience developed during government employment. For example, an enforcement lawyer at the Securities and Exchange Commission could become a valued private practitioner. Although that lawyer may have acquired extremely sensitive information about the targets of Commission investigations, she may under Rule 1.11 join a firm defending such targets in Commission proceedings as long as she is appropriately screened. The Committee is unaware of evidence that governmental clients have seen their confidences eroded through breaches of the screen. The protections of confidential information afforded to the government client should work equally well for private clients. The growing number of states that endorse screening for lawyers in both contexts suggests a growing acceptance of this analysis. . . .

"Substantial Involvement" as a Factor in Determining Imputation. Of the 23 states that permit private lateral screening, a majority have rules substantially similar to the proposal. Two states permit screening unless the disqualified lawyer had played a "primary" role in the former matter, and a significant minority permits private lateral screening unless the disqualified lawyer either had played a "substantial" role or has acquired "substantial" confidential information. The Committee considered, and rejected, the suggestion that prohibiting screening when the lawyer had been "substantially involved" should be the ABA model. It concluded, among other things, that the possibility of disqualification by a tribunal adequately addresses the unusual cases in which the extent of a disqualified lateral lawyer's role in a matter of the amount of the material confidential information possessed by that lawyer raises legitimate doubts about the efficacy of screening. . . .

The Committee's invitation for comments on its proposal also drew some advocates of this position, but the proposed tests for "substantial involvement" all involved balancing a series of facts and circumstances. Such balancing tests do not provide clear guidance for prospective behavior, although courts may use them in making disqualification judgments.

The Committee believes that adoption of a substantial involvement test implies that lawyers in private practice cannot be trusted to adhere to the Model Rules and to report honestly that they have conducted themselves in accordance with both the Rules and with established screening procedures. It suggests that screening should be sanctioned only where it is not likely to be needed (the transferring lawyer has no material confidential information or had only a slight involvement in the matter). This limitation to screening is not the rule in the situations governed by Rules 1.11(b) or 1.12, or with respect to nonlawyers moving from one firm to another. . . .

American Bar Association Standing Committee on Ethics and Professional Responsibility Minority Report to the House of Delegates
February 2009

We dissent from the Committee's Report with Recommendations because we believe that screening of the lateral hire should remain ineffective to avoid imputation under Model Rule 1.10 unless the lateral lawyer's former client consents. The Committee's proposal departs substantially from the rules in thirty-nine jurisdictions, twenty-three of which permit only consensual screening, and eleven more that permit nonconsensual screens only when a laterally hired lawyer had no substantial responsibility or acquired no significant confidential information in a previous adverse response.

We believe that the current Model Rules serve lawyers and clients well by providing a bright line rule that protects both. When a lawyer leaves a firm, Model Rule 1.9 prevents that lawyer from acting adverse to her former clients in the same or substantially related matters. Model Rule 1.10 prohibits that lawyer's new firm from the same representations without the consent of the migrating lawyer's former client. Former clients can condition consent on a screen of the lateral lawyer. These consensual screens are becoming more common, and they protect the new firm, the new firm's current clients and the former client's interest.

Fiduciary duty is the foundation of both of these rules. Rule 1.9 prohibits the lateral lawyer from using or disclosing confidential information of former clients. Rule 1.10 imputes this obligation to the new law firm because it presumes that lawyers in firms interact for the benefit of their current clients. Both of these conflict of interest rules derive from centuries old agency rules that require client consultation and consent to keep a lawyer-agent focused on the client-principal's interests.

The current articulation of these principles in the Model Rules protects lawyers against our own judgment when it might be impaired by our own or some other client's interests. The lateral lawyer interested in changing law firms and the clients at the new firm have interests of their own which well might conflict with those of the former client. It is this conflict which endows those clients with the right recognized by agency law and the current rules to determine their own best interests.

Consider for example, that in all of the following circumstances, the proposed rules would allow an involuntary screen when a former client reasonably might refuse consent.

1. A lawyer with a significant role in a matter who leaves a law firm while the matter is pending to join the firm representing the opposing party in the same matter.

2. A lawyer who billed no hours to a client matter, but spent a two hour lunch discussing it in detail with the lead lawyer on the case now has joined the firm representing the other side in the same matter.

3. A lawyer who gained significant information about a wife's business transactions soon thereafter joins the law firm representing the same woman's husband in a divorce.

We do not agree that Rule 1.10 should allow firms to set up nonconsensual screens in circumstances like these, where a lateral lawyer who joins the firm has been exposed to substantial material information or has had a significant involvement in the same or substantially related prior representation. In these circumstances and many more, the committee's proposal replaces the necessity of former client consultation and consent with a nonconsensual screen and notice provision. From the former client's perspective, the proposal allows a nonvoluntary screen of a lateral lawyer when the former client would not have consented if consulted. Also, the proposal potentially confuses lawyers, because it invites them to establish nonconsensual screens in situations where courts in disqualification motions may not recognize them. When this occurs, current clients of the firm involuntarily lose their counsel of choice.

The Committee's proposal rests on newly added procedural requirements to foster the former client's comfort with a nonconsensual screen. Yet, former clients may reasonably refuse consent when their lawyer had either a significant role or exposure to material confidential information in the prior representation. We do not dispute the good will of most lawyers who believe that they can establish and maintain effective screens, even in these circumstances. In fact, the committee's proposal acknowledges that the courts may grant disqualification relief to former clients, which puts current clients of the firm at risk. But lawyers and clients recognize that both are human, and that law firm systems can break down. When lawyers and clients differ in their estimation of these risks, the client's view should prevail.

Current Rule 1.10 protects former clients against the risk of adverse use or disclosure of confidential information. The proposed amendment substitutes the law firm's resolution of this risk for the client's. It catapults the lawyer's interests over the former client's determination at precisely the time the lateral lawyer and the new firm have their own and their client's interests understandably in mind. Lawyers should consult with former clients about these matters and be bound by the client's determination, which is precisely what current Model Rule 1.10 requires.

———

Commenting on the "lack of evidence that screening doesn't work" argument that supporters of screening make, Andrew Kaufman responded, in the context of the Ethics 2000 screening proposals:

> I have had several lawyers tell me confidentially that when there is only one screen in place in their firms, things are manageable, but they often have a dozen or more and then breaches are inevitable. Those stories are not real evidence and I could not testify to their accuracy. But I believe that they indicate that there is a problem, and that if screening becomes the norm, the problem will be like an iceberg. Most of it will be hidden.
>
> But my real objection here is to the notion that the objections to screening are obsolete in our modern world of national and international law practice, that screening has become the desirable norm, and that the burden is on opponents to produce factual evidence that screening is problematic. On that basis, I don't know why the Commission did not provide for screening as a solution to simultaneous representation conflict problems as well as successive representation conflicts problems. Perhaps that is next.
>
> I do not understand the Commission's "factual basis" reasoning. The Commission is proposing many changes in the rules for which it has no "factual basis." Putting aside the question whether the Commission itself has a factual basis for its leap of faith with respect to the changes it is proposing with regard to screening, I would ask the Commission to state the factual basis for its proposals to expand the exceptions to the confidentiality rule. That a majority of jurisdictions have adopted such exceptions?
>
> Whether "lack of evidence that a problem exists" is a persuasive reason depends on the circumstances. Lack of a complaint about six inches of legroom between airplane seats would be persuasive evidence that there is no problem—because those subject to the practice would be expected to complain. But lack of evidence about a problem with screening does not fall in that category. Whom did the commission expect to complain? Clients? They are unlikely to know enough to complain. How about law firms that have used screens, either in jurisdictions that permit them or in situations of client consent? Did the Commission really expect firms to confess to negligence or worse, with loss of business and lawsuits to follow? Really?
>
> The Commission apparently ignored some cases that analyzed screening attempts in Pennsylvania firms in which courts found that screens had in fact leaked—sometimes quite badly. I am of course referring to *Maritrans* and Steel v. GM. And there is also Lord Jefri v. KPMG from the House of

Lords.[1] If the Commission had been interested in what affected clients thought, it could have devised a client survey that might have produced such information. The reasonable perceptions of clients about the efficacy of screening is a relevant datum, especially when the actuality of the effectiveness of screening is not easy to determine.

Kaufman, "Ethics 2000 — Some Heretical Thoughts," The Professional Lawyer 1 (2001 Symposium issue).

Notes

1. It remains to be seen whether the majority of the states that do not currently permit screening will be convinced by the Majority or by the Minority Reports from the ABA's Standing Committee on Ethics and Professional Responsibility. So far, states have been slow to adopt the ABA's newly permissive view of screening. Readers of these materials should develop their own views on the issue.

2. Given the composition of the ABA, it is easy to understand why the Majority Report objects that framing the issue as a choice between client protection and lawyer mobility is a false choice. It urges that the issue is how client protection should be accomplished. If that is the issue, one might have expected substantial, if not conclusive, input from a variety of client representatives. That was not the case.

3. The Majority Report, which chastises the supporters of a "substantial involvement" provision for implying a distrust of lawyers, itself implies distrust of clients by suggesting that they have no obligation to refrain from withholding consent to screening unreasonably. If there is conflict over whom to distrust more, why should the principal architect of Rule change be a body composed entirely of lawyers?

4. The Kaufman article excerpted above proposed a cooperative effort between federal and state courts through the Judicial Conference of the United States and the Conference of State Court Chief Justices, with the ABA in an advisory role, as the appropriate mechanism for providing a model code of professional responsibility. Such a process would be less dominated by the practicing bar and would have a greater chance of producing more uniformity. Is that idea pie in the sky?

O'Donnell v. Robert Half International, Inc., Corp.
641 F. Supp. 2d 84 (D. Mass. 2009)

ROBERT B. COLLINGS, U.S.M.J.

I. Background

The plaintiffs in this case have been and are represented by the law firm of Lichten & Liss-Riordan, P.C. ("Lichten firm"). The defendants have been and are

---

1. Maritrans v. Pepper, Hamilton & Scheetz; Steel v. General Motors Corp.; Prince Jefri Bolkiah v. KPMG, p. 252, 279, and 260 Note 3.

represented by the law firm of Seyfarth Shaw LLP ("Seyfarth firm"). The plaintiffs'
claims arise under the Fair Labor Standards Act. . . .

The prayer for the disqualification of plaintiffs' counsel . . . concerns an attorney,
Sarah Getchell, Esquire, who . . . began working for the Seyfarth firm in October,
2008. In May, 2009, due to a reduction in force at the Seyfarth firm, Attorney Getchell was laid off and began to seek other employment. She explored an opportunity
to work at the Lichten firm, and on May 28, 2009, Attorney Liss-Riordan from that
firm confirmed that the firm had hired Attorney Getchell. Because Attorney Liss-
Riordan had sought a reference from the Seyfarth firm, the Seyfarth firm knew about
the possibility that Attorney Getchell would be hired by the Lichten firm. The Seyfarth firm notified Attorney Liss-Riordan that because of the work Attorney Getchell had done while at the Seyfarth firm on the instant case, "serious conflicts" would
arise which would require the Lichten firm to be disqualified from further representing the plaintiffs in the instant case. Attorney Liss-Riordan on behalf of the Lichten firm took the position that no conflict existed and that Attorney Getchell would
have nothing to do with the instant case while at the Lichten firm.

II. Procedural History

. . . Judge Gorton ordered that the Lichten firm institute a "Chinese wall" so that
henceforth Attorney Getchell would have no exposure whatever to the instant case. . . .
[A] dispute arose as a result of plaintiffs' attorneys' claim that the material submitted by the defendants *in camera* in support of the motion to disqualify should be disclosed to them. . . .

. . . [T]he undersigned issued a Memorandum holding that plaintiffs' counsel
would not be allowed to have access to the materials submitted *in camera*. . . .

III. Applicable Law

There does not seem to be a dispute between the parties that Attorney Getchell
herself is disqualified from representing the plaintiffs in this matter. The dispute is
whether the Lichten firm itself is also disqualified. That issue is governed by Rule
1.10 of the Massachusetts Rules of Professional Conduct which provides:

> When a lawyer becomes associated with a firm, the firm may *not* undertake
> to or continue to represent a person in a matter that the firm knows or rea-
> sonably should know is the same or substantially related to a matter in which
> the newly associated lawyer (the "personally disqualified lawyer"), or a firm
> with which that lawyer was associated, had previously represented a client
> whose interests are materially adverse to the person unless:
>
> (1) the personally disqualified lawyer has no information protected by Rule
> 1.6 or Rule 1.9 that is material to the matter ("material information"); or
>
> (2) the personally disqualified lawyer (i) had neither substantial involvement
> nor substantial material information relating to the matter and (ii) is screened
> from any participation in the matter in accordance with paragraph (e) of
> this Rule and is apportioned no part of the fee therefrom.

Mass. R. Prof. C. 1.10(d) (emphasis added).

IV. Applying the Rule to the Instant Case—The Relevant Factors

. . . [T]he essential question is whether the exception under subpart (2)(i) can be applied to this case. Subpart (1) is inapplicable because based on the *in camera* submissions, I find that Attorney Getchell did receive information protected by Rule 1.6 of the Massachusetts Rules of Professional Conduct which is "material" to the case at hand.

Moving to subpart (2)(i), I find that Attorney Getchell did not have "substantial involvement" in the litigation of this case. The fact is that she spent a total of 7.2 hours on March 23 and 24, 2009 researching a discrete legal issue related to the case for which she wrote a one and one-half page single spaced memorandum summarizing her research. This was the only work she did on the case, and while she can be said to have had "involvement in the matter" to this extent, the Court finds that the involvement was not "substantial."[2] . . . On the record before me, I do not find her involvement to have been "substantial."

The much more difficult and close question is whether, during the course of her employment at the Seyfarth firm, she received "substantial material information." As noted, supra, the Court has found that Attorney Getchell did receive information protected by Rule 1.6 of the Massachusetts Rules of Professional Conduct which is "material" to the case at hand. The question then becomes whether that "material information" was "substantial."

Again, the use of the word "substantial" indicates that the exception will not be foreclosed in all situations in which the attorney has received "material information"; rather, the exception is foreclosed only when the extent of the material information disclosed is "substantial." The Court then is faced with the task of deciding when the line is crossed from "material information" to "substantial material information." The late Judge Keeton made the point extremely well in a case decided ten years ago. In discussing the terms used in the Rule, including "substantial material information," he wrote:

> These are phrases that require a decision-maker to make an evaluative rather than bright-line determination. They require an exercise of discretion leading to a single choice after taking into account an array of factors.

United States Filter Corporation, U.S. v. Ionics, Inc., 189 F.R.D. 26, 30 (D. Mass. 1999).

---

2. The defendants concede that Attorney Getchell was not on the RHI (Robert Half International) "team" and never entered an appearance on behalf of the defendants in this case. The Court does not view her attendance at a meeting of the Wage and Hour Practice Group at which the case was discussed or the other activities listed in the *in camera* submissions to amount to "substantial involvement" in the instant case; rather, they are relevant on the question, discussed infra, as to whether, while at the Seyfarth firm, she received "substantial material information" as a result of those activities.

Further, in making the decision on this aspect, the Court is faced with somewhat of a dilemma. The evidence on which such a finding is to be made has been submitted to the Court *in camera* and has not been disclosed to either Attorney Getchell or any member of the Lichten firm. In addition, Attorney Getchell, in testimony at an evidentiary hearing before me on July 24, 2009, asserted that she had absolutely no memory of ever having worked on the instant case or of having received information about this case while at the Seyfarth firm. The Court credits her testimony. In a situation in which a new attorney is receiving different assignments from different attorneys on an almost daily basis over a period of seven or so months and is being briefed on numerous cases at various practice group sessions, it is not surprising that the attorney would lack a specific memory of specific cases or issues on which he or she might have worked. But the end result is that the Court is left to rely on the materials submitted *in camera* by counsel for the defendants without the benefit of cross-examination. . . .

The first time Attorney Getchell was exposed to confidential information was at a practice group meeting in November, 2008 at which the instant case was discussed. It is asserted that the subject of the discussion was the strategy which the defendants would pursue in this case going forward . . . . The Court infers that the discussion involved no revelation of confidential information received from the clients but rather the type of material protected by the work-product doctrine, which, in the words of Rule 26(b)(3)(B), Fed. R. Civ. P., include the "mental impressions, conclusions, opinions, or legal theories" of defendants' counsel at the Seyfarth firm.

Another time when Attorney Getchell was exposed to confidential information was when she worked with one of defendants' attorneys, Richard L. Alfred, Esq., on an article "on the retroactivity of the treble damages bill in Massachusetts" which was later published . . . . Again, it does not appear that any confidential information of the client was revealed to Attorney Getchell during this process; rather, the revelations were of the work-product of the client's attorneys at the Seyfarth firm. . . .

. . . Attorney Getchell did do a research project on the instant case for Attorney Eaton on a discrete issue in the case and billed the defendants for 3.8 hours of time on March 23, 2009 and 3.4 hours of time on March 24, 2009. In briefing Attorney Getchell on the assignment, Attorney Eaton did divulge confidential information of the client—it was a single fact clearly relevant to the issue being researched. Further, Attorney Eaton divulged the legal strategy which she was pursuing with respect to that issue on behalf of the defendants.

V. Applying the Rule to the Instant Case—The Result

Although the question is admittedly close, the Court is compelled to conclude that in the aggregate, the material information which was communicated to Attorney Getchell is more accurately described as "substantial" as opposed to "insubstantial." The Court emphasizes that it must look at the totality of the material information which Attorney Getchell received while at the Seyfarth firm about the defense of this case. During the November meeting, she received confidential information as to the strategy the defense was going to pursue as a result of Judge Gorton's October 21st Order. In connection with the article she helped prepare . . . , she was briefed on the legal strategy which the defense was going to pursue with respect to the issue which was the subject of the article. Lastly, she actually worked on a project and billed the defendants for work on yet another legal aspect and in so doing, received confidential client information as well as information about the legal strategy the defense was going to pursue with respect to that issue. Given this record, the Court cannot find that the "material information" Attorney Getchell learned about the case while at the Seyfarth firm was not "substantial." . . .

There is another aspect to this issue which bears noting. Both the defendants and counsel for the defendants are entitled to rely on the Rule in regulating the extent to which confidential information is shared with the firm, whether that be with partners or associates. More specifically, they are entitled to rely on an assurance that the Rule will be enforced, and that they will not have to face a law firm on the other side of the case at which a former partner or associate who has been privy to substantial material information is employed.

There is no question that the Rule is rather strict. It involves ". . . the lawmaking choice of the Supreme Judicial Court to promulgate [Rule 1.10] with its single choice standard . . . ." *United States Filter Corp*, supra, 189 F.R.D. at 30. The single choice is to disqualify or not disqualify a firm. But this follows logically from the reasons behind the Rule as explicated by Judge Gorton in the case of Rodriguez v. Montalvo, 337 F. Supp. 2d 212 (D. Mass. 2004) as follows:

> Massachusetts courts have . . . explain[ed] that under the 'substantial relationship' test, a subsequent representation is proscribed on the grounds that the later suit, by virtue of its relationship to the former suit, exposes the attorney to 'an intolerably strong temptation to breach his duty of confidentiality to the former client.' E.g. Bays v. Theran, 418 Mass. 685, 691 . . . (1994) . . . . The former client is not required to prove that the attorney actually misused the information, but only need show that the tempting situation existed because of an attorney-client relationship that was established in the former representation, and that the 'former and current representations are both adverse and substantially related.' *Bays*, 418 Mass. at 691.

Id. at 218. . . .

Lastly, the Court cannot help but comment that the Lichten firm took an enormous risk when they hired Attorney Getchell knowing that she had worked for the Seyfarth firm and knowing that the Seyfarth firm took the position that based on what was disclosed to her, the Lichten firm would be disqualified if they hired her. Just as the Seyfarth firm was entitled to rely on the Rule in disclosing confidential information to associates in the firm, the Lichten firm was on notice that if they hired Attorney Getchell, they would have to meet a challenge to their continued participation in the case. Hopefully, they thoroughly researched the law with respect to the

Rule before hiring Attorney Getchell so that they were aware of the risk they were taking.

It is ORDERED that Defendants' Emergency Motion to Disqualify Plaintiffs' Counsel be, and the same hereby is, ALLOWED

A purpose of the ABA's amendment of Rule 1.10 in situations of lateral movement of lawyers from firm to firm was to enable the new employer to avoid disqualification in such cases. Consider how you would handle the following situation in a jurisdiction that has adopted the ABA Model Rule.

Problem 4–18

You are Ethics Counsel at Lichten and Liss-Riordan, P.C. Shannon Liss-Riordan, the Lichten firm attorney handling O'Donnell v. Robert Half International (p. 324) on behalf of the plaintiffs, has come to you seeking advice. The O'Donnell case is still at the deposition phase and she has scheduled depositions of key employees of the defendants for later in the week. The factual situation with respect to Sarah Getchell is as described in Magistrate Collings's opinion with the following additions and exceptions:

- In her hiring interview with the Lichten firm, Sarah Getchell remembered her involvement in all the events in the O'Donnell litigation that are set forth in Magistrate Collings's opinion. She stated that she had no other involvement in the litigation and was aware of the issues involved in only that one segment of the case in which she was involved. She also stated that she has not disclosed any confidential information relating to that representation to anyone other than in connection with the work she did at Seyfarth Shaw.

- The Lichten firm hired Sarah Getchell, and Getchell and the firm have complied to date with the various screening procedures set forth in Rule 1.10. Seyfarth Shaw therefore has not sought to disqualify the Lichten firm.

Liss-Riordan further reported that there was a lunch meeting yesterday of the employment section of the Lichten firm and Sarah Getchell was in attendance. There was no discussion of the O'Donnell case. The subject matter of the lunch was recent developments in employment law of which the firm needed to be aware and the uses to which these new developments might be put in the firm's practice. Sarah Getchell participated in the discussion.

Liss-Riordan tells you that she found herself lying awake last night thinking about this week's upcoming depositions in O'Donnell. She suddenly realized that something Getchell said about a recent California case suggested a promising line of inquiry in the O'Donnell case on an issue that apparently had nothing to do with the part of the case that Getchell said she worked on. Liss-Riordan said that she had not thought of pursuing that line herself. She could, however, pursue it with the witnesses scheduled for deposition this week. Furthermore, she was quite excited because if the depositions produced the necessary evidence, as she thought was quite likely, this new idea would turn what looked like a losing case into a winning case.

What issues of professional responsibility does the Liss-Riordan story suggest to you? How will you advise her? Does the firm need to reconsider for the future how it will handle lateral hiring decisions? Does new Model Rule 1.6(b)(7) help? How do the interviewing and interviewed lawyers decide whether any revealed information would "prejudice the client"?

F. Class Actions and Conflicts of Interest for Counsel

Problem 4–19

A lawyer was approached by several freelance investigators of the effectiveness of commercial products about their belief that a widely used rat exterminating product had lost all, or a substantial part, of its effectiveness because rats had developed an immunity to it. They had failed in their efforts to convince the manufacturer that their evidence demonstrated their view. They were interested in putting together a class of consumers to file a class action lawsuit that would have as its main objective getting the manufacturers to do all or some of the following: change their label and advertising claims about the product's worth; fund research by themselves or others to test the product; improve the product; or refund consumers who used the product unsuccessfully. The lawyer put together the required class of at least 100 named plaintiffs under the Magnuson Moss Warranty Act. After months of depositions, the lawyers for the manufacturer indicated that they were ready to talk settlement. How does class counsel decide which of the objectives to pursue when the named plaintiffs have very different notions about which are the most important? While the negotiations are pending, the manufacturers' lawyers indicate to class counsel that they favor a refund solution combined with the payment of a fee of $500,000 to class counsel. How do class counsel proceed?

In addition to mediating the conflicts within a class, a lawyer for a class action must also confront various ethical challenges in representation of a class as such. Consider the following story by Professor Susan Koniak, who was an expert witness for the objectors to the settlement, regarding her observation and involvement with the asbestos-related class action litigation.

Susan P. Koniak[*]
Feasting While the Widow Weeps:
Georgine v. Amchem Products, Inc.
80 Cornell L. Rev. 1045 (1995)

This article tells the story of Georgine v. Amchem Products, Inc. [521 U.S. 591 (1997)], a class action involving asbestos-related personal injury claims. *Georgine* was filed in federal district court on January 15, 1993. On the same day, class counsel and the lawyers for the defendants filed a proposed settlement with the court. The court authorized notice to the class, allowed a period for opt-outs, recognized objectors to the settlement, ordered discovery proceedings, held a fairness hearing, and, in August 1994, approved the settlement. The objectors to the settlement retained me to testify as an expert witness on the ethics of class counsel.

The *Georgine* defendants were nineteen financially viable companies and one company now in bankruptcy. The class action was brought on behalf of all people who had *not* filed suit against the twenty corporate defendants by January 15, 1993, and who had been occupationally exposed to the asbestos products of the defendants or who had been exposed to asbestos from those products through the occupational exposure of a family member. The class thus included all the people who are well now but may someday get sick from their past exposure to the defendants' products and *some* of the people who are sick now from that exposure—that is, the sick people who did not file suit by January 15, 1993.

It is a huge class. Although no one knows precisely how large the class is, this suit may be one of the largest mass tort class actions ever filed. *Georgine* is an important case for that reason alone, but it is especially important because it is already serving as a model for other class actions, and the model is fundamentally flawed. *Georgine* is important because it is big, because it is being copied, and because it is wrong.

I write to bear witness to what went wrong in this case: the collusion between class counsel and the defendants; the district court's willingness to turn a blind eye to the facts and neglect the law; the spectacle of lawyers telling contradictory stories about their actions to a tribunal that didn't seem to care which story the lawyers told or how often the story changed; the presentation and admission of testimony at the fairness hearing on what result other federal judges might like to see in this case; and the mistreatment of the widows who served as named representatives for the class— people whose experiences illustrate how the interests of class members were

---

* ... I served as an expert witness on the ethics of class counsel in this matter, testifying for the objectors to the settlement. I worked many hours on this case, reading stacks of documents, reviewing case law, writing a report with Professor Roger Cramton, and testifying both in a deposition and at the fairness hearing. I was paid for those hours and made what for me is a great deal of money....

subordinated to the interests of persons not parties to this suit. I also write to expose the serious defects in the *Georgine* model, a model that invites defendants who harm large groups of people to pay a premium to the first victims who file claims in exchange for lower and more limited liability to all future claimants.

I also make several proposals and suggest some new areas of academic and judicial inquiry. For example, I propose that underinclusive class definitions, now mentioned by courts only as a problem that might plague defendants, be considered by courts as a sign of collusion. I argue that courts should replace ad hoc review of the adequacy of class counsel with more general prohibitions, such as a ban on simultaneous representation of two classes against a common defendant. I propose that the ethics rules be read to require an increased duty of candor to the court on the part of lawyers presenting settlements that require court approval, and that before granting approval, courts should demand forthright responses from the settling lawyers on matters within their personal knowledge. I also question what role, if any, malpractice suits against class counsel might play in assuring counsel's fidelity to the class, a possibility that the law and economics crowd might fruitfully examine. However, my primary goal in this Article is not to make proposals, but to point out abuse in the hope of inspiring others to make proposals or to rethink proposals already made.

I write neither to condemn nor praise the efficiency arguments that might be made to justify the use of class actions to resolve mass tort claims. I do not urge that class actions never be used to resolve mass tort claims, nor do I denounce all class actions that are filed and settled on the same day (known as "settlement class actions"). I do not condemn all uses of class actions to resolve the claims of those who have not yet manifested injury. Finally, I do not write to propose some macro solution to the ethical problems that plague class action suits. Instead, I write to describe how empty the following safeguards proved to be in one case: adequacy of representation, class counsel's ethical obligations, and the court's duty to review class action settlements. I write to challenge the academics and judges who justify their positions by leaning on one or more of those supposed safeguards. I write to draw attention to the failure of these safeguards and to stimulate new thought on how more meaningful protections might be substituted for empty promises. . . .

Once upon a time, not so long ago, twenty companies faced the prospect of defending against millions of legal claims brought in connection with their asbestos products. Many thousands of these cases were already pending. The rest would be filed in years to come. The companies wanted out of this mess, and they found a way. They settled almost all of these claims—most of those that were pending and almost all of those that had not yet been filed. The key was to craft two deals: a class action and another deal. Two deals to cover so many claims may sound like a triumph of efficiency, but it was one deal too many, and therein lies the tale.

These twenty companies formed the Center for Claims Resolution (CCR) to coordinate their legal response. In 1992 the CCR lawyers from Shea & Gardner approached plaintiffs' lawyers Gene Locks, Ronald L. Motley, and Joseph Rice, and suggested working out a deal to resolve the CCR defendants' asbestos liability. Mr. Locks practiced in the firm Greitzer and Locks; Mr. Motley and Mr. Rice were partners in Ness, Motley, Loadholt, Richardson & Poole. These firms together represented over 14,000 asbestos claimants.

The lawyers sat down and worked out two deals: the class action settlement that became *Georgine* and another deal. Both deals covered people with a wide range of diseases caused by asbestos: mesothelioma, lung cancer, and the full range of non-malignant asbestos diseases—from disease that seriously affects one's ability to breathe to disease that leaves marks on the lungs but does not result in severe breathing impairment. Although the deals covered the same sorts of people with the same sorts of diseases, the deals had different terms. For example, it appears that the people covered by the class action got considerably less money than the people with the same diseases who were covered by the other deal.

Who ended up outside the class—with the other deal? Messrs. Locks, Motley, and Rice designed a class that excluded over fourteen thousand of their clients and many, if not most, of the clients of other asbestos lawyers. These clients—and their lawyers—got the deal with more money.

Before *Georgine*, the CCR companies saw no end to potential lawsuits against them. In the first years of its existence, CCR made "inventory settlements." An inventory settlement is an agreement with a plaintiffs' law firm to settle the firm's inventory of cases according to specified terms. These settlements typically involved large blocks of cases, but as soon as one inventory was settled, the plaintiffs' law firm would start building another inventory of cases. CCR thus changed its settlement strategy in 1991. Although it was willing to settle the relatively small number of asbestos cases that could get scheduled for trial, it now refused to settle the bulk of the existing cases without some guarantee about the future. The CCR companies did not want to continue paying people who had marks on their lungs caused by asbestos but who had no significant breathing impairment—the so-called pleural plaintiffs. They also wanted control over the number of cases they would face each year and, preferably, control over how much money they would have to pay out each year. They determined that the best way to get what they wanted was through a "settlement class action"—a class action put together solely for the purpose of achieving settlement. CCR approached Messrs. Locks, Motley, and Rice, who agreed to serve as class counsel in such an action.

Messrs. Locks, Motley, and Rice wanted their existing inventory of cases settled, but apparently not on the terms proposed by CCR for the class. They agreed that pleural class members would receive no cash, but they disassociated their own pleural clients from the class and got cash for them. This would assure Messrs. Locks, Motley, and Rice a return of thirty-three percent of their pleural clients' awards, instead of some percentage of nothing on their pleural clients' claims. Acting as counsel for the class, they agreed to require class members with lung cancer to establish by objective evidence that their cancer was caused by asbestos, while their own clients did not have to produce that proof. By disassociating all their lung cancer clients from the class and insisting that CCR pay them without objective evidence of causation, more of class counsel's lung cancer patients would be paid money than might be paid under the class settlement.

Class counsel also agreed with CCR that under the class settlement the average payment made to class members each year must fall within a negotiated range for each disease category. By disassociating their clients from the class and insisting that the class ranges not be used to settle their clients' claims, class counsel could make a lot more money overall than they would make if their clients were treated as class members. These are reasons to keep as many of one's own clients out of the class as possible, and that's what class counsel did. Class counsel accomplished all this by carefully drafting the class definition. They gerrymandered the class for profit.

Why did CCR agree to treat class counsel's clients and the clients of other asbestos lawyers more generously than the class? This generosity was simply part of the price CCR had to pay to get the class settlement it wanted. CCR needed two deals to accomplish its goal because plaintiffs' lawyers, including class counsel, would not accept for their own clients the terms CCR was prepared to offer the largest group of asbestos victims, the future claimants.

Why would class counsel and CCR define a class that excluded the clients of *other* asbestos lawyers? Because by offering more generous terms to the clients of other asbestos lawyers CCR could buy third-party support for the settlement among the asbestos bar. The more members of the asbestos bar who supported the class settlement, the better CCR's chances would be of getting the resolution it wanted. The gerrymandered class, the separate client settlements, and the substantial differences between the class settlement and the inventory settlements can all be explained in this way: CCR paid class counsel on the side, by which I mean outside the class action proceeding through the client settlements, for agreeing to support the class settlement. Or to put it even more bluntly, CCR bought off the class lawyers.

Why would a district court accept such a tainted settlement on behalf of so many absent class members? To help rid the court system of the terrible burden imposed by what appears to be interminable asbestos litigation. To accomplish this end, the court deliberately closed its eyes to the evidence that CCR and the lawyers for the putative class had colluded. The court also ignored other serious legal problems with this tainted deal. That the court would approve such a deal, despite its obligation to protect the interests of class members who were not present to protect themselves, is shameful. Without the court's blessing, the lawyers for the settling parties could not have affected the rights of the class members. Responsibility for this corruption of justice must therefore rest, in the end, with the court.

Notes

1. The issue of conflict of interest within the membership of the class came up often in the context of desegregation litigation for thirty years and produced a classic article on the subject. See Derrick Bell, "Serving Two Masters: Integration Ideals and Client Interests in School Desegregation Litigation," 85 Yale L.J. 470 (1976); the more general situation was canvassed in Deborah Rhode, "Class Conflicts in Class Actions," 34 Stan. L. Rev. 1183 (1982). Professor Rhode references Professor Derrick Bell's critique of the actions of civil rights lawyers in the Atlanta and Detroit desegregation cases. In both cases, lawyers from the national offices of the NAACP and the Legal Defense Fund urged courts to reject compromise desegregation plans that had been worked out between community leaders (including the local president of the NAACP in the Detroit case, whom the national office subsequently removed) and school officials because the plans concentrated on improving predominantly black schools and did not require busing white students into predominantly black schools in order to achieve full integration. Although Professor Bell made it clear that he supported desegregation class actions, he nevertheless criticized the NAACP and LDF for allowing their "commitment to an integrated society" to interfere with their obligation to provide full representation to their clients.

What should the NAACP and LDF lawyers have done in these cases? Is it wrong for a public interest organization to be committed to an ideal such as creating "an integrated society"? Isn't fighting for such an ideal—even in the face of internal opposition—exactly what a public interest organization should do? Or does such an organization have an obligation to see that substantial opposition within the class it represents has its views heard through separate representation?

2. In the course of his critique, Professor Bell cites approvingly Justice Harlan's dissent in NAACP v. Button, 371 U.S. 415 (1963), in which the Supreme Court held that the First Amendment prohibits a state from enforcing its rules of professional responsibility to prohibit the NAACP from soliciting clients and coordinating a national litigation strategy. We will return to *Button* and the Supreme Court's subsequent decision in *In re Primus*, in which the Court again created a special exception to the rules of professional responsibility for public interest lawyers, in Chapter 8.

3. A study of civil rights and poverty lawyers in Chicago sheds some interesting light on how civil rights lawyers might minimize (even if they cannot avoid) the kinds of conflicts identified by Professors Rhode and Bell. See Ann Southworth, "Collective Representation for the Disadvantaged: Variations in Problems of Accountability," 67 Fordham L. Rev. 2449 (1999). Based on interviews with 69 lawyers who regularly litigate class actions and other forms of litigation on behalf of groups of clients, the author concluded that lawyers are significantly less likely to impose their own views on their clients or to ignore important conflicts among clients when the group in question is an organization where internal governance structures tend to bring conflicts to the surface and to generate decisionmaking criteria. As a result, when a lawyer represents an organization (which Professor Southworth found to be

more common than traditional class action representation of diffuse groups) clients participate "more actively in setting goals and strategy than did clients who were individuals or plaintiff classes." Id., at 2454. Moreover, Professor Southworth found that civil rights lawyers often facilitated group organizing efforts and helped these organizations to run effectively. She therefore concludes that ethics rules should encourage—or at the very least, avoid discouraging—"lawyers from helping clients build organizations and institutions serving clients' collective as well as individual needs." Id., at 2473.

4. Given the problems Professor Koniak documents, should courts simply prohibit so-called "settlement" class actions?

G. Confidences and Conflicts Among Co-Clients

It would be a mistake to think that conflict of interest or confidentiality problems arise neatly packaged as such. What follows is a Problem combining elements of both. It raises issues that many, if not most, law firms with multiple clients in a single matter have failed to face carefully.

Problem 4–20

You are a new associate in a law firm. The senior partner has left you the following memorandum.

"The following sticky situation confronts me. Two years ago, H, a long-standing client of mine, asked me to review his financial situation and to prepare an estate plan for him and his wife, W. They had been married for some years; both had worked; their assets had been largely commingled; and some were being held in joint name. I interviewed H and W and together we worked out an estate plan, making use of the marital deduction, that basically left property to one another, part outright and part in trust, with remainder to their children. H has just called me and asked me to revise his will and trust, substantially reducing W's interests. H said that he has not discussed the matter with W. He asked me not to inform W of the request or of the action he proposes to take.

"Is there any problem with my complying with H's wishes? If so, what is it? What are the various alternatives that are open to me? What are the pros and cons of each alternative and which alternative do you recommend? Do you have any views as to how we should handle situations like this to avoid this kind of problem in the future?"

How do you respond to this memorandum?

———————

There is relatively little "law" on the disclosure problem involved in Problem 4–20, but there are two major points of view. Both are expressed in the following case.

A. v. B. v. Hill Wallack

158 N.J. 51 (1999)

POLLOCK, J.

This appeal presents the issue whether a law firm may disclose confidential information of one co-client to another co-client. Specifically, in this paternity action, the mother's former law firm, which contemporaneously represented the father and his wife in planning their estates, seeks to disclose to the wife the existence of the father's illegitimate child.

A law firm, Hill Wallack, (described variously as "the law firm" or "the firm") jointly represented the husband and wife in drafting wills in which they devised their respective estates to each other. The devises created the possibility that the other spouse's issue, whether legitimate or illegitimate, ultimately would acquire the decedent's property.

Unbeknown to Hill Wallack and the wife, the husband recently had fathered an illegitimate child. Before the execution of the wills, the child's mother retained Hill Wallack to institute this paternity action against the husband. Because of a clerical error, the firm's computer check did not reveal the conflict of interest inherent in its representation of the mother against the husband. On learning of the conflict, the firm withdrew from representation of the mother in the paternity action. Now, the firm wishes to disclose to the wife the fact that the husband has an illegitimate child. To prevent Hill Wallack from making that disclosure, the husband joined the firm as a third-party defendant in the paternity action.

In the Family Part, the husband, represented by new counsel, Fox, Rothschild, O'Brien & Frankel ("Fox Rothschild"), requested restraints against Hill Wallack to prevent the firm from disclosing to his wife the existence of the child. The Family Part denied the requested restraints. The Appellate Division reversed and remanded "for the entry of an order imposing preliminary restraints and for further consideration." . . .

In October 1997, the husband and wife retained Hill Wallack, a firm of approximately sixty lawyers, to assist them with planning their estates. On the commencement of the joint representation, the husband and wife each signed a letter captioned "Waiver of Conflict of Interest." In explaining the possible conflicts of interest, the letter recited that the effect of a testamentary transfer by one spouse to the other would permit the transferee to dispose of the property as he or she desired. The firm's letter also explained that information provided by one spouse could become available to the other. Although the letter did not contain an express waiver of the confidentiality of any such information, each spouse consented to and waived any conflicts arising from the firm's joint representation.

Unfortunately, the clerk who opened the firm's estate planning file misspelled the clients' surname. The misspelled name was entered in the computer program that the firm uses to discover possible conflicts of interest. The firm then prepared reciprocal wills and related documents with the names of the husband and wife correctly spelled.

In January 1998, before the husband and wife executed the estate planning documents, the mother coincidentally retained Hill Wallack to pursue a paternity claim against the husband. This time, when making its computer search for conflicts of interest, Hill Wallack spelled the husband's name correctly. Accordingly, the computer search did not reveal the existence of the firm's joint representation of the husband and wife. As a result, the estate planning department did not know that the family law department had instituted a paternity action for the mother. Similarly, the family law department did not know that the estate planning department was preparing estate plans for the husband and wife.

A lawyer from the firm's family law department wrote to the husband about the mother's paternity claim. The husband neither objected to the firm's representation of the mother nor alerted the firm to the conflict of interest. Instead, he retained Fox Rothschild to represent him in the paternity action. After initially denying paternity, he agreed to voluntary DNA testing, which revealed that he is the father. Negotiations over child support failed, and the mother instituted the present action.

After the mother filed the paternity action, the husband and wife executed their wills at the Hill Wallack office. The parties agree that in their wills, the husband and wife leave their respective residuary estates to each other. If the other spouse does not survive, the contingent beneficiaries are the testator's issue. The wife's will leaves her residuary estate to her husband, creating the possibility that her property ultimately may pass to his issue. Under N.J.S.A. 3B:1–2; :2–48, the term "issue" includes both legitimate and illegitimate children. When the wife executed her will, therefore, she did not know that the husband's illegitimate child ultimately may inherit her property.

The conflict of interest surfaced when Fox Rothschild, in response to Hill Wallack's request for disclosure of the husband's assets, informed the firm that it already possessed the requested information. Hill Wallack promptly informed the mother that it unknowingly was representing both the husband and the wife in an unrelated matter.

Hill Wallack immediately withdrew from representing the mother in the paternity action. It also instructed the estate planning department not to disclose any information about the husband's assets to the member of the firm who had been representing the mother. The firm then wrote to the husband stating that it believed it had an ethical obligation to disclose to the wife the existence, but not the identity, of his illegitimate child. Additionally, the firm stated that it was obligated to inform the wife "that her current estate plan may devise a portion of her assets through her spouse to that child." The firm suggested that the husband so inform his wife and stated that if he did not do so, it would. Because of the restraints imposed by the Appellate Division, however, the firm has not disclosed the information to the wife.

II.

This appeal concerns the conflict between two fundamental obligations of lawyers: the duty of confidentiality, Rules of Professional Conduct (RPC) 1.6(a), and the duty to inform clients of material facts, RPC 1.4(b). The conflict arises from a law firm's joint representation of two clients whose interests initially were, but no longer are, compatible.

Crucial to the attorney-client relationship is the attorney's obligation not to reveal confidential information learned in the course of representation. Thus, RPC 1.6(a) states that "[a] lawyer shall not reveal information relating to representation of a client unless the client consents after consultation, except for disclosures that are impliedly authorized in order to carry out the representation." . . .

A lawyer's obligation to communicate to one client all information needed to make an informed decision qualifies the firm's duty to maintain the confidentiality of a co-client's information. RPC 1.4(b), which reflects a lawyer's duty to keep clients informed, requires that "[a] lawyer shall explain a matter to the extent reasonably necessary to permit the client to make informed decisions regarding the representation." . . . In limited situations, moreover, an attorney is permitted or required to disclose confidential information. Hill Wallack argues that RPC 1.6 mandates, or at least permits, the firm to disclose to the wife the existence of the husband's illegitimate child. RPC 1.6(b) requires that a lawyer disclose "information relating to representation of a client" to the proper authorities if the lawyer "reasonably believes" that such disclosure is necessary to prevent the client "from committing a criminal, illegal or fraudulent act that the lawyer believes is likely to result in death or substantial injury to the financial interest or property of another." RPC 1.6(b)(1). Despite Hill Wallack's claim that RPC 1.6(b) applies, the facts do not justify mandatory disclosure. The possible inheritance of the wife's estate by the husband's illegitimate child is too remote to constitute "substantial injury to the financial interest or property of another" within the meaning of RPC 1.6(b).

By comparison, in limited circumstances RPC 1.6(c) permits a lawyer to disclose a confidential communication. RPC 1.6(c) permits, but does not require, a lawyer to reveal confidential information to the extent the lawyer reasonably believes necessary "to rectify the consequences of a client's criminal, illegal or fraudulent act in furtherance of which the lawyer's services had been used." RPC 1.6(c)(1). Although RPC 1.6(c) does not define a "fraudulent act," the term takes on meaning from our construction of the word "fraud," found in the analogous "crime or fraud" exception to the attorney-client privilege. N.J.R.E. 504(2)(a) (excepting in the course of legal service sought or obtained in the aid of the commission of a crime or fraud") . . . . When construing the "crime or fraud" exception to the attorney-client privilege, "our courts have generally given the term 'fraud' an expansive reading." Fellerman v. Bradley, 99 N.J. 493, 503–04 (1985).

We likewise construe broadly the term "fraudulent act" within the meaning of RPC 1.6(c). So construed, the husband's deliberate omission of the existence of his illegitimate child constitutes a fraud on his wife. When discussing their respective estates with the firm, the husband and wife reasonably could expect that each would disclose information material to the distribution of their estates, including the existence of children who are contingent residuary beneficiaries. The husband breached that duty. Under the reciprocal wills, the existence of the husband's illegitimate child could affect the distribution of the wife's estate, if she predeceased him. Additionally, the husband's child support payments and other financial responsibilities owed to the illegitimate child could deplete that part of his estate that otherwise would pass to his wife.

From another perspective, it would be "fundamentally unfair" for the husband to reap the "joint planning advantages of access to information and certainty of outcome," while denying those same advantages to his wife. . . . In effect, the husband has used the law firm's services to defraud his wife in the preparation of her estate. . . .

Under RPC 1.6, the facts support disclosure to the wife. The law firm did not learn of the husband's illegitimate child in a confidential communication from him. Indeed, he concealed that information from both his wife and the firm. The law firm learned about the husband's child through its representation of the mother in her paternity action against the husband. Accordingly, the husband's expectation of nondisclosure of the information may be less than if he had communicated the information to the firm in confidence.

In addition, the husband and wife signed letters captioned "Waiver of Conflict of Interest." These letters acknowledge that information provided by one client could become available to the other. The letters, however, stop short of explicitly authorizing the firm to disclose one spouse's confidential information to the other. Even in the absence of any such explicit authorization, the spirit of the letters supports the firm's decision to disclose to the wife the existence of the husband's illegitimate child.

Neither our research nor that of counsel has revealed a dispositive judicial decision from this or any other jurisdiction on the issue of disclosure of confidential information about one client to a co-client. Persuasive secondary authority, however, supports the conclusion that the firm may disclose to the wife the existence of the husband's child.

The forthcoming Restatement (Third) of the Law Governing Lawyers § 112 comment 1 (Proposed Final Draft No. 1, 1996) ("the Restatement") [§ 60 in the published version] suggests, for example, that if the attorney and the co-clients have reached a prior, explicit agreement concerning the sharing of confidential information, that agreement controls whether the attorney should disclose the confidential information of one co-client to another. Ibid. ("Co-clients . . . may explicitly agree to share information" and "can also explicitly agree that the lawyer is not to share certain information . . . with one or more other co-clients. A lawyer must honor such agreements."); see also Report of the ABA Special Committee on Professional Responsibility: Comments and Recommendations on the Lawyer's Duties in Representing

Husband and Wife, 28 Real Prop. Prob. Tr. 765, 787 (1994) ("Although legally and ethically there is no need for a prior discussion and agreement with the couple about the mode of representation, discussion and agreement are the better practice. The agreement may cover . . . the duty to keep or disclose confidences."); American College of Trust and Estate Counsel, ACTEC Commentaries on the Model Rules of Professional Conduct 65–66 (2d ed. 1995) ("When the lawyer is first consulted by the multiple potential clients the lawyer should review with them the terms upon which the lawyer will undertake the representation, including the extent to which information will be shared among them.").

As the preceding authorities suggest, an attorney, on commencing joint representation of co-clients, should agree explicitly with the clients on the sharing of confidential information. In such a "disclosure agreement," the co-clients can agree that any confidential information concerning one co-client, whether obtained from a co-client himself or herself or from another source, will be shared with the other co-client. Similarly, the co-clients can agree that unilateral confidences or other confidential information will be kept confidential by the attorney. Such a prior agreement will clarify the expectations of the clients and the lawyer and diminish the need for future litigation.

In the absence of an agreement to share confidential information with co-clients, the Restatement reposes the resolution of the lawyer's competing duties within the lawyer's discretion:

> [T]he lawyer, after consideration of all relevant circumstances, has the . . . discretion to inform the affected co-client of the specific communication if, in the lawyer's reasonable judgment, the immediacy and magnitude of the risk to the affected co-client outweigh the interest of the communicating client in continued secrecy.

[Restatement (Third) of the Law Governing Lawyers, {§ 60} comment *l*.]

Additionally, the Restatement advises that the lawyer, when withdrawing from representation of the co-clients, may inform the affected co-client that the attorney has learned of information adversely affecting that client's interests that the communicating co-client refuses to permit the lawyer to disclose. Ibid.

In the context of estate planning, the Restatement also suggests that a lawyer's disclosure of confidential information communicated by one spouse is appropriate only if the other spouse's failure to learn of the information would be materially detrimental to that other spouse or frustrate the spouse's intended testamentary arrangement. Id. {§ 60} comment *l*, illustrations 2, 3. The Restatement provides two analogous illustrations in which a lawyer has been jointly retained by a husband and wife to prepare reciprocal wills. The first illustration states:

> Lawyer has been retained by Husband and Wife to prepare wills pursuant to an arrangement under which each spouse agrees to leave most of their property to the other [compare {§ 130}, Comment c, Illustrations 1–3].

Shortly after the wills are executed, Husband (unknown to Wife) asks Lawyer to prepare an inter vivos trust for an illegitimate child whose existence Husband has kept secret from Wife for many years and about whom Husband has not previously informed Lawyer. Husband states that Wife would be distraught at learning of Husband's infidelity and of Husband's years of silence and that disclosure of the information could destroy their marriage. Husband directs Lawyer not to inform Wife. The inter vivos trust that Husband proposes to create would not materially affect Wife's own estate plan or her expected receipt of property under Husband's will, because Husband proposes to use property designated in Husband's will for a personally favored charity. In view of the lack of material effect on Wife, Lawyer may assist Husband to establish and fund the inter vivos trust and refrain from disclosing Husband's information to Wife.

[Id. {§ 60} comment *l*, illustration 2.]

In authorizing non-disclosure, the Restatement explains that an attorney should refrain from disclosing the existence of the illegitimate child to the wife because the trust "would not materially affect Wife's own estate plan or her expected receipt of property under Husband's will." Ibid.

The other illustration states:

Same facts as [the prior Illustration], except that Husband's proposed inter vivos trust would significantly deplete Husband's estate, to Wife's material detriment and in frustration of the Spouses' intended testamentary arrangements. If Husband will neither inform Wife nor permit Lawyer to do so, Lawyer must withdraw from representing both Husband and Wife. In the light of all relevant circumstances, Lawyer may exercise discretion whether to inform Wife either that circumstances, which Lawyer has been asked not to reveal, indicate that she should revoke her recent will or to inform Wife of some or all the details of the information that Husband has recently provided so that Wife may protect her interests. Alternatively, Lawyer may inform Wife only that Lawyer is withdrawing because Husband will not permit disclosure of information that Lawyer has learned from Husband.

[Id. {§ 60} comment *l*, illustration 3.]

Because the money placed in the trust would be deducted from the portion of the husband's estate left to his wife, the Restatement concludes that the lawyer may exercise discretion to inform the wife of the husband's plans. Ibid.

An earlier draft of the Restatement described the attorney's obligation to disclose the confidential information to the co-client as mandatory. Id. (Council Draft No. 11, 1995); cf. Collett, [28 Real Prop. Prob. Tri. J.] at 743 (arguing that nature of joint representation of husband and wife supports mandatory disclosure rule). When reviewing the draft, however, the governing body of the American Law

Institute, the Council, modified the obligation to leave disclosure within the attorney's discretion.

Similarly, the American College of Trust and Estate Counsel (ACTEC) also favors a discretionary rule. It recommends that the "lawyer should have a reasonable degree of discretion in determining how to respond to any particular case." American College of Trust and Estate Counsel, [Commentaries on the Model Rules of Professional Conduct,] at 68. The ACTEC suggests that the lawyer first attempt to convince the client to inform the co-client. Ibid. When urging the client to disclose the information, the lawyer should remind the client of the implicit understanding that all information will be shared by both clients. The lawyer also should explain to the client the potential legal consequences of non-disclosure, including invalidation of the wills. Ibid. Furthermore, the lawyer may mention that failure to communicate the information could subject the lawyer to a malpractice claim or disciplinary action. Ibid.

The ACTEC reasons that if unsuccessful in persuading the client to disclose the information, the lawyer should consider several factors in deciding whether to reveal the confidential information to the co-client, including (1) duties of impartiality and loyalty to the clients; (2) any express or implied agreement among the lawyer and the joint clients regarding the subject of the representation would be shared with the other client; (3) the reasonable expectations of the clients; and (4) the nature of the confidence and the harm that may result if the confidence is, or is not, disclosed. Id. at 68–69.

The Section of Real Property, Probate and Trust Law of the American Bar Association, in a report prepared by its Special Study Committee on Professional Responsibility, reached a similar conclusion:

> Faced with any adverse confidence, the lawyer must act as a fiduciary toward joint clients. The lawyer must balance the potential for material harm to the confiding spouse caused by disclosure against the potential for material harm to the other spouse caused by a failure to disclose.

[Report of the Special Study Committee on Professional Responsibility: Comments and Recommendations on the Lawyer's Duties in Representing Husband and Wife, 28 Real Prop. Prob. Tr. J. at 787.] . . .

The Professional Ethics Committees of New York and Florida, however, have concluded that disclosure to a co-client is prohibited. New York State Bar Ass'n Comm. on Professional Ethics, Op. 555 (1984); Florida State Bar Ass'n Comm. on Professional Ethics, Op. 95-4 (1997).

The New York opinion addressed the following situation:

> A and B formed a partnership and employed Lawyer L to represent them in connection with the partnership affairs. Subsequently, B, in a conversation with Lawyer L, advised Lawyer L that he was actively breaching the partnership agreement. B preceded this statement to Lawyer L with the statement

that he proposed to tell Lawyer L something "in confidence." Lawyer L did not respond to that statement and did not understand that B intended to make a statement that would be of importance to A but that was to be kept confidential from A. Lawyer L had not, prior thereto, advised A or B that he could not receive from one communications regarding the subject of the joint representation that would be confidential from the other. B has subsequently declined to tell A what he has told Lawyer L.

[New York State Bar Ass'n Comm. on Professional Ethics, Op. 555.]

In that situation, the New York Ethics Committee concluded that the lawyer may not disclose to the co-client the communicating client's statement. The Committee based its conclusion on the absence of prior consent by the clients to the sharing of all confidential communications and the fact that the client "specifically in advance designated his communication as confidential, and the lawyer did not demur." Ibid.

The Florida Ethics Committee addressed a similar situation:

Lawyer has represented Husband and Wife for many years in a range of personal matters, including estate planning. Husband and Wife have substantial individual assets, and they also own substantial jointly-held property. Recently, Lawyer prepared new updated wills that Husband and Wife signed. Like their previous wills, their new wills primarily benefit the survivor of them for his or her life, with beneficial disposition at the death of the survivor being made equally to their children. . . . Several months after the execution of the new wills, Husband confers separately with Lawyer. Husband reveals to Lawyer that he has just executed a codicil (prepared by another law firm) that makes substantial beneficial disposition to a woman with whom Husband has been having an extra-marital relationship.

[Florida State Bar Ass'n Comm. on Professional Ethics, Op. 95-4.]

Reasoning that the lawyer's duty of confidentiality takes precedence over the duty to communicate all relevant information to a client, the Florida Ethics Committee concluded that the lawyer did not have discretion to reveal the information. In support of that conclusion, the Florida committee reasoned that joint clients do not necessarily expect that everything relating to the joint representation communicated by one co-client will be shared with the other co-client.

In several material respects, however, the present appeal differs from the hypothetical cases considered by the New York and Florida committees. Most significantly, the New York and Florida disciplinary rules, unlike RPC 1.6, do not except disclosure needed "to rectify the consequences of a client's . . . fraudulent act in the furtherance of which the lawyer's services had been used." RPC 1.6(c). But see New York Code of Professional Responsibility DR 4-101; Florida Rules of Professional Conduct 4-1.6. Second, Hill Wallack learned of the husband's paternity from a third party, not from the husband himself. Thus, the husband did not communicate anything to the law firm with the expectation that the communication would be kept confidential. Finally, the husband and wife, unlike the co-clients considered by the New York and Florida Committees, signed an agreement suggesting their intent to share all information with each other.

Because Hill Wallack wishes to make the disclosure, we need not reach the issue whether the lawyer's obligation to disclose is discretionary or mandatory. In conclusion, Hill Wallack may inform the wife of the existence of the husband's illegitimate child.

Finally, authorizing the disclosure of the existence, but not the identity, of the child, will not contravene N.J.S.A. 9:17-42, which provides:

> All papers and records and any information pertaining to an action or proceeding held under [the New Jersey Parentage Act] which may reveal the identity of any party in an action, other than the final judgement or the birth certificate, whether part of the permanent record of the court or of a file with the State registrar of vital statistics or elsewhere, are confidential and are subject to inspection only upon consent of the court and all parties to the action who are still living, or in exceptional cases only upon an order of the court for compelling reason clearly and convincingly shown.

The law firm learned of the husband's paternity of the child through the mother's disclosure before the institution of the paternity suit. It does not seek to disclose the identity of the mother or the child. Given the wife's need for the information and the law firm's right to disclose it, the disclosure of the child's existence to the wife constitutes an exceptional case "for compelling reason clearly and convincingly shown."

The judgment of the Appellate Division is reversed and the matter is remanded to the Family Part.

Notes

1. The court's conclusion in *Hill Wallack* turned on the parties' expectations in light of both the letter they signed and the amended version of Rule 1.6 in force in New Jersey. Many jurisdictions have adopted provisions like New Jersey's RPC 1.6(c)(1). How would such a provision affect a situation like Problem 4–20? Would the subsequent disclosure by the husband that he planned to alter his will without telling his wife trigger the lawyer's discretion under a provision like RPC 1.6.(c)(1)? Is Comment 31 to Model Rule 1.7, added by the ABA in 2002, helpful in a situation like *Hill Wallack*? The Restatement, which was cited heavily in the opinion above, also addresses a situation in which two individuals retain the lawyer to form a business partnership, and one of the partners soon tells the lawyer that the partner had recently been convicted of defrauding business associates (but in an unrelated venture). As a public record of conviction, is the conviction confidential? Is it generally known? If it is confidential information, should the lawyer nevertheless have discretion to disclose the conviction to the other partner?

2. Following the advice of the New York and Florida ethics opinions cited in *Hill Wallack* that the lawyer should not reveal one co-client's confidence to the other does not necessarily mean that the lawyer who followed such advice would be exempt from a malpractice action or would even be exempt from a finding of ethical impropriety. The issue still remains whether the lawyers were responsible for the situation in which they found themselves by reason of their failure to have an appropriate discussion about the problem of disclosure of confidences at the beginning of the relationship with the co-clients.

3. At the end of its opinion, the New Jersey Supreme Court stated that it did not have to answer the question whether the law firm's obligation to disclose was discretionary or mandatory because the firm had expressed its desire to disclose. What would be the basis for finding a mandatory requirement? The court had already stated that the mandatory requirement of RPC 1.6(b)(1) did not apply.

Chapter 5

The Lawyer's Responsibility to Some Special Clients

The previous Chapters have discussed issues of lawyers' responsibilities in the context of situations where it was generally quite clear who the clients were to whom the lawyers had fiduciary relationships. There are, however, situations where that is a problem. This Chapter deals with three of them—the lawyer for a corporation, for the government, and for an individual who is or may be "incompetent." Those wishing to learn more about the context in which these problems arise should read them in conjunction with the materials in Chapter 12. As we have throughout, we reference those materials where appropriate. In any event, before reading part A, look at Model Rule 1.13 and Part 5 of the Sarbanes–Oxley Act.

A. The Lawyer for the Corporation

Problem 5–1

a) Same facts as Problem 2–9, except that you, the lawyer with the engineer friend, go to your boss, the company's general counsel, with the concerns raised by your friend. The general counsel shrugs it off saying: "Counsel in companies that manufacture products get warnings like this from employees several times a year on average. They even have a name: 'The Cover My Butt' warning. Some employees, at the slightest whiff of any kind of problem, immediately report so that no one can say that they are responsible for not having done something if a problem ever arises. I have actually heard this rumor before; I talked with the chief engineer and he has assured me that we have tested our product to the nth degree and it is safe." You reply that you have known your friend for a long time and know that he is not the nervous type. Moreover, he has told you that his concerns are shared by others in his department. General counsel says: "I have heard you. You should return to your job and not spread these rumors any further. Period." Now what do you do?

Your jurisdiction has the current version of Model Rule 1.13 and the rest of the Model Rules word for word, so far as this issue is concerned. Given the fact that you don't "know" very much in this scenario, does Model Rule 1.13 permit, require, or forbid any reporting upward in this situation? Comment 4 states: "Even in circumstances where a lawyer is not obligated by Rule 1.13 to proceed, a lawyer may bring to the attention of an organizational client, including its highest authority, matters

349

that the lawyer believes to be of sufficient importance to warrant doing so in the best interests of the organization." Suppose you are not sure what "the best interests of the organization" are in these circumstances? Who defines them anyhow? Is this Comment consistent with Rule 1.4?

Compare the policy behind the exceptions to Rule 1.6 with the policy that animates 1.13. The exceptions to 1.6 exist largely to protect persons other than the client. The policy behind 1.13 seems designed to protect "the client." Isn't it true that the higher in the organizational hierarchy that one goes, the closer one gets to "the client"? Why then does 1.13 put high hurdles in front of reporting upwards?

Note that Model Rule 1.13(c) contains a provision permitting disclosure outside the organization, even if not permitted by Rule 1.6, to "prevent substantial injury to the organization." In that situation California's Rule 3-600 limits the lawyer's response to "the right, and, where appropriate, the duty to resign." Which of those solutions is preferable? Or should an organization's lawyer be required (not just permitted) to disclose confidential information in order to prevent substantial injury to the organization?

b) Would your response be different if the company is covered by the requirements of Sarbanes–Oxley?

United States v. Quest Diagnostics, Inc.
734 F.3d 154 (2d Cir. 2013)

José A. Cabranes, Circuit Judge:

Plaintiff appeals from the July 12, 2011 judgment of the United States District Court for the Southern District of New York dismissing this *qui tam* action and disqualifying plaintiff, its individual members—including a former general counsel to defendant—and its outside counsel from bringing a subsequent *qui tam* action on the basis that the suit was brought in violation of the general counsel's ethical obligations under the New York Rules of Professional Conduct (the "N.Y. Rules").[1] The issues on appeal arise out of the tension between an attorney's ethical duty of confidentiality and the federal interest in encouraging "whistleblowers" to disclose unlawful conduct harmful to the government.

We consider here two questions: (1) whether the District Court correctly held that the former general counsel to defendant violated his ethical obligations under the N.Y. Rules by participating in this *qui tam* action; and, if so, (2) whether the District Court erred in dismissing the complaint and disqualifying plaintiff, all of its general

---

1. The current version of the New York Rules of Professional Conduct took effect on April 1, 2009, and is reprinted with amendments in N.Y. Jud. Law App. (McKinney 2013). The District Court evaluated this claim under a version of the New York Code of Professional Responsibility which has since been replaced by the current N.Y. Rules cited in this opinion, and relied upon by the parties in their briefs. The rules are substantively unchanged, but the language of the earlier version applied by the District Court is noted for reference throughout the opinion.

partners including the former general counsel, and its outside counsel from brining any subsequent *qui tam* action based on similar facts.

We agree that the attorney in question, through his conduct in this *qui tam* action, violated N.Y. Rule 1.9(c) which, in relevant part, prohibits lawyers from "us[ing] confidential information of [a] former client protected by Rule 1.6 to the disadvantage of the former client," N.Y. Rule 1.9(c), except "to the extent that the lawyer reasonably believes necessary . . . to prevent the client from committing a crime," id. 1.6(b)(2).

In addition, we hold that the District Court did not err by dismissing the complaint as to all defendants, and disqualifying plaintiff, its individual relators, and its outside counsel on the basis that such measures were necessary to avoid prejudicing defendants in any subsequent litigation on these facts. . . .

BACKGROUND

Plaintiff-appellant Fair Laboratory Practices Associates ("FLPA" or "plaintiff") brought this *qui tam* action[2] pursuant to the federal False Claims Act ("FCA"),[3] 31 U.S.C. §§ 3729–3733, against defendants-appellees Quest Diagnostics Incorporated ("Quest") and Unilab Corporation ("Unilab") for alleged violations of the federal Anti-Kickback Statute, 42 U.S.C. § 1320a–7b ("AKS").[5] One of FLPA's general partners, Mark Bibi, was formerly General Counsel to defendant Unilab. The facts set forth are drawn from the record on appeal, including the account of facts found by the District Court.

A. The Parties

Quest is a Delaware corporation founded in 1996 and headquartered in New Jersey that provides diagnostic medical testing services for managed care organizations ("MCOs") and independent practice associations ("IPAs") nationwide. In

---

2. . . . The False Claims Act's *qui tam* provision allows "a private plaintiff, known as a relator, [to] bring[ ] suit on behalf of the [g]overnment to recover a remedy for a harm done to the [g]overnment." . . . As the "real party in interest" in a *qui tam* action, the government may intervene and take over prosecution of the lawsuit. . . . In such cases, however, the relator is still entitled to a share of any recovery. 31 U.S.C. § 3730(d).

3. The FCA creates a cause of action against one who "knowingly presents, or causes to be presented, a false or fraudulent claim for payment or approval." 31 U.S.C. § 3729(a)(1). Plaintiff also brought claims under the false claims statutes of several states.

5. Title 42 U.S.C. § 1320a–7b(b)(2) provides that

whoever knowingly and willfully offers of pays any remuneration (including any kickback, bribe, or rebate) directly or indirectly, overtly or covertly, in cash or in kind to any person to induce such person—(A) to refer an individual to a person for the furnishing or arranging for the furnishing of any item or service for which payment may be made in whole or in part under a Federal health care program, or (B) to purchase, lease, order, or arrange for or recommend purchasing, leasing, or ordering any good, facility service, or item for which payment may be made in whole or in part under a Federal health care program, shall be guilty of a felony and upon conviction thereof, shall be fined not more than $25,000 or imprisoned for not more than five years, or both.

2003, Quest acquired Unilab—a clinical laboratory company headquartered in California—through a "cash tender offer." Unilab became a wholly-owned subsidiary of Quest through a subsequent merger.

FLPA, the "relator" in this *qui tam* action, is a Delaware general partnership formed in 2005 by three former Unilab executives, Andrew Baker ("Baker"), Richard Michaelson ("Michaelson"), and Mark Bibi ("Bibi" and jointly, the "individual relators") for the purpose of bringing this *qui tam* action. The individual relators worked for Unilab prior to its acquisition by Quest in 2003. Baker was Unilab's Chairman and Chief Executive Officer from 1993 to about December 1996. Michaelson was Unilab's Chief Financial Officer from 1993 to January 1998, and was a director of and consultant to Unilab from January 1998 to November 1999. Bibi was Unilab's Vice President, Executive Vice President, Secretary, and General Counsel from November 1993 to March 2000, and then served only as an Executive Vice President through June 2000, after which he was retained as a consultant by Unilab until December 2000.

Bibi's role as Unilab's General Counsel is central to the issues presented on appeal. Bibi, who has been practicing law in New York since 1985, was Unilab's sole "in-house" lawyer from 1993–2000. In that capacity, he was responsible for all of Unilab's legal and compliance affairs, such as advising Unilab on matters relating to its MCO contracts and managing all litigation against the company.

B. The Alleged Scheme

FLPA alleges that "[f]rom at least 1996 through at least 2005, Unilab and Quest violated the AKS by operating a 'pull-through' scheme by which they charged MCOs and IPAs commercially unreasonable discounted prices [on non-federal business] to induce referrals of Medicare and Medicaid business and then billed the Medicare and Medicaid business to the Government at dramatically higher prices than those charged to the MCOs and IPAs [on the non-federal business]." . . . Specifically, FLPA argues that the "commercially unreasonable discounted prices" constituted "kickback[s], bribe[s] or rebate[s]" insofar as they were designed to induce referrals of Medicare and Medicaid business. . . .

Between 1993 and 1996, the individual relators began to question whether Unilab's pricing structure violated the AKS. For example, as Chief Financial Officer, Michaelson allegedly knew that Unilab often charged its MCO clients prices that were sometimes less than 50% of Unilab's actual testing costs. And Bibi allegedly advised Baker that Unilab's pricing structure, as it was then formulated, potentially facilitated "kickbacks."

In response to these concerns about Unilab's pricing structure, "Unilab, under its then-CEO [Baker], established a new pricing policy . . . that included negotiated increases to the rates under its existing contracts." Specifically, in 1996 Unilab delivered a letter to its MCO and physician-association customers "stating that it was reserving its contractual right to terminate its contract with that customer and would, in thirty days, cease providing laboratory services to any customer that did not agree to a price increase." Following Unilab's notice that it was raising its prices, some of Unilab's "customers began to slowly slip away to [its] competitors." . . .

FLPA asserts that Baker's tenure as CEO ended in 1997 as a result of the falling profits caused by this increase in Unilab's prices. When Baker left, Unilab's shares were selling for less than $3 per share. In 1999, Kelso & Co. completed a leveraged buy-out of Unilab for $5.85 per share and installed a new management team, including Robert Whalen as CEO. Whalen reversed course from Baker's pricing policy, informing other executives that "Baker's increased pricing had been a mistake, and that Unilab needed to (i) accept commercially unreasonable contracts with MCOs and physician associations and (ii) implement a strategy that required physicians to refer, and the MCOs to arrange for or recommend that physicians refer, fee-for-service business, including Medicare and Medicaid-reimbursable business, to Unilab." . . .

In December 1999, the U.S. Department of Health and Human Services Office of the Inspector General ("OIG") published Advisory Opinion ("AO") 99–13, which addressed the pricing practices of clinical pathologists. In particular, AO 99–13 indicated that if the prices offered to MCOs on non-federal business were below "actual cost," such an arrangement "might" violate the AKS because the OIG would infer that such discounts were offered for the purpose of inducing physicians to refer their Medicare and Medicaid business.

The month after AO 99–13 was published, Bibi had a meeting with Whalen during which Bibi stated his "personal opinion," that AO 99–13 created an inference of illegality with respect to Unilab's existing pricing structure. Whalen allegedly instructed Bibi to work with outside counsel to "find a way around" AO 99–13. In response Bibi obtained an opinion letter from an outside law firm, Winston & Strawn, on this issue. Bibi never reported his concerns to the Unilab Board.

FLPA alleges that Bibi was subsequently "frozen out" by Unilab's management as a result of his concerns related to Unilab's pricing structure and was no longer asked for advice on compliance matters. By March 2000, Bibi had been replaced as General Counsel.

After the individual relators left Unilab, the company allegedly "continued its illegal pull-through strategy and as a result significantly improved its profitability." . . . In 2003, Quest acquired Unilab at a price of $26.50 per share. According to Bibi, Baker—who had sold his remaining Unilab shares for $5.85 per share three years earlier—felt "shortchanged." Baker contacted Jeffrey Lanzolatta, a longtime Unilab executive, who allegedly told Baker that Unilab "had become very profitable engaging in the pull-through practice." . . . Baker relayed this information to Bibi, stating that he was in a tax dispute with Unilab/Quest and "wanted to go after them . . . [t]hrough a *qui tam* lawsuit." . . .

C. Procedural History

Baker initiated the filing of this *qui tam* action and invited Michaelson and Bibi to join him as individual relators; in particular, he believed Bibi's status as a lawyer "would improve our credibility with the government." . . . Recognizing the potential ethical implications of a former general counsel bringing a *qui tam* lawsuit against his former company and client, Bibi consulted the N.Y. Rules and the American Bar Association's Model Rules of Professional Conduct to determine whether he could participate. Bibi concluded that certain exceptions to the attorney-client confidentiality rules permitted his participation, and "did not feel it was necessary" to verify his understanding with the New York state bar. . . .

On January 1, 2005, FLPA was formed for the purpose of acting as a relator in one or more *qui tam* actions against defendants for alleged violations of the AKS. Pursuant to the FLPA partnership agreement, Bibi stands to collect 29% of any *qui tam* recovery, while Baker and Michaelson would receive 57% and 14%, respectively. On June 7, 2005, FLPA filed this *qui tam* action in the Southern District of New York. After FLPA filed the operative Second Amended Complaint ("Complaint") on May 18, 2010, the District Court permitted defendants to take discovery regarding whether Bibi and FLPA had improperly used or disclosed Unilab's confidences in this lawsuit. Following the completion of this discovery, defendants filed a motion to dismiss the Complaint, arguing that Bibi's participation in this *qui tam* action violated two provisions of the N.Y. Rules.

First, defendants argued that Bibi violated N.Y. Rule 1.9(a), known as the "side-switching" rule, which provides that

> [a] lawyer who has formerly represented a client in a matter shall not thereafter represent another person in the same or a substantially related matter in which that person's interests are materially adverse to the interests of the former client unless the former client gives informed consent, confirmed in writing.

N.Y. Rule 1.9(a). Defendants asserted that, by acting as an individual relator in this *qui tam* action, Bibi essentially "switched sides" and represented the government against Unilab, his former client.

Second, defendants argued that Bibi violated the N.Y. Rules by making use of Unilab's confidential information for this litigation. . . .

On March 24, 2011, the District Court granted defendants' motion to dismiss, presumably pursuant to the "inherent power . . . necessarily vested in courts to manage their own affairs." Chambers v. NASCO, Inc., 501 U.S. 32, 49 (1991). The District Court concluded that the FCA did not preempt applicable state ethical rules, and that Bibi's participation in this action violated Rule 1.9(a) — the "side-switching rule" — and Rule 1.9(c)'s prohibition on disclosing client confidences beyond what was "necessary," within the meaning of Rule 1.6(b), to prevent the commission of a crime. . . .

In light of these conclusions, the District Court held that the appropriate remedy was to (1) dismiss the Complaint as to all defendants, and (2) disqualify FLPA, each of the individual relators, and FLPA's counsel from bringing this suit or any subsequent suit based on the same facts. The District Court reasoned that these measures were "necessary to protect Defendants from the use of their confidential information against them." . . . The District Court clarified that the dismissal in no way affected the right of the United States to intervene and bring an action against defendants. . . . On July 5, 2011, however, the United States gave notice that it was declining to intervene. Judgment was entered on July 12, 2011.

This appeal followed.

DISCUSSION

On appeal, FLPA argues principally that (1) the District Court erred in holding that Bibi violated his ethical duties under the N.Y. Rules; and (2) the District Court erred in granting an overly broad remedy in favor of the defendants. We consider each argument in turn.

A. Bibi Violated N.Y. Rule 1.9(c) by Disclosing Unilab's Confidential Information

. . .

1. The FCA Does Not Preempt State Ethical Rules

As a general matter, the "salutary provisions [of New York's ethical rules] have consistently been relied upon by the courts of this district and circuit in evaluating the ethical conduct of attorneys." Hull v. Celanese Corp. 513 F.2d 568, 571 n.12 (2d Cir. 1975). Nothing in the False Claims Act evinces a clear legislative intent to preempt state statutes and rules that regulate an attorney's disclosure of client confidences. See Bates v. Dow Agrosciences LLC, 544 U.S. 431, 449 (2005) ("In areas of traditional state regulation, we assume that a federal statute has not supplanted state law unless Congress has made such an intention clear and manifest." (internal quotation marks omitted)). As one court recognized, "[w]hile the [FCA] *permits* any person . . . to bring a *qui tam* suit, it does not authorize that person to violate state laws in the process." United States ex rel. Doe v. X. Corp., 862 F. Supp. 1502, 1507 (E.D. Va 1994) (emphasis supplied).

At the same time, we are mindful that the central purpose of the N.Y. Rules—to protect client confidences—can be "inconsistent with or antithetical to federal interests." Grievance Comm. for S.D.N.Y. v. Simels, 48 F.3d 640, 646 (2d Cir. 1995), which under the FCA, are to "'encourage private individuals who are aware of fraud being perpetrated against the [g]overnment to bring such information forward,'" U.S. ex rel. Dick v. Long Island Lighting Co., 912 F.2d 13, 18 (2d Cir. 1990). In such instances courts must interpret and apply the N.Y. Rules in a manner that "balancing the varying *federal* interests at stake." *Simels*, 48 F.3d at 646. We conduct the following analysis with these principles in mind.

2. Bibi Violated Rule 1.9(c) by Disclosing Confidential Information Beyond What Was "Necessary" Within the Meaning of N.Y. Rule 1.6(b)

FLPA concedes that N.Y. Rule 1.9(c) governs Bibi's conduct in this case. As noted above, N.Y. Rule 1.9(c) provides that

[a] lawyer who has formerly represented a client in a matter . . . shall not thereafter:

(1) use confidential information of the former client protected by Rule 1.6 to the disadvantage of the former client, except as these Rules would permit

or require with respect to a current client or when the information has become generally known; or

(2) reveal confidential information of the former client protected by Rule 1.6 except as these Rules would permit or require with respect to a current client.

N.Y. Rule 1.6(b)(2), in turn, authorizes a lawyer to "reveal or use confidential information to the extent that the lawyer reasonably believes necessary: . . . (2) to prevent the client from committing a crime. . . ."

Accordingly, review of the District Court's determination that Bibi's participation in the *qui tam* action violated Rule 1.9(c) requires us to decide whether Bibi reasonably believed that (1) the defendants intended to commit a crime when FLPA filed this action in 2005, and (2) the disclosures were necessary to prevent the defendants from committing a crime.

a.

We agree with the District Court that "Bibi could have reasonably believed in 2005 that [d]efendants had the intention to commit a crime." . . . The District Court made specific factual findings as to what Bibi knew about defendants' alleged violations of the AKS. . . . Defendants do not argue that any finding made by the District Court in this regard was erroneous. Finding no error based on the record before us, we affirm the judgment of the District Court insofar as it rests on its conclusion that Bib reasonably could have maintained such a belief.

b.

The second question is whether Bibi reasonably believed that his disclosures were necessary to prevent defendants from committing a crime. FLPA asserts that it was "necessary"—within the meaning of N.Y. Rule 1.6(b)—for Bibi to reveal the confidential information disclosed in this lawsuit because the terms of the FCA required Bibi to make "'written disclosure of substantially all material evidence and information the person possesses'" to the government. Thus, FLPA argues, "[u]nder elementary principles of the supremacy of federal law, the FCA preempts application of Rule 1.6. . . ." We disagree, in light of the balancing principles set forth in Part A.1.

Rule 1.6(b)(2) implicitly accounts for the federal interests at stake in the FCA by permitting disclosure of information "necessary" to prevent the ongoing commission of a crime. As illustrated by this very case, Rule 1.6's prohibition on Bibi's disclosures could not have undermined the *qui tam* action in light of the alternative means, discussed below, of exposing the alleged kickback scheme. Because Rule 1.6 itself balances the interests at stake, it need not give way to section 3730(b)(2)'s requirement of full disclosure of material evidence.

Alternatively, FLPA contends that even if Rule 1.6(b) does not give way to section 3730, Bibi complied with its requirements by "tempering his disclosures" until his deposition, when he finally testified as to the details of his conversations with

Whalen and revealed the existence of the Winston & Strawn opinion letter upon solicitation by Unilab. FLPA argues further that the ongoing nature of the alleged crime necessitated the broad disclosures.

The District Court concluded that "[e]vidence of the continuing crime in 2005 could be shown by evidence of Quest's pricing agreements with MCOs and IPAs in effect in 2005 and not, for example, through Bibi's disclosures [confidential information]." . . . Thus, the Court reasoned, the confidential information divulged by Bibi, dating back to 1996, went beyond what was reasonably necessary to prevent any alleged ongoing crime in 2005, when the suit was filed. . . .

We agree with the District Court that the confidential information Bibi revealed was greater than reasonably necessary to prevent any alleged ongoing fraudulent scheme in 2005. By FLPA's own admission, it was unnecessary for Bibi to participate in this *qui tam* action at all, much less to broadly disclose Unilab's confidential information. ("Baer and Michaelson each has ample relevant information to bring this case.") FLPA could have brought the *qui tam* action based on the information that Baker and Michaelson possessed as former executives of Unilab, or, *if necessary*, Bibi could have made limited disclosures. Instead, Bibi chose to participate in the action and disclose protected client confidences, in violation of N.Y. Rule 1.9(c).

Because we affirm the judgment of the District Court on the grounds that Bibi violated N.Y. Rule 1.9(c), we need not consider whether Bibi also violated N.Y. Rule 1.9(a) — the "side-switching" rule — by participating in this *qui tam* action.

B. The District Court Did Not Err or "Abuse Its Discretion" in Dismissing the Complaint and Disqualifying FLPA and Its Counsel

Having affirmed the judgment of the District Court insofar as it concluded that Bibi violated N.Y. Rule 1.9(c), we must decide whether the District Court's remedy — dismissing the complaint and disqualifying FLPA, FLPA's counsel, and the individual relators from bringing this action or any subsequent action based on the same facts — was proper.

We review a district court's decision on remedies for ethical violations for "abuse of discretion." See W. T. Grant Co. v. Haines, 531 F.2d 671, 676 (2d Cir. 1976) . . . . A district court has abused its discretion if it "(1) based its ruling on an erroneous view of the law, (2) made a clearly erroneous assessment of the evidence, or (3) rendered a decision that cannot be located within the range of permissible decisions." NML Capital, Ltd. v. Republic of Argentina, 680 F.3d 254, 257 (2d Cir. 2012) (internal quotation marks omitted).

We have long recognized "the power of trial judges to disqualify [attorneys] where necessary to preserve the integrity of the adversary process . . ." — most commonly "where the attorney is at least potentially in a position to use privileged information concerning the other side through prior representation . . . ." Bd. of Ed. of New York v. Nyquist, 590 F.2d 1241, 1246 (2d Cir. 1979) (internal quotation marks omitted).

Dismissal of a complaint prepared in reliance on privileged information may also be an appropriate remedy. . . .

We are conscious that, notwithstanding any salutary effect on attorney ethics or the appearance of fairness, dismissal or disqualification for violations of ethical rules may impede the pursuit of meritorious litigation to the detriment of the justice system. . . . Accordingly, courts must balance these competing concerns by limiting remedies for ethical violations to those necessary to avoid "taint[ing] the underlying trial." . . .

We have repeatedly cautioned that, "[w]hen dealing with ethical principles, we cannot paint with broad strokes." . . . In evaluating the remedies ordered here, we note FLPA's unusual posture in this litigation by virtue of its status as relator. While FLPA stands to benefit from any recovery in this case, it brings this suit on behalf of the United States government. As such, it acts neither as the real party in interest nor in a representative capacity. In addition, we recognize the particularly strong federal interest underpinning *qui tam* litigation pursuant to the FCA.

1. Dismissal of the Complaint and Disqualification of FLPA

We first address the District Court's decision to dismiss the Complaint as to all defendants and disqualify FLPA and its individual relators. In ordering remedies for Bibi's violation of the N.Y. Rules, the District Court correctly recognized that "[n]ot all violations of the legal code of ethics require dismissal or disqualification of counsel," and that the relevant inquiry was the "possibility of prejudice at trial." . . . After considering lesser alternatives, the District Court concluded that because FLPA "pursued this litigation on the basis that Bibi could 'spill his guts' and freely disclose Unilab's confidential information," it would be "virtually impossible to identify and distinguish each improper disclosure." . . . Furthermore, given the concessions by Baker and Michaelson that Bibi had revealed information about confidential communications with Whalen, "[a]llowing Baker and Michaelson to proceed with the suit would allow that taint to proceed into trial."

We do not conclude that the District Court erred or "abused its discretion" in finding that, in view of Bibi's unrestricted sharing of confidential information with the other individual relators, permitting FLPA or any of its individual relators to proceed with the suit would taint the trial proceedings and prejudice defendants. Moreover, FLPA is not the real party in interest here, and, as the District Court emphasized, its decision did not foreclose the *government* (or, for that matter, a different relator) from bringing suit. Accordingly, dismissal of the Complaint and disqualification of FLPA does not significantly impair the federal interests embodied in the FCA.

Alternatively, FLPA argues that it should be permitted to proceed against Quest, if not Unilab, because Bibi never owed any duty to Quest. This argument ignores the fact that "when control of a corporation passes to new management [as a result of, *inter alia*, a merger], the authority to assert and waive the corporation's attorney-client privilege passes as well." Commodity Futures Trading Comm'n v. Weintrab, 471 U.S.

343, 349 (1985). The District Court thus correctly held that "any obligation Bibi had to Unilab was transferred to Quest upon its purchase." . . . We hold that it was not error for the District Court to conclude that "simply dismissing Unilab from this action would not fully purge the taint associated with Bibi's unethical disclosures of Unilab confidences."

2. Dismissal of FLPA's Counsel

We next consider whether the District Court abused its discretion by *sua sponte* disqualifying FLPA's counsel . . . on the basis that such dismissal was "necessary to protect [d]efendants from the use of their confidential information against them." . . .

We note at the outset that the ethical violations at issue here were committed by Bibi, a general partner of the *client*, FLPA, and not by counsel in this case. As such, the circumstances of this disqualification do not lend themselves to the "precise application of precedent." . . . We have, however, previously found it necessary to dismiss counsel who had themselves committed no ethical violation, on the basis that "confidences . . . could have been revealed [to them]" that would prejudice a party in litigation. . . .

Here, the District Court concluded that, by virtue of the confidential information likely revealed to them, counsel for FLPA "are in a position to use [defendants' confidential information] to give present or subsequent clients an unfair, and unethical, advantage." . . . Moreover, FLPA's disqualification, by virtue of the intimate collaboration with Bibi in the ethics violations, *alleviates* the concern that "[t]he sins of counsel should not be visited upon his client so as to vitiate the latter's cause of action." . . . In sum, the District Court's decision to disqualify FLPA's counsel was not based on any error of law or fact, and is "located within the range of permissible decisions." . . .

CONCLUSION

To summarize:

(1) The False Claims Act does not preempt state ethical rules governing the disclosure of client confidences; therefore N.Y. Rule 1.9(c), which generally prohibits disclosure of confidential information of a former client, governs a New York attorney's conduct as relator in a *qui tam* action under the False Claims Act.

(2) N.Y. Rule 1.6(b)(2), which permits a lawyer to reveal or use confidential information to the extent that the lawyer reasonably believes necessary to prevent the client from committing a crime, does not justify Bibi's disclosures in this case: Bibi reasonably could have believed in 2005 that defendants intended to commit a crime. His disclosure of Unilab's confidential information, however, went well beyond what was "necessary" within the meaning of N.Y. Rule 1.6(b)(2) to prevent Unilab from committing a crime inasmuch as there was ample non-confidential information on which to bring an FCA action. Therefore, Bibi's conduct in this *qui tam* action violated his ethical obligaitons under N.Y. Rule 1.9(c).

(3) The District Court did not err or "abuse its discretion" in dismissing the Complaint and disqualifying FLPA, all of its general partners, and its outside counsel from brining any subsequent related *qui tam* action, on the basis that such measures were necessary to prevent the use of Bibi's unethical disclosures against defendants.

Accordingly, the judgment of the District Court is AFFIRMED.

Notes (on exam)

Give them a try for feedback

1. The court read New York's versions of Rules 1.9(c) and 1.6(b)(2) together to conclude that Bibi had revealed more confidential information than necessary to prevent his client's commission of a crime. Would that conclusion have been the same if the court had applied the Model Rules' version of Rule 1.6, which contains subparagraph (b)(3), which permits disclosure of confidential information "to prevent, mitigate or rectify substantial injury to the financial interests or property of another that is reasonably certain to result or has resulted from the client's commission of a crime or fraud in furtherance of which the client has used the lawyer's services"? What argument would FLPA have made under that provision? Given the fact that the matter was in federal court and involved a cause of action under a federal statute, should the federal district court have considered itself bound by the state rules of professional conduct? Is that issue governed by preemption doctrine?

2. If Bibi practiced in a jurisdiction whose version of Rule 1.6 permitted him to reveal the confidential information that he did, would that answer the question whether his participation as a plaintiff in the litigation violated the governing rules of professional conduct? Note that the court did not directly address that question. How would you answer it?

3. The court's conclusions might shield significant corporate misconduct, at least to the extent that the court has effectively deterred lawyers (who often are in good positions to discover the misconduct) from reporting. Do the policies driving lawyers' duties of loyalty and confidentiality justify this result?

4. What is the relevance of the discussion of preemption under the False Claims Act to a similar discussion with respect to the Sarbanes–Oxley Act where its requirements differ from those under the disciplinary rules of particular states?

5. The Dodd–Frank Act, 15 U.S.C. § 78u-6, provides bounties to whistleblowers for providing relevant information derived from independent knowledge or independent analysis. Regulations under the Act tell whistleblowers:

> (4) The Commission will not consider information to be derived from your independent knowledge or independent analysis in any of the following circumstances:

> (i) If you obtained the information through a communication that was subject to the attorney-client privilege, unless disclosure of that information would otherwise be permitted by an attorney pursuant to

§ 205.3(d)(2) [SOX Rules] of this chapter, the applicable state attorney conduct rules, or otherwise;

(ii) If you obtained the information in connection with the legal representation of a client on whose behalf you or your employer or firm are providing services, and you seek to use the information to make a whistleblower submission for your own benefit, unless disclosure would otherwise be permitted by an attorney pursuant to § 205.3(d)(2) of this chapter, the applicable state attorney conduct rules, or otherwise . . . 17 C.F.R. § 240.21F-4(b)(4).

In a jurisdiction whose version of Rule 1.6(b) or Rule 1.13 would permit disclosure of confidential information, would efforts by lawyers to take advantage of the bonus provisions of Dodd–Frank be prohibited by Rule 1.7 or Rule 1.9?

6. In Danon v. Vanguard Group, Inc., 2015 N.Y. Misc. LEXIS 4239 (N.Y. Super. Ct. 2015), the judge dismissed the complaint of a Vanguard lawyer whistleblower under the New York False Claims Act that alleged that the company had operated an illegal tax shelter for almost forty years by not dealing with its affiliated advisory services at arm's length, as required by Treasury Rules, by not charging them fees for advisory services. The complaint charged that Vanguard had avoided payments of a billion dollars in federal taxes and $20 million in state taxes over the previous ten-year period. A subsequent submission of its tax expert raised the amount of unpaid federal taxes in the period 2007–2014 to $34.6 billion. The trial judge dismissed the complaint on the basis that the lawyer had insufficiently alleged a nexus between his firing and his whistleblower activities. In addition, relying substantially on *Quest*, he concluded that the lawyer had disclosed more confidential information than necessary to prevent the company from continuing its alleged tax violations. He concluded that the disclosures to the tax authorities were not protected by the explicit whistleblower protections in the state False Claims Act because they were not alleged to be necessary to prevent future violations. The court did not discuss the effect of the nonstandard Comment 6D to Rule 1.6 of New York's Rules of Professional Conduct, which states: "Some crimes, such as criminal fraud, may be ongoing in the sense that the client's past material false representations are still deceiving new victims. The law treats such crimes as continuing crimes in which new violations are constantly occurring. The lawyer whose services were involved in the criminal acts that constitute a continuing crime may reveal the client's refusal to bring an end to a continuing crime, even though that disclosure may also reveal the client's past wrongful acts, because refusal to end a continuing crime is equivalent to an intention to commit a new crime." A subsequent suit in federal district court by the lawyer under the Sarbanes–Oxley and Dodd–Frank Acts and the Pennsylvania Whistleblower statute was dismissed on the grounds of collateral estoppel. Danon v. Vanguard Grp., Inc., 2016 U.S. Dist. LEXIS 67773, remanded for consideration of Dodd–Frank claim and affirmed in other respects, 2017 U.S. App. LEXIS 6260 (3d

Cir.). See Dennis Ventry, "Stitches for Snitches: Lawyers as Whistleblowers," 50 U.C. Davis L. Rev. 1455 (2017) for a very critical analysis of the New York lawsuit.

Problem 5–2

Corporation, which is about to file a disclosure statement with the SEC, has its main production facilities on a piece of real estate that has been discovered by Lawyer to contain a defect in title. Lawyer has advised Corporation that since it has occupied the property for nineteen years, Corporation will own the piece of property by adverse possession free and clear of any claim if no suit is filed within the next year. If the defect is discovered by the adjoining landowner, however, it would at the very least cause a great deal of expense to the Corporation and, at the very worst, it could be disastrous. It is unlikely, however, that anyone will discover the defect within the year. What advice does Lawyer give with respect to the disclosure statement?

———

This factual example and others like it have been used by many for a long time as illustrative of the difficulty of this field. See William T. Coleman, "The Different Duties of Lawyers and Accountants," 30 Bus. Law. 91, 92 (Special Issue March 1975). See also Loss, *Fundamentals of Securities Regulation* 1269 (1983), which points out that it is a crime willfully to fail to file a required report or to file it late and that it is also a crime willfully and knowingly to make any statement in a required report that is "false or misleading as to any material fact."

Suppose that it was not a registration statement that was involved but rather that Lawyer had received a request from Corporation's accountants to list "all contingent liabilities of the Corporation of which you have knowledge." How should Lawyer respond? This is the substantive issue faced by Anita Charles in Problem 1–2, p. 32. Suppose that the discovery that Lawyer had made involved (a) payment of bribes to government officials, either in the United States or abroad, or (b) payment of an apparently exorbitant salary to the agent in charge of a foreign subsidiary, when Lawyer's suspicion is that the salary includes a bribe fund. What should Lawyer do in such cases when an annual report is to be filed with the SEC, assuming that the payments were made with the knowledge of the board of directors?

An interesting review of various models when corporate counsel are chosen to investigate possible violations of law, either by voluntary or involuntary request of the corporation, is contained in Gruenbaum and Oppenheimer, "Special Investigative Counsel: Conflicts and Roles," 33 Rutgers L. Rev. 865 (1981).

Problem 5–3

Lawyer is a member of the corporate legal staff of Steel Corporation, which is under a court order obtained at the instigation of Agency to reduce smoke emissions to a designated level at its Springfield plant. It has spent $5 million on new equipment to comply with the order. Lawyer's major corporate responsibility is to give legal advice to the Springfield plant manager. Lawyer inquires about the status of the plant's compliance. Plant Manager replies happily, "Our new equipment is working wonderfully. Except on the 'worst' days of summer and a few days in winter, we are well within the requirements of the order. But the problems occur only about 5% of the time and, while the technology exists to achieve 100% compliance, it would cost an astronomical amount to buy that equipment." What does Lawyer do next? She knows, but has never told Plant Manager, that Agency monitors compliance on one of the first three business days of the month. Compare your view in this case with the advice you decided to give in Problem 2–9, p. 68. In the Problem 2–9 situation, at what point would you have communicated your fears about flaws in the company's alloy to the board of directors?

Problem 5–4

You are an associate in Big & Little, a two-hundred-person law firm located in a Model Rules jurisdiction. A senior partner has left you the following email:

"I hope that you are not too busy because I need some advice from you in a hurry. I am preparing the Douglas matter for appeal. That's of course the one on which you did some brief work for me last month—where our client Douglas Inc. bought a $120 million piece of property from Ticktock Industries in 2005 and within six months had to pay $10 million in cleanup costs from a spill that must have occurred several years before. Douglas has sued on alternative theories of misrepresentation and failure to disclose information that Ticktock had a duty to disclose. Ticktock said it did make disclosure at the time of our purchase and produced an unsigned copy of a disclosure letter addressed to Suzanne Green, Douglas's general counsel, from its files. All Douglas employees involved in the purchase, including Suzanne Green and the outside lawyer who handled the deal (not from our firm), testified at the trial that they never saw that letter and could not find it in their files. Our theory is that either it was lost in transmission or perhaps even never sent, with a copy left in the Ticktock files to create the impression that it had been sent. The jury returned a verdict of $10 million in our favor plus $15 million in punitive damages, and Ticktock has filed a notice of appeal. After the notice of appeal was filed, Ticktock's insurer submitted an offer of $7.5 million to settle the case. Yesterday Suzanne Green, Douglas's general counsel, told me to reject the offer. One reason is that Douglas is counting on as large a verdict as possible to offset expected losses that, without payment of the judgment, would throw Douglas into the red for the next quarter for the first time in twenty-five years. Obviously, they would rather not have to deal with the issues that would raise, and the expectations for the following quarters are quite good. I have not yet communicated with Ticktock's lawyers.

"This morning I was visited by John Azera, Douglas's assistant general counsel. He told me that while looking for the latest SEC filing, he opened Green's desk. Picking up the filing, he noticed underneath it a post-it in Green's handwriting saying "Sharon, please get rid of this now" attached to a letter. Sharon is Ms. Green's longtime assistant. The letter was dated six months before the Ticktock–Douglas property closing, was addressed to Green, and disclosed the spill that is the subject of this litigation. Azera has not talked to Green about the letter and is not planning to do so. He said to me that 'Green is a wonderful person and a wonderful lawyer. There must be some explanation for her testimony and that note, even though I can't think of one. Anyhow, I can't afford to cross her. I don't want to lose my job. I don't want to know any more than I know already. But I thought that someone should know and that someone is you. But keep me out of this from now on.' I didn't know quite what to say to Azera, and he really didn't want me to say anything and so we ended the conversation.

"I need to get the ball rolling on handling this issue quickly. I therefore need you to lay out a scenario or possibly several scenarios for me of all the things I need to have in mind, all the things I need to consider doing in the various likely eventualities. One thing that occurs to me is simply making everything go away by leaning on Green—carefully—to accept the settlement offer or possibly even by withdrawing from representation immediately. But even if either of those possibilities is the way to go, I need to have a road map from you about all the things I should be considering and the various alternatives. You know the drill—first the issues, then the possible resolutions of those issues, then the alternative courses of action, and then your recommendations. If you think you need additional factual information, tell me what you need to know and why different factual assumptions would make a difference in your conclusions."

There is a large volume of literature on these Problems. In addition to the other articles cited in this part of the Chapter, see Maupin, "Environmental Law, The Corporate Lawyer, and The Model Rules of Professional Conduct," 36 Bus. Lawyer 431 (1981); Lorne, "The Corporate Securities Adviser, The Public Interest, and Professional Ethics," 76 Mich. L. Rev. 423 (1978). For an examination of some of these issues by the Reporter for the ABA's Ethics 2000 Commission, see Nancy J. Moore, "Conflicts of Interest for In-House Counsel: Issues Emerging From the Expanding Role of the Attorney-Employee," 39 S. Tex. L. Rev. 497 (1998).

Whenever in the corporate context lawyers become aware that there is a possibility that crimes or fraud may have been, or may be about to be, committed, they have two immediate matters to consider. With whom in the corporate hierarchy should they pursue the issue? What is their obligation or discretion to disclose the information outside the corporate hierarchy if the issue cannot be resolved internally?

Identification of the client became very important with the emergence in the courts and especially in the Securities and Exchange Commission of "new" theories of the attorney's responsibility in the late twentieth century. Garner v. Wolfinbarger, 430 F.2d 1093 (5th Cir. 1970), cert. denied, 401 U.S. 974 (1971), was the landmark case.

It was a stockholders' derivative suit based on alleged violations of the securities acts in connection with sale of stock by the corporation to them. The plaintiffs sought discovery of the advice given by the corporate attorney to the corporation. The court did not hold that the would-be stockholders were "clients" of the corporation's attorney in connection with advice he gave to the corporation regarding the sale, although it did refer to the joint client exception to the attorney-client privilege as "instructive." But without supplying any logical connection between the joint client exception and the situation in *Garner*, the court did hold that the corporation would be precluded from asserting the attorney-client privilege in this stockholders' derivative suit arising out of their transaction with the corporation if they showed good cause for obtaining the information. See, e.g., Fausek v. White, 965 F.2d 126 (6th Cir. 1992) (following *Garner* and barring a corporation from asserting attorney-client privilege against minority shareholder plaintiffs). The logical connection must be some notion of responsibility of the corporation toward would-be purchasers of its stock. If the corporation has that responsibility, can the responsibility of the attorney be far behind?

The corporate world changed considerably at the beginning of the twenty-first century following the Enron and Arthur Andersen scandals (among others). The fallout ultimately brought substantial changes in the rules and attitudes governing corporate lawyers. The Sarbanes–Oxley Act was Congress's response to these scandals. It represents yet another national layer of professional responsibility law. The Sarbanes–Oxley Act led the ABA to alter Rule 1.13 somewhat and to expand the exceptions to confidentiality in Rule 1.6 to conform more closely to changes that had already been made by most states. Compare the difference in the triggers for "reporting up the corporate ladder" in the congressional statue and in the Model Rules. Lawyers need to keep both sets of triggers in mind. Note also that Rule 1.13(c) adds an additional ground to Rule 1.6(b) for disclosure of confidential information; note also the explicit statement in Comment 6 to that Rule stating that Rule 1.13 does not preempt Rule 1.6 in the corporate context. We shall consider several more "Enron effects" in the following pages.

Should the confidentiality rules for corporate clients be different from those for individuals? If so, should the rules be *more* or *less* restrictive for corporate lawyers? Consider this question again after you have read the excerpt from Professor Simon later on in this section and the accompanying Notes.

————————

The issue of a corporate lawyer's obligations within the corporate hierarchy was the subject of litigation pursued by the SEC in a proceeding to discipline two partners of a well-known Wall Street law firm. In re Carter and Johnson, 1981 Fed. Sec. L. Rep. ¶82,847 (SEC 1981), was a proceeding instituted by the SEC pursuant to Rule 2(e) of its Rules of Practice, 17 C.F.R. §201(e)(1), which provided:

The Commission may deny, temporarily or permanently, the privilege of appearing or practicing before it in any way to any person who is found by the Commission after notice of and opportunity for hearing in the matter (i) not to possess the requisite qualifications to represent others, or (ii) to be lacking in character or integrity or to have engaged in unethical or improper professional conduct, or (iii) to have willfully violated, or willfully aided and abetted the violation of any provision of the Federal securities laws. [Current Rule 102(e)(1) is virtually the same.]

Carter and Johnson (and Socha, a third lawyer not involved in the proceeding) were partners in the New York firm of Brown, Wood, Ivey, Mitchell & Perry, which represented National Telephone Company, a lessor of sophisticated telephone equipment systems. National's business required enormous amounts of capital to finance purchases of equipment whose rental would cover the cost only over an extended period of time. The principal shareholder, president, treasurer, and chairman of the board of National at the relevant time was Sheldon Hart. For the year prior to the filing of National's bankruptcy, the company was faced with enormous financial pressure. Hart and his in-house counsel, Lurie, were consistently uncooperative in following the advice of Carter and Johnson concerning the disclosure requirements of federal securities laws. The lawyers were aware that National's press releases and letters and reports to stockholders contained insufficient disclosures of its financial troubles and they knew that their recommendations regarding disclosures in the Annual Report and letters to stockholders had been ignored. Later when National was required to implement the so-called LMP, a plan to curtail activity because certain conditions outlined in its loan agreements with its lenders had occurred, Hart refused for a month to follow the lawyers' advice that disclosure of these occurrences was required. Only after Hart's resignation was disclosure made.

The trial judge suspended the lawyers from appearing or practicing before the Commission for a period of time. The Commission first upheld the validity of its disciplinary authority by rejecting an attack upon its authority to promulgate Rule 2(e). It then reversed the findings of statutory violation.

The SEC reviewed the evidence relating to all these events in great detail and concluded that although it was a "close judgment," the evidence was "insufficient to establish that either respondent acted with sufficient knowledge and awareness or recklessness to satisfy the test for willful aiding and abetting liability." It also stated that since the Commission had not adopted applicable standards of professional conduct and since there were no unambiguous professional norms of conduct in the situation presented, it would reverse the findings of unethical and improper professional conduct. But it then stated a rule for the future:

> The Commission is of the view that a lawyer engages in "unethical or improper professional conduct" under the following circumstances: When a lawyer with significant responsibilities in the effectuation of a company's compliance with the disclosure requirements of the federal securities laws

becomes aware that his client is engaged in a substantial and continuing failure to satisfy those disclosure requirements, his continued participation violates professional standards unless he takes prompt steps to end the client's noncompliance.

It continued:

We do not imply that a lawyer is obliged, at the risk of being held to have violated Rule 2(e), to seek to correct every isolated disclosure action or inaction he believes to be at variance with applicable disclosure standards, although there may be isolated disclosure failures that are so serious that their correction becomes a matter of primary professional concern. It is also clear, however, that a lawyer is not privileged to unthinkingly permit himself to be co-opted into an ongoing fraud and cast as a dupe or a shield for a wrongdoing client.

Initially, counseling accurate disclosure is sufficient, even if his advice is not accepted. But there comes a point at which a reasonable lawyer must conclude that his advice is not being followed, or even sought in good faith, and that his client is involved in a continuing course of violating the securities laws. At this crucial juncture, the lawyer must take further, more affirmative steps in order to avoid the inference that he has been co-opted, willingly or unwillingly, into the scheme of nondisclosure.

The lawyer is in the best position to choose his next step. Resignation is one option, although we recognize that other considerations, including the protection of the client against foreseeable prejudice, must be taken into account in the case of withdrawal. A direct approach to the board of directors or one or more individual directors or officers may be appropriate; or he may choose to try to enlist the aid of other members of the firm's management. What is required, in short, is some prompt action that leads to the conclusion that the lawyer is engaged in efforts to correct the underlying problem, rather than having capitulated to the desires of a strong-willed, but misguided, client.

Some have argued that resignation is the only permissible course when a client chooses not to comply with disclosure advice. We do not agree. Premature resignation serves neither the end of an effective lawyer-client relationship nor, in most cases, the effective administration of the securities laws. The lawyer's continued interaction with his client will ordinarily hold the greatest promise of corrective action. So long as a lawyer is acting in good faith and exerting reasonable efforts to prevent violations of the law by his client, his professional obligations have been met. In general, the best result is that which promotes the continued, strongminded and independent participation by the lawyer.

We recognize, however, that the "best result" is not always obtainable, and that there may occur situations where the lawyer must conclude that the misconduct is so extreme or irretrievable, or the involvement of his client's management and board of directors in the misconduct is so thorough-going and pervasive that any action short of resignation would be futile. We would anticipate that cases where a lawyer has no choice but to resign would be rare and of an egregious nature.

Notes

1. While much of the discussion about this case concerned possible violation of the rules of professional conduct, note that that was not the lawyers' only concern. The Commission indicated that the lawyers had come quite close to aiding and abetting criminal violations. See the *National Student Marketing* litigation, discussed below, where such violations were found.

2. Rule 1.13 and In re Carter and Johnson both assume that a corporate lawyer faced with a situation where management refuses to follow his advice about disclosure should take the matter to the entity's "highest authority," which in most cases is the board of directors. What happens, however, when the lawyer is himself a member of the board? Should the lawyer recuse himself from the board's decision? Or should the lawyer use his board role to push vigorously for his position? Should lawyers who represent corporations serve on their clients' boards at all? Does it make a difference whether the lawyer in question works in-house or for a private firm that represents the company? Accountants, for example, are barred from serving on the boards of companies they represent. Should lawyers be governed by the same rules? For an argument that lawyers should be barred from corporate boards, see Susanna M. Kim, "Dual Identities and Dueling Obligations: Preserving Independence in Corporate Representation," 68 Tenn. L. Rev. 179 (2001).

Lawyers must pay close attention to an array of sources of law regulating the conduct of lawyers, including those of statutory law. In SEC v. National Student Marketing Corp., the court scrutinized the obligations of lawyers for both the acquiring and the acquired publicly owned companies in a merger when on the day of closing information was transmitted by accountants that indicated that interim financial statements of the acquiring company were erroneous. The executives of the acquired company made a business decision to close the deal anyway. The SEC filed complaints against both sets of lawyers, charging various violations of the securities acts. The lawyers for the acquiring company entered into a consent decree. The case against the lawyers for the acquired company proceeded to trial. The District Court for the District of Columbia stated that the lawyers should have refused to proceed with the merger absent disclosure to, and resolicitation of, the shareholders of their client because of the materiality of the adjustments required to be made in the interim financial statements. It held that their actions constituted an aiding and abetting of the violations of the antifraud provisions of § 17a of the Securities Act of 1933 and § 10b and Rule 10b-5 of the Securities Exchange Act of 1934 by the defendant executives of their client. The court, however, refused to enter the injunction sought for the SEC because of the unlikelihood of repetition of the conduct. 457 F. Supp. 682 (D.D.C. 1978).

In considering the *National Student Marketing* litigation, it should be emphasized that although the case provoked several years of discussion about the corporate lawyer's obligation to disclose confidences in order to protect what were at least arguably "third parties," namely the stockholders of their client, the case was decided not on the basis of violation of rules of professional conduct but rather on the basis of lawyers' violation of criminal statutes.

———————

The new theory of lawyer obligation that surfaced in the 1970s in SEC complaints and in some court opinions had a variety of effects. Some lawyers were made quite cautious, causing loud complaints that the unprofessionalism being exhibited was the exact opposite of what some observers were complaining about: lawyers were in fact breaking their obligations of zealous representation and confidentiality by giving in to SEC pressure. See Freedman, *Lawyers' Ethics in an Adversary System* 20–24 (1975). The ABA's House of Delegates took the extraordinary step of adopting a Statement of Policy setting forth a view of the lawyer's confidentiality obligation that implicitly rejected the "auditor" notion advanced by Commissioner Sommer. (The Statement is published in full in 31 Bus. Law. 543 (Nov. 1975).)

Are the fears expressed by the ABA plausible in the context of securities work? Is there really a danger that securities lawyers will give overly cautious advice because they fear SEC enforcement efforts? Is there anything that corporate clients can do to protect themselves against such under-zealousness? Does your answer depend upon whether you are imagining the client to be a large publicly traded corporation or a small limited partnership? Keep these questions in mind when you read Professor Wilkins' argument about client ethics in the next section and the materials on corporate lawyers in Chapter 12.

The ABA also addressed another problem involving the same area of confidential and potentially detrimental information possessed by lawyers. This problem was the bounds of appropriate questioning by accountants and appropriate responses by a lawyer with respect to loss contingencies (potential liabilities of a client) about which the lawyer had confidential information. (Recall that deciding how to respond to such a letter was the source of the dispute between Steve Langford and Anita Charles in Problem 1–2.) In December 1975 the ABA Board of Governors approved a Statement of Policy on this matter. A coordinated Statement on Auditing Standards (known as Financial Accounting Standards 5) was approved by the American Institute of Certified Public Accountants' Auditing Standards Executive Committee in January 1976. In pertinent part, the joint statement provides that a lawyer should only inform an auditor about those possible unasserted claims that the client has specifically identified as being probable of assertion, that are material to its financial condition and, in addition, there is a reasonable possibility of an unfavorable outcome. Moreover, although the statement requires that the lawyer consult with the client regarding questions of disclosure, and allows her to resign if her advice on this subject is disregarded by the client, such resignation is not mandatory unless it is clear that (1) the undisclosed matter is of material importance and (2) there can be no reasonable doubt that nondisclosure in the client's financial statement would be a violation of law giving rise to material claims.

The Statement on Auditing Standards is an important effort to set forth a professional view of the extent of desirable disclosure by clients, via lawyers, of their contingent liabilities. In particular, the Statement suggests an answer to Problem 5–2. Lawyers who accept and attempt to follow the ABA recommendations, however, should be aware that the Statement is not "law" and that its particular accommodation is not necessarily the one that the SEC will, or will always, accept. See, however, Tew v. Arky, Freed, Stearns et al., 655 F. Supp. 1571, 1573 (S.D. Fla. 1987), both aff'd without published opinion, 846 F.2d 753 (11th Cir. 1988), in which the court relied in part on the ABA Statement in dismissing a malpractice complaint against a lawyer for failure to disclose his alleged knowledge of a company's financial difficulties to its auditors when the lawyer and his firm were not retained with respect to the company's financial problems and the company did not identify its financial problems in the auditors' inquiry letters or request the firm to comment on them.

In June 2008, the Financial Accounting Standards Board proposed a replacement for FASB Statement No. 5 that would enlarge the disclosure requirements with respect to loss contingencies. It would require disclosure of an unasserted claim and prediction concerning the outcome if the assertion of the claim was not remote, as opposed to not "probable" under the present standard, and even if the likelihood of assertion was remote, disclosure would be required if the contingency "could have a severe impact on the entity's financial position, cash flows, or results of operations." This proposal was, not unexpectedly, quite controversial, but it has not been adopted.

The last quarter of the twentieth century did not see a showdown between the profession and the SEC because, with a change in the composition of the SEC in the 1980s, the SEC backed away from treating the lawyer in some circumstances as an "auditor," a position towards which it seemed to be edging in the 1970s. That does not mean, however, that lawyers on the firing line need not be concerned about the issue or that students of professional responsibility should conclude that the problem of the appropriate obligation to be imposed on lawyers has been resolved. For one thing, a change in emphasis that comes from a change in political administration may change once again with a new political administration. For another, a view of lawyer obligation so powerfully focused on protection of the consumer public, once loosened, is not likely to be suppressed so easily. Also, there are other agencies besides the SEC, with power to affect, if not to control, the conduct of lawyers.

The legal profession has also been made increasingly aware, from within, of lawyers' exposure to liability by reason of their clients' exposure. There has been a large increase in litigation against lawyers. That litigation has resulted not only in judgments against lawyers but also in settlements entered into by insurance companies fearful of new opinions finding liability that would only highlight the new vulnerability of lawyers. The consequence has been an enormous increase in the cost of malpractice insurance, especially for lawyers practicing in the securities field. A result of that increase has been the growing decision of many lawyers to "go bare," that is, to practice without the protection of any malpractice insurance. The consequences of those decisions, both for lawyers and for parties injured by the misconduct of lawyers, are bound to be quite serious.

It was the actions of the SEC that focused attention on the corporate lawyer's role in the 1970s and early 1980s. But the SEC did not pursue its agenda, and debate over the lawyer's role quieted. The savings and loan crisis of the late 1980s and early 1990s produced another spate of examination of the role of lawyers. The Office of Thrift Supervision, successor to the Federal Home Loan Bank Board as regulator of savings and loan institutions, took a stern attitude toward lawyers who, in its view, had failed in their ethical duty to their clients and to the public. The most notable litigation arose out of the spectacular demise of the Lincoln Savings Bank, due to the activities of its president, Charles Keating. Representation of the bank proved very costly to two major law firms, as the following materials demonstrate. It also rekindled the debate about the responsibilities of law firms representing companies whose activities raise suspicion about their compliance with the law.

William H. Simon
The Kaye Scholer Affair: The Lawyer's Duty of Candor and the Bar's Temptations of Evasion and Apology
23 Law and Social Inquiry 243 (No. 2 Spring 1998)

For three years, lawyers from the New York firm of Kaye, Scholer, Fierman, Hays, & Handler devoted themselves to keeping the government off the back of Charles Keating while he engaged in financial and political exploits that eventuated in criminal convictions for Keating and several of his associates, billions of dollars in civil liability for Keating and a larger group of associates, formal criticism by the United States Senate of five of its members, and a loss to the federal banking insurance system estimated at $3.4 billion.

Of course, this fact alone is no discredit to the lawyers. The legality of Keating's conduct was then—and in some aspects remains today—a matter of dispute. (Both [of] Keating's own criminal convictions have been reversed, though billions of dollars in civil judgments against him and various civil and criminal judgments against his associates still stand.) Moreover, as the bar often reminds us, "unpopular" people are entitled to representation too, even people who are unpopular because they are crooks.

But this case took an unusual turn. Succeeding Keating to ownership of the defunct Lincoln Savings & Loan, the banking agencies found themselves with access to records of confidential communications between the Keating crowd and the Kaye Scholer lawyers and, from this intimate vantage point, concluded that some of the lawyers' conduct went beyond the legitimate bounds of representation. The Office of Thrift Supervision (OTS) charged the lawyers with misconduct in a case the firm settled for $41 million and injunctive relief.

Although widely publicized, these charges against the best-known lawyers for the most notorious figure in the largest financial scandal in American history have received little direct discussion within the profession. Not that the bar doesn't have a lot to say about Kaye Scholer. Lawyers like to talk about the "freeze" of the firm's assets that OTS, on questionable grounds, mandated. They like to talk about how the agency's authority to regulate lawyers relates to that of the bar and the courts. They like to talk about what the case has done to insurance rates. But they don't particularly care to talk about what OTS alleged Kaye Scholer did and whether such conduct is wrong.

Unpleasant as some may find the prospect, there are good reasons to consider the charges against Kaye Scholer in detail. First, the effort can help clarify the issues. OTS's charges were widely portrayed as radical and, in particular, as challenging traditional notions of confidentiality. In fact, as I show in part I, though the charges were occasionally ambiguous and innovative, most rested in substantial part on the notion that a lawyer who cannot do anything for a client that would not further his frauds should withdraw. This proposition is in no way radical, but the Kaye Scholer debate has left great confusion as to whether the mainstream bar rejects it as a matter of principle, disputes its applicability to the particulars of the Kaye Scholer matter, or simply emotionally resists its enforcement against prominent lawyers.

Second, the bar's performance in the Kaye Scholer affair should be counted as a large mark against it in the current debate over the appropriate allocation of regulatory responsibilities between public authorities and professional institutions. Kaye Scholer indicates limitations on the profession's willingness and ability to set and enforce plausible standards of practice. Its instincts throughout the affair appear to have been self-protective rather than self-regulatory. Part II shows that a broad range of professional leaders and institutions failed to seriously confront the issues raised by the OTS complaint, instead producing a panoply of evasions.

Third, the case raised important issues about the participation of lawyers in the kinds of events that turn out to be major scandals. Professional responsibility discussions most often focus on discrete episodes of lawyer behavior in relatively clearly and narrowly defined practice contexts. Issues that arise from lawyer involvement in financial and political scandals typically involve longer courses of conduct in broader and more ambiguous contexts. In such situations, disputes can arise both about the proper characterization of relevant norms and conduct and about allocations of responsibility to individual lawyers for outcomes that result from complex interactions of many people. Kaye Scholer's partisans deserve credit for raising a variety of issues of this sort that are rarely discussed, but ... their arguments have been often unpersuasive.

A major obstacle to appraising Kaye Scholer's conduct that may have inhibited discussion, especially by those inclined to be sympathetic to the charges, is that we have limited knowledge of the facts. Thus, one risks both doing an injustice to Kaye Scholer and looking foolish in the event one's inferences prove mistaken. Nevertheless, the issues are too important to pass over. The stakes in the immediate case are large; the charges are representative of those found in several S&L failures, and the alleged conduct is emblematic for many of a morally disturbing style of professional conduct.

Moreover, it's not unusual in our system for important points to be established on the basis of pleadings, and most of the arguments defending Kaye Scholer have challenged the facial validity of OTS's charges rather than disputed the facts. Thus, throughout most of the article I focus simply on the OTS allegations and their prima facie validity.

Kaye Scholer does, however, dispute many of OTS's factual allegations, and in an appendix [not reproduced here], I report and briefly appraise the firm's claims. Kaye Scholer's response asserts important mitigating facts, identifies key ambiguities in the charges, and denies many of the particulars of the charges. It seems impossible to reach definite conclusions about the ultimate merits on this mooted record, but the firm's response, even if assumed to be factually accurate, leaves standing at least some of the concerns raised by the charges.

I. OTS'S DUTY-OF-CANDOR CHARGES AGAINST KAYE SCHOLER

A. Some Background

Lincoln Savings & Loan was a California-chartered bank wholly owned by American Continental Corporation (ACC), a holding company headquartered in Phoenix controlled by Charles Keating. The charges against Kaye Scholer arose from its representation of Lincoln and ACC between 1986 and 1989 in connection with examinations by the Federal Home Loan Bank Board, the predecessor of OTS. This work was supervised by two Kaye Scholer partners—Peter Fishbein and Karen Katzman—who were members of the firm's litigation department and had no prior experience with banking law.

The Bank Board administered a pervasive regulatory scheme designed to protect depositors and the Federal Savings and Loan Insurance Corporation (FSLIC), which guaranteed nearly all savings-and-loan (S&L) deposits. The banking field has long been subject to intense regulation. The Bank Board, moreover, had the status, not only of regulator but, as FSLIC's affiliate, of guarantor of most of the banks' debts. The banking laws thus gave the agency almost unrestricted access to information about insured banks and imposed on the banks and their agents unusually strong duties of candor.

In 1986 when the Kaye, Scholer litigators went to work, the S&L industry was in the midst of a crisis of astonishing magnitude. Two important problems arose from the structure of the thrift industry created by the New Deal banking legislation. The first was a mismatch in the "term structure" of the thrifts' liabilities and assets. Thrifts were envisioned as community banking centers, drawing their deposits from local residents and lending to them primarily for home mortgages. A thrift's typical liabilities—savings deposits—were short term, but its typical assets—home mortgages—were long term. This meant that when rates went up, its depositors could insist on the current rates, but its borrowers continued to pay at the old rates. Thus, when the tight-money policies of the late 1970s generated large interest-rate shocks, the thrifts were thrown into turmoil. By some estimates the entire industry was insolvent by the early 1980s.

The second structural problem was the incentive structure created by federal deposit insurance. Since their money was insured, depositors were indifferent to the soundness of the banks. Shareholders had an interest in preserving their capital, but once the banks neared insolvency, this interest became limited and skewed. Since income went first to creditors, relatively high-risk/high-return projects would have the strongest appeal to shareholders, though such projects would not be in the interests of creditors or the insurance fund. In situations of insolvency the insurance fund was the real residual claimant (owner) and entitled to take control. But such situations might be difficult to identify (or acknowledge), and until then, the operators could gamble with what was effectively the public's money. If they hit the jackpot, they could pay off the depositors and make themselves rich; if they lost, the public would bear the cost. The main safeguards against such strategies were the regulatory limits on deposit interest rates, restrictions of investments to relatively safe areas, and licensing requirements that inhibited competition. These constraints were swept away by the reform legislation of 1980 and 1982.

Congress saw an industry dying from an interest-rate squeeze and competition from new financial products, such as money market funds. It responded to these problems by deregulation, lifting restrictions in order to foster competitiveness. In doing so it aggravated the incentive problem. Operators could attract deposits by raising interest rates and put them in relatively high-risk/high-return types of investments, knowing that the government bore much of the risk.

Confronting the incentive problem would have required raising insurance premia or capital requirements for relatively risky institutions, and this would have pushed many into explicit insolvency. While the costs of doing so would have been far less than the costs of not doing so turned out to be, the former costs seemed too large for the Reagan administration and the Congress, which in the early 1980s were struggling to justify tax cuts.

One consequence of the reforms was . . . [a "new breed of thrift owners"]. The worst of this new breed displayed to breathtaking extremes speculative passion, contempt for law and government, dishonesty, and brazen arrogance. Some of them got away with murder until the drop in the real estate and junk bond markets at the end of the 1980s and then succumbed. In doing so they contributed a major fraction of the $200 billion cost to the public of the S&L crisis.

B. The Allegations

The Kaye Scholer litigators were asked to represent Lincoln in its dealings with the Bank Board in June 1986, after examiners had raised what turned out to be largely valid concerns about the soundness of the bank and the propriety of some of its practices. They represented the bank until it was finally seized in 1989. Kaye Scholer immediately set an aggressive tone and asserted a degree of control that everyone agrees was unusual in the bank examination process. It wrote the Bank Board insisting that all requests for information be funneled through its lawyers. The firm billed Lincoln $13 million for work done between 1985 and 1989.

Here are the principal specific instances of misconduct toward the Bank Board alleged in OTS's Notice of Charges.

1. *The "Grandfathered" Loans.* Kaye Scholer made misleading representations regarding whether certain otherwise-prohibited Lincoln investments were allowed under a "grandfathering" exception. Whether the investments were grandfathered depended on whether Lincoln had made "definitive plans" for them by a cutoff date. Many documents Lincoln used to support its grandfathering claim had been prepared after the cutoff date in a manner designed to give the impression that they were contemporaneous records of a pre-cutoff decision. They were backdated and written in the present tense. Unauthorized signatures were appended to some documents, and some falsely recited that other documents had been presented to the Board prior to the cutoff date.

Beside its general participation in the examination, Kaye Scholer associated itself with Lincoln's fraud in two specific ways. First, it gave Lincoln an opinion, which it knew Lincoln intended to use to shore up its position with the Bank Board, that various investments met the "definite plans" requirement of the grandfathering exception. The opinion recited as grounds for its conclusion that the "Board of Directors had directed" that the investments be made prior to the relevant date. In fact, the documentation of Board action provided to the examiners consisted of the written consents that were prepared after the grandfathering date but backdated to before it. Second, the lawyers transmitted the misleading documents to the Bank Board and asserted repeatedly that they supported Lincoln's position, again without disclosing the circumstances of their preparation.

2. *The Arthur Andersen Resignation.* Kaye Scholer transmitted a Lincoln SEC "8-K" filing requested by the Bank Board that reported the resignation of its accounting firm, Arthur Andersen, and stated that the resignation "was not the result of any concern by AA [Arthur Andersen] with [ACC/Lincoln's] operations . . . or asset/liability management." Although the Arthur Andersen firm approved this statement, members of the firm had expressed concerns about operations and asset/liability

management, and Kaye Scholer was aware of at least one of these statements. A few days before transmitting the form to the Bank Board, Fishbein wrote to Keating, enclosing a memorandum of a conversation with a senior Andersen partner named Joseph Kresse, which he characterized as containing "some insight into what may have motivated Andersen's decision [to resign]." The memo reports various reservations about Lincoln's operations, for example, "Lincoln looks like most of the other S&L's that have failed. . . . Andersen views Lincoln as a high risk client." Kaye Scholer did not disclose this statement in connection with its transmission of the SEC form.

3. *The "Linked" Transactions.* Keating inflated the book value of Lincoln's assets by a series of "linked" transactions. He would sell property to an ally for a price higher than Lincoln had paid for it, recording the increase as a capital gain. In fact, Lincoln or ACC sometimes had loaned the ally the money to buy the property, promised to repurchase it, or simultaneously purchased an overvalued property from the ally. The records of the sale would be separated from the records of the loan, repurchase obligation, or concurrent purchase in the hope that the regulators would not notice the "link." These practices were a major focus of the criminal charges that resulted in Keating's federal conviction, as well as various civil charges against Lincoln executives.

Kaye Scholer was aware of this activity and repeatedly expressed concern internally that the regulators would discover it, once for example referring to "Linked transactions" as "a powder keg which could explode if FHLBB analyzes them carefully."[5] The firm made general representations to the Bank Board about Lincoln's financial circumstances that were misleading without disclosure of the links. For example, they argued that the earnings figures on Lincoln's financial statements demonstrated "managerial skill" and "prudent underwriting," knowing that these figures reflected the "linked transactions."

4. *Underwriting Defects.* Kaye Scholer's study of Lincoln's records revealed a pattern of loans made without formal loan applications, with little or no analysis of collateral, with unexplained negative-credit-verification material, and without

---

5. The full passage as quoted in the Notice of Charges reads: " 'Linked transactions' remain the greatest area of concern. These are the transactions such as the recent Crown-Zellerbach deal and the past Crowder ranch deal. We know that Charlie [Keating] will continue to do these transactions to support ACC's real estate business, but these deals may be a powder keg which could explode if the FHLBB analyzes them carefully. The number of such transactions appears to have increased dramatically since the completion of the last exam."

Another excerpt, this from a memo from Kaye Scholer to ACC's General Counsel, also suggests an attitude toward impropriety preoccupied with the possibility of discovery: "Although the file itself does not document how the $10 million of the purchase price of the GOSLP stock was paid, it is possible that the linkage with the acquisition of the Garcia notes can be determined, and as discussed below, giving rise to question of the soundness of each portion individually. A further concern is that the discovery of one linked transaction may cause the investigators to uncover other linked transactions."

appraisals or cash-flow histories. In an internal memo, a firm lawyer characterized one set of loan files as running "the spectrum from disaster to non-existent." Yet in defending the firm's underwriting to the Bank Board, the firm made statements such as the following: "In making real estate loans, Lincoln has always undertaken very careful and thorough procedures to analyze the collateral and the borrower. What is unusual about Lincoln's underwriting is its particular emphasis on, and the thoroughness of, its underwriting of the collateral."

Similarly, Kaye Scholer lawyers had privately concluded that Lincoln's junk bond underwriting was "very weak, and there is little or no evidence in the files of proper underwriting." Yet they made representations to the Board to the effect that there was "no basis for the . . . conclusion that Lincoln's high yield bond underwriting is inadequate." The lawyers used as examples two junk bond investments that they had selected privately "to show Lincoln's underwriting in its best possible light" but represented to the Board that "a similar process is undertaken for all of Lincoln's investments."

5. *The Doctored Loan Files.* Kaye Scholer knew but failed to disclose that Lincoln had altered loan documentation files produced for the examiners. Information that reflected negatively on loans had been removed. Information supporting the loans had been added subsequent to the decisions to make them. Much of this information had not been obtained from borrowers or verified in accordance with customary underwriting practices but had been pulled from the borrowers' advertising and the public media. "Repayment analyses" coinciding with the payment obligations of the loan were invented without analysis and verification of the borrowers' actual circumstances. Underwriting summaries prepared after the decisions were written in the present tense, as if they were contemporaneous with the loan decision, and placed, undated, in the files.

Kaye Scholer transmitted some of the misleading documents to the Board and made numerous representations defending Lincoln's underwriting without disclosing these facts (though the Notice of Charges concedes that the principal written responses to the 1986 examination report did acknowledge briefly that some material had been added to some files subsequent to the loans).

6. *Rancho Vistoso.* Kaye Scholer made misleading representations about a large land development transaction that Lincoln had classified as a loan in an effort to comply with limits on equity investments. In fact, Kaye Scholer knew facts suggesting that the classification was improper, and many people within Lincoln had expressed doubts about it.

Arthur Andersen and its successor, Arthur Young, had signed off on the classification, but Kaye Scholer knew that they did so in ignorance of the facts, first, that Lincoln controlled the project, and second, that the putative borrower was dependent on further uncollateralized loans and "sham land 'purchases'" by Lincoln in order to make the payments. Without noting either these facts or the accountants' lack of awareness of them, Kaye Scholer repeatedly asserted that the opinions of the accountants, whom they described as having "carefully reviewed" and "closely scrutinized" the transactions, established the validity of the classifications.

7. *Hotel Ponchartrain.* Kaye Scholer made misrepresentation about a $20 million line of credit granted by a Lincoln subsidiary to a limited partnership formed by Keating and other ACC insiders to hold the Hotel Ponchartrain. The loan was an illegal "affiliated transaction." It was made without collateral to an entity experiencing serious operating losses at a below-market interest rate. A Kaye Scholer internal memo reported these facts and noted that the "[f]ile lacks virtually all required materials" and the "loan has serious problems concerning (a) safety and soundness and (b) affiliate transactions."

Kaye Scholer securities lawyers prepared SEC filings, which by law had to be filed with the Board as well, from which several specific facts reflecting on the quality and legality of the loan were misleadingly omitted. These facts included the liberal terms of the loan, which the internal memo had suggested might make it a "gift of assets," and the severe operating losses and negative net worth of the borrower.

When the California Department of Savings and Loan questioned Lincoln's disclosure, Kaye Scholer wrote a letter insisting that it was adequate and specifically referring to a letter from Lincoln that asserted that the borrower was running an operating profit, when in a nearly contemporaneous in-house memo one of its lawyers noted that "although an 'operating profit' of $60,037 was achieved, this failed to account for $2,192,760 of expenses for interest, property taxes, depreciation, management fees and other expenses.... It seems disingenuous to fail to deduct [these expenses] when the relevant figures are so easily obtainable."

C. Standards

The OTS charges have been portrayed as based on novel, even radical, conceptions of professional responsibility. While some of the agency's contentions did depend on innovative legal propositions, many did not. Most of the conduct OTS alleged seems wrongful in terms of familiar, mainstream notions of deceit that legal ethics rules, and in turn the Bank Board's regulations, incorporated.[6]

---

6. OTS invoked two sets of banking norms. First, its regulations prescribe that "any person practicing before it" refrain from, inter alia, "unethical or improper professional conduct" or from aiding and abetting violations of the banking laws. 12 C.F.R. 513.4(a)(3) (1986). OTS interpreted this regulation to incorporate the state professional responsibility codes. See ABA Working Group 1993, 144 (quoting OTS General Counsel Harris Weinstein). It remains ambiguous whether this means the requirements of a particular state (say, of the licensing state) or a "federal common law" consisting of norms that have been generally adopted or are considered relatively sound by the regulators. This issue, however, does not seem important in Kaye Scholer, since the relevant provisions are substantially the same in all the potentially relevant jurisdictions. In particular, they prohibit fraud, misrepresentation, and assisting illegal client conduct....

Second, OTS invoked a series of disclosure, record keeping, and antifraud norms, including a conventional prohibition of statements "false or misleading with respect to a material fact," 12 C.F.R. 563.18(b) (1988) (now 563.180[b]). Two of these norms are arguably more demanding than

Claims under disclosure or misrepresentation norms typically require an element of knowledge and an element of conduct. Claims against lawyers most often fail for want of proof that the defendants understood that the statements or conduct in question were misleading. Nonclient claimants have little access to relevant evidence, most of which is shielded by confidentiality commitments. The Kaye Scholer case was extraordinary in this respect because, by virtue of Lincoln's bankruptcy, the deposit insurance system had been transformed from a party adverse to Lincoln into Lincoln's institutional successor. It thus had access to the confidential communications of its lawyers.

For the few who have read it, OTS's Notice of Charges is likely to have had a dramatic impact because of its extensive quotations from memos that the Kaye Scholer lawyers never expected outsiders to see indicating detailed knowledge of—and suggesting a complacent attitude toward—Lincoln's reckless and deceptive practices. To be sure, the evidence of the memos is not conclusive, and Kaye Scholer disputes many of OTS's allegations about the extent of its knowledge. But the Notice of Charges states an unusually powerful prima facie case on the issue of knowledge.

Turning from knowledge issues to conduct issues, we find some ambiguity about the levels and kinds of lawyer conduct that incur liability under disclosure and misrepresentation norms. We can distinguish three standards that might be applied.

At one pole, a minimal standard prohibits only explicit misrepresentation and direct assistance in explicit representation. An example of such direct assistance might be drafting a document incorporating client statements that the lawyer knows to be false. No one doubts that at least this minimal duty applied to the Kaye Scholer lawyers.

---

conventional antifraud prohibitions: (i) a prohibition of any statement that "omits to state a material fact concerning any matter within the jurisdiction of the Board," id.; (ii) a requirement that insured institutions "establish and maintain such accounting and other records as will provide an accurate and complete record of all business it transacts," 12 C.F.R. 563.17-1(c) (1988) (now 562.1).

It is undisputed that the requirements of the first set of norms—those prohibiting "unethical or improper professional conduct"—applied to Kaye Scholer. However, the sanctions for violation of this section are limited to censure, suspension, or disbarment from practice before the agency. The second set of norms are enforceable by civil penalties and injunctive relief but only against banks and "institution-affiliated parties." Amendments effective since the events involved in Kaye Scholer specify that this term includes lawyers who participate in breaches of law or fiduciary duty. 12 U.S.C. 1813(u)(4). The law applicable at the time of the Kaye Scholer events did not mention lawyers, but it did include both an "agent" of an insured institution and a person "who participated in the conduct of [its] affairs." 12 U.S.C. 1730(g) (1988). Kaye Scholer argued that it did not fit either of these definitions. With respect to the "participates in the conduct" language, it has found some support in cases interpreting similar language of the RICO statute not to apply to the work of an organization's outside accountants. . . . OTS might have sought to distinguish these cases on the basis of either the unusual degree of Kaye Scholer's involvement with Lincoln or the distinctive protective concerns of the banking laws, as opposed to RICO. Even if it lost this point, it would still have had the argument that the lawyers were "agent[s]," which seems strong.

Whatever the outcome of these arguments, Kaye Scholer was subject to the substantive professional responsibility norms of section 513. . . .

At the other pole, we have a maximal standard that would require the lawyers to themselves fulfill the client's affirmative disclosure duties, or at least resign if the client refused either to authorize them to do so or to do so itself. In the banking context, this would entail exceptionally strong duties, because banking regulations require banks not only to respond to regulatory requests for information, but to volunteer information even if it's not asked for. The Notice of Charges could be read to suggest that Lincoln's lawyers had such a duty, and this suggestion provoked a good deal of controversy. There are two arguments for applying such a maximal standard to the Kaye Scholer lawyers.

First, OTS argued that Kaye Scholer acquired its client's disclosure duties by virtue of having taken control of the examination process or having "interposed" itself between its client and the regulators. This seems plausible in principle. Indeed, participation considerably short of complete control or "interposition" should be sufficient to impute the client's duty to the lawyer. The critical factor is whether the lawyers were making the relevant compliance decision themselves on behalf of the client or were executing decisions made by officers. If the lawyers accepted or exercised decision-making responsibility for the client with respect to a particular compliance matter, they should be held to the client's duty on that matter regardless of whether they had control over other matters and regardless of whether the regulators had independent access to the client. The major problems with such claims in Kaye Scholer are factual. The lawyers denied that they took control of the examination process, or precluded access to Lincoln, or had decision-making responsibility with respect to Lincoln's noncompliance.

The second argument for the maximal standard is that as long as Lincoln was violating its duty of disclosure to the regulators, any assistance Kaye Scholer gave Lincoln in dealing with the regulators should be deemed assisting illegal activity, which lawyers are forbidden to do. This argument suggests that the lawyer assists illegal activity even when the activity is merely passive noncompliance with affirmative disclosure duties and even when the lawyer's assistance is not directly related to the noncompliance — for example, if the lawyer is facilitating full and accurate disclosure over matters different from the ones with respect to which the client is withholding information. In this view, if the lawyer finds the client engaging in any noncompliance — or at least any clear noncompliance affecting matters of substantial importance — the lawyer has to see that the client rectifies, or withdraw from any representation involving dealings with the agency. In the banking context, this means that the lawyer who comes across a piece of undisclosed material information has to press the client to disclose.

This seems extreme; it comes close to saying that insured banks must waive confidentiality vis-à-vis the regulators in order to obtain legal representation. However, the apparent extremity is partly a function of the unusually strong disclosure duties of insured banks, which are in turn a function of the government's unusually strong stake, as both regulator and insurer, in their soundness. If lawyers are rarely obliged to press their clients to volunteer information to adverse parties, that is partly because clients usually do not have duties to volunteer such information.

As a matter of policy, the maximal duty seems defensible in the banking context. However, neither before nor since the Kaye Scholer case has such a duty been proclaimed.[11] Where lawyers themselves make compliance decisions on behalf of the client, such a duty would find some support in general agency principles and in professional responsibility norms in analogous contexts, including civil discovery. However, if we credit Kaye Scholer's insistence that its role was more executory, the maximal standard would seem anomalous in this case.

In any event, none of the duty-of-candor charges depends on this standard. All of them allege either active deception by the lawyers or lawyer assistance to active deception by Lincoln. Not a single charge suggests that Lincoln should have resigned because of client wrongdoing consisting solely of the passive nondisclosure of material information to the Board.

Now consider an intermediate standard that would prohibit the lawyer from both directly and indirectly misleading conduct and from providing any services substantially related to active unlawful client conduct. The intermediate standard differs from the minimal one in prohibiting indirect as well as direct deception and assistance to client wrongdoing. It differs from the maximal standard in limiting liability to situations where the wrongdoing involves more than passive nondisclosure and the assistance bears a substantial relation to the wrongdoing.

Obviously, this standard requires difficult judgments about what conduct is indirectly misleading and about how closely related the lawyer's services have to be to the client's illegality. But these judgments are of the sort that the law makes routinely in many areas. Indeed the intermediate standard represents substantially the requirements of the tort law of deceit, which are applicable to our context both directly and by virtue of their incorporation in both the banking law and the professional responsibility codes. It approximates as well disclosure duties supported by authority under the securities acts.[15] Although applications of this intermediate standard

---

11. Note that extreme as the maximal claim may appear, it does not completely abrogate traditional confidentiality notions. The demand, if the client refuses to comply, is for the lawyer to withdraw, not disclose.

15. E.g., . . . SEC v. National Student Mktg. Corp. [457 F. Supp. 682, 712–715 (D.D.C. 1978)] (lawyers wrongfully assisted violations by closing transaction without disclosing material new information); In re Carter & Johnson ("When a lawyer with significant responsibilities in the effectuation of a company's compliance with the disclosure requirements of the federal securities law becomes aware that his client is engaged in a substantial and continuing failure to satisfy those disclosure requirements, his continued participation violates professional standards unless he takes prompt steps to end the client's noncompliance.")

On the other hand, there is authority suggesting more limited duties (e.g., Rubin v. Schottenstein [143 F.3d 263 (1997)] [lawyer who gave opinion not in itself misleading and made vaguely misleading statements knowing of client fraud not liable]). . . .

To be sure, most securities act claims against lawyers have failed. However, the problem is most often insufficient proof of *scienter*, rather than of substantial assistance. . . .

will often be controversial, there is nothing remotely radical about its invocation in the Kaye Scholer context.

The duty-of-candor allegations of the Notice of Charges state a weak case under the minimal standard and a strong case under the maximal standard. However, it is most plausible to read the allegations as invoking something like the intermediate standard. I think the allegations make out a moderately persuasive prima facie case under the intermediate standard.[16]

Three sorts of activity can be distinguished: First, the allegations indicate that the lawyers made their own misrepresentations. Their statements about Lincoln's "definite plans" for the allegedly grandfathered investments (the "Grandfathered" Investments), Lincoln's "careful underwriting" (Underwriting Defects), the accountants' "careful review" and approval of the loan classification (Rancho Vistoso), a losing investment showing an "operating profit" (Hotel Ponchartrain), and the inflated accounting figures reflecting "managerial skill" (the "Linked Transactions") seem to have been statements the lawyers knew "to be materially misleading because of [their] failure to state additional or qualifying matter." Such statements are fraudulent misrepresentations within the meaning of ordinary tort law [Restatement of Torts 2d § 529 (1977)].

That some statements might be true in light of some interpretation the lawyers did not assert at the time would not necessarily excuse them. Substantial (though not uncontested) authority suggests that if the lawyers knew — or under some authority, were simply indifferent to the possibility — that the regulators would understand the statements in a misleading way, the statements were misrepresentations. Nor is the conclusion affected by the fact that some of Kaye Scholer's statements involved opinions as well as factual assertions. In these cases, it's the implied factual assertions, not the opinions, that constitute the misconduct. Thus, when the lawyers argue that fraudulently inflated accounting figures show "managerial skill," they imply that they have no strong reason unknown to the recipient to doubt that the figures are legitimate, and that's the misrepresentation.

As we will see, some of Kaye Scholer's defenders have treated these statements as argumentative rather than factual assertions. Argumentative assertions are characterizations of circumscribed bodies of fact or evidence available to the people to whom the assertions are addressed — for example, a closing argument at trial. Because they

---

16. See In re American Continental/Lincoln S&L Sec. Litig. [794 F. Supp. 1424, 1450–52 (D. Ariz. 1992)] which denied summary judgment to Kaye Scholer's predecessor, Jones, Day, Reavis, & Pogue, in a private damage action that included claims for common law and securities act fraud based on allegations that the lawyers "provided hands-on assistance in hiding loan file deficiencies from the regulators, . . . reviewed SEC registration statements and prospectuses [containing false statements], and lent its name to a misleading legal opinion." [Id. at 52.] See also Hazard, Koniak, and Cramton [*The Law and Ethics of Lawyering* 757 n.8 (3d ed. 1999)] (OTS's allegations against Kaye Scholer "were at least as strong as those in the case involving Jones, Day and would probably have established a prima facie case against Kaye, Scholer of professional negligence, breach of fiduciary obligations to the entity client and aiding and abetting client illegalities.")

do not imply, and even disclaim, any independent knowledge of the underlying facts, such statements are not considered misrepresentation, even when erroneous or in bad faith. The Lincoln bank examination, however, was not a formal, trial-like proceeding with a clearly defined record. OTS alleged that the Kaye Scholer lawyers had acquired extensive independent knowledge about Lincoln, and the statements quoted in the Notice of Charges seem to imply the authority of such knowledge. If the Board reasonably understood them that way, they should be treated as factual rather than argumentative assertion.

Second, allegedly, the lawyers knowingly transmitted misleading material prepared by Lincoln concerning Arthur Andersen's resignation, the grandfathered loans, underwriting, and the Hotel Ponchartrain. This conduct seems like the kind of direct assistance to client illegality forbidden by ethical and tort norms.

Third, some of Kaye Scholer's alleged activities wrongfully assisted Lincoln's frauds indirectly. This is the most controversial claim, and the one most difficult to delimit. However, it rests on the solid intuition that activities, though innocent when viewed in isolation, are culpable when the actor knows they are integral to client wrongdoing.

Take, for example, Lincoln's conduct in doctoring files to obscure underwriting failures and the relation between the parts of the "linked" transactions. Assume that the transactions involved a large number of files and a large amount of money, but that Kaye Scholer scrupulously avoided participating in the transactions or their documentation and made no representations relevant to them. Would Kaye Scholer's pervasive involvement in other aspects of the examination be acceptable (if it involved no separate wrongdoing)? Though the answer is not certain, I'd say such involvement should not be acceptable, even under the intermediate standard. The examination, after all, is an integral process. The acceptability of lawyer participation ought to be assessed with reference to the whole process, and large-scale client wrongdoing ought to preclude even indirect lawyer participation.

On the whole then, the OTS allegations of breach of duty of candor toward the Bank Board seem prima facie valid under the most strongly supported substantive standard—the intermediate one. . . .

[The remainder of this article deals with the bar's response, or lack thereof, to the issues involved in the Office of Thrift Supervision's litigation against Kaye Scholer.]

———————

A different perspective on Kaye Scholer's actions was provided in a response to Professor Simon by Professor Donald Langevoort:

> As the representation evolved, I suspect that Fishbein and the other Kaye Scholer lawyers might have come to a contemporaneous impression of Keating and his associates somewhat along the following lines: Keating was an

aggressive banker who liked to go close to the line of legality and might from time to time have crossed it. He was not particularly sensitive to conflicts of interest so far as Lincoln's money was concerned. But he was also talented, and running a largely legitimate institution whose problems were mostly caused by difficult marketplace and regulatory circumstances. Client officials had justifications and excuses for everything they were doing. Keating was being targeted aggressively by the Bank Board, not without reason, but maybe without a balanced understanding of context. Certainly many Bank Board officials suspected the worst about Keating, and already had a good deal of knowledge of where problem areas were.

Against this backdrop, how would most lawyers apply the ban against knowing assistance of client fraud? I suspect, first, that they would doubt that they *knew* much of anything for sure, and for this reason alone would be reluctant to pass adverse judgment on the client, absent clear knowledge of document tampering or affirmative misstatements. Second, they would be disinclined to characterize their client's behavior as pervasively fraudulent (even if it is hardly a model of cooperation) given the technical comfort they were getting from the accountants, the extent of the government's knowledge and suspicions, and the way fraud is restrictively understood in adversary settings. Even if the lawyers were aware that the client was not being entirely forthcoming with respect to occasional files or documentation, they might perceive such actions as either aberrant or immaterial, maybe even justifiable given the circumstances (especially if information was added rather than removed). If so, they would probably continue an aggressive representation without serious ethical guilt. . . .

Langevoort, "What Was Kaye Scholer Thinking?," 23 J. Am. Bar Fdn. 297 (1998). That same issue contains several other commentaries on Professor Simon's article.

Notes

1. The "interposition" between client and regulators that Professor Simon and the OTS refer to was contained in a letter from Kaye Scholer to the Federal Home Loan Bank Board. It stated, in part, "During the extended course of this examination, Lincoln has been increasingly disturbed at the extraordinary burden in officer and employee time and expense that has been imposed on the Association. . . . In these circumstances, Lincoln has asked this firm to coordinate examination requests so as to make the process as efficient as possible and limit the burden on its officers and employees. Therefore, would you please have any Bank employee engaged in the examination who desires any documents or information from Lincoln contact Ms. Karen Katzman of our office with the request. . . . She will arrange for an appropriate response. We fully intend to cooperate with legitimate examination requests in a way that will not unduly burden the Association or detract from its ability to operate its regular business."

2. A large part of the law firm's "defense" consisted of a claim that the Federal Home Loan Bank Board's examination had proceeded to a stage that was adversarial and that the bank's lawyers were required to proceed on behalf of their client as if they were engaged in litigation. Any duties that might have been imposed on them by involvement in the regulatory process were therefore superseded. A large problem with that argument is that the Board's examination proceeded year by year. Even if, say, the 1986 examination had reached an adversarial stage when the 1987 or 1988 examination began, the Bank had regulatory duties that had to be complied with. But it was required to disclose in 1987 and 1988 information about transactions that were the subject of controversy in the still pending 1986 examination. How does the law firm square its claim about an adversary stance in the earlier year with its obligations to give regulatory advice with respect to the new year's examination?

3. Which of the standards of misrepresentation and disclosure set forth by Professor Simon has been adopted in the Model Rules? See Rules 1.2(d), 3.3(a), 4.1, and 8.4(c) and the Comments thereto.

4. An even more radical argument might be that corporations, as "artificial persons," are entitled to neither the attorney-client privilege nor the duty of confidentiality. The philosopher David Luban, for example, argues that neither of the most persuasive arguments for confidentiality apply in the corporate context. See David Luban, *Lawyers and Justice: An Ethical Study* 228–233 (1988). Corporations, he argues, have no legal or moral claim to the kind of dignitary interests that underlie the privilege against self-incrimination and other similar protections that prevent individuals from being put to the choice of either lying or becoming active instruments in their own self-destruction. Individual corporate officers and employees, of course, do have dignitary rights, but as we saw in Chapter 3, the corporation's attorney represents the "entity" and not (at least without express consent) the corporation's employees. Nor is the standard utilitarian claim that confidentiality is necessary to ensure frank discussions between attorney and client valid because, unlike individuals, corporations already have extensive disclosure requirements and, as we have said, the interests of individual corporate employees are not served by the corporate privilege because the corporation can always decide to disclose whatever employees tell to corporate counsel if it is in the entity's best interest.

A recent resurrection of an alternative to traditional "shareholder" theories of corporate ownership arguably points to a similar conclusion. Professors Margaret Blair and Lynn Stout argue "that a public corporation is best understood as a nexus of team-specific assets invested by shareholders, managers, employees, and others who hope to profit from team production." 24 Iowa J. Corp. L. 743, 746 (1999). In this model, "control over the entity rests not with the shareholders, but with a board of directors that serves as a trustee for the firm as a whole." Id. "Stakeholder theory"— the argument that corporations owe a duty to all those who have a "stake" in the corporation—is a longstanding argument in the business literature that has typically been employed to justify corporate social responsibility. See William M. Evans & R. Edward Freeman, "A Stakeholder Theory of the Modern Corporation: Kantian Capitalism," in *Ethical Theory in Business* 100 (Beauchamp & Bowie eds., 3d ed. 1988). To the extent that the board of directors owes obligations to managers, employees, and perhaps even suppliers and consumers, the argument that board members, or derivatively their lawyers, should be authorized to conceal information that might harm the interests of these various constituencies is considerably weakened. For an argument applying the "team production model" to argue for greater monitoring and disclosure duties by in-house lawyers, see Peter C. Kostant, "Breeding Better Watchdogs: Multidisciplinary Partnerships in Corporate Legal Practice," 84 Minn. L. Rev. 1213 (2000). What do you think of these approaches to the lawyer's duty of confidentiality to the corporate client? Are "dignitary interests" the basis of confidentiality? The only basis? Should protection of "stakeholder" interests be viewed as the key to understanding the obligations of corporate managers?

5. Both Professors Simon and Langevoort assume that Kaye Scholer should be judged by the same rules that would apply to lawyers in other areas of practice. This is not surprising, given that any indication that the OTS was applying new or different rules to the firm's actions raises obvious issues of notice, fairness, and authority. Moreover, as we have seen, the claim that lawyers are governed by a single, unitary code of conduct is one of the profession's most important normative ideals. Both sides in the Kaye Scholer case have an interest in invoking this traditional vision. For the government, the image of a unitary legal community supports the claim that lawyers, as "learned professionals," have a unique responsibility to place principle before profit. At the same time, firms being investigated by the OTS utilize the image of a unitary profession to rally lawyers from diverse professional backgrounds to their defense by invoking the profession's long-standing opposition to government control.

The actual arguments advanced by both the government and Kaye Scholer, however, frequently rest on claims about the significance of specific aspects of the context in which Kaye Scholer represented Lincoln. Thus, as we saw in Note 2, Kaye Scholer stressed that it was Lincoln's "litigation counsel" and therefore not covered by the restrictions that might apply to "regulatory counsel." Similarly the OTS relies heavily on Lincoln's status as a federally insured depository institution to justify the disclosure obligations that it claims the firm was under. Critics of the government's decision to "freeze" Kaye Scholer's assets also frequently ground their objections in contextual terms by arguing that such draconian measures, even if authorized by the banking laws, are not appropriate for a law firm of Kaye Scholer's size and stature.

Should the rules of professional conduct formally incorporate distinctions such as these? One of the biggest complaints about the Model Code was that it did not distinguish between "litigation" and "counseling" in defining a lawyer's ethical duties. The Model Rules specifically move in this direction, but do they go far enough? If you favor drawing a sharper distinction between these two tasks, how should the rules define the border between the two fields of lawyer activity? Is the threat of litigation enough to move the lawyer from the "counseling" to the "litigation" side of the ledger? Similarly, should the rules make distinctions based on the substantive area in which a lawyer is practicing? Recall the *Carter and Johnson* case. Should lawyers who represent clients in regulated industries be subject to different ethical rules from those governing lawyers who represent clients in other contexts? If so, which regulated areas would you include: securities? banking? tax? social security or welfare? Finally, should either the rules or enforcement officials pay any attention to the size or the stature of lawyers or firms that might be subject to professional discipline or other sanctions? If so, should high status lawyers be given more or less deference under the rules or by enforcement officials? You should reconsider these issues after you have read the materials in Chapter 12. For an argument about the importance of context to the Kaye Scholer case, see David B. Wilkins, "Making Context Count: Regulating Lawyers After Kaye Scholer," 66 S. Cal. L. Rev. 1145 (1993).

6. The Departmental Disciplinary Committee of the First Judicial Department of the Appellate Division filed a complaint against Mr. Fishbein and conducted an investigation limited to three specific areas set forth in the OTS charges against Mr. Fishbein. In a brief written disposition, it found "no basis for taking any disciplinary action" and the complaint was therefore dismissed. What conclusion about the lawyers' performance should one draw from the combined action of the federal government and the New York disciplinary system?

7. A decade later, an arguably larger scandal rocked the legal world—Enron. See generally Milton C. Regan, Jr., "Teaching Enron," 74 Fordham L. Rev. 1139 (2005). Enron's primary outside counsel, Vinson & Elkins and Kirkland & Ellis, found themselves targeted for their role in Enron's accounting fantasies. In a lengthy opinion, the federal district court concluded that the class action plaintiff had stated a cause of action against Vinson & Elkins under §10b of the Securities Exchange Act of 1934. In re Enron Corp., 235 F.Supp.2d 549 (S.D. Tex. 2002). The litigation cost Vinson & Elkins millions of dollars (not including additional payouts in related cases, such as the $30 million it agreed to pay to settle claims in Enron's bankruptcy proceedings). The Enron collapse was part of the background for adoption of the Sarbanes–Oxley Act of 2002, 15 U.S.C. §7245, and the ABA's amendment of both Model Rules 1.13 and 1.6.

8. Read that part of the SOX regulation relating to attorney conduct, 17 C.F.R. Part 205, 68 Fed. Reg. 6296, and consider whether and how it applies to Problem 5–3.

9. While the new version of Model Rule 1.13 is similar to the SEC's rules of practice, it differs in important respects. For example, Model Rule 1.13(b) requires a lawyer to go up the ladder when he or she "knows" of a violation of a legal duty "reasonably likely" to result in substantial corporate injury, whereas Rule 205 is triggered by "credible evidence, based upon which it would be unreasonable . . . for a prudent attorney not to conclude that it is reasonably likely that a material violation has occurred, is ongoing, or is about to occur." 17 C.F.R. §205.2(e). Which standard do you feel is more manageable (or even comprehensible) for an attorney?

Which is better designed to combat corporate misconduct? How would you improve either, if at all?

10. Will business executives and accountants continue to confide in the corporation's attorneys once they realize that the attorneys must report the matter up the chain of command? This question is by no means limited to the business context; in fact, it forms the primary, but somewhat untested, justification for attorney-client privilege and the confidentiality obligation of lawyers.

———

It has been said that, with heightened regulation, in-house counsel for public corporations are in a dangerous business. While that sentiment may be an overstatement, consider the fate of the following in-house counsel.

The SEC brought a civil case against John Isselmann, Jr., for his actions as general counsel of Electro Scientific Industries. Importantly, the SEC did *not* claim that Isselmann took part in fraud—or even knew about it. In order to boost the corporation's quarterly income statement, top executives cut employee benefits and improperly accounted for the resulting savings. The executives did not tell Isselmann that they had, in fact, made the cut; they merely asked him to get an opinion from an outside law firm discussing whether the decision would be permissible. Outside counsel advised Isselmann that the corporation could not legally terminate the benefits. Isselmann tried to raise the objection at the corporation's disclosure meeting, but the CFO would not let Isselmann speak. The corporation then filed its disclosure statement with the improper accounting. When Isselmann found out, he promptly told the corporation's audit committee. The SEC was not content. It insisted that Isselmann should not have failed to provide the material facts to the corporation's accountants. Isselmann eventually settled the suit for $50,000 and the issuance of a cease-and-desist order against him. In re John Isselmann, Jr., Admin. Proc. File No. 3-11678 (2004).

You would have stood up to your CFO, right? Perhaps lawyers will now do so, knowing that individual liability awaits them. (The preceding case also is one of the many examples of the difficulties inherent in the fact that the client is the non-existent corporation—not the living, breathing "boss" with whom you interact. See Model Rule 1.13(a).) The following example presents the issue on a much larger scale.

Enron's auditors, Arthur Andersen, obviously had a large hand in Enron's accounting treatment. In fact, Arthur Andersen had "truckloads" of documents relating to the transactions and their accounting treatment. Realizing that Enron (and perhaps Andersen itself) was on the verge of a large SEC investigation, one of Andersen's in-house counsel, Nancy Temple, among others, sent e-mails and prompted training sessions to encourage employees to follow Andersen's "document retention policy." See Arthur Andersen LLP v. United States, 544 U.S. 696 (2005). The "encouragement" resulted in the destruction of a large number of documents. The conduct resulted in Andersen's criminal obstruction of justice indictment in federal court. The jury convicted Andersen and the Court of Appeals affirmed. The Supreme Court ultimately reversed, however, on the ground that the jury instructions (among other flaws) did not convey the proper mens rea for the crime (i.e., that an Andersen employee "'*knowingly* . . . corruptly persuad[ed]' another" to destroy documents to be used in an official proceeding). Id. By the time of reversal, however, Arthur Andersen had been dismantled; the conviction resulted in a market death sentence that could not be reversed.

For present purposes, what is even more remarkable about the Arthur Andersen saga is the apparent basis of its conviction. Andersen's in-house counsel, Nancy Temple, played a central role. According to reports from some jurors, however, it was not Temple's insistence on following the document retention policy that caused the jury to convict Andersen of obstruction of justice. It was another matter entirely.

When Enron could no longer hide its huge losses, it disclosed a $1.01 billion charge to earnings. Enron erroneously characterized the charge as "non-recurring," meaning that the earnings would not be charged again as a result of Enron's behavior. Before Enron released its statement, Andersen told Enron that it was inaccurate to characterize the debt as non-recurring, but Enron did not change the release. Andersen's advice was contemporaneously recorded in an internal memorandum "suggest[ing]" that Andersen had "concluded that the release is misleading." Nancy Temple advised the author of the memorandum to edit it because she was uncomfortable with that conclusion from a liability standpoint, and the document was revised. The jury reportedly convicted Andersen not for the vast document shredding but for Temple's advice to edit the memorandum. Stephen Gillers, "The Flaw in the Andersen Verdict," New York Times, June 18, 2002.

Lawyers edit client documents all the time and often instruct that outdated drafts be discarded. What is the appropriate standard for deciding whether Temple's advice was improper? See Jonathan Weil et al., "Shredding Wasn't a Factor in Verdict, Jurors Say; A Single E-Mail Was," Wall Street Journal, June 17, 2002. As you can see, in-house and outside counsel indeed may face heightened scrutiny of advice given to clients in these changing times. Is that a change for the better? For lawyers? For the public?

Is there any room left for attorney-client confidentiality in this field? After the fact (whatever that problematic fact may be), the corporation may have to waive its attorney-client privilege in order to avoid the government's wrath. The DOJ (through the "Thompson" and "McNulty" Memoranda), the SEC, and the United States Sentencing Guidelines have often conditioned favorable treatment on waiver. E.g., U.S. Sentencing Guidelines Manual § 8C2.5, Application Note 12 (requiring waiver for cooperation credit in certain corporate sentencings; now withdrawn). It is a tough position, indeed, because some courts have held that turning the information over to the government to assist its investigation may also waive the privilege with respect to private plaintiffs who later want the information. E.g., In re Qwest Communications Int'l Inc., 450 F.3d 1179 (10th Cir. 2006) (rejecting controversial "selective waiver" doctrine). These issues are the subject of much controversy and many proposals for change have been made. In the face of considerable criticism from the segments of the bar and from members of Congress, the Bush Administration retreated. In the "Filip Memorandum," the Justice Department in 2008 issued a new set of guidelines for federal lawyers operating under its jurisdiction. The guidelines, among other things, provide that in assessing whether corporations have "cooperated" with criminal investigations, cooperation will be measured by disclosure of relevant facts and not by waiver of the attorney-client or work product protection. Among other things, disclosure of relevant facts may well be interpreted as including items that would otherwise be protected confidential information. A second Justice Department policy relating to attorney-client relationships was tested in court. The Department had secured indictments against the accounting firm KPMG and thirteen of its employees. In attempting to avoid prosecution, KPMG, under government pressure, terminated its practice of advancing attorneys fees and other defense costs to the indicted employees. The district court viewed that pressure as interfering with the individual defendants' constitutional right to assistance of counsel and dismissed the indictments. The Court of Appeals for the Second Circuit affirmed. United States v. Stein, 541 F.3d 130 (2008). Then in 2015, the Justice Department acted again, with yet another memorandum, the Yates Memorandum, providing further guidance for federal prosecutors. The most important revision provides that "To be eligible for any cooperation credit, corporations must provide to the Department all relevant facts about the individuals involved in corporate misconduct." Department of Justice: Sally Quillian Yates, Memorandum Re Individual Accountability for Corporate Wrongdoing. September 9, 2015, available at <http://www.justice.gov/dag/file/769036/download>. With the change in administration, further action by the Justice Department is expected.

Scandals such as Enron and Kaye Scholer have caused many in the legal academy to rethink how the lawyer-client relationship between companies and their lawyers (both in-house counsel and outside firms) should be conceptualized. The following two excerpts present two attempts to characterize these important relationships in light of recent changes in the market and regulatory conditions faced by both clients and lawyers.

John C. Coffee, Jr.
Gatekeepers: The Professions and Corporate Governance (2006)
pp. 192–195, 198

Law is an old profession, but the idea of the attorney as a gatekeeper for parties other than the attorney's direct client is far more recent. Indeed, the concept has never truly been accepted by the organized bar, which prefers to view the attorney as an advocate, whose sole duty is the zealous representation of the client. Few attorneys probably consider themselves gatekeepers. Still, presenting the attorney as primarily an advocate profoundly misrepresents the functional activity of the corporate lawyer.

The corporate lawyer functions in a very different capacity from the advocate in at least two important respects. First, the corporate lawyer acts principally as a transaction engineer. Corporate lawyers . . . rarely appear in court and have little direct contact with litigation. Essentially, their real work is the planning, structuring and negotiating of transactions for their largely corporate and institutional clientele. Second, the special skill of the corporate lawyer has been drafting and disclosure, including the special verification skills—known as "due diligence" work with the profession—that accompany the preparation of disclosure documents. . . . [O]ver time, the process of preparing disclosure documents for public offerings evolved into an often elaborate "due diligence" investigation, jointly conducted by counsel for the issuer and counsel for the underwriters. Characteristically, both counsel approached this task not as "zealous advocates," but as careful factfinders, seeking to reduce the risk of liability by verifying the essential facts. From this starting point, investors too came to rely on the corporation's outside counsel to assure full disclosure. But while investors may have expectations, they have few, if any, rights against the attorneys for the corporation.

The differences between the corporate lawyer and the litigator all suggest that the corporate lawyer is well positioned to serve as a gatekeeper. As transaction engineers, corporate lawyers have a skill set focused on negotiation, drafting, business planning, and the ability to maintain a comprehensive, almost encyclopedic, understanding of extremely complex and integrated business transactions. . . . In truth, the world of the corporate lawyer probably more closely borders on that of the accountant than that of the litigator/advocate. For example, in practice, corporate lawyers are likely to be far more familiar with "generally accepted accounting principles" than with the Federal Rules of Civil Procedure . . . .

. . . Not only do litigators inhabit a more adversarial environment, but they generally are consulted by their clients on an ex post basis after trouble has arisen. In contrast, corporate lawyers tend to advise on an ex ante basis and accordingly envision themselves as "wise counselors," who gently guide their clients toward law compliance by pointing out the risks of alternative courses of action. . . .

This picture is changing, [however], and it is increasingly debatable whether the corporate lawyer can either monitor the corporate client to the same extent as in the past or gently dissuade it from illegal or reckless action. . . .

. . . The key actor in this process is the in-house general counsel, who has every incentive to break down the traditional one-to-one relationships between his client and its primary outside counsel. From our perspective, this relative shift in the balance of power between outside and inside counsel raises a basic question: can the in-house counsel replace the outside lawyer/statesman as a gatekeeper? Here, it is difficult to be optimistic. While the outside attorney has been increasingly relegated to a specialist's role and is seldom sought for statesman-like advice, the in-house general counsel seems even less suited to play a gatekeeping role. First, the in-house counsel is less an independent professional — indeed he is far more exposed to pressure and reprisals than even the outside audit partner. Second, the in-house counsel is seldom a reputational intermediary . . . because the in-house counsel cannot easily develop reputational capital that is personal and independent from the corporate client. . . .

. . . Put bluntly, the social and economic circumstances that placed [lawyers such as Louis] Brandeis in a position where he could be both professionally independent and counsel broadly "for the situation," have probably gone with the wind. . . . [But there is] a narrower . . . role that can realistically be mandated for the corporate lawyer. . . . [T]he independent lawyer could be asked to monitor the corporation's disclosures in a functionally similar fashion to the manner in which the independent auditor monitors the corporation's financial performance. . . .

[Coffee goes on to propose that the SEC require that all disclosure documents be certified by an independent "disclosure counsel" who would acknowledge his or her responsibility for the preparation or review of the documents. To ensure independence, "the attorney could neither be an employee of the corporation; nor could the attorney's firm receive more than some specified percentage of its revenues from the corporation whose disclosures the attorney was reviewing."]

David B. Wilkins
Team of Rivals?
Toward A New Model of the Corporate Attorney-Client Relationship
78 Fordham L. Rev. 2067 (2010)

. . . There is arguably no more quoted, or in the minds of many lawyers beloved, understanding of the duties owed by an advocate to his or her client than [Lord Henry] Brougham's legendary speech in defense of Queen Caroline. Speaking on the floor of the House of Lords in 1820, Lord Brougham eloquently stated what many still believe to be the essence of the lawyer's role:

> [A]n advocate, in the discharge of his duty, knows but one person in all the world, and that person is his client. To save that client by all means and expedients, and at all hazards and costs to other persons, and, amongst them, to himself, is his first and only duty; and in performing this duty he must not regard the alarm, the torments, the destruction which he may bring upon others. Separating the duty of a patriot from that of an advocate, he must go on reckless of the consequences, though it should be his unhappy fate to involve his country in confusion.[1]

---

1. See Monroe H. Freedman, "Henry Lord Brougham, Written by Himself," 19 Geo. J. Legal Ethics 1215 (2006) (quoting 2 The Trial of Queen Caroline 3(1821)).

For almost two centuries, these words have stood as the embodiment of the ideal of zealous advocacy that lawyers owe to their clients. But of late, there have also been many who have questioned whether such an extreme standard of partisanship—ignoring the "alarm," "torment," and "destruction" of others—is the proper standard for lawyers to take in all circumstances. Specifically, I and others have argued that whatever the value of Brougham's conception in the context in which he made his famous claim—i.e., the representation of an individual criminal defendant facing the unchecked power of the King in circumstances where the defendant's head was quite literally on the line—this understanding has much less to recommend it when we consider how corporate lawyers ought to conceive of their duties, particularly in the area of regulatory compliance.

Today, these concerns are especially salient. As the spotlight of blame shines its accusatory light on the cast of characters involved in the current economic meltdown, it is only a matter of time before the inside and outside lawyers who represented the banks and other financial institutions we are currently bailing out will be called upon to take their turn in the dock. When they do, it is unlikely enforcement officials or the public will have much sympathy for an ethic that appears to commend lawyers for these powerful clients to proceed "reckless of the consequences" even if it means casting "the country in confusion"—let alone bankruptcy. Given the current mood, there may be little the bar can do to avoid this "unhappy fate" this time around. But as we prepare to enter into a brave new world in which all corporate actors—lawyers included—will almost certainly face increased scrutiny, I want to suggest that the profession and those we purport to serve would do well to consider whether there is something more fundamentally wrong with applying Brougham's conception of the lawyer's role to the corporate context than the conflation of the standards of advocacy appropriate to the criminal context with those that should govern in civil or regulatory matters.

At the heart of Brougham's understanding of the lawyer's role stands a simple but powerful assumption: that the attorney-client relationship is essentially one of agency. Of course a lawyer "knows but one person in all the world" and is required to promote that person's interests "by all means and expedients and at all hazards and costs to other persons," even "to himself," Brougham would likely say. These are simply the duties that an agent owes to his or her principal. Lawyers are doing no more—and should be entitled to do no less—than others who are engaged by principals to protect their interests and pursue their goals.

It is this traditional idea that I intend to question here. . . .

Specifically, I will argue that for all of its intuitive appeal, the agency model is no longer a helpful template for understanding the relationship between corporations and their outside firms. Instead, expanding on ideas that I first put forward in 1998,[11]

_____

   11. See generally David B. Wilkins, "Do Clients Have Ethical Obligations to Lawyers? Some Lessons from the Diversity Wars," 11 Geo. J. Legal Ethics 855 (1998).

I will argue that the relationship between these large and sophisticated clients and their increasingly large and sophisticated counsel is better conceptualized as a new kind of strategic alliance or partnership—or, to borrow a phrase that has been used to describe the long-term strategic partnerships between Japanese automakers and their suppliers, a new kind of "legal *keiretsu*"—than as the typical agent-principal relationship envisioned by Brougham. . . .

Collectively . . . five interlocking trends—convergence of work in the hands of a limited number of "preferred" firms; consolidation of the firms themselves through merger and acquisition; greater integration and knowledge transfer between companies and firms; changes in the organizational structure of companies that promote integration and blur the boundaries between the inside and the outside; and increasing instability and contraction in general counsel offices—are spurring the creation of a new working partnership between companies and their primary outside firms. Although general counsels continue to insist that they "hire lawyers not firms," in reality their relationship with their primary firms is a good deal stickier than this standard slogan would suggest.

To be sure, this is not the old fashioned marriage that firms and clients entered into during the Golden Age. Firms that manage to make it on a company's preferred provider list can lose their privileged status for reasons of incompetence or disloyalty. Even if they perform well, most companies still put the arrangement up for periodic review and renegotiation. And firms still compete with others on the list for particular assignments, or to grow their share of the relationship.

More fundamentally, outside firms and in-house lawyers still actively compete with each other for both work and influence. Companies compete by taking their work in-house or by switching (or threatening to switch) their business to other law firms. Firms compete by selling the knowledge they gain through their representation to others and by "firing" existing clients in favor of new ones who can provide more lucrative work. . . .

Indeed, it is precisely this paradoxical element of simultaneous cooperation and competition—"co-option," to use a phrase deployed by management scholars—that defines the modern relationship between companies and firms. As a result, these relationships increasingly have come to resemble the kind of strategic alliances or partnerships that companies have entered into with other long-term suppliers in order to achieve common objectives. Like the partners in these arrangements, both corporations and law firms depend on each other to provide crucial information and expertise if the purposes of the cooperative venture—i.e., winning the case, successfully completing the deal, etc.—are to be achieved. Corporations depend upon their lawyers to supply specialized legal knowledge; to gather information; to interface with competitors, consumers and government officials; and to monitor and mediate conflicts within the organization. For their part, firms depend upon their corporate clients to supply accurate information about corporate goals and practices, to follow the firm's instructions on matters of legal compliance; and, of course, to provide the firm with the capital that it needs for its survival, including reputational capital in the form of referral to other potential clients. In return for receiving these goods, each partner demands a certain level of control over the other partner's internal affairs. As Richard Painter argues, in their roles as "monitors" and "dealmakers," outside counsel exercise substantial control over the corporation's internal affairs.[131] For the reasons set out above, corporate clients now exercise similar control over the internal affairs of outside firms. . . .

The Ethics of Alliance

. . .

To . . . create effective collaborative relationships, companies and firms will have to develop what Gomes-Casseres calls "relationship capital" by honoring their stated commitments and adhering to norms of "fairness" and "reciprocity."[235] Although the parties can achieve a good deal of what is required by contractual means, for example by moving to fixed fees, supporting the broader normative aspects of the relationship . . . will require ethical as well as contractual support. This, in turn, will require revisiting the standard principal-agent conception of the attorney-client relationship.

As indicated above, in theory the agency model gives clients near plenary control over the terms and conditions of the lawyer-client relationship. Although this helps to ensure loyalty by lawyers, it raises significant problems for developing and preserving a relationship of mutual trust—particularly one that incorporates public-regarding commitments on both sides.[236]

Consider the client's unqualified right to dismiss a lawyer for any reason. This right is a natural outgrowth of the agency model. It also hands corporate clients a potent sword to pressure lawyers into engaging in risky or unethical conduct. In the infamous Lincoln Savings and Loan debacle, for example, Charles Keating deftly used this authority to put pressure on lawyers from the law firm of Kaye, Scholer, Fierman, Hays & Handler not to question his actions regarding the management of the thrift. Thus, when the law firm initially handling the regulatory audit insisted that Lincoln disclose certain questionable transactions to regulators, Keating fired it and

---

131. See Richard Painter, "The Moral Interdependence of Corporate Lawyers and their Clients," 67 S. Cal. L. Rev. 507, 520–553 (1994).

235. See [Benjamin] Gomes-Casseres, [*The Alliance Revolution: The New Shape of Business Rivalry* (1996)] at 87.

236. Jack Coffee cites exactly this problem as the reason for dismissing legal ethics as a plausible foundation for establishing an effective gatekeeping role for corporate counsel:

> Because legal ethics at its core views the attorney as a client-serving professional who is not permitted to dominate the relationship (and because market conditions make it unlikely that lawyers could do so today), legal ethics does not hold out a practical remedy for gatekeeper failure. One must therefore look beyond legal ethics and the moral exhortations it provides to find a realistic means to empower the attorney as gatekeeper.

Coffee, *Gatekeepers* 229 (2005). The fact that the move toward strategic alliances between lawyers and firms alters the market conditions that inhibit gatekeeping implies that a move away from the client-serving agency model might actually produce real results.

brought in Kaye Scholer. The lesson was not lost on lawyers at the newly hired firm, who vowed to avoid the "situation of mutual distrust and animosity" that was caused by the prior firm's tough stance regarding Keating's questionable practices. To make matters worse, under the governing ethical rules applicable at the time the prior firm not only had no power to contest the dismissal on grounds of public policy, but was equally powerless to disclose what it almost certainly suspected to be criminal or fraudulent conduct by Lincoln — even to Kaye Scholer.

Nor was this the only way in which Keating sought to exploit his power as principal in Lincoln's relationship with its lawyer-agents. In addition to holding the sword of Damocles over Kaye Scholer's head, Keating also assiduously controlled the information that was given to any of the many firms representing the thrift. As a result, no single law firm working for the thrift — let alone any single lawyer — had a complete understanding of Lincoln's practices, thereby making it easier for Keating to hide his illegal conduct. Reports about the conduct of company officials at Enron and WorldCom suggest that Keating was far from alone in using this power to ensure that legal work is sufficiently fragmented that no one can take the long view, and "the broader interests of the corporation . . . go unrepresented." Although critics of these practices have urged lawyers to reject this kind of narrow framing,[243] as John Coffee accurately notes, such calls "exist in considerable tension with traditional legal ethics," which, consistent with the agency model, gives clients sole authority to "define the objectives of representation."[244] Consequently, as Coffee concludes, in many recent scandals the problem is not so much that lawyers were at the scene of the crime but chose to look the other way, but rather that "lawyers were nowhere near the scene of the crime, thereby enabling others to orchestrate the fraud."[245]

To move beyond this state of affairs, it is necessary to construct an account of legal ethics that helps to place lawyers in a position to detect client misconduct — and to give them the power to do try to deter what they see. Structurally, as indicated above, the new strategic alliances between companies and firms are likely to place lawyers in a better position to be at the "scene of the crime" — or better yet, the place where the crime may be averted — than the spot-contracting model manipulated by Charles Keating. But if the lawyers are to utilize their newfound knowledge, the ethical restrictions that discourage them from doing so ought to be removed. The logic of embeddedness that characterizes these cooperative relationships suggests that parties should not engage in deception, coercion, or other forms of pressure tactics designed to force the other partner into violating a legal or ethical duty. To the extent that a company

---

243. See, e.g., Robert Gordon, "A New Role for Lawyers? The Corporate Counselor after Enron," 35 Conn. L. Rev. 1185 (2003).

244. See Coffee, *Gatekeepers*, at 226 (citing Model Rules of Prof'l Conduct R. 1.2 (2003)). As Coffee goes on to say, "If the organization as client wants to use outside counsel in a narrow fashion, asking them only technical questions and structuring the relationship so that outside counsel is neither invited nor equipped to provide 'holistic' advice, the organization would seem entitled to do so." Id.

245. Coffee, *Gatekeepers*, at 231.

has breached this ethical duty to its outside firm, there would seem to be little reason to reward it for transgressing such a fundamental part of the joint relationship. Although a contrary rule surely raises difficult questions about how such an obviously strained attorney-client relationship will be managed, courts do not hesitate to compel lawyers to continue representing clients in circumstances where the *lawyer* does not want to continue because of a disagreement with the client.[247] At a minimum, the logic of these new relationships suggests that clients should pay some penalty for dismissing an attorney for failing to breach one of the lawyer's own ethical duties.

Indeed, one can see the recent changes in the confidentiality rules enacted by the American Bar Association as nodding in the direction of acknowledging the fundamental unfairness of the traditional agency model in a world in which lawyers are almost as vulnerable to client manipulation as the other way around. After steadfastly resisting the imposition of all but the most minimal gatekeeping—let alone whistleblowing—duties, the ABA amended the Model Rules in 2002 and 2003 to give lawyers significantly greater latitude to disclose client fraud. Thus, Model Rule 1.6 governing confidentiality has been changed to allow lawyers to disclose information when reasonably necessary to prevent a client from "committing a crime or fraud that is reasonably certain to result in substantial injury to the financial interests or property of another" or to "prevent, mitigate or rectify" financial injury "that is reasonably certain to result or has resulted from the client's commission of a crime or fraud." In both of these instances, however, the lawyer can only blow the whistle if the client has used the lawyer's services in furtherance of the criminal or fraudulent conduct. In other words, clients like Charles Keating who involve their lawyers unknowingly in their fraudulent schemes, or who dismiss their lawyers for failing to cooperate in further misconduct, risk empowering their former advisors to disclose the fraud in order to protect themselves from the deleterious consequences of their client's overreaching.

The amendments to Model Rule 1.13, which governs the duties of lawyers who represent "organizational" clients such as corporations, arguably go even further. Beginning in 2003, lawyers who believe that a corporate manager has, or is about to, act—or refuse to act—in a manner that constitutes "a violation of a legal obligation to the organization" or that may result in a "violation of law that reasonably might be imputed to the organization" are given three interlocking protections against being ensnared in the client's wrongdoing. First, the lawyer is required to report what he knows to "higher authority in the organization, including, if warranted . . . to the

---

247. See Bd. of Prof'l Responsibility of the Supreme Court of Tenn., Formal Ethics Op. 96-F-140 (1996) (refusing to allow a lawyer appointed to represent a minor seeking an abortion to resign because the lawyer was morally opposed to the procedure under any circumstances). Given that corporate clients are sophisticated repeat players who must operate every day in relationships that are less than ideal, the argument that the rule allowing clients to fire their lawyers for any reason is necessary to preserve the client's right to effective legal representation rings hollow in the face of cases that require individual lawyers with strong moral objections to do otherwise.

highest authority that can act on behalf of the organization as determined by applicable law." Secondly, if that authority "insists upon or fails to address in a timely and appropriate manner" conduct that the lawyer believes is "clearly a violation of law" *and* is "reasonably certain to result in substantial injury to the organization," the lawyer "may reveal" whatever information the lawyer "reasonably believes necessary to prevent substantial injury" to her organizational client. Finally, a lawyer who "reasonably believes that he or she has been discharged" or "forced to withdraw" for reporting conduct under either of the above two provisions, "shall proceed as the lawyer reasonably believes necessary to assure that the organization's highest authority is informed of the lawyer's discharge or withdrawal." Collectively, these three provisions both require that lawyers ensure that the their real client—the "organization" (at least as represented by the board)—is aware of any potential misconduct by corporate managers or employees that might harm the organization's real long-term interests, while giving them at least some leverage against retaliation by those who might be tempted to ignore the lawyer's advice or punish him or her for trying to give it.

To be sure, these reforms continue to leave the heart of the agency model in place. None of these changes, for example, alter a corporate client's fundamental right to exclude lawyers from the venues where important decisions are made or to strategically manipulate the information the lawyer receives. A complete account of the ethics of lawyer-client strategic alliances would have to define client obligations as well as lawyer rights. To begin to articulate such an account of "client ethics," however, necessarily requires moving beyond the domain of legal ethics. Whatever their other virtues, the Model Rules of Professional Conduct cannot bind non-lawyers. Although one can try to infer client duties from either the general moral commitments that all members of society share, or the special responsibilities that corporations owe to society, any system that purports to bind credibly companies to adhere to norms of trust and reciprocity with law firms that acknowledge that lawyers have public duties to the legal framework as well as private obligations to clients will inevitably require an engagement with substantive law.

Regulating Reciprocity

Even the modest progress that the profession has achieved since 2002 in moving away from a completely client-centric agency model of legal ethics toward one that gives lawyers at least some tools to protect themselves against client opportunism can be traced to the threat of state regulation. The rules permitting lawyers to disclose contemplated or completed financial frauds were proposed as part of the original text for the Model Rules of Professional Conduct in 1981, only to be repeatedly and vociferously voted down for almost twenty years. Only the public outcry over Enron and related scandals and the threat of the imposition of even more fulsome reporting requirements by Congress galvanized the bar to adopt these provisions. Indeed, the ABA's House of Delegates refused to impose mandatory "up-the-ladder" reporting requirements in Model Rule 1.13 until the beating of the wings of the Sarbanes–Oxley Act (SOX) made it painfully clear that in the absence of some amendment, the profession's entirely discretionary version of that rule would soon be rendered entirely superfluous. Even then, the bar adopted a version of Rule 1.13 that is significantly weaker than the statutory duty imposed by SOX.[255]

It is not surprising that Congress passed rules of conduct creating more stringent gatekeeping duties on lawyers than the profession was inclined to impose on itself. The bar is well aware that what I have elsewhere called "institutional controls," such as SEC enforcement, are far more likely to detect a lawyer's violation of public gatekeeping duties than the profession's own disciplinary system, and, even more importantly, to impose significant sanctions when violations are brought to the surface.... The question remains, however, whether these and other recent statutory attempts to regulate lawyer conduct can play a positive role in encouraging lawyers to take their public gatekeeping roles seriously, notwithstanding the fact that the developments described in this paper are likely to place outside counsel in long-term relationships with clients that blur the traditional boundary between law and business.

Although the evidence is both preliminary and mixed, there is at least some indication that these regulatory changes are having a positive effect on lawyer independence. Tanina Rostain, for example, reports that interviews with ten general counsels from large companies revealed a much higher commitment by respondents to assert "jurisdiction over questions of legal risk," and to embrace broad gatekeeping duties than reported in earlier studies.[258] ... Surveys of the attitudes of general counsel after the passage of the Act appear to support this conclusion, as does the fact that many companies increased their spending on outside counsel during this period.[260]

---

255. Although the trigger for up-the-ladder reporting under SOX is notoriously murky, the Act nevertheless sets an objective standard for defining the lawyer's duties in this area. See § 307 ... (mandating up-the-ladder reporting if there is "credible evidence based upon which it would be unreasonable ... for a prudent and competent attorney not to conclude that it is reasonably likely that a material violation has occurred"). Model Rule 1.13, on the other hand, still requires that the lawyer has actual knowledge of a material violation before he or she is required to report conduct to a higher authority in the organization. Model Rules of Prof'l Conduct 1.13 (2007); see also id. R. 1.0(f) (defining "knows" as "denot[ing] actual knowledge of the fact in question").

258. See Tanina Rostain, "General Counsel in the Age of Compliance, Preliminary Findings and New Research Questions," 21 Geo. J. Legal Ethics 465, 473 (2008). Rostain compares her results to the relative unwillingness by general counsels to act as "cops" found in studies conducted by Nelson and Neilsen and Robert Rosen in the 1990s and 1980s respectively. See generally Nelson & Nielsen, ["Cops, Counsel, and Entrepreneurs: Constructing the Role of Inside Counsel in Large Corporations," 34 Law & Soc'y Rev. 457 (2000)]; Robert Rosen, ["The Inside Counsel Movement, Professional Judgment and Organizational Representation," 64 Ind. L.J. 479 (1989)].

260. See Martin C. Daks, "Compliance, Not Legal Fees, Named as GC's Chief Concern," N.J. L.J., Nov. 1, 2006 (reporting that in a survey of general counsel in 169 companies, 86% listed "keeping track of company activities that might have legal implications" as their number one concern); see also [Janet] Conley, ["GC's 'Can't Get No Satisfaction' from Outside Counsel," GC S., Mar. 2006] (reporting that "GCs—buffeted by regulatory changes from the Sarbanes–Oxley Act, an increasingly risk-averse corporate environment and CEOs who want cost containment and more value from in-house departments—are turning to outside lawyers with greater frequency").

This dynamic highlights a key feature of the current approach to regulating corporate conduct. In addition to setting out mandates and penalties, contemporary regulatory schemes governing corporate conduct employ incentives to encourage companies to create internal compliance regimes that diffuse regulatory norms throughout the organization. As Rostain explains, in these new regulatory schemes "[c]orporations are expected to install controls—including ethics codes, self-audit mechanisms, compliance training, whistleblower protections, and the designation of compliance personnel—at every organizational level to minimize the risk of unlawful and unethical behavior."[261]

These regulatory regimes make it clear that responsibility for compliance will be jointly shared between lawyers, managers, and other professionals who possess relevant technical competence or expertise. The growth of the kind of strategic alliances between companies and law firms discussed above further highlights that the "lawyers" helping to establish and operate these new compliance mechanisms will come from both inside and outside the company. All of this underscores the need to develop an account of how these diverse professionals can collaborate in ways that further, rather than frustrate, the public goals underlying these new compliance systems.

John Coffee, for example, proposes that companies be required to have their annual and quarterly disclosure documents reviewed by an "independent" attorney from outside the company, who, "after reasonable inquiry," would then be required to certify that the disclosures were not materially misleading.[262] Lawyers who failed to discharge this new duty competently under Coffee's proposal could be sued under the securities laws for aiding and abetting their client's fraud.

By highlighting how regulation can be used to impose duties on clients that in turn support the public gatekeeping duties of outside counsel, Coffee's proposal is a step in the right direction. But in trying to "restor[e] the principal-agent relationship between lawyers and investors" by creating a special role for "disclosure counsel," while keeping the traditional "hired gun" model of the lawyer-agent endorsed by Lord Brougham in place for the rest of the company's counsel, Coffee risks minimizing the effectiveness of the former while exacerbating the problems of the latter. Although companies would presumably have to share information with their disclosure counsel, these same clients would have no incentive to do so with all of the other lawyers involved in the company's complex compliance machinery. Nor would the hired-gun agents have any power or incentive to protest this fate. Indeed, it is entirely possible that Coffee's proposal could drive the vast majority of lawyers not acting as disclosure counsel to give up their gatekeeping roles altogether

---

261. Rostain, supra note 258, at 480. Examples of this new regulatory approach can be found in fields as diverse as environmental protection policy to antiterrorism and employment discrimination regulation. See id., at 466–467.

262. See Coffee, *Gatekeepers*, at 349.

while at the same time encouraging the company to treat their disclosure counsel as little more than an agent of the government . . . .[265]

Moreover, as important as the goal of ensuring proper disclosure under the securities laws is to the overall functioning of our market economy, this is hardly the only place where we want lawyers act as public gatekeepers. As indicated above, the new regulatory focus on compliance has resulted in the creation of numerous gatekeeping regimes. It is difficult to see, however, how Coffee's proposal could be replicated across all of these diverse regulatory domains. Should Congress seek to create a dedicated "compliance counsel" in every instance in which the statutory scheme contemplates public gatekeeping? If so, how would these new compliance specialists interact with each other, and with lawyers not in this role who, according to Coffee, would continue to operate under Brougham's hired-gun agency model? As others have noted, there is already a burgeoning industry of "law consultants" claiming to assist companies in defining and operationalizing these new compliance mandates.[266] Although creating a separate "compliance counsel" might prevent the legal profession from losing market share to these new competitors (many of whom, as Rostain notes, are themselves lawyers), it might also entrench the kind of turf wars that will only work to obscure the fundamental purpose underlying these regulatory schemes — that achieving effective compliance is the joint responsibility of legal and business professionals. To achieve this goal it is necessary to move beyond a regulatory focus that assumes that gatekeeping duties are the sole responsibility of a single actor.

Notes

1. What do you think of the two approaches suggested by Coffee and Wilkins? Should corporate lawyers be expected to act as public-regarding "gatekeepers"? Even if it would be desirable for them to do so, is Coffee correct that neither law firms nor in-house counsel are any longer in a position to do so? Will the new "strategic alliances" between large companies and their law firms identified by Professor Wilkins change this dynamic? For an argument made more than 15 years before Coffee's that market conditions had significantly curtailed the ability of outside counsel to act as

---

265. Although any proposal to create a class of specialists with enhanced responsibilities for gatekeeping runs the risk of diminishing the importance that lawyers not in this role place on these public duties, Coffee's proposal seems particularly likely to produce this result. A law firm general counsel, for example, is specifically charged with interacting with the firm's partners and associates in order to remind them of their individual professional obligations. See generally [Anthony] Davis, ["Legal Ethics and Risk Management: Complementary Visions of Lawyer Regulation," 21 Geo. J. Legal Ethics 95 (2008)]. Coffee's proposal, on the other hand, seems to contemplate that disclosure counsel, who by definition will come from a different law firm than the other lawyers working for the corporation, should perform their role independently without seeking to influence what the company's other lawyers are doing. . . .

266. See Christine Parker, *The Open Corporation: Effective Self-Regulation and Democracy* (2002); Tanina Rostain, "The Emergence of 'Law Consultants,'" 75 Fordham L. Rev. 1397 (2006).

public regarding gatekeepers, see Ronald Gilson, "The Devolution of the Legal Profession: A Demand Side Perspective," 49 Md. L. Rev. 869 (1990). For the classic text on gatekeeping, see Reinier H. Kraakman, "Gatekeepers: The Anatomy of a Third-Party Enforcement Strategy," 2 J. L. Econ & Org. 53 (1986). We will return to these issues in Chapter 12.

2. Assuming that Professor Wilkins is correct that big companies and their principal law firms are moving toward relationships that are closer and more enduring, is this a good development for both parties? Professor Wilkins borrows the phrase "legal kieretsu" from the description of the "American Kieretsus" that U.S. automobile companies Chrysler and Ford formed with their primary suppliers to compete with the close working relationships that their Japanese competitors had with their suppliers. See Jeffrey Dyer, "How Chrysler Created an American Keiretsu," 74 Harv. Bus. Rev. 42, July/Aug 1996. Given what has happened within the automobile industry and its suppliers in recent years — exploding air bags, faulty ignition switches, manipulated emission results — should companies and firms be cautious about entering into a similar relationship? Studies have suggested, for example, that immersion in such a culture reduces ethical sensitivity and objectivity. As corporations continue (for cost and other reasons) to bring more lawyers in-house, what antidotes would you propose?

3. If clients do have ethical obligations to lawyers, do such obligations call for a new conception of legal ethics? Does Professor Wilkins (and perhaps Professor Coffee as well) underestimate the extent to which the current framework can accommodate the objectives he seeks? Professor Wilkins characterizes the "legal keiretsu" model as one in which firms "depend upon their corporate clients to supply accurate information about corporate goals and practice, to follow the firm's instructions on matters of legal compliance and, of course, to provide the firm with the capital that it needs for survival, including reputational capital in the form of referrals to other potential clients." Would a firm in a traditional agency status depend on the client in any different way?

4. Do you agree with the way that Professor Wilkins has characterized the amendments to Model Rules 1.6 and 1.13? Does the way he describes these changes make it appear that they were designed primarily to benefit lawyers and not the public?

5. If the principal–agent relation is not entirely correct in capturing the client-lawyer relationship and corporate governance more generally, then how should we begin to conceptualize the obligations that might attach to these relationships? Is it clear that even if we move away from this traditional model that corporate clients should have an ethical obligation to assure the profitability of the firm it hires? Does that include subsidizing very high levels of pay for new associates and seven-figure incomes for partners?

6. As a lawyer, which status — agent or strategic alliance partner — would you rather occupy?

7. In discussing the Kaye Scholer affair, Professor Wilkins states that the dismissed law firm was powerless to disclose information about suspected criminal or fraudulent behavior of its client, if it had such information, to its successor counsel. Is that clear? As a matter of the law of the confidentiality obligation, should that be the rule? As a practical matter, couldn't the successor law firm have conditioned its acceptance of the retainer on being permitted to talk to previous counsel?

B. The Government Lawyer

This section highlights some challenging issues facing government lawyers, e.g., who is their actual client? Reaching definitive (or even somewhat helpful) answers has plagued government lawyers and scholars. We first raise some key problems relating to the role of prosecutors in criminal practice and then government lawyers generally in civil practice.

1. Prosecutors and Prosecutorial Discretion

Problem 5–5

You are a prosecutor. As a practical matter, in most cases where the defendant has no prior record, your office has for many years treated as misdemeanors certain kinds of cases that could have been prosecuted as felonies. However, your office also charges a felony in all cases where a felony charge is possible because there is insufficient time to make a thorough enough investigation to be sure that discretion should be exercised to treat the case as a misdemeanor. When, at plea bargaining time in a particular case, you conclude that the case should be treated as a misdemeanor, should you disclose that fact to defense counsel immediately, or should you use the presence (and threat) of the felony charge to obtain a misdemeanor plea more readily?

Problem 5–6

You are a prosecutor, and your first assistant has just reported that she is about to file criminal charges in the following circumstances. The defendant has been arrested many times in connection with a variety of theft and assault situations but has never been convicted. The police have been working on a very large robbery case and have discovered some evidence linking the defendant to it but not enough, in her opinion, to make out a case of probable cause. The statute of limitations is about to run and the detective in charge of the case has just been given a tip that he believes will provide the needed evidence. Do you authorize the filing of charges? Is Rule 3.8(a) conclusive? Suppose there is enough evidence to support a finding of probable cause but not enough to convict. Do you authorize the filing of charges then? Suppose that there is enough to convict but you are doubtful whether you would convict if you were a juror. Do you authorize the filing of charges then?

Problem 5–7

You are a prosecutor who has been investigating a suspected gang member for years. Finally, acting on a tip, you have the suspect's car seized and some heroin is found. The car is registered in the name of the suspect's wife. Would you threaten to charge the suspect's wife unless the suspect agrees to plead guilty to a variety of drug-related charges?

Problem 5–8

You are a prosecutor with a drug case in which the defendant was attempting to sell to an undercover officer two-and-one-half kilograms of heroin. The case has been progressing through pretrial proceedings for nearly a year and recently you and the defense have agreed to a plea bargain to eight years in prison, which you consider to be a very lenient offer given the large amount of heroin involved and the defendant's lengthy criminal record. A week before sentencing, however, you learn that the undercover officer, whose testimony would have been important were a trial necessary, has died. Must you tell the defense about the officer's death? What if, instead of losing the witness, you discover that the heroin has been somehow lost or stolen from the evidence lockup: must you disclose that fact to the defense? Regardless of your disclosure decision under either scenario, should you lower your offered prison sentence?

Problem 5–9

You are still a prosecutor, and ten years ago, you successfully prosecuted Jeb Mallory for the cold-blooded murder of a young mother. At trial, you called two eyewitnesses who testified consistently that a man who looked just like Mallory walked into the mother's house at virtually the exact time (as the autopsy would later reveal) that the victim was murdered. There were also bite marks on the victim and shoe prints at the scene of the crime, both of which appeared to match Mallory's physical attributes. Moreover, Mallory had been with the victim a few weeks earlier, and his alibi on the night of the murder was uncorroborated. You were, and remain, convinced that Mallory was responsible for this heinous murder. Last week, however, you received a letter from the state innocence project on Mallory's behalf, demanding Mallory's immediate release. The letter enclosed DNA test results from a reputable lab indicating strongly that Mallory could not have been the one who committed the murder. While you have no reason to question the test results, you are not inclined to do anything about the results for two reasons: (1) even with the results, Mallory could still have been at the scene at the time of the crime as an accomplice or mastermind—the results indicate only that Mallory did not strike the deadly blow; and (2) the victim's children and former husband could not withstand the emotional pain and suffering that would attend a reopening of this gruesome, long-closed case—they (and the criminal justice system) need closure and finality. What, if anything, *should* you do?

Owing in part to prosecutors' power effectively to imprison citizen-defendants (or at least ruin their reputations) and to prosecutors' unique role as "ministers of justice," prosecutors are the only class of lawyers with their own specific Model Rule guiding their conduct. See Model Rule 3.8. As the Supreme Court famously noted some eighty years ago:

> The [prosecutor] is the representative not of an ordinary party to a controversy, but of a sovereignty whose obligation to govern impartially is as compelling as its obligation to govern at all; and whose interest, therefore, in a criminal prosecution is not that it shall win a case, but that justice shall be done. As such, he is in a peculiar and very definite sense the servant of the law, the twofold aim of which is that guilt shall not escape or innocence suffer. He may prosecute with earnestness and vigor—indeed, he should do so. But, while he may strike hard blows, he is not at liberty to strike foul ones. It is as much his duty to refrain from improper methods calculated to produce a wrongful conviction as it is to use every legitimate means to bring about a just one.

Berger v. United States, 295 U.S. 78, 88 (1935); see also Bennett L. Gershman, "'Hard Strikes and Foul Blows': Berger v. United States 75 Years After," 42 Loy. U. Chi. L.J. 177, 206 (2010) (exploring *Berger*'s context and concluding that "[g]iven the prosecutor's increasing domination of criminal law, his unilateral control of proof, his virtually unfettered power to charge, bargain, and give immunity, and the deference given to his hard blows to convict guilty people, it is hardly surprising that *Berger*'s rhetoric would be summoned, however wistfully, to express an ideal of justice," but despite *Berger*'s increasing citation by courts and scholars, its rhetoric is "too weak to be a meaningful limit" on prosecutorial conduct).

Notwithstanding the Model Rule and the Supreme Court's rhetoric, however, problems of wrongful convictions and prosecutorial misconduct persist. As DNA evidence has exonerated innocent defendants, many of whom spent years or even decades in prison or even on death row, the prosecutor's role in those wrongful convictions has been exposed. Ellen Yaroshefsky, "Wrongful Convictions: It Is Time to Take Prosecution Discipline Seriously," 8 U. D.C. L. Rev. 275 (2004); Keith Swisher, "Prosecutorial Conflicts of Interest in Post-Conviction Practice," 41 Hofstra L. Rev. 181, 198–201 (2012) (noting several examples of prosecutors who, even in the face of clear evidence that they had convicted the wrong person, refused to believe the evidence or to help the innocent person be released from prison). In addition, prosecutors have rarely been disciplined for misconduct (although there are some preliminary indications that prosecutorial discipline may finally be on the rise). See generally Angela J. Davis, "The Legal Profession's Failure to Discipline Unethical Prosecutors," 36 Hofstra L. Rev. 275 (2007); Lara Bazelon, "For Shame: The Public Humiliation of Prosecutors by Judges to Correct Wrongful Convictions," 29 Geo. J. Legal Ethics 305 (2016); Hon. Alex Kozinski, "Criminal Law 2.0," 44 Geo. L.J. Ann. Rev. Crim. Proc. III, viii–x (2015) (observing that prosecutors do not always play fair and noting an "epidemic of *Brady* violations").

Additional guidance is thus needed to address the prosecutor's delicate role. The National District Attorneys Association and the ABA, among others, have attempted to provide specific guidance. The ABA Standards for the Prosecution Function (1992 ed.) provide the following guidance with respect to Problems 5–5 to 5–7 above:

Standard 3-3.9. Discretion in the Charging Decision

(a) A prosecutor should not institute, or cause to be instituted, or permit the continued pendency of criminal charges when the prosecutor knows that the charges are not supported by probable cause. A prosecutor should not institute, cause to be instituted, or permit the continued pendency of criminal charges in the absence of sufficient admissible evidence to support a conviction.

(b) The prosecutor is not obliged to present all charges which the evidence might support. The prosecutor may in some circumstances and for good cause consistent with the public interest decline to prosecute, notwithstanding that sufficient evidence may exist which would support a conviction. Illustrative of the factors which the prosecutor may properly consider in exercising his or her discretion are:

(i) the prosecutor's reasonable doubt that the accused is in fact guilty;

(ii) the extent of the harm caused by the offense;

(iii) the disproportion of the authorized punishment in relation to the particular offense of the offender;

(iv) possible improper motives of a complainant;

(v) reluctance of the victim to testify;

(vi) cooperation of the accused in the apprehension or conviction of others; and

(vii) availability and likelihood of prosecution by other jurisdictions.

(c) A prosecutor should not be compelled by his or her supervisor to prosecute a case in which he or she has a reasonable doubt about the guilt of the accused.

(d) In making the decision to prosecute, the prosecutor should give no weight to the personal or professional advantages or disadvantages which might be involved or to a desire to enhance his or her record of convictions.

(e) In cases which involve a serious threat to the community, the prosecutor should not be deterred from prosecution by the fact that in the jurisdiction juries have tended to acquit persons accused of the particular criminal act in question.

(f) The prosecutor should not bring or seek charges greater in number or degree than can reasonably be supported with evidence at trial or than are necessary to fairly reflect the gravity of the offense.

(g) The prosecutor should not condition a dismissal of charges, nolle prose-
qui, or similar action on the accused's relinquishment of the right to seek civil
redress unless the accused has agreed to the action knowingly and intelligently,
freely and voluntarily, and where such a waiver is approved by the court.

———————

Professor Richard Uviller, who has written extensively about the prosecutor's role
and the criminal justice system, has produced a snapshot of his views in the following excerpt.

H. Richard Uviller
The Neutral Prosecutor:
The Obligation of Dispassion in a Passionate Pursuit
68 Fordham L. Rev. 1695 (2000)

Introduction

When I was a young prosecutor in New York County, the most baffling part of
my job was the decision—which I was regularly required to make: what was the case
at hand really worth? Two notches below the grade charged in the top count in
the indictment? Half the maximum prison time the legislature had prescribed for
cases of this sort? Crimes are described in the penal law in their worst manifestation. Indictments often comprise a network of accusations in the most serious degrees
and combinations that the facts might conceivably support. Occasionally—very
rarely—a case comes along that fits the most aggravated accusation the prosecutor
can devise. On such cases, the subsequent appraisal was easy: "top count; max
time." But even in the deliberate homicides, the major robberies, and the brutal rapes,
there was usually some room for a reconsideration of the true gravity of the case. I
have since come to understand that these appraisals, or re-appraisals, of the worth
of a case are an indispensable—and largely healthy—part of the process. No less
than the power to charge, to dismiss charges, and to immunize witnesses, the power
to tailor a charge to the gravity of a particular offense and the deserts of a particular
offender is the essence of the executive function in the prosecution of crime. At this
point in my tour, I was not assigned to try the cases I evaluated for disposition. So I
could ponder the elusive appraisal of worth in its full mystery.

As a trial Assistant, thumbing through the case jacket, talking to witnesses, I could
focus on only one question: what were my chances of persuading a jury of twelve
at a full—and fully contested—trial that my charges were in all likelihood true?
But even as I revisited the plea offer with only the "triability" of the case in mind, I
knew, and still believe, that reading these portents is not the whole story. It is not
enough to say, as some have, that the just disposition of a criminal charge is the
point at which the interests of the state in conviction and of the accused in the light-
est possible punishment intersect. There is another, less pragmatic, element in the
assessment of worth. . . .

It is not easy to describe this normative element in the appraisal of a case. It is in part a calibration of the level of contextual social outrage. In part, it is the location of the particular instance of the crime on a moral spectrum of similar crimes. In part, it is a reflection of the customary level of punishment for crimes of the same category. But, thankfully, I have no purpose here to attempt to discern — or to defend — the retributive valence as it contributes to the resolution of a criminal accusation. Rather, I hope to describe the process by which the evaluation is made, and to call it "adjudicative" as distinct from "adversary." And inasmuch as this adjudicative task is part of the public prosecutor's executive function, I will argue that it should be performed by members of the staff who are detached from the demands of zealous advocacy.

As I shall describe the prosecutor's responsibilities, a third aspect will emerge. Long before setting a date for trial, very likely before opening discussions about disposition by guilty plea, the prosecutor will be asking questions, possibly directing further interviews with witnesses, examining documents, experts, reports; in short, investigating the case. Overlapping somewhat with the adjudicative function, this investigative responsibility also requires a level of neutrality quite different from the attitude with which the prosecutor prepares for trial. At the pre-adversary stage, I shall contend, the prosecutor should be schooled in the detached exercise of discretion. As facts are sifted and weighed, as the resulting accusation is assessed for gravity, neutrality is a critical component of diligence. The abandoned investigation, the light plea offer — these are no less worthy accomplishments than the selection of a suspect to prosecute to the fullest.

In that connection, I shall ask, too, whether the virtuous prosecutor is not ethically constrained — if not legally[3] — to inform the grand jury to whom he submits inculpatory evidence that there is support for a conflicting hypothesis. Neutrality, I will suggest, puts the prosecutor in the position of advocate for all the people — including the person against whom the evidence has been accumulating. Thus, I will urge, whatever the court's role might be in supervising the prosecutor before the grand jury, the ethical imperatives require full and balanced prosecutorial presentation. Finally, I will ask whether we have imposed fundamentally inconsistent obligations on our prosecutors, bending them into psychological pretzels by requiring them to be the neutral investigator and the "quasi-judicial" adjudicator while at the same time imagining themselves as the zealous courtroom advocate.

---

3. The United States Supreme Court decision in United States v. Williams, 504 U.S. 36 (1992), relieved the prosecutor of any legal obligation to present exculpatory evidence to a grand jury. In that case, the Court declined to exercise its supervisory powers to direct the prosecutor's performance before a grand jury, apparently leaving the matter of fairness beyond legal control. See id. at 54–55. . . . However, a recent statute, known as the McDade Law, provides that U.S. government prosecutors must abide by local rules regarding the ethical obligations of counsel. See 28 U.S.C. § 530B (Supp. 1999). This, the government now fears, may have overruled *Williams* in those jurisdictions where the state prosecutor is under some obligation to present exculpatory evidence to the grand jury, thus converting the local ethical rule into a federal obligation of law.

I. The Role of the Prosecutor in the American Model

In the American model of criminal justice—in contrast to the British, for example—the prosecutor is not just a lawyer assigned to represent the interests of the government in the trial of a criminal case. The American prosecutor, state or federal, is a public official, elected or appointed to exercise executive authority. The prosecutor doesn't have a client; he has a constituency. The local prosecutor is not responsible to the state government but to the people directly. The federal prosecutor is affiliated with, and in some sense subject to, a department of the central government, the Department of Justice. And the DOJ exercises a certain amount of supervisory control over its far-flung district prosecutors. But essentially, all prosecutors—unlike lawyers generally—enjoy independence in the exercise of discretion. Free of client control, they have the luxury and burden of developing the standards for the exercise of public authority. While they function within the adversary system, they function also as administrative policy makers. And, as such, they allocate resources in the pursuit and disposition of cases according to their own best judgment of the demands of justice.

As Americans have long known, and are beginning to acknowledge openly, our system of criminal justice is compound and complex. Only a relatively small proportion—an extremely important, but small portion—of criminal cases are disposed of in anything resembling the simple, traditional adversary mode of which we have been so inordinately proud down through the centuries. The pristine paradigm has, essentially, three sequential and interwoven phases. The first is the commencement. Following an arrest predicated on probable cause—and often very little more—or a grand jury indictment, the formal charge is lodged. Normally, the charge is the result of the prosecutor's judgment, confirmed (usually pro forma) by the grand jury in those jurisdictions that maintain the relic for the ordinary felony case.[5] That judgment takes heavily into consideration the likely outcomes of succeeding phases.

Phase two is investigation and trial preparation. Here, the prosecutor begins the arduous process of getting all his witnesses and documents in order, perhaps conducting supplementary forays to patch and mend, to fill and brace, to trim and align the diverse, faint, and chaotic traces of the facts clinging to the bare beams of the counts in the indictment. In this, the prosecutor gets no help from the accused, nor does he expect any. And in this old-fashioned paradigm, the prosecutor does not share his discoveries with defense counsel, who would be a fool if she did not react to such advance intelligence by devising evasions and rehearsing counter-thrusts. If the

---

5. Twenty-three states and the District of Columbia have retained the indicting grand jury for certain offenses. See Susan W. Brenner, "The Voice of the Community: A Case for Grand Jury Independence," 3 Va. J. Soc. Pol'y & L. 67, 101 (1995). These jurisdictions generally require an indictment for capital crimes and/or serious offenses. See id. . . . All 50 states have preserved the investigative grand jury. See Kathryn E. White, "What Have You Done With My Lawyer?: The Grand Jury Witness's Right to Consult with Counsel," 32 Loy. L.A. L. Rev. 907, 925 (1999). England abolished the grand jury system in 1933. . . .

defendant has any colorable defense, let him develop it on his own. For his response to the evidence adduced against him, he can wait for phase three, the trial. After all, that's what a trial is for: to display in neat and persuasive array the case against the defendant.

So the final phase is the adversary encounter. The . . . prosecutor parades his best case before a neutral and attentive panel of citizens, each witness subject to vigorous challenge, perhaps impeachment. The defense receives a full opportunity to contradict the prosecutor's evidence, and the issue is finally submitted to the jury for their secret and dutiful deliberation and (let us hope) their indelible verdict. Through this critical third stage, the judge—fair, detached, and in all likelihood ignorant of the facts—exercises her passive control over the proceedings, maintaining order and assuring the appearance of justice, while taking some pains to exhibit fidelity to applicable law. But even the most participatory judge does not presume to present or evaluate the evidence. There is some room in this idealized version of the adversary confrontation for appellate review, but not too much stress is laid upon it. It should be but an emergency procedure to correct grievous and devastating deviations from legal protocol by a foolish or foolhardy trial judge, or an impulsive or ignorant prosecutor.

Add to this paradigm a dollop of discovery and a robust helping of pre-trial motion practice and you have a recipe for a procedure resembling today's trial regime. But what has been airbrushed out of this adversary myth is adjudication by agreement, the so called "plea-bargaining" and the demands it makes on the prosecutor to resolve the case she intended merely to try. It is difficult, even in this record-saturated world, to know precisely what percentage of the trial docket is disposed of by guilty plea. Different jurisdictions vary in their plea policies, and keep their records by significantly different schemes for counting: if you include misdemeanors and petty offenses in the "trial docket," the disposition-by-verdict column will shrink dramatically; so too, if you include dismissals and consolidations with the guilty pleas, the proportion of verdicts is further reduced. A crudely calculated number that many commentators take as an honest estimate is 80% to 90% dispositions by guilty plea. Even at the high end of the estimate, the cases that are tried to verdict remain a very important component in the system, both for themselves (they are likely to be cases involving major factual disputes or extremely serious crimes), and for the influence they exert on the disposition policies regarding the others (a couple of jury verdicts convicting tavernkeepers as accessories to drunk driving will raise the plea offers in future prosecutions). Thus, neither concern about the inefficiencies and inequities of the adversary paradigm, nor efforts to improve upon the method of adjudication of contested cases should be disparaged because of the relatively few cases affected. At the same time, we would do well to pay greater attention to the problems of prosecutor as adjudicator.

Today, I believe things are much as they were in my time as a prosecutor over 30 years ago. Young Assistants think of themselves primarily as advocates. The case they make, or (more likely) inherit from a law enforcement unit, is cast immediately as a trial scenario. It is refined and amplified—as it usually requires—in preparation for exposure to a jury. In this posture, of course, the Assistant cares a good deal more for supplementary information that fortifies the case against the defendant than new data that call his thesis into question. What is shared with the defense is shared reluctantly and only because of the law's stern injunction,[11] and what is received from the defense is taken with suspicion and the assumption that, insofar as it contradicts the prosecution version, counsel is likely to be disingenuous, misinformed, or naive.

If and when the overture is made for a possible disposition by guilty plea, the young gladiator is ready. It is all but routine. As others have noted, the term "plea bargaining" or even "negotiating" is misleading. Having spent several years in the process, I can vouch that little, if any, haggling goes on in these sessions. For the most part, the prosecutor announces to defense counsel the counts or crimes to which he would accept a guilty plea in satisfaction of the entire accusation, and perhaps—implicitly or explicitly—the sentence that he would recommend or not object to. The announcement is not likely to surprise experienced defense counsel. The proposal is the composite of several factors: the stress of the docket backlog (a parameter), the strength of the evidence (suspected by diligent counsel), and a conventional "market price" for the particular constellation of facts in the case. A robbery with a weapon but no injuries by a defendant with only minor offenses on his record may go for three years regardless of the legislative maximum for first degree robberies. Counsel may argue: "This is no robbery! Your victim—no winner himself—and my client had been drinking together and were both drunk when my client got a little too insistent in trying to collect an old gambling debt from his buddy." But the prosecutor has probably already heard this story, and factored it into the winability equation. So the offer stands, take it or leave it.

What is going on here? And how does it comport with our picture of the prosecutor as advocate? Prosecutorial discretion in general and the practice of plea bargaining in particular have attracted the attention of generations of scholars and commentators. It is not my present purpose to summarize—or to quarrel—with their work. Rather, I propose to devote some paragraphs to the second question, the

---

11. See Jencks Act, 18 U.S.C. § 3500 (1994) (requiring the government to produce upon demand any available statement, made by its own witness, which relates to the subject matter of such witness's testimony at trial); Brady v. Maryland, 373 U.S. 83, 87 (1963) (holding that "the suppression by the prosecution of evidence favorable to an accused upon request violates due process where the evidence is material either to guilt or to punishment, irrespective of the good faith or bad faith of the prosecution"); Fed. R. Crim. P. 16(a) (setting forth five categories of information which must be disclosed by the government upon defendant's request). The Jencks Act and Rule 16 apply in the federal courts, and similar statutes have been enacted in most states. The *Brady* rule applies in all criminal cases.

Another former prosecutor remembers that plea-inducing inculpatory information was more readily imparted than potentially damaging exculpatory data. Maybe so. But I still recall the sense that even inculpatory details, served up to wily counsel in advance of trial, might well stimulate the artful construction of an evasive defense.

role of the prosecutor, of which her performance in the drama of plea bargaining is only a part. It is my thesis that we need to reconceptualize the prosecutor to take account of her substantial responsibility as investigator and, in a real sense, arbiter of the accusation. Discharge of this major obligation, the wise exercise of virtually unilateral discretion in the matter, demands neutrality, the suspension of the partisan outlook, and at least until the case passes to the adversarial stage, dedication to interests that may prove antithetical to her ultimate position. And because these conflicting obligations may impair quasi-judicial detachment, I will propose a structural change that might better accommodate the neutrality of the prosecutor in the pre-adversary mode.

I start with the faith that thorough investigation by a detached and dedicated investigator is the best assurance of a conclusion that comports with historical truth.[14] I do not mean to say that the clash of thesis and antithesis in a courtroom setting has not on occasion revealed the truth. And I take full account of the social importance of the public forum for dispute, and of the shows and trappings of the law's dispassion. But I am far from confident that the devoted pursuit of inconsistent contentions in the artificial setting of a trial readily allows a naive and sheltered fact-finder to distinguish truth from dissimulation, to tell the sturdy inference from the artful.[15] Still, I share with many observers some distrust of the free-ranging exercise of official discretion. First, let us acknowledge that not all prosecutors are up to the task they have undertaken. Not all are diligent, learned, or wise. And even the best of the prosecutors—young, idealistic, energetic, dedicated to the interests of justice—are easily caught up in the hunt mentality of an aggressive office.

Yet, I confess that notwithstanding the sporadic wimps and whiners, the occasional Batmen and blockheads, from what I have known of prosecutors and former prosecutors, I consider them by and large the flower of the bar. At a critical stage in their careers, they have, or have had, the supreme professional luxury known to the practice of law: the blessing of working without regard to the interests of a single-minded client. Virtually alone among their classmates—most of whom were laboring in the competitive world of billable hours and client promiscuity—they were told by their superiors: "Do only what you think is right; bend every professional effort to achieve an outcome that you think best comports with justice within the constraints of law." And the instruction was sincere. Heady wine, especially for a newly fledged lawyer. And in the best of the breed—perhaps in most of them—assimilation of this extraordinary mission gave rise to a conscious and conscientious project to refine their judgment, to define for themselves the just provinces of law, and to temper all with an acute appreciation for the demands of reality. If discretion is to

---

14. I have elsewhere expounded on this faith at somewhat greater length. See H. Richard Uviller, *The Tilted Playing Field: Is Criminal Justice Unfair?* 73–112 (1999).

15. I should note here (with some astonishment) that judges with whom I am well acquainted do not seem to share my misgivings, being, by and large, thoroughly content that the adversary process delivers a close approximation of the truth in most cases. See H. Richard Uviller, *Virtual Justice: The Flawed Prosecution of Crime in America* 279–305 (1996).

be lodged anywhere in the system — as it must be — I tend to favor the prosecutor's office.

But, as I say, I am wary. I know that the earnest effort to do justice is easily corrupted by the institutional ethic of combat. So long as the prosecutor is primarily an advocate, sees himself, armor-clad, prepared to do battle for what is right, detachment falters. I am, then, seeking a way to capture the neutrality implicit in the mission as first declared without undermining the adversary posture of the courtroom advocate that the prosecutor may ultimately become. . . .

A prosecutor's first contact with a case comes in one of two ways. Most commonly, and particularly on the state side (where the overwhelming proportion of criminal prosecutions are found), criminal cases begin with an arrest. The prosecutor greets the case, along with the arresting officer, at the courthouse door. Some of these arrests may be the product of long and painstaking investigation by the law enforcement corps. In some jurisdictions, the custom may be to consult with the prosecutor long before arrest in these protracted police investigations flipping the case into my second category. But often — particularly where the local police have experience and pride in their detection skills, the investigation that precedes the arrest is a police operation exclusively. In these cases, the police like to say: the case comes to the prosecutor "trial ready." This is rarely the prosecutor's view, however.

Most of the other cases that come in for arraignment — cases in which a more modest investigation, if any, preceded arrest — are grand jury ready or information ready. An alert prosecutor at the arraignment desk, however, will not automatically process what the line officer brings in. At the very least, the complainant should be interviewed first hand. Too, the facts must be reviewed to make sure the officer has not mis-designated the offense. The result is that the prosecutor, on first contact, does provide some filtration and a number of these cases do wash out at the first stage.[16] Arraignment must be prompt so the prosecutor has little time for preliminary investigation. But between arraignment and accusation, the prosecutor has an opportunity for some further inquiry. Prosecutors realize that an indictment is more than a mere accusatory formality — a piece of paper that serves only to bring the case to court, as judges like to instruct juries. To the accused, it is an instrument of terror, to say nothing of a major incision in the pocketbook (if the accused has one). The conscientious prosecutor, then, will not be content with "technical" sufficiency for the commencement of a criminal prosecution. The prosecutor should be assured to a fairly high degree of certainty that he has the right person, the right crime, and a

---

16. In the federal system, from Oct. 1, 1995 through Sept. 30, 1996, of the 98,454 suspects in criminal matters, 58% were prosecuted in district courts, 33% were declined for prosecution, and 9% were referred to federal magistrate judges. See Bureau of Justice Statistics, U.S. Dep't of Justice, Compendium of Federal Justice Statistics, 1996, 16 (1999). Of the 32,832 declinations, 27% occurred because of case-related reasons (such as weak evidence); 23% occurred because there was no crime or criminal intent; and 19% occurred for other reasons, such as agency requests and lack of federal interest. See id. at 17. These statistics are also available in Bureau of Justice Statistics, U.S. Dep't of Justice (visited Feb. 1, 2000) <http://www.ojp.usdoj.gov/bjs/>.

good chance of success with a petit jury. To reach that point of assurance, the prosecutor should approach the case handed to him with a working degree of suspicion. The good prosecutor—like any good trial lawyer—is skeptical of what appears patent to others, and curious concerning details that seem trivial to the casual observer. . . .

The point being that even the cases presented wrapped and tied with a ribbon—"we've got a positive ID by the complainant, an independent witness who puts him at the scene, a patently incredible story from the perp, and a handsome criminal record"—deserves further investigation. Positive IDs are frequently mistaken, on-the-scene presence may explain his arrest but does not necessarily attest to his culpability, "patently incredible" stories are sometimes true, and there are many innocent people walking around out there with criminal records. The mindset with which the prosecutor should approach this task is different from the advocate shoring up a somewhat equivocal case; it is the mindset of the true skeptic, the inquisitive neutral.

Following a judgment of conviction, the prosecutor should maintain her adversary stance, fighting off motions, writs, and appeals with which the judgment is besieged: one juror told another juror during a lunch break that the accused looked like a liar to her; during deliberations, one juror shook his fist in the face of another; defense counsel came back from lunch smelling of booze and dozed through the afternoon; during her summation, the prosecutor hinted that she and her office believed the testimony of the accusing witnesses; in his charge to the jury, the judge hiccoughed meaningfully. All such attacks on an adverse disposition must be resisted with full adversary zeal.

But where a post-judgment motion goes directly to the issue of guilt, the prosecutor is returned to the pre-adversary mode, and neutrality must resurface. A critical prosecution witness recants; a cop is accused of fabricating evidence in another case; a DNA test discloses that the defendant could not have been the rapist. Upon tenable grounds for such allegations, the prosecutor must resume the role of neutral investigator. A thorough and dispassionate investigation of the new development must be made and, where the result warrants, the prosecutor must not hesitate to cancel the victorious judgment and see that justice is done in the light of the amplified or revised facts. We have read of instances in which DNA evidence has unequivocally contradicted eyewitness testimony, and the prosecutor refuses to join in the motion to set aside the prior judgment or to move to dismiss the charges after the court does so. This seems to me a grievous deviation from the role of neutral servant of justice, which the prosecutor is duty-bound to fulfill. I do not say that the prosecutor should cave at the first allegation of miscarriage; the government's case, presumably, strong and convincing when tried, does not become instantly so weak it can no longer support the verdict. But a firmly based charge that a woeful mistake was made, that an innocent person was convicted, is not to be taken lightly. We know such mistakes are made (though we have no inkling how frequently) and each one threatens the probity of the entire system. All efforts must be bent to the diligent investigation of the claim and, if substantiated, it is incumbent upon the people's representative, the guardian of the integrity of the process, to urge immediate remedy to assist the court in righting the wrong. . . .

[In the omitted section Professor Uviller discusses the extent to which, in his view, prosecutors have an *ethical* duty to disclose exculpatory evidence to a grand jury, notwithstanding the holding of the Supreme Court of the United States that they have no *constitutional* duty to do so.]

III. The Duality of the Prosecutor's Responsibility

To return, then, to the bifurcated responsibilities of the prosecutor, what sort of mindset is called for by this extraordinary task? Can we expect a dispassionate investigator to maintain the initiative, to persist in the pursuit of elusive veils of suspicion, to summon the energy to pore through cartons of documents, interview dozens of reluctant and prevaricating participants in the hope of finding a case buried in the haystack? Or is it only the taste of the trial to come that fires the soul of the investigator? It may well be the latter, I know. But my experience is that, in the investigative bureaus of my shop—especially the commercial frauds bureau—the prosecutors did not really expect that a trial would result from their prodigious labors. By the time they had assembled a case warranting indictment, the guilty plea was virtually assured. Indeed, the object was to close every loophole so securely, to knit the skein so tightly, that surrender was the defendant's only option. And of course, from the purely tactical standpoint, one way to assure the guilty plea was to cut loose any suspects who had a tenable defense. That requires an open mind and a relentless pursuit of possible defenses not only to destroy the untenable, but to honor the tenable.

For the cases in which the prosecutor expects a resolution of the accusation by guilty plea, as well as for the ordinary case working its way up the docket toward a jury trial, the prosecutor must pause and consider what is the just disposition of the case by agreement? Since docket economy is an ongoing imperative, some discount is probably granted solely in exchange for bypassing the trial and appeal. Projected success with a jury counts too. But underlying the state's accord to a reduction in the top count penalty must be a defensible assessment of the gravity of the crime and the deserts of the defendant.

This process looks a lot like adjudication. Not the familiar adversary process of adjudication, but a model closer to the civil law system. In the European model— sometimes called, disparagingly, "inquisitorial" by those in our "adversarial" tradition—a semi-judicial figure (called in some places a *juge d'instrucion*) supervises the investigation and prepares the detailed, all-but-dispositive accusation in the dossier. In the prevalent mode of American adjudication, the prosecutor emerges from her role as ex parte investigator to preside over the disposition of the accusation she has brought. Of course, the judge will actually preside, ultimately reviewing the case and authorizing the agreed upon resolution. But, if the parties have done their work truly and well, there will be little left for the court to adjudicate beyond signing off on the disposition approved by the prosecutor.

Again, we see our prosecutor in a role quite different from that of the gladiator, his mind set on the public exposure of his skills and the mettle of his cause in the colonnaded arena. Is this, should this be, can this be the same person imbued with the same ethic of the same office?

I think it would be well if we recognized the difficulty of sustaining the detachment of an adjudicator with the commitment of an advocate. Prosecutors were not designed to be both simultaneously. The adjudicatory function evolved from the simple surrender of a guilty plea—a matter between the confessing defendant and the judgmental court. With increasing regularity, counsel for the penitent began to visit the prosecutor's office in search of some extra consideration in exchange for the client's guilty plea. As long as pleading guilty meant only throwing oneself upon the mercy of the court—meaning, hoping for leniency within the court's sentencing discretion—the prosecutor was no part of the transaction. But where the prosecution's recommendation was solicited in support of the bid for lenity or, more likely, some adjustment in the accusation was sought to facilitate the award of a lighter sentence, the prosecutor became a critical player in the disposition drama. Under federal and many state constitutions, the grand jury was the accusing authority, and even the court, alone, could not redact their charge. Traditionally, pardon and clemency were reserved to the executive, descendant of the divinely-endowed monarch. And modifications to a less from a more serious charge are variants on the forgiveness power. Hence, laws such as New York's[46] specifically require the consent of the executive officer, the prosecutor, for dismissal or acceptance of a plea to a charge less than the grand jury's top count. So, as courts increasingly deferred to the judgment of the prosecutor who, presumably, represented the interests of the law-abiding community, the prosecutor gradually displaced the court as the arbiter of a just resolution.[47]

How does the prosecutor meet the demands for quasi-judicial performance? As others have noted, and many lawyers know from personal experience, prosecutors perform this prerogative largely by unarticulated, unreviewed, intuitive standards proudly designated "the interests of justice." The question of whether these standards should be written and promulgated, and thereby somehow achieve the status of law is a difficult and debatable point. . . . It is sufficient for present purposes to note that in the performance of the quasi-judicial role, the prosecutor should be sufficiently detached from his prospects as an advocate to reach a dispassionate appraisal of the interests of justice.

---

46. See N.Y. Crim. Proc. §§ 210.20, 210.40, 220.10, 220.50 (McKinney 1993).

47. Of course, the prosecution cannot *enter* the guilty plea, but with some judicial input, the recommendation of the prosecutor usually becomes the disposition of the court.

I believe that for the office of prosecutor faithfully to discharge the incompatible roles of advocate and arbiter, the investigators and adjudicators should be segregated from the advocates. . . . I . . . think that those who investigate, assess, and negotiate settlement should belong to a different cadre from those who try the cases that fail to reach accord. Since the disposition of a charge should never ignore entirely the trial potential of the case, I would staff my adjudicative team with trial veterans. And insofar as the trial process may abort at any time and the question of a fair disposition raise its head anew deep into the trial process, I would have stage one and stage two prosecutors collaborate on its resolution. With these and other adjustments for overlap, I would encourage my adjudicators to celebrate their dispassion, to relish their role not only as the fact-seekers initially, but the justice-seekers ultimately. These people should be honored by defense counsel and judges, along with their colleagues, for their devotion to the right result regardless of adversarial considerations. And where they find it impossible, for one reason or another, to adjudicate the case by accord, they should step out of it and turn the cause over to a warrior to take into battle.

There is some (though inadequate) recognition of the importance of these values in the bureaucratic arrangement in some large offices that disempowers trial assistants from granting immunity to witnesses, dismissing indictments, or accepting pleas to reduced charges. These adjudicative decisions must be approved by senior supervisors. One may assume that the supervisors are trial veterans with some degree of detachment, if not neutrality. It's the right idea. But such supervision is often nominal at best since the senior assistant knows only what the young trial assistant tells him and is inclined to approve any reasonable course the trial assistant advises. As I envision the ideal arrangement, the senior "adjudicative assistant" would have exclusive control of the case from inception, through investigation and accusation, and into plea assessment and whatever negotiation accompanies it. The case would be surrendered to the young gladiator — the "adversary assistant" — only when all else fails. And any future plea overtures would be considered only with the advice of the adjudicative assistant.

I am told that the glamour factor cuts against this scheme. Trial assistants are the stars of an office and the most desirable recruits to the private sector to which they will, most likely, graduate. Under my regime, investigators and plea bargainers would be seen as mere clerks. . . . [F]rom my own experience I believe that if the normal routine was to put juniors in court and to reserve the more mature and experienced assistants for the pretrial stage, the office ethic would soon reflect the fact — especially since the assistants themselves would recognize the just allocation of responsibility. . . .

More troublesome in my plan is a factor I have tried to ignore, but every experienced trial dog will attest to its importance. The strongest impetus to disposition by guilty plea is the imminence of trial. Any well-run prosecutor's office hates the last minute, eve-of-trial repentance, the desperate attempt (often abetted by the judge) to revive a lapsed offer as the prospective jurors file into the courtroom. Defendants are told in the strongest language that an offer must be seized at once or lost forever. But I am forced to conclude there is something about the criminal mentality that blocks reception of the message. . . . It is only at the very last minute, as the jury is being empanelled, that the accused will face the inevitability of judgment; only at this point is he ready to accept the fact that surrender is the wisest course. And I well remember my reluctance to revive the offer when my defendant belatedly faces the music . . . . But it is hard to fight with a judge who urges you to relent, arguing: if the disposition was right last week, it must be right today.

My plan virtually ignores the imminence factor insofar as it assumes that the evaluation of the case will be done well before the jury call goes out. And I should recognize that there will inevitably be many cases in which the first serious approach to the prosecutor regarding disposition will be made to the trial assistant. Yet, I maintain that the position of the trial assistant if and when she gets that telephone call will be greatly aided, and office policy will be stabilized by the earlier work done by the adjudicator. There is no reason that I can imagine why the late broach of the possibility of plea should not return the case to the pre-adversary mode, with the added factor that the trial assistant can now offer the additional input that she wants very much to go to trial—or is reluctant to do so.

Conclusion

So, in sum, I see prosecutors as executing multiple functions within three general categories: investigative, adjudicative, and adversary. The first two of these call for a quality of professional disposition different from the last. Investigation and adjudication call for neutrality, while the trial mode of the advocate demands full partisan commitment. Passion and dispassion are not cut from the same mentality. Dedicated detachment is a precious quality in a public prosecutor, difficult to cultivate and best developed at some remove from the adversary zeal that characterizes the trial phase. Conscientious commitment to an office policy or tradition goes a long way toward the ideal of quasi-judicial performance. So, too, effective and devoted supervision can imbue the line assistance with an appreciation of his or her dual responsibilities. But neither commitment nor supervision of this sort can be generally assumed. Indeed, enjoining the same person to be at once neutral and contentious may induce some discomfort. So I propose that some structural reflection of the bifurcation in prosecutorial function might encourage development of both orientations. Recognition of the division by separating the Assistants who assemble and evaluate evidence from those who present it in adversary form to a factfinder might enhance both commitments.

————————

Professor Uviller's suggestions, designed in part to infuse more "neutrality" into the prosecutor's role, line up nicely with recent studies suggesting that the partisan effect skews our best judgment. See, e.g., Andrew M. Perlman, "A Behavioral Theory of Legal Ethics," 90 Ind. L.J. 1639 (2015). But the use of the term "neutrality" has generally provoked criticism, as too vague to be helpful; prosecutors instead need to develop workable principles to guide their discretion, a task rarely completed. See, e.g., Bruce A. Green & Fred C. Zacharias, "Prosecutorial Neutrality," 2004 Wis. L. Rev. 837, 903 ("It is neither helpful simply to ask prosecutors to be 'neutral' nor fair to criticize prosecutors for alleged failures to act 'neutrally.' Indeed, the neutrality rhetoric is singularly unpersuasive as criticism, because even the most egregious prosecutorial decisions can ordinarily be defended as 'neutral' in some sense of the term."). See also Peter Joy and Kevin McMunigal, "Different Rules for Prosecutors?," 31 Crim. Just. 43 (Summer 2016).

Professor Uviller also suggests that if "defense counsel came back from lunch smelling of booze and dozed through the afternoon," the prosecutor should resist "with full adversary zeal" any appeal seeking to reverse the defendant's conviction on that basis. For an informative and critical discussion about the responsibilities of prosecutors in cases where the defendant is represented by incompetent counsel, see Vanessa Merton, "What Do You Do When You Meet 'A Walking Violation of the Sixth Amendment' if You're Trying to Put that Lawyer's Client in Jail?," 69 Fordham L. Rev. 997 (2000) and Bruce A. Green, "Criminal Neglect: Indigent Defense from A Legal Ethics Perspective," 52 Emory L.J. 1169 (2003).

Finally, we conclude this brief exploration of the unique role of prosecutors and their broad and powerful discretion with the following critical article, based in part on the fallout from the "war on drugs":

Abbe Smith
Can You Be a Good Person and a Good Prosecutor?
14 Geo. J. Legal Ethics 355 (2001)

[T]he citizen's safety lies in the prosecutor who tempers zeal with human kindness, who seeks truth and not victims, who serves the law and not factional purposes, and who approaches his task with humility.

— Robert H. Jackson, former prosecutor

Somehow, it is understood that prosecutors have the high ground. Most people simply assume that prosecutors are the good guys, wear the white hats, and are on the "right" side. Most law students contemplating a career in criminal law seem to think this. It could be that most practicing lawyers think this, as well.

Prosecutors represent the people, the state, the government. This is very noble, important, and heady stuff. Prosecutors seek truth, justice, and the American way. They are the ones who stand up for the victims and would-be victims, the bullied and battered and burgled. They protect *all of us*.

Meanwhile, defenders are always on the defensive. In a social climate that exalts crime control over everything else, defenders are barely tolerated. It is sometimes hard for the public to distinguish defenders from the "scum" we represent. We are often seen as our clients' accomplices or, at best, their apologists. When defenders are asked, as we often are, "How can you defend those people?," there is an assumption that there is something wrong with "those people" and something wrong with those of us who choose to defend them. Although high profile cases usually enhance the image of prosecutors, they don't often help the public image of defenders. We are lawyers for the mob and the murderer and the molester. Too often we are seen muttering "no comment" as we stand beside clients desperately attempting to hide from view.

Defenders become accustomed to having our morals challenged; it is an occupational hazard. We have been called all sorts of things by all sorts of people: "sleazy," "slick," egomaniacal, hateful, and worse. Just listen to any radio talk show and you can hear defenders denigrated, derided, and denounced. To many, the work defenders do is inherently disreputable.

It doesn't matter how lofty the lawyers. Consider, for example, Senator Orrin Hatch disparaging Harvard law professor and former public defender Charles Ogletree as a "two-bit slick lawyer." The conduct that gave rise to Hatch's outburst was Ogletree's disclosure during the 1991 Senate confirmation hearings for Supreme Court nominee Clarence Thomas that Anita Hill had passed a polygraph exam. Ogletree, one of Hill's lawyers, devised the polygraph idea in response to Thomas supporters' fierce attack on his client's character and credibility.

The current popular culture doesn't help. The television series, *The Practice*, although acclaimed by both viewers and critics, is mostly about the questionable ethics of defense lawyers. There is the constant suggestion that, by definition, zealous advocacy on behalf of the accused crosses some ethical—or certainly *moral*—line. Gone are the days when defenders were heroes, the days of Clarence Darrow and Atticus Finch. Who do we have now? Johnnie Cochran, the guy who got O.J. Simpson off. . . .

Even respected law scholars have described defenders as "amoral," "immoral," or otherwise ethically suspect. The most generous commentators suggest that defenders "detach themselves from difficult moral questions."

Much has been written about whether you can be a good person and a good *defender*—that is, whether it is morally acceptable to defend people who do bad things—and what the personal and professional dilemmas are for those who engage in such work.

Meanwhile, almost nothing has been written about whether you can be a good person and a good *prosecutor*—that is, whether it is morally acceptable to prosecute people who do bad things. At the heart of this question is the reality that prosecution inevitably leads to punishment, which, in recent times, means locking people up (especially *some people*) for very long periods of time, and, with increased regularity, executing them.

I want to turn the tables and at least *ask the question about prosecution*. I believe it is an important question. In this Article, I will examine the morality of prosecution. First, I will explore the context of criminal lawyering at the millennium and what it means to prosecute under current conditions. Then, I will discuss whether it is possible to do "good" in this context — that is, whether a well-intentioned prosecutor can temper the harsh reality of the criminal justice system — in view of the institutional and cultural pressures of prosecutor offices. I will conclude by answering the question I pose in the title of this Article and addressing some likely objections.

I. THE CONTEXT: LOCK 'EM UP AND THROW AWAY THE KEY

. . .

> If we look squarely at the present state of crime and punishment in America . . . it is difficult to avoid the recognition that something is terribly wrong; that a society that incarcerates such a vast and rapidly growing part of its population — but still suffers the worst violent crime in the industrial world — is a society in trouble, one that, in a profound sense, has lost its bearings.
>
> — Elliot Currie

> [The prosecutor] wields the most terrible instruments of government.
>
> — Felix Frankfurter

THE JAILING OF AMERICA

In the past two decades, this country has turned to imprisonment like never before. As of December, 1999, more than two million people were behind bars, an increase of 3.4% from the year before. In the past ten years, the incarcerated population has grown at an average rate of 5.7% a year, resulting in a rise in the total number of people in custody by 711,818 inmates, the equivalent of 1,607 new inmates a week. Between 1990 and 1999, the rate of incarceration has increased from 1 in every 218 residents of the United States to 1 in every 147 residents.

There is no other developed nation that compares to the United States when it comes to locking up its residents. The United States is second only to Russia in its rate of incarceration. The rate of incarceration in this country is six to ten times higher than that of other comparable industrialized nations, such as England, France, Germany, and Switzerland.

Incarceration rates are so high — largely due to sentencing for drug offenses, but also because of increased severity in sentencing, the abolition of parole, and other "reforms" such as "truth in sentencing" — that the prison system has become an industry of its own. And by all accounts, these are boom times for the "prison-industrial complex."

We look to prisons as the answer to a host of complex social problems borne of poverty, inequality, isolation, and drugs. There is no mystery about the demographics of who is incarcerated in this country or the path that leads most would-be prisoners to prison. They are the deprived, the afflicted, and the forgotten. And they are disproportionately non-white.

Among the tangible harms caused by massive imprisonment is the spread of disease and poor health. The conditions of confinement in our jails and prisons—overcrowding, inadequate ventilation, physical and sexual abuse, poor medical systems—have led to the spread of infectious diseases among inmates and those with whom they come into contact. As of 1992, there were more than 48,000 tuberculosis cases reported in the state and federal prison systems. Because of the dramatic escalation in the incarceration of drug offenders—many of whom use intravenous drugs, share needles, and exchange sex for drugs—the rate of HIV infection in prison is nearly thirteen times that of the non-prison population. Those unlucky enough to be ill in prison receive horrible medical care, if they receive treatment at all. . . .

There is no question that a term of imprisonment can seriously impair an inmate's future ability to obtain and hold a job. Many people who serve time in prison already have a marginal relationship to legitimate employment; ousting them from the work force and failing to provide training or work experience that reflects current workplace needs all but guarantees a dismal employment future. . . .

DISPROPORTIONATE IMPACT ON AFRICAN AMERICANS

As inner city areas have become more isolated from the social and economic changes happening elsewhere, unprecedented numbers of African American men have become entangled in the criminal justice system. By the mid-1990s, half of the nation's prisoners were African American even though they comprise only 13% of the general population. No one who works in the criminal justice system could fail to notice that our jails and prisons have become repositories for young black men. As one researcher starkly put it: "[F]or African American males, the rates of incarceration can only be described as catastrophic."

Indeed, the data paint a bleak reality: 11% of African American males in their twenties and early thirties were incarcerated as of mid-1999. On any given day, one in fourteen adult black males is locked up in a prison or jail. One in three black males between the ages of twenty and twenty-nine is under some form of criminal justice supervision, either in prison or jail, or on probation or parole. In some cities, including our nation's capital, *one in two* young African American men are under the control of the criminal justice system.

The picture of the future is equally harrowing: Three out of ten African American baby boys will grow up and spend some time in prison. A black boy born in 1991 stands a 29% chance of being imprisoned at some point in his life, compared to a 16% chance for a Hispanic boy and a 4% chance for a white boy.

Although the number of African American women in prison is substantially less than that of African American men, the trends are troubling. From 1985 to 1995, there was a 204% growth in the number of African American women in federal and state prisons compared to the 143% increase for black males and the 126% increase in the overall prison population. . . .

The virtual banishment of an entire generation of black males has widespread social consequences. It is not simply a criminal justice problem, it is a *civil rights* problem: The legal gains African Americans have made in this country are seriously threatened by the current incarceration rate. And yet, in our rush to get these people off the streets, no one except for a handful of criminal justice researchers is willing to *pause* and contemplate these consequences. Unfortunately, the situation is getting worse, not better. In the face of what we know about the race-based nature of crime control we continue to embrace policies that perpetuate the problem.

To add to the symbolic loss of citizenship that banishment implies, there is actual loss. Across the nation, criminal disenfranchisement laws have led to the loss of voting rights for millions of Americans. . . .

IMPLICATIONS FOR PROSECUTORS

Prosecutors and would-be prosecutors must acknowledge *who it is* they are seeking to lock up and for *what*. They must acknowledge that those who are locked up remain there for longer and longer periods of time, no matter the circumstance: drug users and drug sellers, first-time offenders and those who have been in trouble before, the violent and nonviolent. Although prosecutors are not responsible for the conditions that spawn crime, the criminal laws that unfairly penalize conduct engaged in by some citizens and not others, the race-based nature of law enforcement, diminished constitutional protection from race-based law enforcement, or racism in American society generally, prosecutors routinely validate and perpetuate this sorry state of affairs.

Prosecutors uphold the banishment of a generation of African American men simply by playing their role in the context of today's criminal justice system. The government has devoted an arsenal of resources to a mean-spirited and misguided criminal justice policy that has literally stolen hope for the next generation from entire communities. There is no redemption under this policy, no belief that people who have done wrong could ever rise above their pasts and contribute something of value. There is only the prison cell. It is the role of the prosecutor, the *government's lawyer*, to carry out these policies.

The most mundane prosecutorial duties maintain the current regime: charging decisions, plea offers, disclosure of evidence, pretrial and trial advocacy, and sentencing arguments. This is so for prosecutors who see themselves as mere players in an imperfect system, hard-working government lawyers just trying to do their jobs. Because of the context in which they are practicing, even prosecutors who claim to be concerned about racial and social justice are helping to lock up scores of young black men for years.

I believe there are moral implications to choosing sides in this context. The only question is whether well-intentioned prosecutors—prosecutors who are "conscientious," "prudent," and socially conscious—can make enough of a difference to overcome this context.

II. THE CORRUPTION OF GOOD INTENTIONS

> [Your] true purpose is to convict the guilty man who sits at the defense table, and to go for the jugular as viciously and rapidly as possible . . . You must never forget that your goal is total annihilation.
>
> —Senior prosecutor lecturing his fellow prosecutors

> Case law says that the object of selecting a jury is to get one that's competent, fair, and impartial. Well, that's ridiculous. You're not trying to get that. If you go in there thinking you're some noble civil libertarian, you'll lose. You're there to win, and the only way to do that is to get jurors that are unfair and likely to convict.
>
> —Training tape in a prestigious prosecutor's office

> At one point I didn't care who went to jail, because everybody was guilty of something. It was just a matter of winning. I just had to win.
>
> —Former prosecutor

THE DUTY TO SEEK JUSTICE AND THE TENDENCY TOWARD SELF-IMPORTANCE

Ethical standards, rules, and codes all proclaim that the central duty of prosecutors is to "seek justice [and] not merely . . . convict." This overarching and "rigorous" duty, which has been recognized for well over a century, requires that prosecutors "do the right thing," not merely the easy or popular thing. It is a righteous exaltation, a call to rise above the Machiavellian, win-at-all-costs nature of ordinary law practice. While these same standards, rules, and codes also acknowledge the multiple roles of prosecutors as "administrators of justice," "advocates," and "officers of the court," the duty to seek justice is the chief and abiding ethic, marking prosecution as a grand and noble vocation, unlike any other.

But, what does it mean to be both an advocate and an administrator of justice? How does one balance these competing and sometimes inconsistent obligations? And how much do prosecutors actually care about—or even think about—their competing duties, especially when they are immersed in a case? The reality is most don't.

And what does it mean to "seek justice"? The concept could not be more ambiguous and subject to multiple interpretations.

Moreover, what prosecutor doesn't think that he or she is "seeking justice," doing "right," or doing "good"? Perhaps this sense of righteousness is a good thing; it might reflect awareness on the part of an individual prosecutor that he or she is *obliged* to be righteous, no matter the competing impulses. But too often righteousness becomes *self*-righteousness. Too often prosecutors believe that because it is their *job* to do justice, they have extraordinary in-born wisdom and insight. Too often prosecutors believe that they *and only they* know what justice is.

There is an inherent vanity and grandiosity to this aspect of the prosecution role. Many prosecutors genuinely believe they are motivated only by conscience and principle. But many prosecutors come to believe they are the only forces of good in the system.

The reality is that justice is an elusive and difficult concept. Most defenders recognize this on a daily basis. Wise prosecutors do, too. Justice, like many an abstract notion, is in the eye of the beholder. It can mean one thing in one case and something totally different in another. Ethical standards are turned on their heads, however, when prosecutors claim with confidence to have a special understanding of the meaning of justice.

THE TENDENCY TOWARD NARROWNESS AND CYNICISM

Prosecutors have a tendency to see things as black and white, right or wrong, guilty or not guilty. There is little interest in the various shades of grey that color most people's lives. Both as interpreters and enforcers of the law, prosecutors have a preference for the literal over the figurative, for *what* happened over *why* it happened, for the trees over the forest.

To prosecutors, the record is everything: police reports, criminal records, chemical analysis, physical evidence, documentary evidence. This is the stuff you can put your hands on; it speaks for itself. The fact that the record may not tell the whole story, or that there is another story altogether, is a complicating detail to be dealt with at trial or sentencing.

Most prosecutors believe that if someone breaks the law, he or she ought to be prosecuted. Individual accountability is everything. Individual circumstances, the forces that cause an event to happen, and the broad context of the matter only clutters things up. If the law is sometimes harsh, this is the responsibility of those who make the law, not those who enforce it.

This tendency to see things in black and white may be related to prosecutors not having clients. Prosecutors represent the government, not a flesh-and-blood client. They represent an abstract entity, not someone with frailties, weaknesses, vulnerabilities. Although some prosecutors claim to be "representing victims"—and some prosecutors may develop close bonds with some victims—the relationship between prosecutors and alleged victims is a complicated one, not fairly analogized to the lawyer-client relationship. The reality is that alleged victims are prosecution *witnesses*, not clients.

Defenders, on the other hand, undertake the representation of *people* in all their ugliness and splendor. We represent clients who have made mistakes, who have problems, and who may have done some terrible things—but who didn't arrive at that point from nowhere. In order to effectively represent a client, a lawyer must understand the client in all his or her complexity and make an effort to walk in the client's shoes.

The best lawyers are those who are able to "submerge" themselves in the client—at least for a time.

The ability to submerge oneself in another is related to the capacity for empathy. In the context of criminal law practice, empathizing with the client—connecting with and embracing the client no matter what he or she is alleged to have done, and no matter whether he or she is guilty or innocent—can be difficult. It requires both generosity and the suspension of *judgment*. It also requires acknowledging the random nature of good and bad fortune in life.

But prosecutors are in the business of *judging*, of upholding standards, of exacting penance. To prosecutors, luck is irrelevant. People make choices. The humility and liberation that defenders experience when they connect with a client may be antithetical to what prosecutors need to do. Compassion, while laudable, may not be something prosecutors can afford on a regular basis.

Perhaps to compensate for the lack of knowledge that comes from working closely with clients, prosecutors often act as if they have heard it all before no matter how inexperienced they may be. Too often, a prosecutor's immediate reaction to an alternative version of the facts—an exonerating or mitigating circumstance, or simply a different perspective—is to reject it. What defender hasn't begged, pleaded, explained, or cajoled, only to be told, "I don't buy it, counselor"?

For many prosecutors, cynicism takes over in both style and substance. In order not to be played for a fool, taken for a ride, considered a *sucker*—a nightmarish reputation for a prosecutor—prosecutors often become suspicious, untrusting, disbelieving. Notwithstanding the legal presumption of innocence, the cultural and institutional presumption in most prosecutor offices is that *everybody is guilty*.

At its best, there is a clarity and consistency in a narrow, letter-of-the-law approach and perspective of prosecutors; if the focus is on the act and not the actor there is less opportunity for prejudice or unfairness. At its worst, however, there is a kind of moral fascism.

THE PARADOX OF DISCRETION

Many commentators have noted the discretionary power of prosecutors. Prosecutors have the power to direct investigations, define the crime to be charged, affect punishment both in plea offers and sentencing arguments, and decide whether or not to prosecute at all. Indeed, this power is an enormous draw for many would-be prosecutors. The well-intentioned believe they will have the power to do good, to make a difference, or, at the very least, to moderate the excesses of the system.

The truth is most prosecutors have very little discretion. For newer prosecutors and those at the lower levels in an office, there is often little autonomy and independence. This is not necessarily different for more experienced prosecutors. As often as not, there is someone higher up in the office hierarchy who must be consulted before a prosecutor can act.

There are some cases in which prosecutors, no matter how experienced, often have no discretion at all. Cases alleging assault on a police officer are a prime example. High profile cases are another. However, sometimes prosecutors abdicate—or at best share—their discretionary authority even in ordinary cases.

Although prosecutors have discretion to go forward with a prosecution and may decline to prosecute for any number of reasons, there is generally not a lot of soul searching about the decision to prosecute. Too often, prosecutors decide *not to decide* and cede responsibility to the fact-finder. This is an especially troubling occurrence.

When prosecutors *do* have power, they too often abuse it. They throw their weight around to show defense lawyers who is the boss. They throw their weight around to show defendants that they are prosecutor, judge, and jury rolled into one. They throw their weight around because they *can*.

WINNING

In view of the institutional culture of prosecutor's offices and the culture of the adversary system generally, it is perhaps inevitable that the overriding interest of prosecutors would be winning. This is so notwithstanding the prosecutor's ethical obligation to embrace justice over winning, or the ambiguity of what it means to "win."

There is a courthouse saying—known by anyone who has ever practiced criminal law—that expresses the ethos of winning over everything else in a grisly, sardonic way: "Any prosecutor can convict the guilty. It takes real talent to convict the innocent." This would be just another cheap (but clever) shot about prosecutors if there weren't so many cases in which prosecutors *have proudly convicted the innocent* and refused to back down even upon compelling proof that the conviction was wrongful.

It is not just the big, high profile cases—too frequently capital cases—that create pressure on prosecutors to win. The same pressure is present in ordinary, run-of-the-mill cases. The pressure is both external, the result of the inherently political nature of prosecution, and internal, the result of policies relating to salary and promotion.

The desire to win inevitably wins out over matters of procedural fairness, such as disclosure. It is remarkable from the standpoint of both fairness and *efficiency* how reluctant most prosecutors are to provide meaningful discovery in advance of trial, and how little the situation has changed in the past forty years. The concealment of exculpatory evidence by prosecutors remains a serious problem.

The desire to win takes over and corrupts the plea negotiation process as well. There is no other explanation for the frequent, troubling occurrence of prosecutors making generous plea offers when a case is weak. The practice is troubling because it puts pressure on innocent people to plead guilty and avoid the cost and uncertainty of a trial. No doubt, prosecutors come to believe that the defendants to whom they make such offers are guilty of *something*, and the deal simply reflects problems of proof, not truth. . . .

THE LONELY AND DIFFICULT LIFE OF THE WHISTLE-BLOWER

For the idealistic would-be prosecutor who intends to do things differently and resist the corrupting influences, the road ahead may be hard. It takes courage, "strength of character," and a willingness to endure a certain amount of loneliness in order to "do justice" in any meaningful sense.

But a prosecutor cannot really stand *alone* and effectively prosecute. Prosecution is a team effort. Prosecutors have to rely on other prosecutors, police officers, other law enforcement personnel, and a variety of witnesses in order to do their job.

The prosecutor who becomes known for questioning police officers' honesty, or worse, for dismissing cases or seeking sanctions against lying cops is not going to get a lot of police cooperation in his or her other cases. Unfortunately, too many prosecutors go the other way: They unwittingly collude with lying and abusive police officers by allowing cases to go forward that should not. The typical instance is the defendant who is beaten by the police but is charged with assaulting an officer and resisting arrest.

Some well-intentioned would-be prosecutors genuinely believe they are going to grapple with the problem of police perjury, by recognizing it when it arises, declining to prosecute the cases infected by it, and seeking appropriate sanctions for the offending officer. Then, why is it that in eighteen years of law practice I have yet to encounter a single prosecutor who even acknowledges the possibility of police perjury in a case? If police perjury is as widespread as it is believed to be, why is it that prosecutors never encounter it? . . .

Many well-intentioned prosecutors also believe that their presence alone will ensure fairness and decency. If they are in the courtroom, none of the horrible inequities or indignities that sometimes befall the poor and forsaken will happen. Yet, again, why have I never encountered—or even heard of—a single prosecutor who has come forward to halt a trial in the face of plainly incompetent defense counsel? The right to competent counsel is central to every other right of the criminally accused, and the denial of that right threatens the foundation of adversarial justice.

Surely, prosecutors have an ethical obligation to do something—and not just take advantage—when they encounter a plainly ineffective defense lawyer. There are instances of incompetent, drunk, hung-over, and sleeping lawyers representing the indigent accused in every courthouse in the country, but there is never any mention of the other institutional actors who are present doing anything about it. The prosecutor clearly knows what is going on—among those of us who labor in criminal court, everyone knows who the terrible lawyers are, the lawyers who make you cringe and thank your lucky stars that you're not the poor schlub being represented by them—why don't they at least approach the bench and make a record of the incompetence they observe?

From a narrow perspective of *winning*, the convictions obtained here are just fine. Most of the defendants are probably guilty anyway, and, so long as the prosecutor is otherwise "ethical," what difference does it make that defense counsel is lacking? After all, the constitutional requirement of effective assistance of counsel doesn't require that defense counsel be *good*. But this is the sort of thing that strikes at the heart of our system of justice, raising questions about its legitimacy. These are also the convictions that stick.

Would-be heroic prosecutors should acknowledge how difficult it is to be a whistle blower. Glory is rare and fleeting for those who blow the whistle on co-workers, associates or powers-that-be in most settings; instead, there is resentment and hostility. The righteous are as often shunned as embraced. Most people want to do well and be accepted, whatever the setting. It is especially difficult for prosecutors with ideals *and* ambition to resist the pressure to adapt, conform, and be part of the team.

CONCLUSION

> I have never yet tried a case where the state's attorney did not say that it was the most cold-blooded, inexcusable, premeditated case that ever occurred. If it was murder, there never was such a murder, If it was robbery, there never was such a robbery. If it was a conspiracy, it was the most terrible conspiracy that ever happened since the Star Chamber passed into oblivion. If it was a larceny, there never was such a larceny.
>
> —Clarence Darrow

My answer to the question, "Can You Be a Good Person and a Good Prosecutor?" is now probably evident. But, let me say it plainly and then attempt to address some of the objections to my position. My answer is both harsh and tempered: I hope so, but I think not.

My position is rooted in this time and place. We live in an extraordinarily harsh and punitive time, a time we will look back on in shame. The rate of incarceration in this country, the growing length of prison terms, the conditions of confinement, and the frequency with which we put people to death have created a moral crisis. Although, arguably, all those who work in the criminal justice system have something to do with its perpetuation and legitimacy, prosecutors are the chief legal enforcers of the current regime.

My respect and fondness for my prosecution-bound students accounts for my "hope." By and large, their intentions are pure and they are headed into prosecution with greater awareness and sensitivity than most. My admiration for the handful of prosecutors I have faced who embody the qualities extolled by Justice Jackson also allow me some hope. . . .

———————

A rather different view is expressed in the following excerpt:

Charles E. MacLean, James Berles, and Adam Lamparello
Stop Blaming the Prosecutors:
The Real Causes of Wrongful Convictions
and Rightful Exonerations
44 Hofstra L. Rev. 151 (2015)

The primary responsibility of a prosecutor is to seek justice, which can only be achieved by the representation and presentation of the truth.

—National Prosecution Standards

I. INTRODUCTION

Wrongfully convicted and rightfully exonerated criminal defendants spent an average of ten years in prison before exoneration, and the ramifications to the defendants, the criminal justice system, and society are immeasurable. Prosecutorial misconduct, however, is not the primary cause of wrongful convictions. To begin with, although more than twenty million new adult criminal cases are opened in state and federal courts each year throughout the United States, there have been only 1702 total exonerations over the last twenty-five years. In only six percent of those cases was prosecutorial misconduct the predominant factor resulting in those wrongful convictions. In cases where DNA has resulted in exoneration, the most frequent causes of the underlying wrongful convictions are eyewitness misidentifications, improper forensics, false confessions, and informants. Certainly, one could argue that prosecutorial misconduct is inextricably linked to this problem because prosecutors may knowingly rely on this evidence at trial despite its unreliability. That assertion, however, ignores the fact that judges, not prosecutors, determine whether evidence should be admitted into the record and amounts to a claim that prosecutors rely on evidence and elicit testimony that they know is false. As discussed below, such a categorical claim of unethical behavior by prosecutors is not supported by the record.

Of course, even when prosecutorial misconduct is not the driving force behind wrong convictions, prosecutors can—and should—be part of a comprehensive solution that reduces the likelihood of wrongful convictions. This Article proposes the following solutions: DNA testing and functional magnetic resonance imaging ("fMRI") should be available to defendants who demonstrate a likelihood of proving by a preponderance of the evidence that such testing could demonstrate their innocence. When DNA samples are too degraded to permit genotyping, investigators should increasingly use DNA phenotyping to create a profile of the likely perpetrator and thereby exclude certain classes of people. Appellate courts should focus on the second prong of the Anti-Terrorism and Effective Death Penalty Act ("AEDPA"), which permits reversal of a conviction where a district court's decision constitutes an unreasonable application of clearly established federal law, even if the decision itself is not contrary to that law. In applying Strickland v. Washington's ineffective assistance of counsel standard, courts should focus more heavily on whether defense counsel's performance fell below an objectively reasonable standard of care. The qualified immunity doctrine should be applied uniformly, and supervisory prosecutors should be vicariously liable for a deputy prosecutor's unethical behavior. Simply put, lawmakers, courts, and prosecutors have the power and obligation to reduce the number of wrongful convictions by, among other things, ensuring a fair trial and meaningful appellate review.

To be sure, the term "wrongful conviction" should not be limited to the question of whether a defendant is innocent or guilty. Wrongful convictions should include those where the crime with which a defendant is convicted *or* the resulting sentence does not accurately reflect the defendant's culpability. This definition is consistent with the criminal justice system's commitment to due process and will lead to procedures that enhance the fairness and reliability of a defendant's sentence. Ultimately, where prosecutors, courts, and legislators exercise their power ethically, justice can be achieved; where that power is exercised in a manner that ignores pervasive flaws in the criminal justice system, justice is compromised. . . .

2. Government Lawyers: Civil

Problem 5–10

(a) City Solicitor, under the city's charter, is the attorney for the Mayor. While discussing a contract that the city had just awarded, after negotiations in which the Mayor took an important part, the Mayor mentioned to the City Solicitor that he owned a small amount of stock in the winning bidder. The participation of the Mayor in that award violated the state's conflict of interest statute and the City Solicitor has so advised the Mayor. The Mayor professed ignorance of the statute, expressed concern for his political future, promised never to violate the statute again and to sell his stock, but refused to take any action to undo what he had done because that would make the conflict public. What should City Solicitor do?

(b) City Solicitor, under the city's charter, is also the attorney for all city agencies and officials as well as the City Council, which is the governing body of the city. Solicitor is defending the city Planning Board in its refusal to grant City University permission to build a twenty-story dormitory. The Planning Board has just granted permission to David Developer to build a big mixed office and residential development in the city's historic district. The City Council has directed the City Solicitor to file suit against Developer and the Planning Board to overturn that decision. May City Solicitor do that?

Problem 5–11

a) Under Title IV of the Civil Rights Act of 1964, the Attorney General is authorized to bring suit if a complaint is made by parents that their schoolchildren as members of a class are being denied equal protection and if the Attorney General determines that the signers of the complaint are unable to initiate and maintain a suit on their own. §407(a), 78 Stat., at 248. Suppose that the Attorney General begins a lawsuit pursuant to that statute and the court finds de jure segregation in a particular town. When the time comes to decide what remedy should be sought, how does the Attorney General decide whose interests to consider and what weight to give them? Does the Attorney General in a sense represent all citizens' interests, including those who prefer racial separation? Does the Attorney General represent only the interests of the children on behalf of whom the Department of Justice originally brought suit? If the latter group is not regarded as the client, or as the only client, who will represent their interests before the court? Cf. United States v. Allegheny-Ludlum Industries, Inc., 517 F.2d 826 (5th Cir. 1975).

If there is a charge of discrimination and the Attorney General concludes that the metropolitan remedy being advocated by the United States is unwise, may the Attorney General cause the United States to switch sides? Must there be consultation with the plaintiffs first? Cf. Washington v. Seattle School District No. 1, 458 U.S. 457 (1982). See Note, "Professional Ethics in Government Side-Switching," 96 Harv. L. Rev. 1914 (1983).

b) Suppose that a claim is brought by a federal employee against the United States under the Federal Tort Claims Act for severe injuries caused by the negligent conduct of another employee of the United States. The case has received considerable publicity in the local press. You are the local United States Attorney, and the Assistant United States Attorney in charge of the case informs you that there is no doubt that claim is clearly meritorious and without any defense except that the applicable statute of limitations has run. She asks whether she should assert that defense on behalf of the United States. What do you reply and why? If you tell her to assert the defense, but before she takes action you are informed by political leaders in your party that they are working on presenting a "kind face" for the upcoming election, would you take that into account in deciding whether to countermand your order? See Lanctot, "The Duty of Zealous Advocacy and the Ethics of the Federal Government Lawyer: The Three Hardest Questions," 64 S. Cal. L. Rev. 951 (1991).

Problem 5–12

Under state law the Attorney General of the State is the chief law officer, with responsibility to advise various state agencies. The State Personnel Board was considering holding a closed meeting in a controversial disciplinary matter involving a member of the State Police. At the direction of the Attorney General, an Assistant Attorney General attended a board meeting at which the matter was discussed. The discussion necessarily included the matters uncovered by the Board's investigation. The Assistant Attorney General reported the Attorney General's opinion that there should be an open meeting and advised it most strongly to follow that advice. When the Board held a closed meeting, the Attorney General brought suit to invalidate its decision because it had been rendered after an illegal closed meeting. The Board then hired private lawyers to file a complaint with the State Bar charging that the Attorney

General's actions violated his duties under the Code of Professional Responsibility with respect to maintaining his client's confidences and avoiding conflicts of interest. The Attorney General then brought suit in state court to enjoin the proceedings on the ground that the primary obligation of the Attorney General was owed to the public as his client and that he was not bound by all the professional rules that apply to private attorneys. How should that case be decided? Compare People ex rel. Deukmajian v. Brown, 29 Cal. 3d 150 (1981), with State Bar Rule 4-102, Standard 69 (1988), as promulgated by the Georgia Supreme Court after an attempt by the State Bar's Disciplinary Board to proceed with disciplinary action against the state Attorney General. The latter took legal action against a state agency that acted contrary to advice given by his office after it had been consulted by the agency. The Supreme Court adopted retroactively a standard that first set forth the general rule that a lawyer may not represent a client against a former client in a substantially related matter without the former client's consent. It then excepted from the definition of "client" a public agency, officer or employee represented by a lawyer who is a full-time public official.

United States v. John Doe

399 F.3d 527 (2d Cir. 2005)

JOHN M. WALKER, JR., Chief Judge:

This opinion follows our expedited order of August 25, 2004, reversing an order of the United States District Court for the District of Connecticut that would have compelled the former chief legal counsel in the Office of the Governor of Connecticut to reveal to a federal grand jury the contents of private conversations she had with the Governor and various members of his staff for the purpose of providing legal advice. We now explain the reasoning in support of the order.

BACKGROUND

On February 19, 2004, in the course of investigating possible criminal violations by Connecticut public officials and employees, and by private parties with whom the state had done business, a federal grand jury subpoenaed the testimony of Anne C. George, former chief legal counsel to the Office of the Governor of Connecticut. George served in that position from August 2000 to December 2002 and before that as deputy legal counsel. During the period leading up to issuance of the subpoena, the U.S. Attorney's Office ("the Government") had been investigating, in particular, whether Governor Rowland and members of his staff had received gifts from private individuals and entities in return for public favors, including the favorable negotiation and awarding of state contracts. The Government had sought, through direct contact with Governor Rowland, to gain access to specified communications between Rowland, his staff, and legal counsel, all to no avail. The Government had also asked George herself to submit to a voluntary interview. She declined, however, after the Office of the Governor notified her that it believed that the information the Government was seeking was protected by the attorney-client privilege.

On March 3, 2004, prior to George's appearance before the grand jury, the Government moved in the district court to compel George to testify about the contents of confidential communications between George and Governor Rowland and members of his staff. The district court withheld decision pending George's actual appearance and assertion of the privilege before the grand jury.

On April 7, 2004, when George appeared before the grand jury, she testified that in her capacity as legal counsel to the Governor she had engaged in numerous conversations with Rowland and other members of his staff on the subject of the receipt of gifts and the meaning of related state ethics laws. George also stated that she had spoken with Rowland's former co-Chief of Staff about a practice of state contracts being sent to the Governor's Office for approval. She testified, however, that because all of these conversations were in confidence and conducted for the purpose of providing legal advice, the Office of the Governor was of the view that they were protected by the attorney-client privilege, which it declined to waive. Accordingly, asserting the privilege on behalf of her client, George refused to answer questions pertaining to the content of the conversations.

On April 26, 2004, the district court entered an order compelling George's testimony. After noting that it was "undisputed that the grand jury need[ed] the information it [sought] to obtain from Ms. George," the district court concluded that "reason and experience dictate that, in the grand jury context, any governmental attorney-client privilege must yield because the interests served by the grand jury's fact-finding process clearly outweigh the interest served by the privilege." The district court distinguished the "governmental" attorney-client privilege from the privilege in the context of a private attorney-client relationship, by explaining that "unlike a private lawyer's duty of loyalty to an individual client, a government lawyer's duty does not lie solely with his or her client agency," but also with the public.

Both the Office of the Governor and Rowland, as interested parties, appealed the district court's decision. We granted the Government's motion to expedite the appeal.

On June 21, 2004, one day prior to oral argument, Governor Rowland announced that he would resign as Governor, effective July 1, 2004. At argument, we asked the parties to address the question of whether Rowland's resignation would affect our disposition of the appeal. The Government subsequently informed us that it had asked Rowland's successor, Governor M. Jodi Rell, to consider waiving the privilege insofar as the privilege was held by the Office of the Governor, and requested that we defer our disposition of the appeal pending Governor Rell's decision. On August 6, 2004, the newly appointed counsel to the Office of the Governor informed us that Governor Rell declined to waive the privilege.

On August 25, 2004, for reasons we now explain, we issued an order reversing the district court.

DISCUSSION

Federal Rule of Evidence 501 governs the nature and scope of a privilege claimed in proceedings before a federal grand jury. See In re Katz, 623 F.2d 122, 124 n.1 (2d Cir. 1980). The rule instructs that "the privilege of a witness, person, government, State, or political subdivision thereof shall be governed by the principles of the common law as they may be interpreted by the courts of the United States in the light of reason and experience." Fed.R.Evid. 501. Our determination of whether the Office of the Governor may claim a privilege, then, requires us to ascertain "the principles of the common law" and to apply them "in the light of reason and experience." In doing so, while we may draw on the law of privilege as it has developed in state courts, we are not bound by it. In criminal cases, Rule 501 plainly requires that we apply the federal law of privilege. See United States v. Gillock, 445 U.S. 360, 368 (1980).

Although there is little case law addressing the application of the attorney-client privilege in the specific circumstances presented here, we are nonetheless dealing with a well-established and familiar principle. "The attorney-client privilege is one of the oldest recognized privileges for confidential communications," Swidler & Berlin v. United States, 524 U.S. 399, 403 (1998), one that for centuries has been a part of the common law, in one form or another. While the privilege has a long history, understandings of its purpose and scope have varied over time. Compare 1 John W. Strong, *McCormick on Evidence* § 87, at 343–46 (5th ed. 1999) (summarizing view that privilege, as it first appeared in Elizabethan England, was linked to barrister's code of honor, but rationale behind it later developed a more utilitarian bent) with 24 Charles Alan Wright & Kenneth W. Graham, Jr., *Federal Practice and Procedure* § 5472, at 71–77 (1986) (characterizing as "highly questionable" the view that a rationale predicated on notions of honor, loyalty, and fairness gradually gave way to a utilitarian rationale for privilege, and arguing that during the modern period both rationales have coexisted). Today, the generally acknowledged purpose of the privilege is "to encourage 'full and frank communication between attorneys and their clients and thereby promote broader public interests in the observance of law and the administration of justice.'" *Swidler*, 524 U.S. at 403 (quoting Upjohn Co. v. United States, 449 U.S. 383, 389 (1981)) . . . .

The idea that a robust attorney-client privilege will in fact "promote broader public interests" does not mean that application of the privilege will render justice in every single case. Nevertheless, courts have by reason and experience concluded that a consistent application of the privilege over time is necessary to promote the rule of law by encouraging consultation with lawyers, and ensuring that lawyers, once consulted, are able to render to their clients fully informed legal advice. . . .

In light of the common-law roots of the attorney-client privilege and the attendant principle (evident in case law stretching back at least a century, see Hunt v. Blackburn, 128 U.S. 464, 470 (1888)) that safeguarding client confidences promotes, rather than undermines, compliance with the law, we believe it best to proceed cautiously when asked to narrow the privilege's protections in a particular category of cases. We are aware, of course, that even existing privileges are not to be "expansively construed," as they "are in derogation of the search for truth," United States v. Nixon, 418 U.S. 683, 710 (1974), and that the attorney-client privilege, in particular, "applies only where necessary to achieve its purpose," Fisher v. United States, 425 U.S. 391, 403 (1976). But this admonishment does not invite a wholesale reassessment of the privilege's utility whenever it is invoked under previously unexplored circumstances. Instead, our application of the privilege in a "new" context remains informed by the longstanding principles and assumptions that underlie its application in more familiar territory.

There is no dispute in this case that these principles and assumptions apply to government lawyers and their clients under certain circumstances. The Government concedes, for instance, both that a governmental attorney-client privilege exists generally, and that it may be invoked in the civil context. Ample authority supports both propositions. In 1972, the Supreme Court promulgated Federal Rules of Evidence setting forth nine specific categories of privileges, including an attorney-client privilege. Proposed Federal Rule 503, defining the privilege, included public officers and public entities within its definition of "client," see Proposed Fed.R.Evid. 503(a)(1), reprinted in 56 F.R.D. 183, 235 (1972); commentary accompanying the proposed rule, moreover, provided that the "definition of 'client' includes governmental bodies," id. at 236. While Proposed Rule 503 was not adopted by Congress, courts and commentators have treated it as a source of general guidance regarding federal common law principles. . . . ("They are the culmination of three drafts prepared by an Advisory Committee consisting of judges, practicing lawyers and academicians."); 3 Jack B. Weinstein & Margaret A. Berger, *Weinstein's Federal Evidence*, § 503.02, at 503–10 (2d ed. 1997) ("[Proposed Rule 503] restates, rather than modifies, the common-law lawyer-client privilege. Thus, it has considerable utility as a guide to the federal common law.") . . . . Similarly, section 74 of the Restatement (Third) of the Law Governing Lawyers provides that the "attorney-client privilege extends to a communication of a governmental organization" as it would to a private organization. The commentary to that section notes that "the privilege aids government entities and employees in obtaining legal advice founded on a complete and accurate factual picture." Id. cmt. b. While these authorities are not conclusive as to the existence at common law of a governmental attorney-client privilege, they demonstrate that serious legal thinkers, applying "reason and experience," have considered the privilege's protections applicable in the government context.

The case law, as well, while not extensively addressing the issue, generally assumes the existence of a governmental attorney-client privilege in civil suits between government agencies and private litigants. See, e.g., In re Lindsey, 158 F.3d 1263, 1268 (D.C. Cir. 1998) ("Courts, commentators, and government lawyers have long recognized a government attorney-client privilege in several contexts."). . . . The privilege has arisen in a number of these cases in the context of Exemption 5 of the Freedom of Information Act, 5 U.S.C. § 552(b)(5), which allows a federal government agency to withhold from requests under the Act "inter-agency or intra-agency memorandums or letters which would not be available by law to a party other than an agency in litigation with the agency." Courts have construed Exemption 5 as covering materials protected by the attorney-client privilege and, in doing so, have assumed that such a privilege attaches when the attorney is a government lawyer and the client a government entity. See, e.g., Coastal States Gas Corp. v. Dep't of Energy, 617 F.2d 854, 862 (D.C. Cir. 1980) ("Exemption 5 protects, as a general rule, materials which would be protected under the attorney-client privilege.") . . . .

There is, then, substantial authority for the view that the rationale supporting the attorney-client privilege applicable to private entities has general relevance to governmental entities as well. The Government argues that while this authority may establish a privilege of some kind, recent case law in other circuits supports its view that the attorney-client privilege in the government context is weaker than in its traditional form. It cites In re: A Witness Before the Special Grand Jury, 288 F.3d 289 (7th Cir. 2002) ("*Ryan*"); In re Lindsey, 158 F.3d 1263 (D.C. Cir. 1998) ("*Lindsey*"); and In re Grand Jury Subpoena Duces Tecum, 112 F.3d 910 (8th Cir. 1997) ("*Grand Jury*"), for the proposition that the "governmental" attorney-client privilege must give way where a federal grand jury seeks access to otherwise privileged statements in order to further a criminal investigation. While *Lindsey* and *Grand Jury* involved applications of the privilege to communications by a *federal* executive, and thus involved statutes and considerations unrelated to this case, all three decisions broadly questioned the relevance of the traditional rationale supporting the privilege to the government context. See *Ryan*, 288 F.3d at 293; *Grand Jury*, 112 F.3d at 921; *Lindsey*, 158 F.3d at 1272–73.

Drawing on these decisions, the Government contends that the reasons for the traditional attorney-client privilege do not apply with the same force in the circumstances presented by this case: a federal grand jury investigation into potentially criminal government conduct. It argues, first, that George, as a government attorney, has a fundamentally different relationship with her client, the Office of the Governor, than does a private attorney representing a private individual. George's client is a public entity, accountable to the general citizenry. As the Office of the Governor serves the public, the Government argues, so too must George as counsel to that office. Her loyalty to the Governor, the Government contends, must yield to her loyalty to the public, to whom she owes ultimate allegiance when violations of the criminal law are at stake. Accordingly, the Government argues that the privilege should not be used as a shield to permit George, as a government attorney, to withhold client confidences, when revealing them would be in the public interest. Implicit in the Government's argument is the presumption that the public interest in the present circumstances lies with disclosure and the furtherance of the "truth-seeking" function of the grand jury. "To allow the Governor's Office to interpose a testimonial privilege 'as a shield against the production of information relevant to a federal criminal investigation,'" the Government concludes, "'would represent a gross misuse of public assets.'" (Gov't Brief at 23 (quoting *Grand Jury,* 112 F.3d at 921)).

We cannot accept the Government's unequivocal assumption as to where the public interest lies. To be sure, it is in the public interest for the grand jury to collect all the relevant evidence it can. However, it is also in the public interest for high state officials to receive and act upon the best possible legal advice. Indeed, the people of Connecticut have deemed the latter interest more important than the former: if *state* prosecutors had sought to compel George to reveal the conversations at issue, there is little doubt that the conversations would be protected. The Connecticut legislature has enacted a statute specifically providing that

> [i]n any civil or criminal case or proceeding or in any legislative or administrative proceeding, all confidential communications shall be privileged and a government attorney shall not disclose any such communications unless an authorized representative of the public agency consents to waive the privilege and allow such disclosure.

Conn. Gen. Stat. § 52-146r(b). The people of Connecticut, then, acting through their representatives, have concluded that the public interest is advanced by upholding a governmental privilege even in the face of a criminal investigation. We do not suggest, of course, that federal courts, charged with formulating federal common law, must necessarily defer to state statutes in determining whether the public welfare weighs in favor of recognizing or dissolving the attorney-client privilege. But we cite the Connecticut statute to point out that the public interest is not nearly as obvious as the Government suggests. One could as easily conclude, with the Connecticut legislature, that the protections afforded by the privilege ultimately promote the public interest, even when they might impede the search for truth in a particular criminal investigation.

We believe that, if anything, the traditional rationale for the privilege applies with special force in the government context. It is crucial that government officials, who are expected to uphold and execute the law and who may face criminal prosecution for failing to do so, be encouraged to seek out and receive fully informed legal advice. Upholding the privilege furthers a culture in which consultation with government lawyers is accepted as a normal, desirable, and even indispensable part of conducting public business. Abrogating the privilege undermines that culture and thereby impairs the public interest. . . .

We are aware, of course, that the relationship between a government attorney and a government official or employee is not the same as that between a private attorney and his client. For one, in the government context, the individual consulting with his official attorney may not control waiver of the privilege. Even if he does control waiver during his time in government, the possibility remains that a subsequent administration might purport to waive the privilege exercised by a predecessor. Thus, some commentators (and presumably the Government, here) question whether application of the attorney-client privilege in the government context will in fact encourage public officials and employees to confide in counsel. See, e.g., Melanie B. Leslie, "Government Officials as Attorneys and Clients: Why Privilege the Privileged?," 77 Ind. L.J. 469, 507 (2002). While encouraging little in the way of legal consultation and disclosure, their argument goes, the privilege engenders significant costs by frustrating the "search for truth."

Whatever merit there is to this reasoning, we think it insufficient to jettison a principle as entrenched in our legal tradition as that underlying the attorney-client privilege. Such reasoning amounts to little more than speculation over the way in which the privilege functions in the government context. Cf. *Swidler*, 524 U.S. at 410 ("A 'no harm in one more exception' rationale could contribute to the general erosion of the privilege, without reference to common-law principles or 'reason and experience.'"). We also reject the idea that because government employees can confer with private counsel to represent their own, individual interests, the privilege is somehow less important when applied to government counsel. The privilege serves to promote the free flow of information to the attorney (and thereby to the client entity) as well as to the individual with whom he communicates. See *Upjohn*, 449 U.S. at 390. The government attorney requires candid, unvarnished information from those employed by the office he serves so that he may better discharge his duty to that office.

Having determined that the attorney-client privilege applies to the communications at issue in this case, we decline to fashion a balancing test, or otherwise establish a rule whereby a "generalized assertion of privilege must yield to the demonstrated, specific need for evidence . . . ." *Nixon*, 418 U.S. at 713 (establishing balancing test with regard to executive privilege). The Supreme Court has instructed that, where the attorney-client privilege applies, its protections must be reliably enforced in order to effectuate its goal of promoting compliance with the law. See *Swidler*, 524 U.S. at 409 ("Balancing *ex post* the importance of the information against client interests, even limited to criminal cases, introduces substantial uncertainty into the privilege's application. For just that reason, we have rejected use of a balancing test in defining the contours of the privilege."); see also *Upjohn*, 449 U.S. at 393 ("An uncertain privilege, or one which purports to be certain but results in widely varying applications by the courts, is little better than no privilege at all."). We see no persuasive reason to abandon that logic here. Of course, nothing we hold today derogates from traditional doctrines, such as the crime-fraud exception, that apply to the private attorney-client relationship and that courts have developed, through reason and experience, to limit egregious abuses of the protections that the privilege affords. See [In re] *John Doe, Inc.*, 13 F.3d [633 (2d Cir. 1994)] at 636 ("The crime-fraud exception strips the privilege from attorney-client communications that relate to client communications in furtherance of contemplated or ongoing criminal or fraudulent conduct.") (internal quotation marks and citation omitted).

In arguing that we ought not "extend" the attorney-client privilege to the present situation, the Government asks us, in essence, to assign a precise functional value to its protections and then determine whether, and under what circumstances, the costs of these protections become too great to justify. We find the assumptions underlying this approach to be illusory, and the approach itself potentially dangerous. The Government assumes that "the public interest" in disclosure is readily apparent, and that a public official's willingness to consult with counsel will be only "marginally" affected by the abrogation of the privilege in the face of a grand jury subpoena. Because we cannot accept either of these assumptions, we decline to abandon the attorney-client privilege in a context in which its protections arguably are needed most.[4] In the end, we do not view the question before us as whether to "extend" the privilege to the government context, and our decision today does no such thing. Rather, we have simply refused to countenance its abrogation in circumstances to which its venerable and worthy purposes fully pertain.

For the foregoing reasons, we REVERSE the order of the district court.

Notes

1. A quite different approach to the ethical responsibilities of government counsel was taken by the Court of Appeals for the District of Columbia in In re Lindsey, referred to in the principal case. The investigation of President Clinton by Independent Counsel Kenneth Starr produced two important decisions concerning the protection of confidential discussions between the President and members of the White House staff on the one hand and White House counsel on the other. Each case involved conversations in which the government "client" had both personal and official concerns. Swidler & Berlin v. United States, discussed at the beginning of Chapter 2, was the first. *Lindsey* was the second. It involved a whole variety of complex attorney-client privilege issues that arose out of the efforts of the Independent Counsel to obtain the testimony of Bruce Lindsey, Deputy White House Counsel and Assistant to the President, in connection with the investigation of the grand jury looking into the relationship between President Clinton and Monica Lewinsky. The majority regarded the existence of a government attorney-client privilege in the grand jury context as a matter of first impression and concluded that "the Office of the President is a part of the federal government, consisting of government employees doing government business, and neither legal authority nor policy nor experience suggests that a federal government entity can maintain the ordinary

---

4. Our decision is in conflict with the Seventh Circuit's decision in *Ryan*, and is in sharp tension with the decisions of the Eighth (*Grand Jury*) and the D.C. Circuits (*Lindsey*). We are mindful that uniformity among the circuits fosters predictability in the invocation of the privilege and suppresses forum shopping. See also Boren v. Sable, 887 F.2d 1032, 1038 (10th Cir. 1989) ("The Federal Rules of Evidence are intended to have uniform nationwide application . . . ."); Matinchek v. John Alden Life Ins. Co., 93 F.3d 96, 101 (3d Cir. 1996) ("We must attempt, to the extent possible, to harmonize our own federal common law rules with those of other federal courts of appeals."). We are in no position, however, to resolve this tension in the law.

common law attorney-client privilege to withhold information relating to a federal criminal offense." The rest of the opinion dealt with the extent of President Clinton's personal attorney-client privilege.

In connection with its conclusion concerning the non-existence of a government attorney-client privilege in a grand jury setting, the majority argued that the rule announced would chill only those communications relating to possible criminal wrongdoing. Moreover, in those circumstances the government official could always consult private counsel. Given the large number of criminal laws that surround government officials and the possible approach to boundaries in the course of carrying out lawful official activities, is the absolute rule announced by the court the most desirable public policy? Is it realistic to expect government officials to pay their own money and to reveal confidential government information to private counsel in order to get legal advice that will be protected from disclosure? See Note, "Maintaining Confidence in Confidentiality: The Application of the Attorney-Client Privilege to Confidentiality," 112 Harv. L. Rev. 1995 (1999).

2. As to any discussions between Mr. Lindsey and the President that related to the activities of then-Governor Clinton in connection with the so-called Whitewater land transaction, in which Governor and Mrs. Clinton were involved, or to any personal sexual encounter between the Governor and Paula Jones, should those discussions be protected either by the attorney-client privilege or by the ethical confidential obligation of Mr. Lindsey acting as his government lawyer?

3. How much of Mr. Lindsey's confidentiality problem, in your view, was caused by the fact that he held the position of Assistant to the President, a nonlegal position, as well as Deputy White House Counsel? If you believe that some of his conversations with the President could have been protected by the attorney-client privilege, would that privilege have been lost if Mr. Lindsey intermixed government legal, personal legal, and general political advice?

4. Judge Tatel's dissenting opinion suggested that the unique position of the Presidency and its unique need for legal advice is an independent reason for rejecting the majority's view that there is no attorney-client privilege with respect to information relating to the possible commission of crime when sought by a federal grand jury. Is the Presidency so unique as to this issue as to justify a different rule on attorney-client privilege from other government officials? In the state context, should there be a different rule for Governors from other state officials?

5. In the principal case, if Governor Rell had waived the attorney-client privilege on behalf of the Office of the Governor, should Attorney George have been compelled to testify about legal advice given to former Governor Rowland?

A Piece of History — Watergate

In conjunction with the proceedings looking toward the impeachment of President Nixon, Mr. James St. Clair was hired to represent the President and was paid with public funds. He was quoted as saying that he represented "the office of the Presidency," not the occupant of that office "individually." (New York Times, March 13, 1974, p. 1 at col. 7.) What does that concept mean? If Mr. Nixon had wished to follow a particular line of defense that would hurt the Presidency, could Mr. St. Clair have declined to pursue that defense on the ground that the Presidency and not Mr. Nixon was his client? If Mr. St. Clair represented the Presidency, what was the relation between his duties and those of the Attorney General? In the case of a public official, is it a beneficent or dangerous notion that a lawyer who represents the official as far as official actions are concerned has a duty to the public that may transcend the duty to the official? Who could hire a lawyer to fulfill such a role? Who could give him or her instructions?

Compare the views of Dean Freedman attacking New York Times columnist Anthony Lewis's criticism of Mr. St. Clair for making the statement quoted above. "Was Mr. St. Clair representing 'the Office of the Presidency'? Obviously, Mr. Lewis did not think so, nor did I. But there are people who, in good faith, did think so . . . . For those who believe in the need for a strong presidency, at any cost, Mr. St. Clair's assertion was certainly not frivolous. Nor was Mr. St. Clair's contention even an uncommon one. A lawyer seeking to exclude unlawfully seized evidence against a client in a narcotics prosecution, for example, would similarly stress that the true issue is not the guilt or innocence of the defendant, but the integrity of the law enforcement under the Constitution — in short, that the lawyer is not representing a heinous criminal, but the Fourth Amendment." Freedman, *Lawyers' Ethics in an Adversary System* 13 (1975). Is there a difference between claiming to represent the Fourth Amendment and Mr. Nixon's lawyer claiming to represent the office of the Presidency?

Regardless of its applicability to the St. Clair case, do you find Freedman's distinction between "representing a heinous criminal" and "representing the Fourth Amendment" persuasive on its own terms? What is the purpose of drawing such a distinction? Is it to allow lawyers to distance themselves from their clients and their clients' actions? If so, is it clear that this is in the client's interests? Is it even possible? We will return to this issue in Chapter 7 when we examine lawyers who represent unpopular clients.

Recent History — The "Torture Memos"

In the months after the attacks on the World Trade Center and the Pentagon, the government proposed and/or implemented a number of restrictions or modifications on traditional legal practices, including: 1) detaining indefinitely and in secret non-U.S. citizens who the government has "reasonable grounds to suspect" are engaged in "any activity that endangers the national security of the United States"; 2) instructing the FBI to investigate young Middle Eastern men who fit a certain profile and to gather information about them and ask them to submit to a "voluntary" interview without first demonstrating that there is reason to believe that they may be involved in criminal activity; 3) trying foreigners accused of terrorism in special military courts, where traditional protections such as the defendant's right to advance knowledge of the charges and evidence against him, to a public trial, to confront adverse witnesses, to be convicted only upon proof beyond a reasonable doubt, and perhaps even to the counsel of his choice would not apply; 4) sanctioning eavesdropping on attorney/client conversations of those in federal custody when the Attorney General concludes that there is reasonable suspicion that the communications are related to future terrorist acts; and 5) a variety of restrictions on the right to sue airlines, aircraft makers, airports—and even, for a brief time, Osama bin Laden—in connection with the September 11 attacks, and perhaps with respect to future attacks as well. See, e.g., Matthew Purdy, "Bush's New Rules to Fight Terror Transform the Legal Landscape," New York Times, November 25, 2001; Bob Van Voris, "Sept. 11 Laws Raise Fears of Tort Reform: Is Ground Zero a Slippery Slope?," Nat'l L. J., November 27, 2001.

Not surprisingly, each of these measures proved controversial, triggering a substantial debate about whether the "war on terrorism" justifies infringements on traditional civil liberties. Resolving this complex question is plainly beyond the scope of a course on professional responsibility. Nevertheless, the current debate highlights a fundamental issue that is at the core of this subject: do *lawyers* have special grounds for either supporting or opposing governmental measures that purport to promote national security at the expense of traditional legal rights in times of crisis?

For example, one of the most controversial actions taken by the Bush Justice Department relates to a series of memos written by the lawyers at the Office of Legal Counsel (OLC), the section of the department charged with signing off on the legality of government action. Shortly after 9/11, Assistant Attorney General Jay S. Bybee and his chief deputy John Yoo wrote a series of memoranda and legal opinions claiming that the United States was not subject to the restrictions of various international conventions (including the Geneva Convention and the International Convention Against Torture) and that the President alone had sole responsibility for deciding the fate of "enemy combatants" arrested or otherwise detained in the "war on terror." See David Luban, *Legal Ethics and Human Dignity* 162–205 (2007) (describing the memos in detail); *The Torture Papers: The Road to Abu Ghraib* (Karen J. Greenberg and Joshua L. Dratel eds., 2005) (compiling the actual work product of Bush Administration lawyers). On the basis of these memos, military and CIA officers working in the U.S. detention center in Guantanamo Bay, Cuba and elsewhere engaged in a variety of conduct—including subjecting detainees to waterboarding, sleep deprivation, beatings, and sexual and psychological manipulation—that many now consider to fit the definition of torture under various international agreements. See, e.g., Luban, supra at 197 (arguing that "crucial arguments in the torture memos" authored by Bybee, Yoo, and others "are frivolous" and that the approved conduct clearly amounted to torture under the relevant conventions). In addition, administration officials relied on these and other legal opinions to authorize a variety of other practices, including warrantless searches, "extraordinary rendition," under which suspected terrorists were sent to countries where it was likely that they would be tortured, and indefinite detention of those suspected of collaborating with Al Qaeda or other groups hostile to the United States. See Philippe Sands, *Torture Team: Rumsfeld's Memo and the Betrayal of American Values* (2008); David Cole & Jules Lobel, *Less Safe, Less Free: Why America is Losing the War on Terror* (2007). Beginning in 2003, Jack Goldsmith, who succeeded Bybee as the head of OLC, issued a series of opinions repudiating or withdrawing some of the opinions drafted by Bybee and Yoo. See Jack Goldsmith, *The Terror Presidency* (2007).

Notwithstanding this action, however, many of the actions described above continued throughout the duration of the Bush presidency. Shortly after taking office, President Obama and his new Attorney General, Eric Holder, issued a series of orders and opinions repudiating the use of most of the interrogation techniques authorized by the Bybee/Yoo memos as well as ordering the closure of the detention center in Guantanamo Bay and ordering the release of several additional Bush Justice Department memos. See Editorial, "Dealing with a Disgrace," Washington Post, Apr. 17, 2009.

There continues to be significant controversy surrounding both the underlying legality of the original "torture memos" and the adequacy of the Obama Administration's response. Although the President and Attorney General Holder announced that they would not seek to prosecute military and CIA officers who relied on the Bush administration lawyers' memos, Bybee and Yoo (as well as others ranging from lawyers in the departments of state and defense to former Secretary of Defense Donald Rumsfeld and Vice President Richard Cheney) were offered no such immunity. Many Americans, including the New York Times editorial page, called on the Obama administration and others to take further action. See Editorial, "The Torturer's Manifesto," New York Times, April 19, 2009 (calling on the Obama administration to investigate and possibly prosecute those responsible for authorizing torture and proposing that the Senate consider impeaching Bybee from his position as a judge on the U.S. Court of Appeals for the Ninth Circuit). See also Firejohnyoo.net (an entire website devoted primarily to having John Yoo fired from his position as a Professor at the University of California at Berkeley School of Law). But see Christopher Edley, Jr., "The Torture Memos and Academic Freedom," Berkeley Law News, Apr. 10, 2008 (letter by the Dean disagreeing with Yoo's substantive judgment but rejecting calls that he be fired). Yoo did not lose his position as a tenured professor at Berkeley, and neither Yoo nor Bybee was ultimately disciplined by the Department of Justice. See Associate Deputy Attorney General David Margolis, United States Dep't of Justice, Memorandum of Decision Regarding the Objections to the Findings of Professional Misconduct in the Office of Professional Responsibility's Report of Investigation into the Office of Leal Counsel's Memoranda Concerning Issues Relating to the Central Intelligence Agency's Use of "Enhanced Interrogation Techniques" on Suspected Terrorists, at 68

(Jan. 5, 2010) ("Margolis Memorandum") (reversing finding of misconduct but noting that Bybee and Yoo used "poor judgment"). Should either or both have been disciplined by the states in which they are licensed? Even though no disciplinary action was taken with respect to those who authorized or sanctioned these policies, however, the conduct that was alleged raises important issues about the proper role for lawyers working in the Justice Department and similar agencies. The following excerpt explores these questions.

Norman W. Spaulding
Professional Independence in the Office of the Attorney General
60 Stan. L. Rev. 1931 (2008)

There is now a burgeoning literature on the conduct of lawyers for the Bush administration, particularly the role of the lawyers who offered formal opinions purporting to confer legal authority for torture. The literature is, for the most part, roundly condemnatory. While I share the conviction that the work of lawyers for the Bush administration warrants censure for setting us on a path away from our most fundamental democratic and constitutional commitments, the assumptions about professional independence underlying the discourse of condemnation are, I believe, falsely reassuring. That false comfort is dangerous to the extent that it distorts debate about the source of professional failure and possible reform measures.

A. Independence as Moral Activism

One set of criticisms aimed at the Bush administration's lawyers is grounded in the assumption that the advice sanctioning extralegal conduct in response to the attacks of September 11, 2001, was the product of coldly neutral amoral legal advice. The lawyers in the Department of Justice, on this view, gave distorted advice either because they wrongly imported adversarial ideology about their role obligations into a counseling function in which there is no adversary, or because, caught up in disciplinary indifference to social ends, they simply lacked the character and integrity to avoid complicity in immoral and inhumane conduct. . . .

Properly independent lawyers, on either account, would have been moral activists. They would have rejected the rigid separation of conscience from professional duty. . . . By hypothesis, the opinions offered by such lawyers would have been more balanced . . . and, if the administration persisted after remonstration, the lawyers would have been self-reliant enough to withdraw or resign, and perhaps even disclose consequences . . . if necessary to prevent criminal conduct with life-threatening consequences to third parties.

B. Independence as Legal Positivism

A second set of arguments critical of the Bush administration lawyers draws . . . on the duty of fidelity to positive law. On this view, any properly trained, responsible lawyer would have identified and respected the clear legal boundaries prohibiting torture, domestic surveillance, indefinite detention and extraordinary rendition, the classification of prisoners of war, etc. Even if the administration lawyers lacked all moral scruples, so the argument goes, they should not have disregarded the unequivocal mandates of positive law. . . .

C. Independence as Civic Republicanism

A third set of arguments draws on the civic republican tradition of disinterested professional service. Here, the problem with the Bush administration lawyers is conceived not just as a failure to respect positive legal boundaries as such, but a failure to approach the counseling function from a perspective that consciously incorporates the general interests of the rule of law. Lawyers, all the more so lawyers representing the state, have a duty not only to provide disinterested advice, but also to be "public sentinels" . . . .

On this account, the administration lawyers were not only complicit in extralegal conduct, the conduct they endorsed and the form of their endorsement can be seen as undermining the rule of law itself . . . .

D. Independence as Political Accountability

Each of these critiques has its appeal, and some foundation in the facts. But the fit is hardly perfect. First, notice that the problem in each approach is primarily one of character, how lawyers define and internalize professional norms, not one of institutional design, how the structure of the office of the Attorney General and the Department of Justice supports or suppresses compliance with norms. An ethic of responsibility (morally activist, positivist, or civic republican) thus stands or falls with the integrity of individual role actors. Second, the core problem appears to lie in the general standards of the professional conduct applicable to all lawyers which, role critics claim, endorse (over) zealous client-centered lawyering. Professional failure in the Department of Justice is but one more piece of evidence that the lawyering role as it is conventionally played is morally corrupt and that "good" lawyers who know this must uphold their own higher standards.

. . . [T]he problem appears to be correctable primarily through Congress. Above all, the Senate must take care to ensure that only truly upstanding lawyers are appointed and confirmed to hold leadership positions. . . .

. . . However reassuring it may be to believe that character and the ideology of advocacy account for the professional failure of these lawyers, the available evidence suggests a more complex set of sources. Both the moral activism and civic republican critiques resonate in part by discounting the possibility that administration lawyers were animated by deep personal and professional enthusiasm for the administration's foreign policy agenda. But . . . I think [it] quite likely that, whatever their post hoc statements to the contrary, these lawyers were in fact operating consistently with conscience. That is to say, they acted as moral activists or "cause lawyers," seeking to vindicate, not disregard, their own strongly held moral, political, and legal views. If that is right . . . the general professional standards of neutral, morally humble advocacy critics attack might actually have provided a check that conscience could not.

Against the civic republican concern that the ideology of advocacy does not foster respect for the architecture of the rule of law must be weighed the possibility that these lawyers (perhaps naively or too easily) believed the conduct their advice sanctioned was fundamental to generating an appropriate new legal framework for handling the distinctive issues presented by terrorism in the twenty-first century. If so, the problem may have been an excess of purposivism, not an excess of narrowly client-centered lawyering. . . .

I think the positivist claim that the administration lawyers violated black letter law is quite right. Several of the central positions taken by the administration are legally frivolous. Or rather they *were* frivolous. In a structure that subordinates law to politics, it is always possible that initially extralegal acts will be ratified in the new political environment they help to create. . . . [President] Lincoln and [Secretary] Bates' suspension of the writ of habeas corpus and defiance of [Justice] Taney's opinion in Ex parte Merryman were followed by congressional suspension in 1863. With respect to the Bush administration's antiterrorism policy, Congress has acquiesced on a number of important fronts and looks to be acquiescing on others—even to the point of conferring retroactive immunity on complicit third parties. . . .

To be sure, not all extralegal projects "succeed," and not all should. But if success brings with it the imprimatur of new law, and if failure has the effect of reaffirming the legitimacy of existing law, why not simply embrace political accountability and the subordination of independence it demands? . . . If we value independence, if we want government lawyers to embody an ethic of responsibility, genuine independence requires structural support. And we would have to be willing to relinquish some of the flexibility for change—more baldly put, the room for lawlessness—which the current framework allows.

Specifying the structural changes that would enhance independence without compromising the positive aspects of political accountability is, of course, a surpassingly important question. . . . [S]ome things can be done to enhance accountability to Congress and the public. For instance, with respect to the advisory function of the Attorney General (now vested in the Office of Legal Counsel) formal opinions should be made public, subject to very narrow exceptions. . . .

. . . [H]istory and structure strongly suggest that the political accountability to the President is most likely to compromise professional independence in precisely those areas where secrecy and/or political disempowerment of affected groups forestall meaningful congressional oversight and public scrutiny. . . . Leaks to the media and post hoc congressional oversight are woefully inadequate substitutes for ex ante, structural guarantees of independence in the advisory function performed by the Office of Legal Counsel. . . .

Notes

1. What do you think of Professor Spaulding's critique of the various arguments that were made against the conduct of Bush administration lawyers? Is his criticism of the three positions internally consistent? Does it matter whether these lawyers *actually* believed that what they were doing was right, either as a matter of conscience or because it was consistent with what they believed to be the purposes underlying the rule of law, or should the standard be whether their belief was *reasonable* as measured against some objective standard? If the latter, what should that standard be and how should we define it? Recall the debate among Professors Pepper, Luban, and Kaufman in Chapter 3. Do Spaulding's criticisms raise questions about encouraging lawyers to be "moral activists," "positivists," or "civic republicans" outside of the government context? Should the legal profession itself have more "political accountability"? We will return to this issue in Chapters 8 and 10.

2. Do you favor greater "political accountability" for the Department of Justice? Do you favor accomplishing this objective by making the department more "structurally independent"? For example, should all of the Attorney General's advice to the President be made public, except perhaps in extraordinary circumstances? Should the Office of Legal Counsel be taken out of the Department of Justice and made an independent agency not subject to control by either the President or the Attorney General? Or more radically still, should the entire Department of Justice be independent? Indeed, should the United States move to create a fully professionalized and independent bureaucracy of the kind that arguably exists in many European and Asian countries?

3. Professor Spaulding argues that any "properly trained, responsible lawyer" should have understood that many of the positions advanced by the Bush administration lawyers were legally frivolous. But what about the many military and civilian lawyers who were enlisted in the administration's campaign to interrogate and prosecute suspected terrorists who were not "properly trained" in international law? Consider, for example, Lieutenant Colonel Diane Beaver, a lawyer in the Judge Advocate General corps. In her capacity as the chief legal advisor at Guantanamo, Beaver wrote a memorandum authorizing specific interrogation techniques that now are widely considered to constitute torture. As a result, many commentators have condemned Beaver, placing her in the same category as Bybee and Yoo. See David Luban, *Legal Ethics and Human Dignity* 182–184 (discussing Beaver's memo in the context of those written by Bybee and Yoo and concluding that "her memo on the legality of interrogation techniques concludes by recommending government approval of a felony"). Philippe Sands, however, demonstrates that Beaver's situation is more complex than this simple account would suggest. After extensive interviews with Beaver and her military and civilian superiors, Sands reports that Beaver, who had no experience in international law, was given absolutely no guidance before assuming her post. More importantly, when Beaver repeatedly sought guidance from her superiors about which interrogation techniques should be

allowed, her requests went unanswered and she was told to "give it her best shot." See Philippe Sands, *Torture Team: Rumsfeld's Memo and the Betrayal of American Values* 48–49 (2008). As Sands concludes:

> Apart from Diane Beaver's legal input, no one else seemed to have provided any detailed legal advice on the new techniques. . . . [T]here was no written legal advice from General Hill's lawyers at SOUTHCOM, or from the General Counsel to the Joint Chiefs of Staff. It seemed strange that on so important a decision the legal advice of a relatively junior lawyer, with limited experience of these issues, could be definitive. Why did [Defense Department General Counsel] Haynes not require anything more? The question kept coming up.

Id., at 448–49.

Why do you think Haynes or other high level lawyers left such an important decision in the hands of a junior lawyer like Beaver? Should senior lawyers have an ethical obligation not to put such important matters in the hands of someone with little or no experience?

4. Diane Beaver was far from the only military or civilian lawyer put in a difficult position as a result of the legal advice given (or not given) by more senior Bush administration lawyers. Consider the following affidavit filed by a career JAG lawyer explaining why he resigned his position as the lead prosecutor in the military commission trial of a Guantanamo detainee named Mohammed Jawad:

> My ethical qualms about continuing to serve as a prosecutor relate primarily to the procedure for affording defense counsel discovery. I am highly concerned, to the point that I believe I can no longer serve as a prosecutor at the Commissions, about the slipshod, uncertain "procedure" for affording defense counsel discovery. . . .
>
> In my view, evidence we have an obligation as prosecutors and officers of the court to produce has not been made available to the defense. Potentially exculpatory evidence has not been provided. My own practice has been to relinquish immediately any piece of evidence I have come across to the defense, even at the peril of the case against Mohammed Jawad, and even though I sympathize and identify with the victims in the case. To take only one example, when I discovered that Mr. Jawad had been placed in the "frequent flyer" program,[2] I notified the defense, sought an investigation, spoke to witnesses who had not been identified by the law enforcement agencies assisting us, and, in the end, conceded in a court filing that I had been wrong in denouncing Mr. Jawad when he complained of the conduct toward him in one of the first Commission proceedings. My personal

---

2. The term refers to a technique of interrogation in which the detainee is awakened repeatedly during the night and made to walk for long distances in order to induce sleep deprivation and exhaustion. Many consider this practice to be torture.

practice of disclosing exculpatory or mitigating evidence is not universally practiced at OMC-P [Office of Military Commissions—Prosecution].

I have previously declined to share the foregoing information with the defense because I believe I have some justifiable concern of retaliation if I am seen as being too cooperative with the defense and because I had hoped to change and improve things from within OMC-P. Other officers who have displeased the powers that be have been subject to treatment that in my opinion was retaliatory in nature . . . . I have decided to come forward at this point and share some of my reasons for offering my resignation because I believe I have an obligation to provide truthful information to the court regardless of which side calls me as a witness.

United States v. Mohammed Jawad, Declaration of Lieutenant Colonel Darrel J. Vandeveld, Sept. 22, 2008.[3]

In a series of emails with Slate.com, Vandeveld states that in addition to becoming convinced that Jawad had been subjected to various forms of mental and possibly even physical abuse (including long periods of isolation and allegations that he was hooded, shackled, beaten, and made to stand for long periods of time[4]), Vandeveld also began to have grave doubts about whether Jawad was in fact guilty of the crime for which he had been charged—and even if he was, whether there were important mitigating factors. However, because of Vandeveld's fears of retaliation from commanding officers who had already reprimanded him for stating in a filing before the commission that Jawad had been subject to "some abuse," he did not provide any of the relevant evidence to the defense. As Slate reports:

Vandeveld said he did not provide the defense with information the government had about another suspect in U.S. custody who had confessed to the same crime Jawad is alleged to have committed. Nor did Vandeveld provide the defense with a report by a U.S. government intelligence analysis stating that Jawad may have been forcibly recruited into a militia group that targets young men,[5] sexually abuses them and drugs them before forcing them to engage in violence—a report that appears to have been corroborated as part of the defense counsel's case.

---

3. We are grateful to Catherine Rogers for bringing Mr. Vandeveld's case to our attention.

4. During the period in which he was in isolation, Jawad tried to commit suicide "first by banging his head against the metal structures in his cell, then by hanging himself." "Confessions of a former Guantanamo Prosecutor: The Inside Story of a Military Lawyer Who Discovered Stunning Injustice at the Heart of the Bush Administration's Military Commissions," Slate.com, Oct. 23, 2008.

5. There were allegations that Jawad was only 17 at the time he was detained, which was an independent cause for concern by Vandeveld since minors were supposed to be segregated from adult detainees, which Jawad was not.

"Confessions of a Former Guantanamo Prosecutor: The Inside Story of a Military Lawyer who Discovered Stunning Injustice at the Heart of the Bush Administration's Military Commissions," Slate.com, Oct. 23, 2008.

What should be the obligations of a lawyer who is asked to participate in a military proceeding in which a defendant is not entitled to the full range of procedural protections that he or she would be entitled to if prosecuted in a civilian court of law? See David Luban, "Lawfare and Legal Ethics in Guantanamo," 60 Stan. Law. Rev. 1981 (2008) (detailing the many differences between the procedural protections afforded defendants in Military Commission trials and those conducted in civilian courts). Should the answer to this question be different for military lawyers than for those not in the military who are asked to participate in such proceedings? Did Lieutenant Colonel Vandeveld do the right thing in resigning his commission and disclosing what he knew to the defense? If Vandeveld had sought to continue as a JAG officer after disclosing information to Jawad's defense team, would the military have been justified in dismissing him? For an informative discussion of the many legal ethics issues faced by both military and civilian lawyers in Guantanamo, see David Luban, id. See also Alexandra Lahav, "Portraits of Resistance: Lawyer Responses to Unjust Proceedings," 57 UCLA L. Rev. 725 (2010) (using the Guantanamo case and other examples to develop a general theory about how lawyers should respond to "unjust" legal proceedings).

5. It is clear that Lt. Colonel Vandeveld's deeply held religious faith played a crucial role in his decision to resign. As he told Slate.com, "I am a resolute Catholic and take as an article of faith that justice is defined as reparative and restorative, and that Christ's most radical pronouncement—command, if you will—is to love one's enemies." "Confessions of a Former Guantanamo Prosecutor," id. As his doubts about the fairness of the process mounted, Vandeveld sent an email to Father John Dear, a priest known for his social activism with an on-line ministry expressing both his concerns and his fears. "I am beginning to have grave misgivings about what I am doing, and what we are doing as a country," Vandeveld wrote. "I no longer want to participate in the system, but I lack the courage to quit. I am married, with four children, and not only will they suffer, I will lose a lot of friends." Father Dear responded by encouraging Vandeveld to quit: "God does not want you to participate in injustice, and GITMO is so bad, I hope and pray you will quietly, peacefully, prayerfully, just resign, and start your life over." Id. Was it appropriate for Vandeveld to rely on his religious beliefs in reaching his decision whether to continue to serve as a military prosecutor or to disclose information to the defense? Should he have consulted a priest for guidance? Isn't it true that for many people, their deeply held religious convictions are what gives them the strength to do what they believe to be right in the face of grave personal risk? Isn't this also true of many of the detainees in Guantanamo? Is there any way to distinguish between these two uses of religion? Should we? We will return to the question of the role of religion and other forms of identity in the professional lives of lawyers in Chapter 12.

C. The Client Under a Disability

Problem 5–13

You are a new associate in a law firm. The senior partner has left you the following memorandum:

"I was appointed to represent a 13-year-old young woman who is the subject of an ongoing proceeding brought by the state Division of Social Services. I am her attorney, not her guardian, in this proceeding. My client was removed from her home and placed in a residential setting as a result of a determination that her mother was unfit to care for her. There is no guardian, but the state, in the form of a very overworked social worker, is monitoring her case. While the residential setting appears to have worked very well, my client has recently expressed a desire to return home and be reunited with her mother. The state's social worker believes that such a reunion would be inappropriate. I have learned from my client that the real reason she wants to return home is to reestablish contact with the friends whose drug habits got her in trouble in the first place. Whether the social worker is correct or not on the information the state has, I agree with the state's conclusion based upon what the client has told me. I have not been able to persuade my client that it is in her best interest to remain in her present setting. She wishes me to file a motion seeking the court's permission for her to return home.

"I need some help in deciding how to respond to her. Would you list the issues that I need to decide and give me a brief memorandum telling me how to go about reaching a decision."

"Ethical Issues in the Legal Representation of Children," 64 Fordham L. Rev. 1279 (1996) is a symposium on the issues contained in this Problem. For one proposed solution, see Kaufman, "Representing a Minor: A Shared Dilemma in Ontario and Massachusetts," 46 Osgoode Hall L.J. 159 (2008). How helpful is Model Rule 1.14?

Problem 5–14*

A district court judge who knows your interest in mental health matters has appointed you as counsel for the respondent in an involuntary commitment proceeding to be held before him in fourteen days. Your client is fifty-seven years of age and has a history of mental illness. He is presently an inmate in a locked ward in a state institution where he was brought on an emergency commitment after his brothers reported to his doctor that he was beginning to hear voices and get into trouble again as a result, apparently, of not taking his medication. When you visit the institution to see your client, the nurses tell you that he is having an anxiety attack, but that you

---

* This problem was prepared largely by Professor Charles H. Baron, Boston College Law School, with some assistance from Professor Kaufman, in connection with their participation in a conference held at Boston College Law School, February 21, 1980, under the auspices of the Mental Health Legal Advisors Committee of the Supreme Judicial Court of Massachusetts. It is reproduced here with the permission of Professor Baron.

are welcome to see him if you like. When you go into his room, he is startled by your entry, backs into a corner, and makes it clear that he is not interested in talking. The nurse with you attempts an introduction, but your client starts chanting "No, I don't want to see this man. He's not a lawyer. No, I don't want to see him." You decide to leave for the moment and take the time to check your client's records.

The records reveal several previous commitments at the same institution starting at the age of 16. All of the previous institutionalizations have been voluntary, but he has refused consent this time. Each time, he has been released after the proper balance of medication has been found for him and he has been sent back to live with his brothers, where he occupies himself in assisting one brother in his work as a plumber. So long as he stays on medication, he seems to function well. However, he has a tendency to develop side effects if the medication is not closely monitored. Each time he had been committed it had been because he stopped taking his medication, and he was released ultimately after he "recompensated" on a new regimen of medication. However, on two occasions he spent as long as two years in the institution.

After another vain attempt to communicate with the client, you return to your office to pursue other lines in the case. Telephone discussions with the brothers reveal evidence which is likely to provide the judge with a sufficient basis for an involuntary commitment. However, the brothers would prefer that an involuntary commitment not be on their brother's "record," and they believe that he would prefer that too. A discussion with the lawyer for the Department of Public Health indicates that he believes that he has an open-and-shut case, but would prefer a voluntary commitment, and is willing to agree to extended continuances until the respondent gets to the point where he is willing to consent or is released to a less restrictive alternative.

The next day you return to the institution to review records, speak to the medical personnel, and make another attempt to communicate with your client. You discover that he is still highly delusional but less anxious. You also discover that the hospital is understaffed with doctors and lacks the medical personnel to make sure that his medication is as closely monitored as it needs to be to get him recompensated as quickly as possible. It seems to you that the best course might be to have the client put under the guardianship of one of the brothers. This would provide him with a competent and caring person who might force the medical staff to discuss and justify plans for a medical regimen in a way which would get him the attention he needs. It would also provide you with someone who could advise you as to whether you should agree to a continuance. However, the irony of suggesting a guardianship for your own client does not escape you. In hopes of avoiding this problem, you make an effort to speak to the client again. This time he is quiet but looks suspicious. You explain that you are his lawyer and try to explain what is going on. When you are finished he says, "Who says you're my lawyer, anyway? You're not my lawyer. You're trying to commit me. I'm represented by Bill Clinton. Go away. I don't want to see you." You leave.

The following day you receive a call from the hospital telling you that your client has signed a voluntary commitment.

1. Do you still represent the client?

2. Suppose that you had not been appointed counsel by the district court but that you were regular counsel for that patient. After the conversation reported above, would you still regard yourself as representing the client?

3. Assuming that you are still counsel, do you challenge a voluntary commitment on the ground that your client was not competent to consent? Do you challenge the giving of medication on that ground?

4. If there is to be a hearing on the petition for involuntary commitment, do you ask for the appointment of a guardian ad litem who can give you direction as to whether you can seek an indefinite continuance?

5. Do you seek to initiate or have initiated a proceeding for the appointment of one of the brothers as guardian for the purpose of consenting to medical care?

6. If a guardian ad litem is appointed and wishes to approve a particular course of medication that your "client" rejects, do you still regard yourself as representing your "client"?

7. Suppose that the situation was just at the point where a brother of your client reported that your client had ceased taking medication and was beginning to act peculiarly, in much the same fashion as had occurred before prior commitments. You talk to your client who says that he does not want your help or counsel. His brother seeks your advice about getting help for your client. What do you do?

8. If there is to be a hearing on the petition for involuntary commitment and an attorney for the hospital says that she proposes to call you as a witness to testify about your observation of the client's conduct—but not any communications—may you continue as attorney in the matter?

9. After considering this Problem, reconsider Problem 2–20, p. 106. Is the "solution" to that Problem to be found in Rule 1.14? In Rule 1.14 only?

––––––––––

The lawyer faced with a situation like that depicted in Problem 5–14 must deal with the combination of new developments in the substantive law about clients' choices with regard to their own medical needs—refusal to undertake medical treatment, whether it is psychiatric care or blood transfusions, or the so-called right to die—and the uncertain professional duties of lawyers. The importance of the problem for lawyers is recognized in Model Rule 1.14 and its Comment. The drafters have recognized the complexity of the issues and have highlighted the difficulty of the lawyers' situation. They are advised that they should maintain as much of a lawyer-client relation as possible, even if there is a guardian, that they may (and therefore need not) seek the appointment of a guardian when the client appears unable to act in his or her own interest, that they should be concerned about disclosure of a client's disability, and that "ordinarily" (but not always) they should look to an appointed guardian for instructions. Compare In re Runge, 858 N.W.2d 901, 905 (N.D. 2015) (noting that "a lawyer's overriding directive in representing a client with limited capacity is to 'as far as reasonably possible, maintain a normal client-lawyer relationship with the client'" and refusing to discipline a lawyer who, believing his client to be competent, drafted a revocation of a power-of-attorney without first contacting the holder of the client's POA), with In re Jarvis, 349 P.3d 445, 457 (Kan. 2015) (suspending indefinitely a lawyer who, while representing a long-time client suffering from dementia and seeking to protect that client's best interests, interfered with both "the temporary guardian and conservator's management of [the client']s estate" and the court's orders in the guardianship proceedings).

Much is therefore left to the lawyer's discretion, including an overall choice of theory: whether the lawyer is to be guided by the "best interests" of the client or whether the lawyer should whenever possible and as soon as possible look to someone else, a guardian or the court, for instructions whenever there is doubt about the appropriate course of action. The selections that follow address that issue. See also Perlin and Sadoff, "Ethical Issues in the Representation of Individuals in the Commitment Process," 45 Law & Contemp. Probs. 161 (No. 3 1982). The Fordham symposium referred to at the end of Problem 5–13 contains 850 pages of articles on this subject. Two older articles that briefly set forth quite contrasting points of view still relevant today follow.

Neil H. Mickenberg
The Silent Clients: Legal and Ethical Considerations
in Representing Severely and Profoundly
Retarded Individuals[*]
31 Stan. L. Rev. 625 (1979)

A basic tenet of legal ethics requires lawyers to zealously represent their clients' interests. Ordinarily, of course, the client determines the nature and scope of his or her interest, and the lawyer merely uses special skills and training to achieve the goals defined by the client. Yet this principle, so rarely a problem in attorney-client relationships, presents great difficulties when the client is severely or profoundly retarded and lacks the mental capacity and skills in communication to provide the necessary guidance to the attorney. This article identifies some of these difficulties and suggests ways of ensuring effective legal representation of severely and profoundly retarded persons. . . .

THE ROLE OF THE ATTORNEY REPRESENTING A SEVERELY OR
PROFOUNDLY RETARDED PERSON

Reports on the quality of legal representation provided to retarded clients . . . tell of inadequate effort, unjustified compromise of clients' rights, and distorted perceptions of legal ethics. Although a "new breed" of mental health and mental retardation lawyers is emerging, advocates in this area are inevitably exposed to

---

* [The terminology in this article is dated. In 2010, Congress passed "Rosa's Law," replacing the term "mental retardation" with the term "intellectually disabled." — Eds.]

influences which discourage aggressive advocacy: In bringing litigation, the attorney must, for example, maintain good relationships with adverse government officials whose cooperation will be needed later to secure legislative reform and with service agencies with whom the attorney will be dealing in informal negotiations in later cases.[41]

Another barrier to effective representation is the apparently widespread belief that courts have failed to define the role of the attorney in representing mentally retarded clients. In fact, the courts repeatedly have made clear that the attorney with a mentally disabled client must not only act as an adversary counsel, but must "represent his client as zealously as the bounds of ethics permit."[43] . . . The attorney cannot waive any substantial rights of an incompetent client, or take any action that is prejudicial to the client's interests.

The requirement of zealous advocacy of course requires that the attorney advance the interests and goals of the "client" — the mentally retarded person — and not those of the parent, guardian, or other third-party representative. When an attorney is first contacted by a third-party representative, the attorney should carefully explain that it is the handicapped person who is the "client" and whose interest will govern the course of litigation. As long as the attorney is satisfied that the third-party representative — whether a legal or natural guardian, close relative, or friend — is guided by the best interests of the retarded person, the attorney can expect the third-party representative to protect and help define the goals of the retarded person. Legal and ethical principles require that the attorney obtain a guardian ad litem whenever a severely or profoundly retarded person lacks a third-party representative or has a representative whose interests conflict with his own. But what is the responsibility of counsel when he or she disagrees with the course designated by the guardian ad litem? Even the most concerned representative may project his own views and prejudices into the "best interests" of a mentally disabled person, and the possibility of disagreement will be great as both guardian and counsel attempt to define and pursue those interests. . . .

. . . [W]hile the guardian ad litem or other representative will have the ultimate responsibility for defining the goals of representation, the lawyer is not required to meekly succumb to any course of action suggested by the client-representative.

Occasionally, disagreements may arise between the attorney and the guardian ad litem. In Vermont, for example, the courts in civil commitment proceedings for mentally retarded and mentally ill persons appoint a guardian ad litem whenever the

---

41. Other factors include the attorney's likely ignorance of a field pervaded with medical and psychological experts, the complexity and ambiguity in this evolving area of the law, the inability of clients to guide counsel or to protest unreasonable accommodations by counsel, and the close professional and personal ties that often exist among advocates, service agencies, and state officials in this narrow field. See Bellow, ["Turning Solutions into Problems: The Legal Aid Experience," 34 Nat'l Legal Aid & Defender A. Briefcase 108 (1977)] . . . .

43. State ex rel. Hawks v. Lazaro, 202 S.E.2d 109, 126 (W.Va. 1974). . . .

client cannot communicate with counsel. Typically, the guardian will meet with the client, review the client's records, and thereafter discuss the case with counsel. In most cases, the attorney suggests an approach which he or she perceives as best for the client, and the guardian concurs. Occasionally, however, the attorney and guardian disagree over such things as community placement. These disagreements are usually resolved without referring to the court, but that option is available to either representative. Case law in other jurisdictions makes clear that whenever an attorney feels that a guardian ad litem is advancing goals that are not in the best interest of the client, he can seek judicial removal of the present guardian and appointment of a new guardian ad litem. If the guardian ad litem is acting generally in the interests of the retarded person but insists upon a particular course of action that the attorney feels is unwise, then the attorney can seek judicial resolution of the disagreement with the guardian, or can withdraw from the case.

A relationship between a client-representative and lawyer in which neither side dominates will most closely achieve the goals the client would have sought, had he or she been able to communicate directly with counsel. . . .

Alan A. Stone, M.D.*
The Myth of Advocacy
30 Hospital & Community Psychiatry 819 (No. 12 Dec. 1979)

Several years ago, a congressman wrote to me asking if I would testify on behalf of a bill he had filed. His staff, with the assistance of the Department of Health, Education, and Welfare and the Library of Congress, had determined that it would cost $60 million a year to provide every psychiatric inpatient in the United States with a lawyer. In his letter, he claimed that he had read my book, *Mental Health and Law: A System in Transition* [1975], and he was confident that I would support his bill on behalf of patient advocates. I responded by return mail that I would be delighted to testify if he would amend his bill to ask for $120 million so that there would be good legal representation on both sides. I never heard from the congressman again. But recently legislation providing for federally funded advocates for patients has surfaced again in Congress, with no recognition of the need for legal representation on the other side.

This is the era of advocacy. We have consumer advocates, child advocates, and patient advocates. The American Psychiatric Association has even amended its constitution and bylaws so that psychiatry too has an advocacy mission. Like the Congress, we want to climb on the bandwagon; we want the public to know we are for advocacy. Advocacy is by no means a new idea. One of the eponyms for Jesus Christ was "the Advocate," but surely his version of salvation was different than the one the

---

* Dr. Stone, 108th president of [the American Psychiatric Association], is the Touroff-Glueck Professor of Law and Psychiatry at Harvard University. . . .

lawyers have recently proposed for our patients and for us. It is time to unpack this buzzword, this slogan of advocacy.

The APA's notion of advocacy is that we will champion the medical needs of our patients. The lawyers' notion of advocacy is that they will champion the legal rights of their clients. Where we want the best treatment setting for our patients, they want the least restrictive alternative. Where we want careful treatment planning and continuity of care, they want immediate deinstitutionalization and maximum liberty. Where we are concerned about access to treatment, they are concerned about stigma and the right to refuse treatment. Where we are trying to salvage what is salvageable in the state hospital system, they are trying to close down the state hospital system. Where we want to advocate the medical model, they want to advocate the legal model. Our advocacy and theirs conflict more often than not, but for those who know little about the mental health system, the buzzword "advocacy" suggests both kinds with no conflict.

The root problem of the conflict is only understood when the last difference I mentioned, the legal model versus the medical model, is examined not in terms of goals but of procedures. The lawyers' notion of advocacy comes naturally; it is part of the Anglo-American adversarial system of justice. Each side is meant to have a zealous advocate. The work of the court advances as these advocates joust with each other.

The lawyers' canons of ethics give great importance to this duty to be a zealous advocate. Indeed, it would be fair to say that the basic credo of legal ethics is that the lawyer should feel free to proceed almost unrestrained as an advocate because there is a zealous advocate on the other side. This is the very basis of our adversarial system of justice. It is not a search for truth. Rather, each side struggles for an advantage, and out of the struggle the judge and jury pluck the just resolution.

The lawyers, then, have a long tradition of advocacy. It combines a notion of rights and a professional way of doing things. When their form of advocacy is applied in the political arena, it can become a formidable tool for achieving change. During the past decade, such advocacy has been the means for giving power to the powerless. Consumer advocates have given consumers who as individuals had no power the ability to assert their common demands. Civil rights advocates have done the same for minority groups. Advocates for welfare recipients and the aged have been able to have an impact on the entrenched federal bureaucracies. These advocates use the courts, the class-action suit, the media, and the political process to advance the needs and interests of the group they represent. They do so by presenting the needs and interests of their group as legal rights.

Given the success of this kind of advocacy, one can easily understand how advocacy has become a buzzword and a slogan appealing to liberals and populists alike. But it is crucial to recognize that where advocacy has really worked, it has worked because, first, the group's needs and interests could be readily defined; second, the interests could be formulated as some legal right; and third, paradoxically to us but basic to the system of law, the legal adversary had a powerful opponent, an adversary who had something to lose. Without an adversarial struggle, the judge has no real ability to find a resolution that is balanced.

None of these crucial elements have been present in most of the litigation in the field of mental health over the past decade. Legal advocates for the mentally ill have not been willing to consider seriously the needs of the mentally ill and to formulate those needs as legal rights. Instead they have done the reverse. They have treated rights as if they constituted the needs of the mentally ill.

And who is the powerful adversary for the mental health advocate to attack? There is none. Instead, mental health advocates, with the assistance of the radical anti-psychiatrists, had to invent a powerful adversary—the psychiatric establishment. But the last decade has made it clear that psychiatrists are anything but a powerful adversary. Wherever the mental health advocate pressed, the psychiatric profession gave way. In the courtrooms, there was almost never a zealous legal advocate to oppose the self-appointed patient advocate.

Consider the kind of case in which Congress wants to provide legal advocates for the patient who may be involuntarily confined. Take for example, a prototypical patient, named Mr. Jones. He has, for the past month, been increasingly agitated. For some time he has been convinced that people at work were conspiring against him. Last week he decided people were reading his mind, and he began to hear voices accusing him of sexual perversity. Since then, he has been unable to sleep and has stopped going to work. He now refuses to communicate with his wife or children. He paces up and down with a pained expression on his face; he is obviously suffering. He is now either crazy, or, as his legal advocate might argue, exercising his right to be different.

Mrs. Jones begs and cajoles her husband to come with her to the emergency room of the nearby community hospital. He reluctantly agrees. There he sees a psychiatrist who, after interviewing Mr. Jones and getting a history from Mrs. Jones, makes a diagnosis of acute paranoid schizophrenia and recommends hospitalization. Mr. Jones adamantly refuses any treatment at all. Mrs. Jones begs the doctor to do something: she is afraid her husband will lose his job, and she worries about the effect of this strange behavior on the children.

The question is, What does Mr. Jones need? What should happen now? The following is what the legal advocates believe should happen before Mr. Jones' psychiatric needs can even be considered.

First, Mr. Jones must be provided with his own lawyer, presumably paid for by the federal government, whose duty is to advocate Mr. Jones' freedom. Second, he must have a hearing before a judge within 48 hours and, no matter how disturbed he may get, the doctors are not to begin treatment until that hearing. At that hearing, his lawyer will argue that he should not be further confined and that, if confined, he has a right to refuse treatment. Third, the lawyer will insist that the psychiatrist must inform Mr. Jones of his right to remain silent and his fifth-amendment privilege against self-incrimination.

Fourth, Mr. Jones and his lawyer must be given timely notice of the charges justifying his confinement so that they can prepare a defense. Fifth, he must have notice of the right to a jury trial. Sixth, he is entitled to a full hearing, a trial with the right to cross-examine Mrs. Jones and his doctors, who must testify about the details of his illness and his dangerous behavior. Seventh, it must be proved by clear and convincing evidence that Mr. Jones is mentally ill and dangerous. And, finally, there must be inquiry into whether some less restrictive alternative can be found for Mr. Jones before involuntary inpatient care is ordered. "Less restrictive" for the lawyer will mean least loss of freedom and not "best treatment setting."

I have already mentioned that the estimated cost of these legal procedures was $60 million several years ago; it is undoubtedly much more today. That covers only the cost of lawyers for all of the Joneses; it does not include the court costs, the time of the hospital staff who must testify, and the lawyers, if any, for the other side.

The total costs will far exceed $60 million, and if the federal government doesn't pay it, who will? Why should any state or prosecutor want to go to all that trouble and expense? The state is being asked to use all that money and all those legal resources to justify putting Mr. Jones in a hospital so that the state can spend still more to treat him. What is in it for the state? Prosecutors have all sorts of incentives for putting away criminals, but what is their incentive for putting away Mr. Jones? And what about the incentives of the psychiatrist? Experience demonstrates that psychiatrists have always disliked being involved in civil commitment; with these new procedures, that dislike has become abhorrence.

In sum, legal advocacy is proposed to advance the interests of the patients against a powerful adversary, but it turns out that no one but Mrs. Jones really has an incentive to confine Mr. Jones. The powerful adversary of the mental patient turns out to be a paper tiger, and the psychiatrist is soft as a grape. Nor is it clear that the advocate is concerned or will care about Mr. Jones' needs in all this rhetoric of rights.

There are two important points I want to make here. The first is that the legal adversary system doesn't work well unless there are adversaries on both sides. But you won't have adversaries on both sides unless both sides have an incentive. In the ordinary psychiatric case, the state and the prosecutor have no real incentive, and the psychiatrist doesn't either. Thus in most states today, given the existing statutes and the lack of any real adversary, a conscientious legal advocate should be able to prevent all involuntary confinement. Many lawyers who work as members of the mental health bar candidly admit this to be the case, and some acknowledge that even they sometimes question the value of what they do.

Let me briefly mention another striking example of how the adversary legal model goes astray in our field. During the Supreme Court's deliberation of the need for legal advocates for children who are to be admitted to treatment facilities, a startling case was presented as an example of a violation of rights indicating the need for a lawyer. A child with Down's syndrome was being reared at home with the assistance of various professional programs. His parents, under a respite program, were to take the other children on a one-week vacation while the retarded child was placed temporarily in a facility. This kind of respite program is thought to be one good way to support families of retarded children and to encourage them to keep their children at home rather than abandon them. The legal advocates insisted that the child should be provided with a lawyer whose obligation it would be to resist this one-week respite program, using most of the procedures I described for Mr. Jones.

Once again, the question arises about what incentive the state has to use its lawyers to resist such advocacy. In the end, the kind of legal advocacy the Congress wants to provide every patient would destroy the respite program in the name of children's rights, ignoring the fact that the child needs a family and the family needs the support they get from the respite program.

Some lawyers may insist that I am drawing a caricature of legal advocacy rather than a true picture. One distinguished lawyer, for example, sees the advocacy role as one that tries to place the retarded child in the best facility available during the respite. He sees the lawyer's role as getting Mr. Jones into the best treatment setting with the least loss of freedom. His kind of advocacy is my kind of advocacy, and I can find it nowhere in the lawyers' canons of ethics. He would have the legal advocate take on the duties of the expert in access to mental health facilities. His kind of advocacy looks to needs, as well as rights.

But when I describe this kind of advocacy to the lawyers who are increasingly being recruited to the mental health bar, they generally resist it. In the first place, they don't want to be social workers, and they don't want to be responsible for taking care of clients' nonlegal problems. Their vision of advocacy is the lawyer as adversary, providing a limited legal service: Mr. Jones and the retarded child have a right to be free; it is their job to see to that freedom, and what happens afterward is not their business.

When legal advocates listen to my arguments and hear them, and admit that a system of legal advocates on one side won't work, they usually come to the conclusion that it is up to psychiatrists to see that the hospitals and the state supply lawyers to the other side. Theoretically they are right, and that is why I was willing to write the congressman to ask for $120 million. That would restore the integrity of the adversarial system; the two sides of the argument could be heard.

But no one has ever said that providing lawyers for alleged criminals would reduce the problem of crime in the streets or assist in the rehabilitation of criminals. At best, it ensures that alleged criminals obtain justice from the courts. Similarly, no one can deny that providing individual legal advocates for psychiatric patients will reduce mental illness or assist in the treatment of mental patients. The best it can do is to see that alleged patients get justice in the courts. But it is not at all clear what justice is in this context.

When the Congress supports legal advocacy for mental patients, it ignores the distinction and the conflict between advocacy of rights and advocacy of needs. But that distinction is crucial to the future of effective mental health care in this country. How can we make that distinction clear to the courts, to the legislatures, and to the public? How can we make them realize that legal advocacy will mean that lawyers and courts will be telling us how to practice our profession?

Here we confront a paradox that many psychiatrists do not appreciate. If the American Psychiatric Association is to become an advocate for patients, then to be at all effective, we too have to hire lawyers and learn to work with them, for better or worse. There is no alternative; we will have to do it their way. We have no tradition of advocacy of our own, and without legal advocacy we are helpless. The central task of working with lawyers is to create new laws that will reverse the trend of making rights into needs. We have begun to do that in the last few years and with growing success, as illustrated by the following comment about recent Supreme Court decisions[2,3] in the Mental Disability Law Reporter, a publication that has frequently been a critic of the psychiatric establishment:

> The Supreme Court's decisions seem to be signaling de-emphasis of procedural due process and a new awareness of the right to treatment in a broad medical as well as legal sense. The Supreme Court has also discussed the tragic implications of denying proper care to those who actually need that care, saying a person who "is suffering from a debilitating mental illness, and in need of treatment is neither wholly at liberty nor free of stigma." Now one sees a new emphasis that promotes the need to allow psychiatrists to practice their profession unhindered by time-wasting legal procedures. There can be little doubt that the American Psychiatric Association through its amicus briefs has made a significant impact upon the legal profession.

Perhaps the author goes too far in saying that we have made an impact on the legal profession, but we have made a significant impact on the future of our own profession and our capacity to treat our patients. With the help of our lawyers, we have taken our professional destiny into our own hands, and surely that is a good thing.[4]

2,3. Addington v. Texas, 441 U.S. 418 (1979); Parham v. R., 442 U.S. 584 (1979).

4. "Historic Supreme Court Decision on the Voluntary Admission of Minors Issued," Mental Disability Law Reporter, Vol. 3, July–August 1979, pp. 231–234.

Chapter 6

Everyday Problems of the Practicing Lawyer

This Chapter continues our discussion of specific problems that may come up in handling contested matters in our adversary system, either in the office or in court. In other words, many of the problems that follow address recurring ethical issues in litigation. The Model Rules contain a good deal of general language, but also some specific prohibitions, in connection with many of these situations. See Rules 3.1–3.4, 3.6, 3.8, 4.1, and 4.4.

Many of the Problems that follow relate to criminal matters, and in fact one way to consider the materials in the Chapter is to treat the criminal and civil matters as separate groups. A special note, however, should be added about the former. There has been a wealth of writing in recent years about the professional responsibility of prosecutors and defense counsel. The Model Rules address criminal matters directly in a number of places, but their coverage of specific problems that arise in the criminal context is spotty.

A. Investigation: Possession of Tangible Evidence by a Lawyer

Problem 6–1

Your client, Paula Bryce, has been questioned repeatedly about stealing $500,000 in a bank robbery. One day she hurries into your office and hands a parcel to you. You ask what's going on and she replies that she believes that the police are about to arrest her, that the parcel contains money from the robbery, that she wants you to return the money anonymously by dumping it down the night depository box, and that if you will not, she will go to the ladies' room and destroy the money. What do you do? Would it make any difference if the money had been stolen not from a bank but from the mattress of an aged couple and represented their life savings? Would it make any difference if it was the Mona Lisa and not money that had been stolen?

What lawyers should do with physical evidence that comes into their possession has become a subject of considerable interest. See Stephen Gillers, "Guns, Fruits, Drugs, and Documents: A Criminal Defense Lawyer's Responsibility for Real

Evidence," 63 Stan. L. Rev. 813 (2011); Note, "Ethics, Law and Loyalty: The Lawyer's Duty to Turn Over Incriminating Physical Evidence," 32 Stan. L. Rev. 977 (1980). The issue may have constitutional dimensions, raising questions of the privilege against self-incrimination, as when a client gives written information to a lawyer. The Supreme Court dealt in part with the problem in Fisher v. United States, 425 U.S. 391 (1976), where it held that compelled production of documents from an attorney did not "implicate whatever Fifth Amendment privilege the [client] might have enjoyed from being compelled to produce them himself," id. at 402, but that the attorney-client privilege would apply to documents possessed by an attorney that would have been privileged under the Fifth Amendment in the hands of the client. *Fisher*, however, did not address the lawyer's more general obligation apart from the evidentiary issue of the scope of the attorney-client privilege. Does the obligation to maintain a client's confidences and secrets and the obligation to represent a client zealously permit or require lawyers to refrain from transmitting to the police evidence that has come into their possession? Is there a difference between possession of a letter from a client containing a confession and possession of a letter containing a map of the bank's premises detailing the planned holdup? Is there a difference between possession of a parcel containing stolen goods and possession of a parcel containing a murder weapon? Does the source of evidence—the client or a third party—make a difference?

Some of the issues discussed in the preceding paragraph are suggested by the following case, especially as one considers variations of its facts.

Morrell v. State

575 P.2d 1200 (Alaska 1978)

[Cline, a lawyer representing Morrell, who was charged with kidnapping and rape, was given a pad containing a written kidnapping plan by Wagner, a friend of Morrell. Wagner had found it in one of Morrell's vehicles after Morrell had asked him to clean it out. Cline arranged to have Wagner turn the pad over to the police. On appeal from his conviction, Morrell claimed that the admission of the pad into evidence denied him the effective assistance of counsel because the pad was obtained through improper behavior by Cline.]

RABINOWITZ, Justice

. . . As Morrell notes, authority in this area is surprisingly sparse. The existing authority seems to indicate, however, that a criminal defense attorney has an obligation to turn over to the prosecution physical evidence which comes into his possession, especially where the evidence comes into the attorney's possession through the acts of a third party who is neither a client of the attorney nor an agent of a client. After turning over such evidence, an attorney may have either a right or a duty to remain silent as to the circumstances under which he obtained such evidence, but Morrell presents no authority which establishes that a criminal defendant whose attorney chooses to testify regarding to these matters is denied effective assistance of counsel.

Most of the decisions which discuss the situation in question involve bar disciplinary proceedings or contempt proceedings against the attorney for refusing to answer questions or to turn over evidence. In State v. Olwell, 64 Wash. 2d 828 (1964), an order holding an attorney in contempt was reversed. The attorney had refused to comply with a subpoena duces tecum or answer questions at a coroner's inquest concerning a knife owned by a client. The Washington Supreme Court assumed for purposes of its decision that the attorney had obtained the knife in question as a result of a confidential communication with his client. The court stated that if the evidence had been obtained from a third party with whom no attorney-client relationship existed, communications concerning the knife would not be privileged.

The Court in *Olwell* held that incriminating objects delivered to a criminal defense attorney by his client may be withheld by the attorney for a reasonable time to help the attorney prepare his case, and then they must be given to the prosecution. In addition, the court held that in order to protect the attorney-client relationship, the prosecution must not reveal the source of such evidence in the presence of the jury when it is introduced at trial. In discussing the scope of this limited privilege, the court stated that to be protected as a privileged communication at all, the subjects obtained by the attorney must have been delivered to the attorney by the client or have been acquired as a direct result of information communicated by the client and not merely have been obtained by the attorney while acting in that capacity for the client. In short, the *Olwell* rule requires a criminal defense attorney to turn over to the prosecution physical evidence that the attorney obtains from his client. This rule requires the defense attorney to avoid giving to investigating or prosecuting authorities any information concerning the source of the evidence or the manner in which it was obtained. Finally, if the evidence is obtained from a non-client third party who is not acting as the client's agent, even the privilege to refuse to testify concerning the manner in which the evidence was obtained is inapplicable.

In People v. Lee, 3 Cal. App. 3d 514 (1970), a district attorney obtained a search warrant for a pair of blood-stained shoes held by a judge pursuant to an agreement between the district attorney and the public defender. The judge and the two attorneys had agreed that the judge would hold the shoes pending a judicial determination of the proper disposition of the shoes. The public defender later testified at his client's trial that he had received the shoes from his client's wife and that he had delivered the shoes to the judge.

In both the *Lee* case and the case at bar a criminal defendant sought suppression of evidence delivered by his attorney to the authorities. The attorney obtained the evidence not from his client, but from a person with whom his client had a close personal relationship. Further, the attorney testified at the defendant's trial concerning the circumstances under which he obtained the evidence.

The court in *Lee* held that the attorney-client privilege does not give an attorney the right to withhold evidence. The court stated that it would be an abuse of a lawyer's duty of professional responsibility to knowingly take possession of and secrete instrumentalities of a crime. (The shoes were an instrumentality because the defendant had allegedly kicked the victim in the head.) In dicta, the court noted that although a client's delivery of evidence to the attorney may be privileged, the object itself does not become privileged. Thus, the California court held that seizure of the shoes by warrant was proper and that the objection to introduction of the shoes as evidence was properly overruled.

Further, the *Lee* court held that the attorney-client privilege did not cover the trial testimony of the attorney concerning the circumstances under which he obtained the shoes because he received the shoes from his client's wife rather than from his client. The court stated that the attorney-client privilege does not protect information which comes to an attorney unless the third party is acting as the client's agent. Although the attorney in *Lee* had obtained the shoes from his client's wife, the court found that she was not acting as the client's agent in turning the shoes over to the attorney.

Also of significance is In re Ryder, 263 F. Supp. 360 (E.D. Va. 1967), aff'd 381 F.2d 713 (4th Cir. 1967). *Ryder* involved a proceeding to determine whether an attorney should be suspended or disbarred. The attorney had taken possession from his client of stolen money and a sawed-off shotgun, knowing that the money was stolen and that the gun had been used in an armed robbery. The attorney intended to retain the property until after his client's trial and then to return the money to its rightful owner.

The client in *Ryder* had put the money and the gun in his safe deposit box. The attorney, knowing that the money in the box was marked and disbelieving his client's story about how the client had acquired the money, went to the bank to transfer the money to his own safe deposit box. Upon opening the client's box, the attorney discovered the shotgun and transferred both the money and the gun to his own box. The court stated in dicta that the attorney's state of mind when he transferred the evidence demonstrated sufficient knowledge to fall within the statute prohibiting knowing concealment of stolen property.

The court in *Ryder* suspended the attorney, holding that his actions did not fall within the protection of the attorney-client privilege. The court noted, however, that neither the client nor his attorney could be compelled to produce merely evidentiary articles, as opposed to fruits or instrumentalities of the crime. This dictum was based on the notion that such merely evidentiary articles could not even be seized in a legal search; and, therefore, their production could not be compelled. . . . The rule that mere evidence may not be seized in a lawful search has since been disapproved. Warden v. Hayden, 387 U.S. 294, 306–307 (1967). Therefore, we think that no distinction should be drawn in the privilege context between physical evidence obtained by a criminal defense attorney which is "mere evidence" of a client's crime and that which may be said to be either a fruit of all instrumentality of the crime. . . .

From the foregoing cases emerges the rule that a criminal defense attorney must turn over to the prosecution real evidence that the attorney obtains from his client. Further, if the evidence is obtained from a non-client third party who is not acting for the client, then the privilege to refuse to testify concerning the manner in which the evidence was obtained is inapplicable. We think the foregoing rules are sound, and we apply them in reaching our resolution of the effective-assistance-of-counsel issue in the case at bar.

Morrell correctly cites cases which establish that misprision statutes are generally interpreted to require an affirmative act of concealment in addition to a failure to disclose a crime to the authorities. See United States v. Daddano, 432 F.2d 1119 (7th Cir. 1970), cert. denied, 402 U.S. 905 (1971). However, the cases disciplining attorneys for failing to turn over evidence or upholding denials of motions to suppress evidence turned over by attorneys do not rest alone on the notion that an attorney who does not turn over such evidence may be guilty of a crime. The cases cited are also based on the proposition that it would constitute unethical conduct for an attorney—an officer of the court—to knowingly fail to reveal relevant evidence in a criminal case.

We believe that Cline would have been obligated to see that the evidence reached the prosecutor in this case even if he had obtained the evidence from Morrell. His obligation was even clearer because he acquired the evidence from Wagner, who made the decision to turn the evidence over to Cline without consulting Morrell and therefore was not acting as Morrell's agent.

Since Cline was obligated to see that the evidence reached the prosecutor, Morrell cannot have been deprived of effective assistance of counsel by Cline's decision to return the evidence to Wagner. Further, Cline's efforts to aid Wagner's transfer of the evidence to the police appear to have been within the scope of Cline's obligation. Cline could have properly turned the evidence over to the police himself and would have been obliged to do so if Wagner had refused to accept the return of the evidence.[17]

One additional aspect of this issue remains for discussion. As was noted earlier, the Ethics Committee of the Alaska Bar Association gave Cline an advisory opinion as to what to do with the questioned legal pad. The Opinion advised Cline to return the subject papers to Wagner, to explain to Wagner the law on concealment of

17. The only remaining question is whether Cline's testimony concerning the Wagner incident was within the attorney-client privilege and, if it was, whether the testimony deprived Morrell of his rights to effective assistance of counsel and to a fair trial. While the *Olwell* rule might have imposed a duty on Cline to remain silent as to these matters if Cline had obtained the evidence from Morrell, the acquisition of incriminating evidence from a nonclient third party who is not acting as a client's agent falls outside the attorney-client privilege. Cline could not have claimed that the attorney-client privilege precluded him from testifying as to his acquisition of the evidence from Wagner. Therefore, Morrell cannot have been deprived of effective assistance of counsel by Cline's testimony.

evidence,[18] and to withdraw from the case if it later became obvious to Cline that a violation of ethical rules would result from his continued representation of Morrell. On June 6, 1977, the Board of Governors of the Alaska Bar Association adopted Ethics Opinion 76-7 which embodied the advice the Ethics Committee had earlier given Cline. The Opinion also stated, however, that Cline would be ethically obligated not to reveal the existence of the physical evidence "unless required to do so by statute." The Bar Association declined to render an opinion as to the applicability of AS 11.30.315 or other state law.

We think Cline followed the advice of the Bar Association in relation to his dealings with Wagner. It also appears to us that Cline could have reasonably concluded that AS 11.30.315 required him to reveal the existence of the physical evidence; and thus, although he affirmatively involved himself in the revelation of the evidence's existence, he did follow the advice of the Bar Association as it dealt with his obligation to preserve his client's secrets.

Assuming Ethics Opinion 76-7 is a correct statement of the law, whether Cline rendered effective counsel then turns on whether he could reasonably have concluded that AS 11.30.315 required him to reveal the existence of the evidence. Otherwise, the opinion states that he had an ethical obligation not to reveal the evidence. AS 11.30.315 makes it a crime to willfully destroy, alter or conceal evidence concerning the commission of a crime or evidence which is being sought for production during an investigation, inquiry or trial, with the intent to prevent the evidence from being discovered or produced. While statutes which address the concealing of evidence are generally construed to require an affirmative act of concealment in addition to the failure to disclose information to the authorities, taking possession of evidence from a non-client third party and holding the evidence in a place not accessible to investigating authorities would seem to fall within the statute's ambit. Thus, we have concluded that Cline breached no ethical obligation to his client which may have rendered his legal services to Morrell ineffective. . . .

Notes

1. The court in *Morrell* discusses many of the major cases that have considered the issue of lawyers' obligations when physical evidence comes into their possession. Some of these cases involved receipt of the evidence from a third party and some involved receipt of the evidence from the defendant. *Morrell* and the cases it discusses hold that lawyers have an obligation to turn over physical evidence in both situations. The only situation in which it might make a difference is the evidentiary

---

18. AS 11.30.315 provides:

Destroying, altering or concealing evidence. A person who wilfully destroys, alters or conceals evidence concerning the commission of a crime or evidence which is being sought for production during an investigation, inquiry or trial, with the intent to prevent the evidence from being discovered or produced, is guilty of a misdemeanor and upon conviction is punishable by imprisonment for not more than one year, or by a fine of not more than $1,000, or by both.

issue of testimony by lawyers as to how they obtained the evidence. See footnote 17, p. 467.

2. Note that it has not seemed to the courts to make a difference whether the physical evidence possessed by the lawyer was the instrumentality of the crime (the knife with which a homicide was committed), the fruits of the crime (the stolen money), or evidence that would link the defendant with the crime (bloodstained shoes or a kidnapping plan). But suppose that Morrell had shown up in Cline's office bringing with him a statement of how he had committed the crime so that his lawyer should know everything? Would Cline be obligated to turn that statement over to the police? Suppose Morrell said that he didn't have to prepare a statement because he had already written out in his diary how the crime occurred and had brought the diary with him. The diary even contained a map. Does Cline have an obligation to turn the diary over to the police?

3. How should the lawyer in *Ryder* have behaved if his client, Cook, had appeared in his office, dumped the shotgun on his desk, and headed for the door saying that he was getting out while he still had a chance?

4. If Cook had mailed the money to Ryder, saying that he was fleeing and leaving no return address, what should Ryder have done with the money?

5. Suppose that Cook had written to Ryder saying that he was about to flee and directing Ryder to a rural area where he would meet Ryder. Ryder went and found not Cook but several sacks of money in Bank of Virginia wrappers. What should he do with them? If snow was beginning to cover the sacks and it seemed likely that the money would be destroyed in the coming winter, what should he do with it? If it was not money that Ryder found but a distinctive sawed-off shotgun that fit the description of the one carried by the robber, what should Ryder do? Does Model Rule 3.3(a)(2) or 3.4(a) answer the question?

6. An interesting debate on the lawyer's obligation with respect to physical evidence occurred in Hitch v. Pima County Superior Court, 708 P.2d 72 (Ariz. 1985). The majority held that a lawyer may return physical evidence to the source (in this case the woman companion of the client) instead of turning it over to the police, if and only if the lawyer reasonably believes that it will not be destroyed and if the lawyer explains the law on concealment and destruction of evidence. That possibility adds yet another element of risk to the lawyer's decision: the element of retroactive second-guessing of the reasonableness of his or her belief. The dissenters, however, would have permitted the item to be returned if the lawyer's purpose in having accepted it had been legitimate, as it was in that case because it was important for the lawyer to examine the item. The only exception would be for items that were contraband or dangerous. The dissenters, however, also advised against seeking to obtain possession of exculpatory physical evidence except in special circumstances. See Commonwealth v. Stenhach, 356 Pa. Super. 5 (1986), petition for allowance of appeal denied, 534 A.2d 769 (1987), for a prosecution of two lawyers for a variety of crimes relating to tampering with evidence and hindering prosecution. Counsel,

believing that the attorney-client privilege applied, had been led by defendant to a broken rifle stock used in the homicide but did not turn it over to the prosecution. The court held that the stock should have been turned over but reversed their conviction because the statutes under which they were prosecuted were vague and overbroad as applied to defense attorneys.

A different kind of issue with respect to lawyers' possession of evidence has been presented by the growing use, by state and federal prosecutors, of the subpoena power to seize and examine lawyers' files and to force lawyers to testify before grand juries in connection with matters in which they are currently representing clients. See Suni, "Subpoenas to Criminal Defense Lawyers," 65 Or. L. Rev. 215 (1986). Responding to the complaint that such actions and the threat of such actions seriously impinged upon the ability of lawyers to defend those accused of crime, the Model Rules were amended in 1990 to follow the substance of rules previously adopted in Massachusetts and Pennsylvania that forbade a prosecutor from issuing a subpoena to an attorney requiring testimony in a grand jury proceeding about past or present clients without meeting several conditions and, in addition, without obtaining prior judicial approval. See Model Rule 3.8(e). The Department of Justice has argued strongly that the application of such rules, even if adopted by federal district courts, is beyond the authority of the district courts and when enforced as state law, violates the Supremacy Clause. The Court of Appeals for the Third Circuit agreed, Baylson v. The Disciplinary Board, 975 F.2d 102 (3d Cir. 1992), but the Rules were originally upheld in the First Circuit. Whitehouse v. United States District Court for the District of Rhode Island, 53 F.3d 1349 (1st Cir. 1995). Subsequently, however, that Court held that the Rules' conditions on obtaining subpoenas affected both grand jury and trial proceedings too substantially to fall within local rule-making power. The McDade Amendment, see p. 20, did not save the local rule because the rule was not a rule of ethics, which is the subject matter of the Amendment. Stern v. United States District Court for the District of Massachusetts, 214 F.3d 4 (1st Cir. 2000), petition for rehearing denied by an equally divided court. Id. at 15 (2000). But the controversy continues unabated. See, e.g., United States v. Supreme Court of New Mexico, 839 F.3d 888 (10th Cir. 2016) (concluding that even though the rule is indeed one of ethics covered by the McDade amendment, the rule nevertheless is preempted with respect to federal prosecutors practicing before grand juries, but is not preempted outside of the grand-jury context).

B. Destruction of Evidence

Problem 6–2

Client has consulted Lawyer about possible antitrust liability in connection with certain business practices. No suits, either public or private, have been brought or threatened. In reviewing the files, Lawyer points out certain internal memoranda that are likely to be damaging if litigation ever ensues. Does Lawyer have any obligation if, without any further advice, Client says he will destroy paper copies and will activate the program that will delete them from his company's computers, including backups? May Lawyer advise that they be destroyed? May Lawyer advise the establishment of a policy of destruction of all memoranda older than a certain date (which includes the damaging memoranda)? May Lawyer advise the establishment of a policy of destruction of all computer-generated material, including emails and backup computer drives, at regular intervals? What would be legitimate reasons for doing so?

Arthur Andersen LLP v. United States
544 U.S. 696 (2005)

Chief Justice REHNQUIST delivered the opinion of the Court.

As Enron Corporation's financial difficulties became public in 2001, petitioner Arthur Andersen LLP, Enron's auditor, instructed its employees to destroy documents pursuant to its document retention policy. A jury found that this action made petitioner guilty of violating 18 U.S.C. §§ 1512(b)(2)(A) and (B). These sections make it a crime to "knowingly use intimidation or physical force, threaten, or corruptly persuade another person . . . with intent to . . . cause" that person to "withhold" documents from, or "alter" documents for use in, an "official proceeding." The Court of Appeals for the Fifth Circuit affirmed. We hold that the jury instructions failed to convey properly the elements of a "corrup[t] persua[sion]" conviction under § 1512(b), and therefore reverse.

Enron Corporation, during the 1990's, switched its business from operation of natural gas pipelines to an energy conglomerate, a move that was accompanied by aggressive accounting practices and rapid growth. Petitioner audited Enron's publicly filed financial statements and provided internal audit and consulting services to it. Petitioner's "engagement team" for Enron was headed by David Duncan. Beginning in 2000, Enron's financial performance began to suffer, and, as 2001 wore on, worsened. On August 14, 2001, Jeffrey Skilling, Enron's Chief Executive Officer (CEO), unexpectedly resigned. Within days, Sherron Watkins, a senior accountant at Enron, warned Kenneth Lay, Enron's newly reappointed CEO, that Enron could "implode in a wave of accounting scandals." She likewise informed Duncan and Michael Odom, one of petitioner's partners who had supervisory responsibility over Duncan, of the looming problems.

On August 28, an article in the Wall Street Journal suggested improprieties at Enron, and the SEC opened an informal investigation. By early September, petitioner had formed an Enron "crisis-response" team, which included Nancy Temple, an in-house counsel. On October 8, petitioner retained outside counsel to represent it in any litigation that might arise from the Enron matter. The next day, Temple discussed Enron with other in-house counsel. Her notes from that meeting reflect that "some SEC investigation" is "highly probable."

On October 10, Odom spoke at a general training meeting attended by 89 employees, including 10 from the Enron engagement team. Odom urged everyone to comply with the firm's document retention policy.[4] He added: "'[I]f it's destroyed in the course of [the] normal policy and litigation is filed the next day, that's great. . . . [W]e've followed our own policy, and whatever there was that might have been of interest to somebody is gone and irretrievable.'" 374 F.3d 281, 286 (CA5 2004). On October 12, Temple entered the Enron matter into her computer, designating the "Type of Potential Claim" as "Professional Practice—Government/Regulatory Investigation." Temple also e-mailed Odom, suggesting that he "'remin[d] the engagement team of our documentation and retention policy.'"

On October 16, Enron announced its third quarter results. That release disclosed a $1.01 billion charge to earnings.[5] The following day, the SEC notified Enron by letter that it had opened an investigation in August and requested certain information and documents. On October 19, Enron forwarded a copy of that letter to petitioner.

On the same day, Temple also sent an e-mail to a member of petitioner's internal team of accounting experts and attached a copy of the document policy. On October 20, the Enron crisis-response team held a conference call, during which Temple instructed everyone to "make sure to follow the [document] policy." On October 23, Enron CEO Lay declined to answer questions during a call with analysts because of "potential lawsuits, as well as the SEC inquiry." After the call, Duncan met with other Andersen partners on the Enron engagement team and told them that they should ensure team members were complying with the document policy. Another meeting for all team members followed, during which Duncan distributed the policy and told everyone to comply. These, and other smaller meetings, were followed by substantial destruction of paper and electronic documents.

On October 26, one of petitioner's senior partners circulated a New York Times article discussing the SEC's response to Enron. His e-mail commented that "the problems are just beginning and we will be in the cross hairs. The marketplace is going to keep the pressure on this and is going to force the SEC to be tough." On

---

4. The firm's policy called for a single central engagement file, which "should contain only that information which is relevant to supporting our work." The policy stated that, "[i]n cases of threatened litigation . . . no related information will be destroyed." It also separately provided that, if petitioner is "advised of litigation or subpoenas regarding a particular engagement, the related information should not be destroyed. See Policy Statement No. 780—Notification of Litigation." (emphasis deleted). Policy Statement No. 780 set forth "notification" procedures for whenever "professional practice litigation against [petitioner] or any of its personnel has been commenced, has been threatened or is judged likely to occur, or when governmental or professional investigations that may involve [petitioner] or any of its personnel have been commenced or are judged likely."

5. The release characterized the charge to earnings as "non-recurring." Petitioner had expressed doubts about this characterization to Enron, but Enron refused to alter the release. Temple wrote an e-mail to Duncan that "suggested deleting some language that might suggest we have concluded the release is misleading."

October 30, the SEC opened a formal investigation and sent Enron a letter that requested accounting documents.

Throughout this time period, the document destruction continued, despite reservations by some of petitioner's managers.[6] On November 8, Enron announced that it would issue a comprehensive restatement of its earnings and assets. Also on November 8, the SEC served Enron and petitioner with subpoenas for records. On November 9, Duncan's secretary sent an e-mail that stated: "Per Dave — No more shredding. . . . We have been officially served for our documents." [Brief for United States] at 10. Enron filed for bankruptcy less than a month later. Duncan was fired and later pleaded guilty to witness tampering.

In March 2002, petitioner was indicted in the Southern District of Texas on one count of violating §§ 1512(b)(2)(A) and (B). The indictment alleged that, between October 10 and November 9, 2001, petitioner "did knowingly, intentionally and corruptly persuade . . . other persons, to wit: [petitioner's] employees, with intent to cause" them to withhold documents from, and alter documents for use in, "official proceedings, namely: regulatory and criminal proceedings and investigations." A jury trial followed . . . and . . . the jury returned a guilty verdict. The District Court denied petitioner's motion for a judgment of acquittal.

The Court of Appeals for the Fifth Circuit affirmed. 374 F.3d at 284. It held that the jury instructions properly conveyed the meaning of "corruptly persuades" and "official proceeding"; that the jury need not find any consciousness of wrongdoing; and that there was no reversible error. Because of a split of authority regarding the meaning of § 1512(b), we granted certiorari. 543 U.S. 1042 (2005).

Chapter 73 of Title 18 of the United States Code provides criminal sanctions for those who obstruct justice. Sections 1512(b)(2)(A) and (B), part of the witness tampering provisions, provide in relevant part:

> Whoever knowingly uses intimidation or physical force, threatens, or corruptly persuades another person, or attempts to do so, or engages in misleading conduct toward another person, with intent to . . . cause or induce any person to . . . withhold testimony, or withhold a record, document, or other object, from an official proceeding [or] alter, destroy, mutilate, or conceal an object with intent to impair the object's integrity or availability for use in an official proceeding . . . shall be fined under this title or imprisoned not more than ten years, or both.

---

6. For example, on October 26, John Riley, another partner with petitioner, saw Duncan shredding documents and told him "this wouldn't be the best time in the world for you guys to be shredding a bunch of stuff." On October 31, David Stulb, a forensics investigator for petitioner, met with Duncan. During the meeting, Duncan picked up a document with the words "smoking gun" written on it and began to destroy it, adding "we don't need this." Stulb cautioned Duncan on the need to maintain documents and later informed Temple that Duncan needed advice on the document retention policy.

In this case, our attention is focused on what it means to "knowingly . . . corruptly persuade" another person "with intent to . . . cause" that person to "withhold" documents from, or "alter" documents for use in, an "official proceeding."

"We have traditionally exercised restraint in assessing the reach of a federal criminal statute, both out of deference to the prerogatives of Congress, Dowling v. United States, 473 U.S. 207 (1985), and out of concern that 'a fair warning should be given to the world in language that the common world will understand, of what the law intends to do if a certain line is passed,' McBoyle v. United States, 283 U.S. 25, 27 (1931)." United States v. Aguilar, 515 U.S. 593, 600 (1995).

Such restraint is particularly appropriate here, where the act underlying the conviction—"persua[sion]"—is by itself innocuous. Indeed, "persuad[ing]" a person "with intent to . . . cause" that person to "withhold" testimony or documents from a Government proceeding or Government official is not inherently malign.[8] Consider, for instance, a mother who suggests to her son that he invoke his right against compelled self-incrimination, see U.S. Const., Amdt. 5, or a wife who persuades her husband not to disclose marital confidences, see Trammel v. United States, 445 U.S. 40 (1980). . . .

"Document retention policies," which are created in part to keep certain information from getting into the hands of others, including the Government, are common in business. See generally Chase, "To Shred or Not to Shred: Document Retention Policies and Federal Obstruction of Justice Statutes," 8 Ford. J. Corp. & Fin. L. 721 (2003). It is, of course, not wrongful for a manager to instruct his employees to comply with a valid document retention policy under ordinary circumstances.

Acknowledging this point, the parties have largely focused their attention on the word "corruptly" as the key to what may or may not lawfully be done in the situation presented here. Section 1512(b) punishes not just "corruptly persuad[ing]" another, but "*knowingly* . . . corruptly persuad[ing]" another. (Emphasis added.) . . .

. . . Only persons conscious of wrongdoing can be said to "knowingly . . . corruptly persuad[e]." And limiting criminality to persuaders conscious of their wrongdoing sensibly allows § 1512(b) to reach only those with the level of "culpability . . . we usually require in order to impose criminal liability." United States v. Aguilar, 515 U.S., at 602; see also Liparota v. United States, [471 U.S. 419 (1985)], at 426.

The . . . jury instructions at issue simply failed to convey the requisite consciousness of wrongdoing. Indeed, it is striking how little culpability the instructions required. For example, the jury was told that, "even if [petitioner] honestly and sincerely believed that its conduct was lawful, you may find [petitioner] guilty." The

---

8. Section 1512(b)(2) addresses testimony, as well as documents. Section 1512(b)(1) also addresses testimony. Section 1512(b)(3) addresses "persuade[rs]" who intend to prevent "the communication to a law enforcement officer or judge of the United States of information" relating to a federal crime.

instructions also diluted the meaning of "corruptly" so that it covered innocent conduct. . . .

The instructions also were infirm for another reason. They led the jury to believe that it did not have to find *any* nexus between the "persuasion" to destroy documents and any particular proceeding. In resisting any type of nexus element, the Government relies heavily on § 1512(e)(1), which states that an official proceeding "need not be pending or about to be instituted at the time of the offense." It is, however, one thing to say that a proceeding "need not be pending or about to be instituted at the time of the offense," and quite another to say a proceeding need not even be foreseen. A "knowingly . . . corrup[t] persuade[r]" cannot be someone who persuades others to shred documents under a document retention policy when he does not have in contemplation any particular official proceeding in which those documents might be material. . . .

For these reasons, the jury instructions here were flawed in important respects. The judgment of the Court of Appeals is reversed, and the case is remanded for further proceedings consistent with this opinion.

It is so ordered.

Notes

1. The principal case involved prosecution of a major accounting firm for the activities of several of its employees, including one lawyer, in connection with destruction of documents relating to its auditing duties to a client. The Supreme Court reversed the conviction because the jury was incorrectly led to believe that it could convict a defendant under a statute requiring knowingly corrupt persuasion when the conduct in question was "innocent" and when the persuader did not have any particular proceeding in mind in which the shredded documents might be relevant. It is difficult to know whether the Court meant to imply that the statute would not have been violated if there was a document destruction policy in place and the lawyer knew that her instructions to follow the policy would result in destruction of documents material to an investigation that she believed was highly likely to ensue. Whatever the criminal statute means, should the same standard be applied in interpreting the "counsel or assist" language in Rule 3.4(a) of the Model Rules?

2. Recall the "Case of the Shredded Memo" in Problem 1–2 (p. 32). Is there any difference between Temple's actions and Steve Langford's request that Anita Charles collect all of the copies of her memo and "shred them"?

3. In United States v. IBM Corp., 58 F.R.D. 556 (S.D.N.Y. 1973), the court dealt with an unusual question of destruction of records. During lengthy proceedings in a private antitrust action against IBM, a lawyer for Control Data Corporation prepared a computerized "database" that was an essential feature of CDC's ability to locate documents in the vast IBM files. At the same time, the United States was pursuing an antitrust action against IBM based on the same events that gave rise to the private action. An order was entered in that suit requiring both parties to preserve

"all documents, writings, recordings or other records of any kind whatsoever which relate in any way to electronic data processing." Id. at 557 n.1. IBM settled its lawsuit with Control Data, and as part of the settlement the parties agreed to destroy "work product generated in support of the litigation." Id. at 558. As a result of that agreement, the computerized database was destroyed. The government claimed that the database, or one like it, was indispensable to its preparation for trial and sought to force IBM to pay for the cost of reconstructing a database.

While the court did not grant that particular relief because it regarded its order as preserving documents and not as adjudicating whether any particular documents were discoverable, it condemned the "unseemly behavior" of "respected members of the bar" for the action they took without informing the court. Id. at 559. The court rejected as irrelevant "affidavits from many distinguished lawyers which affirm the ethical propriety of destroying work product prepared during the course of litigation at the time of settlement of the suit" because the affidavits did not deal with a situation where there was a document preservation order. Would the position taken in the affidavits be sound if there were no such order? Does it depend upon whether it is clear that the documents destroyed are not discoverable because they are work product? Does it depend on whether the parties seeking destruction know that the documents might be discoverable and will be, or are likely to be, sought by another party?

4. A comprehensive description and analysis of the various civil and criminal liabilities for intentional destruction of evidence by clients and lawyers is contained in Solum and Marzen, "Truth and Uncertainty: Legal Control of the Destruction of Evidence," 36 Emory L.J. 1085 (1987). The authors discuss the general provisions of the Model Code and the general and specific provisions of the Model Rules, especially Rule 3.4(a), that relate to destruction of evidence by attorneys and their obligation to reveal destruction of evidence by clients. See id. at 1125–1137.

5. Several jurisdictions have recognized a tort for "spoliation of evidence," which imposes liability for intentional or negligent destruction of evidence. But California, which led the way in creation of the tort, has retreated. The California Supreme Court refused to recognize the tort where the victim knows or should have known of the spoliation before trial or other disposition of the case. It concluded that the many nontort remedies were sufficient. Cedars Sinai Medical Center v. The Superior Court, 18 Cal. 4th 1 (1998). See Solum and Marzen, supra Note 4, at 1100–1106.

6. Another line of attack in destruction, or nonproduction, of documents cases is suggested by Cresswell v. Sullivan & Cromwell, 668 F. Supp. 166 (S.D.N.Y. 1987). Claiming that they were induced to settle earlier litigation against Prudential-Bache Securities because that company and its lawyers intentionally failed to produce a document called for by a document request, plaintiffs chose not to attempt to reopen the former settlement under Fed. R. Civ. P. 60(b) but instead brought an action in fraud against that company and its lawyers. The court denied a motion to dismiss on the ground that Rule 60(b) provided the exclusive remedy and permitted the

action to proceed. The Court of Appeals held that the cause of action should be tried in federal court as a federal equitable cause of action and not remanded to the state court as a common law fraud case. 922 F.2d 60 (2d Cir. 1990). On retrial, the district court dismissed the complaint on the ground that the plaintiffs had failed to prove that the claimed damage had been caused by the alleged negligence of Sullivan & Cromwell and not by the negligence of their own lawyers. 771 F. Supp. 580 (1991).

7. An interesting twist on the destruction of documents problem is prescribed by Herbster v. North American Company, 150 Ill. App. 3d 21 (1986). The court refused to extend the tort of retaliatory discharge to a company's chief legal officer, who was employed under a contract at will and who alleged that he was discharged because he refused to destroy or remove from company files documents requested by plaintiffs in a pending lawsuit. The court believed that extension of the tort would have too severe an impact on the special attributes of the attorney-client relationship. See Chapter 10, Section D, for issues relating to whistleblowing by lawyers against their own firms.

C. Investigation: Talking with a "Party"

1. Rule 4.2 and Civil Cases

Problem 6–3

Your firm represents the insurance carrier of a surgeon sued by a patient for malpractice. The hospital in which the malpractice is alleged to have occurred was joined as a co-defendant and cross claims have been filed by the surgeon and the hospital against one another. You have been told to interview the head nurse of the hospital to get her version of what happened in the operating room. What problems of professional responsibility do you want to consider before you go to see her? Would it make any difference if the interview was about to take place at a time when the suit had not yet been brought?

Problem 6–4

Your firm is representing a plaintiff in a class action gender discrimination suit attacking an employer's hiring and promotion policies. The assistant personnel manager of the defendant has said to a friend who is a member of the class that he is willing to talk with plaintiff's counsel about defendant's informal hiring and promotion policies and has indicated that he knows "where the bodies are buried." He says, however, that he will not talk in the presence of defendant's counsel. May the lawyer have such a discussion without permission of defendant's counsel? May the lawyer avoid any problem by telling the member of the class who brought him the information that she should get the relevant information from her friend and then tell the firm?

In virtually every jurisdiction, lawyers are prohibited from contacting represented parties directly or through their agents (e.g., paralegals or private investigators). According to its drafters, the rule (Model Rule 4.2) protects "a person who has chosen to be represented by a lawyer in a matter against possible overreaching by other lawyers who are participating in the matter, interference by those lawyers with the client-lawyer relationship and the uncounselled disclosure of information relating to the representation." To speak with a represented "party" (previous language) or "person" (current language), the lawyer must first gain permission from the opposing lawyer, seek a court order, or await formal (and often slow and expensive) discovery procedures (most commonly a deposition). The represented person's consent to speak with the lawyer is insufficient under the rule; only that person's lawyer may provide consent. Is this restriction necessary in the context of a corporate executive or even just a competent adult? Is it there for the lawyer's convenience or does it actually protect the client (who might, for example, inadvertently reveal privileged communications to the opposing lawyer)?

Although restrictive, the rule is relatively clear when the represented person is actually a person. When the person is an entity, however, determining which employees and other agents may be contacted can be a difficult and sometimes risky task. Should the rule prohibit contact with a former employee or other agent (or just current ones)? See Note 4, p. 492.

There are many issues to be considered in the typical fact situations involved in Problems 6–3 and 6–4, which deal with current employees. Under Rule 4.2, a major question is whether the head nurse is to be regarded as a person known to be represented by counsel for purposes of application of the rule as opposed to being viewed as a witness, as she would be if an accident had happened in a doctor's office and she were simply an employee who saw, but had no other involvement in, the incident. There was a good deal of litigation over the reach of this anti-communication provision under the prior Model Code provision, Rule 7-104(A), which was quite similar in wording except that it used the term "party" instead of "person." Some courts saw the prohibition as threatening the ability of litigants to obtain needed information and read the prohibition narrowly to exclude communication only with members of the so-called "control group" of the corporation. Others saw the purpose of the rule as designed to prevent lawyers from interfering with opposing counsel's ability to advise their clients and read the prohibition broadly to include employees who, in the scope of their employment, had participated in the conduct involved in the litigation.

While the text of Rule 4.2 and its predecessor 7-104(A) of the Model Code has remained substantially the same since 1969, the interpretation has been varied by changes in the Comments. The drafters of the original version of the Model Rules in Comment 4 to Rule 4.2 spoke to the issue by stating that the prohibition against communication extended to "any other person whose act or omission in connection with that matter may be imputed to the organization for purposes of civil or criminal liability or whose statement may constitute an admission on the part of the organization." The Comment thus refers lawyers seeking guidance to the substantive law of corporations, agency, and evidence. The last category—those whose statements may constitute an admission of the organization—has been the most problematic. How is the lawyer to make a judgment before speaking with an employee? Does the term "may constitute an admission" mean that a particular statement of the employee is simply evidence that may be used against the employer? Does it mean that the particular statement may be conclusive against the employer? Does it mean that the employee's status is such with respect to the specific matter that whatever the employee says will be either evidence or conclusive? Cf., e.g., Paris v. Union Pac. R. Co., 450 F. Supp. 2d 913, 915 (E.D. Ark. 2006) (noting that the Arkansas Supreme Court rejected the admission language based on similar concerns with its breadth). The American Law Institute's Restatement (Third) of the Law Governing Lawyers seeks to answer this question by applying this branch of the anti-contact rule only to employees whose statements would actually bind the organization with respect to proof of the particular matter. § 100(2)(c). The case law interpreting Rule 4.2 and its predecessor DR 7-104(A) of the Model Code with respect to its reach to corporate employees varies widely. The Comments were revised in 2002 to eliminate the reference to statements that may constitute an admission on the part of the organization but many jurisdictions still retain the former wording. In addition, the language of current Model Rule Comment 7 prohibiting contact with those "whose act or omission may be imputed to the organization for purposes of civil or criminal liability" may well be interpreted to overlap a good deal with the former "admission" language. In considering Problem 6–3, how much difference does it make that the jurisdiction has or has not removed the "admission" standard from its version of the anti-contact rule?

The following case discusses the variety of interpretations of the anti-contact provision.

Messing, Rudavsky & Weliky, P.C.
v.
President and Fellows of Harvard College
436 Mass. 347 (2002)

COWIN, J.

The law firm of Messing, Rudavsky & Weliky, P.C. (MR&W), appeals from an order of the Superior Court sanctioning the firm for violations of Mass. R. Prof. C. 4.2 . . . and its predecessor, S.J.C. DR 7-104(A)(1) . . . . Both versions of the rule prohibit attorneys from communicating with a represented party in the absence of that party's attorney. This appeal raises the issue whether, and to what extent, the rule prohibits an attorney from speaking ex parte to the employees of an organization represented by counsel. A judge in the Superior Court interpreted the rule to prohibit communication with any employee whose statements could be used as admissions against the organization pursuant to Fed. R. Evid. 801(d)(2)(D), and sanctioned MR&W for its ethical breach. We vacate the order and remand for entry of an order denying the motion for sanctions. . . .

1. *Facts and procedural history.* From the stipulated facts, we distill the following. In August of 1997, MR&W filed a complaint against the President and Fellows of Harvard College (Harvard) with the Massachusetts Commission Against Discrimination (commission) on behalf of its client, Kathleen Stanford. Stanford, a sergeant with the Harvard University police department (HUPD), alleged that Harvard and its police chief, Francis Riley, discriminated against her on the basis of gender and in reprisal for earlier complaints of discrimination. MR&W represented Stanford . . . . Following the institution of the suit, MR&W communicated ex parte with five employees of the HUPD: two lieutenants, two patrol officers, and a dispatcher. Although the two lieutenants had some supervisory authority over Stanford, it was not claimed that any of the five employees were involved in the alleged discrimination or retaliation against her or exercised management authority with respect to the alleged discriminatory or retaliatory acts.

In response to a motion by Harvard, the commission ruled that MR&W's ex parte contacts with all five employees violated rule 4.2, but declined to issue sanctions for these violations. MR&W removed the case to the Superior Court, where Harvard filed a motion seeking sanctions for the same violations of rule 4.2 on which the commission had previously ruled. The Superior Court judge then issued a memorandum of decision and order holding that MR&W violated the rule with respect to all five employees, prohibiting MR&W from using the affidavits it had procured during the interviews, and awarding Harvard the attorney's fees and costs it had expended in litigating the motion, in a later order calculated as $94,418.14. . . .

3. Interpretation of Rule 4.2 of the Massachusetts Rules of Professional Conduct.

a. *An overview.* . . .

The rule has been justified generally as "preserv[ing] the mediating role of counsel on behalf of their clients . . . protect[ing] clients from overreaching by counsel for adverse interests," Pratt v. National R.R. Passenger Corp., 54 F. Supp. 2d 78, 79 (D. Mass. 1999), and "protecting the attorney-client relationship." In re Air Crash Disaster near Roselawn Ind., 909 F. Supp. 1116, 1121 (N.D. Ill. 1995). . . .

Neither version of the rule explicitly addresses the scope of the prohibition when the represented person is an organization. When the represented person is an individual, there is no difficulty determining when an attorney has violated the rule; the represented person is easily identifiable. In the case of an organization, however, identifying the protected class is more complicated.

Because an organization acts only through its employees, the rule must extend to some of these employees. However, most courts have rejected the position that the rule automatically prevents an attorney from speaking with all employees of a represented organization. . . .

Most of MR&W's contacts with the Harvard employees took place in late 1997, when DR 7-104(A)(1) was still the operative rule. However, the Superior Court found that MR&W also made "minimal communication" in early 1998, and sanctioned MR&W for violations of both the old and new versions of the rule. Rule 4.2 uses the phrase "person the lawyers knows to be represented," while DR 7-104(A)(1) uses the phrase "party [a lawyer] knows to be represented." By replacing the word "party" with "person," the drafters of rule 4.2 arguably intended to prohibit contact with a broader class than did DR 7-104(A)(1). However, both versions of the rule consider an organization to be a "person" or "party," and thus prohibit ex parte contact with at least some of the organization's employees. . . . See . . . Mass. R. Prof. C. 9.1(h), 426 Mass. 1432 (1998) (defining "[p]erson" to include a corporation, association, trust, partnership, and any other organization or legal entity). In the context of contact with the employees of a represented organization, courts have interpreted the two versions of the rule to prohibit the same conduct. . . .

The comment to rule 4.2 provides guidance in the case of a represented organization. Because both versions of the rule prohibit essentially the same conduct, the comment is instructive (although not controlling) in determining the scope of both the old and new versions of the rule. See Mass. R. Prof. C. Scope [9], 426 Mass. 1305 (1998) ("The Comments are intended as guides to interpretation, but the text of each Rule is authoritative").

According to comment [4] to rule 4.2, an attorney may not speak ex parte to three categories of employees: (1) "persons having managerial responsibility on behalf of the organization with regard to the subject of the representation"; (2) persons "whose act or omission in connection with that matter may be imputed to the organization for purposes of civil or criminal liability"; and (3) persons "whose statement may constitute an admission on the part of the organization." . . .

b. *The Superior Court judge's decision.* The judge held that all five employees interviewed by MR&W were within the third category of the comment. He reached this result by concluding that the phrase "admission" in the comment refers to statements admissible in court under the admissions exception to the rule against hearsay. The Commonwealth's version of this rule was defined in Ruszcyk v. Secretary of Pub. Safety, 401 Mass. 418 (1988), where we held that a court may admit a "statement by [the party's] agent or servant concerning a matter within the scope of [the] agency or employment, made during the existence of the relationship." Id. at 420, quoting Proposed Mass. R. Evid. 801(d)(2)(D). This rule is identical to Fed. R. Evid. 801(d)(2)(D). Because the comment includes any employee whose statement *may* constitute an admission, this interpretation would prohibit an attorney from contacting any current employees of an organization to discuss any subject within the scope of their employment. This is, as the Superior Court judge admitted, a rule that is "strikingly protective of corporations regarding employee interviews."

c. *Other interpretations of rule 4.2.* Harvard contends that the third category of the comment is an unambiguous reference to the admissions exception to the hearsay rule. However, other jurisdictions that have adopted the same or similar versions of rule 4.2 are divided on whether their own versions of the rule are properly linked to the admissions exception to the hearsay rule, and disagree about the precise scope of the rule as applied to organizations. . . .

Some jurisdictions have adopted the broad reading of the rule endorsed by the judge in this case. See, e.g., Weibrecht v. Southern Ill. Transfer, Inc., 241 F.3d 875 (7th Cir. 2001); Cole v. Appalachian Power Co., 903 F. Supp. 975 (S.D.W. Va. 1995); Brown v. St. Joseph County, 148 F.R.D. 246, 254 (N.D. Ind. 1993). Courts reaching this result do so because, like the Superior Court, they read the word "admission" in the third category of the comment as a reference to Fed. R. Evid. 801(d)(2)(D) and any corresponding State rule of evidence. Id. This rule forbids contact with practically all employees because "virtually every employee may conceivably make admissions binding on his or her employer." *In re Air Crash Disaster near Roselawn, Ind.* at 1121. However, some of the courts that have adopted this interpretation have expressed reservations. See Pratt v. National R.R. Passenger Corp., 54 F. Supp. 2d 78, 80 (D. Mass. 1999) ("This [c]ourt has previously highlighted some of the negative aspects of ethical rules prohibiting ex parte communications with individuals in the corporate context"); Hurley v. Modern Cont. Constr. Co., [1999 WL 95723 (D.Mass. Feb. 19, 1999) (stating that linking rule to rule of evidence may frustrate "truth-seeking process").

At the other end of the spectrum, a small number of jurisdictions have interpreted the rule narrowly so as to allow an attorney for the opposing party to contact most employees of a represented organization. These courts construe the rule to restrict contact with only those employees in the organization's "control group," defined as those employees in the uppermost echelon of the organization's management. See Johnson v. Cadillac Plastic Group, Inc., 930 F. Supp. 1437, 1442 (D. Colo. 1996); Fair Automotive Repair, Inc. v. Car-X Serv. Sys., Inc., 128 Ill. App. 3d 763, 771 (1984) (applying rule only to "top management persons who had the responsibility of making final decisions"); Wright v. Group Health Hosp., 103 Wash. 2d 192, 200 (1984) (applying rule only to "those employees who have the legal authority to 'bind' the corporation in a legal evidentiary sense, i.e., those employees who have 'speaking authority' for the corporation").

Other jurisdictions have adopted yet a third test that, while allowing for some ex parte contacts with a represented organization's employees, still maintains some protection of the organization. The Court of Appeals of New York articulated such a rule in Niesig v. Team I, 76 N.Y.2d 363 (1990), rejecting an approach that ties the rule to Fed. R. Evid. 801(d)(2)(D). Instead, the court defined a represented person to include "employees whose acts or omissions in the matter under inquiry are binding on the corporation . . . or imputed to the corporation for purposes of its liability, or employees implementing the advice of counsel." Id. at 374. Other jurisdictions have subsequently adopted the *Niesig* test. See, e.g., Weider Sports Equip. Co. v. Fitness First, Inc., 912 F. Supp. 502 (D. Utah 1996); Branham v. Norfolk & W. R.R., 151 F.R.D.

67, 70–71 (S.D.W.Va. 1993); State v. CIBA–GEIGY Corp., 247 N.J. Super. 314, 325 (1991); Dent v. Kaufman, 185 W.Va. 171 (1991); Strawser v. Exxon Co., U.S.A., 843 P.2d 613 (Wyo. 1992). In addition, the Restatement (Third) of the Law Governing Lawyers endorses this rule. See Restatement (Third) of Law Governing Lawyers § 100 Reporter's Note comment e, at 98 (1998).

d. *Our interpretation of rule 4.2.* We adopt a test similar to that proposed in Niesig v. Team I, supra. Although the comment's reference to persons "whose statement may constitute an admission on the part of the organization" was most likely intended as a reference to Fed. R. Evid. 801(d)(2)(D), this interpretation would effectively prohibit the questioning of all employees who can offer information helpful to the litigation. We reject the comment as overly protective of the organization and too restrictive of an opposing attorney's ability to contact and interview employees of an adversary organization.

We instead interpret the rule to ban contact only with those employees who have the authority to "commit the organization to a position regarding the subject matter of representation." See Johnson v. Cadillac Plastic Group, Inc., supra at 1442; Restatement (Third) of Law Governing Lawyers, supra at § 100 comment e. See also Ethics 2000 Commission Draft for Public Comment Model Rule 4.2 Reporter's Explanation of Changes (Feb. 21, 2000) (recommending deletion of the third category of the comment). The employees with whom contact is prohibited are those with "speaking authority" for the corporation who "have managing authority sufficient to give them the right to speak for, and bind, the corporation." Wright v. Group Health Hosp., supra at 201. Employees who can commit the organization are those with authority to make decisions about the course of the litigation, such as when to initiate suit, and when to settle a pending case. See Restatement (Third) of the Law Governing Lawyers, supra at § 100 comment e, at 93 (employees who have the power to make binding evidentiary admissions are "analogous to . . . person[s] who possess[ ] power to settle a dispute on behalf of the organization"). We recognize that this test is a retrenchment from the broad prohibition on employee contact endorsed by the comment.

This interpretation, when read in conjunction with the other two categories of the comment, would prohibit ex parte contact only with those employees who exercise managerial responsibility in the matter, who are alleged to have committed the wrongful acts at issue in the litigation, or who have authority on behalf of the corporation to make decisions about the course of the litigation. This result is substantially the same as the *Niesig* test because it "prohibit[s] direct communication . . . 'with those officials . . . who have the legal power to bind the corporation in the matter or who are responsible for implementing the advice of the corporation's lawyer . . . or whose own interests are directly at stake in a representation.'" Niesig v. Team I, supra at 374, quoting C. Wolfram, *Modern Legal Ethics* § 11.6, at 613 (1986).

Our test is consistent with the purposes of the rule, which are not to "protect a corporate party from the revelation of prejudicial facts," Dent v. Kaufman, supra at

175, quoting Wright v. Group Health Hosp., supra at 200, but to protect the attorney-client relationship and prevent clients from making ill-advised statements without the counsel of their attorney. Prohibiting contact with all employees of a represented organization restricts informal contacts far more than is necessary to achieve these purposes. See Niesig v. Team I, supra at 372–373. The purposes of the rule are best served when it prohibits communication with those employees closely identified with the organization in the dispute. The interests of the organization are adequately protected by preventing contact with those employees empowered to make litigation decisions, and those employees whose actions or omissions are at issue in the case. We reject the "control group" test, which includes only the most senior management, as insufficient to protect the "principles motivating [Rule 4.2]." See id. at 373. The test we adopt protects an organizational party against improper advances and influence by an attorney, while still promoting access to relevant facts. See id. at 373–374. The Superior Court's interpretation of the rule would grant an advantage to corporate litigants over nonorganizational parties. It grants an unwarranted benefit to organizations to require that a party always seek prior judicial approval to conduct informal interviews with witnesses to an event when the opposing party happens to be an organization and the events at issue occurred at the workplace.

While our interpretation of the rule may reduce the protection available to organizations provided by the attorney-client privilege, it allows a litigant to obtain more meaningful disclosure of the truth by conducting informal interviews with certain employees of an opposing organization. Our interpretation does not jeopardize legitimate organizational interests because it continues to disallow contacts with those members of the organization who are so closely tied with the organization or the events at issue that it would be unfair to interview them without the presence of the organization's counsel. Fairness to the organization does not require the presence of an attorney every time an employee may make a statement admissible in evidence against his or her employer. The public policy of promoting efficient discovery is better advanced by adopting a rule which favors the revelation of the truth by making it more difficult for an organization to prevent the disclosure of relevant evidence.

Harvard argues that adopting the Superior Court's interpretation of rule 4.2 will not prevent parties from conducting informal interviews with an organization's employees, but will instead simply force them to seek prior judicial approval. However, if we adopt such a rule, too often in cases involving a corporate party the court will be asked to decide the extent of informal interviews permitted. This will result in extensive litigation before the underlying case even begins, and would clearly favor the better-financed party. . . .

Our decision may initially result in some increased litigation to define exactly which employees fall within the bounds of the rule. Although "a bright-line rule" in the form of a "control group" test or a blanket ban on all employee interviews would be easier to apply, the rule we adopt is, as discussed above, fair, and will allow for ex parte interviews without prior counsel's permission when an employee clearly falls outside of the rule's scope. . . .

The dissent argues that the *Niesig* test is not transferable to this jurisdiction because the test was adopted in the context of New York's narrower rule on employee admissions, which allows fewer employee statements to be admitted as admissions against the employer than the Massachusetts rule. See Niesig v. Team I, supra at 374. The limits of the ethical rule are not dictated by the breadth or narrowness of local evidentiary rules. While it is true that New York has adopted a more limited rule of evidence regarding admissions, this fact does not mandate that we adopt a rule with greater protection of organizational employees. The *Niesig* court adopted the test after balancing the competing interests of organizational litigants and the interests of the parties who oppose them; the court's decision was not rooted in its recognition that New York has a more limited rule of evidence. Id. at 373–375. For the reasons described above, the *Niesig* test is sound regardless of its basis.

The dissent also complains of "a distinct disadvantage to the organizational parties" as a result of our construction of the rule because "[i]n the nonorganizational context, a witness's hearsay statement could not be a vicarious admission of the defendant, yet in the organizational context it could." . . . We do not discern a meaningful distinction. The otherwise hearsay statements of the hypothetical witnesses posited by the dissent become admissible in evidence because of an agency relationship that exists between the witness and the party against whom the statement is offered. It is because of that agency relationship that the witness's statement is deemed to be the statement of his principal and is thus admissible. This is true both in an organizational as well as a nonorganizational context, given that individuals as well as organizations can have agents who may make statements attributable to them. If such agents come within the protected categories that we have delineated, their principals may insist that they not be approached by adverse counsel without prior permission. If they do not come within such categories, then they may provide information without such restriction whether they are agents of an organization or of an individual. The fact that organizations more often use agents who make admissible statements means only that there may be more people who may speak authoritatively for organizations than for individuals. It does not alter the principles that underlie what we believe is a desirable shift in emphasis in the direction of truth seeking.

4. *Applying rule 4.2 to the employees interviewed by MR&W.* The five Harvard employees interviewed by MR&W do not fall within the third category of the comment as we have construed it. As employees of the HUPD, they are not involved in directing the litigation at bar or authorizing the organization to make binding admissions. In fact, Harvard does not argue that any of the five employees fit within our definition of this category.

The Harvard employees are also not employees "whose act or omission in connection with that matter may be imputed to the organization for purposes of civil or criminal liability." Mass. R. Prof. C. 4.2 comment [4]. Stanford's complaint does not name any of these employees as involved in the alleged discrimination. In fact, in an affidavit she states that the two lieutenants "had no role in making any of the decisions that are the subject of my complaint of discrimination and retaliation," and Harvard does not refute this averment. All five employees were mere witnesses to the events that occurred, not active participants.

We must still determine, however, whether any of the interviewed employees have "managerial responsibility on behalf of the organization with regard to the subject of the representation." Mass. R. Prof. C. 4.2 comment [4]. Although the two patrol officers and the dispatcher were subordinate to Stanford and had no managerial authority, the two lieutenants exercised some supervisory authority over Stanford. However, not all employees with some supervisory power over their coworkers are deemed to have "managerial" responsibility in the sense intended by the comment. . . . Even if the two lieutenants are deemed to have managerial responsibility, the Massachusetts version of the comment adds the requirement that the managerial responsibility be in "regard to the subject of the representation." Mass. R. Prof. C. 4.2 comment [4]. Thus, the comment includes only those employees who have supervisory authority over the events at issue in the litigation. There is no evidence in the record that the lieutenants' managerial decisions were a subject of the litigation. The affidavits of the two lieutenants indicate that they did not complete any evaluations or offer any opinions of Stanford that Chief Riley considered in reaching his decisions.

5. *Conclusion.* Because we conclude that rule 4.2 did not prohibit MR&W from contacting and interviewing the five HUPD employees, we vacate the order of the Superior Court judge and remand the case for the entry of an order denying the defendant's motion for sanctions.

CORDY, J. (concurring in part and dissenting in part).

I concur that the financial sanction levied against Messing, Rudavsky & Weliky, P.C., must be set aside, but do so for reasons different from those set forth in the court's opinion. I disagree with the court's interpretation of Mass. R. Prof. C. 4.2, 426 Mass. 1402 (1998), and its comment that became effective on January 1, 1998, and therefore dissent from its holding in that regard.

Rule 4.2. Whatever the merits of the interpretation that the court today gives rule 4.2, it is not consistent with the rule and the comment that we adopted in 1998, or its predecessor, S.J.C. Rule 3:07, Canon 7, DR 7-104(A)(1), as appearing in 382 Mass. 786 (1981), and creates a troubling inconsistency in the way we treat organizations in our adversary system.

I begin with the premise that organizations have the right to be represented effectively by counsel to the same extent as individuals, while recognizing that organizations act through agents and employees, thus complicating the question of who the represented party is when it becomes, or is about to become, the subject of a legal proceeding. In this context the answer to the question has significant implications for defining and establishing the parameters of the attorney-client relationship, and for determining whether and to what extent actions and statements of individuals will be imputed to it in the legal proceedings. The answer to the same question also informs the meaning of the provision in our code of professional conduct that prohibits attorneys from having ex parte communication with opposing parties (or persons) they know to be represented by counsel (the no-contact rule), the essence of DR 7-104(A)(1) and rule 4.2.

It strikes me that the answer ought to be as close to being a single and consistent one as we can make it. This is particularly critical in the context of determining on the one hand whose actions and statements will be attributed to the organization in litigation, and on the other hand who in the organization is represented by counsel for purposes of the no-contact rule now embodied in rule 4.2. The purpose of the no-contact rule, after all, is to ensure the effective assistance of counsel by preserving counsels' mediating role on behalf of their clients, protecting clients from overreaching by counsel for adverse interests, and protecting the attorney-client relationship by preventing clients from making ill-advised statements without the advice of their attorney. There are few responsibilities more central to the effective representation of organizations (or individuals) than being in a position to advise and counsel them when they are being asked by opposing counsel to make statements that can be used against them to establish liability in litigation.

It is in this framework that, in 1982, the Committee on Professional Ethics of the Massachusetts Bar Association issued Opinion No. 82-7, interpreting DR 7-104(A)(1), as it applied to ex parte contacts by opposing counsel with employees of an organization. The opinion concluded that a lawyer could not interview current employees of such a party without the consent of opposing counsel "where the proposed interview concerns matters within the scope of the employee's employment." The ethics committee reasoned that the principal interest reflected in DR 7-104(A)(1) is the party's right to "effective representation of counsel" that can be guarded adequately only by viewing all present employees of an organization as parties where the proposed interview concerned matters within the scope of their employment. It further reasoned that effective representation requires that the attorney aid his client both to avoid procedural pitfalls and to present truthful statements in the most effective manner. Finally, it underscored that the position it was adopting was in accord with the law of evidence "which recognizes an exception to the hearsay rule as to 'a statement by [an] agent or servant concerning the matter within the scope of his agency or employment.'" "This rule binds the corporation with respect to admissions by employees far beyond the 'control group' of the corporation." Accordingly, it concluded that the definition of a "represented party" for purposes of DR 7-104(A)(1) needed to be consistent with the reach of the evidentiary rule.

This opinion, while it made eminent sense, was not fully embraced by the few Massachusetts courts (all Federal) which had occasion to consider DR 7-104(A)(1) in the context of petitions by parties to allow or prohibit ex parte communication with employees during discovery. These courts, while generally acknowledging the reasoning of Opinion No. 82-7, often concluded that in the absence of specific language in the rule regarding this subject, the better test was to balance, on a case by case basis, the competing interests of "effective representation," and the need, largely by plaintiffs, to gather facts informally, unpolished or influenced by counsel for the corporate opposition. This case-by-case balancing was eventually criticized in 1990 in Siguel v. Trustees of Tufts College, U.S. Dist. Ct., Civ. A. No. 88-0626-Y (D. Mass. 1990), as being wasteful of judicial resources, running the risk of treating similarly situated parties differently, and, most importantly, providing no clear guidance on ethical behavior to attorneys who needed to act and rely on that guidance every day. The court called on the Supreme Judicial Court to address the issue and provide clarity to the rule.

Although it took several years, this court eventually addressed the issue when, after comment and hearings, it adopted rule 4.2 and its comment. The rule was adopted with the full knowledge of Opinion No. 82-7 and its interpretation of DR 7-104(A)(1), with full knowledge of its 1988 decision in Ruszcyk v. Secretary of Pub. Safety, 401 Mass. 418 (1988), adopting those portions of Proposed Mass. R. Evid. 801(d)(2)(D) that made hearsay statements of employees admissible as vicarious admissions of their employers, and after hearing and considering the concerns of many lawyers (including the plaintiff law firm), that, if the court adopted rule 4.2 and its comment without amendment it would be adopting the view expounded in Opinion No. 82-7. Even the court acknowledges that the adopted language in the comment prohibiting contact with persons "whose statement may constitute an admission on the part of the organization" was "most likely" intended as a reference to Fed. R. Evid. 801(d)(2)(D). . . .

In this context it is painful to see the court now claim that, when it adopted the commentary, it did not intend its consequence; a consequence that merely ensures that organizations are as effectively represented by counsel as individuals. We should not shrink from what is a perfectly reasonable balancing of the equities.

In its opinion, the court states that to interpret the rule and commentary as adopted would grant an advantage to organizational litigants over nonorganizational litigants because, inter alia, as concerns a nonorganizational defendant, witnesses to an event could be interviewed without court approval, but if the defendant were an organization and the witnesses were employees, those witnesses could not be interviewed without court approval (assuming the interview concerned matters within the scope of their employment). . . . This observation misses the point. The reason that witnesses to an event would be, and should be, treated differently is precisely because the consequences of their interviews are treated differently. In the nonorganizational context, a witness's hearsay statement could not be a vicarious admission of the defendant, yet in the organizational context it could. The scope of the no-contact rule should be tailored to the legal consequences of the contact because the purpose of the rule is to ensure the effective legal representation of counsel. Our ruling today upsets the balance created by the rule and commentary and creates a distinct disadvantage to the organizational parties.

The Niesig v. Team I test. For purposes of the no-contact rule, the court now adopts the definition of a represented party explicated by the New York Court of Appeals in Niesig v. Team I, 76 N.Y.2d 363 (1990). That definition, in the organizational context, includes only those "employees whose acts or omissions in the matter under inquiry are binding on the corporation . . . or imputed to the corporation for purposes of its liability, or employees implementing the advice of counsel." Id. at 374. The court also notes that the *Niesig* test is consistent with the position taken in the Restatement (Third) of the Law Governing Lawyers § 100 Reporter's Note comment e (1998). The Restatement, in turn, also relies largely on the *Niesig* opinion to justify its position.

A close reading of the *Niesig* case, however, casts doubt on the transferability of its test to Massachusetts. First, the *Niesig* court was interpreting DR 7-104(A)(1), not rule 4.2 and its comment. Second, as the New York court points out, the rule it adopts "is rooted in developed concepts of the law of evidence and the law of agency," as those concepts have developed under New York law. For this reason, it cites and specifically rejects the breadth of the rule described in Opinion No. 82-7, which the Massachusetts Bar Association justified, in part, by reference to Massachusetts' rules of evidence permitting statements of employees, made within the scope of their employment, to operate as admissions of their employer. In rejecting Opinion No. 82-7, the New York Court simply states that the rule of evidence in New York is different on this point, id. at 374, citing Loschiavo v. Port. Auth. of N.Y. & N.J., 58 N.Y.2d 1040 (1983). There, the *Loschiavo* court held that under New York Rules of Evidence, "the hearsay statement of an agent is admissible against his employer under the admissions exception to the hearsay rule only if the making of the statement is an activity within the scope of his authority." Id. at 1041. In other words, only if the employee has the authority to speak for the organization. The *Niesig* court, therefore, did not have to grapple with or even consider the challenges posed to providing effective assistance of counsel to an organization, in the context of a State which has a far more expansive rule concerning what constitutes an admission of an organization for evidentiary purposes. . . .

In these circumstances, it seems to me that we should not be so quick to adopt the position of States with very different jurisprudential landscapes, and disown a rule that makes good sense in the Commonwealth. Rather, we should work to ensure that the reach of the rule does not exceed the limits necessary to its purpose. This can be accomplished in two ways. First, by making it clear that the prohibition against communicating with persons whose statements may constitute an admission on the part of their organization (1) does not preclude counsel from contacting all employees of a represented organization and (2) only applies to communications with employees about matters within the scope of their employment that would be admissible as vicarious admissions of the organization in the particular controversy that is the subject of the representation. Second, by demonstrating that we intend narrowly to interpret the qualifying factor, i.e., what matters are within the scope of an individual's employment, for purposes of this rule and the common-law rule of evidence announced in Ruszcyk v. Secretary of Pub. Safety, 401 Mass. 418 (1988).

Applying these limiting factors to the prohibition, I would not, for example, conclude that the plaintiff's communications with the Harvard patrol officers and dispatcher would have been impermissible. Observations by an employee of apparent wrongful conduct by other employees ought not generally be construed to be within the scope of an employee's employment unless it was their responsibility to observe or investigate such conduct. Consequently, hearsay statements about such observations should not be admissible against the organization under the admissions exception to the hearsay rule.

I view the plaintiff's communications with the Harvard police lieutenants, however, as more problematic. Those employees clearly had a measure of supervisory responsibility over Stanford, whose job performance was to be a central issue in her discrimination litigation. Thus, those interviews run afoul not only of the prohibition against communicating with employees about matters within the scope of their employment but also the prohibition against communicating with employees having managerial responsibility regarding the subject of the representation.

Sanctions. I fully support the imposition of sanctions by trial judges against litigants who violate or abuse the discovery rules, obstruct the efficient exchange of discoverable information, or who take and litigate frivolous positions. The use of the cost of litigating such matters as a measure of the appropriate sanction also makes a great deal of sense. But DR 7-104(A)(1) and rule 4.2 are ethical rules, not discovery rules. In addition, the position taken and arguments made by the plaintiff law firm were not frivolous, and its actions were not clearly violative of the ethical rules at the time, in light of the state of the law regarding the reach and meaning of DR 7-104(A)(1). Therefore, notwithstanding my view that some of the plaintiff's actions violated DR 7-104(A)(1) and rule 4.2, as I would interpret them, I would vacate the financial sanctions as an abuse of discretion. I would leave the remainder of the motion judge's order in effect.

Notes

1. An interesting feature of this opinion is that the Supreme Judicial Court had just recently revised the state's rules of professional responsibility and had promulgated in its "legislative" capacity the very Comment that it rejected in its judicial capacity. It is perhaps a good example of how focus on a specific problem in its factual setting leads to different decision-making from focusing on a general situation in the context of a whole revision of a set of rules. Another feature of the case is that the plaintiff's lawyers seemed to have been very much aware that they were engaging in conduct that was in violation of the Comment's interpretation of Rule 4.2 but were willing to take the risk of a substantial sanction in the name of what they saw as far-reaching principle. The opinion does not say whether they obtained the consent of their client in conducting the interviews of the Harvard police. Was client consent required?

2. In Pratt v. AMTRAK, 54 F. Supp. 2d 78 (D. Mass. 1999), at a time when the Massachusetts version of the Comment to Rule 4.2 contained the "admission" language, the federal court considered the validity of an ex parte deposition of the

foreman of a railroad being sued under the Federal Employers' Liability Act (FELA). The lawyer for an employee who had been hurt opening a baggage car took the deposition ex parte because the railroad had refused to produce the foreman. The court concluded that, unless the lawyer's conduct was "authorized by law," the deposition was a violation of Rule 4.2 because Massachusetts and federal courts would admit against the railroad any statement by its current agent that related to the scope of the agent's employment. Section 10 of the FELA makes void "any rule . . . or device whatsoever . . . the effect of which shall be to prevent employees of any common carrier from voluntarily furnishing information to a person in interest as to the facts incident to the injury or death of any employee." Recognizing that section 10 did not explicitly refer to ex parte conversations and noting an almost even split among the fifteen cases that had considered the issue, the court used the legislative history to conclude that the purpose of the section was to level the playing field in the conduct of litigation. It viewed Rule 4.2 as creating just the kind of inequity that section 10 was designed to correct and concluded that section 10 authorized the ex parte communication. Contra, Weibrecht v. Southern Illinois Transfer, Inc., 241 F.3d 875 (7th Cir. 2001).

3. Model Rule 8.4(a) makes it professional misconduct to violate the rules of professional conduct "through the acts of another." In what the court described as a "close case," it found that the lawyer for a plaintiff in an age discrimination case had violated the combination of Rule 4.2 and Rule 8.4(a) by encouraging his client, successfully, to obtain sworn statements from coworkers who had made favorable comments about his factual evidence. Holdren v. General Motors Corp., 13 F. Supp. 2d 1192 (D. Kan. 1998). Some authorities would reach the opposite conclusion. A sentence was added to Comment 4 in 2002 stating that "a lawyer is not prohibited from advising a client concerning a communication that the client is legally entitled to make." Would that Comment permit the lawyer to ghostwrite the client's letter or script the telephone conversation seeking sworn statements? Would these actions constitute "advising a client"? A controversial ABA Ethics Opinion addressed the issue in Formal Opinion 11-461. It concluded that too stringent a definition of "scripting" "would unduly inhibit permissible and proper advice to the client regarding the content of the communication." After telling lawyers that they may afford clients "substantial assistance" in preparing to communication with the other side, the Opinion then went on to caution lawyers against violating the underlying purpose of Rule 4.2: to prohibit overreaching. "Prime examples of overreaching include assisting the client in securing from the represented person an enforceable obligation, disclosure of confidential information, or admissions against interest without the opportunity to seek the advice of counsel. To prevent such overreaching, a lawyer must, at a minimum, advise her client to encourage the other party to consult with counsel before entering into obligations, making admissions or disclosing confidential information. If counsel has drafted a proposed agreement for the client to deliver to her represented adversary for execution, counsel should include in such agreement conspicuous language on the signature page that warns the other party to consult with his lawyer before signing the agreement."

4. Another issue presented by Rule 4.2 is the reach of the prohibition to former employees. There was a split under the Model Code, with the majority of jurisdictions taking the position that the purpose of the prohibition was to protect the principal–agency relation between the organization and its employees. Hence the prohibition did not apply to conversations with a former employee. The jurisdictions that have passed on this question under the Model Rule as written prior to 2002 are still split. Compare, e.g., Camden v. Maryland, 910 F. Supp. 1115, 1124 (D. Md. 1996) (granting disqualification because the attorney contacted a former employee of the moving party and obtained confidential information), with Lang v. Superior Court, 826 P.2d 1228, 1233 (Ariz. Ct. App. 1992) (reversing sanctions against counsel who contacted former employees of the defendant corporation and concluding that the rule "does not bar counsel from having *ex parte* contacts with a former employee of an opposing party where the former employer is represented by counsel *unless* the acts or omissions of the former employee gave rise to the underlying litigation or the former employee has an ongoing relationship with the former employer in connection with the litigation."). Some argued that although the text of the Rule is unchanged insofar as it affects this issue, the Comments suggested a broader purpose to the Rule. To the extent that the statements of a former employee may constitute an admission by, or may be imputed to, the organization, the prohibition covers those employees. When the ABA amended the Comments to eliminate the "admission" standard, it also added a sentence in Comment 7 stating that consent of the organization's lawyer was not needed for communication with a former employee. Is that distinction fair to corporate entities, which of course can speak or act only through agents? In other words, should the plaintiff's lawyer have direct access to a former high-level executive of the represented corporate defendant simply because that executive chose to move to another corporation?

5. A court, quite persuasively, refused to apply Rule 4.2 literally and held that it "cannot apply where lawyers and/or their investigators, seeking to learn about current corporate misconduct, act as members of the general public to engage in ordinary business transactions with low-level employees of a represented corporation." In the particular case, the lawyers were seeking to learn whether the company was violating a consent decree prohibiting it from selling certain memorabilia relating to the Beatles to the general public. The court also refused to apply literally the language of Rule 8.4(c), which prohibits lawyers from engaging in "conduct involving dishonesty, fraud, deceit or misrepresentation." It concluded that the concealment of identity for the purpose of engaging in a sale in order to detect violation of law was generally approved conduct and did not rise to the level of misrepresentation or deceit that raised a question of the lawyers' professional fitness. Apple Corps v. International Collectors Society, 15 F. Supp. 2d 456 (D.N.J. 1998). There are a variety of ethics opinions across the country on the similar use of "testers," who are employed to detect discrimination (among other violations) in housing, employment, and other markets. In analyzing the ethics of deceiving others as to one's identity or purpose, the jurisdictions wrestle less with Rule 4.2 and more with Rule 8.4(c), as noted above. See generally David B. Isbell & Lucantonio N. Salvi, "Ethical Responsibility

of Lawyers for Deception by Undercover Investigators and Discrimination Testers: An Analysis of the Provisions Prohibiting Misrepresentation Under the Model Rules of Professional Conduct," 8 Geo J. Legal Ethics 791, 792 (1995).

6. Contact with government officials may be "authorized by law" even though a government agency may be a party to the litigation. See Comment 1 to Rule 4.2; ABA Formal Opinion 97-408; and American Canoe Ass'n v. City of St. Albans, 18 F. Supp. 2d 620 (S.D. W.Va. 1998).

7. A far-reaching attack on the anti-contact rule as overly protective of lawyers' interests is contained in Leubsdorf, "Communicating with Another Lawyer's Client: The Lawyer's Veto and the Client's Interests," 127 U. Pa. L. Rev. 683 (1979); see also Geoffrey C. Hazard, Jr. & Dana Remus Irwin, "Toward A Revised 4.2 No-Contact Rule," 60 Hastings L.J. 797 (2009) (arguing that Rule 4.2 should be repealed or, failing that, amended to narrow its scope and increase its clarity).

2. Rule 4.2 and Criminal Cases

Problem 6–5

A defendant in a drug case being prosecuted by the federal government wants to talk to the Assistant United States Attorney (AUSA) in charge of the case about a plea bargain. He is afraid to do so in the presence of his lawyer, who is being paid by the defendant's employer. May the AUSA talk with the defendant without saying anything to the defendant's lawyer?

Model Rule 4.2 also applies in criminal cases. The Michigan Supreme Court was sharply divided in fashioning a remedy when a defendant while in custody voluntarily made a statement to investigating officers accompanied by an assistant prosecutor who had not obtained prior consent to the interview from defense counsel. All agreed that the anti-contact rule had been violated. Four judges refused to apply a prophylactic exclusionary rule suppressing the statement, holding that the Model Code represented simply self-imposed internal regulations that did not govern rules of evidence. They found no constitutional violation and held that bar disciplinary action was the appropriate remedy. Three judges would have suppressed the evidence. Two focused heavily on that remedy as the appropriate remedy for violation of the court's own rules of practice. People v. Green, 405 Mich. 273 (1979).

In United States v. Hammad, 846 F.2d 854, petition for reh'g denied with Opinion, 855 F.2d 36, opinion revised, 858 F.2d 834 (1988), the Court of Appeals for the Second Circuit dealt with the applicability of the anti-contact rule in the context of a case in which a prosecutor had supplied an informant with a fictitious subpoena and had then "wired" him and recorded his conversation with the defendant, knowing that the defendant was represented by counsel. The Court agreed with the district court that the Disciplinary Rule was not coextensive with the Sixth Amendment and hence applied at the investigation stage. However, it rejected the district court's limitation of the Rule to situations where the defendant "had retained counsel specifically for representation in conjunction with the criminal matter in which he is held suspect." The Court responded that such a limitation might restrict the government's ability to conduct criminal investigations "in that small but persistent number of cases where a career criminal has engaged 'house counsel' to represent him in conjunction with an ongoing fraud or criminal enterprise." Id. at 839. The Court then stated that it regarded legitimate use of informants as falling within the "authorized by law" exception in the Rule. In the present case, however, the Court regarded the use of a counterfeit grand jury subpoena with a false signature of the clerk of the court as egregious misconduct making the informant the alter ego of the prosecutor so that a violation of the Rule followed. It also held that suppression of the evidence would be an appropriate remedy, although it reversed the suppression in the instant case because the law had previously been so unsettled. For our purposes, however, the bottom line is that the court did not craft a rule to deal just with the "house counsel" problem. It stated a broad rule that absent egregious misconduct, the use of informants in pre-indictment, noncustodial situations will generally not constitute a violation of the anti-contact rule.

Many other courts have interpreted the anti-contact rule as not being applicable before indictment. See, e.g., United States v. Balter, 91 F.3d 427 (3d Cir. 1996), cert. denied, 519 U.S. 1011 (1996). Thereafter a federal district court, interpreting California's Rule 2-100, its version of Rule 4.2, held that the Rule applied to a pre-indictment situation where an Assistant United States Attorney refused to allow the target company's lawyer to attend her interview with its bookkeeper, who had been subpoenaed to appear before a grand jury. The AUSA had taken the bookkeeper to a room in the courthouse because he wanted to interview her outside the lawyer's presence. The district court found a violation of Rule 2-100 by the AUSA. The court of appeals reversed, relying on the circumstances under which contact had occurred. The employee had approached the AUSA claiming that her employer was pressuring her to perjure herself and stating that she did not want to be represented by company counsel. She had also rejected the AUSA's suggestions that she hire independent counsel. United States v. Talao, 222 F.3d 1133 (9th Cir. 2000).

The Justice Department has taken the position that the anti-contact rule of Model Rule 4.2 hampers law enforcement efforts greatly, especially when applied to pre-arrest investigation, and has sought, in a variety of ways, to prevent its application to its lawyers. See generally Bruce A. Green, "Prosecutors and Professional Regulation," 25 Geo. J. Legal Ethics 873, 878–79 (2012) (noting prosecutors' various attempts to avoid professional regulation, including the no-contact rule). The most far-reaching effort began in 1989 when Attorney General Thornburgh issued a memorandum declaring that Justice Department lawyers were exempt from both state and federal anti-contact rules. This memorandum provoked considerable controversy, but the Justice Department promulgated its own regulations governing whether and when its attorneys may contact represented persons and represented parties. Those regulations were the subject of attack in the following case.

United States ex rel. O'Keefe

v.

McDonnell Douglas Corporation

The Conference of Chief Justices, Amicus Curiae
132 F.3d 1252 (8th Cir. 1998) (rehearing en banc denied)

HANSEN, Circuit Judge

The United States of America appeals the district court's protective order preventing government attorneys from engaging in ex parte communications with current employees of the defendant, McDonnell Douglas Corporation (McDonnell Douglas). The government also appeals restrictions placed upon its investigation of former employees. We affirm.

I.

This action arose as a qui tam action brought by Daniel O'Keefe under the False Claims Act, 31 U.S.C. §§ 3729–33, alleging mischarging of labor hours by employees of McDonnell Douglas Corporation (McDonnell Douglas) while working on United States military contracts. The United States subsequently intervened in the suit pursuant to 31 U.S.C. § 3730(b)(4) and (c). On behalf of the United States, the Department of Justice (DOJ) began its pretrial investigation. In particular, investigative agents of the DOJ began making ex parte contacts with various present and former lower-level employees of McDonnell Douglas without the consent of McDonnell Douglas's counsel.

McDonnell Douglas brought a motion for a protective order preventing such contacts, arguing that such ex parte contacts were barred by Missouri Supreme Court Rule 4-4.2. Missouri Supreme Court Rule 4-4.2 provides, "in representing a client, a lawyer shall not communicate about the subject of the representation with a party the lawyer knows to be represented by another lawyer in the matter, unless the lawyer has the consent of the other lawyer or is authorized by law to do so." The official comment explains that where the opposing party is an organization, Rule 4-4.2 bars ex parte communications with "persons having the managerial responsibility on behalf of the organization, and with any other person whose act or omission in connection with that matter may be imputed to the organization for purposes of civil or criminal liability or whose statement may constitute an admission on the part of the organization." This comment was adopted by the Supreme Court of Missouri in State ex rel. Pitts v. Roberts, 857 S.W.2d 200, 202 (Mo. 1993) (en banc). The Supreme Court of Missouri's ethical rules have in turn been adopted by the United States District Court for the Eastern District of Missouri. See E.D. Mo. L.R. 12.02 ("The Code of Professional Responsibility adopted by this Court is the Code of Professional Responsibility adopted by the Supreme Court of Missouri, as amended from time to time, except as may otherwise be provided by this Court's Rules of Disciplinary Enforcement.").

The government argues that a protective order was not warranted because the ex parte contacts it engaged in are expressly authorized by 28 C.F.R. § 77.10(a), a rule promulgated by the Attorney General of the United States. This rule provides as follows:

> A communication with a current employee of an organization that qualifies as a represented party or represented person shall be considered to be a communication with the organization for purposes of this part only if the employee is a controlling individual. A "controlling individual" is a current high level employee who is known by the government to be participating as a decision maker in the determination of the organization's legal position in the proceeding or investigation of the subject matter.

28 C.F.R. § 77.10(a). The Government argues that section 77.10(a) supersedes the local rules of the Eastern District of Missouri. In the alternative, the government argues that, in light of section 77.10(a), the disputed ex parte contacts by DOJ attorneys were "authorized by law," and thus fell under the express exception to Rule 4-4.2 which states that ex parte contacts are permissible if "authorized by law." McDonnell Douglas responds to both arguments by asserting that the Attorney General lacked the statutory authority to issue 28 C.F.R.§ 77.10(a), and that this provision is therefore invalid and of no effect.

The district court concluded that section 77.10(a) fell beyond the limits of the Attorney General's statutory authority. Accordingly, it granted the protective order in part, finding that the government's ex parte contacts with current McDonnell Douglas employees violated Missouri Supreme Court Rule 4-4.2 as adopted by the Eastern District of Missouri. It ordered the government to cease such contacts and to provide discovery of information obtained from those contacts already made. The court also imposed conditions on ex parte contacts with former McDonnell Douglas employees. At the government's request, we stayed that portion of the district court's order that requires the government to provide discovery of information obtained from its ex parte contacts.

II.

"It is axiomatic that an administrative agency's power to promulgate legislative regulations is limited to the authority delegated by Congress." Bowen v. Georgetown Univ. Hosp., 488 U.S. 204, 208 (1988); see also Louisiana Pub. Serv. Comm'n v. FCC, 476 U.S. 355, 374 (1986) ("an agency literally has no power to act . . . unless and until Congress confers power upon it."). The government claims that 5 U.S.C. § 301 and various sections of Title 28 of the United States Code grant the Attorney General the authority to promulgate 28 C.F.R. § 77.10(a). We address each assertion in turn.

A. The Housekeeping Statute

The government relies primarily on 5 U.S.C. § 301 (1994). Section 301, better known as the "Housekeeping Statute," was passed in 1789 "to help General Washington get his administration underway by spelling out the authority for executive officials to set up offices and file government documents." H.R.Rep. No. 85-1461 (1958), reprinted in 1958 U.S.C.C.A.N. 3352. The current version of the Housekeeping Statute provides as follows:

The head of an Executive department or military department may prescribe regulations for the government of his department, the conduct of its employees, the distribution and performance of its business, and the custody, use, and preservation of its records, papers, and property. This section does not authorize withholding information from the public or limiting the availability of records to the public.

5 U.S.C. § 301 (1994).

The government's argument that the Housekeeping Statute authorizes the Attorney General's promulgation of 28 C.F.R. § 77.10(a) contradicts the plain meaning of the statute and the jurisprudence of the Supreme Court. In Chrysler Corp. v. Brown, 441 U.S. 281, 310 (1979), the Supreme Court examined the Housekeeping Statute and held that it *does not* provide statutory authority for substantive regulations. After a brief historical analysis of the provision, the Court wrote:

> Given this long and relatively uncontroversial history, and the terms of the statute itself, it seems to be simply a grant of authority to the agency to regulate its own affairs. . . . It is indeed a "housekeeping statute," authorizing what the APA terms "rules of agency organization, procedure or practice" as opposed to "substantive rules."

Id. at 309–10. In so ruling, the Court noted that Congress had looked carefully at the statute in 1958, that the Special Subcommittee on Government Information had "unanimously agreed that [§ 301] originally was adopted in 1789 to provide for the day-to-day office housekeeping in the Government departments," and that attempts to construe it as something more was "misuse" which "twisted" the statute. *Chrysler Corp.*, 441 U.S. at 310 n.41 (quoting H.R. Rep. No. 85-1461 at 7 (1958)) (alterations in original).

In recent years, several agencies have unsuccessfully attempted to find statutory authority for substantive regulations in the Housekeeping Statute. See In re Bankers Trust Co., 61 F.3d 465, 470 (6th Cir. 1995) (Federal Reserve Board regulation requiring subpoenaed party to refuse production of confidential FRB information, contrary to Federal Rule of Civil Procedure 34, was not authorized by the Housekeeping Statute and "exceed[ed] the congressional delegation of authority"), cert. dismissed, 517 U.S. 1205 (1996); Exxon Shipping Co. v. United States Dep't of Interior, 34 F.3d 774, 776–78 (9th Cir. 1994) (Housekeeping Statute did not authorize regulations allowing agency to withhold deposition testimony of federal employees); In re Cincinnati Radiation Litig., 874 F. Supp. 796, 826–27 (S.D. Ohio 1995) (Housekeeping Statute did not authorize 1953 Defense Department directive on the use of human volunteers in experimental research); McElya v. Sterling Med. Inc., 129 F.R.D. 510, 514 (W.D. Tenn. 1990) (Housekeeping Statute did not give Department of Navy authority to create general discovery privilege for persons under its jurisdiction). The government's argument in the case at bar is simply one more attempt to twist this simple administrative statute into an authorization for the promulgation of substantive rules. . . .

B. Title 28

The government relies additionally on various sections of Title 28 of the United States Code (sections 509, 510, 515(a), 516, 519, 533, and 547) which, it argues, collectively authorize 28 C.F.R. § 77.10(a). We reject this contention because none of these is any more than a general enabling statute, see United States v. Lopez, 4 F.3d 1455, 1461 (9th Cir. 1993) (rejecting claim that §§ 509, 515, 516, 533, and 547 authorized similar DOJ policy), and because no reviewing court could "reasonably . . . conclude that the grant of authority contemplates the regulations issued." See *Chrysler Corp.*, 441 U.S. at 308. Sections 509, 510, 515(a), 516, 519, and 533 define the duties of the Attorney General, grant her the power to appoint inferior officers and to delegate power to these officers, and provide that these officers shall answer to her.

Section 547 simply defines the role of United States Attorneys who, although appointed by the President and removable by him, are nonetheless directed by the Attorney General in the discharge of their duties pursuant to section 519. The district court correctly concluded that nothing in any of these sections expressly or impliedly gives the Attorney General the authority to exempt lawyers representing the United States from the local rules of ethics which bind all other lawyers appearing in that court of the United States.

III.

An agency's promulgation of rules without valid statutory authority implicates core notions of the separation of powers, and we are required by Congress to set these regulations aside. 5 U.S.C. § 706(2)(C) (1994) ("The reviewing courts shall . . . hold unlawful and set aside agency action, findings and conclusions found to be . . . in excess of statutory jurisdiction, authority, or limitations, or short of statutory right . . . .") . . .

Because we cannot reasonably conclude that the grants of authority in the statutory provisions cited by the government contemplate the issuance of anything resembling 28 C.F.R. § 77.10(a), we find this regulation to be invalid. Accordingly, we reject the government's argument that its ex parte contacts are "authorized by law" and therefore satisfy Rule 4-4.2. Moreover, because invalid promulgations of the Attorney General can neither preempt nor supersede the local federal rules for the Eastern District of Missouri, we reject the government's supersession/preemption argument as well. Because the government's position has no remaining legs on which to stand, we lift the stay and affirm the order of the district court.

IV.

The district court determined that Missouri Supreme Court Rule 4-4.2 does not require the DOJ to obtain the consent of McDonnell Douglas's counsel before initiating ex parte contacts with McDonnell Douglas's *former* employees, unless such former employees are currently represented by counsel. However, it ordered the government to keep a list of the names of the former employees it interviews and the dates on which it interviews them. The court further ordered the government to preserve all statements, notes, and answers to questions obtained as a result of these contacts, and to make these documents available to McDonnell Douglas for review upon request, subject to work-product limitations.

The government appeals the imposition of these conditions upon its investigation of the former employees. We review discovery matters only for "gross abuse of discretion resulting in fundamental unfairness in the trial of the case." Prow v. Medtronic, Inc., 770 F.2d 117, 122 (8th Cir. 1985). Since the district court created safeguards to protect government attorney work-product from discovery, and since the non-privileged information would be subject to normal discovery in any case, we find no gross abuse of discretion....

For the reasons stated above, we lift the stay and affirm the judgment of the district court.

Notes

1. The struggle over Rule 4.2 has also led to a jurisdictional battle regarding state efforts to discipline federal prosecutors for violation of the Rule. See In re Doe, 801 F. Supp. 478 (D.N.M. 1992) (federal district court would not remove from state disciplinary board a proceeding against state-licensed federal prosecutor for violating District of Columbia anti-contact rule); United States v. Ferrara, 54 F.3d 825 (D.C. Cir. 1995) (refusing to enjoin New Mexico disciplinary proceeding against that same federal prosecutor arising out of the same conduct); see also generally In re Kline, 113 A.3d 202, 213 (D.C. 2015) (noting prosecutors' attempts in several states not to follow the broad disclosure requirements as written in the ethical rules and instead to follow the more lax requirements imposed by the Constitution and holding that Rule 3.8 "requires a prosecutor to disclose all potentially exculpatory information in his or her possession regardless of whether that information would meet the materiality requirements of" constitutional law).

2. When the ABA revised the Comments to Rule 4.2 in 2001, the drafters decided not to address the concerns of the Justice Department about the effect of Rule 4.2 upon its ability to investigate illegal activities, concluding that the Rule struck "the proper balance between effective law enforcement and the need to protect client-lawyer relationships."

D. Litigation Tactics

Problem 6–6

Lawyer is representing a man charged with passing a forged check. The only substantial issue at trial is identification. The bank teller to whom the check was passed identified the defendant, who was sitting at counsel table, as the person who deposited the forged check. During a recess in the trial, the lawyer had his client switch clothes with another man who bore a superficial resemblance to the defendant. That person then replaced the defendant at the counsel table. On cross-examination, the lawyer specifically directed the witness' attention to the man sitting at the counsel table and asked if he was sure that this was the person who deposited the forged check. The witness answered that he was. Was that a proper tactic?

A serious problem of professional responsibility was involved in the course of trial in In re Metzger, 31 Haw. 929 (1931), where defense counsel (later a United States District Judge) in a capital case was cross-examining an expert handwriting witness who had testified that the same hand (admittedly that of one of the defendants) that had written Exhibit E, a certain card, also had written a crucial letter. During a recess, counsel forged Exhibit E and then cross-examined the witness again, taking him carefully through the details of the writing contained in it. The expert failed to note the substitution; subsequently, the defendants were acquitted. Defense counsel was then charged with misconduct before the Supreme Court of Hawaii in an information by the attorney general. The court, in suspending counsel from practice for ten days, stated, in an opinion by Chief Justice Perry:

> . . . The plan had been carefully devised. His express purpose, as he admitted at the hearing in this Court in answer to a question by a member of the Court, was, in saying what he said and in doing what he did, to deceive the witness into thinking that he was handing him the genuine exhibit "E." The plan devised and followed was well calculated to accomplish that purpose; and succeeded. The respondent first deceived the clerk by failing to return to him, as was his duty, the precise paper (exhibit "E") which he had received from him and for which he had given him a receipt and by the method pursued made the clerk an innocent and unwitting participant in the misrepresentation and deception, to the witness, which followed. When, after a lengthy examination and a lengthy cross-examination of the handwriting of the letter, the envelope and the genuine card, the clerk, in answer to the cross-examining attorney's request, produced the letter and a card, the witness had a right to believe, and could only believe, that the card was the genuine exhibit "E." The presentation by the respondent to the witness of a card as exhibit "E" was a deliberate misrepresentation. If the representation had been made in words, e.g., "this is exhibit 'E,'" instead of by acts, it would have been a deliberate falsehood. So, also, forgery of the clerk's signature (by initials), for the purpose of conveying to the witness the clerk's apparent certification of the genuineness of the card, was in itself an offense which cannot be ignored.

> There can be no doubt that it was the right and the duty of the respondent, who was entrusted with the defense of two men who were on trial for their lives, to expose if he could what he believed to be a lack of ability and a lack of reliability or accuracy on the part of the witness who had testified as an expert on handwriting; but there was a limitation upon that right and that duty and the limitation was that the test and the exposure must be

accomplished by fair and lawful means, free from falsehood and misrepresentation. The so-called "necessities of the case," the keenness of the desire of the attorney to defend the accused to the best of his ability, cannot in our judgment justify falsehood or misrepresentation by the attorney to a witness or to the clerk of the court, whether that falsehood or misrepresentation be expressed in direct language or be conveyed by artful subterfuge. We are unwilling to certify to the younger attorneys who are beginning their experience at the bar of this court, or to any of the attorneys of this Territory, that it is lawful and proper for them to defend men, even though on trial for their lives, by the use of falsehood and misrepresentation, direct or indirect. The conduct of the respondent was unethical and unprofessional.

With reference to the action to be taken in consequence of this finding and this ruling, it is proper to consider the surrounding circumstances. The responsibility of an attorney who is defending men in a capital case is a serious one. Right and justice require that he should be zealous and active in securing all proper evidence in behalf of the accused and in cross-examining as effectively as may be the witnesses produced by the prosecution. The respondent testifies that when he devised and executed his plan he was not conscious of the fact that it might be deemed unethical or unprofessional. We accept his statement. The two attorneys whom he consulted as to the probable success of the plan did not utter any caution as to its possible impropriety. These are considerations tending towards leniency. [However, in] order to give emphasis to our disapproval of the respondent's conduct, we feel that it is our duty to suspend his license for a brief period of time.

Justice Banks, in dissent, commented as follows:

Metzger's right to impeach by every proper means Bailey's [the expert's] opinion that the letter, envelope and card were written by the same hand it seems to me must be conceded. Indeed it was not only his right to do this but his duty to do so—his duty to his clients, to the jury, and to the court. Of course if he had known that the letter and the envelope were in the handwriting of one of his clients, as he knew that the writing on the card was, the situation would be quite different. Under such circumstances his effort would have been not to destroy what he believed to be false but to destroy what he knew to be true. I think a lawyer, even if his zeal to extricate his client from a serious position, may not ethically go so far. This, however, was not the case. At the hearing of the instant proceeding Metzger testified that having had considerable experience in chirography he believed that the writing on the card was not by the same person as the writing on the envelope and the letter. There is no apparent reason for disbelieving him. His purpose therefore was not the evil one of misleading the jury as to a fact which he knew existed but the laudable one of exposing what he believed to be an erroneous opinion. This was in the interest of justice and not against it. Metzger also testified that he had been unable after a long cross-examination of Bailey to discredit his opinion and that there was no other handwriting expert available whom he could consult or to whose opinion he could submit the writings. His only alternative therefore was in some way to lead Bailey to disclose his own fallibility. The question that remains is whether the means he used to accomplish his purpose were unethical.

I do not think that his treatment of the witness was unfair. A cross-examiner is certainly under no professional obligation to warn an expert witness, whose opinion he wishes to test, of the pit which has been dug for him and into which he will fall unless he has sufficient technical learning to discover and avoid it. Nor do I think it a violation of legal ethics to withhold from such witness a fact which, if he knew it, would enable him to discover the pit independent of his technical knowledge. It is a principle peculiar to the cross-examination of expert witnesses that in order to evaluate their opinions, things may be assumed as facts which are not facts. This is all that Metzger really did. He in effect assumed, in the presence of the witness, the court and the jury, that the fabricated card was the real exhibit about which the witness had already testified and proceeded to ascertain by cross-examination whether he was capable of discovering that the assumption was false. In doing this he was entirely fair to the witness. According to his testimony he required Bailey to subject the fabricated card to the same tests to which he had subjected the real exhibit and to compare it with the writing on the envelope and the letter just as he had compared the real exhibit. It was an acid test of the value of Bailey's opinion, but no more severe than that that to which a handwriting expert may properly be put.

Under the evidence in this proceeding I likewise see no disregard of legal ethics on Metzger's part in delivering to the clerk the fabricated card instead of the original exhibit, without informing him of the substitution. I think the ethical quality of everything that Metzger did in carrying out the plan he devised for testing the accuracy of Bailey's opinion must be judged by the motive that actuated him to make the test, *unless what he did was otherwise inherently wrong*. His motive in making the test was to discredit an opinion that had been given by a putative expert, which opinion he believed to be erroneous. I see nothing *inherently wrong* in his temporarily withholding from the clerk the fact that the fabricated card which he delivered was not the original exhibit. That he only intended to temporarily withhold this fact from the clerk is shown by Metzger's testimony that when he handed the clerk the simulated card together with two of the exhibits he had withdrawn the clerk said to him, "I will destroy your receipt," and that he told the clerk not to do this because there would be further transactions with respect to these papers. He did in fact return the original exhibit to the clerk after he had concluded his cross-examination of Bailey. His purpose in withholding the fact from the clerk was to guard against the danger of having his plan for testing the value of Bailey's opinion frustrated by a premature exposure. This was not in my opinion a fraud on the clerk nor was it a fraud on the court, nor was it inimical to the cause of justice. It was done not to defeat a fair trial but to promote it. If it had not been done the weakness of Bailey's opinion might not have been revealed and men whom the jury found to be innocent might have been found guilty and sent to the gallows.

Notes

1. Is the only vice in Mr. Metzger's plan that he did not seek the trial judge's approval? If you were seeking such approval, would you invite the prosecutor to accompany you to see the trial judge? See Model Rule 3.5(b).

2. If you had been the trial judge in State v. Poai and Spalding (the name of the case Mr. Metzger defended), and defense counsel had sought your permission to try the handwriting switch, would you have permitted it? Why?

3. Note that the dissenting judge makes the belief of the attorney in his client's innocence the crucial point. Do you agree?

4. Meek v. Fleming, 3 All E.R. 148 (C.A. 1961), involved an action by a newspaper photographer against a police officer for assault and battery. The defendant was demoted from chief inspector to station sergeant while the case was pending because he had deceived a court in another matter. This was known to defendant's counsel who decided that the matter should not be revealed to the court. In pursuit of that decision, counsel had defendant appear at the trial in plain clothes, did not ask defendant his name and rank when he took the stand, and consistently referred to him as "Mr." In addition, neither he nor defendant corrected the judge or plaintiff's counsel when they referred to him as "chief inspector" and on cross-examination defendant gave the answer, "Yes, that is true," to the question, "You are a chief inspector, and you have been on the force, you told us, since 1938." A jury verdict was given for defendant, but on appeal a new trial was granted because of the conduct of defendant and counsel when the true facts later became known. What conduct of counsel was improper? (1) Failure to inform plaintiff's counsel of the demotion as soon as it occurred? (2) Instructing defendant to appear in plain clothes and addressing him as "Mr."? (3) Failing to correct plaintiff's counsel and the judge when they addressed defendant as "chief inspector"? (4) Failing to have defendant correct inaccurate testimony on cross-examination or, if defendant would not do so, failing to correct the testimony himself?

How different is Meek v. Fleming from the case where the lawyer provides a client with shirt, tie, and a dark suit to wear at his trial for a particularly ugly murder? Where the prosecutor tells the victim witness in a rape case to wear more conservative clothing? Consider the conduct of O. J. Simpson's lawyers, who did some "redecorating" before the mostly African-American jurors were scheduled to conduct an onsite visit of O. J.'s house: "They took away the picture that Mr. Simpson kept near the fireplace in his bedroom showing his white girlfriend of the time in a nude pose; they put a photograph of him and his mother on his bedside table. Then, to give Mr. Simpson's home 'something depicting African-American history,' aimed at arousing the sympathy of the mostly black jury, they brought in a Norman Rockwell 1963 painting, 'The Problem We All Live With,' showing a black grade school girl walking to class surrounded by Federal marshals." Richard Bernstein, "Shedding Light on How Simpson's Lawyers Won," N.Y. Times, Oct. 16, 1996 (reviewing Lawrence Schiller & James Willwerth, *American Tragedy* (1996)). Did the lawyers' "redecorating" violate Rules 3.3 or 3.4? Was it deceptive? See Rule 8.4(c).

5. It is not only criminal defense counsel who get involved in deceptive methods of seeking truth. In Nigrone v. Murtagh, 46 App. Div. 2d 343 (2d Dept. 1974), aff'd. in part and appeal dismissed in part without reaching the issue of prosecutorial misconduct, 36 N.Y.2d 421 (1975), the Appellate Division considered the conduct of Maurice Nadjari, a special prosecutor appointed by the governor to investigate corruption in New York City's criminal justice system. Acting on allegedly specific information about corruption in the system, Nadjari caused a fake indictment to be returned by a grand jury against an undercover agent who then contacted Judge Rao of the United Customs Court and was put in touch with defendant lawyers, one of whom was Judge Rao's son. Subsequently, an Extraordinary Special Grand Jury, investigating whether defendants had conspired with a second judge to bribe a third judge in connection with the fake case, called defendants to testify. Based on discrepancies between their testimony and taped recordings of conversations between defendants and the undercover agent, defendants were indicted for perjury. They moved to have the indictments dismissed.

The Appellate Division was unanimous in condemning Mr. Nadjari's conduct in the strongest terms for numerous improprieties committed in the course of setting up a sham case, including deceiving various judges at the arraignment and setting of bail, the grand jury that returned the indictment, and the Assistant District Attorney who thought a real case was being presented. Nevertheless, the Appellate Division, on a 3–2 vote, denied the relief. The majority noted that the investigation in which the perjury was allegedly committed was before a different grand jury from the one that returned the fake indictment and refused to legitimate any reason to lie to a grand jury. It viewed an extension of the exclusionary rule to this "sui generis case" as an unwarranted interference into the investigation, and believed its condemnation of the conduct would be sufficient to prevent its repetition. 46 App. Div. 2d at 349.

The dissenters would have granted the motion on the ground that (1) the conduct occurred after the Second Circuit had condemned similar conduct of other prosecutors in United States v. Archer, 486 F.2d 670 (1973), a case in which Mr. Nadjari appeared as amicus curiae, and therefore condemnation was not an effective deterrent; (2) the events before the two grand juries cannot be separated because the second grand jury was investigating a case that was a sham and did not exist; and (3) most importantly, that outrageous governmental misuse of power and of the purposes of the criminal justice system corrupts the system and that the courts should announce that they will "not approve indictments resulting from an 'unprecedented' and illegal exercise of power by the Special Prosecutor." 46 App. Div. 2d at 358. On remand, however, Justice Murtagh of the Supreme Court on his own motion dismissed the indictments, on other evidentiary grounds. The Appellate Division, however, reversed this order and remanded the case for a hearing. 53 App. Div. 2d 904 (2d Dept. 1976). On remand, Justice Sandler dismissed the indictment against Judge Rao but upheld the indictment against his son and another lawyer. Lawyer Rao was convicted, but on appeal that conviction was reversed. The Appellate Division concluded that misconduct of the prosecutors constituted a denial of due process. The court's opinion supported its conclusion by reference to the original misconduct and further prosecutorial misconduct at the grand jury proceedings, including suppression of exculpatory evidence. 73 A.D.2d 88 (2d Dept. 1980).

6. An attorney discipline proceeding in Oregon tested the meaning of the professional rules prohibiting dishonesty, fraud, deceit and misrepresentation—see Model Rule 8.4(c)—and frightened both private and public lawyers in that state. An attorney's complaint against deceptive investigative practices by state attorneys was dismissed by the state Professional Responsibility Board as not violating the ethics rules. The attorney then engaged in similar deceptive tactics in investigating one of his own matters. He was publicly reprimanded by the Oregon Supreme Court, which declined to read an "investigation exception" into the disciplinary rules and a statute authorizing imposition of discipline for willful deceit. In re Gatti, 330 Or. 517 (2000). Referring to the prior dismissal of charges against government lawyers, the court went on to say that the rule applies to the investigatory activities of government attorneys as well and that any exceptions would have to be created by changes in the statute and judicial rules. The Department of Justice then brought suit to enjoin the Oregon State Bar, the disciplinary arm of the court, from trying to discipline government lawyers engaging in such investigative activities (17 ABA/BNA Manual on Professional Conduct 407 (July 4, 2001)) and the Oregon Supreme Court amended its professional responsibility rules to permit lawyers to advise clients about, or to supervise, lawful cover activities to investigate violations of civil or criminal law or constitutional rights. Oregon Rule of Professional Conduct 8.4(b).

7. People v. Pautler (Colo. Office of Presiding Disciplinary Judge 2001) presents another twist on the issue of deception. A prosecutor who pretended to be a public defender in order to get a confessed murderer to turn himself in was suspended for three months by a divided disciplinary board. It concluded that the prosecutor's conduct was not only a deception but included a purpose to keep the murderer talking about his criminal activities, and it refused to accept a justification defense. 17 ABA/BNA Lawyers Manual on Judicial Conduct 258 (April 25, 2001). The Colorado

Supreme Court ultimately affirmed the violation and the discipline. Paulter was given a stay of the suspension conditioned on his successful completion of the terms of his probation (which among other things required him to retake the MPRE) within one year. In re Pautler, 47 P.3d 1175 (Colo. 2002).

Another example of aggressive litigation tactics that misfired is In re Beiny, 129 App. Div. 2d 126, on motion for reargument or renewal and leave to appeal, 132 App. Div. 2d 190 (1st Dept. 1987). In connection with a trust accounting proceeding, the law firm for a beneficiary desired to obtain the files of a liquidated law firm that had represented the settlor of the trust. The factual situation was described in the opinion of the court on the motion for reargument:

> Petitioner's counsel, Sullivan & Cromwell, believing that the liquidator of the law firm of Greenbaum, Wolff & Ernst had factual information concerning the property at issue, served a subpoena duces tecum and notice of deposition directing the liquidator to appear for examination with all the papers concerning certain clients, including trustee Beiny. No notice was given by Sullivan & Cromwell to the other parties. The subpoena was knowingly aimed at privileged materials, and no court would have sustained its broad demand. In order to give the subpoena a sharper edge, Sullivan & Cromwell enclosed it in a letter that deceptively represented to the liquidator that Sullivan & Cromwell's client, petitioner Wynyard, was the executor of the estate of a former client of the Greenbaum firm. Sullivan & Cromwell, having thereafter received from the liquidator the mass of papers to which no law but only its deceit entitled it, then canceled the day fixed for the liquidator's examination. Within weeks, the trustee, ignorant of the raid upon Greenbaum's papers, was examined in London by Sullivan & Cromwell who not only used those papers to surprise her but refused to disclose how the papers had been obtained. When the trustee's counsel learned how Sullivan & Cromwell had obtained the papers, they asked for their production, but Sullivan & Cromwell refused, unless the trustee made concessions in discovery. Only after the trustee was driven to obtain an order of the Surrogate in December 1985, granting the trustee access to the papers, did the trustee learn the extent of Sullivan & Cromwell's massive intrusion into the trustee's privileged papers; and not until July 1986 did the trustee have in hand an order of the Surrogate suppressing all but 7 of 114 documents as to which the trustee claimed privilege. . . .

The Surrogate suppressed most of the documents but refused to disqualify the law firm. The Appellate Division affirmed the suppression but also found that the abuse of the confidential information had been so great that disqualification was required not only to sanitize the proceeding but also to prevent the firm from deriving further benefit from its misconduct. On motion for reargument, the court focused its entire attention on the conduct of the law firm.

In re Beiny

132 App. Div. 2d 190 (1st Dept. 1987)

MURPHY, P. J.

We refer this proceeding to the Departmental Disciplinary Committee for investigation, including an inquiry by the Committee into the August 3, 1987 report of the Wall Street Journal that Donald Christ, a member of Sullivan & Cromwell, allegedly assaulted an attorney for trustee Beiny in the Surrogate's Court at a conference in this case. . . .

In ending this appeal, it might be useful to trace the lines of certain features of the case for they show how this court, faced each moment with matters involving profound issues of liberty and property, can be burdened by an appeal such as that at bar, an appeal that is before us solely because of the misconduct of lawyers in pursuit of a fee. We speak of the matter because it extends beyond the ownership and transfer of porcelains, and well beyond the interest of a law firm in its reputation. Our consideration of the case is enlarged by issues involving the ethical norms required of attorneys as advocates. . . .

In consequence of Sullivan & Cromwell's conduct, this court has had placed before five of its Justices about 1,700 pages of record and briefs, to say nothing of paper footage given to motions that have since slid into the dark of appellate memory. Petitioner Wynyard's case, which may be one involving substantial merit, has been delayed by about 2½ years given over to the legal debris that now lies before us. He has been left by Sullivan & Cromwell's conduct to search for other counsel who will probably bill him for the reading of the lengthy record generated by Sullivan & Cromwell's misconduct. Trustee Beiny has been driven down a legal gauntlet, arched by fees of expensive counsel and hedged by the anxiety to which Bench and Bar are often insensible. In short, upon facts that should have led Sullivan & Cromwell to a prompt, practical resolution, one that would have avoided delay, fees and the worrying of court and clients, Sullivan & Cromwell chose instead to drive the trustee toward the steps of the Surrogate's Court and, ultimately, both petitioner and the trustee to the steps of this court. Having arrived in this court, Sullivan & Cromwell, in protection of its reputation, then set about the making of arguments that, startlingly curious in design, required the time of this much pressed court to identify and answer. . . .

Sullivan & Cromwell argued on the appeal that its associate, Garrard Beeney, who had engineered the acquisition of the now suppressed documents, was procedurally correct in his obtaining of the papers without notice to the parties. The argument was notable if only because it might have caused an applicant's failure upon the Bar examination, to say nothing of its use against Sullivan & Cromwell by its adversaries in other actions. On reargument, petitioner's additional counsel, retained for the motions at bar, made for safer waters, conceding that Beeney was in error but that Beeney had acted innocently. In short, Beeney had known what he was doing but did not know that it was wrong. As far as our research has gone this is the first instance, at least in this court, in which a breach of the Civil Practice Law and Rules has been met with the defense raised in 1843 in *M'Naghten's Case* (8 Eng Rep 718), a fact that would have startled poor M'Naghten as he stood acquitted in the dock. The record shows that Beeney indeed knew what he was about when he palmed off petitioner as the executor of the estate of a decedent whose will was never probated, and when he canceled a deposition that he never intended to conduct. The record shows that even though Donald Christ, a senior partner at Sullivan & Cromwell, must have known at the very least of the way Beeney had acquired the privileged papers, still nothing was done to right what must have seemed to Mr. Christ to have been wrong. Instead, Sullivan & Cromwell in their prosecution of the case thereafter used the papers against the trustee. As for the argument that the liquidator was in substance a volunteer in need of a subpoena as a kind of receipt for his files, we give to it the same value that we have given to Beeney's singular belief that petitioner was the executor of an estate unknown to any probate court.

Petitioner's claim that the trustee and he had been jointly represented by the Greenbaum firm, a claim unproved before the Surrogate, can hardly be a foothold in justification of Sullivan & Cromwell's raid upon the Greenbaum files. Our cachet of approval upon such a primitive notion of discovery, to say nothing of the extension of such a principle throughout our law, would entice the invasive, disorderly mind in an area in which rights must be judicially or consensually fixed before parties proceed in the gathering of facts.

Last, it is disingenuous for petitioner's counsel to argue that we did not find that the suppressed documents were substantially related to the issues. We suppose that petitioner's counsel read our statement that "among the matters to which the documents refer are transactions involving the disposition of the very assets whose ownership is at issue in this proceeding," or if they did not read our plain statement, they surely must have recalled their own repeated statements concerning the probative value of the suppressed documents. Nor do we think it an exercise in candor for petitioner's counsel to say on this motion that the suppressed documents are not substantially related to the issues before us when the record shows that, among other things, petitioner's counsel themselves characterized those documents as proof that the trustee unlawfully transferred the property at issue to entities in her control, defrauded the petitioner, violated her fiduciary duties to him and is a perjurer.

In sum, this appeal is an example of the accidental subversion of the interests of a client by his own advocates who acted as if the law did not apply to them. . . .

Notes

1. The Departmental Disciplinary Committee, to which the proceeding was referred by the Appellate Division, investigated and dismissed the charges. It issued no opinion explaining its decision not to follow the Appellate Decision's lead.

2. Are you surprised that the disciplinary committee took no action in this case? Do you think Sullivan & Cromwell's status as a large, prestigious law firm helped to protect it from discipline? Should it? Or should the law firm's size and status be factors that ought to argue *against* leniency? Recall that Kaye, Scholer was also not disciplined by bar officials notwithstanding being fined $41 million by the Office of Thrift Supervision for its actions representing Lincoln Savings and Loan. Does the fact that courts and administrative agencies seem more prepared to sanction lawyers from large law firms than do disciplinary officials suggest anything to you about the claim that professional discipline should be the sole—or even the primary—means of controlling lawyer misconduct? We will return to these questions in Chapter 10.

3. In Cleary Gottlieb Steen & Hamilton LLP v. Kensington International Ltd., 2008 U.S. App. Lexis 13812 (2d Cir. 2008), the Second Circuit affirmed sanctions of $165,000 in attorneys' fees and costs against a major New York law firm for attempting in bad faith to dissuade a non-party witness from attending a post-judgment deposition.

4. A startling case of deception resulted in the disbarment of two lawyers, one a partner in a major Boston law firm, and a three-year suspension of a third lawyer, a former president of the Massachusetts Bar Association. The lawyers had become convinced that the trial judge had predetermined the outcome of a major civil case. They concocted an elaborate subterfuge to induce the judge's law clerk to make statements discrediting the judge and casting doubt on her impartiality and finally threatened the law clerk if he did not cooperate with them. See Matter of Curry, 450 Mass. 503 (2008) and Matter of Crossen, 450 Mass. 533 (2008).

5. For a comprehensive discussion of the apparent increase in aggressive, deceptive, and manipulative litigation tactics that nevertheless may not expressly be prohibited by the rules, see Symposium, "Ethics Beyond the Rules," 67 Fordham L. Rev. 691 (1998). For example, do the rules cover the following tactics, which recently occurred in the middle of a lengthy and highly publicized trial? You hear that the opposing counsel has had a DUI and continues to this day to drink and drive regularly. You also know that virtually each night after trial, opposing counsel has dinner at a bar near the courthouse. You decide to send your paralegal to the bar after trial tonight to spy on opposing counsel, strike up a conversation with him, and to drink with him. You then call your friend, who is a member of the local police department, to be on the lookout in front of the bar for a drunk driver and you give your officer-friend a description of opposing counsel's vehicle. Opposing counsel is successfully arrested for drunk driving and now cannot appear at court for trial the following day. For this conduct (and more), the lead attorney was disbarred. Florida Bar v. Diaco, No SC14-1052, Report of Referee (Aug. 27, 2015); Florida Bar v. Diaco, No. SC14-1052, 2016 WL 374277, at *1 (Fla. Jan. 28, 2016) (adopting referee's report and permanently disbarring counsel). The conduct was obviously unseemly, but which specific rules prohibited it?

6 · EVERYDAY PROBLEMS OF THE PRACTICING LAWYER

E. Negotiations and Plea Bargaining

Problem 6–7

During the course of settlement negotiations, D's lawyer makes a third and "final" offer to P's attorney who replies, "It's no better than any of the others. You are so low that I haven't even bothered my client with any of your other offers, and I'm not going to pass this one along either. I'll have my client consider an offer when you come into the ballpark." What course of conduct may D's lawyer pursue in order to have the offer considered by P? (Recall Rule 4.2 above in your consideration.)

Problem 6–8

You are a prosecutor and there is a case in your office in which an indictment for aggravated assault has been returned by the grand jury. You are about to conclude a plea bargain with the defendant and his attorney when you learn that your main witness, without whose testimony there is only a weak case, has died. Do you reveal this information to counsel for the defendant?

Notes

1. In Brady v. Maryland, 373 U.S. 83, 87 (1963), the Supreme Court held that "suppression by the prosecution of evidence favorable to an accused upon request violates due process where the evidence is material either to guilt or to punishment, irrespective of the good faith or bad faith of the prosecution." The awkwardness of the phrase limiting the holding to situations where the evidence is requested by defense counsel suggests that the limitation may have been inserted "upon request" of a member of the Court who might not otherwise have joined the opinion. In any event, the limitation does not appear in the Model Rule's statement of the applicable disciplinary rule. See In re Kline, 113 A.3d 202 (D.C. 2015); Model Rule 3.8(d); ABA Ethics Op. 09–454 (2009). But does that provision or the *Brady* rule explicitly cover Problem 6–8? See also Moore v. Illinois, 408 U.S. 786 (1972), reaffirming and elaborating the *Brady* rule; United States v. Agurs, 427 U.S. 97 (1976), holding that constitutional error is to be found in nondisclosure even without a request for the information when the nondisclosed evidence creates a reasonable doubt that did not otherwise exist; and United States v. Bagley, 473 U.S. 667 (1985), holding that a conviction must be reversed for failure to comply with the *Brady* rule only if the nondisclosed evidence "is material in the sense that its suppression undermines confidence in the outcome of the trial."

2. A notorious case involved a prosecution of Duke University lacrosse players for alleged rape, followed by eventual dismissal of all charges. Michael Nifong, the prosecutor, was then disbarred after the North Carolina State Bar, the disciplinary authority in that jurisdiction, conducted a hearing and determined that, among other disciplinary violations, Mr. Nifong had failed to disclose, and indeed had concealed, substantial amounts of evidence that were specifically exculpatory.

Disciplinary action against prosecutors, however, is a relatively rare phenomenon. See also generally Chapter 5, Section B (discussing prosecutorial ethics).

3. Yet another high-profile case in which prosecutors (this time federal prosecutors) failed to disclose exculpatory evidence led Attorney General Holder, in the spring of 2009, to move to dismiss certain corruption charges against Alaska Senator Ted Stevens, who had been convicted the previous fall and subsequently was defeated for reelection. District Judge Sullivan, in granting the government's motion, was quoted as saying that he had never seen anything like the "mishandling and misconduct" of the government's lawyers.

Problem 6–9

Insurance company counsel (ICC) and plaintiffs' counsel (PC) are attempting to negotiate a settlement of an automobile accident case. ICC realizes from statements made by PC that one reason PC is willing to settle more reasonably than expected is that PC has misunderstood the facts of the relationship between the driver of the truck and its insured. PC appears to be concerned that a master–servant relationship might not exist when in fact ICC knows quite clearly that it does. Should ICC correct PC's misunderstanding? In summarizing her client's position, may ICC allude to the likelihood that PC will not be able to prove the existence of a master–servant relationship?

PC, on the other hand, has just learned that a main witness, without whose testimony there will be only a weak case, has just died. PC knows that this witness gave the insurance company adjuster a statement that is quite favorable to his client, but that ICC does not know of her death. Should PC reveal that fact to ICC?

Problem 6–10

You represent a company that has just discovered that a trusted employee has embezzled $50,000. The company president wants to get as much of the money back as possible and is determined to get rid of the employee. On the other hand, having consulted the board, she believes that it would be very bad publicity for the company to have a criminal trial splashed all over the papers. She has therefore instructed you to threaten the employee's attorney that you will go to the prosecutor unless the employee immediately discloses to your satisfaction how every penny was spent, turns over as much cash as is unaccounted for and everything bought with the embezzled funds, plus whatever other assets that you can reasonably squeeze out of him. A number of jurisdictions have adopted the language of former Model Code DR 7-105(A) that prohibits a lawyer from presenting or threatening to present criminal charges "solely" to obtain an advantage in a civil matter. In such a jurisdiction could you follow your client's instructions to threaten the employee's attorney? If you are in a jurisdiction that has no such provision, does that mean that you have no problem? See Livermore, "Lawyer Extortion," 20 Ariz. L. Rev. 403 (1978), for a discussion of the relevance of extortion statutes to problems like this. See also generally Comm.

on Legal Ethics of the W. Virginia State Bar v. Printz, 416 S.E.2d 720 (W. Va. 1992) (concluding that "(1) attorney who tells client's employee that unless he makes restitution of amounts embezzled from client, attorney will press criminal charges, does not violate Disciplinary Rules, and (2) attorney could not be prosecuted under statute which prohibits offer not to prosecute crime in exchange for return of funds lost due to crime").

The following excerpts present differing approaches to problems of professional responsibility that arise in the negotiation context. The idea that professional responsibility requires some role-specific code of conduct is not limited to law. The first excerpt presents a relevant perspective in the context of business ethics by Albert Carr. Written almost fifty years ago, the article has been a standard text in business ethics. In reading Carr's argument, ask yourself what in his view are the rules of the "business game"? What justifies these rules? Do you find these justifications persuasive? If so, do the examples Carr gives fit the justifications?

The second excerpt, by Judge Alvin Rubin of the Court of Appeals for the Fifth Circuit, should be compared with the views expressed by Marvin Frankel with respect to the lawyer's obligation to truth in our adversary system. (See Frankel's excerpted article in Chapter 3.) The final excerpt in this section, by Professor James J. White of the Michigan Law School, surveys the scene from the perspective of a very practical teacher of negotiation skills and theory.

Albert Z. Carr
Is Business Bluffing Ethical?
46 Harv. Business Rev. 143 (1968)

The ethics of business are not those of society, but rather those of the poker game

A respected businessman with whom I discussed the theme of this article remarked with some heat, "You mean to say you're going to encourage men to bluff? Why, bluffing is nothing more than a form of lying! You're advising them to lie!"

I agreed that the basis of private morality is a respect for truth and that the closer a businessman comes to the truth, the more he deserves respect. At the same time, I suggested that most bluffing in business might be regarded simply as game strategy — much like bluffing in poker, which does not reflect on the morality of the bluffer.

I quoted Henry Taylor, the British statesman who pointed out that "falsehood ceases to be falsehood when it is understood on all sides that the truth is not expected to be spoken" — an exact description of bluffing in poker, diplomacy, and business. I cited the analogy of the criminal court, where the criminal is not expected to tell the truth when he pleads "not guilty." Everyone from the judge down takes it for granted that the job of the defendant's attorney is to get his client off, not to reveal the truth; and this is considered ethical practice. I mentioned Representative Omar

Burleson, the Democrat from Texas, who was quoted as saying, in regard to the ethics of Congress, "Ethics is a barrel of worms" — a pungent summing up of the problem of deciding who is ethical in politics.

I reminded my friend that millions of businessmen feel constrained every day to say *yes* to their bosses when they secretly believe *no* and that this is generally accepted as permissible strategy when the alternative might be the loss of a job. The essential point, I said, is that the ethics of business are game ethics, different from the ethics of religion.

He remained unconvinced. Referring to the company of which he is president, he declared: "Maybe that's good enough for some businessmen, but I can tell you that we pride ourselves on our ethics. In 30 years not one customer has ever questioned my word or asked to check our figures. We're loyal to our customers and fair to our suppliers. I regard my handshake on a deal as a contract. I've never entered into price-fixing schemes with my competitors. I've never allowed my salesmen to spread injurious rumors about other companies. Our union contract is the best in our industry. And, if I do say so myself, our ethical standards are of the highest!"

He really was saying, without realizing it, that he was living up to the ethical standards of the business game — which are a far cry from those of private life. Like a gentlemanly poker player, he did not play in cahoots with others at the table, try to smear their reputations, or hold back chips he owed them.

But this same fine man, at that very time, was allowing one of his products to be advertised in a way that made it sound a great deal better than it actually was. Another item in his product line was notorious among dealers for its "built-in obsolescence." He was holding back from the market a much-improved product because he did not want it to interfere with sales of the inferior item it would have replaced. He had joined with certain of his competitors in hiring a lobbyist to push a state legislature, by methods that he preferred not to know too much about, into amending a bill then being enacted.

In his view these things had nothing to do with ethics; they were merely normal business practice. He himself undoubtedly avoided outright falsehoods — never lied in so many words. But the entire organization that he ruled was deeply involved in numerous strategies of deception.

Pressure to deceive

Most executives from time to time are almost compelled, in the interests of their companies or themselves, to practice some form of deception when negotiating with customers, dealers, labor unions, government officials, or even other departments of their companies. By conscious misstatements, concealment of pertinent facts, or exaggeration — in short, by bluffing — they seek to persuade others to agree with them. I think it is fair to say that if the individual executive refuses to bluff from time to time — if he feels obligated to tell the truth, the whole truth, and nothing but the truth — he is ignoring opportunities permitted under the rules and is at a heavy disadvantage in his business dealings. . . .

The game is played at all levels of corporate life, from the highest to the lowest. At the very instant that a man decides to enter business, he may be forced into a game situation, as is shown by the recent experience of a Cornell honor graduate who applied for a job with a large company:

This applicant was given a psychological test which included the statement, "Of the following magazines, check which ones that you have read either regularly or from time to time, and double-check those which interest you most. Reader's Digest, Time, Fortune, Saturday Evening Post, The New Republic, Life, Look, Ramparts, Newsweek, Business Week, U.S. News & World Report, The Nation, Playboy, Esquire, Harper's, Sports Illustrated."

His tastes in reading were broad, and at one time or another he had read almost all of these magazines. He was a subscriber to The New Republic, an enthusiast for Ramparts, and an avid student of the pictures in Playboy. He was not sure whether his interest in Playboy would be held against him, but he had a shrewd suspicion that if he confessed to an interest in Ramparts and The New Republic, he would be thought a liberal, a radical, or at least an intellectual, and his chances of getting the job, which he needed, would greatly diminish. He therefore checked five of the more conservative magazines. Apparently it was a sound decision, for he got the job.

He had made a game player's decision, consistent with business ethics. . . .

The Poker Analogy

We can learn a good deal about the nature of business by comparing it with poker. While both have a large element of chance, in the long run the winner is the man who plays with steady skill. In both games ultimate victory requires intimate knowledge of the rules, insight into the psychology of the poker players, a bold front, a considerable amount of self-discipline, and the ability to respond swiftly and effectively to opportunities provided by chance.

No one expects poker to be played on the ethical principles preached in churches. In poker it is right and proper to bluff a friend out of the rewards of being dealt a good hand. A player feels no more than a slight twinge of sympathy, if that, when — with nothing better than a single ace in his hand — he strips a heavy loser, who holds a pair, of the rest of his chips. It was up to the other fellow to protect himself. In the words of an excellent poker player, former President Harry Truman, "If you can't stand the heat, stay out of the kitchen." If one shows mercy to a loser in poker, it is a personal gesture, divorced from the rules of the game.

Poker has its special ethics, and here I am not referring to rules against cheating. The man who keeps an ace up his sleeve or who marks the cards is more than unethical; he is a crook, and can be punished as such — kicked out of the game or, in the Old West, shot.

In contrast to the cheat, the unethical poker player is one who, while abiding by the letter of the rules, finds ways to put the other players at an unfair disadvantage. Perhaps he unnerves them with loud talk. Or he tries to get them drunk. Or he plays in cahoots with someone else at the table. Ethical poker players frown on such tactics.

Poker's own brand of ethics is different from the ethical ideals of civilized human relationships. The game calls for distrust of the other fellow. It ignores the claim of friendship. Cunning deception and concealment of one's strength and intentions, not kindness and openheartedness, are vital in poker. No one thinks any the worse of poker on that account. And no one should think any the worse of the game of business because its standards of right and wrong differ from the prevailing traditions of morality in our society. . . .

The point was forcefully made to me by a Midwestern executive who has given a good deal of thought to the question:

> "So long as a businessman complies with the laws of the land and avoids telling malicious lies, he's ethical. If the law as written gives a man a wide-open chance to make a killing, he'd be a fool not to take advantage of it. If he doesn't, somebody else will. There's no obligation on him to stop and consider who is going to get hurt. If the law says he can do it, that's all the justification he needs. There's nothing unethical about that. It's just plain business sense." . . .

Among the most respected of our business institutions are the insurance companies. A group of insurance executives meeting recently in New England was startled when their guest speaker, social critic Daniel Patrick Moynihan, roundly berated them for "unethical" practices. They had been guilty, Moynihan alleged, of using outdated actuarial tables to obtain unfairly high premiums. They habitually delayed the hearings of lawsuits against them in order to tire out the plaintiffs and win cheap settlements. In their employment policies they used ingenious devices to discriminate against certain minority groups.

It was difficult for the audience to deny the validity of these charges. But these men were business game players. . . . But morally they have in their view done nothing wrong. As long as they comply with the letter of the law, they are within their rights to operate their businesses as they see fit. . . .

I think it is fair to sum up the prevailing attitude of businessmen on ethics as follows:

We live in what is probably the most competitive of the world's civilized societies. Our customs encourage a high degree of aggression in the individual's striving for success. Business is our main area of competition, and it has been ritualized into a game of strategy. The basic rules of the game have been set by the government, which attempts to detect and punish business frauds. But as long as a company does not transgress the rules of the game set by law, it has the legal right to shape its strategy without reference to anything but its profits. If it takes a long-term view of its profits, it will preserve amicable relations, so far as possible, with those with whom it deals. A wise businessman will not seek advantage to the point where he generates dangerous hostility among employees, competitors, customers, government, or the public at large. But decisions in this area are, in the final test, decisions of strategy, not of ethics. . . .

If a man plans to take a seat in the business game, he owes it to himself to master the principles by which the game is played, including its special ethical outlook. He can then hardly fail to recognize that an occasional bluff may well be justified in terms of the game's ethics and warranted in terms of economic necessity. Once he clears his mind on this point, he is in a good position to match his strategy against that of the other players. He can then determine objectively whether a bluff in a given situation has a good chance of succeeding and can decide when and how to bluff, without a feeling of ethical transgression.

To be a winner, a man must play to win. This does not mean that he must be ruthless, cruel, harsh, or treacherous. On the contrary, the better his reputation for integrity, honesty, and decency, the better his chances of victory will be in the long run. But from time to time every businessman, like every poker player, is offered a choice between certain loss or bluffing within the legal rules of the game. If he is not resigned to losing, if he wants to rise in his company and industry, then in such a crisis he will bluff—and bluff hard. . . .

Notes

1. Consider the rhetorical posture adopted in Carr's exposition of the poker analogy in business: So long as the law is not broken, then anything goes to secure a business advantage. How persuasive do you think the analogy between business and a poker game is? Do you think business itself has changed in the almost fifty years since Carr's essay was published? See Ben W. Heineman, Jr., *High Performance With High Integrity* (Memo to the CEO) (2008) (arguing that global companies must have both performance and integrity to compete effectively in the global economy). For example, recent writing in welfare economics argues that "trust" is socially productive by encouraging people to interact without incurring expensive monitoring and enforcement costs. See, e.g., Stephen Knack & Philip Keefer, "Does Social Capital Have an Economic Payoff? A Cross-Country Investigation," 112 Q.J. Econ. 1251 (1997) (finding that societies with higher civic norms of trust and reciprocity have higher economic performance than those that do not). Such research has led some legal scholars to conclude that trust is an important foundation of corporate well-being. See Margaret M. Blair & Lynn Stout, "Trust, Trustworthiness, and the Behavioral Foundations of Corporate Law," 149 U. Pa. L. Rev. 1735 (2001). Indeed, some argue that an over-reliance on legal enforcement can actually undermine the conditions that foster efficient trust between contracting parties, for example, by introducing grounds for distrust (i.e., the potential that sophisticated parties will use legal protections intended to safeguard vulnerable parties opportunistically to defeat legitimate expectations by those with whom they deal) or undermining the social conditions necessary to generate trust in the first instances (i.e., by turning "voluntary" compliance into "legally imposed" compliance, which may not be forthcoming in the absence of the threat of legal sanction). See Larry E. Ribstein, "Law v.

Trust," 81 B.U. L. Rev. 553 (2001). Does this research affect your view of how the "business game" should be played? See Lynn Sharp Paine, "Moral Thinking in Management: An Essential Capability," in *Ethics in Practice: Lawyers' Roles, Responsibilities and Regulation* 59 (Deborah L. Rhode, ed. 2000).

2. What in Carr's view are the "ethics," as opposed to the "rules" of the business game? For an extended argument that lawyers can learn a great deal from poker and other card games, see Steven Lubet, *Lawyer's Poker: 52 Lessons that Lawyers Can Learn from Card Players* (2008).

3. Consider Professor Freedman's argument in Chapter 2. To what extent are the rules of the "adversary system" game similar to Carr's rules for the business game? Is this the same game Anita Charles (Problem 1–2, p. 32) was encouraged or required to play? Is "trust" as important to the proper functioning of the legal system? Recall Judge Frankel's argument in Chapter 3 that current conceptions of the adversary system placed too low a value on truth from a systemic perspective. Is there also an argument that lawyers who play the "law" game the way Carr argues that the "business" game should be played are also hurting their clients? See, e.g., Peter Kostant, "Paradigm Regained: How Competition from Accounting Firms May Help Corporate Attorneys to Recapture the Ethical High Ground," 20 Pace L. Rev. 43 (1999); John A. Humbach, "The National Association of Honest Lawyers: An Essay on Honesty, 'Lawyer Honesty' and Public Trust in the Legal System," 20 Pace L. Rev. 93 (1999).

4. Is there any similarity between Carr's portrayal of the "ethics" of the business game and Professor Pepper's first-class citizenship model for lawyers (in Chapter 3)?

5. Carr's piece arguably reflects a very culturally gendered view of business as a poker game. How might the surge in women's participation in business and law alter the rules of the game described by Carr? We will return in Chapter 12 to the question whether and how the increase in the number of women lawyers might affect the way law is practiced.

Alvin Rubin
A Causerie on Lawyers' Ethics in Negotiation
35 La. L. Rev. 577 (1975)

... Taken together, [the rules of the Model Code],* interpreted in the light of that old but ever useful candle, ejusdem generis, imply that a lawyer shall not himself engage in illegal conduct; since the meaning of assisting a client in fraudulent conduct is later indicated by the proscription of *other* illegal conduct. As we perceive, the lawyer is forbidden to make a false statement of law or fact *knowingly*. But nowhere is it ordained that the lawyer owes any general duty of candor or fairness to members of the bar or to laymen with whom he may deal as a negotiator or of honesty or of good faith insofar as that term denotes generally scrupulous activity.

---

* [and the Model Rules too. — Eds.]

Is the lawyer-negotiator entitled, like Metternich, to depend on "cunning, precise calculation, and a willingness to employ whatever means justify the end of policy"? Few are so bold as to say so. Yet some whose personal integrity and reputation are scrupulous have instructed students in negotiating tactics that appear tacitly to countenance that kind of conduct. In fairness it must be added that they say they do not "endorse the *propriety*" of this kind of conduct, and indeed even indicate "grave reservations"[20] about such behavior; however, this sort of generalized disclaimer of sponsorship hardly appears forceful enough when the tactics suggested include:

— Use two negotiators who play different roles. (Illustrated by the "Mutt and Jeff" police technique: "Two lawyers for the same side feign an internal dispute . . .")

— Be tough — especially against a patsy.

— Appear irrational when it seems helpful.

— Raise some of your demands as the negotiations progress.

— *Claim* that you do not have authority to compromise. (Emphasis supplied.)

— After agreement has been reached, have your client reject it and raise his demands.[21]

Another text used in training young lawyers commendably counsels sincerity, capability, preparation, courage and flexibility. But it also suggests "a sound set of tools or tactics and the know how to use (or not to use) them."[22] One such tactic is, "Make false demands, bluffs, threats; even use irrationality."[23] . . .

Let us consider the proper role for a lawyer engaged in negotiations when he knows that the opposing side, whether as a result of poor legal representation or otherwise, is assuming a state of affairs that is incorrect. Hypothesize: L, a lawyer, is negotiating the sale of his client's business to another businessman who is likewise represented by counsel. Balance sheets and profit and loss statements prepared one month ago have been supplied. In the last month, sales have fallen dramatically. Counsel for the potential buyer has made no inquiry about current sales. Does L have a duty to disclose the change in sales volume?

Some lawyers say, "I would notify my client and advise him that *he* has a duty to disclose," not because of ethical considerations but because the client's failure to do so might render the transaction voidable if completed. If the client refused to sanction disclosure, some of these lawyers would withdraw from representing him *in this matter* on ethical grounds. As a practical matter (i.e., to induce the client to accept

---

20. M. Meltsner & P. Schrag, *Public Interest Advocacy: Materials for Clinical Legal Education* 232 (1974) (emphasis in original).

21. Id. at 236–238. Regarding the tactic of having the client reject the agreement and raise his demand, the authors add, "This is the most ethically dubious of the tactics listed here, but there will be occasions where a lawyer will have to defend against it or even to employ it." Id. at 238.

22. H. Freeman & H. Weihofer, *Clinical Law Training* 122 (1972).

23. Id.

their advice) they say, in consulting with the client, the lawyer is obliged to present the problem as one of possible fraud in the transaction rather than of lawyers' ethics.

In typical law school fashion, let us consider another hypothet[ical]. L, the lawyer, is representing C, a client, in a suit for personal injuries. There have been active settlement negotiations with LD, the defendant's lawyer. The physician who has been treating C rendered a written report, containing a prognosis stating that it is unlikely that C can return to work at his former occupation. This has been furnished to LD. L learns from C that he has consulted another doctor who has given him a new medication. C states that he is now feeling fine and thinks he can return to work, but he is reluctant to do so until the case is settled or tried. The next day, L and LD again discuss settlement. Does L have a duty either to guard his client's secret or to make a full disclosure? Does he satisfy or violate either duty if, instead of mentioning C's revelation he suggests that D require a new medical examination?

Some lawyers avoid this problem by saying that it is inconceivable that a competent LD would not ask again about C's health. But if the question as to whether L should be frank is persistently presented, few lawyers can assure that they would disclose the true facts.

Lawyers whose primary practice is corporate tend to distinguish the two hypotheticals, finding a duty to disclose the downturn in earnings but not the improvement in health. They may explain the difference by resorting to a discussion of the lower standards (expectations?) of the bar when engaged in personal injury litigation. "That's why I stay away from that kind of work," one lawyer said. The esteem of a lawyer for his own profession must be scant if he can rationalize the subclassifications this distinction implies. Yet this kind of gradation of professional ethics appears to permeate the bar.

Lawyers from Wall Street firms say that they and their counterparts observe scrupulous standards, but they attribute less morality to the personal injury lawyer, and he, in turn, will frequently point out the inferiority of the standards of those who spend much time in criminal litigation. The gradation of the ethics of the profession by the area of law becomes curiouser and curiouser the more it is examined, if one may purloin the words of another venturer in wonderland.

None would apparently deny that honesty and good faith in the sale of a house or a security implies telling the truth and not withholding information. But the [rules do] not exact that sort of integrity from lawyers who engage in negotiating the compromise of a law suit or other negotiations. . . .

Do the lawyer's ethics protest more strongly against giving false information? [Model Rule 3.3(a)(1)] forbids the lawyer to "knowingly make" a false statement of law or fact. Most lawyers say it would be improper to prepare a false document to deceive an adversary or to make a factual statement known to be untrue with the intention of deceiving him. But almost every lawyer can recount repeated instances where an adversary of reasonable repute dealt with facts in such an imaginative or hyperbolic way as to make them appear to be different from what he knew they were. . . .

To most practitioners it appears that anything sanctioned by the rules of the game is appropriate. From this point of view, negotiations are merely, as the social scientists have viewed it, a form of game; observance of the expected rules, not professional ethics, is the guiding precept. But gamesmanship is not ethics. . . .

The courts have seldom had occasion to consider these ethical problems, for disciplinary proceedings have rarely been invoked on any charge of misconduct in the area. But where settlements have in fact been made when one party acted on the basis of a factual error known to the other and this error induced the compromise, courts have set releases aside on the basis of mistake, or, in some cases, fraud. . . .

If he is a professional and not merely a hired, albeit skilled, hand, the lawyer is not free to do anything his client might do in the same circumstances. The corollary of that proposition does set a minimum standard: the lawyer must be at least as candid and honest as his client would be required to be. The agent of the client, that is, his attorney-at-law, must not perpetrate the kind of fraud or deception that would vitiate a bargain if practiced by his principal. Beyond that, the profession should embrace an affirmative ethical standard for attorneys' professional relationships with courts, other lawyers and the public: *The lawyer must act honestly and in good faith.* Another lawyer, or a layman, who deals with a lawyer should not need to exercise the same degree of caution that he would if trading for reputedly antique copper jugs in an oriental bazaar. . . .

Since bona fides and truthfulness do not inevitably lead to fairness in negotiations, an entirely truthful lawyer might be able to make an unconscionable deal when negotiating with a government agency, or a layman or another attorney who is representing his own client. Few lawyers would presently deny themselves and their clients the privilege of driving a hard bargain against any of these adversaries though the opponent's ability to negotiate effectively in his own interest may not be equal to that of the lawyer in question. . . .

This raises the problem inevitable in an adversary profession if one opponent obeys a standard the other defies. As Countryman and Finman inquire,

> How is a lawyer who looks at himself as "an instrument for the furtherance of justice" likely to fare when pitted against an attorney willing to take whatever he can get and use any means he can get away with?[56]

While it might strain present concepts of the role of the lawyer in an adversary system, surely the professional standards must ultimately impose upon him a duty not to accept an unconscionable deal. While some difficulty in line-drawing is inevitable when such a distinction is sought to be made, there must be a point at which the lawyer cannot ethically accept an arrangement that is completely unfair to the other side, be that opponent a patsy or a tax collector. So I posit a second precept: *The lawyer may not accept a result that is unconscionably unfair to the other party.*

---

56. V. Countryman & T. Finman, *The Lawyer in Modern Society* 281 (1966). . . .

A settlement that is unconscionable may result from a variety of circumstances. There may be a vast difference in the bargaining power of the principals so that, regardless of the adequacy of representation by counsel, one party may simply not be able to withstand the expense and bear the delay and uncertainty inherent in a protracted suit. There may be a vast difference in the bargaining skill of counsel so that one is able to manipulate the other virtually at will despite the fact that their framed certificates of admission to the bar contain the same words.

The unconscionable result in these circumstances is in part created by the relative power, knowledge and skill of the principals and their negotiators. While it is the unconscionable result that is to be avoided, the question of whether the result is indeed intolerable depends in part on examination of the relative status of the parties. The imposition of a duty to tell the truth and to bargain in good faith would reduce their relative inequality, and tend to produce negotiation results that are within relatively tolerable bounds. . . .

The lawyer should not be free to negotiate an unconscionable result, however pleasing to his client, merely because it is possible, any more than he is free to do other reprobated acts. He is not to commit perjury or pay a bribe or give advice about how to commit embezzlement. These examples refer to advice concerning illegal conduct, but we do already, in at least some instances, accept the principle that some acts are proscribed though not criminal; the lawyer is forbidden to testify as a witness in his client's cause[61] or to assert a defense merely to harass his opponent;[62] he is enjoined to point out to his client "those factors that may lead to a decision that is morally just."[63] Whether a mode of conduct available to the lawyer is illegal or merely unconscionably unfair, the attorney must refuse to participate. This duty of fairness is one owed to the profession and to society; it must supersede any duty owed to the client. . . .

Notes

1. How would Judge Rubin's test answer his own hypotheticals? How would it answer Problems 6–8 and 6–9? Does Problem 6–9 present an issue of professional responsibility at all? If a client would not have to make any disclosure under the common law of fraud, what would be the justification for putting a greater responsibility on the attorney?

2. There is some substantive law imposing obligations on lawyers to reveal certain kinds of factual information in negotiations or litigation. See Virzi v. Grand Trunk Warehouse and Cold Storage Co., 571 F. Supp. 507 (E.D. Mich. 1983) and In re Forrest, 158 N.J. 428 (1999) (death of a client); Kath v. Western Media, Inc., 684 P.2d 98 (Wyo. 1984) (perjury of a witness during depositions); Nebraska State Bar Assn. v. Addison, 226 Neb. 585 (1987) (in negotiating with hospital for release of its lien against proceeds of settlement with insurance companies, plaintiff's lawyer had

---

61. [Model Rule 3.7.]
62. [Model Rules 3.1 and 4.4.]
63. [Model Rule 2.1.]

a duty to disclose the existence of an unknown umbrella policy and to correct known misapprehension by hospital as to number of relevant insurance policies; lawyer suspended for failure to comply with this duty); and Naposki v. First National Bank, 18 App. Div. 3d 835 (2d Dept. 2005) (law firm sanctioned for failure to notify court that California case with identical claims had been settled).

3. In Spaulding v. Zimmerman, 116 N.W.2d 704 (1962), which is Problem 1–1, p. 15 supra, the Minnesota Supreme Court held that there was no duty on defense counsel to disclose the aneurysm to plaintiff during the course of their negotiations. However, the trial court had discretion to vacate a settlement on behalf of a minor, even without a showing of fraud or bad faith, when the opposing side had important knowledge that it concealed. It did so in this case and the Minnesota Supreme Court affirmed.

4. If his propositions are to be adopted only as ethical considerations, how does Judge Rubin resolve the problem he refers to on p. 520, that of the opponent obeying a standard the other defies?

5. Would adoption of Judge Rubin's proposed standards achieve his goal? If not, what would you suggest if you agree with his general propositions?

6. Is the general negotiation framework that Judge Rubin envisages preferable to the one currently in vogue in the profession, assuming the general accuracy of his description?

7. In order to reach a conclusion with respect to Notes 5 and 6, one needs some background in the art of negotiation. A few sentences or even a few pages cannot supply it. It must be said, however, that at its best, negotiation represents a process in which lawyers for adverse parties test one another's positions in an effort to narrow differences and to perceive the basis upon which agreement may be reached. The kind of openness advocated by Judge Rubin appears as each lawyer achieves better understanding of his or her own position and that of his or her adversary and, just as importantly, achieves confidence in one another. At its worst, however, negotiation involves lawyers one or both of whom are unskilled or too busy, or afraid, to contemplate going to trial. One wonders whether busyness, fear, and lack of skill are not in fact far greater obstacles to proper working of the negotiation process than lack of honesty.

The drafters of the Model Rules sought to meet the challenge posed by Judge Rubin and others. The first public draft, the Discussion Draft of Jan. 30, 1980, contained a provision plainly directed to the conduct of negotiations. Rule 4.2 of that draft provided:

4.2 Fairness to Other Participants

(a) In conducting negotiations, a lawyer shall be fair in dealing with other participants.

(b) A lawyer shall not make a knowing misrepresentation of fact or law, or fail to disclose a material fact known to the lawyer, even if adverse, when disclosure is:

(1) Required by law or the rules of professional conduct; or

(2) Necessary to correct a manifest misapprehension of fact or law resulting from a previous representation made by the lawyer or known by the lawyer to have been made by the client, except that counsel for an accused in a criminal case is not required to make such a correction when it would require disclosing a misrepresentation made by the accused.

(c) A lawyer shall not:

(1) Engage in the pretense of negotiating with no substantial purpose other than to delay or burden another party;

(2) Illegally obstruct another party's rightful access to information relevant to the matter in negotiation;

(3) Communicate directly with another party which the lawyer knows is represented by other counsel, except with the consent of the party's counsel or authorized by law.

The draft was attacked as impractical, ill-conceived, and destructive of the adversary system and in the end the attempt to require more truthtelling in negotiations failed. The current Model Rules 4.1 and 4.2 contain all that is left of the substance of the earlier proposed Rule and represents no advance over the provisions of the Model Code. The Comment to Model Rule 4.1 seeks to answer doubts raised about certain negotiating methods: "Under generally accepted conventions in negotiation, certain types of statements ordinarily are not taken as statements of material fact. Estimates of price or value placed on the subject of a transaction and a party's intentions as to an acceptable settlement of a claim are ordinarily in this category." Professor White's article on lawyers' standards of conduct in negotiation was written against the backdrop of the change in attitude proposed by draft Model Rule 4.2. While the draft was not adopted, Professor White's comments about general standards, specific cases, and the desirability of changes in current standards are still timely.

James J. White
Machiavelli and the Bar:
Ethical Limits on Lying in Negotiation
1980 Am. B. Found. Res. J. 926

. . . The difficulty of proposing acceptable rules concerning truthfulness in negotiation is presented by several circumstances. First, negotiation is nonpublic behavior. If one negotiator lies to another, only by happenstance will the other discover the lie. If the settlement is concluded by negotiation, there will be no trial, no public testimony by conflicting witnesses, and thus no opportunity to examine the truthfulness of assertions made during the negotiation. Consequently, in negotiation, more than in other contexts, ethical norms can probably be violated with greater confidence that there will be no discovery and punishment. Whether one is likely to be caught for violating an ethical standard says nothing about the merit of the standard. However, if the low probability of punishment means that many lawyers will violate the standard, the standard becomes even more difficult for the honest lawyer to follow, for by doing so he may be forfeiting a significant advantage for his client to others who do not follow the rules.

The drafters appreciated, but perhaps not fully, a second difficulty in drafting ethical norms for negotiators. That is the almost galactic scope of disputes that are subject to resolution by negotiation. One who conceives of negotiation as an alternative to a lawsuit has only scratched the surface. Negotiation is also the process by which one deals with the opposing side in war, with terrorists, with labor or management in a labor agreement, with buyers and sellers of goods, services, and real estate, with lessors, with governmental agencies, and with one's clients, acquaintances, and family. By limiting his consideration to negotiations in which a lawyer is involved in his professional role, one eliminates some of the most difficult cases but is left with a rather large and irregular universe of disputes. Surely society would tolerate and indeed expect different forms of behavior on the one hand from one assigned to negotiate with terrorists and on the other from one who is negotiating with the citizens on behalf of a governmental agency.[3] The difference between those two cases illustrates the less drastic distinctions that may be called for by differences between other negotiating situations. Performance that is standard in one negotiating arena may be gauche, conceivably unethical, in another. More than almost any other form of lawyer behavior, the process of negotiation is varied; it differs from place to place and from subject matter to subject matter. It calls, therefore, either for quite different rules in different contexts or for rules stated only at a very high level of generality.

A final complication in drafting rules about truthfulness arises out of the paradoxical nature of the negotiator's responsibility. On the one hand the negotiator must be fair and truthful; on the other he must mislead his opponent. Like the poker player, a negotiator hopes that his opponent will overestimate the value of his hand. Like the poker player, in a variety of ways he must facilitate his opponent's inaccurate assessment. The critical difference between those who are successful negotiators and those who are not lies in this capacity both to mislead and not to be misled.

Some experienced negotiators will deny the accuracy of this assertion, but they will be wrong. I submit that a careful examination of the behavior of even the most forthright, honest, and trustworthy negotiators will show them actively engaged in misleading their opponents about their true positions. That is true of both the

---

3. For a discussion of the circumstances that might justify a lie, even for one with an extraordinary commitment to truthfulness, see Sissela Bok, ch. 8, *Lies in a Crisis in Lying: Moral Choice in Public and Private Life* 107–122 (New York: Pantheon Books, 1978).

plaintiff and the defendant in a lawsuit. It is true of both labor and management in a collective bargaining agreement. It is true as well of both the buyer and the seller in a wide variety of sales transactions. To conceal one's true position, to mislead an opponent about one's true settling point, is the essence of negotiation.

Of course there are limits on acceptable deceptive behavior in negotiation, but there is the paradox. How can one be "fair" but also mislead? Can we ask the negotiator to mislead, but fairly, like the soldier who must kill, but humanely?

The obligation to behave truthfully in negotiation is embodied in the requirement of Rule 4.2(a) that directs the lawyer to "be fair in dealing with other participants." Presumably the direction to be fair speaks to a variety of acts in addition to truthfulness and also different from it. At a minimum it has something to say about the threats a negotiator may use, about the favors he may offer, and possibly about the extraneous factors other than threats and favors which can appropriately be used in negotiating. . . .

Pious and generalized assertions that the negotiator must be "honest" or that the lawyer must use "candor" are not helpful. They are at too high a level of generality, and they fail to appreciate the fact that truth and truthful behavior at one time in one set of circumstances with one set of negotiators may be untruthful in another circumstance with other negotiators. There is no general principle waiting somewhere to be discovered, as Judge Alvin B. Rubin seems to suggest in his article on lawyer's ethics. Rather, mostly we are doing what he says we are not doing, namely, hunting for the rules of the game as the game is played in that particular circumstance.

The definition of truth is in part a function of the substance of the negotiation. Because of the policies that are behind the securities and exchange laws and the demands that Congress has made that information be provided to those who buy and sell, one suspects that lawyers engaged in SEC work have a higher standard of truthfulness than do those whose agreements and negotiations will not affect public buying and selling of assets. Conversely, where the thing to be bought and sold is in fact a lawsuit in which two professional traders conclude the deal, truth means something else. Here truth and candor call for a smaller amount of disclosure, permit greater distortion, and allow the other professional to suffer from his own ignorance and sloth in a way that would not be acceptable in the SEC case. In his article Rubin recognizes that there are such different perceptions among members of the bar engaged in different kinds of practice, and he suggests that there should not be such differences. Why not? Why is it so clear that one's responsibility for truth ought not be a function of the policy, the consequences, and the skill and expectations of the opponent?

Apart from the kinds of differences in truthfulness and candor which arise from the subject matter of the negotiation, one suspects that there are other differences attributable to regional and ethnic differences among negotiators. Although I have only anecdotal data to support this idea, it seems plausible that one's expectation concerning truth and candor might be different in a small, homogeneous community from what it would be in a large, heterogeneous community of lawyers. For one thing, all of the lawyers in the small and homogeneous community will share a common ethnic and environmental background. Each will have been subjected to the same kind of training about what kinds of lies are appropriate and what are not appropriate.

Moreover, the costs of conformity to ethical norms are less in a small community. Because the community is small, it will be easy to know those who do not conform to the standards and to protect oneself against that small number. Conversely, in the large and heterogeneous community, one will not have confidence either about the norms that have been learned by the opposing negotiator or about his conformance to those norms. . . .

If the Comments or the body of the Model Rules are to refer to truthfulness, they should be understood to mean not an absolute but a relative truth as it is defined in context. That context in turn should be determined by the subject matter of the negotiation and, to a lesser extent, by the region and the background of the negotiators. Of course, such a flexible standard does not resolve the difficulties that arise when negotiators of different experience meet one another. I despair of solving that problem by the promulgation of rules, for to do so would require the critics of these rules to do something that they obviously could not wish to do. That is, unless they wish to rely on the norms in the various subcultures in the bar to flesh out the rules, they will have to draft an extensive and complex body of rules.

Although it is not necessary to draft such a set of rules, it is probably important to give more than the simple disclaimer about the impossibility of defining the appropriate limits of puffing that the drafters have given in the current [proposed but never adopted] Comments.[15] To test these limits, consider five cases. Easiest is the question that arises when one misrepresents his true opinion about the meaning of a case or a statute. Presumably such a misrepresentation is accepted lawyer behavior both in and out of court and is not intended to be precluded by the requirement that the lawyer be "truthful." In writing his briefs, arguing his case, and attempting to persuade the opposing party in negotiation, it is the lawyer's right and probably his responsibility to argue for plausible interpretations of cases and statutes which favor his client's interest, even in circumstances where privately he has advised his client that those are not his true interpretations of the cases and statutes.

A second form of distortion that the Comments plainly envision as permissible is distortion concerning the value of one's case or of the other subject matter involved in the negotiation. Thus the Comments make explicit reference to "puffery." Presumably they are attempting to draw the same line that one draws in commercial law

---

15. "The precise contours of the legal duties concerning disclosure, representation, puffery, overreaching, and other aspects of honesty in negotiations cannot be concisely stated." Comment to Rule 4.2, Model Rules . . . .

between express warranties and "mere puffing" under section 2-313 of the Uniform Commercial Code."[17] . . .

A third case is related to puffing but different from it. This is the use of the so-called false demand. It is a standard negotiating technique in collective bargaining negotiation and in some other multiple-issue negotiations for one side to include a series of demands about which it cares little or not at all. The purpose of including these demands is to increase one's supply of negotiating currency. One hopes to convince the other party that one or more of these false demands is important and thus successfully to trade it for some significant concession. The assertion of aloof argument for a false demand involves the same kind of distortion that is involved in puffing or in arguing the merits of cases or statutes that are not really controlling. The proponent of a false demand implicitly or explicitly states his interest in the demand and his estimation of it. Such behavior is untruthful in the broadest sense; yet at least in collective bargaining negotiation its use is a standard part of the process and is not thought to be inappropriate by any experienced bargainer.

Two final examples may be more troublesome. The first involves the response of a lawyer to a question from the other side. Assume that the defendant has instructed his lawyer to accept any settlement offer under $100,000. Having received that instruction, how does the defendant's lawyer respond to the plaintiff's question, "I think $90,000 will settle this case. Will your client give $90,000?" Do you see the dilemma that question poses for the defense lawyer? It calls for information that would not have to be disclosed. A truthful answer to it concludes the negotiation and dashes any possibility of negotiating a lower settlement even in circumstances in which the plaintiff might be willing to accept half of $90,000. Even a moment's hesitation in response to the question may be a nonverbal communication to a clever plaintiff's lawyer that the defendant has given such authority. Yet a negative response is a lie.

It is no answer that a clever lawyer will answer all such questions about authority by refusing to answer them, nor is it an answer that some lawyers will be clever enough to tell their clients not to grant them authority to accept a given sum until the final stages in negotiation. Most of us are not that careful or that clever. Few will routinely refuse to answer such questions in cases in which the client has granted a much lower limit than that discussed by the other party, for in that case an honest answer about the absence of authority is a quick and effective method of changing the opponent's settling point, and it is one that few of us will forego when our authority is far below that requested by the other party. Thus despite the fact that a clever negotiator can avoid having to lie or to reveal his settling point, many lawyers, perhaps most, will

---

17. Section 2-313(2) of the Uniform Commercial Code [in 1980 and still in 2016] reads in part as follows: "It is not necessary to the creation of an express warranty that the seller use formal words . . . but an affirmation merely of the value of the goods or a statement purporting to be merely the seller's opinion or commendation . . . does not create a warranty." Put another way, puffing is permitted.

sometime be forced by such a question either to lie or to reveal that they have been granted such authority by saying so or by their silence in response to a direct question. Is it fair to lie in such a case?

Before one examines the possible justification for a lie in that circumstance, consider a final example recently suggested to me by a lawyer in practice. There the lawyer represented three persons who had been charged with shoplifting. Having satisfied himself that there was no significant conflict of interest, the defense lawyer told the prosecutor that two of the three would plead guilty only if the case was dismissed against the third. Previously those two had told the defense counsel that they would plead guilty irrespective of what the third did, and the third had said that he wished to go to trial unless the charges were dropped. Thus the defense lawyer lied to the prosecutor by stating that the two would plead only if the third were allowed to go free. Can the lie be justified in this case?[21]

How does one distinguish the cases where truthfulness is not required and those where it is required? Why do the first three cases seem easy? I suggest they are easy cases because the rules of the game are explicit and well developed in those areas. Everyone expects a lawyer to distort the value of his own case, of his own facts and arguments, and to deprecate those of his opponent. No one is surprised by that, and the system accepts and expects that behavior. To a lesser extent the same is true of the false demand procedure in labor–management negotiations where the ploy is sufficiently widely used to be explicitly identified in the literature. A layman might say that this behavior falls within the ambit of "exaggeration," a form of behavior that while not necessarily respected is not regarded as morally reprehensible in our society.

The last two cases are more difficult. In one the lawyer lies about his authority; in the other he lies about the intention of his clients. It would be more difficult to justify the lies in those cases by arguing that the rules of the game explicitly permit that sort of behavior. Some might say that the rules of the game provide for such distortion, but I suspect that many lawyers would say that such lies are out of bounds and are not part of the rules of the game. Can the lie about authority be justified on the ground that the question itself was improper? Put another way, if I have a right to keep certain information to myself, and if any behavior but a lie will reveal that information to the other side, am I justified in lying? I think not. Particularly in the case in which there are other avenues open to the respondent, should we not ask him to take those avenues? That is, the careful negotiator here can turn aside all

---

21. Consider a variation on the last case. Assume that the defense lawyer did not say explicitly that the two would plead only if the third were allowed to go free but simply said, "If you drop the charges against one, the other two will plead guilty." In that case the lie is not explicit but surely the inference which the defense lawyer wishes the prosecutor to draw is the same. Should that change the outcome?

such questions and by doing so avoid any inference from his failure to answer such questions.

What makes the last case a close one? Conceivably it is the idea that one accused by the state is entitled to greater leeway in making his case. Possibly one can argue that there is no injury to the state when such a person, particularly an innocent person, goes free. Is it conceivable that the act can be justified on the ground that it is part of the game in this context, that prosecutors as well as defense lawyers routinely misstate what they, their witnesses, and their clients can and will do? None of these arguments seems persuasive. Justice is not served by freeing a guilty person. The system does not necessarily achieve better results by trading two guilty pleas for a dismissal. Perhaps its justification has its roots in the same idea that formerly held that a misrepresentation of one's state of mind was not actionable for it was not a misrepresentation of fact.

In a sense rules governing these cases may simply arise from a recognition by the law of its limited power to shape human behavior. By tolerating exaggeration and puffing in the sales transaction, by refusing to make misstatement of one's intention actionable, the law may simply have recognized the bounds of its control over human behavior. Having said that, one is still left with the question, Are the lies permissible in the last two cases? My general conclusion is that they are not, but I am not nearly as comfortable with that conclusion as I am with the conclusion about the first three cases.

Taken together, the five foregoing cases show me that we do not and cannot intend that a negotiator be "truthful" in the broadest sense of that term. At the minimum we allow him some deviation from truthfulness in asserting his true opinion about cases, statutes, or the value of the subject of the negotiation in other respects. In addition some of us are likely to allow him to lie in response to certain questions that are regarded as out of bounds, and possibly to lie in circumstances where his interest is great and the injury seems small. It would be unfortunate, therefore, for the rule that requires "fairness" to be interpreted to require that a negotiator be truthful in every respect and in all of his dealings. It should be read to allow at least those kinds of untruthfulness that are implicitly and explicitly recognized as acceptable in his forum, a forum refined both by the subject matter and by the participants. . . .

To draft effective legislation is difficult; to draft effective ethical rules is close to impossible. Such drafters must walk the narrow line between being too general and too specific. If their rules are too general, they will have no influence on any behavior and give little guidance even to those who wish to follow the rules. If they are too specific, they omit certain areas or conflict with appropriate rules for problems not foreseen but apparently covered.

There are other, more formidable obstacles. These drafters are essentially powerless. They draft the rules; but the American Bar Association must pass them, and the rules must then be adopted by various courts or other agencies in the states.

Finally the enforcement of the rules is left to a hodgepodge of bar committees and grievance agencies of varied will and capacity. Thus the drafters are far removed from and have little control over those who ultimately will enact and enforce the rules. For that reason, even more than most legislators, drafters of ethical rules have limited power to influence behavior. This weakness presents a final dilemma and one they have not always faced as well as they should, namely, to make the appropriate trade-off between what is "right" and what can be done. To enact stern and righteous rules in Chicago will not fool the people in Keokuk. The public will not believe them, and the bar will not follow them. What level of violation of the rules can the bar accept without the rules as a whole becoming a mockery? I do not know and the drafters can only guess. Because of the danger presented if the norms are widely and routinely violated, the drafters should err on the conservative side and must sometimes reject better and more desirable rules for poorer ones simply because the violation of the higher standard would cast all the rules in doubt.

Notes

1. There is a clear relation between Professor White's views about the utility of general negotiation rules and the appropriateness of particular conduct on the one hand and, on the other, his answers to the specific hypotheticals he poses. In answering the third case, he appears to find it conclusive that the specific "untruthful" behavior "is not thought to be inappropriate by any experienced bargainer." If that factual assertion is accurate and conclusive, how do standards of conduct change? Much that was not thought inappropriate in the days when caveat emptor was supreme is no longer thought appropriate today. How did we get from there to here? Is it relevant that the "false demand" that takes the form of prosecutorial overcharging of defendants is under heavy attack today? Or should the different circumstances of the criminal justice system cause us to draw a sharp line between the false demand there and in civil negotiation?

2. Note that the drafters of the Comment to Rule 4.1 of the Model Rules have addressed Professor White's fourth case and imply that what Professor White calls "a lie" is actually not a statement of "material fact." See also generally ABA Ethics Op. 06–439 (2006) (discussing so-called puffery); Cal. Ethics Op. 2015–194.

3. Does your reading of the way courts have interpreted the provisions of the Model Rules lead you to agree with Professor White's view about the powerlessness of drafters? That is quite a different point from the one that he makes in conjunction with it — that the danger of wholesale disobedience to a particular rule ought to cause a drafting committee to be quite conservative in its attempt to alter "ethical" behavior. Does his observation account for or justify, say, the original effort of the drafters of the Model Rules to provide a nearly absolute principle of confidentiality in Model Rule 1.6? And how would he characterize the retreat after the passage of the

Sarbanes–Oxley Act? Does his argument sufficiently take account of the nonlawyer interests that are vastly underrepresented in the drafting process?

––––––––––

Problem 6–11

A prosecutor in a capital offense case has offered to reduce the charge to one carrying a maximum six month sentence on a plea of guilty. Although there is some evidence of guilt, the defendant maintains his innocence. Does the lawyer have an obligation to disclose the defendant's statement of innocence to the court when the plea is to be entered? How does the lawyer advise the client to respond to a trial judge's inquiry to tell how the crime occurred, when the lawyer knows that if the client states his innocence, the plea will not be accepted?

Former Chief Justice (then Judge) Warren Burger addressed the issue in "Standards of Conduct for Prosecution and Defense Personnel," 5 Am. Crim. L.Q. 11, 15 (1966):

> ... A judge may not properly accept a guilty plea from an accused who denies the very acts which constitute the crime. However, he may do so if the matter is in such dispute or doubt that a jury might find him guilty in spite of his denials. When an accused tells the court he committed the act charged to induce acceptance of the guilty plea, the lawyer to whom contrary statements have been made owes a duty to the court to disclose such contrary statements so that the court can explore and resolve the conflict. The key lies in the obligation to be candid with the court, and no plea of guilt should be accepted except upon a full disclosure which permits the court to make an informed and intelligent decision in acting on the plea. ...

Professor Addison Bowman took a different view in "Standards of Conduct ... An Attorney's Viewpoint," 5 Am. Crim. L.Q. 28, 31 (1966):

> counsel ... should advise the defendant that the latter may attempt to enter a plea of guilty to assault and battery, and that the plea may be accepted if counsel points out to the court that the evidence against the defendant is sufficient to justify a jury verdict of guilty. However, counsel should also advise his client that the plea may not be accepted without an acknowledgement of guilt, whereupon the latter may suggest that he can tell the court he is guilty even though this is not true.

See North Carolina v. Alford, 400 U.S. 25 (1970), holding that it was not constitutional error for a judge to accept a guilty plea voluntarily and understandingly made, when the record contained strong evidence of guilt notwithstanding the defendant's protestation that he was innocent. The court went on to state that it was not holding that a state had to afford a criminal defendant the right to have a guilty plea accepted. Id. at 38. Cf. Fed. R. Crim. Proc. 11(b)(3), providing that "[b]efore entering judgment on a guilty plea, the court must determine that there is a factual basis for the plea."

The ABA Standards Relating to the Defense Function originally provided in § 5.3:

> If the accused discloses to the lawyer facts which negate guilt and the lawyer's investigation does not reveal a conflict with the facts disclosed but the accused persists in entering a plea of guilty, the lawyer may not properly participate in presenting a guilty plea, without disclosure to the court.

It is interesting to note the reasoning stated in the commentary to this section:

> In many, perhaps most, situations the accused is simply not capable of relating his conduct to the legal conclusion of guilt or innocence. The law does not permit his opinion on the ultimate and often complex question of his guilt as a matter of law to control the judgment of the court. That judgment can only be made in accordance with the processes of the law. . . . The essence of the principle . . . is that a court considering the acceptance of a plea of guilty should be fully informed and never misled and that both counsel have a duty in this respect.

The Standard's analysis of the problem seemed to ignore the lawyer's obligation not to reveal the client's confidential information. Would Model Rule 3.3 justify Standard 5.3? Standard 5.3 was eliminated in the 1979 revision of the Standards. The reason given is interesting for its lack of much reliance on the confidentiality obligation.

> If . . . a so called *Alford* plea is either not accepted by the court or is not offered by the defendant, it does not follow that defense counsel should be required to reveal to the court that the defendant privately denies guilt to counsel. As long as the defendant openly acknowledges guilt to the court and a factual basis for the plea is present, this is deemed sufficient. If counsel were to tell the court that the defendant privately insists that he or she is innocent the result is likely to be unsatisfactory. The defendant will most likely insist to the court that he or she is, in fact, guilty because the defendant wants the plea to be accepted, and that any statements previously made to counsel were false. It is probable, moreover, that prior to entry of the guilty plea, defense counsel will have devoted considerable effort to convincing the defendant to do just what the defendant has finally done — to openly admit wrongdoing. When the defendant finally does plead guilty, and defense counsel then reports to the court that the defendant privately maintains innocence, the defendant is likely to find counsel's actions baffling. Meanwhile, acceptance of the guilty plea will be jeopardized, despite the presence of a factual basis and the defendant's public admission of guilt. The attorney-client relationship will also probably have been destroyed. As a matter of practice among defense counsel, it is believed that adherence to original standard 5.3 was virtually

non-existent. Under no circumstances, however, should a lawyer recommend to a defendant acceptance of a plea unless a full investigation and study of the case has been completed, including an analysis of controlling law and the evidence likely to be introduced at trial. See Standards 4-4.1, 4-5.1(a), and 4-6.1(b).

If the defendant is placed under oath when the plea is offered, the problem for defense counsel seemingly becomes more difficult because the defendant's statements will be perjurious. This situation obviously is similar to that confronted when a defendant seeks to lie under oath at his or her trial. . . .

Over a half century has passed since this issue first became a subject of serious discussion. It is still a subject of controversy among lawyers and judges.

F. Lawyers and Their Own Speech and Conduct

A theme in discussion of issues of professional responsibility is the extent to which lawyers lose the freedom of action or non-action that ordinary citizens have. Recall that in seeking representation to defend the Defense of Marriage Act (DOMA), the House of Representatives sought to prohibit any "advocacy against DOMA by any lawyer affiliated with the firm," including the exercise of free speech outside a legal forum. The issue is often framed in terms of "extent" rather than in terms of whether there is any difference at all because it is quite clear that lawyers do have some special obligations. For example, there is no doubt that as citizens we are free to reveal our friends' confidences without incurring any legal consequences, whereas as lawyers we are not free as a general rule to reveal our clients' confidences. And so the issue is "When and under what circumstances should professional requirements impose a special obligation to act or not to act where no such obligation is imposed on nonlawyers?" The question in each situation is whether the special privileges that are given to lawyers in connection with their "monopoly" of representation require or justify putting special obligations upon them to speak in a certain way or to remain silent.

Problem 6–12

(a) At a meeting with clients Lawyer is asked why they lost their case at trial. May he respond: "I think we'll have a much better chance on appeal because the trial judge is stupid, prejudiced against you and the minorities whose rights were involved in this case, and it wouldn't surprise me if he had been talked to by the powers that be in this town," if Lawyer honestly believes this to be the case? Does it make a difference if this statement is made to a newspaper reporter? Does Lawyer need "evidence" of some kind before he makes those charges? What kind of evidence? Does he need different "evidence" when talking to his clients from what he needs when talking to the reporter? If he has "evidence," is he precluded from talking to either the clients or the reporter until he has taken the matter up with the appropriate disciplinary body? Does it make any difference whether the case is civil or criminal? See Model Rules 3.6, 8.2(a), and 8.3(b).

(b) Suppose that it is your observation (and that of others) that a lawyer is much more likely to receive favorable treatment, and probably even to win cases, before Judge X if he or she is part of the same political clique that was responsible for Judge X's elevation to the bench. Is it appropriate for you to tell this to your client when that judge is assigned to hear your client's case? Should you go further and suggest that your client associate a lawyer member of that clique with you at the trial? What other alternatives are open to you, assuming that you don't have sufficient evidence to prove corrupt conduct by the judge? See Model Rule 8.4(e).

Problem 6–13

For several years Lawyer has been conducting a class action suit against the state mental health department. There are many aspects to the suit, but its principal thrust attacks the inadequate treatment given to mental patients confined to state hospitals pursuant to court order. A judgment has been entered in favor of plaintiffs, finding inadequacy of treatment, but the case has dragged on with respect to implementation of the original judgment. Many unresolved matters are still pending with respect to the plans being proposed by the state regarding different classes of patients and different hospitals. Lawyer has been asked to address a society of medical and legal personnel interested in mental health matters about the situation as she views it in state mental hospitals. Obviously, the case will have to be discussed and, in addition, Lawyer would like to advocate that the audience urge certain specific reforms on the appropriate state agencies. May Lawyer make the speech she wants to make?

Gentile v. State Bar of Nevada
501 U.S. 1030 (1991)

[Dominic Gentile, attorney for the defendant, held a press conference the day after his client, Grady Sanders, had been indicted for stealing drugs and travelers' checks that had been stored by the police in safe deposit boxes in his company's vault. After Sanders was acquitted, the Supreme Court of Nevada reprimanded Mr. Gentile for violation of its disciplinary rules relating to trial publicity. He appealed to the Supreme Court, which reversed. There were two majority opinions, one by Chief Justice Rehnquist, upholding that part of the Nevada disciplinary rule modeled on Model Rule 3.6 against First Amendment attack as applied to Gentile's speech, and one by Justice Kennedy for a different majority, striking down the Nevada Rule as applied for vagueness. We have reorganized the opinions to put factual material from

Justice Kennedy's opinion first and then to print excerpts from the majority and dissenting opinions on each issue together.]

Justice KENNEDY:

Hours after his client was indicted on criminal charges, petitioner Gentile, who is a member of the Bar of the State of Nevada, held a press conference. He made a prepared statement . . . and then he responded to questions. . . .

Some six months later, the criminal case was tried to a jury and the client was acquitted on all counts. The State Bar of Nevada then filed a complaint against petitioner, alleging a violation of Nevada Supreme Court Rule 177, a rule governing pretrial publicity almost identical to ABA Model Rule of Professional Conduct 3.6.

[Nevada Supreme Court Rule 177, as in effect prior to January 5, 1991.

Trial Publicity

1. A lawyer shall not make an extrajudicial statement that a reasonable person would expect to be disseminated by means of public communication if the lawyer knows or reasonably should know that it will have a substantial likelihood of materially prejudicing an adjudicative proceeding.

2. A statement referred to in subsection 1 ordinarily is likely to have such an effect when it refers to a civil matter triable to a jury, a criminal matter, or any other proceeding that could result in incarceration, and the statement relates to:

(a) the character, credibility, reputation or criminal record of a party, suspect in a criminal investigation or witness, or the identity of a witness, or the expected testimony of a party or witness;

(b) in a criminal case or proceeding that could result in incarceration, the possibility of a plea of guilty to the offense or the existence or contents of any confession, admission, or statement given by a defendant or suspect or that person's refusal or failure to make a statement;

(c) the performance or results of any examination or test or the refusal or failure of a person to submit to an examination or test, or the identity or nature of physical evidence expected to be presented;

(d) any opinion as to the guilt or innocence of a defendant or suspect in a criminal case or proceeding that could result in incarceration;

(e) information the lawyer knows or reasonably should know is likely to be inadmissible as evidence in a trial and would if disclosed create a substantial risk of prejudicing an impartial trial; or

(f) the fact that a defendant has been charged with a crime, unless there is included therein a statement explaining that the charge is merely an accusation and that the defendant is presumed innocent until and unless proven guilty.

536 · EVERYDAY PROBLEMS OF THE PRACTICING LAWYER

3. Notwithstanding subsection 1 and 2(a–f), a lawyer involved in the investigation or litigation of a matter may state without elaboration:

(a) the general nature of the claim or defense;

(b) the information contained in a public record;

(c) that an investigation of the matter is in progress, including the general scope of the investigation, the offense or claim or defense involved and, except when prohibited by law, the identity of the persons involved;

(d) the scheduling or result of any step in litigation;

(e) a request for assistance in obtaining evidence and information necessary thereto;

(f) a warning of danger concerning the behavior of a person involved, when there is reason to believe that there exists the likelihood of substantial harm to an individual or to the public interest; and

(g) in a criminal case:

(i) the identity, residence, occupation and family status of the accused;

(ii) if the accused has not been apprehended, information necessary to aid in apprehension of that person;

(iii) the fact, time and place of arrest; and

(iv) the identity of investigating and arresting officers or agencies and the length of the investigation.]

Following a hearing, the Southern Nevada Disciplinary Board of the State Bar found that Gentile had made the statements in question and concluded that he violated Rule 177. The board recommended a private reprimand. Petitioner appealed to the Nevada Supreme Court, waiving the confidentiality of the disciplinary proceeding, and the Nevada court affirmed the decision of the board. . . .

Pre-Indictment Publicity. On January 31, 1987, undercover police officers with the Las Vegas Metropolitan Police Department (Metro) reported large amounts of cocaine (four kilograms) and travelers' checks (almost $300,000) missing from a safety deposit vault at Western Vault Corporation. The drugs and money had been used as part of an undercover operation conducted by Metro's Intelligence Bureau. Petitioner's client, Grady Sanders, owned Western Vault. John Moran, the Las Vegas sheriff, reported the theft at a press conference on February 2, 1987, naming the police and Western Vault employees as suspects.

Although two police officers, Detective Steve Scholl and Sergeant Ed Schaub, enjoyed free access to the deposit box throughout the period of the theft, and no log reported comings and goings at the vault, a series of press reports over the following year indicated that investigators did not consider these officers responsible. Instead, investigators focused upon Western Vault and its owner. Newspaper reports quoted the sheriff and other high police officials as saying that they had not lost confidence in the "elite" Intelligence Bureau. From the beginning, Sheriff Moran had "complete faith and trust" in his officers. . . .

Initial press reports stated that Sanders and Western Vault were being cooperative; but as time went on, the press noted that the police investigation had failed to identify the culprit and through a process of elimination was beginning to point toward Sanders. Reports quoted the affidavit of a detective that the theft was part of an effort to discredit the undercover operation and that business records suggested the existence of a business relation between Sanders and the targets of a Metro undercover probe.

The deputy police chief announced the two detectives with access to the vault had been "cleared" as possible suspects. According to an unnamed "source close to the investigation," the police shifted from the idea that the thief had planned to discredit the undercover operation to the theory that the thief had unwittingly stolen from the police. The stories noted that Sanders "could not be reached for comment."

The story took a more sensational turn with reports that the two police suspects had been cleared by police investigators after passing lie detector tests. The tests were administered by one Ray Slaughter. But later, the Federal Bureau of Investigation (FBI) arrested Slaughter for distributing cocaine to an FBI informant, Belinda Antal. It was also reported that the $264,900 seized from the unrented safety deposit box at Western Vault had been stored there in a suitcase owned by one Tammy Sue Markham. Markham was "facing a number of federal drug-related charges" in Tucson, Arizona. Markham reported items missing from three boxes she rented at Western Vault, as did one Beatrice Connick, who, according to press reports, was a Colombian national living in San Diego and "not facing any drug related charges." (As it turned out, petitioner impeached Connick's credibility at trial with the existence of a money laundering conviction.) Connick also was reported to have taken and passed a lie detector test to substantiate her charges. Finally, press reports indicated that Sanders had refused to take a police polygraph examination. The press suggested that the FBI suspected Metro officers were responsible for the theft, and reported that the theft had severely damaged relations between the FBI and Metro.

The Press Conference. Petitioner is a Las Vegas criminal defense attorney, an author of articles about criminal law and procedure, and a former associate dean of the National College for Criminal Defense Lawyers and Public Defenders. Through leaks from the police department, he had some advance notice of the date an indictment would be returned and the nature of the charges against Sanders. Petitioner had monitored the publicity surrounding the case, and, prior to the indictment, was personally aware of at least 17 articles in the major local newspapers, the Las Vegas Sun and Las Vegas Review-Journal, and numerous local television news stories which reported on the Western Vault theft and ensuing investigation.

Petitioner determined, for the first time in his career, that he would call a formal press conference. He did not blunder into a press conference, but acted with considerable deliberation.

[From the Appendix: Mr. Gentile's statement at the press conference]

Mr. Gentile: I want to start this off by saying in clear terms that I think that this indictment is a significant event in the history of the evolution of the sophistication of the City of Las Vegas, because things of this nature, of exactly this nature have happened in New York with the French Connection case and in Miami with cases—at least two cases there—have happened in Chicago as well, but all three of those cities have been honest enough to indict the people who did it; the police department, crooked cops.

When this case goes to trial, and as it develops, you're going to see that the evidence will prove not only that Grady Sanders is an innocent person and had nothing to do with any of the charges that are being leveled against him, but that the person that was in the most direct position to have stolen the drugs and money, the American Express Travelers' checks, is Detective Steve Scholl.

There is far more evidence that will establish that Detective Scholl took these drugs and took these American Express Travelers' checks than any other living human being.

And I have to say that I feel that Grady Sanders is being used as a scapegoat to try to cover up for what has to be obvious to people at the Las Vegas Metropolitan Police Department and at the District Attorney's office.

Now, with respect to these other charges that are contained in this indictment, the so-called other victims, as I sit here today I can tell you that one, two—four of them are known drug dealers and convicted money launderers and drug dealers; three of whom didn't say a word about anything until after they were approached by Metro and after they were already in trouble and are trying to work themselves out of something.

Now, up until the moment, of course, that they started going along with what detectives from Metro wanted them to say, these people were being held out as being incredible and liars by the very same people who are going to say now that you can believe them.

Another problem that you are going to see develop here is the fact that of these other counts, at least four of them said nothing about any of this, about anything being missing until after the Las Vegas Metropolitan Police Department announced publicly last year their claim that drugs and American Express Travelers' checks were missing.

Many of the contracts that these people had show on the face of the contract that there is $100,000 in insurance for the contents of the box.

If you look at the indictment very closely, you're going to see that these claims fall under $100,000.

Finally, there were only two claims on the face of the indictment that came to our attention prior to the events of January 31 of '87, that being the date that Metro said that there was something missing from their box.

And both of these claims were dealt with by Mr. Sanders and we're dealing here essentially with people that we're not sure if they ever had anything in the box. . . .

Chief Justice REHNQUIST delivered the opinion of the Court with respect to [the First Amendment issues raised by the application of Nevada's rule to Mr. Gentile's comments]. . . .

Gentile asserts that the same stringent standard applied in Nebraska Press Assn. v. Stuart, 427 U.S. 539 (1976), to restraints on press publication during the pendency of a criminal trial should be applied to speech by a lawyer whose client is a defendant in a criminal proceeding. . . . Respondent, on the other hand, relies on statements in cases such as Sheppard v. Maxwell, 384 U.S. 333 (1966), which sharply distinguished between restraints on the press and restraints on lawyers whose clients are parties to the proceeding . . . .

In the United States, the courts have historically regulated admission to the practice of law before them and exercised the authority to discipline and ultimately to disbar lawyers whose conduct departed from prescribed standards. "Membership in the bar is a privilege burdened with conditions," to use the oft-repeated statement of Cardozo, J., in In re Rouss, 221 N.Y. 81, 84 (1917) . . . . [The Chief Justice then reviewed 100 years of history of professional rules governing lawyers' speech about pending trials.]

When the Model Rules of Professional Conduct were drafted in the early 1980's, the drafters . . . adopted the "substantial likelihood of material prejudice" test. Currently, 31 States in addition to Nevada have adopted—either verbatim or with insignificant variations—Rule 3.6 of the ABA's Model Rules. Eleven States have adopted Disciplinary Rule 7-107 of the ABA's Code of Professional Responsibility, which is less protective of lawyer speech than Model Rule 3.6, in that it applies a "reasonable likelihood of prejudice" standard. Only one State, Virginia, has explicitly adopted a clear and present danger standard, while four States and the District of Columbia have adopted standards that arguably approximate "clear and present danger."

Petitioner maintains, however, that the First Amendment to the United States Constitution requires a State, such as Nevada in this case, to demonstrate a "clear and present danger" of "actual prejudice or an imminent threat" before any discipline may be imposed on a lawyer who initiates a press conference such as occurred here. . . .

Respondent State Bar of Nevada points out, on the other hand, that none of these cases involved lawyers who represented parties to a pending proceeding in court. . . .

These opposing positions illustrate one of the many dilemmas which arise in the course of constitutional adjudication. . . . The outcome of a criminal trial is to be decided by impartial jurors, who know as little as possible of the case, based on material admitted into evidence before them in a court proceeding. Extrajudicial comments on, or discussion of, evidence which might never be admitted at trial and ex parte statements by counsel giving their version of the facts obviously threaten to undermine this basic tenet.

At the same time, however, the criminal justice system exists in a larger context of a government ultimately of the people, who wish to be informed about happenings in the criminal justice system, and, if sufficiently informed about those happenings, might wish to make changes in the system. The way most of them acquire information is from the media. The First Amendment protections of speech and press have been held, in the cases cited above, to require a showing of "clear and present danger" that a malfunction in the criminal justice system will be caused before a State may prohibit media speech or publication about a particular pending trial. The question we must answer in this case is whether a lawyer who represents a defendant involved with the criminal justice system may insist on the same standard before he is disciplined for public pronouncements about the case, or whether the State instead may penalize that sort of speech upon a lesser showing.

It is unquestionable that in the courtroom itself, during a judicial proceeding, whatever right to "free speech" an attorney has is extremely circumscribed. An attorney may not, by speech or other conduct, resist a ruling of the trial court beyond the point necessary to preserve a claim for appeal. . . . Even outside the courtroom, a majority of the Court in two separate opinions in the case of In re Sawyer, 360 U.S. 622 (1959), observed that lawyers in pending cases were subject to ethical restrictions on speech to which an ordinary citizen would not be. . . .

We think that the quoted statements . . . rather plainly indicate that the speech of lawyers representing clients in pending cases may be regulated under a less demanding standard than that established for regulation of the press in Nebraska Press Assn. v. Stuart, 427 U.S. 539 (1976), and the cases which preceded it. Lawyers representing clients in pending cases are key participants in the criminal justice system, and the State may demand some adherence to the precepts of that system in regulating their speech as well as their conduct. As noted by Justice Brennan in his concurring opinion in *Nebraska Press*, which was joined by Justices Stewart and Marshall, "[a]s officers of the court, court personnel and attorneys have a fiduciary responsibility not to engage in public debate that will redound to the detriment of the accused or that will obstruct the fair administration of justice." Id., at 601, n.27. Because lawyers have special access to information through discovery and client communications, their extrajudicial statements pose a threat to the fairness of a pending proceeding since lawyers' statements are likely to be received as especially authoritative. . . . We agree with the majority of the States that the "substantial likelihood of material prejudice" standard constitutes a constitutionally permissible balance between the First Amendment rights of attorneys in pending cases and the State's interest in fair trials.

When a state regulation implicates First Amendment rights, the Court must balance those interests against the State's legitimate interest in regulating the activity in question. . . . The "substantial likelihood" test embodied in Rule 177 is constitutional under this analysis, for it is designed to protect the integrity and fairness of a State's judicial system, and it imposes only narrow and necessary limitations on lawyers' speech. The limitations are aimed at two principal evils: (1) comments that are likely to influence the actual outcome of the trial, and (2) comments that are likely to prejudice the jury venire, even if an untainted panel can ultimately be found. Few, if any, interests under the Constitution are more fundamental than the right to a fair trial by "impartial" jurors, and an outcome affected by extrajudicial statements would violate that fundamental right. . . . Even if a fair trial can ultimately be ensured through voir dire, change of venue, or some other device, these measures entail serious costs to the system. Extensive voir dire may not be able to filter out all of the effects of pretrial publicity, and with increasingly widespread media coverage of criminal trials, a change of venue may not suffice to undo the effects of statements such as those made by petitioner. The State has a substantial interest in preventing officers of the court, such as lawyers, from imposing such costs on the judicial system and on the litigants.

The restraint on speech is narrowly tailored to achieve those objectives. The regulation of attorneys' speech is limited—it applies only to speech that is substantially likely to have a materially prejudicial effect; it is neutral as to points of view, applying equally to all attorneys participating in a pending case; and it merely postpones the attorneys' comments until after the trial. While supported by the substantial state interest in preventing prejudice to an adjudicative proceeding by those who have a duty to protect its integrity, the Rule is limited on its face to preventing only speech having a substantial likelihood of materially prejudicing that proceeding.

[Justice Kennedy argued in dissent that Nevada's application of Rule 177 violated the First Amendment. In his view, petitioner was punished for pure political speech seeking to counter prejudicial pretrial publicity. His speech was directed at public officials "at a time and in a manner that neither in law nor in fact created any threat of real prejudice to his client's right to a fair trial or to the State's interest in the enforcement of its criminal laws." He included the following statement justifying Mr. Gentile's statement: "An attorney's duties do not begin inside the courtroom door. He or she cannot ignore the practical implications of a legal proceeding for the client. Just as an attorney may recommend a plea bargain or civil settlement to avoid the adverse consequences of a possible loss after trial, so too an attorney may take reasonable steps to defend a client's reputation and reduce the adverse consequences of indictment, especially in the face of a prosecution deemed unjust or commenced with improper motives. A defense attorney may pursue lawful strategies to obtain dismissal of an indictment or reduction of charges, including an attempt to demonstrate in the court of public opinion that the client does not deserve to be tried." Justice Kennedy made a further argument with respect to the relevance of the First Amendment.]

... Five Members of the Court ... endorse an extended discussion which concludes that Nevada may interpret its requirement of substantial likelihood of material prejudice under a standard more deferential than is the usual rule where speech is concerned. It appears necessary, therefore, to set forth my objections to that conclusion and to the reasoning which underlies it.

Respondent argues that speech by an attorney is subject to greater regulation than speech by others, and restrictions on an attorney's speech should be assessed under a balancing test that weighs the State's interest in the regulation of a specialized profession against the lawyer's First Amendment interest in the kind of speech that was at issue. The cases cited by our colleagues to support this balancing, Bates v. State Bar of Arizona, 433 U.S. 350 (1977); Peel v. Attorney Registration and Disciplinary Comm'n of Ill., 496 U.S. 91 (1990); Ohralik v. Ohio State Bar Assn., 436 U.S. 447 (1978); and Seattle Times Co. v. Rhinehart, 467 U.S. 20 (1984), involved either commercial speech by attorneys or restrictions upon release of information that the attorney could gain only by use of the court's discovery process. Neither of those categories, nor the underlying interests which justified their creation, were implicated here. Petitioner was disciplined because he proclaimed to the community what he thought to be a misuse of the prosecutorial and police powers. Wide-open balancing of interests is not appropriate in this context.

Respondent would justify a substantial limitation on speech by attorneys because "lawyers have special access to information, including confidential statements from clients and information obtained through pretrial discovery or plea negotiations," and so lawyers' statements "are likely to be received as especially authoritative." Rule 177, however, does not reflect concern for the attorney's special access to client confidences, material gained through discovery, or other proprietary or confidential information. We have upheld restrictions upon the release of information gained "only by virtue of the trial court's discovery processes." Seattle Times Co. v. Rhinehart, supra, 467 U.S., at 32. And Seattle Times would prohibit release of discovery information by the attorney as well as the client. Similar rules require an attorney to maintain client confidences. . . .

This case involves no speech subject to a restriction under the rationale of Seattle Times. Much of the information in petitioner's remarks was included by explicit reference or fair inference in earlier press reports. Petitioner could not have learned what he revealed at the press conference through the discovery process or other special access afforded to attorneys, for he spoke to the press on the day of indictment, at the outset of his formal participation in the criminal proceeding. We have before us no complaint from the prosecutors, police, or presiding judge that petitioner misused information to which he had special access. And there is no claim that petitioner revealed client confidences, which may be waived in any event. Rule 177, on its face and as applied here, is neither limited to nor even directed at preventing release of information received through court proceedings or special access afforded attorneys. . . . It goes far beyond this. . . .

At the very least, our cases recognize that disciplinary rules governing the legal profession cannot punish activity protected by the First Amendment, and that First Amendment protection survives even when the attorney violates a disciplinary rule he swore to obey when admitted to the practice of law. We have not in recent years accepted our colleagues' apparent theory that the practice of law brings with it comprehensive restrictions, or that we will defer to professional bodies when those restrictions impinge upon First Amendment freedoms. And none of the justifications put forward by respondent suffice to sanction abandonment of our normal First Amendment principles in the case of speech by an attorney regarding pending cases.

[Justice Kennedy then turned to the vagueness issue on which he spoke for the majority.]

As interpreted by the Nevada Supreme Court, the Rule is void for vagueness, in any event, for its safe harbor provision, Rule 177(3), misled petitioner into thinking that he could give his press conference without fear of discipline. Rule 177(3)(a) provides that a lawyer "may state without elaboration . . . the general nature of the . . . defense." Statements under this provision are protected "[n]otwithstanding subsection 1 and 2(a–f)." By necessary operation of the word "notwithstanding," the Rule contemplates that a lawyer describing the "general nature of the . . . defense" "without elaboration" need fear no discipline, even if he comments on "[t]he character, credibility, reputation or criminal record of a . . . witness," and even if he "knows or reasonably should know that [the statement] will have a substantial likelihood of materially prejudicing an adjudicative proceeding."

Given this grammatical structure, and absent any clarifying interpretation by the state court, the Rule fails to provide "'fair notice to those to whom [it] is directed.'" Grayned v. City of Rockford, 408 U.S. 104, 112 (1972). A lawyer seeking to avail himself of Rule 177(3)'s protection must guess at its contours. The right to explain the "general" nature of the defense without "elaboration" provides insufficient guidance because "general" and "elaboration" are both classic terms of degree. In the context before us, these terms have no settled usage or tradition of interpretation in law. The lawyer has no principle for determining when his remarks pass from the safe harbor of the general to the forbidden sea of the elaborated.

Petitioner testified he thought his statements were protected by Rule 177(3). A review of the press conference supports that claim. He gave only a brief opening statement, and on numerous occasions declined to answer reporters' questions seeking more detailed comments. . . .

Nevertheless, the disciplinary board said only that petitioner's comments "went beyond the scope of the statements permitted by SCR 177(3)," and the Nevada Supreme Court's rejection of petitioner's defense based on Rule 177(3) was just as terse. The fact that Gentile was found in violation of the Rules after studying them and making a conscious effort at compliance demonstrates that Rule 177 creates a trap for the wary as well as the unwary.

The prohibition against vague regulations of speech is based in part on the need to eliminate the impermissible risk of discriminatory enforcement . . . for history shows that speech is suppressed when either the speaker or the message is critical of those who enforce the law. The question is not whether discriminatory enforcement occurred here, and we assume it did not, but whether the Rule is so imprecise that discriminatory enforcement is a real possibility. The inquiry is of particular relevance when one of the classes most affected by the regulation is the criminal defense bar, which has the professional mission to challenge actions of the State. Petitioner, for instance, succeeded in preventing the conviction of his client, and the speech in issue involved criticism of the government.

Chief Justice REHNQUIST, joined by Justice WHITE, Justice SCALIA, and Justice SOUTER, dissented on the vagueness issue.

[In this part of his opinion, the Chief Justice concluded that Model Rule 3.6 was neither overbroad nor vague.]

. . . It is of course true, as the majority points out, that the word "general" and the word "elaboration" are both terms of degree. But combined as they are in the first sentence of § 3, they convey the very definite proposition that the authorized statements must not contain the sort of detailed allegations that petitioner made at his press conference. No sensible person could think that the following were "general" statements of a claim or defense made "without elaboration": "the person that was in the most direct position to have stolen the drugs and the money . . . is Detective Steve Scholl"; "there is far more evidence that will establish that Detective Scholl took these drugs and took these American Express Travelers' checks than any other living human being"; "[Detective Scholl] either had a hell of a cold, or he should have seen a better doctor"; and "the so-called other victims . . . one, two — four of them are known drug dealers and convicted money launderers." Section 3, as an exception to the provisions of §§ 1 and 2, must be read in the light of the prohibitions and examples contained in the first two sections. It was obviously not intended to negate the prohibitions or the examples wholesale, but simply intended to provide a "safe harbor" where there might be doubt as to whether one of the examples covered proposed conduct. These provisions were not vague as to the conduct for which petitioner was disciplined . . . .

. . . The State Bar of Nevada, which made its own factual findings, and the Supreme Court of Nevada, which upheld those findings, were in a far better position than we are to appreciate the likely effect of petitioner's statements on potential members of a jury panel in a highly publicized case such as this. The board and the Nevada Supreme Court did not apply the list of statements likely to cause material prejudice as presumptions, but specifically found that petitioner had intended to prejudice the trial, and that based upon the nature of the statements and their timing, they were in fact substantially likely to cause material prejudice. We cannot, upon our review of the record, conclude that they were mistaken. . . .

Justice O'Connor concurred in the Chief Justice's opinion on the First Amendment issue and in Justice Kennedy's opinion on the vagueness issue.

Notes

1. The greatest likelihood of material prejudice to an adjudicative proceeding derives from the effect of pretrial publicity on the trier of the fact. Since the purpose of the voir dire is to root out bias, how can a lawyer ever "know" or "reasonably should know" that an extrajudicial statement will violate Rule 3.6? Wouldn't the lawyer have to assume that the voir dire would fail to achieve its purpose? See also Rule 3.8(f), which places some additional obligations on prosecutors, including an obligation to take reasonable steps to prevent law enforcement personnel from making extrajudicial statements about a matter that the prosecutor would be forbidden to make by Rule 3.6.

2. Note the revised version of Rule 3.6(c). Does this exception substantially undercut the main thrust of the Rule? Note also that since *Gentile*, Rule 3.6(a) has changed the standard for judging the likelihood that a statement will be publicized and its potential for prejudice from that of the "reasonable person" to that of the "reasonable lawyer." The concept of a "reasonable person" has a long, if not wholly clear, history in legal analysis. But after one rejects the notion that a "reasonable lawyer" is an oxymoron as a concept, just what characteristics do you associate with "reasonable lawyer" when contemplating making an extrajudicial statement? Zealous advocate? Cautious counselor?

3. In the bracketed material at the opening of Justice Kennedy's opinion with respect to the First Amendment issues, he makes much of the lawyer's obligation to defend his or her client outside the courtroom door. Does that view undercut the whole purpose of Rule 3.6 to protect the fairness of the trial? Does Rule 3.6 strike a fair accommodation between the needs of a fair trial and free speech? How would you revise it, if at all?

4. In In re Snyder, 472 U.S. 634 (1985), a lawyer's request for a fee of approximately $1800 was twice rejected by an administrator due to insufficient documentation. In response to an invitation by the administrator to put his views in writing, the lawyer wrote:

> In the first place, I am appalled by the amount of money which the federal court pays for indigent criminal defense work. The reason that so few attorneys in Bismarck accept this work is for that exact reason. We have, up to this point, still accepted the indigent appointments, because of a duty to our profession and the fact that nobody else will do it.
>
> Now, however, not only are we paid an amount of money which does not even cover our overhead, but we have to go through extreme gymnastics even

to receive the puny amounts which the federal courts authorize for this work. We have sent you everything we have concerning our representation, and I am not sending you anything else. You can take it or leave it.

Further, I am extremely disgusted by the treatment of us by the Eighth Circuit in this case, and you are instructed to remove my name from the list of attorneys who will accept criminal indigent defense work. I have simply had it.

Thank you for your time and attention. . . .

After some exchange of correspondence with the Chief Judge of the Court of Appeals of the Eighth Circuit in which the lawyer refused to apologize for his letter, the Court of Appeals found his conduct contumacious and suspended him from practice in the federal courts for six months. On appeal, the Supreme Court reversed: "even assuming that the letter exhibited an unlawyer-like rudeness, a single incident of rudeness or lack of professional courtesy—in this context—does not support a finding of contemptuous or contumacious conduct, or a finding that a lawyer is 'not presently fit to practice law in the federal courts.' Nor does it rise to the level of 'conduct unbecoming a member of the bar' warranting suspension from practice."

5. Compare Matter of Erdmann, 33 N.Y.2d 559 (1973), where a divided New York Court of Appeals in a brief per curiam opinion reversed a judgment of censure of a legal services attorney who referred to the judicial system of New York's First Department, in an interview given to *Life* magazine, in the following language (301 N.E.2d at 560):

There are so few trial judges who just judge, who rule on questions of law, and leave guilt or innocence to the jury. And Appellate Division judges aren't any better. They're the whores who became madams.

I would like to [be a judge] just to see if I could be the kind of judge I think a judge should be. But the only way you can get it is to be in politics or buy it—and I don't even know the going price.

The Court of Appeals stated that while perhaps persistent or general courses of conduct that were "degrading to the law, the Bar, and the courts, and are irrelevant or grossly excessive would present a different issue," "isolated instances of disrespect for the law, judges and courts expressed by vulgar and insulting words or other incivility, uttered, written, or committed outside the precincts of a court are not subject to professional discipline." Do you agree? Do the Court of Appeals' words— "general," "grossly excessive," or "isolated"—raise similar "insufficient guidance" questions to those raised by Justice Kennedy in *Gentile* regarding Nevada Supreme Court Rule 177?

6. The issue of lawyers' free speech has been severely tested in a number of cases with strongly political overtones. In re Sawyer, 360 U.S. 622 (1959) is a major precedent. Defense counsel in a Smith Act prosecution of Communist leaders for conspiracy to advocate violent overthrow of the government made a speech while the trial was still going in which she referred, among other things, to the "shocking and

horrible" things that were going on at the trial and the impossibility of getting a fair trial in a Smith Act case. After a close reading of the reported speech, a bare majority of the court concluded that the record did not support the findings that the impartiality and character of the trial judge had been impugned. While the Court's opinion is presented primarily in terms of the specific facts of the case, there are overtones, which bothered the dissenters and at least one member of the majority, of a constitutional dimension to the right of a lawyer to make rather sharp attacks on the conduct of a pending trial.

7. The ability of courts to punish lawyers engaging in harsh criticism of judges and courts continues to divide courts. Compare Grievance Administrator v. Fieger, 476 Mich. 231 (2006) (not a violation of the First Amendment to discipline a lawyer who called Court of Appeals judges a jackass court and referred to them as Hitler, Goebbels, and Eva Braun) with Oklahoma ex rel. Oklahoma Bar Assn v. Porter, 766 P.2d 958 (1988) (First Amendment violation to discipline a lawyer for charging in the media that the federal district judge who sentenced his client was racist).

8. Constand v. Cosby, 229 F.R.D. 472 (E.D. Pa. 2005) is an example of a civil case where a court explicitly adopted Model Rule 3.6 as the standard for decision in addressing a motion by a defendant sued for sexual assault for a gag order limiting the ability of parties and counsel to make extrajudicial statements. The court noted constitutional issues posed by such an order, found that most of the media coverage was based on the parties' assertions in their pleadings, and stated explicitly that statements by counsel were already subject to sanction, "albeit seldom enforced," under Pennsylvania's disciplinary Rule 3.6. Noting the high profile status of the litigation, the court stated that after-the-fact discipline would not be effective. However, it stated its own readiness to enforce the Rule itself under provisions of the Federal Rule of Civil Procedure or its own inherent powers if need be.

9. In Maldonado v. Ford Motor Co., 476 Mich. 372 (2006), the plaintiff's sexual harassment suit was dismissed after plaintiff and her counsel repeatedly referred in public statements and on TV to a conviction for indecent exposure by the defendant supervisor notwithstanding expungement of the conviction and a court warning that that evidence of the prior conviction was inadmissible and should not be referred to publicly. A bitterly divided Michigan Supreme Court concluded that the publicity was designed to influence the potential jury pool and therefore constituted a violation of Rule 3.6. The court also concluded that dismissal of the suit did not violate the First Amendment.

10. Notwithstanding *Maldonado*, there is some increasing judicial receptiveness or simply surrender to the notion that the First Amendment protects lawyers' public statements about public (including court) records. See, e.g., Dwyer v. Cappell, 762 F.3d 275, 276 (3d Cir. 2014) ("Attorney Andrew Dwyer, lauded by New Jersey judges in separate judicial opinions, published on his law firm's website those complimentary remarks. One of the judges objected to this, and ultimately the New Jersey Supreme Court adopted an attorney-conduct guideline that bans advertising with

quotations from judicial opinions unless the opinions appear in full. Is the guideline an unconstitutional infringement on speech as applied to the advertisements of Mr. Dwyer and his firm? We believe it is . . ."); Hunter v. Virginia State Bar ex rel. Third Dist. Comm., 744 S.E.2d 611 (Va. 2013) (concluding that "State Bar's interpretation of professional conduct rule relating to confidentiality of information, as barring attorney from reporting on his blog what transpired in concluded public judicial proceedings, violated First Amendment"). Is there a compelling or at least significant state interest in nevertheless suppressing lawyers' speech about court proceedings? Do you think that the public believes lawyers more than others in this regard? Even if so (which would seem a bit questionable given the general public opinion of lawyers), should truth be a complete defense? When lawyers who advertise tout their acquittals or their praise from judges in opinions or hearings, do they imply an improper ability to influence the court?

11. Traditionally, it was only lawyers involved in criminal cases and plaintiffs' lawyers who attempted to "try their cases in the press." In recent years, however, it has become increasingly common for defense lawyers to attempt to influence the court of public opinion. In the recent legal controversy involving the withdrawal of the drug Vioxx from the market amid allegations that it was responsible for causing a variety of health problems, the drug's manufacturer Merck & Co. was primarily represented in the press by its general counsel. See "Merck & Co.: Communication Lessons from the Withdrawal of Vioxx," 27 J. Bus. Strategy 11 (2006). Does this trend raise issues that are different from those discussed in *Gentile* and *Ruggieri*? Does it matter whether the lawyer is the actual spokesperson or simply working behind the scenes with the company's internal or external public relations specialists to craft the company's message? Should corporate lawyers have an ethical obligation to help their clients craft their legal public relations strategy? Does the trend toward lawyers being involved in these issues pose any special risks for lawyer, clients, or the public? For an interesting examination of this important but underappreciated set of issues, see Michele DeStefano Beardslee, "Advocacy in the Court of Public Opinion Part I: Broadening the Role of Corporate Attorneys," 22 Geo. J. Legal Ethics 1119 (2010).

Gentile concerns the speech rights of lawyers in their traditional roles as client representatives. In recent years, however, lawyers and law professors are increasingly engaged in new roles that present novel challenges to the goal of striking a proper balance between the First Amendment and the right to a fair trial.

The first is the burgeoning demand for legal commentators. Lawyers, of course, have always been asked to comment on newsworthy legal events. The O. J. Simpson murder case, however, turned this occasional practice into a cottage industry. Dozens of lawyers and law professors now appear regularly on television to analyze developments in the latest "trial of the century." Many more are anxious to join their ranks.

What are the ethical obligations of legal commentators? Should lawyers who serve as commentators be governed by ethical standards applicable to journalists, lawyers, or some new hybrid standard? Does your answer depend upon whether a lawyer-commentator is a full time commentator or a practicing lawyer or professor who comments on the side? A paid consultant or a volunteer? What, if any, obligations do lawyer-commentators have regarding confidentiality and conflicts of interest? For example, what happens when a lawyer acting in this role receives non-public information from a lawyer or judge involved in the case that may bear upon the party's strategy or the just resolution of the case? Similarly, should a lawyer comment on an issue that might affect the interests of one of the lawyer's other cases or clients? Must the lawyer disclose that he or she may have an interest in the issue involved, and if so to whom? Finally, do lawyer-commentators have any special obligations to the public in virtue of their status as lawyers? Are lawyers who engage in this activity under a *professional* obligation to ensure that they are sufficiently knowledgeable about both the facts and the law in a particular area to render a competent opinion? Must they ensure that their comments contribute to the fair and efficient administration of justice? Is there an obligation to make "commenting" services widely available so that those who do paid commentary should also have to do some on a "pro bono" basis? For a thoughtful account of the ethics of legal commentators by two law professors who participate extensively in this activity, see Erwin Chemerinsky and Laurie Levenson, "The Ethics of Being a Commentator," 69 S. Cal. L. Rev. 1303 (1996). The next year, Professors Chemerinsky and Levenson addressed the ethics of commentators in trials that are closed to the media, such as the Simpson civil case. See Erwin Chemerinsky and Laurie Levenson, "The Ethics of Being a Commentator II," 37 Santa Clara L. Rev. 913 (1997).

Similar concerns are raised by the second role (other than advocate) that lawyers and law professors increasingly are playing in trials and other legal proceedings: consultant or expert witness. Once again, lawyers have always consulted with clients and other lawyers on complex legal issues and served as expert witnesses, particularly in malpractice cases. The explosion in the number of actions against lawyers (including regulatory enforcement actions of the kind at issue in the *Merrill Lynch* case discussed in Chapter 4 (p. 229)), however, has significantly increased the number of lawyers and law professors who consult or testify as well as the cumulative impact of their new roles. Law professors—particularly those who teach or write in the area of professional ethics—are especially in demand.

What are the obligations of lawyers or law professors who serve as consultants or expert witnesses? Are consultants or witnesses permitted—or perhaps even obligated—to give any opinion that favors the interests of those who hire them so long as there is a good faith basis for doing so under the applicable legal rules? Does the answer depend upon whether the person is acting as a consultant or a witness? See generally ABA Ethics Op. 97–407 (1997) (discussing these differences). Does it matter whether the lawyer in question is a practitioner or an academic?

Does testifying as an expert pose a threat to the scholarly independence of lawyers? Should professors only give opinions or testimony consistent with what they would say in a scholarly article? Is it possible to hew to that line consistently under the pressures of testifying, especially as new facts or issues may arise in the course of litigation? Do ethics professors have a special obligation to make consulting and expert witnesses services "widely available" by devoting some portion of the time they spend consulting or testifying for pro bono clients or causes? Should there be any ethical restrictions on the fees that ethics professors and others charge for these services? How is the increasing use of ethics consultants likely to affect the overall distribution of legal resources between plaintiffs and defendants, individuals and corporations? For a heated exchange on this question between law professors who served as experts on opposing sides of a case, see William H. Simon, "The Market for Bad Legal Advice: Academic Professional Responsibility Counseling as an Example," 60 Stan. L. Rev. 1555 (2008); Bruce A. Green, "Reply—The Market for Bad Legal Scholarship: William H. Simon's Experiment in Professional Regulation," 60 Stan. L. Rev. 1605 (2008); William H. Simon, "Response—Transparency Is the Solution, Not the Problem: A Reply to Bruce Green," 60 Stan L. Rev. 1673 (2008). Return to this question after you have considered the materials on the distribution of lawyer services in Chapter 12.

Finally, what effect might the growing demand for ethics professors to act as consultants or expert witnesses have on legal teaching or scholarship? Is there a danger that professors will shade what they say or write in order to attract (or at a minimum, not to discourage) lucrative consulting or witness fees? Will wealthy litigants involved in high-stakes disputes attempt to sway scholarly support for their position by commissioning papers by leading academics on topics important to their positions? Is it enough that the academics who accept such engagements assert that their professional integrity would never allow them to compromise their scholarly judgment simply because they are being paid to write about a particular topic? Should they also have to disclose that the work has been commissioned, and if so what exactly should be disclosed: i.e., the name of the organization commissioning the paper; the real parties in interest; the amount the academic has been paid? Should professors who have acted as consultants or expert witnesses regarding particular issues be required to disclose this fact in articles on the same subject which have not been commissioned by the party for whom they worked? Should they be required to disclose such participation to their students in courses they teach on the subject? Should there be an ethical code for ethics experts, and if so who should draft it: the ABA? the American Association of Law Schools? individual law school deans and faculty? the Judicial Conference of the United States or the Conference of Chief Justices? So far the ABA's House of Delegates has refused to adopt anything formal, even though its Litigation Section has thrice submitted proposed ethical rules for adoption.

The fact that law professors are (for the most part) also lawyers presents a number of other potential conflicts between teaching and scholarship, on the one hand, and professional ethics on the other. For example, may professors use cases in which they have participated as lawyers as hypotheticals in class or in articles? See Carrie Menkel-Meadow, "Telling Stories in School: Using Case Studies and Stories to Teach Legal Ethics," 69 Fordham L. Rev. 787 (2000). Must a professor who advises current or former students on ethics or legal issues be licensed to practice law in the jurisdiction in which he or she teaches? Should professors be obligated to perform pro bono work in courts where such work is mandatory? For an argument that law professors are first and foremost members of the *legal* profession as opposed to the *academic* profession, and therefore subject to the duties and responsibilities of lawyers, see David Luban, "Faculty Pro Bono and the Question of Identity," 49 J. Legal Educ. 58 (1999).

Note: The Integrated Bar and Lawyer Freedom

A very different issue with respect to lawyers' speech is presented by the combination of three Supreme Court cases, Lathrop v. Donohue, 367 U.S. 820 (1961); Abood v. Detroit Board of Education, 431 U.S. 209 (1977); and Keller v. State Bar of California, 496 U.S. 1 (1990). In *Lathrop*, the Court rejected an attack on an order of the Wisconsin Supreme Court creating an "integrated" bar by requiring every lawyer admitted to practice to join, and pay dues to, the State Bar. The court held that such compulsion did not violate any associational rights of lawyers. The issue in *Lathrop* was limited to the requirement to pay dues. There was no decision whether compelled dues could be spent to advocate legislation and programs to which specific lawyers objected. That issue was finally addressed in *Abood*, in the context of an agency shop agreement between Detroit teachers and the Board of Education. The court held that notwithstanding ideological objections of specific teachers to union activities as their exclusive representative, such interference was constitutionally justified so long as the union's activities related to "collective bargaining, contract administration, and grievance adjustment purposes." The Court noted the difficulty of "drawing lines between collective bargaining activities, for which contributions may be compelled, and ideological activities unrelated to collective bargaining, for which such compulsion is prohibited." Id. at 236. It noted the complaint about union sponsorship of social activities, but, lacking specificity about the activities, it left that question to be resolved first by the state courts. It did, however, specifically forbid compulsion to contribute to support of political candidates and views.

Whether compelled dues may be spent to advocate "political" or "ideological" goals, in the context of an integrated state bar association, was finally addressed by the Supreme Court in *Keller*. The petitioners were twenty-one members of the State Bar of California who, in common with all members of the California bar, had been compelled to pay dues as a condition of practicing law in California. The dues were used both for "self-regulating" functions, such as lawyer discipline, as well as for other activities, including lobbying for and against specific legislation and the sponsoring of gun control and nuclear freeze initiatives. The petitioners filed suit, claiming that mandatory dues that financed "ideological and political" activities to which they were opposed violated their First Amendment free speech rights. The Supreme Court agreed, rejecting the state bar's argument that it was a governmental agency and therefore free to engage in such activities as a matter of their own First Amendment rights. Relying on *Lathrop* and *Abood*, the Court concluded that "the guiding standard must be whether the challenged expenditures are necessarily or reasonably incurred for the purpose of regulating the legal profession or 'improving the quality of the legal service available to the people of the State.'" 496 U.S. at 14. The constitutionality of integrated bar regulation remains unsettled after the decisions in Harris v. Quinn, 134 S.Ct. 2618 (2014), striking down on First Amendment grounds an Illinois law requiring payment of union agency fees by non-member home health providers and Friedrichs v. California Teachers Ass'n, 136 S.Ct. 1089 (2016), affirming, by an equally divided court, California's agency shop law requiring non-member public school teachers to pay union dues to support normal collective bargaining activities.

Even the limited standard chosen to define the purposes for which mandatory dues may be spent leaves many problems. Consider the following bar association activities: providing budgets for standing committees on substantive areas of law; supporting a change from election to appointment of judges; rating judges, both elected and appointed; sponsoring "Law Day" activities on television and in the schools; sponsoring pro-abortion or anti-abortion legislation; opposing legislation to regulate fees, or to bring lawyers under Social Security; sponsoring annual dinners and a golf tournament for lawyers, to which judges are invited as nonpaying guests. Is the Court's standard to be preferred to one that focuses on concern for the "administration of justice," which would support a broader panoply of activities?

The controversy about the appropriate role of integrated bars, which exist in a majority of the jurisdictions in the United States, came to a head in the District of Columbia. Following a proposal for increasing lawyers' dues, opponents of programs initiated by the Bar sponsored a referendum of the members of the Bar to limit mandatory dues and assessments to "admission of attorneys; their continued registration; discipline of attorneys; and, client security fund." The referendum passed by a vote of 6,721 to 5,189. The District of Columbia Court of Appeals, under whose jurisdiction the District of Columbia Bar functions as an official arm of the court, stayed operation of the referendum to consider whether it conflicted with its Rules organizing the Bar and if so, whether those Rules should be amended. When the Court divided four to four on whether it should override the referendum, Chief Judge Newman, who would have overridden it, nevertheless voted to vacate the stay because a majority of the court was not prepared to override. On Petition to Amend Rule 1, 431 A.2d 521 (1981).

The effect of the referendum on existing activities was characterized by one of the dissenters, Judge Ferren.

> Almost precipitously, therefore, funding no longer is assured for virtually the entire program of professional and community activities overseen

by the Board of Governors. These include continuing legal education (CLE) to help maintain lawyer competence; an array of 17 membership divisions and 11 standing committees (as well as special committees) to study and recommend improvements in the administration of justice; an Office of Public Service Activities to provide lawyer referral and information services, including help for the indigent; a major Bar publication, the District Lawyer, to report on local professional issues and on significant national trends; and a Citizens Advisory Committee to help assure lawyer accountability by putting hard questions from the client perspective. . . .

It is difficult to imagine, for example, an effective organized bar without membership divisions and study committees. Over the years, the courts, the professional, and the community have benefited enormously from the unified Bar's study of justice-related issues. For example, Division 2 (Antitrust, Trade Regulation and Consumer Affairs) issued a major report on consumer protection; Division 5 (Criminal Law and Individual Rights) scrutinized Superior Court appropriations; and Division 4 (Courts, Lawyers, Administration of Justice) has contributed a number of important evaluations on the unauthorized practice of law, six- and twelve-member juries, District Court rules, reciprocal admission to federal courts, fee arbitration, and lawyer competency requirements for the federal courts.

Bar committees have provided equally significant service. Recently, the Horsky Committee completed a comprehensive study of the local court system, released in ten volumes over a two-year period. In earlier years, committees have issued special reports on criminal defense services, complaints about ineffective assistance of counsel, the proposed transfer of prosecutive and judicial-appointive powers from the federal to the District of Columbia government, and the prospects for arbitration in conjunction with Superior Court proceedings. Important standing committees, such as the Committee on Legal Ethics, have made similar contributions.

The diversity of the Bar adds significant strength to the work of its divisions and committees. Recently, for example, this court received a comprehensive report on a matter of substantial professional and public concern from a Bar committee comprised of 19 lawyers engaged in a wide variety of fields. There were 4 lawyers from large firms, 3 from medium firms, 4 from small firms, 5 sole practitioners, 1 from a prepaid legal service plan, 1 law professor, and 1 federal administrative law judge. The makeup of this committee enhanced the quality and credibility of the report; such diversity reflects a special contribution that a unified bar assuredly can make.

There is another threatened program, the Office of Public Service Activities, which is of particular significance to the public. Through its Lawyer Referral and Information Service (LRIS) and related programs, this office has been handling approximately 20,000 calls a year from persons in need of information or a lawyer's help. Last year, trained Bar staff, after carefully screening each matter, were able to assist 43% of the callers without need for referral. Of the others, the staff directed 18% to lawyers on a regular or reduced fee basis and referred the other 39%—unable to afford a fee—to legal aid organizations, pro bono lawyers, government agencies, community programs, and the courts. In addition, LRIS maintains a branch at the Landlord–Tenant Division of Superior Court, providing conciliation as well as referral service.

The Bar's ability to provide such comprehensive assistance has depended, in substantial measure, on full-time staff equipped not only to relay information about community resources, but also to recruit pro bono lawyers to sponsor training for these lawyers in fields (such as Landlord–Tenant court) which do not easily generate paid CLE subscribers, and to match indigent clients with volunteer lawyers having particular interests and skills. These coordinated programs of the Office of Public Service Activities require money—$385,000 in 1980–81, of which $360,000 or $11.22 per lawyer are budgeted from Bar dues. In contrast with the outlook for certain other Bar programs, the prospect is dim for increased user charges to sustain this essentially pro bono service.

The four judges who voted to uphold the referendum concluded that it was essential to uphold the democratic procedures it had provided in the Rules promulgated to govern the Bar. While noting that a referendum may not infringe members' constitutional rights or amend the court's Rules governing the Bar without its permission, they found no such case since it read the Rules as not obligating the Bar to perform any of the functions whose funding out of mandatory dues was forbidden. They noted that on the contrary it had been argued that the funding of certain programs out of mandatory dues had violated members' constitutional rights but they did not discuss that argument any further. The four dissenters agreed, in separate opinions, that the Court's Rules required the Bar to perform certain public and professional duties that were prohibited by the referendum. The major opinion was written by Judge Ferren, who would have continued the stay and created a task force to identify those Bar programs that are essential to the bar and public because they are "inherent Bar responsibilities." He viewed his court's original decision to create a unified bar as a decision to assure that the Bar would carry out certain public responsibilities and he was ready to have the court identify them. Indeed, he thought open-ended delegation of regulatory authority to lawyers themselves was improper. (See pp. 767–773 for discussion of the similar issues of mandatory pro bono service on an individual basis.)

Chapter 7

Lawyers' Obligations to the Legal System, to the Public, and to Legal Institutions

The profession has long recognized (at least as an ideal) duties not only to clients, but also to the legal system and to the public. The first comment to the Model Rules states that "A lawyer is a representative of clients, an officer of the legal system and a public citizen having special responsibility for the quality of Justice." Duties to the legal system and the public entail affording representation to all persons in need of it, and that obligation has been constitutionalized to a very large extent for criminal matters. Gideon v. Wainwright, 372 U.S. 335 (1963); Argersinger v. Hamlin, 407 U.S. 25 (1972); Model Rule 6.2 ("A lawyer shall not seek to avoid appointment by a tribunal to represent a person except for good cause . . ."). On the other hand, generally there is no right to counsel in civil matters, where many cannot afford legal services. We explore the important issues concerning access to law, lawyers and legal services in Chapter 8.

What other duties, if any, do lawyers owe to the legal system and the public?

While the Model Rules describe the practice of law as a three-legged stool, deeming the lawyer's roles as officer of the legal system and as public citizen to be on equal footing with the lawyer's role as a representative of clients, in practice lawyers' duties to the legal system and the public are very limited. The duty to the legal system includes an obligation to represent unpopular clients, to act with civility and to otherwise practice law professionally. Duties to the public and to legal institutions are as important, but are even less well-defined than duties to the legal profession.

A. Lawyers' Obligations to the Legal System

1. The Duty to Represent Unpopular Clients

The obligation to represent unpopular clients is not without its problems. First, it raises complex questions about the allocation of authority, legal and moral, between client and attorney in the relationship, explored by Professor Wilkins below. Second, it entails striking a balance between access to lawyers and justice, on the one hand, and other values, such as national security (examined in U.S. v. Reid, p. 562), on the other. Finally, the representation of unpopular clients triggers institutional tensions, for example, when a partner seeks to represent a client but her firm disagrees.

David B. Wilkins
Race, Ethics, and the First Amendment:
Should a Black Lawyer Represent the Ku Klux Klan?
63 Geo. Wash. L. Rev. 1030 (1995)

The headline in The New York Times read: "A Klansman's Black Lawyer, and a Principle." The black lawyer in question is Anthony Griffin, a cooperating attorney in the Texas Chapter of the American Civil Liberties Union ("ACLU") and, until the events described in the Times article, the General Counsel for the Port Arthur Branch of the National Association for the Advancement of Colored People ("NAACP"). In his former capacity, Griffin agreed to represent Michael Lowe, the grand dragon of the Texas Knights of the Ku Klux Klan ("KKK" or "Klan"), against efforts by the Texas Commission on Human Rights ("Commission") to compel Lowe to turn over the Klan's membership list. This action eventually cost Griffin his position with the NAACP.

The Times headline succinctly sums up the issues presented in this controversial case. As the first clause suggests, Griffin's decision to represent the Klan raises important questions about the relationship between personal identity and professional role. Why would a *black* lawyer (particularly one with such a demonstrated commitment to civil rights) agree to represent an organization that has brutalized and intimidated African-Americans for more than a century? The underlying facts of this case make this concern particularly salient.

The Klan is engaged in a systematic campaign to terrorize the handful of blacks who were moved into an all-white housing project in all-white Vidor, Texas. This attempt to desegregate Vidor is in turn based on a federal court's explicit finding of blatant and widespread discrimination by state and federal officials responsible for the distribution of public housing in Texas. The Texas Commission on Human Rights contends that it needs the Klan's membership list in order to prosecute those Klansmen who have sought to shield their illegal activities by wearing hooded sheets and by enforcing a code of silence through threats and intimidation. By opposing the State's request, isn't Griffin helping to perpetuate the very racist practices that, in his capacity as General Counsel to the NAACP, he has fought so long to eradicate?

As the Times headline's second clause implies, the solution proposed by Griffin and his supporters for this seeming paradox is a legal principle: the First Amendment. The conventional wisdom is that the Constitution's guarantee of free expression, and the corollary right to associate freely with like-minded individuals, entitles the Klan to keep its membership list confidential. It is this constitutional principle, the argument goes, and not the Klan's atrocities, that Griffin is defending. According to this line of thinking, the true irony is the NAACP's failure to appreciate the importance of these First Amendment concerns—particularly in light of the Supreme

Court's 1958 decision in *NAACP v. Alabama* [357 U.S. 449 (1958)], which upheld the NAACP's right to keep *its* membership list private on First Amendment grounds.

These competing characterizations of Griffin—as either an apologist for the Klan or the defender of First Amendment freedoms—are the latest installment in a familiar debate over how the public should regard a lawyer who represents a client whose views the lawyer opposes (or ought to oppose). . . .

Canon 2 of the Model Code of Professional Responsibility ("Model Code") instructs lawyers to "assist the legal profession in fulfilling its duty to make legal counsel available." This injunction, however, has never been interpreted to require a lawyer to accept any particular case that might come to her attention. To the contrary, a lawyer is free to turn down a given case for any reason, including the most banal (and undoubtedly the most common) reason of all: the client can't afford to pay the freight. From the perspective of the individual practitioner, therefore, the ethical commitment to make legal counsel available is a background norm that does not compel a specific decision in any particular case. In other words, no individual lawyer has an ethical obligation to represent the Klan.[34]

The issue becomes more complicated, however, when a lawyer refuses to take on a client because he disagrees with the client's views. The rules of professional conduct urge lawyers not to turn away unpopular clients or causes. In order to facilitate this objective, the Model Rules of Professional Conduct ("Model Rules") specifically state that a "lawyer's representation of a client . . . does not constitute an endorsement of the client's political, economic, social or moral views or activities." Nor, in an implicit rebuke of the effects thesis, do the rules hold lawyers legally or morally accountable for wrongful actions that a client might take as a result of their legal advice, so long as they do not actively assist in the wrongdoing or otherwise transgress the bounds of the law. Instead, lawyers who represent unpopular clients are celebrated in professional lore for providing a vital service to society. Ironically, one of the most commonly cited examples in this lore is the fictional lawyer Atticus Finch who, in the 1950s book and film *To Kill A Mockingbird*, braved the bigoted fury of his small town neighbors to defend a black defendant falsely accused of rape.[*]

The profession has good reasons for being worried about unpopular clients gaining access to legal services. Standing up to public pressure invariably is difficult. A doctor, for example, can render medical assistance to someone who has become a social outcast without becoming directly implicated in that person's antisocial views.

---

34. As famed criminal defense lawyer William Kuntsler succinctly put the matter when explaining why he would not represent the Klan even though he represented the accused [1993] World Trade Center bombers: "[E]veryone has a right to a lawyer, that's true. But they don't have a right to me." . . .

[*] In a subsequent book, *Go Set a Watchman* (2016), Harper Lee offers a darker, more complex Atticus Finch, who was or has become, at least outside of his practice, as bigoted as some of his neighbors.

The lawyer who actively advocates that same person's legal rights and interests is unlikely to be able to do so. At the same time, lawyers depend on the community's goodwill for their economic survival. If history is any indication, few lawyers will be willing to confront these twin dangers.

The real question, therefore, is why the obligation to take on these cases is not mandatory. To be sure, not every unpopular client is like the black defendant in *To Kill A Mockingbird*, that is, both factually innocent and a victim of racial prejudice. Nevertheless, once we concede that even factually guilty people who advocate views that society ought to reject are entitled to a lawyer, the question remains why the profession should count on the aspirational pull of professional honor to ensure that these services are provided rather than directly ordering lawyers to do so.

It is possible to offer two quite different justifications for the . . . decision to treat the representation of unpopular clients as a professional honor rather than a mandatory duty. The most commonly articulated ground rests on the client's interest. Thus, the Model Rules specifically allow lawyers to refuse to accept a court appointment in circumstances where "the client or the cause is so repugnant to the lawyer as to be likely to impair the client-lawyer relationship or the lawyer's ability to represent the client." The second ground, offered primarily by commentators, focuses on the lawyer's moral right to control his or her own labor.

Important consequences flow from the choice between these two rationales. The first ground implies that clients ought to be given the final word. If the possibility of poor service is the only reason why a lawyer should refuse to take a controversial case, then a fully informed client ought to have the right to consent to that risk. Although we might believe that few clients will take advantage of this right, there will certainly be circumstances where it would be prudent for a particular client to do so. The most obvious case is when the client has no other alternative. In circumstances where the choice is between potentially poor representation and no representation at all, a rational client will, in all likelihood, choose the former. As a result, a lawyer who believes that he may only conscientiously object when it is in the client's best interest to do so should feel compelled to take the case despite his misgivings.

Moreover, an unpopular client might rationally choose to press a particular lawyer to accept his case even in circumstances other than the classic "last lawyer in town" scenario. Michael Lowe's delight in being represented by a black lawyer nicely illustrates the point. As Lowe told the reporter from The New York Times: "'The way I look at it, he has to do a good job for me . . . . If he doesn't win, people are going to say, "Yup, that's what you get for taking an African-American lawyer." Everybody will know I got sold down the river by the A.C.L.U.'" In other words, even though there is no evidence that Lowe could not have obtained another lawyer to represent him if Griffin had declined to take the case, he is happy with the arrangement *precisely because* of Griffin's opposition to the Klan. At the same time, Griffin (assuming that he was forced to take the case against his wishes) could be disbarred or sued for malpractice if he were to fail to pursue zealously the Klan's objectives to the full extent permitted by law. Under these circumstances, it might be perfectly rational for the Klan to consent to be represented by a black lawyer even though the Klan is, in the *lawyer's* view, "so repugnant to the lawyer as to be likely to impair . . . the lawyer's ability to represent the client."

Although courts have occasionally compelled a lawyer to represent clients against the lawyer's will, it is highly unlikely that any court or bar association would give clients plenary power over the formation of attorney-client relationships. The second justification for making the duty to represent unpopular clients honorific as opposed to mandatory—that a lawyer has a moral right to control his or her own labor—helps to explain this intuition. Given our society's commitment to both individual autonomy and moral pluralism, it would be fundamentally wrong for the state (or the profession) to compel an individual to commit a moral wrong for the sake of the greater good. These grounds underlie our willingness to excuse from military service those citizens who are sincerely opposed to killing. Similarly, a lawyer who believes that it would be morally wrong to lend her professional skill to a particular cause ought not to be forced to do so just because the client can see some strategic advantage in the arrangement.

The state may legitimately impose adverse consequences on those who exercise this option. Conscientious objectors to the draft may be compelled to provide nonlethal support to the war effort, just as a lawyer who refuses to take one case may be obligated to demonstrate in some other way that he is not shirking his baseline obligation to help make legal counsel widely available. In extreme cases, either the state or the profession might conclude that a particular individual's moral objection to the role of "citizen" or "lawyer" is so pervasive that he or she should be forced to leave the country or resign from the bar. It would be wrong, however, to impose such a draconian penalty on a lawyer whose only transgression is that she is unwilling to represent a particular client because of a sincere moral disagreement with that individual's views or objectives.

Once we accept this justification, however, it is no longer possible to contend that lawyers bear no moral responsibility for their decision to represent particular clients. To this extent, effects theorists are right. If a lawyer has the moral right to refuse to accept a case, then the decision not to exercise this option—in other words, to agree to take the case—also carries moral significance. Even if one accepts that there is a morally significant distinction between committing a harmful act and failing to do something morally praiseworthy, representing a client in the face of strong moral argument to the contrary is to *act*. Moreover, one cannot justify this action solely by referring to the demands of the role itself because, as we have seen, that role specifically allows for conscientious objection. Nor does the "right to counsel" provide a sufficient independent ground unless (perhaps) the lawyer is the last lawyer in town. The claim that "this person deserves legal representation" is fundamentally different from the argument that "*I* should provide that service." In order to arrive at the latter conclusion, a lawyer must examine the specific legal and moral considerations at issue in the particular case. . . .

The limitations that Griffin places on his willingness to be the Klan's lawyer also underscore the delicate balance he is attempting to strike [between his professional commitment to defend first amendment rights and his personal commitment to the black community]. For example, Griffin states that he would not feel obligated to defend Lowe or any other Klan member against criminal charges involving threats to blacks living in Vidor. Nor is Griffin willing to become friends with Lowe or refrain from strongly criticizing the Klan's objectives or actions. Finally, Griffin has neither asked for, nor in all probability would he accept, any money for representing the Klan. As he has repeatedly stated, his sole interest is in defending the constitutional principle that the government cannot interfere with associational rights by obtaining membership lists that might be used to harass or intimidate those with unpopular beliefs. . . .

Notes

1. We will return to other questions raised by this fascinating case—including whether Griffin's race should influence our (or his) judgment about his decision to represent the Klan, and whether the NAACP was justified in dismissing Griffin for agreeing to take the case—in Chapters 12 and 9 respectively. For the moment, consider Professor Wilkins' claim that because lawyers have a moral right *not* to represent a given client, the decision to undertake a particular representation carries "moral weight." Are you persuaded by this argument? What exactly is the moral component of agreeing to represent a given client? How should a lawyer go about "weighing" its significance? What other factors should a lawyer take into account in reaching this judgment: the merits of the case? the willingness of other lawyers to take the case? the potential harm to third parties? the resources of the legal system? Do you think that encouraging lawyers to engage in this kind of moral calculus would lead to a more equitable distribution of legal services or otherwise improve the functioning of the legal system? Are there reasons to allow (or perhaps even to encourage) lawyers to consider the moral, legal, or human costs of client selection that go beyond whether such a calculus is likely to improve the legal system? For an argument that the zero-sum nature (the more one side gains, the more the other loses) of many legal issues creates, in a society characterized by economic inequality, an ethical obligation on the part of lawyers to evaluate the "relative merits" of the cases they take on vis-à-vis other potential uses of their time, see William H. Simon, "Ethical Discretion in Lawyering," 101 Harv. L. Rev. 1083 (1988).

2. What do you think about the limitations that Griffin placed on his willingness to represent Michael Lowe or the Ku Klux Klan? Consider them one at a time. Would the "moral weight" of his decision to represent the Klan be different if he were defending Michael Lowe in a criminal prosecution based on the violence in Vidor? Don't criminal cases present constitutional issues as important as protecting First Amendment rights? Recall Professor Monroe Freedman's contention in Chapter 5, p. 442, that a criminal defense lawyer seeking to suppress evidence "is not representing a heinous criminal, but the Fourth Amendment." Is this claim any less persuasive in

the criminal context than in the First Amendment context? By making a distinction between representing the Klan's First Amendment rights and asserting, for example, that evidence against the Klan should be suppressed in a criminal prosecution, is Griffin implicitly asserting that speech, no matter how repugnant, is less harmful than the kinds of violence for which the Klan might be prosecuted in this case? For a critique of the view that speech is inherently less harmful than action, see Frederick Schauer, "The Phenomenology of Speech and Harm," 103 Ethics 635 (1993).

3. What about Griffin's refusal to become "friends" with Lowe and continued criticism of the Klan and its conduct? What is Griffin trying to accomplish by making this distinction? More to the point, is it ethical for Griffin to refer to his "client" as a "terrorist organization"? Should a lawyer representing an unpopular client be allowed to express publicly his distaste for his client's goals or ideals? Griffin's conduct certainly runs counter to the vision of the lawyer as full service public relations firm currently espoused by many prominent attorneys. For example, Floyd Abrams, a prominent First Amendment attorney, argued that criminal defense lawyers have an ethical obligation to publicly proclaim their client's innocence, whether or not the lawyer knows this to be the case, in order to overcome the inevitable public presumption that the client is guilty. Floyd Abrams, "Why Lawyers Lie," N.Y. Times Mag., Oct. 9, 1994, at 54. Many argue that this is particularly true when the client is unpopular. One lawyer who often represents those accused of being members of organized crime families argues that a lawyer who keeps her distance from an unpopular client will inevitably reinforce the prevailing perception that the client is subhuman and therefore does not deserve legal protection. See Fredric Dannen, "Defending the Mafia," New Yorker, Feb. 2, 1994, at 64 (reporting the views of a prominent criminal defense attorney). See also Charles J. Ogletree, "Beyond Justification: Seeking Motivations to Sustain Public Defenders," 106 Harv. L. Rev. 1239 (1993) (urging public defenders to become actively involved in their clients' lives in order to avoid adopting society's view that criminal defendants are unworthy of care or empathy).

4. Should lawyers be obligated to be "public relations" specialists for their clients? Should speaking to the press be discretionary or mandatory? Should the rules be different for lawyers who represent "unpopular clients"? Whatever obligations or permissions we place on lawyers in this regard, are lawyers permitted—or even obliged—to make statements about their clients' innocence?

5. Whatever the rules require or permit, can lawyers really distance themselves from their clients and their goals? Recall Professor Wasserstrom's worry in Chapter 1, see p. 14, that a lawyer's "professional" role can come to define his or her whole personality. Theories of "cognitive dissonance" underscore this worry. It is a familiar truth that those who are called upon to support positions that they initially find morally abhorrent will search for ways to reduce the distance between their beliefs and their practices. Empirical studies suggest that lawyers may be susceptible to this pressure. For example, in a study of corporate lawyers in Chicago, Robert Nelson found that the lawyers in his sample rarely disagreed with their clients' intentions or goals. See Robert L. Nelson, *Partners with Power: Social Transformation of the Large*

Law Firm 231–270 (1988). This result was at odds with the fact that these same lawyers held views about public policies (such as the value of government regulation) that differed in important ways from those of the typical corporate client. Id. Although one might explain this disparity on the ground that the clients of large law firms rarely pursue objectives that threaten the underlying goals of regulatory policy, it is equally (if not more) plausible that lawyers who work closely with — and receive generous remuneration from — powerful clients will gradually find themselves agreeing more and more with the interests of those clients. Notwithstanding his critical statements about the Klan, Anthony Griffin also characterized the government investigation into Klan violence as a "witch hunt." Wilkins, supra, at 1056. In light of the undisputed record of Klan violence in Vidor, isn't this kind of inflammatory statement exactly what one would expect to hear from a "full service" advocate?

6. What difference does it make that Griffin was representing the Klan pro bono? Is it any less admirable to defend First Amendment rights on behalf of unpopular clients for a fee? For those citizens who disagree with Griffin's decision — particularly black citizens — is it arguably an even greater insult that he was willing to do so for free? Do lawyers who represent unpopular clients pro bono have greater freedom to restrict their participation to protecting the Constitution, allowing them to disassociate themselves from their clients' more unsavory characteristics? If so, is this good for the clients? When answering this last question, reconsider Professor Bell's critique (p. 334, Note 1) of public interest lawyers who put their ideological principles above the interests of their clients.

7. Why do you think that Anthony Griffin decided to represent the Klan in this case? Recall Professor Pepper's claim that lawyers surrender their moral autonomy by becoming lawyers. Does Griffin's case suggest that recognizing a certain amount of moral autonomy on behalf of individual lawyers might actually support, rather than undermine, a lawyer's willingness to defend unpopular clients or causes? We will return to the related questions about the significance of Griffin's identity as a black lawyer in Chapter 12.

The "war on terror" has created special problems for lawyers seeking to represent alleged terrorists, pitting representation of unpopular clients against national security and patriotism.

United States v. Reid

214 F. Supp. 2d 84 (D. Mass. 2002)

YOUNG, C.J.

[. . . [The defendant Richard] Reid is alleged to have attempted to blow American Airlines Flight 63 ("Flight 63") out of the sky with bombs concealed in his shoes on December 22, 2001, while over the Atlantic Ocean en route from Paris to Miami. The plane was immediately diverted to Boston, where it landed in the early afternoon. Reid was turned over to the F.B.I. at that time. . . . An American grand jury sitting in the District of Massachusetts promptly indicted Reid on a variety of federal charges. Reid was arraigned and ordered detained after a hearing before Magistrate Judge Judith Dein. Prior to the hearing, Magistrate Judge Dein appointed the Federal Defender Office in the District as Reid's counsel, having found that Reid was unable to retain counsel. . . .]

. . . [T]he Attorney General [has] promulgated emergency regulations which allow the imposition of "Special Administrative Measures" ("SAMs") upon any federal prisoner as to whom he finds that "there is a substantial risk that a prisoner's communications or contacts with persons could result in death or serious bodily injury to persons . . . ." 28 C.F.R. § 501.3(a) ("Prevention of acts of violence and terrorism.") (1996). The Attorney General has issued such SAMs against Richard C. Reid ("Reid"), the defendant in this case, under the authority of section 501.3.

SAMs issued pursuant to section 501.3 are implemented "upon written notification to the Director, Bureau of Prisons, by the Attorney General or, at the Attorney General's direction, by the head of a federal law enforcement agency, or the head of a member agency of the United States intelligence community." Id. § 501.3(a). SAMs may be imposed for up to a one-year period upon the approval of the Attorney General, and may be renewed. Id. § 501.3(c). The power of the Attorney General to impose SAMs derives mainly from 5 U.S.C. § 301, which grants the heads of executive departments the power to create regulations designed to assist them in fulfilling their official functions and those of their departments, and 18 U.S.C. § 4001, which vests control of federal prisons in the Attorney General and allows him to promulgate rules governing those prisons.

SAMs are prisoner-specific; that is, each prisoner upon whom SAMs are imposed has a set of SAMs issued for him, and him alone, based on the circumstances of his case. This Memorandum discusses, to the extent necessary, the SAMs issued with respect to Reid, a foreign national detained under order of this Court and awaiting trial on serious charges, and explains this Court's orders in light of the SAMs.

On March 4, 2002, this Court held an initial scheduling conference pursuant to Local Rule 116.5(A). . . .

On that day, however, unbeknownst to the Court, the SAMs began to play a significant role in this case. Two weeks earlier, on February 19, 2002, the Marshals Service unilaterally, without seeking the Court's prior permission, imposed case-specific SAMs on the detention of Reid. The portion of these SAMs concerning Reid's attorney-client communications reads:

> d. Defense Counsel May Disseminate Inmate Conversations—The inmate's attorney may disseminate the contents of the inmate's communications to third parties for the sole purpose of preparing the inmate's defense—and not for any other reason—on the understanding that any such dissemination shall be made solely by the inmate's counsel, and not by the counsel's staff.

"Attorney" is defined as the inmate's attorney or attorneys of record, verified and documented by the government. "Staff" is meant to refer to "Pre-cleared" staff members of Reid's defense team: co-counsel, paralegals, investigators, or translators actively engaged in his defense, who have submitted to a background check by the F.B.I. and the United States Attorney for the District of Massachusetts and have been successfully cleared, and who have agreed to adhere to the SAMs by signing the affirmation required of all those engaged in Reid's defense. Co-counsel, i.e., other lawyers engaged in Reid's defense, and the attorneys' paralegal staff, may meet with Reid face to face without Reid's attorneys being present, but the government seeks completely to prohibit the nonlawyer staff of the public defenders office, translators, potential fact witnesses and prospective defense experts, such as a psychiatrist, from meeting with Reid without his attorneys. Such persons are permitted to talk with the defendant on the telephone as long as Reid's attorneys participate in the call, and presumably these properly designated individuals may meet with Reid if accompanied by his attorneys of record. Paragraph 2(j) of the SAMs allows Reid to provide written documents and drawings to his attorney for the purposes of preparing his defense, but require counsel to retain these documents and not disseminate them to anyone not engaged in Reid's defense; paragraphs 2(i) and (k) require that the attorneys show Reid only documents related to his defense and that they not, under any circumstances, divulge, forward, or send the contents of his mail to any third parties. Paragraph 2(h) outlines Reid's privileged telephone conversations for the purpose of conducting his own defense, and requires that these conversations not be overheard by any third parties not engaged in his defense. Finally, Paragraph 2(a) requires Reid's attorneys, their paralegal staff, designated co-counsel, and investigators to acknowledge and sign off on the SAMs. This paragraph reads as follows:

a. Attorney Affirmation of Receipt of the SAM Restrictions Document—The inmate's attorney (or counsel)—individually by each if more than one— must sign an affirmation acknowledging receipt of the SAM restrictions document. The Federal Government expects that the attorney, the attorney's staff, and anyone else at the behest of, or acting on behalf of, the attorney, will fully abide by the SAM outlined in this document; that expectation is set forth in the SAM restrictions document.

i. The [United States Attorney for the District of Massachusetts] shall present, or forward, the "attorney affirmation of receipt of the SAM restrictions document" to the inmate's attorney.

ii. After initiation of SAM and prior to the inmate's attorney being permitted to have attorney/client-privileged contact with the inmate, the inmate's attorney shall execute a document affirming the receipt of the SAM restrictions document and return the original to the [United States Attorney].

iii. The [United States Attorney] shall maintain the original of the SAM acknowledgment document and forward a copy of the signed document to OEO in Washington, DC.

On March 4, 2002, Reid's attorneys informed the government that they had no intention of signing any such affirmation. Approximately six days later, the government entirely cut off defense counsels' communication with their client.

On March 25, 2002, defense counsel filed an emergency motion to enjoin the Attorney General and the United States Attorney from barring their communication with Reid. . . .

. . . On March 25, 2002, the Court issued the following order (the "Emergency Order"):

> Subject to reconsideration upon further briefing: . . .
>
> 2. Tamar Birckhead and Owen Walker shall have access to the defendant at all reasonable times and dates consistent with the security of the institution and the pre-existing regulations of the institution.
>
> 3. There will be no monitoring of the defendant while in the presence of the attorneys.
>
> 4. The substance of what the defendant has to say is confidential to his attorneys and must be held inviolate and not communicated to anyone. . . .

No one appealed the Emergency Order and it took effect in accordance with its terms. Defense counsel thus secured its goal of obtaining relatively unfettered access to their client. The Court, however, went further and ordered a number of other things as well. . . .

Paragraph 3 — prohibiting government monitoring of face-to-face attorney-client communications — is unnecessary because the government has never sought to infringe on the attorney-client privilege in this way with these particular SAMs. . . .

. . . At a hearing on April 22, 2002 concerning the steps to be followed under the Classified Information Procedures Act, 18 U.S.C. app. 3, § 3, defense counsel objected strenuously to a continuation of Paragraph 4 of the Emergency Order which restricted dissemination by Reid's attorneys of communications from Reid to anyone. Citing national security concerns, the Court demurred.

Still, the argument made by defense counsel resonated, and both parties agreed at that hearing that the government had never sought such a sweeping restriction. Indeed, for years I have taught trial lawyers that:

> When you get a case, shop your ideas. Ask someone, "What about this? . . . Have you ever had a case where . . . ? What if I argued . . . ? How do you think this would work?" This is still a profession.

William G. Young, *Reflections of a Trial Judge* 102 (1998). Paragraph 4 prevented precisely this type of trial preparation generally deemed necessary for a proper defense.

On May 7, 2002, Reid moved to dissolve the protective order placing limits upon counsel's disclosure of information received from him. The Court established a briefing schedule and heard oral argument on June 3, 2002. Defense counsel launched their main attack on the blanket prohibition the Court had imposed on their dissemination of data received from Reid in order to prepare his defense. The government did not support the Court's blanket prohibition but, instead, proffered a more limited proposed protective order which, after argument, the Court adopted.

For its part, the government sought an order requiring defense counsel, as a condition of continued access to their client, to sign an affirmation that they have received the SAMs and understand that the SAMs apply to them. On this point, issue was genuinely joined.... [D]efense counsel ... immediately argued that to impose any such affirmation requirement on the defense would violate Reid's Sixth Amendment right to counsel.

The Court took this aspect of the matter under advisement. From the bench, the Court modified the Emergency Order by entering the following modified order (the "June 3 Order"):

> ...
>
> Two: Defense counsel for Mr. Reid are to be provided access to their client for the purpose of engaging in confidential oral conversations and exchanging written communications solely for the purpose of preparing Mr. Reid's defense and reviewing the conditions of his confinement.
>
> Three: Defense counsel may share the substance of their oral conversations with Mr. Reid, and the written communications sent to or received from Mr. Reid, pertaining to the substance of the charges against him, only with each other and third parties who are engaged in the preparation of Mr. Reid's defense or providing information which is necessary and helpful to that defense. Such exchange of information shall be for the sole purpose of preparing Mr. Reid's defense.
>
> Four: Mr. Reid's conversations and written communications with defense counsel are subject to the Procedural Statement and Security Regulations of the Massachusetts Correctional Institution at Cedar Junction for so long as Mr. Reid shall be housed there, and otherwise applicable policies or regulations of the United States Marshals Service that were in effect prior to February 19, 2002 — prior to the February 19, 2002 issuance of the Special Administrative Measures in this case.
>
> ...
>
> Five: ... The United States shall not require from defense counsel any specific undertaking or affirmation without express order of this Court.
>
> Six: Nothing herein precludes either party from moving this Court to modify the terms and conditions of this protective order or any of the SAMs deemed to be applicable.

On June 19, 2002, the government informed the Court that it had modified the SAMs applicable to Reid to conform to the Court's order. With respect to the affirmation requirement, Reid's SAMs now state:

a. Attorney Affirmation of Receipt of the SAM Restrictions Document—The inmate's attorney (or counsel)—individually by each if more than one—must sign an affirmation acknowledging receipt of the SAMs restrictions document, *except where such affirmation is excused, precluded, or barred by judicial determination. . . .*

A. Constitutional Limitations on Reid's SAMs

While I have acknowledged that Reid's SAMs are presumptively valid once he has been properly placed in the custody of the executive as a pre-trial detainee, as noted earlier, the executive's control is not absolute. . . . Most pertinent to this case, pre-trial strictures on a detainee cannot unduly burden Reid's fundamental constitutional right to a vigorous defense by an independent attorney under the Sixth Amendment.

When I left the bench on June 3rd, I thought I had been presented with a significant constitutional question under the Sixth Amendment. Then, sixteen days later, the government backed off. Modifying the SAMs applicable to Reid, the government now makes the affirmation requirement applicable *unless* "excused, precluded, or barred by judicial determination." SAMs Renewal ¶ 2(a). As a consequence of this modification, the government subordinates its SAMs with respect to Reid to the exercise of the Court's discretion, and the constitutional issue evaporates.

Nevertheless, a decent respect for the arguments of counsel requires me to explain why, after considerable reflection, this Court (in the exercise of its discretion and not as a matter of Sixth Amendment constitutional interpretation), has determined not to require an affirmation from Owen Walker, Esq., Tamar Birckhead, Esq., and Elizabeth Prevett, Esq. Here is why: "[S]o vital is the role of the advocate that all judicial systems in the western world are today 'adversary' in the sense that parties in contention, including parties contending with the state, are entitled to be heard through independent, trained, partisan legal representatives." Marvin Frankel, *Partisan Justice* 7 (1978). . . .

The affirmation here unilaterally imposed by the Marshals Service as a condition of the free exercise of Reid's Sixth Amendment right to consult with his attorneys fundamentally and impermissibly intrudes on the proper role of defense counsel. They are zealously to defend Reid to the best of their professional skill without the necessity of affirming their bona fides to the government. As trusted officers of this Court, in their representation of Reid they are subordinate to the existing laws, rules of court, ethical requirements, and case-specific orders of this Court—and to nothing and no one else. If the government feels the need for specific protective orders applicable to all counsel alike, it may make application to the Court.

Nor is this all. The Court takes judicial notice, pursuant to Federal Rule of Evidence 201, that the government has indicted attorney Lynne Stewart, Esq. for violating 28 U.S.C. § 1001, in that having signed the required affirmation, she violated the SAMs applicable to one Sheikh Abdel Rahman, and therefore knowingly made a false statement. . . . Evidently, the government theorizes that the affirmation was knowingly false when made.[8] Whatever the merits of this indictment, its chilling effect on those courageous attorneys who represent society's most despised outcasts cannot be gainsaid. . . .

. . . As the government has conceded in its renewal of the SAMs, Reid's attorneys are not required to sign any affirmation that they will abide by the SAMs or a receipt of their acknowledgment where this Court has barred such an affirmation. SAMs Renewal ¶ 2(a). Insofar as the Emergency Order placed limitations on attorney-client communications, as explained previously, the Emergency Order was modified on June 3, 2002, to remove the limits it imposed upon counsel's disclosure of information received from Reid and its limitations upon the people with whom Reid could communicate as part of his defense. This modification stands and Reid's Sixth Amendment rights are thereby fully vindicated. In all other respects, the existing SAMs apply to Reid and his counsel; in addition, all otherwise applicable policies or regulations of the United States Marshals Service in effect at MCI/Cedar Junction that were in effect prior to February 19, 2002 — prior to the February 19, 2002 issuance of the SAMs in this case, are applicable to Reid so long as he shall be housed there pending trial.

Notes

1. Chief Judge Young raised, but did not need to decide, the Sixth Amendment issue with respect to the original requirement in the SAM that cut off the ability of defense counsel to communicate the defendant's communications to third parties. Was there also a problem of professional responsibility for defense counsel in agreeing to limit that aspect of their representation? May they waive that right? Do the government attorneys encounter a professional responsibility problem of their own when they seek to compel the defendant and his counsel to waive that right as a condition of furnishing counsel? Is this issue the same as the issue involved in the Thornburgh, McNulty, Reno, Filip, and Yates Memoranda discussed in Chapter 5? Suppose the SAM requires that the defendant and counsel agree to permit attorney-client conversations to be recorded by the government?

2. The indictment of Lynne Stewart, referred to in Chief Judge Young's opinion, resulted in a conviction of the lawyer for Sheik Abdul Rahman (who had been convicted of plotting terrorist bombings). Fearful that Abdul Rahman would direct terrorist activities from prison, the Attorney General had imposed SAMs limiting his communications with the outside world and Stewart had signed an affirmation that she would comply with them. She was prosecuted under 18 U.S.C. § 2339A, which makes it a crime to provide support or resources "knowing or intending that

---

8. While the indictment is unclear on this point, if the government complains only that she violated her affirmation and that this violation transgresses 28 U.S.C. § 1001, serious constitutional issues might arise in that the Attorney General would himself be criminalizing a variety of conduct by imposing the SAMs and then seeking indictments for their violation. It is constitutional bedrock that only the Congress can enact federal criminal statutes. . . .

they are to be used in preparation for, or in carrying out" various terrorist crimes. Following her conviction Stewart was disbarred.

(3.) In January 2007, Charles Stimson, Deputy Assistant Secretary of State for Detainee Affairs, made the following statement on a local talk radio program in Washington, D.C.:

> As a result of a FOIA request through a major news organization, somebody asked, "Who are the lawyers around this country representing detainees down there?" And you know what, it's shocking. The major law firms in this country—Pillsbury Winthrop; Jenner & Block; Wilmer Cutler Pickering; Covington & Burling here in D.C.; Sutherland Asbill & Brennan; Paul Weiss Rifkind; Mayer Brown; Weill Gotschal; Pepper Hamilton; Venable, Alston & Bird; Perkins Coie; Hunton & Williams; Fulbright Jaworski, all the rest of them—are out there representing detainees, and I think quite honestly, when corporate CEOs see that these firms are representing the very terrorists who hit their bottom line back in 2001, these CEOs are going to make those law firms choose between representing terrorists or representing reputable firms, and I think that is going to have major play in the next few weeks. It's going to be fun to watch this play out.

David Luban, "Lawfare and Legal Ethics in Guantanamo," 60 Stan. L. Rev. 1981 (2008) (quoting Stimson). As it turned out, Stimson had substantially less fun than he anticipated. His statement was roundly condemned by editorial and bar organizations as a blatant attack on lawyers who were upholding the highest ideals of the profession. See, e.g., Charles Fried, Op-Ed, "Mr. Stimson and the American Wall," Wall St. Journal, Jan. 16, 2007; John Heilprin, "Views on Detainee Representation Draw Fire; Pentagon Official's Suggestion of a Boycott is Irresponsible, Legal Groups Say," Washington Post, Jan. 14, 2007. Notwithstanding his apology, three weeks later Stimson was out of a job. See "Pentagon Official Who Criticized Detainee Lawyers Quits," Washington Post, Feb. 3, 2007.

Although it is easy to dismiss the gratuitous nature of Assistant Secretary Stimson's criticism, he was far from the only person to suggest that the "normal" rules of ethics and legality did not apply in times of war. As we saw in Chapter 5, lawyers for the Bush administration took a similar view with respect to the standards for interrogating detainees. Similarly, in the days following 9/11, the president of the Association of Trial Lawyers of America called for a moratorium on civil lawsuits arising out of the tragedy and urged its members to "support our government so it can fully gather all the evidence needed quickly to identify and prosecute the terrorists." See letter from Leo V. Boyle, "ATLA Joins Nation in Mourning, Calls for Moratorium in the Time of National Crisis on Civil Lawsuits That May Arise From Tragedy," September 13, 2001 (on file with the authors). Many other prominent attorneys who had in the past strongly supported civil liberties or defended those accused of crimes against the government publicly stated that they were "rethinking" their original positions and decided to endorse the use of extraordinary measures— ranging from military tribunals, to using racial and/or religious profiling as a means of identifying individuals who may be subject to heightened scrutiny, to "torture warrants" allowing judges to grant authorities the legal right to torture suspected terrorists—as necessary and appropriate in the war against international terrorism. Indeed, when former American Bar Association president James Brosnahan agreed to represent John Walker Lindh, the so-called "American Taliban" picked up by U.S. forces in the early days of the Afghan war, Brosnahan's law firm Morrison & Foerster—where he had been a partner for more than 20 years—required that he make it clear that the firm was not involved in the representation. See Brenda Sandburg, "MoFo's Distance No Big Deal, Brosnahan Claims," The Recorder, Jan. 29, 2002.

Indeed, notwithstanding its rhetoric about the duty to represent unpopular clients, the profession's record on fulfilling this mandate is decidedly mixed. History is replete with examples of individual lawyers from John Adams to Thurgood Marshall who have been willing, often at great personal cost, to challenge government action on the ground that it infringes on important constitutional rights or to defend those accused of heinous crimes. The profession as a whole, however, has been considerably less forthcoming in its defense of individual liberty—particularly during what are perceived as times of crisis. For example, few lawyers were willing to represent accused Communists during the McCarthy era, and the ABA and other organizations were generally silent on issues such as blacklisting suspected Communists or the internment of Japanese-Americans during World War II. See Deborah L. Rhode, "Ethical Perspectives on Legal Practice," 37 Stan. L. Rev. 589, 630 (1985). As the Japanese example makes plain, the Supreme Court has frequently endorsed the government's claim that extraordinary measures are called for in extraordinary times. As Justice Black wrote for the majority in the case upholding the internment order: "There was evidence of disloyalty on the part of some, the military authorities considered that the need for action was great, and time was short. We cannot—by availing ourselves of the calm perspective of hindsight—now say that at that time these actions were unjustified." See Korematsu v. United States, 323 U.S. 414 (1944). Given this record, it should be a point of pride for the bar that Stimson was able to name so many prominent law firms that were involved in the representation of detainees.

Moreover, to the extent that representing unpopular clients embodies the role of lawyers as officers of the legal system, it is noteworthy that the obligation applies only, practically speaking, to trial lawyers. But most U.S. attorneys are not trial lawyers or litigators. Does it mean that the majority of lawyers have no real role to play as officers of the legal system?

----

2. Civility

A general view has become accepted by the bar and the judiciary that "hardball" tactics of practice, always present in certain situations, have overwhelmed the practice of law to the point that not only is there widespread unpleasantness in lawyer dealings but that common courtesies that used to be exchanged as a matter of routine were disappearing. The result has been a spate of "civility codes" coming from courts and bar associations. See Monroe Freedman, "Civility Runs Amok," Legal Times, Aug. 14, 1995 at 54 (referencing "100 courtesy codes and civility guidelines throughout the country"). The status of the codes is uncertain. In the majority of the states these codes are not part of the codes of professional conduct that form the basis for professional discipline, but a few states have incorporated civility provisions into their Rules such that incivility may result in disciplinary action, and others include civility commitments as part of the oath taken by newly admitted members of the bar. Moreover, civility codes are usually stated in such broad terms that they do not give much notice of what is and what is not permissible conduct, in part because of the difficulty of drawing a line between permitted zealous advocacy and prohibited incivility. Nonetheless, such codes are beginning to be referred to in court opinions for their general statements about unacceptable conduct.

The following case is much cited because of the prominence of the case that was involved and the lawyer whose conduct was criticized. The case involved the effort of QVC Network to prevent the acquisition of Paramount Networks by Viacom so that it could acquire Paramount itself. Paramount Communications v. QVC Network, 637 A.2d 34 (Del. 1994). After disposing of the case on the merits, the Delaware Supreme Court appended an Addendum in order to criticize severely the conduct in particular of Joseph Jamail, a well-known Texas litigator who had handled many high-profile cases, among them the enormous judgment he won for Pennzoil against Texaco in connection with its acquisition of Getty Oil.

Addendum to
Paramount Communications v. QVC Network
637 A.2d 34 (Del. Sup. Ct. 1994)

VEASEY, C.J.:

The Court is constrained, however, to add this Addendum. Although this Addendum has no bearing on the outcome of the case, it relates to a serious issue of professionalism involving deposition practice in proceedings in Delaware trial courts.[23]

The issue of discovery abuse, including lack of civility and professional misconduct during depositions, is a matter of considerable concern to Delaware courts and courts around the nation. One particular instance of misconduct during a deposition in this case demonstrates such an astonishing lack of professionalism

---

23. We raise this matter *sua sponte* as part of our exclusive supervisory responsibility to regulate and enforce appropriate conduct of lawyers appearing in Delaware proceedings. . . . Normally our supervision relates to the conduct of members of the Delaware Bar and those admitted *pro hac vice*. Our responsibility for supervision is not confined to lawyers who are members of the Delaware Bar and those admitted *pro hac vice*, however. . . . Our concern, and our duty to insist upon appropriate conduct in any Delaware proceeding, including out-of-state depositions taken in Delaware litigation, extends to all lawyers, litigants, witnesses, and others.

and civility that it is worthy of special note here as a lesson for the future—a lesson of conduct not to be tolerated or repeated.

On November 10, 1993, an expedited deposition of Paramount, through one of its directors, J. Hugh Liedtke, was taken in the state of Texas. The deposition was taken by Delaware counsel for QVC. Mr. Liedtke was individually represented at this deposition by Joseph D. Jamail, Esquire, of the Texas Bar. Peter C. Thomas, Esquire, of the New York Bar appeared and defended on behalf of the Paramount defendants. It does not appear that any member of the Delaware bar was present at the deposition representing any of the defendants or the stockholder plaintiffs.

Mr. Jamail did not otherwise appear in this Delaware proceeding representing any party, and he was not admitted *pro hac vice*. Under the rules of the Court of Chancery and this Court, lawyers who are admitted *pro hac vice* to represent a party in Delaware proceedings are subject to Delaware Disciplinary Rules,[28] and are required to review the Delaware State Bar Association Statement of Principles of Lawyer Conduct (the "Statement of Principles").[29] During the Liedtke deposition, Mr. Jamail abused the privilege of representing a witness in a Delaware proceeding, in that he: (a) improperly directed the witness not to answer certain questions; (b) was extraordinarily rude, uncivil, and vulgar; and (c) obstructed the ability of the questioner to elicit testimony to assist the Court in this matter.

To illustrate, a few excerpts from the latter stages of the Liedtke deposition follow:

A. [Mr. Liedtke] I vaguely recall [Mr. Oresman's letter] .... I think I did read it, probably.

---

28. It appears that at least Rule 3.5(c) of the Delaware Lawyer's Rules of Professional Conduct is implicated here. It provides: "A lawyer shall not ... (c) engage in conduct intended to disrupt a tribunal or engage in undignified or discourteous conduct which is degrading to a tribunal."

29. The following are a few pertinent excerpts from the Statement of Principles:

The Delaware State Bar Association, for the Guidance of Delaware lawyers, **and those lawyers from other jurisdictions who may be associated with them**, adopted the following Statement of Principles of Lawyer Conduct on [November 15, 1991] .... The purpose of adopting these Principles is to promote and foster the ideals of **professional courtesy, conduct and cooperation** .... A lawyer should develop and maintain the qualities of integrity, compassion, learning, civility, diligence and public service that mark the most admired members of our profession .... [A] lawyer ... **should treat all persons, including adverse lawyers and parties, fairly and equitably** .... **Professional civility is conduct that shows respect not only for the courts and colleagues, but also for all people encountered in practice** .... Respect for the court requires ... emotional self-control; [and] the absence of scorn and superiority in words [or] demeanor .... A lawyer should use pre-trial procedures, including discovery, solely to develop a case for settlement or trial. **No pre-trial procedure should be used to harass an opponent or delay a case** .... **Questions and objections at deposition should be restricted to conduct appropriate in the presence of a judge** .... Before moving the admission of a lawyer from another jurisdiction, a Delaware lawyer should make such investigation as is required to form an informed conviction that the lawyer to be admitted is ethical and competent, and should furnish the candidate for admission with a copy of this Statement.

(Emphasis supplied.)

. . . .

Q. (By Mr. Johnston [Delaware counsel for QVC]) Okay. Do you have any idea why Mr. Oresman was calling that material to your attention?

MR. JAMAIL: Don't answer that. How would he know what was going on in Mr. Oresman's mind? Don't answer it. Go on to your next question.

MR. JOHNSTON: No, Joe—

MR. JAMAIL: He's not going to answer that. Certify it. I'm going to shut it down if you don't go to your next question.

MR. JOHNSTON: No. Joe, Joe—

MR. JAMAIL: Don't "Joe" me, asshole. You can ask some questions, but get off of that. I'm tired of you. You could gag a maggot off a meat wagon. Now, we've helped you every way we can.

MR. JOHNSTON: Let's just take it easy.

MR. JAMAIL: No, we're not going to take it easy. Get done with this.

MR. JOHNSTON: We will go on to the next question.

MR. JAMAIL: Do it now.

MR. JOHNSTON: We will go on to the next question. We're not trying to excite anyone.

MR. JAMAIL: Come on. Quit talking. Ask the question. Nobody wants to socialize with you.

MR. JOHNSTON: I'm not trying to socialize. We'll go on to another question. We're continuing the deposition.

MR. JAMAIL: Well, go on and shut up.

MR. JOHNSTON: Are you finished?

MR. JAMAIL: Yeah, you—

MR. JOHNSTON: Are you finished?

MR. JAMAIL: I may be and you may be. Now, you want to sit here and talk to me, fine. This deposition is going to be over with. You don't know what you're doing. Obviously someone wrote out a long outline of stuff for you to ask. You have no concept of what you're doing. Now I've tolerated you for three hours. If you've got another question, get on with it. This is going to stop one hour from now, period. Go.

MR. JOHNSTON: Are you finished?

MR. THOMAS: Come on, Mr. Johnston, move it.

MR. JOHNSTON: I don't need this kind of abuse.

MR. THOMAS: Then just ask the next question.

Q. (By Mr. Johnston) All right. To try to move forward, Mr. Liedtke . . . I'll show you what's been marked as Liedtke 14 and it is a covering letter dated October 29 from Steven Cohen of Wachtell, Lipton, Rosen & Katz including QVC's Amendment Number 1 to its Schedule 14D-1, and my question—

A. No.

Q.—to you, sir, is whether you've seen that?

A. No. Look, I don't know what your intent in asking all these questions is, but, my God, I am not going to play boy lawyer.

Q. Mr. Liedtke—

A. Okay. Go ahead and ask your question.

Q.—I'm trying to move forward in this deposition that we are entitled to take. I'm trying to streamline it.

MR. JAMAIL: Come on with your next question. Don't even talk with this witness.

MR. JOHNSTON: I'm trying to move forward with it.

MR. JAMAIL: You understand me? Don't talk to this witness except by question. Did you hear me?

MR. JOHNSTON: I heard you fine.

MR. JAMAIL: You fee makers think you can come here and sit in somebody's office, get your meter running, get your full day's fee by asking stupid questions. Let's go with it.

Staunch advocacy on behalf of a client is proper and fully consistent with the finest effectuation of skill and professionalism. Indeed, it is a mark of professionalism, not weakness, for a lawyer zealously and firmly to protect and pursue a client's legitimate interests by a professional, courteous, and civil attitude toward all persons involved in the litigation process. A lawyer who engages in the type of behavior exemplified by Mr. Jamail on the record of the Liedtke deposition is not properly representing his client, and the client's cause is not advanced by a lawyer who engages in unprofessional conduct of this nature. It happens that in this case there was no application to the Court, and the parties and the witness do not appear to have been prejudiced by this misconduct.[31]

---

31. We recognize the practicalities of litigation practice in our trial courts, particularly in expedited proceedings such as this preliminary injunction motion, where simultaneous depositions are often taken in far-flung locations, and counsel have only a few hours to question each witness. Understandably, counsel may be reluctant to take the time to stop a deposition and call the trial judge for relief. Trial courts are extremely busy and overburdened. Avoidance of this kind of misconduct is essential. If such misconduct should occur, the aggrieved party should recess the deposition and engage in a dialogue with the offending lawyer to obviate the need to call the trial judge. If all else fails and it is necessary to call the trial judge, sanctions may be appropriate against the offending lawyer or party, or against the complaining lawyer or party if the request for court relief

Nevertheless, the Court finds this unprofessional behavior to be outrageous and unacceptable. If a Delaware lawyer had engaged in the kind of misconduct committed by Mr. Jamail on this record, that lawyer would have been subject to censure or more serious sanctions. While the specter of disciplinary proceedings should not be used by the parties as a litigation tactic, conduct such as that involved here goes to the heart of the trial court proceedings themselves. As such, it cries out for relief under the trial court's rules, including Ch. Ct. R. 37. Under some circumstances, the use of the trial court's inherent summary contempt powers may be appropriate. See In re Butler, Del. Supr., 609 A.2d 1080, 1082 (1992).

Although busy and overburdened, Delaware trial courts are "but a phone call away" and would be responsive to the plight of a party and its counsel bearing the brunt of such misconduct. It is not appropriate for this Court to prescribe in the abstract any particular remedy or to provide an exclusive list of remedies under such circumstances. We assume that the trial courts of this State would consider protective orders and the sanctions permitted by the discovery rules. Sanctions could include exclusion of obstreperous counsel from attending the deposition (whether or not he or she has been admitted *pro hac vice*), ordering the deposition recessed and reconvened promptly in Delaware, or the appointment of a master to preside at the deposition. Costs and counsel fees should follow.

As noted, this was a deposition of Paramount through one of its directors. Mr. Liedtke was a Paramount witness in every respect. He was not there either as an individual defendant or as a third party witness. Pursuant to Ch. Ct. R. 170(d), the Paramount defendants should have been represented at the deposition by a Delaware lawyer or a lawyer admitted *pro hac vice*. A Delaware lawyer who moves the admission *pro hac vice* of an out-of-state lawyer is not relieved of responsibility, is required to appear at all court proceedings (except depositions when a lawyer admitted *pro hac vice* is present), shall certify that the lawyer appearing *pro hac vice* is reputable and competent, and that the Delaware lawyer is in a position to recommend the out-of-state lawyer. Thus, one of the principal purposes of the *pro hac vice* rules is to assure that, if a Delaware lawyer is not to be present at a deposition, the lawyer admitted *pro hac vice* will be there. As such, he is an officer of the Delaware Court, subject to control of the Court to ensure the integrity of the proceeding.

Counsel attending the Liedtke deposition on behalf of the Paramount defendants had an obligation to ensure the integrity of that proceeding. The record of the deposition as a whole demonstrates that, not only Mr. Jamail, but also Mr. Thomas (representing the Paramount defendants), continually interrupted the questioning, engaged in colloquies and objections which sometimes suggested answers to questions, and constantly pressed the questioner for time throughout the deposition. As to Mr. Jamail's tactics quoted above, Mr. Thomas passively let matters proceed as they

---

is unjustified. See Ch.Ct.R. 37. It should also be noted that discovery abuse sometimes is the fault of the questioner, not the lawyer defending the deposition. These admonitions should be read as applying to both sides.

did, and at times even admitted his own voice to support the behavior of Mr. Jamail. A Delaware lawyer or a lawyer admitted *pro hac vice* would have been expected to put an end to the misconduct in the Liedtke deposition.

This kind of misconduct is not to be tolerated in any Delaware court proceeding, including depositions taken in other states in which witnesses appear represented by their own counsel other than counsel for a party in the proceeding. Yet, there is no clear mechanism for this Court to deal with this matter in terms of sanctions or disciplinary remedies at this time in the context of this case. Nevertheless, consideration will be given to the following issues for the future: (a) whether or not it is appropriate and fair to take into account the behavior of Mr. Jamail in this case in the event application is made by him in the future to appear *pro hac vice* in any Delaware proceeding;[38] and (b) what rules or standards should be adopted to deal effectively with misconduct by out-of-state lawyers in depositions in proceedings pending in Delaware courts.

As to (a), this Court will welcome a voluntary appearance by Mr. Jamail if a request is received from him by the Clerk of Court within thirty days of the date of this Opinion and Addendum. The purpose of such voluntary appearance will be to explain the questioned conduct and to show cause why such conduct should not be considered as a bar to any future appearance by Mr. Jamail in a Delaware proceeding. As to (b), this Court and the trial courts of this State will undertake to strengthen the existing mechanisms for dealing with the type of misconduct referred to in this Addendum and the practices relating to admissions *pro hac vice*.

Notes

1. Jamail was asked whether he intended to accept the Court's invitation to appear to explain his conduct. His reported response was "I'd rather has [*sic.*, have] a nose on my ass than go to Delaware for any reason . . . I don't intend to explain my behavior to that court ever. . . . It's their behavior that's become suspect." The article quotes a Texas federal judge and a Texas law professor who agreed with the Delaware Supreme Court's position but also cites the view of Professor Buford of the South Texas College of Law, who thought the opinion was like "a trip back in time to the Victorian Age" and that while "Jamail was probably impolite" and "may have been impatient," he saw nothing that rose to the level of "improper conduct." Texas Lawyer, p. 11, February 14, 1994. What characterization of Mr. Jamail's conduct would you adopt and, if you were a Delaware judge, would you grant his application for admission *pro hac vice* in a subsequent case?

---

38. The Court does not condone the conduct of Mr. Thomas in this deposition. Although the Court does not view his conduct with the gravity and revulsion with which it views Mr. Jamail's conduct, in the future the Court expects that counsel in Mr. Thomas's position will have been admitted *pro hac vice* before participating in a deposition. As an officer of the Delaware Court, counsel admitted *pro hac vice* are now clearly on notice that they are expected to put an end to conduct such as that perpetrated by Mr. Jamail on this record.

2. A federal district court took the suggestion of the Delaware Supreme Court seriously and denied admission *pro hac vice* to a lawyer whose past behavior when admitted *pro hac vice* had been "uncivilized and unprofessional." The court drew a distinction between uncivilized and unethical conduct but concluded that "repeated, documented, instances of uncivilized behavior, whether or not rising to the level of a disbarable offense, strips him of the privilege of *pro hac vice* admission." Kohlmayer v. AMTRAK, 124 F. Supp. 2d 877 (D.N.J. 2000).

3. What lies behind the proliferation of civility codes? Are lawyers really less "civil" to each other than they were in the past? Certainly, many observers, including many lawyers and judges, believe so, although there is little in the way of hard empirical evidence bearing on the question. See, e.g., Robert W. Gordon, "The Ethical World of Large Law Firm Litigators: Preliminary Observations," 67 Fordham L. Rev. 709 (1999) (reporting a general feeling among lawyers that incivility is on the rise but also noting the absence of any clear definition of the problem and the danger that a rise in reporting may say more about reporting or enforcement than about underlying behavior). To the extent that civility has declined, what explains this trend? Many commentators place the blame on the increasing size and heterogeneity of the profession. The larger the profession, the argument goes, the less likely it is that lawyers will encounter one another on a repeat basis, thereby limiting the effectiveness of informal norms and sanctions as a means of controlling overreaching. Moreover, the argument continues, the more diverse the profession becomes, the more fragile these informal regulatory processes will be since lawyers will share fewer social and communal ties that make such norms and sanctions possible in the first place. Do you find this explanation persuasive? Are there other causes not captured by this explanation? For example, isn't it true that civility standards have declined in many other areas of American life, for example, in politics? Does this suggest that the decline in civility among lawyers is primarily related to issues external to the legal profession?

Moreover, to the extent that homogeneity reinforces civility, does it also lead to a clubby insularity that excludes "outsiders" from meaningful participation, reinforces existing power inequalities, and stifles innovation? In reporting on the views on civility of a sample of litigators from large law firms, Professor Robert Gordon notes that women lawyers registered a "partial dissent" from the view that a weakening of "solidarity bonds" was the primary cause of incivility on the ground that "the old solidarities had excluded them, and that the new conditions of practice opened up more opportunities for them to cultivate valuable long-term relationships — both with partners and with house counsel (often staffed by other women)." Gordon, supra, at 718. Or consider the claim by plaintiffs' lawyers in the same study that they are "forced" to use aggressive litigation tactics as a means of overcoming the defendants' inherent advantage stemming from their ability continuously to delay the case by hiding or withholding documents. As one plaintiff lawyer put it: "You have to get to the point where the defendant's lawyers respect you. To get to that point you have to keep on attacking." Austin Sarat, "Enactments of Professionalism: A Study of Judges' and Lawyers' Accounts of Ethics and Civility in Litigation," 67 Fordham L. Rev. 809, 831 (1999).

4. Is civility necessarily inconsistent with zealous advocacy? Does the decline of civility reflect the supremacy of the lawyer's role as a representative of clients over her roles as an officer of the legal system and as a public citizen? See Russell G. Pearce & Eli Wald, "The Obligation of Lawyers to Heal Civic Culture: Confronting the Ordeal of Incivility in the Practice of Law," 34 U. Ark. Little Rock L. Rev. 1 (2011).

B. Lawyers' Obligations to the Public

As we have seen, while lawyers' obligations to clients are broad and numerous, lawyers' obligations to the legal system are quite limited. Some commentators assert that obligations to the public fare even worse, and amount to little more than a rhetorical tool used by lawyers to justify their status.

Deborah L. Rhode
Lawyers as Citizens
50 Wm. & Mary L. Rev. 1323 (2009)

> If we judge by wealth and power, our times are the best of times; if the times have made us willing to judge by wealth and power, they are the worst of times.

> —Randall Jarrell

The Preamble to the American Bar Association's Model Rules of Professional Conduct declares: "A lawyer, as a member of the legal profession, is a representative of clients, an officer of the legal system and a public citizen having special responsibilities for the quality of justice." In the absence of empirical evidence, it is at least a useful thought experiment to ask whether attorneys view themselves in those terms. What exactly are the "special responsibilities" of lawyers as "public citizens"? Does that question ever occur to a practicing attorney? Or even to the drafters of the bar's Multistate Professional Responsibility Exam? Are these phrases simply ceremonial folklore, embellishments reserved for celebratory speeches and academic symposia? If those questions seem rhetorical, perhaps they are the wrong questions, and far too dispiriting for occasions like this. The more useful inquiry might be: What responsibilities *should* lawyers assume for the quality of justice? And what would it take to get lawyers to take those responsibilities seriously? ...

... [T]his Essay assesses three fundamental obligations of the lawyer's civic role. The first involves developing and sustaining legal frameworks, including those that govern the profession's own behavior. The second grows out of lawyers' relationships with clients and entails some responsibility for the quality of justice that results from

[handwritten margin note at top: ③ Access to justice = pro bono not enough; make legal services accessible to who need them the most]

legal assistance. The third obligation involves access to justice, and the bar's responsibilities not only to engage in pro bono work, but also to support a system that makes legal services widely available to those who need them most.

The foundations for the American bar's civic role are generally traced to the lawyer statesmen who helped shape American governance structures in the late eighteenth century and legal reforms during the early twentieth century. Alexander Hamilton, in *The Federalist Papers*, offered one of the earliest expressions of this idealized portrait: "Will not the man of the learned profession, who will feel a neutrality to the rivalships between different branches of industry, be likely to provide an impartial arbiter between them . . . conducive to the general interests of society?"

Alexis de Tocqueville and Louis D. Brandeis similarly stressed lawyers' capacity to serve as "arbiters between the citizens," and independent intermediaries "between the wealthy and the people, prepared to curb the excesses of either . . . ." According to Woodrow Wilson, "[p]ublic life was a lawyer's forum," with both opportunities and obligations to shape "matters of common concern."

A related responsibility involves the bar as an intermediary between client and societal interests. As Brandeis famously argued, the issues that arise for lawyers guiding private affairs are often "questions of statesmanship." To nineteenth-century legal ethics experts like George Sharswood, as well as twentieth-century sociologists like Talcott Parsons, the attorney served a crucial role in compliance counseling, and in providing a "kind of buffer between the illegitimate desires of his client and the social interest." *[handwritten margin note: → Bar = inter. b/t client & social interests]*

A third aspect of the lawyer's civic role involves making legal services available to clients and causes pro bono publico. . . .

The extent to which lawyers' actual practices reflected these public responsibilities has been a matter of extended debate that need not be recounted at length here. There is, however, little doubt that on most dimensions, the profession's performance has fallen considerably short. . . .

. . . [C]ontemporary historians have found relatively little evidence of lawyers' compliance counseling during the allegedly golden ages of civic virtue; in fact, many of the bar's institutional reform initiatives were made necessary by the lawyers' own complicity in client misconduct. Recent competitive pressures and bottom-line orientations have compounded the problem . . . . *[handwritten margin note: Bar Reforms stemmed from lawyers' failure or participation in misconduct]*

According to the recent Report of the ABA's Commission on Renaissance of Idealism in the Legal Profession, "while it is undeniably true that the pace and pressures of modern practice pose serious challenges to the values of the profession, it is equally true that the spirit of idealism needed to meet those challenges is alive and well." If so, more efforts will be necessary than the largely exhortatory initiatives chronicled in the Report, such as public service awards, model powerpoints, billboard campaigns, continuing education programs, advisory resolutions, and "I Am an Idealist" buttons. Translating the bar's civic obligations into daily practices will require less aspirational rhetoric and more structural reform.

This is not the occasion for a full-scale blueprint, but the general direction of change is clear. In essence, the bar needs to become more publicly accountable for its public responsibilities. If, as lawyers often lament, the profession has become more like a business, then it needs to be regulated more like a business. Although some measure of professional independence remains necessary, models from other nations suggest that it can be maintained under governance systems that have greater distance from the self-interests of the organized bar. At a minimum, such systems need to provide more transparency regarding lawyer performance and stiffer sanctions for those complicit in client misconduct.

The profession's regulatory structures and workplace norms also must provide more support for lawyers' public responsibilities in representing private clients. One of those responsibilities is to foster compliance with the purposes as well as letter of the law and with core principles of honesty and fairness on which legal processes depend. That, in turn, will require better oversight structures in law firms and corporate counsel offices, and stiffer liability standards for lawyers who fall short. Everyone's ethical compass benefits from some external checks; clients need pressure from attorneys, and attorneys need pressure from each other.

With respect to pro bono services, lawyers need not just exhortation but enforceable expectations, imposed by courts, bar associations, or legal employers. More information should be widely available about lawyers' contributions and the quality of services provided. Since Florida has required reporting of pro bono work, the number of lawyers providing assistance to the poor has increased by 35 percent, the number of hours has increased by 160 percent, and financial contributions have increased by 243 percent. The American Lawyer's rankings of pro bono contributions by large firms, and the special visibility that it gives to high performers and "cellar dwellers," also has had a significant impact. But more efforts are necessary, and enlisting law students and clients in the demand for better public service records should be a high priority.

Law schools also need to become more active partners in this effort. In too many institutions, issues of professional responsibility are relegated to a single required course, which focuses largely on the minimum requirements of the ABA's Model Rules of Professional Conduct. The result is legal ethics without the ethics and little attention to broader issues of access to justice. The Carnegie Foundation's recent overview of legal education found that issues such as social responsibility or matters of justice rarely received significant coverage in the core curriculum; when the issues arose they were "almost always treated as addenda." . . .

Notes

1. Professor Rhode argues that the profession must be held accountable to its public responsibilities. As an example, she advocates for regulatory reforms, such as moving away from regulating lawyers to regulating service providers and allowing non-lawyers to offer some legal services to increase access. See ABA Resolution 105 (Feb. 2016), which includes "Meaningful access to justice and information about the

law, legal issues, and the civil and criminal justice systems," "Transparency regarding the nature and scope of legal services to be provided, the credentials of those who provide them, and the availability of regulatory protections," and "Delivery of affordable and accessible legal services."

2. Professor Rhode believes that one public responsibility of lawyers is "to foster compliance with the purposes as well as letter of the law and with core principles of honesty and fairness on which legal processes depend." Should lawyers advise clients to comply with the letter of the law or should they also explain the purpose and spirit of the law?

3. Revised Model Rule 8.4(g) states that "It is professional misconduct for a lawyer to engage in conduct that the lawyer knows or reasonably should know is harassment or discrimination on the basis of race, sex, religion, national origin, ethnicity, disability, age, sexual orientation, gender identity, marital status or socioeconomic status in conduct related to the practice of law." The comment explains the rule in terms of obligations to the public: "Discrimination and harassment by lawyers in violation of paragraph (g) undermine confidence in the legal profession and the legal system." Some commentators, however, object to 8.4(g) on the ground that it violates lawyers' free speech. Professor Ron Rotunda, for example, has opined that "when one lawyer tells another, in connection with a case, 'I abhor the idle rich. We should raise capital gains taxes,' [t]he lawyer has just violated the ABA rule by manifesting bias based on socioeconomic status." Ron Rotunda, "The ABA Overrules the First Amendment," The Wall Street J. (Aug. 16, 2016). Is Rule 8.4(g) a legitimate obligation lawyers owe as public citizens? Does it infringe on lawyers' free speech? A lengthy defense of Revised Rule 8.4(g) is Gillers, "A Rule to Forbid Bias and Harassment in Legal Practice," 30 Georgetown J. Legal Ethics ___ (2017).

4. The Preamble to the Model Rules states that "A lawyer should be mindful of deficiencies in the administration of justice and of the fact that the poor, and sometimes persons who are not poor, cannot afford adequate legal assistance. Therefore, all lawyers should devote professional time and resources and use civic influence to ensure equal access to our system of justice for all those who because of economic or social barriers cannot afford or secure adequate legal counsel." This language is usually construed to encourage lawyers to devote professional time to providing pro bono legal services to those who cannot afford to pay for them. In the following excerpt, Professor Eli Wald calls for a very different kind of lawyers' investment of time and resources to ensure equal access.

Eli Wald
Serfdom Without Overlords:
Lawyers and the Fight Against Class Inequality
54 U. Louisville L. Rev. 269 (2016)

Lawyers are not very engaged in the public discourse about the growing class inequality in America. In part, lawyers' silence may be reflective of the taboo against acknowledging class in American society, or the belief that class inequality is primarily an economic and political problem rather than a legal one. Of course, some public interest lawyers directly combat class inequality; other lawyers routinely deal with some of the legal aspects of the growing class inequality—criminal defense, legal aid, immigration, welfare, housing and bankruptcy, to name a few. Yet, because law and lawyers are not commonly perceived to be a cause of the class problem, some may believe that lawyers are not, and should not be, part of the solution. This article challenges the legal profession's passive stance on class inequality, arguing that even if attorneys are not a cause of the problem, all lawyers have an important role to play in the fight against inequality.

Our Kids and the Legal Profession:
The Likely Rise of a Stratified Elitist Legal Profession

. . . Poor kids are increasingly less likely to graduate from ever more segregated high schools, less likely to go to college, and therefore less likely to attend law schools (let alone elite law schools) which value the very extra-curricular activities poor kids are less likely to be exposed to. Putnam explains, for example, that while more poor kids attend college in recent years, the gain is mostly explained in attendance at less selective colleges—community colleges with a two-year degree, or for-profit institutions—whereas the class gap has widened in selective institutions. Worse, the class gap in graduation has increased. . . .

Over time, the growing opportunity gap among our kids is going to have a significant, distinct impact on the composition of the legal profession: it is going to grow increasingly less class-diverse and more stratified along socioeconomic lines. Specifically, even as the profession continues to grow more gender- and racially-diverse among affluent women and minorities, the opportunity gap will result in two related phenomena. First, fewer poor kids will be able to meet the admission criteria of law schools (such as graduating from a four-year college degree [program]) or [will be able to] afford [to enroll] when admitted, resulting in a diminished pool of lawyers from low socioeconomic backgrounds. Second, if admitted and enrolled, fewer poor kids will be admitted into elite law schools, which tend to feed elite legal institutions and produce elite lawyers, because they will not satisfy the demanding admission criteria of these institutions, which treat academic excellence at elite colleges as a necessary but insufficient condition and scrutinize extra-curricular interests, hobbies, and social and cultural capital the poor increasingly lack. The result is an increasingly class-stratified profession, with a diminishing pool of poor lawyers relegated to the low-end, individual hemisphere of law practice.

Our Lawyers: The Consequences of a Class-Based Stratified Legal Profession

. . . While this vast and growing opportunity gap constitutes serfdom without overlords, or, in Putnam's words, inequality "without upper-class villains," in the sense that privilege is self-perpetrating and requires no overt intentional discrimination against the poor, it nonetheless imposes costs on all Americans. First, the opportunity gap impedes economic growth for all and levies both real costs (such as welfare programs) and opportunity costs (such as keeping disadvantaged work-ers out of the workforce). Second, the opportunity gap results in widespread and growing political estrangement, which in turn renders our political system less rep-resentative and more alienating to those who are increasingly excluded from it. "In short," Putnam writes, "the opportunity gap undermines political equality and thus democratic legitimacy," and if not addressed, may result in political instability. Thus, the opportunity gap undermines the American Dream because it violates basic equal-ity, rendering the poor second-class citizens.

The same equality, democracy, and legitimacy concerns apply with even greater force to our lawyers and increased class stratification in the legal profession for at least two related reasons. First, in America "Law is King," and lawyers are high priests of a civic religion, an aristocracy, a governing class. Lawyers may well already be an unelected, undemocratic, self-appointed upper-class elite, but increased class strati-fication renders the profession even more illegitimate and undemocratic. It is one thing to have an elite class if everyone can join it by graduating from law school. Indeed, such an open and meritocratic legal profession would constitute a means of climbing up the socioeconomic ladder and leveling the playing field for all. It is alto-gether another to have an elite club whose members play a significant role in Ameri-can private and public lives and exert ample power when, de facto, only the affluent can join it. The latter would turn the legal profession into part of the problem, part and parcel of the serfdom without overlords system.

Second, a stratified profession is increasingly less likely to be able to effectively serve the interests of all those with legal needs. While it was never the case that only women (or minorities) could or should represent women (or minorities), the increased gender and racial diversity of the profession has been a desirable phenomenon. It meant, for example, that a women seeking a divorce or taking a stand against domes-tic abuse could choose to be represented by a female lawyer, and that a man of color facing criminal prosecution could choose to be defended (and may be prosecuted and judged) by a minority lawyer. Moreover, the increased diversity of the profes-sion has been desirable not only symbolically, but rather it helped make lawyers more effective because they were more culturally competent, empathetic, and understand-ing of their clients' backgrounds and objectives. Ample research suggests that empa-thetic lawyers who actively listen to their clients, as opposed to imputing to them generic goals, in part because they do not understand their clients, their goals, their backgrounds, and their ways of reasoning, offer more effective representation. As I observe elsewhere, "while all lawyers, irrespective of their identities, could do their jobs effectively, a diverse bar, class diversity included, is more likely to be able to meet and be perceived as able to meet the goals of access to lawyers, justice, and effective representation."

In contrast, increased class stratification makes the profession less effective and, worse, tends to disfavor the most vulnerable of clients and would-be clients—the underprivileged and underrepresented poor. In turn, a profession that is perceived to be, and is, less effective and representative is going to be less legitimate and less democratic. Worse still, in a highly-regulated society, access to law and lawyers is a condition precedent for first-class citizenship. Systematically denying the poor both access to membership in the legal profession and access to lawyers who are likely to be effective in representing their needs undermines equality as well as the legitimacy of the profession. Thus, the growing opportunity gap among our kids, in turn resulting in a growing opportunity gap among our lawyers and the increased underrepresentation of the underprivileged among our lawyers, constitutes a significant challenge to equality within the profession and to access to lawyers, law and justice. . . .

What Can Lawyers do about the Opportunity Gap?

Holding.

As citizens, active members of a governing affluent class, and as public citizens, lawyers can and should take an active role in leading the campaign to turn our kids into a high-priority public policy issue. Similarly, as participants in the very legal system that subjects lawyers of poor backgrounds and as officers of the legal system, lawyers are duty-bound to lead the battle against increased class stratification in their own backyard. . . . If lawyers have a duty to help our kids and our lawyers, the question then becomes how exactly might they live up to their obligation?

All Lawyers — A Capital Campaign that is Not about Money

Lawyers have access to social & cultural capital assets thru 1st class c-ship

. . . [O]ur kids' and our lawyers' opportunity gaps are a function not only of possessing less economic capital but of having fewer and less valuable social and cultural capital assets, which is exactly where lawyers can and should come into play: while some lawyers are not affluent, all lawyers are well-endowed with social and cultural capital. Because in America "Law is King," first-class citizenship requires a nuanced understanding of the law and access to lawyers. It is exactly the kind of place where lawyers possess ample social and cultural capital assets, both the relationships and the knowhow and sophistication about the workings of America's elite institutions. And it is this capital that lawyers possess and that the underprivileged so desperately need in order to narrow the opportunity gap which makes lawyers so well-positioned for the task.

The lack of social and cultural capital endowments results, to use Ta-Nehisi Coates' words, in our kids having stunted imagination. "It never occurred to me," writes Coates, to think outside the box: "I always thought I was destined to go back home after college — but not simply because I loved home but because I could not imagine much else for myself." Yet possession of social and cultural capital assets may make all the difference in the world for our kids' imagination and future: "And yet some of us really do see more[;] . . . others who, having gotten a boost from a teacher, an aunt, an older brother, had peered over the wall as children, and as adults became set on seeing the full view." The value of noneconomic capital, of mentors and supports who provide knowledge, guidance and understanding simply cannot be overstated. "I didn't always have things, but I had people — *I always had people.*"

Lawyers as public citizens can make a difference for our kids. If lawyers, a class of over one million, were to commit themselves to our kids by serving as mentors and role models, educating and informing our poor kids about civics and life, educating and informing their parents, and acting as leaders in their communities to help stabilize the home environments of vulnerable kids, their contributions could impact the opportunity gap. Opportunities to serve our kids abound, from organizations sponsoring one-on-one relationships, such as Big Brothers Big Sisters of America, to programs bringing lawyers into underprivileged classrooms, such as Lawyers in the Classroom.

Of course, as Putnam points out, the last thing our vulnerable kids need is another disappointing adult in their lives. Serving our kids as public citizens cannot be a haphazard temporary commitment, a pastime during the downtime following the Great Recession, a résumé builder for lawyers. Instead, what our kids need is a sustainable commitment, reliable access to knowledgeable mentors and information, and repeated opportunities to identify, explore, and vet relevant information, which are exactly the kinds of opportunities lawyers have been searching for to infuse their role as public citizens with meaningful content.

To be sure, acting as public citizens to serve our kids and their parents is not going to be easy. Lawyers are not social workers and especially those who are not parents may have a hard time interacting with kids and their parents, even with the assistance of intermediary organizations. Next, lawyers may be viewed with suspicion by underprivileged parents who may mistrust them as officers of the legal system. And lawyers, their rhetorical commitment to the role of public citizenship notwithstanding, may find it imposing in an increasingly competitive and time-consuming market for legal services. Yet lawyers qua lawyers do have ample social and cultural capital, the essential components needed to combat the opportunity gap, which positions them well to help our kids, real constraints notwithstanding.

Notably, while all lawyers, and lawyers as a class, possess ample social and cultural capital, context would matter greatly in how different lawyers go about living up to their duty as public citizens to help our kids. To begin, consider lawyers populating the individual hemisphere. Some, for example, rural lawyers, may be well-positioned to play the role of mentors to kids, their parents and local communities. As Lisa Pruitt and Bradley Showman document, rural lawyers are "also neighbors, acquaintances, and even friends or family," who benefit from "familiarity and visibility" that may allow them to build the trust needed to act as mentors and overcome the culture of law avoidance and suspicion of lawyers common in rural communities. On the other hand, rural lawyers' very position within their communities imposes on them "accompanying accountability," while dealing with the significant challenges of the economic viability of their law practices, which forces understandable constraints on the time resources rural attorneys can dedicate to their role as public citizens.

Other individual hemisphere attorneys, such as lawyers practicing in exurbia or in the metropolitan periphery, may be well-positioned to mentor and help build capital for kids from both dense metropolitan areas and the suburbs. Yet relative geographical proximity and more stable law practices compared with their rural counterparts notwithstanding, solo practitioners and attorneys from small law firms practicing in the metropolitan periphery may experience significant challenges establishing trusting relationships with kids and parents from large metropolitan areas, and may benefit from assistance from intermediary organizations, such as bar organizations.

Large law firms' attorneys, while bringing to the table the most resources, face imposing competitive pressures and billable expectations that may undercut commitments to acting as public citizens, and likely possess particular social and capital assets that may be suited for public citizenship other than in one-on-one interfaces with kids. At the same time, however, all lawyers must act as public citizens and help close the opportunity gap and the profession must guard against opting out by its most elite members.

Similarly, and perhaps more intuitively, the legal profession can and must make a difference with regard to the opportunity gap affecting our lawyers. Lawyers can reduce the opportunity gap by reaching out to potential law students in non-elite colleges, community colleges, and high schools or educating high school and college students from poorer backgrounds about the law, law schools, the admission process, and how to finance an increasingly expensive legal education. Once the less-affluent enter law schools, lawyers' contributions can again make all the difference in the world, providing access to information and experience about how to succeed in law school, how to pursue valuable extra-curricular activities, how to form valuable relationships, and how to identify and position oneself as a compelling candidate for a job after graduation. Moreover, lawyers can help poor law students invest in and build networks of relationships, which will help such students overcome the all-important deficit in social capital.

A significant body of work documents the role of social and cultural capital in lawyers' careers. Members of the legal profession can help colleagues who hail from disadvantaged backgrounds and who possess fewer capital assets close the opportunity gap by lending their social and cultural capital, for example, by serving as mentors, helping such lawyers build professional networks and by explaining and advising regarding the workings of the legal system and the legal profession. Indeed, some jurisdictions have recently begun to acknowledge and sponsor mentorship programs to support newcomers to the profession, and these programs can be expanded to acknowledge and encourage mentoring of lawyers who possess lesser capital endowments.

The legal profession is in the midst of experiencing a significant structural transformation against a background of increased competition. In a day and age in which many newcomers to the profession struggle to find a job and others struggle to keep their practices afloat, advocating a new robust — and admittedly imposing — role for lawyers as public citizens and officers of the legal system who contribute and share their social and cultural capital with our kids may seem counterintuitive to some members of the bar. Indeed, in the short-run, this new role and accompanying commitment may seem, and will be, imposing. Yet in the long-run active public citizenship is likely to be both rewarding and self-serving.

Notes

1. Professor Wald believes that lawyers, as public citizens, must actively fight inequality as mentors to underprivileged kids and underprivileged lawyers. Note that unlike Rule 8.4(g), which imposes nondiscrimination principles on lawyers' conduct while practicing law, Professor Wald advocates for duties imposed on lawyers outside of their practice. Yet such broad reach is not unprecedented under the Rules. For example, Rule 8.4(b) deems misconduct "a criminal act that reflects adversely on the lawyer's honesty, trustworthiness or fitness as a lawyer in other respects," and Rule 8.4(c) states that "conduct involving dishonesty, fraud, deceit or misrepresentation," including conduct unrelated to the practice of law, constitutes professional misconduct.

[handwritten: Holding]

2. In his book *Between the World and Me* (2016), public intellectual Ta-Nehisi Coates asserts that injustice prevails in the U.S. because while Caucasians get a chance to pursue the American Dream, "[f]ear is omnipresent for blacks." Injustice, however, is not merely the result of individual indifference to the fear of blacks. Rather, such injustice is necessary to maintain the Dream: "[t]he Dreamers accept this as the cost of doing business, accept our bodies as currency. . . . Our bodies have refinanced the Dream of being white." Indeed, "[t]he forgetting is habit, is yet another necessary component of the Dream. . . . They have forgotten, because to remember would tumble them out of the beautiful Dream and force them to live down here with us, down here in the world." And so fears are left unquestioned. As a result, "[s]ome of us make it out. But the game is played with loaded dice . . . ." "I felt myself to be among the survivors of some great natural disaster." Id. at 14, 131–32, 143, 124.

[handwritten: → Injustice is needed to pursue the US Dream.]

Justice, asserts Coates, requires constant use of the tools of questioning. It demands being "politically conscious" as a state of being. Equality for all means an ongoing individualized critical scrutiny of hierarchy, of feeling "discomfort" with every dream. Such questioning and critical scrutiny, struggling against the Dream, has a meaning, argues Coates. Indeed, it is *the* meaning. The hope of having a just society depends on our ability "to awake the Dreamers, to rouse them to the facts of what their need to be white . . . [h]as done to the world." Justice depends on our ability to wake up, to question our Dream and overcome our fears. Id. at 29–30, 34, 53, 69, 71, 146.

[handwritten: Justice demands political conscious ↓ It depends on our ability to Q the Dream.]

That Ta-Nehisi Coates explores injustice in America and does not even mention lawyers is arguably a sad statement about how irrelevant lawyers have become to the cause of justice. Yet members of the legal profession, who define their calling as public citizens having a special responsibility to the quality of justice, can prove Coates wrong. Justice requires ongoing individualized critical scrutiny of hierarchy and lawyers as public citizens can model and teach such critical scrutiny.

While Coates, in his exploration of injustice in America, does not mention the role of lawyers, shouldn't members of the legal profession, who proclaim their role as public citizens, have a special responsibility to examine critically (and to educate the public about) the quality of justice, however they define it?

C. Lawyers' Obligations to Legal Institutions

David B. Wilkins & Eli Wald
The Fourth Responsibility

(forthcoming 2017)

"A lawyer," states the American Bar Association Model Rules of Professional Conduct ("Rules"), "is a representative of clients, an officer of the legal system and a public citizen having special responsibility for the quality of justice." These three traditional core responsibilities of lawyers, to clients, the legal system and the public, neglect, however, to discuss any duty owed by lawyers to legal institutions, such as law firms, governmental agencies, and in-house legal departments, and a corresponding duty owed by legal institutions to their lawyers. This is a significant oversight because for many lawyers legal institutions shape and inform their conduct and are the constituent with which they interact most often and most extensively professionally. The failure to identify any responsibility owed to firms and a corresponding duty they owe their lawyers sends the implied and misleading message that lawyers owe the institutions in which they practice no such duty.

The Fourth Responsibility

Duties of Lawyers to their Firm

Lawyers have responsibilities to the institution in which they work. These responsibilities have two bases: lawyers' role as professionals, which imposes on lawyers certain duties; and lawyers' role as agents of law firms. Some of the duties of lawyers to their firm are both intuitive and uncontroversial. Lawyers owe their firm a (thin) duty of loyalty, to avoid acting in ways contrary to the best interests of the firm. . . . Next, because lawyers' efforts, work ethos and quality of work are relatively hard to directly monitor at least in the short-run, as opposed to their input in terms of billable hours, lawyers owe their firm a duty to avoid shirking and meet billable expectancies and other firm specified objectives in good faith. Law firms are not without recourse if they perceive that their lawyers are shirking. Firms may withhold bonuses for underperforming attorneys and may of course terminate shirking lawyers. . . . Lawyers also owe their firm a duty to act competently.

In addition to these intuitive duties, lawyers owe their firm a responsibility to reasonably contribute to the firm's human capital and its culture. Contributing to the firm's human capital includes, for partners, training and mentoring junior lawyers, as well as sharing with more junior partners and senior associates business development opportunities and assets, including referrals and gradual transfer of client relationships. For associates, the duty includes training and respectfully working with staff attorneys as well as investing, as a mentee, in relationships with more senior firm lawyers and in getting to know other firm lawyers and staff.

Contributions to firm culture include service on firm committees, such as hiring, promotion, diversity and management committees (this is especially important in the case of powerful partners and rainmakers), participating in firm sponsored events, and volunteering on behalf of the firm. For partners, support of firm culture includes learning about colleagues' work and offering feedback, and actively participating in group and departmental meetings as well as in firm retreats. For all firm lawyers and staff, the duty to contribute to firm culture includes acting with civility, indeed, being nice to colleagues. Because the firm is the place where many lawyers spend so much time, civility and courtesy in the workplace are of particular significance. It is also important exactly because not all partners can and will invest equally in the culture of the firm, not only because they are busy developing business and billing but also because of competing personal and familial obligations. Yet, especially those who invest less in firm culture must be visibly courteous.

Of course, we are not naïve about the decline of training, mentoring and substantive evaluations at large law firms, nor about the declined ability and inclination of firms to reign in rainmakers who insufficiently contribute to the firm's human capital and culture, in a day and age in which firms are worried about star partners moving elsewhere. At the same time, we are mindful of the substantive and symbolic value of ensuring this very participation by star equity partners in terms of ensuring equality within the firm.

Even before the recent expansion of tiers and tracks, indeed even in the lockstep compensation era, not all large law firm partners were created equal, with some partners concentrating on rainmaking while others supporting their work, and we are not arguing that all firm lawyers must equally contribute to the firm's human capital and culture at all times. Yet we insist that not training, mentoring and evaluating members of one's legal institution, and failing to reasonably contribute to the firm culture is a betrayal of a professional responsibility. As a matter of understanding one's professional role and corresponding professional responsibilities, all firm lawyers owe the firm a responsibility—the fourth responsibility—to reasonably contribute to its human capital and culture. Failing to reasonably contribute is a breach of a professional duty, while still acknowledging that the meaning of reasonableness may vary depending on the circumstances.

Suppose an AM200 law firm has 200 partners. Our point is that all the firm's partners owe it a duty to contribute to its human capital and culture, including the 20–30 powerful rainmakers at the top. Yet, while the firm may creatively structure and accommodate the contributions of its top rainmakers, it is important not to lose sight of the remaining 170–80 partners who we insist owe a duty to the firm. If, for example, only a handful of partners, say 5–10, shoulder the burden of firm human capital and culture then the breach of the fourth responsibility is systemic. If a minority of contributing partners fulfills institutionally designated roles, such as the Pro Bono Coordinating Partner and the Diversity Partner, legitimizing the failure of all other partners to contribute to its capital and culture, then implicitly and unintentionally the firm may be aggravating the challenge by letting its partners off the hook too easily. Even worse, if the minority of contributing partners happens to disproportionally consist of women and minorities, the firm may be obscuring and collapsing different challenges—a universal duty to contribute to the firm's human capital and culture with a commitment to equality, diversity and inclusiveness.

Duties of a Firm to Its Lawyers

Transparency

Large law firm practice has become more transparent. Firms' salaries are often a matter of public record, and so is information about firms' various tracks (although in recent years some firms have refused to share information about, for example, the gender breakdown of their various partnership tiers). Staff attorneys, associates, of counsel and partners at firms usually have, at least formally, a solid grasp of their position and role, institutional expectations and targets, and prospects for retention and promotion. Rich scholarship supplements formal knowledge, breaking down firms' complex practice realities and explaining in context the practical imperatives of social capital (mentoring), cultural capital (training) and identity capital.

Yet, core aspects of firms' hiring, evaluation, retention and promotion policies and practices remain opaque and inaccessible. In particular, there is a gap between formal policies and practical realities, with the less savvy left to fend for themselves. Consider hiring practices. Entry-level associates usually know the size of their class, the department they will work for, and the formal billable targets as well as formal career development markers. They do not know, however, how many partners the firm expects to make at the end of their probation period (nor is relevant past information readily available), details about the workflow within their departments, how work will be assigned and monitored to them and their counterparts over time and what are some of the implicit cultural expectations within and outside their departments. Some of this information can be observed and gathered before joining and while at the firm but astute associates may have a significant advantage accumulating and acting on this knowledge compared to the less savvy outsiders.

Evaluations, retention and promotion policies and realities are no less opaque. Associates and partners are likely to be aware of formal policies but access to valuable informal information varies greatly, such as whether one is actually making sufficient progress on one's track, how specifically to improve on weaknesses and whether such improvements are likely to suffice, and whether one's mentors occupy a position of power and influence within the department and at the firm to help effectuate future promotion. Notably, relative gaps in possession of material information are as important here as absolute gaps. That is, some firms are more forthcoming than others in terms of sharing or restricting access to proprietary information, yet irrespective of a particular firm's stance, some tend to have better access to information than others.

Moreover, some information may be quite hard to collect and process. BigLaw has long made diversity a priority in terms of both hiring and promotion, yet its commodification of its lawyers' identity capital has mostly been implicit and difficult to assess. Latina associate has been hired by a large law firm. Have diversity priorities played any role in the hiring decision? If so, to what extent? And does the firm have any expectations regarding associate's identity work? These and related questions are never addressed to the determent of the firm and its lawyers. Lack of transparency may lead to compromised self-esteem, underperformance, speculation and stereotyping.

Law firms' fourth responsibility includes a duty to act transparently, and their duty of transparency to their lawyers consists of two components. Substantive transparency would provide lawyers with as much information as possible about why they were hired, including perceived strengths and weaknesses, informal institutional expectations and career development markers and means of pursuing them, and gradual access to information about firm practice realities, politics and culture. For example, some law firms engage, to varying degrees of formality, in seeding and ranking of their lawyers based on factors such as billable expectancies, participation in high-profile matters and profitability. Routine dissemination of such information may allow firm lawyers to monitor their progress and take steps to proactively manage their career trajectory and prospects. As importantly, law firms must mind relative transparency, ensuring that whatever level of substantive transparency they adopt, they provide equal access to information to all their lawyers.

Fair Shot / Equal Opportunity for All

Law firms' fourth responsibility to their lawyers includes a duty to give all lawyers a fair shot at succeeding within their ranks. This used to mean, in the days of explicit discrimination, equal treatment, that is, a commitment to assess the work product of all lawyers based on merit and to treat all lawyers equally in terms of access to high quality assignments irrespective of one's identity and personal traits. But today a commitment to equality must mean a move from difference blindness to bias-awareness, and extending equal opportunity to all, with regard to retention, evaluation, distribution of work, and promotion.

To begin with, firms must ensure that early on all of their lawyers receive an equal opportunity to experience similar work loads and quality assignments. Of course, firms' organic workflow will play a significant role in specific work assignments in any given point in time. But firms must be sensitive to the fact that lawyers equipped with better relationships and knowledge about firms' inner-workings will tend to secure over time more and better work assignments. Thus, a difference blindness/ equal treatment approach, for example, formally assigning all entry-level associates a certain mix of matters over a set timeframe may be unfair. Instead, firms ought to monitor the actual workflow of their associates to ensure that the less savvy receive equal opportunities to develop their professional skills.

Similarly, subjecting all firm lawyers to the same formal evaluation policies, an example of equal treatment, ignores our growing body of knowledge about systematic and pervasive biases in assessment, disproportionately and negatively affecting women and minority lawyers. Instead, in addition to effectively and repeatedly educating all firm lawyers about reducing instances and the impact of implicit bias, firms ought to develop equal opportunity assessment and evaluation tools that mitigate the impact of implicit bias on evaluations.

Relatedly, firms must carefully monitor the allocation of their training and mentoring resources to ensure equal opportunity for all lawyers. Once again, alluring equal treatment policies might result in counter-intuitive and unintended consequences. For example, random assignment of formal mentors to new lawyers based on the availability of partners and senior associates in the department ignores the reality that associates possessing superior endowments of social and cultural capital will tend over time to acquire more powerful mentors. As importantly, the pairing up of associates with partners based on affinity and personal identity traits, while well-intentioned and an example of bias-awareness may at the same time ignore the impact of social and cultural capital and the ability of the savvy to secure powerful mentors irrespective of personal identity traits. Instead, firms ought to match lawyers with lesser capital assets with their most powerful partners not only as formal mentors but in assignments to ensure that all firm lawyers enjoy a fair shot and an equal opportunity to succeed.

This, to be clear, does not mean that every staff lawyer must be given a shot as an associate or that every salaried partner must be promoted to equity partner if they only work hard enough. Nor does it mean that firms cannot seed and track, or gradually acknowledge and act on merit, assessing work product. But it does mean that law firms owe their lawyers a duty of giving everybody an equal opportunity to succeed, grounded in transparency.

Thus, for example, a Latina associate who is hired in part based on her identity capital and the diversity benefit to the firm ought to be made aware of the weight identity capital played in her hiring decision and be given a fair and equal opportunity to succeed at the firm. If associate has lower endowments of social and cultural capital compared with her white male counterparts, she ought to be given opportunities to acquire and develop capital assets such that she can be assessed and evaluated over time on equal terms with other associates. Such capital opportunities include equal opportunity access to powerful mentors and workload.

In turn, providing all lawyers equal opportunities to develop capital assets means that firms must assess, record and act according to the various capital endowments of their lawyers. Firms committed to giving all of their lawyers a fair shot at success and to retaining and promoting the best lawyers must acknowledge the interplay of merit and capital and do their best to provide all lawyers opportunities to acquire and develop the requisite capital assets for success.

Culture and Ethical Infrastructure

Evolving doctrines of Corporate Social Responsibility are premised on the realization that powerful corporations have duties to the public, the public interest, the communities where they do business, their neighbors, customers and their employees. More generally, analysis of the institutional duties of entities recognizes the role of institutions such as law firms in the lives of their clients, lawyers and the legal profession. The fourth responsibility, encompassing a duty to build and maintain an appropriate ethical infrastructure and firm culture, similarly recognizes that given the dominant role law firms play in the professional and personal lives of their lawyers, firms have a duty with regard to offering a suitable ethical infrastructure and culture. We argue that because of the ways in which law firms' ethical infrastructure and culture shape and inform the conduct, professional and personal, of their lawyers, law firms owe their lawyers a duty to build and maintain appropriate ethical infrastructure and culture.

Furthermore, such a duty acknowledges that firm lawyers may otherwise have a hard time living up to their obligations as officers of the legal system and public citizens without the firm's assistance, for example, with pro bono. Put differently, as individual attorneys, firm lawyers have duties as officers of the legal system and as public citizens, obligations they may have a hard time meeting as individuals because of competing commitments to the firm and its clients.

In this context, the firm has a duty to its lawyers to offer an ethical infrastructure and culture that not only avoids standing in the way of such individual professional commitments but affirmatively assists firm lawyers to meet their professional obligations.

As public citizens, lawyers owe a special responsibility for the quality of justice. Law firms' duty to justice is thus a derivative duty to the quality of justice originating from the duty of their lawyers and owed to their lawyers, a duty to foster a culture that will allow lawyers to live up to their special responsibility to the quality of justice. In addition, as professional entities, law firms owe a direct duty to the quality of justice in addition to their duty to their lawyers. Thus, law firms' culture must embody a commitment to justice, including, but not limited to pro bono, equality, diversity, and inclusiveness.

Specifically, we argue that in addition to self-interested diversity arguments (the so-called business case for diversity), and general moral arguments in favor of diversity (it's the right thing to do), law firms have an obligation to pursue diversity that is grounded in their responsibility to their lawyers to offer and maintain a culture that helps realize the duties of individual lawyers to justice, equality and diversity. For example, firms must ensure that powerful partners serve on their diversity committees, such that associates (minority and others) who are asked to serve on it have a meaningful opportunity to form mentorships with powerful partners. And firms must develop visible policies that encourage and reward their lawyers who contribute to their culture.

Moreover, firms must put in place policies that incentivize all lawyers to contribute and disincentivize ignoring firm culture. More generally, a firm has a duty to ensure that its culture respects and effectuates its commitment to justice, equality, diversity and inclusiveness.

Next, firms' fourth responsibility includes a commitment to invest in its lawyers' human capital and ensure that all of its lawyers contribute to it. A culture that regards training and mentoring as its cornerstone, a manifestation of the firm's professional responsibility to its lawyers, and that demands it from all of its members stands a better chance at combating the well-documented decline of mentoring and training at BigLaw.

Of course, different firms will have different cultures, and all cultures will reflect a strong commitment to client service and maximizing the financial bottom line of the firm and its members. Importantly, however, we insist that training and mentoring, as well as a firm's more general commitment to the human capital of its lawyers and its culture is not and cannot be thought of as an afterthought or a charitable, voluntary feature that may be sacrificed or downsized at will in competitive economic times. Rather, commitments to human capital and firm culture, mentoring and training included, are part of the professional responsibility law firms owe their lawyers.

Conclusion

In contemporary law practice, a lawyer is not only a representative of clients, an officer of the legal system and a public citizen, but also a member of legal institutions. A lawyer's practice, as well as exercise of professional judgment, is shaped and formed by firms, and, in turn, informs and impacts firms' performance and culture. This symbiotic relationship entails corresponding duties — the fourth responsibility. Law firms and their lawyers have long acknowledged, informally, the fourth responsibility, in the form of thick fiduciary duties of loyalty. But, as traditional informal fiduciary duties decline, a more formal fourth responsibility that reflects the relationship between legal institutions and their lawyers must be recognized.

Notes

1. Professors Wilkins and Wald advance the notion of a fourth responsibility (in addition to a lawyer's traditional three responsibilities to clients, the legal system and the public) owed to legal institutions, such as law firms. What responsibilities, if any, do government lawyers owe the institutions in which they practice? Do in-house lawyers owe a fourth responsibility? If so, is the duty owed to the legal in-house department or to the employer-entity?

2. Do solo practitioners who practice in a law firm of one owe a duty to the institution? What is the nature of the duty? Is it akin to the duty of officers and directors

in closely held corporations to maintain the separate and distinct legal identity of the entities to avoid having courts pierce the corporate veil?

D. Conflicting Obligations

Taking seriously lawyers' obligations as officers of the legal system and as public citizens must entail acknowledging the possibility that those obligations may conflict with lawyers' obligations to clients. The Rules state that "[i]n the nature of law practice . . . conflicting responsibilities are encountered. Virtually all difficult ethical problems arise from conflict between a lawyer's responsibilities to clients, to the legal system and to the lawyer's own interest in remaining an ethical person while earning a satisfactory living."

Resolving such conflicting obligations when they do arise is a daunting challenge. The Rules note, somewhat unhelpfully, that such conflicts "must be resolved through the exercise of sensitive professional and moral judgment guided by the basic principles underlying the Rules. These principles include the lawyer's obligation zealously to protect and pursue a client's legitimate interests, within the bounds of the law, while maintaining a professional, courteous and civil attitude toward all persons involved in the legal system." In practice, these conflicts are often resolved in favor of clients, revealing an understanding of lawyers' role as predominantly representatives of clients. In the exchange below, David Dudley Field, one of the outstanding lawyers of his era, advances this very understanding in this debate that took place over 145 years ago between himself and his son Dudley on one side and Samuel Bowles, one of the leading newspaper publishers of the nineteenth century, on the other. The issue was Field's representation of James Fisk and Jay Gould, well-known figures in several celebrated market manipulations in the 1860s and 1870s.

The Lawyer and his Clients:
Correspondence of Messrs. David Dudley and Dudley Field
of the New York Bar,
with Mr. Samuel Bowles, of the Springfield Republican*
[privately printed 1871]

I. DAVID DUDLEY FIELD TO SAMUEL BOWLES

December 27, 1870.

Dear Sir:

I address you thus, taking it for granted that the scurrilous attack upon me in the form of a letter, published in a late number of the Springfield Republican, was inserted

---

* A more complete version was printed in the first and second editions of this work.

without your consent or knowledge. Allow me to call your attention to this attack, and ask you for a public disavowal of it. . . .

Yours very truly,
David Dudley Field

IV. SAMUEL BOWLES TO DUDLEY FIELD (SON)

December 29, 1870.

Dear Sir: . . .

. . . [T]he Republican had long ago maintained, and applied to cases in Massachusetts, the doctrine that a lawyer was responsible, in a decided degree, for the character of his clients and the character of the suits which he undertook in their behalf; and I believe your professional conduct is more open to criticism, in this respect, than that of your father. If he is no more guilty than other prominent gentlemen of the New York bar, so much the worse for the New York bar. But whether correctly or not, the public have identified your father especially with the more desperate and notorious causes of your distinguished Erie clients, and are disposed, it would seem, to concentrate upon him a responsibility, which, perhaps, should be shared, in some degree, by others. . . .

Yours very truly and very gratefully,
Samuel Bowles

V. DAVID DUDLEY FIELD TO SAMUEL BOWLES

December 30, 1870.

Dear Sir:

Your letter of the 29th, in answer to mine of the 27th, was received this morning. . . .

You assail me for what you call my "professional association with notorious parties, [Messrs. Gould and Fisk] with generally conceded corrupt schemes." Your meaning is cloudy, since I am not sure whether it be that I have a professional association with notorious parties who have "generally conceded corrupt schemes," or a "professional association with notorious parties" and also "with generally concealed corrupt schemes." . . . I must ask you what you mean by "professional association." Is it giving them legal opinions and arguing cases for them in court? Or is it something else? If it be something else, I must ask you what that something is, as I do not know. If it be only giving them legal opinions, and arguing cases for them, all that I need say is, that I have done not only what I had a right, but what I was bound to do. If, in giving an opinion, I have perverted or misunderstood the law, point out the instance, and I will admit myself wrong. If, in arguing a cause, I have suppressed evidence or misled the court, point out an instance of that also, and I will again admit myself wrong. I deny that I have done any of these things in any one instance. If you say I have, mention the instance, or admit yourself a false accuser.

You must realize that a lawyer, who is denied the shelter of his professional character, is necessarily put to great disadvantage. His communications with his client are confidential. He cannot in most cases say what advice he has given, because he cannot disclose the information which his client has given him. In that respect his lips are sealed. . . .

The storm of abuse, that is poured upon me, is really, however designed, an attack upon the independence of the bar. Such abuse of an advocate is not a new thing in the world. They who hate a client fancy, in their folly, that if they can frighten his advocate, they may destroy the client, not reflecting that they would thus weaken their own security. When Erskine, defending Thomas Paine, rose to address the jury, he said: "Every man, within hearing at this moment, nay, the whole people of England, have been witnesses to the calumnious clamor, that by every art has been raised against me. In every place, where business or pleasure collects the public together, day after day my name and character have been the topics of injurious reflection." "And for what?" he asked, and thereupon replied that it was due to the fact that he had not shrunk from the discharge of a duty "which no personal advantages recommended and which a thousand difficulties repelled." Then he boldly vindicated himself, saying, "I will forever, at all hazards, assert the dignity, independence and integrity of the English bar, without which impartial justice, the most valuable part of the English constitution, can have no existence." Do not mistake me by supposing that I am likening myself to Erskine, or my clients to Paine. I am stating a principle in better terms than I can state it myself.

I am not insensible to the respect of my fellow-men, and especially of my fellow members of the bar, who are in the main a noble but much calumniated body of men; but I value still more my own self-respect, and if I were to be driven by clamor or by any means whatever short of absolute force to abandon my clients, I should lose my self-respect. That I will not do, be the consequences what they may. I am resolved, that so far as I am able to effect it, my clients shall be judged according to the law of the land. I shall, whenever I speak for them in the courts of the country, stand between them and popular clamor, just as I would stand between them and power, if they were menaced by power of any kind, monarchical or republican. I have never cared for popularity. I have met many a scowl in my day; as when I defended the fugitive slave, or when I inveighed against arrests without legal warrant, under color of the war power, or when I denied the legality of test oaths, or argued against the constitutionality of the military governments in the South. . . .

Very truly yours,
David Dudley Field

VI. SAMUEL BOWLES TO DAVID DUDLEY FIELD

January 3, 1871.

Dear Sir: . . .

[Y]our . . . position . . . certainly, is entitled to every possible respect; and I have neither the disposition nor the power to criticise it in detail. I have "walked

backward with averted eyes" through much of the history of your professional association with those notorious clients that have dragged down your professional
fame;—and I cannot measure the precise extent or character of the services you have
rendered them. I can only say, my judgment has been formed from the general observation of your name in connection with their most desperate causes, and with some
of the more extraordinary proceedings which have been had in their behalf in the
New York courts,—as well as from the testimony of some of the local public journals, and of prominent members of your local bar;—as likewise, further, from gentlemen of your profession in this state,—any of whom would naturally watch the
details with greater closeness and discrimination, than either my ability or inclination allowed. I am glad that you are able to satisfy yourself of the propriety of your
conduct,—I hope you may be able to satisfy your friends, your profession and the
public. But I must tell you, frankly, that if you are right, they are widely and deeply
wrong, and you are one of the most misunderstood and best abused men in the
country. . . .

The province of professional duty, to causes and to clients, is, I believe, an open
question among lawyers themselves. Even the principles of it have never been stated
to general acceptance; but it is much easier to agree upon a principle than to decide
upon practice under it. Perhaps none would dispute the statements of Erskine. Certainly posterity honors him for the defense of a man, who was arraigned for opinions on abstract questions. But your clients, for whom you have incurred deep
responsibilities and dared professional dishonor, are no martyrs to opinions, and are
not arraigned for a bold adherence to, and publication of, unpopular principles. Their
offenses are against the peace and integrity of business. They have achieved and hold
possession of a railroad by means little short of robbery itself. They have sought, for
mere purposes of personal aggrandizement, to corrupt the very health of the nation.
And they have, with like purposes in view, brought temporary disorder into the
financial condition of the country, and spread ruin, with a wanton hand, among its
people. It is in assisting or defending these men in such plans and in such operations; in bestowing the forms and technicalities of law to sustain them in their
positions, or to screen them from justice; it is in lending your great ability and your
legal knowledge, either to the concoction or the defense of gross schemes of stock
speculation or railroad and business aggrandizement, at the expense of innocent
parties and the public; it is in interposing yourself and your professional services,
between men, whom the nation supposes, rightly or wrongly, aye *believes*, with a
faith that cannot be readily shaken, are men of public corruption and men of business dishonor,—between such men and their dispossession of their ill-gotten gains
and power, and the relief of the business of the country from such paralyzing control and corrupting example;—it is for acts and influences like these, that you have
been arraigned before the public, and that not only professional but popular opinion sits in judgment upon you. . . .

I am, sir, yours very truly,
Samuel Bowles

VII. DAVID DUDLEY FIELD TO SAMUEL BOWLES

January 5, 1871.

Dear Sir:

In this state of things I know no better general rule than this: that the lawyer, being intrusted by government with the exclusive function of representing litigants before the courts, is bound to represent any person who has any rights to be asserted or defended. If a person has no rights, the lawyer is not bound to assist. If he has any rights, the lawyer is bound to see them respected if he can. Let me apply this rule to . . . my clients. . . . Suppose them . . . to be guilty of all the wrongs you charge them with, have they still no rights? If a ruffian beats one of them in the street, may he be sued for it? If he utter a falsehood concerning them, may he be prosecuted? Or suppose one, who has a spite against them, to buy a share or two of stock in the Erie railway company for the purpose of harassing them with a lawsuit, is it lawful to defend them against such a suit? Or suppose a speculator, who has sold stocks on time, to bring a suit, for the purpose of affecting the price, may such a suit be resisted? Or suppose an enemy, unwilling to take the responsibility himself, brings forward a third person, to bring suits against them, and keep them in continued litigation, for the gratification of revenge, are these suits to go on without resistance? Or suppose them to have enough of the stock of a corporation to give them the majority at an election, and the managers to manufacture secretly new stock to overcome their majority, using the property of the company to pay for it, and making away with the books to complete the secrecy,—must the wrong be acquiesced in and redress by the courts given up? Or suppose still further, that actions are brought against them for damages on alleged sales of gold, which they say they never bought, is it unprofessional to put in their answers and try the causes for them? These are not imaginary cases. They are mainly real cases for engaging in which I am assailed. . . .

Let us look at the question from another point of view. It is lawful to advocate what it is lawful to do. Would you have a judge decide against these men, because he thinks them of bad repute or of bad lives or of evil example? What would you think of him if, in pronouncing judgment, he were to say, I do not think the proof sustains the charges of this complaint, but the defendants are outraging decency and corrupting justice, and I shall decide against them? Nay, suppose you were a juror, trying one of the suits for damages on alleged gold contracts, would you violate your oath and find a verdict against them, contrary to the evidence, because they "have sought, for mere purposes of personal aggrandizement, to corrupt the very head of the nation," or because "they have, with like purposes in view, brought temporary disorder into the financial condition of the country, and spread ruin with a wanton hand among its people"? Of course you answer, that you are not a knave or a dog, that you should do this thing. But how in the name of all that is reconcilable, are you to be informed of the real case before you, if nobody may explain it to you; how is the evidence to be forthcoming, if they cannot have the aid of the law in obtaining it; how are they to get the facts fairly before you, if they are denied the privilege of counsel?

. . . Let me tell you that you had better at once confess yourself wrong, and accept the theory that the lawyer is responsible, not for his clients, nor for their causes, but for the manner in which he conducts their causes. Here I admit the fullest responsibility. I do not assert to the theory of Brougham that the lawyer should know nobody but his client. I insist that he should defend his client per fas and not per nefas. By this rule, I am willing to be judged. . . . You applaud Erskine. Yet he defended a man who was believed by nearly the whole people of England to be undermining the foundations of religion and all morality, aiming to subvert the throne and blot out the name of God. All that Messrs Gould and Fisk are charged with is as nothing, in quality or in consequence, compared with what he was charged with. His advocate was denounced, hunted, dismissed from office, for defending him. Now you say, "posterity honors him for the defense." . . .

Your obedient servant,
David Dudley Field

VIII. SAMUEL BOWLES TO DAVID DUDLEY FIELD

January 10, 1871.

My Dear Sir:

I have read with profound attention yours of the 5th, received yesterday in the hope to find some reason for the modification of my judgment in the matter between us, even if not to "confess myself wrong." But I am utterly unable to do so. I am only impressed with the fact that you believe yourself right, and that you are acting sincerely, if not intelligently. But the grounds of your action, as of your defense, seem to me purely technical and altogether narrow. They do not reach the question, as it lies in my mind, and as it presents itself to the mind of the great public. It is not a question of law, or even of abstract individual right, but of a broad public morality. You have sinned against no statute; I will not undertake to say, even, that you have violated any prescript of the code professional. Within those lines you are wiser than I, and I shall not follow you. But that you have offended the moral sense of the public, — that is what I insist upon, is what, in my duty as a journalist, I have proclaimed to the public. If I am wrong, it is simply in reading wrongly the public judgment, — in transcribing incorrectly its verdict. Time and the developments of public testimony will judge between us here.

Thus I dismiss the most of your argument as purely technical, and not pertinent to my view of the subject. Still, let me say, that your assumption that your clients are not to suffer for their bad character is neither good law nor good sense. Hardly a cause is tried, where the character of the parties for good or bad is not an element in the argument of the counsel, in the opinion of the judge, in the conclusion of the jury. It should, if it does not, go back to the assumption of the case by the counsel. A man *should* suffer for his bad character, as he should gain for his good character; and nothing more convinces me of the perverted views, which you take of your conduct and of the province of your professional duty, than your more than ignoring this consideration,—your denial of it. . . .

I am yours very truly,
Samuel Bowles

IX. DUDLEY FIELD (SON) TO SAMUEL BOWLES

January 9, 1871.

Dear Sir: . . .

The rest of your letter amounts to this: . . .

Sixth,—That "The Republican has long ago maintained, and applied to cases in Massachusetts, the doctrine that a lawyer was responsible in a decided degree for the character of his clients and the character of the suits which he undertook in their behalf." . . . Shades of Webster, Choate and the numberless great Massachusetts advocates, that have passed away, defend us! Most of these men, whom Massachusetts delighted to honor, defended and prosecuted at divers times divers men accused of crime. When they represented the accused, and he was found guilty, did they share his guilt? When they represented the prosecution, and the accused was acquitted, did they share in the guilt of the wrongful prosecution? In almost all criminal prosecutions, there is a right and a wrong. In a large proportion of civil suits, there is also an absolute moral right and wrong. Where the right rests is determined by a jury, and upon your doctrine their verdict determines the moral character of the counsel for the defeated party. Now, as in almost all cases there are two lawyers, and as in all cases, where the jury do not disagree, there is a verdict one way or the other, and as every lawyer of any considerable practice loses and wins a number of cases each year, it follows that all lawyers must necessarily be wicked men. . . . If a lawyer on A.'s behalf brings an action against B. on a promissory note, and A. has been guilty of bigamy, the lawyer should go to the state prison, or, to put it in the most favorable terms for your theory, if on the trial B. proves that the note was procured by fraud, and defeats A., the lawyer is as guilty as A. . . .

Your obedient servant,
Dudley Field

Notes

1. The Field–Bowles controversy and correspondence has been commented on by George Martin in *Causes and Conflicts—The Centennial History of the Association of the Bar of the City of New York, 1870–1970*, at 55–56 (1970):

> Field was a man who loved controversy, and he rushed into this one. . . . After Field and his son, Dudley, had exchanged several letters apiece with Bowles, Field had the lot printed as a pamphlet, which he first distributed privately and then gave to the World to publish.

The letters debated the ancient question which, like the moon, is constantly renewed: Must a lawyer concern himself with the social and economic effects of his legal actions? Bowles argued in essence that Field had bad men as clients and that he helped them to rob the public; Field argued that he was not responsible for the character of his clients.

Field won the exchange, at least in the opinion of most lawyers, if only because many of them had themselves been employed at one time by Fisk, Gould, or the Erie Railroad. . . . On this particular issue, at least—the question of a lawyer's responsibility for the character of his client (which was taking Bowles's argument at its narrowest)—the bar as a whole, however, reluctantly was with Field.*

2. The Field–Bowles correspondence has also been dealt with in Michael Schudson, "Public, Private and Professional Lives," 21 Am. Leg. Hist. 191 (1977). Schudson sees the exchange as representing an older pre–Civil War view of professional morality represented by Bowles's view of the public responsibility of the professional and Field's movement toward a more neutral amoral professional position focusing on the private relationship between lawyer and client. More historical research is required to discuss the accuracy of his view of the pre–Civil War stance of the legal profession and of the dominance of the "neutral" view in the period since the Civil War. Schudson's view of the modern stance of the profession's rules finds support in Bellow & Kettleson, "The Mirror of Public Interest Ethics: Problems and Paradoxes," in *Professional Responsibility: A Guide for Attorneys*, 219, 258–265 (1978) and Schwartz, "The Missing Rule of Professional Conduct," 52 L.A. B. J. 10, 11–12, 15 (1976). For a view that modern professional rules still embody, albeit in somewhat obscured fashion, the tension between a professional devotion owed to a client and a professional responsibility owed to society, see Andrew Kaufman, "A Professional Agenda," 6 Hofstra L. Rev. 619, 621–623 (1978).

The articles referred to in the preceding paragraph were substantially based on the professional norms embodied in the Model Code. Obviously, a more complete study would require a careful look at other sources—the current Model Rules of Professional Conduct, court and ethics committee opinions, statutes, and most

---

* The problem is truly perennial. Several generations later, for example, writing of business and legal practice in the country after the Spanish–American War, Robert T. Swaine stated: "Holding companies, with inflated capitalizations top-heavy with debt, popped up like puffballs, controlling production and distribution in many industries, with little concern for the anti-trust laws. Those critics who ascribe to the corporate executives and bankers of the day and to their lawyers moral turpitude in these transactions are wrong, and unfairly so. Mistaken judgment there may have been—but not dishonesty or deliberate flouting of the law. As to lawyers, they did not regard the social and economic problems as theirs." Robert T. Swaine, *The Cravath Firm and Its Predecessors, 1819–1947* (New York, Ad Press Ltd., 1946), Vol 1, p. 667. But a large portion of the public would ask Swaine: Why not? Why don't lawyers regard the social and economic problems as theirs? Is a lawyer truly divisible? Does membership in the legal profession bestow a right to loose vicious dogs on the public? And the suspicion remains that many lawyers think as they do on this point because it is convenient for their pocketbooks.

important and most difficult to ascertain, the actual practice of lawyers. But the disciplinary rules are important in forming a judgment about the professional stance on the role of lawyers because they represent the one effort to make a comprehensive professional statement. Thus the text, for convenience, discusses the provisions of the "Model Rules." It is, however, also important to understand that when we talk about the stance of the "profession," we need to remember that while there is certainly a common approach to many, if not most, problems throughout the country, there are many important differences among the various jurisdictions. These are reflected in the different rules they have adopted, different answers given by courts and advisory ethics committees on particular issues, and different practices in different communities and different segments of the practice.

The tension between the professional devotion owed to clients and the professional responsibility to third parties, the profession, and society continues under the Model Rules, especially in the variety of forms in which they have been amended in the adopting jurisdictions. The materials in this book have commented rather heavily on aspects of the Rules where the primary focus is on duties to clients. But there are reminders of other responsibilities as well. See the Preamble to the Model Rules entitled "A Lawyer's Responsibilities," the discussion about objectives and means in Rule 1.2 and its Comment, and the requirement for, and purposes of, communication set forth in Rule 1.4. The lawyer's right to follow personal choices was specifically recognized in additions made to Rule 1.16, the section governing withdrawal, by the ABA in 1983. That section has been criticized for upsetting the delicate balance between confidentiality and disclosure recommended by the Kutak Commission by restricting the number of situations in which disclosure was possible. See Chapter 2. At the same time, however, the delegates widened greatly the lawyer's ability to withdraw. They added two situations to that portion of Rule 1.16(b) permitting withdrawal without the condition of lack of material adverse effect on the client's interest: (1) where the client has used the lawyer's services to perpetrate a crime or fraud, and, more importantly for this discussion, (2) where the client "insists upon pursuing an objective that the lawyer considers repugnant or imprudent." Whatever one may think of allowing withdrawal where a client has simply been "imprudent," allowing it when a client's conduct has been "repugnant" certainly bespeaks concern for the lawyer's personal moral integrity. When the Restatement of the Law Governing Lawyers was being drafted, there was debate over inclusion of a "repugnance" standard for withdrawal. A minority thought such a standard gave lawyers carte blanche to withdraw, but Section 32(3) permits withdrawal on such a basis.

The obvious question to ask with regard to these materials is whether each of us prefers the Bowles view or the Field view of the duty of the individual lawyer. Are there other positions that might be taken? Is there a difference between representation in the civil and in the criminal context? Between representation in connection with past events only and representation in connection with past events that have obvious future consequences, such as control of the Erie Railroad? If we assume that the machinations of Fisk and Gould were notorious, should that have imposed any additional duty of inquiry on Field? Does the nature of the inquiry as to duty change as the representations grow in number?

Chapter 8

Access to Legal Services:
The Traditional Model

This Chapter deals with the traditional model of access to legal services, pursuant to which legal services are delivered through the marketplace. Gideon v. Wainwright, 372 U.S. 335 (1963). The traditional model consists of two premises. As a default, clients pay for legal services; and those who cannot afford to pay for legal services are considered the exception to the rule, the marginalized afterthought. Both premises are problematic. Historically, the marketplace premise was never fully embraced. Lawyers were never thought of as mere service providers engaged in arm's length transactions with clients. Instead, as professionals, lawyers were thought of as special agents of clients, fiduciaries who owe their clients special duties. Moreover, law was never conceived as a mere service or commodity. Rather, it was and is still considered a public good, the delivery of which entails unique considerations and regulations. In addition, unlike ordinary markets, the practice of law was never fully open for competition. These issues concerning the delivery of legal services by lawyers are examined in Chapter 9. In the twenty-first century, approximately three-quarters of individual clients in the U.S. are priced out and cannot afford to pay for legal services. Yet three-quarters of Americans cannot be thought of as exceptions to the rule. Accordingly, Chapter 9 will revisit the traditional model and its treatment of those who cannot afford to pay for legal services.

A. Fees

While the traditional model embraces a market approach to the delivery of legal services, the approach is qualified by notions of professionalism. Lawyers are not conceived as mere service providers but rather as fiduciaries who owe special duties to clients. For example, whereas ordinary agents can charge clients whatever fees the market will bear, lawyers may only charge clients a reasonable fee. The basic rationale for Rule 1.5 is that setting the fee for legal services entails an inherent conflict of interest between attorney and client, and that addressing the conflict in a manner that acknowledges a lawyer's duty of loyalty to a client requires imposing a constraint—reasonableness—on the fee an attorney may charge. Moreover, the reasonableness constraint presumably embodies a commitment to providing access to legal services by keeping the fees at a reasonable and thus affordable level. Whether the Rules meet these professional objectives or whether they amount to mere self-interested rhetoric is debatable: the elements of Rule 1.5(a) do not construe reasonableness in terms of client affordability and, as we shall see, many individuals and small businesses are de facto priced out of the market for legal services.

Problem 8–1

You and Counsel were classmates in law school and assistant district attorneys together for two years in the local district attorney's office. The two of you have recently opened your own law office. One of the first items on your agenda for discussion of partnership business is the matter of criteria for charging fees. Neither of you has any experience in private practice; between you, you have isolated the following questions to be answered:

(a) Is it proper to ascertain from other attorneys in town the customary range of fees they charge for certain kinds of business? *yes, but should consider exp.*

(b) Do certain kinds of services—for example, real estate title closings, uncontested divorce proceedings—have something that more or less approximates a market worth?

(c) Is it also proper to take into account, in setting a fee, the overhead of a particular office?

(d) Should an attorney establish a basic hourly rate for his or her time—to be used in matters where billing is done at least partly on that basis, and as a guideline in other matters? How does the lawyer go about establishing such a rate? Should such a rate be seen as an estimate of the lawyer's own intrinsic worth, using other lawyers' hourly rates as a starting point? What factors determine a lawyer's "intrinsic worth"? Or should a lawyer project yearly overhead, desired net income, and then establish an hourly rate on the basis of a reasonable estimate of billable hours—perhaps after some experience with actual figures for a year or two?

(e) Is it appropriate for a lawyer who does a large amount of pro bono work to charge somewhat higher fees to his or her non–pro bono clients? What kind of disclosure should be made to the client about this practice? When?

(f) What kind of explanation ought a lawyer to make to a client about fees, and especially about the basis on which charges are set?

Problem 8–2

You are a partner in a large firm that has a highly specialized corporate acquisition practice. Corporation X has offered the firm a large annual retainer. Although Corporation X does not expect to require any legal work from your firm, it wants to prevent any corporation attempting to take it over from utilizing your firm's services. If any legal work were actually done for Corporation X by your firm, however, it would be billed against the retainer.

At a partnership meeting to discuss whether or not to accept the retainer, what position will you take? Does it matter to you whether there are a large number of corporations offering such a retainer instead of just Corporation X?

Problem 8–3

(a) Lawyers are representing a class of emotionally and mentally handicapped children who have been placed in the custody of state officials pursuant to state law. They are litigating a suit on behalf of the class, alleging that state officials have violated the class's federal constitutional rights because of a variety of deficiencies in the educational and health services provided to the class. One week before trial, after three years of pretrial discovery and endless negotiations, the defendants have put forth a settlement plan offering virtually everything requested in the complaint. The condition to the offer, however, is that lawyers agree to waive any fee to which they might be entitled pursuant to the Civil Rights Attorney's Fee Award Act of 1976. What should the lawyers do? Is it relevant that fee awards under the statute are made to the client, although for the benefit of the lawyer?

(b) Next time the lawyers agree to handle an action in which the Civil Rights Attorney's Fee Award Act is relevant, may they at the outset of the action have the client agree, with court approval if necessary, that the client will not bargain away the lawyer's fee to get a better substantive result?

The subject of fees affects access to the legal system in two ways. The availability of legal services is affected by the basic premise of our system that each party in a private dispute should pay its own counsel, in contrast to the British system, which provides that losers pay the costs, including attorneys' fees, of the winners. (Reforms in Great Britain now require a court awarding costs to consider, apart from who won, the conduct of all the parties with respect to the manner of pursuing their claims or asserting their defenses.) In certain situations, however, as a matter of equitable principle, a court may order payment of attorneys' fees out of a "common fund" involved in the litigation. See Dawson, "Lawyers and Involuntary Clients," 87 Harv. L. Rev. 1597 (1974), 88 Harv. L. Rev. 849 (1975). In a variety of other situations a court may order payment of attorneys' fees by one party to another as a matter either of statutory interpretation or of equitable doctrine. The number of federal statutes under which fee awards may be made has expanded greatly, probably exceeding one hundred. This combination of statute and equitable principles proceeded to the point where some commentators noted that our system was approaching the British system to a great extent. However, in Alyeska Pipeline Service Co. v. Wilderness Society, 421 U.S. 240 (1975), the Supreme Court cut back considerably on the ability of federal courts to order one party to pay the other's legal fees without statutory authority, except in a few well-defined situations. In those situations, however, the Court has still been sympathetic to the equitable notions underlying the common fund doctrine. See Boeing Co. v. Van Gemert, 444 U.S. 472 (1980). And after *Alyeska*, Congress enacted a very broad statute authorizing the award of a reasonable attorney's fee to the prevailing party in civil rights litigation, 42 U.S.C. § 1988. But the term "prevailing party" does not include the plaintiff whose lawsuit is the catalyst for change, but that change is accomplished without a final judgment or consent decree. Buckhannon Bd. & Care Home, Inc. v. West Va. Dep't of Health, 532 U.S.

598 (2001). See the 2007 Open Government Act, 5 U.S.C. § 552(a)(4)(E)(ii), reviving the catalyst doctrine in Freedom of Information Act cases.

The standards governing payment of fees to a successful plaintiff who is enforcing statutory policy against one who violated it are quite different from those applied in favor of a successful defendant. In the former case, fees are awarded in all cases except where payment would be unjust, Newman v. Piggie Park Enterprises, 390 U.S. 400 (1968), although in determining the amount of the award, the extent of the success is crucial. Hensley v. Eckerhart, 461 U.S. 424 (1983); Ruckelshaus v. Sierra Club, 463 U.S. 680 (1983). Indeed, under that formulation the Court has held that fees might be awarded against members of a state supreme court if they exercise enforcement as opposed to adjudicatory functions regarding discipline of lawyers, although it held that it was an abuse of discretion to award fees against them for acts of omission in their legislative function of promulgating a code of professional responsibility. Supreme Court of Virginia v. Consumers Union, 446 U.S. 719 (1980), on remand, 688 F.2d 218 (4th Cir. 1982) (affirming district court fee award against Virginia Supreme Court judges). Where it is a successful defendant, however, who is seeking an award of legal fees, the Court has held that an award is to be made only when the action brought is "frivolous, unreasonable, or without foundation." Christianburg Garment Co. v. E.E.O.C., 434 U.S. 412, 421 (1978). The Supreme Court has held, however, that if a vexatious lawsuit is knowingly brought, such an abuse of judicial process justifies a fee award even against plaintiff's attorneys. Roadway Express Co. v. Piper, 447 U.S. 752 (1980).

[handwritten margin notes: "Fees maybe awarded against state Supreme Ct. Judges."; "Claim frivolous, unreasonable, or w/o foundation → D can seek legal fees."; "↑ Abuse of Jud. resources by P lawyer."]

The arguments concerning who should bear the burden of fees have been canvassed thoroughly in legal literature. One article discussing the British and American rules, and pro-plaintiff and pro-defendant models, from an economic standpoint is Shavell, "Suit, Settlement, and Trial: A Theoretical Analysis Under Alternative Methods of Legal Costs," 11 J. Legal Stud. 55 (1982). Another piece discussing the conceptual underpinnings, or lack thereof, is Rowe, "The Legal Theory of Attorney Fee Shifting: A Critical Overview," 1982 Duke L.J. 651. These are important issues and if one wishes to pursue them, those two articles are worth reading at this point.

The size of lawyers' fees obviously affects access to legal services. Newspapers, magazines, and even books have discussed the subject, sometimes in sensational terms that highlight the seven- (or even eight-) figure fees that have been received by particular law firms from large corporations or as a result of victories in particular lawsuits. The settlement of major tobacco litigation produced claims for legal fees in the billions of dollars. The size of fees, especially those of the largest law firms, has played an important role in the strengthening of inside corporate law departments and in the parceling out of law business to many firms, often by competitive bidding, as a replacement for an older practice of very large companies, which used to rely on a single firm to provide a wide variety of services, including service on the company's board of directors. The conceptual underpinnings of the fee system and the payment of very large fees, however, raise issues that are quite different from the ordinary problems that lawyers' fees present to both lawyer and client. We will therefore take these issues up in Chapter 12.

A common situation for most lawyers involves a client who cannot pay the lawyer's charge easily, has difficulty appreciating the worth of the service performed, and is not overly happy about the necessity to pay for it. Another kind of size of fee problem was dealt with by the Supreme Court in Walters v. National Association of Radiation Survivors, 473 U.S. 305 (1985), upholding a Civil War statute that limited the fee of a lawyer who appeared before the Veterans Association in a matter relating to a service-connected disability claim to $10.

It is therefore understandable that one of the lawyer's most difficult tasks, perhaps the most difficult routine task, is the sending of a bill to a client. At that time, the lawyer must step out of the role of adviser-confidant and take what is essentially an adversary stand against the client. Moreover, the matter of the fee is typically a constant source of worry and irritation between attorney and client from the beginning to the very end of the relationship. Yet except in very standardized situations or in situations where a contingent fee is appropriate and agreed on, the uncertain nature of most legal services often makes it very difficult to give a client more than a very general notion of the possible range of the fee that will be involved. But see Model Rule 1.5(b).

Model Rule 1.5 sets out a series of factors to be kept in mind in fixing a fee. Recognizing the difficulty of setting fees, the provision obviously gives lawyers a great deal of discretion although, theoretically at least, it subjects the lawyer to disciplinary action for violation of the rule. Model Rule 1.5(a) has changed the standard for discipline from the "clearly excessive" fee of the Model Code to a fee that is not "reasonable." Several jurisdictions, however, have amended their Rule to use an "excessive" or "clearly excessive" standard. These jurisdictions do not mean to be understood as telling lawyers that they can charge an unreasonable fee so long as it is not excessive. The disciplinary standard doubtless does not change the substantive common law rule that requires lawyers' fees to be reasonable. It just leaves a little breathing room between a finding that a particular fee has crossed the line of reasonableness and the consequence that the lawyer has therefore committed a disciplinary violation. A case in which the theoretical possibility of discipline became actual follows.

In the Matter of Fordham

423 Mass. 481 (1996)

O'CONNOR, J. This is an appeal from the Board of Bar Overseers' (board's) dismissal of a petition for discipline filed by bar counsel against attorney Laurence S. Fordham. On March 11, 1992, bar counsel served Fordham with a petition for discipline alleging that Fordham had charged a clearly excessive fee in violation of S.J.C. Rule 3:07, DR 2-106, as appearing in 382 Mass. 772 (1981), for defending Timothy Clark (Timothy) in the District Court against a charge that he operated a motor vehicle while under the influence of intoxicating liquor (OUI) and against other related charges. Fordham moved that the board dismiss the petition and the board chair recommended that that be done. Bar counsel appealed from the chair's decision to the full board, and the board referred the matter to a hearing committee.

After five days of hearings, and with "serious reservations," the hearing committee concluded that Fordham's fee was not substantially in excess of a reasonable fee and that, therefore, the committee recommended against bar discipline. Bar counsel appealed from that determination to the board. By a vote of six to five, with one abstention, the board accepted the recommendation of the hearing committee and dismissed the petition for discipline. Bar counsel then filed . . . a claim of appeal from the board's action. . . .

We summarize the hearing committee's findings. On March 4, 1989, the Acton police department arrested Timothy, then twenty-one years old, and charged him with OUI, operating a motor vehicle after suspension, speeding, and operating an unregistered motor vehicle. At the time of the arrest, the police discovered a partially full quart of vodka in the vehicle. After failing a field sobriety test, Timothy was taken to the Acton police station where he submitted to two breathalyzer tests which registered .10 and .12 respectively.

Subsequent to Timothy's arraignment, he and his father, Laurence Clark (Clark) consulted with three lawyers, who offered to represent Timothy for fees between $3,000 and $10,000. Shortly after the arrest, Clark went to Fordham's home to service an alarm system which he had installed several years before. While there, Clark discussed Timothy's arrest with Fordham's wife who invited Clark to discuss the case with Fordham. Fordham then met with Clark and Timothy.

At this meeting, Timothy described the incidents leading to his arrest and the charges against him. Fordham, whom the hearing committee described as a "very experienced senior trial attorney with impressive credentials," told Clark and Timothy that he had never represented a client in a driving while under the influence case or in any criminal matter, and he had never tried a case in the District Court. The hearing committee found that "Fordham explained that although he lacked experience in this area, he was a knowledgeable and hard-working attorney and that he believed he could competently represent Timothy. Fordham described himself as 'efficient and economic in the use of [his] time.' . . .

"Towards the end of the meeting, Fordham told the Clarks that he worked on [a] time charge basis and that he billed monthly. . . . In other words, Fordham would calculate the amount of hours he and others in the firm worked on a matter each month and multiply it by the respective hourly rates. He also told the Clarks that he would engage others in his firm to prepare the case. Clark had indicated that he would pay Timothy's legal fees." After the meeting, Clark hired Fordham to represent Timothy.

According to the hearing committee's findings, Fordham filed four pretrial motions on Timothy's behalf, two of which were allowed. One motion, entitled

"Motion in Limine to Suppress Results of Breathalyzer Tests," was based on the theory that, although two breathalyzer tests were exactly .02 apart, they were not "within" .02 of one another as the regulations require. See 501 Code Mass. Regs. § 2.56(2) (1994). The hearing committee characterized the motion and its rationale as "a creative, if not novel, approach to suppression of breathalyzer results." Although the original trial date was June 20, 1989, the trial, which was before a judge without jury, was held on October 10 and October 19, 1989. The judge found Timothy not guilty of driving while under the influence.

Fordham sent the following bills to Clark:

1. April 19, 1989, $3,250 for services rendered in March, 1989.

2. May 15, 1989, $9,850 for services rendered in April, 1989.

3. June 19, 1989, $3,950 for services rendered in May, 1989.

4. July 13, 1989, $13,300 for services rendered in June, 1989.

5. October 13, 1989, $35,022.25 revised bill for services rendered from March 19 to June 30, 1989.

6. November 7, 1989, $15,000 for services rendered from July 1, 1989 to October 19, 1989.

The bills totaled $50,022.25, reflecting 227 hours of billed time, 153 hours of which were expended by Fordham and seventy-four of which were his associates' time. Clark did not pay the first two bills when they became due and expressed to Fordham his concern about their amount. Clark paid Fordham $10,000 on June 20, 1989. At that time, Fordham assured Clark that most of the work had been completed "other than taking [the case] to trial." Clark did not make any subsequent payments. Fordham requested Clark to sign a promissory note evidencing his debt to Fordham and, on October 7, 1989, Clark did so. In the October 13, 1989, bill, Fordham added a charge of $5,000 as a "retroactive increase" in fees. On November 7, 1989, after the case was completed, Fordham sent Clark a bill for $15,000.

Bar counsel and Fordham have stipulated that all the work billed by Fordham was actually done and that Fordham and his associates spent the time they claim to have spent. They also stipulated that Fordham acted conscientiously, diligently, and in good faith in representing Timothy and in his billing in this case. . . .

The board dismissed bar counsel's petition for discipline against Fordham because it determined, relying in large part on the findings and recommendations of the hearing committee, that Fordham's fee was not clearly excessive. Pursuant to S.J.C. Rule 3:07, DR 2-106(B), "a fee is clearly excessive when, after a review of the facts, a lawyer of ordinary prudence, experienced in the area of the law involved, would be left with a definite and firm conviction that the fee is substantially in excess of a reasonable fee." The rule proceeds to list eight factors to be considered in ascertaining the reasonableness of the fee:

(1) The time and labor required, the novelty and difficulty of the questions involved, and the skill requisite to perform the legal service properly.

(2) The likelihood, if apparent to the client, that the acceptance of the particular employment will preclude other employment by the lawyer.

(3) The fee customarily charged in the locality for similar legal services.

(4) The amount involved and the results obtained.

(5) The time limitations imposed by the client or by the circumstances.

(6) The nature and length of the professional relationship with the client.

(7) The experience, reputation, and ability of the lawyer or lawyers performing the services.

(8) Whether the fee is fixed or contingent.

In concluding that Fordham did not charge a clearly excessive fee, the board adopted, with limited exception, the hearing committee's report. The board's and the hearing committee's reasons for dismissing the petition are as follows: Bar counsel and Fordham stipulated that Fordham acted conscientiously, diligently, and in good faith in his representation of the client and his billing on the case. Although Fordham lacked experience in criminal law he is a "seasoned and well-respected civil lawyer." The more than 200 hours spent preparing the OUI case were necessary, "in part to educate [Fordham] in the relevant substantive law and court procedures," because he had never tried an OUI case or appeared in the District Court. The board noted that "although none of the experts who testified at the disciplinary hearing had ever heard of a fee in excess of $15,000 for a first-offense OUI case, the hearing committee found that [Clark] had entered into the transaction with open eyes after interviewing other lawyers with more experience in such matters." The board also thought significant that Clark "later acquiesced, despite mild expressions of concern, in [Fordham's] billing practices." Moreover, the Clarks specifically instructed Fordham that they would not consider a guilty plea by Timothy. Rather, they were interested only in pursuing the case to trial. Finally, Timothy obtained the result he sought: an acquittal.

Bar counsel contends that the board's decision to dismiss the petition for discipline is erroneous on three grounds: First, "the hearing committee and the Board committed error by analyzing only three of the factors set out in DR 2-106(B)(1)–(8), and their findings with regard to these criteria do not support their conclusion that the fee in this case was not clearly excessive"; second, the board "misinterpreted [DR 2-106's] prohibition against charging a clearly excessive fee by reading into the rule a 'safe harbor' provision"; and third, "by allowing client acquiescence as a complete defense."

In reviewing the hearing committee's and the board's analysis of the various factors, as appearing in DR 2-106(B), which are to be considered for a determination as to whether a fee is clearly excessive, we are mindful that, although not binding on this court, the findings and recommendations of the board are entitled to great weight. Matter of Hiss, 368 Mass. 447, 461 (1975). We are empowered, however, to review the board's findings and reach our own conclusion. Matter of Anderson, 416

Mass. 521, 525 (1993). In the instant case we are persuaded that the hearing committee's and the board's determinations that a clearly excessive fee was not charged are not warranted.

The first factor listed in DR 2-106(B) requires examining "the time and labor required, the novelty and difficulty of the questions involved, and the skill requisite to perform the legal service properly." Although the hearing committee determined that Fordham "spent a large number of hours on [the] matter, in essence learning from scratch what others . . . already know," it "[did] not credit Bar Counsel's argument that Fordham violated DR 2-106 by spending too many hours." The hearing committee reasoned that even if the number of hours Fordham "spent [were] wholly out of proportion" to the number of hours that a lawyer with experience in the trying of OUI cases would require, the committee was not required to conclude that the fee based on time spent was "clearly excessive." It was enough, the hearing committee concluded, that Clark instructed Fordham to pursue the case to trial, Fordham did so zealously and, as stipulated, Fordham spent the hours he billed in good faith and diligence. We disagree.

Four witnesses testified before the hearing committee as experts on OUI cases. One of the experts, testifying on behalf of bar counsel, opined that "the amount of time spent in this case is clearly excessive." He testified that there were no unusual circumstances in the OUI charge against Timothy and that it was a "standard operating under the influence case." The witness did agree that Fordham's argument for suppression of the breathalyzer test results, which was successful, was novel and would have justified additional time and labor. He also acknowledged that the acquittal was a good result; even with the suppression of the breathalyzer tests, he testified, the chances of an acquittal would have been "not likely at a bench trial." The witness estimated that it would have been necessary, for thorough preparation of the case including the novel breathalyzer suppression argument, to have billed twenty to thirty hours for preparation, not including trial time.

A second expert, testifying on behalf of bar counsel, expressed his belief that the issues presented in this case were not particularly difficult, nor novel, and that "the degree of skill required to defend a case such as this . . . was not that high." He did recognize, however, that the theory that Fordham utilized to suppress the breathalyzer tests was impressive and one of which he had previously never heard. Nonetheless, the witness concluded that "clearly there is no way that [he] could justify these kind of hours to do this kind of work." He estimated that an OUI case involving these types of issues would require sixteen hours of trial preparation and approximately fifteen hours of trial time. He testified that he had once spent ninety hours in connection with an OUI charge against a client that had resulted in a plea. The witness explained, however, that that case had involved a second offense OUI and that it was a case of first impression, in 1987, concerning new breathalyzer equipment and comparative breathalyzer tests.

An expert called by Fordham testified that the facts of Timothy's case presented a challenge and that without the suppression of the breathalyzer test results it would have been "an almost impossible situation in terms of prevailing on the trier of fact." He further stated that, based on the particulars in Timothy's case, he believed that Fordham's hours were not excessive and, in fact, he, the witness, would have spent a comparable amount of time. The witness later admitted, however, that within the past five years, the OUI cases which he had brought to trial required no more than a total of forty billed hours, which encompassed all preparation and court appearances. He explained that, although he had not charged more than forty hours to prepare an OUI case, in comparison to Fordham's more than 200 expended hours, Fordham nonetheless had spent a reasonable number of hours on the case in light of the continuance and the subsequent need to reprepare, as well as the "very ingenious" breathalyzer suppression argument, and the Clarks' insistence on trial. In addition, the witness testified that, although the field sobriety test, breathalyzer tests, and the presence of a half-empty liquor bottle in the car placed Fordham at a serious disadvantage in being able to prevail on the OUI charge, those circumstances were not unusual and in fact agreed that they were "normal circumstances."

The fourth expert witness, called by Fordham, testified that she believed the case was "extremely tough" and that the breathalyzer suppression theory was novel. She testified that, although the time and labor consumed on the case was more than usual in defending an OUI charge, the hours were not excessive. They were not excessive, she explained, because the case was particularly difficult due to the "stakes [and] the evidence." She conceded, however, that legal issues in defending OUI charges are "pretty standard" and that the issues presented in this case were not unusual. Furthermore, the witness testified that challenging the breathalyzer test due to the .02 discrepancy was not unusual, but the theory on which Fordham proceeded was novel. Finally, she stated that she thought she may have known of one person who might have spent close to one hundred hours on a difficult OUI case; she was not sure; but she had never heard of a fee in excess of $10,000 for a bench trial.

In considering whether a fee is "clearly excessive" within the meaning of S.J.C. Rule 3:07, DR 2-106(B), the first factor to be considered pursuant to that rule is "the novelty and difficulty of the questions involved, and the skill requisite to perform the legal service properly." DR 2-106(B)(1). That standard is similar to the familiar standard of reasonableness traditionally applied in civil fee disputes. See . . . Restatement (Third) of the Law Governing Lawyers § 46 comment f (Proposed Final Draft 1996) ("The standards that apply when fees are challenged as unreasonable in fee disputes are also relevant in the discipline of lawyers for charging unreasonably high fees"). Based on the testimony of the four experts, the number of hours devoted to Timothy's OUI case by Fordham and his associates was substantially in excess of the hours that a prudent experienced lawyer would have spent. According to the evidence, the number of hours spent was several times the amount of time any of the witnesses had ever spent on a similar case. We are not unmindful of the novel and successful motion to suppress the breathalyzer test results, but that effort cannot justify a $50,000 fee in a type of case in which the usual fee is less than one-third of that amount.

The board determined that "because [Fordham] had never tried an OUI case or appeared in the district court, [Fordham] spent over 200 hours preparing the case, in part to educate himself in the relevant substantive law and court procedures." Fordham's inexperience in criminal defense work and OUI cases in particular cannot justify the extraordinarily high fee. It cannot be that an inexperienced lawyer is entitled to charge three or four times as much as an experienced lawyer for the same service. A client "should not be expected to pay for the education of a lawyer when he spends excessive amounts of time on tasks which, with reasonable experience, become matters of routine." Matter of the Estate of Larson, 103 Wash. 2d 517, 531 (1985). "While the licensing of a lawyer is evidence that he has met the standards then prevailing for admission to the bar, a lawyer generally should not accept employment in any area of the law in which he is not qualified. However, he may accept such employment if in good faith he expects to become qualified through study and investigation, as long as such preparation would not result in unreasonable delay or expense to his client." Model Code of Professional Responsibility EC 6-3 (1982). . . .

DR 2-106(B) provides that the third factor to be considered in ascertaining the reasonableness of a fee is its comparability to "the fee customarily charged in the locality for similar legal services." The hearing committee made no finding as to the comparability of Fordham's fee with the fees customarily charged in the locality for similar services. However, one of bar counsel's expert witnesses testified that he had never heard of a fee in excess of $15,000 to defend a first OUI charge, and the customary flat fee in an OUI case, including trial, "runs from $1,000 to $7,500." Bar counsel's other expert testified that he had never heard of a fee in excess of $10,000 for a bench trial. In his view, the customary charge for a case similar to Timothy's would vary between $1,500 and $5,000. One of Fordham's experts testified that she considered a $40,000 or $50,000 fee for defending an OUI charge "unusual and certainly higher by far than any I've ever seen before." The witness had never charged a fee of more than $3,500 for representing a client at a bench trial to defend a first offense OUI charge. She further testified that she believed an "average OUI in the bench session is two thousand [dollars] and sometimes less." Finally, that witness testified that she had "heard a rumor" that one attorney charged $10,000 for a bench trial involving an OUI charge; this fee represented the highest fee of which she was aware. The other expert witness called by Fordham testified that he had heard of a $35,000 fee for defending OUI charges, but he had never charged more than $12,000 (less than twenty-five per cent of Fordham's fee).

Although finding that Fordham's fee was "much higher than the fee charged by many attorneys with more experience litigating driving under the influence cases," the hearing committee nevertheless determined that the fee charged by Fordham was not clearly excessive because Clark "went into the relationship with Fordham with open eyes," Fordham's fee fell within a "safe harbor," and Clark acquiesced in Fordham's fee by not strenuously objecting to his bills. The board accepted the hearing committee's analysis apart from the committee's reliance on the "safe harbor" rule.

The finding that Clark had entered into the fee agreement "with open eyes" was based on the finding that Clark hired Fordham after being fully apprised that he lacked any type of experience in defending an OUI charge and after interviewing other lawyers who were experts in defending OUI charges. Furthermore, the hearing committee and the board relied on testimony which revealed that the fee arrangement had been fully disclosed to Clark including the fact that Fordham "would have to become familiar with the law in that area." It is also significant, however, that the hearing committee found that "despite Fordham's disclaimers concerning his experience, Clark did not appear to have understood in any real sense the implications of choosing Fordham to represent Timothy. Fordham did not give Clark any estimate of the total expected fee or the number of $200 hours that would be required." The express finding of the hearing committee that Clark "did not appear to have understood in any real sense the implications of choosing Fordham to represent Timothy" directly militates against the finding that Clark entered into the agreement "with open eyes."

That brings us to the hearing committee's finding that Fordham's fee fell within a "safe harbor." The hearing committee reasoned that as long as an agreement existed between a client and an attorney to bill a reasonable rate multiplied by the number of hours actually worked, the attorney's fee was within a "safe harbor" and thus protected from a challenge that the fee was clearly excessive. The board, however, in reviewing the hearing committee's decision, correctly rejected the notion "that a lawyer may always escape discipline with billings based on accurate time charges for work honestly performed."

The "safe harbor" formula would not be an appropriate rationale in this case because the amount of time Fordham spent to educate himself and represent Timothy was clearly excessive despite his good faith and diligence. Disciplinary Rule 2-106(B)'s mandate that "[a] fee is clearly excessive when, after a review of the facts, a lawyer of ordinary prudence, experienced in the area of the law involved, would be left with a definite and firm conviction that the fee is substantially in excess of a reasonable fee," creates explicitly an objective standard by which attorneys' fees are to be judged. We are not persuaded by Fordham's argument that "unless it can be shown that the 'excessive' work for which the attorney has charged goes beyond mere matters of professional judgment and can be proven, either directly or by reasonable inference, to have involved dishonesty, bad faith or overreaching of the client, no case for discipline has been established." Disciplinary Rule 2-106 plainly does not require an inquiry into whether the clearly excessive fee was charged to the client under fraudulent circumstances, and we shall not write such a meaning into the disciplinary rule. . . .

Finally, bar counsel challenges the hearing committee's finding that "if Clark objected to the numbers of hours being spent by Fordham, he could have spoken up with some force when he began receiving bills." Bar counsel notes, and we agree, that "the test as stated in the DR 2-106(A) is whether the fee 'charged' is clearly excessive, not whether the fee is accepted as valid or acquiesced in by the client." Therefore, we conclude that the hearing committee and the board erred in not concluding that Fordham's fee was clearly excessive.

Fordham argues that our impositions of discipline would offend his right to due process. A disciplinary sanction constitutes "a punishment or penalty" levied against the respondent, and therefore the respondent is entitled to procedural due process. In re Ruffalo, 390 U.S. 544, 550 (1968). Matter of Kenney, 399 Mass. 431, 436 (1987) ("attorney has a substantial property right in his license to practice law"). Fordham contends that the bar and, therefore, he, have not been given fair notice through prior decisions of this court of the express language of DR 2-106 that discipline may be imposed for billing excessive hours that were nonetheless spent diligently and in good faith. . . . It is true, as Fordham asserts, that there is a dearth of case law in the Commonwealth meting out discipline for an attorney's billing of a clearly excessive fee. There is, however, as we have noted above, case law which specifically addresses what constitutes an unreasonable attorney's fee employing virtually the identical factors contained within DR 2-106. . . . More importantly, the general prohibition in DR 2-106(A) that "[a] lawyer shall not enter into an agreement for, charge, or collect an illegal or clearly excessive fee," is followed by eight specific, and clearly expressed, factors, to be evaluated by the standard of "a lawyer of ordinary prudence," in determining the propriety of the fee. . . . In addition, nothing contained within the disciplinary rule nor within any pertinent case law indicates in any manner that a clearly excessive fee does not warrant discipline whenever the time spent during the representation was spent in good faith. The fact that this court has not previously had occasion to discipline an attorney in the circumstances of this case does not suggest that the imposition of discipline in this case offends due process. . . .

In charging a clearly excessive fee, Fordham departed substantially from the obligation of professional responsibility that he owed to his client. The ABA Model Standards for Imposing Lawyer Sanctions § 7.3 (1992) endorses a public reprimand as the appropriate sanction for charging a clearly excessive fee. We deem such a sanction appropriate in this case. . . .

Notes

1. Part of the opinion suggests that there was a disciplinary violation because the client was not fully informed about the possible extent of the fee and therefore that the consent was not effective. What more should the lawyer have done by way of informing the client?

2. Another part of the opinion suggests that a clearly excessive fee is a clearly excessive fee, and no amount of consent will save the lawyer from a disciplinary violation. Consider the following scenario. Client desperately does not want a criminal conviction for driving under the influence of alcohol, with the consequent loss of his driver's license. All the lawyers who routinely handle that kind of case say that given the open bottle of alcohol on the front seat and the results of the breathalyzer test, he doesn't have a chance and had better plead guilty. Client then goes to one of the best trial lawyers in the state and says, "I know you don't handle this kind of case,

but I am desperate. Money is no object. I'll pay the hourly fees you charge your rich corporate clients. But help me." The lawyer yields to his pleas, devotes an enormous amount of time to this otherwise routine case, comes up with an innovative defense that gets the client acquitted on the criminal charges and saves his license. He sends a bill for $50,000 when the normal fee an ordinary lawyer would charge in a case like this would be in the $5000 range. Under the court's theory, has the lawyer committed a disciplinary violation? Even if the client were Bill Gates or Warren Buffett or Rupert Murdoch? Why is the principal case different?

3. Shortly after deciding the principal case, which evidenced great concern for fees charged to clients, the same Justices adopted a new set of disciplinary rules based on the Model Rules. At the time, Massachusetts had, and still has, a rule that was the most permissive in the nation regarding the forwarding fee. Under the rule, a lawyer is permitted to take such a fee without doing any work or accepting any responsibility, providing only that the client consents to the employment of the other lawyer and to the joint participation in the fee. The Massachusetts Supreme Judicial Court made numerous changes in the Model Rules in revising its disciplinary rules, but it specifically refused to adopt the suggestion of its own Model Rules Committee that lawyers splitting a fee in a referred case tell the client what the split will be. That information would seem to be important for effective consent, and the Court did add a Comment to the rule stating that a lawyer must inform a client who asks. Is there any justification for that decision? After the revised Rules were adopted, the Chief Justice (who had recused himself in the *Fordham* case) wrote an article candidly stating that to win the support of the state bar association for its project of revising the rules, the justices had indicated that they "would agree in advance that they would make no substantive change in the rule governing the division of fees." Herbert Wilkins, "The New Massachusetts Rules of Professional Conduct," 82 Mass. L. Rev. 261 (1997).

Model Rule 1.5(e) permits the payment of a forwarding fee to a lawyer who does not work on a matter so long as the client does not object to the participation of all the lawyers and, by written agreement with the client, all lawyers assume joint responsibility for the representation. What is the justification for allowing the referring lawyer who does no work to be paid a substantial referral fee?

———————

The Model Rules also address the subject of the contingent fee, which has, after great professional struggle, become accepted in civil litigation, except perhaps in divorce litigation. See Model Rule 1.5(d)(1). While the contingent fee has been extolled for its role in achieving access to the courts for poor people, especially injured poor people, its exacerbation of the already present economic conflict that exists between lawyer and client continues to cause concern. A related criticism, most prominently expressed by Lester Brickman, is that "standard" contingent fees (i.e., 33% of the total recovery) ought to be viewed as unethical in cases, for example airplane accident litigation, where the lawyer faces little or no risk that the claim will not be successful. See, e.g., Lester Brickman & Lawrence A. Cunningham, "Nonrefundable Retainers: A Response to Critics of the Absolute Ban," 64 U. Cin. L. Rev. 11 (1995); Lester Brickman & Lawrence A. Cunningham, "Nonrefundable Retainers: Impermissible Under Fiduciary, Statutory and Contract Law," 57 Fordham L. Rev. 149 (1988).

Efforts to replace or modify standard contingent fees have been made in a number of states. See, for example, the limits on contingent fee charges imposed by the Appellate Division of the New York Supreme Court, except in special circumstances; these survived determined challenge in Gair v. Peck, 6 N.Y.2d 97 (1959), cert. denied, 361 U.S. 374 (1960); see also McCreary v. Joel, 186 So. 2d 4 (Fla. 1966), holding an agreement for a 66.7% contingent fee to be unconscionable; and Roa v. Lodi Medical Group, 37 Cal. 3d 920 (1985), appeal dismissed, 474 U.S. 990 (1985), upholding California's statutory sliding scale limitation on contingent fees in medical malpractice cases against attack on due process, equal protection, and separation of powers grounds. With the rise of the class action, bringing more and more fees under direct court supervision, the attitude of courts is becoming crucial. This potential impact exists not only in matters like probate, juvenile proceedings, and bankruptcy, where courts have direct supervision over fees, but also throughout the private practice of law because of the courts' power, albeit rarely invoked, to rule on the reasonableness of all legal charges.

Do you think that modifying or eliminating standard contingent fees would affect the incentives of plaintiff's lawyers or the distribution of legal services? Do plaintiffs' lawyers already have market incentives to reduce the percentage of the recovery that they take as their fee in cases where liability is certain and damages are potentially high? We will discuss these and other similar questions when we examine the structure of the plaintiff bar in Chapter 12.

The following opinion discusses one approach to fee awards and a particularly difficult professional responsibility problem that arises in connection with statutory fee awards.

Prandini v. National Tea Co.

557 F.2d 1015 (3d Cir. 1977)

WEIS, Circuit Judge

In certain types of litigation, a successful plaintiff may receive attorneys' fees in addition to the customary damages for his claim. Although the negotiation of a fee contemporaneously with the evaluation of damages may be conducted with diligence and honesty, the potential for impropriety gives rise to possible misunderstanding by the public. We agree with the district court's disapproval of the procedure, but remanded for further findings of fact necessary in calculation of reasonable fees. . . .

The awarding of counsel fees is a matter of discretion with the trial court, but we have provided objective standards to guide and facilitate the sound exercise of that discretion. Lindy Bros. Builders, Inc. of Phila. v. American Radiator & Standard Sanitary Corp., 487 F.2d 161 (3d Cir. 1973) (*Lindy I*), and Lindy Bros. Builders, Inc. of Phila. v. American Radiator & Standard Sanitary Corp., 540 F.2d 102 (3d Cir. 1976) (*Lindy II*). The district court is required to employ the formula we devised and to articulate the values of its variable components. The total time expended and a reasonable hourly rate are the elements of the initial computation. That calculation in turn must be adjusted to reflect the quality of the work, benefit to the client, and contingency of the result in order to arrive at a reasonable value of the attorneys' services. . . .

. . . [T]he district court was doubtful that hours expended is always a fair measurement of the value of legal services, stating at the hearing: "I know many attorneys achieve results in two hours that takes another a week to get." We do not disagree, and observe that the "quality" factor requires the court to adjust a fee on the basis of results of the work performed. Quality in this sense includes efficiency. If the attorney achieves good results with a minimum time expenditure, the total award may be increased to reflect efficiency and benefit to the client. . . . Conversely, emphasis on the objective quantity of time spent should not shield wasteful or inefficient logging of hours from scrutiny, and the court should reduce the compensation when that practice occurs. Similarly, hours spent on purely clerical matters, easily delegable to non-professional assistants, should not be valued at legal service rates. *Lindy* does not fetter a trial judge's ability to arrive at a reasonable fee but offers a principled means of achieving that result and, at the same time, provides an adequate record for appellate and public review. . . .

We are aware of the differences in rationale underlying the award of fees from a fund produced for the benefit of a class and those provided by statute. In the former case, the court exercises its equitable jurisdiction over the relationship between an attorney and his amorphous client, and factors which would appropriately have influenced the fee arrangement made between private parties, such as the contingency of litigation, are relevant. In the latter case, the statutory fee is often a part of the defendant's penalty for violating the applicable law. Contingency may be of little significance in that situation if the result is to give a smaller fee to the plaintiffs' lawyer who recovers from a defendant in flagrant violation than the attorney who succeeds in establishing liability in a very close case. The contingency factor would be less where the liability is easily proved than when it is questionable. Hence, the penalty fastened on the defendant would vary in inverse proportion to the strength of the case against him. . . .

The respective interests of lawyer and client may also vary, depending on whether the fee comes from a recovered fund or directly from the defendant in satisfaction of a separate obligation. In the common fund situation, the adverse interests are patent and the necessity for a court to recognize the equities of the absent and passive members of a class is obvious. When the statute provides that a fee is to be paid as a separate item, the conflict between client and attorney may not be as apparent, particularly in the event of settlement. It is often present nonetheless.

The district court concluded that it had been a mistake to approve the payment to the class separately because there was, in reality, only one fund for both the class and attorneys' fees. Reasoning that in cases of this nature a defendant is interested only in disposing of the total claim asserted against it, the court noted that the allocation between the class payment and the attorneys' fees is of little or no interest to the defense. As the court phrased it:

> The defendant is not faced with a group of claimants who are personally involved in the litigation, but only with one or a few representative parties whose award can be greatly increased over that of individual class members because of personal participation in the preparation of the case. In this case the sole representative plaintiff was awarded $15,000.00 for her initiation of the case and participation therein. The defendant deals with the representative party or parties and counsel who also represents the class. The impulse to treat opposing counsel and the representative party generously is an element that cannot be ignored.

The court went on to explain the unpleasant situation in which it found itself:

> Therefore, as devil's advocate, we must look at an agreement by defendants to pay counsel for the class a fee up to a certain maximum, as determined by the court, as having the potentiality of what is known in the labor field as a "sweetheart contract." This puts the judge who must determine its reasonableness and fairness in the posture of a "bad guy." None of the class members complained; counsel for the defendant does not complain; why should he inject himself into the arrangement?

We are placed in the similar unfortunate position of considering an appeal ex parte and are thus deprived of adversarial presentations.

The district judge's sentiments about the conflict of interest and "sweetheart contract" problems have been expressed in other cases. . . . The articulated difficulties are real and practical — present in all cases where the defendant pays the plaintiff's lawyers and particularly so in class actions. The court does have the duty to see to it that the administration of justice has the appearance of propriety as well as being so in fact. In this case the district court properly exercised its responsibility by requiring public disclosure of the basis for the fees even though the defendant had agreed to the amount.

However, we recognize that with the increasingly heavy burden upon the courts, settlements of disputes must be encouraged and in the absence of special circumstances, such as those mentioned by the district court in this case, we doubt the necessity to completely exclude statutorily authorized attorneys' fees from that policy. A reasonable solution, we suggest, is for trial courts to insist upon settlement of the damage aspect of the case separately from the award of statutorily

authorized attorneys' fees. Only after court approval of the damage settlement should discussion and negotiation of appropriate compensation for the attorneys begin. This would eliminate the situation found in this case of having, in practical effect, one fund divided between the attorney and client.

This procedure may not be particularly appealing to the parties, but it preserves the benefits of the adversary system since the defendant continues to have an economic interest. Moreover, the merits of fee disputes become separated from those of damages, thus reducing the conflict between client and attorney. This procedure would make the court's task less burdensome and remove a source of uneasiness over the settlement procedure without in any way impairing the power to set a proper fee. . . .

Notes

1. Another aspect of the relationship between fees and class counsel has also spawned a per se rule in some jurisdictions that forbids attorneys from becoming class counsel if they have certain relationships with a class representative: "No member of the bar either maintaining an employment relationship, including a partnership or professional corporation, or sharing office or suite space with an attorney class representative during the preparation or pendency of a Rule 23(b)(3) class action may serve as counsel to the class if the action might result in the creation of a fund from which an attorneys' fee award would be appropriate." Kramer v. Scientific Control Corp., 534 F.2d 1085, 1093 (3d Cir.), cert. denied, 429 U.S. 830 (1976); accord, Zylstra v. Safeway Stores, Inc., 578 F.2d 102 (5th Cir. 1978); Jacobs v. Citibank, 2003 U.S. Dist. Lexis 2880 (S.D.N.Y.), appeal dismissed, 72 Fed. Appx. 735 (2d Cir. 2003) (plaintiff class representative may not act as class counsel). The fear is that attorneys' interest in the fee award might compromise their zeal for obtaining the most favorable settlement for the class. In *Kramer*, the rule was applied even though the class representative stated that he would not share in any fee award.

2. The *Lindy* opinions, which are referred to in *Prandini*, are very important in the history of fee determination in class action cases. Prior to *Lindy*, class action fee awards were generally made on a percentage, contingency basis. *Lindy* established time worked and an hourly rate as the "lodestar" for awarding fees. It has been followed by almost all the courts of appeals. It has, however, been attacked as inhibiting early settlements and as inducing wasteful expenditure of time, especially as settlement neared. See Solovy and Mendillo, "Calculating Class Action Awards," 4 Nat'l L. J. 20 (May 2, 1983). See also Hensley v. Eckerhart, 461 U.S. 424 (1983). In Pennsylvania v. Delaware Valley Citizens' Council for Clean Air, 483 U.S. 711 (1987), the Supreme Court held it was appropriate under the relevant statute to increase the "lodestar" to compensate for the risk of losing, although not in the circumstances of that case. See also Pierce v. Underwood, 487 U.S. 552 (1988), where the Supreme Court found that the "special circumstances" exception to the $75 per hour cap on lawyers' fees in the Equal Access to Justice Act had not been met.

[handwritten margin note: some jx. don't allow lawyer for class if r-ship w/member — B/c]

3. Very much related to the issue of fee sharing is the ability of a lawyer, or the estate of a lawyer, to sell the good will of a practice to an attorney with whom the seller (or deceased attorney) never practiced. Such sales used to be forbidden on the twin notions that clients could not be sold and that sale of good will was really a forbidden division of future legal fees. Model Rule 1.17 specifically permits the sale of good will under stated conditions.

4. For many years prior to 1975, local, county, and state bar associations published minimum fee schedules for a whole variety of standard legal services, from title closings and forming corporations, to writing simple wills and making court appearances. While these schedules were justified as providing information and guidance to lawyers about common charges and reasonable fees, they also served at many times in many places as implicit and explicit efforts to set floors on charges so as to avoid price cutting. An attack on a minimum fee schedule that operated in such a fashion was mounted in Goldfarb v. Virginia State Bar, 421 U.S. 773 (1975). The Supreme Court held that price fixing was involved; that interstate commerce was sufficiently affected to bring the price fixing activities within section 1 of the Sherman Act; and that they were not exempt either because of a "learned profession" exclusion in that Act or because they constituted "state action" within the meaning of Parker v. Brown, 317 U.S. 341 (1943).

[margin note: Fee schedules for certain legal services.]

5. The billable hour as a standard basis for charging fees periodically comes under scrutiny and attack. The presiding partner at the major New York firm of Cravath, Swaine & Moore proposed the standard of Joe the contractor remodeling a kitchen. "For reasonable periods of time during the life of a lawsuit, say three months at a time, I should do what Joe does: identify the client's objectives, measure, calculate, build in a contingency and come back with a price." He would deal with the problem of the lawyer tempted to cut corners to save on costs by adding on a success fee just as a contractor should be rewarded with a bonus for doing a good job ahead of schedule. Evan Chesler, "Kill the Billable Hour," Forbes.com (Jan. 12, 2009). Some major British firms follow just that practice, at least with some clients.

The Supreme Court in Goldfarb was careful to say that it was not dealing with a purely advisory fee schedule but only with one that set a fixed price floor. Nevertheless, the Court's action, together with developments in advertising and the rise of legal clinics, has led to a virtual demise of the promulgation of minimum fee schedules. Of equal interest is what Goldfarb meant for the future of professional regulation. The Court did specifically state that professional practices were not to be equated automatically with business practices, thus leaving open the possibility of greater immunity from Sherman Act regulation for the profession. Yet when dealing with the state agency exemption from anticompetitive practices that it created in Parker v. Brown, the Court adverted specifically to the fact that it intended "no diminution of the authority of the State to regulate its professions."

[margin note: Prof. practices ≠ Business practices]

Note: Conflict Between Lawyer and Client with Respect to Fees

As noted before, it is apparent that there is a conflict of interest that is inherent in the setting of a price for lawyers' service. The court in *Prandini* noted that there is an additional difficulty when the lawyer is awarded a fee by the court out of a common fund created or preserved by the lawyer. It then observed that when a fee award is based on statutory authority, the conflict is less apparent because it is added to damages.

But the court went on to point out that conflict might still exist in two forms. One is the situation suggested in *Prandini*. The defendants made a $15,000 payment to the named plaintiff and offered what appears to have been a generous fee settlement to class counsel. This raises, as the court noted, the problem of a "sweetheart contract," and the possibility that the interests of the unnamed members of the class might not have been pursued sufficiently. Generous offers of this kind certainly create problems of conflict between named plaintiff and class counsel on the one hand and the remainder of the class on the other.

A second opportunity for conflict between counsel and client is presented when the defendants offer a satisfactory settlement to the class conditioned on waiver by class counsel of their statutory fee award. That is the issue presented by Problem 8–3 and by *Prandini*. As we saw in Chapter 4, in cases where the settlement is a monetary payment, such an offer forces counsel to seek its fee from the award. The resulting conflict created for counsel and class is just the problem that the statutory fee award was designed to avoid. In cases where the settlement consists not of a damage payment but of an agreement to undertake, or to desist from, certain conduct, the conditional offer is likely to mean that class counsel will get no fee at all if the offer is accepted. Needless to say, it is very difficult for class counsel to advise their clients in that situation.

The response of the *Prandini* court was an effort to effectuate the legislative policy embodied in the statutory fee award and to minimize the adversary relationship into which the fee problem puts plaintiff class and its lawyer. Efforts were made to incorporate the *Prandini* result into the Model Rules. They failed largely because of the perceived unfairness in forbidding defendants from making a settlement on the basis of its total liability for both damages and fees at the same time. The *Prandini* solution therefore continues to be problematic.

It is worthwhile to note that the facts of Problem 8–3 are the facts of Evans v. Jeff D., 475 U.S. 717 (1986). In the actual case, the lawyer for the class signed the stipulation accepting the settlement proposal, which contained a fee waiver. He then petitioned the district court to approve the settlement except for the fee waiver. The district court approved the settlement and denied the lawyer's motion to be permitted to present a request for a statutory fee. The Court of Appeals, however, citing *Prandini*, invalidated the fee waiver. The Supreme Court reversed, finding nothing in the language or policy of the Fee Act requiring that it be construed as embodying a general rule prohibiting settlements conditioned on fee waiver. The Court also did not regard the lawyer as having any "ethical dilemma"; no rule of ethics required the lawyer to seek a fee. Finally, the Court found no abuse of discretion in the approval by the district court of a settlement with a complete fee waiver. The Court suggested the possibility that approval might not be justified if the defendants had no realistic defense or if they had adopted a vindictive policy of forcing fee waiver to inhibit counsel from bringing such cases.

While the *Jeff D.* case settles the interpretation of the Fee Act, it does not remove the ethics problem for plaintiff counsel. While it is true that there is no ethical dilemma in the sense that counsel violated no ethical rule by waiving a fee, counsel who need to earn a living certainly have an ethical dilemma both in trying to decide whether they must accept the fee waiver if the settlement is good for the client class and in trying to decide what to do the next time they are asked to take on representation in a situation where the problem seems likely to arise. And so *Jeff D.* has not made the ethics issue that the *Prandini* court grappled with obsolete. It has simply added another dimension to the problem. See Pinto v. Spectrum Chemicals, 200 N.J. 580 (N.J. 2008), adopting the Brennan dissent position under a state fee-shifting statute.

Note: Emerging New Fee Arrangements

Consider the fee arrangement described in the below excerpt.

David B. Wilkins
Team of Rivals?
Toward a New Model of the Corporate
Attorney-Client Relationship

78 Fordham L. Rev. 2067 (2010)

. . .

When Trevor Faure took over the legal department of Tyco International's operations for Europe, the Middle East, and Asia in 2004, the department was in a state of total disarray. Fresh from the major accounting scandal that nearly destroyed the parent company, Faure was given explicit instructions to improve the competence and integrity of the legal function. To achieve this objective, Faure instituted a systematic examination of how the company was spending its legal resources, both internally and with outside firms. What he quickly discovered was that notwithstanding significant increases in spending on both internal and external resources, the legal department was doing a poor job of managing its known legal expenses—and an even worse job of providing the kind of comprehensive legal coverage that could prevent legal problems from occurring in the first place.

Armed with this knowledge, Faure developed a plan to reallocate the company's legal spending in a manner that better protected its interests. At the core of Faure's strategy was a proposal to achieve the ultimate in convergence by slashing the number of outside firms the company used from 250 to a single provider. After interviewing several candidates, Faure settled on the 2000-lawyer U.K. firm Eversheds. The two-year deal covered a wide range of work, including labor and employment, IP, compliance, and litigation. All told, Eversheds was expected to gross $20 million per year in fees.

Implementing this plan, however, proved more difficult than either Tyco or Eversheds anticipated. Indeed, after the first year, Faure almost pulled the plug on the arrangement because Eversheds had not yet learned how to control the company's legal costs. For its part, the law firm claimed that the sheer volume of work—1000 live matters followed by 100 new matters a month, spread over thirty jurisdictions—was simply too much for even such a large global firm to absorb. In the end, however, because of the significant investment that both parties had already made in the new relationship, the company and the law firm chose voice rather than exit and agreed to a new deal that brings the sides even closer together.

Specifically, the new deal makes it even clearer than before that the company and firm will share both the risks and the rewards of Tyco's legal fate. To accomplish this objective, the company and the firm have agreed to a set of benchmarks for specific kinds of cases. For basic "commodity work," the company agrees to pay Eversheds for 10,000 hours of work at reduced rates. If the firm exceeds this preset number of hours, it will receive nothing for the first 1250 hours, and a dramatically reduced rate for any hour thereafter. If, on the other hand, the firm is able to complete the tasks in under the prescribed amount of time, the company will allow Eversheds to bill for fifty percent of the hours that it *did not work* up to the 10,000 hours agreed upon to achieve this objective. For all litigation under $1 million, the firm will receive a twenty-five percent success premium on top of its discounted fees for any case it wins—and will suffer a ten percent penalty from its discounted rates if the case is lost. With respect to higher-value litigation and transactional work, the deal provides that Eversheds be paid its standard fees minus a smaller discount. Finally, premium work, such as "bet-the-company" litigation and structuring transactions, is expressly not included in the deal, but Eversheds will be given an opportunity to compete for these matters along with other firms.

The most innovative aspects of the new arrangement between Tyco and Eversheds, however, fall outside of these typical parameters. These terms provide that in addition to making money on the fees the company pays it for its work, Eversheds can also profit if the firm hits a number of additional targets designed by the company to further what it considers to be important objectives. For example, the deal specifies that the firm will pocket a bonus in excess of $100,000 if the firm improves Tyco's "client satisfaction" as measured by a survey given to the company's senior managers every October. The firm will also take home a six-figure bonus if it meets certain targets for diversifying its legal and support staff. Finally, the arrangement contains an incentive for Eversheds to help Tyco avoid getting into legal trouble in the first place. The firm will take home another six-figure bonus if it is able to reduce the number of lawsuits filed against Tyco by fifteen percent over the number filed in the previous year. To give Eversheds the chance to meet this target, Tyco promises to give the firm access (at the law firm's expense) to Tyco's business processes and people.

By providing specific rewards for helping the company to achieve its own objectives, Faure hopes to create a "win-win" mentality between the company and Eversheds. As he told The American Lawyer, he hoped to avoid the "winner-take-all" mentality that typically characterizes the relationship between outside counsel and firms and to create a relationship "that encourages the right behaviors from both sides." As the editors of the magazine note, the result is a unique "two-way partnership [that] ties the firm to the client but . . . [also] ties the client to the firm."

As indicated above, the Tyco/Eversheds deal is indeed unique in both its scope and innovation. But it is also clear that other companies are looking closely at Tyco's experience. Since news of Faure's SMARTER model hit the press, a steady stream of general counsel have beaten a path to his door to see if they can adopt some or all of his methods. In 2008, Tyco's Trevor Faure was named "In-House Lawyer of the Year" by The Lawyer, which specifically praised the company's creation of "win-win" incentives such as paying the firm a bonus for reducing litigation against the company. Given the overall trend toward convergence, it is only a matter of time before aspects of Faure's model will be copied by other companies. Even companies that do not embrace all aspects of the SMARTER model are increasingly exploring mechanisms to encourage "risk sharing" by their primary law firms through mechanisms like "value billing" and the delivery of "products" that standardize templates and tools in ways that are guaranteed to produce results.

Notes

1. Historically, contingency fee arrangements were thought of as a means of increasing access to legal services to clients who could not otherwise afford to pay for legal services, with a typical example being a victim of an automobile accident who had a potentially meritorious claim but no means to pay for representation. Note some of the implicit aspects of this typical example: contingency arrangements were usually limited to litigation, and featured a solo practitioner or a small litigation firm and a client with limited means. More recently, contingency arrangements have become more common outside of litigation, for example, in business transactions, where a law firm will be paid only a fraction of its fees if the deal does not close, and a markup above its fees if the deal does close. They have also become more commonly utilized by mid-size and large law firms to benefit a whole range of clients, including those who can otherwise afford to pay for legal services.

2. As Professor Wilkins explains, at least in certain parts of legal practice, the basic rationale for emerging fee arrangements is changing, moving away from access to legal services measured in terms of clients' ability to pay and toward focusing more on risk sharing among clients and lawyers.

B. Advertising and Solicitation

Just as lawyers in the traditional model were not thought of as mere service providers, law was not conceived of as an ordinary service. Although the traditional access to legal services model purportedly embraced the market approach, historically information about legal services was not readily available to clients.

Problem 8–4

7.1
yes, given that
not m.rep or misleading

Law Firm wishes to advertise itself as "Best Lawyers in Town," or "Best lawyers, lowest fees in Town," or "Best lawyers, lowest fees, best results achieved in Town." May it do so under the Model Rules? Whatever the answer in a particular jurisdiction, should such advertising be forbidden?

Problem 8–5

(1) isn't it live?

yes. this fine
nothing consists
of live person
to person contact
7.3(b) & 7.2(a)

Law Firm, which does substantial advertising in the media of its personal injury practice, wishes to expand its business. It proposes to do the following: (1) have a partner offer free seminars to workers under the auspices of the local Council of Unions; (2) leave brochures describing its practice, expertise, and fees for display to patients in the offices of doctors who do substantial personal injury work; (3) mail those brochures to all the members of several local unions; (4) subscribe to a newspaper clipping service, send the brochures to all persons identified as accident victims, and follow up with a telephone call or email or even a visit offering the firm's services; and (5) put the contents of the brochures on its website with an email link permitting the viewer to contact a member of the firm directly. May it do so under the Model Rules? Whatever the answer in a particular jurisdiction, should such practices be forbidden?

Good practice
for MPRE
←

← Problem 8–6   *?? 7 No-But pecuniary gain*

yes- 7.2(b)(5)
←

For many years Lawyer has been a good friend of the Assistant Administrator of the Emergency Room of the local Hospital. Her law business has fallen off recently, and she asks Administrator if he would keep her in mind if accident victims ever ask his advice about a lawyer. Does that request subject the lawyer to discipline? When Christmas approaches, Lawyer realizes that she has had a good year financially. May she give Administrator a Christmas present without violating a disciplinary rule? May she propose to the Hospital a plan whereby she will perform legal services for employees of the Hospital at reduced rates and the Hospital will make that offer known by providing her literature, describing her services and the discounted rates, to its employees? *It depends if there was a relationship b/t lawyer & hospital.*

Problem 8–7

A & B, a national law firm, with its main office in Washington, D.C. and offices in fifteen other cities in the United States and in seven foreign countries, has established its own website. With whose disciplinary rules must it comply? Is its website in violation of an applicable disciplinary rule that prohibits all "in-person" solicitation of legal business?

Note: A Few Generalities

There are two aspects to the profession's rules governing advertising and solicitation. The first is the rules' efforts to control the methods by which lawyers get business. The second is the rules' impact on the ability of the general populace to obtain legal services and to select a particular lawyer. This Chapter does not purport to cover the myriad situations involving professional concern with advertising and solicitation by lawyers. We will make a few general observations and then consider some of the controversial aspects of the present rules.

The rules relating to advertising and solicitation used to be what many people thought about when the subject of ethics was mentioned. They were the stereotype of the perceived pettiness and self-protective nature of the profession's rules. And there was some truth to that view. Passing judgment on the size of business cards, the propriety of sending Christmas cards to clients, and the like was grist for the mills of many ethics committees. Sometimes, a novel problem surfaced and a committee decided whether a news story about a law firm and the unusual office building it built (State ex rel. Florida Bar v. Nichols, 151 So. 2d 257 (Fla. 1963)); or the laudatory article in Life Magazine in which the law firm cooperated (In re Connelly, 18 App. Div. 2d 466 (1st Dept. 1963)); or a lawyer's endorsement of a brand of Scotch (Belli v. State Bar of California, 10 Cal. 3d 824 (1974)) constituted a violation of the professional rules.

The triviality of some of the matters covered by the rules, however, should not obscure the serious professional concerns that led to regulation. Those concerns reflect in part a view of the practice of law as a profession, with no place for extravagant, misleading, deceptive, or outright false claims, and with no place for sensational methods of drawing attention to oneself.

The ideal was that business came to the lawyer and not vice versa. The rules prohibiting lawyers from engaging in activities that might draw attention to themselves have, however, never been absolute. Lawyers were never required to be hermits and to refrain from all activities that might draw attention to themselves. They traditionally engaged in all sorts of public and private community activities that were good for their business as well as for their community. But the policy considerations favoring involvement in this sort of activity so outweighed its mercenary aspects that rules against solicitation and advertising were not invoked against such activities, and lawyers were not required to forswear practical reasons for engaging in them. Thus in codifying the generally accepted prohibitions, the drafters of the former Model Code accepted the distinction between getting business through self-praise and through doing good works.

Those rules, however, came under attack more and more from a variety of quarters. Justice Stewart of the Supreme Court made some remarks at the 1975 meeting of the ABA that instantly became quite controversial.* He first expressed the view that *Goldfarb*, discussed earlier in this Chapter, "says that lawyers are primarily economic actors, men and women who perform a service, for profit. . . . And the members of the public, the consumers of lawyers, are best served if there is true competition among lawyers for their patronage." He then went on to make some more general remarks about the nature of a lawyer's professional responsibility:

> In this view of the legal profession, what is left for a code of professional responsibility for the business lawyer? Are professional ethics now to be no more elevated than the standards of a Better Business Bureau? Are we now to exalt the morals of the market place into a model of professional respectability? These are fundamental and difficult questions, but I submit that affirmative answers to them, rhetoric aside, may not be so calamitous as might be supposed.

> It goes without saying, of course, that every lawyer has a duty to keep the confidences of his client, that every lawyer in whom is confided a trust must conduct himself as a trustee, that every lawyer should keep his word and deal honorably in all his associations. And it certainly is the duty of every lawyer, and of every association of lawyers, to denounce and to eliminate from our midst those who have betrayed our profession for their own ugly or dishonest purposes.

> But beyond these and a few other self-evident precedents of decency and common sense, a good case can be made, I think, for the proposition that the ethics of the business lawyer are indeed, and perhaps should be, no more than the morals of the market place. The first rule for a business lawyer is to provide his total ability and effort to his client. But is this an ethical standard, or no more than a response to the economic forces of the market place? After all, the first rule in *any* occupation is to be competent. The business lawyer is in the business of providing legal advice for a businessman. If he performs that job with diligence, conscientiousness, and knowledgeable ability, his client will reap the benefits and will reward him accordingly. If not . . . the lawyer will find his client less than eager to retain indefinitely a professional adviser who habitually leads him down the wrong path.

> In short, it can fairly be argued that many aspects of what we call "ethics" are not really ethics at all, but are merely corollaries of the axiom of the better mousetrap, an axiom that is itself derived from enlightened self-interest.

---

* Stewart, "Professional Ethics for the Business Lawyer: The Morals of the Market Place," 31 Bus. Law. 463, 466–467 (1975).

While one may engage in endless argument about what Justice Stewart meant to say, his remarks appear to deemphasize the special ideals that have been associated with the most service-oriented concept of professionalism.

A second attack on the rules came from civil libertarians who focused on the effect of the restrictions on lawyers' speech and the public's access to information. They relied on the quartet of legal services cases discussed in the next Chapter, together with *Goldfarb* and Bigelow v. Virginia, 421 U.S. 809 (1975) (holding unconstitutional a Virginia statute as applied to forbid advertising of a legal New York abortion referral service in a Virginia newspaper).

A third line of attack focused primarily on the effect of the rules on informed access by the public to legal services. It pointed to the Model Code, which noted that changed conditions "have seriously restricted the traditional selection process" because of the disappearance of the former knowledge that potential clients had of the reputation of local lawyers for competence and integrity. (See EC 2-6, 2-7, and 2-8.) But beyond noting that the selection is often the result of recommendation by third parties and that it should be disinterested and informal, neither the Model Code nor the Model Rules offer very much in the way of new means for the client to acquire the information that they assume was formerly available.

At a time when there was a great deal of ferment for change of the advertising and solicitation rules, the Supreme Court lifted the discussion to the level of constitutional law, deciding a whole series of cases that put severe limits on the ability of the states to regulate advertising and, to a much lesser extent (for the time being), solicitation.

The major case was Bates v. State Bar of Arizona, 433 U.S. 350 (1977). It involved two lawyers who were disciplined for placing a newspaper advertisement offering "legal services at very reasonable fees," and listing fees for certain specified services.

The discipline was based on the admitted violation of a disciplinary rule that forbade newspaper or other media advertising by lawyers. The Supreme Court held, 5–4, that the First Amendment prohibits blanket suppression of advertising in general and this advertisement in particular. It rejected arguments in support of the rule that were based on an adverse effect on professionalism; the inherently misleading nature of lawyer advertising; the adverse effect on the administration of justice; the undesirable economic effects of advertising; and the adverse effect of advertising on the quality of services rendered. The court went on to note that it was dealing only with suppression of advertising; states were free to regulate advertising, especially with respect to those advertisements that are likely to mislead. The dissenters disagreed very strongly with the Court's analysis, arguing that it had unnecessarily weakened the supervisory authority of the courts and the states over "officers of the court." It believed that most advertising of legal services was susceptible of being seriously misleading and that enforcement of rules based on deception was going to be very difficult.

The states have responded to *Bates* with a spectrum of regulatory efforts, ranging from rules that largely prohibit only false, fraudulent, deceptive or misleading advertisements to those that contain a whole series of regulations attempting to add specificity to those terms, for example, by forbidding dramatizations and comparative advertising, or by requiring disclaimers thought to be needed to make general language accurate, such as disclosing possible hidden costs in an advertisement of "free" services. The debate over these proposals has focused on three issues. First, what is the purpose of advertising legal services? Is it to safeguard the rights of lawyers and others to provide information about legal services and hence to safeguard consumers' rights to receive that information? That view is grounded both in "robust" First Amendment and in "robust" competitive antitrust theories. Or is it to ensure that members of the public receive the most useful information to help them select lawyers? That view is grounded in a "functional" view of the First Amendment and of professional rules. Or is it that unrestrained advertising contributes to an increasing trend in the profession to emphasize commercialism rather than professionalism? That view is grounded as an aspirational ideal for lawyering that is controversial both in descriptive and normative terms.

———————

Shortly after it decided the *Bates* case, the Supreme Court turned its attention to the constitutional aspects of the profession's solicitation rules in the following two opinions. "Solicitation" is that subdivision of advertising where the lawyer seeks business from specific persons on an individualized basis, either in person or by telephone or mail.

Ohralik v. Ohio State Bar Association

436 U.S. 447 (1978)

Mr. Justice POWELL delivered the opinion of the Court....

I

Appellant, a member of the Ohio Bar, ... while picking up his mail at the ... Post Office ... learned from the postmaster's brother about an automobile accident ... in which Carol McClintock, a young woman with whom appellant was casually acquainted, had been injured. Appellant made a telephone call to Ms. McClintock's parents, who informed him that their daughter was in the hospital. Appellant suggested that he might visit Carol in the hospital. Mrs. McClintock assented to the idea, but requested that appellant first stop by at her home.

During appellant's visit with the McClintocks, they explained that their daughter had been driving the family automobile on a local road when she was hit by an uninsured motorist. Both Carol and her passenger, Wanda Lou Holbert, were injured and hospitalized. In response to the McClintocks' expression of apprehension that they might be sued by Holbert, appellant explained that Ohio's guest statute would preclude such a suit. When appellant suggested to the McClintocks that they hire a lawyer, Mrs. McClintock retorted that such a decision would be up to Carol, who was 18 years old and would be the beneficiary of a successful claim.

Appellant proceeded to the hospital, where he found Carol lying in traction in her room. After a brief conversation about her condition,[1] appellant told Carol he would represent her and asked her to sign an agreement. Carol said she would have to discuss the matter with her parents. She did not sign the agreement, but asked appellant to have her parents come to see her.[2] Appellant also attempted to see Wanda Lou Holbert, but learned that she had just been released from the hospital. He then departed for another visit with the McClintocks.

On his way appellant detoured to the scene of the accident, where he took a set of photographs. He also picked up a tape recorder, which he concealed under his raincoat before arriving at the McClintocks' residence. Once there, he re-examined their automobile insurance policy, discussed with them the law applicable to passengers, and explained the consequences of the fact that the driver who struck Carol's car was an uninsured motorist. Appellant discovered that the McClintocks' insurance policy would provide benefits of up to $12,500 each for Carol and Wanda Lou under an uninsured motorist clause. Mrs. McClintock acknowledged that both Carol and Wanda Lou could sue for their injuries, but recounted to appellant that "Wanda swore up and down she would not do it." The McClintocks also told appellant that Carol had phoned to say that appellant could "go ahead" with her representation. Two days later appellant returned to Carol's hospital room to have her sign a contract, which provided that he would receive one-third of her recovery.

In the meantime, appellant obtained Wanda Lou's name and address from the McClintocks after telling them he wanted to ask her some questions about the accident. He then visited Wanda Lou at her home, without having been invited. He again concealed his tape recorder and recorded most of the conversation with Wanda Lou.[3] After a brief, unproductive inquiry about the facts of the accident, appellant told Wanda Lou that he was representing Carol and that he had a "little tip" for Wanda Lou: The McClintocks' insurance policy contained an uninsured motorist clause which might provide her with a recovery of up to $12,500. The young woman, who was 18 years of age and not a high school graduate at the time, replied to the appellant's query about whether she was going to file a claim by stating that she really did

---

1. Carol also mentioned that one of the hospital administrators was urging a lawyer upon her. According to his own testimony, appellant replied: "Yes, this certainly is a case that would entice a lawyer. That would interest him a great deal."

2. Despite the fact that appellant maintains that he did not secure an agreement to represent Carol while he was at the hospital, he waited for an opportunity when no visitors were present and then took photographs of Carol in traction.

3. Appellant maintains that the tape is a complete reproduction of everything that was said at the Holbert home. Wanda Lou testified that the tape does not contain appellant's introductory remarks to her about his identity as a lawyer, his agreement to represent Carol McClintock, and his availability and willingness to represent Wanda Lou as well. Appellant disputed Wanda Lou's testimony but agreed that he did not activate the recorder until he had been admitted to the Holbert home and was seated in the living room with Wanda Lou.

not understand what was going on. Appellant offered to represent her, also, for a contingent fee of one-third of any recovery, and Wanda Lou stated "O.K."[4]

Wanda's mother attempted to repudiate her daughter's oral assent the following day, when appellant called on the telephone to speak to Wanda. Mrs. Holbert informed appellant that she and her daughter did not want to sue anyone or to have appellant represent them, and that if they decided to sue they would consult their own lawyer. Appellant insisted that Wanda had entered into a binding agreement. A month later Wanda confirmed in writing that she wanted neither to sue nor to be represented by appellant. She requested that appellant notify the insurance company that he was not her lawyer, as the company would not release a check to her until he did so.[5] Carol also eventually discharged appellant. Although another lawyer represented her in concluding a settlement with the insurance company, she paid appellant one-third of her recovery in settlement of his lawsuit against her for breach of contract.[7]

Both Carol McClintock and Wanda Lou Holbert filed complaints against appellant with the Grievance Committee of the Geauga County Bar Association. The County Bar Association filed a formal complaint with the Board of Commissioners on Grievance and Discipline of the Supreme Court of Ohio.[8] After a hearing, the Board found that appellant had violated Disciplinary Rules (DR) 2-103(A) and 2-104(A) of the Ohio Code of Professional Responsibility. The Board rejected appellant's defense that his conduct was protected under the First and Fourteenth Amendments. The Supreme Court of Ohio adopted the findings of the Board,[10] reiterated that appellant's conduct was not constitutionally protected, and increased

---

4. Appellant told Wanda that she should indicate assent by stating, "O.K.," which she did. Appellant later testified: "I would say that most of my clients have essentially that much of a communication. . . . I think most of my clients, that's the way I practice law."

In explaining the contingency fee arrangement, appellant told Wanda Lou that his representation would not "cost [her] anything" because she would receive two-thirds of the recovery if appellant were successful in representing her but would not "have to pay [him] anything" otherwise.

5. The insurance company was willing to pay Wanda Lou for her injuries but would not release the check while appellant claimed, and Wanda Lou denied, that he represented her. Before appellant would "disavow further interest and claim" in Wanda Lou's recovery, he insisted by letter that Wanda Lou first pay him the sum of $2,466.66, which represented one-third of his "conservative" estimate of the worth of her claim.

7. Appellant represented to the Board of Commissioners at the disciplinary hearing that he would abandon his claim against Wanda Lou Holbert because "the rules say that if a contract has its origin in a controversy, that an ethical question can arise." Yet in fact appellant filed suit against Wanda for $2,466.66 after the disciplinary hearing. Ohralik v. Holbert, Case No. 76-CV-F-66, filed February 2, 1976, Chardon Mun.Ct., Geauga County, Ohio. Appellant's suit was dismissed with prejudice on January 27, 1977, after the decision of the Supreme Court of Ohio had been filed.

8. The Board of Commissioners is an agent of the Supreme Court of Ohio. Counsel for appellee stated at oral argument that the Board has "no connection with the Ohio State Bar Association whatsoever."

10. The Board found that Carol and Wanda Lou "were, if anything, casual acquaintances" of appellant; that appellant initiated the contact with Carol and obtained her consent to handle her claim; that he advised Wanda Lou that he represented Carol, had a "tip" for Wanda, and was prepared to represent her, too. The Board also found that appellant would not abide by Mrs. Holbert's

the sanction of a public reprimand recommended by the Board to indefinite suspension.

The decision in *Bates* was handed down after the conclusion of proceedings in the Ohio Supreme Court. We noted probable jurisdiction in this case to consider the scope of prosecution of a form of commercial speech, and an aspect of the State's authority to regulate and discipline members of the bar, not considered in *Bates*. 434 U.S. 814 (1977). We now affirm the judgment of the Supreme Court of Ohio.

II

The solicitation of business by a lawyer through direct, in-person communication with the prospective client has long been viewed as inconsistent with the profession's ideal of the attorney-client relationship and as posing a significant potential for harm to the prospective client. It has been proscribed by the organized Bar for many years. . . . The balance struck in *Bates* does not predetermine the outcome in this case. The entitlement of in-person solicitation of clients to the protection of the First Amendment differs from that of the kind of advertising approved in *Bates*, as does the strength of the State's countervailing interest in prohibition.

A

Appellant contends that his solicitation of the two young women as clients is indistinguishable, for purposes of constitutional analysis, from the advertisement in *Bates*. Like that advertisement, his meetings with the prospective clients apprised them of their legal rights and of the availability of a lawyer to pursue their claims. According to appellant, such conduct is "presumptively an exercise of his free speech rights" which cannot be curtailed in the absence of proof that it actually caused a specific harm that the State has a compelling interest in preventing. But in-person solicitation of professional employment by a lawyer does not stand on a par with truthful advertising about the availability and terms of routine legal services, let alone with forms of speech more traditionally within the concern of the First Amendment.

Expression concerning purely commercial transactions has come within the ambit of the Amendment's protection only recently. In rejecting the notion that such speech "is wholly outside the protection of the First Amendment," *Virginia* [State Board of] *Pharmacy* [v. Virginia Citizens Consumer Council], 425 U.S. [748 (1976)], at 761, we were careful not to hold "that it is wholly undifferentiable from other forms" of speech. Id., at 771 n.24. We have not discarded the "common-sense" distinction between speech proposing a commercial transaction, which occurs in an area traditionally subject to government regulation, and other varieties of speech. Ibid. To require a parity of constitutional protection for commercial and noncommercial speech alike could invite dilution, simply by a leveling process of the force of the Amendment's guidance with respect to the latter kind of speech. Rather than

---

request to leave Wanda alone, that both young women attempted to discharge appellant, and that appellant sued Carol McClintock.

subject the First Amendment to such a devitalization, we instead have afforded commercial speech a limited measure of protection, commensurate with its subordinate position in the scale of First Amendment values, while allowing modes of regulation that might be impermissible in the realm of noncommercial expression. . . .

In-person solicitation by a lawyer of remunerative employment is a business transaction in which speech is an essential but subordinate component. While this does not remove the speech from the protection of the First Amendment, as was held in *Bates* and *Virginia Pharmacy*, it lowers the level of appropriate judicial scrutiny.

As applied in this case, the Disciplinary Rules are said to have limited the communication of two kinds of information. First, appellant's solicitation imparted to Carol McClintock and Wanda Lou Holbert certain information about his availability and the terms of his proposed legal services. In this respect, in-person solicitation serves much the same function as the advertisement at issue in *Bates*. But there are significant differences as well. Unlike a public advertisement, which simply provides information and leaves the recipient free to act upon it or not, in-person solicitation may exert pressure and often demands an immediate response, without providing an opportunity for comparison or reflection. The aim and effect of in-person solicitation may be to provide a one-sided presentation and to encourage speedy and perhaps uninformed decisionmaking; there is no opportunity for intervention or counter-education by agencies of the Bar, supervisory authorities, or persons close to the solicited individual. The admonition that "the fitting remedy for evil counsels is good ones" is of little value when the circumstances provide no opportunity for any remedy at all. In-person solicitation is as likely as not to discourage persons needing counsel from engaging in a critical comparison of the "availability, nature, and prices" of legal services, cf. *Bates*, at 364; it actually may disserve the individual and societal interest, identified in *Bates*, in facilitating "informed and reliable decisionmaking." Ibid.

It also is argued that in-person solicitation may provide the solicited individual with information about his or her legal rights and remedies. In this case, appellant gave Wanda Lou a "tip" about the prospect of recovery based on the uninsured motorist clause in the McClintocks' insurance policy, and he explained that clause and Ohio's guest statute to Carol McClintock's parents. But neither of the Disciplinary Rules here at issue prohibited appellant from communicating information to these young women about their legal rights and the prospects of obtaining a monetary recovery, or from recommending that they obtain counsel. DR 2-104(A) merely prohibited him from using the information as bait with which to obtain an agreement to represent them for a fee. The Rule does not prohibit a lawyer from giving unsolicited legal advice; it proscribes the acceptance of employment resulting from such advice.

Appellant does not contend, and on the facts of this case could not contend, that his approaches to the two young women involved political expression or an exercise of associational freedom, "employ[ing] constitutionally privileged means of expression to secure constitutionally guaranteed civil rights." NAACP v. Button, 371 U.S. 415, 442 (1963); see In re Primus, [p. 640]. Nor can he compare his solicitation to the mutual assistance in asserting legal rights that was at issue in United Transportation Union v. Michigan Bar, 401 U.S. 576 (1971), Mine Workers v. Illinois Bar Assn., 389 U.S. 217 (1967), and Railroad Trainmen v. Virginia Bar, 377 U.S. 1 (1964) [discussed in Chapter 9]. A lawyer's procurement of remunerative employment is a subject only marginally affected with First Amendment concerns. It falls within the State's proper sphere of economic and professional regulation. . . . While entitled to some constitutional protection, appellant's conduct is subject to regulation in furtherance of important state interests.

B

The state interests implicated in this case are particularly strong. In addition to its general interest in protecting consumers and regulating commercial transactions, the State bears a special responsibility for maintaining standards among members of the licensed professions. . . . "The interest of the States in regulating lawyers is especially great since lawyers are essential to the primary governmental function of administering justice, and have historically been 'officers of the courts.'" Goldfarb v. Virginia State Bar, 421 U.S. 773 (1975). While lawyers act in part as "self-employed businessmen," they also act "as trusted agents of their clients, and as assistants to the court in search of a just solution to disputes." Cohen v. Hurley, 366 U.S. 117 (1961).

As is true with respect to advertising . . . it appears that the ban on solicitation by lawyers originated as a rule of professional etiquette rather than as a strictly ethical rule. See H. Drinker, *Legal Ethics* 210–211, and n.3 (1953). . . . But the fact that the original motivation behind the ban on solicitation today might be considered an insufficient justification for its perpetuation does not detract from the force of the other interests the bar continues to serve. . . . While the Court in *Bates* determined that truthful, restrained advertising of the prices of "routine" legal services would not have an adverse effect on the professionalism of lawyers, this was only because it found "the postulated connection between advertising and the erosion of *true professionalism* to be severely strained." 433 U.S., at 368 (emphasis supplied). The *Bates* Court did not question a State's interest in maintaining high standards among licensed professionals. Indeed, to the extent that the ethical standards of lawyers are linked to the service and protection of clients, they do further the goals of "true professionalism."

The substantive evils of solicitation have been stated over the years in sweeping terms: stirring up litigation, assertion of fraudulent claims, debasing the legal profession, and potential harm to the solicited client in the form of overreaching, overcharging, underrepresentation, and misrepresentation. The American Bar Association, as amicus curiae, defends the rule against solicitation primarily on three broad grounds: It is said that the prohibitions embodied in Disciplinary Rules 2-103(A) and 2-104(A) serve to reduce the likelihood of overreaching and the exertion of undue influence on lay persons; to protect the privacy of individuals; and to avoid situations where the lawyer's exercise of judgment on behalf of the client will be clouded by his own pecuniary self-interest.

We need not discuss or evaluate each of these interests in detail as appellant has conceded that the State has a legitimate and indeed "compelling" interest in preventing those aspects of solicitation that involve fraud, undue influence, intimidation, overreaching, and other forms of "vexatious conduct." We agree that protection of the public from these aspects of solicitation is a legitimate and important state interest.

III

Appellant's concession that strong state interests justify regulation to prevent the evils he enumerates would end this case but for his insistence that none of those evils was found to be present in his acts of solicitation. He challenges what he characterizes as the "indiscriminate application" of the rules to him and thus attacks the validity of DR 2-103(A) and DR 2-104(A) not facially, but as applied to his acts of solicitation. And because no allegations or findings were made of the specific wrongs appellant concedes would justify disciplinary action, appellant terms his solicitation "pure," meaning "soliciting and obtaining agreements from Carol McClintock and Wanda Lou Holbert to represent each of them," without more. Appellant therefore argues that we must decide whether a State may discipline him for solicitation per se without offending the First and Fourteenth Amendments. . . .

. . . [A]ppellant errs in assuming that the constitutional validity of the judgment below depends on proof that his conduct constituted actual overreaching or inflicted some specific injury on Wanda Holbert or Carol McClintock. His assumption flows from the premise that nothing less than actual proven harm to the solicited individual would be a sufficiently important state interest to justify disciplining the attorney who solicits employment in person for pecuniary gain.

Appellant's argument misconceives the nature of the State's interest. The rules prohibiting solicitation are prophylactic measures whose objective is the prevention of harm before it occurs. The rules were applied in this case to discipline a lawyer for soliciting employment for pecuniary gain under circumstances likely to result in the adverse consequences the State seeks to avert. In such a situation, which is inherently conducive to overreaching and other forms of misconduct, the State has a strong interest in adopting and enforcing rules of conduct designed to protect the public from harmful solicitation by lawyers whom it has licensed.

The State's perception of the potential for harm in circumstances such as those presented in this case is well-founded. The detrimental aspects of face-to-face selling even of ordinary consumer products have been recognized and addressed by the Federal Trade Commission, and it hardly need be said that the potential for overreaching is significantly greater when a lawyer, a professional trained in the art of persuasion, personally solicits an unsophisticated, injured, or distressed lay person. Such an individual may place his or her trust in a lawyer, regardless of the latter's qualifications or the individual's actual need for legal representation, simply in response to persuasion under circumstances conducive to uninformed acquiescence. Although it is argued that personal solicitation is valuable because it may apprise a victim of misfortune of his or her legal rights, the very plight of that person not only makes him or her more vulnerable to influence but also may make advice all the more intrusive. Thus, under these adverse conditions the overtures of an uninvited lawyer may distress the solicited individual simply because of their obtrusiveness and the invasion of the individual's privacy, even when no other harm materializes. Under such circumstances, it is not unreasonable for the State to presume that in-person solicitation by lawyers more often than not will be injurious to the person solicited.

The efficacy of the State's effort to prevent such harm to prospective clients would be substantially diminished if, having proved a solicitation in circumstances like those of this case, the State were required in addition to prove actual injury. Unlike the advertising in *Bates*, in-person solicitation is not visible or otherwise open to public scrutiny. Often there is no witness other than the lawyer and the lay person whom he has solicited, rendering it difficult or impossible to obtain reliable proof of what actually took place. This would be especially true if the lay person were so distressed at the time of the solicitation that he or she could not recall specific details at a later date. If appellant's view were sustained, in-person solicitation would be virtually immune to effective oversight and regulation by the State or by the legal profession, in contravention of the State's strong interest in regulating members of the Bar in an effective, objective, and self-enforcing manner. It therefore is not unreasonable, or violative of the Constitution, for a State to respond with what in effect is a prophylactic rule.

On the basis of the undisputed facts of record, we conclude that the disciplinary rules constitutionally could be applied to appellant. He approached two young accident victims at a time when they were especially incapable of making informed judgments or of assessing and protecting their own interests. He solicited Carol McClintock in a hospital room where she lay in traction and sought out Wanda Lou Holbert on the day she came home from the hospital, knowing from his prior inquiries that she had just been released. Appellant urged his services upon the young women and used the information he had obtained from the McClintocks, and the fact of his agreement with Carol, to induce Wanda to say "O.K." in response to his solicitation. He employed a concealed tape recorder, seemingly to insure that he would have evidence of Wanda's oral assent to the representation. He emphasized that his fee would come out of the recovery, thereby tempting the young women with what sounded like a cost-free and therefore irresistible offer. He refused to withdraw when Mrs. Holbert requested him to do so only a day after the initial meeting between appellant and Wanda Lou and continued to represent himself to the insurance company as Wanda Holbert's lawyer.

The court below did not hold that these or other facts were proof of actual harm to Wanda Holbert or Carol McClintock but rested on the conclusion that appellant had engaged in the general misconduct proscribed by the Disciplinary Rules. Under our view of the State's interest in averting harm by prohibiting solicitation in circumstances where it is likely to occur, the absence of explicit proof or findings of harm or injury is immaterial. The facts in this case present a striking example of the potential for overreaching that is inherent in a lawyer's in-person solicitation of professional employment. They also demonstrate the need for prophylactic regulation in furtherance of the State's interest in protecting the lay public. We hold that the application of Disciplinary Rules 2-103(A) and 2-104(A) to appellant does not offend the Constitution.

Accordingly, the judgment of the Supreme Court of Ohio is Affirmed.

In re Primus

436 U.S. 412 (1978)

Mr. Justice POWELL delivered the opinion of the Court.

We consider on this appeal whether a State may punish a member of its Bar who, seeking to further political and ideological goals through associational activity, including litigation, advises a lay person of her legal rights and discloses in a subsequent letter that free legal assistance is available through a nonprofit organization with which the lawyer and her associates are affiliated. Appellant, a member of the Bar of South Carolina, received a public reprimand for writing such a letter. The appeal is opposed by the State Attorney General, on behalf the Board of Commissioners on Grievances and Discipline of the Supreme Court of South Carolina. . . .

I

Appellant, Edna Smith Primus, is a lawyer practicing in Columbia, S.C. During the period in question she was associated with the "Carolina Community Law Firm,"[1] and an officer of and cooperating lawyer with the Columbia branch of the American Civil Liberties Union (ACLU).[2] She received no compensation for her work on behalf of the ACLU,[3] but was paid a retainer as a legal consultant for the South Carolina Council on Human Relations (Council), a nonprofit organization with offices in Columbia.

---

1. The court below determined that the Carolina Community Law Firm was "an expense sharing arrangement with each attorney keeping his own fees." 268 S.C. 259, 261 (1977). The firm later changed its name to Buhl, Smith & Bagby.

2. The ACLU was organized in 1920 by individuals who had worked in the defense of the rights of conscientious objectors during World War I and political dissidents during the postwar period. It views itself as a "national non-partisan organization defending our Bill of Rights for all without distinction or compromise." ACLU, *Presenting the American Civil Liberties Union* 2 (1948). The organization's activities range from litigation and lobbying to educational campaigns in support of its avowed goals. . . .

3. Although all three lawyers in the Carolina Community Law Firm maintained some association with the ACLU—appellant and Carlton Bagby as unsalaried cooperating lawyers, and

During the summer of 1973, local and national newspapers reported that pregnant mothers on public assistance in Aiken County, S.C. were being sterilized or threatened with sterilization as a condition of the continued receipt of medical assistance under the "Medicaid" program. Concerned by this development, Gary Allen, an Aiken businessman and officer of a local organization serving indigents, called the Council requesting that one of its representatives come to Aiken to address some of the women who had been sterilized. At the Council's behest, appellant, who had not known Allen previously, called him and arranged a meeting in his office in July 1973. Among those attending was Mary Etta Williams, who had been sterilized by Dr. Clovis H. Pierce after the birth of her third child. Williams and her grandmother attended the meeting because Allen, an old family friend, had invited them and because Williams wanted "[t]o see what it was all about . . . ." At the meeting, appellant advised those present, including Williams and the other women who had been sterilized by Dr. Pierce, of their legal rights and suggested the possibility of a lawsuit.

Early in August 1973 the ACLU informed appellant that it was willing to provide representation for Aiken mothers who had been sterilized. Appellant testified that after being advised by Allen that Williams wished to institute suit against Dr. Pierce, she decided to inform Williams of the ACLU's offer of free legal representation. Shortly after receiving appellant's letter dated August 30, 1973[6] — the centerpiece of

---

Herbert Buhl as staff counsel — appellant testified that "the firm did not handle any litigation for [the] ACLU."

6. Written on the stationery of the Carolina Community Law Firm, the letter stated:

August 30, 1973

Mrs. Marietta Williams
347 Sumter Street
Aiken, South Carolina 29801

Dear Mrs. Williams:

You will probabl[y] remember me from talking with you at Mr. Allen's office in July about the sterilization performed on you. The American Civil Liberties Union would like to file a lawsuit on your behalf for money against the doctor who performed the operation. We will be coming to Aiken in the near future and would like to explain what is involved so you can understand what is going on.

Now I have a question to ask of you. Would you object to talking to a women's magazine about the situation in Aiken? The magazine is doing a feature story on the whole sterilization problem and wants to talk to you and others in South Carolina. If you don't mind doing this, call me *collect* at 254-8151 on Friday before 5:00, if you receive this letter in time. Or call me on Tuesday morning (after Labor Day) *collect*.

I want to assure you that this interview is being done to show what is happening to women against their wishes, and is not being done to harm you in any way. But I want you to decide, so call me collect, and let me know of your decision. This practice must stop.

About the lawsuit, if you are interested, let me know, and I'll let you know when we will come down to talk to you about it. We will be coming to talk to Mrs. Waters at the same time; she has already asked the American Civil Liberties Union to file a suit on her behalf.

Sincerely,
s/Edna Smith

this litigation—Williams visited Dr. Pierce to discuss the progress of her third child who was ill. At the doctor's office, she encountered his lawyer and at the latter's request signed a release of liability in the doctor's favor. Williams showed appellant's letter to the doctor and his lawyer, and they retained a copy. She then called appellant from the doctor's office and announced her intention not to sue. There was no further communication between appellant and Williams.

On October 9, 1974, the Secretary of the Board of Commissioners on Grievances and Discipline of the Supreme Court of South Carolina (Board) filed a formal complaint with the Board, charging that appellant had engaged in "solicitation in violation of the Canons of Ethics" by sending the August 30, 1973 letter to Williams. Appellant denied any unethical solicitation and asserted, inter alia, that her conduct was protected by the First and Fourteenth Amendments and by Canon 2 of the Code of Professional Responsibility of the American Bar Association (ABA). The complaint was heard by a panel of the Board on March 20, 1975. The State's evidence consisted of the letter, the testimony of Williams,[7] and a copy of the summons and complaint in the action instituted against Dr. Pierce and various state officials, Doe v. Pierce, . . . aff'd in part and rev'd in part. Walker v. Pierce, 560 F.2d 609 (CA4 1977), cert. denied, 434 U.S. 1075 (1978).[8] Following denial of appellant's motion to dismiss, she testified in her own behalf and called Allen, a number of ACLU representatives, and several character witnesses.

The panel filed a report recommending that appellant be found guilty of soliciting a client on behalf of the ACLU, in violation of Disciplinary Rules (DR) 2-103(D)(5)(a) and (c) and 2-104(A)(5) of the Supreme Court of South Carolina, and that a private reprimand be issued. It noted that "[t]he evidence is inconclusive as to whether [appellant] solicited Mrs. Williams on her own behalf, but she did solicit Mrs. Williams on behalf of the ACLU, which would benefit financially in the event of successful prosecution of the suit for money damages." The panel determined

---

Edna Smith
Attorney-at-law

7. Williams testified that at the July meeting appellant advised her of her legal remedies, of the possibility of a lawsuit if her sterilization had been coerced, and of appellant's willingness to serve as her lawyer without compensation. Williams recounted she had told appellant that because her child was in critical condition, she "did not have time for" a lawsuit and "would contact [appellant] some more." She also denied that she had expressed to Allen an interest in suing her doctor. . . . On cross-examination, however, Williams confirmed an earlier statement she had made in an affidavit that appellant "did not attempt to persuade or pressure me to file [the] lawsuit." . . .

8. This class action was filed on April 15, 1974, by two Negro women alleging that Dr. Pierce, in conspiracy with state officials, had sterilized them, or was threatening to do so, solely on account of their race and number of children, while they received assistance under the Medicaid program. The complaint sought declaratory and injunctive relief, damages, and attorney's fees, and asserted violations of the Constitution and 42 U.S.C. §§ 1981, 1983, 1985(3) and 2000d.

Bagby, one of appellant's associates in the Carolina Community Law Firm and fellow cooperating lawyer with the ACLU, was one of several attorneys of record for the plaintiffs. Buhl, another of appellant's associates and a staff counsel for the ACLU in South Carolina, also may have represented one of the women.

that appellant violated DR 2-103(D)(5) "by attempting to solicit a client for a non-profit organization which, as its primary purpose, renders legal services, where respondent's associate is a staff counsel for the non-profit organization." Appellant also was found to have violated DR 2-104(A)(5) because she solicited Williams, after providing unsolicited legal advice, to join in a prospective class action for damages and other relief that was to be brought by the ACLU.

After the hearing on January 9, 1976, the full Board approved the panel report and administered a private reprimand. On March 17, 1977, the Supreme Court of South Carolina entered an order which adopted verbatim the findings and conclusions of the panel report and increased the sanction, sua sponte, to a public reprimand. 268 S.C. 259. . . .

II

. . .

Unlike the situation in *Ohralik* . . . appellant's act of solicitation took the form of a letter to a woman with whom appellant had discussed the possibility of seeking redress for an allegedly unconstitutional sterilization. This was not in-person solicitation for pecuniary gain. Appellant was communicating an offer of free assistance by attorneys associated with the ACLU, not an offer predicated on entitlement to a share of any monetary recovery. And her actions were undertaken to express personal political beliefs and to advance the civil-liberties objectives of the ACLU, rather than to derive financial gain. The question presented in this case is whether, in light of the values protected by the First and Fourteenth Amendments, these differences materially affect the scope of state regulation of the conduct of lawyers. . . .

. . . The Supreme Court of South Carolina found appellant to have engaged in unethical conduct because she " 'solicit[ed] a client for a non-profit organization, which, as its primary purpose, renders legal services, where respondent's associate is a staff counsel for the non-profit organization.' " 268 S.C., at 269. It rejected appellant's First Amendment defenses by distinguishing *Button* [discussed in Chapter 9] from the case before it. Whereas the NAACP in that case was primarily a " 'political' " organization that used " 'litigation as an adjunct to the overriding political aims of the organization,' " the ACLU " 'has as one of its primary purposes, the rendition of legal services.' " Id., at 268, 269. The court also intimated that the ACLU's policy of requesting an award of counsel fees indicated that the organization might " 'benefit financially in the event of successful prosecution of the suit for money damages.' " Id., at 263.

Although the disciplinary panel did not permit full factual development of the aims and practices of the ACLU, the record does not support the state court's effort to draw a meaningful distinction between the ACLU and the NAACP. From all that appears, the ACLU and its local chapters, much like the NAACP and its local affiliates in *Button*, "[engage] . . . in extensive educational and lobbying activities" and "also [devote] . . . much of [their] funds and energies to an extensive program of assisting certain kinds of litigation on behalf of [their] declared purposes." 371 U.S., at

419–420. . . . The court below acknowledged that "'the ACLU has only entered cases in which substantial civil liberties questions are involved . . . .'" 268 S.C., at 263. . . . It has engaged in the defense of unpopular causes and unpopular defendants and has represented individuals in litigation that has defined the scope of constitutional protection in areas such as political dissent, juvenile rights, prisoners' rights, military law, amnesty, and privacy. . . . For the ACLU, as for the NAACP, "litigation is not a technique of resolving private differences"; it is "a form of political expression" and "political association." 371 U.S., at 429, 431.[20]

We find equally unpersuasive any suggestion that the level of constitutional scrutiny in this case should be lowered because of a possible benefit to the ACLU. The discipline administered to appellant was premised solely on the possibility of financial benefit to the organization, rather than any possibility of pecuniary gain to herself, her associates, or the lawyers representing the plaintiffs in the Doe v. Pierce litigation. It is conceded that appellant received no compensation for any of the activities in question. It is also undisputed that neither the ACLU nor any lawyer associated with it would have shared in any monetary recovery by the plaintiffs in Doe v. Pierce. If Williams had elected to bring suit, and had been represented by staff lawyers for the ACLU, the situation would have been similar to that in *Button*, where the lawyers for the NAACP were "organized as a staff and paid by" that organization. 371 U.S., at 434. . . .

Contrary to appellee's suggestion, the ACLU's policy of requesting an award of counsel fees does not take this case outside the protection of *Button*. Although the Court in *Button* did not consider whether the NAACP seeks counsel fees, such requests are often made both by that organization . . . and by the NAACP Legal Defense Fund, Inc. . . . In any event, in a case of this kind there are differences between counsel fees awarded by a court and traditional fee-paying arrangements which mitigate against a presumption that ACLU sponsorship of litigation is motivated by considerations of pecuniary gain rather than by its widely recognized goal of vindicating civil liberties. Counsel fees are awarded in the discretion of the court; awards are not drawn from the plaintiff's recovery, and are usually premised on a successful outcome; and the amounts awarded often may not correspond to fees generally obtained in private litigation. Moreover, under prevailing law during the events in question, an award of counsel fees in federal litigation was available only in limited circumstances. And even if there had been an award during the period in question, it would have gone to the central fund of the ACLU.[24] Although such benefit to the

---

20. There is nothing in the record to suggest that the ACLU or its South Carolina affiliate is an organization dedicated exclusively to the provision of legal services. Nor does the record support any inference that either the ACLU or its affiliate "is a mere sham to cover what is actually nothing more than an attempt," Eastern Railroad President Conf. v. Noerr Motor Freight, 365 U.S. 127, 144 (1961), by a group of attorneys to evade a valid state rule against solicitation for pecuniary gain. . . .

24. Appellant informs us that the ACLU policy then in effect provided that cooperating lawyers associated with the ACLU or with an affiliate could not receive an award of counsel fees for services rendered in an ACLU-sponsored litigation. . . .

organization may increase with the maintenance of successful litigation, the same situation obtains with voluntary contributions and foundation support, which also may rise with ACLU victories in important areas of the law. That possibility, standing alone, offers no basis for equating the work of lawyers associated with the ACLU or the NAACP with that of a group that exists for the primary purpose of financial gain through the recovery of counsel fees.

Appellant's letter of August 30, 1973 to Mrs. Williams thus comes within the generous zone of First Amendment protection reserved for associational freedoms. The ACLU engages in litigation as a vehicle for effective political expression and association, as well as a means of communicating useful information to the public. . . .

V

South Carolina's action in punishing appellant for soliciting a prospective litigant by mail, on behalf of the ACLU, must withstand the "exacting scrutiny applicable to limitations on core First Amendment rights . . . ." Buckley v. Valeo, 424 U.S. 1, 44–45 (1976). . . .

Appellee contends that the disciplinary action taken in this case is part of a regulatory program aimed at the prevention of undue influence, overreaching, misrepresentation, invasion of privacy, conflict of interest, lay interference, and other evils that are thought to inhere generally in solicitation by lawyers of prospective clients, and to be present on the record before us. We do not dispute the importance of these interests. . . .

A

The disciplinary rules in question sweep broadly. Under DR 2-103(D)(5), a lawyer employed by the ACLU or a similar organization may never give unsolicited advice to a lay person that he or she retain the organization's free services, and it would seem that one who merely assists or maintains a cooperative relationship with the organization also must suppress the giving of such advice if he or anyone associated with the organization will be involved in the ultimate litigation. Notwithstanding appellee's concession in this Court, it is far from clear that a lawyer may communicate the organization's offer of legal assistance at an informational gathering such as the July 1973 meeting in Aiken without breaching the literal terms of the Rule. Moreover, the Disciplinary Rules in question permit punishment for mere solicitation unaccompanied by proof of any of the substantive evils that appellee maintains were present in this case. In sum, the Rules in their present form have a distinct potential for dampening the kind of "cooperative activity that would make advocacy of litigation meaningful," *Button*, 371 U.S., at 438, as well as for permitting discretionary enforcement against unpopular causes.

This policy was changed in 1977 to permit local experimentation with the sharing of court-awarded fees between state affiliates and cooperating attorneys. The South Carolina chapter has not exercised that option. We express no opinion whether our analysis in this case would be different had the latter policy been in effect during the period in question.

B

Even if we ignore the breadth of the Disciplinary Rules and the absence of findings in the decision below that support the justifications advanced by appellee in this Court, we think it clear from the record—which appellee does not suggest is inadequately developed—that findings compatible with the First Amendment could not have been made in this case. . . .

Where political expression or association is at issue, this Court has not tolerated the degree of imprecision that often characterizes government regulation of the conduct of commercial affairs. The approach we adopt today in *Ohralik* . . . that the State may proscribe in-person solicitation for pecuniary gain under circumstances likely to result in adverse consequences, cannot be applied to appellant's activity on behalf of the ACLU. Although a showing of potential danger may suffice in the former context, appellant may not be disciplined unless her activity in fact involved the type of misconduct at which South Carolina's broad prohibition is said to be directed.

The record does not support appellee's contention that undue influence, overreaching, misrepresentation, or invasion of privacy actually occurred in this case. Appellant's letter of August 30, 1973, followed up the earlier meeting—one concededly protected by the First and Fourteenth Amendments—by notifying Williams that the ACLU would be interested in supporting possible litigation. The letter imparted additional information material to making an informed decision about whether to authorize litigation, and permitted Williams an opportunity, which she exercised, for arriving at a deliberate decision. The letter was not facially misleading; indeed, it offered "to explain what is involved so you can understand what is going on." The transmittal of this letter—as contrasted with in-person solicitation—involved no appreciable invasion of privacy; nor did it afford any significant opportunity for overreaching or coercion. Moreover, the fact that there was a written communication lessens substantially the difficulty of policing solicitation practices that do offend valid rules of professional conduct. . . . The manner of solicitation in this case certainly was no more likely to cause harmful consequences than the activity considered in *Button*.

Nor does the record permit a finding of a serious likelihood of conflict of interest or injurious lay interference with the attorney-client relationship. . . .

The State's interests in preventing the "stirring up" of frivolous or vexatious litigation and minimizing commercialization of the legal profession offer no further justification for the discipline administered in this case. The *Button* Court declined to accept the proffered analogy to the common-law offenses of maintenance, champerty, and barratry, where the record would not support a finding that the litigant was solicited for a malicious purpose or "for private gain, serving no public interest," 371 U.S., at 440. The same result follows from the facts of this case, and considerations of undue commercialization of the legal profession are of marginal force where, as here, a nonprofit organization offers its services free of charge to individuals who may be in need of legal assistance and may lack the financial means and sophistication necessary to tap alternative sources of such aid.[31]

At bottom, the case against appellant rests on the proposition that a State may regulate in a prophylactic fashion all solicitation activities of lawyers because there may be some potential for overreaching, conflict of interest, or other substantive evils whenever a lawyer gives unsolicited advice and communicates an offer of representation to a layman. Under certain circumstances, that approach is appropriate in the case of speech that simply "propose[s] a commercial transaction," Pittsburgh Press Co. v. Human Relations Comm'n, 413 U.S. 376, 385 (1973). . . . In the context of political expression and association, however, a State must regulate with significantly greater precision.[32]

VI

The State is free to fashion reasonable restrictions with respect to the time, place, and manner of solicitation by members of its Bar. . . . The State's special interest in regulating members of a profession it licenses, and who serve as officers of its courts, amply justifies the application of narrowly drawn rules to proscribe solicitation that in fact is misleading, overbearing, or involves other features of deception or improper influence. . . . [A] State also may forbid in-person solicitation for pecuniary gain under circumstances likely to result in these evils. And a State may insist that lawyers not solicit on behalf of lay organizations that exert control over the actual conduct of any ensuing litigation. See *Button*, 371 U.S., at 447 (Mr. Justice White, concurring in part and dissenting in part). Accordingly, nothing in this opinion should be read to foreclose carefully tailored regulation that does not abridge unnecessarily the associational freedom of nonprofit organizations, or their members, having characteristics like those of the NAACP or the ACLU.

---

31. . . . In recognition of the overarching obligation of the lawyer to serve the community, see Canon 2 of the ABA Code of Professional Responsibility, the ethical rules of the legal profession traditionally have recognized an exception from any general ban on solicitation for offers of representation, without charge, extended to individuals who may be unable to obtain legal assistance on their own. See, e.g., In re Ades, 6 F. Supp. 467, 475–476 (Md. 1934); Gunnels v. Atlanta Bar Assn., 191 Ga. 366 (1940); American Bar Association, Committee on Professional Ethics and Grievances, Formal Opinion 148, at 416–419 (1967).

32. Normally the purpose or motive of the speaker is not central to First Amendment protection, but it does bear on the distinction between conduct that is "an associational aspect of 'expression,'" Emerson, "Freedom of Association and Freedom of Expression," 74 Yale L.J. 1, 26 (1964), and other activity subject to plenary regulation by government. *Button* recognized that certain forms of "cooperative, organizational activity," 371 U.S., at 430, including litigation, are part of the "freedom to engage in association for the advancement of beliefs and ideas," NAACP v. Alabama, 357 U.S. 449, 460 (1958), and that this freedom is an implicit guarantee of the First Amendment. See Healy v. James, 408 U.S. 169, 181 (1972). As shown above, appellant's speech—as part of associational activity—was expression intended to advance "beliefs and ideas." In Ohralik v. Ohio State Bar Assn., the lawyer was not engaged in associational activity for the advancement of beliefs and ideas: his purpose was the advancement of his own commercial interests. The line, based in part on the motive of the speaker and the character of the expressive activity, will not always be easy to draw . . . but that is no reason for avoiding the undertaking.

We conclude that South Carolina's application of its Disciplinary Rules 2-103(D) (5)(a) and (c) and 2-104(A)(5) to appellant's solicitation by letter on behalf the ACLU violates the First and Fourteenth Amendments. The judgment of the Supreme Court of South Carolina is Reversed.

Mr. Justice MARSHALL, concurring in part and concurring in the judgments. . . .

What is objectionable about Ohralik's behavior . . . is not so much that he solicited business for himself, but rather the circumstances in which he performed that solicitation and the means by which he accomplished it. Appropriately, the Court's actual holding in *Ohralik*, 48 Ohio St. 2d 217, is a limited one: that the solicitation of business under circumstances—such as those found in this record—presenting substantial dangers of harm to society or the client independent of the solicitation itself, may constitutionally be prohibited by the State. In this much of the Court's opinion in *Ohralik*, I join fully.

II

The facts in *Primus*, 268 S.C. 259, by contrast, show a "solicitation" of employment in accordance with the highest standards of the legal profession. Appellant in this case was acting not for her own pecuniary benefit, but to promote what she perceived to be the legal rights of persons not likely to appreciate or to be able to vindicate their own rights. The obligation of all lawyers, whether or not members of an association committed to a particular point of view, to see that legal aid is available, "where the litigant is in need of assistance, or where important issues are involved in the case," has long been established. In re Ades, 6 F. Supp. 467, 475 (Md. 1934) . . . .

In light of this long tradition of public interest representation by lawyer volunteers, I share my Brother Blackmun's concern with respect to Part VI in the Court's opinion, and believe that the Court has engaged in unnecessary and unfortunate dicta therein. It would be most undesirable to discourage lawyers—so many of whom find time to work only for those clients who can pay their fees—from continuing to volunteer their services in appropriate cases. Moreover, it cannot be too strongly emphasized that, where "political expression and association" are involved, "a State may not, under the guise of prohibiting professional misconduct, ignore constitutional rights." NAACP v. Button, [p. 727]. For these reasons, I find particularly troubling the Court's dictum that "a State may insist that lawyers not solicit on behalf of lay organizations that exert control over the actual conduct of any ensuing litigation." This proposition is by no means self-evident, has never been the actual holding of this Court, and is not put in issue by the facts presently before us. . . .

III

Our holdings today deal only with situations at opposite poles of the problem of attorney solicitation. In their aftermath, courts and professional associations may reasonably be expected to look to these opinions for guidance in redrafting the disciplinary rules that must apply across a spectrum of activities ranging from clearly protected speech to clearly proscribable conduct. A large number of situations falling between the poles represented by the instant facts will doubtless occur. In considering the wisdom and constitutionality of rules directed at such intermediate situations our fellow members of the Bench and Bar must be guided not only by today's decisions, but also by our decision last Term in Bates v. State Bar of Arizona. . . . In that context we rejected many of the general justifications for rules applicable to one intermediate situation not directly addressed by the Court today—the commercial but otherwise "benign" solicitation of clients by an attorney.[3] . . .

A

Like rules against advertising, rules against solicitation substantially impede the flow of important information to consumers from those most likely to provide it—the practicing members of the Bar. Many persons with legal problems fail to seek relief through the legal system because they are unaware that they have a legal problem, and, even if they "perceive a need," many "do not obtain counsel . . . because of an inability to locate a competent attorney." Bates v. State Bar of Arizona. Notwithstanding the injurious aspects of Ohralik's conduct, even his case illustrates the potentially useful, information-providing aspects of attorney solicitation: Motivated by the desire for pecuniary gain, but informed with the special training and knowledge of an attorney, Ohralik advised both his clients (apparently correctly) that, although they had been injured by an uninsured motorist, they could nonetheless recover on the McClintocks' insurance policy. The provision of such information about legal rights and remedies is an important function, even where the rights and remedies are of a private and commercial nature involving no constitutional or political overtones. . . .

In view of the similar functions performed by advertising and solicitation by attorneys, I find somewhat disturbing the Court's suggestion in *Ohralik* that in-person solicitation of business, though entitled to some degree of constitutional protection as "commercial speech" is entitled to less protection under the First Amendment than is "the kind of advertising approved in *Bates*." The First Amendment information interests served by solicitation, whether or not it occurs in a purely commercial context, are substantial, and they are entitled to as much protection as the interests we found to be protected in *Bates*.

The impact of the nonsolicitation rules, moreover, is discriminatory with respect to the suppliers as well as the consumers of legal services. Just as the persons who suffer most from lack of knowledge about lawyers' availability belong to the less privileged classes of society, so the disciplinary rules about solicitation fall most heavily on those attorneys engaged in a single practitioner or small partnership form of

---

3. By "benign" commercial solicitation, I mean solicitation by advice and information that is truthful and that is presented in a noncoercive, nondeceitful and dignified manner to a potential client who is emotionally and physically capable of making a rational decision either to accept or reject the representation with respect to a legal claim or matter that is not frivolous. . . .

practice[7]—attorneys who typically earn less than their fellow practitioners in larger, corporate-oriented firms. . . . Indeed, some scholars have suggested that the rules against solicitation were developed by the professional bar to keep recently immigrated lawyers, who gravitated toward the smaller, personal injury practice, from effective entry into the professions. See J. Auerbach, *Unequal Justice* 42–62, 126–129 (1976). In light of this history, I am less inclined than the majority appears to be to weigh favorably in the balance of the State's interests here the longevity of the ban on attorney solicitation. . . .

C

By discussing the origin and impact of the nonsolicitation rules, I do not mean to belittle those obviously substantial interests that the State has in regulating attorneys to protect the public from fraud, deceit, misrepresentation, overreaching, undue influence, and invasions of privacy. But where honest, unpressured "commercial" solicitation is involved—a situation not presented in either of these cases—I believe it is open to doubt whether the State's interests are sufficiently compelling to warrant the intrusion on the free flow of information which results from a sweeping nonsolicitation rule and against which the First Amendment ordinarily protects. While the State's interest in regulating in-person solicitation may, for reasons explained in *Ohralik*, be somewhat greater than its interest in regulating print advertisements, these concededly legitimate interests might well be served by more specific and less restrictive rules than a total ban on pecuniary solicitation. For example, the Justice Department has suggested that the disciplinary rules be reworded "so as to *permit* all solicitation and advertising except the claims that are false, misleading, undignified or champertous."[8]

To the extent that in-person solicitation of business may constitutionally be subjected to more substantial state regulation as to time, place, and manner than printed advertising of legal services, it is not because such solicitation has "traditionally" been banned, nor because one form of commercial speech is of less value than another under the First Amendment. Rather, any additional restrictions can be justified only to the degree that dangers which the State has a right to prevent are actually presented by conduct attendant to such speech, thus increasing the relative "strength of the State's countervailing interest in prohibition." As the majority notes, and I wholeheartedly agree, these dangers are amply present in the *Ohralik* case. . . .

Mr. Justice REHNQUIST, dissenting.

In this case and the companion case of Ohralik v. Ohio State Bar Assn., the Court tells its own tale of two lawyers: One tale ends happily for the lawyer and one does not. If we were given the latitude of novelists in deciding between happy and unhappy

---

7. According to the American Bar Foundation, 72.7% of all lawyers were in private practice in 1970; of these, over half practiced as individual practitioners. The 1971 Lawyer Statistical Report 10 (1972).

8. Remarks of L. Bernstein, Chief, Special Litigation Section, Antitrust Division, Department of Justice, reprinted in 5 CCH Trade Reg. Rep. ¶50,197 (1974) (emphasis added). . . .

endings for the heroes and villains of our tales, I might well join in the Court's disposition of both cases. But under our federal system it is for the States to decide which lawyers shall be admitted to the bar and remain there; this Court may interfere only if the State's decision is rendered impermissible by the United States Constitution. We can of course develop a jurisprudence of epithets and slogans in this area, in which "ambulance-chasers" suffer one fate and "civil liberties lawyers" another. But I remain unpersuaded by the Court's opinions in these two cases that there is a principled basis for concluding that the First and Fourteenth Amendments forbid South Carolina from disciplining Primus here, but permit Ohio to discipline Ohralik in the companion case. I believe that both South Carolina and Ohio are well within the limits prescribed by those Amendments, and I would therefore affirm the judgment in each case. . . .

In distinguishing between Primus' protected solicitation and Ohralik's unprotected solicitation the Court lamely declares, "We have not discarded the 'common-sense' distinction between speech proposing a commercial transaction, which occurs in an area traditionally subject to government regulation, and other varieties of speech." Yet to the extent that this "common-sense" distinction focuses on the content of the speech, it is at least suspect under many of this Court's First Amendment cases, see, e.g. Police Dept. of Chicago v. Mosley, 408 U.S. 92, 96–98 (1972), and to the extent it focuses upon the motive of the speaker, it is subject to manipulation by clever practitioners. If Albert Ohralik, like Edna Primus, viewed litigation "'not [as] a technique of resolving private differences,'" but as "'a form of political expression' and 'political association,'" for all that appears he would be restored to his right to practice. And we may be sure that the next lawyer in Ohralik's shoes who is disciplined for similar conduct will come here cloaked in the prescribed manner of "political association" to assure that insurance companies do not take unfair advantage of policyholders. . . .

I do not believe that any State will be able to determine with confidence the area in which it may regulate prophylactically and the area in which it may regulate only upon a specific showing of harm. Despite the Court's assertion to the contrary, the difficulty of drawing distinctions on the basis of the content of the speech or the motive of the speaker *is* a valid reason for avoiding the undertaking where a more objective standard is readily available. I believe that constitutional inquiry must focus on the character of the conduct which the State seeks to regulate, and not on the motives of the individual lawyers or the nature of the particular litigation involved. The State is empowered to discipline for conduct which it deems detrimental to the public interest unless foreclosed from doing so by our cases construing the First and Fourteenth Amendments. . . .

Here, South Carolina has not attempted to punish the ACLU or any layman associated with it. Gary Allen, who was the instigator of the effort to sue Dr. Pierce, remains as free as before to solicit potential plaintiffs to future litigation. Likewise, Primus remains as free as before to address gatherings of the sort described in *Button* to advise potential plaintiffs of their legal rights. Primus' first contact with Williams took place at such a gathering, and South Carolina evidently in response to *Button*, has not attempted to discipline her for her part in that meeting. It has disciplined her for initiating further contact on an individual basis with Williams, who had not expressed any desire to become involved in the collective activity being organized by the ACLU. While *Button* appears to permit such individual solicitation for political purposes by lay members of the organization, it nowhere explicitly permits such activity on the part of lawyers.

As the Court understands the Disciplinary Rule enforced by South Carolina, "a lawyer employed by the ACLU or a similar organization may never give unsolicited advice to a lay person that he or she retain the organization's free services." That prohibition seems to me entirely reasonable. A State may rightly fear that members of its Bar have powers of persuasion not possessed by laymen and it may also fear that such persuasion may be as potent in writing as it is in person. Such persuasion may draw an unsophisticated layman into litigation contrary to his own best interests and it may force other citizens of South Carolina to defend against baseless litigation which would not otherwise have been brought.

I cannot agree that a State must prove such harmful consequences in each case simply because an organization such as the ACLU or the NAACP is involved. I cannot share the Court's confidence that the danger of such consequences is minimized simply because a lawyer proceeds from political conviction rather than for pecuniary gain. A State may reasonably fear that a lawyer's desire to resolve "substantial civil rights questions," 268 S.C. 259, 263 (1976), may occasionally take precedence over his duty to advance the interests of his client. It is even more reasonable to fear that a lawyer in such circumstances will be inclined to pursue both culpable and blameless defendants to the last ditch in order to achieve his ideological goals. Although individual litigants, including the ACLU, may be free to use the courts for such purposes, South Carolina is likewise free to restrict the activities of the members of its Bar who attempt to persuade them to do so.

I can only conclude that the discipline imposed upon Primus does not violate the Constitution, and I would affirm the judgment of the Supreme Court of South Carolina.

[Justice Blackmun's concurring opinion is omitted.]

Notes

1. Recall Derrick Bell's claim, discussed in Chapter 4, that civil rights lawyers in Atlanta and Detroit allowed their personal commitment to integration to take precedence over their professional obligations to their clients. Would Bell agree with Rehnquist that there was a similar danger in *Primus* and that therefore the state should be entitled to draft prophylactic rules to prevent it? Are there important differences between the ACLU lawyer's actions in *Primus* and the actions Professor Bell attributes to the NAACP lawyers in Atlanta and Detroit?

2. What about the ethics of the *doctor's* lawyer in *Primus*? Did the doctor's lawyer violate the Model Rules when he confronted Ms. Smith in the doctor's office and "asked" her to sign a release absolving the doctor of any liability? See Model Rule 4.3, especially its Comment.

Note: The Aftermath of Bates, Ohralik, *and* Primus

While the decisions in *Ohralik* and *Primus* established constitutional rules at the ends of the spectrum of solicitation, it was immediately apparent that not only was there a great deal of room left in between but also, as indicated by the opinions of Justices Marshall and Rehnquist, that it remained to be seen whether the distinctions set forth in those cases could be maintained. Even the holding of *Bates* left many questions as to state regulatory power unanswered. The Court has continued to address issues of advertising and solicitation in the context of its own varying attitudes toward commercial speech and the First Amendment, as expressed in the hesitations various members of the Court have expressed about the efficacy of the standard stated in Central Hudson Gas & Elec. Corp. v. Public Serv. Comm'n of N.Y., 447 U.S. 557 (1980).

The Court has reconsidered the area in three major opinions: Zauderer v. Office of Disciplinary Counsel of Supreme Court of Ohio, 471 U.S. 626 (1985); Shapero v. Kentucky Bar Association, 486 U.S. 466 (1988); and Florida Bar v. Went For It, Inc., 515 U.S. 618 (1995). In *Zauderer*, the Supreme Court struck down a rule that prohibited an attorney from targeted and illustrated newspaper advertising, in this case an advertisement in a local newspaper that specifically sought employment from women injured by using the Dalkon Shield, a drawing of which was included in the advertisement. The Court, distinguishing in-person solicitation, refused to allow the state to apply a prophylactic rule to newspaper advertising that was not deceptive. The Court did, however, uphold certain disclosure requirements that the state had imposed on such advertising, specifically the obligation on clients to pay costs when they hire a lawyer on a contingent fee basis.

While *Zauderer* settled the issue of targeted newspaper advertising, a major solicitation issue was mail solicitation targeted to specific people or groups of people, especially those known to need legal services of the kind being offered. Model Rule 7.3, for example, prohibited the latter kind of solicitation. The Supreme Court addressed that issue in Shapero v. Kentucky Bar Association, which reviewed the refusal, by Kentucky's Attorneys Advertising Commission, to approve a solicitation letter that a lawyer proposed to send to persons who had foreclosure suits filed against them. The Court held that nondeceptive, targeted mail solicitation was entitled to the same protection as targeted newspaper advertising had received in *Zauderer*. The Court found that the potential for overreaching and undue influence that had justified the prophylactic rule in the circumstances of in-person solicitation in *Ohralik* was not present in personalized mail solicitation where abuses could be reached by regulation less restrictive than a ban. The possibility of regulation by requiring filing of solicitation letters with a state agency was suggested.

Justice O'Connor, joined by Chief Justice Rehnquist and Justice Scalia in dissent, agreed that the result in *Shapero* was a logical extension of the decision in *Zauderer*. Nevertheless, she objected to the whole line of commercial speech cases relating to lawyer advertising that began with *Bates*. In particular, she believed that the Court had undervalued the state interests in regulation:

> Even if I agreed that this Court should take upon itself the task of decid-ing what forms of attorney advertising are in the public interest, I would not agree with what it has done. The best arguments in favor of rules permit-ting attorneys to advertise are founded in elementary economic principles. See, e.g., Hazard, Pearce, & Stempel, "Why Lawyers Should Be Allowed to Advertise: A Market Analysis of Legal Services," 58 N.Y.U. L. Rev. 1084 (1983). Restrictions on truthful advertising, which artificially interfere with the ability of suppliers to transmit price information to consumers, presumably reduce the efficiency of the mechanisms of supply and demand. Other factors being equal, this should cause or enable suppliers (in this case attorneys) to maintain a price/quality ratio in some of their services that is higher than would otherwise prevail. Although one could probably not test this hypoth-esis empirically, it is inherently plausible. Nor is it implausible to imagine that one effect of restrictions on lawyer advertising, and perhaps sometimes an intended effect, is to enable attorneys to charge their clients more for some services (of a given quality) than they would be able to charge absent the restrictions.
>
> Assuming *arguendo* that the removal of advertising restrictions should lead in the short run to increased efficiency in the provision of legal services, I would not agree that we can safely assume the same effect in the long run. The economic argument against these restrictions ignores the delicate role they may play in preserving the norms of the legal profession. While it may be difficult to defend this role with precise economic logic, I believe there is a powerful argument in favor of restricting lawyer advertising and that this argument is at the very least not easily refuted by economic analysis.
>
> One distinguishing feature of any profession, unlike other occupations that may be equally respectable, is that membership entails an ethical obli-gation to temper one's selfish pursuit of economic success by adhering to standards of conduct that could not be enforced either by legal fiat or through the discipline of the market. There are sound reasons to continue pursuing the goal that is implicit in the traditional view of professional life. Both the special privileges incident to membership in the profession and the advan-tages those privileges give in the necessary task of earning a living are means to a goal that transcends the accumulation of wealth. That goal is public ser-vice, which in the legal profession can take a variety of familiar forms. This

favor of rest.
lawyer ads-

view of the legal profession need not be rooted in romanticism of self-serving sanctimony, though of course it can be. Rather, special ethical standards for lawyers are properly understood as an appropriate means of restraining lawyers in the exercise of the unique power that they inevitably wield in a political system like ours.

It is worth recalling why lawyers are regulated at all, or to a greater degree than most other occupations, and why history is littered with failed attempts to extinguish lawyers as a special class. . . . Operating a legal system that is both reasonably efficient and tolerably fair cannot be accomplished, at least under modern social conditions, without a trained and specialized body of experts. This training is one element of what we mean when we refer to the law as a "learned profession." Such knowledge by its nature cannot be made generally available and it therefore confers the power and the temptation to manipulate the system of justice for one's own ends. Such manipulation can occur in at least two obvious ways. One results from overly zealous representation of the client's interests; abuse of the discovery process is one example whose causes and effects (if not its cure) is [*sic*, are] apparent. The second, and for present purposes the more relevant, problem is abuse of the client for the lawyer's benefit. Precisely because lawyers must be perceived with expertise that is both esoteric and extremely powerful, it would be unrealistic to demand that clients bargain for their services in the same arms-length manner that may be appropriate when buying an automobile or choosing a dry cleaner. Like physicians, lawyers are subjected to heightened ethical demands on their conduct towards those they serve. These demands are needed because market forces, and the ordinary legal prohibitions against force and fraud, are simply insufficient to protect the consumers of their necessary services from the peculiar power of the specialized knowledge that these professionals possess.

Imbuing the legal profession with the necessary ethical standards is a task that involves a constant struggle with the relentless natural force of economic self-interest. It cannot be accomplished directly by legal rules, and it certainly will not succeed if sermonizing is the strongest tool that may be employed. Tradition and experiment have suggested a number of formal and informal mechanisms, none of which is adequate by itself and many of which may serve to reduce competition (in the narrow economic sense) among members of the profession. A few examples include the great efforts made during this century to improve the quality and breadth of the legal education that is required for admission to the bar; the concomitant attempt to cultivate a sub-class of genuine scholars within the profession; the development of bar associations that aspire to be more than trade groups; strict disciplinary rules about conflicts of interest and client abandonment; and promotion of the expectation that an attorney's history of voluntary public service is relevant in selecting judicial candidates.

Restrictions on advertising and solicitation by lawyers properly and significantly serve the same goal. Such restrictions act as a concrete, day-to-day reminder to the practicing attorney of why it is improper for any member of this profession to regard it as a trade or occupation like any other. There is no guarantee, of course, that the restrictions will always have the desired effect, and they are surely not a sufficient means to their proper goal. Given their inevitable anticompetitive effects, moreover, they should not be thoughtlessly retained or insulated from skeptical criticism. Appropriate modifications have been made in the light of reason and experience, and other changes may be suggested in the future.

In my judgment, however, fairly severe constraints on attorney advertising can continue to play an important role in preserving the legal profession as a genuine profession. Whatever may be the exactly appropriate scope for these restrictions at a given time and place, this Court's recent decisions reflect a myopic belief that "consumers," and thus our nation, will benefit from a constitutional theory that refuses to recognize either the essence of professionalism or its fragile and necessary foundations. . . . In one way or another, time will uncover the folly of this approach. I can only hope that the Court will recognize the danger before it is too late to effect a worthwhile cure. [Id. at 448–491.]

Justice O'Connor was the author of the following solicitation opinion, which upheld the constitutionality of a Florida rule prohibiting direct mail solicitation of personal injury or wrongful death clients within thirty days of the accident. Florida Bar v. Went For It, Inc., 515 U.S. 618 (1995). Justice O'Connor's majority opinion held that the intrusive nature of such solicitation on vulnerable individuals was a substantial interest justifying a rule designed to preserve the integrity of the legal profession. Justice Kennedy's dissent argued that in view of the important speech interests involved in connection with the often urgent need to take rapid action to protect victims' rights, the interests identified by the majority were not sufficiently substantial to prohibit mail solicitation.

Notes

1. In her *Shapero* dissent, Justice O'Connor assumes that removing restrictions on lawyer advertising would probably result in lower prices to consumers, although she believes that such short-term gains might be negated in the long run by the erosion of lawyer professionalism. But how persuasive are the economic arguments in favor of lawyer advertising? As Justice O'Connor predicts, the few empirical studies of the effects of lawyer advertising fail to provide conclusive evidence one way or the other. Nevertheless, according to one influential summary of the available empirical data in the mid-1980s, some patterns have emerged. See Stewart Macauley, "Lawyer Advertising, Yes But . . . ," Working Papers/Institute for Legal Studies: 2 (Dispute

Processing Research Program: Working Paper 7-3) (1985). First, the vast majority of lawyers do not advertise at all, and those who do mainly use the yellow pages of the telephone directory. Only a tiny percentage advertise on radio or television. And many firms that advertise extensively say nothing about the fees that they will charge for specific services and instead make general claims about their competence, hard work, or effectiveness. However, consistent with the "elementary economic principles" Justice O'Connor cites, advertising does appear to have lowered fees for certain basic legal services — uncontested divorces, name changes, simple wills, etc. — in large metropolitan areas. At the same time, fees for more complex matters and for personal injury litigation appear to be unaffected. Indeed, firms that advertise personal injury services appear to charge *higher* contingent fees for cases that are settled before trial than firms that do not advertise — even though some of these same firms are also charging *lower* fees than their competitors for other advertised services.

What accounts for these complex effects? Are there some "elementary economic principles" of advertising that help to explain why firms might simultaneously charge lower fees for uncontested divorces and name changes while charging higher rates for personal injury cases? Does the existence of this pattern affect your judgment about whether lawyers should be allowed to advertise?

2. Since Macauley's summary of the literature, an important change in lawyer advertising has been the increasing number of large law firms who now advertise in print, radio, and even on television. Prior to the 1970s, the practices of large law firms were shrouded in secrecy. As one legal journalist reported, in the early 1970s, "law firms were reluctant to part with even the most harmless information" such as the number of lawyers who worked for the firm. See Tom Goldstein, "Review: The American Lawyer," 83 Colum. L. Rev. 1351, 1353 (1983). As we noted above, this reticence was reinforced by ethical rules that seemed to brand any contact with the press as unethical. Beginning in 1978, however, national publications such as the National Law Journal and the American Lawyer created a new kind of legal journalism. Freed from the fear of disciplinary sanction (or more likely public embarrassment) by *Bates*, law firms became active participants in an unprecedented stream of disclosures about firm structure, hiring policy, marketing strategies, clients, fees, and compensation. Moreover, in addition to actively seeking to be profiled as having the "biggest deals" or the most impressive litigation victories, big firms began producing brochures, sending out newsletters, conducting seminars, and retaining public relations firms to sell themselves to potential clients.

Although most large law firms had wholeheartedly joined the marketing age by the close of the 1980s, few were ready to join the growing number of personal injury lawyers marketing their wares in newspapers, television, and billboards. See Marc Galanter and Thomas Palay, *Tournament of Lawyers: The Transformation of the Big Law Firm* 72 (1991) (reporting that mass media advertising was for lawyers who represent "individual" clients). In the twenty-first century, this last vestige of the traditional culture of law firms is also beginning to give way. Beginning in the 1990s, law firms began advertising extensively in publications aimed at their two most important constituents—clients, in publications such as Corporate Counsel Magazine, and law students, in law school newspapers and the Student Lawyer. By the decade's close, several firms had expanded their advertising to mainstream media outlets, including billboards in airports, print ads in general business publications, and traditional 30-second spots on radio and television. See Crystal Nix Hines, "A Legal Eagle (His Ad Claims): With Mascots and Slogans, Lawyers Turn to Advertising," N.Y. Times, Nov. 15, 2001; Chris Reidy, "A Case for Advertising: Boston Law Firms Turn Back on Stodgy Image in Bid to be More Competitive with Global Business," Boston Globe, March 25, 2001. These ads have come complete with slogans (Boston's Hale & Dorr: "When Success Matters"), symbols (San Francisco's Orrick, Herrington & Sutcliffe's campaign revolves around the letter "O"), and even mascots (Winston-Salem's Womble, Carlyle, Sandridge & Rice illustrates its slogan "Our Lawyers Mean Business" with a bulldog). What they do not include, however, is any discussion of price. Indeed, many offer almost no specific information at all. For example, in one of the television commercials run by San Francisco's Brobeck, Phleger & Harrison that shocked even seasoned observers of the profession, a computer-animated train speeding through a mountain pass (produced by the company responsible for effects in movies such as "Titanic" and "The Matrix") is aided in its journey by a benevolent hand that appears from the sky to straighten out the track ahead. The only information about the firm conveyed by the ad comes in the form of a voice-over reciting a series of statistics about the number of deals the firm has done in particular areas, followed by the tag line "Brobeck. When your future is at stake." Ironically, the Brobeck train crashed when the dot-com bubble burst in 2002, and the firm was dissolved in bankruptcy a year later. See generally, David Parnell, *The Failing Law Firm: Symptoms and Remedies* (ABA 2015).

Why do you think large law firms are turning aggressively to advertising? What do firms expect to receive for the substantial expenditures—in the case of Brobeck's television campaign, an estimated $3.5 million—that they are investing in advertising? Why do the ads contain so little in the way of substantive information about services or price? Does the fact that many large law firms are now enthusiastically embracing commercial advertising provide additional support for Justice O'Connor's concerns in her *Shapero* dissent? We will return to the question of whether "market values" have undermined professionalism—or alternatively, whether such values have established a new and better paradigm for the legal profession—in Chapter 12.

3. Shortly after the Court's decision in *Went for It*, Congress passed a statute prohibiting lawyers from approaching the families of air crash victims for 45 days after the accident. This statute, like the Florida statute at issue in *Went for It*, was justified on the ground that it was necessary to protect families at a time in which they are particularly vulnerable. Both the federal and Florida statutes, however, only apply to contact by plaintiffs' lawyers. They do not cover the actions of other actors who

might try to contact family members during this period. For example, following the tragic events of September 11, 2001, 76 families of passengers killed in the four hijackings received packets "stuffed with $50 to $200 in cash, prepaid calling cards, and the names of four law firms with 'extensive experience in major airline and other similar mass disasters.'" Jonathan Glater and Diana B. Henriques, "Company Tried to Capitalize on Sept. 11," N.Y. Times, October 13, 2001. The packets, however, did not come from the lawyers whose names were included, all of whom claimed that they were unaware of the mailing. Instead, the mailing was done by a company that specialized in lending money to accident victims in anticipation of awards from a subsequent lawsuit. The company employs no lawyers and is therefore arguably not covered by the federal statute. Similarly, airlines routinely assign representatives to assist the families of crash victims. In addition to helping with funeral arrangements and emergency expenses, these representatives are also in a position to "counsel" family members that it is not necessary for them to hire a lawyer because the airline "will take care of them" and to collect information about crash victims that may be relevant to any subsequent litigation that may develop between family members and the airline. Are there reasons why plaintiff lawyers should be treated differently from these other actors?

4. Prior to *Went for It*, the Supreme Court, in Edenfeld v. Fane, 507 U.S. 761 (1993), held unconstitutional a broad Florida regulation prohibiting accountants from soliciting business in person. Do you think that the Court had said in *Ohralik* that substantial state interests justified a prophylactic rule banning all in-person solicitation? Or did it only say that the likelihood of overreaching was so substantial in the circumstances of that case that a prophylactic rule could be applied to Mr. Ohralik without the need to show actual injury?

Relying on *Edenfeld*, two lawyers in Georgia, wanting to continue their practice of having doctors recommend their personal injury services to patients and their families, attacked the state's ethics rules prohibiting such solicitation. The Court of Appeals for the Eleventh Circuit upheld the Georgia regulation. It distinguished *Edenfeld* on the ground that that case involved solicitation of businesses for services involving independence and objectivity and not solicitation of injured individuals for services involving advocacy, which was the complaining lawyers' stock in trade. State Bar of Georgia v. Falanga, 150 F.3d 1333 (11th Cir. 1998), rehearing en banc denied, cert. denied, 526 U.S. 1087 (1999).

5. Even in a jurisdiction that follows *Falanga*, should the result be different if the lawyer is attempting personal solicitation of a person engaged in business? Suppose the business being solicited is a "Mom and Pop" business? See In re Amendment to S.J.C. Rule 3:07, DR 2-103 and DR 2-104, 398 Mass. 73 (1986), where the Massachusetts Supreme Judicial Court, by a vote of 4–3, refused to adopt a rule permitting in-person solicitation of persons engaged in trade or commerce. Ten years later the same court appointed a new committee to study the advertising rules. That Committee voted to permit in-person solicitation by communications to "publicly held

entities, non-profit entities or governmental entities for purposes related to the solicitation of professional employment by such entities." Ten members of the twenty-two person committee would have broadened the business exemption to all organizations engaged in trade or commerce. The limited exemption voted by the majority was to prevent in-person solicitation of "Mom and Pop" businesses. If we put constitutional considerations aside, would you vote as a matter of public policy to permit in-person solicitation of all businesses? Some businesses? Or would you prohibit all in-person solicitation? Does your answer depend upon whether lawyers who represent large corporations are ever disciplined for solicitation? The Supreme Judicial Court adopted the views of the dissenters on its committee. 430 Mass. 1309–1310 (1999) (in the interest of full disclosure we note that one of the authors of this casebook, Professor Kaufman, was a member of the S.J.C. Advisory Committee). We take up the differences between lawyers who represent corporations and those who represent individuals in Chapter 12.

6. The Court's holdings in *Ohralik* and *Edenfeld* and other recent developments in advertising and solicitation raise interesting questions for the debate over multidisciplinary practice. For example, does the fact that courts appear to treat solicitation by accountants differently from similar conduct by lawyers bear on whether lawyers should be allowed to form partnerships with accountants? Similarly, recent print and television advertisements by large law firms are strikingly similar to those run by large accounting and consulting firms and by investment banks. Does the MDP debate suggest why large law firms may be investing in such campaigns? Does the convergence between the marketing of law firms and other professional service providers affect your views about the propriety of multidisciplinary partnerships between lawyers and these other professionals? Keep these questions in mind when we take up MDPs at the end of this Chapter.

7. One situation where solicitation rules are having an increasing, but uncertain, impact is when partners or associates leave a firm to join another or to start their own. Such an event does not just happen all at once. The process of decision-making may take a long time. Indeed, an important consideration may be whether clients with whom the departing lawyer has a relationship will choose to stay with the departing lawyer or with the firm. The departing lawyer, however, may fear, and quite rightly, that to mention the possibility of departure will lead to immediate dismissal. Thus, the lawyer who is thinking about or planning a departure must worry about what it is permissible to say and do with respect to clients of the firm with whom he or she has a working relationship.

There is a growing amount of law with respect to this problem. Four associates of a law firm determined to leave and establish their own firm. They prepared letters to clients of the firm with open matters on which they had worked while employees of the firm. The letters informed Clients that they were leaving or had left the firm and that Clients could choose to be represented by them, by Law Firm, or by any other attorney. Enclosed were a blank form discharging Law Firm and a contingent fee agreement. Some telephone calls and personal contacts were made with Law Firm clients to the same effect. A line of credit was obtained from a bank using as collateral Law Firm's cases on which they had worked and had not yet been turned over to them. The trial court enjoined the former associates from communicating with those persons who up to the date of their departure had active matters in which they were represented by Law Firm except that they could send out professional cards. Clients of Law Firm were not precluded from discharging Law Firm and hiring the former associates. The injunction was reversed in the Superior Court and reinstated in the Pennsylvania Supreme Court. It found a clear violation of the anti-solicitation disciplinary rules and a clear interference with Law Firm's existing contractual relations with its clients. It found that the "contacts too easily could overreach and unduly influence . . . clients with active cases" and hence fell within the area of unprotected conduct outlined in *Ohralik*. Adler, Barish, Daniels, Levin, and Creskoff v. Epstein, 393 A.2d 1175 (1978). In Dowd & Dowd Ltd. v. Gleason, 181 Ill. 2d 460 (1998), the Illinois Supreme Court held that departing lawyers could make pre-departure arrangements for space and supplies but predeparture solicitation of firm clients would constitute a breach of fiduciary duty and could also constitute a tortious interference with the firm's economic advantage and a civil conspiracy. See also Meehan v. Shaughnessy, 404 Mass. 419 (1989); Hillman, "Law Firms and their Partners: The Law and Ethics of Grabbing and Leaving," 67 Tex. L. Rev. 1 (1988); Johnson, "Solicitation of Law Firm Clients by Departing Partners and Associates," 50 U. Pitt. L. Rev. 1 (1998).

In Gibbs v. Breed, Abbott & Morgan, 271 A.D.2d 180 (App. Div. 2000), the court confronted the question of whether a departing partner's solicitation of other partners and associates to join him in leaving the firm violated the partner's fiduciary duty to his old firm. Holding that employee recruitment is permitted on even narrower ground than client recruitment, since lawyers have no countervailing fiduciary duty to employees that would limit their duty of loyalty to the firm, the Appellate Division concluded that pre-withdrawal recruitment is generally allowed only after the firm has been given notice of the lawyer's intention to withdraw. Although this limitation did not preclude a partner from discussing his plans with another partner so long as the second partner formed an independent intention to leave, it did preclude the departing partners from preparing and circulating to other law firms a list of associates (complete with salaries and billing rates) that the partners would like any new firm to recruit. See also Hillman, "Loyalty in the Firm: A Statement of General Principles on the Duties of Partners Withdrawing from Law Firms," 55 Wash. & Lee L. Rev. 997 (1998).

8. Another important change in access to information about legal services has been the advent of social media. According to the 2016 ABA Legal Technology Survey Report, more lawyers than ever are interacting online: 85% of law firms have a website and 76% of law firms now maintain an online presence, compared to only 55% in 2012. Lawyers report that they interact online for a variety of reasons, with career development and networking leading the way (71%), followed by client development

(48%), education and current awareness (45%), and case investigation (24%). The Report found that 57% of law firms report a presence on LinkedIn, 35% of firms have a Facebook page, and 21% of firms use Twitter. See generally Michael E. Lackey Jr. & Joseph P. Minta, "Lawyers and Social Media: The Legal Ethics of Tweeting, Facebooking and Blogging," 28 Touro L. Rev. 149 (2012).

9. New sources of information about legal services, such as private ranking systems, supplement traditional means of advertisement. AVVO, for example, was launched in 2006 as an online directory of lawyers offering potential clients access to lawyers' profiles and rating the lawyers' quality. AVVO has since expanded its services to offer prospective clients a platform on which they can connect with lawyers. See Alberto Bernabe, "AVVO Joins the Legal Market; Should Attorneys Be Concerned?," 104 Geo. L.J. Online 184 (2016). On the rise of rating agencies, see Renee Newman Knake, "The Commercialization of Legal Ethics," 29 Geo. J. Legal Ethics 715 (2016).

C. Monopoly Over the Provision of Legal Services: Who May Practice Law

Another aspect of the traditional model's market approach is a two-fold barrier to entry into the legal service marketplace: restricting admission to the bar and prohibiting non-lawyers from practicing law.

1. Admission to the Bar

Problem 8–8

You are General Counsel to the Committee on Admissions appointed by the supreme court of your state. The President of the Committee has given you the job of preparing a questionnaire designed to be answered by every applicant for admission to the bar. The President's memorandum to you states:

"We are not interested in revising those portions of the questionnaire that ask the standard questions about residence, education, jobs, and the like. I have asked the Secretary of the Committee to look at those questions. What I am concerned about is fulfilling our statutory duty to satisfy ourselves that the applicant is of 'good moral character.'

"I have requested that committee members submit to me sample questions for our questionnaire. Here is the first group that I have received. With respect to each question, I would like you to tell me whether you think it should be on our questionnaire. If any question seems too general, please rephrase it to be more precise if you think it seeks information we should have. I am not asking for your opinion as a matter of constitutional law. I want you to forget constitutional law. I want your judgment about how far our Committee on Admissions ought to go in satisfying itself on an applicant's good moral character, while at the same time respecting individual dignity and privacy.

"There is one thing we both should keep in mind. There is a big difference between asking for information and deciding what to do with information that is supplied. You should not assume that unfavorable responses to any of these questions will be used automatically to deny admission to the bar. Each case will be handled on an individual basis and, of course, your advice will be sought in each of the cases as it arises.

"Here are some of the questions I received:

(1) Have you ever been convicted of a crime, other than a minor traffic offense punishable by a fine of $500 or less? If so, please give details, date and place for each such conviction.

(2) Have you ever been charged with, arrested or questioned regarding any of the crimes reportable under question 1? If so, please give details, date, and place for each such charge, arrest, or questioning.

(3) To your knowledge, have you within the past three years violated any law, other than traffic and motor vehicle laws or laws carrying no possibility of imprisonment or fines greater than $500?

(4) Have you within the past five years received any traffic or parking summons to which you did not respond? If the answer is yes, please give details with respect to each summons, including approximate dates and places to the best of your memory.

(5) Were you the subject of any disciplinary charge, formal or informal, while in college or law school relating to any academic or nonacademic matter? What was the charge and what action was taken by the school? Please give details, date, and school.

(6) While you were at law school, did you ever fail to observe any rule or requirement set by the school or by an individual professor with respect to the taking of any examination? If the answer is yes, please give details including whether or not the matter came to the school's attention and action taken, if any.

(7) Have you ever sold any of the following drugs (listing every drug whose sale is illegal in the state)? If the answer is yes, please give details.

(8) To your knowledge, have you taken or used any of the drugs listed in question 7 within the past year? If the answer is yes, please give details.

(9) Have you consulted a psychologist or psychiatrist during the past three years? If the answer is yes, do not give details, but be prepared to discuss with the Committee in a general way any condition from which you were found to be suffering. In the alternative, please indicate whether you would

permit the Committee to inquire of the psychologist or psychiatrist whether any condition he or she found would have a substantial effect on your conduct or ability as a lawyer. See In re Applicant, 443 So. 2d 71 (Fla. 1984).

(10) Have you read the disciplinary rules applicable to lawyers that are in force in this state? If the answer is yes, do you accept the principles and prohibitions set forth in the disciplinary rules as the guides to your professional conduct? If the answer to the latter question is no, please set forth which principles or prohibitions you do not accept and the reasons for your rejection.

"As you think about these questions, let me solicit your advice about how we should handle the following four cases pending before the Committee."

Problem 8–9

Case # 1: We have received a letter from the law school professor who had supervisory responsibility for the legal aid program in which this applicant participated for the last two years of law school. The crucial sentence of the letter states: "I believe that I should tell you that despite constant warnings from me and from others, this student would continuously talk about his clients' affairs, including the revealing of confidential matters at cocktail parties and in informal conversations with other students who were not members of the legal aid office."

Problem 8–10

Case #2: The question on our current form does not ask about minor traffic violations, but we received information, which we have verified, indicating that while Ms. Student was at law school, she collected and ignored 25 parking tickets. We have spoken with her about it and she offered as an explanation the fact that she was incensed at the police because they always came around to ticket right at the end of a morning class hour so as to catch students but never checked these meters at other hours of the days when townspeople occupied them. Yesterday our state Supreme Court handed down an opinion in In re X, also involving deliberate nonpayment of parking tickets, 23 of them, by a practicing lawyer of twenty-five years' standing. The court viewed the offense as very serious, suspended the lawyer for six months, and said that except for the lawyer's previous long unblemished record, the suspension would have been considerably longer.

Problem 8–11

Case #3: The applicant is the state leader of an aggressive white supremacist group, who has taken a leading role in public, nonviolent demonstrations in which he has preached hatred against a wide variety of racial and religious minorities. Our Rules of Professional Conduct prohibit lawyers in their professional capacity from engaging in conduct manifesting bias or prejudice on account of race, sex, religion, national origin, disability, age, or sexual orientation except that they do not preclude legitimate advocacy when such matters are an issue in the legal matter in which the lawyer is acting. At its last meeting, after a hearing, a majority of the Committee concluded that the applicant's views were so strongly held that he was bound to violate our anti-discrimination rules. The applicant, however, denied that he would violate the anti-discrimination rules while he was acting as an attorney. The Committee has decided to defer action on whether to deny him admission until it had heard your views.

Problem 8–12

Case #4: We have an applicant who allegedly lied on her financial aid application for the first two years of law school in order to obtain larger awards. The student never admitted that her applications were deliberately falsified, and advanced all sorts of explanations to justify the figures in her applications. Nevertheless, after a hearing, a law school faculty-student committee found that the applications had been deliberately falsified. The student was suspended for two years, but was later readmitted and awarded her degree. In her application to us, she still asserts that she did nothing wrong and told no falsehoods on her financial aid applications. Some members of our committee believe that it is important that we reach a judgment as to whether the original financial aid applications were falsified so as to be able to test her current sincerity. Others believe that her current "moral character" is the crucial question, that a suspension from law school should not automatically prevent her admission four years later, and that we should simply accept and not reexamine the law school determination. What do you think we should do?

The materials in this section are concerned almost exclusively with the issue of "moral character." Admission to the bar raises another crucial question, that of competence. That issue is discussed in Chapter 10, and the materials of these two Chapters should therefore be considered together.

Over the years, admission to the bar has been the province of the apparatus established in each state, subject to any limitations imposed by the Constitution. Educational prerequisites, residence and apprentice requirements, even the ability to practice statewide, have been treated as matters of purely local concern, and the practices have varied greatly.

Admission to federal practice in a particular state has tended to follow the state practice, as has disbarment, although in the last several decades there has been some movement in the federal courts away from automatic following of state practice. See Spanos v. Skouras, 364 F.2d 161 (2d Cir. 1966), cert. denied, 385 U.S. 987 (1966) (state may not constitutionally prohibit citizen with a federal claim or defense from engaging an out-of-state lawyer to collaborate with an in-state lawyer); Theard v. United States, 354 U.S. 278 (1957) (lawyer's disbarment by federal district court upon disbarment by state court reversed; federal court should give respect to state action but is not bound by it); but see In re Abrams, 521 F.2d 1094 (3d Cir.

1975), cert. denied with two dissents, 423 U.S. 1038 (1975) (reversing federal district court's disbarment of lawyer suspended for one year for same conduct by New Jersey Supreme Court; when district court relied on record in state court proceeding, it could not base its action in part on a charge that had been withdrawn in the state proceeding; nor could it rely on a state court precedent that had been distinguished by the state Supreme Court). In Leis v. Flynt, 439 U.S. 438 (1979), the Supreme Court, following the theory of procedural due process enunciated in Paul v. Davis, 424 U.S. 693 (1976), held that an out-of-state attorney has no property interest in appearing *pro hac vice* in a local court. The local court therefore need not accord the attorney any procedural due process before denying an application to appeal.

For 165 years, however, federal interference with state control over the profession was almost nonexistent. There were only rare decisions like Cummings v. Missouri, 71 U.S. 277 (1866), holding unconstitutional Missouri's test oath for lawyers and other groups, requiring them to deny previous actions, words, or sympathies on behalf of those engaged in rebellion against the United States. In a series of decisions beginning in the mid-1950s, however, the Supreme Court manifested greater concern with what the states were doing with their freedom to regulate the profession. The Court's increasing activity was in a sense reflective of its constitutional agenda at that time. It is also indicative perhaps of the Court's growing concern over the performance of the profession and the balance the profession had struck between the rights of individual lawyers and its own needs in the context of service to clients and society.

Most of the relevant Supreme Court cases, especially those of the late 1950s and early 1970s, focused on the kinds of preliminary inquiries the state bar committees could make to test ultimate statements in one form or another of nonparticipation in revolutionary activity looking to the violent overthrow of the government. Schware v. Board of Bar Examiners, 353 U.S. 232 (1957); Konigsberg v. State Bar, 353 U.S. 252 (1957) and 366 U.S. 36 (1961); Anastaplo v. Illinois, 366 U.S. 82 (1961); In re Stolar, 401 U.S. 23 (1971); and Baird v. State Bar, 401 U.S. 1 (1971). In all of the cases, however, the Court recognized the general supervisory powers of the state over admission to the bar and, more particularly, its authority to set standards relating to character. See Law Students Civil Rights Research Council, Inc. v. Wadmond, 401 U.S. 154 (1971), upholding New York's requirement that applicants for admission to the bar must possess "the character and general fitness requisite for an attorney and counsellor-at-law." The Supreme Court has not revisited these issues since then.

A large number of cases have raised a different constitutional issue: the ability of states to impose residence or domicile requirements as a condition of taking a bar examination or of being admitted. The Supreme Court has consistently held that such requirements violate the Privileges and Immunities Clause of Article 4 of the Constitution because of the burden imposed and the failure of the restrictions to meet any substantial state interest. E.g., Supreme Court of Virginia v. Friedman, 487 U.S. 59 (1988), and Supreme Court of New Hampshire v. Piper, 470 U.S. 274 (1985).

A whole variety of other constitutional issues have also been raised about admission requirements. See, e.g., Application of Hansen, 275 N.W.2d 790 (Minn. 1978), appeal dismissed for want of a substantial federal question, 441 U.S. 938 (1979) (denial of right to take bar examination because applicant did not attend ABA-accredited school upheld); Younger v. Colorado State Bd. of Bar Examiners, 625 F.2d 372 (10th Cir. 1980) (limitation on number of times bar examination may be taken upheld). Numerous other challenges have been made to grading practices on the bar examinations by minority groups and by others alleging antitrust violations because of limitations on numbers of attorneys admitted. See Hoover v. Ronwin, 466 U.S. 558 (1984). The Court in that case held that members of the bar examination committee appointed by the Arizona Supreme Court who failed the applicant and whose recommendation that he be denied admission to the bar was accepted by the Arizona Supreme Court were immune from Sherman Act liability under the state action doctrine. See p. 692, Note 5. The Court noted that the Arizona Supreme Court had approved the Committee's grading formula, closely supervised its activities, and was the body that actually granted or denied admission to the bar.

More recently, federal interference with state control over the profession has dramatically increased via federal statutes and federal agencies' regulations. For a thorough review of this development, see Daniel R. Coquillette & Judith A. McMorrow, "Zacharias's Prophecy: The Federalization of Legal Ethics through Legislative, Court, and Agency Regulation," 48 San Diego L. Rev. 123 (2011).

An important aspect of the admission process generally involves an assessment of the applicant's "moral character," a process that has become increasingly controversial. Excerpts from Supreme Court opinions discussing the requirement and a case applying it follow.

Schware v. Board of Bar Examiners

353 U.S. 232, 247 (1957)

Justice FRANKFURTER, whom Justice CLARK and Justice HARLAN join, concurring.

Certainly since the time of Edward I, through all the vicissitudes of seven centuries of Anglo-American history, the legal profession has played a role all its own. The bar has not enjoyed prerogatives; it has been entrusted with anxious responsibilities. One does not have to inhale the self-adulatory bombast of after-dinner speeches to affirm that all interests of man that are comprised under the constitutional guarantees given to "life, liberty and property" are in the professional keeping of lawyers. It is a fair characterization of the lawyer's responsibility in our society that he stands "as a shield," to quote Devlin, J., in defense of right and to ward off wrong. From a profession charged with such responsibilities there must be exacted those qualities of truth-speaking, of a high sense of honor, of granite discretion, of the strictest observance of fiduciary responsibility, that have, throughout the centuries, been compendiously described as "moral character."

From the thirteenth century to this day, in England the profession itself has determined who should enter it. In the United States the courts exercise ultimate control. But while we have nothing comparable to the Inns of Court, with us too the profession itself, through appropriate committees, has long had a vital interest, as a sifting agency, in determining the fitness, and above all the moral fitness, of those who are certified to be entrusted with the fate of clients. With us too the requisite "moral character" has been the historic unquestioned prerequisite of fitness. . . .

Konigsberg v. State Bar
353 U.S. 252 (1957)

Mr. Justice BLACK delivered the opinion of the Court.

A. *Good Moral Character.* — The term "good moral character" has long been used as a qualification for membership in the Bar and has served a useful purpose in this respect. However the term, by itself, is unusually ambiguous. It can be defined in an almost unlimited number of ways for any definition will necessarily reflect the attitudes, experiences, and prejudices of the definer. Such a vague qualification, which is easily adapted to fit personal views and predilections, can be a dangerous instrument for arbitrary and discriminatory denial of the right to practice law.

While we do not have the benefit of a definition of "good moral character" by the California Supreme Court in this case, counsel for the State tells us that the definition of that term adopted in California "stresses elements of honesty, fairness and respect for the rights of others and for the laws of the state and nation." The decisions of California courts cited here do not support so broad a definition as claimed by counsel. These cases instead appear to define "good moral character" in terms of an absence of proven conduct or acts which have been historically considered as manifestations of "moral turpitude." To illustrate, California has held that an applicant did not have good character who had been convicted of forgery and had practiced law without a license, or who had obtained money by false representations and had committed fraud upon a court, or who had submitted false affidavits to the Committee along with his application for admission. It should be emphasized that neither the definition proposed by counsel nor those appearing in the California cases equates unorthodox political beliefs or membership in lawful political parties with bad moral character. Assuming for purposes of this case that counsel's broad definition of "good moral character" is the one adopted in California, the question is whether on the whole record a reasonable man could fairly find that there were substantial doubts about Konigsberg's "honesty, fairness and respect for the rights of others and for the laws of the state and nation." . . .

Notes

1. The Bankruptcy Code provides that "a governmental unit may not deny . . . a license, permit, charter, franchise, or other similar grant to . . . a person that . . . has been . . . a bankrupt or debtor under the Bankruptcy Act . . . solely because such debtor or bankrupt . . . has not paid a debt . . . that was discharged under the Bankruptcy Act" (11 U.S.C. § 525). It also provides, however, that an educational loan is not dischargeable under the Code unless the court finds that excepting the debt from discharge imposes undue hardship on the debtor and the debtor's dependents (11 U.S.C. § 523(a)). The crucial word in § 525 is "solely." The court in In re W.D.P., 91 P.3d 1078, 1088–89 (2004) affirmed denial of an applicant's admission to the bar in part on the ground of bankruptcy discharge of student loans stating that the "bankruptcy laws do not prohibit examination of the circumstances surrounding bankruptcy, as these circumstances illustrate an applicant's judgment in handling serious financial obligations." Suppose that a lawyer contemplating leaving her public interest firm to try to obtain a job with a large law firm in another jurisdiction commences a case in bankruptcy under the "undue hardship" exception to get rid of her student loans before leaving her present job. What should be the result when she applies for admission in the jurisdiction where the large law firm is located?

2. In In re Batali, 98 Wash. 2d 610 (1983), the Washington Supreme Court ruled that the Supremacy Clause did not permit the imposition of a condition on readmission of a suspended lawyer that he pay federal income taxes that had been discharged in bankruptcy. However, in Brookman v. The State Bar, 46 Cal. 3d 1004 (1988), the California Supreme Court held that imposition of a requirement that a disciplined lawyer repay $48,900 to the state's Client Security Fund as a condition of disciplinary probation did not contravene the purposes of § 525(a) of the Bankruptcy Code. The purpose of the disciplinary requirement was not to penalize the lawyer but to protect the public and rehabilitate the lawyer.

In the Matter of Harvey Prager

422 Mass. 86 (1996)

LIACOS, C.J. On June 13, 1994, Harvey Prager applied for admission to the bar of the Commonwealth. The Board of Bar Examiners (board) held a hearing on his application and on January 6, 1995, reported to this court, pursuant to G. L. c. 221 § 37 (1994 ed.), that the applicant is of "good moral character and sufficient acquirements and qualifications and recommends his admission." . . . We deny Prager's application for admission to the bar with leave to reapply in five years from the date of this opinion.

The record reveals the following facts. Prager was born in 1947, the son of immigrants. He attended Bowdoin College from 1965 to 1969, where he was a member of Phi Beta Kappa and was graduated summa cum laude. From 1971 to 1972, Prager attended Harvard University as a graduate student. While at Harvard, it appears that he began smoking marihuana regularly, which he claims subsequently led him into the illegal sale and distribution of marihuana. Over a period of approximately six years, Prager organized and led a large-scale international drug smuggling operation. Much of the marihuana smuggled into the country came by boat from South America into Maine, New York, and other points along the eastern coast of the United States. Over the course of Prager's dealings, he used several aliases, including "Jack," "John Stead," "Steven Shane," and "Jack Harvey."

Prager testified before the board that he stopped smoking marihuana in 1981, at which time he also ceased his smuggling operation. However, he continued to sell marihuana in the United States for two more years. In 1983, Prager was indicted by a Federal grand jury in the district of Maine. On learning of the indictment, Prager fled the country and lived as a fugitive until he was extradited from Great Britain in 1987. The record is sparse in relation to Prager's activities during the years before 1987. Following his flight from the United States, it appears he spent some time in the Caribbean, where he owned investment property presumably purchased with proceeds from his illegal activities. Also, he owned a $400,000 apartment in Paris, where he met and married his wife. He was known in London, under the name "Harvey Israel," as a reputable art dealer. In 1987, Scotland Yard was investigating a bank robbery when they came upon a safe deposit box identifying Harvey Israel as Harvey Prager. Prager remained incarcerated (in London and the United States) six months while awaiting extradition and trial.

On January 29, 1988, Prager pleaded guilty to, inter alia, conspiracy to import into the United States a large quantity of marihuana, possession with intent to distribute a large quantity of marihuana, aiding and abetting the commission of this crime, and conspiracy to possess with intent to distribute in excess of 1,000 pounds of marihuana. He received a suspended sentence with probation for five years on special conditions of probation. These conditions, which Prager helped negotiate, required Prager to reside and maintain employment in Maine, volunteer a minimum of forty-five hours each week toward assisting those with acquired immune deficiency syndrome (AIDS), and to create and maintain a free-standing hospice unit for persons in the terminal stages of AIDS. Prager was unable to develop a free-standing hospice, due in part to his inability as a convicted felon to obtain Medicare certification. In 1989, the sentencing judge modified the terms of Prager's probation. Prager was to provide care in his home to AIDS patients in the terminal stages of the disease.

In 1991, Prager sought and received permission from the Federal court to apply to the University of Maine School of Law. He enrolled as a full-time student in the fall of 1991. In Prager's absence, nurses cared for Prager's clients in his home during daytime hours. Prager was named to the dean's list in his first year, and was selected as a staff member on the Law Review. . . . In 1993, Prager applied for and was accepted to a judicial clerkship for the Supreme Judicial Court of Maine.[9] In August, 1993, Prager was granted permission to complete his third year of law school as a student at Northeastern University School of Law in Massachusetts, and relocated the last of his AIDS clients out of his home in August, 1993. His probationary period ended on October 10, 1993. Prager graduated summa cum laude from the University of Maine School of Law in May, 1994. He began clerking for Associate Justice Howard H. Dana, Jr., in 1994.

Prager applied for admission to the Massachusetts bar in June, 1994. He sat for the bar examination in July, 1994. Having passed the written examination, Prager was invited to appear at an oral interview before the board. A hearing, at which Prager testified, was held on December 22, 1994. The board reported that "Prager has so rehabilitated himself since the time of his criminal activities thirteen years ago that he is of present good moral character," and recommended Prager's admission to the bar of the Commonwealth.

The license to practice law may not be withheld arbitrarily or discriminatorily. While deference is given to the decision of the board, this court retains ultimate authority to decide a person's fitness to practice law in the Commonwealth. . . .

A prior conviction is not an absolute bar to admission. We have stated that no offense is so grave as to preclude a showing of present moral fitness. The commission of a felony is, however, conclusive evidence of lack of good moral character at the time of the offense. The test is whether at the present time the applicant has so rehabilitated himself by "[leading] a sufficiently exemplary life to inspire public confidence once again, in spite of his previous actions." Matter of Hiss [368 Mass. 447 (1975)], at 452. As stated by the board in the instant case, "the law rightfully requires us to focus upon the question of Prager's rehabilitation. The concept that

---

9. At this time Prager's criminal activity and perceived favored treatment by the United States District Court for the District of Maine became the subject of great publicity and attention in Maine. The article entitled "Unequal Justice," [*Times* (Brunswick, Me.), Sept. 29, 1993] outlined the perceived disparate treatment of Prager ("gentleman, scholar . . . released to the comfort of his Maine home to serve his sentence in a Victorian mansion with skylights and a harbor view") and Jim Henry, a struggling lobsterman from a poor family who assisted in two of Prager's smuggling operations in exchange for the promise of his own fishing boat. Henry surrendered after he learned of Prager's guilty plea and punishment. The same organization that helped craft Prager's sentence proposed to the court that Henry teach troubled youths marine science and fishing as a substitute for incarceration. The same judge who sentenced Prager refused Henry's alternative sentence. Instead, he sentenced Henry to nine years imprisonment, despite a prosecution request for from seven to eight years. Prager's other associates received sentences of from three to ten years. In response to questions about the disparity in sentences, Prager stated, "I don't think my sentence was easy. I think many people are angry that it did not include time in prison. And to the extent that it didn't include time in prison, it was easier than spending time in prison. On the other hand, most of my co-defendants, their prison time was spent in minimum security camps."

The article generated substantial media attention, resulting in many letters to both the Supreme Judicial Court of Maine and the board expressing outrage that Prager would be allowed to hold a prestigious clerkship or be admitted to the practice of law in Massachusetts. Prager did not apply for admission to the bar of Maine.

human redemption is possible and valuable is both well established in law and premised upon long-standing, even ancient traditions." Thus, the issue before us is whether the applicant has sufficiently proved such rehabilitation that he currently possesses the necessary moral character to be admitted to the bar of the Commonwealth.

As in a case of reinstatement after disbarment, the burden of showing good moral character after conviction of a felony is on the applicant. This court has clearly established the standard of rehabilitation required for reinstatement after disbarment. "Whatever the offense for which a judgment of disbarment was entered, the person disbarred has a heavy burden on a subsequent petition for admission to the bar to overcome by evidence the weight of the facts adjudicated by such judgment and to establish affirmatively that since his disbarment he has become 'a person proper to be held out by the court to the public as trustworthy.'" Matter of Hiss, supra at 460–461, quoting Matter of Keenan, 313 Mass. 186, 219 (1943) (*Keenan I*). The factors to be considered in reinstatement hearings are as follows: "(1) the nature of the original offense for which the petitioner was disbarred, (2) the petitioner's character, maturity, and experience at the time of his disbarment, (3) the petitioner's occupations and conduct in the time since his disbarment, (4) the time elapsed since the disbarment, and (5) the petitioner's present competence in legal skills" (footnotes omitted).

The test of fitness for reinstatement is two pronged. Not only must a petitioner demonstrate the requisite moral qualifications and learning in the law, but he also must show that his resumption of the practice of law will not be detrimental to the integrity of the bar, the administration of justice, or the public interest. S.J.C. Rule 4:01, § 18(5), as amended, 394 Mass. 1106 (1985). The rules governing original admissions to the bar, promulgated prior to development of the rules governing reinstatement, have no reference to the integrity of the bar or the public interest. See G. L. c. 221, § 37; S.J.C. Rule 3:01, § 1.3, as appearing in 382 Mass. 753 (1981). These directives set out a procedural scheme rather than substantive guidelines for bar admissions. Thus, it is appropriate, despite the lack of specific directives, to consider the public perception of and confidence in the bar when determining the fitness of original applicants to practice law in the Commonwealth. . . . The protection of the public is universally recognized as a significant and central goal of admitting only qualified persons to the practice of a particular profession. See Rhode, "Moral Character as a Professional Credential," 94 Yale L.J. 491, 507–512 (1985). Reinstatement "amounts to a certification to the public that the attorney is a person worthy of trust." Matter of Gordon [385 Mass. 48 (1982)], at 54. The allowance of an applicant's original admission to the bar is logically a similar endorsement that the applicant is worthy of the public trust. We would be remiss were we not to recognize the role of the public interest in these proceedings.

Although we have not enunciated clearly a quantum of proof necessary to prevail in a showing of good moral character by an applicant for original admission, we note that several jurisdictions require a showing of clear and convincing evidence where the applicant has been convicted of a felony. . . . We conclude that the standard we have adopted in reinstatement proceedings is adequately amenable to the fitness inquiry of original applicants. The *Hiss* factors allow the court to balance circumstances surrounding the misconduct against the action the applicant has taken to show his rehabilitation. Such an approach better serves the interests of the public than would an inflexible quantum of proof requirement. We thus apply the *Hiss* factors to the inquiry whether a bar applicant has demonstrated the requisite rehabilitation since his crime.

It is appropriate to consider in a reinstatement proceeding the amount of time that has elapsed since the disbarment or suspension. An applicant to the bar, however, has not been the subject of a disbarment or suspension proceeding, and thus we must decide the date from which it is appropriate to commence measuring the time that has elapsed. The date here most closely analogous to the date a person might have been disbarred is the date of adjudication of the latest offense. Prager was indicted in 1983 and pleaded guilty to criminal charges in January, 1988. Prager does not benefit from the fact that his indictment occurred more than ten years ago. His flight from the country, for which he did not face prosecution, was none the less a wrong which continued until 1987. We consider then, whether Prager has established affirmatively that since his conviction in January, 1988, he "has become 'a person proper to be held out by the court to the public as trustworthy.'" Matter of Hiss, supra at 460–461, quoting *Keenan I*, supra at 219.

Prager's offenses were not minor. He not only participated in, but masterminded an international marihuana smuggling operation. He shipped eleven tons of marihuana into the United States. He enlisted others to carry out the day-to-day operations of this illegal enterprise. His smuggling operation spanned a period of approximately six years. It was large in scale and operated for profit. It was a freely-chosen commercial venture, generating millions of dollars which Prager amassed in multiple countries. When he learned of his grand jury indictment, Prager became a fugitive from justice. He lived under various aliases. He admitted that, if his identity had not been accidentally discovered, he probably would not have returned to the United States. Although he states he was unhappy as a fugitive, "ultimately [he] lacked the courage to come back at that time in [his] life." . . .

Although not an attorney at the time, Prager's conduct was the product of neither inexperience nor immaturity. Prager's use and large scale sale and distribution of marihuana spanned a period in which Prager was in his mid-twenties to mid-thirties. He lived as a fugitive from justice for an additional four years, until the age of forty. He returned involuntarily and only when his true identity was discovered. Prager was, by his own admission, "mature enough and bright enough to have known better." His actions were not the result of economic or emotional necessity. He was well-educated and not without adequate resources to choose from a variety of paths of conduct. Prager's offenses were multiple, of lasting duration, deliberate, and motivated by personal gain. . . .

The record shows that since Prager's conviction, he successfully completed the terms of his probation. He testified to the chastening effect working with those in the terminal stages of AIDS had on him. He has not been the subject of further criminal proceedings. He successfully completed law school, and took and passed the Massachusetts bar examination. In the year following his graduation from law school, the same year in which these proceedings commenced, Prager clerked for the Supreme Judicial Court of Maine. While his employment record to date appears to be without blemish, we note that his work experience includes solely jobs of relatively short duration, mostly designed to further his own self-interest. It does not appear that Prager has continued his work with AIDS patients in either Maine or in Massachusetts, despite his assertions to the board of his intent to continue to assist those in need. No other evidence has been presented to show Prager's present involvement in civic activities. Indeed, the seven-year period since his conviction has been spent almost entirely serving his sentence and achieving his law degree. "[P]assage of time alone is insufficient to warrant [admission]." Matter of Hiss, supra at 460 n.19. It is premature at this time, given the severity and length of Prager's misbehavior, to conclude that Prager has shown he is now fully rehabilitated and worthy of the public trust....

We cannot say at this time that Prager's admission would not be detrimental to the integrity of the bar or the public interest. Prager's flight from the country undermined the integrity of judicial process. It is a wrong directly related to the practice of law and Prager's ability to act as an officer of the court. Additionally, although we cannot say that Prager was dishonest with the board or with this court, the absence in the record of information central to Prager's misconduct and rehabilitation creates some concern about his forthrightness. We are confident that Prager's admission at this time would reflect poorly on the integrity of the bar.

Prager presented numerous letters in his support from various persons associated with him. While we are impressed by the number of recommendations and the conviction of their authors, we are not persuaded by their pleas. Many of those writing on Prager's behalf have known Prager only a short time.... Other letters attest to Prager's compassion when dealing with AIDS patients in his care. We do not question that the work Prager did with those with AIDS was difficult and that Prager maintained true compassion for those he came to know. We do take into account, however, that Prager's work with AIDS patients constituted his alternative sentence, in the design of which he participated. We are not surprised that Prager would carry out his functions in a diligent manner, with the utmost respect and care for his patients. This is precisely what was required of him by his sentence. "Merely showing that an individual is now living as and doing those things he or she should have done throughout life, although necessary to prove rehabilitation, does not prove that the individual has undertaken a useful and constructive place in society.... The requirement of positive action is appropriate for applicants for admission to the bar because service to one's community is an implied obligation of members of the bar."...

The applicant may be on a course of conduct conducive to a future finding of rehabilitation. We conclude, however, that seven years of a creditable work history, successful completion of law school, and compliance with the terms of a five-year probationary period, are insufficient to show good moral character when balanced against approximately sixteen years of marihuana use, international smuggling, and living as a fugitive. . . . The applicant here was released from probation only two years ago. He applied for admission to the bar just eight months after the termination of his probationary period. This is not the case where "no purpose would be served by requiring a more extended demonstration of worthiness for admission." In re Polin, 630 A.2d 1140, 1142 (D.C.App. 1993) (admitting applicant six and one-half years after release from halfway house; first application rejected as four and one-half years from date of release insufficient time). The applicant is free to petition for admission to the bar in five or more years hence, at which time a more complete record of the applicant's activities since his conviction should be available, including his work history, any criminal involvement, and his contributions to society.

We feel it appropriate at this juncture to provide guidance on character inquiries to the board and to future applicants. It is the obligation of an applicant to assure the members of the board and, ultimately, this court that he or she possesses the necessary qualifications to practice law in the Commonwealth. Such a showing requires a full and exhaustive disclosure of prior wrongdoing, including all relevant circumstances surrounding the conduct, both militating and mitigating, and official documentation where appropriate. It requires the same vigorous disclosure with respect to relevant conduct since the wrongdoing, in order that a determination of rehabilitation may be openly and satisfactorily made. "A hearing to determine character and fitness should be more of a mutual inquiry for the purpose of acquainting this court with the applicant's innermost feelings and personal views on those aspects of morality, attention to duty, forthrightness and self-restraint which are usually associated with the accepted definition of 'good moral character.'" In re Application of Davis, 38 Ohio St. 2d 273, 274 (1974). The approach should not be that of the adversarial nature of bar discipline cases, but rather should be one of cooperation by the applicant.

The information provided by the applicant in the record must be sufficient to ensure that this court can independently assure the public that the applicant is trustworthy and "that the guilty person can . . . inspire the public confidence necessary to the proper performance of the duties of an attorney at law." Matter of Keenan, 314 Mass. 544, 549 (1943). Such an inquiry, where a hearing is held pursuant to G. L. c. 221, § 37, and S.J.C. Rule 3:01, § 5, as appearing in 411 Mass. 1321 (1992), requires a thorough investigation into facts presented by the applicant as well as satisfaction that the applicant has indeed presented all material facts and supporting information. It would be helpful to the court if the board should additionally make factual findings regarding the five factors enunciated in Matter of Hiss, supra at 460. . . .

The public welfare demands that this court be certain that the "elaborate machinery" designed to ensure the standards of the profession fully operates. That machinery requires an applicant to the bar who has a criminal past strive diligently to overcome the burden he placed on himself when he violated the laws of the society he later seeks to uphold. Although we recognize rehabilitation when an applicant proves his changed character, the applicant has not done so here.

The petitioner's application is to be denied.

O'CONNOR, J. (dissenting).

In Matter of Gordon, 385 Mass. 48, 58 (1982), a bar discipline case, the court observed, "We have given respect and close attention to the conclusions of the Board of Bar Overseers. The Board is dedicated to the public interest, as commissioned in the words of the rules of this court, and as demonstrated in the high standards of performance of the members of the Board in the several years of its existence." The same observation appropriately may be made regarding the board of Bar Examiners (board). For that reason alone, significant weight should be accorded to the findings and recommendation of the board in this case. In addition, significant weight should be given to the findings of the board because the board, not the court, heard the testimony and observed the witnesses at the hearing on Prager's application. The board, "by virtue of this firsthand observation, is better able than a reviewing court to judge the relative credibilities of witnesses and to assign weight to the evidence they give." Matter of Hiss, 368 Mass. 447, 461 (1975). Matter of Gordon, supra at 55.

In its unanimous report, the board summarized Prager's criminal history, indictment, flight, six-months' incarceration while awaiting extradition and trial, guilty pleas and convictions. The board reported that, on conviction, Prager "was admitted to probation for a term of five years, upon special conditions of probation which required him to open and operate a residential hospice care facility for AIDS sufferers in their terminal state. He was also required to make restitution to the United States for all of the substantial profits he had made from his illegal activities. In October, 1989, the United States District Judge (Gene Carter) determined after a hearing that, in spite of Prager's performance 'in every respect as the Court expected in attempting to bring about the opening of a hospice facility,' he was unable to accomplish it. The Court stated: 'Indeed, it appears that his efforts in this regard have been the principal catalyst to the newly undertaken initiative to accomplish Medicare certification of AIDS patients in Maine.' Prager subsequently provided care to 15 AIDS patients in his own home."

The board's report continues:

"Testimony from a referring physician, two nurses who assisted him, the stepmother of one of his patients and a letter to the board from another nurse all clearly established that Prager's care of the patients was diligent, considerate, empathic and moving. Prager testified convincingly to the deep impression and chastening effect his experience had upon him.

"On October 10, 1993, Prager's probation period ended. The chief probation officer of the United States District Court wrote a lengthy letter to the board commending the 'extreme effort Prager had brought to his special conditions of probation,' and concluded: 'Harvey Prager has complied with the sanctions imposed by our Court and redeemed his status as a responsible and highly productive citizen.' The Assistant United States Attorney who prosecuted the case wrote a lengthy letter describing his experiences with Prager, and concluded as follows: 'I am convinced that the Harvey Prager of the late 1970s and early 1980s is not the Harvey Prager who now desperately wants to contribute to society. In short, I am convinced that he has regained his moral rudder and now again is on the path of being an American success story. I believe that there can be justifiable faith in the Harvey Prager who is now husband, father and care provider.'

"Prager was given permission by Judge Carter to apply for admission to the University of Maine Law School. An Admissions Committee interviewed him and made extensive inquiries which resulted in a decision to admit him. The Chairperson of the Admissions Committee testified before the board and recommended him. Letters were received from other faculty members and the Director of The Cumberland Legal Aid Clinic, where Prager was a student attorney providing services to indigent clients. In detailed descriptions of their experiences with Prager, they uniformly concluded with unqualified recommendations for his admission.

"Prager was selected by the Supreme Judicial Court of Maine to be one of its eleven law clerks. Justice Howard H. Dana, Jr. testified before the board to his unqualified confidence in Prager and to his opinion that he was of good moral character.

"As a result of Prager's selection to be a law clerk in Maine, he became the subject of widespread, constant notoriety. That, in turn, generated many letters to the board in opposition to his admission. While a few writers thought that his rehabilitation should be recognized, the vast majority of correspondents bitterly complained that his crime was unforgivable, that he had been given unfairly favorable treatment by Judge Carter, that he should not be favorably considered merely because of his outstanding academic record at Bowdoin College and at law school and that his admission would do great harm to the public image of the Bar of this Commonwealth.

"While the publicity engendered opposition letters, it did not result in the presentation to us by the correspondents, or by others of any factual evidence that would seriously bring into question the validity of the observations and recommendations of the chief probation officer, the federal prosecutor, the nurses who worked with him, the law school faculty members and Justice Dana. Those recommendations were reinforced by Prager's testimony before us.

"It is the unanimous opinion of the board of Bar Examiners that Prager has so rehabilitated himself since the time of his criminal activities thirteen years ago that he is of present good moral character. While we recognize and respect the force of the arguments presented to us that rehabilitation should not be the basis of our report, the law rightfully requires us to focus upon the question of Prager's rehabilitation. The concept that human redemption is possible and valuable is both well established in law and premised upon long-standing, even ancient traditions. The public interest would be ill-served if we refused to recognize rehabilitation when it is adequately proved. Avoidance by us of making a judgment concerning rehabilitation would itself be an act which would tarnish the image of the Bar. . . ."

The court concludes, "Although we recognize rehabilitation when an applicant proves his changed character, the applicant has not done so here." I think differently. I agree with the chairman of the admissions committee at the University of Maine School of Law: "If [Prager] hasn't established that he is rehabilitated, then it's hard for me to see how anyone ever could." The court's conclusion appears to rest in substantial part, if not entirely, on its perception that Prager's work experience since his conviction in January, 1988, "includes solely jobs of relatively short duration, *mostly designed to further his own self-interest*" (emphasis added). The court notes that "[n]o other evidence has been presented to show Prager's present involvement in civic activities. Indeed, the seven-year period since his conviction has been spent almost entirely serving his sentence and achieving his law degree." Whether the court's "finding" that Prager's postconviction activities were "mostly designed to further his own self-interest" is warranted, is doubtful. In any event, I do not agree that substantial self-interest is antithetical to true rehabilitation, or that conversion to good moral character is not demonstrated when a man who had been convicted of serious crime turns to a legitimate and socially productive life because of his desire for self-respect, the respect of others, and other material or spiritual rewards. The court states that the "applicant is free to petition for admission to the bar in five or more years hence" (when he will be in his mid-fifties). Is it realistic or fair to expect that then, or at any time, Prager will be able to prove that his "civic activities" or other good works were free from the "taint" of substantial self-interest?

The court "take[s] into account . . . that Prager's work with AIDS patients constituted his alternative sentence, in the design of which he participated." "We are not surprised," the court says, "that Prager would carry out his functions in a diligent manner, with the utmost respect and care for his patients. This is precisely what was required of him by his sentence." The court, in my view, unfairly minimizes Prager's extraordinary compassion and immensely difficult hands-on service to the dying AIDS patients. Mr. Gillis's observation to the board, set forth above, that, to be able to appreciate that service, a person "should try caring for a patient dying with this kind of disease for one week," is on the mark. Even if Prager's service was no more than what was required of him by his sentence, Prager surely demonstrated his good moral character by fulfilling a most unique and extraordinarily demanding sentence to the complete satisfaction of those who might be expected to be tough task masters; the chief probation officer, the prosecuting assistant United States Attorney, and the trial judge. . . .

The court rightfully does not wish to send the wrong message to the bar or to the public. The court is very properly concerned about the public perception of the integrity of the bar and public confidence in the administration of justice. I respect-fully suggest, however, that this court's order denying Prager's application to the bar of this Commonwealth delivers the wrong message. "'A fundamental precept of our system . . . is that men can be rehabilitated. "Rehabilitation . . . is a 'state of mind' and the law looks with favor upon rewarding with the opportunity to serve, one who has achieved 'reformation and regeneration.'"' March v. Committee of Bar Examiners, 67 Cal. 2d 718, 732 (1967)." Matter of Allen, [400 Mass. 417 (1987)] at 425. Matter of Hiss, supra at 454. Recognizing that principle, the board stated, "The concept that human redemption is possible and valuable is both well established in law and premised upon longstanding, even ancient traditions. The public interest would be ill-served if we refused to recognize rehabilitation when it is adequately proved. Avoidance by us of making a judgment concerning rehabilitation would itself be an act which would tarnish the image of the Bar." This case presents an appropriate opportunity for the court to deliver to the bar and the public the encouraging and humane message that the court will recognize and support a wrongdoer's rehabilitation when it has been fairly proved as it was here. The court fails to do so and therefore conveys the opposite, discouraging, message. I respect-fully dissent from the court's order.

Notes

1. Prager did wait the prescribed time, reapplied for admission to the Massachu-setts bar in 2003, and is currently practicing in Massachusetts. His law firm's website recites that he "focuses his practice in matters concerning legal professional respon-sibility and ethics," see <http://www.pragerlegal.com/profile/>.

2. In *Prager*, the decision to deny admission was based on long-lasting criminal activity. A different basis was the critical factor in Matter of Ronwin, 136 Ariz. 566 (1983). In *Ronwin*, a graduate of Arizona State Law School was admitted to the bar in Iowa but denied admission in Arizona. He then commenced a long series of law-suits in which he ended up suing not only the Arizona Bar Examiners but also his own and opposing lawyers, the dean of his Law School, student law review editors who had written about his cases, clerks of court, and every judge who heard any of his cases as all engaged in a conspiracy to deny him admission. The Arizona court twice denied him admission, concluding that he had a personality disorder leading him to engage in grossly improper behavior. The *Ronwin* court rejected the free speech claim by finding "habitual unreasonable reaction to adverse rulings" in courtroom settings. There is an obvious relation between the holding in *Ronwin* and the earlier material in Chapter 6 that considered the freedom of lawyers to speak their minds. There is also a relation between *Ronwin* and the material of the next Chapter relating to discipline. *Ronwin* is not unique. See, e.g., the similar holdings in In re Converse, 258 Neb. 159 (1999), and In re McLaughlin, 144 N.J. 133 (1996).

3. Very critical analyses of the operation of state admissions procedures are con-tained in Fortney, "Law Student Admissions and Ethics," 45 S. Tex. L. Rev. 983 (2004)

and Rhode, "Moral Character as a Professional Credential," 94 Yale L.J. 491 (1984). Their conclusions are that the whole process of character assessment should be abolished except perhaps for a few specific offenses and that the resources thus saved should be refocused on regulation of professional misconduct. If you agree with the authors in theory, would your conclusion be affected if the applicant had been convicted of first-degree murder? See In re Hamm, 123 P. 3d 652 (Ariz. 2005) (denying admission to applicant who had committed an execution-style murder during a drug deal over twenty years earlier). What about attempted murder? See In re King, 136 P. 3d 878 (Ariz. 2006) (same result with respect to attempted murder with a firearm almost twenty years earlier, even though applicant had been admitted in Texas twelve years earlier and had practiced there without any disciplinary complaint).

4. Issues of "moral character" also arise in connection with petitions for readmission to practice after a lawyer has been disbarred or suspended indefinitely. One of the more famous cases was In re Alger Hiss, 368 Mass. 447 (1975), where Mr. Hiss was readmitted 22 years after having been disbarred upon conviction for perjury in his testimony to a congressional committee denying that he had turned over State Department documents to a Communist spy ring. Despite the fact that he refused to admit guilt and therefore was unable to urge rehabilitation of character, the court found that he was presently of good moral character and that readmission would "not be detrimental to the integrity and standing of the bar, the administration of justice, or to the public interest." The court reached its conclusion despite the fact that it viewed the crime of which he was convicted as "a direct and reprehensible attack on the foundations of our judicial system," and "one that is further tainted by the breach of confidence and trust which underlay his conviction." Compare In re Braverman, 271 Md. 196 (1974) (reinstating a lawyer disbarred after conviction of violation of the Smith Act, 18 U.S.C. § 2385 (1940), which criminalized advocacy of violent overthrow of the government, on a finding of current good moral character and a further finding that there was insufficient evidence to have supported his conviction under the standard of proof subsequently required) with In re Braverman, 399 F. Supp. 801 (1975) (same lawyer not reinstated by divided United States District Court for the District of Maryland).

5. Problem 8–11 tracks the facts regarding the application of Matthew Hale for admission to the Illinois Bar. The Illinois Supreme Court's Character and Fitness Committee denied his application because of his very strongly expressed hatred for blacks and Jews, predicting that he would behave the same way as a lawyer, notwithstanding Hale's repeated claims that he would abide by the rules of professional conduct—including the rule prohibiting discrimination—until such time as he could change the law to eliminate equal protection for blacks and other minorities by peaceful means. The Committee concluded:

> [A] lawyer cannot, as his life's mission, do all in his power to incite racial and religious hatred among the populace so that it will peaceably abolish the rule of law for all persons save those of the "white race." Instead, and by

rejecting Matthew Hale's application, let it be said that the Bar and our courts stand committed to [the fundamental truth that] all persons are possessed of individual dignity [and] the enforcement and application of [this value] to specific cases has been entrusted to our courts and its officers—the lawyers—a trust that lies at the heart of our system of government.... If the civilized world had no experience with Hitler, Matthew Hale might be dismissed as a harmless "crackpot." However, history teaches a different lesson.... While Hale has not yet threatened to exterminate anyone, history tells us that extermination is sometimes not far behind when governmental power is held by persons of his racial views. The Bar of Illinois cannot certify someone as having good moral character and general fitness to practice law who has dedicated his life to inciting racial hatred for the purpose of implementing those views.

In re Hale, Committee on Character and Fitness for the Third Appellate District of the Supreme Court of Illinois (1998). One member of the panel dissented on the ground that "[t]ime will tell if Matthew Hale can in fact practice law in accordance with his oath while holding extremist views" and that "[t]he Rules of the Attorney Registration and Disciplinary Commission of the Illinois Supreme Court are the profession's and the public's protection against any abuse." Id. The Illinois Supreme Court denied review. The one dissenting judge believed that the court should consider the First Amendment issue, among others, raised by the case. 723 N.E.2d 206 (1999). The United States Supreme Court denied certiorari. 530 U.S. 1261 (2000).

Which position do you find more persuasive, the majority's or the dissent's? Does the majority's position imply that an applicant's membership in any organization committed to overthrowing the current government of the United States and replacing it with a regime that would not recognize some or all or our existing constitutional rights is a sufficient ground for excluding him or her from the bar? Would you apply this criterion to membership in the Communist Party? Do Hale's racist and anti-Semitic views arguably imply something different about his conduct as a lawyer than membership in the Communist Party? To the extent that conduct, not views, is what is at issue, isn't the dissent correct that such questions should be handled by the disciplinary process, not the admissions process? Are violations of Illinois' rules prohibiting lawyers from engaging in "adverse discriminatory treatment of litigants, jurors, witnesses, lawyers, and others, based on race, sex, religion, or national origin" likely to come to the attention of disciplinary officials? Illinois Model Rules of Professional Conduct, Rule 8.4(a)(5). Reconsider this question after you have read the materials on professional discipline in Chapter 10.

What should we make of the majority's references to the "lessons" of Nazi Germany? As the majority concedes, the First Amendment protects even the most extreme views. The majority suggests, however, that there is a difference when people with such views hold "governmental power." Do you agree? Should Hale's extremist beliefs bar him from holding elected or appointed office? Or from being a judge? Do lawyers hold the same kind of "governmental power" as office holders or judges? Is there an argument that it is important to our constitutional framework that there be lawyers with extremist beliefs in order to insure that citizens with similar beliefs will be able to find a lawyer when the state seeks to prosecute them for allegedly acting on their radical views? Or that there be lawyers to represent them even in unrelated matters? Does your answer depend upon whether you believe that lawyers without such views are likely to take seriously their professional aspiration to represent "unpopular" clients? For an argument about the importance of providing radicals such as those in the "militia movement" with adequate legal representation, see Susan P. Koniak, "When Law Risks Madness," 8 Cardozo Stud. L. & Lit. 65 (1996). To the extent that you believe that Hale should be admitted—either to safeguard the rights of unpopular clients or because you fear giving licensing boards unfettered discretion to determine which views should not be tolerated in the profession—does this affect your view about Professor Rhode's proposal in the article cited in Note 3 to confine character and fitness review to examining whether the applicant has violated certain narrowly proscribed legal rules?

In a tragic postscript to the Hale case, Benjamin Nathaniel Smith, an avowed white supremacist and devoted member of World Church of the Creator, the white supremacist organization headed by Matthew Hale, embarked on a killing spree shortly after Hale was denied admission to the bar. Carrying two rifles and his copy of the "White Man's Bible," Smith indiscriminately targeted blacks, Asians, and Orthodox Jews, eventually killing two and wounding 15 others before turning the gun on himself. When asked whether he was concerned about Smith's actions, Hale responded that although he did not advocate violence, "as far as we're concerned, the loss is one white man." Stephanie Simon, "Leader of Hate's Church Mourns 'One White Man,'" L.A. Times, July 6, 1999. Six months later, Hale remained unrepentant, noting that Smith "died for our cause" and boasting that "[m]embership [in the World Church of the Creator] has increased about 50%" since the shootings "[a]nd we've sold more copies of the 'White Man's Bible' in the last six months than in the previous three years." Kirsten Scharberg, "A Supremacist's Shots Still Echo Across Midwest," Boston Globe, January 16, 2000. If the relevant issue is "moral character," do these remarks shed any light on whether Hale should have been admitted to the bar? If not, is there any difference between "moral character" and simply being "law-abiding"?

Following those events, Hale and his church lost a trademark case involving ownership of the title World Church of the Creator. He was then indicted, convicted, and sentenced in 2005 to 40 years in prison for having solicited an undercover FBI agent to kill federal judge Joan Lefkow, who had ruled against him in the trademark matter. See United States v. Hale, 448 F.3d 971 (7th Cir. 2006) (affirming Hale's conviction).

6. The issue of mental competence of lawyers has traditionally been seen as a relevant area of inquiry for state bar admission. See Problem 8–8. More recently, however, after several states have begun asking questions about applicants' mental health and demanding additional detailed medical information, the Department of

Justice stepped in, advising states that such inquiries, as opposed to questions about past conduct, violated provisions of the Americans with Disabilities Act. See Anna Stolley Persky, "State Bars May Probe Applicants' Behavior, But Not Mental Health Status," ABA Journal (June 1, 2014).

7. While significant attention has been given to the issue of moral character, two other developments regarding admission to the bar warrant attention. First, as of 2016, approximately half of the states have adopted the Uniform Bar Examination ("UBE"), an admission test "uniformly administered, graded, and scored by user jurisdictions [that] results in a portable score that can be transferred to other UBE jurisdictions." See <http://www.ncbex.org/exams/ube/>. While the UBE is a long way from nationalizing bar admission—takers still need to be individually admitted in adopting jurisdictions—it is certainly a step in that direction. Second—and following repeated scholarly criticism of standardized testing (and in particular criticism of multiple choice questions) as the predominant means of regulating admission to the bar, many jurisdictions have begun incorporating additional testing into the bar exams, supplementing the traditional standardized Multistate Bar Examination with the Multistate Performance Examination. See Marjorie M. Shultz & Sheldon Zedeck, "Predicting Lawyer Effectiveness: Broadening the Basis for Law School Admission Decisions," 36 Law & Soc. Inquiry 620 (2011).

2. The Unauthorized Practice of Law

Closely related to problems of admission to the bar is the matter of what acts constitute the practice of law; in other words, which acts require a license? There has been a great deal of litigation in the field and many cases have gone quite far in prohibiting lay people, such as real estate brokers and title companies, from selecting and filling in the blanks on preprinted forms to consummate agreements among their customers. The issue has returned to prominence recently. Unauthorized practice restrictions have been seen as raising serious antitrust problems, because they limit competition in the provision of legal services. They have also been seen as constituting barriers to access, especially inexpensive access, to legal rights of poor people. A comprehensive, critical study of unauthorized practice regulation is Deborah Rhode, "Policing the Professional Monopoly: A Constitutional and Empirical Analysis of Unauthorized Practice Prohibitions," 34 Stan. L. Rev. 1 (1981).

Problem 8–13

Services have sprung up all over the country that want to help individuals who cannot afford lawyers to obtain various kinds of benefits and entitlements. Some want to help fill out forms in uncontested divorce cases. Others want to be able to meet with government officials to help clients obtain veterans' benefits, Social Security payments, and the like. Still others want to be able to negotiate disputes with landlords. Shall the professional rules be changed to permit persons who are not members of the bar to render such services?

Florida Bar v. Brumbaugh

355 So. 2d 1186 (Fla. 1978)

PER CURIAM

The Florida Bar has filed a petition charging Marilyn Brumbaugh with engaging in the unauthorized practice of law, and seeking a permanent injunction prohibiting her from further engaging in these allegedly unlawful acts. We have jurisdiction under our constitutional authority to adopt rules for the practice and procedure in all the courts of this state. Article V, Section 2(a), Florida Constitution (1968). We now issue an injunction, delineating in this opinion those acts of respondent which we deem to constitute the unauthorized practice of law, and ordering her to stop such activities.

Respondent, Marilyn Brumbaugh, is not and has never been a member of the Florida Bar, and is, therefore, not licensed to practice law within this state. She has advertised in various local newspapers as "Marilyn's Secretarial Service" offering to perform typing services for "Do-It-Yourself" divorces, wills, resumes, and bankruptcies. The Florida Bar charges that she performed unauthorized legal services by preparing for her customers those legal documents necessary in an uncontested dissolution of marriage proceeding and by advising her customers as to the costs involved and the procedures which should be followed in order to obtain a dissolution of marriage. For this service, Ms. Brumbaugh charges a fee of $50.

Of course, we must determine whether the Florida Bar has presented sufficient evidence in the record before us to prove that respondent has engaged in the unauthorized practice of law. But, in cases such as this, the Florida Supreme Court is not confined to act solely in its judicial capacity. In addition, it acts in its administrative capacity as chief policy maker, regulating the administration of the court system and supervising all persons who are engaged in rendering legal advice to members of the general public. Such authority carries with it the responsibility to perform this task in a way responsive to the needs and desires of our citizens. . . .

The Florida Bar, as an agent of this court, plays a large role in the enforcement of court policies and rules and has been active in regulating and disciplining unethical conduct by its members. Because of the natural tendency of all professions to act in their own self interest, however, this Court must closely scrutinize all regulations tending to limit competition in the delivery of legal services to the public, and determine whether or not such regulations are truly in the public interest. Indeed, the active role of state supreme courts in the regulation of the practice of law (when such regulation is subject to pointed reexamination by the state court as policy maker) is accorded great deference and exemption from federal interference under the Sherman Act. Bates v. State Bar of Arizona. [See p. 631.]

The United States Supreme Court has recently decided issues which may drastically change the practice of law throughout the country, especially with regard to advertising and price competition among attorneys. Bates v. State Bar of Arizona;

Goldfarb, et al. v. Virginia State Bar, [see p. 623, Note 4]. In addition, the Supreme Court has affirmed the fundamental constitutional right of all persons to represent themselves in court proceedings. Faretta v. California, 422 U.S. 806 (1975). In *Faretta*, the Supreme Court emphasized that an attorney is merely an assistant who helps a citizen protect his legal rights and present his case to the courts. A person should not be forced to have an attorney represent his legal interests if he does not consent to such representation. It is imperative for us to analyze these cases and determine how their holdings and the policies behind them affect our regulation of the legal profession in this state.

With regard to the charges made against Marilyn Brumbaugh, this court appointed a referee to receive evidence and to make findings of fact, conclusions of law, and recommendations as to the disposition of the case. The referee found that respondent, under the guise of a "secretarial" or "typing" service prepares, for a fee, all papers deemed by her to be needed for the pleading, filing, and securing of a dissolution of marriage, as well as detailed instructions as to how the suit should be filed, notice served, hearings set, trial conducted, and the final decree secured. The referee also found that in one instance, respondent prepared a quit claim deed in reference to the marital property of the parties. The referee determined that respondent's contention that she merely operates a typing service is rebutted by numerous facts in evidence. Ms. Brumbaugh has no blank forms either to sell or to fill out. Rather, she types up the documents for her customers after they have asked her to prepare a petition or an entire set of dissolution of marriage papers. Prior to typing up the papers, respondent asks her customers whether custody, child support, or alimony is involved. Respondent has four sets of dissolution of marriage papers, and she chooses which set is appropriate for the particular customer. She then types out those papers, filling in the blank spaces with the appropriate information. Respondent instructs her customers how the papers are to be signed, where they are to be filed, and how the customer should arrange for a final hearing.

Marilyn Brumbaugh, who is representing herself in proceedings before this court, has made various objections to the procedure and findings of fact of the referee. . . . Respondent argues that she has never held herself out as an attorney, and has never professed to have legal skills. She does not give advice, but acts merely as a secretary. She is a licensed counselor, and asserts the right to talk to people and to let her customers make decisions for themselves. Finally, respondent contends that her civil rights have been violated, and that she has been denied the right to make an honest living.

This case does not arise out of a complaint by any of Ms. Brumbaugh's customers as to improper advice or unethical conduct. It has been initiated by members of The Florida Bar who believe her to be practicing law without a license. The evidence introduced at the hearing below shows that none of respondent's customers believed that she was an attorney, or that she was acting in their behalf. Respondent's advertisements clearly addressed themselves to people who wish to do their own divorces.

These customers knew that they had to have "some type of papers" to file in order to obtain their dissolution of marriage. Respondent never handled contested divorces. During the past two years respondent has assisted several hundred customers in obtaining their own divorces. The record shows that while some of her customers told respondent exactly what they wanted, generally respondent would ask her customers for the necessary information needed to fill out the divorce papers, such as the names and addresses of the parties, the place and duration of residency in this state, whether there was any property settlement to be resolved, or any determination as to custody and support of children. Finally, each petition contained the bare allegation that the marriage was irretrievably broken. Respondent would then inform the parties as to which documents needed to be signed, by whom, how many copies of each paper should be filed, where and when they should be filed, the costs involved, and what witness testimony is necessary at the court hearing. Apparently, Ms. Brumbaugh no longer informs the parties verbally as to the proper procedures for the filing of the papers, but offers to let them copy papers described as "suggested procedural education."

The Florida Bar argues that the above activities of respondent violate the rulings of this Court in The Florida Bar v. American Legal and Business Forms, Inc., 274 So. 2d 225 (Fla. 1973), and The Florida Bar v. Stupica, 300 So. 2d 683 (Fla. 1974). In those decisions we held that it is lawful to sell to the public printed legal forms, provided they do not carry with them what purports to be instructions on how to fill out such forms or how to use them. We stated that legal advice is inextricably involved in the filling out and advice as to how to use such legal forms, and therein lies the danger of injury or damage to the public if not properly performed in accordance with law. In *Stupica*, supra, this court rejected the rationale of the New York courts in New York County Lawyer's Association v. Dacey, 28 A.D.2d 161, reversed and dissenting opinion adopted 21 N.Y.2d 694 (N.Y. 1967), which held that the publication of forms and instructions on their use does not constitute the unauthorized practice of law if these instructions are addressed to the public in general rather than to a specific individual legal problem. The Court in *Dacey* stated that the possibility that the principles or rules set forth in the text may be accepted by a particular reader as a solution to his problem does not mean that the publisher is practicing law. Other states have adopted the principle of law set forth in *Dacey*, holding that the sale of legal forms with instructions for their use does not constitute unauthorized practice of law. See State Bar of Michigan v. Cramer, 399 Mich. 116 (1976); Oregon State Bar v. Gilchrist, 272 Or. 552 (1975). However, these courts have prohibited all personal contact between the service providing such forms and the customer, in the nature of consultation, explanation, recommendation, advice, or other assistance in selecting particular forms, in filling out any part of the forms, suggesting or advising how the forms should be used in solving the particular problems.

Although persons not licensed as attorneys are prohibited from practicing law within this state, it is somewhat difficult to define exactly what constitutes the practice of law in all instances. This Court has previously stated that: "if the giving of such advice and performance of such services affect important rights of a person under the law, and if the reasonable protection of the rights and property of those advised and served requires that the persons giving such advice possess legal skill and knowledge of the law greater than that possessed by the average citizen, then the giving of such advice and the performance of such services by one for another as a course of conduct constitute the practice of law." [State v. Sperry, 140 So. 2d 587, 591 (Fla. 1962).] . . .

In determining whether a particular act constitutes the practice of law, our primary goal is the protection of the public. However, any limitations on the free practice of law by all persons necessarily affects important constitutional rights. Our decision here certainly affects the constitutional rights of Marilyn Brumbaugh to pursue a lawful occupation or business. . . . Our decision also affects respondent's First Amendment rights to speak and print what she chooses. In addition, her customers and potential customers have the constitutional right of self-representation and the right of privacy inherent in the marriage relationship. All citizens in our state are also guaranteed access to our courts by Article I, Section 21, Florida Constitution (1968). Although it is not necessary for us to provide affirmative assistance in order to ensure meaningful access to the courts to our citizens, as it is necessary for us to do for those incarcerated in our state prison system . . . we should not place any unnecessary restrictions upon that right. We should not deny persons who wish to represent themselves access to any source of information which might be relevant in the preparation of their cases. There are numerous texts in our state law libraries which describe our substantive and procedural law, purport to give legal advice to the reader as to choices that should be made in various situations, and which also contain sample legal forms which a reader may use as an example. We generally do not restrict the access of the public to these law libraries, although many of the legal texts are not authored by attorneys licensed to practice in this state. These texts do not carry with them any guarantees of accuracy, and only some of them purport to update statements which have been modified by subsequently enacted statutes and recent case law.

The policy of this Court should continue to be one of encouraging persons who are unsure of their legal rights and remedies to seek legal assistance from persons licensed by us to practice law in this state. However, in order to make an intelligent decision as whether or not to engage the assistance of an attorney, a citizen must be allowed access to information which will help determine the complexity of the legal problem. Once a person has made the decision to represent himself, we should not enforce any unnecessary regulation which might tend to hinder the exercise of this constitutionally protected right. However, any restriction of constitutional rights must be "narrowly drawn to express only the legitimate state interests at stake." Roe v. Wade [410 U.S. 113 (1973)] . . . . "And if there are other reasonable ways to achieve those goals with a lesser burden on constitutionally protected activity, a state may not choose the way of greater interference. If it acts at all, it must choose less drastic means." Shelton v. Tucker, 364 U.S. 479 (1960).

It is also important for us to consider the legislative statute governing dissolution of marriage in resolving the question of what constitutes the practice of law in this area. Florida's "no fault" dissolution of marriage statute clearly has the remedial purpose of simplifying the dissolution of marriage whenever possible. Section 61.001, Florida Statutes (1975) states:

(1) This chapter shall be liberally construed and applied to promote its purposes.

(2) Its purposes are:

(a) To preserve the integrity of marriage and to safeguard meaningful family relationships;

(b) To promote the amicable settlement of disputes that have arisen between parties to a marriage;

(c) To mitigate the potential harm to the spouses and their children caused by the process of legal dissolution of marriage.

Families usually undergo tremendous financial hardship when they decide to dissolve their marital relationships. The Legislature simplified procedures so that parties would not need to bear the additional burden of expensive legal fees where they have agreed to the settlement of their property and the custody of their children. This Court should not place unreasonable burdens upon the obtaining of such divorces, especially where both parties consent to the dissolution.

Present dissolution procedures in uncontested situations involve a very simplified method of asserting certain facts required by statute, notice to the other parties affected, and a simple hearing where the trial court may hear proof and make inquiries as to the facts asserted in those pleadings.

The legal forms necessary to obtain such an uncontested dissolution of marriage are susceptible of standardization. This Court has allowed the sale of legal forms on this and other subjects, provided that they do not carry with them what purports to be instructions on how to fill out such forms or how they are to be used. . . . These decisions should be reevaluated in light of those recent decisions in other states which have held that the sale of forms necessary to obtain a divorce, together with any related textual instructions directed towards the general public, does not constitute the practice of law. The reasons for allowing the sale of such legal publications which contain sample forms to be used by individuals who wish to represent themselves are persuasive. State Bar of Michigan v. Cramer, supra, reasoned that such instructional material should be no more objectionable than any other publication placed into the stream of commerce which purports to offer general advice on common problems and does not purport to give a person advice on a specific problem particular to a designated or readily identified person. . . .

Although there is a danger that some published material might give false or misleading information, that is not a sufficient reason to justify its total ban. We must assume that our citizens will generally use such publications for what they are worth in the preparation of their cases, and further assume that most persons will not rely on these materials in the same way they would rely on the advice of an attorney or other persons holding themselves out as having expertise in the area. The tendency of persons seeking legal assistance to place their trust in the individual purporting to have expertise in the area necessitates this Court's regulation of such attorney-client relationships, so as to require that persons giving such advice have at least a minimal amount of legal training and experience. Although Marilyn Brumbaugh never held herself out as an attorney, it is clear that her clients placed some reliance upon her to properly prepare the necessary legal forms for their dissolution proceedings. To this extent we believe that Ms. Brumbaugh overstepped proper bounds and engaged in the unauthorized practice of law. We hold that Ms. Brumbaugh, and others in similar situations, may sell printed material purporting to explain legal practice and procedure to the public in general and she may sell sample legal forms. To this extent we limit our prior holdings in *Stupica* and *American Legal and Business Forms, Inc.* Further, we hold that it is not improper for Marilyn Brumbaugh to engage in a secretarial service, typing such forms for her clients, provided that she only copy the information given to her in writing by her clients. In addition, Ms. Brumbaugh may advertise her business activities of providing secretarial and notary services and selling legal forms and general printed information. However, Marilyn Brumbaugh must not, in conjunction with her business, engage in advising clients as to the various remedies available to them, or otherwise assist them in preparing those forms necessary for a dissolution proceeding. More specifically, Marilyn Brumbaugh may not make inquiries nor answer questions from her clients as to the particular forms which might be necessary, how best to fill out such forms, where to properly file such forms, and how to present necessary evidence at the court hearings. Our specific holding with regard to the dissolution of marriage also applies to other unauthorized legal assistance such as the preparation of wills or real estate transaction documents. While Marilyn Brumbaugh may legally sell forms in these areas, and type up instruments which have been completed by clients, she must not engage in personal legal assistance in conjunction with her business activities, including the correction of errors and omissions.

Accordingly, having defined the limits within which Ms. Brumbaugh and those engaged in similar activities may conduct their business without engaging in the unauthorized practice of law, the rule to show cause is dissolved.

Judge KARL concurs specially.

There is a popular notion that every attempt to define the practice of law and restrict the activities within the definition to those who are authorized to practice law is nothing more than a method of providing economic protection for lawyers. I recognize that a small number of attorneys who advocate a broad definition of the practice coupled with severe penalties for those who encroach are motivated by economic self-interest. Indeed, regardless of motive, any law or rule that stakes out an area "for lawyers only" will result in some incidental benefit to those who are authorized to practice law—a form of serendipity for them.

What is often lost in the rush to condemn members of the legal profession for alleged selfishness is the existence of a genuine need to protect the public from those who are willing to give legal advice and render legal service, for their own profit, without being competent to do so and without being subject to restraint and punishment if they cause damage to some unsuspecting and uninformed persons in the process. Just as the public must be protected from physical harm inflicted by those who would prescribe drugs and perform surgery without proper training, so must we provide protection from financial and other damage inflicted by pseudo-lawyers.

We could develop a perfect set of disciplinary rules for attorneys and establish a procedure that quickly disbars and delicenses those who violate the rules, but if we should then permit nonmembers of the bar, including those who have been disbarred, to engage in the same activities as lawyers, we would have accomplished nothing. The members of the public would still be in serious jeopardy.

The problem, so well articulated in the majority opinion, is where to draw the lines between activities that constitute the practice of law and those that do not. There must be a balancing of constitutional rights with the recognized need to protect the public. The broader the definition, the more effective are the disciplinary rules and the greater is the public protection, but the need for protection must give way to rights guaranteed by the Constitution.

I concur with the majority because I am persuaded that the definition of the practice of law developed in The Florida Bar v. American Legal and Business Forms, Inc., 274 So. 2d 225 (Fla. 1973), and The Florida Bar v. Stupica, 300 So. 2d 683 (Fla. 1974), is too broad to withstand an attack based on the provisions of the First Amendment of the United States Constitution and must, therefore, be contracted. I reject as specious the argument that constitutionally permissible restrictions on activities defined as the practice of law are designed solely to produce high legal fees by discouraging competition and encouraging legal featherbedding.

Notes

1. Following *Brumbaugh*, the Florida Bar sought to enjoin Rosemary Furman, owner of a secretarial service that also helped people obtain uncontested divorces and a leading opponent of unauthorized practice rules, from practicing law. Ms. Furman attacked the *Brumbaugh* restrictions, arguing that because so many of her clients were uneducated, it was necessary to have some oral conversation with them. Moreover, the prohibition against oral communication wastes judicial resources because papers are improperly filed, and is generally inhibiting to people who want to handle their own cases. She further argued that in many places a service like hers is the only place where poor people needing help can go; legal aid does not exist or has put a limit on matrimonial matters because of the workload, and the Bar has

provided no other help. In addition, Ms. Furman contended that the *Brumbaugh* rules violated the First Amendment and the Equal Protection Clause. They impinged on poor people's access to the courts by limiting their right to receive, and her right to disseminate, relevant information. Without even addressing the constitutional issues, the court found Ms. Furman guilty of unauthorized practice of law. The court also directed the Florida Bar to begin a study and report to the court its findings regarding better ways to provide legal services to the poor, The Florida Bar v. Furman, 376 So. 2d 378 (1979), appeal dismissed for want of a substantial federal question, 444 U.S. 1061 (1980), and in fact a simplified procedure for dissolution of marriages without need for participation by lawyers was put into effect by the Florida Supreme Court in June 1984. Subsequently, however, Ms. Furman was found in contempt on testimony of her customers that not only had she undertaken activity in violation of the court order but also that she had advised customers to falsify and conceal information in marriage dissolution documents on several occasions. Florida Bar v. Furman, 451 So. 2d 808 (Fla. 1984), appeal dismissed for want of a substantial federal question, 469 U.S. 925 (1984). Governor Graham, however, commuted her jail sentence on the condition that she successfully complete the remaining two years of the court's injunction. 71 A.B.A. J. 19 (1985).

2. Should the answer to whether Ms. Furman was practicing law without a license have turned on the availability of affordable legal services? If that lack of availability is not conclusive, what should be? Is the line drawn in *Brumbaugh* about right? Does its justification lie in its definitional quality of the practice of law or in its prophylactic quality in stopping lay assistance at the point where policing becomes difficult? What is the difference between *Brumbaugh* and filling out someone's tax return? Or telling a sick friend to take some aspirin and go to bed? Is that practicing medicine? The issue of non-lawyers practicing poverty law is discussed in a 1998 symposium. See, e.g., "Report of the Working Group on the Use of Non-Lawyers," 67 Fordham L. Rev. 1813 (1999); Alex Hurder, "Nonlawyer Legal Assistance and Access to Justice," 67 Fordham L. Rev. 2241 (1999); and Derek Denckla, "Nonlawyers and the Unauthorized Practice of Law," 67 Fordham L. Rev. 2581 (1999).

3. Suppose the case involved a contest over custody and the lawyer for the other side called Ms. Brumbaugh to the stand and asked her to relate everything her "client" said. Would that be privileged? /Vo -

4. One of Ms. Furman's lawyers in the Florida proceeding was Alan Morrison, then director of the Public Citizen Litigation Group, members of which were popularly known at one time as Ralph Nader's lawyers. Mr. Morrison has taken a crack at answering some of the questions in Notes 2 and 3 in "Defining the Unauthorized Practice of Law: Some New Ways of Looking at an Old Question," 4 Nova L.J. 363 (1980). The Florida Supreme Court has revisited and consistently followed the *Brumbaugh* approach many times. See The Florida Bar v. We The People Forms and Service Center of Sarasota, Inc., 883 So.2d 1280 (Fla. 2004) (reaffirming *Brumbaugh* and citing numerous Florida cases since *Brumbaugh*).

5. The earlier discussion of Bates v. State Bar of Arizona, p. 631, omitted consideration of an antitrust issue that is relevant here. The disciplined lawyers in that case attacked the application of the advertising rules of the Code of Professional Responsibility to their activities as a violation of sections one and two of the Sherman Act. The Supreme Court rejected that attack, holding that the doctrine of Parker v. Brown, 317 U.S. 341 (1943), exempted certain state action from the coverage of that act. The Court viewed as crucial the fact that the Arizona Supreme Court had "adopted the rules, and it is the ultimate trier of fact and law in the enforcement process." 433 U.S. at 361. Since the state's policy is so clearly expressed and its supervision was so active, the Parker v. Brown exemption applied.

Remember that prior to the decision in *Bates*, the Supreme Court had already held that the Sherman Act did apply in an analogous situation when the state had not prescribed and supervised the activities of the bar alleged to be anticompetitive. See Goldfarb v. Virginia State Bar, p. 623, Note 4. The combination of *Goldfarb* and *Bates* made dubious the practice of many state bar associations of issuing advisory opinions relating to ethical practices, and especially unauthorized practice of the law, when coupled with a threat of disciplinary proceedings. After *Goldfarb* and before *Bates*, one court held that the Parker v. Brown exemption did not shield a state bar from the Sherman Act even though it was required to issue advisory opinions by the state supreme court. Advisory opinions relating to unauthorized practice were not seen as sufficiently related to the state's interests in granting lawyers a monopoly of the practice of law to justify their anticompetitive effects. Surety Title Ins. Agency, Inc. v. Virginia State Bar, 431 F. Supp. 298 (E.D. Va. 1977). After *Bates*, the court of appeals vacated this decision in order that a companion state proceeding brought by the state attorney general charging the same title insurance companies with unauthorized practice could be decided first. Virginia State Bar v. Surety Title Ins. Agency, 571 F.2d 205 (4th Cir. 1978). The Supreme Court denied certiorari, 436 U.S. 941 (1978). The Supreme Court of Virginia, on motion of the bar, then issued new rules with respect to issuance of advisory opinions that required all opinions finding that particular conduct constituted unauthorized practice eventually to be reviewed by that court. See Rule 10, Virginia State Bar, 219 Va. 367 (1979). The applicability of the Parker v. Brown exemption to lawyer disciplinary rules and boards is still uncertain as a result of the Supreme Court's opinion in North Carolina Board of Dental Examiners v. FTC, 135 S. Ct. 1101 (2015), summarized at p. 815, infra.

6. How are developments in information technology, particularly the internet, likely to affect unauthorized practice issues such as those raised in *Brumbaugh* and *Furman*? Consider the story of Marcus Arnold, a fifteen-year-old high school student who became one of the top purveyors of legal advice on a popular legal internet bulletin board. See Michael Lewis, "Faking It," New York Times Magazine, July 15, 2001, at 32. Using the handle "lawguy," Marcus dispensed answers to a broad range of legal questions ranging from whether it is legal to keep a dog that wanders on to your property even if the owners want it back ("no") to whether a parolee can be

prevented from marrying by his parole officer (not "unless the parolee has 'no marriage' under the special conditions in which he is released"). In less than a year, answers such as these made "lawguy" one of the top legal analysts on the site—a site that featured advice from several licensed lawyers. When Marcus eventually revealed the fact that he was 15, most of the complaints he received were from lawyers and other competitors on the site. Although some of his former "clients" also registered complaints, many came to his defense. Two weeks later, he became the site's number one rated legal analyst.

LegalZoom, a website founded in 2001, offers inexpensive template legal documents, such as wills and incorporation documents for people who cannot afford to purchase legal services from lawyers. While several bar associations have taken the position that LegalZoom is engaged in the unauthorized practice of law, some commentators have argued that the prevailing realities of insufficient access to legal services under the traditional model render entities like LegalZoom both necessary and desirable. See Cody Blades, "Crying Over Spilt Milk: Why the Legal Community is Ethically Obligated to Ensure LegalZoom's Survival in the Legal Services Marketplace," 38 Hamline L. Rev. 31 (2015). Notably, just as LegalZoom far exceeds anything Marcus Arnold could have offered, developments in artificial intelligence may soon dwarf the capabilities of LegalZoom, radically changing the landscape of access to legal services and the unauthorized practice of law. See John O. McGinnis & Russell G. Pearce, "The Great Disruption: How Machine Intelligence Will Transform the Role of Lawyers in the Delivery of Legal Services," 82 Fordham L. Rev. 3041 (2014).

What do Marcus Arnold's and LegalZoom's stories say about the public's view of the unauthorized practice rules? Whether or not these rules serve the public interest, is it possible to enforce them in cyberspace? Does your answer to this question have implications for legal practice that go beyond unauthorized practice issues? Return to this last question after you have considered the materials on multidisciplinary practice at the end of this Chapter.

7. In late 2012, Washington state authorized the practice of Limited License Legal Technicians ("LLLT"), meant to "offer an affordable legal support option to help meet the needs of those unable to afford the service of an attorney. Legal Technicians . . . are trained and licensed to advise and assist people going through divorce, child custody and other family-law matters in Washington." See WSBA, <http://www.wsba.org/licensing-and-lawyer-conduct/limited-licenses/legal-technicians>. Hailed by early commentators as the next big thing in access to legal services, the LLLT movement has since lost some steam, in part because following the Great Recession of 2008–2009 some bar associations, arguably self-interestedly, have opposed the authorization of LLLTs on the ground that insufficient access to legal services ought to be met from within the ranks of unemployed and under-employed lawyers as opposed to from non-lawyers.

Problem 8–14

Jones & Smith, a very large law firm with offices in many major cities in the United States and throughout the world, represents Worldwide Builders, the construction subsidiary of a major international conglomerate. Reginald Jones, the partner in charge of the contract work of Worldwide, is admitted to practice only in New York. In the past year he has performed the following tasks for Worldwide:

1. Issued an opinion about Worldwide's responsibility to pay certain taxes under Louisiana law in connection with a recently completed drydock construction project in New Orleans. All employees with whom he consulted met with him in New York.

2. Negotiated a contract with a major concrete supplier in North Dakota. Jones spent a week in Fargo with employees of Worldwide negotiating the contract with supplier's lawyers. The contract states that North Dakota law applies.

3. Negotiated a second contract with the concrete supplier's Wyoming subsidiary, located in Casper. All negotiations were done by email and telephone between New York City and Casper. The contract states that Wyoming law applies.

4. Investigated a claim by Worldwide for extra compensation on a road building contract in Illinois. Jones spent two weeks in Illinois over a four-month period, and submitted a memorandum to Worldwide's general counsel. If suit is instituted in Illinois, in either state or federal court, Jones expects to handle it and will ask to be admitted *pro hac vice* to the appropriate court.

Has Jones engaged in the unauthorized practice of law in any of these situations? Would it make any difference if Jones were inside general counsel of Worldwide? See Model Rules 5.5 and 8.5.

Problem 8–15

House counsel is admitted only in the District of Columbia but spends all of her professional time advising Company and its subsidiaries at its main office in New Jersey, mostly about federal and New Jersey law. She learns that a New Jersey subsidiary of the Company is engaged in illegal activities likely to cause substantial financial harm to a New Jersey company. Under the District of Columbia's professional responsibility rules, she must keep the confidences although she may "withdraw," whatever that means in these circumstances. Under New Jersey law, she must reveal the fraud to prevent the harm to the victim. Whose law should govern her conduct?

The case that follows discusses the issue of unauthorized practice in the context of multistate practice.

Birbrower v. Superior Court of Santa Clara County

17 Cal. 4th 119 (Cal. 1998), cert. denied, 525 U.S. 920 (1998)

[The "essentially undisputed" facts of the case, as summarized by the majority of the court, are as follows:

The defendant law firm Birbrower, Montalbano, Condon & Frank, P.C. (Birbrower) is a professional law corporation incorporated in New York with its principal place of business in New York. During 1992 and 1993, Birbrower attorneys, defendants Kevin F. Hobbs and Thomas A. Condon (Hobbs and Condon), performed substantial work in California relating to the law firm's representation of ESQ Business Services, Inc. (ESQ). Neither Hobbs nor Condon has ever been licensed to practice law in California. None of Birbrower's attorneys were licensed to practice law in California during Birbrower's ESQ representation.

ESQ is a California corporation with its principal place of business in Santa Clara County. In July 1992, the parties negotiated and executed the fee agreement in New York, providing that Birbrower would perform legal services for ESQ, including "All matters pertaining to the investigation of and prosecution of all claims and causes of action against Tandem Computers Incorporated [Tandem]." The "claims and causes of action" against Tandem, a Delaware corporation with its principal place of business in Santa Clara County, California, related to a software development and marketing contract between Tandem and ESQ dated March 16, 1990 (Tandem Agreement). The Tandem Agreement stated that "The internal laws of the State of California (irrespective of its choice of law principles) shall govern . . . this Agreement . . . ." Birbrower asserts, and ESQ disputes, that ESQ knew Birbrower was not licensed to practice law in California.

While representing ESQ, Hobbs and Condon traveled to California on several occasions. In August 1992, they met in California with ESQ and its accountants. During these meetings, Hobbs and Condon discussed various matters related to ESQ's dispute with Tandem and strategy for resolving the dispute. They made recommendations and gave advice. During this California trip, Hobbs and Condon also met with Tandem representatives on four or five occasions during a two-day period. At the meetings, Hobbs and Condon spoke on ESQ's behalf. Hobbs demanded that Tandem pay ESQ $15 million. Condon told Tandem he believed that damages would exceed $15 million if the parties litigated the dispute.

Around March or April 1993, Hobbs, Condon, and another Birbrower attorney visited California to interview potential arbitrators and to meet again with ESQ and its accountants. Birbrower had previously filed a demand for arbitration against Tandem with the San Francisco offices of the American Arbitration Association (AAA). In August 1993, Hobbs returned to California to assist ESQ in settling the Tandem matter. While in California, Hobbs met with ESQ and its accountants to discuss a proposed settlement agreement Tandem authored. Hobbs also met with Tandem representatives to discuss possible changes in the proposed agreement. Hobbs gave ESQ legal advice during this trip, including his opinion that ESQ should not settle with Tandem on the terms proposed.

ESQ eventually settled the Tandem dispute, and the matter never went to arbitration. But before the settlement, ESQ and Birbrower modified the contingency fee agreement. The modification changed the fee arrangement from contingency to fixed fee, providing that ESQ would pay Birbrower $1 million. The original contingency fee arrangement had called for Birbrower to receive "one third (1/3) of all sums received for the benefit of the Clients . . . whether obtained through settlement, motion practice, hearing, arbitration, or trial by way of judgment, award, settlement, or otherwise . . . ."

In January 1994, ESQ sued Birbrower for legal malpractice and related claims in Santa Clara County Superior Court. Birbrower removed the matter to federal court and filed a counterclaim, which included a claim for attorney fees for the work it performed in both California and New York. The matter was then remanded to the superior court. There ESQ moved for summary judgment and/or adjudication on the first through fourth causes of action of Birbrower's counterclaim, which asserted ESQ and its representatives breached the fee agreement. ESQ argued that by practicing law without a license in California and by failing to associate local counsel while doing so, Birbrower violated section 6125, rendering the fee agreement unenforceable.]

CHIN, J. with George C.J., Mosk, Baxter, Werdegar, and Brown, JJ., concurring.

Business and Professions Code section 6125 states: "No person shall practice law in California unless the person is an active member of the State Bar." We must decide whether an out-of-state law firm, not licensed to practice law in this state, violated section 6125 when it performed legal services in California for a California-based client under a fee agreement stipulating that California law would govern all matters in the representation.

Although we are aware of the interstate nature of modern law practice and mindful of the reality that large firms often conduct activities and serve clients in several states, we do not believe these facts excuse law firms from complying with section 6125. Contrary to the Court of Appeal, however, we do not believe the Legislature intended section 6125 to apply to those services an out-of-state firm renders in its home state. We therefore conclude that, to the extent defendant law firm [Birbrower] practiced law in California without a license, it engaged in the unauthorized practice of law in this state. . . . We also conclude that Birbrower's fee agreement with real party in interest ESQ is invalid to the extent it authorizes payment for the substantial legal services Birbrower performed in California. If, however, Birbrower can show it generated fees under its agreement for limited services it performed in New York, and it earned those fees under the otherwise invalid fee agreement, it may, on remand, present to the trial court evidence justifying its recovery of fees for those New York services. . . .

II. DISCUSSION

A. The Unauthorized Practice of Law

The California Legislature enacted section 6125 in 1927 as part of the State Bar Act (the Act), a comprehensive scheme regulating the practice of law in the state. . . . Since the Act's passage, the general rule has been that, although persons may represent themselves and their own interests regardless of State Bar membership, no one but an active member of the State Bar may practice law for another person in California. The prohibition against unauthorized law practice is within the state's police power and is designed to ensure that those performing legal services do so competently.

A violation of section 6125 is a misdemeanor. (§ 6126) Moreover, "No one may recover compensation for services as an attorney at law in this state unless [the person] was at the time the services were performed a member of The State Bar." (Hardy v. San Fernando Valley C. of C., 99 Cal. App. 2d 572, 576 (1950).)

Although the Act did not define the term "practice law," case law explained it as "'the doing and performing services in a court of justice in any matter depending therein throughout its various stages and in conformity with the adopted rules of procedure.'" . . .

In addition to not defining the term "practice law," the Act also did not define the meaning of "in California." In today's legal practice, questions often arise concerning whether the phrase refers to the nature of the legal services, or restricts the Act's application to those out-of-state attorneys who are physically present in the state.

Section 6125 has generated numerous opinions on the meaning of "practice law" but none on the meaning of "in California." In our view, the practice of law "in California" entails sufficient contact with the California client to render the nature of the legal service a clear legal representation. In addition to a quantitative analysis, we must consider the nature of the unlicensed lawyer's activities in the state. Mere fortuitous or attenuated contacts will not sustain a finding that the unlicensed lawyer practiced law "in California." The primary inquiry is whether the unlicensed lawyer engaged in sufficient activities in the state, or created a continuing relationship with the California client that included legal duties and obligations.

Our definition does not necessarily depend on or require the unlicensed lawyer's physical presence in the state. Physical presence here is one factor we may consider in deciding whether the unlicensed lawyer has violated section 6125, but it is by no means exclusive. For example, one may practice law in the state in violation of section 6125 although not physically present here by advising a California client on California law in connection with a California legal dispute by telephone, fax, computer, or other modern technological means. . . . We must decide each case on its individual facts. . . .

If we were to carry the dissent's narrow interpretation of the term "practice law" to its logical conclusion, we would effectively limit section 6125's application to those cases in which nonlicensed out-of-state lawyers appeared in a California courtroom without permission. . . .

Exceptions to section 6125 do exist, but are generally limited to allowing out-of-state attorneys to make brief appearances before a state court or tribunal. They are narrowly drawn and strictly interpreted. For example, . . . with the permission of the California court in which a particular cause is pending, out-of-state counsel may appear before a court as counsel *pro hac vice* . . . if the out-of-state attorney is a member in good standing of another state bar and is eligible to practice in any United States court or the highest court in another jurisdiction. . . . The out-of-state attorney must also associate an active member of the California Bar as attorney of record and is subject to the Rules of Professional Conduct of the State Bar. . . .

The Act does not regulate practice before United States courts. Thus, an out-of-state attorney engaged to render services in bankruptcy proceedings was entitled to collect his fee. . . .

Finally, California Rules of Court, rule 988, permits the State Bar to issue registration certificates to foreign legal consultants who may advise on the law of the foreign jurisdiction where they are admitted. These consultants may not, however, appear as attorneys before a California court or judicial officer or otherwise prepare pleadings and instruments in California or give advice on the law of California or any other state or jurisdiction except those where they are admitted.

The Legislature has recognized an exception to section 6125 in international disputes resolved in California under the state's rules for arbitration and conciliation of international commercial disputes. . . . This exception states that in a commercial conciliation in California involving international commercial disputes, "The parties may appear in person or be represented or assisted by any person of their choice. A person assisting or representing a party need not be a member of the legal profession or licensed to practice law in California."

B. The Present Case

The undisputed facts here show that neither *Baron*'s definition [Baron v. City of Los Angeles, 2 Cal. 3d 535 (1970), which stated that in defining the practice of law, the cases "uniformly hold that the character of the act, and not the place where it is performed, is the decisive element, and if the application of legal knowledge and technique is required, the activity constitutes the practice of law, even if conducted before an administrative board or commission"] nor our "sufficient contact" definition of "practice law in California" would excuse Birbrower's practice in this state. Nor would any of the limited statutory exceptions to section 6125 apply to Birbrower's California practice. As the Court of Appeal observed, Birbrower engaged in unauthorized law practice *in California* on more than a limited basis, and no firm attorney engaged in that practice was an active member of the California State Bar. . . . As the Court of Appeal concluded, "the Birbrower firm's in-state activities clearly constituted the [unauthorized] practice of law" *in California*.

Birbrower contends, however, that section 6125 is not meant to apply to *any* out-of-state *attorneys*. Instead, it argues that the statute is intended solely to prevent nonattorneys from practicing law. The contention is without merit because it contravenes the plain language of the statute. Section 6125 clearly states that *no person* shall practice law in California unless that person is a member of the State Bar. The statute does not differentiate between attorneys or nonattorneys, nor does it excuse a person who is a member of another state bar. . . .

Birbrower next argues that we do not further the statute's intent and purpose — to protect California citizens from incompetent attorneys — by enforcing it against out-of-state attorneys. Birbrower argues that because out-of-state attorneys have been licensed to practice in other jurisdictions, they have already demonstrated sufficient competence to protect California clients. But Birbrower's argument overlooks the obvious fact that other states' laws may differ substantially from California law. Competence in one jurisdiction does not necessarily guarantee competence in another. By applying section 6125 to out-of-state attorneys who engage in the extensive practice of law in California without becoming licensed in our state, we serve the statute's goal of assuring the competence of all attorneys practicing law in this state. . . .

California is not alone in regulating who practices law in its jurisdiction. Many states have substantially similar statutes that serve to protect their citizens from unlicensed attorneys who engage in unauthorized legal practice. Like section 6125, these other state statutes protect local citizens "against the dangers of legal representation and advice given by persons not trained, examined and licensed for such work, whether they be laymen or lawyers from other jurisdictions." [The court cited cases from New York and North Dakota.]

Assuming that section 6125 does apply to out-of-state attorneys not licensed here, Birbrower alternatively asks us to create an exception to section 6125 for work incidental to private arbitration or other alternative dispute resolution proceedings. Birbrower points to fundamental differences between private arbitration and legal proceedings, including procedural differences relating to discovery, rules of evidence, compulsory process, cross-examination of witnesses, and other areas. . . .

We decline Birbrower's invitation to craft an arbitration exception to section 6125's prohibition of the unlicensed practice of law in this state. Any exception for arbitration is best left to the Legislature, which has the authority to determine qualifications for admission to the State Bar and to decide what constitutes the practice of law. . . . Even though the Legislature has spoken with respect to *international* arbitration and conciliation, it has not enacted a similar rule for private arbitration proceedings. Of course, private arbitration and other alternative dispute resolution practices are important aspects of our justice system. . . . Section 6125, however, articulates a strong public policy favoring the practice of law in California by licensed State Bar members. In the face of the Legislature's silence, we will not create an arbitration exception under the facts presented. . . .

Finally, Birbrower urges us to adopt an exception to section 6125 based on the unique circumstances of this case. Birbrower notes that "Multistate relationships are a common part of today's society and are to be dealt with in commensense fashion." (In re Estate of Waring, 47 N.J. 367 (1966).) In many situations, strict adherence to rules prohibiting the unauthorized practice of law by out-of-state attorneys would be "'grossly impractical and inefficient.'" (Ibid.; see also Appell v. Reiner, 43 N.J. 313 (1964) (strict adherence to rule barring out-of-state lawyers from representing New Jersey residents on New Jersey matters may run against the public interest when case involves inseparable multistate transactions).)

Although, as discussed, we recognize the need to acknowledge and, in certain cases, to accommodate the multistate nature of law practice, the facts here show that Birbrower's extensive activities within California amounted to considerably more than any of our state's recognized exceptions to section 6125 would allow. Accordingly, we reject Birbrower's suggestion that we except the firm from section 6125's rule under the circumstances here.

C. Compensation for Legal Services

Because Birbrower violated section 6125 when it engaged in the unlawful practice of law in California, the Court of Appeal found its fee agreement with ESQ unenforceable in its entirety. . . .

Birbrower asserts that . . . it should be permitted to recover fees for those limited services it performed exclusively *in New York* under the agreement. . . .

We agree with Birbrower that it may be able to recover fees under the fee agreement for the limited legal services it performed for ESQ in New York to the extent they did not constitute practicing law in California, even though those services were performed for a California client. Because section 6125 applies to the practice of law in California, it does not, in general, regulate law practice in other states. [The court then considered the issue of severability, finding that the portion of the parties' contract concerning services performed for ESQ in New York (and the fees relating thereto) could be severed from the otherwise unenforceable agreement.]

III. DISPOSITION

We conclude that Birbrower violated section 6125 by practicing law in California. To the extent the fee agreement allows payment for those illegal local services, it is void, and Birbrower is not entitled to recover fees under the agreement for those services. The fee agreement is enforceable, however, to the extent it is possible to sever the portions of the consideration attributable to Birbrower's services illegally rendered in California from those attributable to Birbrower's New York services. Accordingly, we . . . remand for further proceedings consistent with this decision.

KENNARD, J., dissenting

. . . In this case, New York lawyers who were not members of the California Bar traveled to this state on several occasions, attempting to resolve a contract dispute between their clients and another corporation through negotiation and private arbitration. Their clients included a New York corporation and a sister corporation incorporated in California; the lawyers had in previous years represented the principal owners of these corporations. The majority holds that the New York lawyers' activities in California constituted the unauthorized practice of law. I disagree.

The majority focuses its attention on the question of whether the New York lawyers had engaged in the practice of law *in California*, giving scant consideration to a decisive preliminary inquiry: whether, through their activities here, the New York lawyers had engaged in the practice of law *at all*. In my view, the record does not show that they did. In reaching a contrary conclusion, the majority relies on an overbroad definition of the term "practice of law." I would adhere to this court's decision in Baron v. City of Los Angeles, 2 Cal. 3d 535 (1970), more narrowly defining the practice of law as the representation of another in a judicial proceeding or an activity requiring the application of that degree of legal knowledge and technique possessed only by a trained legal mind. Under this definition, this case presents a triable issue of material fact as to whether the New York lawyers' California activities constituted the practice of law. . . .

In 1970, in *Baron* . . . [w]e were quick to point out . . . however, that "ascertaining whether a particular activity falls within this general definition may be a formidable endeavor." *Baron* emphasized "that it is not the whole spectrum of professional services of lawyers with which the State Bar Act is most concerned, but rather it is the smaller area of activities defined as the 'practice of law.'" (Ibid.) It then observed: "In close cases, the courts have determined that the resolution of legal questions for another by advice and action is practicing law 'if difficult or doubtful legal questions are involved which, to safeguard the public, reasonably demand the application of a *trained legal mind*.'" . . . *Baron* added that "if the application of legal knowledge and technique is *required*, the activity constitutes the practice of law." . . .

The majority asserts that the definition of practice of law I have stated above misreads this court's opinion in *Baron*. But what the majority characterizes as "the dissent's fanciful interpretation of the [*Baron* court's] thoughtful guidelines" consists of language I have quoted directly from *Baron*.

The majority also charges that the narrowing construction of the term "practice of law" that this court adopted in *Baron* "effectively limit[s] section 6125's application to those cases in which nonlicensed out-of-state lawyers appeared in a California courtroom without permission." Fiddlesticks. Because the *Baron* definition encompasses all activities that "'reasonably demand application of a trained legal mind'" (*Baron*, at 543), the majority's assertion would be true only if there were no activities, apart from court appearances, requiring application of a trained legal mind. Many attorneys would no doubt be surprised to learn that, for example, drafting testamentary documents for large estates, preparing merger agreements for multinational corporations, or researching complex legal issues are not activities that require a trained legal mind.

According to the majority, use of the *Baron* definition I have quoted would undermine protection of the public from incompetent legal practitioners. The *Baron* definition provides ample protection from incompetent legal practitioners without infringing upon the public's interest in obtaining advice and representation from other professionals, such as accountants and real estate brokers, whose skills in specialized areas may overlap with those of lawyers. This allows the public the freedom to choose professionals who may be able to provide the public with needed services at a more affordable cost. . . .

The majority's overbroad definition would affect a host of common commercial activities. On point here are comments that Professor Deborah Rhode made in a 1981 article published in the Stanford Law Review: "For many individuals, most obviously accountants, bankers, real estate brokers, and insurance agents, it would be impossible to give intelligent counsel without reference to legal concerns that such statutes reserve as the exclusive province of attorneys. As one [American Bar Association] official active in unauthorized practice areas recently acknowledged, there is growing recognition that ' "all kinds of other professional people are practicing law almost out of necessity." ' Moreover, since most legislation does not exempt gratuitous activity, much advice commonly imparted by friends, employers, political organizers, and newspaper commentators constitutes unauthorized practice. For example, although the organized bar has not yet evinced any inclination to drag [nationally syndicated advice columnist] Ann Landers through the courts, she is plainly fair game under extant statutes [proscribing the unauthorized practice of law.]" (Rhode, "Policing the Professional Monopoly: A Constitutional and Empirical Analysis of Unauthorized Practice Prohibitions," 34 Stan. L. Rev. 1, at 47, fns. omitted.)

Unlike the majority, I would for the reasons given above adhere to the more narrowly drawn definition of the practice of law that this court articulated in *Baron*: the representation of another in a judicial proceeding or an activity requiring the application of that degree of legal knowledge and technique possessed only by a trained legal mind. Applying that definition here, I conclude that the trial court should not have granted summary adjudication for plaintiffs based on the Birbrower lawyers' California activities. That some or all of those activities related to arbitration does not necessarily establish that they constituted the practice of law, as I shall explain.

[Judge Kennard reviewed several differences between the arbitration and the judicial processes.] . . .

To summarize, under this court's decisions, arbitration proceedings are not governed or constrained by the rule of law; therefore, representation of another in an arbitration proceeding, including the activities necessary to prepare for the arbitration hearing, does not necessarily require a trained legal mind. . . .

In this case, plaintiffs have not identified any specific California activities by the New York lawyers of the Birbrower firm that meet the narrow definition of the term "practice of law" as articulated by this court in *Baron*. Accordingly, I would reverse the judgment of the Court of Appeal and direct it to remand the matter to the trial court with directions to vacate its order granting plaintiff's motion for summary judgment and to enter a new order denying that motion.

Notes

1. Which definition of "practicing law" do you prefer: the majority's expansive definition or the more narrow definition of Justice Kennard in dissent? Whatever your preferred definition, who should be the final defining authority? The majority suggests that the legislature should be the entity that defines the "practice of law" and the requirements for admission to the bar. Why not the judiciary?

2. If what the Birbrower firm did constituted the practice of law in California, why would associating local California counsel with it make its practice any less the practice of law in California? Or is it that out-of-state lawyers may practice law in California in association with California counsel? Why is this case different from others for which the court, as it acknowledges, might make an exception?

3. Immediately after *Birbrower*, an intermediate appellate court limited its holding to out-of-state lawyers who represented California clients, holding that its policy was inapplicable to lawyers who "practiced" California law for out-of-state clients. Condon v. McHenry, 65 Cal. App. 4th 1138 (1998).

4. Since *Birbrower*, the California legislature has addressed the unauthorized practice problem several times. The current version of Cal. Civ. Proc. Code § 1282.4 allows out-of-state lawyers to appear in California arbitration matters under strict regulation.

5. A Colorado Appeals Court decision reached the same result as *Birbrower* with respect to work done by a Wisconsin lawyer in connection with Colorado state law claims prior to his admission *pro hac vice* by the Colorado federal court as co-counsel in federal aspects of the same matter. The court required a refund of all of the fees paid on the state matters under a statute requiring a refund by an "unlicensed person." Koscove v. Bolte, 2001 Colo. App. Lexis 290 (Colo. Ct. App. 2001), pet. for cert. to Colo. Sup. Ct. denied, 2001 Colo. Lexis (2001). The Supreme Court of Wisconsin later publicly reprimanded the lawyer for the same conduct. In re Bolte, 699 N.W.2d 914 (2005). More recently, the Minnesota Supreme Court followed *Birbrower* in a case where a Colorado lawyer trying to negotiate a settlement of an outstanding Minnesota judgment sent emails to a Minnesota lawyer representing the plaintiff. The Court held that advising Minnesota clients on Minnesota law with respect to a Minnesota lawsuit constituted the unauthorized practice of law in Minnesota which was not protected as "temporary" practice under Rule 5.5. In re Charges of Unprofessional Conduct in Panel File No. 39302, No. A15-2078 (Minn. 2016).

6. The *Birbrower* result poses additional problems for transactional lawyers who are not able to be admitted *pro hac vice*, as litigation lawyers may be. Many cases that

raise the problem of unauthorized practice arise because of a dispute over fees. But there are occasional cases in which state authorities institute direct suits alleging unauthorized practice of law. See Attorney Grievance Commission v. Harper, 356 Md. 53 (1999), in which the Maryland Court of Appeals dealt with the case of a lawyer admitted in the District of Columbia and the federal district court in Maryland, but not in the Maryland courts themselves, who nevertheless operated a law office in Maryland with a Maryland lawyer. The court permanently barred the lawyer from practicing in Maryland. See also the similar result in Cleveland Bar Association v. Misch, 82 Ohio St. 3d 256 (1998). Moreover, In re Jackman, 165 N.J. 580 (2000), concluded that a seven-year associate of a New Jersey firm, who was licensed only in Massachusetts (and was on "inactive" status) and did only transactional work in New Jersey, had engaged in unauthorized practice in New Jersey and delayed his admission to the New Jersey bar for 18 months. The court was unimpressed by the advice given by the firm's managing partner that admission in New Jersey was not necessary.

7. The federal courts have divided on whether admission to the state bar is a prerequisite to regular practice in the federal courts. Compare In re Poole, 222 F.3d 618 (9th Cir. 2000), with In re Lite Ray Realty Co., 257 B.R. 150 (Bankr. S.D.N.Y. 2001).

8. The potential use of the internet to deliver services to individuals was discussed earlier in this Chapter. What effect would a broad application of *Birbrower* and other similar cases have on the ability of lawyers to offer on-line legal advice? Must such an entity employ lawyers who are licensed in every state? Is this economically viable?

Note: Multijurisdiction Practice — For Both U.S. and Foreign Lawyers

Aside from appointing the Ethics 2000 Commission, the ABA also appointed a Commission on Multijurisdictional Practice to study and make recommendations with respect to issues like those involved in Problem 8–14. Model Rule 5.5 and the associated choice of law provision Model Rule 8.5, both of which have been widely adopted, are the result of that Commission's work. Note that Rule 5.5, in permitting the performance of some legal services by lawyers not admitted in the jurisdiction, still requires a jurisdiction to decide what constitutes the provision of legal services "in this jurisdiction." The *Birbrower* issue still lives.

Rule 5.5. accommodates, to a limited extent at least, the nationalization of law practice in the United States. Large and mid-size law firms represent clients all over the country. Aside from worrying about the issue that burst upon the profession with the decision in *Birbrower*, lawyers must worry about the law that governs their conduct when the clients they serve or the subject matter of the representation involves jurisdictions in which they are not licensed to practice. Whether the lawyer on the other side of the transaction is governed by different law may also be a matter of concern. The issues are not abstract. Lawyers often need to decide which of two or more different rules governs a question of confidentiality, a question of the ability to avoid a conflict of interest by screening, the ability to represent the affiliate of a corporation against a parent or a subsidiary, or the ability of a party to communicate with an employee or former employee of an opposing party. While such matters have not yet become questions of disciplinary enforcement, they have become important questions for many lawyers trying to decide what is or is not an appropriate course of action.

Rule 8.5 of the Model Rules, as originally promulgated in 1983, stated in its entirety only that "A lawyer admitted to practice in this jurisdiction is subject to the disciplinary authority of this jurisdiction although engaged in practice elsewhere." The ABA redrafted Rule 8.5 in 1993 to add a subsection (b) making the governing law the rules of the jurisdiction where a lawyer was licensed to practice or, if licensed to practice in more than one jurisdiction, then the rules of the jurisdiction where the lawyer principally practiced. A proviso, however, stated that "if the particular conduct clearly has its predominant effect in another jurisdiction in which the lawyer is licensed to practice, the rules of that jurisdiction shall be applied to that conduct."

In 2002, the ABA's Commission on Multijurisdictional Practice recommended, and the ABA adopted, a major change. It eliminated, in transactional matters and in litigation matters before a suit has been filed, the references to the jurisdiction of licensing and principal practice. Model Rule 8.5(b) now states with respect to such conduct that the governing law is "the rules of the jurisdiction in which the lawyer's conduct occurred, or, if the predominant effect of the conduct is in a different jurisdiction, the rules of that jurisdiction shall be applied to that conduct." The Rule goes on to provide a partial safe harbor for lawyers by providing that "A lawyer shall not be subject to discipline if the lawyer's conduct conforms to a rule of a jurisdiction in which a lawyer reasonably believes the predominant effect of the lawyer's conduct will occur."

The 1993 version, making the lawyer's licensing or principal office jurisdiction the default choice of law jurisdiction, comported with the natural expectation of practicing lawyers. Those are the Rules that lawyers will or should know and abide by. As the default rule, it seems highly preferable to the current ABA Model Rule's default rule of "the jurisdiction where the lawyer's conduct occurred." In today's legal world, quite often the jurisdiction where a lawyer's conduct occurs is difficult to discern or has only a limited relationship to the transaction, and the ABA Model Rule and its Comments give little guidance to the meaning of the text. The Model Rule suggests that different rules might apply if a lawyer licensed in State A gives advice to a client in State B by telephone from an office in State A or in person in State B. And good luck on figuring out if the "predominant effect" of the conduct will occur in a different jurisdiction. What does that expression mean? If the Montana employee of an Illinois-based client tells New York lawyers of an environmental spill in Montana, and the lawyers must decide whether they must not, may, or must disclose that confidential information, is the predominant effect of the conduct in the New York office where the disclosure decision will be made, in Illinois where the client is located, or in Montana where the physical damage is occurring? One could further complicate the problem by making the client a Delaware corporation, by having the disclosure made by telephone or email, and by having the lawyers sitting around the table be members of several different bars. Given the variety of confidentiality rules in the United States, and the variety of other situations mentioned above where the disciplinary rules differ, we should not be surprised that ethics committees in many law firms are being increasingly asked for advice about choice of law matters.

As complex as the rules regarding multijurisdictional practice are when applied to purely domestic issues, they become even more problematic when an international element is added to the equation. When Rule 8.5 was originally enacted in 1983, a comment to the Rule expressly exempted "transnational practice." See Catherine A. Rogers, "Lawyers without Borders," 30 U. Pa. J. Int'l L. 1035, 1041 (2009). In 2002, however, this comment was deleted from the Rule at the request of the American Bar Association's International Law Section. Id. As a result, U.S. lawyers practicing abroad are now also governed by the Rule. In Chapter 12, we will return to the difficulties of interpreting Rule 8.5 in the context of litigation before various foreign and international tribunals. For present purposes, however, we want to highlight the problem that the Rules on multijurisdictional practice pose for foreign lawyers practicing in the United States.

As part of its package of recommendations, the Multijurisdiction Practice Commission urged all states to adopt rules permitting foreign lawyers who are fully qualified in their home jurisdiction to be allowed to practice as Foreign Legal Consultants without taking a U.S. bar exam. See Laurel S. Terry, Carol Silver, Ellyn Rosen Carol Needham, Robert E. Lutz, Peter D. Ehrenhaft, "Transnational Legal Practice: 2006–07 Year in Review," 42 J. Int'l L. 833, 843–844 (2008). Thereafter, in 2013, this recommendation, which had already been adopted by a majority of states, was incorporated into the Model Rules by including foreign lawyers in the exceptions contained in Rule 5.5(d). See also Rule 5.5(e) for the eligibility requirements for foreign lawyers. Nevertheless, the fact that non-U.S. lawyers continue to be subject to a patchwork of state-by-state regulation that does not allow them free access to the U.S. market as a whole "has been discussed during the GATS [General Agreement on Trade and Services] legal services negotiations and cited as a request of our trading partners in the Doha Round negotiations." Id.

In addition to frustrating our trading partners—and providing justification for other countries to continue keeping their domestic markets closed to U.S. and other "foreign lawyers"—the fact that states retain the power to exclude non-U.S. lawyers under their unauthorized practice rules can also invite the kind of viewpoint-based manipulation that we saw some commentators complaining about with respect to the character and fitness rules described in the preceding section. Consider, for example, the decision by the Louisiana Supreme Court to reverse what had been a 20-year-long practice of permitting "non-immigrant aliens"—those who have the right to live and work in the United States but who are not planning to live here permanently—to take the bar and practice in the state. The decision came in the context of an Australian lawyer seeking to take the Louisiana bar in order to work with a public interest organization opposed to the death penalty, where he would join several other foreign trained lawyers who had previously passed the exam. See Elizabeth Amon, "Raising the Bar," Nat'l L. J., Feb. 14, 2003. The Louisiana Supreme Court, it should be noted, has a history of this kind of restriction. See Southern Christian Leadership Conference v. Supreme Court, 252 F.3d 781 (5th Cir. 2001) (affirming the decision by the Louisiana Supreme Court to change the state's student practice rules even though there was evidence that the decision was intended to make it more difficult for the Tulane Environmental Law clinic to bring litigation against business and governmental interests in the state).

3. The Future of MDPs

The issues of multijurisdictional practice are of obvious relevance to the issues of multidisciplinary practice, which are discussed immediately following Problem 8–16.

Problem 8–16

After merging with Arthur Small & Co. (a large international consulting firm), ACCT (one of the Big Four accounting firms) wants to be able to offer legal services as part of a package it offers its clients, mostly large international firms. To that end it wants to create a legal department not to do its own legal work but to serve as part of combined teams of accountants, economists, engineers, business consultants, and lawyers that would offer integrated services, including litigation services, for a single fee to meet complex client needs. Should professional rules be changed to permit lawyers to operate in this fashion?

At the end of the twentieth century, it looked as if the multidisciplinary juggernaut was about to result in a vast and immediate change in the organization of the large units of law practice. After a decade of debate, the ABA's Commission on Multidisciplinary Practice recommended in 2000 that the ABA "amend the Model Rules of Professional Conduct consistent with the following principles":

> 1. Lawyers should be permitted to share fees and join with nonlawyer professionals in a practice that delivers both legal and nonlegal professional services (Multidisciplinary Practice), provided that the lawyers have the control and authority necessary to assure lawyer independence in the rendering of legal services. "Nonlawyer professionals" means members of recognized professions or other disciplines that are governed by ethical standards.

2. This Recommendation must be implemented in a manner that protects the public and preserves the core values of the legal profession, including competence, independence of professional judgment, protection of confidential client information, loyalty to the client through the avoidance of conflicts of interest, and pro bono publico obligations.

3. Regulatory authorities should enforce existing rules and adopt such additional enforcement procedures as are needed to implement these principles and to protect the public interest.

4. The prohibition on nonlawyers delivering legal services and the obligations of all lawyers to observe the rules of professional conduct should not be altered.

5. Passive investment in a Multidisciplinary Practice should not be permitted.

———————

At the annual meeting of the American Bar Association in July 2000, the following resolution on the subject of multi-disciplinary practice was submitted by the Bar Associations of Illinois, New Jersey, New York, Florida, and various state and local bar associations in Ohio to the House of Delegates and adopted overwhelmingly:

RESOLVED, that each jurisdiction is urged to revise its law governing lawyers to implement the following principles and preserve the core values of the legal profession:

1. It is in the public interest to preserve the core values of the legal profession, among which are:

a. the lawyer's duty of undivided loyalty to the client;

b. the lawyer's duty competently to exercise independent legal judgment for the benefit of the client;

c. the lawyer's duty to hold client confidences inviolate;

d. the lawyer's duty to avoid conflicts of interest with the client; and

e. the lawyer's duty to help maintain a single profession of law with responsibilities as a representative of clients, an officer of the legal system, and a public citizen having special responsibility for the quality of justice;

f. the lawyer's duty to promote access to justice.

2. All lawyers are members of one profession subject in each jurisdiction to the law governing lawyers.

3. The law governing lawyers was developed to protect the public interest and to preserve the core values of the legal profession that are essential to the proper functioning of the American justice system.

4. State bar associations and other entities charged with attorney discipline should reaffirm their commitment to enforcing vigorously their respective law governing lawyers.

5. Each jurisdiction should reevaluate and refine to the extent necessary the definition of the "practice of law."

6. Jurisdictions should retain and enforce laws that generally bar the practice of law by entities other than law firms.

7. The sharing of legal fees with non-lawyers and the ownership and control of the practice of law by nonlawyers are inconsistent with the core values of the legal profession.

8. The law governing lawyers, that prohibits lawyers from sharing legal fees with nonlawyers and from directly or indirectly transferring to nonlawyers ownership or control over entities practicing law, should not be revised.

FURTHER RESOLVED that the Standing Committee on Ethics and Professional Responsibility of the American Bar Association shall, in consultation with state, local and territorial bar associations and interested ABA sections, divisions, and committees undertake a review of the Model Rules of Professional Conduct ("MRPC") and shall recommend to the House of Delegates such amendments to the MRPC as are necessary to assure that there are safeguards in the MRPC relating to strategic alliances and other contractual relationships with nonlegal professional service providers consistent with the statement of principles in this Recommendation.

FURTHER RESOLVED that the American Bar Association recommends that in jurisdictions that permit lawyers and law firms to own and operate nonlegal businesses, no nonlawyer or nonlegal entity involved in the provision of such services should own or control the practice of law by a lawyer or law firm or otherwise be permitted to direct or regulate the professional judgment of the lawyer or law firm in rendering legal services to any person.

FURTHER RESOLVED that the Commission on Multidisciplinary Practice be discharged with the Association's gratitude for the Commission's hard work and with commendation for its substantial contributions to the profession.

This Resolution of the American Bar Association has of course no binding effect on any jurisdiction, lawyer, or nonlawyer in the United States. It is merely one development in the ongoing efforts of accounting firms and some other professional groups to offer more comprehensive services, including legal services, to their clients. Various states have amended their rules of professional conduct to allow MDPs, at least to some extent. See, e.g., Lucci, Note, "New York Revises Ethics Rules to Permit Limited MDPs," 8 Fordham J. Corp. & Fin. L. 151 (2003); D.C. Rules Prof. Conduct 5.4 (permitting certain forms of MDPs). There is also an ongoing debate over the kinds of conditions that ought to be imposed on "alliances" between accountants or consulting firms and lawyers. One current issue that has divided the ABA's Standing Committee on Ethics and Professional Responsibility and the New York State Bar Association, one of the leaders in the fight over multidisciplinary practice, is whether mutual referral arrangements between accounting and law firms may be "exclusive." The former committee has said no, but the latter has said yes. What is the justification for the latter position?

The most important developments regarding the future of multidisciplinary practice—and indeed, about the future of the regulation of the legal profession along many important dimensions—is now happening outside the United States. Before examining these developments, however, it is important to note that it is not only large law firms and their corporate clients that are interested in multidisciplinary practice.

Louise G. Trubek and Jennifer J. Farnham
Social Justice Collaboratives:
Multidisciplinary Practices for People
7 Clinical L. Rev. 227 (2000)

The four main areas where [social justice collaboratives] cope with the tensions within the regulatory system are confidentiality, unauthorized practice, undivided loyalty to the client and conflicts. The mandatory reporting of child abuse is an example of an apparently intimidating conflict between the code provision and the reality of collaborative practice. The collaboratives that work with social workers revisit the issue often and are frequently in doubt about how to properly interpret the rules. Unauthorized practice has been an unresolved concern for many years. For the collaboratives, this ambivalence is very disturbing. They realize the importance of simplifying forms and encouraging nonlawyer access to law. They also understand that movement in this direction requires an interpretation of unauthorized practice restrictions. Practices dealing with families see the difficulty of providing legal assistance to families while constrained by the code limits on single client representation. Again, commentators have suggested alternative approaches but little assistance is being provided. Conflicts concerns are a major tension for the social justice collaboratives, as they are for large firms. Waivers are useful but do not resolve the issue of the lack of availability of lawyers for the unrepresented party.

The practices are evolving interesting ways of dealing with the tensions. These include written documents such as protocols and waivers. They also include the institution of quality systems that allow them to demonstrate client satisfaction and responsive service. The current ethics regulatory system cannot respond appropriately to the emerging practices developing within the collaboratives for two reasons: the system does not engage with their concerns and does not value their innovations. This lack of fit causes nervousness and excessive time spent by collaborators in working within a framework not relevant to their practices. The regulatory and enforcement system is in place to locate the "bad lawyer" rather than encouraging quality and best practices.

Proponents of multidisciplinary practices for people can endorse two alternative approaches in the debate on reforming the ethics regulatory system: a separate system for social justice collaboratives or unified revision for all MDPs. The first approach is the easiest to conceptualize and most likely to succeed. It would create safe havens for "approved social justice collaboratives." Collaboratives who meet criteria for providing services for people unable to pay the full cost of legal services could apply. The criteria would not require nonprofit status or links with legal aid programs. The key eligibility criteria would be a percent of service to assist low-income programs. . . . When a practice was approved as a "social justice collaborative" it would be subject to a different set of procedures. Code provisions would be modified to include carve-outs for particular code sections; at least one state has enacted these exceptions for certain provisions. The Committee on Legal Services of the ABA has proposed a special code provision for legal service–sponsored hotlines that includes variation for the conflicts requirements. The approved practices would also qualify for a set of "certified" protocols in the areas of greatest concern, such as mandatory reporting. There would also be a special provision for unauthorized practice indicating that is not a violation for the approved practices that demonstrate how their programs serve underserved people. Quality elements would also be integrated into the procedures. Every approved practice would have to incorporate client satisfaction surveys and other forms of client participation. Participation by other appropriate professional groups would also have to be documented. The committee developed by the state regulatory agency would have to survey the approved organizations regularly for "best practices" and issue an annual report describing the work of the approved practices. There are existing models allowing special treatment for practices engaged in serving people of low and moderate incomes. Wisconsin, for example, has a special regulatory system for group and pre-paid programs. This system has its own quality control through a consumer complaint system and an oversight committee that reviews ethics problems and monitors how well the plans serve the public.

The second strategy is to reform the entire legal system. This approach accepts the validity of the ABA position that, in order for professional values to endure, the unified bar must be maintained. The advantage of this approach is that it would bring together advocates for consumers and low income people with business consultancies. It also unites scholars like Tanina Rostain who propose systems where all aspects of the bar incorporate social commitments, and bar leaders who want to display the "good lawyers." Redoing the infrastructure for all lawyers, however, is a daunting task and this article is not the place to do it. However, we have some preliminary thoughts. The easiest place to start is exploring systems for quality. Business consultancy firms are constructing their own evaluation system for the lawyers they employ. Ruffalo, in describing the business consultancy firms, discusses the importance of evaluation—measuring client satisfaction—in staying competitive. The consultancies use client surveys, review of files and employment of evaluators as tools for feedback and benchmarking. He points out that the goal of quality through extensive evaluation distinguishes consultancies from traditional legal practice where client satisfaction is only judged by keeping the client and by the absence of complaints filed in the disciplinary system. There is evidence that, in response to consumer dissatisfaction with the performance of lawyers, legal institutions are revising the disciplinary system to include potential quality measures. Colorado has initiated a computerized system for immediate response to client complaints. The system attempts to educate the lawyer as well as solve the client grievance. Other states seem to be taking note; Wisconsin is proposing an extensive revamping to emulate the Colorado system.

Notes

1. Which of these two approaches do you favor? Should bar leaders consider enacting special rules for "social justice collaboratives"? Would such rules threaten professional values by undermining the image of a unitary bar? Do we have a unitary bar in any meaningful sense? If we do, or if we want to preserve whatever unity currently exists, should the rules governing MDPs be ones that favor the needs of corporate clients and those who seek to serve them or ones that respond to the social justice needs of MDPs for individuals? Revisit these questions after you have read the materials in Chapter 12 concerning the systemic differences between lawyers who represent corporations and those who represent individuals. See generally Deborah Rhode, "Access to Justice: Connecting Principles to Practice," 17 Geo. J. Legal Ethics 369 (2004).

2. The term "collaborative law" has become a term of art for a species of alternate dispute resolution. ABA Ethics Opinion 07-447, which considered its ethical propriety, described its main features:

> Collaborative law is a type of alternative dispute resolution in which the parties and their lawyers commit to work cooperatively to reach a settlement. It had its roots in, and shares many attributes of, the mediation process. Participants focus on the interests of both clients, gather sufficient information to ensure that decisions are made with full knowledge, develop a full range of options, and then choose options that best meet the needs of the parties. The parties structure a mutually acceptable written resolution of all issues without court involvement. The product of the process is then submitted to the court as a final decree. The structure creates a problem-solving atmosphere with a focus on interest-based negotiation and client empowerment. . . . Although there are several models of collaborative practice, all of them share the same core elements that are set out in a contract between the clients and their lawyers (often referred to as a "four-way" agreement). In that agreement, the parties commit to negotiating a mutually acceptable settlement without court intervention, to engaging in open communication and information sharing, and to creating shared solutions that meet the needs

of both clients. To ensure the commitment of the lawyers to the collaborative process, the four-way agreement also includes a requirement that, if the process breaks down, the lawyers will withdraw from representing their respective clients and will not handle any subsequent court proceedings.

The Ethics Committee of the Colorado Bar Association in its Opinion 115 (2007) concluded that the required withdrawal provision in the four-way agreement in the event that the process is unsuccessful created a conflict of interest that could not be waived by the client. The ABA's Committee on Ethics and Professional Responsibility reached the opposite conclusion, because it viewed the four-way agreement as a species of permissible limited scope representation under Rule 1.2(c).

As we indicated, the most important developments concerning multidisciplinary practice are happening outside the United States. No country has gone further than the United Kingdom. The following excerpt describes the UK's recent regulatory changes, collectively referred to as the "Clementi Reforms."

John Flood
Will There Be Fallout from Clementi?
The Repercussions for the Legal Profession
after the Legal Services Act 2007
2012 Mich. St. L. Rev. 537

. . .

Sir David Clementi is an accountant, a former deputy governor of the Bank of England, chairman of Prudential—one of the UK's largest insurance companies, and now chairman of a new bank, Virgin Money. In 2003, he was chosen by Lord Falconer, the Lord Chancellor . . .

> To consider what regulatory framework would best promote competition, innovation and the public and consumer interest in an efficient, effective and independent legal sector.

> To recommend a framework which will be independent in representing the public and consumer interest, comprehensive, accountable, consistent, flexible, transparent, and no more restrictive or burdensome than is clearly justified.[3]

These innocuous terms of reference gave rise to one of the most far-reaching analyses and sets of proposals for reforming the legal profession that the UK, or indeed,

---

3. Sir David Clementi, Review of the Regulatory Framework for Legal Services in England and Wales: Final Report, Dec. 2004 at 1 . . . .

the world, had ever seen. The culmination of this work was the Legal Services Act 2007.

This Article explores the genesis of the Act and its consequences both actual and anticipated. I argue that the present trend of the legal profession is moving away from traditional conceptions of professionalism to a commercialized and industrialized alternative. In speculating about the potential outcomes, with the use of hypotheticals and real case studies, I suggest that de-skilling and de-professionalization will be among the logical outcomes. Yet in spite of this dystopian view, which among other things will compromise the role of the law school, there are signs of optimism to be found among the newer generation's—that is Generation Y's—approach to work-life practices that signal the tendency towards immaterial labor as the descriptive metaphor for the new world.

I. HOW THE CLEMENTI REVIEW CAME ABOUT

. . . Two converging processes were in play. The first was a product of complaints about lawyers' services. The second was an investigation by the UK competition authority, the Office of Fair Trading, into the restrictive practices of professions: were they able to justify their restrictions on entry and modes of practice as in the public interest?

A. Profile of the Legal Profession

Let me take another step back. The UK has a population of around 62 million people, which is serviced by 316,373 legal services providers in total. What does the English legal profession look like? The 169,002 lawyers comprise 150,128 solicitors and 15,387 barristers. There are around 10,400 solicitor's firms, most of which have four partners or fewer (over 8,800, 84.8%). Firms with over 80 partners only number 57. There are roughly 750 barristers' chambers and most of those are small organizations. Approximately 31,000 solicitors and 3,000 barristers work outside private practice as in-house counsel or government lawyers. The UK also exports lawyers and over 6,600 work overseas.

In 2009, legal services generated about $36 billion of the UK's gross domestic product (1.8%), and $5 billion worth of legal services were exported compared to imports of legal services of $800 million. The UK is a net exporter of legal services to the value of $3 billion.

As in the U.S., the UK legal profession is predominantly made up of small law firms with an increasing number of large law firms. Although aspects of the profession are quite specialized, there are essentially two hemispheres of lawyers who practice for individual clients and corporate clients. The corporate sector includes a number of international law firms including DLA Piper, with over 4,000 lawyers, and Clifford Chance, with 3,200 lawyers, making them the largest law firms in the world along with Baker & McKenzie with 3,750 lawyers. Yet it is the individual sector that gives rise to the greatest number of complaints. Individual clients are typically one-shot clients with little knowledge of or expertise in legal matters. Corporate clients tend to be more sophisticated and are knowledgeable repeat players in their use of lawyers and law firms and know how to sanction untoward behavior effectively.

B. Complaints Against Lawyers

What does the profile of complaints look like? . . . It looked similar to the types of complaints made against lawyers in the U.S. In 2005, the Law Society received over 17,000 complaints. And *Which?* [The Law Society] reported that a third of people considered they received poor service from their lawyer. Complaints included lawyers not telling their clients about how much they would be charged and being dilatory about giving estimates, with few given in writing. Other complaints included rudeness, arrogance, lack of communication, delays, getting higher bills than expected, and incompetence. . . .

Unfortunately for lawyers, the high number of complaints was accompanied by an inefficient and inept system of handling complaints, which included three levels for the client to go up before a final resolution might be achieved and multiple entry points. Because of this, the backlog of complaints has been rising year after year. And the government-established Legal Services Commissioner began fining the lawyers' professional bodies for not keeping their houses in order.

Complaints against lawyers grew with an attendant rise in the consumerism movement. . . . If lawyers had been able to clear up these backlogs of complaints or had listened to the claims of consumer watchdogs, they might have postponed what was to come.

C. Is the Legal Profession Anti-Competitive?

The second strand that led to Clementi was the investigation by the Office of Fair Trading (OFT) into whether restrictive practices were distorting professional competition. This investigation was promoted by the UK Treasury and included the professions of architects, lawyers, and accountants. The OFT focused on three themes: restrictions on entry, restrictions on conduct, and restrictions on methods of supply, which included aspects of price competition, advertising, and types of business organizations through which professions deliver their services.[37] . . .

The OFT argued that the conveyance and probate markets should be liberalized to remove the lawyer's monopoly. Cold-calling by lawyers should be permitted, and the Law Society changed its rules here. Multidisciplinary practices should be permitted: it should be possible, for example, for lawyers and accountants to merge, or for real estate entities to practice together. Moreover, lawyer-client privilege should be curtailed to those areas where other professionals could not give cognate advice. The government agreed with all except the restricting of legal privilege, much to the annoyance of accountants who were advocating either an extension of the same rights to them or a shrinking of lawyers' rights. Finally, the OFT pointed out that there was

---

37. See Office of Fair Trading, Competition in Professions: A Report by The Director General of Fair Trading 6–7 (2001) . . . .

a regulatory maze surrounding lawyers, having identified that twenty-two regulators, which were incoherent, did not interface easily, and that there were gaps between them. . . .

Shortly afterwards the government decided to establish the Clementi review.

II. CLEMENTI REVIEW

Many government commissions are passive, inviting interested parties to contribute evidence, then pondering among themselves and producing a report. Clementi was different. His team engaged in outreach: they sought out lawyers, consumers, policy wonks, academics, and more. . . .

A. Regulating the Legal Profession

In a report of nearly 200 pages, Clementi examined the regulation and structures of the legal profession. He identified six key objectives for a regulator of legal services. They were:

1. Maintaining the rule of law

2. Access to justice

3. Protection and promotion of consumer interests

4. Promotion of competition

5. Encouragement of a confident, strong and effective legal profession

6. Promoting public understanding of the citizen's legal rights

These objectives were to be allied to a set of principles and precepts, which included:

- Independence

- Integrity

- The duty to act in the best interests of the client

- Confidentiality

. . .

According to Clementi, current regulation mixed its aims. Some were devoted to professional bodies and others to activities. Moreover, there was an emphasis on the individual lawyer rather than the law firm or economic unit. Clementi proposed that the economic unit should be the primary focus of regulation, not the individual. Interestingly, Clementi thought that regulation should promote a strong and healthy profession because of the legal profession's success in promoting itself outside the UK. Globalization was included in the menu.

B. Organizational Structure of the Legal Profession

With this in mind, Clementi tackled the organization of the delivery of legal services. He deemed them as unnecessarily restrictive, with, for example, solicitors in partnerships and barristers as solo practitioners. Freedom to organize as professionals would assist the promotion of competition. In order to ensure standards would not drop, Clementi proposed that an organization delivering legal services should have a head of legal practice and a head of finance and administration, which could be the same person. These individuals would be responsible for reporting to the regulators, that is, the entity not the individual lawyer.

Clementi did not accept any of the arguments put forward by lawyers about their respective styles of organization. He argued they should be opened up. His proposals included two stages.

First would be the emergence of legal disciplinary practices (LDP), which would be composed of different types of lawyers. The form could be corporate, partnership, or otherwise. Lawyers or non-lawyers could manage it. And, quite radically, it could have outside owners, as long as they passed a "fitness to own" test. Lawyers would have to constitute the majority of the managers. Outside owners would not be permitted to interfere with individual cases or have access to client files. And there would be conflicts of interest rules against taking clients when the outside owner has an adverse interest in the outcome.

LDPs were only the first step. The second would be to permit multidisciplinary practices (MDP) where lawyers and non-lawyers work together and share fees. Clementi could see lawyers and accountants practicing together delivering tax advice and investment services; lawyers and real estate specialists, surveyors, and architects providing construction packages; motoring organizations offering legal, insurance, health, and property repair services; and labor unions packaging legal services with health and employment issues. The potential range of MDPs could run from the needs of the individual client to the large corporate client. Integrated service would be seamless: one-stop shopping.

Clementi identified a number of issues with MDPs including the extent of regulatory reach (would a single frontline regulator deal with all professionals or would it be by sector?), the extent of legal privilege (who would be bound by what rules?), and whether there would necessarily be a dominant profession. Unlike LDPs where lawyers would be in the majority of practitioners, they could easily be in the minority in an MDP. What would the role of outside owners be?

Clementi noted that instances already existed. Law firms gave financial advice and as such were regulated by the Financial Services Authority. . . . Clementi understood that the issues with MDPs were complex and so agreed that LDPs should be the first incarnation of the new organization with MDPs, or Alternative Business Structures as they were to become named, coming on stream later.

III. THE WHITE PAPER: THE FUTURE OF LEGAL SERVICES: PUTTING CONSUMERS FIRST

Following the Clementi review, the government produced a White Paper, which was consumerist in orientation . . . . It essentially followed the Clementi recommendations. This was a lively period of debate and lobbying by the legal profession. Finally, the Legal Services Act came into being after prolonged scrutiny by Parliament.

IV. THE LEGAL SERVICES ACT 2007

The Act was signed into law at the end of 2007. Again it followed the course set by the OFT, Clementi, and the White Paper. It created a Legal Services Board (LSB), which would also have a Consumer Panel, and there would be an Office of Legal Complaints. The frontline authorized regulators would be under the LSB.

But it was in the sphere of "Alternative Business Structures" that the Act took a more radical view than its predecessors. The new structure could be an LDP or MDP: there would be no intermediate step as recommended by Clementi. As long as the new structure obtained a license from its regulator, it could exist. . . .

The Legal Services Act has sanctioned both the partial and complete ownership of legal practices by external investors. The way forward for a supermarket or investment bank to own a law practice has been opened. The SRA has licensed the first set of ABS in 2012, which included the supermarket, the Cooperative, which now runs Cooperative Legal Services.

V. THE FUTUROLOGY OF THE LEGAL SERVICES ACT

What then are the consequences of the Act? For U.S. lawyers, they are potentially hazardous because they will place them at a competitive disadvantage in the global marketplace. Before I detail some of the changes, let me conduct a thought experiment, namely, "Tesco Law" and "Goldman Sachs Skadden." . . .

A. Tesco Law

Tesco recently opened its U.S. branch of supermarkets in California. It was able to do this because it is the most profitable supermarket in the UK. It already runs in-store pharmacies and doctors' walk-in surgeries. Both are popular. The stores are situated in middle class and working class areas of cities and Tesco runs the most successful loyalty card in retail history. Tesco has been able to mine the data—more rigorously than any other store—gained through its loyalty card, not only to increase the sales of its products in store and online, but also to generate huge revenues from providing financial services—credit cards, insurance, banking. It gives consumers what they want and what they think they might want, where they can get it easily, and at attractive prices.

Imagine the typical High Street or Main Street lawyer: a dull office, rather forbidding, no list of prices, no discounts, slow responses to queries. All of this is quite off-putting to the average consumer who cannot understand why lawyers are so inefficient and yet so expensive.

Suppose Tesco decides to offer legal services. It could have a section near the doctor and pharmacy, brightly lit, a warm welcome, comfy chairs, and familiar surroundings. Prices would be clearly marked along with the month's special offers. And there would be no mention anywhere of billable hours. Even the checkout clerks could be primed to spot potential customers and proffer specials on legal services. Imagine a credit card rejected at the cash desk, which could be the stimulus for assistance with debt management and bankruptcy. This could generate a raft of special offers after the Christmas big spend. For someone with bruises, a bit of help on the domestic relations front, perhaps. [An] analysis of Facebook statistics showed that most breakups occurred in the two weeks prior to Christmas and during Spring Break (March), which demonstrates how these kinds of data can be deployed by marketers in organizations like Tesco to cross-sell all kinds of services, including legal. Moreover, quality controls would ensure satisfaction, most likely money-back guarantees. It is a captive market that no lawyer can compete with on price or range of service.

The work would be commoditized, based around the use of intelligent software, possibly outsourced (to India), and referred out if specialist help is needed. Lawyers, or even paralegals, would be hired at cheap rates—it would be a competitive market after all.

B. Goldman Sachs Skadden

Mergers and acquisitions is lucrative work. In 2007, Goldman Sachs' revenues were over $69 billion with 30,000 employees (3,000 in India). In 2007, Skadden Arps finally broke through the $2 billion revenue mark with approximately 2,000 lawyers. Suppose Goldman Sachs were to acquire Skadden and then offer a total M&A package at rates that would not depend on variable professional fees, but straightforward value billing instead, just as banks already do. They could offer a seamless service that might even undercut in-house legal rates; it could be attractive to corporate clients. Perhaps it could lead to conflicts rules becoming a thing of the past. For the law firm it could potentially be a rewarding marriage, one that reaches across the globe without having to worry about opening offices in strange places. Moreover, all the difficulties that arise in decision making in partnerships would disappear because there would be no need for partners and associates, only employees and those fortunate enough to convert equity into cash and stocks. . . .

However, to comprehend the kinds of changes that are being wrought on the legal industry, it is necessary to understand how the conventional image of the law firm has altered. We need to look at the redesigned law firm.

C. In the Redesigned Law Firm

Robert Rosen, in his seminal article, "We're All Consultants Now," speculated on how the changes in companies would affect the way legal services are contracted for and delivered. Gone are the days of the wise counselor advising the CEO on his next strategic move; instead there are teams, amoeba-like, that shape-shift to incorporate skills and competencies as they are required for the project. And lawyers are part of these teams, whether in-house or external lawyers. The redesigned company is permeable and malleable, no longer quite a fixed entity with a uniform identity.

The Legal Services Act is stimulating the production of the redesigned law firm. There is no requirement for the redesigned law firm to adhere to the Cravath model of law firm growth and design. In fact there is every commercial reason for the redesigned law firm to move away from that model to a more easily controlled and controllable corporate structure where accountabilities are calibrated and audited.

The redesigned law firm is, in effect, continuing changes that have been occurring. Partnerships are rarely single tier equity structures; they are two-tiered or more. Partners are placed under enormous pressures to bill hours and generate business. The large UK law firm, Eversheds, introduced, for example, a system of soccer red and yellow cards to warn partners of when they are slacking. There is no security in being a law firm partner any more.

The Cravath model of law firm development . . . was predicated on the idea that associates' investment in their probation (a form of deferred gratification) could lead to the reward of partnership. In the redesigned law firm, the ideal of permanent partnership is fast disappearing. Wilkins & Gulati [see Chapter 12, p. 981] have demonstrated that partners must be selective about which associates they choose to train on the path to partnership. Because of the pressures on partners, they can't encircle the entire cohort of associates. This division between the trained and the non-trained establishes two-tier associateships aligned with two-tier partnerships. Those in the latter class are consigned to high-turnover paperwork until burnt out. They are never considered for partnership. Add to this class the group who become "staff attorneys" or "contract attorneys" and one sees a fragmentation of the composition of the law firm and the legal profession emerging with dynamic force. In one sense we see the de-skilling of the workforce or the de-professionalization of law.

Let me mention two further points in relation to the redesigned law firm. In 2004, Baker & McKenzie decided to cease being an Illinois partnership because of the difficulties and obstacles the law firm encountered with this structure in the light of its global organization. It reorganized as a Swiss *verein*. The second point relates to the ability of Washington DC law firms to run wholly owned subsidiaries engaged in other businesses, such as health economics or financial consulting. . . .

E. Generation Y and Immaterial Labor

Other forces are at play in the redesigned law firm. The discussion above looks at the process of the division of labor in the law firm from the top down. What is happening from the bottom up? Is it any different? Is there reason for optimism in dystopia?

Sometimes we elide one generation with another without distinguishing their characteristics, their expectations, and their choices. There is a strong argument put forward that the millennial generation, known as Generation Y (born in early 1980s), has a different perspective on life choices as compared with earlier generations. The general emphasis of the research shows that careers are viewed quite differently by Generation Y than the way that "Baby Boomers" perceive them. Careers are seen as discrete moments rather than as ladders naturally joined. These discrete moments are composed of three to four year periods. For example, one study suggests only two percent of Generation Y believed a career was for life.

It is in this context we see the establishment of ventures such as Axiom Law, a company that hires associates eight to ten years into their careers who have made a choice to abandon the partnership tournament in favor of a more relaxed life-work balance. They are employed to work in in-house legal departments for however long the client wants them present. The knowledge base is provided by Axiom, but they work in the teams of the client. They are cheaper than a law firm, but of course their salaries are lower too. But they are the repositories of knowledge, skills, and competencies that law firms agonize over how to retain, but don't. In the redesigned law firm there will evolve a concordance of styles that will accelerate convergence towards the new law firm.

How will legal education as presently structured and taught by mostly non-Generation Y professors evolve? Is it trapped in a time warp? Does it perhaps represent the last stronghold of values that seem to be slipping out of the legal system? ...

F. The Decline of Professionalism?

Professions have been characterized in a number of ways over the years, some laudatory, others skeptically. ...

Professionalism is now assuming the role of a folk term, a taxonomic trope, which triggers set responses without reflection. In the redesigned law firm, the ascendance of technical expertise is trumping and exiling symbolic functions. The result of the move to the technical is the abandonment of the mythic power of law in favor of the application of rules, regulation, and audit. ...

De-skilling is an essential component of deprofessionalization. It is the reformulation of time, space, and action, which tries to internalize new concepts without detracting from the old, but nevertheless supplanting them. Somehow a concept of profession might endure, but it will bear little resemblance to its precursors. It is the deliberate erasure of the past and we are left wondering what values, if any, have persisted. The history of the redesigned law firm (or, more likely, legal services provider) will be an interesting text to read.

Notes

1. What do you think of the Clementi Reforms? Should the United States consider implementing some or all of these proposals? Could this country implement such sweeping reforms, even if it wanted to? Are there aspects of the way we regulate lawyers in the United States that would make it much more difficult to implement this kind of fundamental restructuring?

2. Regardless of whether eliminating the restrictions on multidisciplinary practice or other forms of non-lawyer ownership would be good for lawyers and clients in this country, will the U.S. legal profession be able to stop these Clementi reforms from crossing the Atlantic? Although it has received almost no attention in the legal or popular press, the General Agreement on Trade in Services, the North American Free Trade Agreement, and other similar international conventions purport to set standards for the terms on which member states govern trade or provision of

services, including legal service. As a result, regardless of the ABA's rules, states may be powerless, for example, to exclude lawyers from a publicly traded Australian law corporation from "practicing law" in the United States if the GATS Council for Trade deems such a prohibition an illegitimate restraint on free trade in services. See Laurel S. Terry, "GATS' Applicability to Transnational Lawyering and Its Potential Impact on U.S. State Regulation of Lawyers," 34 Vand. J. Transnat'l L. 989 (2002). A 2002 opinion in a case before the European Court of Justice, however, concluded it was not a violation of the various competition-protective provisions of the European Community Treaty for the Dutch bar to have prohibited lawyers practicing in the Netherlands from entering into multidisciplinary partnerships with accountants if that prohibition was necessary to ensure the independence and professional secrecy of lawyers. The opinion in Case 99/309 may be viewed at <http://curia.eu.int>. Nevertheless, if a publicly traded Australian or British law firm could operate in the United States, will professional rules prohibiting American lawyers from following suit continue to garner support in the bar or in the courts?

3. Australia already allows publicly traded law firms. In May 2007, the Australian law firm of Slater & Gordon floated an initial public offering and became the first law firm to be listed on the Australian stock exchange—or as far as we know, any other. Alexia Garamfalvi, "In a First, Law Firm Goes Public," Legal Times, May 22, 2007. The shares opened at 1 Australian dollar per share. By the end of trading, the price had risen to AU$1.40, generating AU$49 million in proceeds. Although there has been some fluctuation, the firm's share price has remained relatively strong. See Milton C. Regan, Jr., "Lawyers, Symbols, and Money: Outside Investment in Law Firms," 27 Penn. St. Int'l L. Rev. 407, 409–412 (2008) (describing the offering); "Slater & Gordon Announces 56 Percent Profit Growth," The Lawyer, Feb. 22, 2008 (reporting that the firm had "increased profits more than half since its IPO"). It should be noted, however, that the jury is still out on the Slater & Gordon experiment. Only a few Australian law firms attempted to follow in its footsteps and the firm has experienced significant losses and discontent by its shareholders.

4. Why do law firms want to go public? Given that many law firms have gross revenues of over $1 billion a year, is it clear that they need to raise capital in this way? Are there reasons why even firms with significant gross revenues might nevertheless want access to the capital markets? Is raising equity capital preferable to other ways that law firms have traditionally raised money, including borrowing from banks? Does the experience of some of the law firms that have failed in recent years bear on this questions? For an examination of the role that bank debt may have played in the demise of San Francisco's Heller Ehrman, see Amanda Royal, "Banks and Landlord Blamed in Heller Bankruptcy," The Recorder, Dec. 30, 2008.

5. Slater & Gordon is primarily a plaintiff-side law firm. Does that suggest any reasons why it was particularly interested in the capital markets? In its first year as a publicly traded entity, Slater & Gordon acquired six other smaller plaintiff-side firms in Australia. Does that suggest another reason why law firms might want to access

the capital markets? Jon Parker, "Is Slater's IPO a Model that UK Firms Could Follow? Ambitious Law Firms are Nothing New, but Six Mergers in Nine Months is Plenty by Anyone's Standards," The Lawyer, March 3, 2008. See generally, Edward S. Adams, "Rethinking the Law Firm Organizational Form and Capitalization Structure," 78 Mo. L. Rev. 777 (2013).

6. Is it clear that even if law firms decide to go public, their clients will follow them down that path? Are there any dangers for clients in publicly traded firms? Are there regulations that could be put in place to mitigate these dangers? Are there any benefits that clients might receive from the institutional structures and accountability that might come through public ownership? For a thoughtful discussion of the pros and cons of outside investment in firms, see Regan, "Lawyers, Symbols, and Money," Note 3 supra. See also Christopher J. Whelan, "The Paradox of Professionalism: Global Law Practice Means Business," 27 Penn. St. Int'l L. Rev. 465 (2008); Tonio D. DeSorrento and Geoffrey R. Thompson, "Something Short of Selling Out: Derivatives-Based Innovation in the Legal Profession and Capital Markets," 21 Geo. J. Legal Ethics 577 (2008).

7. Setting aside the question of institutional structure, is it clear that either clients or firms will benefit from the move to multidisciplinary organizations? Have client interests and the demands of globalization resulted in the need to expand our traditional approach to the practice of law? Is law unique in this respect or is the move toward consolidation and multidisciplinary practice in the legal services market part of a more general trend concerning the erosion of traditional categories and boundaries? Or have such concerns been substantially overrated? Consider the following skeptical view expressed by the Economist during the heyday of debate over MDPs in the U.S. and Europe in 2001:

> For years, stock markets have applied a "conglomerate discount": they value diversified manufacturing conglomerates at some 20% less, on average, than the value of the sum of their parts. The discount still applies, in good times and bad. Extraordinary manufacturers (like GE) can defy it for a while; more ordinary ones (like Philips and Siemens) cannot. The "synergy" that these groups invoked at their birth was supposed to make two plus two equal five; more often than not, it made them equal three.

Special Report, "Spoilt for Choice," Economist, July 5, 2001. Given this history, isn't it likely that law firms that stick to their "core business" will have a competitive advantage? Does your answer depend upon what the firm's "core business" is? Are some firms better positioned to withstand the challenge of globally integrated MDPs than others? By the same token, are there some firms—or some lawyers in firms—who will *want* to be acquired by an MDP?

8. If law firms do decide to become multidisciplinary organizations—or go further and become public—will it make any sense to continue to talk about law as being an "autonomous profession"? Would anything be lost if we fail to do so? Should we instead think of law as simply one part of the "professional services industry"?

See, e.g., Mark C. Scott, *The Intellect Industry: Profiting and Learning from Professional Services Firms* xi–xii (1998). What would this mean for legal ethics and the regulation of the profession? Does Clementi provide any important clues? We will return to the "paradox of professional distinctiveness"—whereby lawyers both understandably want to be like other service providers (or indeed, like their corporate clients), but by so doing risk losing their unique status with potential clients and recruits, and the public at large—in Chapter 12.

9. District of Columbia Rule of Professional Conduct 5.4(b) allows lawyers to practice law in organizations in which nonlawyers hold financial interests or exercise managerial authority. The rule states that

> A lawyer may practice law in a partnership or other form of organization in which a financial interest is held or managerial authority is exercised by an individual nonlawyer who performs professional services which assist the organization in providing legal services to clients, but only if:
>
> (1) The partnership or organization has as its sole purpose providing legal services to clients;
>
> (2) All persons having such managerial authority or holding a financial interest undertake to abide by these Rules of Professional Conduct;
>
> (3) The lawyers who have a financial interest or managerial authority in the partnership or organization undertake to be responsible for the nonlawyer participants to the same extent as if nonlawyer participants were lawyers under Rule 5.1;
>
> (4) The foregoing conditions are set forth in writing.

The rule is predominantly used to allow lobbyists to become partners in DC law firms. Why is the rule limited in application to traditional law firms? Should law firms supplement subsection 5.4(b)(2) with contractual obligations such that nonlawyers who violate it can be held accountable for breach of contract? How should lawyer-partners supervise the work of nonlawyer-partners? To the same extent they supervise the conduct of lawyer-partners?

10. In early 2016 the House of Delegates adopted the ABA Model Regulatory Objectives for the Provision of Legal Services. Objective D, which states as a regulatory objective "Transparency regarding the nature and scope of legal services to be provided, the credentials of those who provide them, and the availability of regulatory protections," is commonly understood as the first step toward opening the door to the provision of legal services by nonlawyers. See Resolution 105 (February 2016).

Should nonlawyers be allowed to offer all legal services to clients as long as they are transparent about their credentials? What regulatory protections ought to apply to nonlawyer service providers? The Model Rules? Other rules? Who should regulate nonlawyer service providers?

Chapter 9

Access to Legal Services in the Twenty-First Century

At this point in our discussion of professional responsibility it seems appropriate to consider the manner in which the profession provides legal services to the public. One reason for doing so here is to recognize that in a day and age in which many individuals and small businesses are priced out of legal services, it makes little sense to think of non-paying clients as an exception to the traditional model of access to legal services. Instead, the profession must face the immense challenges of insufficient access to legal services, which the materials in this Chapter introduce. A second reason is to take up some different issues of professional responsibility — issues that concern lawyers as a group instead of lawyers individually. A third reason is to reconsider a number of issues previously discussed in the context of legal assistance and group legal services offices. A fourth reason is to lay a foundation for subsequent topics in these materials, since much of the controversy concerning them has arisen in the context of the difficulty of obtaining legal services encountered by so many people.

In considering the issues in this Chapter, keep in mind the following findings from a 2016 ABA report on the future of legal services in the United States.

> Despite sustained efforts to expand the public's access to legal services, significant unmet needs persist.
>
> 1. Most people living in poverty, and the majority of moderate-income individuals, do not receive the legal help they need.
>
>> a. Funding of the Legal Services Corporation and other legal aid providers remains insufficient and will continue to be inadequate in the future.
>>
>> b. Pro bono alone cannot provide the poor with adequate legal services to address their unmet legal needs.
>>
>> c. Efforts targeting legal assistance for moderate-income individuals have not satisfied the need.
>
> 2. The public often does not obtain effective assistance with legal problems, either because of insufficient financial resources or a lack of knowledge about when legal problems exist that require resolution through legal representation.

[handwritten margin notes:] Poor & Mid Class people are still priced out of legal.

People don't get LA b/c: ① insuff. $; ② Lack of K

3. The vast number of unrepresented parties in court adversely impacts all litigants, including those who have representation.

4. Many lawyers, especially recent law graduates, are unemployed or underemployed despite the significant unmet need for legal services.

5. The traditional law practice business model constrains innovations that would provide greater access to, and enhance the delivery of, legal services.

6. The legal profession's resistance to change hinders additional innovations.

7. Limited data has impeded efforts to identify and assess the most effective innovations in legal services delivery.

Report on the Future of Legal Services in the United States, Commission on the Future of Legal Services, ABA (2016). For a complete analysis of the many ways that the legal system fails to provide access to justice, see Deborah H. Rhode, *Access to Justice* (2004).

A. Private/Market Programs for Paying Clients

This section of materials is designed to present information and highlight current issues in attempts of group legal service programs to provide access to the legal system. One issue to keep in mind in reading the materials is: If cost, quality of service, and the ability to obtain information about lawyers are important to would-be clients, which of the described forms of group legal service programs seems more likely to be helpful in those regards?

Note: A Survey of the Scene

A great deal of attention has been paid since the mid-1960s to the needs of that large segment of the population who are not eligible for free legal services because they are above the "indigent" income level but who nevertheless cannot (or think they cannot) afford a lawyer and who, whether or not they can afford a lawyer, have great difficulty finding one who is ready, willing, and able to handle their problems competently. Since that time, and indeed, for a considerable time before it, a variety of lay organizations—unions, automobile clubs, civil rights organizations, and corporate law departments—sought to meet the public's need with a variety of formal and informal ways of providing group legal services. In addition, the bar provided lawyer referral programs as a method of assisting people to find lawyers. More recently, legal clinics and prepaid legal service plans have been added to the collection of alternate methods of affording access to the legal system.

Despite considerable criticism, lawyer referral services have shown substantial staying power and figures show increasing use of their programs. Indeed, with the diminution of federal funds for legal services in the early 1980s and the institution of poverty programs by some referral services, the concept of the lawyer referral service regained a certain vitality. Nevertheless, the concept of the referral program waiting passively for the public to come to it and the failure of most programs to provide sufficient information about the individual lawyers participating in the program have hurt their image as an effective force for providing legal services.

As far as group legal services are concerned, for a long time they were assumed to be operating on the low end of the scale of professional respectability because the very concept of group legal services was assumed to be condemned by the principles of the former Canons of Ethics. This assumption was based either on the existence of specific abuses or on the general prohibition in ethics rules against interference by "lay intermediaries" with the professional judgment of the lawyer. The relationship between the lawyer and the sponsoring organization, often a union, was generally believed to involve, explicitly or implicitly, such interference. Nonetheless, a surprising number of what were essentially group legal service organizations continued to operate, often unknown to the profession at large. The awakening of professional conscience to the needs of that vast body of the populace that cannot afford legal services easily or at all has changed the professional attitude to a substantial extent. Group legal services have become respectable, though their respectability has been only grudgingly recognized. An important aspect of this growing recognition has been the prodding of the Supreme Court, which became interested in the subject via the civil rights movement of the 1960s but has since taken substantial interest in constitutional aspects of the bar's attempts to restrict group legal services. The growth in the numbers of people whose legal needs are covered at least to some extent by prepaid plans has been enormous. A study conducted by the National Resource Center for Consumers of Legal Services concluded that in 1995 between 85 and 90 million Americans were covered by such a plan.

[margin note: Interference w/ lawyer's judg.]

Until recently federal constitutional principles played almost no role in regulation of the practice of law. What little constitutional law there was developed with respect to efforts by states to restrict membership in the bar — usually because of a person's beliefs or membership in an organization (see the materials on admission to the bar in Chapter 8), but sometimes on an even more discriminatory basis (see, e.g., Bradwell v. State, 83 U.S. 130 (1872) (gender)). During the civil rights movement of the 1960s, however, efforts to restrict the activities of the NAACP legal staff resulted in a landmark opinion that led the Supreme Court to scrutinize other regulatory efforts of the state and of the profession, with state acquiescence.

NAACP v. Button, 371 U.S. 415 (1963), overturned Virginia's attempt to forbid the NAACP from seeking plaintiffs to institute civil rights suits and supplying lawyers for such suits when plaintiffs (whether members of the NAACP or not) were found. The Supreme Court soon made it quite clear that *Button* was relevant to conventional attempts by unions to obtain the benefits of group legal services. Brotherhood of Railroad Trainmen v. Virginia State Bar, 377 U.S. 1, reh'g denied, 377 U.S. 960 (1964). The Brotherhood of Railroad Trainmen had been in the business of referring injured railroad employee union members to selected lawyers called Regional Counsel for years. The terms and conditions of these referral plans had been the subject of professional and judicial inquiry from 1932 on. See Norman Riedmueller, "Group Legal Services and the Organized Bar," 10 Colum. J.L. & Soc. Probs. 228, 232–245 (1974), for a description of the major cases. In *BRT*, Virginia enjoined the union "from holding out the lawyers selected by it as the only approved lawyers to aid . . . members . . . or in any other manner soliciting or encouraging such legal employment of the selected lawyers," 377 U.S. at 4.

The Court refused to distinguish *Button* on the basis that First Amendment principles controlled in that case only because of the important civil and political rights that were involved. The Court held that the desire of workers to counsel one another in the selection of a lawyer implicated First Amendment rights of speech, assembly, and petition. Relying also on the protective statutory policies enacted in the Federal Employers' Liability Act and the Federal Safety Appliance Act, and finding no substantial countervailing state policy involved, the Court reversed the Virginia decree. But cf. discussion in *Ohralik* and *Primus*, pp. 632–656.

The *BRT* case was extended in UMW v. Illinois State Bar Assn., 389 U.S. 217 (1967), to a plan in which the union employed a lawyer on a salaried basis to handle members' workers' compensation claims. Illinois had enjoined this practice as involving the unauthorized practice of law by the union, but the Court found that the same First Amendment principles that were controlling in *BRT* governed this case as well.

Some of the possibilities for abuse that exist in group legal service plans emerge from Justice Harlan's description of the plan in his dissent in the *UMW* case, 389 U.S., at 225. Although the original letter of employment of the lawyer stated, "You will receive no further instructions or directions and have no interference from the District, nor from any officer, and your obligations and relations will be to and with only the several persons you represent," id. at 220, it also appeared that "[i]njured union members are furnished by the Union with a form which advises them to send the form to the Union's legal department. Upon receipt . . . the attorney assumes it to constitute a request that he file on behalf of the injured member a claim with the Industrial Commission, though no such explicit request is contained in the form. . . . In most instances, the attorney has neither seen nor talked with the union member at this stage. . . . Ordinarily the member and this attorney first meet at the time of the hearing before the Commission." Id. at 230. Justice Harlan also stated: "Evidently, he [the attorney] negotiates with the employer's counsel about many claims at the same time," and the UMW attorney was "also an Illinois state senator." Id. at 231.

Assembly-line handling of cases, lack of contact with the client, and settlement of claims en masse are all problems that exist in the profession today. The apprehension even among many persons sympathetic to group legal service programs is that the likelihood that these problems will occur is greater in group legal service programs. These fears also exist with respect to public defender programs in the criminal law sphere. The reasonableness of these fears was seen by Justice Harlan as sufficient to support the conclusion of the Illinois court. Although not mentioned by Justice Harlan, the problems of conflict that any lawyer-legislator must face in accommodating his or her duties to the public and to private clients are enhanced in a situation like the *UMW* case where the legislative interests of the union may exert pressures on the lawyer-legislator that might affect the handling of particular cases for individual union members.

The Supreme Court also dealt with group legal services in United Transportation Union v. State Bar of Michigan, 401 U.S. 576 (1971), in which the court struck down portions of a Michigan decree which had been based on the injunction entered on remand after the Supreme Court opinion in the *BRT* case. The Court held that the decree interpreted prior Supreme Court cases too narrowly and emphasized that the "common thread" running through those decisions was that "collective activity undertaken to obtain meaningful access to the courts is a fundamental right within the protection of the First Amendment." Id. at 585.

The developing professional recognition of the importance of group legal services was given impetus by the quartet of Supreme Court decisions, and by pressure from various groups and lawyers interested in exploring the potential of group legal service programs.

In California, where hundreds of group legal services programs were operating, usually with very little public awareness, see Progress Report of the Standing Committee on Group Legal Services of the State Bar of California, 39 Cal. State B.J. 639 (1964), the California Supreme Court finally responded to recommendations of the State Bar and adopted a rule validating participation by lawyers in group legal service plans so long as the group had been "formed principally for common purposes other than the rendering of legal services," whose furnishing must be "merely incidental." 1 Cal. 3d Rules 56 (1970).

The ABA was split in its views on the subject of group legal services when it approved the Code of Professional Responsibility, and it debated the relevant Code provisions throughout the 1970s. The provisions of Model Rules 7.2 and 7.3 were drafted to avoid most of the problems that plagued prepaid services under the Model Code. See Comment 7 to Rule 7.2.

One final issue relating to group legal services remains to be discussed—the relation between a large unmet need for legal services and different delivery systems for such services. The existence of "unmet legal needs" has itself been controversial. The American Bar Association and the American Bar Foundation collaborated all through the 1970s on a nationwide survey designed to determine the facts about the public's need for, and use of, lawyers and also about the public's attitude toward lawyers. The efforts produced a report by Barbara Curran entitled *The Legal Needs of the Public* (1977); A Final Report of the ABA Special Committee to Survey Legal Needs; and Curran ed., *The Lawyer Statistical Report* (American Bar Foundation 1985); and a Supplement to that Report (American Bar Foundation 1986).

In the late 1970s, legal clinics aimed at middle income clients appeared to be a promising way to bridge the gap between legal "haves" and "have nots." The plan was straightforward. Clinics would provide routine legal services most in demand by middle-class individuals: wills, bankruptcies, divorces. Attorneys at the clinics would benefit by coordinated advertising and a recognized brand name and in return would be expected to generate new business, keep current with reports to management, and supply a high volume of efficient, quality legal services at reasonable prices.

Attempts to implement this strategy, however, have not been wholly successful. In the 1980s two firms, Jacoby & Meyers and Hyatt Legal Services grew into huge interstate chains based upon this model. At its peak, Hyatt Legal Services had 200 offices nationwide. Nevertheless, by 1999 Hyatt Legal Services had sold its interests to local attorneys and cancelled its charter. As of the same time, Jacoby & Meyers had 17 remaining offices in various metropolitan areas in the Northeast and on the west coast, but it has since expanded, with 300 lawyers and offices in 28 states in early 2017. See Report of the New York State Bar Association Special Committee on the Law Governing Structure and Operation, *Preserving the Core Values of the American Legal Profession: The Place of Multidisciplinary Practice in the Law Governing Lawyers* 58–61 (2000) (describing the history of franchise law firms).

The history of both Hyatt Legal Services and Jacoby & Meyers suggests a mixed message with regard to the effectiveness of national organizations operating local law offices on the clinic approach. We will return to some of these issues in Chapter 12. For the moment, consider the ethical problems associated with legal clinics. Are legal clinics likely to provide quality legal services to clients? Are these services likely to be better or worse than those provided by the average solo practitioner? Should legal clinics monitor the quality of the services provided by their lawyers and, if so, how should they accomplish that objective? What other monitoring mechanisms do you expect these organizations to adopt? Are these additional systems consistent with a lawyer's professional independence? Are lawyers who work in legal clinics any less independent than those who work in large law firms or corporate legal departments? Should they be less independent?

The other principal development in service to moderate income individuals is prepaid legal insurance plans in which individuals or groups pay a monthly fee which entitles them to obtain access to a lawyer for low or no cost when they have certain kinds of legal problems. In the 1970s, pre-paid plans were purchased largely by labor unions as a benefit for their members. As the following excerpt indicates, however, legal insurance has recently become big business—for both lawyers and investors.

Brian Heid and Eitan Misulovin
The Group Legal Plan Revolution: Bright Horizon or Dark Future?
18 Hofstra Lab. & Emp. L.J. 335 (2000)

Mention the words "group legal plan" or "prepaid legal plan," and lawyers and laymen alike may say, "I've never heard of them." This is surprising, however, since this form of legal services is quickly becoming an integral part of the American legal landscape. Estimates as of April 1999 place the number of Americans covered by some type of legal coverage plan at approximately 110 million people. A study undertaken by Hewitt Associates, a management consulting firm based in Illinois, predicts that as many as one in five large companies nationwide will be offering group legal plans by the end of the year 2000.

Group legal plans are becoming big business, as exemplified by one of its largest publicly traded companies, Pre-Paid Legal Services, Inc. which has seen its stock price soar, almost doubling in less than one year. Insurance companies are also getting into the picture due in part to the demand for group legal plans from their larger institutional clients. Furthermore, profit margins on group legal services are estimated to hover around fifteen percent, a number that is nearly four times greater than that for group health plans. Thus, the president of Pre-Paid Legal Services, Inc. may not have been exaggerating when he stated that the company's motto is "[w]e're an idea whose time has come." . . .

The cost of a group legal plan varies depending upon the range of services offered and the size of the workforce that enrolls in the program. In order to accommodate a particular employer, most providers are willing to design a plan that is tailored to meet the needs of the company's workforce. A group legal plan's premiums can range from as low as $1 to as high as $25 per month. However, monthly premiums paid by legal plan members are, on average, between $12 and $20. Once these fees have been paid, there are no additional charges for those benefits included in the plan, with the exception of certain co-payments and deductibles that may apply.

Most prepaid legal service plans rely on a panel of lawyers in private practice. These panels may vary from one attorney or firm servicing a small group under formal contract, to a national network of law firms that have agreed to provide services for all plan subscribers. The lawyers enrolled in the various plans are often required to meet certain qualification procedures that may include a minimum number of years in active practice, academic requirements, and screening processes that investigate the potential network member with the state and local bar associations. Additionally, networks may require their members to carry professional liability insurance with a minimum of $100,000 coverage for legal malpractice.

These plans can be described as legal preferred provider organizations (PPO), much like their equivalents in the healthcare field. For example, the subscriber often has the option to choose either an in-network or out-of-network attorney. When the employee decides to use an attorney within the preferred directory of legal service providers, the plan user does not incur any out-of-pocket expenses. However, when the user decides that he or she would prefer to go outside the plan, perhaps to a life-long family lawyer not enrolled in the network, the plan will reimburse the user for their out-of-pocket expenses at a pre-negotiated rate. This is very similar to the manner in which a patient who is part of a healthcare PPO would be reimbursed if the patient went beyond the network to an outside doctor.

The most basic form of group legal service is usually referred to as the access/discount plan. It provides an employee, their spouse, and any dependents, with accessible legal guidance and consultation. This service is usually available over the telephone and is limited to simple legal issues. If an employee is interested, they may call a toll-free number to access the provider's program. The program administrator may then route the call, perhaps by using the employee's zip code, to locate the nearest attorneys participating in the plan. This is actually a reasonable proposition, since group legal plan providers have found that as many as seventy percent of the situations that plan members call about are resolved over the telephone.

This type of plan may also include such services as the examination of basic legal documents, the drafting of simple wills, and short correspondences, written or by phone, to an opposing party. Additional representation or in-office service is available to all plan members at a discounted rate from a selection of attorneys belonging to the provider's network. Some plans provide many of these benefits without restrictions and at no additional price. Costing $5 to $10 a month, access/discount plans have the lowest monthly fees.

At a slightly higher monthly premium, usually ranging from $13 to $23, the employee is eligible to receive a more expansive level of services usually referred to as a comprehensive plan. In addition to the services provided by the access/discount plan, a comprehensive plan provides for personal legal consultation at the attorney's office, preparation of more complex legal documents, and both trial and negotiation representation. Some of the common legal issues covered by a more comprehensive legal plan include adoption, consumer protection, credit problems, debt collection, divorce, juvenile court proceedings, property protection, real estate transactions, traffic matters, and will preparation. Moreover, if the subscriber wishes to obtain legal services beyond those covered in their plan, they may be able to obtain this extended representation at a discounted rate.

Many consumers are delighted with the services provided by both plans, describing in glowing terms how group legal plan lawyers have represented their children in criminal proceedings, forced out-of-state rental tenants to pay back rent and fees, and led courts to dismiss traffic violations. Individual corporate employees are not the only groups to enroll in these plans, as small businesses are also being enticed to become independent members of legal plan networks.

However, it should be noted that most plans prohibit employees from using group legal services against their employer. This limitation is usually recommended to corporate benefits directors when setting up a group legal plan since companies would not want to offer a service that could be used against them. These situations may also be restricted by legislation.

Plan coverage may also be restricted for other legal actions. Generally, plans limit their coverage of members facing criminal charges and those with pre-existing cases. The reasons for these restrictions are that it would be too cost prohibitive to offer such services at the low monthly premiums of the plans. Services that are limited or excluded for economic reasons, or to avoid abuses of the benefit packages, include "representation in business matters, legal services related to class actions, patents or copyrights, appeals, small claims court actions and tax preparation." Matters stemming from an employee's abuse of drugs or alcohol are also rarely covered.

Moreover, plans usually do not cover any legal action where the member is in a position that they acquire legal reimbursement or representation from other sources, such as an insurance policy or a government sponsored legal service program. Further, any legal action in which a contingent fee is customarily the method of payment to an attorney is also excluded from the plan.

For a slightly higher monthly premium, employers can bargain for plans to extend to certain crimes that are rarely included, such as vehicular homicide or even a loss of driving privileges due to a charge of driving while intoxicated. A higher fee or deductible may also be required for contested divorce proceedings and civil law suits. In an action that requires extended litigation, the plan member may be required to contribute both a deductible payment to the service plan attorney, as well as an additional percentage of the cost of the entire litigation, up to the amount covered by the member's legal plan.

What the plans ultimately offer is 24-hour access to legal consultants who are capable of providing simple, though often highly important, legal services to the group legal plan member without delivering the anxiety of huge legal bills or the daunting task of choosing a lawyer out of the yellow pages. Although the response of individuals who take advantage of their services is generally positive, the plans do not offer anything truly unique. Most of the extended legal services require additional fees and contain cost ceilings, and therefore, offer only limited savings to the consumer. As a result, the members needing these services find themselves in a position that is of little difference from the one they were in without the plan.

The Flaws of Group Legal Plans

Although the plans are structured so as to satisfy the needs of both the employer and the employee, there are several issues of concern that may arise. Many critics of group legal plans have argued that the low costs to the employees may pose problems to the quality and efficiency of the plan. These opponents claim that the plans do not offer the type or quality of service that the employees would normally get on their own. Thus, the plans create a conflict between the services provided and the services that the employees are both entitled to and expect to receive.

First, the low fees charged to the groups have forced attorneys to try and maximize their profits by servicing as many claims as possible. As a result, these attorneys often find themselves to be overloaded. In an effort to handle their excessive responsibilities, attorneys are inclined to expedite those clients who are covered by group legal services. This churning of clients can result in both the rapid preparation of documents and premature settlements; neither of which is in the best interest of the client. The client may also need or require face-to-face consultation or other additional services that are not available without extra costs in many of the basic plans.

Another problem of group legal plans may be that as employees become more dependent on these services, they may be more likely to bring the smallest of problems to the attorney's attention. People would want to get the most use and service from the small amount of money that they spend on the plan. For example, many claims, which members would have simply disregarded in the past, would be brought to an attorney at no extra effort or cost to the employee. Therefore, by making it so easy to access these services, the legal community may be creating a more litigious society. The effects of increased claims would also put additional strains on the already stressed judicial system.

The attempt to maintain balance between an attorney's own needs and his obligation to the client's best interests may create ethical dilemmas for the practicing attorney. In this situation, the attorney has a duty to service all the clients enrolled in the program. Realistically, however, the attorney in the network must service enough clients in order to remain profitable. Thus, profitable firms may be saturated with prepaid clients' claims, and new claims may have to take a back seat or existing claims will have to be expedited, often in a less effective manner.

Moreover, many critics argue that by charging such modest fees, the service providers are "primarily attract[ing] inexperienced lawyers." Since these plans are often limited to personal services and representation for minor claims and actions, the attorneys associated with these networks rarely face complex or challenging litigation. Consequently, the low fees and less demanding work have caused typical corporate law firms and large firms with established practices, which often employ the most reputable and qualified attorneys, to express little or no interest in associating themselves with these programs.

Essentially, what group legal plans seem to be offering, rather than a new service or a revolutionary way of handling society's legal concerns, is simply a different way of marketing lawyers and law firms to the public-at-large. Rather than making a name for themselves in the local community by attending practice-building functions, such as civic clubs or business meetings, attorneys can instead be guaranteed a steady source of income from a prepaid legal plan.

It has been argued that many of the services that are offered by group legal plans are available elsewhere, often at no cost at all. For example, many attorneys already provide for free consultations. Some organizations offer legal phone advice through monthly free-of-charge "Call-A-Lawyer" programs. Further, when it comes to the actual fees, in order to attract potential clients, most lawyers will negotiate payment plans that are both convenient and fit their clients' personal needs. By offering these features, an attorney who is not a member of a group legal plan can be just as cost effective for clients as an attorney who is part of a legal plan network.

As a result of this core marketing function, small to medium sized law firms, as well as some insurance providers have become the main suppliers of group legal services. Law firms enter this emerging field because it enables them to establish a name for themselves while attaining greater visibility and, therefore, demand through a constant flow of clients. The emergence of group legal benefits from insurance and financial institutions is due to their desire to offer a full line of insurance and other employment benefits from only one source.

This co-marketing venture benefits both the attorneys and the insurance companies. Lawyers benefit since they are often restricted from openly advertising themselves due to court rules and ethics codes, even in this period of relaxing regulations in those areas. Similarly, insurance companies are enthusiastic to market and advertise group legal plans due to the high profit margins of such plans, despite the substantial effort and capital required. Insurance companies are also interested in becoming major subsidizers of group legal plans because they are often the underwriters of these plans. As a result, insurance companies bear the risks of the plan and guarantee the payment of the legal fees to the lawyers.

The entrance of these new legal service providers into the legal community poses an unexpected concern because of the effects that they may have on the entire legal field. As people will be more likely to turn to the attorneys authorized in their provider's network there may no longer be a niche for local legal practitioners. After all, since many minor services may be provided on a pre-paid basis, the local legal practitioners and other attorneys not part of an existing practice may be forced to join these networks in order to attract and maintain clients. This concern is most apparent in communities that are situated near large companies that provide group legal benefits to much of the locally employed populace. This may force attorneys to change the way they have chosen to practice their profession. . . .

Notes

1. What, if anything, can the legal profession learn from the country's experience with third-party payment systems in the health care field? From your experience, are doctors particularly satisfied with HMOs? Are patients? On the other hand, is medical care more widely available to those with moderate incomes than legal services? See Susan B. Garland, "The H.M.O. Approach to Choosing a Lawyer," New York Times, Jan. 11, 2004.

2. Group and prepaid legal services have continued to expand in the first two decades of the twenty-first century. See Jeremy Bryant Tomes, "The Emergence of Group and Prepaid Legal Services: Embracing A New Reality," 16 Transactions: Tenn. J. Bus. L. 25 (2014). What are the primary obstacles encountered by providers and clients of group legal services? Regulatory constraints imposed by the Model Rules? Administrative and management challenges? Perceptions?

B. Public/Government Programs
for Non-Paying Clients

Problem 9–1

You are charged with formulating policy recommendations for a group of legal assistance organizations with a dozen operating branches and a central administrative office. The following issues are on the agenda for discussion:

1) Whether and to what extent the individual branches should be allowed to make their own policy decisions.

2) What is your preferred resolution of each of the following policy issues:

(a) Should each office take clients on a first-come, first-served basis, or should priority be given to suits that may be labeled "law reform"? Such a choice must be made because it is anticipated that, like most other legal assistance organizations, these offices will not have sufficient resources to handle the caseload.

(b) If law reform is given priority, what criteria should be established for determining when a suit is "law reform"?

(c) Even if law reform issues are given priority, does the office have an obligation to try to handle as many cases as possible?

(d) What attitude should each office take toward the local bar? Should local bar leaders be involved in policy-making or advisory functions? Should general policy be established for all offices, or should an assessment be made of the local bar in each community before reaching a decision? For an informative discussion of these issues in the context of the public defenders' service, see Kim Taylor-Thompson, "Effective Assistance: Reconceiving the Role of the Chief Public Defender," 2 J. Inst. Stud. Legal Ethics 199 (1999); Kim Taylor-Thompson, "Individual Actor v. Institutional Player: Alternative Visions of the Public Defender," 84 Geo. J. Legal Ethics 2419 (1999).

1. Legal Aid

As we consider the substantive issues of the direction that a legal services program should take, as presented by Problem 9–1, we should have in mind some of the history of the provision of legal services in this country.

The first systematic efforts to provide legal services to those who could not afford them began with the legal aid movement. The best known study is Emory Brownell, *Legal Aid in the United States* (1951 and Supp. 1961). A briefer, more critical assessment is contained in Chapter 1 of *Justice and Reform* (1974) by Earl Johnson, Jr., former director of the Legal Services Program of the Office of Economic Opportunity. See also Auerbach, *Unequal Justice* 53–62 (1976).

Throughout its history, as the Brownell and Johnson books demonstrate, the legal aid movement has encountered both conceptual and financial difficulties. To a large extent it tied itself to local bar associations for professional assistance and to private charity for financial assistance. A trend in the 1920s toward municipally funded legal assistance ended abruptly with the Depression. The tie to the local bar and private charity led to a conclusion that the great need was the provision of legal services to individuals who needed them. There was no focus on remedying the economic or social forces that produced the need. The result was that a group of underfinanced, overworked legal aid offices and lawyers handled an enormous number of cases for individual clients. As Johnson points out, at the beginning of the 1960s, "the equivalent of 400 full-time lawyers was available to serve almost 50 million Americans [who could not afford a lawyer] (a ratio of one lawyer for 120,000 persons), as compared with almost 250,000 full-time attorneys to take care of the remaining 140 million (a ratio of one lawyer for every 560 persons)." Johnson, supra, at 9. The concept of using a lawsuit as part of a general reform movement on behalf of the class of poor people—whom, as Abraham Lincoln put it, God must have loved because he made so many of them—became an issue in the provision of legal services only with President Johnson's "War on Poverty" in the 1960s.

2. The OEO Legal Services Program and the Legal Services Corporation

The following article, written some time ago, raises a number of important issues that continue to fuel the current debate over the provision of legal services to people who cannot afford them.

Roger C. Cramton
Crisis in Legal Services for the Poor
26 Villanova L. Rev 521 (1981)

Four eras in civil legal aid in the United States may be identified. Prior to 1875, legal aid was left to the unorganized and voluntary activities of individual lawyers. Although occasional representation was provided, the pro bono efforts of American lawyers were directed largely to the defense of indigents charged with crime, in itself no small task.

The rise of voluntary organizations—a typically American response to a tough social problem—characterizes the second era. The year 1875 marked the beginning of traditional legal aid through private organizations financed by charitable contributions, staffed by a small number of full-time lawyers, and assisted by the volunteered time of lawyers in private practice. Through the efforts of such pioneers as Reginald Heber Smith, and with the support of the organized bar, legal aid offices were established in most large metropolitan areas by 1962.

Traditional legal aid was oriented toward individual client service, helping individuals with legal problems, such as landlord–tenant controversies, family quarrels, and consumer affairs. The implicit assumption was that justice was a civil right, not a commodity to be purchased.

A more controversial approach to legal aid characterized the third era, which began in 1965 with the legal services program of the now defunct Office of Economic Opportunity (OEO). The *Gideon* case had recognized a constitutional right to appointed counsel in criminal cases; a period of destructive urban riots had suggested the desirability of providing more peaceful methods of handling the grievances of the urban poor; and President Johnson, with large congressional support, had embarked on his War on Poverty.

The OEO legal services program did not reject the client-service objective of traditional legal aid, but it included an emphasis on two additional objectives: 1) social justice through law reform and income redistribution; and 2) political organization of the poor. . . .

Political interference with the program began during the Johnson years and during the early '70s the program was fighting for its life. At one point President Nixon decided to dismantle the program and Howard Phillips, a young political lieutenant, was dispatched to the OEO to carry out the task. A series of bruising battles in Congress and the courts left the program in place but crippled in morale and funding. The American Bar Association . . . fought hard for the establishment of a permanent legal services program in a form that would remove it from the immediate supervision of the President and vicissitudes of politics. When President Nixon shifted ground and supported this approach, the Legal Services Corporation Act was signed into law,[22] beginning the fourth era in civil legal aid. . . .

The Legal Services Corporation Act (Act) contained two features that were designed to cure most of the deficiencies of its OEO predecessor. The first was independence, both from political control by politicians and from political use by legal service attorneys; and the second was a strong focus on professionalism — delivering quality legal services in accordance with the best traditions of the profession. The creation of a new quasi-governmental body governed by an independent and nonpartisan board of electors was designed to insulate legal services programs from the kind of political intervention that had troubled the OEO program. Statutory prohibitions prevented legal service grantees from using program funds or personnel for political purposes, organizational activities, or participation in strikes, picketing, and demonstrations.

On the major issue of the nature and scope of representation to be provided to poor clients, the Act smothered quite different perspectives and objectives under a soothing new slogan: access to justice for all. This neutral principle clearly encompassed the individual-client service of traditional legal aid. It also included the law reform objective of the OEO program so long as the significant issues to be litigated arose out of client service in actual cases.

The governing principle was that a lawyer for the poor should do the best he can for his client, just as the lawyer for Exxon or anyone else does. If the zealous and complete representation required by the Code of Professional Responsibility leads the lawyer to believe that framing a test case, pursuing extensive discovery, or participating in administrative or legislative proceedings will best advance the interests of the client, then these activities should be undertaken. The explicit statutory proviso was that the legal services attorney cannot dream up the law suit and then solicit the client; the law suit must emerge out of routine client service. Nor could the legal

---

22. Legal Services Corporation Act, Pub. L. No. 93-355, 88 Stat. 378 (1974) (codified at 42 U.S.C. § 2996 (1976 & Supp. 1979)). . . .

services attorney organize a client group so that he could litigate its rights. But education of poor clients concerning their legal rights, including their right to organize, was not precluded. . . .

Hence the present framework for legal services authorizes the full armory of legal techniques and procedures to be brought to bear on behalf of poor clients, as required in the particular case. Impact litigation and lobbying activities are indicated insofar as they arise out of client representation. But the more frankly political objectives of the OEO program — to organize the poor or constituent subjects as effective pressure groups — are excluded by statute. . . .

DESCRIPTION OF THE CURRENT PROGRAM

Until the crisis precipitated by President Reagan's . . . decision to eliminate the program, legal services prospered under the new structural arrangement. In 1975, when the Corporation came into being, the legal services program was clustered in major cities of the North and far West; and the programs in these areas were starved and demoralized from five years of static funding and constant attack. In five short years, legal services [became] a national program providing a minimum level of service to poor people in all parts of the country. Funding grew rapidly from $70 million in 1975 to $321 million in 1981.

The structure of the program is worth a brief explanation. The Corporation is not empowered to provide legal services to anyone. It is a grant-making and regulatory organization that funds and supervises community-based organizations which hire attorneys to represent eligible poor persons. The Corporation is governed by an eleven-member board of directors which selects a president, who in turn supervises an administrative staff. The Corporation issues regulations governing the program (for example, defining the group eligible for service pursuant to general statutory guidelines), makes grants to the local program for the delivery of legal services, audits and activities of these programs, and carries on general support activities such as training and research that assist the program as a whole.

Representation of poor clients is carried on by 323 local programs funded by the Corporation. They include a few specialized litigation organizations (referred to as support centers and having a national scope), a small number of specialized client programs for Native Americans and migrants, and a large number of community-based programs scattered throughout the country, each serving a particular geographic area. Each local program is a separate non-profit corporation, with its own board of directors and staff. . . .

The 323 independent programs funded by the Corporation are staffed by about 6,200 attorneys, 2,800 paralegals, and a large number of secretaries and clerks. They handle more than 1,000,000 poor clients a year through about 1,200 local offices. Although the independent programs receive support from other sources, over two-thirds of the total funding comes from the Corporation. Other federal funding sources provide about 22%, with private contributions and state and local government contributing the remaining 11%.

The staff lawyers employed by the local programs are generally relatively young and low paid; entering salaries average about $14,000 per year and average salaries for all lawyers are less than $17,000; both figures are well below compensation provided by private law firms or other government offices. Caseloads are large, ranging up to 150–250 open cases per attorney. The new attorneys are generally liberal and idealistic, and there is a high turnover. About one-fourth of new attorneys leave the program in a year or less; more than 80% are gone after three years. Those who survive more than three years are likely to make a career of legal services; they become the leaders and supervisors of the more inexperienced attorneys who join the program, work with a burst of enthusiasm for a year or two, and leave "burned out" by the constant pressure of handling a large volume of generally routine cases. . . .

[In 1980] the legal services program handled about one and one-half million matters for over a million poor persons. The average cost of each matter handled is about $200. The program's clients are 51% white, 30% black, and 10% Hispanic. Only one-fifth of them are employed; most are living on welfare or Social Security.

The types of cases fall into expected categories. Thirty-four percent involve family matters; 17% involve landlord–tenant or other housing problems; 14% are concerned with income maintenance; and 12% involve consumer disputes. The rest involve an enormous variety of subjects.

CRITICISMS OF THE LEGAL SERVICES PROGRAM

Criticisms of the current legal services program fall into three categories: 1) the program is a political instrument of activist lawyers; 2) it is not a poor people's program but a lawyers' program; and 3) it is inefficient both in assisting poor people and in the costs it places on others. Each of these charges deserves examination.

A. POLITICAL ACTIVISM

The most common criticism of the legal services program is that it embodies or encourages activism by staff attorneys who seek to stir up litigation to force judicial resolution of matters that should be left to elected officials. Even the statement of the criticism raises fundamental questions not limited to legal aid, concerning the appropriate role of courts, legislatures, and the executive in a democratic society, to say nothing of the difficulty of characterizing particular issues as "political" or "activist." . . .

The "political activism" critique, insofar as it does not overlap with more general concern about judicial activism, appears to involve two subthemes: the propriety of the government funding law suits against itself, and the relative emphasis in the legal services program of impact litigation as against individual client service.

Should the federal legal services program permit representation involving suits against governmental units or before legislative bodies, including administrative rulemaking? It is apparent that the program as we now know it would be crippled if these forms of representation were to be prohibited. Poor people would have effective recourse against merchants, landlords, and other private persons, but not against governmental agencies or officers. . . .

The second subtheme concerns the relative emphasis of the legal services program on impact litigation rather than individual client service. The critics of the legal services program talk as if the only cases that a program should handle are those that are routine and unimportant, affecting the individual client and no one else. The normal rules of stare decisis and res judicata make that an impossible goal since a judicial precedent affects all persons similarly situated and res judicata may bind the same defendant when sued by other plaintiffs . . . .

Moreover, whether the result in a law suit will turn out to be significant cannot be determined at its commencement. The importance of a decision results from the particular findings of fact and rulings of law that a court makes at the conclusion of a case. . . .

Aside from these practical and philosophical difficulties with the concern about law reform, there is an efficiency concern. Repetitive litigation of the same problem in one-by-one litigation is wasteful of private and public resources. The disposition of significant issues in a manner that affects a large number of people provides a much more efficient use of taxpayer funds for legal services. Any other approach would be wasteful and duplicative, even if feasible.

The concern about impact litigation also rests on an inaccurate perception of the underlying facts. The critics of legal services have been mesmerized by the publicity given to a small number of highly visible controversies and by the ambitious rhetoric of an occasional legal services lawyer, who may talk enthusiastically and unrealistically about changing the world through test cases or class actions. The reality of day-by-day work in a legal services office, however, is far different. . . .

B. A LAWYERS' PROGRAM, NOT A POOR PEOPLES' PROGRAM

A more fundamental but less common critique of the legal services program is that, despite its noble pretense, its benefits go largely to lawyers instead of poor people. The argument has been most fully stated by Stephen Chapman.[69] Mr. Chapman raises provocative questions concerning the purposes and effects of the legal services program. . . .

The legal services program, according to Mr. Chapman, is a full employment bill for lawyers. The ABA and other bar associations support the program because it provides employment for the current overflow of young lawyers from the law schools, who would otherwise be in competition with the existing private bar. Since legal services programs are prohibited from taking fee-generating cases, they do not compete with private lawyers. Even more important, every case handled by a legal services lawyer creates new business for other lawyers, since the opposing

---

69. See Chapman, "The Rich Get Rich, and the Poor Get Lawyers," The New Republic, Sept. 24, 1977, at 9, reprinted in 126 Cong. Rec. 14688 (1980) (remarks of Sen. Helms).

parties need the services of a lawyer. Thus the program has a tremendous multiplier effect; it not only relieves the competitive pressures of new lawyers entering the legal market, but also requires additional compensated lawyer time to defend the claims brought by legal services lawyers. . . .

The second wing of Mr. Chapman's argument characterizes the program as paternalistic and doubts the importance of the public provision of legal services in contrast to other possible benefits for the poor, especially money. Mr. Chapman argues that lawyers exaggerate the importance of legal counsel, regarding it, "like food, shelter, and medical care, as a basic right, the lack of which makes life practically intolerable." . . .

The issues presented by these arguments are very broad, and far beyond the scope of this discussion, but a brief response is required.

First, the opportunity to enforce legal rights and responsibilities involves more than just economics and efficiency. It is a question of the moral tone of a society and the legitimacy of its institutions. . . .

Second, the economic arguments in favor of distribution of money rather than legal services assume that substantial amounts of money would be available for distribution and that market imperfections do not prevent rational choices by poor people. Both assumptions are dubious. The current appropriation for the national legal services program amounts to only about ten dollars per eligible poor person. That amount of money will not purchase much in the way of legal services or anything else. . . .

Finally, especially in situations in which poor people are affected, but each only with respect to a small amount, there is a free-rider problem.[77] No one has an incentive to expend the amount necessary to litigate a $100 claim, but the pooling effect of legal services operates to confer a benefit on all members of the group by supporting litigation based on the aggregated value of the claims, which may be very large.

C. ECONOMIC EFFICIENCY

Arguments that the legal services program is paternalistic and lawyer-oriented are closely related to attacks on the program on grounds of economic efficiency. Professor [now Judge] Posner, for example, states some of the same points made by Chapman in language more familiar to economists.[78] Providing legal services to the poor at no price, he argues, "prevents many poor people from achieving their

---

77. "Free riders" are those who receive the benefits of successful litigation although they bear none of the costs. For discussion of the "free ride" problem in the administrative law field, see Cramton, "The Why, Where, and How of Broadened Public Participation in the Administrative Process," 60 Geo. L.J. 525 (1972). For discussion of the alternative of aggregating numerous small claims through class action proceedings, see R. Posner, *Economic Analysis of Law* 449–450 (2d ed. 1977).

78. See R. Posner, supra note 77, at 355–359.

most efficient pattern of consumption." A poor person will accept free legal services unless their value to him is outweighed by the lost time and other inconvenience of dealing with a lawyer. The demand for free legal services will invariably exceed the available supply, creating a serious rationing problem. Since the value to some recipients will be less than its cost to the taxpayers, the distribution of free services is wasteful. It is better, in his view, to give poor persons $100 and let them decide how to spend it. . . .

Arguments concerning the efficiency effects of the legal services programs fail to reflect the benefits provided to poor people as a class when small claims, uneconomic to be litigated individually by any claimant, are pursued systematically on behalf of such persons as consumers or tenants. Moreover, one of the great advantages of the program is that substantial benefits accrue even to those who are not represented. To the extent that legal rules and procedures are modified in favor of welfare recipients, consumers, tenants, and other classes, everyone in the class, even those not eligible for free legal services, is benefitted. . . .

Supporters and critics of the legal services program do not question its effectiveness as an instrument for enforcing the legal rights of the poor. Both agree that it produces substantial results. The criticisms, rather, are that the assertion of these claims tempts judges to do things they shouldn't do, benefits lawyers more than clients, or misallocates resources in the community. . . .

The claims brought by legal services programs on behalf of poor people are decided by judges, not by legal services lawyers. Approximately 85% of all matters are resolved favorably to the program's clients, a remarkably high success rate. The rub about the legal services program may be that it is successful, and its very success creates opposition among interests adversely affected. "Political activism" and similar slogans may be code words for another complaint: "their just claims have been upheld against us and we resent it." . . .

Crippling Restrictions

Another mode of attack on legal services is to cripple it with demeaning or inappropriate restrictions. . . . The harmful effect of such restrictions turns entirely on the content and effects of the particular restriction.

The Act has always contained restrictions on the availability and type of service. Questions of policy in the provision of publicly-funded services are appropriate for legislative resolution, especially when choices as to who enjoys a social benefit must inevitably be made. Examples of longstanding restrictions are those relating to criminal cases and fee-generating cases, which prevent the use of Corporation funds in situations in which representation is available from other sources. More controversial are present restrictions on handling school desegregation cases, draft matters, abortion cases, and cases involving homosexual rights. The ABA, the Corporation, and the legal services community have opposed such restrictions, but the existing restrictions have not been especially troublesome because their scope is so limited and most programs are inactive in the areas involved. . . .

WHY LEGAL SERVICES FOR THE POOR?

The legal services program is commonly viewed by its proponents, as well as its critics, as a mechanism for redistribution of social wealth to the poor. There are three difficulties with this view: 1) economic theory often denies that changing a legal rule will have the effect of redistributing income within the larger community; 2) the redistribution theory invites courts to decide issues that are more properly left to resolution by policy makers; and 3) it is inconsistent with the facts, both in respect to the bulk of the activities of legal service programs and in its overestimation of the capacity of litigation to perform such dramatic changes in economic well-being.

. . . [But] [g]lobal changes such as large-scale redistribution of income within the community cannot be accomplished by lawsuit except in rare and limited situations. The cooperation and action of legislative bodies is required for accomplishments of this character. . . .

So far, my justification for publicly-funded legal services has been negative in character, expressing doubts that broad claims of social justice are an achievable and appropriate goal of the national legal services program. But much of a positive nature needs to be said as to why publicly-funded legal assistance for the poor is an essential buttress of our enduring values. The arguments will be marshalled under three heads: 1) access to justice, 2) the bias of law against the unrepresented, and 3) helping individuals to help themselves.

A. ACCESS TO JUSTICE

Provision of legal services for the poor is a conservative program in the sense that it helps preserve the enduring values of our republican form of government — access to justice on reasonably equal terms, and due process and equal justice for all. . . .

B. THE BIAS OF THE LAW AGAINST THE UNREPRESENTED

The legal services program improves legal rules and procedures so that poor people get a fairer break. The thought behind this assertion is the reality that all of our institutions tend to respond to the interests that are present and represented. Just as regulatory agencies, if they are closeted with industry representatives for a period of years are frequently captured by them, so legislatures, courts, and administrative bodies respond to the viewpoints that are presented and the arguments that are made. . . .

Legal services for the poor offer an effective and efficient remedy. It is an efficient remedy because it is not essential that representation be provided to every tenant, consumer, borrower or the like in order for beneficent effects to be felt. Provision of legal services for some of the poor changes rules and procedures that benefit everyone in the affected class, even those who are not poor. . . .

C. HELPING THE HURT AND SUFFERING

Finally, in a society that values the dignity of the individual, the role of legal services in helping the poor to help themselves must remain the basic justification. The legal services program helps bring justice to individuals who are hurt, troubled, unfortunate, and dispossessed. What further justification is required other than: "Because they need it and they are important"? . . .

Notes

1. Professor Cramton argues that a major purpose of the OEO legal services program was not merely to achieve "social justice through law reform and income redistribution" but that it also envisaged and in many places undertook "political organization of the poor." It was this feature of the program—the actual organization and politicization of community groups through use of government money—that sparked a great deal of political opposition that attacked not only the overt political activities but also the legal manifestation of those activities, especially the class action suits against governmental entities. See Agnew, "What's Wrong With the Legal Services Program," 58 A.B.A. J. 930, 931 (1972): "What we may be on the way to creating is a federally funded system manned by ideological vigilantes, who owe their allegiance not to a client, not to the citizens of a particular state or locality and not to the elected representatives of the people, but only to a concept of social reform." For a response, see Klaus, "Legal Services Program: Reply to Vice President Agnew," 58 A.B.A. J. 1178 (1972).

It was criticism of this sort that partly explains some of the restrictions on the activities of grantees of the Legal Services Corporation that are referred to by Professor Cramton and further elaborated in Notes 2, 3, and 4. They are also partly the product of the negotiations that led to support of the organized bar for the "depoliticized" Legal Services Corporation. The main casualty of the change in direction of legal services after the establishment of the Legal Services Corporation was not the class action suit against the government but rather the political organization of the local client community that had been the hallmark of many OEO legal services programs. Some have seen a potential for renewal of community political organization through the growing clinical education programs at law schools. That perception has been fueled by a movement of legal services attorneys into such programs.

2. Professor Cramton refers to some of the original restrictions on use of funds that were imposed by Congress on grantees from the Legal Services Corporation. They have been described in summary form in a Note in the American Bar Association Journal, 60 A.B.A. J. 1045 (1974):

> The act contains many restrictions, which for convenience may be classified as restrictions (1) on the corporation itself; (2) on the corporation and recipients; (3) on recipients and staff attorneys (a "staff attorney" being a lawyer who receives more than a half of his annual professional income from a recipient); (4) on employees of the corporation and recipients; (5) on attorneys employed full time; (6) on "all attorneys engaged in legal assistance activities supported in whole or in part" by L.S.C.; and (7) on the use of funds.

Restrictions on the corporation—The corporation may not participate in litigation on behalf of clients other than itself, and it may not undertake to influence legislation, except that personnel of L.S.C. may testify or make other "appropriate communication" when requested to do so by a legislative body or a member of one or in connection with legislation or appropriations affecting the corporation.

Restrictions on the corporation and recipients—Neither the L.S.C. nor a recipient may contribute or make available corporate funds or program personnel or equipment for political parties or candidates or to advocate or oppose "any ballot measures, initiatives, or referendums." The act adds at this point: "However, an attorney may provide legal advice and representation as an attorney to any eligible client with respect to such client's legal rights." . . .

Restrictions on employees of the corporation and of recipients—This broad category of persons is prohibited from intentionally identifying the corporation or a recipient with any "partisan or nonpartisan political activity associated with a political party or association, or the campaign of any candidate for public or private office." They also are enjoined, while carrying out legal assistance activities, not to engage in or encourage others to engage in public demonstrations, picketing, boycotts, strikes, riots, civil disturbances, violations of injunctions, or "any other illegal activity."

Restrictions on attorneys employed full time—Full-time lawyer employees must refrain from compensated outside practice and may engage in uncompensated outside practice only as authorized under L.S.C. policies.

Restrictions on "all attorneys"—All attorneys, while engaged in legal assistance activities, must refrain from "any political activity" and from providing voter transportation or engaging in voter registration activity. However, the phrase "(other than legal advice and representation)" is attached to the prohibitions relating to voter transportation and registration.

Restrictions on the use of funds—No funds made available by the corporation, either by grant or contract, may be used

(1) to provide legal assistance in a "fee-gathering" case, except in accordance with guidelines established by the corporation;

(2) for "any political activity";

(3) in criminal proceedings;

(4) in civil actions brought by a person convicted of a crime against court or law enforcement officials;

(5) to provide legal assistance to unemancipated persons under eighteen, except (a) on written request of parents or guardians, (b) on request of a

court, or (c) in child abuse, persons-in-need-of-supervision, and institutionalization proceedings;

(6) to support or conduct training programs for the purpose of advocating particular public policies, or encouraging political, labor, or antilabor activities, or demonstrations, as distinguished from the dissemination of information;

(7) to organize or assist in the organization of any entity except one for the provision of legal assistance to eligible clients;

(8) in proceedings or litigation relating to the desegregation of elementary or secondary schools;

(9) in proceedings or litigation seeking to procure a nontherapeutic abortion or to compel an abortion when it is contrary to the "religious bounds or moral convictions" of the individual or institution involved;

(10) in proceedings or litigation arising from a violation of the Military Selective Service Act or of desertion from the armed forces;

(11) to influence the issuance, amendment, or revocation of executive orders or "similar promulgations" of any governmental agency; and

(12) to undertake to influence legislation, except in the representation of a client or when requested to make representations by a legislative body or governmental agency. . . .

3. Efforts were made to remove some of the restrictions on the Legal Services Corporation, especially those relating to abortion and school desegregation cases, at the time funding was renewed for three years in December 1977. Those efforts failed, although a number of changes were made, including removal of restriction (5), supra, and addition of a provision permitting use of funds for lobbying when necessary for representation of a client, so long as the client was not solicited in violation of "professional responsibilities." In addition, attorneys were brought under the Hatch Act, which does not prohibit seeking election to non-partisan political office. 91 Stat. 1619 (Dec. 28, 1977). See 64 A.B.A. J. 189 (Feb. 1978).

4. In 1982, some additional restrictions were added in the Joint Resolution of Congress providing continuing appropriations for a number of government agencies for fiscal year 1983. The expenditure of funds to provide legal assistance for most aliens unlawfully in the United States was prohibited. The ability of funded programs to lobby government was also restricted. Finally, only private attorneys or nonprofit legal service organizations governed by a board of directors, a majority of whom are attorneys appointed by bar associations representing a majority of the attorneys practicing in the area served by the recipient, may receive funds as a grantee of the Legal Services Corporation. These restrictions were substantially continued in succeeding authorizations throughout the 1980s.

5. Is the Legal Services Corporation idea preferable to the OEO Legal Services idea? Should the goals and policies of a legal services program be set by governmental bodies, professionals, or clients? Does it depend whether the issue is involvement in law

reform and lobbying, or management of caseloads, or selection of clients and categories of legal problems?

6. Which of the listed restrictions do you think are appropriate to a legal services program funded with government funds?

7. Note that Problem 9–1 may be discussed in terms of the Legal Services Corporation's policy-setting role for recipient organizations. How would you resolve those issues in this setting? The Act does not resolve the issue of the Corporation's role in "law reform," but it prohibits grants to public interest law firms. 42 U.S.C. §2996(f)(b)(5).

The two-term administration of President Reagan saw a struggle over the very existence of the Legal Services Corporation and the programs that it funds. While the friends of local legal services programs in Congress, with the strong support of the organized bar, fought off the effort to abolish the LSC entirely, there was initially a sharp reduction of funding for LSC programs, followed by a continuing struggle to restore lost funding and even increase it. LSC's FY 2009 budget request pointed out that if its funding "had just kept pace with inflation with its FY 1980 funding levels, LSC would be receiving 765 million today." <http://www.lsc.gov/about/budget.php> In fact, FY 2016 funding was approximately $385 million whereas FY 1980 funding had been $303 million. As this book goes to press, President Trump has said that he wants to eliminate LSC funding entirely.

While the appropriations for LSC dropped sharply after 1981 before recovering, it should also be noted that nonfederal resources devoted to civil legal services for the poor grew rapidly during the 1980s. State and local government grants and funds from private sources mushroomed from about $10 million in 1980 to nearly $100 million in 1988. In the same period, the number of lawyers contributing their services pro bono also expanded greatly, reaching perhaps 100,000 lawyers who provided some free service in 1988.

President Reagan's 1981 attack on LSC had a dramatic effect on the relationship of private lawyers to local legal services programs. The support given by the organized bar to LSC led, at least in part, to congressional legislation that gave local bar associations control over the boards of directors of local programs and required LSC to ensure private attorney involvement in delivery of services. Over the next seven years, more than 400 new pro bono and judicare programs were developed by legal services programs and state and local bar associations, usually working through cooperative agreements. These private attorney involvement programs, in turn, recruited tens of thousands of local lawyers to take on cases for poor clients.

LSC itself, however, continued to be quite hostile to "reform" activity of its grantees during the 1980s. In addition, it developed an extremely inquisitorial process for monitoring the behavior of grant recipients, exploring possible technical violations of regulations in great depth but rarely investing energy in questions about the quality or effectiveness of local advocacy for clients. Congress reacted by including riders to appropriation bills that forbade LSC from enforcing regulations with respect to legislative advocacy by local programs, local board composition, and even committee activity dealing with such minutiae as LSC's Audit Guide, computer purchases, and small experimental grants to law school clinics.

A major factor in the increase of non-federal funds was the adoption since 1979 in all states and the District of Columbia of some kind of IOLTA (Interest on Lawyers' Trust Accounts) plan as a way of raising money to support legal services programs. The IOLTA programs permit or require lawyers to deposit trust funds that would otherwise not generate interest for clients (because they are too small or they are held for too short a time) into pooled interest-drawing trust accounts. The IOLTA programs follow three major patterns: mandatory, sometimes called "comprehensive," i.e., all lawyers must join; mandatory but with an opt-out provision; and voluntary. The mandatory programs have naturally raised the largest amounts of money and in some states the amount of money that has been raised is impressive. The National Association of IOLTA Programs reported that in fiscal 2007, $240 million was awarded to legal services by all the IOLTA programs. With the falling interest rates and the economic recession at the end of the first decade of the twenty-first century, the money available to legal services from IOLTA programs fell precipitously. Moreover, the backers of IOLTA tell us that this program is only a short-term aid for legal services, for more sophisticated technology is making it more and more administratively feasible for banks to pay interest to individual clients on short-term funds in relatively small amounts.

Almost from their inception the IOLTA programs came under constitutional attack. Finally, in 1998, in Phillips v. Washington Legal Foundation (524 U.S. 156) the Supreme Court held (5–4) that the clients whose funds produced the interest turned over to the Texas IOLTA program had a property interest in those funds on the general principle that ownership of the interest followed from ownership of the principal. It remanded the case for a determination whether the IOLTA program worked as a "taking" of the clients' funds and, if so, whether the clients were entitled to compensation for the taking. Subsequently, in Brown v. Legal Foundation of Washington, 538 U.S. 216 (2003), the Court held, also by a 5–4 vote, that there was no Fifth Amendment violation. Requiring that certain client funds be placed in an IOLTA account did not confiscate any client interest and did not effect any regulatory taking because there was no economic impact on the client. Moreover, even if there was a taking, there was no requirement to compensate because the pecuniary loss to the client was zero. The dissenters believed that once interest was in fact earned on the accounts—through IOLTA pooling—it belonged to the clients and that therefore client property had been taken without just compensation.

As for the fate of the Legal Services Corporation, the 1996 Act introduced nineteen further restrictions on the grantees of LSC funds. One set of restrictions prohibits grantees from all kinds of legislative advocacy and from attempting to influence any adjudicatory proceeding involving an "agency policy of general applicability and future effect." Grantees may seek relief from an agency as long as existing laws and interpretations of laws are not challenged. The statute also forbids the representation of a variety of clients: illegal aliens, and some legal aliens as well; tenants evicted from public housing on allegation of involvement in drug crimes; and prisoners. The Act increases the kinds of cases that grantees may not handle to include redistricting, abortion-related cases, assisted suicide, and welfare-reform litigation. Finally, class action lawsuits may not be instituted and attorneys fees may not be recovered under federal or state statutes. Moreover, the restrictions also apply to the grantees' use of non-LSC funds, both public and private, and to all organizations that receive funds from grantees.

Some of these last restrictions were enjoined preliminarily in Legal Aid Society v. Legal Services Corp., 961 F. Supp. 1402 (D. Haw. 1997). LSC thereupon rewrote the restrictions relating to non-LSC funds to assure that recipients of LSC funds have "objective integrity and independence from any organization that engages in restricted activities." The new restrictions were upheld in a second round of litigation in the Hawaii suit. 145 F.3d 1017 (1998), cert. denied, 525 U.S. 1015 (1998). These restrictions and also the direct restriction on the use of federal funds by the grantees themselves were also mostly upheld in Velazquez v. Legal Services Corp., 164 F.3d 757 (2d Cir. 1999). One provision, however, forbidding LSC grantees to represent clients attempting to amend or challenge welfare laws, was held unconstitutional. The Supreme Court affirmed, 531 U.S. 533 (2001) (5–4). Oregon attacked the "objective integrity and independence" requirement on the Tenth Amendment ground that the LSC regulations interfered with Oregon's sovereignty in preventing an Oregon proposal to combine an Oregon-funded and an LSC-funded legal aid program into one organization. The court, however, held that Oregon lacked standing because it could not demonstrate any state interest separate from that of the legal service provider. Oregon was free to fund its own programs free from LSC restrictions. Oregon v. Legal Services Corp., 552 F.3d 965 (9th Cir. 2009). For a collection of materials relating to the issues of this topic, see Conference on the Delivery of Legal Services to Low-Income Persons: Professional and Ethical Issues, 67 Fordham L. Rev. 1713 (1999).

C. Public–Private Initiatives

Problem 9–2

Community Law Firm, Inc., a "public interest law firm," has been approached by two environmental groups that want to attack a decision of a state Forestry Department to open a piece of state forest to multiple use. One environmental group wishes the area to be kept forever wild. The other is willing to permit certain kinds of controlled camping, but opposes the Forestry Department's plans as too extensive. How does Community Law Firm, Inc. decide which client to represent?

Problem 9–3

Community Law Firm represents a local action group that has been fighting the construction of a highway through a portion of city parkland. As the suit is about to come to trial, the Highway Department proposes an alternate route that would take the road through a relatively sparsely settled but poor neighborhood. The local action group wants to accept the proposal, but there is opposition from the people whose homes would be condemned and from the neighborhood generally. The members of Community Law Firm believe that acceptance of the alternate route is not in the public interest, but are unable to convince their client. What courses of action are open to Community Law Firm, and which one do you, as a member of the Firm, think it should follow?

Problem 9–4

The Committee for the Preservation of Civil Rights (CPCR), a non-profit corporation with a civil rights agenda, is experiencing financial difficulties like those of many similar organizations. At a board meeting, a lawyer member noted that on several occasions in recent years it had forwarded litigation to lawyers to whom statutory fee awards had been made upon the successful conclusion of the cases. The lawyer suggested that in the future CPCR could receive considerable income if it persuaded the lawyers to whom it referred such cases to contribute a considerable percentage of any fees earned from the litigation. Should such a sharing of fees constitute a violation of disciplinary rules? See Model Rule 5.4(a)(3). Should a law school clinic, a relief organization, or a political organization be permitted to raise funds for its operations by operating a referral business under that Rule's fee-sharing provision?

The practice of "public interest" law by private entities outside the government-financed network has not been without controversy. One of the most thoughtful critiques, by a veteran of the public interest movement, follows. The issues he raises persist in much of so-called public interest work.

Kenney Hegland
Beyond Enthusiasm and Commitment
13 Ariz. L. Rev. 805 (1971)

The image: A large reception office, beige carpet, xerox machine, IBM electric typewriters, a tasteful peace poster on one wall, a bright Picasso on the other. Activity, noise, movement—phones ringing, the hum of the typewriters; a young man, sleeves up, collar loose, looking over a secretary's desk, dictating a hurried memo. In the inner offices, talking, writing, reading, stretching, the "Experts": lawyers, sociologists, economists, political scientists, ecologists, planners. An efficient, organized and highly competent team. The goal: The "public interest."

The image excites—the sense of commitment, action, progress—but it also disturbs. While others in this symposium will focus on the excitement, here let us ask why the image is also disturbing.

The basic goal of the public interest law movement is to assure adequate representation of currently unrepresented or underrepresented interests and peoples. Democratic theory and the adversary system require that all be heard. All are not. Thus, the large "public interest" umbrella encompasses such diverse interests as racial equality, consumer protection, poverty and ecology.

While agreeing totally that a vast amount of legal talent must be shifted to the unrepresented, this article questions whether the public interest firm, as presently conceived, can accomplish this goal. First, the rhetoric of the movement, its seizure of the coveted mantle of "public interest," may in fact reduce the net pool of legal manpower available to the unrepresented. Such rhetoric alienates the private bar whose support and involvement is needed by the movement. Perhaps a greater challenge with such rhetoric, however, is that it will be believed. When lawyers proclaim that they are the protectors of blacks, of the poor, and of the environment, the rest of the bar might conclude that these matters are no longer their concern. The result, therefore, would be a reduction of the number of lawyers involved in public interest work. Second, the public interest movement has generally failed to distinguish between unrepresented interests and peoples in terms of their relative need for legal manpower. It will be asserted that there is often adversity between those interests currently lumped together under the public interest label (racism, poverty, ecology) and that lawyers, because of the unique role of the law, should be concerned more with some than with others.

In addition to its rhetoric and its failure to focus—both of which are counterproductive to the goal of increased representation of the unrepresented—there are at least two other disturbing aspects of the public interest law movement. First, although the movement is in essence an attempt to make the adversary system more representative of all interests, its politicalization of the practice of law—the assertion that lawyers represent "interests" rather than people—may undermine the keystone of that system: the public's confidence, already shaky, that the law will protect the individual even if he is unpopular. Finally, and most fundamentally, there is the problem of the attorney-client relationship. Given the vast numbers of unrepresented interests and peoples, the public interest practitioner, to increase his effectiveness, attempts to assert generalized interests rather than specific interests; to view clients as representatives of large nebulous classes (blacks, the poor, consumers, ecologists) rather than as individuals. The attorney's role consequently shifts from that of advocate to that of planner. This is regrettable. First, there is the problem of the accountability of these new planners. Second, there is the notion that our major problems cannot be solved by planners and experts; that they can be solved only by returning decision making to the individual. That planning is the cure-all is an extremely dangerous trap for lawyers. Only lawyers are capable of protecting the rights of the individual against those who would plan for his happiness. . . .

The solution [to the problem of unrepresented interests] . . . advocated by the public interest movement is to have more attorneys represent the poor and, similarly, blacks, consumers and ecologists. Given the vast numbers of unrepresented individuals and the magnitude of their interests (racial equality, consumer protection, poverty and ecology), the public interest movement simply cannot succeed by the infusion of small bands of dedicated attorneys. What is needed is the active support and involvement of the private bar.[4]

Viewed from the perspective of allocation, what of the sign on the door, "Public Interest Law Firm"? It tends to reduce the net pool of legal help available. The assertion, represented both by the sign and much of the rhetoric of the movement, that there are two kinds of practitioners—public interest practitioners ("good guys") and other practitioners ("bad guys")—is bad politics. It undercuts the goal of representation of the unrepresented by alienating the "bad guys" so that they will not support, help or even possibly become "good guys." No one likes the black hat and this may explain much of the hostility that the private bar harbors for the public interest movement.[5] The assertion, however, has a greater danger: it may make the "bad guys" even worse by allowing them an easy way out of their professional

---

4. As to the need of involving private practitioners in public interest law and the unique contribution they can make, see Cahn & Cahn, "Power to the People or to the Profession?—The Public Interest in Public Interest Law," 79 Yale L.J. 1005, 1031–1037 (1970).

Many private practitioners are anxious to involve themselves in public interest law. The major impediment to the solo practitioner's or small firm's participation is the lack of an effective mechanism that limits the attorney's commitment so to assure that he will not be flooded with free work. An attorney is not like a physician who can "give" a couple of hours a week in a free clinic, knowing that that will be the end of it. Each time an attorney sees a client, there is no way of predicting how much time his case will require. . . .

5. Those who oppose the public interest law movement should ask themselves just why they do so. Upon analysis, I believe, most objections disappear or are greatly weakened. Some may object that the goals sought by public interest firms are essentially political and hence not the proper subject of judicial redress. When one realizes that all judicial decisionmaking is ultimately based on political premises, this objection disappears. Public interest firms are simply asserting new political premises. See note 6 infra. Others may object to the active stance of public interest firms such as their greater willingness to seek cases, to attack traditional standing requirements and, generally, to force the courts into more active roles. This active stance is, however, inevitable in a society in which the rate of change is continually quickening and the time lag between problem and crisis is continually shortening. The job of lawyers and courts is to resolve conflict: they can no longer afford the luxury of passivity. . . . A third objection may stem from disagreement with the substantive claims asserted by public interest firms. If this is the objection, members of a profession committed to the right of all to be heard cannot oppose the mere existence of the public interest firm but could only oppose its substantive arguments in court. . . . A final objection is that of the different nature of the attorney-client relationship in public interest law firms. As the text will indicate, I believe that this objection has merit.

responsibilities. One of the basic ideals of the legal profession is that of public service. While the very need for the public interest firm stems from the failure of the bar to conform to that ideal, the public interest firm may end in killing it. For example, the mere existence of legal aid has allowed many attorneys who previously did free work to now refer that work to legal aid and, with a clear conscience, focus on paying clients. . . . Has the private bar represented people? Clearly not in the area of criminal justice—there the bar has presented only facets of the client's problems. The criminal defendant does not have a "bail problem" or a "plea problem"; he has the problem of surviving the criminal justice system. Yet lawyers routinely part company with their clients at the prison door—what happens inside is "someone else's" problem. Other examples could be given—the divorce lawyer who shrugs when told the police cannot protect his client from physical assaults by her husband and the trial attorney who, while waiting for his case to be called, studiously examines his shoes while the magistrate runs rampant over the rights of an unrepresented defendant.

The danger with the assertion that there are two kinds of legal practice—public interest and private interest—is that the public interest law firm may become the institutionalized conscience of the bar. For the traditional practitioner, justice may become, even more than it is today, "someone else's" problem.

Further, the sign on the door, "Public Interest Law Firm," clouds the basic issues and hence prevents the movement from allocating help on a "greatest need" basis. Loggers, gleefully stripping the forest, are working for a public interest: cheaper operating costs means cheaper lumber, means cheaper houses. Under traditional economic theory (the public good being that which the public is willing to pay for) the loggers may have a stronger claim to the "public interest" than do the ecologists: people are clearly willing to pay for their product.

Quite simply the public interest law movement is the assertion of special interests which are currently slighted or ignored by decision makers in defining the "public interest."[6] This elemental proposition is worth noting. Recognition that public interest law firms are really asserting special interests underscores the fact that there will

---

6. It will be objected that these other interests—interests in the quality of the environment, interests in . . . equality . . . —are essentially political and hence ones which the courts cannot properly handle. This can be best answered by the simple recognition that all judicial and legal decisions are based on political interests as broadly understood. Take, for example, the classic case of a man leaving his watch with a jeweler for repair. The jeweler sells it. Between the owner and the purchaser, who prevails? The decision will turn on the court's conception of which alternative before it will better aid commerce, protecting "title" or protecting "transactions." The goal is pure political theory: it is best to aid commerce because this will create more goods and the public good is served by the creation of more goods. "Public interest" or "other interest" is simply an assertion that other interests, interests in the past not generally asserted, must be taken into account. The traditional job of law is the balance of competing interests. This job will be made more difficult as qualitative, as well as quantitative, demands are made. The job must be done, however. It is the function of law. . . . As the Cahn article suggests, supra note 4, lawyers, and especially the law schools, must work to relieve the pressure on the courts by developing alternative dispute-resolving

be conflicts between public interest firms. The clearest example is the conflict between ecology firms and poverty firms. Insistence on strict conservation measures will raise the cost of low cost housing; curtailment of pollution causing power generation will mean that many poor families will go without heat.

As noted by Jean and Edgar Cahn,[7] there is a more subtle competition between various public interests. The basic thrust of the public interest movement is to represent people who currently do not have legal representatives. Given the fact that legal manpower is a scarce commodity, it should be allocated to those interests which have least chance of success without it. As the politically powerful—the upper and middle classes—cannot escape breathing smog and drinking impure water, the ecology movement can be expected to achieve its goal (if it is achievable at all) politically, without massive legal help. Indeed, the executive and legislative branches of government are expressly designed to respond to majority movements, which the ecology movement is fast becoming. Compare the "political muscle" of the black welfare recipient. Her goals cannot be achieved politically because the majority feels its interests are adverse to hers. Her problems, such as feeding, clothing and sheltering herself and her child . . . do not directly affect the majority. The governmental institution designed to protect the individual from the majority is the judiciary. Quite simply, the fight against poverty cannot be won without attorneys whereas the fight against pollution may be. Hence, under this analysis, the ecology movement, by drawing off legal talent, is adverse to the interests of the black welfare recipient. This should be remembered by law students planning their careers and by practitioners desiring to participate in "public interest" work.

Only one further comment on the sign, "Public Interest Law Firm." What does it tell the public? The traditional sign, "X & Y Law Firm" asserts that either X or Y will handle your case. The public interest firm label, however, adds a qualification—your case will be handled only if it is in the "public interest." The traditional ideal of the attorney is that he is a professional—one who will put aside personal belief in the practice of his skills. The ideal is currently under attack in the law schools where one repeatedly hears students assert that they will never work for a prosecutor or for a huge corporation. Further, it is debatable whether the public ever really believed the image of the lawyer as the nonpolitical technician. Finally, on the basis of the old saying that actions speak louder than words, it can be asserted that lawyers have always represented interests, since the majority has traditionally worked for primarily one interest—the rich and powerful.

Upon analysis, the image proves more of a mirage. Does this mean we disregard it and simply put "Public Interest" or "X Interest" on the door? There is no doubt that the practice of public interest law in such areas as civil rights, poverty and consumer fraud has greatly enhanced the image of the lawyer as the defender of the

---

institutions such as community landlord-tenant courts, and by expanding the pool of legal manpower such as by the use of paraprofessionals.

7. See note 4 supra.

downtrodden, as opposed to that of the mere spokesman for vested interests. But what of the sign or, more basically, the assertion that lawyers represent interests rather than individuals? There are dangers.

To lawyers, the practice of law may mean several things: money, excitement, power to bring social change, the ability to help others. In the current debate among lawyers as to what the practice of law should mean to them, it is easy to forget what it means to the public. To the individual in trouble, a lawyer is often his only hope. From such a person's standpoint, the role of the lawyer is simply to help him, even though the attorney does not agree with him or relate to him. For the members of the public, the bar should be striving to make the old ideal of the "professional" a reality, not casting it aside because it has often proven to be a sham. For practitioners and especially for law students, it must be affirmed that the role of the attorney is not to work out his own political philosophy or even to sleep well at night. It is to help others not as interests, but as individuals. It must be remembered that lawyers have a monopoly and that monopolies have a duty to serve all; to coin a phrase, it's in the "public interest."[9]

Having finally gotten beyond the door of the Public Interest Law Firm, let us continue our tour. Everything seems in order—conference room, library, coffee pot. But still, something seems to be missing. Suddenly, it hits us: "Where are the clients?"

Of course, there will be clients, but not traditional ones. By definition, the public interest law firm begins with a concept of the public interest and fashions its clients around that. This reverses the traditional process where attorneys begin with clients and then fashion a concept of the public interest to correspond to the interests of their clients. This is not to say, as is frequently alleged, that public interest law firms use their clients as pawns. There is enough "lawyer" in public interest practitioners

---

9. The problem of a lawyer as a "mere spokesman" versus a lawyer as an independent actor is an extremely difficult one. At the one extreme, few would defend the proposition that the lawyer must cease to be a moral being and assert any claim his client wishes. . . .

The current reaction against the "mere spokesman" function stems from the belief that attorneys, in the past, have given up their morality to serve their clients. In many areas of law, I feel that the breakdown has occurred for the opposite reasons—the failure of lawyers to vigorously assert their clients' interests. This is clearly true in the area of criminal law where defense counsel have known for years the deplorable conditions of the prisons, but have done relatively nothing about them. What is needed is not a pronouncement that the lawyer should remain a moral being, but rather a pronouncement that lawyers represent people, not just cases. For example, the lawyer's responsibility extends beyond the guilt or innocence stage of a criminal proceeding to the human being whose sole interest is coming out of the criminal system whole.

There is a danger that the pendulum will swing too close to the other extreme, with lawyers, as moral beings, asserting only that with which they agree. It is good to alert practitioners that they cannot hide behind the adversary model. The danger lies in the assertion of this as a governing principle, the result of which will be that lawyers will become judges rather than advocates and the unpopular will find it even more difficult to obtain representation.

to prevent them from sacrificing a client's interests on the altar of the higher good.[10] A more accurate view of public interest clients is that they are "tickets"—without which the firm could not play the law game.

So why should attorneys have clients—shouldn't they just be issued free passes allowing them to play? The question may sound flip, but raised is a fundamental question concerning the role of the courts. Traditionally, courts have existed to keep the peace. A did X to B. If the courts didn't do something about it, A and B might just fight it out in the street. . . .

As the rate of social change increases, the time lag between problem and crisis decreases; to effectively cope with the problem, the courts simply must get involved at an earlier stage. So what's wrong with the "free pass" concept—groups of attorneys deciding, on their own motion, what suits should be filed and what suits vindicated? There are valid interests of society which should be considered in defining the "public good"—should they not be heard simply because they have not been verbalized by a traditional off-the-street client? Surely the magnitude of the conflicting interests in society means that the courts must become more active, must do away with technical standing requirements, case and controversy requirements, and bans against some forms of solicitation. But does this mean we should do away with clients?

Without clients, what are we doing? Without clients, we are setting up a law office that is indistinguishable from a good governmental bureaucracy. A governmental agency, whether concerned with housing, welfare or the environment, brings together diverse experts whose job is to define and implement the "public interest." Those advocating public interest law firms correctly argue that these governmental agencies have often failed. It is, however, ironic that they would adopt, as the means of solution, the governmental model. How are they to succeed where government has failed? Better experts? Bigger hearts?

By viewing clients as tickets rather than as individuals, the lawyer becomes a planner rather than an advocate. The planner begins with a nebulous class, such as blacks, consumers, the poor, and then generalizes and distills the interests of that class, projects goals and finally adopts strategies. The advocate, on the other hand, begins with specific individuals or specific groups within the generalized class (Welfare Rights Association, C.O.R.E., the Black Panthers) and thereafter simply acts as their advocate, allowing them to define their interests, formulate their goals, and adopt methods of achieving them.[13]

---

10. There are problems, however. Even the most careful attorney, in presenting his client alternatives, will favor the one he thinks best. The attorney who begins with a concept of the public interest, as opposed to a commitment to his individual client, cannot help but let his preconception influence the kind of advice he gives the client. The attorney may not even be conscious of this. . . .

13. This does not mean, however, that the advocate representing specific individuals or groups within the generalized class (poor, blacks, consumers) will practice in the same manner as does the traditional practitioner. An attorney representing a group of poor persons, for example, will

The shift from advocacy to planning has been justified on the basis that it is the best way to allocate limited legal manpower; there are just too many blacks, too many poor people, too many consumers to treat them as individuals. To maximize the effectiveness of the limited number of attorneys involved, it is reasoned, they must focus on issues common to the generalized class rather than on problems of individuals or specific groups within the generalized class. This reasoning, for example, leads many legal services programs to reject service cases, such as divorce and bankruptcy, in favor of law reform — a focused attack on statutes which adversely affect the generalized class of poor persons.[14]

While the allocational analysis seems to demand the new role, there are dangers when lawyers become planners rather than advocates. Immediately, there arises the problem of accountability. How can one assume that these new planners truly represent the interests of blacks, consumers or the poor? Moreover, there is the basic problem of planning itself — to the degree that planners make decisions, the individual does not. This, in turn, contributes to the individual's sense that he has less and less control over his life. Perhaps the basic problem of our time, as well as the root cause of many others is precisely this: the individual's growing sense of loss of control, of lack of worth. Finally, there is the issue of the institutionalized role of law and of lawyers. The law is perhaps the only profession capable of protecting the individual in our ever increasingly planned society. While many can plan, only lawyers can protect the rights of the individual in the process.

Once the attorney breaks the moorings of a specific client's interests, how can he be held accountable? How can the attorney be sure of the correctness of his concept of the interests of a generalized class of people such as the poor? Take, for example,

---

behave differently than the attorney representing a corporation: the client's interests, and hence the method of best serving those interests, differ. The attorney-client commitment, however, is the same. Thus, the poverty attorney helps organize groups and may engage in "direct action" such as picketing. For the details of such a practice, see Wexler, "Practicing Law for Poor People," 79 Yale L.J. 1049 (1970).

14. At the other extreme from law reform there are those legal aid offices which, realizing that they do not have adequate legal manpower to serve all potential clients, attempt to stretch that manpower by offering the poor a watered down form of service. For example, many legal aid attorneys have open caseloads numbering in the hundreds; their clients cannot help but receive inadequate legal representation. This is grossly unjust to the client and to the attorney — a young attorney, given such a caseload, cannot help but develop habits which will likely prevent him from becoming truly competent. The argument for taking more cases than one can properly handle is powerful: "Look, I'm the only attorney who will help these people. They need help desperately. Something is better than nothing." Upon analysis, however, "something" proves worse than "nothing." That something means that all the clients receive less than they are entitled. Further, that something deludes the poor into believing that the "system" is protecting their legal rights. Obviously, the system is not . . . guaranteeing "equal justice under law." Those committed to the poor should not conceal this from them: glossing over injustice, even in the best of motives, perpetuates it. Legal aid attorneys must realize that it is not their fault that many go without legal assistance. They should not assume the responsibility and feel compelled to help everyone. It is unfair both to the attorney and the client and it is counter-productive to the proper solution of the ultimate problem.

Shapiro v. Thompson,[15] the successful culmination of the attack on welfare residency laws. Does that decision further the interest of the poor? It undoubtedly helps many poor—those wishing to move to another state. It may, however, also harm others [who] if there is a great influx of recipients in those states may find their benefits reduced and their state taxes increased.

To cope with the accountability problem, many legal services programs and public interest law firms have created advisory bodies composed of representatives of the client community. Whether such bodies can achieve accountability is questionable. There is the danger that such lay bodies will be consciously or unconsciously manipulated by professional staff which has its own concept of its function: law reform versus servile work. Further, there is the problem of just how representative the representatives are. Initial selection will tend to favor the more militant—those who have already taken on a "spokesman's" role. Even if selected in a manner to assure representativeness, they may quickly become an elite group, identifying more closely with the interests of the public interest firm than with those of their theoretical constituents.

It should be remembered that a major professed goal of public interest firms is to make government accountable to the individual. By adopting the governmental model of planning for generalized classes of individuals, however, the public interest firms may themselves become unaccountable to their "clients." If they do, all that has been accomplished is to subject the individual to the whims of yet another group of professionals. Nevertheless, even if a mechanism could be devised to assure that the attorney-planner was truly planning to achieve the best interests of the generalized group, the fundamental question remains whether the basic problem of our society has been inadequate planning or too much planning.

Our society has grown more complex; so too has our reliance on experts. When faced with a difficult problem, we turn to those who gave us penicillin and radar. Given our apparent inability to solve our critical problems—racism, pollution, poverty—it is tempting to conclude that there are simply not enough experts working on them or that those who are on the wrong side. This appears to be the conclusion of the public interest law movement. Its thrust is to create groups of "counter-experts" who will be plugged into decision-making bodies. From heated yet scholarly debate (outsiders cannot be expected to understand their jargon), the true "public interest" will emerge—Joe's, yours, mine. In the pitched battle between urbanologist and ecologist, the insistence on clients seems rather picayunish—what, after all, do they know? . . .

This tension between "expert" decision making and individual decision making is more acute for the lawyer attempting to define his proper role than it is for other professionals. The institution of law is probably the only one capable of protecting the individual in the planned society. There are simply enough

---

15. 394 U.S. 618 (1969).

experts and planners deciding the greatest good for the greatest number; once lawyers start playing that game, the individual suffers the hazard of escalating dehumanization.

The law has a unique role to play in society—the protection of the rights of the individual *against* the greatest good for the greatest number. Jerome Carlin provides an extremely helpful analysis.[21] There are, he believes, two models of justice, the adversary model and the welfare model. Under the adversary concept, individuals are deemed to have rights against each other and against the state. Not so under the welfare concept which recognizes no conflict between the interests of the individual and those of the state. Hence the state is free, even required, to control the individual for his own best interest. Typically, the welfare model is employed when dealing with the poor, as in the juvenile court where the judge does not act as referee between two competing interests, but rather adopts the role of parent to the child, looking to his needs rather than to his rights. Given the non-adversary framework, it is not surprising to find a loosening of procedural guarantees and the seed of total government control.

Public interest firms, viewing clients as tickets rather than as individuals, tend to adopt the welfare model. The question becomes "What are the needs of blacks?" rather than "What are the rights of this specific black man?" There are many experts asking the first question; lawyers are the only ones capable of asking the second. In a planned society, the law must not forget its fundamental mission: protecting the individual as the possessor of given rights, rights which he can assert even if not in the best interests of society; indeed, even if not in his own best interest.

Notes

1. Do you agree with Professor Hegland's vision of the "public interest," particularly as discussed in his article at footnote 9? Compare his vision with those that follow.

2. Since this article was written in the early 1970s, public interest law has expanded dramatically. Consider the following assessment based on a study of 51 public interest organizations conducted by Professor Deborah Rhode:

> The public interest legal movement at midlife has much to celebrate. It has increased dramatically in numbers, scale and scope. . . . Thirty years ago, only ten percent of the nation's public interest organizations had budgets that, adjusted for inflation, come close to the norm of today's organizations. Fewer still had leadership with the experience, expertise, or strategic vision now common in the field.
>
> The movement's strength is also reflected in its concrete achievements. . . . The movement has changed not just law but "lawyers' approach to the law." By representing causes as well as clients, public interest organizations have made

---

21. J. Carlin, J. Howard & S. Messinger, *Civil Justice and the Poor* 24–34 (1966).

clear the capacity of legal strategies in promoting social change. Law reform has been both an end in itself and a vehicle for raising public awareness, mobilizing political support, and giving communities a voice in the policies that affect them. In virtually every major American social reform movement of the last half century, cause lawyers have played an important role.

Yet as public interest legal organizations have grown in size and scale, so too have most of the problems they seek to address[,] . . . far outpac[ing] legal resources.

Further challenges arise from the growing conservatism of the courts and the public on many issues involving social justice and judicial remedies. In this climate, the limits of litigation have become pronounced. . . .

In the face of these pressures, lawyers committed to social causes have grown more strategic, proactive, and collaborative. They are less reliant on litigation, and more innovative in their use of multiple legal, political and educational approaches. Coalitions with grassroots, governmental, and other public interest organizations have become increasingly common and effective. The same is true of partnerships with pro bono counsel. Although these relationships are not always free from difficulty, they have enabled most organizations to greatly expand their resources, influence, and credibility.

Deborah H. Rhode, "Public Interest Law: The Movement at Midlife," 60 Stan. L. Rev. 2027, 2075–2076 (2008).

Although Professor Rhode's assessment of the state of public interest law is primarily positive, do you see any potential dangers with the picture she describes? For example, are there any potential ethical implications of public interest law firms moving away from traditional impact litigation toward "strategic" and "proactive" measures outside of the courts? Are there any risks to public interest organizations — or the clients they represent — of forming more "collaborative" working relationships with private law firms? Professor Rhode reports that some public interest organizations complained that some of the law firms with whom they partnered had "very aggressive public relations departments" which sought to take all of the credit for the matter, id., at 2071. Might such actions undermine the ability of public interest organizations to raise money or recruit lawyers? More generally, is there a danger that public interest organizations will grow too dependent on the resources of private law firms? Could this prove problematic in times of economic downturn?

3. What does it mean that the public interest law movement "has changed not just law but 'lawyers' approach to law'"? Once again, although Professor Rhode intends this as a compliment, are there any dangers inherent in encouraging all lawyers to approach legal practice like traditional public interest lawyers? Is there a danger that lawyers for corporate interests have absorbed too many of the lessons of public interest law by engaging in "grassroots mobilization" in the form of sophisticated marketing campaigns to promote corporate interests, and "impact" litigation

in the form of "SLAPP" (Strategic Lawsuit Against Public Participation) suits designed to quell opposition before it starts? For an argument that corporations are seeking to both hijack and silence the public interest movement, see George W. Pring and Penelope Canan, *SLAPPs: Getting Sued for Speaking Out* (1996); Ralph Nader and Wesley J. Smith, *No Contest: Corporate Lawyers and the Perversion of Justice in America* (2006).

4. Another manifestation of the growing convergence of "public interest" and "private practice" is the growing number of "private public interest" law firms. As Scott Cummings and Ann Southworth argue: "The private public interest law firm has emerged as a practice site that attempts to marry 'profit and principle' on very different economic and political terms than the large commercial law firm — providing an alternative way for lawyers to pursue public ends through private means that challenges the conventional pro bono model." See Scott L. Cummings and Ann Southworth, "Between Profit and Principle: The Private Public Interest Law Firm," in *Private Lawyers and the Public Interest: The Evolving Role of Pro Bono in Legal Education* 183 (2009). Although the authors concede that there is no definitive database of such firms, the authors report that searching the "Law Firm-Public Interest Focus/Practice" database on a popular public interest web site uncovered 464 firms nationwide that were pursuing this model, "with 187 in California, and only 117 in New York, Massachusetts, and Washington, D.C. collectively." Id., at 20.

5. Indeed, has the "public interest" movement itself been captured by those who initially opposed its goals? Although most commentators speak about "public interest" law as if it is comprised exclusively of organizations on the political left, the most important growth in the public interest law community in the last decade has been among organizations affiliated with the political right. As Ann Southworth points out, "conservative and libertarian legal advocacy organizations now rival their liberal counterparts in size and resources." See Ann Southworth, *Lawyers of the Right: Professionalizing the Conservative Coalition* 35 (2008). As Southworth goes on to note, these conservative organizations have attained this status by mimicking — and then exceeding — the techniques invented by the traditional organizations on the political left:

> Some methods used by conservative public interest law groups to identify and recruit clients and to shape public opinion make liberal groups' outreach and public education strategies look narrow and modest. Jay Sekulow, for example, finds new cases for the American Center for Law and Justice through his radio show *Jay Sekulow Live!* Michael Farris, chairman of the Home School Legal Defense Association, teaches an online high school-level constitutional law course, whose required text is his own *Constitutional Law for Christian Students* . . . .
>
> Conservative and libertarian public interest law groups also have expanded the cooperating attorney model pioneered by the ACLU. The Institute for

Justice holds seminars on public interest litigation for hundreds of students, policy activists, and lawyers, and it invites graduates of these programs to join its "Human Action Network." ADF [Alliance Defense Fund] runs week long training programs—"National Litigation Academies"—to "train a generation of attorneys" to "restore America's legal system . . . ." Each lawyer who attends the academy commits to provide 450 hours of pro bono legal work "on behalf of the Body of Christ." As of August 2007, one thousand lawyers had graduated from twenty-eight of these training sessions and contributed $70 million worth of pro bono legal services.

Id., at 34. As Southworth concludes: "The creation of conservative legal advocacy groups to compete with liberal public interest law groups has eliminated the equation between public interest law and liberal politics and dramatically increased the number and diversity of nonprofit organizations that seek to influence public policy making." Id., at 32.

6. As contested as the domain of "public interest law" has become in the U.S. context, it is likely to be even more so as the movement goes global. As Scott Cummings and Louise Trubek document, "public interest law has been pulled from its American roots, becoming a crucial element of building Rule of Law systems in developing and transitional countries—thus tying public interest law more closely to the concept of economic development and incorporating it into pre-existing activist networks organized around human rights." Scott L. Cummings and Louise G. Trubek, "Globalizing Public Interest Law," 13 U.C.L.A. J. Int'l L. & For. Aff. 1, 6 (2008). At the same time, the fact that these projects have been funded by global institutions such as the World Bank and the United Nations has created a "distinct global role for public interest law, which is integrated into transnational campaigns that seek to hold international finance and trade institutions accountable for their distributional impacts, challenge the deregulation of global markets through multi-level advocacy efforts, and leverage the power of the human rights system to strengthen domestic social justice movements and build transnational solidarity." Id. The result, Cummings and Trubek argue, is that public interest law is emerging as both a global institution and a process for negotiating global governance. How the various local and transnational constituencies will shape these two dimensions will determine whether public interest lawyers of the kind who have proven so influential in the American context play a similar role on the world stage.

———————

Should public interest lawyers have different conflict of interest rules from those that apply to "private" lawyers? Does your answer depend upon whether we are thinking about traditional issues relating to the simultaneous or successive representation of clients with conflicting interests or to so-called "positional" conflicts that arise when a lawyer represents a client who advocates positions on legal or factual questions that conflict with the interests or goals of one of the lawyer's other clients? In the context of public interest representation, is it harder to tell the difference between these two kinds of conflicts than it is in other areas?

The case discussed in Professor Wilkins' excerpt in Chapter 7 involving a black lawyer who agreed to represent the Ku Klux Klan in its efforts to resist a government request for the Klan's membership list provides an interesting window into these questions. As Professor Wilkins notes, at the time Anthony Griffin agreed to represent the Klan, he was also the unpaid general counsel of the Port Arthur Branch of the NAACP. When NAACP officials discovered that Griffin was defending the Klan, they demanded that he resign from that representation. When he refused, the head of the Port Arthur Branch dismissed him from his position as general counsel.

NAACP officials might offer two distinct justifications for their decision to fire Griffin. The first would be grounded in the substantive claim that it was morally wrong for Griffin to represent the Klan and therefore he was not fit to serve as the civil rights organization's general counsel. The second sounds in process and professional ethics. The claim would be that it was wrong for Griffin to represent the Klan *at the same time* that he was representing the NAACP. Because he was unwilling to resign from the former representation, the NAACP was justified in removing him as their lawyer. Both arguments have important implications for the ethics of public interest lawyers.

The first argument equates *representing* the Klan with *joining* the Klan—an action that no person should take even if we are unprepared to ban Klan activity altogether. The logic of this position not only supports the NAACP's decision to fire Griffin from his position as General Counsel, but would also justify his expulsion from the organization as well. Someone who is the equivalent of a Klan member should be shunned by people of good will everywhere and certainly has no place in an organization devoted to championing the rights of black Americans.

How persuasive do you find this claim? Griffin argued that his decision to represent the Klan was perfectly consistent with the NAACP's commitment to racial justice. Thus, Griffin repeatedly pointed out that the legal principle he was defending—that the First Amendment protects membership lists from government scrutiny—was first established by the Supreme Court in a case involving the NAACP's efforts to keep *its* membership list confidential. See NAACP v. Alabama, 357 U.S. 449 (1958). NAACP officials countered that the Klan ought not to be entitled to the protection afforded by this case because the Klan, unlike the NAACP, is nothing more than a terrorist organization with a demonstrated history of violence and intimidation—a distinction, the NAACP argued, that was expressly recognized when the court in NAACP v. Alabama approved a prior Supreme Court decision that relied on the Klan's violent history to justify a New York statute requiring the Klan to disclose its membership list to state authorities. See Bryant v. Zimmerman, 278 U.S. 63 (1928). Regardless of whether NAACP officials ultimately have the right to reject Griffin's claims about what is best for the organization, do those who run public interest organizations committed to producing social change through law have something like an ethical duty to at least consider legal arguments in favor of pursuing a course different from the one the organization's leadership currently favors?

NAACP officials might assert that the previous arguments are irrelevant because Griffin was not fired for his dissenting views. Instead, officials might claim, he was fired because he was simultaneously representing the Klan and the NAACP. Is this the kind of simultaneous representation that is—or should be—prohibited by the conflict rules? If so, what is the exact nature of conflict of interest? Did Griffin violate Rule 1.7 when he agreed to represent the Klan? Are there additional facts about the case that you would need to know in order to answer this question? If there is a violation of Rule 1.7, is it likely to be one that falls under 1.7(a) or 1.7(b)? If neither provision has clearly been violated, is there nevertheless an argument that Griffin's dual representation of the Klan and the NAACP implicates important conflict of interests concerns? If so, what is the nature of these concerns and what weight should they be given by NAACP officials? Is there an argument that public interest lawyers should be held to stricter standards about representing clients with conflicting, but arguably not "directly adverse," interests than lawyers engaged in commercial practice? Is there something about public interest practice that makes so-called positional conflicts more problematic here than in other areas? Would your assessment of the NAACP's actions be the same if Griffin were simply one of many lawyers who volunteer to take cases for the NAACP from time to time as opposed to the organization's "general counsel"?

More generally, do (or should) public interest lawyers understand their ethical responsibilities—to clients, adversaries, the legal system, or to each other—in ways that differ from the understanding of their peers in "private" practice? Consider the following account of the professional ideology of "cause lawyers" based on a study of lawyers who specialize in representing death row inmates in appellate and post-conviction proceedings:

> Cause lawyers use their professional skills to move law away from the daily reality of violence and toward a particular vision of the Good. For them, the Good is known in the causes for which they work even as its realization may be deferred. It is their work to give content to the "impossibility" of Justice. In so doing, they reject what David Luban calls "the principle of professional nonaccountability," namely the view that a lawyer is "responsible neither for the means used nor the ends achieved in legal representation." Cause lawyers refuse to use their skills indiscriminately, to be the "hired gun" of anyone able to pay for their services. They also reject the alternative role of the "lawyer-statesman" because it is elitist and disconnected from any conception of substantive justice. Instead, they self-consciously politicize their professional lives, and make lawyering a vocation of Justice rather than technique, of moral engagement rather than moral neutrality.

Austin Sarat, "Between (the Presence of) Violence and (the Possibility of) Justice: Lawyering Against Capital Punishment," in *Cause Lawyering: Political Commitments and Professional Responsibilities* 318–319 (Austin Sarat and Stuart Scheingold, eds. 1998).

In his book, *The Lost Lawyer* (1993), Dean Anthony Kronman put forth the ideal of the "lawyer-statesman" and asserted that this ideal was—and should be—the essence of lawyer professionalism. For the moment, consider the conflicting implications that the existence of a group of lawyers who reject any vision of lawyering that is not directly connected to ideas about substantive justice creates for the bar's traditional account of lawyer professionalism. On the one hand, cause lawyers are tangible proof that the legal profession is committed to ideals that go beyond the "hired gun" imagery that frequently dogs the profession. At the same time, these lawyers also pose a constant challenge to the traditional understanding that lawyers should be, as Professor Pepper argued in Chapter 3, "amoral" advocates whose moral worth lies solely in facilitating their clients' autonomy. See p. 123. Does this tension help to explain why cause lawyers are both venerated in professional lore and after-dinner speeches while at the same time perpetually marginalized and underfunded within the bar? Does it help to explain the constant tension between "public interest" students and their classmates in law schools? Are any of these issues likely to affect who becomes a public interest lawyer and what role such lawyers will play in the legal profession and in society more generally? For an excellent collection of essays about the ideals, practices, and professional ideology of cause lawyers in the United States and elsewhere around the world, see Southworth, *Lawyers of the Right*, p. 762, Note 5.

Finally, given the unique and passionate commitment of lawyers who consider themselves "cause lawyers," are there likely to be important differences in the manner in which these lawyers and other members of the private bar represent similar clients in similar cases? Recall Professor Derrick Bell's criticism of the actions of NAACP lawyers in school desegregation cases. See p. 336, Notes 1 and 2. Although Professor Bell underscores the danger that a cause lawyer's passionate commitment might cause him to ignore his client's true interests, are there ways in which having an advocate who is committed to a particular vision of substantive justice might also lead to better service for the client than if the same person were represented by an equally competent private lawyer who subscribed to Professor Pepper's amoral vision of lawyering? For an informative study of the differing approaches to lawyer/client decisionmaking taken by full-time civil rights lawyers, lawyers working in a law school clinic, and private practitioners working pro bono, see Ann Southworth, "Lawyer-Client Decisionmaking in Civil Rights and Poverty Practice: An Empirical Study of Lawyers' Norms," 9 Geo. J. Legal Ethics 1 (1996).

The following Problem and accompanying materials raise additional questions about pro bono representation by the private bar.

Problem 9–5

Law Firm has nearly decided that it is going to become general counsel to a cigarette manufacturer when it discovers that on her own time, Associate (with firm knowledge) has been doing pro bono legal work for the Citizens' Lobby Against Smoking and through that connection is assisting in a lawsuit brought by a lung cancer victim against the cigarette manufacturer. Must Law Firm decline the position of general counsel? If Associate ceases to work on the case, may the firm accept the representation? Suppose that instead of doing legal work for the Lobby, Associate was president of the organization? Should the combination of Rule 1.7(b) and Rule 1.10(a) of the Model Rules preclude Law Firm from accepting the position of general counsel?

The private bar has been seen by many as an important source of public interest support. Indeed, as we have seen, the Reagan administration saw the private bar as capable of replacing in substantial part the programs funded by the Legal Services Corporation. Starting in the middle of the 1970s, important parts of the organized bar have sought to make pro bono services by lawyers into a mandatory obligation.

There has been fairly general agreement that lawyers ought to feel a professional obligation on an individual basis to render pro bono service. The struggle has been over proposals that would require it. The arguments for mandatory service have stressed the effect of the inability of so many to use the justice system and the obligation of service owed by professionals with state-granted privileges. The arguments against mandatory service have centered on the undesirability of singling out lawyers for compulsory service and the difficulty and inefficiency in a time of growing specialization of forcing lawyers with no experience in poverty practice to engage in it on a very partial basis.

The House of Delegates of the American Bar Association in 1975 voted a resolution stating that "it is a basic professional responsibility of each lawyer to provide public interest services." The resolution went on to define public interest services as falling into the areas of poverty law, civil rights law, public rights law, charitable organization representation, and activity improving the administration of justice. The report accompanying the resolution suggested the provision of 5%–10% of billable time but then modified the notion of individual responsibility by suggesting not only that a law firm might meet its obligation on a group basis but also that a financial substitute for service might also be considered.

Responding to that proposal, a Special Committee of the Association of the Bar of the City of New York on the Lawyer's Pro Bono Obligations recommended a general minimum contribution by lawyers on a mandatory basis, with some flexibility for individual exemptions, of 30 to 50 hours of service per year, with the potential for later increase to a 40 to 60 or 50 to 70 range. Shortly thereafter early drafts of the Kutak Commission's Model Rules of Professional Responsibility contained mandatory pro bono requirements in a series of differing proposals, one of which stated a 40-hour minimum, and others of which contained a financial alternative, reporting requirements, and a variety of definitions of pro bono service.

These proposals provoked enormous controversy and opposition. The result was that first the Executive Committee of the Association of the Bar of the City of New York rejected, in part, its Committee's proposal. It proposed an ethical obligation, backed not by disciplinary sanctions or reporting but by self-evaluations, that could be satisfied with a financial contribution. Subsequently, the Kutak Commission retreated to a position now set forth in Model Rule 6.1 that states the lawyer's responsibility in the aspirational sense of "should" rather than the disciplinary rule sense of "shall." A thorough analysis of the history of pro bono "requirements," and the constitutional, economic, and policy considerations related thereto is contained in David Shapiro, "The Enigma of the Lawyer's Duty to Serve," 55 N.Y.U. L. Rev. 735 (1980). He concludes that the position embodied in the Model Rules with respect to the general principle of pro bono service is about right. Others disagree. See, e.g., David Luban, *Lawyers and Justice: An Ethical Study* 277–289 (1988).

A number of courts, however, including courts in El Paso, Texas; Westchester County, New York; and the federal district court in eight districts in Arkansas, Illinois, Iowa, and Texas adopted mandatory programs requiring pro bono service in civil cases, and so has the California Supreme Court, on an ad hoc basis. See Payne v. Superior Court, 17 Cal. 3d 908 (1976). Bar associations in counties in Florida, Texas, Illinois, and Wisconsin have also imposed similar requirements on their members. At the same time, however, some courts have held that it is unconstitutional under both federal and state constitutions to order lawyers to represent indigents, even in criminal cases, without providing adequate compensation. E.g., State ex rel. Stephan v. Smith, 242 Kan. 336 (1987) (collecting numerous cases). The issues for all lawyers are how much of a commitment to pro bono work they are willing and able to make, how they will define pro bono work, whether they favor imposing a mandatory pro bono requirement on all lawyers, and if so, on what terms. These continue to be important questions, but no state has yet imposed a requirement of mandatory annual pro bono service on its lawyers. Florida has instituted a mandatory annual reporting requirement of pro bono services performed, and in many states pro bono assignments are made by courts in particular cases on an ad hoc basis. See, e.g., Madden v. Delran, 126 N.J. 591 (1992), spelling out New Jersey's assignment system. As of 2017, New York requires 50 hours of pro bono service as a condition for bar applicants to become licensed. See Section 520.16(a) of New York's Rules of the Court of Appeals for the Admission of Attorneys and Counselors at Law.

Regardless of whether one favors mandatory pro bono service, however, the fact remains that relatively few lawyers come close to meeting the Model Rules' aspirational requirement of rendering "at least 50 hours of pro bono publico legal services a year" primarily "to persons of limited means or to organizations assisting such persons." Model Rule 6.1. Deborah Rhode's summary in 2000 is still relevant:

> [A]bout half of attorneys perform no pro bono work and the average contribution is less than half an hour a week. Much of the uncompensated assistance that lawyers do goes not to low-income clients but to family, friends, clients who fail to pay their fees, and middle-class organizations like hospitals and schools that might become paying clients. Involvement in public interest and poverty law programs remains minimal at many of the nation's leading law firms and in-house corporate counsel's offices. Only about a third of the nation's five hundred largest firms have agreed to participate in the ABA Pro Bono Challenge, which requires a minimum annual contribution of 3 percent of the firm's total billable hours. Attorneys at these firms often would like to pursue such work but are deterred by policies that fail to count pro bono activity toward billable hour requirements or to value it in promotion and compensation decisions.

Deborah L. Rhode, *In the Interest of Justice: Reforming the Legal Profession* 37 (2000).

Notwithstanding these numbers, pro bono has become a crucial part of the way that legal services are delivered to those who could not otherwise afford them. Equally as important, the manner in which these services are delivered by law firms has also changed dramatically since 2000. The following excerpt explains these important changes.

Scott L. Cummings
The Politics of Pro Bono
52 U.C.L.A. L. Rev. 1 (2004)

The dominant narrative of pro bono over the past decade was one of a professional ideal under siege. Particularly as law firms experienced fantastic growth in the late 1990s, lawyers became subject to market pressures that placed strains on their capacity to engage in pro bono service. The dot-com boom created a market bubble at the nation's biggest law firms, where spiraling profits were met by increasing billable hour demands. Pro bono suffered under the new law firm economics, as lawyers sacrificed public service in the name of ballooning salaries and bigger year-end bonuses. Even as the blistering pace of Internet deal-making screeched to a halt and volunteerism was resurrected in the new millennium, pro bono failed to regain its previous standing, as associates fearful of looming lay-offs were reluctant to appear too consumed with non-billable work. The professional elite condemned pro bono's retrenchment in the face of law firm commercialization, giving official sanction to the discourse of pro bono's decline.

Yet all the fervor over pro bono's plight seemed disconnected from the bigger picture of professional service. Although American lawyers had always provided some services for free, they were never generous in their gratuity, which often simply involved helping out friends, relatives, and groups such as the local church, Little League, or opera. In fact, the very concept of "pro bono"—understood as a professional duty, discharged outside the normal course of billable practice, to provide free services to persons of limited means or to clients seeking to advance the public interest—did not exist until quite recently. Service to the individual poor client had historically been treated as charity to be dispensed by organizations like legal aid, while the free representation of public interest groups was sporadic and controversial. Indeed, it was not until the 1980s that the profession's ethical rules even referred to the term "pro bono" in discussing a lawyer's public service responsibility.

Behind the headlines and hand-wringing over decreasing big-firm pro bono, a much more important story was in fact taking shape—one which was transforming the nation's system for delivering free legal services to poor and underserved clients. The defining feature of the 1990s' boom was not that private lawyers were prioritizing profit over pro bono service. This had, to some degree, always been the case. Instead, the real story was the radical change taking place in *how pro bono services were being dispensed*. Whereas pro bono had traditionally been provided *informally*—frequently by solo and small firm practitioners who conferred free services as a matter of individual largesse—by the end of the 1990s pro bono was regimented and organized, distributed through a network of structures designed to facilitate the mass provision of free services by law firm volunteers acting out of professional duty.

This transformation was apparent at multiple levels. The American Bar Association campaigned to make "pro bono a priority," revising the ethical rules on pro bono service, challenging the nation's biggest law firms to step up their pro bono commitments, and supporting the development of a pro bono infrastructure in nonprofit groups, law firms, and law schools. Local bar associations, public interest organizations, and legal services groups expanded programs designed to link unrepresented clients with pro bono volunteers. Big law firms, in turn, augmented their own pro bono systems, creating new pro bono positions, developing innovative projects, and sending their associates to staff public interest organizations and poverty law clinics. Private foundations turned their attention to funding pro bono programs, new ranking systems emerged to track pro bono performance, and states experimented with pro bono reporting requirements. As pro bono infiltrated corporate legal departments and business law practice groups, penetrated small-town communities, and shot across national borders, its transformation could not be ignored. Once confined to the margins of professional practice, pro bono had become radically *institutionalized*, emerging as the dominant model of delivering free legal services. Viewed in this light, the loud outcry over declining pro bono in the 1990s did not miss the point of pro bono's institutional ascendance, but rather constituted its central expression reflecting the power of newly formed pro bono constituencies to promote their agenda and protect their institutional investments.

———————

Assessing the consequences of this dramatic shift is a difficult task and depends to some degree on one's vantage point. The power of pro bono as a way of mobilizing large amounts of resources to help those in need is undeniable. The response of the New York City bar in the aftermath of 9/11 is a case in point, providing a microcosm of the vitality and flexibility of the new pro bono system. In its report on the legal community's response to the 9/11 attacks, the New York City Bar Association described the huge need for help as over 4000 individuals and families struggled to arrange funerals and burials, apply for aid, administer estates, find new homes and jobs, and deal with a range of other issues stemming from the disaster.

To respond to the crisis, the City Bar convened a meeting with leaders from pro bono programs such as Volunteers of Legal Service and the Lawyers Alliance, public interest and legal services groups, probono.net, and other legal organizations. The outcome of the meeting was the development of a "coordinated and collaborative [response] among all [the legal community's] elements, including the courts, bar associations, legal service organizations, the private bar, in-house counsel, government attorneys, and law schools."

The centerpiece was the creation of the "Facilitator Project," which provided clients with an individual lawyer to give comprehensive, ongoing representation on all legal issues arising from 9/11. To launch this project, a meeting was arranged by the City Bar at the law office of Chadbourne & Park, which was attended by major partners from all the city's big firms, as well as prominent in-house counsel. All agreed to designate a "September 11 Coordinator" to organize attorneys within their firms and corporations, and to serve as a liaison with the City Bar. Two firm attorneys were assigned as "case managers" at the City Bar to implement the Facilitator Project, which commenced a comprehensive training program on topics such as death certificates, probate, public aid, unemployment assistance, life insurance, retirement benefits, family law, personal finance, tax, immigration, and landlord-tenant issues. More than 800 lawyers took the facilitator training course, in which they learned how to "conduct a legal inventory, prioritize the client/family's needs, act as a problem solver to represent or refer the client in an exemplary and expeditious manner, and find other experts to assist with special legal needs." In meeting the needs, law firms provided the most volunteers, drawing upon preexisting pro bono structures and combining their resources to develop "economies and efficiencies in their representations." Technology was key, as probono.net provided document storage and interactive messaging, while the City Bar used a web-based case referral system. In addition, firms developed a range of written material like the "Helping Handbook— Legal Resources for Families of Victims of the World Trade Center Disaster," to assist Facilitators in their charge. The City Bar trumpeted the spirit of stakeholder collaboration and deemed the project an extraordinary success, providing "a comprehensive textbook on how best to deliver pro bono services!"

However, the reach of pro bono only goes so far. Indeed, what is striking about the 9/11 example is not just the power of professional service, but also the narrowness of its scope. There, the focus was on brief service, referrals, and individual representation in areas where firms had little at stake from a business perspective. To underscore this, the City Bar crafted an engagement letter for the Facilitator Project "that defined the scope of the representation to allow law firms to represent 9/11 clients on a range of issues, while simultaneously limiting representation for tort claims and giving the individual client fair notice of that limitation." Thus, while law firms diligently assisted individuals and families probating estates and applying for public benefits, they ruled out the prospect of litigation against possible business targets.

A similar story emerged in New York City's civil lawsuit against the gun industry alleging that its marketing and distribution practices fostered an illegal market in firearms. To match the gun industry's muscle, the City retained New York heavyweight firm Weil, Gotshal & Manges to represent it on a pro bono basis. However, after more than two years of work, the law firm withdrew on the eve of trial in 2004, citing "positional conflicts." Apparently, a Smith & Wesson lawyer contacted a corporate client of Weil, Gotshal, & Manges, who immediately "raised questions . . . about whether the gun case might lead to precedents that could later be used against them. With the gun case heating up . . . the Weil, Gotshal lawyers privately told the city's lawyers that they could no longer continue to work on the case." New York Times, April 17, 2004.

Of course, most pro bono cases are not so dramatic. Outside of this type of conflict, private lawyers do a tremendous service representing individual poor clients in routine matters and lending their institutional resources to support the reform agendas of public interest groups. Their volunteer work ranges from the mundane to the transformative and includes matters of intense personal interest and immense social import. But the central dilemma of pro bono remains: A system that depends on private lawyers is ultimately beholden to their interests. This means not just that private lawyers will avoid categories of cases that threaten client interests, but also that they will take on pro bono cases for institutional reasons that are disconnected from the interests of the poor and underserved—and often contrary to them. This is most apparent in the use of pro bono for law firm associate training: Associates who gain skills in the volunteer context spend most of their time using them to vigorously advocate against the interests served through pro bono representation. In so doing, they become zealous partisans for corporate clients—defending them from tort claims, consumer suits, employment and labor grievances, and environmental challenges. The time they spend engaged in pro bono work provides a respite from this world, but does not change it.

There are other drawbacks to the pro bono system. Pro bono lawyers do not invest heavily in gaining substantive expertise, getting to know the broader public interest field, or understanding the long-range goals of client groups. Particularly in contrast to the way big-firm lawyers seek to understand and vigorously advance the goals of their client community, the partiality and narrowness of pro bono representation is striking. And the disparity of the resources devoted to billable versus pro bono work—which, even at the most generous firm, rarely constitutes more than 5 percent of total hours—underscores the vast inequality in legal services that persists. Indeed, there are no parallel resources available to press the interests of marginalized social groups. Legal services are too restricted and nonprofit groups are too financially constrained. This is not accidental. Opponents of the reformist agenda of legal services have championed pro bono as an acceptable alternative, knowing that it does not pose the threat to business interests that an unrestricted legal services program would. Marginalized groups, then, are left to depend heavily on volunteer efforts to respond to their needs—a fact that distinguishes them from all of their adversaries, who spend lavishly to purchase the best legal counsel money can buy.

The story of pro bono is still being written. As trends of privatization, volunteerism, and globalization press forward, one can expect pro bono to be a growth industry in the years to come, not simply shaping the American system of free legal services, but informing the discussion about equal access to justice around the world. Questions about pro bono's effectiveness as a model for meeting the legal needs of poor and underserved groups will therefore take center stage. It is important that the advantages of pro bono—its decentralized structure, collaborative relationships, pragmatic alliances, and flexible approaches—receive full attention. Yet these advantages must be carefully weighed against the systemic challenges that pro bono poses: its refusal to take on corporate practice and its dilettantish approach to advancing the interests of marginalized groups. Instead of professional platitudes about the virtues of volunteerism, robust debate is therefore in order—debate that includes a full airing of both the promise and perils of pro bono, and provides a rigorous account of what equal access to justice looks like in practice. To avoid this debate invites the uncritical expansion of pro bono as a stop-gap measure rather than a thoughtful response to the dilemma of unequal legal representation. More fundamentally, the failure to confront pro bono's limitations risks privileging professional interests over concerns of social justice—promoting the image of equal access without the reality.

Jeanne Charn & Richard Zorza
Civil Legal Assistance for All Americans
Bellow-Sacks Access to Civil Legal Services Project
pp. 14–17, 18, 19–23 (2005)

A. Re-imagining the Access to Justice Agenda

Envisioning a new access to justice agenda in the United States requires us to challenge some commonly held views about the nature of the access problem. Free of these constricting and untenable assumptions, we will be in a position to design a functional system that affords Americans full access to legal advice and assistance. Specifically, we challenge the following five truisms:

Assumption 1: Money Alone Will Produce Access

We have been too quick to assume that all we need is money to solve the access problem. No doubt we need more resources, but we cannot insist on universal access at any cost regardless of the size of the ultimate bill. We cannot view concerns with cost constraints or cost effectiveness as antithetical to access ideals. Rather, we should embrace the concept of assuring value for every dollar spent as a core principle, and view *how much we have* as no more important than *how we use what we have*.

Assumption 2: Money Is the Only Barrier to Access

From the perspective of consumers of legal services, common sense as well as international and U.S. studies tell us that people face many non-financial barriers in accessing legal services. These barriers range from language and mobility problems to a shortage of lawyers, for pay or otherwise, in many rural areas. Other subtle but nonetheless significant barriers exist as well. These include consumer doubt that legal help would "make a difference," concerns about losing control over a problem, lack of understanding of how to use legal services, unwillingness to assert claims in an adversarial way and mistrust of lawyers and the legal system. Money alone will not address these barriers. We must invest in understanding how ordinary Americans recognize and deal with legal problems, what types of help they find most useful, including less adversarial help, and we must design gateways to legal assistance that consumers recognize and find easy to use.

Assumption 3: All Legal Needs Are Equal

We often do not differentiate among legal needs. It has become conventional in the United States to conduct studies to demonstrate the extent of unmet needs experienced by low- and moderate-income Americans. These studies usually take the broadest possible approach to defining legal problems and show that two-thirds or more of people with needs do not get legal help of any kind. The result is a chasm of undifferentiated, unmet legal need with no suggestions, other than infusions of vast amounts of money, for how to begin to close such a daunting gap.

We should not treat all legal needs as equivalent. Instead, we can and should identify types of problems, or clusters of problems, where legal help demonstrably protects and enhances the real-world situation of those served. These priority areas would define the coverage of the system. In these covered areas, which might differ among states or regions, assistance would be available to everyone who is eligible. As resources expand and service delivery approaches become more efficient, the coverage of the system could be expanded.

Assumption 4: Lawyers Will Provide Most of the Service

Lawyers must abandon the assumption that they will be the primary source of advice and assistance in a bigger legal services system. Providing an experienced attorney for every client who is not served by the market is unrealistic. If attorneys were fairly compensated the costs would be enormous. Nor would such a "lawyered-up" society be in our interest. Skilled attorneys will always be needed to represent clients on legally complex problems, but many straightforward matters can be addressed by law students or recent graduates. Moreover, other matters might not require the services of an attorney at all. Technology, knowledgeable lay advisors, paraprofessionals and consumer self-help tools will all play a part in a cost- and quality-effective system.

Sectors of the bar may resist encroachments on their monopoly, claiming not guild but quality and client protection concerns. The response is that a well-designed, client-centered and quality-assured system will address these concerns whether the service provider is a lawyer or a lay advisor. Far-sighted lawyers recognize that solving the access problem will help to preserve the bar's autonomy and protect its interests more effectively than aggressively policing non-lawyer services.

Assumption 5: The Access Problem Can Be Solved Solely by Providing Consumers with More Assistance

We will not solve the access problem by focusing exclusively on getting help to consumers while ignoring the ways in which legal rules, procedures, courts and agencies make resolving legal problems unnecessarily complex, time-consuming and opaque. Simplifying, explaining, and de-mystifying legal processes may turn out to be one of the most cost- and outcome-effective strategies for increasing access to justice.

B. A Policy Framework for Full Access to Legal Services

We propose a policy agenda that is comprehensive, practical and flexible. We call for better coordination among providers, more integration with courts and stronger management and accountability at federal, state and local levels. We believe that by deploying existing resources more effectively we can expand access in the short term. As we make the delivery system more accountable, efficient and transparent — and as we demonstrate that we have wrung out every bit of quality service from the existing resource base — we will gain the broad support that will eventually generate resources from legislatures and private funders to build a full-access delivery system. . . .

1. The Scope and Coverage of a Full-Access Legal Services System

We begin with policies that define the scope and coverage of a full access legal services system. These include: Who will be entitled to assistance? What will be the scope of entitlement to assistance? Will consumers be entitled to assistance from an attorney?

Who will be entitled to assistance?
An expanded delivery system should serve low- and moderate-income people.

The 1994 ABA Comprehensive Civil Legal Needs Study showed that moderate-income people have legal needs and access problems similar to those of low-income people. Not only are the legal needs of moderate-income people similar in nature to those of poorer households and individuals, but moderate-income people may also be similarly vulnerable. Domestic violence doesn't disappear above the poverty line. Job loss, marital break-up or a family member's illness can generate a downward spiral that tumbles a household into poverty or dependency on public assistance. Preventive legal counseling, advice and planning may help people protect themselves in hard times. Greater equity of access also has the potential to increase consumer support for the program.

For these reasons, we believe that a full-access system should serve moderate- as well as low-income people. We do not propose specific eligibility criteria, but it is likely that individuals and households with income as high as three or even four times the poverty level will need some subsidy to obtain decent legal assistance. In high cost-of-living areas, the eligibility level might be higher.

In some peer nations more than 40% of the population is eligible for government-subsidized legal assistance. In the United States, there are already many examples of legal services efforts that reach moderate- as well as low-income people. For example, many AARP legal service programs serve a mixed-income population, as do legal services funded by the federal Older Americans Act, the Violence Against Women Act and the Ryan White/Living Legacy Act (assistance for households and individuals impacted by AIDS and HIV). Some law school clinics, such as Harvard Law School's Legal Services Center, serve mixed-income populations as do some pro bono and volunteer lawyer programs.

What types of legal problems will be covered or given priority?
The types of legal needs for which assistance will be provided should be defined as a matter of policy. Specific service priorities, within broad categories, should be determined locally.

While we do not specify the types of legal problems on which consumers will be entitled to assistance, we recognize that defining the coverage of a full access system is an essential task, one that should reflect local social, economic and demographic considerations. Setting substantive priorities is necessary because consumers' legal needs are elastic. Almost any problem can be dealt with legally, but resorting to the law is sometimes an implausible or ineffective option. For example, a tenant could sue a noisy neighbor for interference with quiet enjoyment, but a more effective response might be to talk to the neighbor, complain to the landlord or call the police. As indicated earlier, full access does not and should not mean that everyone who is financially eligible is entitled to subsidized assistance on any problem.

Coverage for broad categories of legal matters should be determined as a matter of policy. Domestic relations matters, the largest single category of service in the programs of both the United States and peer nations, would surely be an important area of coverage. Coverage would also be likely to include assistance relating to: maintaining a secure residence, whether rented or owned; employment and educational opportunities; health, disability, pension and other benefits both private and public; and protecting and enhancing assets. Other substantive areas may be significant depending on the age, health status and economic circumstances of local populations.

Coverage policies should be informed by periodic surveys of consumer needs and preferences. The Legal Services Research Centre, part of the Legal Services Commission of the United Kingdom, has developed state-of-the-art surveys of legal needs and of the public's perceptions and use of legal services. These studies inform funder-driven service priorities developed in collaboration with community partners. See *Project Findings* for more information on these impressive efforts.

Will consumers be entitled to assistance from an attorney?
Consumers will be entitled to advice and assistance, but an attorney's services would be available only when lawyers provide the highest-quality and most cost-effective response.

An expanded system will entitle eligible clients to legal advice and assistance but not necessarily to the services of an attorney. Because client needs vary greatly, services should vary accordingly. A comprehensive system will offer advice; web-based information and document preparation; assistance in self-representation; lay/paralegal advisors; "unbundled" (less than full) representation from attorneys; mediation, collaborative lawyering and other ADR services; and representation by law students, recent graduates and experienced lawyers. The goal of the system will be to match clients' needs to the most cost-effective intervention that meets that need. The types of service available to an individual will depend on the nature of the legal problem and the capacity and circumstances of the applicant. Therefore, one of the system's crucial functions will be to assess requests for service and make referrals to appropriate providers.

Diversity of providers, to a greater or lesser extent, already exists in most areas of the country. Many legal aid offices employ paralegal or other non-lawyer advocates. AARP has pioneered the use of lay volunteers as "navigators" to assist clients using computer information programs. Non-lawyers often provide mediation and alternative dispute resolution services. Unbundled legal services have been pioneered in the private sector, aided in several states by court and ethics rule changes.

Problem 9–6

Legal aid offices and legal services programs have struggled for a long time with the conflicting aims of providing first-class legal service and of providing as much legal service as possible to the client community. One result has been an enormous caseload problem in some offices, with the whole variety of problems that come in its wake: inability to handle cases requiring the expenditure of a great deal of time, often cases that potentially present important issues of law reform involving a large segment of the "client community"; inability to spend sufficient time on cases actually in the office, with the result that lawyers come to feel they are providing insufficient representation; and various office management techniques that prevent continuity of representation of a client throughout a given matter.

Problems like this resulted in two strikes within a year in the Legal Aid Society of New York. The lawyers, who were unionized, also struck for higher wages. The Presiding Justices of the First and Second Departments of the Appellate Division were reported to have characterized the strike as "palpably unprofessional conduct." New York Times, September 27, 1974.

Is that characterization appropriate? What other alternatives were available to the lawyers? Would it be unprofessional for the lawyers to file affidavits in connection with petitions seeking post-conviction relief, asserting inadequacy of their own representation or of the representation by other Legal Aid Society lawyers because of the caseload problem?

————————

The New York County Lawyers Association issued an opinion dealing with this strike in response to an inquiry (Question 645). The opinion follows (N.Y.L.J., June 5, 1975):

> This Committee does not pass on issues of law, but for the purposes of this opinion it does not question the right of lawyer employees to belong to a labor union composed of lawyers or to engage in collective bargaining through such a union for the purpose of negotiating wages, hours and conditions of employment. It may also be true that the employees have the right, through their union (i) to negotiate with the employer with regard to the terms and conditions on which the society should deal with the municipality or the manner in which, as a matter of management, the society carries out its contractual obligations to supply legal services to indigent defendants, or (ii) to exert pressure on the municipality to supply more funds to the society to permit it to manage its affairs in the manner urged by the union. The latter activities may, however, be outside the scope of the employees' collective bargaining rights.
>
> Also, the Committee does not question that lawyer employees have the legal right to strike. But, as in the case of all rights, the right to strike is not an absolute and wholly unrestricted right exercisable irrespective of rights possessed by others and respective of the duties and obligations assumed by the person who has the right. The public interest dictates that some rights and duties take precedence over others depending on the circumstances. Also, restraints may be imposed on the manner in which the right to strike is exercised. It cannot legally be exercised by violence or in any other manner that encroaches seriously on the fundamental rights of others.
>
> When a lawyer elects to become a member of the bar he becomes an officer of the court and a part of the judicial system and he thereby assumes obligations, not imposed on other citizens, both to the court system and to the public. One of these is the duty not to "engage in conduct that is

prejudicial to the administration of justice." DR 1-102(A)(5) [Model Rule 8.4(d) has the same language]. This duty is also imposed in the same language in Section 90(2) of the Judiciary Law of the State of New York. Also, when a lawyer undertakes to represent a client he may "not withdraw from employment until he has taken reasonable steps to avoid foreseeable prejudice to the rights of his client, allowing time for employment of other counsel." DR 2-110(A)(2) [See Model Rule 1.16(b) and (d)]. In addition DR 6-101(A)(3) forbids a lawyer to "[n]eglect a legal matter entrusted to him." [See Model Rules 1.1 and 1.3.]

In our opinion these duties, being obligations to the judicial system, to the public and to clients, take precedence over any right of lawyers to strike against their employer. Also, once a particular indigent client has been assigned to a staff lawyer by his employer he may not refuse to take whatever steps are reasonably necessary to protect the client from foreseeable prejudice.

But beyond these duties, it must be recognized that the society is a unique organization. By reason of its purpose to afford legal services to the poor of the municipality it owes an obligation, not alone to persons for whom it is already engaged on specific matters, but also to persons who are relying on it for professional services in the future. This obligation is shared by the individual members of the professional staff of the society. The staff lawyers also have a duty to the judicial system which makes them ethically obligated not to participate in action either individually or in concert with others which materially interferes with the operation of the courts.

Accordingly, staff lawyers of a legal aid society cannot ethically exercise their right to strike if doing so either disrupts the proper functioning of the courts and the judicial system or deprives indigent defendants of their right to proper representation and a speedy trial.

Notes

1. Although private insurance pays for the majority of health care services, this country also has a number of publicly funded insurance programs, including Medicare and Medicaid at the federal level. Why is there no comparable "legal insurance" program? In England, for example, poor and moderate income individuals needing legal services are entitled to public funds (typically on a sliding scale according to need) to help them pay for private lawyers who agree to handle their cases at rates set by the state. Similar state sponsored programs, often called "judicare," are available in several European countries as well. Why is there no similar program in the United States? Do you think it has something to do with Professor Wasserstrom's argument in Chapter 1 about the intrinsic moral value of "health" as opposed to "law"? Are there reasons to think that Americans may be more skeptical about the

value of providing universal access to legal services than citizens of other countries? If so, how does this square with America's professed commitment to the "rule of law"?

2. Would you favor "judicare" over the current legal aid system described in the preceding section? Assuming equal funding levels, how might moving to a judicare system affect the quality of legal services delivered to poor and moderate income individuals? Would a shift in judicare be likely to affect the kinds of disputes that are brought on behalf of this group? Overall, would judicare improve access to justice for individuals of modest means? Does your answer depend upon whether we focus on individuals with moderate incomes or those who are truly poor? Does your answer similarly depend upon what one means by "access to justice"?

3. What role might the internet play in providing access to legal services on behalf of low- and moderate-income individuals? Consider the following possibilities:

> The Web adds several important elements to the existing technological mix. First, websites permit significantly increased customization to individual users, thereby bridging the gap between electronic and personal advice. Just as Amazon can tell users what books they are likely to want based on what books they have indicated they wanted, a legal website might be able to tell "clients" what decisions they are likely to want to make by comparing information provided by the network of users. . . . Second, websites such as free-advice.com, laws.com, and americounsel.com can convey large quantities of legal information directly to consumers by posting the information itself or providing links to other websites. Although this information is not itself advice, like the Web generally it has the potential for educating consumers enough to reduce their dependence on professional advice. . . . Third, Web services can combine these capabilities with links to individual lawyers in various forms, including face to face representation, email and voice consultation, all with electronic transfer of relevant documents.

Larry E. Ribstein, "Lawyers' Property Rights in State Law," Law and Economics Working Paper Series, Working Paper No. 00-43 (Nov. 2000), at 9. We will return to the potential role of the internet in providing legal services in Chapter 12.

4. Can any of the new initiatives discussed in this Chapter succeed in providing poor and moderate-income individuals meaningful access to the legal system if lawyers continue to maintain their monopoly over the delivery of legal services? What would it mean to provide access to law without lawyers?

Chapter 10

Discipline, Competence, Malpractice, and Whistleblowing

A. Discipline

This Chapter and Problems 10–1 through 10–4 raise a number of important issues in the discipline process: Should the major focus of a disciplinary system be on lawyers' professional conduct or on lawyers' performance of their contractual obligations toward their clients? Should the discipline system be largely in professional control, through judicial supervision of boards staffed entirely or largely by lawyers? Or should the discipline system fall under more traditional legislative-executive control? The materials in this Chapter attempt to give a sense of the way various systems are operating and to offer controversial solutions to some of the shortcomings. They are a starting point for discussion and are intended to be read critically.

There is one additional point you should keep in mind when reading through these materials. Whatever disciplinary system the profession adopts will have to deal with a pervasive problem among lawyers that, by all accounts, underlies many of the ethical and legal violations that currently come to the attention of the bar: the high rates of depression, alcoholism, and drug abuse among practicing lawyers. Study after study has found that lawyers suffer disproportionately from these problems, and that this is particularly true with respect to the lawyers who end up before disciplinary agencies or as defendants in malpractice litigation. See G. Andrew Benjamin, Elaine Darling, and Bruce Sales, "The Prevalence of Depression, Alcohol Abuse, and Cocaine Abuse Among United States Lawyers," 13 Int'l J.L. & Psychiatry 223 (1990); Patrick Krill, Ryan Johnson, and Linda Albert, "The Prevalence of Substance Abuse and Other Mental Health Concerns Among American Lawyers," 10 J. Addiction Medicine 46 (Feb. 2016). To cope with this problem, there are now lawyer assistance programs in every jurisdiction, many of which allow lawyers to seek out confidential help with their problems. Nevertheless, one of the most wrenching—but also most important—ways in which you may have to interact with the disciplinary system is to help a colleague or friend face up to his or her problems and get help. To borrow a maxim from the successful campaign to reduce drunk driving: Friends don't let friends practice law drunk (or otherwise impaired).

Problem 10–1

Assume the same factual situation as in Problem 8–10, except that the State Supreme Court, instead of having passed on a disciplinary case, has ruled in an admissions case that an applicant is not automatically disqualified from becoming a member of the bar by reason of having been found guilty of being a "scofflaw" two years previously in connection with 25 unpaid parking tickets. In a disciplinary hearing against a practicing lawyer "scofflaw" with 25 unpaid parking tickets, what effect should the admissions ruling have?

Problem 10–2

Four lawyers have been convicted in separate cases of (a) embezzlement of a client's funds; (b) embezzlement of the funds of a company of which the lawyer is president; (c) willful failure to pay income taxes; and (d) an illegal campaign contribution. Each is appealing the conviction. You are counsel to the disciplinary committee with appropriate jurisdiction. You have been asked by the chairman whether the committee should institute proceedings looking toward at least temporary suspension of the lawyers' licenses to practice pending the appeals, or whether the committee should await final disposition of the appeals, which will likely take at least two years.

Problem 10–3

Client has made a complaint to the disciplinary committee of which you are chief counsel. The gist of the complaint is that he cannot get a proper accounting of funds that he claims Lawyer has been holding. The records that Client gave you seem to indicate that he did not get the money to which he was entitled. You have communicated with Lawyer who has said that since the complaint in effect makes a criminal accusation, she is invoking her constitutional privilege against self-incrimination and, regretfully, will have nothing to say to the disciplinary committee. The committee has asked you whether the failure of Lawyer to respond to the accusation may be taken into account by it in determining what weight should be given to independent evidence that is produced to demonstrate a violation of the disciplinary rules.

Problem 10–4

Counsel has been asked to write a letter of recommendation about Mr. Z, with whom she worked closely when he was in the legal department of one of her clients. Counsel believes that Z is a good lawyer but she knows that since Z left the client's employment, he has been convicted of raping a guest at a party in a friend's house. The job Z seeks is a legal job with an insurance company. Does Counsel have any obligation to mention the conviction—i.e., should she be subject to discipline for failure to do so? Should the answer turn on whether the crime is related to professional competence? See New York Times, Feb. 4, 1982, for the report of censure by the Massachusetts Medical Society of three doctors who failed to make such disclosure to a would-be employer in a similar case. What if aside from the letter of recommendation, Counsel is debating whether to inform the disciplinary authorities of the conviction? Should (or must) Counsel report it?

The issues with respect to discipline are very closely tied to those involved in admission. In some places the same committee screens applications for both admission and disciplinary charges. Issues with respect to "bad moral character" or "unprofessional conduct" are obviously interrelated. Indeed, the same tension exists in both admissions and discipline cases. At the same time that the profession is being attacked for laxness in self-policing and is being exhorted to screen lawyers more carefully and to be more responsive to the unprofessional conduct that exists, courts, including the Supreme Court, have been increasingly protective of the rights of individual applicants seeking admission and of practitioners against whom charges have been levied. The materials later in the Chapter present examples of both these phenomena. Should the same acts that bar admission to practice also mandate disbarment of practicing attorneys? See Deborah L. Rhode, "Moral Character as a Professional Credential," 94 Yale L.J. 491 (1984) (arguing that a double standard exists in which certain types of attorney misconduct are treated more leniently than the same misconduct by bar applicants).

Note: Disciplinary Rules — Problems of Generality

A particular difficulty to be considered in connection with the Model Rules is that the drafters have given us two types of disciplinary rules. First we have the rather specific prohibition of certain types of conduct. This is followed by a very broad catch-all, which is the hallmark of the statutory drafter who does not want to leave anything out. An example is contained in Model Rule 8.4, entitled "Misconduct." Among other things that a lawyer shall not do, we find subsection (c), "Engage in conduct involving dishonesty, fraud, deceit, or misrepresentation," a rather specific prohibition (albeit broadly applicable) followed by subsection (d), a more general prohibition, "Engage in conduct that is prejudicial to the administration of justice."

The use of a very general disciplinary rule as the basis for imposition of discipline presents both a fairness and a notice problem. In re Ruffalo, 390 U.S. 544 (1968), may provide some assistance. The Supreme Court reviewed a disbarment by a federal court of appeals that had been based on a prior state court disbarment. One ground for the state disbarment had been that the lawyer, who handled a lot of Federal Employer's Liability Act cases for plaintiffs, had hired an employee of the B. & O. Railroad as an investigator. He occasionally had the employee investigate suits against the B. & O. There was no evidence that the employee investigated cases in the yard where he worked, or that he used confidential information, or worked for the lawyer on company time.

The Ohio Supreme Court nevertheless concluded that "one who believes that it is proper to employ and pay another to work against the interest of his regular employer is not qualified to be a member of the Ohio Bar." Mahoning County Bar Ass'n v. Ruffalo, 176 Ohio St. 263, 269 (1964). The federal district court found no misconduct, but the lawyer was disbarred by the Court of Appeals for the Sixth Circuit. The Supreme Court reversed the Court of Appeals because its decision was infected by procedural defects amounting to a denial of due process in the state court proceeding. Justices White and Marshall disagreed with the procedural basis for the majority's decision but concurred on the merits. In considering general standards for disbarment, Justice White stated (390 U.S. at 555):

> members of a bar can be assumed to know that certain kinds of conduct, generally condemned by responsible men, will be grounds for disbarment. This class of conduct certainly includes the criminal offenses traditionally known as malum in se. It also includes conduct which all responsible attorneys would recognize as improper for a member of the profession.

He then noted that neither of those situations was present in *Ruffalo*, where reasonable people might, and in fact did, differ, and went on to say (390 U.S. at 556):

> I would hold that a federal court may not deprive any attorney of the opportunity to practice his profession on the basis of a determination after the fact that conduct is unethical if responsible attorneys would differ in appraising the propriety of that conduct.

This view is very helpful to an understanding of those disciplinary rules of the Model Rules that contain very general language. It indicates that there are some categories of conduct for which there can be disciplinary action even though there is only a general prohibitory rule in the Model Rules, or no rule at all, but that when one gets into a doubtful area, there must be specificity—and *Ruffalo* is such a case.

In making these comments about those Disciplinary Rules that are exceedingly broad, such as the ones relating to misconduct just quoted, we do not mean to imply that that such provisions ought to have been omitted. What is needed is that those charged with interpretation and enforcement build up the common law relating to these rules both as a guide to the profession and as a necessary predicate for enforcement. The necessity that these bodies be disinterested, responsible, and enjoy the confidence of the profession and the public is a subject all its own, and it was beyond the scope of the drafters' charge.*

———————

"Self-regulation" by the profession has become a major focus of critical examination of the profession. Many attacks on the profession focusing on this feature, however, reveal a good deal of misunderstanding about the term. Very often the term is used to indicate a belief that the entire structure of professional regulation—admission and discipline—is conducted by the legal profession, free from governmental control or restraint. That view is misleading, for often it fails to take account of the

———————

* In *Ruffalo* itself the Supreme Court noted pointedly, although it did not pass on the issue, that the initial investigation was made by the Association of American Railroads, which referred charges to the president of the local county bar association, who happened to be local counsel to the B. & O. Railroad, and that the county bar association then instituted charges against Mr. Ruffalo with regard to his employment of a B. & O. employee in connection with suits against the B. & O. 390 U.S. at 549. See also In re Gatti, 8 P.3d 966 (Or. 2000) (per curiam) (disciplining attorney, even assuming fact that bar authorities gave attorney misleading ethics advice about the conduct for which he was disciplined).

role that lawyers play in the normal regulatory process when the legal profession is not involved. The crucial question is whether lawyers are involved in the regulatory process merely as representatives of the profession or whether they are involved as government officials in a meaningful way—that is, are they functioning pursuant to relatively specific directions and are they subject to official supervision? The English Inns of Court and the Law Society, which used to manage the whole system for English barristers and solicitors, were the paradigm case of self-regulation. A state agency, appointed by the governor pursuant to a detailed legislative mandate, that used lawyers only as subordinate staff to handle its normal legal work, would be the paradigm example of absence of self-regulation.

All jurisdictions in the United States fall somewhere in between and there is a good deal of diversity. In recent years, however, there has been noticeable movement toward lessening the self-regulation features. While lawyers predominate as the operative personnel even at policy-making levels, the bodies making disciplinary recommendations to the courts are tending more and more to be separated from the local bar associations through appointment by the state courts; their counsel, the "bar counsel," also often hold similar official appointments. Indeed, bar counsel have formed their own association, the National Organization of Bar Counsel, and, as governmental officials charged with policing the profession, they express their own different perspective on professional issues. Thus, while it seems accurate to say that state supreme courts are often passive in supervising the profession, we should not infer that the task of supervision is being exercised by lawyers acting solely in their private capacity. Discipline counsel act in an official governmental capacity and the long-term prospect is for even greater official regulation of the profession.

A second issue in the regulatory process is the desirability of including lay personnel as part of the system. There has been resistance to this proposal on the ground that lay people will not be familiar with the practices of the profession. While lay persons may have difficulty comprehending complicated professional issues, that problem is tolerated with respect to jury trial of complicated cases. Moreover, lay personnel on a discipline committee might well ask the questions that would force the lawyers, in articulating a response, to rethink standards that formerly were automatically accepted. This line of thinking has led several states to reorganize their disciplinary procedures to include lay members on their statewide disciplinary committee. Whether this change in membership makes an appreciable difference in the resolution of disciplinary matters is another matter and difficult to assess.

Note: Who Should Regulate Lawyers: State or Federal Courts, Agencies, or Legislatures?

Another possibility for regulating lawyers would be a more traditional state agency not dominated by lawyers and not operated by the judiciary. In many jurisdictions that solution would present a substantial constitutional problem of violation of separation of powers. See, e.g., Wajert v. State Ethics Comm'n, 420 A.2d 439 (1980) (holding unconstitutional legislation that infringed on the inherent and exclusive power of the judiciary to regulate the legal profession). While most courts have regarded regulation of attorneys as falling within the "inherent" power of the judiciary, not all have been so inflexible as the Pennsylvania court. See Sadler v. Oregon State Bar, 275 Or. 279 (1976) and Opinion of the Justices, 375 Mass. 795 (1978), for opinions upholding legislation similar to that of *Wajert* on the theory that it complemented and did not conflict with ultimate judicial power.

Consideration of the appropriate forum for attorney discipline involves not only issues of separation of powers among branches of government but also division of powers between the federal and state governments. Pieces of this issue have already been presented in Chapters 5 and 6 in the context of the power of federal administrative agencies to regulate the conduct of attorneys who appear before them, the power of state courts to regulate the conduct of federal prosecutors practicing in those states, and the appropriate rule-making authority for federal lawyers or lawyers practicing in federal courts. As we have seen, these matters involve not only procedural questions of the appropriate disciplinary body but substantive questions of the appropriate body to set standards of conduct.

One state supreme court has gone very far in asserting its jurisdiction to discipline federal prosecutors for activities in the federal courts. In Waters v. Barr, 747 P.2d 900 (1987), the Nevada Supreme Court asserted such authority with respect to federal prosecutors admitted (and even those not admitted) to practice in Nevada. In the latter situation, it defined its power as existing at least with respect to misbehavior that occurred in Nevada and that affected other Nevada lawyers or the integrity of the Nevada bar. But see Kolibash v. Committee on Legal Ethics, 872 F.2d 571 (4th Cir. 1989) (allowing removal of state disciplinary proceeding to federal court); U.S. v. Supreme Court of New Mexico, 839 F.3d 888 (10th Cir. 2016) (holding that New Mexico Rule of Professional Conduct 16-308(E)* violates the Supremacy Clause and is preempted with respect to federal prosecutors practicing before grand juries, but is not preempted outside of the grand jury context). See also p. 470, supra.

What ought to be the scope of the judiciary's "inherent power" to regulate the legal profession, and how does this power relate to professional independence and the effectiveness of professional regulation generally? The *Wajert* case is typical of the sweeping language in which courts and bar leaders often discuss this principle. According to this standard line of argument, courts must retain exclusive jurisdiction over the legal profession in order to preserve the "separation of power" among the executive, legislative, and judicial branches of government that underlie our constitutional democracy. As Professor Wolfram argues, this traditional argument contains two distinct claims: an "affirmative" claim that gives courts an inherent right

---

* New Mexico Rule of Professional Conduct 16-308(E) prohibits a prosecutor from subpoenaing a lawyer to present evidence about a past or present client in a grand jury or other criminal proceeding unless such evidence is "essential" and "there is no other feasible alternative to obtain the information."

to regulate lawyers even in the absence of any express statutory or constitutional authority, and a "negative" claim that the judiciary's authority over lawyers must be exclusive. Charles W. Wolfram, "Lawyer Turf and Lawyer Regulation — The Role of the Inherent-Powers Doctrine," 12 U. Ark. Little Rock L.J. 1, 4 (1989–1990). It is this second aspect of the doctrine that defenders of the current disciplinary system assert prevents administrative agencies such as the SEC or the Federal Trade Commission from drafting rules or creating enforcement procedures designed to regulate lawyers.

How persuasive is the claim that separation of powers concerns require that the judiciary have exclusive control over lawyer discipline? Lawyers, after all, play an integral role in executive and administrative agencies as well as in courts. Why doesn't this justify the other branches of government exerting supervisory authority over the lawyers who exercise these functions? Moreover, is it clear that authorizing the legislature or the judiciary to regulate various aspects of lawyer conduct will undermine the judiciary's interest in preserving an "independent" legal profession? Does your answer depend upon whether these other branches are given rulemaking authority to alter the *content* of professional norms, or are simply authorized to enforce rules that are promulgated by the judiciary? Is it possible to separate the content of professional rules from the procedures enacted to ensure their compliance? Even if the two domains cannot be desegregated completely, is there nevertheless an argument that alternative sanctioning systems would be more effective in curbing the kinds of lawyer misconduct most likely to threaten the underlying purposes of our legal system?

Aside from separation of powers concerns, is there anything else to the concept of "professional independence" that might affect the choice among sanctioning systems? Bar officials frequently assert that only an independent legal profession can adequately protect the rights of individuals against state power. The example most frequently invoked is the criminal defense lawyer, who must be able to defend vigorously the rights of accused citizens without fear of retribution by state authorities. At other times, the fact that citizens in a democracy have a right to use the public resources of the state to achieve their private purposes is said to require that lawyers be independent from any source of authority, public or private, that might limit their clients' access to the public goods encoded in law. Here, the example might be a small town lawyer resisting community pressure to assist a local developer in pursuing a controversial project. Still others point to the important role lawyers play in upholding the framework of rules and procedures at the foundation of democratic government. According to this argument, an independent legal profession acts as a mediating force between the interests of private clients and the public purposes of the legal order. A good example of this form of independence is a lawyer who persuades her client not to take advantage of an arguably applicable legal loophole on the ground that it would undermine the policies of the statute and result in unjustified harm to innocent parties.

Each of these "democratic theory" arguments captures important social benefits. The value of a legal profession that is prepared to defy state authority in the name of individual rights, advocate creative solutions to complex problems, and dissuade recalcitrant clients from undermining long-term legal values cannot seriously be disputed. The relationship between the achievement of these valuable social goals and the shape of the enforcement system, however, is more complex than most of the proponents of these independence claims generally suppose.

The claim that a particular enforcement system is the first step toward totalitarianism, although generally cloaked in the language of independence, frequently rests on implicit assumptions about content or compliance. For example, when opponents of state regulation invoke the image of lawyers in Nazi Germany and other authoritarian regimes who were nothing but tools of the government, their claims are plausible only if one assumes either a radical redrafting of professional norms or massive noncompliance with current standards. Is it realistic to consider the kind of institutional enforcement at issue in the *Kaye Scholer* case (p. 371) a similar kind of threat to professional independence? Is it credible to believe that the SEC or the OTS is attempting to turn lawyers into tools of the state?

Even if we put aside the kind of hyperbole often used in this area, there remains a core content to the concept of professional independence. Even in the most carefully drafted rule system, many areas of ambiguity or discretion will remain. Society has an important stake in the content lawyers give to discretionary norms. If lawyers were to comply only with the literal commands of clear rules, and advise their clients to do likewise, many important societal goals would be frustrated. For example, when lawyers refuse to represent political dissidents, as many did in the McCarthy era, they undermine society's commitment to preserving the right to free expression and other important democratic liberties. By the same token, if tax lawyers systematically choose to exploit the indeterminacy of the legal standards regarding what constitutes proper tax advice, the entire revenue collection system would be endangered. Because the lawyer's conduct is discretionary, society must rely on something other than direct enforcement to ensure that the discretion is not abused.

Independence claims seek to occupy this discretionary space. To reach solid judgments about how they should act in ambiguous situations, lawyers must independently assess both their client's "true" (as opposed to merely articulated) interests and the public purposes underlying relevant legal restrictions. From this somewhat detached perspective, the lawyer can work to discover creative avenues for harmonizing competing concerns in a manner that accomplishes as much of the client's purposes as possible while at the same time promoting long-term legal values. Given the inherent ambiguity of the circumstances under which these decisions will be made, there is no a priori method for predicting how particular lawyers will resolve these conflicts in specific cases. Instead, the model is of a person who has fully integrated the values of the legal system—including all of the conflicts and ambiguities—and is honestly struggling to discover and implement the approach that best effectuates its underlying purposes. Independence, therefore, is primarily an "attitude" or a habit of mind as opposed to a structural condition.

Bar officials argue that confining enforcement to the disciplinary system is the best way to preserve this kind of independent judgment. Given what you know about the operation of this system, do you find this argument persuasive? Is there an argument that supplementing the disciplinary system with other enforcement mechanisms might actually give lawyers more of an incentive to maintain an appropriate level of distance from both the state and their clients? Does your answer depend upon whether we imagine a corporate lawyer deciding whether to claim a questionable tax deduction on behalf of a multinational corporation or a legal services lawyer considering whether her client is required to report a particular source of income that might disqualify her for badly needed welfare benefits? To the extent that such considerations are relevant, are we more likely to be able to take them into consideration in an enforcement system that includes "institutional" regulators with jurisdiction over lawyers in particular settings or practice areas or a unitary system in which all cases must go through the disciplinary system? You should return to these questions after you have read the material in Chapter 12.

An important problem with which every disciplinary committee must deal is the meaning of the major Supreme Court decision dealing with the rights of lawyers subjected to disciplinary proceedings. Spevack v. Klein, which follows, was a 5–4 decision that forbade disciplinary committees from imposing discipline for a certain type of non-cooperation by lawyers. It also left an enormous area of uncertainty because of the generality of the language in the opinions making up the majority.

Spevack v. Klein
385 U.S. 511 (1967)

Justice DOUGLAS announced the judgment of the Court and delivered an opinion in which The Chief Justice, Justice BLACK and Justice BRENNAN concur.

This is a proceeding to discipline petitioner, a member of the New York Bar, for professional misconduct. Of the various charges made, only one survived, viz., the refusal of petitioner to honor a subpoena duces tecum served on him in that he refused to produce the demanded financial records and refused to testify at the judicial inquiry. Petitioner's sole defense was that the production of the records and his testimony would tend to incriminate him. The Appellate Division of the New York Supreme Court ordered petitioner disbarred, holding that the constitutional privilege against self-incrimination was not available to him in light of our decision in Cohen v. Hurley, 366 U.S. 117 [1961]. See 24 App. Div. 2d 653. The Court of Appeals affirmed, 16 N.Y.2d 1048, 17 N.Y.2d. 490. . . .

Cohen v. Hurley was a five-to-four decision rendered in 1961. It is practically on all fours with the present case. . . .

In 1964 the Court in another five-to-four decision held that the Self-Incrimination Clause of the Fifth Amendment was applicable to the States by reason of the Fourteenth. Malloy v. Hogan, 378 U.S. 1 [1964]. . . .

And so the question emerges whether the principle of Malloy v. Hogan is inapplicable because petitioner is a member of the Bar. We conclude that Cohen v. Hurley should be overruled, that the Self-Incrimination Clause of the Fifth Amendment has been absorbed in the Fourteenth, that it extends its protection to lawyers as well as to other individuals, and that it should not be watered down by imposing the dishonor of disbarment and the deprivation of a livelihood as a price for asserting it. These views, expounded in the dissents in Cohen v. Hurley, need not be elaborated again.

We said in Malloy v. Hogan: "The Fourteenth Amendment secures against state invasion the same privilege that the Fifth Amendment guarantees against federal infringement—the right of a person to remain silent unless he chooses to speak in the unfettered exercise of his own will, and to suffer no penalty . . . for such silence." 378 U.S., at 8.

In this context "penalty" is not restricted to fine or imprisonment. It means, as we said in Griffin v. California, 380 U.S. 609 [1965], the imposition of any sanction which makes assertion of the Fifth Amendment privilege "costly." Id., at 614. . . . What we said in *Malloy* and *Griffin* is in the tradition of the broad protection given the privilege at least since Boyd v. United States, 116 U.S. 616, 634–635 [1886], where compulsory production of books and papers of the owner of goods sought to be forfeited was held to be compelling him to be a witness against himself. . . .

The threat of disbarment and the loss of professional standing, professional reputation, and of livelihood are powerful forms of compulsion to make a lawyer relinquish the privilege. That threat is indeed as powerful an instrument of compulsion as "the use of legal process to force from the lips of the accused individual the evidence necessary to convict him . . . ." United States v. White, 322 U.S. 694, 698 [1886]. . . . Lawyers are not excepted from the words "No person . . . shall be compelled in any criminal case to be a witness against himself"; and we can imply no exception. Like the school teacher in Slochower v. Board of Education, 350 U.S. 551 [1956], and the policemen in Garrity v. New Jersey . . . lawyers also enjoy first-class citizenship.

The Court of Appeals alternately affirmed the judgment disbarring petitioner on the ground that under Shapiro v. United States, 335 U.S. 1 [1948], and the required records doctrine he was under a duty to produce the withheld records. The Court of Appeals did not elaborate on the point; nor did the Appellate Division advert to it. . . .

The *Shapiro* case dealt with a federal price control regulation requiring merchants to keep sales records. The Court called them records with "public aspects" as distinguished from private papers (335 U.S., at 34); and concluded by a divided vote that their compelled production did not violate the Fifth Amendment. We are asked to overrule *Shapiro*. But we find it unnecessary to reach it.

. . . The Court of Appeals was the first to suggest that the privilege against self-incrimination was not applicable *to the records*. Petitioner, however, had been disbarred on the theory that the privilege was applicable *to the records*, but that the invocation of the privilege could lead to disbarment. His disbarment cannot be affirmed on the ground that the privilege was not applicable in the first place. Cole v. Arkansas, 333 U.S. 196, 201 [1948]. For that procedure would deny him all opportunity at the trial to show that the Rule, fairly construed and understood, should not be given a broad sweep and to make a record that the documents demanded by the subpoena had no "public aspect" within the required records rule but were private papers.

Reversed.

Justice FORTAS, concurring in the judgment.

I agree that Cohen v. Hurley, 366 U.S. 117 (1961), should be overruled. But I would distinguish between a lawyer's right to remain silent and that of a public employee who is asked questions specifically, directly, and narrowly relating to the performance of his official duties as distinguished from his beliefs or other matters that are not within the scope of the specific duties which he undertook faithfully to perform as part of his employment by the State. This Court has never held, for example, that a policeman may not be discharged for refusal in disciplinary proceedings to testify as to his conduct as a police officer. It is quite a different matter if the State seeks to use the testimony given under this law in a subsequent criminal proceeding. Garrity v. New Jersey, 385 U.S. at 493.

But a lawyer is not an employee of the State. He does not have the responsibility of an employee to account to the State for his actions because he does not perform them as agent of the State. His responsibility to the State is to obey its laws and the rules of conduct that it has generally laid down as part of its licensing procedures. The special responsibilities that he assumes as licensee of the State and officer of the court do not carry with them a diminution, however limited, of his Fifth Amendment rights. Accordingly, I agree that Spevack could not be disbarred for asserting his privilege against self-incrimination.

If this case presented the question whether a lawyer might be disbarred for refusing to keep or to produce, upon properly authorized and particularized demand, records which the lawyer was lawfully and properly required to keep by the State as a proper part of its functions in relation to him as licensor of his high calling, I should feel compelled to vote to affirm, although I would be prepared in an appropriate case to re-examine the scope of the principle announced in Shapiro v. United States, 355 U.S. 1 (1948). I am not prepared to indicate doubt as to the essential validity of *Shapiro*. However, I agree that the required records issue is not appropriately presented here, for the reasons stated by my Brother Douglas. On this basis I join in the judgment of the Court.

Justice HARLAN, whom Justice CLARK and Justice STEWART join, dissenting.

This decision, made in the name of the Constitution, permits a lawyer suspected of professional misconduct to thwart direct official inquiry of him without fear of disciplinary action. What is done today will be disheartening and frustrating to courts and bar associations throughout the country in their efforts to maintain high standards at the bar.

It exposes this Court itself to the possible indignity that it may one day have to admit to its own bar such a lawyer unless it can somehow get at the truth of suspicions, the investigation of which the applicant has previously succeeded in blocking. For I can perceive no distinction between "admission" and "disbarment" in the rationale of what is now held. The decision might even lend some color of support for justifying the appointment to the bench of a lawyer who, like petitioner, prevents full inquiry into his professional behavior. And, still more pervasively, this decision can hardly fail to encourage oncoming generations of lawyers to think of their calling as imposing on them no higher standards of behavior than might be acceptable in the general marketplace. The soundness of a constitutional doctrine carrying such denigrating import for our profession is surely suspect on its face. . . .

It should first be emphasized that the issue here is plainly not whether lawyers may "enjoy first-class citizenship." Nor is the issue whether lawyers may be deprived of their federal privilege against self-incrimination, whether or not criminal prosecution is undertaken against them. These diversionary questions have of course not been presented or even remotely suggested by this case either here or in the courts of New York. The plurality opinion's vivid rhetoric thus serves only to obscure the issues with which we are actually confronted, and to hinder their serious consideration. The true question here is instead the proper scope and effect of the privilege against self-incrimination under the Fourteenth Amendment in state disciplinary proceedings against attorneys. In particular, we are required to determine whether petitioner's disbarment for his failure to provide information relevant to charges of misconduct in carrying on his law practice impermissibly vitiated the protection afforded by the privilege. This important question warrants more complete and discriminating analysis than that given to it by the plurality opinion.

This Court reiterated only last Term that the constitutional privilege against self-incrimination "has never been given the full scope which the values it helps to protect suggest." Schmerber v. California, 384 U.S. 757, 762 [1966]. The Constitution contains no formulae with which we can calculate the areas within this "full scope" to which the privilege should extend, and the Court has therefore been obliged to fashion for itself standards for the application of the privilege. In federal cases stemming from Fifth Amendment claims, the Court has chiefly derived its standards from consideration of two factors: the history and purposes of the privilege, and the character and urgency of the other public interests involved. See, e.g., Orloff v. Willoughby, 345 U.S. 83 [1953]; Davis v. United States, 328 U.S. 582 [1946]; Shapiro v. United States, 335 U.S. 1 [1948]. . . .

It cannot be claimed that the purposes served by the New York rules at issue here, compendiously aimed at "ambulance chasing" and its attendant evils, are unimportant or unrelated to the protection of legitimate state interests. This Court has often held that the States have broad authority to devise both requirements for admission and standards of practice for those who wish to enter the professions. E.g., Hawker v. New York, 170 U.S. 189 [1898]; Dent v. West Virginia, 129 U.S. 114 [1889]; Barsky v. Board of Regents, 347 U.S. 442 [1954]. The States may demand any qualifications which have "a rational connection with the applicant's fitness or capacity," Schware v. Board of Bar Examiners, 353 U.S. 232, 239, and may exclude any applicant who fails to satisfy them. In particular, a State may require evidence of good character, and may place the onus of its production upon the applicant. Konigsberg v. State Bar of California, 366 U.S. 36. Finally, a State may without constitutional objection require in the same fashion continuing evidence of professional and moral fitness as a condition of the retention of the right to practice. Cohen v. Hurley, 366 U.S. 117. All this is in no way questioned by today's decision.

As one prerequisite of continued practice in New York, the Appellate Division, Second Department, of the Supreme Court of New York has determined that attorneys must actively assist the courts and the appropriate professional groups in the prevention and detection of unethical legal activities. The Second Department demands that attorneys maintain various records, file statements of retainer in certain kinds of cases, and upon request provide information, all relevant to the use by the attorneys of contingent fee arrangements in such cases. These rules are intended to protect the public from the abuses revealed by a lengthy series of investigations of malpractices in the geographical area represented by the Second Department. It cannot be said that these conditions are arbitrary or unreasonable, or that they are unrelated to an attorney's continued fitness to practice. English courts since Edward I have endeavored to regulate the qualification and practice of lawyers, always in hope that this might better assure the integrity and evenhandedness of the administration of justice. Very similar efforts have been made in the United States since the 17th century. These efforts have protected the systems of justice in both countries from abuse, and have directly contributed to public confidence in those systems. Such efforts give appropriate recognition to the principle accepted both here and in England that lawyers are officers of the court who perform a fundamental role in the administration of justice. The rules at issue here are in form and spirit a continuation of these efforts, and accordingly are reasonably calculated to serve the most enduring interests of the citizens of New York.

Without denying the urgency or significance of the public purposes served by these rules, the plurality opinion has seemingly concluded that they may not be enforced because any consequence of a claim of the privilege against self-incrimination which renders that claim "costly" is an "instrument of compulsion" which impermissibly infringes on the protection offered by the privilege. Apart from brief *obiter dicta* in recent opinions of this Court, this broad proposition is entirely without support in the construction hitherto given to the privilege, and is directly inconsistent with a series of cases in which this Court has indicated the principles which are properly applicable here. The Court has not before held that the Federal Government and the States are forbidden to permit any consequences to result from a claim of the privilege; it has instead recognized that such consequences may vary widely in kind and intensity, and that these differences warrant individual examination both of the hazard, if any, offered to the essential purposes of the privilege, and of the public interests protected by the consequence. This process is far better calculated than the broad prohibition embraced by the plurality to serve both the purposes of the privilege and the other important public values which are often at stake in such cases. It would assure the integrity of the privilege, and yet guarantee the most generous opportunities for the pursuit of other public values, by selecting the rule or standard most appropriate for the hazards and characteristics of each consequence.

One such rule has already been plainly approved by this Court. It seems clear to me that this rule is applicable to the situation now before us. The Court has repeatedly recognized that it is permissible to deny a status or authority to a claimant of the privilege against self-incrimination if his claim has prevented full assessment of his qualifications for the status or authority. Under this rule, the applicant may not both decline to disclose information necessary to demonstrate his fitness, and yet demand that he receive the benefits of the status. He may not by his interjection of the privilege either diminish his obligation to establish his qualifications, or escape the consequences exacted by the State for a failure to satisfy that obligation.

This rule was established by this Court in Orloff v. Willoughby, 345 U.S. 83. The Court there held that a doctor who refused, under a claim of the privilege against self-incrimination, to divulge whether he was a Communist was not entitled by right to receive a commission as an Army officer, although he had apparently satisfied every other prerequisite for a commission. The Court expressly noted that "[n]o one believes he can be punished" for asserting the privilege, but said that it had "no hesitation" in holding that the petitioner nonetheless could not both rely on the privilege to deny relevant information to the commissioning authorities and demand that he be appointed to a position of "honor and trust." 345 U.S., at 91. The Court concluded that "we cannot doubt that the President of the United States, before certifying his confidence in an officer and appointing him to a commissioned rank, has the right to learn whatever facts the President thinks may affect his fitness." Ibid. . . .

. . . [Prior] cases [citations omitted] . . . make plain that so long as state authorities do not derive any imputation of guilt from a claim of the privilege, they may in the course of a bona fide assessment of an employee's fitness for public employment require that the employee disclose information reasonably related to his fitness, and may order his discharge if he declines. Identical principles have been applied by this Court to applicants for admission to the bar who have refused to produce information pertinent to their profession and moral qualifications. Konigsberg v. State Bar of California, 366 U.S. 36; In re Anastaplo, 366 U.S. 82 [1961]. In sum, all these cases adopted principles under the Fourteenth Amendment which are plainly congruent with those applied in Orloff v. Willoughby, supra, and other federal cases to Fifth Amendment claims. . . .

Justice WHITE, dissenting.

In . . . Garrity v. New Jersey, [385 U.S. 493 (1967)], the Court apparently holds that in every imaginable circumstance the threat of discharge issued by one public officer to another will be impermissible compulsion sufficient to render subsequent answers to questions inadmissible in a criminal proceeding. . . .

. . . [W]ith *Garrity* on the books, the Court compounds its error in Spevack v. Klein. . . . The petitioner . . . refused to testify and to produce any of his records. He incriminated himself in no way whatsoever. The Court nevertheless holds that he may not be disbarred for his refusing to do so. Such a rule would seem justifiable only on the ground that it is an essential measure to protect against self-incrimination—to prevent what may well be a successful attempt to elicit incriminating admissions. But *Garrity* excludes such statements, and their fruits, from a criminal proceeding and therefore frustrates in advance any effort to compel admissions which could be used to obtain a criminal conviction. I therefore see little legal or practical basis, in terms of the privilege against self-incrimination protected by the Fifth Amendment, for preventing discharge of a public employee or the disbarment of a lawyer who refuses to talk about the performance of his public duty.* . . .

Notes

1. Justice Fortas's concurrence clearly implies that a public employee may be discharged for invoking the privilege against self-incrimination with respect to "questions specifically, directly, and narrowly relating to the performance of his official duties." He distinguishes the situation of a lawyer who is not a state employee and whose only responsibility to the State "is to obey its laws and the rules of conduct that it has generally laid down as part of its licensing procedures." Unless Justice Fortas intended to include the rules that the profession has imposed on itself—not only rules of behavior but also of responsibility—within the "licensing procedures" of the State, his conception of what it means to become a lawyer is unfortunately narrow. Is it unfair to link Justice Fortas's apparent failure in *Spevack* to acknowledge the responsibilities of lawyers to the public with an insensitivity that later resulted in his own forced resignation from the Court? See MacKenzie, *The Appearance of Justice* 72–76 (1974) and Murphy, *Fortas: The Rise and Ruin of a Supreme Court Justice* (1988), for a discussion of those events. In any event, the relationship between the state and the profession is considerably more intricate than his opinion recognizes. In a thoughtful discussion of *Spevack*, Russell Niles and Judith Kaye (later Chief Judge of the New York Court of Appeals) made the following comments about the Fortas

---

* The opinion of my Brother Douglas professes not to resolve whether policemen may be discharged for refusing to cooperate with an investigation into alleged misconduct. However, the reasoning used to reach his result in the case of lawyers would seemingly apply with equal persuasiveness in the case of public employees.

concurrence (Niles & Kaye, "*Spevack v. Klein*: Milestone or Millstone in Bar Discipline?," 53 A.B.A. J. 1121, 1122 (1967)):

> The practice of law is now, more than ever, a public profession involving a public trust. The Supreme Court has recently gone farther than ever before in insisting on the right to counsel—in calling on lawyers to be the protectors of the accused, the indigent and, most recently, certain juveniles. Merely by reason of license, attorneys are entrusted with the defense for the life and liberty of others. No other citizens have such power.
>
> Other extraordinary powers of lawyers are commonplace in a commercial practice. Only a lawyer can represent in court the interests of other persons and corporations; he can enter into stipulations and settlements and receive money in his client's behalf. In New York a lawyer on his signature alone may issue subpoenas,[11] requiring personal attendance and production of documents; he can cause expense, mental anguish, degradation and even the loss of liberty for anyone who chooses to ignore his subpoena. On his signature alone, he can require the sheriff to seize personal property[12] and he can place an encumbrance on real property.[13] There are many important ex parte orders available to him where without contest or adversary, the court must rely on the attorney's word.[14]
>
> In the interests of the public, these powers presuppose that the attorney is an individual of utmost honesty and good character, that he continues to meet high professional standards. . . .

Once one reaches an opinion about the proper scope of the public responsibilities of a lawyer, however, one is still left to decide the proper scope of *Spevack*, for the former does not automatically decide the latter.

2. The distinction between lawyers and public officials, urged by Justice Fortas in *Spevack*, was adopted, at least in dicta, by the Court in Gardner v. Broderick, 392 U.S. 273 (1968), in an opinion by Justice Fortas.

3. Cohen v. Hurley and Spevack v. Klein both involved situations where the New York courts disbarred lawyers solely on the basis of their assertion of the privilege against self-incrimination. Is the situation in Problem 10–3 sufficiently different that a different result might obtain?

4. Another issue left open by *Spevack* is the effect of the grant of immunity from criminal prosecution given by the state to a lawyer in connection, say, with an investigation of the conduct of a public official. May a disciplinary committee later disbar the attorney solely on the basis of that compelled testimony? A number of cases have held that it may, on the ground that a disciplinary proceeding is not criminal. See,

---

11. New York Civil Practice Laws and Rules [CPLR] §2302(a). In the federal courts the subpoena is technically issued by the clerk, but as a practical matter it is the work of the attorney.

12. CPLR §7102.

13. CPLR §6501.

14. Examples are an order of arrest (CPLR §6111) and an order of attachment (CPLR §6211).

e.g., In re Ungar, 27 App. Div. 2d 925 (1st Dept.), motion for leave to appeal denied, 20 N.Y.2d 642, cert. denied, 389 U.S. 1007 (1967); Anonymous Attorneys v. Bar Assn., 41 N.Y.2d 506 (1977); see also In re Hill, 545 A.2d 1019 (Vt. 1988) (applying similar reasoning in a judicial conduct proceeding). On this whole subject, see Fred C. Zacharias, "The Purposes of Lawyer Discipline," 45 Wm. & Mary L. Rev. 675 (2003).

5. Some courts have also concluded that *Spevack* does not answer conclusively the question of the scope of the immunity that must be given an attorney to compel testimony against another person in a criminal proceeding. The Florida Supreme Court, after first ruling that the immunity must include immunity against disciplinary proceedings, changed its mind on rehearing and held that it need not because disciplinary proceedings were remedial, not criminal. The dissenters thought that *Spevack* had answered that question for this case as well. DeBock v. State, 512 So. 2d 164 (Fla. 1987), cert. denied, 484 U.S. 1025 (1988).

6. The final issue remaining unresolved after *Spevack* relates to the required records doctrine of Shapiro v. United States, 335 U.S. 1 (1947). In that case the Supreme Court held, 5–4, that sales records that sellers of fruits and vegetables were required to keep under the Emergency Price Control Act were "public" documents, at least to the extent that no privilege against self-incrimination attached when sellers were subpoenaed to produce the records, and that the statutorily granted immunity did not follow, and was not constitutionally required to follow, from their production. The *Spevack* Court left open the question whether in an appropriate case the "required records doctrine" could be applied to any lawyers' records. Many states have a variety of requirements with respect to record keeping, not only with respect to certain kinds of fee arrangements, but also with respect to client funds held by the lawyer. See Niles and Kaye, supra Note 1, at 1125. Should the privilege against self-incrimination cover such items? If so, how does the disciplinary committee prove its case?

7. The impact of Supreme Court decisions regarding the privilege against self-incrimination on lawyer discipline in the years after *Spevack* is reviewed in Hazard and Beard, "A Lawyer's Privilege Against Self-Incrimination in Professional Disciplinary Proceedings," 96 Yale L.J. 1060 (1987).

––––––––––

In addition to constitutional questions regarding the power of disciplinary agencies to compel information from individual lawyers, one can also ask whether such agencies should have jurisdiction over *law firms* as well as individual lawyers. Consider the following argument.

Ted Schneyer
Professional Discipline For Law Firms?
77 Cornell L. Rev. 1 (1992)

Consider five well-publicized cases involving misconduct by large law firms:

1. In 1989 a partner at Baker & McKenzie made improper racist and sexist remarks while interviewing a University of Chicago Law School student for a job with the firm.

Shortly after the incident was reported to the firm, the interviewer opted for early retirement. But matters did not end there. Instead of treating the incident as the isolated wrongdoing of a "bad apple," the school insisted that the firm submit a written description of the measures it was taking to prevent similar incidents before the school would allow the firm to recruit on campus again. The firm complied with this demand. Thus, by imposing an informal sanction on the firm, the school promoted appropriate professional behavior by the firm's lawyers.

2. A company represented by Fried, Frank, Harris, Shriver & Jacobson sued the federal government to obtain documents under the Freedom of Information Act. The company's name was to be kept confidential under a protective order. In 1989, Fried, Frank inadvertently filed in court an unredacted document that divulged the client's name. The person or persons in the firm who allowed the document to be submitted were not identified. The mistake involved not only a breach of confidentiality but a possible violation of the ethical requirement that lawyers take reasonable care to prevent their employees or associates from revealing client confidences.

3. Lawyers in the Chicago office of Kirkland & Ellis represented Westinghouse on antitrust claims against its uranium suppliers. At the same time, Kirkland's Washington office represented the American Petroleum Institute in an effort to convince a congressional committee that there was adequate competition among energy suppliers. In preparing a report to the committee, the Washington office gained information in confidence from Institute members who were also adverse parties in the litigation. As a result, the firm was disqualified from further participation in the lawsuit. The firm's two branches had apparently taken on these matters without a coordinated effort to identify possible conflicts of interest.

4. During the pretrial phase of a major antitrust suit against Kodak, the company's lawyer, a senior partner at Donovan, Leisure, Newton & Irvine, lied to opposing counsel and the judge when he told them that documents sought in discovery no longer existed. Though an associate who worked closely with the partner allegedly reminded him that the documents were still at the firm, the partner did not correct his previous statement. The associate kept the partner's lie to himself, but it later came disastrously to light. The law firm had no ethics committee to which the associate could have referred the problem.

5. A federal judge determined that Lord, Bissell & Brook aided in a violation of the antifraud provisions of the securities laws by failing to notify the shareholders of its client company when the firm learned that the earnings of an intended merger target had been grossly inflated in merger documents. A partner working on the case held stock in the target company and was interested in the deal's success. The judge, however, refused to grant the SEC an injunction that would have required Lord, Bissell & Brook to change its internal procedures to discourage such incidents in the future. The court noted the professional duty of the firm's lawyers to "conform their conduct to the dictates of the law" and expressed confidence that the firm would voluntarily take "appropriate steps." But the firm failed to take those steps and was

later sued for securities violations in a similar matter, which resulted in a 24 million dollar settlement.

This article argues that such incidents provide significant insight into the regulation of lawyering in law firms.

Law practice in the United States is regulated in many ways, but most comprehensively through a specialized system that metes out professional discipline to those who violate the rules of legal ethics. Under this system a bar committee or state supreme court agency investigates complaints about the conduct of lawyers licensed in its jurisdiction. If the agency determines that a lawyer may have breached the legal ethics code, it may pursue the case in an administrative hearing or, ultimately, before the state supreme court. If the lawyer is found guilty of code violations, the agency or court may impose the following sanctions: Private reprimand, public censure, probation, payment of restitution and costs, suspension from practice, or disbarment. Disciplinary targets are often afforded procedural protections reminiscent of the criminal process: a right to counsel; a right to reputation-protecting secrecy in preliminary investigations; and a requirement that wrongdoing be shown by clear and convincing evidence or even proof beyond a reasonable doubt, rather than by a mere preponderance of the evidence.

Disciplinary agencies have always taken individual lawyers as their targets. They have never proceeded against law firms either directly, for breaching ethics rules addressed to them, or vicariously, for the wrongdoing of firm lawyers in the course of their work. The traditional focus on individuals has probably resulted from the system's jurisdictional tie to licensing, which the state requires only for individuals, and from the system's development at a time when solo practice was the norm.

Legal practice, however, has changed. While as late as 1951, sixty percent of the bar practiced alone, two-thirds now work in law firms and other organizations; in addition, more lawyers in private practice now work in firms than as sole practitioners. Law firms themselves have also changed. As a result of internal growth and mergers, the top 100 law firms now account for nearly twenty percent of all legal fees. While only thirty-eight American law firms had more than fifty lawyers in the late 1950s, by 1986 over 500 firms did so and over 250 had more than 100 lawyers. As of 1984, 95 of the 100 largest firms had at least one branch office. Branching has made intrafirm coordination both more difficult and more important. Firms have also become highly leveraged — that is, the ratio of relatively inexperienced associates to partners has risen as high as four-to-one. The proportionally larger number of inexperienced lawyers within firms has heightened the need for supervision.

As law firms have grown, firm governance has become more complex. A few large firms may still govern themselves the old-fashioned ways — either as a patriarchy ruled by a single senior partner or as a loose collection of nearly independent practitioners. But most firms now recognize the limits of individual partner control in the face of extensive personal liability for firm malpractice and have adopted a variety of bureaucratic controls to limit their exposure: policy manuals, formal rules, committees, specialized departments, and centralized management. This trend toward law firm bureaucracy is expected to accelerate.

As law firms grow, the potential harm they can inflict on clients, third parties, and the legal process grows as well. At the same time, the law firm, at least the larger firm, is ripening into an institution that presents new opportunities for bureaucratically controlling the technical and ethical quality of law practice. Indeed, the large firm may now be ready to perform the control or monitoring function for its lawyers "that the hospital [or HMO] performs for the medical profession."

So far, however, those who make disciplinary policy have taken little notice of these developments. True, the latest American Bar Association (ABA) code governing lawyer conduct, the Model Rules of Professional Conduct, notes that "the ethical atmosphere of a firm can influence the conduct of its members." The Model Rules also make clear for the first time that supervisory lawyers are responsible for monitoring their subordinates, an obligation with particular significance in the hierarchical setting of the large firm. But the ABA, the state supreme courts that adopt the ABA codes, and the agencies that assist the courts in disciplinary enforcement have yet to confront the infrequency of disciplinary proceedings against lawyers in firms.

Proceedings against lawyers in large or even medium-sized firms are very rare. In 1981–82, for example, more than eighty percent of the lawyers disciplined in California, Illinois, and the District of Columbia were sole practitioners, and none practiced in a firm with over seven lawyers. Yet, judging from the frequency with which larger firms and their lawyers are the targets of civil suits, motions to disqualify, and sanctions under the rules of civil procedure, disciplinable offenses occur with some regularity in those firms. Some observers attribute the paucity of disciplinary actions against larger-firm lawyers to an informal immunity from disciplinary scrutiny that those lawyers, as the most prestigious segment of the bar, supposedly enjoy. Others point out that the types of misconduct that most often generate grievances and disciplinary sanctions—neglect of cases and misappropriation of client property, respectively—occur much more often in small practices than in larger firms. Still others cite the reactive nature of disciplinary enforcement; the authorities do not normally investigate until clients (or, occasionally, nonclients) complain about a lawyer's conduct. On this theory, the businesses that predominate on the client lists of large firms rarely report complaints against their lawyers. Unlike the "one shot" individuals whom sole practitioners tend to represent, regular business clients may not view the disciplinary process as a "governance mechanism" for their relations with lawyers, and may instead rely on their ability to take their business elsewhere to protect them.

These factors may help to explain the infrequency of disciplinary proceedings against large-firm lawyers, but additional explanations, so far neglected, have important implications for disciplinary policy. These explanations stem from the nature of group practice. First, even when a firm has clearly committed wrongdoing, courts may have difficulty, as an evidentiary matter, in assigning blame to particular lawyers, each of whom has an incentive to shift responsibility for an ethical breach onto others in the firm. Many, perhaps most, of the tasks performed in large firms are assigned to teams. Teaming not only encourages lawyers to take ethical risks they would not take individually, but also obscures responsibility, which makes it difficult for both complainants and disciplinary authorities to determine which lawyers committed a wrongful act. The mystery as to just who at Fried, Frank allowed an unredacted document to be submitted to the court illustrates the problem. So might a case in which a law firm filed a frivolous claim or motion within the meaning of Model Rule 3.1. Though a single lawyer signs the complaint or motion, such filings are often the joint product of "background preparation and drafting by several attorneys," not every one of whom—conceivably none of whom—personally has the information needed to recognize their frivolousness.

Second, even when courts and disciplinary agencies can link professional misconduct to one or more lawyers in a firm as an evidentiary matter, they may be reluctant to sanction those lawyers for fear of making them scapegoats for others in the firm who would have taken the same actions in order to further the firm's interests. For example, at a time when lawyers were forbidden to publicize their services, a court refused to discipline associates who had given Life Magazine material for a story on their firm. Although no general defense of superior orders exists in disciplinary proceedings, the court found that the associates were not responsible for the offending publication since the decision to cooperate with the Life reporter was "one for the partnership."

Third and most important, a law firm's organization, policies, and operating procedures constitute an "ethical infrastructure" that cuts across particular lawyers and tasks. Large law firms are typically complex organizations. Consequently, their infrastructures may have at least as much to do with causing and avoiding unjustified harm as do the individual values and practice skills of their lawyers. Lord, Bissell & Brook's re-involvement in securities violations after the *National Student Marketing* case, for example, may well have resulted from the firm's failure to change its procedures for identifying improperly interested firm lawyers. Similarly, in the Westinghouse case, when separate Kirkland & Ellis offices found themselves improperly representing clients with conflicting interests, the lack of an adequate mechanism for identifying conflicts presumably was more to blame than the ethical sensibilities of the lawyers immediately involved. But who was—and who was not—responsible for the arguable failure of these firms to develop the appropriate infrastructure? In such matters, the locus of individual responsibility seems inherently unclear, in part because it is difficult to attribute omissions to specific individuals in a group. Even a firm with a well-defined management structure does not delegate the duty to make firm policy and maintain an appropriate infrastructure solely to management. To varying degrees this remains every partner's business—and sometimes, as a result, no one's. In no aspect of law firm work is teaming, and thus collective responsibility, more important than in the development of firm structure, policy, and procedures.

Given the evidentiary problems of pinning professional misconduct on one or more members of a lawyering team, the reluctance to scapegoat some lawyers for sins potentially shared by others in their firm, and especially the importance of a law firm's ethical infrastructure and the diffuse responsibility for creating and maintaining that infrastructure, a disciplinary regime that targets only individual lawyers in an era of large law firms is no longer sufficient. Sanctions against firms are needed as well.

While there has been little attention to these points in the field of lawyer discipline, scholars and policymakers have given considerable attention to analogous matters. Commentators have considered the significance of bureaucratic or structural variables in accounting for corporate crime; the pros and cons of making corporations, and not just their agents, liable for crimes committed in the furtherance of organizational interests; and the appropriate mix of criminal sanctions for organizational offenders. . . .

Two varieties of corporate criminal liability are of particular note in evaluating whether to implement a system of law firm discipline. First, some penal statutes directly address corporations and impose liability for failure to discharge a "specific duty of affirmative performance," such as a duty to file reports with an administrative agency. Taking this approach, a system of law firm discipline might address to law firms those ethics rules that implicate centralized firm functions, such as rules dealing with the handling of client funds, files, and property. It might also address directly to law firms prophylactic ethics rules dealing with matters of ethical infrastructure; these rules might include a provision such as MR 5.1(a). The disciplinary system might go even further down this road and give specific content to the "reasonable efforts" standard of MR 5.1(a) by, for example, requiring law firms over a certain size to have new-business and ethics committees.

Disciplinary rules that specify monitoring requirements in detail would have the desirable effect of giving law firms notice of their precise ethical obligations. Such prior notice would help foster in the legal community a stronger sense that firms deserve to be disciplined for violations. Specific rules would also help to steer firms toward more ethical conduct without waiting for a long series of "common law" adjudications and ethics opinions to determine whether various monitoring practices satisfy the "reasonable efforts" test of MR 5.1(a). The resulting reduction in adjudications and opinions would preserve disciplinary resources for other purposes.

On the other hand, problems may arise if the specification of law firm monitoring practices becomes a boom industry. Whenever the law tells an enterprise precisely how to monitor its own work, it is "meddling in a process" about which policymakers are likely to know less than the enterprise managers themselves. Given the enormous range in law firm size, as well as the structural diversity that exists among firms of comparable size, few specific monitoring practices are likely to be worthwhile in all firms. Only when a monitoring practice is obviously worthwhile and could be imposed on a sufficiently uniform set of firms should it be crystallized into a disciplinary rule.

The second relevant type of corporate criminal liability is *respondeat superior*. Under federal law, organizations are liable for crimes committed by agents who act within the scope of their employment and with the intention of serving organizational interests. These organizations are vicariously liable for their agents' job-related crimes, even when an agent acts without the knowledge or authorization of management and even if management has forbidden the conduct in question. Moreover, the government need not prove that any specific agent acted illegally, but only that *some* agent committed the underlying crime. Thus, when a corporation is prosecuted on this theory, no individual codefendants are needed. Even when they exist, if a jury convicts the corporation but acquits the individuals, the conviction will stand. Furthermore, a corporation is deemed to have acquired the collective knowledge of its employees; it cannot avoid a guilty verdict by showing that the relevant knowledge "was not acquired by any one individual employee who then would have comprehended its full import."

The case for vicarious corporate criminal liability extends to disciplinary liability for law firms. Authorizing vicarious discipline for law firms when someone in the firm has committed an ethical infraction would enable a court or agency to impose discipline even when it cannot practically determine who committed the underlying offense or it is reluctant to proceed against specific lawyers because such action would amount to scapegoating. If a disciplined *firm* then considered it important to assign individual blame for the underlying infraction, it could do so on the basis of its own internal investigation. Geoffrey Hazard has examined the efficiency of internal firm investigations relative to formal disciplinary proceedings, which are "quasi-criminal, entail an intensely adversary process," and "threaten the [individual] lawyer's livelihood and standing in the community." Assessing the internal investigations that have been prompted by some civil suits against the larger firms, Hazard notes that the firms are in a good position to obtain information from the lawyers in question, have ready access to the necessary records, and know the identity of relevant witnesses.

Some commentators argue that blameworthiness should always be a prerequisite to criminal liability and that an entity cannot be blamed when it has taken reasonable steps to prevent wrongdoing by its agents. These commentators would allow a corporation to show as an affirmative defense in criminal cases based on *respondeat superior* (though not in civil suits, where compensation is involved) that it had implemented "reasonable safeguards designed to prevent [the underlying] crimes." Since this "due diligence" showing would constitute an affirmative defense, the prosecutor would not have to prove the corporation's lack of reasonable preventive measures, but would have to rebut company evidence that reasonable measures were taken.

In designing a system of vicarious law firm discipline, policymakers will have to decide whether to recognize a due diligence defense, which has already been built into the SEC's disciplinary system for broker-dealers. This defense avoids the over-deterrence that might result if sanctions were imposed on law firms which had already taken all cost-justified precautions to promote ethical behavior. Overdeterrence could occur whenever the gravity of the disciplinary sanctions, coupled with any malpractice liability or other nondisciplinary sanctions the firm experiences, is greater than the losses that the underlying ethical infraction has caused. In such cases, the disciplinary system would encourage firms to take monitoring precautions that cost more than they are worth in terms of the harm prevented.

Rather than establishing a due diligence defense to safeguard against overdeterrence, disciplinary authorities would probably do better to seek only modest firm sanctions in many cases and to exercise their discretion in others to proceed solely against individual lawyers and not their firms. In the context of law firm discipline, a major drawback of the due diligence defense is that the decisionmaker would have to determine in each case whether a firm had exercised due diligence. These determinations may often be expensive and unreliable, because law firms have not yet standardized their monitoring techniques nearly to the degree that large brokerage houses and accounting firms have. Although disciplinary agencies are specialists in professional regulation and might eventually become experts on law firm operations and the meaning of due diligence, it seems wiser for now to give the agencies the option of subjecting law firms to vicarious discipline for their lawyers' job-related ethical infractions and to give the firms the discretion to then decide whether to abandon a questionable policy or develop new monitoring programs. For example, if a firm was disciplined because an associate had padded her hours, the firm could decide for itself whether its policy of requiring associates to bill 2300 hours a year posed unacceptable ethical risks.

Alternatively, disciplinary agencies could allow a firm to show that it was exercising due diligence (even if it only began to do so after the underlying infraction occurred), not for purposes of exoneration, but in order to determine the appropriate sanction. If, for example, a firm had a well-structured new-business committee in place (even if the committee only came into being after an improper conflict of interest had occurred), it would be senseless to sanction the firm by putting it on probation pending the creation of a satisfactory conflict-avoidance program.

If a system of law firm discipline provided for vicarious liability without a due diligence defense, one might ask why the system should also include the firm-directed rules calling for reasonable supervision that were suggested earlier. After all, in enforcing those rules the authorities would also have to make difficult determinations of the reasonableness of a firm's monitoring practices. The answer is that those rules would serve an indispensable function when the authorities discovered a clear lack of appropriate firm infrastructure or monitoring, yet lawyers in the firm had not yet committed an underlying ethical infraction. Concededly, such a discovery would be rare in a disciplinary system that has always relied heavily on reactive rather than proactive enforcement. However the system need not remain static in this respect; the authorities could enforce these particular rules proactively. Disciplinary agencies could, for example, require firms to report periodically on the measures they have taken to comply with the duty of reasonable supervision (and proceed against firms whose reports reveal clear inadequacies), much as lawyers in some states must now report the location and nature of client trust accounts and allow those accounts to be audited. If firm infrastructure is clearly deficient, a disciplinary agency should no more wait for harm to result than the police should wait for a driver with obviously poor brakes to hit someone before stopping him. . . .

The criminal sanctions that are recognized as appropriate for convicted corporations can easily be converted into a sensible scheme of disciplinary sanctions for law firms. These sanctions include fines, restitution, adverse publicity, and probation.

Notes

1. In 1996, New York amended its disciplinary rules to impose on law firms the same ethical responsibilities as those imposed on individual lawyers in particular cases. See the New York versions of Model Rules 5.1 and 5.3. In 1998, New Jersey followed New York, when the Supreme Court of New Jersey amended the Rules of Court to allow for the imposition of ethical sanctions on law firms, including fines in "exceptional circumstances." See Rule 1:20-15(j). The amended rules provide that "every attorney and business entity authorized to practice law in the State of New Jersey . . . shall be subject to the disciplinary jurisdiction of the Supreme Court." Rule 1:20-1. See In re Ravich et al., 715 A.2d 216 (N.J. 1998) (reprimanding law firm for in-person solicitation of disaster victims). A proposal to include a similar provision as part of the Ethics 2000 revision of the Model Rules was removed before the proposed rules were sent to the ABA House of Delegates for approval.

2. Notably, Courts of Appeals have split on the issue of whether federal bankruptcy courts have the power under section 1927 of the Bankruptcy Act to sanction law firms as well as individual lawyers for misconduct. See Castellanos Group Law Firm v. FDIC, 545 B.R. 401, 420–21 (Bankruptcy Appellate Panel 1st Cir. 2016) (summarizing the split).

3. What difference would expanding disciplinary authority to law firms make on how these institutions operate and on the lives of partners and associates? See Elizabeth Chambliss and David Wilkins, "A New Framework for Law Firm Discipline," 16 Geo. J. Legal Ethics 335 (2003); Russell G. Pearce & Eli Wald, "The Relational Infrastructure of Law Firm Regulation: Is the Death of Big Law Greatly Exaggerated?," 42 Hofstra L. Rev. 109 (2013).

Does your answer depend upon whether you are imagining a large law firm like the ones at issue in the examples at the beginning of Schneyer's article or a small firm of five lawyers, each of whom primarily practices independently in different substantive areas of law? Which type of firm do you anticipate will be most likely to be sanctioned under this type of expanded disciplinary authority?

4. What are the implications of the debate over professional discipline for law firms in the ongoing MDP debate? Is some form of organizational regulation a necessary part of preserving the professional independence of lawyers working in MDPs? If so, is it clear that the current disciplinary processes should exercise such authority?

5. Schneyer argues that professional discipline for firms would encourage these organizations to develop an "ethical infrastructure" that might prevent misconduct from occurring in the first place. To a large extent, this has already begun. In the 1970s, many firms established "conflicts committees" to deal with the growing problem of preventing different lawyers within the same firm from representing conflicting interests. Several firms gradually expanded the jurisdiction of these committees to include other questions relating to ethics and professional responsibility within the firms, while others established separate "ethics committees." Recently, some firms have gone even further, designating a partner as "counsel to the firm" or "ethics partner," while others have established internal "ombudsmen" to address ethical complaints by associates and partners.

Why have firms moved in this direction and how effective do you anticipate these measures to be in addressing the kinds of issues identified by Professor Schneyer? Does your answer depend upon which measures a firm adopts? For example, are "ethics specialists" likely to be more or less effective than "ethics committees"? If a firm has an ethics specialist, should that person be a partner or an associate? Should he or she be full or part time (i.e., continue to practice law in addition to their duties to the firm)? If the ethics person continues to practice, should he or she represent other lawyers or law firms facing ethics charges? Regardless of whether the ethics partner represents outside clients, should that person also represent lawyers within the firm who are accused of ethics violations? What procedures should an ethics specialist or committee use in investigating complaints or deciding on firm policy? Should the ethics specialist/committee have jurisdiction over all regulatory/liability issues facing the firm or only those that involve violations of the rules of professional responsibility? For a general overview of the work of in-house ethics advisers, see Elizabeth Chambliss, "The Professionalization of Law Firm In-House Counsel," 84 N.C. L. Rev. 1515 (2006); Elizabeth Chambliss and David B. Wilkins, "The Work of In-House Ethics Advisers," 44 Ariz. L. Rev. 449 (2002); Elizabeth Chambliss and David B. Wilkins, "Ethical Infrastructure in Large Law Firms," 30 Hofstra L. Rev. 691 (2002). We will return to the question of how this kind of "ethical infrastructure" might affect the manner in which lawyers perform their public responsibilities in Chapter 12.

6. In addition to in-house ethics experts and ombudsmen, some firms are moving to formalize traditional forms of peer review. Lawyers who practice together in firms have always exercised a certain degree of control and influence over one another's conduct through peer pressure, socialization, and informal monitoring.

See, e.g., Douglas R. Richmond, "Professional Responsibilities of Law Firm Associates," 45 Brandeis L.J. 199 (2007). Indeed, many studies of the ethical conduct of lawyers working in firms have identified a firm's culture as one of the most important factors in determining how individual lawyers working in these organizations identify and interpret ethical rules. See, e.g., Michael J. Kelly, *Lives of Lawyers Revisited: Transition and Resilience in the Organizations of Practice* (2007); Jerome Carlin, *Lawyers' Ethics: A Survey of the New York City Bar* 107–109 (1966). Unfortunately, as the Carlin study demonstrates, a firm's "ethical climate" can undermine as well as reinforce ethical conduct. Indeed, Carlin found that some firms in New York generated a "permissive" atmosphere in which lawyers facing similar problems provided mutual support for the decision to violate ethical norms. Moreover, whatever role informal cultural norms have played in shaping lawyer conduct in the past may be weakening as law firms increase in size and take in lateral hires who have not been raised in the firm's culture. See Carol Messikomer, "Ambivalence, Contradiction, and Ambiguity: The Everyday Ethics of Defense Litigators," 67 Fordham L. Rev. 739, 756 (1999) (reporting that in focus groups among lawyers about discovery abuse, "most defense partners [in large law firms] seemed convinced that the introduction of 'laterals' constitutes a threat to a firm's cultural cohesion").

In an effort to promote a culture that both discourages misconduct and encourages effective client service, many firms have instituted measures to increase the degree of review and control that partners exercise over each other. A recent study of peer review procedures of all Texas law firms with over ten lawyers demonstrates the breadth of approaches that firms are now taking:

> Peer review covers a spectrum of approaches and procedures designed to enable law firm principals to monitor and evaluate their fellow principals. Traditionally, firms have confined partner review to the evaluation of partner productivity and contributions for compensation purposes. Now, an increasing number of firms are setting the stage for peer review by adopting standard procedures and policies applicable to all firm attorneys. For example, firms typically implement policies and procedures relating to conflict checks, engagement letters, and opinion letters. When firms actually monitor principals' compliance with established procedures and policies, they institute a rudimentary form of peer review. Compliance with these technical standards can be determined by auditing selected client files.
>
> Firms also utilize peer review committees to obtain more substantive information on principal performance. The committee solicits information from the firm's principals, and in some cases, its associates. In addition, a peer review committee can obtain client feedback by conducting a client audit. This information helps the committee assess the principal's performance and client satisfaction.

Susan Saab Fortney, "Are Law Firm Partners Islands Unto Themselves? An Empirical Study of Law Firm Peer Review and Culture," 10 Geo. J. Legal Ethics 271, 281 (1996). Although Fortney found that most law firms exercised some form of peer review, these efforts were largely confined to informal discussions by department chairs and formal policies on such matters as serving on a client's board of directors. Less than a third of the firms answering the survey had designated a partner or committee with responsibility for evaluating the manner in which partners handle client matters and less than 10% employed formal procedures for reviewing partner work other than in connection with compensation decisions. See id., at 290.

Why don't law firms engage in more formal peer review? In medicine, formal peer review—for example, morbidity and mortality rounds in hospitals—is quite common. Why haven't law firms instituted similar procedures? Are there reasons why the "practice of law" may be less susceptible to effective peer review than the "practice of medicine"? Are there differences in the professional socialization or external constraints on doctors and lawyers that may affect their respective willingness to embrace peer review? Are changes in law practice—including the growth in legal malpractice litigation and increasing competition among lawyers for clients—likely to spur interest in peer review? If so, do these catalysts provide an important clue about the kind of lawyer conduct that is likely to be the subject of peer review? For more on the legal, ethical, and practical arguments for and against peer review, see Susan Saab Fortney, "Am I My Partner's Keeper? Peer Review in Law Firms," 66 U. Colo. L. Rev. 329 (1995) (discussing the legal, ethical, and practical arguments in favor of peer review).

7. One issue raised by the kind of peer review discussed above is what happens when a law firm determines that one of its partners has violated the firm's (or the profession's) rules. Traditionally, partnership in a law firm—particularly a large law firm—was considered to be the private equivalent of tenure. Partners were rarely "dismissed" and only for egregious violations. See Erwin O. Smigel, *The Wall Street Lawyer: Professional Organization Man?* 259 (1969); Mark Stevens, *The Power of Attorney: The Rise of the Giant Law Firms* 8 (1967). Today, however, partners at even the largest firms may find themselves ousted for reasons ranging from a decline in billings to a disagreement with their peers over a colleague's decisionmaking or the firm's practices. See David B. Wilkins, "Partner Shmartner! EEOC v. Sidley Austin Brown & Wood," 120 Harv. L. Rev. 1264 (2007); Larry E. Ribstein, "Law Partner Expulsion," 55 Bus. Law. 845 (2000). For an example, see p. 839, and we shall see the implications of the decline of partnership-as-tenure for the structure and operation of the internal labor markets of large law firms in Chapter 12.

8. Formal peer review systems tend to concentrate on monitoring the actions of "partners." Regardless of what policies firms implement in this area, however, they have always been responsible for monitoring the conduct of associates and training them to be competent and ethical practitioners. See ABA Comm'n on Professionalism, *In the Spirit of Public Service: A Blueprint for the Rekindling of Lawyer Professionalism* 22 (1986) (noting that firms bear the responsibility for facilitating their associates' "transition into practice"). In Chapter 12, we will discuss whether firms are carrying out this responsibility effectively.

9. Firm culture is not the only informal normative system that shapes and constrains lawyer conduct. Between the formal rules of ethics of the professional community as a whole and the workplace norms of particular firms lies an amorphous but nevertheless powerful system of norms and sanctions that develop around specific institutions and practice areas where lawyers frequently interact with a relatively small and distinct group of peers, adversaries, and officials. These norms can either reinforce or subvert the formal rules of practice. For example, a recent study of divorce lawyers concludes that informal norms within the community of those who routinely handle divorce cases tend to discourage "unreasonable" tactics such as harassing motions and failure to respond to legitimate discovery requests. See Lynn Mather, Craig A. McEwen, and Richard J. Maiman, *Divorce Lawyers at Work: Varieties of Professionalism in Practice* 52–56 (2001). On the other hand, Abraham Blumberg's famous study of criminal defense lawyers in local criminal courts found that these lawyers routinely sacrifice their clients' interests to maintain good relations with police, prosecutors, judges, and other state officials with whom they are locked into long-term relationships. See Abraham Blumberg, "The Practice of Law as Confidence Game: Organizational Cooptation of a Profession," 1 Law & Soc'y Rev. 15 (1967). See also Kenneth Mann, *Defending White-Collar Crime: A Portrait of Attorneys at Work* 234–48 (1985) (describing how the informal norms shared by the community of lawyers who routinely defend white collar criminal cases undermine or circumvent the formal rules of ethics). Any assessment of the effects of "peer control" as a method of enforcing professional norms must therefore come to terms with the manner in which each of these "semi-autonomous social fields"—law firms, specialty bars, institutional repeat players—interact with each other and with the formal rules of professional conduct in shaping the values and conduct of lawyers. See generally Sally Falk Moore, "Law and Social Change: The Semi-Autonomous Social Field as an Appropriate Object of Study," 7 Law & Soc'y Rev. 719 (1973).

Note: Should the Legal Profession Move Toward a Medical Model?

Over the last several decades, the medical profession has devoted enormous energy to trying to decrease the rate and severity of medical errors. Are there lessons in its experience for the legal profession? After an exhaustive study of six disciplinary cases in New York, Professor Richard Abel, one of the country's foremost scholars of the legal profession, believes that there are.

Richard L. Abel
Lawyers in the Dock:
Learning from Attorney Disciplinary Proceedings (2008)
pp. 525–528

Lawyers could draw many useful lessons from doctors. Almost no doctor practices alone today; it is not clear that any lawyer should do so. Litigators need others to make appearances and mind the office.... Multi-lawyer firms would have a reputational interest in preventing misconduct and a financial incentive to ensuring minimum quality (malpractice liability and insurance premium levels). Missed deadlines are the iatrogenic infections of law. Rapid advances in information technology make electronic tickler systems foolproof (except for data entry). There is no more excuse for litigators to operate without them than for car drivers not to buckle up. Legal clinics . . . have demonstrated that standardizing practice can reduce both errors and cost. The quality of a nation's justice is determined less by how it handles the rare high profile case than by how it routinely processes garden variety claims. Compulsory partnership would disproportionately burden minority lawyers, who are overrepresented among sole practitioners, but it also would disproportionately benefit their clients, who are also more likely to be minorities.

Lawyers should be allowed to compete freely. In the 30 years since the U.S. Supreme Court recognized lawyers' First Amendment rights in commercial speech state bars have persisted in restraining advertising. Clients are as needy and deserving of information about the cost and quality of legal services as patients are about medical care. . . . The largest private physicians' practice in California, serving more than 500,000 patients, has posted the price of 58 common procedures on its website; lawyers could do the same. Malpractice claims and disciplinary complaints and their outcomes (including settlements) should be available online.

Medicine began certifying specialists decades ago. Law has been slow to follow suit, often grandfathering in practitioners on the basis of experience without assessing expertise. In Britain, patients first must consult general medical practitioners, who alone can refer them to specialist consultants. . . . Specialization would force lawyers to develop measures of quality. (There is a danger, of course, that it could become yet another restrictive practice, allowing specialists to extract higher monopoly rents.)

Given the difficulty laypeople encounter in evaluating quality, referral sources could play an invaluable role. Merely aggregating client reactions — the equivalent of Zagat's for restaurants, online ratings for hotels, and Angie's List for many other services — risks letting superficial judgments of style eclipse substantive measures of lawyer performance. . . . But for-profit referral sources (perhaps using legally trained evaluators) could assess and monitor the lawyers to whom they make referrals, transforming one-shot clients into repeat players who would have the market power to demand quality (as unions allow members to do). . . . Third-party payers (Medicare, Medicaid, private insurance, and the employers who pay most of the insurance premiums) have long monitored the price and quality of medical services. But there is no realistic prospect of replicating this for legal services. . . .

The boundaries of the legal monopoly (which includes advice) are broader in the United States than anywhere else and should be drastically contracted. Much of what solo and small firm lawyers do badly laypersons could do better and more cheaply. . . .

For more than a decade, American lawyers have bewailed the crisis in their profession, wringing their hands about its bad image. . . . The structural changes described above are first steps in restoring the public trust in lawyers. Can the profession muster the political will to reform?

Notes

1. Do you favor switching to the kind of medical model of professional regulation Professor Abel describes? Have doctors been particularly effective in bringing down either the error rate or the cost of medical services? Would there be any disadvantages for lawyers, clients, or the public in treating lawyers more like doctors?

2. Would you favor eliminating solo practice? Return to these questions after you have read the materials in Chapter 12.

B. Competence

Model Rule 1.1 imposes an "ethical" obligation on lawyers to practice competently. While the subject has arisen at various points throughout these materials, this subsection focuses on the issue of competence, and specifically, remedies for incompetence. Sections A and C of this Chapter, dealing with the discipline system and the action for malpractice, are therefore sections whose subject matter is also "competence," although Section A deals with conduct issues in addition to competence. This subsection, however, sets forth some of the profession's formal efforts to deal with problems of competence once lawyers have been admitted to the bar.

It is difficult to have a sense of the competence of the bar throughout the centuries. In this country in the last century, efforts to open the profession to children of the poor and of the immigrant have entangled the issues of competence and elitism into a hopeless snarl. See Jerold S. Auerbach, *Unequal Justice: Lawyers and Social Change in Modern America* 40–52 (1976), for a view focusing on the "elitist" elements of movements for "higher standards." Indeed, there have been those who have seen a danger that movements for higher standards will not only be elitist but also will have the effect of stifling dissent. See statements of lawyers quoted in Levy, "Is Specialization a Conspiracy?," 4 Juris Dr. 43, 44–45 (December 1974); see also Barton, "Why Do We Regulate Lawyers?," 33 Ariz. State L.J. 429 (2001). Yet complaints about poor lawyering are heard so often that it is difficult to believe that there is not a competence problem of major proportions. Perhaps research projects can be designed that would throw more light on this issue. For the moment, however, we are left to rely by and large on the instinctive judgments of experienced practitioners and students of the profession in whom we have confidence. They tell us that competence is an enormous problem in the profession.

If that is true, then the problem of incompetence affects every other professional issue. It is one thing for us to define problems of professional responsibility when we assume a starting point of competent lawyers. It is quite another when we must assume that we are dealing with a large number of lawyers who are incompetent or who, perhaps because of the press of business, practice incompetently a large part of the time. The same is true when we focus on the availability of legal services. Just what quality of service are we attempting to make available?

This book cannot provide sufficient materials to study the whole problem of lawyers' educations. See Reed, *Training for the Public Profession of Law* (1921); Packer & Ehrlich, *New Directions in Legal Education* (1972); and the Carrington Report on Training for the Public Professions of the Law (1971) (printed as an appendix to the Packer and Ehrlich book) for some exposition of the issue. Likewise, it does not seem advisable to deal with the bar examination as the profession's primary independent method of testing competence.

One approach to the problem of competence is the encouragement, or at least the recognition, of specialization. See Ariens, "Know The Law: A History of Legal Specialization," 45 S.C. L. Rev. 1003 (1994). There were several decades of indecisive debate over the merits of official state recognition of categories of specialists who would be allowed to designate themselves as such. See Model Rule 7.4. Those engaged in the discussion realized that the issue touched a whole variety of professional concerns and a great number of questions were raised and discussed. The following is a partial list: Is the level of professional competence high enough to deal with the increasing complexity of law? If not, how shall it be raised? Is further "academic" training the answer, and if so, who shall administer it? Or is the answer "practical" training and experience? What is the relationship between the answers to these questions and the rules relating to advertising? What is the relation between specialization and cost of legal services? Will specialization and advertising of specialists tend to lead the public to lawyers who can do their work most efficiently and therefore most cheaply, or will it tend to lead the public to lawyers who will charge more for their expertness? Should a condition of certification of a specialist be the devotion of a certain amount of time to free legal "clinics" or some other kind of free representation? And finally, what will specialization do to the profession itself? Will it create, or increase, elitism? Will it mean greater fragmentation of the profession and the end of the general practitioner? Will it discriminate against young and minority members of the bar? Should competence include cultural competence, in terms of developing skills to allow for a more accurate appreciation and understanding of clients' goals, objectives and background information relating to representations? See Susan Bryant, "The Five Habits: Building Cross-Cultural Competence in Lawyers," 8 Clinical L. Rev. 33 (2001).

The organized profession asked questions like these for years, and for years it was so fearful about the answers and about guessing wrong that it preferred the status quo to experimentation. It was uncertain both about the relevance of the medical model, which had existed for years, and about whether it liked the results of specialization in that profession. It also came to realize that limited experimentation was already taking place in the profession because there was an ever-increasing amount of specialization in fact among lawyers. Finally, perhaps spurred by the realization that temporizing was in fact a decision of sorts, but spurred even more by a growing feeling that there was a strong link between the issues involved in the specialization debate and the profession's duty to provide greater public access to legal services, the State Bar of California recommended, and the California Supreme Court in 1974 approved, a pilot specialization program. The California plan adopted a model that provided for official certification of specialists by the state. The pilot program was limited initially to three fields: workers' compensation, taxation, and criminal law. Family law; immigration and nationality law; appellate law; estate planning, trust, and probate law; and personal and small business bankruptcy law were added thereafter.

As implemented by standards promulgated by the Board of Legal Specialization, the program sets forth detailed requirements for certification and recertification every five years that are somewhat different for all five fields. All contain substantial "task and experience" requirements involving participation in specified amounts of litigation and, in the case of tax specialists, preparation of written documents; completion of a specified number of units of educational programs; and either a written examination or completion of a prescribed alternate educational program. In addition, each applicant is required to produce references to attest to his or her level of competence, and the advisory committee that conducts an independent review of each applicant in each specialty field obtains further references on its own. There are also elaborate procedural provisions governing the initial decision and possible review of denial of certification or recertification. In addition, certification may be obtained from private accreditation agencies approved by the Board of Legal Specialization after meeting its standards. Arizona, for example, has adopted a similar system for eight fields of law. See, e.g., State Bar of Arizona, "Standards for Certification of Lawyers Specializing in Criminal Law" (rev. Feb. 25, 2000) (requiring seven years of practice, criminal trial and appellate experience, examination, references, and continuing legal education), available at <http://www.azbar.org/media/93749/criminal _law_standards.pdf>.

The American Bar Association has been active in the specialization debate since 1952 when it established a committee to study the issue. Committee recommendations to encourage or recognize the practice were consistently rejected by the House of Delegates through the 1950s and 1960s. In 1969, the Delegates approved a resolution stating that implementation of a nationwide plan was not desirable at that time and deferring action in favor of experimental state programs. However, the ABA Committee on Specialization did not want too much experimentation either, and its Committee Reports through the early 1970s consistently urged states to await evaluation of programs then in existence and the establishment of uniform standards.

After the decision of the Supreme Court in Bates v. State Bar, p. 631, the ABA Committee, perceiving a close relationship between regulation of specialization and truthful advertising of competence, renewed its interest in development of specialization programs and approved a Model Plan of Specialization that had been developed by its Specialization Committee. The Model Plan sought to steer a middle course between the quality and access focuses of the certification and designation proposals. Calling itself a "recognition program," it would mandate substantial involvement in the given field, continuing legal education, and peer review, but not necessarily examination. It would also provide flexibility in permitting standards to be met by equivalents. This last provision was the Committee's substitute for so-called "grandfather provisions."

It is not easy to classify all the types of specialization programs that have been adopted in the various states. Programs that are basically state-run certification programs have been adopted in Alabama, Arizona, California, Connecticut, Florida, Minnesota, Louisiana, New Jersey, New Mexico, Ohio, Tennessee and Texas. Many other states approve certification by private organizations if they meet certain standards. Generally, the national trend is toward recognizing more specialization. See 2013 Nat'l Roundtable on Specialization, "Lawyer Specialty Certification By the Numbers: 1996–2012" (noting that numbers of certified specialists nearly doubled between 1994 and 2012, with most specialists falling in the categories of civil trial, criminal and family law), available at <http://www.americanbar.org/content/dam /aba/administrative/professional_responsibility/2012_national_certification _census.authcheckdam.pdf>.

Certification ran into substantial opposition in California, especially from younger members of the bar and from minorities. Various proposals to strengthen or weaken the pilot program divided the bar for years until the Supreme Court finally made the program permanent in 1985. The designation programs have encountered difficulty too. A number of states have rejected designation proposals, at least partly on the ground that since the Supreme Court's decision in *Bates*, designation does not seem to amount to much more than advertising by field, which enjoys constitutional protection in any event. Some states have introduced continuing legal education requirements in their programs in order to add a quality component to the plans. Florida has also added a certification program for twenty-six fields of practice. Georgia, on the other hand, terminated its designation program when only 12% of eligible lawyers took advantage of it. See ABA Standing Committee on Specialization, <http://www.americanbar.org/groups/professional_responsibility/committees _commissions/specialization.html> for a listing of the state specialization programs. There is a discussion of the various pros and cons of certification and designation plans at pp. 464–472 and 473–478 of the first edition of this book. An article questioning the whole development of specialization plans is Marvin W. Mindes, "Proliferation, Specialization and Certification: The Splitting of the Bar," 11 U. Tol.

L. Rev. 273 (1980). In a recent notable decision, North Carolina State Board of Dental Examiners v. Federal Trade Commission, 135 S. Ct. 1101 (2015), the Court held that when a controlling number of the decisionmakers on a state licensing board are active participants in the occupation the board regulates, the board can invoke state-action immunity only if it is subject to active supervision by the state. While the implications for lawyers of the decision remain to be seen, the decision implies the narrowing of the legal profession's ability to restrict competition by imposing on lawyers and nonlawyers alike licensing and specialization requirements without appropriate state supervision.

In Peel v. Attorney Reg. and Disc. Comm'n of Ill., 496 U.S. 91 (1990), the Supreme Court overturned the censure of a lawyer who stated truthfully on his letterhead that he was certified as a civil trial specialist by the National Board of Trial Advocacy. The Illinois Supreme Court had held that the letterhead implied state recognition as a specialist and was inherently misleading on a variety of grounds. The United States Supreme Court reversed, on First Amendment grounds, holding that the letterhead was neither actually nor inherently misleading, although the suggestion was made that states could constitutionally require a disclaimer stating that the certification was not that of the government.

It should be added that while continuing legal education requirements are a component of specialization plans, they are also a growing feature in the states wholly apart from the debate over specialization. Starting in Minnesota in 1975, the idea has spread rapidly so that now a large majority of states have imposed such requirements. The constitutionality of the requirements has been upheld against an argument that the requirement violated the Thirteenth and Fourteenth Amendments. Verner v. Colorado, 716 F.2d 1352 (10th Cir. 1983), cert. den., 466 U.S. 960 (1984). A few states, like Ohio and Tennessee, have expanded their continuing legal education programs to encourage and reward mentoring, recognizing that lawyers' conduct in practice, and their competence, is shaped and influenced by the conduct and competence of peers. (Ohio:<http:www.supremecourt.ohio.gov/AttySvcs/CLE/>) (Tennessee:<https://www.tncourts.gov/rules/supreme-court/21>)

In 2015, the ABA revised the comment to Rule 1.1, noting that keeping abreast of changes in the law and its practice include understanding the "benefits and risks associated with relevant technology." Acknowledging the importance of maintaining technological competence as part of professional competence is consistent with the Rules' new emphasis on the relevance of technology to contemporary law practice, for example, in the context of protecting confidentiality against cyber threats per Rule 1.6(c), discussed in Chapter 2.

C. Malpractice

Lack of competence is the principal basis for legal malpractice. Generally, malpractice includes the "negligent rendition of professional services," although in many jurisdictions the concept may also include breach of fiduciary obligation. Ronald E. Mallen and Jeffrey M. Smith, 1 Legal Malpractice §§ 1:1, 8:13 (2008 ed.). The quintessential instance of malpractice is the failure to file the client's action within the deadline prescribed by the statute of limitations. Often malpractice litigation involves the extent, not the existence, of a duty to the client. See 1 id. § 8.2. ("Except where nonclients are involved, the primary issue in a legal malpractice case is not the existence of a duty but the extent of that duty.") The following case illustrates the point.

Procanik v. Cillo

206 N.J. Super. 270 (L. Div. 1985)

BOYLE, J.S.C.

This case involves the pre-termination duties of an attorney who is a specialist in his field arising out of a legal malpractice claim within a medical malpractice suit. The primary issue is whether an attorney, a specialist in malpractice, has the duty, not only to advise his clients on the settled law, but whether he also has a duty to disclose to his clients, clearly and unmistakably, an opinion held by him that the settled law is ripe for reconsideration. The subject matter, therefore, concerns what constitutes a complete, informed judgment. Additionally, there are contentions of a post-termination duty to advise clients of a decision subsequently reported in the advance sheets and whether these duties are mooted by a prospective application thereafter as to the applicable two-year statute of limitations. The issues arise out of a remand of the Supreme Court, Procanik By Procanik v. Cillo, 97 N.J. 339 (1984) (hereinafter cited as *Procanik*). Cross-motions for summary judgment have been made by all parties who agree that there are no genuine issues as to any material fact under R. 4:46-2. . . .

FACTUAL HISTORY

On June 8, 1976, co-plaintiff, Rosemarie Procanik (Procanik), placed herself under the medical care of the co-defendants, Dr. Joseph P. Cillo, Dr. Herbert Langer and Dr. Ernest P. Greenberg, who are board-certified obstetricians and gynecologists who apparently conduct a group practice. Thereafter, Procanik visited the offices of defendant-physicians from time to time. On June 9, 1977, she reported to defendant, Dr. Cillo, that her last menstrual period had been May 4, 1977. She further advised him that she had recently been diagnosed by family-physician as having measles but did not know if it was rubella (German measles). He examined Procanik and ordered "tests for German measles, known as Rubella Titer Test," at Rahway Hospital. The results "were 'indicative of past infection of Rubella.'" Instead of ordering further tests, it is alleged that Dr. Cillo negligently interpreted the results and told Procanik that she "had nothing to worry about because she had become immune to German measles as a child." In fact, the "past infection" disclosed by the tests was the German measles that had prompted Procanik to consult the defendant-physicians. Ignorant of what an accurate diagnosis would have disclosed, Procanik allowed her pregnancy to continue and delivered a son, the infant and incompetent, Peter Procanik; he having been born December 26, 1977. On January 16, 1978, the child was diagnosed as suffering from congenital rubella Down's syndrome.

As a result of the doctors' alleged negligence, Procanik was deprived of the choice of terminating the pregnancy, and Peter was "born with multiple birth defects," including eye lesions, heart disease, and auditory defects.

On April 26, 1978, the co-plaintiffs, Rosemarie Procanik and Michael Procanik, her husband, consulted with defendant-attorney, Harold Sherman (Sherman), regarding a possible claim for personal injuries as a result of the alleged medical malpractice of defendant-physicians. As a result of the consultation, Sherman determined that an opinion was necessary from a specialist in medical malpractice. Plaintiffs concede Sherman is a general practitioner in law. On November 6, 1978, Sherman consulted with Lee S. Goldsmith (Goldsmith), who was "of counsel" to the firm of Greenstone, Greenstone & Naishuler (Greenstone), a professional corporation specializing in medical malpractice claims. Goldsmith and Greenstone are also defendant-attorneys in this action. Goldsmith, in addition to being an attorney is a medical doctor. Answers to interrogatories disclosed that he had handled 300 cases involving medical malpractice. He specializes in medical malpractice cases. It was also conceded that Goldsmith, being "of counsel" (although not an employee of the Greenstone firm) acted as its agent.

Sherman collected plaintiffs' records and any other information regarding this matter and passed them along to defendants, Greenstone and Goldsmith. It was understood that Goldsmith would review the matter and render an opinion to Sherman.

Subsequently, Goldsmith referred the file to Dr. Leslie Iffy, professor of obstetrics and gynecology and director, division of maternal-fetal medicine at the New Jersey University of Medicine and Dentistry, for an expert medical opinion. Discovery revealed various correspondence between Goldsmith, Greenstone and Sherman. Of significance is a letter dated January 29, 1979 from Goldsmith to Greenstone.[1] It is clear from that letter that Goldsmith was aware of Gleitman v.

---

1. January 29, 1979

Gentlemen:

   We have, in the office, a Procanik file. This is a case in which a woman had a last menstrual period in May, measles at the end of May, then went to a gynecologist at the beginning of June; rubella test done, showed that she did have antibodies to it and apparently never informed of this so as to get an abortion. Gave birth to a deformed child in the following year.

   This case would fall into the area of Gleitman v. Cosgrove, 227 Atlantic 2d 689. The decision in this case was in 1967, at a time when abortions were still illegal. The decision was 4 to 3, and was, in part, based on the fact that abortions were illegal.

   Recently in New York, (and a copy of this decision is enclosed) there were two cases decided. Becker v. Schwartz and Park v Jessin [*Chessin*, 46 N.Y.2d 401], which in effect reverses Gleitman v. Cosgrove, and the New York case, Stuart v. Long Island Hospital. I think that now, at this time, it is an appropriate time to determine clearly whether or not we wish to take on Gleitman v. Cosgrove,

Cosgrove, 49 N.J. 22 (1967), which precluded wrongful birth actions. Goldsmith indicated that in his opinion the Procanik case was an appropriate one to reverse *Gleitman*. The letter stated "I think the time is right, and think we have a good shot at reversal." On February 7, 1979, Goldsmith and Greenstone received Dr. Iffy's medical report. In March 1979, Goldsmith delivered the entire file to Greenstone for his review. In a letter to Sherman dated April 26, 1979, Goldsmith and Greenstone decided not to accept the case.[2] They concluded that: (1) Gleitman "prohibits

---

going up to the Supreme Court. I think the time is right, and I think we have a good shot at reversal. The reason for the memo, then, is please read Becker v. Schwartz which is enclosed as well as *Gleitman*, so that we can discuss it and discuss our options. The damages are heavy.

> Cordially,
> */s/ Lee*
> Lee S. Goldsmith

2. April 26, 1979

Dear Harold:

We have finally come to a decision as to what to do with the Procanik case, after a great deal of discussion here in the office because of the problems presented by the case. Let me outline those problems to you as this forms the basis of our turning down the case.

The Procanik case basically falls into the area of a woman who had measles which was not definitively diagnosed, and, at approximately the same time was diagnosed as being pregnant. No steps were taken at that time. We are aware that Mrs. Procanik indicated that had she known of the potential problem, she would have undergone an abortion. We sent out the questions in the form of a possible malpractice case to an obstetrician/gynecologist, who felt that it was an extremely difficult position to put an obstetrician/gynecologist in. We did, however, decide not to leave it there and went ahead and reviewed the following:

1) Gleitman v. Cosgrove, 49 N.J. 22 (1967). As you are probably aware, this case prohibits the kind of action that would have to be brought herein. In other words, that type of action would either be a wrongful birth or an action for the purpose of trying to obtain damages for children who were born, and who would otherwise not have been born.

2) In January, 1979 two cases came down, reported as Nos. 559 and 560 of the Court of Appeals, New York entitled, Becker v. Schwartz and Park v. Chessin. These actions both are similar to Gleitman v. Cosgrove, and in effect, in New York, render a different opinion. It is possible that *Gleitman* could be reversed and it is further possible that the New Jersey courts could follow Becker v. Schwartz and Park v. Chessin. These cases do allow a person to sue under the circumstances of Procanik, and would allow the possibility of damages for life. It would mean, however, in Procanik, that the case would have to be started, face a dismissal at this level, and then obviously be appealed to the Supreme Court in the hopes of obtaining a reversal of Gleitman v. Cosgrove.

Considering the fact that the expert is somewhat weak on the case and considering the fact that it would have to be taken to the Supreme Court in order to obtain a reversal before a valid case could be brought, we have decided not to proceed. *The law is dead against us in the State and the reversal would be necessary.*

I am returning herewith all the hospital records that you were kind enough to send us. I will, if you like, send you a copy of the report of the expert. We have checked out every avenue and I think in all probability Mrs. Procanik did have measles, did become pregnant while she had the measles, and was not so informed. But because of the many and sundry other problems, we would not proceed.

Will you please be good enough to inform the Procaniks.

> Cordially,
> */s/ Lee*

the kind of action that would have to be brought herein"; (2) "It is possible that *Gleitman* could be reversed"; (3) "that it would have to be taken to the Supreme Court in order to obtain a reversal"; and (4) "The law is dead against us in the State and the reversal would be necessary."

As a result of this letter, Sherman determined to terminate the attorney-client relationship with Procanik. A meeting took place at his office with the Procaniks present. He discussed with them Goldsmith's letter of April 26, 1979, and reviewed a letter with them dated May 2, 1979[3] which constituted a termination of his services for the Procaniks. The letter indicated that Goldsmith was not interested in handling the case, and "his judgment is one on which I would certainly rely." It also advised the Procaniks "that you are free to consult another attorney, who after all, might feel differently about the case." It also advised the Procaniks of the applicable statute of limitations both as to the parents' claims and that of the infant, Peter. It also suggested "that if you want to pursue this matter further, you contact another attorney immediately." After Sherman had been originally retained and before termination of that relationship, the Supreme Court granted certification on September 5, 1978 in Berman v. Allan, 80 N.J. 421 (1979), which was reported in the New Jersey Law Journal (Law Journal), 102 N.J.L.J. 576 (1978).

LEE S. GOLDSMITH

3. May 2, 1979

Dear Mr. & Mrs. Procanik:

This will confirm that we have had a personal meeting to discuss the letter which I received from Mr. Lee Goldsmith, to whom I had referred the possible malpractice claims, along with the materials and records collected up to this point.

The sad truth is that while the probabilities are that the facts you relate are true, that under the law of New Jersey as it presently stands, the case would not survive a dismissal at the trial level. For your information, Mr. Goldsmith is not interested in handling the matter, and his judgment is one on which I would certainly rely.

Accordingly, I have returned the materials to you with the caution that you are free to consult another attorney, who after all, might feel differently about the case. You are also advised that, while the infant's claim survives until two years from attaining his 18th birthday, it is advisable to bring these cases within two years after the parents know or should have known that there was a possible malpractice claim, because the parents' claims for loss of services and medical expenses may be barred within two years, even though the infant's claim for injury might survive, as previously stated. It is also true that witnesses become less available, including doctors, and the same applies to records and other necessary documents.

I would, therefore, suggest that if you want to pursue this further, you contact another attorney immediately. I will provide any such attorney with a copy of Mr. Goldsmith's letter, should this request be made.

You will recall that you advanced us $200.00 towards costs, which were as follows:

Rahway Hospital Records:	$54.00
Presbyterian Hospital Records:	48.00
Children's Hospital Records:	18.00
Total:	$120.00

Accordingly, enclosed find our check for $80.00.

Very truly yours,
HAROLD A. SHERMAN

Although all of the defendant-attorneys were readers of the Law Journal, none of them had read this certification in that publication. On February 26, 1978, *Berman* was argued before the Supreme Court. On July 5, 1979, shortly after the attorney-client relationship had been terminated and memorialized by letter of May 2, 1979, the Law Journal established the notification of the decision of Berman v. Allan, 104 N.J.L.J. 1 (1979), which was decided on June 26, 1979. On July 26, 1979, the full text of the opinion in *Berman* appeared in the Law Journal, 104 N.J.L.J. 73 (1979). The *Berman* decision was then published in the advance sheets on August 31, 1979. In Berman v. Allan, 80 N.J. 421 (1979), the Court recognized that parents may recover for emotional distress for the "wrongful birth" of a child born with birth defects. The defendant-attorneys had not read the certification in *Berman*, reported in the Law Journal prior to termination with the Procaniks, nor, it was revealed by answers to interrogatories, could they recall with specificity when, after termination, they had become aware of the reported decision. Consequently, defendant-attorneys never advised the Procaniks that they had a cause of action, and the two-year statute of limitations expired on their claims on January 16, 1980. However, after January 16, 1980, the Procaniks engaged new counsel and a complaint was filed on April 8, 1981, almost 15 months after the statute of limitations had expired and nearly 3½ years after the infant was diagnosed as suffering from congenital rubella Down's syndrome.

Specifically, plaintiffs' complaint alleges that defendant-physicians negligently failed to diagnose a rubella infection early in plaintiff-mother's pregnancy, as a result of which infant-plaintiff was born with multiple birth defects. This medical malpractice cause them to suffer emotional injury and to incur medical expenses. Plaintiffs also assert that their defendant-attorneys undertook to investigate plaintiffs' potential malpractice claims and, in the course of that undertaking, negligently discharged their professional responsibilities in several ways: (1) by failing to become aware of an appeal pending before the Supreme Court which implicated the areas of medical malpractice law; (2) by advising them that the then settled law in this State precluded their contemplated action without further advising them that "a decision [of the unrelated pending appeal in *Berman*, supra] could be expected shortly"; (3) if not, that a "precautionary suit" should be instituted; and (4) in failing to advise them, months after their professional relationship had terminated, of the publication of the Court's decision in *Berman* and its recognition of the actionability of their claim.

Defendant-attorneys, on the other hand, maintain that no duty existed and that the actions exercised by defendant-attorneys were within the standard of care of the legal profession. . . .

In order to find defendant-attorneys liable for negligence, a legal duty must be found to exist and there must have been a breach of that duty. . . .

The standard for determining legal malpractice is that an attorney is obligated to exercise that degree of reasonable knowledge and skill that lawyers of ordinary ability and skill possess. . . . Our Supreme Court has adopted a North Carolina court's definition of the standard of care in legal malpractice actions . . . when it quoted Hodges v. Carter, 239 N.C. 517 (1954):

> Ordinarily when an attorney engaged in the practice of law and contracts to prosecute an action in behalf of his client, he impliedly represents that (1) he possesses the requisite degree of learning, skill and ability necessary to the practice of his profession and which others similarly situated ordinarily possess; (2) he will exert his best judgment in the prosecution of litigation entrusted to him; and (3) he will exercise reasonable and ordinary care and diligence in the use of his skill and in the application of his knowledge to his clients' cause. [239 N.C. at 519]

PRE-TERMINATION DUTY

Plaintiffs contend that Goldsmith and Greenstone were negligent by not being aware of the *Berman* certification reported in the Law Journal which, by implication, requires a finding of a duty to read or be aware of the Law Journal. Plaintiffs also claim that upon the publication of the certification in the Law Journal the law on wrongful birth claims became unsettled.

Since there is no dispute factually that Goldsmith and Greenstone, at the time of the rendering of the opinion and before termination of the attorney-client relationship ended, had not read the *Berman* certification, this Court must find whether a duty existed to nevertheless read the certification. This Court finds that the specialists had no duty to read the Law Journal and the specific certification that implicated this area of medical malpractice law.

R. 2:12-1 states that the Supreme Court may, on its own motion, certify any action or class of actions for appeal. While it is apparent to this Court: (1) That the issue in *Berman* presented a question of general public importance even though *Gleitman* had been previously settled by the Supreme Court as to wrongful birth claims; and (2) the decision under review was in potential conflict with the *Gleitman* doctrine and called for an exercise of the Supreme Court's supervision and other matters in the interest of justice, the certification did not render the law unsettled on wrongful birth claims. . . . Although the Law Journal publishes decisions of the courts, it is an unofficial publication in that regard. Reports of cases argued and determined in the courts are officially reported in the advance sheets and subsequently in the bound volumes of the New Jersey Reports and the New Jersey Superior Court Reports. A certification is a signal that the Supreme Court may be reconsidering settled law, not a final decision that the law, in fact, will change. . . .

This court holds, therefore, that *Gleitman* was the settled law at the time of the rendering of the opinion letter from Goldsmith to Greenstone dated April 26, 1979 as conveyed to the Procaniks May 2, 1979. This court also finds that the specialists had the right to decline the Procanik case. The closer question is whether the specialists' opinion reflected complete informed judgment. Their opinion certainly gave the settled law, but it did not convey to Sherman for the benefit of Procanik, what the specialists knew, i.e., that *Gleitman* was ripe for reconsideration. An examination of the Goldsmith letter to Sherman of April 26, 1979 omits that vital piece of information. It is known that this opinion was held and conveyed by Goldsmith to Greenstone in his letter of January 29, 1979. This court holds that a lawyer has a duty to disclose to his client, clearly and unmistakably, a complete opinion giving his full informed judgment that the settled law is ripe for reconsideration, particularly when one is held out as a specialist in the complicated field of medical malpractice.

. . . However . . . the advice was not based upon the exercise of an informed judgment, limited to the facts in this case. In Boss-Harrison Hotel Company v. Barnard, 148 Ind. App. 406 (1971), the court found that good appellate advocacy demands the regular reading of the advance sheets and that these advance sheets constitute central law since they are cases which have yet to be bound in their final volumes.

. . . This court agrees that liability should attach in such a situation. Attorneys are absolutely responsible for case law decisions as well as all temporary supplemental office texts of the case law such as an advance sheet. . . .

An examination of the letter of April 26, 1979 from Goldsmith to Sherman states: "It is possible that *Gleitman* could be reversed . . . ." In the last paragraph, the letter says: "The law is dead against us in the state and a reversal would be necessary." This court finds that although Goldsmith correctly and fully set forth the settled law in New Jersey, he failed to indicate in his letter to Sherman the clear opinion that he had given Greenstone, which stated: "and I think we have a good shot at reversal." A fair reading of that phrase indicates an anticipation that the *Gleitman* doctrine is ripe for reconsideration. On the other hand, Goldsmith's letter to Sherman, while admittedly stating that *Gleitman* could possibly be reversed, is not in the same context. The former is affirmative; the latter is negative. Furthermore and more importantly, Goldsmith's letter to Sherman of April 26, 1979 is an incomplete informed judgment and opinion. While complete as to the settled law, it is incomplete with respect to the posture for change. Realistically, a client not informed of this additional and vital element of information that *Gleitman* is ripe for reversal could reasonably allow a jury to conclude that the Procaniks, based upon this advice and counsel of a specialist, would decide that their claim was almost hopeless, and would discourage them from seeking a second opinion.

An attorney's stock in trade is his counsel and advice. The duty involved here is to give the client all of the information in complete form. Here, we had those ingredients in which Greenstone and Goldsmith were perceptive as specialists. *Gleitman* was a doctrine of long standing. At the time of that holding, abortions were not legal. Subsequently, it was held that abortions were legal. Roe v. Wade, 410 U.S. 113 (1973). Goldsmith was aware of the then favorable New York decisions which caused him to be optimistic in this case. Both specialists knew this even without the benefit of the *Berman* certification.

The law is perpetually in regeneration. This duty does not include predicting with any certainty whether the change will, in fact, occur nor when. A specialist in his field has a duty to be alert, aware and sensitive to the fact that his counsel and advice will have substantial weight and influence on any subsequent decisions that a client might make in pursuing the engagement of another attorney for a second opinion. Historically, we know that the final decision as to *Berman* was officially reported only a few months after the termination of the attorney-client relationship and well within the two-year statute of limitations applied retrospectively.

A legal expert in medical malpractice, securely perched on the summit of his specialty, must give a complete, informed opinion to the referring attorney for conveyance to the client. He must do no less, nor is more demanded. A specialist has a multi-tier standard of duty. It not only includes the duty generally applicable to those attorneys in the general practice of law, but also a duty of counsel and advice in the specialty involved, here — medical malpractice. . . .

This duty is not one to guaranty a change in the law, but rather to be aware that a realistic probability exists that the settled law is likely to be reconsidered.

It should be clear that this duty is not to be confused with hindsight or prescience. This duty does not require clairvoyance or the ability to predict as a prophet that the change in the law, in fact, will occur. It has been conceded by plaintiffs that if such a duty exists, it only applied to Greenstone and Goldsmith since they were specialists. Plaintiffs further conceded that Sherman, not being a specialist in medical malpractice, would not have a concurrent duty. Discovery and Sherman's termination letter of May 2, 1979 shows clearly that he, in fact, met the standard of reasonable care applicable to an admitted general practitioner as to this case. He discussed with the Procaniks Goldsmith's letter to him of April 26, 1979. He clearly relied on the judgment of Goldsmith. He advised his clients "you are free to consult another attorney, who after all, might feel differently about the case." He advised them as to the statute of limitations. He also stated "I would, therefore, suggest that if you want to pursue this matter further, you contact another attorney immediately." Based on the foregoing, this court holds that Sherman exercised the knowledge, skill and ability ordinarily possessed and exercised by members of the legal profession similarly situated, and he exercised reasonable care and prudence in relying upon the advice of the specialists.

POST-TERMINATION DUTY

Plaintiffs contend that defendants, Greenstone and Goldsmith, were negligent in not calling back their clients (presumably via Sherman) after the Law Journal published the *Berman* decision on January 26, 1979. For the reasons previously expressed, this court holds that they had no duty to do so since the Law Journal is not an official publication on adjudicatory decisions by the Supreme Court. However, it raises the question as to whether said defendants were negligent in failing to contact their clients after the *Berman* decision was reported in the advance sheets and subsequently the bound volumes in the New Jersey Reports. *Boss-Harrison Hotel Company*, supra.

Berman was published in the advance sheets on August 31, 1979, well within the remaining period of the statute of limitations. It is contended by the plaintiffs that the nature of the fiduciary relationship between Greenstone and Goldsmith and the Procaniks continued in force and did not terminate on May 2, 1979. They state that just as the obligation of confidentiality remains after termination, so does the duty of care remain as to relevant matters between the clients and the attorneys. Therefore, by not calling their clients to advise them of the *Berman* decision, said defendants were negligent.

"Generally, absent death or legal insanity of either party, the (attorney-client) relationship terminates only upon the accomplishment of the purpose for which the attorney was consulted, or upon mutual agreement of the parties." Tormo v. Yormark, 398 F. Supp. [1159 (1975)] at 1173. Therefore, the test regarding the termination of an attorney-client relationship asks (1) if there was a clear and unmistakable termination by the attorney, or (2) whether the purpose for which the attorney has been retained has been fulfilled. . . .

Here, the termination was clear and unmistakable. However, there is an additional ingredient: the attorney-specialists' opinion lacked full disclosure and was an incomplete conveyance of their opinion to their clients. Therefore, the second criterion in terminating an attorney-client relationship was not met in that they did not accomplish the purpose for which they were hired. Plaintiffs contend that Greenstone and Goldsmith had a post-termination duty. A jury could find that their relationship with the clients never terminated because the purpose of their retention was not fulfilled and, therefore, a pre-termination duty merely continued. Under the facts of this case, if the specialists are found to have breached a duty in the pretermination stage, they cannot utilize that wrong in evading responsibility subsequently.

The second criterion which this court imposes upon the specialists is not without precedent in the medical profession. In the case Tresemer v. Barke, 86 Cal. App. 3d 656 (1978), the court held that a physician had a duty to notify his client two years after the insertion of a dalcon shield that it could cause medical complications. The court stated that the patient had a cause of action by virtue of a confidential relationship between doctor and patient. The malpractice action was imposed from the continuing status of the physician-patient where the danger arose from that relationship. The situation in *Tresemer* is analogous to the case at bar. Although *Tresemer* involved a physician-patient relationship, the courts have continually held that similar rules of law and duties are applicable to physicians and attorneys. McCullough v. Sullivan, 102 N.J.L. 381, 384 (E. & A. 1926); Stewart v. Sbarro, 142 N.J. Super. 581, 590 (App. Div. 1976).

Accordingly, questions for the jury exist in that they might find: (1) a breach of the pre-termination duty involving an obligation to advise the clients that their case was ripe for reconsideration; (2) a breach of the post-termination duty involving an obligation to advise the clients of the favorable decision in *Berman* which would have prevented their medical malpractice claim from being time barred; and (3) that if there was a pre-termination duty that was breached by Greenstone and Goldsmith; the fiduciary relationship, limited to full disclosure, continued after the termination. . . .

For the reasons expressed herein, Sherman's motion for summary judgment is granted and all cross-claims against him are hereby dismissed. The summary judgment motion brought by Greenstone and Goldsmith is denied. An appropriate order consistent with this opinion shall be submitted.

Procanik v. Cillo

226 N.J. Super. 132 (App. Div. 1988)

PRESSLER, P.J.A.D.

. . .

With respect to the trial judge's conclusion on the summary judgment motion that an attorney-client relationship existed between Goldsmith and plaintiffs, we point out first that that ruling was, insofar as we are able to determine, based on a fact which later turned out to be incorrect. The trial court's factual recitation noted that Sherman had engaged Goldsmith to give his opinion and advice as to the Procaniks' prospective cause. By the time of trial it appeared that that characterization was not accurate. Sherman had not submitted the matter to Goldsmith for a specialist's opinion but had rather asked Goldsmith if he would be interested in accepting the representation. The relational posture was therefore not that of an undertaking to render advice by a "specialist" attorney but merely his declination to accept a proffered representation. It is clear that an attorney must affirmatively accept a professional undertaking before the attorney-client relationship can attach, whether his acceptance be by speech, writing, or inferred from conduct. . . . This case is about an affirmative refusal of a professional undertaking, not its acceptance. There was thus no attorney-client relationship . . . .

We nevertheless do not intend to suggest that threshold communications between attorney and prospective client do not impose certain obligations upon the attorney. But it is only the nature of the attorney's obligation in that threshold context, an obligation we address hereafter, which we must consider, not the whole panoply of fiduciary responsibilities and duties which come into play when an attorney-client relationship is formed. Thus, the sole dispositive issue as we perceive it is whether, based on the undisputed facts and plaintiffs' proofs at trial, plaintiffs established a prima facie case of attorney negligence against Goldsmith in that context.

That issue is narrowly focused. First, plaintiff contends that the Greenstone firm committed no act of independent or separate attorney negligence. Its liability is predicated exclusively on principles of agency and *respondeat superior*. Second, plaintiffs concede that Goldsmith was not guilty of any intentional conduct against them but only of negligent conduct. Third, plaintiffs concede that in declining to take the case, Goldsmith had no obligation to state any reason at all for his decision. What this case is consequently about is plaintiffs' theory, accepted by the trial judge both on the summary judgment motion and at trial, that if an attorney, and particularly a specialist, undertakes to give any reason at all for declining the case, he must give his full, complete and informed judgment. Plaintiffs assert that Goldsmith failed to do so.

The entire factual predicate on which plaintiffs construct their theory of Goldsmith's professional negligence is based on two alleged flaws in his letter of April 26, 1979 to Sherman . . . . The first flaw was Goldsmith's failure to iterate in his letter to Sherman the statement made in his January 29, 1979 memorandum to Greenstone respecting *Gleitman*, namely, that "I think the time is right, and I think we have a good shot at reversal." Their point is that Goldsmith thereby misled them respecting the strength of their case on appeal. [The second alleged flaw is irrelevant to the issues under consideration in this Chapter.] We reject both of these theses.

While we agree with the proposition that an attorney, in declining a representation, need give no reason at all, we disagree with the notion that if he gives any reason, it must fully explain his entire mental processes. In our view, if an attorney, including a specialist, voluntarily undertakes to give any reason for declining a case, whatever he does say must be professionally reasonable in the circumstances. We are also persuaded that there is not a scintilla of proof in this case that Goldsmith failed to comply with that standard.

We consider first the reason given by Goldsmith to Sherman respecting the state of the law on wrongful birth and wrongful life. Plaintiffs concede that Goldsmith's letter to Sherman was entirely accurate. They acknowledge, moreover, that the letter not only correctly stated the then settled law in New Jersey, but also explained that the law was evolving elsewhere and hence that "it is possible that *Gleitman* could be reversed and it is further possible that the New Jersey courts could follow" the recent New York decision. And, they acknowledge, the letter correctly outlined the appellate procedure which would have to be prosecuted "in the hopes of obtaining a reversal of Gleitman v. Cosgrove." They complain only that Goldsmith did not say to Sherman, as he had to Greenstone, that the chances for reversal were good and the time was right for a change.

We regard the letter in this respect to be entirely reasonable and adequate as a matter of law. We wholly disagree with the trial judge's conclusion that Goldsmith was obligated to convey any private thoughts he might have had about the prospect of the success of an appeal seeking an overhauling of the clearly stated decisional law. . . . [A] lawyer who correctly explains the existing decisional law of the jurisdiction, the recent disparate view of a sister jurisdiction, the consequent fact of potential change of decisional law on appeal, and the procedures for obtaining change has fulfilled any obligation he may have to explain his state-of-the-law reasons for declining the case. It is not a professional dereliction for him to withhold his gratuitous prediction of the prospect of success of an appeal which would be taken to obtain a change in the law.

Our conclusion is based on what we believe to be established principle governing an attorney's communication respecting the state of the law whether to a client or a prospective client. First, where, as here, there is no attorney-client relationship, an attorney is free to decline the representation without stating any reason at all. He is not, however, without obligation with respect to a reason he does undertake to give. . . . [I]n In re Gavel, 22 N.J. 248, 265 (1956) . . . Justice Vanderbilt . . . concluded that the attorney's fiduciary obligation extends to "persons who, although not strictly clients, he has or should have reason to believe rely on him." Ibid. . . . We have no doubt that when an attorney, and particularly one specializing in a specific area of the law, declines a representation because of the state of the law which he undertakes to express, he knows or should know that the prospective client will depend on the reliability of that expression. Nor is there any doubt there that Goldsmith knew that plaintiffs would so rely on his letter to Sherman. Indeed he asked Sherman to "please be good enough to inform the Procaniks."

We also regard as well settled the scope and nature of the duty of a lawyer who does undertake to state the law to a client or a prospective client. If the law is settled, he is expected to know what it is and to state it accurately. . . . If the law is unsettled, debatable or doubtful, he is not required to be correct, usually determinable only by hindsight, but only to exercise an informed judgment based on a reasoned professional evaluation. . . . Nor is an attorney obliged to anticipate a change in settled law. . . . And if, as here, the attorney has a degree of expertise in a complex and volatile area of the law which leads him to believe, because of developments elsewhere, that change in settled law is possible, it is surely enough for him to point that that is so and why—just as Goldsmith did here. That explanation need not and perhaps ought not be accompanied by a prediction of the likelihood that he can effect that change in the decisional law in that very case. Surely any experienced practitioner must understand the uncertainty of that prospect even if he believes that the time for seeking change is right and the chances reasonably good. And it is that very uncertainty which ultimately precludes imposition of liability based on his withholding of such a prediction. . . . Nor . . . can a lawyer be penalized when he not only accurately states the existing rule of law but also points out a reasoned basis supporting the possibility of its change. There was, in sum, nothing actionable in Goldsmith's legal explanation to Sherman.

Notes

1. The Supreme Court of New Jersey declined to review the decision of the Appellate Division. 113 N.J. 357 (1988). Note that the issues presented by the motions for summary judgment are related to one another. The first issue is whether the plaintiffs were "clients" of the specialists in the five-month period before the specialists turned down the case. The second issue, whether attorneys who turn down a case have an obligation to state their real reasons for so doing if they give any reasons at

all, is affected by the reasonable beliefs of the client as to their relationship because of the length of time during which the specialists were considering the matter. In other words, the time lag is important on both issues.

2. It is worth noting that the plaintiffs alleged, and the trial court found, two kinds of incompetence. The first was incompetence of the specialists in failing to communicate their original views accurately and in failing to mention the new decision of the New Jersey Supreme Court. The second, however, is incompetence with respect to their expertness—the failure to keep up with the current decisions if in fact they did not become aware of the critical case in time. The trial court simply stated that good appellate advocacy required keeping up with the advance sheets. That issue apparently was never presented to the Appellate Division.

3. While the more common basis for a malpractice claim is in tort, the courts have also recognized a contract basis when an attorney fails to perform a task that a client has specifically instructed him or her to perform or when an attorney fails to keep a specific promise that was reasonably relied on by the client. E.g., Sherman Indus., Inc. v. Goldhammer, 683 F. Supp. 502 (E.D. Pa. 1988).

4. In Russo v. Griffin, 147 Vt. 20 (1986), the court held that the geographical standard for measuring a lawyer's standard of care in a professional malpractice case was statewide and not limited to that of the locality in which the lawyer practiced. The court noted that the standards for admission and the rules of practice were statewide and that a limitation of the standard of care to the locale of practice would make it harder to get expert witnesses and indeed could lead to a "conspiracy of silence." Does that rationale seem applicable to large legal markets, such as New York City, Chicago, or Los Angeles? See Chapman v. Bearfield, 207 S.W.3d 736 (Tenn. 2006), citing numerous cases applying statewide standards and relying on use of the internet as a primary legal research tool for additional justifications.

The problem in *Procanik* involved the duty owed by an attorney to a potential client whom the lawyer eventually decided not to represent. In the following case, the issue is whether an attorney had agreed to represent the client in the specific aspect of the transaction in which the client suffered damage.

Lane v. Cold

882 So. 2d 436 (Fla. Ct. App. 2004)

VAN NORTWICK, J.

Gary Lane appeals a final summary judgment entered in favor of Kathleen Holbrook Cold . . . in Lane's legal malpractice action against Cold based upon her alleged failure to prepare a buy-sell agreement. . . .

Cold prepared the necessary documents for the incorporation of Bobcat of North Florida, Inc., with Lane and his now deceased brother, Bobby Lane, as sole shareholders. Lane argues that genuine issues of material fact are in dispute as to whether Cold was negligent in failing to prepare a buy-sell agreement when she incorporated Bobcat to assure a plan of succession for the corporation in the event of the death of one of the brothers. The facts are undisputed that Cold had prepared a buy-sell agreement at the time of the incorporation of another corporation wholly-owned by the Lanes; that, at the time of the incorporation of Bobcat, Cold inquired of the Lanes as to whether they wished her to prepare a buy-sell agreement; and that no one requested Cold to prepare a buy-sell agreement relating to Bobcat. Although Gary Lane and the Lanes' accountant stated that the Lanes wanted a buy-sell agreement, Lane produced no evidence that either the Lanes, their accountant or anyone acting on their behalf had requested Cold to prepare the agreement or expressed to Cold an interest in having a buy-sell agreement in connection with Bobcat.

To recover in a legal malpractice action, the plaintiff must show (1) the attorney's employment, (2) the attorney's neglect of a reasonable duty, and (3) such negligence was the proximate cause of loss to the plaintiff. . . . With respect to establishing the first element, it is not sufficient merely to show that an attorney-client relationship existed between the parties, it is essential that the plaintiff show that the relationship existed with respect to the acts or omissions upon which the malpractice claim is based. Here, Lane has presented no evidence that Cold was retained to prepare a buy-sell agreement or that she otherwise agreed, expressly or implicitly, to undertake that responsibility.

Further, although an attorney's negligent act or omission in connection with a client's business planning may be the basis for a malpractice action . . . Lane does not allege that Cold gave him negligent advice. It is undisputed that Cold counseled with her clients with respect to the buy-sell agreement and asked her clients whether they wished one to be prepared. Cold's professional inquiry concerning the desire for a buy-sell agreement, without more, did not create a duty on her part to prepare the agreement. See Boyd v. Brett-Major, 449 So.2d 952, 954 (Fla. Ct. App. 1984) ("It is not the role of an attorney acting as counsel to independently determine what is best for his client and then act accordingly. Rather, such an attorney is to allow the client to determine what is in the client's best interests and then act according to the wishes of that client within the limits of the law." (quoting Orr v. Knowles, 337 N.W.2d 699, 702 (Neb. 1983)).

Where a movant for summary judgment (here, Cold) offers sufficient evidence to support her claim of the nonexistence of a genuine issue of material fact, the opposing party (in this case, Lane) must demonstrate the existence of an issue or issues either by countervailing facts or justifiable inferences from the facts presented. . . . Here, Lane failed to present to the trial court any evidence showing that Cold was employed to prepare or otherwise had a professional obligation to prepare a buy-sell agreement for the Lanes and Bobcat. Accordingly, we find that there is no genuine issue of material fact as to one of the essential elements of Lane's cause of action and we affirm the final summary judgment.

Note

Is it clear that drafting the agreement was not part of the purpose for which Cold was employed? After all, she had done so before for these same clients in an apparently similar transaction, and plaintiff did present evidence that the clients "wanted" such an agreement here. One possible explanation is that plaintiff's lawyer simply neglected to introduce evidence that his client communicated that desire to Cold. Another possibility is that the plaintiff and his brother saw no need to go to the extra expense of having Cold draft an extra document. If that was the case, consider how wise Cold was to take the time to put her request in writing. When trouble comes, a lawyer and a client may have quite different memories about whether a lawyer gave specific advice orally. A lawyer cannot reduce every bit of advice to writing, but sometimes it is worth the time to put particular items in writing.

The *Procanik* case dealt with the standard of care owed by a lawyer to a client, and indeed that is the setting in which claims about negligent practice are usually made. Occasionally, however, the claim of negligent practice is made by someone who is not a client, as in the following case.

Angel, Cohen & Rogovin v. Oberon Investment, N.V.

512 So. 2d 192 (Fla. 1987)

PER CURIAM

We review Oberon Investments v. Angel, Cohen and Rogovin, 492 So. 2d 1113 (Fla. 3d DCA 1986), because of direct and express conflict with Amey, Inc. v. Henderson, Franklin, Starnes & Holt, P.A., 367 So. 2d 633 (Fla. 2d DCA), cert. denied 376 So. 2d 68 (Fla. 1979) and Drawdy v. Sapp, 365 So. 2d 461 (Fla. 1st DCA 1978). Art. V, § 3(b)(3), Fla. Const.

This case deals with the actions of petitioner in its representation of one Leonard Treister. Respondent brought suit against Treister alleging that, while acting as attorney and agent for respondent, Treister arranged a transaction whereby respondent sold its wholly-owned subsidiary to an undisclosed principal, actually Treister, for a certain sum while concurrently arranging a second transaction reselling the same property to a third-party buyer for a larger sum, thus defrauding respondent. In a separate count, respondent Oberon alleged that the petitioner law firm represented Treister in preparing the sale documents and should have foreseen the damage to Oberon; ergo the petitioner was negligent in preparing the documents or failing to inform respondent of the nature and extent of the transactions or in permitting Treister to use the document for defrauding [respondent]. There was no allegation that the petitioner engaged in fraudulent or conspiratorial conduct. The trial court granted summary judgment in favor of the petitioner. On appeal, the district court reversed, holding that a lack of privity did not bar recovery if petitioner knew that Treister was a fiduciary for respondent and knew of the potential conflict between the interests of Treister and respondent. The court reasoned that should the issues of fact be resolved in respondent's favor, petitioner had a duty to act in the best interest of respondent. Accordingly, because there were material facts in dispute relative to Treister's capacity and petitioner's knowledge, the summary judgment was reversed and the case remanded.

Assuming as we must in the posture of the case that the petitioner was aware that Treister was a fiduciary of respondent and was obligated to act in the best interests of respondent, the issue before this Court is whether such knowledge subjects the petitioner to an action in negligence brought by the third-party respondent.

Florida courts have uniformly limited attorneys' liability for negligence in the performance of their professional duties to clients with whom they share privity of contract.... The only instances in Florida where this rule of privity has been relaxed is where it was the apparent intent of the client to benefit a third party. The most obvious example of this is the area of will drafting.... Florida courts have refused to expand this exception to include incidental third-party beneficiaries. For the beneficiaries' action in negligence to fall within the exception to the privity requirement, testamentary intent as expressed in the will must be frustrated by the attorney's negligence and as a direct result of such negligence the beneficiaries' legacy is lost or diminished. We see no reason to expand this limited exception and specifically reject the invitation to adopt California's balancing of factors test. Biakanja v. Irving, 320 P.2d 16 (1958).

In the instant case, respondent was not the client of the petitioner and thus lacked the requisite privity customarily required to maintain an action sounding in negligence against an attorney. Nor does the respondent, as an incidental third party beneficiary, fit within Florida's narrowly defined third-party beneficiary exception. Respondent's assertion that the petitioner knew or should have known of potential conflict between the interests of Treister and the respondent further undercuts his reliance on the third-party beneficiary exception. If, as respondent alleges, the petitioner knew of the conflict of interest between Treister and respondent, it was equally apparent that the professional services rendered Treister were not to benefit respondent. If, on the other hand, the petitioner did not know of the conflicting interest of Treister and respondent, petitioner's only duty was to its client, Treister. Accordingly, even should the material facts in dispute be resolved in the respondent's favor, they would not support its cause of action. The trial court correctly granted summary judgment. The district court's opinion is quashed and the case remanded for proceedings consistent with this opinion.

Notes

1. The court referred to California's balancing of facts test. The formulation in the *Biakanja* case, to which the court referred, was as follows:

The determination whether in a specific case the defendant will be held liable to a third person not in privity is a matter of policy and involves the balancing of various factors, among which are the extent to which the transaction was intended to affect the plaintiff, the foreseeability of harm to him, the degree of certainty that the plaintiff suffered injury, the closeness of the connection between the defendant's conduct and the injury suffered, the moral blame attached to the defendant's conduct, and the policy of preventing future harm.

How would you decide the principal case using the *Biakanja* formula?

2. While it is true that *Oberon* refused to relax the privity requirement to allow a third party to sue an attorney for negligent performance of his duty to a client, it should not be understood as meaning that a lawyer is not liable to a third party on the same basis that an ordinary citizen would be liable. See Riggs Nat'l Bank v. Freeman, 682 F. Supp. 519 (S.D. Fla. 1988) (noting that an attorney may be liable to a third party for negligent misrepresentation). The court stated that there was no allegation of "fraudulent or conspiratorial" conduct by the law firm. There was an allegation of negligence because the law firm prepared the documents that Treister used to defraud his client.

3. Judge Posner discussed the doctrinal underpinnings of the causes of action against lawyers for professional malpractice and negligent misrepresentation in Greycas v. Proud, 826 F.2d 1560 (7th Cir. 1987), cert. denied, 484 U.S. 1043 (1988). He related developments in those fields to general developments in torts, and his opinion is an interesting exposition of the approach of a judge whose former academic interest in the relation between economics and law has carried over into his judicial work.

D. Whistleblowing on Other Lawyers

Problem 10–5

Without asking you for any advice, a lawyer who has been your close friend for many years tells you that he has learned that his partner has paid, on request, a kickback to a judge who named her a guardian in an estate matter. The judge has recently been assigned to another county; the partner is enormously upset at having given in to the judge's hard luck story that led her to give him the money; and your friend tells you he has decided to do nothing. Must you report the conduct of the judge and lawyers to the local discipline committee?

Problem 10–5 invokes Model Rule 8.3(a), with its premise that the obligation of self-discipline that the profession has undertaken involves self-policing, which in turn requires reporting of unprofessional conduct by other lawyers. The requirement has been controversial, and its opponents call it the "rat rule." Perhaps predictably critics have claimed that the requirement is not enforced, see Arthur E. Greenbaum, "The Attorney's Duty to Report Professional Misconduct," 16 Geo. J. Legal Ethics 259 (2003), but there are a few cases in which violation of a reporting requirement has figured in discipline of a lawyer. See In re Himmel, 125 Ill. 2d 531 (1988) (lawyer suspended for one year for failure to report another lawyer's conversion of the funds of his client); In re Riehlmann, 891 So.2d 1239 (La. 2005) (citing additional Louisiana cases). And see Spencer v. Gavin, 946 A.2d 1051 (App. Div. 2008) (remanding case for trial as to extent of the accused's knowledge). Among other problems with the rule, it is triggered only when an attorney "knows" of another attorney's significant misconduct. Actual knowledge can be hard to come by, particularly given the natural disinclination to report misconduct. (Of course, sometimes the opposite may be the case; knowledge may come easily when Rule 8.3 seems a useful litigation tactic.) A number of courts have set the knowledge standard as "more likely than not that a violation had occurred." See In re Riehlmann, cited above.

Proponents of the Rule have successfully argued in most jurisdictions that given the prerogatives of the license to practice law, a reporting requirement is both appropriate and necessary. The requirement also connects with the discussion of attorneys' alcoholism and substance abuse. Consider whether you would, or will, be able to report your alcoholic or substance abusing partner or associate to the disciplinary authorities. See ABA Comm. on Ethics and Prof'l Responsibility Formal Op. 03-431 (2003) (requiring reporting). Many states now have instituted a temporary "disability inactive" status for such attorneys, perhaps reducing potential damage to reputation.

A second aspect of the responsibility of lawyers for the conduct of other lawyers arises in the context of a law firm. The issue is part of the more general issue of whistleblowing that we also saw when discussing the issue of confidentiality (pp. 39ff.) and document destruction in the *Herbster* case, p. 477, Note 7. Several cases followed the *Herbster* result, but then the New York Court of Appeals decided in Wieder v. Skala, 80 N.Y.2d 628 (1992), that if a law firm fired an associate because he reported an ethics violation by a member of the firm, the associate had a cause of action for unlawful dismissal even though he was only an employee at will. There was an implied understanding in his contract of employment that he would abide by the disciplinary rules of the profession, which mandated the reporting of serious ethical violations. See also General Dynamics Corp. v. Superior Court, 7 Cal. 4th 1164 (1994), in which the California Supreme Court recognized the right of an attorney to sue for wrongful discharge when dismissed for performing an act compelled by state public policy. The Ethics Opinion that follows Problem 10–7 deals with the obligations of whistleblowing.

Model Rules 5.1 and 5.2 address the responsibilities of partners, supervising lawyers, and subordinates for the conduct of one another. Note that Rule 5.2(a) expressly states the obligations of a subordinate to obey the Rules but Rule 5.2(b) then protects subordinates who obey a supervisory lawyer's reasonable resolution of an arguable question of professional duty. But note that violation of Rule 5.1(c)(2) imposes disciplinary liability on the supervising lawyer who doesn't supervise for the disciplinary violations of the lawyer being supervised. See In re Cohen, 847 A.2d 1162 (D.C. Ct. App. 2004), suspending a lawyer for thirty days for failure to supervise.

Problem 10–6

You are an associate in the law firm involved in the OPM fraud, pp. 96–97, Note 5, and you were present when the company officers admitted their fraud to the firm. When you are instructed to prepare the papers to close new loans, you are horrified because you do not believe the company officers who have assured the firm that its fraudulent practices have ceased. You state your beliefs to the partner in charge, who repeats his instructions saying that on the basis of the disclosures and having pushed the company officers hard, he believes that these loans are genuine. You are not at all convinced. What do you do?

Problem 10–7

You were an associate assigned to work on the plaintiff's case by your law firm in the *IBM* case, p. 207. You stated that it was clear that the firm was disqualified and that there was insufficient disclosure and consent to cure the disqualification. The partner in charge disagreed and instructed you to start work on the case. What do you do?

Massachusetts Committee on Professional Ethics
Opinion 99-2
(July 15, 1999)

Facts:

A lawyer (L) has discovered that several of her partners intentionally misrepresented material facts to state and federal agencies (which are not tribunals) in explaining the lawyers' failure to file on time required reports of firm clients. The clients had no knowledge of the fraud. The state agency has not yet acted on a request to forego substantial penalties. The federal agency, relying on the false explanations, did not assess penalties on the clients. L asks whether she has ethical obligations to report her partners' misconduct to the affected clients, the state and federal agencies, and Bar Counsel. L was not representing her partners when she learned of their fraudulent conduct.

Discussion:

1. Disclosure To the Clients. Mass. R. Prof. C. 1.4(a) states:

A lawyer shall keep a client reasonably informed about the status of a matter and promptly comply with reasonable requests for information.

Comment [1] to Rule 1.4 commences with:

The client should have sufficient information to participate intelligently in decisions concerning the objectives of representation and the means by which they are to be pursued . . .

Clearly the lawyers who committed fraud on the agencies are obligated to tell the clients how their matters have been handled. Without this information the clients can hardly "participate intelligently in decisions concerning the objectives of the representation and the means by which they are to be pursued." If the partners who perpetrated the fraud are unwilling to disclose their wrongdoing to the clients, Rule 5.1(c)(2) imposes on L responsibility for their ethical violations:

(c) A lawyer shall be responsible for another lawyer's violations of the Rules of Professional Conduct if: . . .

(2) the lawyer is a partner in the law firm in which the other lawyer practices . . . and knows of the conduct at a time when its consequences can be avoided or mitigated but fails to take reasonable remedial action.

This rule places on the innocent partner the ethical obligation to act to avoid or mitigate the acts of the wrongdoing partners. In the present circumstances that clearly includes contacting the clients, if the wrongdoers will not, and disclosing the fraud to the clients. Because L was not acting as counsel to her partners when she learned of their fraud, her disclosing the fraud to the clients does not raise any issue of confidentiality under Rule 1.6.

2. Obligation to the Agencies. In reliance upon the fraudulent filings by L's partners, the agencies have suffered or will suffer substantial injury to their financial interests by not asserting penalties against the clients. Rule 4.1 states:

In the course of representing a client a lawyer shall not knowingly:

(a) make a false statement of material fact or law to a third person. . . .

L's partners have violated Rule 4.1(a). By reason of Rule 5.1(c)(2), quoted above, L as their partner is responsible for their violations if she "fails to take reasonable remedial action." Disclosure to the affected agencies, however, unlike disclosure to the clients, would involve revealing confidential information of the clients.

Rule 1.6(a) requires that a lawyer "not reveal confidential information relating to the representation of a client unless the client consents after consultation . . . except as stated in paragraph (b)." Comment [5] to Rule 1.6 provides that "confidential information" includes both confidences protected by the attorney/client privilege and "secrets" as defined in an earlier rule. Included within the concept of secret is information disclosure of which would be embarrassing or likely be detrimental to the client. Thus, the information concerning the fraud on the agencies is within "confidential information" and protected by Rule 1.6(a), unless revelation of that information is permitted by Rule 1.6(b), which in relevant part states:

A lawyer may reveal and to the extent required by Rule 3.3, Rule 4.1(b), or Rule 8.3 must reveal, such information:

(1) to prevent the commission of a criminal or fraudulent act that the lawyer reasonably believes is likely to result in death or substantial bodily harm, or in substantial injury to the financial interests or property of another, or to prevent the wrongful execution or incarceration of another.

Thus, Rule 1.6(b)(1) gives L discretion to reveal the unconsummated fraud to the state agency, which has not yet acted on the fraudulent information supplied by L's partners. As noted in Comment [13A] to Rule 1.6, Massachusetts in adopting the Model Rules of Professional Conduct explicitly changed the language of this rule "to permit disclosure of a client's confidential information when the harm will be the result of the activities of third persons as well as of the client." In addition, we believe that the conduct here meets the further requirement that the act to be prevented must be "likely to result . . . in substantial injury to the financial interests . . . of another." While Rule 1.6(b)(1) only gives L discretion to reveal the fraud to the state agency, we believe that Rule 5.1(c)(2) requires her to act to avoid or mitigate the consequences of her partners' fraud. For example, L might withdraw the papers filed by her partners with, but not yet acted upon by, the state agency, or L might under the circumstances have to disclose the fraud to the agency.

Whether Rule 1.6(b)(1) would permit reporting the completed fraud to the federal agency raises a more difficult question, which in the absence of knowing all the facts, we do not at this time address.

3. Disclosure to Bar Counsel. Last we address whether Rule 8.3 imposes upon L an obligation to report her partners' fraudulent conduct to Bar Counsel. Rule 8.3(a) states:

> A lawyer having knowledge that another lawyer has committed a violation of the Rules of Professional Conduct that raises a substantial question as to that lawyer's honesty, trustworthiness or fitness as a lawyer in other respects, shall inform Bar Counsel's office of The Board of Bar Overseers. . . .

> (c) This rule does not authorize disclosure of information otherwise protected by Rule 1.6. . . .

The Office of Bar Counsel has issued a statement of policy asserting that the kinds of violation that raise a "substantial question as to [a] lawyer's honesty, trustworthiness or fitness as a lawyer in other respects" include "at a minimum, any matter that would result in a suspension or disbarment." MBA Lawyers' Journal (March 1999). In our view, no matter what definition of reportable conduct is selected, L has set forth facts that fall within the core area of lawyer misconduct that must be reported under Rule 8.3. On the facts as given, L knows that her partners have engaged in fraud, deceit, and misrepresentation in violation of at least Rule 4.1(a), quoted above, Rule 8.4(c), and perhaps other rules as well.

Rule 8.3(c) excepts from disclosure information "protected by Rule 1.6." As Comment [2] explains, "A report about misconduct is not required or permitted where it would involve violation of Rule 1.6." In this inquiry, however, a report would not violate Rule 1.6 because, as discussed above, L has discretion to reveal the fraud. Since the information is not protected, L must inform Bar Counsel's office of the violation. That is the meaning of the language in Rule 1.6(b) that a "lawyer may reveal, *and to the extent required by . . . Rule 8.3, must reveal*, such information . . . ." (emphasis added). Indeed, Comment [21] to Rule 1.6 states, "The reference to Rules 3.3, 4.1(b), and 8.3 in the opening phrase of Rule 1.6(b) has been added to emphasize that Rule 1.6(b) is not the only provision of these rules that deals with the disclosure of confidential information and that in some circumstances disclosure of such information may be required and not merely permitted."

Ordinarily, assuming that she does not fear for her safety, compare Mass. R. Prof. C. 1.6, Comment 19A, L should urge her partners to disclose to the firm's clients what they have done. If they refuse to do so, L should discuss the fraud with the clients herself. In any event, she should reveal to the clients her ethical obligations to act to avoid consequences of the fraud on the state agency and to report her partners' misconduct to Bar Counsel. L should not be dissuaded from meeting these obligations by the clients, but they have the right to know what she intends to do because they may well be injured by her actions through no fault of their own, and they may wish to seek counsel on how best to protect their interests.

Notes

1. There are a number of interesting features to this opinion. It is crucial to the committee's conclusion that Massachusetts, like many other states, amended its version of the Model Rules to give a lawyer discretion to reveal confidential information to prevent the commission of fraud "likely to result . . . in substantial injury to the financial interests . . . of another." But, as the committee also points out, Massachusetts amended its rules to allow the information to be revealed when the fraudulent act is that of a third person, here the client's lawyer. Was that a desirable change to the Model Rules?

2. In a jurisdiction that does not permit a lawyer to reveal confidential information to prevent client fraud, would Rule 5.1(c)(2) require revelation anyhow if the client acquiesced in the lawyer's fraud on the client's behalf?

3. The committee did not answer the question whether the lawyer was permitted or required to report the completed fraud to the federal agency. Under what factual circumstances do you think the partner might have such an obligation or such discretion in the circumstances of Opinion 99-2? Does your answer turn on whether the client acquiesces in the partners' deception?

4. The Opinion refers to a Comment that deals with the obligation of lawyers to tell clients in advance that they are about to reveal confidential information. Comment 17A to Massachusetts Rule 1.6 states:

> [17A] Whenever the rules permit or require the lawyer to disclose a client's confidential information, the issue arises whether the lawyer should, as a part of the confidentiality and loyalty obligation and as a matter of

competent practice, advise the client beforehand of the plan to disclose. It is not possible to state an absolute rule to govern a lawyer's conduct in such situations. In some cases, it may be impractical or even dangerous for the lawyer to advise the client of the intent to reveal confidential information either before or even after the fact. Indeed, such revelation might thwart the reason for creation of the exception. It might hasten the commission of a dangerous act by a client or it might enable clients to prevent lawyers from defending themselves against accusations of lawyer misconduct. But there will be instances, such as the intended delivery of whole files to prosecutors to convince them not to indict the lawyer, where the failure to give notice would prevent the client from making timely objection to the revelation of too much confidential information. Lawyers will have to weigh the various policies and make reasonable judgments about the demands of loyalty, the requirements of competent practice, and the policy reasons for creating the exception to confidentiality in order to decide whether they should give advance notice to clients of the intended disclosure.

In the circumstances described in Opinion 99-2, should the lawyer have warned both the firm's client and her partners that she was about to reveal confidential information to at least the state agency?

5. Would the analysis in the Massachusetts Bar Association's Ethics Opinion 99-2 be different if the lawyer involved were not a partner at the firm, but rather an associate? Do different considerations apply? If so, should they? Consider, for example, the conduct of Eastman Kodak's counsel in the infamous 1978 Kodak–Berkey antitrust case. During the deposition stage of the matter, a member of Kodak's team of counsel, Mahlon Perkins, falsely represented to counsel for Berkey that certain key documents relevant to the opinion and testimony of Kodak's expert had been inadvertently destroyed and were therefore unavailable for production. Perkins' associate, Joseph Fortenberry, may have been aware of the fact that the documents had not been destroyed, but were in fact in a briefcase back at their office. If that were the case, he did not disclose this information to his colleagues, the court, or to the disciplinary authorities. Was there any basis for his silence? Berkey Photo, Inc. v. Eastman Kodak Co., 457 F. Supp. 404 (1978), aff'd in part, rev'd in part, 603 F.2d 263 (1979), cert. denied, 444 U.S. 1093 (1980). The existence of the documents ultimately came to the attention of Berkey's counsel following the cross-examination of Kodak's expert. Subsequently, Perkins confessed to his perjury. He spent 30 days in jail for the offense, but was not disbarred. For interesting accounts of this incident, see James D. Stewart, *The Partners: Inside America's Most Powerful Law Firms* 327–365 (1983) and Deborah L. Rhode, *Professional Responsibility* 74 and 82–86 (2d ed. 1998).

6. See In re Cohen, 847 A.2d 1162 (D.C. Ct. App. 2004), for a case in which a partner was suspended for inadequate supervision of an associate (his son) who committed several serious disciplinary violations. The District of Columbia version of Rule 5.1(c)(2) adds a "reasonably should know" standard to the Model Rules' knowledge requirement. See also In re Mandelman, 290 Wis. 2d 158 (2006).

Bohatch v. Butler & Binion

977 S.W.2d 543 (Texas 1998)

CRAIG T. ENOCH, J.

Partnerships exist by the agreement of the partners; partners have no duty to remain partners. The issue in this case is whether we should create an exception to this rule by holding that a partnership has a duty not to expel a partner for reporting suspected overbilling by another partner. The trial court rendered judgment for Colette Bohatch on her breach of fiduciary duty claim against Butler & Binion and several of its partners (collectively, "the firm"). The court of appeals held that there was no evidence that the firm breached a fiduciary duty and reversed the trial court's tort judgment; however, the court of appeals found evidence of a breach of the partnership agreement and rendered judgment for Bohatch on this ground. 905 S.W.2d 597. We affirm the court of appeals' judgment.

I. FACTS

Bohatch became an associate in the Washington, D.C. office of Butler & Binion in 1986 after working for several years as Deputy Assistant General Counsel at the Federal Energy Regulatory Commission. John McDonald, the managing partner of the office, and Richard Powers, a partner, were the only other attorneys in the Washington office. The office did work for Pennzoil almost exclusively.

Bohatch was made partner in February 1990. She then began receiving internal firm reports showing the number of hours each attorney worked, billed, and collected. From her review of these reports, Bohatch became concerned that McDonald was overbilling Pennzoil and discussed the matter with Powers. Together they reviewed and copied portions of McDonald's time diary. Bohatch's review of McDonald's time entries increased her concern.

On July 15, 1990, Bohatch met with Louis Paine, the firm's managing partner, to report her concern that McDonald was overbilling Pennzoil. Paine said he would investigate. Later that day, Bohatch told Powers about her conversation with Paine.

The following day, McDonald met with Bohatch and informed her that Pennzoil was not satisfied with her work and wanted her work to be supervised. Bohatch testified that this was the first time she had ever heard criticism of her work for Pennzoil.

The next day, Bohatch repeated her concerns to Paine and to R. Hayden Burns and Marion E. McDaniel, two other members of the firm's management committee, in a telephone conversation. Over the next month, Paine and Burns investigated Bohatch's complaint. They reviewed the Pennzoil bills and supporting computer print-outs for those bills. They then discussed the allegations with Pennzoil in-house counsel John Chapman, the firm's primary contact with Pennzoil. Chapman, who had a long-standing relationship with McDonald, responded that Pennzoil was satisfied that the bills were reasonable.

In August, Paine met with Bohatch and told her that the firm's investigation revealed no basis for her contentions. He added that she should begin looking for other employment, but that the firm would continue to provide her a monthly draw, insurance coverage, office space, and a secretary. After this meeting, Bohatch received no further work assignments from the firm.

In January 1991, the firm denied Bohatch a year-end partnership distribution for 1990 and reduced her tentative distribution share for 1991 to zero. In June, the firm paid Bohatch her monthly draw and told her that this draw would be her last. Finally, in August, the firm gave Bohatch until November to vacate her office.

By September, Bohatch had found new employment. She filed this suit on October 18, 1991, and the firm voted formally to expel her from the partnership three days later, October 21, 1991.

The trial court granted partial summary judgment for the firm on Bohatch's wrongful discharge claim, and also on her breach of fiduciary duty and breach of the duty of good faith and fair dealing claims for any conduct occurring after October 21, 1991 (the date Bohatch was formally expelled from the firm). The trial court denied the firm's summary judgment motion on Bohatch's breach of fiduciary duty and breach of the duty of good faith and fair dealing claims for conduct occurring before October 21, 1991. The breach of fiduciary duty claim and a breach of contract claim were tried to a jury. The jury found that the firm breached the partnership agreement and its fiduciary duty. It awarded Bohatch $57,000 for past lost wages, $250,000 for past mental anguish, $4,000,000 total in punitive damages (this amount was apportioned against several defendants), and attorney's fees. The trial court rendered judgment for Bohatch in the amounts found by the jury, except it disallowed attorney's fees because the judgment was based in tort. After suggesting remittitur, which Bohatch accepted, the trial court reduced the punitive damages to around $237,000.

All parties appealed. The court of appeals held that the firm's only duty to Bohatch was not to expel her in bad faith. The court of appeals stated that "'[b]ad faith' in this context means only that partners cannot expel another partner for self-gain." Finding no evidence that the firm expelled Bohatch for self-gain, the court concluded that Bohatch could not recover for breach of fiduciary duty. However, the court concluded that the firm breached the partnership agreement when it reduced Bohatch's tentative partnership distribution for 1991 to zero without notice, and when it terminated her draw three months before she left. The court concluded that Bohatch was entitled to recover $35,000 in lost earnings for 1991 but none for 1990, and no mental anguish damages. Accordingly, the court rendered judgment for Bohatch for $35,000 plus $225,000 in attorney's fees.

II. BREACH OF FIDUCIARY DUTY

We have long recognized as a matter of common law the "[t]he relationship between . . . partners . . . is fiduciary in character, and imposes upon all the participants the obligation of loyalty to the joint concern and of the utmost good faith, fairness, and honesty in their dealings with each other with respect to matters pertaining to the enterprise." Fitz-Gerald v. Hull, 150 Tex. 39 (Tex. 1951) (quotation omitted). Yet, partners have no obligation to remain partners; "at the heart of the partnership concept is the principle that partners may choose with whom they wish to be associated." Gelder Med. Group v. Webber, 41 N.Y.2d 680 (N.Y. 1977). The issue presented, one of first impression, is whether the fiduciary relationship between and among partners creates an exception to the at-will nature of partnerships; that is, in this case, whether it gives rise to a duty not to expel a partner who reports suspected overbilling by another partner.

At the outset, we note that no party questions that the obligations of lawyers licensed to practice in the District of Columbia—including McDonald and Bohatch—were prescribed by the District of Columbia Code of Professional Responsibility in effect in 1990, and that in all other respects Texas law applies. Further, neither statutory nor contract law principles answer the question of whether the firm owed Bohatch a duty not to expel her. . . . Therefore, we look to the common law to find the principles governing Bohatch's claim that the firm breached a duty when it expelled her.

Courts in other states have held that a partnership may expel a partner for purely business reasons. . . . Further, courts recognize that a law firm can expel a partner to protect relationships both within the firm and with clients. . . . Finally, many courts have held that a partnership can expel a partner without breaching any duty in order to resolve a "fundamental schism." . . .

The fiduciary duty that partners owe one another does not encompass a duty to remain partners or else answer in tort damages. Nonetheless, Bohatch and several distinguished legal scholars urge this Court to recognize that public policy requires a limited duty to remain partners—i.e., a partnership must retain a whistleblower partner. They argue that such an extension of a partner's fiduciary duty is necessary because permitting a law firm to retaliate against a partner who in good faith reports suspected overbilling would discourage compliance with rules of professional conduct and thereby hurt clients.

While this argument is not without some force, we must reject it. A partnership exists solely because the partners choose to place personal confidence and trust in one another. . . . Just as a partner can be expelled, without a breach of any common law duty, over disagreements about firm policy or to resolve some other "fundamental schism," a partner can be expelled for accusing another partner of overbilling without subjecting the partnership to tort damages. Such charges, whether true or not, may have a profound effect on the personal confidence and trust essential to the partner relationship. Once such charges are made, partners may find it impossible to continue to work together to their mutual benefit and the benefit of their clients.

We are sensitive to the concern expressed by the dissenting Justices that "retaliation against a partner who tries in good faith to correct or report perceived misconduct virtually assures that others will not take these appropriate steps in the future." . . . However, the dissenting Justices do not explain how the trust relationship necessary both for the firm's existence and for representing clients can survive such serious accusations by one partner against another. The threat of tort liability for expulsion would tend to force partners to remain in untenable circumstances — suspicious of and angry with each other — to their own detriment and that of their clients whose matters are neglected by lawyers distracted with intra-firm frictions.

Although concurring in the Court's judgment, Justice Hecht criticizes the Court for failing to "address amici's concerns that failing to impose liability will discourage attorneys from reporting unethical conduct." To address the scholars' concerns, he proposes that a whistleblower be protected from expulsion, but only if the report, irrespective of being made in good faith, is proved to be correct. We fail to see how such an approach encourages compliance with ethical rules more than the approach we adopt today. Furthermore, the amici's position is that a reporting attorney must be in good faith, not that the attorney must be right. In short, Justice Hecht's approach ignores the question Bohatch presents, the amici write about, and the firm challenges — whether a partnership violates a fiduciary duty when it expels a partner who in good faith reports suspected ethical violations. The concerns of the amici are best addressed by a rule that clearly demarcates an attorney's ethical duties and the parameters of tort liability, rather than redefining "whistleblower."

We emphasize that our refusal to create an exception to the at-will nature of partnerships in no way obviates the ethical duties of lawyers. Such duties sometimes necessitate difficult decisions, as when a lawyer suspects overbilling by a colleague. The fact that the ethical duty to report may create an irreparable schism between partners neither excuses failure to report nor transforms expulsion as a means of resolving that schism into a tort.

We hold that the firm did not owe Bohatch a duty not to expel her for reporting suspected overbilling by another partner. . . .

Justice HECHT, concurring in the judgment.

[Judge Hecht gave his own version of the facts. In the process, he made the following observations about the firm's report to Pennzoil and the aftermath.

Robert Burns, a member of Butler & Binion's management committee, told John Chapman, the Pennzoil in-house attorney who dealt most directly with Butler & Binion's Washington office, of Bohatch's assertions and asked him to review the firm's bills. Chapman confirmed to Burns that he had complained to McDonald several months earlier about the quality of Bohatch's work, and Burns intimated that Bohatch's assertions might have been in response to such complaints. Chapman discussed the matter with his immediate superior and with Pennzoil's general counsel. The three of them reviewed Butler & Binion's bills for the preceding year and concluded that they were reasonable. After Chapman's superior discussed their conclusions with Pennzoil's president and chief executive officer, Chapman told Burns that Pennzoil was satisfied that the firm's bills were reasonable.

Bohatch expected that Paine would ask her for additional information, and when he did not do so, she wrote him that she believed McDonald had overcharged Pennzoil $20,000 to $25,000 per month for his work. In fact, in the preceding six months McDonald had billed Pennzoil on average less than $24,000 per month for his work, so that if Bohatch had been correct, McDonald should have billed Pennzoil almost nothing. On August 23, 1990, a few weeks after their initial meeting, Paine told Bohatch that he had found no evidence of overbilling. Since he did not see how Bohatch could continue to work for McDonald or Pennzoil under the circumstances, given the rifts her allegations had caused, Paine suggested that she begin to look for other employment. . . .]

The Court holds that partners in a law firm have no common-law liability for expelling one of their number for accusing another of unethical conduct. The dissent argues that partners in a law firm are liable for such conduct. Both views are unqualified; neither concedes or even considers whether "always" and "never" are separated by any distance. I think they must be. The Court's position is directly contrary to that of some of the leading scholars on the subject who have appeared here as amici curiae. The Court finds amici's arguments "not without some force," but rejects them completely. I do not believe amici's arguments can be rejected out of hand. The dissent, on the other hand, refuses even to acknowledge the serious impracticalities involved in maintaining the trust necessary between partners when one has accused another of unethical conduct. In the dissent's view, partners who would expel another for such accusations must simply either get over it or respond in damages. The dissent's view blinks reality.

The issue is not well developed; in fact, to our knowledge we are the first court to address it. It seems to me there must be some circumstances when expulsion for reporting an ethical violation is culpable and other circumstances when it is not. I have trouble justifying a 500-partner firm's expulsion of a partner for reporting overbilling of a client that saves the firm not only from ethical complaints but from liability to the client. But I cannot see how a five-partner firm can legitimately survive one partner's accusations that another is unethical. Between such two extreme examples I see a lot of ground.

This case does not force a choice between diametrically opposite views. Here, the report of unethical conduct, though made in good faith, was incorrect. That fact is significant to me because I think a law firm can always expel a partner for bad judgment, whether it relates to the representation of clients or the relationships with other partners, and whether it is in good faith. I would hold that Butler & Binion did not breach its fiduciary duty by expelling Colette Bohatch because she made a good-faith but nevertheless extremely serious charge against a senior partner that threatened the firm's relationship with an important client, her charge proved groundless, and her relationship with her partners was destroyed in the process. I cannot, however, extrapolate from this case, as the Court does, that no law firm can ever be liable for expelling a partner for reporting unethical conduct. Accordingly, I concur only in the Court's judgment. . . .

. . . I am troubled by the arguments of the distinguished amici curiae that permitting a law firm to retaliate against a partner for reporting unethical behavior would discourage compliance with rules of conduct, hurt clients, and contravene public policy. Their arguments have force, but they do not explain how a relationship of trust necessary for both the existence of the firm and the representation of its clients can survive such serious accusations by one partner against another. The threat of liability for expulsion would tend to force partners to remain in untenable circumstances—suspicious of and angry with each other—to their own detriment and that of their clients whose matters are neglected by lawyers distracted with intra-firm frictions. If "at the heart of the partnership concept is the principle that partners may choose with whom they wish to be associated" . . . surely partners are not obliged to continue to associate with someone who has accused one of them of unethical conduct.

This very difficult issue need not be finally resolved in this case. Bohatch did not report unethical conduct; she reported what she *believed*, presumably in good faith, but nevertheless mistakenly, to be unethical conduct. At the time, the District of Columbia Code of Professional Responsibility provided that "[a] lawyer shall not . . . collect a[ ] . . . clearly excessive fee." D.C. Code of Prof'l Resp. DR 2-106(a) (1990). Pennzoil's conclusion that Butler & Binion's fees were reasonable, reached after being made aware of Bohatch's concerns that McDonald's time was overstated, establishes that Butler & Binion did not collect excessive fees from Pennzoil. A fee that a client as sophisticated as Pennzoil considers reasonable is not clearly excessive simply because a lawyer believes it could have been less. Bohatch's argument that Pennzoil had other reasons not to complain of Butler & Binion's bills is simply beside the point. Whatever its motivations, Pennzoil found the bills reasonable, thereby establishing that McDonald had not overbilled in violation of ethical rules. Bohatch's argument that Pennzoil's assessment of the bills was prejudiced by Butler & Binion's misrepresentations about her is implausible. There is nothing to suggest that Pennzoil would have thought clearly excessive legal fees were reasonable simply because it did not like Bohatch.

Bohatch's real concern was not that fees to Pennzoil were excessive—she had never even seen the bills and had no idea what the fees, or fee arrangements, were—but that McDonald was misrepresenting the number of hours he worked. The District of Columbia Code of Professional Responsibility at the time also prohibited lawyers from engaging in "conduct involving dishonesty, fraud, deceit or misrepresentation." Id. DR 1-102(A)(4). But there is no evidence that McDonald actually engaged in such conduct. At most, Bohatch showed only that McDonald kept sloppy time records, not that he deceived his partners or clients. Neither his partners nor his major client accused McDonald of dishonesty, even after reviewing his bills and time records. Bohatch complains that Butler & Binion did not fully investigate McDonald's billing practices. Assuming Butler & Binion had some duty to investigate Bohatch's charges, it discharged that duty by determining that Pennzoil considered its bills reasonable. (The district court, as the court of appeals noted, excluded evidence that Paine and McDonald himself went so far as to report the charges against McDonald to the lawyer disciplinary authority, which exonerated him. 905 S.W.2d at 607.)

Even if expulsion of a partner for reporting unethical conduct might be a breach of fiduciary duty, expulsion for *mistakenly* reporting unethical conduct cannot be a breach of fiduciary duty. At the very least, a mistake so serious indicates a lack of judgment warranting expulsion. No one would argue that an attorney could not be expelled from a firm for a serious error in judgment about a client's affairs or even the firm's affairs. If Bohatch and McDonald had disagreed over what position to take in a particular case for Pennzoil, or over whether Butler & Binion should continue to operate its Washington office, the firm could have determined that she should be expelled for the health of the firm, even if Bohatch had acted in complete good faith. Reporting unethical conduct where none existed is no different. . . .

Butler & Binion's expulsion of Bohatch did not discourage ethical conduct; it discouraged errors of judgment, which ought to be discouraged. Butler & Binion did not violate its fiduciary duty to Bohatch. . . .

The dissent would hold that "law partners violate[ ] their fiduciary duty by retaliating against a fellow partner who ma[kes] a good-faith effort to alert her partners to the possible overbilling of a client." . . . In fact, the dissent would adopt the broader proposition that a partner could not be expelled from a law firm for reporting any suspected ethical violation, regardless of how little evidence there might be for the suspicion:

> Even if a report turns out to be mistaken or a client ultimately consents to the behavior in question, as in this case, retaliation against a partner who tries in good faith to correct or report perceived misconduct virtually assures that others will not take these appropriate steps in the future. Although I agree with the majority that partners have a right not to continue a partnership with someone against their will, they may still be liable for damages directly resulting from terminating that relationship.

. . .

The dissent finds no support in any authority in any jurisdiction. Furthermore, the argument that allowing expulsion of a partner who incorrectly reports unethical conduct impairs Rule 8.03(a) of the Texas Disciplinary Rules of Professional Conduct is equally unfounded. That rule states in part that "a lawyer having knowledge that another lawyer has committed a violation as to that lawyer's honesty, trustworthiness or fitness as a lawyer in other respects, shall inform the appropriate disciplinary authority." Tex. Disciplinary R. Prof'l Conduct 8.03(a), reprinted in Tex. Gov't Code Ann., tit. 2, subtit. G app. A (Vernon Supp. 1997) (Tex. State Bar R. art X, § 9). A lawyer's duty under this rule is only triggered by (1) knowledge of (2) a rules violation that (3) raises a substantial question about a lawyer's honesty, trustworthiness, or fitness. Bohatch's suspicions do not meet these requirements.

Even if they did, the dissent fails to make a convincing argument for liability in every situation in which a lawyer reports a suspected ethical violation. The dissent does not even acknowledge the tensions that would plainly arise between partners making and denying charges of unethical behavior. These tensions might easily prevent proper representation of clients. "[P]artners have a right not to continue a partnership with someone against their will," the dissent concedes, but if their will is based on a partner's assertions of unethical conduct, then they must pay to exert it. Not even lawyers should be forced to choose *in every instance* between maintaining an untenable partnership and paying for its termination over ethical disagreements however serious and sincere.

The dissent's reference to Twain to say that the "wages" of "right" and "wrong" in disagreements over ethics "is just the same" is clever, but it ignores the practicalities of maintaining a relationship of trust and confidence, and it glibly expresses a much too cynical view of the entire problem presented here. Acknowledging that some law partnerships cannot legitimately be expected to survive internecine quarrels over ethics simply does not spell the end of an attorney's responsibility to professional obligations and standards. Thus it is just not true, as the dissent asserts, that "this case sends an inappropriate signal to lawyers and to the public that the rules of professional responsibility are subordinate to a law firm's other interests." The matter is not so simple. A lawyer cannot simply enshroud any complaint against his colleagues in the mantle of obedience to rule of professional responsibility. The toll such a complaint makes is also important. The dissent's added charge that the result in this case "leaves an attorney who acts ethically and in good faith without recourse," assumes incorrectly that the only "recourse" is an action for damages. Twain suggests that righteousness has its own rewards. The dissent argues that those rewards must be monetary to be real. . . .

Justice SPECTOR, joined by Chief Justice PHILLIPS, dissenting.

> [W]hat's the use you learning to do right when it's troublesome to do right and ain't no trouble to do wrong, and the wages is just the same?
>
> — *The Adventures of Huckleberry Finn*

The issue in this appeal is whether law partners violate a fiduciary duty by retaliating against one partner for questioning the billing practices of another partner. I would hold that partners violate their fiduciary duty to one another by punishing compliance with the Disciplinary Rules of Professional Conduct. Accordingly, I dissent. . . .

The court of appeals held that under the Texas Uniform Partnership Act and the common law, partners violate a fiduciary duty in expelling another partner only if they act in bad faith for self-gain. . . . It concluded that the record in this suit contains no evidence of a breach of fiduciary duty because there was no evidence that the partners expelled Bohatch for self-gain. . . . This Court, however has never limited claims for a breach of fiduciary duty to circumstances in which a partner acts for self-gain. . . . Today, the Court should have followed the advice of several leading legal scholars and disapproved of the court of appeals' opinion.[1] Instead, this court, by affirming the court of appeals' judgment, discards the jury's conclusion that the partners violated their fiduciary duty.

The majority views the partnership relationship among lawyers as strictly business. I disagree. The practice of law is a profession first, then a business. Moreover, it is a self-regulated profession subject to the Rules promulgated by this Court.

As attorneys we take an oath to "honestly demean [ourselves] in the practice of law; and . . . discharge [our] duty to [our] *client[s]* to the best of [our] ability." Tex. Gov't Code § 82.037 (emphasis added). This oath of honesty and duty is not mere "self-adulatory bombast" but mandated by the Legislature. See Schware v. Board of Bar Exam'rs, 353 U.S. 232, 247 [1957] (Frankfurter, J. concurring) (noting that the rhetoric used to describe the esteemed role of the legal profession has real meaning). As attorneys, we bear responsibilities to our clients and the bar itself that transcend ordinary business relationships.

Certain requirements imposed by the Rules have particular relevance in this case. Lawyers may not charge unconscionable fees. Tex. Disciplinary R. Prof'l Conduct 1.04(a) . . . ; see D.C. R. Prof'l Conduct 1.5(1) (West 1997). Partners and supervisory attorneys have a duty to take reasonable remedial action to avoid or mitigate the consequences of known violations by other lawyers in their firm. Tex. Disciplinary R. Prof'l Conduct 5.01; see D.C. R. Prof'l Conduct 5.1. Lawyers who know that another lawyer has violated a rule of professional conduct in a way that raises a substantial question as to that lawyer's honesty or fitness as a lawyer must report that violation. Tex. Disciplinary R. Prof'l Conduct 8.03(a); D.C. R. Prof'l Conduct 8.3. In Texas, Rules 5.01 and 8.03 are essential to the self-regulatory nature of the practice of law and the honor of our profession itself.

This Court has the exclusive authority to issue licenses to practice law. Tex. Gov't Code § 82.021. This Court also has the jurisdiction to discipline errant attorneys and establish procedures for doing so. Id. §§ 81.071, 81.072(a)–(c). Attorneys, whether

---

1. Professors Richard L. Abel (University of California at Los Angeles School of Law), Leonard Gross (Southern Illinois University School of Law), Robert W. Hamilton (University of Texas Law School), David J. Luban (University of Maryland School of Law), Gary Minda (Brooklyn Law School), Ronald D. Rotunda (University of Illinois College of Law), Theodore J. Schneyer (University of Arizona College of Law), Clyde W. Summers (University of Pennsylvania School of Law), and Charles W. Wolfram (Cornell Law School) offered their analyses as amici curiae, concluding that self-gain is not the sole element of a breach of fiduciary duty among partners.

they are sole practitioners, employees, or partners, are still "officers of the court." In re Snyder, 472 U.S. 634, 644 (1985) (quoting People ex rel. Karlin v. Culkin, 248 N.Y. 465 (N.Y. 1928)) . . . .

In sum, attorneys organizing together to practice law are subject to a higher duty toward their clients and the public interest than in other occupations. As a natural consequence, this duty affects the special relationship among lawyers who practice law together.

It is true that no high court has considered the issue of whether expulsion of a partner for complying with ethical rules violates law partners' fiduciary duty. The dearth of authority in this area does not, however, diminish the significance of this case. Instead, the scarcity of guiding case law only heightens the importance of this Court's decision.

I believe that the fiduciary relationship among law partners should incorporate the rules of the profession promulgated by this Court. . . . Although the evidence put on by Bohatch is by no means conclusive, applying the proper presumptions of a no-evidence review, this trial testimony amounts to some evidence that Bohatch made a good-faith report of suspected overbilling in an effort to comply with her professional duty. Further, it provides some evidence that the partners of Butler & Binion began a retaliatory course of action *before* any investigation of the allegation had begun.

In light of this Court's role in setting standards to govern attorneys' conduct, it is particularly inappropriate for the Court to deny recourse to attorneys wronged for adhering to the Disciplinary Rules. I would hold that in this case the law partners violated their fiduciary duty by retaliating against a fellow partner who made a good-faith effort to alert her partners to the possible overbilling of a client.

The duty to prevent overbilling and other misconduct exists for the protection of the client. Even if a report turns out to be mistaken or a client ultimately consents to the behavior in question, as in this case, retaliation against a partner who tries in good faith to correct or report perceived misconduct virtually assures that others will not take these appropriate steps in the future. Although I agree with the majority that partners have a right not to continue a partnership with someone against their will, they may still be liable for damages directly resulting from terminating that relationship. . . .

The Court's writing in this case sends an inappropriate signal to lawyers and to the public that the rules of professional responsibility are subordinate to a law firm's other interests. Under the majority opinion's vision for the legal profession, the wages would not even be the same for "doing right"; they diminish considerably and leave an attorney who acts ethically and in good faith without recourse. Accordingly, I respectfully dissent.

Notes

1. Which of the three opinions would you join, and why? Do you think that after twenty years practicing law you might change your mind?

2. What do you make of Justice Hecht's suggestion that there is a difference between a claim by a 500-lawyer firm that it ought to be able to dismiss a partner who has raised ethical charges against a fellow partner and a similar claim by a five-partner firm? Are there important differences between large and small firms in this context? If so, should the rules governing a firm's right to dismiss partners vary depending upon the size of the firm? How might recognizing such a distinction affect the functioning of large law firms and compliance with legal norms? Does your answer to these questions depend upon whether you are imagining a "traditional" large law firm—i.e., one characterized by collegial decisionmaking, lock-step partner compensation, and that has grown primarily by promoting partners "through the ranks"—or a "modern" firm, in which a few partners control virtually all important decisions, where partners are compensated largely on the basis of the revenue that they personally generate for the firm, and that has grown primarily by merging with other firms and hiring lawyers away from other firms? Return to this last question after you have considered the materials on large law firms in Chapter 12.

3. Are you surprised about the Pennzoil general counsel's attitude about the potential that the company was being overbilled? If you were in his position, would you want a lawyer who mistakenly (but nevertheless in good faith) sought to bring overbilling by one of her partners to your attention to be fired? Would you continue to send business to a firm who fired a partner in such circumstances? As we will discuss in Chapter 12, overbilling appears to be a serious problem, even in many of the country's leading law firms. Why haven't corporations done more to crack down on this problem? Is that fact, if it is a fact, explained by the further fact that many corporate counsel have, in the majority's words describing the relationship between the Pennzoil's general counsel and the accused lawyer in *Bohatch*, "a long-standing relationship" with their outside counsel?

4. In GTE Products Corp. v. Stewart, 421 Mass. 22 (1995), the court followed the opinion of the California Supreme Court in the *General Dynamics* case, p. 833. It also attempted to lay down some standards for finding a constructive discharge that would be the basis for a claim under the *General Dynamics* principle: the employer's conduct must make the employee's situation so intolerable that a reasonable person would feel forced to resign. A general counsel of a division of GTE whose promotability ranking was changed from the highest to the lowest rating after he repeatedly raised safety and liability issues about company products and who was told to cease his confrontational style and stop being the "social conscience" of the company was held not to have met that standard. His resignation therefore was not the result of a constructive discharge.

5. This subsection began with a discussion of the pathbreaking case of Wieder v. Skala, p. 833, which dealt with a law firm's dismissal of an associate. The next New York case involved an allegation by an unadmitted law school graduate who alleged that the firm had forced him to resign by threatening to withhold a favorable job reference so that he would not report a partner's suspected billing fraud to the disciplinary authorities. In fact, although the firm's internal examination exonerated the partner, he later absconded, leaving behind investors who claimed he had defrauded them of $30 million in a "Ponzi-type" investment fraud. When the former "associate" sued under *Wieder*, the law firm moved for summary judgment, making the breathtaking argument that *Wieder* did not apply because the associate, not being admitted to the bar, was not governed by the disciplinary rules. He therefore had no ethical obligation to report misconduct and was not faced with any dilemma when the firm threatened him with loss of a favorable recommendation. Judge Gleeson, in denying the summary judgment motion, rejected that argument (and others), stating that he found it difficult to believe that the firm would tell its clients and newly hired law graduates that the latter were not bound by the disciplinary rules until they were formally admitted to the bar. Kelly v. Hunton & Williams, 1999 U.S. Dist. Lexis 9139 (E.D.N.Y. 1999).

Chapter 11

Professional Responsibility and the Judicial System

Problem 11–1

Pittman v. Cole, 117 F. Supp. 2d 1285 (S.D. Ala. 2000), dealt with a questionnaire that the Christian Coalition of Alabama wanted to circulate to candidates running for election to Alabama state courts. The CCA planned to circulate the questions and responses in a voters' guide. Its questionnaire asked candidates to respond "Agree," "Disagree," "Undecided," or "Decline" to the following fifteen statements:

(1) "Secondary school–based clinics should dispense birth control devices without requiring prior parental notification and consent."

(2) "The faith or religious beliefs of a judge should play no role whatsoever in her or his judicial decisions."

(3) "Leaving aside entirely the relevant U.S. Supreme Court and/or Alabama Supreme Court precedent about legal status of an unborn child, I as an individual believe that an unborn child is a fellow human being, imbued with a soul by its Creator."

(4) "Setting aside my obvious and acknowledged duty to strictly construe and enforce the acts of the legislature, I am personally opposed for moral and religious reasons to the establishment of gambling in this state for any reason."

5) "The ABA House of Delegates has passed various policy resolutions supporting strong federal gun control measures, to include federal licensing requirements for gun purchasers, increased federal taxes, periodic reviews of the eligibility of handgun owners, and waiting periods for the purchase of firearms. As a general matter, I support the ABA's position on handgun control."

(6) "The state should require the registration of firearms and the licensing requirements of firearms owners."

(7) "The ABA House of Delegates passed a policy resolution in February 1999, supporting the enactment of legislation and public policy providing that adoption shall not be denied on the basis of sexual orientation if in the best interest of the child. I support the ABA's position on this issue."

(8) "Marital benefits provided by employers should be extended to domestic partners regardless of marital status or sexual orientation."

(9) "I support adoption of a federal constitutional amendment permitting officially sanctioned non-coercive student led prayer in public schools and at public school sporting events."

(10) "Several years ago, the ABA House of Delegates passed a policy resolution urging reauthorization of the National Endowment of the Arts (NEA) with no restrictions on the content, subject matter, message or idea of what the endowment may fund. I do not support the ABA's position on reauthorization of the NEA."

(11) "Desecration of the American flag has been determined to be protected political speech under the First Amendment. In order to protect the American flag from desecration I would support adoption of a federal constitutional amendment to that effect."

(12) "Some proof of identification should be required in order to vote."

(13) "As a judge, I would have no philosophical objections to reducing a verdict, which is excessive under the applicable law."

(14) "Alabama's reputation for 'lawsuit abuse' and 'Tort Hell,' as described several years ago in some national publications, has harmed economic development efforts and job creation."

(15) "According to the August 2000 issue of the ABA Journal, 33 states have set caps or limitations on the amount of money that juries can award. Placing limitations on jury awards puts the future of the jury system in serious jeopardy."

As a matter of regulating judicial ethics, wholly apart from constitutional issues, should judicial ethics rules be adopted forbidding candidates or nominees for judicial office from responding to all or any of these questions? Does your answer depend on whether the particular state provides for election of judges or for nomination by the executive, with confirmation by the legislature? After reading Republican Party v. White below, consider whether a state may constitutionally prohibit candidates or nominees for judicial office from answering such questions.

Problem 11–2

Judge, before joining the bench, was an active member of organizations of all different types. She wants to know whether she may join, attend meetings of, donate to, and be an officer of the following organizations:

1) The local branch of the American Civil Liberties Union;

2) The Federalist Society, a prominent conservative organization;

3) The Sierra Club;

4) The local branch of the Boy Scouts, in which her son is a Cub Scout; and

5) The state bar association, which among other things, sponsors a variety of pro bono activities, takes positions on pending legislation, and files amicus curiae briefs in state and federal legislation.

As a general matter, might the judge's involvement with any of the organizations above warrant any objections from a party appearing before that judge? See generally 2007 ABA Model Code of Judicial Conduct Rules 1.2, 2.10, 3.1, 3.2, and 4.1. See also Kaufman, "Judicial Correctness Meets Constitutional Correctness: Section 2C of the Code of Judicial Conduct," 32 Hofstra L. Rev. 1293 (2004).

Problem 11–3

The state supreme court has adopted an outreach program under which all state judges are encouraged to participate in community awareness programs as a way of getting the local judiciary to educate, and be educated by, the local community concerning its problems. Neighborhood citizens' groups, concerned about the existence and consequences of criminal activity, have established task forces all over the state to work on problems associated with crime. They have invited members of the police, the prosecutors' offices, and the local judiciary to meet with them on a regular basis to talk about the issues involved in reducing the impact of crime. May judges participate in these meetings? See 2007 Model Code 1.2, 2.4, 2.10, and 3.1.

Problem 11–4

Judge is a member of a state supreme court. The legislature has before it a proposal to alter substantially its "no fault" auto insurance.

(a) May the judge testify before the appropriate legislative committee about the impact of the proposed changes on the business of the judicial system—the effect on caseload, need for juries, costs, and the like? See 2007 Model Code 3.2.

(b) May the judge express her strongly felt views about the substantive merits of the proposed changes? See 2007 Model Code Rules 2.10(A) and (B), and 3.2.

(c) Judge teaches a torts course at the local law school. May she discuss the merits of the proposed changes in her class? May she express her strongly held views that the changes are highly undesirable? See 2007 Model Code 1.2, 3.1 and Comment 1.

(d) May Judge deliver a public speech or write an article attacking the proposed changes?

(e) If Judge does any of the activities set forth in (a) through (d), should she disqualify herself if the proposed changes are enacted and a suit challenging their constitutionality comes before her court? See 2007 Model Code Rule 2.11.

Problem 11–5

Judge is a member of the court that is reviewing an order of the regulatory commission that has just allowed an increase in the rates of the local electric company.

(a) Judge's wife owns $500 in stock in the local electric company. Her parents gave her the stock as a gift when she was a child. For sentimental reasons, she does not wish to sell it even though it pays only $10 a year in dividends. Must Judge disqualify himself? Does it make any difference whether Judge is a federal or state court judge? Compare 2007 Model Code Rule 2.11(A)(2), with 28 U.S.C. § 455(a). See Huffman v. Arkansas Judicial Discipline and Disability Comm'n, 42 S.W.2d 386 (Ark. 2001), denying a judge's appeal from a decision admonishing him from failing to disqualify himself from a case in which Wal-Mart was involved when the judge and his wife owned $700,000 of Wal-Mart stock.

(b) Suppose that the Judge's parents own a number of rental properties whose electric bills will rise substantially. Should Judge disqualify himself? If he does, should he recuse himself, or should he follow the procedure outlined in 2007 Model Code Rule 2.11(C)? If you were on a committee reviewing the Code of Judicial Conduct, would you retain, amend, or eliminate that procedure? In most states, when a litigant moves to disqualify a judge for a lack of impartiality or other violation of the judicial code, that same judge rules on the motion. Do you believe that it complies with due process for the judge whose impartiality is in question to rule on his ability to be impartial? Should a different judge rule on the motion?

Problem 11–6

Federal District Judge has a case that raises, as a subsidiary issue, a difficult question of professional responsibility, a subject that she has not followed closely. She would like to try out her ideas on one or more of the following friends:

(a) Professor A, her former legal profession teacher;

(b) Judge B, a federal district judge in her district;

(c) Mr. C, Judge B's law clerk;

(d) Judge D, a federal district judge in a neighboring state;

(e) Judge E, a Court of Appeals judge in her circuit;

(f) Judge F, a Court of Appeals judge in another circuit; and

(g) Judge G, a member of the state trial court of general jurisdiction in the state in which she sits.

May she talk to any or all of them about the matter and on what basis? See 2007 Model Code Rule 2.9.

Problem 11–7

Judge Judith is a trial judge sitting in the criminal division of a state court and is assigned to hear bail matters every Friday. She has dozens of matters to dispose of every week and does them expeditiously after considering the papers submitted and listening to the arguments of counsel. She states her conclusion in summary fashion, rarely with more than a sentence of explanation. She almost never has time to deliver an oral "opinion" or a written opinion on these bail dispositions. One Friday she released on personal recognizance pending trial a defendant who had recently completed a sentence for manslaughter. He was awaiting trial for having assaulted a guard but the prosecutors had not introduced evidence of dangerousness or flight risk during the bail hearing. Six months later, the defendant fled to another juris-diction and was charged with murdering two people there. The Governor who had appointed Judge Judith was campaigning to be the nominee of his party for President. He immediately issued a statement declaring that Judge Judith should be impeached. May Judge Judith issue a statement defending her actions and explaining why she released the defendant? See Model Code 2.10. Should judges (including Judge Judith) be required to explain their rulings in writing in the first place? See generally Sarah M. R. Cravens, "Judges as Trustees: A Duty to Account and an Opportunity for Virtue," 62 Wash. & Lee L. Rev. 1637 (2005).

Problem 11–8

Judge is a 54-year-old white male, who grew up primarily in Connecticut and Maine. His father was an attorney, and his mother worked for her family's asset holding company. Judge attended undergrad and law school at Ivy League institutions and then clerked for a judge on the Second Circuit. After clerking, Judge entered private practice at a large firm in Manhattan, where he focused his practice on commercial litigation and civil appeals. Eventually, President Obama nominated and the Senate confirmed his appointment as a District Court Judge. Combined with the income of his spouse (who is also a lawyer), Judge earns approximately $410,000 per year. On the District Court, Judge receives a wide array of cases, including a steady diet of serious criminal matters. Judge is currently considering what sentence to impose in a drug-trafficking matter. Defendant is a 23-year-old half–African-American, half-Hispanic, who grew up in Miami. His mother was a server, and he never saw his father. He was recently convicted in Judge's court of his third offense involving heroin trafficking. He also had a handgun in his possession when he was arrested. The prosecution has asked for a life sentence in prison, while the defense has asked for a four-year sentence. Is Judge qualified to "fairly and impartially" impose a sentence on Defendant? Is Judge's disparate age, experience, race, or socio-economic status likely to increase his implicit bias against the Defendant? Judge, moreover, always had money and family support and always lived in a low-crime neighborhood: will he really be able to understand and fairly assess a drug-dealing, gun-toting defendant's culpability? Are there any steps that Judge can take to minimize any conscious or subconscious biases that he might have?

The subject of judicial ethics can be (and occasionally is) a course in itself. A book focusing on issues of professional responsibility of lawyers can do no more than give a glimpse into the kinds of problems that confront judges. Studying judicial ethics is important for lawyers and future lawyers for a variety of reasons, including that lawyers become judges, that lawyers have to deal with judges who are or appear to be acting unethically, and that judicial ethics is tested in most states (through the MPRE). We have chosen to suggest a few problems of judicial professional responsibility in areas that have substantial professional impact on lawyers generally, including disqualification and other recurring issues. We first provide a brief overview of some of the judicial ethics literature, the values animating the judicial ethics code, and the ways in which jurisdictions choose to select and retain their judges.

Several books and articles deal with more specific problems, a few of which we highlight here for your general reference. John P. MacKenzie's *The Appearance of Justice* (1974) discusses a number of incidents involving judges. An accusation of a particular judicial impropriety is discussed in Preble Stolz, *Judging Judges: The Investigation of Rose Bird and the California Supreme Court* (1981). In 1978, the California Supreme Court issued a controversial decision just after Chief Justice Bird had won the election to confirm her in office. The book both explores the charge that the court had reached a decision prior to the election, but had delayed it in order to assist Bird's confirmation by the electorate, and discusses the formal proceedings that investigated the court's conduct. Thereafter, however, a recall election removed Chief Justice Bird and Associate Justices Reynoso and Grondin from office. See Wold and Culver, "The Defeat of the California Justices: the Campaign, the Electorate, and the Issue of Judicial Accountability," 70 Judicature 348 (No. 6 April–May 1987) and the excerpted panel discussion, "After California, What's Next for Judicial Elections," id., at 356. As a more recent example of judicial independence versus judicial accountability to the people, the Iowa Supreme Court unanimously rejected a state prohibition against same-sex marriage in 2009. In retaliation for this decision (which preceded the Supreme Court's later *Obergefell* decision indirectly but effectively affirming the Iowa Supreme Court's decision), the voters ousted the three Iowa justices who were on the ballot the next year. See generally Witosky & Hansen, *Equal Before the Law: How Iowans Led Americans to Marriage Equality* (2015); James Sample, "Retention Elections 2010," 46 U.S.F. L. Rev. 383 (2011).

Another controversial issue of judicial ethics is presented in a book detailing the extrajudicial activities undertaken by Justice Brandeis during his Supreme Court career both on his own and through the substantial annual financial support he provided for the activities of the then-Professor Felix Frankfurter. A great deal of the book is concerned with Brandeis's efforts with respect to legislation that came, or might have come, before the Court. Murphy, *The Brandeis/Frankfurter Connection* (1982); for a somewhat different position by the same author, see Levy and Murphy, "Preserving the Progressive Spirit in a Conservative Time: The Joint Reform Efforts of Justice Brandeis and Professor Frankfurter, 1916–1933," 78 Mich. L. Rev. 1252 (1980). Critical assessments of Murphy's conclusions are contained in Cover, "The Framing of Justice Brandeis," The New Republic, p. 17 (May 5, 1982) and John Frank's book review in 32 J. Legal Educ. 432 (1982). See p. 224, Note 9 for a citation to Mr. Frank's views on various problems of professional responsibility in Justice Brandeis's career as a practicing lawyer. For a more recent criticism of a more recent justice, Justice Breyer, who served as the "architect" of the United States Sentencing Guidelines and then, after having been appointed to the Supreme Court, voted to protect or at least salvage those Guidelines, see Monroe Freedman, "Judicial Impartiality in the Supreme Court—The Troubling Case of Justice Stephen Breyer," 30 Okla. City U. L. Rev. 513 (2005).

Finally, and more generally, for a thought-provoking reader on a variety of judicial ethics issues, see *The Responsible Judge: Readings in Judicial Ethics* (John Noonan, Jr. & Kenneth Winston eds., 1993). For a comprehensive treatise covering judicial ethics regulation and citing the Codes of Judicial Conduct, judicial ethics opinions, disciplinary and general case law, and offering occasional commentary, see Charles Geyh, James Alfini, Steven Lubet & Jeffrey Shaman, *Judicial Conduct and Ethics* (5th ed. 2013). Finally, for the various bases on which federal judges might be permitted or required to recuse themselves from hearing a case, see Charles Geyh, *Judicial Disqualification: An Analysis of Federal Law* (2d ed. 2010); for a book focusing more on the states, see Richard Flamm, *Judicial Disqualification: Recusal and Disqualification of Judges* (2d ed. 2007).

A. Judicial Ethics, Selection, and Independence: An Overview

1. Judicial Ethics Generally

In the United States (among many other countries), judicial ethics rests on instilling and regulating three "I's"—integrity, impartiality, and independence—in judges.[1] These three judicial values are supposed to ensure that litigants receive a fair shake and that the public has confidence in the courts. As you review the materials in this Chapter, consider whether the current judicial ethics rules advance these three

---

1. See, e.g., ABA Model Code of Judicial Conduct (2007); Model Code of Judicial Conduct Terminology (2004) (emphasizing and requiring impartiality, independence, and integrity in both on- and off-the-bench conduct). In the United States and often elsewhere, judges must also abstain from a negative "I"—the appearance of impropriety. See, e.g., id.; Mark Harrison, "The 2007 ABA Model Code of Judicial Conduct: Blueprint for a Generation of Judges," 28 Just. Sys. J. 257 (2007); Raymond McKoski, "Judicial Discipline and the Appearance of Impropriety: What the Public Sees Is What the Judge Gets," 94 Minn. L. Rev. 1914 (2010). For the virtually identical value of propriety in England and Wales, see *Guide to Judicial Conduct* (2013), <http://www.judiciary.gov.uk/wp-content/uploads/JCO/Documents/Guidance/judicial_conduct_2013.pdf>; for the Scottish principle of propriety, see *State of Principles of Judicial Ethics for the Scottish Judiciary* (May 2013) <http://www.scotland-judiciary.org.uk/Upload/Documents/JudicialEthics2013.pdf>. Although a generally recent phenomenon, even the United Nations has essentially adopted a judicial ethics code of sorts, the Bangalore Principles of Judicial Conduct (2002), available at <http://www.unodc.org/documents/corruption/publications_unodc_commentary-e.pdf>. The *Bangalore Principles* list the following judicial values: independence, impartiality, integrity, propriety, equality, competence and diligence.

values; and whether these values are over- or underinclusive of what is needed for a good judge.

The major judicial ethics document is another project sponsored by the American Bar Association: its Code of Judicial Conduct.[2] The ABA Special Committee on Judicial Standards, under the chairmanship of Chief Justice Traynor of California, was appointed in 1969 following adoption of the lawyers' Code of Professional Responsibility. The ABA's House of Delegates in 1972 adopted the Code of Judicial Conduct and state supreme courts in turn widely adopted the Code. A revised version was adopted in 1990, and most states thereafter revised their Codes of Judicial Conduct using the 1990 version as a starting point. That code in turn was revised in 2007, and the majority of states have since revised their codes on the basis of the 2007 Model Code.

The Judicial Conference of the United States, which had adopted a variety of regulations of its own during the 1960s (see Ainsworth, "Impact of the Code of Judicial Conduct on Federal Judges," 1972 Utah L. Rev. 369), subsequently adopted the ABA-sponsored Code and made it applicable to all federal judges, full-time bankruptcy judges and full-time magistrates, with some modifications and exceptions noted below. 1973 Report of the Judicial Conference of the United States 9–11, 52; 1974 Report of the Judicial Conference of the United States 17. Since that time the Judicial Conference has modified that Code in a number of important respects. The most recent revision, still based on the 1990 ABA Model Code, went into effect on July 1, 2009. Its prohibitions are couched in terms of "should," instead of the more definitive "shall" language of both the 1990 and 2007 ABA Model Codes. The Judicial Conference has also created an Advisory Committee to respond to inquiries from federal judges with respect to matters of their own judicial conduct. It has been issuing Advisory Opinions since 1970 and in 1988 made them public. Perhaps the most notable feature of the federal Judicial Code is that it does not apply to the Justices of the Supreme Court of the United States. Indeed, the Justices remain essentially the only judges in the United States who are not bound by a code of judicial conduct, although the Justices consult the Code for guidance. See John G. Roberts, Jr., 2011 Year-End Report on the Federal Judiciary. Do think that the Justices should be bound by an ethical code? If so, who or what has the authority to bind them? And who could and should decide issues of disqualification and ethical violations where Supreme Court Justices are concerned? Are such decisions likely to become entangled in the reviewer's preferred outcomes in particular pending or impending cases?

---

2. The ABA first turned to the topic of judicial ethics nearly a century ago, culminating in the Canons of Judicial Ethics (1924). Most state courts or legislatures adopted or referenced the Canons on questions of judicial conduct. Because the Canons suffered from various issues relating to their clarity and enforceability, however, the ABA began to develop the Code of Judicial Conduct discussed above.

Chief Judge Howard Markey
The Delicate Dichotomies of Judicial Ethics
101 F.R.D. 373 (1984)

"Judicial Ethics" has become a growth industry. Dean McKay has pointed out that "The ethical expectations of the public have risen more rapidly than the perception of judges of what is expected of them." In 1960 there were five literary articles published on judicial ethics. In 1975, there were thirty. Congress has enacted "The Judicial Councils Reform and Judicial Conduct and Disability Act of 1980," (Discipline Act) establishing a mechanism for receiving and acting on complaints of judicial misconduct. Congress also passed the "Ethics in Government Act," over-named because it requires only that judges and others publicly disclose their financial status and that of their families once a year. The Judicial Conference of the United States has adopted a "Code of Judicial Conduct for United States Judges," and has charged an Advisory Committee of thirteen judges with the triple task of advising inquiring individual judges on ethical questions, publishing opinions on ethics for guidance of all judges, and recommending changes in the Code to the Conference. Many states have established similar advisory bodies.

An expanded, and expanding, public interest in judicial ethics should surprise no one. The federal judiciary is currently at the height of its power and influence. Federal judges not only send people to jail, and make people pay large sums, and decide disputes between A and B—they tell whole classes of people, and cities, and states, and presidents, what they can and cannot do—and they do that almost every day.

It is important to federal judges as well that the public look at judicial ethics and be satisfied with what it sees. It is a requirement absolute that federal judges enjoy a reputation for adherence to the highest ethical standards, for that is the bedrock of their power and influence. Without it they would be impotent. As we all know, the judiciary has no armies. Its ability to render justice, to protect the people's liberties against abuse by any group and by the other branches of government, to cement the public's adherence to the law—all depend on its lifeblood: respect for its moral authority, the only authority it has.

That respect must be earned. It doesn't come with the title, "Judge," or with "Your Honor," or with the robe, or with the Bench, which are but its symbols, important and necessary, but symbols nonetheless. Respect cannot, of course, be ordered, bought, or assumed. It cannot for long be simply granted. Respect must be—and can only be—earned.

Neither is it surprising that every judicial misstep, apparent or real, makes headlines. Nor is that practice all bad. Judges who object should ask themselves whether they would want a federal judiciary in which judicial misconduct was so commonplace as not to be newsworthy. Of course it is sad that, when our burgeoning communications enable the peccadillos of one judge to be seen by millions on TV, the American public's tendency to generalize results in a nationwide tarnishing of the judicial image. That tendency, plus the advent and growth of the investigative reporting phenomenon — reporting only failures, never triumphs — makes the smallest apparent anthill of judicial misconduct a mountain to be climbed by other judges in earning respect for the judiciary. An outstanding judge was denied elevation on the expressed ground that he had reflected an insensitivity to general ethical considerations, by participating in a case in which his family financial interest may have been at least minimally involved. In-house publications, like "Judicature," "The Judges' Journal," and the American and Federal Bar Journals, have periodically carried articles on judicial ethics. The ferment proves the prescience of the Commentary to Canon 2 of the Code of Judicial Conduct in its warning that judges should expect to be "the subject of constant public scrutiny." . . .

It would be comforting, but unrealistic, to suppose that ethical conduct of judges is a subject without issues. Ethical principles, like all true principles, may themselves be unchallengeable. It is in their application to specific conduct that discomforting issues are present. The need for value trade-offs, mostly unforeseen when ethical codes and statutes were being adopted, arises when the judge confronts a match-up of an ethical principle or a Code provision with contemplated conduct. It would be nice to think that promulgation of Codes and Statutes, and expected, rigid adherence thereto by all judges all the time, would solve the problem. It would be easy, in responding to a judge's "can I ethically do this?" to merely read a code or statute and always say "No." In a pluralistic, complex society, with numerous competing interests and values, that easy course is rarely open. There are too many delicate dichotomies. . . .

INDEPENDENCE v. ACCOUNTABILITY

Federal judges are constitutionally appointed to serve "during good behavior." The practical effect of that provision in Article III is that federal judges, absent an impeachable offense, may hold their office "for life." . . .

That judges have adopted a Code and have established and are continuously using an advisory process, and that Congress in the Discipline Act has provided, with formal acquiescence of the judicial branch, a mechanism for public complaints of judicial misconduct, speak well for the notion that judges are presently holding themselves "accountable" for their conduct outside or separate from their decision-making. Though there is no method for removing a federal judge for unethical behavior short of that warranting impeachment, the Discipline Act does provide for public complaint and action by judicial councils against such behavior. In this sense, the Act is designed to spotlight accountability of judges for their ethics, and, at the same time, to preserve the independence and autonomy of the judiciary. The question comes on whether judicial compliance with procedures under the Act . . . will supply sufficient accountability, and be sufficiently seen as doing so, to destroy what is now seen by some as a dichotomy between judicial independence and judicial accountability.

ISOLATION v. INVOLVEMENT

In a seeming paradox, the American public is currently and simultaneously demanding (1) that judges through their judging get more and more involved in the management of society; and (2) that judges, when they are not judging, be more and more isolated from society. . . .

The increased involvement of judges in the management of society's affairs through judicial decisions is not the involvement intended for discussion here. The current reaction to what is viewed in some quarters as "judicial activism" and "the imperial judiciary" will in time work toward some semblance of balance in measuring the roles of our judicial, legislative, and executive branches of government.

The involvement intended for discussion here is that of the individual judge and his family as persons in the everyday affairs of the community. It is from that arena that ethical considerations have served, and are serving, to isolate federal judges. The dichotomy arises from the felt need of judges for familiarity with the affairs of men and women beyond that gleanable from TV and newspapers, and insofar as that familiarity would assist in decisionmaking. Judges in their judging must on occasion ignore public clamor, current fads, and what may be asserted by vociferous groups to be "modern societal mores." To do that they must be independent. But that is not to say that judges should be attempting to interpret and apply the law to a society of strangers. Absent some fair level of familiarity, the language and thrust of judicial decisions could appear to be so far ahead or behind the march of society as to cause the people to be "turned off," to cause the people to simply disregard judicial decisions because they seem just too "far out." It is unlikely, for example, that the people would, or with safety could, put all their eggs in a judicial basket carried by a man or woman from outer space, or newly arrived from outer Mongolia. The example emphasizes with exaggeration, but not too much, for most of the Canons in the Code of Conduct for Federal Judges deal with and tend to limit the involvement of the judge as a person in community affairs. Further, the opinions published by the Advisory Committee of the Judicial Conference have supplied similarly limiting interpretation and applications of the Code.

Under the Code, the Commentaries to the Code, and the published Advisory Opinions, for example, a federal judge should not:

1. Do anything that may interfere with performance of his or her judicial duties.

2. Do anything that may enable others, or appear to enable others, to exploit his or her judicial position.

3. Volunteer as a character witness.

4. Initiate recommendations of others for appointment, promotion, parole, admission to school, etc.

5. Join certain types of clubs.

6. Do any fund raising of any kind for any organization or purpose whatsoever.[*]

7. Join any organization that is a potential litigant or financer of litigation.

8. Increase the bases for disqualification by associating with former partners and lawyer-friends, or by making certain investments.

9. Sit in a case in which his or her impartiality might "reasonably be questioned," and shall absolutely not sit when any one of some 14 specific circumstances exist.

10. Advise a trustee of a family estate on investments, unless the judge had a close familial relationship with the deceased.

11. Testify on legislation as a citizen. Testimony as a judge and on legislation dealing with the courts and administration of justice is alone permissible.

12. Speak, be a guest of honor, or accept an award, at any fund raising event.

13. Engage in financial or business dealings with lawyers or persons likely to come before his or her court.

14. Serve as officer, director, partner, manager, advisor, or employee of a business or corporation.

15. Accept any gift, favor, or loan, except under specified, very limited circumstances.

16. Serve as executor, administrator, trustee, or guardian of any trust or estate, except that of a family member, and then only if the trust or estate is not likely to come before the judge.

17. Act as arbitrator or mediator, or practice law, or accept appointment to a non-judicial governmental committee or commission, local, state, or federal.

18. Advise any member of the legislative or executive branches on any subject.

---

[*] [Judge Markey wrote at a time when the Code was, at least in parts, a bit more restrictive than today. Although his examples are generally correct and usefully thought-provoking, the examples should not be read categorically. Moreover, state judicial ethics rules periodically diverge from federal judicial ethics rules. See, e.g., ABA Ethics Op. 08-452 (2008) (permitting judges to engage in limited fundraising for therapeutic or problem-solving courts, such as drug courts); Raymond J. McKoski, "Charitable Fund-Raising by Judges: The Give and Take of the 2007 ABA Model Code of Judicial Conduct," 2008 Mich. St. L. Rev. 769 (2008); see also generally Dana A. Remus, "The Institutional Politics of Federal Judicial Conduct Regulation," 31 Yale L. & Pol'y Rev. 33, 55–58 (2012) (discussing various differences between the ABA Model Code and the federal judicial code).—Eds.]

19. Serve on the board of a community legal aid bureau.

20. Serve as co-trustee of a pension trust.

21. Fail to report to the public all of his or her income and investments and those of the judge's family.

22. Lead or hold office in any political organization, local, state, or federal.

23. Speak for or endorse any political candidate.

24. Contribute money to any political organization or candidate.

25. Attend or buy tickets for political gatherings.

26. Run for political office without first resigning his or her judicial office.

27. Fail to caution a spouse against appearance of involvement of the judge in the spouse's political activities.

28. Lunch once a year at a political club.

29. Serve as counsel to a local United Way charity.

30. Hire as law clerk the child of another judge of the court.

31. Attend an educational seminar financed by frequently litigating corporations.

The foregoing list is by no means exhaustive. The list of "no-no's" would grow beyond the limits of this short paper if it were to include the advice given in confidence to the hundreds of judges who have submitted specific inquiries to the Advisory Committee, which publishes its opinions only in relation to repetitive situations likely to be encountered by most or all judges. The list appears of sufficient length and breadth, however, to warrant discussion of the isolation-involvement dichotomy.

PRESUMPTION OF IMPARTIALITY v. PRESUMPTION OF PARTIALITY

In talking, about five years ago, with a judge of the High Court of England, an American judge exhibited shock when the British judge said his son had argued a case before him. Noting the American's expression, the British judge in turn expressed shock that anyone might even question the impartiality of a judge of the High Court on the mere and sole premise that his son represented one side. The American responded that the same was probably true in the earlier days of his country, but it is true no more.

The view that justice includes the appearance of justice has increasingly gained adherents over the years, until it is now accepted wisdom. The appearance of justice is today seen not as separate from, but as an integral part of justice itself. John P. MacKenzie, now of the New York Times, set forth the rational basis for that view in the clearest terms in his book "The Appearance of Justice." It simply is not enough that justice be actually done. It must be seen to have been done. Our British friend felt free to sit in his son's case precisely because his public would not, apparently, view that event as raising even the possibility that injustice would be done by the judge. On this side of the Atlantic, the public has acquired what some would call a more realistic view of human nature. Others might call the American view jaundiced. In any case, we seem to think it not only possible but probable, if not certain, that a judge sitting in his son's case would either favor his son's client or, because our public is "realistically suspicious," the judge would lean overmuch the other way to avoid an appearance of doing so. It was not always so.

The great Chief Justice Marshall, without quibble or concern, sat on the appeal of decisions he had rendered as trial judge and served a role as Secretary of State in the midnight Judge Scenario that led to his justly famous decision in Marbury v. Madison, 1 Cranch 137. As now documented by Bruce Murphy in "The Brandeis–Frankfurter Connection," those famous and familiar justices of more recent days apparently felt perfectly free to participate up to their elbows in political appointments and political policy-making while on the Bench. That the latter were active in recent times may account for what may have been an attempt to protect the Court, an attempt evidenced by their yeoman efforts to mask their political activities. Though those efforts may indicate that concern for judicial ethics was beginning to be felt in America during and post World War II, that concern was obviously not yet of sufficient strength, or sufficiently widespread, to cause Justices Brandeis and Frankfurter to refrain from or even limit their political activities. Indeed, Murphy ends "Connection" with a quasi-absolution of the two justices on the ground that they had no reason to expect exposure and thus no reason to fear injury to the Court. Given the absence of investigative reporters and widespread public interest in judicial ethics, such an expectation of the justices was reasonable and the cover-up efforts documented in the book were in fact successful at the time.

What may now be seen as a past public faith in American judges may have been something quite different. It may have been mere apathy, aided by lack of communications and minimal contact with the courts as compared with today's litigious society. In any event if it did previously exist here, a public presumption of impartiality cannot be expected to return as part of America's view of its judges. The problem now is to consider whether we are in danger of going, or may have already gone, too far in the direction of a public presumption of partiality. . . .

Canon 3 C(1) and 28 U.S.C. § 455(a) say, for example, that a judge is disqualified if his or her impartiality might "reasonably" be questioned. What means "reasonably"? 28 U.S.C. § 455(b) says the judge is absolutely disqualified if he or she or a family member in the household has an involved financial interest "however small." Whether it is reasonable to expect that a judge will violate his or her oath of office for ten cents is irrelevant under 28 U.S.C. § 455(b). The irrebuttable presumption of partiality in section (b) thus tends to be carried into applications of the general section (a) and to interpretations of "reasonably" in that section.

It would, of course, be possible to establish a presumption that judges act honorably and ethically. Certainly the vast majority of judges work daily toward that end.

Canon 1 recognizes that it is the conduct of judges that either preserves or destroys the perceived integrity and the continued independence of the judiciary. It does seem unfair, though doubtless inevitable, that "the judiciary," and all its members, are tarnished when one judge goes astray. It seems even more unfair when an individual judge, after twenty-five years of outstanding, totally ethical service, is presumed incapable of rendering justice in a case in which his wife has inherited .00000000012% of the stock of Exxon (an actual case). It may also be unwise, for the taxpayers must arrange to replace that judge in that case, and, multiplied by the hundreds, the time and paperwork costs seem excessive.

Last year, Federal District Judge Muecke was forced by 28 U.S.C. § 455(b) to step aside after years and years of presiding over a complex anti-trust class action, when it was learned that his wife owned a few shares in one of some 2000 corporate parties identified long after the suit was filed. In doing so, he issued a lengthy memorandum opinion outlining what can only be here called the unwisdom of the "however small" provision in section 455(b). He pointed out that a new judge and the parties would have to virtually "start over," down a road already paved with massive expenditures of time and money by the parties and the taxpayers. Having made the calculations, he included in his memorandum a statement that the maximum possible effect on his wife's financial interests could not, under even a worst-case scenario, exceed $4.69!

Because of section 455(b) and the public disclosure of judge-and-family stockholdings required by the "Ethics in Government Act," lawyers are enabled to implead or intervene an applicable corporation, or arrange filing by a corporate amicus curiae, at a late stage, should things appear to be going badly before the presiding judge. Because the judge or the judge's family owns stock in that corporation, the lawyers may thereby acquire a new judge and a fresh start. There are no studies and no proofs that this maneuver is yet widespread, but the events in certain cases raise a strong basis for the belief that it has been carried out in some cases, where the stock ownership of the judge and the availability of the right corporation dovetailed. Whether yet widely used, it is obviously available in some cases, and a lawyer's dedication to what is perceived as the client's interest will lead to its use in some of those cases. . . .

APPEARANCE v. REALITY

The dichotomy between presumptions of impartiality and partiality exists on a "wholesale" level. At the "retail" level, where individual judges confront specific circumstances, a dichotomy between appearance and reality resides.

As above indicated, the appearance of justice cannot be divorced from justice itself. A corollary has grown up: "the appearance of unethical conduct cannot be divorced from the conduct itself." Perhaps ninety-five percent of the work of the Advisory Committee on Codes of Conduct deals with "appearance" questions. When contemplated conduct is advised against, it is almost always because that conduct could reasonably present to a watching and suspicious public, or to a segment thereof, the appearance of impropriety, or the appearance that the judge may be partial, or may be subject to an influence, or may be advancing the private or political interests of a person or party, or may have made an appointment on a basis other than merit, or may have an interest in the outcome of a case before him. Similarly, when the Committee advises that no ethical impediment precludes the conduct, it is almost invariably because no such appearance is reasonably possible.

In either case, the reality is irrelevant. The question is rarely whether the conduct is itself unethical. . . .

Does it matter that judges are precluded from what is otherwise ethical conduct because that conduct might reasonably create an untoward facade or appearance? It does to some judges. In the throes of accepting the code and some of its provisions, some judges, certain of their own rectitude, objected to the very concept of a code. That position was variously stated, extending from an assertion that some provisions violated a judge's First Amendment right of free association, to the more common assertion that the code was simply unnecessary, because the conduct of most judges already matched its provisions, and that any expectedly rare infraction could be dealt with on a case-by-case basis. The last was based on a quasi-burden of proof approach, i.e., if someone had any reason to think a particular judge was acting improperly it was up to that person to come forward and assert such charges as were thought appropriate, while the other judges went on acting properly, without codes, advisory opinions, and committees. . . .

In another part of his article, Judge Markey stated that a then-recent attempt to install a process to review and, if necessary, to discipline federal judges would eventually assure the members of the public that they no longer need to be concerned with appearances, in part because "real" instances of unethical behavior (which he viewed as exceedingly rare) would be discovered and redressed. The public generally still has trust issues with the judiciary, however, and the federal judicial disciplinary process has been consistently criticized for lacking in transparency and for being ineffective. Federal judges largely regulate themselves. What would be a better alternative? Does an appearance-based standard remedy, to some extent, judges' rosy opinions of their own behavior? Does it avoid lawyers and litigants having to call the challenged judge unethical? Instead challengers merely allege that the appearance of impropriety requires the judge to step down from a case.

Judge Markey spelled out many of the various prohibitions on judges' conduct (especially as applied to judges' off-the-bench conduct). Did you notice any prohibitions that seem unnecessary or even detrimental for good judges? More generally, do you think that a system of judicial ethics regulation should be based on actually improper conduct alone or at least partially on the appearance of impropriety created by judges' conduct?

2. Judicial Selection and Independence

To choose lawyers who will exhibit impartiality, integrity, and independence as judges, the manner of judicial selection is important.[3] For federal judges, the Constitution provides the answer of appointment by the President "by and with the Advice and Consent of the Senate." Art. 2, § 2. The states have experimented with a variety of different solutions. In the beginning, the predominant method was appointive judges. Starting with the Jacksonian period and continuing for a large part of the nineteenth century, the trend was more and more to elective judges; since that time there has been some movement away from elective to appointive or hybrid systems, although most states still elect most of their judges. The best known of the hybrid systems is the Missouri Plan, which its proponents have named the "merit" plan of selection or the "merit system." In short, the governor appoints judges from a list of nominees submitted by a nominating commission composed of judges, of lawyers often selected by the bar, and of citizens (usually a minority of the commission) appointed by the governor. At the end of the term, the electorate votes on the question whether Judge X should "be retained in office." The materials urging one plan or another are voluminous. An interesting collection, somewhat weighted toward the Missouri Plan but describing numerous other systems, is contained in Winters ed., *Judicial Selection and Tenure* (rev. ed. 1973), which also contains a lengthy bibliography on the subject. A good historical account of judicial elections versus judicial appointments in this country is Jed Shugerman, *The People's Courts* (2012).

A catalogue of the problems of judicial campaign financing, complete with illustrative statistics showing the amounts of money raised and the roles played by lawyers who practice in the courts to which judges are being elected, is contained in Schotland, "Elective Judges' Campaign Financing," 2 J.L. & Pol. 57–167 (1985); see also generally Keith Swisher, "Legal Ethics and Campaign Contributions: The Professional Responsibility to Pay for Justice," 24 Geo. J. Legal Ethics 225, 228 (2011) (exploring the "professional responsibilities of attorneys who contribute to judges' election campaigns and then appear before those judges"). Schotland also has what he calls modest but feasible proposals for reform that do not eliminate elections. The issue has increased in importance in recent years as various interest groups have sought to influence future litigation results by electing candidates thought likely to favor their views. Many judicial election campaigns now run into the millions of dollars. A high percentage of survey respondents (including judges, lawyers, and members of the public) believe that judicial campaign contributions and other expenditures influence judges' decisions. Some judges also appear to rule differently in election years (e.g., they impose longer sentences). See generally

---

3. As an aside, not all judges are lawyers or former lawyers. Several states do not require either a law degree or a bar license for certain lower court judges. The vast majority of judges, however, have both. All judges (except Supreme Court Justices as noted above) are bound by a version of the judicial ethics code.

Michael Kang & Joanna Shepherd, "Judging Judicial Elections," 114 Mich. L. Rev. 929, 940 (2016) (reviewing Melinda Gann Hall, *Attacking Judges: How Campaign Advertising Influences State Supreme Court Elections* (2015)) (noting that "empirical research on judicial decisionmaking finds that judges sentence criminal defendants more harshly as concerns about their own re-elections become more salient"). Such evidence might seem to point to an appointive, rather than an elective, system, in which judges or their campaign committees do not need money or popular opinion to run for their election, reelection, or retention. Or does the evidence instead suggest, as proponents argue, that elections are making judges appropriately accountable to the public?

A closely related and more common issue is what candidates and nominees for office may say in the process of seeking election or appointment. For years the ABA's Model Code and the judicial conduct codes of many states had two kinds of prohibitions: one forbidding candidates and nominees for office from "announcing" their views on issues that might come before them and another forbidding candidates and nominees from making pledges or promises inconsistent with impartial performance of the judicial office. See 1990 Model Code Canon (A)(2)(d); 2007 Model Code Rule 4.1(A)(13). An "announce" clause was the subject of Republican Party of Minnesota v. White, which follows. The Court in that case did not directly address the constitutionality of a "pledges or promises" prohibition. The tension that exists between the desire to give information to the electorate or to those involved in the appointment process and the need to preserve the actuality and the appearance of judicial impartiality, however defined, has been exemplified over and over again in electoral campaigns and in appointment hearings, especially recently in Senate confirmation hearings for many judicial appointments. As you might imagine, the First Amendment and the Canons are often in direct tension, because the Canons designedly limit the speech and expressive conduct of judges to preserve their actual and apparent impartiality.

Republican Party of Minnesota v. White
536 U.S. 765 (2002)

Justice SCALIA delivered the opinion of the Court.

The question presented in this case is whether the First Amendment permits the Minnesota Supreme Court to prohibit candidates for judicial election in that State from announcing their views on disputed legal and political issues.

I

Since Minnesota's admission to the Union in 1858, the State's Constitution has provided for the selection of all state judges by popular election. Since 1912, those elections have been nonpartisan. Since 1974, they have been subject to a legal restriction which states that a "candidate for a judicial office, including an incumbent judge," shall not "announce his or her views on disputed legal or political issues."

Minn. Code of Judicial Conduct, Canon 5(A)(3)(d)(i) (2000). This prohibition, promulgated by the Minnesota Supreme Court and based on Canon 7(B) of the 1972 American Bar Association (ABA) Model Code of Judicial Conduct, is known as the "announce clause." Incumbent judges who violate it are subject to discipline, including removal, censure, civil penalties, and suspension without pay. Lawyers who run for judicial office also must comply with the announce clause. Those who violate it are subject to, inter alia, disbarment, suspension, and probation.

In 1996, one of the petitioners, Gregory Wersal, ran for associate justice of the Minnesota Supreme Court. In the course of the campaign, he distributed literature criticizing several Minnesota Supreme Court decisions on issues such as crime, welfare, and abortion. A complaint against Wersal challenging, among other things, the propriety of this literature was filed with the Office of Lawyers Professional Responsibility, the agency which, under the direction of the Minnesota Lawyers Professional Responsibility Board, investigates and prosecutes ethical violations of lawyer candidates for judicial office. The Lawyers Board dismissed the complaint; with regard to the charges that his campaign materials violated the announce clause, it expressed doubt whether the clause could constitutionally be enforced. Nonetheless, fearing that further ethical complaints would jeopardize his ability to practice law, Wersal withdrew from the election. In 1998, Wersal ran again for the same office. Early in that race, he sought an advisory opinion from the Lawyers Board with regard to whether it planned to enforce the announce clause. The Lawyers Board responded equivocally, stating that, although it had significant doubts about the constitutionality of the provision, it was unable to answer his question because he had not submitted a list of the announcements he wished to make.

Shortly thereafter, Wersal filed this lawsuit in Federal District Court against respondents, seeking, inter alia, a declaration that the announce clause violates the First Amendment and an injunction against its enforcement. Wersal alleged that he was forced to refrain from announcing his views on disputed issues during the 1998 campaign, to the point where he declined response to questions put to him by the press and public, out of concern that he might run afoul of the announce clause. Other plaintiffs in the suit, including the Minnesota Republican Party, alleged that, because the clause kept Wersal from announcing his views, they were unable to learn those views and support or oppose his candidacy accordingly. The parties filed cross-motions for summary judgment, and the District Court found in favor of respondents, holding that the announce clause did not violate the First Amendment. 63 F.Supp.2d 967 (D.Minn. 1999). Over a dissent by Judge Beam, the United States Court of Appeals for the Eighth Circuit affirmed. [Republican Party of Minnesota v. Kelly,] 247 F.3d 854 (2001). . . .

II

Before considering the constitutionality of the announce clause, we must be clear about its meaning. Its text says that a candidate for judicial office shall not "announce his or her views on disputed legal or political issues." Minn. Code of Judicial Conduct, Canon 5(A)(3)(d)(i) (2002).

We know that "announc[ing] . . . views" on an issue covers much more than *promising* to decide an issue a particular way. The prohibition extends to the candidate's mere statement of his current position, even if he does not bind himself to maintain that position after election. All the parties agree this is the case, because the Minnesota Code contains a so-called "pledges or promises" clause, which *separately* prohibits judicial candidates from making "pledges or promises of conduct in office other than the faithful and impartial performance of the duties of the office"—a prohibition that is not challenged here and on which we express no view.

There are, however, some limitations that the Minnesota Supreme Court has placed upon the scope of the announce clause that are not (to put it politely) immediately apparent from its text. . . . The Judicial Board issued an opinion stating that judicial candidates may criticize past decisions, and the Lawyers Board refused to discipline Wersal for the foregoing statements because, in part, it thought they did not violate the announce clause. . . .

There are yet further limitations upon the apparent plain meaning of the announce clause: In light of the constitutional concerns, the District Court construed the clause to reach only disputed issues that are likely to come before the candidate if he is elected judge. . . .

It seems to us, however, that—like the text of the announce clause itself—these limitations upon the text of the announce clause are not all that they appear to be. First, respondents acknowledged at oral argument that statements critical of past judicial decisions are *not* permissible if the candidate also states that he is against stare decisis. Thus, candidates must choose between stating their views critical of past decisions and stating their views in opposition to stare decisis. Or, to look at it more concretely, they may state their view that prior decisions were erroneous only if they do not assert that they, if elected, have any power to eliminate erroneous decisions. Second, limiting the scope of the clause to issues likely to come before a court is not much of a limitation at all. One would hardly expect the "disputed legal or political issues" raised in the course of a state judicial election to include such matters as whether the Federal Government should end the embargo of Cuba. Quite obviously, they will be those legal or political disputes that are the proper (or by past decisions have been made the improper) business of the state courts. And within that relevant category, "[t]here is almost no legal or political issue that is unlikely to come before a judge of an American court, state or federal, of general jurisdiction." Buckley v. Illinois Judicial Inquiry Bd., 997 F.2d 224, 229 (C.A.7 1993). . . .

In any event, it is clear that the announce clause prohibits a judicial candidate from stating his views on any specific nonfanciful legal question within the province of the court for which he is running, except in the context of discussing past decisions—and in the latter context as well, if he expresses the view that he is not bound by stare decisis.

Respondents contend that this still leaves plenty of topics for discussion on the campaign trail. These include a candidate's "character," "education," "work habits," and "how [he] would handle administrative duties if elected." Indeed, the Judicial Board has printed a list of preapproved questions which judicial candidates are allowed to answer. These include how the candidate feels about cameras in the courtroom, how he would go about reducing the caseload, how the costs of judicial administration can be reduced, and how he proposes to ensure that minorities and women are treated more fairly by the court system. Whether this list of preapproved subjects, and other topics not prohibited by the announce clause, adequately fulfill the First Amendment's guarantee of freedom of speech is the question to which we now turn.

III

As the Court of Appeals recognized, the announce clause both prohibits speech on the basis of its content and burdens a category of speech that is "at the core of our First Amendment freedoms"—speech about the qualifications of candidates for public office. 247 F.3d, at 861, 863. The Court of Appeals concluded that the proper test to be applied to determine the constitutionality of such a restriction is what our cases have called strict scrutiny, id., at 864; the parties do not dispute that this is correct. Under the strict-scrutiny test, respondents have the burden to prove that the announce clause is (1) narrowly tailored, to serve (2) a compelling state interest. E.g., Eu v. San Francisco County Democratic Central Comm., 489 U.S. 214, 222 (1989). In order for respondents to show that the announce clause is narrowly tailored, they must demonstrate that it does not "unnecessarily circumscrib[e] protected expression." Brown v. Hartlage, 456 U.S. 45, 54 (1982).

The Court of Appeals concluded that respondents had established two interests as sufficiently compelling to justify the announce clause: preserving the impartiality of the state judiciary and preserving the appearance of the impartiality of the state judiciary. 247 F.3d, at 867. Respondents reassert these two interests before us, arguing that the first is compelling because it protects the due process rights of litigants, and that the second is compelling because it preserves public confidence in the judiciary. Respondents are rather vague, however, about what they mean by "impartiality." Indeed, although the term is used throughout the Eighth Circuit's opinion, the briefs, the Minnesota Code of Judicial Conduct, and the ABA Codes of Judicial Conduct, none of these sources bothers to define it. Clarity on this point is essential before we can decide whether impartiality is indeed a compelling state interest, and, if so, whether the announce clause is narrowly tailored to achieve it.

A

One meaning of "impartiality" in the judicial context—and of course its root meaning—is the lack of bias for or against either *party* to the proceeding. Impartiality in this sense assures equal application of the law. That is, it guarantees a party that the judge who hears his case will apply the law to him in the same way he applies it to any other party. This is the traditional sense in which the term is used. . . .

We think it plain that the announce clause is not narrowly tailored to serve impartiality (or the appearance of impartiality) in this sense. Indeed, the clause is barely tailored to serve that interest *at all*, inasmuch as it does not restrict speech for or against particular *parties*, but rather speech for or against particular *issues*. To be sure, when a case arises that turns on a legal issue on which the judge (as a candidate) had taken a particular stand, the party taking the opposite stand is likely to lose. But not because of any bias against that party, or favoritism toward the other party. *Any* party taking that position is just as likely to lose. The judge is applying the law (as he sees it) evenhandedly.[7]

B

It is perhaps possible to use the term "impartiality" in the judicial context (though this is certainly not a common usage) to mean lack of preconception in favor of or against a particular *legal view.* This sort of impartiality would be concerned, not with guaranteeing litigants equal application of the law, but rather with guaranteeing them an equal chance to persuade the court on the legal points in their case. Impartiality in this sense may well be an interest served by the announce clause, but it is not a *compelling* state interest, as strict scrutiny requires. A judge's lack of predisposition regarding the relevant legal issues in a case has never been thought a necessary component of equal justice, and with good reason. For one thing, it is virtually impossible to find a judge who does not have preconceptions about the law. As then-Justice Rehnquist observed of our own Court: "Since most Justices come to this bench no earlier than their middle years, it would be unusual if they had not by that time formulated at least some tentative notions that would influence them in their interpretation of the sweeping clauses of the Constitution and their interaction with one another. It would be not merely unusual, but extraordinary, if they had not at least given opinions as to constitutional issues in their previous legal careers." Laird v. Tatum, 409 U.S. 824, 835 (1972) (memorandum opinion). Indeed, even if it were possible to select judges who did not have preconceived views on legal issues, it would hardly be desirable to do so. "Proof that a Justice's mind at the time he joined the Court was a complete *tabula rasa* in the area of constitutional adjudication would be evidence of lack of qualification, not lack of bias." Ibid. . . . .

C

A third possible meaning of "impartiality" (again not a common one) might be described as openmindedness. This quality in a judge demands not that he have no

---

7. Justice Stevens asserts that the announce clause "serves the State's interest in maintaining both the appearance of this form of impartiality and its actuality." We do not disagree. Some of the speech prohibited by the announce clause may well exhibit a bias against parties—including Justice Stevens' example of an election speech stressing the candidate's unbroken record of affirming convictions for rape. That is why we are careful to say that the announce clause is "*barely* tailored to serve that interest" (emphasis added). The question under our strict scrutiny test, however, is not whether the announce clause serves this interest *at all*, but whether it is *narrowly tailored* to serve this interest. It is not.

preconceptions on legal issues, but that he be willing to consider views that oppose his preconceptions, and remain open to persuasion, when the issues arise in a pending case. This sort of impartiality seeks to guarantee each litigant, not an *equal* chance to win the legal points in the case, but at least *some* chance of doing so. It may well be that impartiality in this sense, and the appearance of it, are desirable in the judiciary, but we need not pursue that inquiry, since we do not believe the Minnesota Supreme Court adopted the announce clause for that purpose.

Respondents argue that the announce clause serves the interest in openmindedness, or at least in the appearance of openmindedness, because it relieves a judge from pressure to rule a certain way in order to maintain consistency with statements the judge has previously made. The problem is, however, that statements in election campaigns are such an infinitesimal portion of the public commitments to legal positions that judges (or judges-to-be) undertake, that this object of the prohibition is implausible. Before they arrive on the bench (whether by election or otherwise) judges have often committed themselves on legal issues that they must later rule upon. . . . More common still is a judge's confronting a legal issue on which he has expressed an opinion while on the bench. Most frequently, of course, that prior expression will have occurred in ruling on an earlier case. But judges often state their views on disputed legal issues outside the context of adjudication — in classes that they conduct, and in books and speeches. Like the ABA Codes of Judicial Conduct, the Minnesota Code not only permits but encourages this. See Minn. Code of Judicial Conduct, Canon 4(B) (2002) ("A judge may write, lecture, teach, speak and participate in other extra-judicial activities concerning the law . . ."); Minn. Code of Judicial Conduct, Canon 4(B), Comment (2002) ("To the extent that time permits, a judge is encouraged to do so . . ."). That is quite incompatible with the notion that the need for openmindedness (or for the appearance of openmindedness) lies behind the prohibition at issue here.

The short of the matter is this: In Minnesota, a candidate for judicial office may not say "I think it is constitutional for the legislature to prohibit same-sex marriages." He may say the very same thing, however, up until the very day before he declares himself a candidate, and may say it repeatedly (until litigation is pending) after he is elected. As a means of pursuing the objective of openmindedness that respondents now articulate, the announce clause is so woefully underinclusive as to render belief in that purpose a challenge to the credulous. . . .

Justice Stevens asserts that statements made in an election campaign pose a special threat to openmindedness because the candidate, when elected judge, will have a *particular* reluctance to contradict them. That might be plausible, perhaps, with regard to campaign *promises*. A candidate who says "If elected, I will vote to uphold the legislature's power to prohibit same-sex marriages" will positively be breaking his word if he does not do so (although one would be naive not to recognize that campaign promises are — by long democratic tradition — the least binding form of human commitment). But, as noted earlier, the Minnesota Supreme Court has adopted a separate prohibition on campaign "pledges or promises," which is not challenged here. The proposition that judges feel significantly greater compulsion, or appear to feel significantly greater compulsion, to maintain consistency with *nonpromissory* statements made during a judicial campaign than with such statements made before or after the campaign is not self-evidently true. It seems to us quite likely, in fact, that in many cases the opposite is true. . . . In any event, it suffices to say that respondents have not carried the burden imposed by our strict-scrutiny test to establish this proposition (that campaign statements are uniquely destructive of open-mindedness) on which the validity of the announce clause rests. . . .

Moreover, the notion that the special context of electioneering justifies an *abridgment* of the right to speak out on disputed issues sets our First Amendment jurisprudence on its head. . . . We have never allowed the government to prohibit candidates from communicating relevant information to voters during an election.

. . . [E]lected judges—regardless of whether they have announced any views beforehand—*always* face the pressure of an electorate who might disagree with their rulings and therefore vote them off the bench. . . . So if . . . it violates due process for a judge to sit in a case in which ruling one way rather than another increases his prospects for reelection, then—quite simply—the practice of electing judges is itself a violation of due process. It is not difficult to understand how one with these views would approve the election-nullifying effect of the announce clause. They are not, however, the views reflected in the Due Process Clause of the Fourteenth Amendment, which has coexisted with the election of judges ever since it was adopted. . . .

. . . [W]e neither assert nor imply that the First Amendment requires campaigns for judicial office to sound the same as those for legislative office. What we do assert . . . is that, *even if* the First Amendment allows greater regulation of judicial election campaigns than legislative election campaigns, the announce clause still fails strict scrutiny because it is woefully underinclusive, prohibiting announcements by judges (and would-be judges) only at certain times and in certain forms. . . .

But in any case, Justice Ginsburg greatly exaggerates the difference between judicial and legislative elections. She asserts that "the rationale underlying unconstrained speech in elections for political office—that representative government depends on the public's ability to choose agents who will act at its behest—does not carry over to campaigns for the bench." This complete separation of the judiciary from the enterprise of "representative government" might have some truth in those countries where judges neither make law themselves nor set aside the laws enacted by the legislature. It is not a true picture of the American system. Not only do state-court judges possess the power to "make" common law, but they have the immense power to shape the States' constitutions as well. . . . Which is precisely why the election of state judges became popular.

IV

To sustain the announce clause, the Eighth Circuit relied heavily on the fact that a pervasive practice of prohibiting judicial candidates from discussing disputed legal and political issues developed during the last half of the 20th century. 247 F.3d, at 879–880. It is true that a "universal and long-established" tradition of prohibiting certain conduct creates "a strong presumption" that the prohibition is constitutional . . . . The practice of prohibiting speech by judicial candidates on disputed issues, however, is neither long nor universal.

At the time of the founding, only Vermont (before it became a State) selected any of its judges by election. Starting with Georgia in 1812, States began to provide for judicial election, a development rapidly accelerated by Jacksonian democracy. By the time of the Civil War, the great majority of States elected their judges. We know of no restrictions upon statements that could be made by judicial candidates (including judges) throughout the 19th and the first quarter of the 20th century. Indeed, judicial elections were generally partisan during this period, the movement toward nonpartisan judicial elections not even beginning until the 1870s. Thus, not only were judicial candidates (including judges) discussing disputed legal and political issues on the campaign trail, but they were touting party affiliations and angling for party nominations all the while.

. . . Even today, although a majority of States have adopted either the announce clause or its 1990 ABA successor, adoption is not unanimous. . . . This practice, relatively new to judicial elections and still not universally adopted, does not compare well with the traditions deemed worthy of our attention in prior cases. . . .

The Minnesota Supreme Court's canon of judicial conduct prohibiting candidates for judicial election from announcing their views on disputed legal and political issues violates the First Amendment. Accordingly, we reverse the grant of summary judgment to respondents and remand the case for proceedings consistent with this opinion.

Justice O'CONNOR, concurring.

I join the opinion of the Court but write separately to express my concerns about judicial elections generally. Respondents claim that "[t]he Announce Clause is necessary . . . to protect the State's compelling governmental interes[t] in an actual and perceived . . . impartial judiciary." I am concerned that, even aside from what judicial candidates may say while campaigning, the very practice of electing judges undermines this interest.

We of course want judges to be impartial, in the sense of being free from any personal stake in the outcome of the cases to which they are assigned. But if judges are subject to regular elections they are likely to feel that they have at least some personal stake in the outcome of every publicized case. Elected judges cannot help being aware that if the public is not satisfied with the outcome of a particular case, it could hurt their reelection prospects. . . . Even if judges were able to suppress their awareness of the potential electoral consequences of their decisions and refrain from acting on it, the public's confidence in the judiciary could be undermined simply by the possibility that judges would be unable to do so.

Moreover, contested elections generally entail campaigning. And campaigning for a judicial post today can require substantial funds. . . . Unless the pool of judicial candidates is limited to those wealthy enough to independently fund their campaigns, a limitation unrelated to judicial skill, the cost of campaigning requires judicial candidates to engage in fundraising. Yet relying on campaign donations may leave judges feeling indebted to certain parties or interest groups. . . . Even if judges were able to refrain from favoring donors, the mere possibility that judges' decisions may be motivated by the desire to repay campaign contributors is likely to undermine the public's confidence in the judiciary. . . .

By the beginning of the 20th century, however, elected judiciaries increasingly came to be viewed as incompetent and corrupt, and criticism of partisan judicial elections mounted. . . .

In response to such concerns, some States adopted a modified system of judicial selection that became known as the Missouri Plan (because Missouri was the first State to adopt it for most of its judicial posts). Under the Missouri Plan, judges are appointed by a high elected official, generally from a list of nominees put together by a nonpartisan nominating commission, and then subsequently stand for unopposed retention elections in which voters are asked whether the judges should be recalled. If a judge is recalled, the vacancy is filled through a new nomination and appointment. This system obviously reduces threats to judicial impartiality, even if it does not eliminate all popular pressure on judges. . . .

Thirty-one States, however, still use popular elections to select some or all of their appellate and/or general jurisdiction trial court judges, who thereafter run for reelection periodically. Ibid. Of these, slightly more than half use nonpartisan elections, and the rest use partisan elections. Most of the States that do not have any form of judicial elections choose judges through executive nomination and legislative confirmation.

Minnesota has chosen to select its judges through contested popular elections instead of through an appointment system or a combined appointment and retention election system along the lines of the Missouri Plan. In doing so the State has voluntarily taken on the risks to judicial bias described above. As a result, the State's claim that it needs to significantly restrict judges' speech in order to protect judicial impartiality is particularly troubling. If the State has a problem with judicial impartiality, it is largely one the State brought upon itself by continuing the practice of popularly electing judges.

Justice GINSBURG, with whom Justice STEVENS, Justice SOUTER, and Justice BREYER join, dissenting.

Whether state or federal, elected or appointed, judges perform a function fundamentally different from that of the people's elected representatives. Legislative and executive officials act on behalf of the voters who placed them in office . . . . Unlike their counterparts in the political branches, judges are expected to refrain from catering to particular constituencies or committing themselves on controversial issues in advance of adversarial presentation. . . .

I

The speech restriction must fail, in the Court's view, because an electoral process is at stake; if Minnesota opts to elect its judges, the Court asserts, the State may not rein in what candidates may say. . . .

I do not agree with this unilocular, "an election is an election," approach. Instead, I would differentiate elections for political offices, in which the First Amendment holds full sway, from elections designed to select those whose office it is to administer justice without respect to persons. Minnesota's choice to elect its judges, I am persuaded, does not preclude the State from installing an election process geared to the judicial office. . . .

Judges . . . are not political actors. They do not sit as representatives of particular persons, communities, or parties; they serve no faction or constituency. . . . Even when they develop common law or give concrete meaning to constitutional text, judges act only in the context of individual cases, the outcome of which cannot depend on the will of the public. . . .

. . . Nothing in the Court's opinion convincingly explains why Minnesota may not pursue that goal in the manner it did.

Minnesota did not choose a judicial selection system with all the trappings of legislative and executive races. While providing for public participation, it tailored judicial selection to fit the character of third branch office holding. . . . The balance the State sought to achieve—allowing the people to elect judges, but safeguarding the process so that the integrity of the judiciary would not be compromised—should encounter no First Amendment shoal. . . .

A

All parties to this case agree that, whatever the validity of the Announce Clause, the State may constitutionally prohibit judicial candidates from pledging or promising certain results. . . .

. . . [The] cases establish three propositions important to this dispute. First, a litigant is deprived of due process where the judge who hears his case has a "direct, personal, substantial, and pecuniary" interest in ruling against him. Second, this interest need not be as direct as it was in *Tumey* [v. Ohio, 273 U.S. 510 (1927)], where the judge was essentially compensated for each conviction he obtained . . . . And third, due process does not require a showing that the judge is actually biased as a result of his self-interest. Rather, our cases have "always endeavored to prevent even the probability of unfairness." In re Murchison, 349 U.S. [133], at 136. . . .

The justification for the pledges or promises prohibition follows from these principles. When a judicial candidate promises to rule a certain way on an issue that may later reach the courts, the potential for due process violations is grave and manifest. If successful in her bid for office, the judicial candidate will become a judge, and in that capacity she will be under pressure to resist the pleas of litigants who advance positions contrary to her pledges on the campaign trail. If the judge fails to honor her campaign promises, she will not only face abandonment by supporters of her professed views, she will also "ris[k] being assailed as a dissembler," willing to say one thing to win an election and to do the opposite once in office. . . .

In addition to protecting litigants' due process rights, the parties in this case further agree, the pledges or promises clause advances another compelling state interest: preserving the public's confidence in the integrity and impartiality of its judiciary. . . .

Prohibiting a judicial candidate from pledging or promising certain results if elected directly promotes the State's interest in preserving public faith in the bench. When a candidate makes such a promise during a campaign, the public will no doubt perceive that she is doing so in the hope of garnering votes. And the public will in turn likely conclude that when the candidate decides an issue in accord with that promise, she does so at least in part to discharge her undertaking to the voters in the previous election and to prevent voter abandonment in the next. The perception of that unseemly quid pro quo—a judicial candidate's promises on issues in return for the electorate's votes at the polls—inevitably diminishes the public's faith in the ability of judges to administer the law without regard to personal or political self-interest. . . .

The constitutionality of the pledges or promises clause is thus amply supported; the provision not only advances due process of law for litigants in Minnesota courts, it also reinforces the authority of the Minnesota judiciary by promoting public confidence in the State's judges. The Announce Clause, however, is equally vital to achieving these compelling ends, for without it, the pledges or promises provision would be feeble, an arid form, a matter of no real importance.

Uncoupled from the Announce Clause, the ban on pledges or promises is easily circumvented. By prefacing a campaign commitment with the caveat, "although I cannot promise anything," or by simply avoiding the language of promises or pledges altogether, a candidate could declare with impunity how she would decide specific issues. Semantic sanitizing of the candidate's commitment would not, however, diminish its pernicious effects on actual and perceived judicial impartiality. To use the Court's example, a candidate who campaigns by saying, "If elected, I will vote to uphold the legislature's power to prohibit same-sex marriages," will feel scarcely more pressure to honor that statement than the candidate who stands behind a podium and tells a throng of cheering supporters: "I think it is constitutional for the legislature to prohibit same-sex marriages." Made during a campaign, both statements contemplate a quid pro quo between candidate and voter. Both effectively "bind [the candidate] to maintain that position after election." And both convey the impression of a candidate prejudging an issue to win votes. Contrary to the Court's assertion, the "nonpromissory" statement averts none of the dangers posed by the "promissory" one.

By targeting statements that do not technically constitute pledges or promises but nevertheless "publicly mak[e] known how [the candidate] would decide" legal issues, the Announce Clause prevents this end run around the letter and spirit of its companion provision. No less than the pledges or promises clause itself, the Announce Clause is an indispensable part of Minnesota's effort to maintain the health of its judiciary, and is therefore constitutional for the same reasons.

[Concurring opinion by Justice Kennedy and dissenting opinion by Justice Stevens are omitted.]

Notes

1. Which notion of the content of judicial impartiality do you prefer? Following *White*, the ABA defined impartiality and included the concept of "open-mindedness." Compare *White*, 536 U.S., at 775–78 (defining impartiality as "lack of bias for or against either party" or "as openmindedness," which "in a judge demands, not that he have no preconceptions on legal issues, but that he be willing to consider views that oppose his preconceptions, and remain open to persuasion, when the issues arise in a pending case") with Model Code of Judicial Conduct Terminology (2007) (defining impartiality as the "absence of bias or prejudice in favor of, or against, particular parties or classes of parties, as well as maintenance of an open mind in considering issues that may come before a judge").

2. Are the promises and pledges provisions of the 1990 and 2007 Model Codes of Judicial Conduct still constitutional after the decision in the principal case?

3. *White* caused a wave of lower court litigation on the constitutionality of various canons. See, e.g., Wolfson v. Concannon, 811 F.3d 1176, 1186 (9th Cir. 2016) (en banc) (holding that the "Personal Solicitation Clause, Endorsement Clauses, and Campaign Prohibition all withstand First Amendment analysis under strict scrutiny"); Siefert v. Alexander, 608 F.3d 974, 977 (7th Cir. 2010) ("[T]he district court . . . declared the rules prohibiting a judge or judicial candidate from announcing a partisan affiliation, endorsing partisan candidates, and personally soliciting contributions unconstitutional, and enjoined the defendants from enforcing these rules against Siefert. . . . We affirm the district court's holding on the partisan affiliation ban but reverse the district court's ruling that the bans on endorsing partisan candidates and personally soliciting contributions are unconstitutional"). The outcomes have not been uniform across jurisdictions. Thus, a judge or prospective judge in one circuit may enjoy a constitutional right to certain campaign conduct not recognized (or explicitly rejected) in another circuit. The ABA Model Code has struggled to achieve its once-commendable level of uniformity under these conditions. The ABA generally supports a merit selection system and imposes significant restrictions (some argue overly restrictive) on conduct in judicial elections. Do you think that a judge who publicly announces her views on disputed legal or political issues is more

or less likely to feel compelled to honor those views when an applicable case later comes before her?

4. As the opinions indicate, the Justices had differing views about the desirability of choosing judges through judicial elections. Notwithstanding certain Justices' reservations, almost ninety percent of judges are selected in an elective environment. Given the pressures of elective environments (such as the need to receive campaign contributions and to win votes), are these judges sufficiently independent to uphold the values of judicial impartiality and integrity? Several studies have now indicated that elected judges sentence criminal defendants more harshly in election years. Several studies have also indicated (but have not necessarily proven) that elected judges more often vote in a way that is consistent with their contributors' preferences? Does this indicate a problem of independence?

In the Supreme Court's most recent attempt to referee the fight between the Canons and the First Amendment in elective environments, the Canons won:

Williams-Yulee v. The Florida Bar

135 S.Ct. 1656 (2015)

Chief Justice ROBERTS delivered the opinion of the Court, except as to Part II.

Our Founders vested authority to appoint federal judges in the President, with the advice and consent of the Senate, and entrusted those judges to hold their offices during good behavior. The Constitution permits States to make a different choice, and most of them have done so. In 39 States, voters elect trial or appellate judges at the polls. In an effort to preserve public confidence in the integrity of their judiciaries, many of those States prohibit judges and judicial candidates from personally soliciting funds for their campaigns. We must decide whether the First Amendment permits such restrictions on speech.

We hold that it does. Judges are not politicians, even when they come to the bench by way of the ballot. And a State's decision to elect its judiciary does not compel it to treat judicial candidates like campaigners for political office. A State may assure its people that judges will apply the law without fear or favor—and without having personally asked anyone for money. We affirm the judgment of the Florida Supreme Court.

I

A

When Florida entered the Union in 1845, its Constitution provided for trial and appellate judges to be elected by the General Assembly. Florida soon followed more than a dozen of its sister States in transferring authority to elect judges to the voting public. See J. Shugerman, *The People's Courts: Pursuing Judicial Independence in America* 103–122 (2012). The experiment did not last long in the Sunshine State. The war came, and Florida's 1868 Constitution returned judicial selection to the political branches. Over time, however, the people reclaimed the power to elect the state bench: Supreme Court justices in 1885 and trial court judges in 1942. See Little, "An Overview of the Historical Development of the Judicial Article of the Florida Constitution," 19 Stetson L. Rev. 1, 40 (1989).

In the early 1970s, four Florida Supreme Court justices resigned from office following corruption scandals. Florida voters responded by amending their Constitution again. Under the system now in place, appellate judges are appointed by the Governor from a list of candidates proposed by a nominating committee — a process known as "merit selection." Then, every six years, voters decide whether to retain incumbent appellate judges for another term. Trial judges are still elected by popular vote, unless the local jurisdiction opts instead for merit selection. . . .

Canon 7C(1) governs fundraising in judicial elections. The Canon, which is based on a provision in the American Bar Association's Model Code of Judicial Conduct, provides:

> A candidate, including an incumbent judge, for a judicial office that is filled by public election between competing candidates shall not personally solicit campaign funds, or solicit attorneys for publicly stated support, but may establish committees of responsible persons to secure and manage the expenditure of funds for the candidate's campaign and to obtain public statements of support for his or her candidacy. Such committees are not prohibited from soliciting campaign contributions and public support from any person or corporation authorized by law.

Id., at 38.

Florida statutes impose additional restrictions on campaign fundraising in judicial elections. Contributors may not donate more than $1,000 per election to a trial court candidate or more than $3,000 per retention election to a Supreme Court justice. Fla. Stat. § 106.08(1)(a) (2014). Campaign committee treasurers must file periodic reports disclosing the names of contributors and the amount of each contribution. § 106.07.

Judicial candidates can seek guidance about campaign ethics rules from the Florida Judicial Ethics Advisory Committee. The Committee has interpreted Canon 7 to allow a judicial candidate to serve as treasurer of his own campaign committee, learn the identity of campaign contributors, and send thank you notes to donors. . . .

Like Florida, most other States prohibit judicial candidates from soliciting campaign funds personally, but allow them to raise money through committees. According to the American Bar Association, 30 of the 39 States that elect trial or appellate judges have adopted restrictions similar to Canon 7C(1). . . .

B

Lanell Williams-Yulee, who refers to herself as Yulee, has practiced law in Florida since 1991. In September 2009, she decided to run for a seat on the county court for Hillsborough County, a jurisdiction of about 1.3 million people that includes the city of Tampa. Shortly after filing paperwork to enter the race, Yulee drafted a letter announcing her candidacy. The letter described her experience and desire to "bring fresh ideas and positive solutions to the Judicial bench." The letter then stated:

> An early contribution of $25, $50, $100, $250, or $500, made payable to "Lanell Williams-Yulee Campaign for County Judge," will help raise the initial funds needed to launch the campaign and get our message out to the public. I ask for your support [i]n meeting the primary election fund raiser goals. Thank you in advance for your support.

Yulee signed the letter and mailed it to local voters. She also posted the letter on her campaign Web site.

Yulee's bid for the bench did not unfold as she had hoped. She lost the primary to the incumbent judge. Then the Florida Bar filed a complaint against her. As relevant here, the Bar charged her with violating Rule 4–8.2(b) of the Rules Regulating the Florida Bar. That Rule requires judicial candidates to comply with applicable provisions of Florida's Code of Judicial Conduct, including the ban on personal solicitation of campaign funds in Canon 7C(1).

Yulee admitted that she had signed and sent the fundraising letter. But she argued that the Bar could not discipline her for that conduct because the First Amendment protects a judicial candidate's right to solicit campaign funds in an election. The Florida Supreme Court appointed a referee, who held a hearing and recommended a finding of guilt. As a sanction, the referee recommended that Yulee be publicly reprimanded and ordered to pay the costs of the proceeding ($1,860).

The Florida Supreme Court adopted the referee's recommendations. 138 So.3d 379 (2014). The court explained that Canon 7C(1) "clearly restricts a judicial candidate's speech" and therefore must be "narrowly tailored to serve a compelling state interest." Id., at 384. The court held that the Canon satisfies that demanding inquiry. First, the court reasoned, prohibiting judicial candidates from personally soliciting funds furthers Florida's compelling interest in "preserving the integrity of [its] judiciary and maintaining the public's confidence in an impartial judiciary." Ibid. (internal quotation marks omitted; alteration in original). In the court's view, "personal solicitation of campaign funds, even by mass mailing, raises an appearance of impropriety and calls into question, in the public's mind, the judge's impartiality." Id., at 385. Second, the court concluded that Canon 7C(1) is narrowly tailored to serve that compelling interest because it "'insulate[s] judicial candidates from the solicitation and receipt of funds while leaving open ample alternative means for candidates to raise the resources necessary to run their campaigns.'" Id., at 387 (quoting Simes v. Arkansas Judicial Discipline & Disability Comm'n, 368 Ark. 577, 588 (2007)).

The Florida Supreme Court acknowledged that some Federal Courts of Appeals—"whose judges have lifetime appointments and thus do not have to engage in fundraising"—had invalidated restrictions similar to Canon 7C(1). But the court found it persuasive that every State Supreme Court that had considered similar fundraising provisions—along with several Federal Courts of Appeals—had upheld the laws against First Amendment challenges. Florida's chief justice and one associate justice dissented. We granted certiorari.

II

The First Amendment provides that Congress "shall make no law . . . abridging the freedom of speech." The Fourteenth Amendment makes that prohibition applicable to the States. Stromberg v. California, 283 U.S. 359, 368 (1931). The parties agree that Canon 7C(1) restricts Yulee's speech on the basis of its content by prohibiting her from soliciting contributions to her election campaign. The parties disagree, however, about the level of scrutiny that should govern our review.

We have applied exacting scrutiny to laws restricting the solicitation of contributions to charity, upholding the speech limitations only if they are narrowly tailored to serve a compelling interest. See Riley v. National Federation of Blind of N.C., Inc., 487 U.S. 781, 798 (1988). As we have explained, noncommercial solicitation "is characteristically intertwined with informative and perhaps persuasive speech." Id., at 796 (majority opinion). Applying a lesser standard of scrutiny to such speech would threaten "the exercise of rights so vital to the maintenance of democratic institutions." Schneider v. State (Town of Irvington), 308 U.S. 147, 161 (1939).

The principles underlying these charitable solicitation cases apply with even greater force here. Before asking for money in her fundraising letter, Yulee explained her fitness for the bench and expressed her vision for the judiciary. Her stated purpose for the solicitation was to get her "message out to the public." As we have long recognized, speech about public issues and the qualifications of candidates for elected office commands the highest level of First Amendment protection. . . . Indeed, in our only prior case concerning speech restrictions on a candidate for judicial office, this Court and both parties assumed that strict scrutiny applied. Republican Party of Minn. v. White, 536 U.S. 765, 774 (2002). . . .

In sum, we hold today what we assumed in *White*: A State may restrict the speech of a judicial candidate only if the restriction is narrowly tailored to serve a compelling interest.

III

The Florida Bar faces a demanding task in defending Canon 7C(1) against Yulee's First Amendment challenge. We have emphasized that "it is the rare case" in which a State demonstrates that a speech restriction is narrowly tailored to serve a compelling interest. Burson v. Freeman, 504 U.S. 191, 211 (1992) (plurality opinion). But those cases do arise. . . . Here, Canon 7C(1) advances the State's compelling interest in preserving public confidence in the integrity of the judiciary, and it does so through means narrowly tailored to avoid unnecessarily abridging speech. This is therefore one of the rare cases in which a speech restriction withstands strict scrutiny.

A

The Florida Supreme Court adopted Canon 7C(1) to promote the State's interests in "protecting the integrity of the judiciary" and "maintaining the public's confidence in an impartial judiciary." 138 So.3d, at 385. The way the Canon advances those interests is intuitive: Judges, charged with exercising strict neutrality and independence, cannot supplicate campaign donors without diminishing public confidence in judicial integrity. This principle dates back at least eight centuries to Magna Carta, which proclaimed, "To no one will we sell, to no one will we refuse or delay, right or justice." Cl. 40 (1215), in W. McKechnie, *Magna Carta, A Commentary on the Great Charter of King John* 395 (2d ed. 1914). The same concept underlies the common law judicial oath, which binds a judge to "do right to all manner of people . . . without fear or favour, affection or ill-will," 10 Encyclopaedia of the Laws of England 105 (2d ed. 1908), and the oath that each of us took to "administer justice without respect to persons, and do equal right to the poor and to the rich," 28 U.S.C. § 453. Simply put, Florida and most other States have concluded that the public may lack confidence in a judge's ability to administer justice without fear or favor if he comes to office by asking for favors.

The interest served by Canon 7C(1) has firm support in our precedents. We have recognized the "vital state interest" in safeguarding "public confidence in the fairness and integrity of the nation's elected judges." Caperton v. A.T. Massey Coal Co., 556 U.S. 868, 889 (2009). The importance of public confidence in the integrity of judges stems from the place of the judiciary in the government. Unlike the executive or the legislature, the judiciary "has no influence over either the sword or the purse; . . . neither force nor will but merely judgment." The Federalist No. 78, p. 465 (C. Rossiter ed. 1961) (A. Hamilton). The judiciary's authority therefore depends in large measure on the public's willingness to respect and follow its decisions. As Justice Frankfurter once put it for the Court, "justice must satisfy the appearance of justice." Offutt v. United States, 348 U.S. 11, 14 (1954). It follows that public perception of judicial integrity is "a state interest of the highest order." *Caperton*, 556 U.S., at 889. . . .

The parties devote considerable attention to our cases analyzing campaign finance restrictions in political elections. But a State's interest in preserving public confidence in the integrity of its judiciary extends beyond its interest in preventing the appearance of corruption in legislative and executive elections. As we explained in *White*, States may regulate judicial elections differently than they regulate political elections, because the role of judges differs from the role of politicians. 536 U.S., at 783; id., at 805 (Ginsburg, J., dissenting). Politicians are expected to be appropriately responsive to the preferences of their supporters. . . . The same is not true of judges. In deciding cases, a judge is not to follow the preferences of his supporters, or provide any special consideration to his campaign donors. . . . As in *White*, therefore, our precedents applying the First Amendment to political elections have little bearing on the issues here.

The vast majority of elected judges in States that allow personal solicitation serve with fairness and honor. But "[e]ven if judges were able to refrain from favoring donors, the mere possibility that judges' decisions may be motivated by the desire to repay campaign contributions is likely to undermine the public's confidence in the judiciary." *White*, 536 U.S., at 790 (O'Connor, J., concurring). In the eyes of the public, a judge's personal solicitation could result (even unknowingly) in "a possible temptation . . . which might lead him not to hold the balance nice, clear and true." Tumey v. Ohio, 273 U.S. 510, 532 (1927). That risk is especially pronounced because most donors are lawyers and litigants who may appear before the judge they are supporting. . . .

. . . The Florida Bar's interest is compelling.

B

Yulee acknowledges the State's compelling interest in judicial integrity. She argues, however, that the Canon's failure to restrict other speech equally damaging to judicial integrity and its appearance undercuts the Bar's position. In particular, she notes that Canon 7C(1) allows a judge's campaign committee to solicit money, which arguably reduces public confidence in the integrity of the judiciary just as much as a judge's personal solicitation. Yulee also points out that Florida permits judicial candidates to write thank you notes to campaign donors, which ensures that candidates know who contributes and who does not.

It is always somewhat counterintuitive to argue that a law violates the First Amendment by abridging *too little* speech. We have recognized, however, that underinclusiveness can raise "doubts about whether the government is in fact pursuing the interest it invokes, rather than disfavoring a particular speaker or viewpoint." *Brown* [v. Entertainment Merchants Ass'n, 564 U.S. 786 (2011)] at 802. . . .

Although a law's underinclusivity raises a red flag, the First Amendment imposes no freestanding "underinclusiveness limitation." R.A.V. v. St. Paul, 505 U.S. 377, 387 (1992) (internal quotation marks omitted). A State need not address all aspects of a problem in one fell swoop; policymakers may focus on their most pressing concerns. We have accordingly upheld laws — even under strict scrutiny — that conceivably could have restricted even greater amounts of speech in service of their stated interests. . . .

Viewed in light of these principles, Canon 7C(1) raises no fatal underinclusivity concerns. The solicitation ban aims squarely at the conduct most likely to undermine public confidence in the integrity of the judiciary: personal requests for money by judges and judicial candidates. The Canon applies evenhandedly to all judges and judicial candidates, regardless of their viewpoint or chosen means of solicitation. And unlike some laws that we have found impermissibly underinclusive, Canon 7C(1) is not riddled with exceptions. . . . Indeed, the Canon contains zero exceptions to its ban on personal solicitation.

Yulee relies heavily on the provision of Canon 7C(1) that allows solicitation by a candidate's campaign committee. But Florida, along with most other States, has reasonably concluded that solicitation by the candidate personally creates a categorically different and more severe risk of undermining public confidence than does solicitation by a campaign committee. The identity of the solicitor matters, as anyone who has encountered a Girl Scout selling cookies outside a grocery store can attest. When the judicial candidate himself asks for money, the stakes are higher for all involved. The candidate has personally invested his time and effort in the fundraising appeal; he has placed his name and reputation behind the request. The solicited individual knows that, and also knows that the solicitor might be in a position to singlehandedly make decisions of great weight: The same person who signed the fundraising letter might one day sign the judgment. This dynamic inevitably creates pressure for the recipient to comply, and it does so in a way that solicitation by a third party does not. Just as inevitably, the personal involvement of the candidate in the solicitation creates the public appearance that the candidate will remember who says yes, and who says no. . . .

Likewise, allowing judicial candidates to write thank you notes to campaign donors does not detract from the State's interest in preserving public confidence in the integrity of the judiciary. Yulee argues that permitting thank you notes heightens the likelihood of actual bias by ensuring that judicial candidates know who supported their campaigns, and ensuring that the supporter knows that the candidate knows. Maybe so. But the State's compelling interest is implicated most directly by the candidate's personal solicitation itself. A failure to ban thank you notes for contributions not solicited by the candidate does not undercut the Bar's rationale.

In addition, the State has a good reason for allowing candidates to write thank you notes and raise money through committees. These accommodations reflect Florida's effort to respect the First Amendment interests of candidates and their contributors—to resolve the "fundamental tension between the ideal character of the judicial office and the real world of electoral politics." Chisom v. Roemer, 501 U.S. 380, 400 (1991). They belie the principal dissent's suggestion that Canon 7C(1) reflects general "hostility toward judicial campaigning" and has "nothing to do with the appearances created by judges' asking for money." Post, at 1681. Nothing?

The principal dissent also suggests that Canon 7C(1) is underinclusive because Florida does not ban judicial candidates from asking individuals for personal gifts or loans. But Florida law treats a personal "gift" or "loan" as a campaign contribution if the donor makes it "for the purpose of influencing the results of an election," Fla. Stat. § 106.011(5)(a), and Florida's Judicial Qualifications Commission has determined that a judicial candidate violates Canon 7C(1) by personally soliciting such a loan. . . . In any event, Florida can ban personal solicitation of campaign funds by judicial candidates without making them obey a comprehensive code to leading an ethical life. . . .

Taken to its logical conclusion, the position advanced by Yulee and the principal dissent is that Florida may ban the solicitation of funds by judicial candidates only if the State bans *all* solicitation of funds in judicial elections. The First Amendment does not put a State to that all-or-nothing choice. We will not punish Florida for leaving open more, rather than fewer, avenues of expression, especially when there is no indication that the selective restriction of speech reflects a pretextual motive.

C

After arguing that Canon 7C(1) violates the First Amendment because it restricts too little speech, Yulee argues that the Canon violates the First Amendment because it restricts too much. In her view, the Canon is not narrowly tailored to advance the State's compelling interest through the least restrictive means. . . .

By any measure, Canon 7C(1) restricts a narrow slice of speech. . . . Canon 7C(1) leaves judicial candidates free to discuss any issue with any person at any time. Candidates can write letters, give speeches, and put up billboards. They can contact potential supporters in person, on the phone, or online. They can promote their campaigns on radio, television, or other media. They cannot say, "Please give me money." They can, however, direct their campaign committees to do so. Whatever else may be said of the Canon, it is surely not a "wildly disproportionate restriction upon speech." Post, at 1676 (Scalia, J., dissenting).

Indeed, Yulee concedes—and the principal dissent seems to agree—that Canon 7C(1) is valid in numerous applications. Yulee acknowledges that Florida can prohibit judges from soliciting money from lawyers and litigants appearing before them. In addition, she says the State "might" be able to ban "direct one-to-one solicitation of lawyers and individuals or businesses that could reasonably appear in the court for which the individual is a candidate." She also suggests that the Bar could forbid "in person" solicitation by judicial candidates. [C]f. Ohralik v. Ohio State Bar Assn., 436 U.S. 447 (1978) (permitting State to ban in person solicitation of clients by lawyers). But Yulee argues that the Canon cannot constitutionally be applied to her chosen form of solicitation: a letter posted online and distributed via mass mailing. No one, she contends, will lose confidence in the integrity of the judiciary based on personal solicitation to such a broad audience.

This argument misperceives the breadth of the compelling interest that underlies Canon 7C(1). Florida has reasonably determined that personal appeals for money by a judicial candidate inherently create an appearance of impropriety that may cause the public to lose confidence in the integrity of the judiciary. That interest may be implicated to varying degrees in particular contexts, but the interest remains whenever the public perceives the judge personally asking for money.

Moreover, the lines Yulee asks us to draw are unworkable. Even under her theory of the case, a mass mailing would create an appearance of impropriety if addressed to a list of all lawyers and litigants with pending cases. So would a speech soliciting contributions from the 100 most frequently appearing attorneys in the jurisdiction. Yulee says she might accept a ban on one-to-one solicitation, but is the public impression really any different if a judicial candidate tries to buttonhole not one prospective donor but two at a time? Ten? Yulee also agrees that in person solicitation creates a problem. But would the public's concern recede if the request for money came in a phone call or a text message?

We decline to wade into this swamp. The First Amendment requires that Canon 7C(1) be narrowly tailored, not that it be "perfectly tailored." *Burson*, 504 U.S., at 209. The impossibility of perfect tailoring is especially apparent when the State's compelling interest is as intangible as public confidence in the integrity of the judiciary. . . .

Finally, Yulee contends that Florida can accomplish its compelling interest through the less restrictive means of recusal rules and campaign contribution limits. We disagree. A rule requiring judges to recuse themselves from every case in which a lawyer or litigant made a campaign contribution would disable many jurisdictions. And a flood of post-election recusal motions could "erode public confidence in judicial impartiality" and thereby exacerbate the very appearance problem the State is trying to solve. *Caperton*, 556 U.S., at 891 (Roberts, C.J., dissenting). Moreover, the rule that Yulee envisions could create a perverse incentive for litigants to make campaign contributions to judges solely as a means to trigger their later recusal—a form of peremptory strike against a judge that would enable transparent forum shopping.

As for campaign contribution limits, Florida already applies them to judicial elections. Fla. Stat. § 106.08(1)(a). A State may decide that the threat to public confidence created by personal solicitation exists apart from the amount of money that a judge or judicial candidate seeks. Even if Florida decreased its contribution limit, the appearance that judges who personally solicit funds might improperly favor their campaign donors would remain. . . .

The desirability of judicial elections is a question that has sparked disagreement for more than 200 years. Hamilton believed that appointing judges to positions with life tenure constituted "the best expedient which can be devised in any government to secure a steady, upright, and impartial administration of the laws." The Federalist No. 78, at 465. Jefferson thought that making judges "dependent on none but themselves" ran counter to the principle of "a government founded on the public will." 12 The Works of Thomas Jefferson 5 (P. Ford, ed. 1905). The federal courts reflect the view of Hamilton; most States have sided with Jefferson. Both methods have given our Nation jurists of wisdom and rectitude who have devoted themselves to maintaining "the public's respect . . . and a reserve of public goodwill, without becoming subservient to public opinion." Rehnquist, "Judicial Independence," 38 U. Rich. L. Rev. 579, 596 (2004).

It is not our place to resolve this enduring debate. Our limited task is to apply the Constitution to the question presented in this case. Judicial candidates have a First Amendment right to speak in support of their campaigns. States have a compelling interest in preserving public confidence in their judiciaries. When the State adopts a narrowly tailored restriction like the one at issue here, those principles do not conflict. A State's decision to elect judges does not compel it to compromise public confidence in their integrity.

The judgment of the Florida Supreme Court is Affirmed.

Justice SCALIA, with whom Justice THOMAS joins, dissenting.

An ethics canon adopted by the Florida Supreme Court bans a candidate in a judicial election from asking anyone, under any circumstances, for a contribution to his campaign. Faithful application of our precedents would have made short work of this wildly disproportionate restriction upon speech. Intent upon upholding the Canon, however, the Court flattens one settled First Amendment principle after another.

I

The first axiom of the First Amendment is this: As a general rule, the state has no power to ban speech on the basis of its content. One need not equate judges with politicians to see that this principle does not grow weaker merely because the censored speech is a judicial candidate's request for a campaign contribution. Our cases hold that speech enjoys the full protection of the First Amendment unless a widespread and longstanding tradition ratifies its regulation. . . . No such tradition looms here. Georgia became the first State to elect its judges in 1812, and judicial elections had spread to a large majority of the States by the time of the Civil War. Republican Party of Minn. v. White, 536 U.S. 765, 785 (2002). Yet there appears to have been no regulation of judicial candidates' speech throughout the 19th and early 20th centuries. Ibid. The American Bar Association first proposed ethics rules concerning speech of judicial candidates in 1924, but these rules did not achieve widespread adoption until after the Second World War. Id., at 786.

Rules against soliciting campaign contributions arrived more recently still. The ABA first proposed a canon advising against it in 1972, and a canon prohibiting it only in 1990. Even now, 9 of the 39 States that elect judges allow judicial candidates to ask for campaign contributions. In the absence of any long-settled custom about judicial candidates' speech in general or their solicitations in particular, we have no basis for relaxing the rules that normally apply to laws that suppress speech because of content. . . .

Because Canon 7C(1) restricts fully protected speech on the basis of content, it presumptively violates the First Amendment. We may uphold it only if the State meets its burden of showing that the Canon survives strict scrutiny — that is to say, only if it shows that the Canon is narrowly tailored to serve a compelling interest. I do not for a moment question the Court's conclusion that States have different compelling interests when regulating judicial elections than when regulating political ones. Unlike a legislator, a judge must be impartial — without bias for or against any party or attorney who comes before him. I accept for the sake of argument that States have a compelling interest in ensuring that its judges are *seen* to be impartial. I will likewise assume that a judicial candidate's request to a litigant or attorney presents a danger of coercion that a political candidate's request to a constituent does not. But

Canon 7C(1) does not narrowly target concerns about impartiality or its appearance; it applies even when the person asked for a financial contribution has no chance of ever appearing in the candidate's court. And Florida does not invoke concerns about coercion, presumably because the Canon bans solicitations regardless of whether their object is a lawyer, litigant, or other person vulnerable to judicial pressure. So Canon 7C(1) fails exacting scrutiny and infringes the First Amendment. This case should have been just that straightforward.

II

The Court concludes that Florida may prohibit personal solicitations by judicial candidates as a means of preserving "public confidence in the integrity of the judiciary." It purports to reach this destination by applying strict scrutiny, but it would be more accurate to say that it does so by applying the appearance of strict scrutiny.

A

The first sign that mischief is afoot comes when the Court describes Florida's compelling interest. The State must first identify its objective with precision before one can tell whether that interest is compelling and whether the speech restriction narrowly targets it. In *White*, for example, the Court did not allow a State to invoke hazy concerns about judicial impartiality in justification of an ethics rule against judicial candidates' announcing their positions on legal issues. 536 U.S., at 775. The Court instead separately analyzed the State's concerns about judges' bias against parties, preconceptions on legal issues, and openmindedness, and explained why each concern (and each for a different reason) did not suffice to sustain the rule. Id., at 775–780.

In stark contrast to *White*, the Court today relies on Florida's invocation of an ill-defined interest in "public confidence in judicial integrity." The Court at first suggests that "judicial integrity" involves the "ability to administer justice without fear or favor." As its opinion unfolds, however, today's concept of judicial integrity turns out to be "a mere thing of wax in the hands of the judiciary, which they may twist, and shape into any form they please." 12 The Works of Thomas Jefferson 137 (P. Ford ed. 1905). When the Court explains how solicitation undermines confidence in judicial integrity, integrity starts to sound like saintliness. It involves independence from any "'*possible* temptation'" that "'*might* lead'" the judge, "even unknowingly," to favor one party. Ante, at 1667 (emphasis added). When the Court turns to distinguishing in-person solicitation from solicitation by proxy, the any-possible-temptation standard no longer helps and thus drops out. The critical factors instead become the "pressure" a listener feels during a solicitation and the "appearance that the candidate will remember who says yes, and who says no." But when it comes time to explain Florida's decision to allow candidates to write thank-you notes, the "appearance that the candidate . . . remember[s] who says yes" gets nary a mention. And when the Court confronts Florida's decision to prohibit mass-mailed solicitations, concern about pressure fades away. More outrageous still, the Court at times molds the interest in the perception that judges have integrity into an interest in the perception that judges do not solicit—for example when it says, "all personal solicitations by judicial candidates create a public appearance that undermines confidence in the integrity of the judiciary; banning all personal solicitations by judicial candidates is narrowly tailored to address that concern." This is not strict scrutiny; it is sleight of hand.

B

The Court's twistifications have not come to an end; indeed, they are just beginning. In order to uphold Canon 7C(1) under strict scrutiny, Florida must do more than point to a vital public objective brooding overhead. The State must also meet a difficult burden of demonstrating that the speech restriction substantially advances the claimed objective. The State "bears the risk of uncertainty," so "ambiguous proof will not suffice." [Brown v.] *Entertainment Merchants*, 131 S.Ct. [2729], at 2739. In an arresting illustration, this Court held that a law punishing lies about winning military decorations like the Congressional Medal of Honor failed exacting scrutiny, because the Government could not satisfy its "heavy burden" of proving that "the public's general perception of military awards is diluted by false claims." United States v. Alvarez, 132 S.Ct. 2537, 2549 (2012) (plurality opinion).

Now that we have a case about the public's perception of judicial honor rather than its perception of military honors, the Justices of this Court change the rules. The Court announces, on the basis of its "intuiti[on]," that allowing personal solicitations will make litigants worry that "'judges' decisions may be motivated by the desire to repay campaign contributions.'" But this case is not about whether Yulee has the right to receive campaign contributions. It is about whether she has the right to *ask* for campaign contributions that Florida's statutory law already allows her to receive. Florida bears the burden of showing that banning *requests* for lawful contributions will improve public confidence in judges — not just a little bit, but significantly, because "the Government does not have a compelling interest in each marginal percentage point by which its goals are advanced." *Entertainment Merchants*, supra, 131 S.Ct., at 2741, n.9.

Neither the Court nor the State identifies the slightest evidence that banning requests for contributions will substantially improve public trust in judges. Nor does common sense make this happy forecast obvious. The concept of judicial integrity "dates back at least eight centuries," and judicial elections in America date back more than two centuries — but rules against personal solicitations date back only to 1972. The peaceful coexistence of judicial elections and personal solicitations for most of our history calls into doubt any claim that allowing personal solicitations would imperil public faith in judges. Many States allow judicial candidates to ask for contributions even today, but nobody suggests that public confidence in judges fares worse in these jurisdictions than elsewhere. And in any event, if candidates' appeals for money are "'characteristically intertwined'" with discussion of qualifications and views on public issues, how can the Court be so sure that the public will regard them as improprieties rather than as legitimate instances of campaigning? In the final analysis, Florida comes nowhere near making the convincing demonstration required by our cases that the speech restriction in this case substantially advances its objective.

C

But suppose we play along with the premise that prohibiting solicitations will significantly improve the public reputation of judges. Even then, Florida must show that the ban restricts no more speech than necessary to achieve the objective. . . .

Canon 7C(1) falls miles short of satisfying this requirement. The Court seems to accept Florida's claim that solicitations erode public confidence by creating the perception that judges are selling justice to lawyers and litigants. Yet the Canon prohibits candidates from asking for money from *anybody*—even from someone who is neither lawyer nor litigant, even from someone who (because of recusal rules) cannot possibly appear before the candidate as lawyer or litigant. Yulee thus may not call up an old friend, a cousin, or even her parents to ask for a donation to her campaign. The State has not come up with a plausible explanation of how soliciting someone who has no chance of appearing in the candidate's court will diminish public confidence in judges.

No less important, Canon 7C(1) bans candidates from asking for contributions even in messages that do not target any listener in particular—mass-mailed letters, flyers posted on telephone poles, speeches to large gatherings, and Web sites addressed to the general public. Messages like these do not share the features that lead the Court to pronounce personal solicitations a menace to public confidence in the judiciary. Consider online solicitations. They avoid "'the spectacle of lawyers or potential litigants directly handing over money to judicial candidates.'" People who come across online solicitations do not feel "pressure" to comply with the request. Nor does the candidate's signature on the online solicitation suggest "that the candidate will remember who says yes, and who says no." Yet Canon 7C(1) prohibits these and similar solicitations anyway. This tailoring is as narrow as the Court's scrutiny is strict.

Perhaps sensing the fragility of the initial claim that *all* solicitations threaten public confidence in judges, the Court argues that "the lines Yulee asks [it] to draw are unworkable." That is a difficulty of the Court's own imagination. In reality, the Court could have chosen from a whole spectrum of workable rules. It could have held that States may regulate no more than solicitation of participants in pending cases, or solicitation of people who are likely to appear in the candidate's court, or even solicitation of any lawyer or litigant. And it could have ruled that candidates have the right to make fundraising appeals that are not directed to any particular listener (like requests in mass-mailed letters), or at least fundraising appeals plainly directed to the general public (like requests placed online). . . .

The Court's accusation of unworkability also suffers from a bit of a pot-kettle problem. Consider the many real-world questions left open by today's decision. Does the First Amendment permit restricting a candidate's appearing at an event where somebody *else* asks for campaign funds on his behalf? See Florida Judicial Ethics Advisory Committee Opinion No. 2012–14 (JEAC Op.). Does it permit prohibiting the candidate's *family* from making personal solicitations? See ibid. Does it allow prohibiting the candidate from participating in the creation of a Web site that solicits funds, even if the candidate's name does not appear next to the request? See JEAC Op. No. 2008–11. More broadly, could Florida ban thank-you notes to donors? Cap a candidate's campaign spending? Restrict independent spending by people other than the candidate? Ban independent spending by corporations? And how, by the way, are judges supposed to decide whether these measures promote public confidence in judicial integrity, when the Court does not even have a consistent theory about what it means by "judicial integrity"? For the Court to wring its hands about workability under these circumstances is more than one should have to bear.

D

Even if Florida could show that banning all personal appeals for campaign funds is necessary to protect public confidence in judicial integrity, the Court must overpower one last sentinel of free speech before it can uphold Canon 7C(1). Among its other functions, the First Amendment is a kind of Equal Protection Clause for ideas. The state ordinarily may not regulate one message because it harms a government interest yet refuse to regulate other messages that impair the interest in a comparable way. . . .

Fumbling around for a fig-leaf, the Court says that "the First Amendment imposes no freestanding 'underinclusiveness limitation.'" This analysis elides the distinction between selectivity on the basis of content and selectivity on other grounds. Because the First Amendment does not prohibit underinclusiveness as such, lawmakers may target a problem only at certain times or in certain places. Because the First Amendment *does* prohibit content discrimination as such, lawmakers may *not* target a problem only in certain messages. Explaining this distinction, we have said that the First Amendment would allow banning obscenity "only in certain media or markets" but would preclude banning "only that obscenity which includes offensive political messages." R.A.V. v. St. Paul, 505 U.S. 377, 387–388 (1992) (emphasis deleted). This case involves selectivity on the basis of content. The Florida Supreme Court has decided to eliminate the appearances associated with "personal appeals for money," when the appeals seek money for a campaign but not when the appeals seek money for other purposes. That distinction violates the First Amendment. . . .

Even on the Court's own terms, Canon 7C(1) cannot stand. The Court concedes that "underinclusiveness can raise 'doubts about whether the government is in fact pursuing the interest it invokes.'" Canon 7C(1)'s scope suggests that it has nothing to do with the appearances created by judges' asking for money, and everything to do with hostility toward judicial campaigning. How else to explain the Florida Supreme Court's decision to ban *all* personal appeals for campaign funds (even when the solicitee could never appear before the candidate), but to tolerate appeals for other kinds of funds (even when the solicitee will surely appear before the candidate)? It should come as no surprise that the ABA, whose model rules the Florida Supreme

Court followed when framing Canon 7C(1), opposes judicial elections—preferring instead a system in which (surprise!) a committee of lawyers proposes candidates from among whom the Governor must make his selection. See *White*, 536 U.S., at 787.

The Court tries to strike a pose of neutrality between appointment and election of judges, but no one should be deceived. A Court that sees impropriety in a candidate's request for *any* contributions to his election campaign does not much like judicial selection by the people. One cannot have judicial elections without judicial campaigns, and judicial campaigns without funds for campaigning, and funds for campaigning without asking for them. When a society decides that its judges should be elected, it necessarily decides that selection by the people is more important than the oracular sanctity of judges, their immunity from the (shudder!) indignity of begging for funds, and their exemption from those shadows of impropriety that fall over the proletarian public officials who must run for office. A free society, accustomed to electing its rulers, does not much care whether the rulers operate through statute and executive order, or through judicial distortion of statute, executive order, and constitution. The prescription that judges be elected probably springs from the people's realization that their judges can become their rulers—and (it must be said) from just a deep-down feeling that members of the Third Branch will profit from a hearty helping of humble pie, and from a severe reduction of their great remove from the (ugh!) People. (It should not be thought that I myself harbor such irreverent and revolutionary feelings; but I think it likely—and year by year more likely—that those who favor the election of judges do so.) In any case, hostility to campaigning by judges entitles the people of Florida to amend their Constitution to replace judicial elections with the selection of judges by lawyers' committees; it does not entitle the Florida Supreme Court to adopt, or this Court to endorse, a rule of judicial conduct that abridges candidates' speech in the judicial elections that the Florida Constitution prescribes.

This Court has not been shy to enforce the First Amendment in recent Terms—even in cases that do not involve election speech. It has accorded robust protection to depictions of animal torture, sale of violent video games to children, and lies about having won military medals. See United States v. Stevens, 559 U.S. 460 (2010); *Entertainment Merchants*, 131 S.Ct. 2729; *Alvarez*, 132 S.Ct. 2537. Who would have thought that the same Court would today exert such heroic efforts to save so plain an abridgement of the freedom of speech? It is no great mystery what is going on here. The judges of this Court, like the judges of the Supreme Court of Florida who promulgated Canon 7C(1), evidently consider the preservation of public respect for the courts a policy objective of the highest order. So it is—but so too are preventing animal torture, protecting the innocence of children, and honoring valiant soldiers. The Court did not relax the Constitution's guarantee of freedom of speech when legislatures pursued those goals; it should not relax the guarantee when the Supreme Court of Florida pursues this one. The First Amendment is not abridged for the benefit of the Brotherhood of the Robe.

I respectfully dissent.

Notes

1. Was Justice Scalia correct in noting that judges have been treating themselves differently in terms of First Amendment jurisprudence?

2. Can the result in *Williams-Yulee* be soundly squared with the result in *White*? What distinguishing factor best justifies the diverging results?

B. Judicial Recusal and Disqualification

One consequence of Republican Party of Minnesota v. White has been to make the issue of disqualification more prominent as litigants more and more claim that various views expressed by judicial candidates are grounds for recusal or disqualification in subsequent litigation. The 2007 Model Code addresses the issue directly in Rule 2.11(A)(5). Recusal and disqualification at the state level are usually matters for state law and state judicial ethics codes. Some state judicial elections have featured enormous spending by interest groups to the point where the issue has come before the Supreme Court in a constitutional setting. In almost every jurisdiction (state and federal), judges are required to recuse themselves whenever their "impartiality might reasonably be questioned." How should this universal disqualification rule be applied when litigants or lawyers have spent significant sums of money or devoted significant amounts to time trying to elect or reelect the judge before whom those litigants or lawyers are now appearing?

Problem 11–9

Formal complaints about judges are increasing. In most cases, at least one party (i.e., the losing party) is not happy with the judge, and might complain to the state's judicial conduct commission, which typically acts as both the prosecutor and adjudicator of alleged violations of the Code of Judicial Conduct. (The state courts—often the state supreme court—will later review the matter on appeal if the matter is not dismissed and if the judge or the commission's lawyer appeals.) Some judges represent themselves before the commission, while other judges choose to exercise their right to have an attorney present their side of the story.

Judge was recently accused of engaging in ex parte communications with the side that ultimately prevailed in a tort suit. The firm at which Judge used to work seventeen years ago offered to represent the judge pro bono in the judicial conduct proceeding. The lawyer who will represent Judge has never appeared in Judge's court before and has no plans to do so in the future. Other attorneys in the firm, however, do appear before Judge from time to time. May Judge accept the lawyer's offer to represent Judge pro bono? Or at a reduced rate? If so, may other members of the firm continue to appear before Judge in unrelated matters? If so, must Judge at least make the (somewhat embarrassing) disclosure that a lawyer for the firm is representing Judge in a judicial conduct matter? Must Judge also disclose that the lawyer is representing Judge for free or at a discounted rate? See generally Mass. Judicial Ethics Op. 2013-1; Patrick Marley, "Group Files Formal Request for Gableman Investigation," Milwaukee Journal-Sentinel, Dec. 20, 2011 (recounting the story of Wisconsin Supreme Court Justice Michael Gableman, who received from a law firm essentially free legal defense of an ethics complaint and failed to disclose the full relationship with the firm in other cases in which the same firm was involved).

Problem 11–10

You are the CEO of, and a shareholder in, the largest coal-mining company in the state. As a large company, you frequently face litigation from employees, former employees, state agencies, competing mines, and others. For this reason and others, you have a strong interest in the judges running for election and reelection in your state; their rulings often impact, directly or indirectly, the financial health of your company. In one litigation matter, for example, a competing mine just won a $50 million judgment against your company for allegedly backing out of a purchase contract and engaging in unlawful practices to acquire the competing mine. Considering the importance of such litigation and the numerous other cases in which your company is or might become involved, you contribute the maximum amount of direct contributions ($1,000) to a judicial candidate for the state supreme court who claims to be pro-business. You also spend nearly $3,000,000 in independent expenditures, primarily to buy negative television ads attacking the incumbent judge who has ruled less favorably to business interests. Your preferred judge wins (aided in part by your financial expenditures, which far exceeded the expenditures on behalf of the incumbent). Through the normal appellate process, you have appealed the $50 million judgment to the state supreme court. Your preferred judge ultimately writes the opinion overturning the judgment. Did the judge violate the judicial code by hearing your appeal? Did the other side receive due process?

In Caperton v. A.T. Massey Coal Co., the Supreme Court concluded that the circumstances summarized in the Problem above violated the competing mine's right to due process. 556 U.S. 868 (2009). The Court found "a serious risk of actual bias—based on objective and reasonable perceptions—when a person with a personal stake in a particular case had a significant and disproportionate influence in placing the judge on the case by raising funds or directing the judge's election campaign when the case was pending or imminent." Id. at 884; see also, e.g., James Sample, "Caperton: Correct Today, Compelling Tomorrow," 60 Syracuse L. Rev. 293 (2010); Keith Swisher, "Recusal, Government Ethics, and Superannuated Constitutional Theory," 72 Md. L. Rev. 219 (2012) (discussing the Caperton case and its potentially far-ranging implications). The Court's decision has potentially vast implications, particularly given that the CEO for Massey Coal did not spend much in direct contributions (only the state limit of $1,000) but instead invested in so-called "independent expenditures" to attack the incumbent judge. If those expenditures are independent—in other words, the preferred judge had no say in whether or how those dollars were spent—should the judge be required to recuse himself? What if the judge did not want the support (or even affirmatively disavowed the support or the attack ads against the incumbent)? In dissent, Chief Justice Roberts would have affirmed the state supreme court. He believed that the recusal "standard the majority articulates—'probability of bias'—fails to provide clear, workable guidance for future cases." *Caperton*, at 893–94 (Roberts, C.J., dissenting). He contended that the majority's test does not answer an array of related (but counterfactual) questions:

1. How much money is too much money? What level of contribution or expenditure gives rise to a "probability of bias"?

2. How do we determine whether a given expenditure is "disproportionate"? Disproportionate *to what*?

3. Are independent, non-coordinated expenditures treated the same as direct contributions to a candidate's campaign? What about contributions to independent outside groups supporting a candidate?

4. Does it matter whether the litigant has contributed to other candidates or made large expenditures in connection with other elections?

5. Does the amount at issue in the case matter? What if this case were an employment dispute with only $10,000 at stake? What if the plaintiffs only sought non-monetary relief such as an injunction or declaratory judgment?

6. Does the analysis change depending on whether the judge whose disqualification is sought sits on a trial court, appeals court, or state supreme court?

7. How long does the probability of bias last? Does the probability of bias diminish over time as the election recedes? Does it matter whether the judge plans to run for reelection?

8. What if the "disproportionately" large expenditure is made by an industry association, trade union, physicians' group, or the plaintiffs' bar? Must the judge recuse in all cases that affect the association's interests? Must the judge recuse in all cases in which a party or lawyer is a member of that group? Does it matter how much the litigant contributed to the association?

9. What if the case involves a social or ideological issue rather than a financial one? Must a judge recuse from cases involving, say, abortion rights if he has received "disproportionate" support from individuals who feel strongly about either side of that issue? If the supporter wants to help elect judges who are "tough on crime," must the judge recuse in all criminal cases?

10. What if the candidate draws "disproportionate" support from a particular racial, religious, ethnic, or other group, and the case involves an issue of particular importance to that group? . . .

898 11 · PROFESSIONAL RESPONSIBILITY AND THE JUDICIAL SYSTEM

Id. The Chief Justice continued to spin off another thirty questions. Despite the Chief Justice's concern over these unanswered questions, *Caperton* has not yet caused a flood of recusal motions. Of course, time could bring a different result. See generally Adam Liptak et. al., "*Caperton* and the Courts: Did the Floodgates Open?," 18 N.Y.U. J. Legis. & Pub. Pol'y 481 (2015). In drafting opinions, do judges have a professional responsibility to address related questions (such as the ones that the Chief Justice raises above)? Or would that involve judges in acting more like legislatures, which often enact comprehensive, forward-looking legislation, rather than in the more traditional role of sticking to the facts of the case at hand? See, e.g., Bruce Green, "Fear of the Unknown: Judicial Ethics After *Caperton*," 60 Syracuse L. Rev. 229, 238 (2010) (worrying that "constitutional decision making has devolved into a game in which Supreme Court Justices make whatever contested predictions and unsubstantiated empirical assumptions support their policy preferences"); see also generally Keith Swisher, "The Unethical Judicial Ethics of Instrumentalism and Detachment in American Legal Thought," 43 Willamette L. Rev. 577 (2007) (arguing that "judges should rule equitably and primarily on the facts and circumstances before them, with attention paid less to the systemic and societal effects of decisions and more to the immediate consequences on the parties sub judice").

Disqualification of federal judges is dealt with, in part, by statute in 28 U.S.C. §§ 144 and 455. They are set forth below. Their interpretation has caused enormous difficulty for the courts:

§ 144

Whenever a party to any proceeding in a district court makes and files a timely and sufficient affidavit that the judge before whom the matter is pending has a personal bias or prejudice either against him or in favor of any adverse party, such judge shall proceed no further therein, but another judge shall be assigned to hear such proceeding.

The affidavit shall state the facts and the reasons for the belief that bias or prejudice exists, and shall be filed not less than ten days before the beginning of the term at which the proceeding is to be heard, or good cause shall be shown for failure to file it within such time. A party may file only one such affidavit in any case. It shall be accompanied by a certificate of counsel of record stating that it is made in good faith.

§ 455

(a) Any justice, judge, or magistrate of the United States shall disqualify himself in any proceeding in which his impartiality might reasonably be questioned.

(b) He shall also disqualify himself in the following circumstances:

(1) Where he has a personal bias or prejudice concerning a party, or personal knowledge of disputed evidentiary facts concerning the proceeding;

(2) Where in private practice he served as lawyer in the matter in controversy, or a lawyer with whom he previously practiced law served during such association as a lawyer concerning the matter, or the judge or such lawyer has been a material witness concerning it;

(3) Where he has served in governmental employment and in such capacity participated as counsel, adviser or material witness concerning the proceeding or expressed an opinion concerning the merits of the particular case in controversy;

(4) He knows that he, individually or as a fiduciary, or his spouse or minor child residing in his household, has a financial interest in the subject matter in controversy or in a party to the proceeding, or any other interest that could be substantially affected by the outcome of the proceeding;

(5) He or his spouse, or a person within the third degree of relationship to either of them, or the spouse of such a person:

(i) Is a party to the proceeding, or an officer, director, or trustee of a party;

(ii) Is acting as a lawyer in the proceeding;

(iii) Is known by the judge to have an interest that could be substantially affected by the outcome of the proceeding;

(iv) Is to the judge's knowledge likely to be a material witness in the proceeding.

(c) A judge should inform himself about his personal and fiduciary financial interests, and make a reasonable effort to inform himself about the personal financial interests of his spouse and other children residing in his household. . . .

The federal courts have interpreted Section 144 (which relates to actual bias challenges) so narrowly that the use of the section rarely is the determining factor in disqualification issues. See generally Charles Geyh, *Judicial Disqualification: An Analysis of Federal Law* (2d ed. 2010); United States v. Johnson, 827 F.3d 740, 746 (8th Cir. 2016) ("Johnson did not file a legally sufficient affidavit, which is required to disqualify Judge Harpool from his case. See 28 U.S.C. § 144. . . . Judge Harpool did not abuse his discretion in declining to recuse himself from this case."). Section 455, however, applies more broadly and is frequently a key authority. Although not identical, Section 455 is similar to, and was influenced by, the ABA's Model Code of Judicial Conduct. Virtually every state and the federal judiciary has adopted (but amended in more or less significant ways) the ABA's Model Code.

Another disqualification issue frequently arises when judges speak to the press or post on social media about their cases:

In re Boston's Children First

239 F.3d 59 (1st Cir. 2001); 244 F.3d 164 (1st Cir. 2001)
(opinion amended on denial of motion for rehearing
and suggestion for rehearing en banc)

TORRUELLA, Chief Judge. This petition involves the difficult question of whether a sitting district court judge should have recused herself after commenting publicly on a pending matter. Because we find that it was, in this case, an abuse of discretion for the judge not to recuse herself based on an appearance of partiality, we grant the writ of mandamus. In so doing, we emphasize that such a grant in no way indicates a finding of actual bias or prejudice, nor does it suggest that the trial judge abdicated any of her ethical responsibilities.[*]

BACKGROUND

. . .

Petitioners filed suit challenging Boston's elementary school student assignment process on June 21, 1999, claiming that they had been deprived of preferred school assignments based on their race, in violation of state and federal law. The case was assigned to District Judge Nancy Gertner. On May 19, 2000, the district court addressed a motion to dismiss in which defendants argued that "plaintiffs lack standing to sue because they would not have received their preferred school assignments anyway, even if racial preferences were not used" in the assignment formula. The district court found that five of the ten individual plaintiffs[1] had not applied to change schools for the 1999–2000 school year, and thus lacked standing to seek injunctive relief. Boston's Children First v. City of Boston, 98 F. Supp. 2d 111, 114 (D. Mass. 2000) [hereinafter Boston's Children, Standing Order]. The court allowed the remaining plaintiffs to conduct further discovery prior to determining whether they had standing. The court found that because all of the plaintiffs "may have a claim for damages," it could not dismiss any of the damages claims on standing grounds.

Petitioners also sought class certification. In a June 20, 2000 status conference the court indicated that it would not rule on class certification until it had received a written motion . . . that analyzed how the alleged class complied with the requirements of Federal Rule of Civil Procedure 23. The court also offered petitioners a

---

[*] [The tests and explanations for a judge's disqualification are often "appearance-based." In other words, it just matters that the judge's impartiality might reasonably be questioned (and therefore might undermine confidence in the courts), not whether the judge was actually partial (biased). By focusing on appearances, and not necessarily actualities, litigants and reviewing judges do not have to engage in the awkward and potentially dangerous activity of calling a judge or colleague biased. Thus, reviewing judges can state that their disqualification ruling does not suggest any professional misconduct on the now-disqualified judge's part, just that the appearances conspired to warrant disqualification. — Eds.]

1. The other plaintiff-petitioner, Boston's Children First, is a "self-described membership and advocacy organization."

choice: it would either rule on their pending motion for a preliminary injunction at that time, despite the "relatively truncated record," or it would defer the motion until further discovery had occurred. Petitioners chose to conduct further discovery, and the motion for a preliminary injunction remains pending. In a procedural order dated June 29, 2000, the district court set the course of future litigation: it would allow further discovery on the issue of standing, it would determine standing, and if any of the plaintiffs had standing, class discovery and a hearing with respect to class certification would follow. . . .

Despite the schedule proposed in this procedural order, petitioners filed a motion for class certification dated July 26, 2000. The motion noted the similarity between the present case and Mack v. Suffolk County, 191 F.R.D. 16 (D. Mass. 2000), a case in which class certification had been granted *prior* to the resolution of standing issues. Also on July 26, the Boston Herald printed an article in which counsel for petitioners decried the district court's failure to immediately certify a class. Counsel made the provocative claim that "if you get strip-searched in jail, you get more rights than a child who is of the wrong color," a reference to the facts of the *Mack* case. Dave Wedge, "Lawyer Fights School Ruling," Boston Herald, July 26, 2000, at 5. The article said that:

> According to [counsel's] motion, Gertner refused to hear arguments to expand the school suit to a class action because the affected students may no longer have standing in the case. But in the strip-search case [*Mack*], Gertner held just the opposite opinion.

The article then noted that "Gertner could not be reached for comment."

In a July 28, 2000 letter to the Herald (with copies sent to both parties), Judge Gertner responded to what she viewed as inaccuracies in the July 26 article. She noted, correctly, that she had not denied class certification, but had postponed ruling on class certification until further discovery had occurred. She also noted that, as of the date of the reporter's interview with counsel, counsel for petitioners had not yet filed the motion in question. She included with the letter a copy of her procedural order providing for a hearing on class certification after the issue of standing had been resolved.

On August 4, 2000, the Herald published a follow-up article, which, based on a telephone interview with Judge Gertner, quoted her as saying:

> In the [*Mack*] case, there was no issue as to whether [the plaintiffs] were injured. It was absolutely clear every woman had a claim. This is a more complex case.

Dave Wedge, "Race-based Admissions Case To Be Heard," Boston Herald, August 4, 2000, at 24. . . .

Based on Judge Gertner's comments as reported in the August 4 article, petitioners then moved that the judge recuse herself because her "impartiality might reasonably be questioned." 28 U.S.C. § 455(a). Specifically, petitioners claimed that the ex parte conversation between Judge Gertner and the Herald reporter, in which she described the current proceeding as "more complex" than *Mack*, was "specifically proscribed by the Code of Judicial Conduct," constituted a comment on the merits of a pending motion, and meant that the court had "placed itself in the apparent position of advising the defendants."

Judge Gertner denied the motion. . . . 123 F. Supp. 2d at 36. She acknowledged that she had made the reported statements, characterizing them as attempts to correct a record suffering from gross misrepresentation by counsel for the petitioners. She noted that "nothing in the Code of Judicial Conduct" made such a correction improper; moreover, that it was her "obligation to make certain that people receive accurate information regarding the proceedings over which [she] preside[s]." As to the specific comment about the complexity of the instant case, Judge Gertner admitted that a conversation had taken place, but said:

> My comments in court, in the myriad decisions since the inception of the case, reflected precisely that theme — that the case raised complex questions of standing and liability, and that it deserved careful and thoughtful consideration.

As a result, Judge Gertner concluded that she had simply complied with the judicial canon allowing judges to explain "for public information the procedures of the court."

DISCUSSION

We begin, as we must, with the statute. Section 455(a) requires "any justice, judge or magistrate of the United States [to] disqualify himself in any proceeding in which his impartiality might reasonably be questioned." This statute seeks to balance two competing policy considerations: first, that "courts must not only be, but seem to be, free of bias or prejudice," In re United States, 158 F.3d 26, 30 (1st Cir. 1998) (quoting In re United States, 666 F.2d 690, 694 (1st Cir. 1981)); and second, the fear that recusal on demand would provide litigants with a veto against unwanted judges. We have thus considered disqualification appropriate only when the charge is supported by a factual basis, and when the facts asserted "provide what an objective, knowledgeable member of the public would find to be a reasonable basis for doubting the judge's impartiality." In re United States, 666 F.2d at 695. Moreover, we allow district court judges a "range of discretion" in the decision not to recuse. Id. However, we note that the district court should exercise that discretion with the understanding that, "if the question of whether § 455(a) requires disqualification is a close one, the balance tips in favor of recusal." Nichols v. Alley, 71 F.3d 347, 352 (10th Cir. 1995). . . .

The crux of petitioner's complaint is that Judge Gertner's statement — that the present case is "more complex" than *Mack* because in *Mack* "there was no issue as to whether [the plaintiffs] were injured" — could be construed as a comment on the merits of the pending motions for preliminary injunction and class certification. In other words, by calling this case "more complex," Judge Gertner arguably suggested that the petitioner's claims for certification and temporary injunctive relief were less than meritorious; by comparing the case (less than favorably) to *Mack*, Judge Gertner signaled that relief was unlikely to be forthcoming. Petitioners also argue that Gertner's comments provided defendants with a ready-made argument with which to distinguish the instant case from *Mack*. Given that Judge Gertner's comments *could* be construed in this context, petitioners argue that regardless of her intent,[8] the appearance of partiality created by her public statement required her to recuse herself pursuant to §455(a). . . .

Although Canon 3(A)(6) of the Code of Judicial Conduct instructs that "[a] judge should avoid public comment on the merits of a pending or impending action," it does not extend this proscription to "public statements made in the course of the judge's official duties, to the explanation of court procedures, or to a scholarly presentation made for purposes of legal education." 175 F.R.D. 364, 367 (1998). The commentary to the Code also "counsels that 'particular care' be taken" if a case from the judge's own court is involved, so that the comment "does not denigrate public confidence in the integrity and impartiality of the judiciary in violation of Canon 2A." . . .

We have little guidance on when public comments, even those on the merits of a pending action, create an appearance of partiality for which §455(a) recusal is the appropriate remedy.[9] Judges are generally loath to discuss pending proceedings with the media, even when litigants may have engaged in misrepresentation. See [United States v.] *Cooley*, 1 F.3d [985 (10th Cir. 1993)] at 995 ("[Discussing the case with the media] was an unusual thing for a judge to do."). Thus few reported cases deal with recusal on this basis. The Tenth Circuit has provided at least one example of when media contact mandated judicial disqualification. In *Cooley*, a federal district judge who had issued a preliminary injunction preventing abortion protesters from blocking a Kansas clinic "became 'adamant and vocal' in stating that his order was going to be obeyed" upon learning that protesters intended to willfully violate his orders. Id. at 988. As part of his "campaign" to ensure that his orders would be enforced, the judge appeared on "Nightline," where he stated that "these people are breaking the law." Id. at 990. Five defendants arrested for blocking access to the clinic sought recusal of the district court judge, which he refused to grant.

The Tenth Circuit noted that, in refusing to grant the motion for recusal, the district court had maintained that it "knew nothing about the facts of [the defendants'] cases, and had no predisposition as to their guilt or innocence of the charges." 1 F.3d at 995. The court of appeals saw no reason to find otherwise. Id. at 996 ("The record of the proceedings below . . . discloses no bias. To the contrary, it appears that the

---

8. In her memorandum refusing recusal, Judge Gertner has characterized her aims as explanatory and educational. *Boston's Children*, Motion to Recuse, 123 F. Supp. 2d at 37.

9. In contrast, myriad cases indicate that courts are loath to require recusal based on statements made in a judicial context (e.g., in a status hearing or a decision rendered from the bench), even when such statements might suggest, to some extent, pre-determination of the merits. See, e.g., United States v. Grinnell, 384 U.S. 563, 581–82 (1966); United States v. Lopez, 944 F.2d 33, 37 (1st Cir. 1991).

district judge was courteous to the defendants and sedulously protected their rights."). But the court continued to explain why recusal was necessary nonetheless:

> § 455(a) asks a broader question which, on these facts, makes it impossible to take these cases out of context. . . .
>
> Two messages were conveyed by the judge's appearance on national television in the midst of these events. One message consisted of the words actually spoken regarding the protesters' apparent plan to bar access to the clinics, and the judge's resolve to see his order prohibiting such actions enforced. The other was the judge's expressive conduct in deliberately making the choice to appear in such a forum at a sensitive time to deliver strong views on matters which were likely to be ongoing before him. Together, these messages unmistakenly conveyed an uncommon interest and degree of personal involvement in the subject matter. It was an unusual thing for a judge to do, and it unavoidably created the appearance that the judge had become an active participant in bringing law and order to bear on the protesters, rather than remaining as a detached adjudicator.
>
> We conclude that at least after the judge's volunteer appearance on national television to state his views regarding the ongoing protests, the protesters, and his determination that his injunction was going to be obeyed, a reasonable person would harbor a justified doubt as to his impartiality in the case involving these defendants.

Id. at 995.

Although the media contact in this case was less inflammatory than that in *Cooley*, we see the same factors at work, albeit on a smaller scale. . . . [T]he Boston school assignment program is a matter of significant local concern, generating at least two prominent articles in the Boston Herald. Judge Gertner viewed this prominence as all the more reason to correct misrepresentations by petitioners' counsel. However, *Cooley* counsels that in newsworthy cases where tensions may be high, judges should be particularly cautious about commenting on pending litigation. Interested members of the public might well consider Judge Gertner's actions as expressing an undue degree of interest in the case, and thus pay special attention to the language of her comments. With such public attention to a matter, even ambiguous comments may create the appearance of impropriety that § 455(a) is designed to address. In fact, the very rarity of such public statements, and the ease with which they may be avoided, make it more likely that a reasonable person will interpret such statements as evidence of bias. . . .

The fact that Judge Gertner's comments were made in response to what could be characterized as an attack by counsel on the procedures of her court did not justify any comment by Judge Gertner beyond an explanation of those procedures. . . . Whether counsel for petitioners misrepresented the facts or not is irrelevant: the issue here is whether a reasonable person could have interpreted Judge Gertner's comments as doing more than correcting those misrepresentations and creating an appearance of partiality. We feel that, on these facts, a reasonable person could do so.

Again, we underscore that this ruling in no way intimates any actual bias or prejudice on the part of Judge Gertner. . . . "Such a stringent rule may sometimes bar trial by judges who have no actual bias and who would do their best to weigh the scales of justice equally between contending parties." In re Murchison, 349 U.S. 133, 136 (1955). We have every confidence that Judge Gertner is one such judge. "But to perform its high function in the best way, 'justice must satisfy the appearance of justice,'" id., and thus we must grant the writ.

After this opinion was prepared and initially released, the court received a petition for rehearing en banc from the district judge. Although the basis for filing such a petition may be open to dispute, cf., Fed.R.App.P. 21(b)(4), the panel sua sponte has consulted informally with the three non-panelist active judges, a practice that this court has followed in other cases. E.g., Trailer Marine Transp. Corp. v. Rivera Vazquez, 977 F.2d 1, 9 n.5 (1st Cir. 1992).

Those active judges who are not members of the panel are currently of the view that, even if the district court's statement to the reporter comprised a comment on the merits, it does not create an appearance of partiality such as to require mandatory recusal under 28 U.S.C. § 455(a). They are particularly concerned that section 455(a) not be read to create a threshold for recusal so low as to make any out-of-court response to a reporter's question the basis for a motion to recuse. However, they share fully the panel's view that when a judge makes public comments to the press regarding a pending case, he or she invites trouble, and that this comment was at the very least particularly unwise. . . .

Writ of mandamus granted.

Notes

1. The statute and the Code of Judicial Conduct reflect two important principles that clash in the principal case. The first is the bedrock notion that our judges must not only be impartial in deciding particular cases, but that they must appear to be impartial as well. The second is that we do not want to cut our judges off completely from the public whom they serve, especially with respect to educating the public about what they are doing. Do you think that the panel decision privileged the right principle in this case?

2. A more famous application of the impartiality principle was the disqualification of Judge Thomas Jackson in the Microsoft litigation. United States v. Microsoft Corporation, 253 F.3d 34 (2001). The court concluded that while it found no evidence of actual bias, the judge's interviews with the media and many public "offensive comments" about officers of Microsoft created an appearance of partiality that required disqualification of Judge Jackson from participation in the further proceedings that were required. The court also worried that the judge might have violated the prohibition against ex parte communications.

3. Other provisions of § 455 cause difficulty. In In re Cement and Concrete Anti-trust Litigation, 515 F. Supp. 1076 (D. Ariz. 1981), mandamus denied, 688 F.2d 1297 (9th Cir. 1982), judgment aff'd for lack of a quorum, 459 U.S. 1190 (1983), the per se rule of § 455(b)(4) required a judge who had been handling the case for five years to disqualify himself when he realized that his wife held some stock in corporations that were part of one class although the litigation could not have benefited her by more than $30.

The next case on § 455 reached the Supreme Court in the context of the rather unusual situation where a judge, who was clearly disqualified, sat and decided the case because, as the trial court later found, he had forgotten about the disqualifying circumstances. If the judge did not know about the issue, does the litigant need or deserve a remedy?

Liljeberg v. Health Services Acquisition Corp.
486 U.S. 847 (1988)

Justice STEVENS delivered the opinion of the Court.

. . .

In November 1981, respondent Health Services Acquisition Corp. brought an action against petitioner John Liljeberg, Jr., seeking a declaration of ownership of a corporation known as St. Jude Hospital of Kenner, Louisiana (St. Jude). The case was tried by Judge Robert Collins, sitting without a jury. Judge Collins found for Lilje-berg and, over a strong dissent, the Court of Appeals affirmed. Approximately 10 months later, respondent learned that Judge Collins had been a member of the Board of Trustees of Loyola University while Liljeberg was negotiating with Loyola to pur-chase a parcel of land on which to construct a hospital. The success and benefit to Loyola of these negotiations turned, in large part, on Liljeberg prevailing in the liti-gation before Judge Collins.

Based on this information, respondent moved pursuant to Federal Rule of Civil Procedure 60(b)(6) to vacate the judgment on the ground that Judge Collins was dis-qualified under § 455 at the time he heard the action and entered judgment in favor of Liljeberg. Judge Collins denied the motion and respondent appealed. The Court of Appeals determined that resolution of the motion required factual findings con-cerning the extent and timing of Judge Collins' knowledge of Loyola's interest in the declaratory relief litigation. Accordingly, the panel reversed and remanded the matter to a different judge for such findings. On remand, the District Court found that based on his attendance at Board meetings Judge Collins had actual knowledge of Loyola's interest in St. Jude in 1980 and 1981. The court further concluded, however, that Judge Collins had forgotten about Loyola's interest by the time the declaratory judgment suit came to trial in January 1982. On March 24, 1982, Judge Collins reviewed mate-rials sent to him by the Board to prepare for an upcoming meeting. At that time—just a few days after he had filed his opinion finding for Liljeberg and still within the 10-day period allowed for filing a motion for a new trial—Judge Collins once again obtained actual knowledge of Loyola's interest in St. Jude. Finally, the District Court found that although Judge Collins thus lacked actual knowledge during trial and prior to the filing of his opinion, the evidence nonetheless gave rise to an appearance of impropriety. However, reading the Court of Appeals' mandate as limited to the issue of actual knowledge, the District Court concluded that it was compelled to deny respondent's Rule 60(b) motion.

The Court of Appeals again reversed. The court first noted that Judge Collins should have immediately disqualified himself when his actual knowledge of Loyola's interest was renewed. The court also found that regardless of Judge Collins' actual knowledge, "a reasonable observer would expect that Judge Collins would remember that Loyola had some dealings with Liljeberg and St. Jude and seek to ascertain the nature of these dealings." 796 F.2d 796, 803 (1986). Such an appearance of impropriety, in the view of the Court of Appeals, was sufficient ground for disqualification under § 455(a). Although recognizing that caution is required in determining whether a judgment should be vacated after becoming final, the court concluded that since the appearance of partiality was convincingly established and since the motion to vacate was filed as promptly as possible, the appropriate remedy was to vacate the declaratory relief judgment. . . .

In considering whether the Court of Appeals properly vacated the declaratory relief judgment, we are required to address two questions. We must first determine whether § 455(a) can be violated based on an appearance of partiality, even though the judge was not conscious of the circumstances creating the appearance of impropriety, and second, whether relief is available under Rule 60(b) when such a violation is not discovered until after the judgment has become final.

Title 28 U.S.C. § 455 provides in relevant part:

> (a) Any justice, judge, or magistrate of the United States shall disqualify himself in any proceeding in which his impartiality might reasonably be questioned.

> (b) He shall also disqualify himself in the following circumstances: . . .

> (4) He knows that he, individually or as a fiduciary, or his spouse or minor child residing in his household, has a financial interest in the subject matter in controversy or in a party to the proceeding, or any other interest that could be substantially affected by the outcome of the proceeding. . . .

> (c) A judge should inform himself about his personal and fiduciary financial interests, and make a reasonable effort to inform himself about the personal financial interests of his spouse and minor children residing in his household.

Scienter is not an element of a violation of § 455(a). The judge's lack of knowledge of a disqualifying circumstance may bear on the question of remedy, but it does not eliminate the risk that "his impartiality might reasonably be questioned" by other persons. To read § 455(a) to provide that the judge must know of the disqualifying facts requires not simply ignoring the language of the provision—which makes no mention of knowledge—but further requires concluding that the language in subsection (b)(4)—which expressly provides that the judge must *know* of his or her interest—is extraneous. A careful reading of the respective subsections makes clear that Congress intended to require knowledge under subsection (b)(4) and not to require knowledge under subsection (a). Moreover, advancement of the purpose of the provision—to promote public confidence in the integrity of the judicial process, see S. Rep. No. 93-419, p. 5 (1973); H. R. Rep. No. 93-1453, p. 5 (1974)—does not depend upon whether or not the judge actually knew of facts creating an appearance of impropriety, so long as the public might reasonably believe that he or she knew. As Chief Judge Clark of the Court of Appeals explained:

> The goal of section 455(a) is to avoid even the appearance of partiality. If it would appear to a reasonable person that a judge has knowledge of facts that would give him an interest in the litigation then an appearance of partiality is created even though no actual partiality exists because the judge does not recall the facts, because the judge actually has no interest in the case or because the judge is pure in heart and incorruptible. The judge's forgetfulness, however, is not the sort of objectively ascertainable fact that can avoid the appearance of partiality. . . . Under section 455(a), therefore, recusal is required even when a judge lacks actual knowledge of the facts indicating his interest or bias in the case if a reasonable person, knowing all the circumstances, would expect that the judge would have actual knowledge.

796 F.2d, at 802.

Contrary to petitioner's contentions, this reading of the statute does not call upon judges to perform the impossible—to disqualify themselves based on facts they do not know. If, as petitioner argues, § 455(a) should only be applied prospectively, then requiring disqualification based on facts the judge does not know would of course be absurd; a judge could never be expected to disqualify himself based on some fact he does not know, even though the fact is one that perhaps he should know or one that people might reasonably suspect that he does know. But to the extent the provision can also, in proper cases, be applied retroactively, the judge is not called upon to perform an impossible feat. Rather, he is called upon to rectify an oversight and to take the steps necessary to maintain public confidence in the impartiality of the judiciary. If he concludes that "his impartiality might reasonably be questioned," then he should also find that the statute has been violated. This is certainly not an impossible task. No one questions that Judge Collins could have disqualified himself and vacated his judgment when he finally realized that Loyola had an interest in the litigation. The initial appeal was taken from his failure to disqualify himself and vacate the judgment *after* he became aware of the appearance of impropriety, not from his failure to disqualify himself when he first became involved in the litigation and lacked the requisite knowledge.

In this case both the District Court and the Court of Appeals found an ample basis in the record for concluding that an objective observer would have questioned Judge Collins' impartiality. Accordingly, even though his failure to disqualify himself was the product of a temporary lapse of memory, it was nevertheless a plain violation of the terms of the statute.

A conclusion that a statutory violation occurred does not, however, end our inquiry. As in other areas of the law, there is surely room for harmless error committed by busy judges who inadvertently overlook a disqualifying circumstance. There need not be a draconian remedy for every violation of § 455(a). It would be equally wrong, however, to adopt an absolute prohibition against any relief in cases involving forgetful judges.

Although § 455 defines the circumstances that mandate disqualification of federal judges, it neither prescribes nor prohibits any particular remedy for a violation of that duty. . . .

. . . We conclude that in determining whether a judgment should be vacated for a violation of § 455, it is appropriate to consider the risk of injustice to the parties in the particular case, the risk that the denial of relief will produce injustice in other cases, and the risk of undermining the public's confidence in the judicial process. . . .

Like the Court of Appeals, we accept the District Court's finding that while the case was actually being tried Judge Collins did not have actual knowledge of Loyola's interest in the dispute over the ownership of St. Jude and its precious certificate of need. When a busy federal judge concentrates his or her full attention on a pending case, personal concerns are easily forgotten. The problem, however, is that people who have not served on the bench are often all too willing to indulge suspicions and doubts concerning the integrity of judges. The very purpose of § 455(a) is to promote confidence in the judiciary by avoiding even the appearance of impropriety whenever possible. See S. Rep. No. 93-419, at 5; H. R. Rep. No. 93-1453, at 5. Thus, it is critically important in a case of this kind to identify the facts that might reasonably cause an objective observer to question Judge Collins' impartiality.

[The Court then noted that it was remarkable that the judge who had regularly attended meetings that discussed the University's interest in St. Jude's Hospital should have forgotten about it; that it was unfortunate that although before he entered judgment he had received minutes of a meeting that he did not attend at which the subject was discussed, he did not open the envelope in time; that it was remarkable and inexcusable that when he did have actual knowledge, within 10 days after entering judgment, he did not recuse himself and said nothing; and finally that when he denied the motion to vacate the judgment, he did not mention that he had known of the University's interest both shortly before and shortly after the trial.]

These facts create precisely the kind of appearance of impropriety that § 455(a) was intended to prevent. The violation is neither insubstantial nor excusable. Although Judge Collins did not know of his fiduciary interest in the litigation, he certainly should have known. In fact, his failure to stay informed of this fiduciary interest may well constitute a separate violation of § 455. See § 455(c). Moreover, providing relief in cases such as this will not produce injustice in other cases; to the contrary, the Court of Appeals' willingness to enforce § 455 may prevent a substantive injustice in some future case by encouraging a judge or litigant to more carefully examine possible grounds for disqualification and to promptly disclose them when discovered. It is therefore appropriate to vacate the judgment unless it can be said that respondent did not make a timely request for relief; or that it would otherwise be unfair to deprive the prevailing party of its judgment. . . .

The judgment of the Court of Appeals is accordingly Affirmed.

[The dissents of Justice O'Connor and then–Chief Justice Rehnquist, with whom Justices Scalia and White joined, have been omitted.]

Notes

1. Four dissenters argued that the judge's disqualification should depend on what the judge knew, not what he should have known, but note that the focus of § 455(a) is not on either of those facts but rather on the appearance to third parties. Looked at that way, the majority's point ought to be that the parties or the public would have questioned the judge's impartiality if they had known all the circumstances, and the dissent's point ought to be that it would not be reasonable to question the impartiality of the judge when the judge does not have the disqualifying factors in mind during the trial. That is where Judge Stevens' recitation of the facts becomes quite relevant. The parties and the public might well question the impartiality of a judge who knew about the disqualifying factors just before and just after the trial even if he did not "know" of them during the trial. Those factors might well be feared to be operating in the judge's subconscious.

That brings us to the other possible interpretation of Judge Stevens' remarks — that they are a signal that although the Court was not prepared to reverse the finding about the trial judge's lack of knowledge, it was sufficiently doubtful about it that it was willing to give § 455(a) something of a retroactive reading so that it could be applied to a case whose facts were perceived as giving rise to reasonable fear of partiality.

2. There are some lessons in this case for judges. The first is that their judicial obligations require them to pay very close attention to the details of their extrajudicial activities. The second is that when their extrajudicial activities have widespread ramifications throughout the community in which they live, they ought at least to consider whether those ramifications are consistent with their judicial duties — that is, their obligation not to put themselves in situations that will require their disqualification. See, e.g., Model Code of Judicial Conduct R. 3.1, 3.11. One may also wonder why the lawyers were not aware of the judge's position on the board of trustees of the University. Were the lawyers obligated, under their duties of competence and diligence, to discover the judge's connection to the University?

3. In Liteky v. United States, 510 U.S. 540 (1994), a divided Supreme Court concluded that when § 455(b) dealt with a particular subject, it limited the potential reach of § 455(a). Does the text of the statute (quoted above) justify this conclusion?

4. Another kind of recusal problem arose in *Matter of Ronwin*, which was discussed at p. 679, Note 2. The Arizona Supreme Court was faced with deciding an admissions to the bar problem in the context of a situation in which the applicant had already sued the members of the Court in connection with those problems. The Court responded as follows:

Recusal Problems

Yet another problem arises. One member of this court recused himself after oral argument because he felt too personally involved in the case to participate in the decision. That leaves four members of this court. Each has been made a defendant by Ronwin in various actions. If we are to recuse ourselves simply because we have been sued by the applicant, then who is left to decide this case? As the Ninth Circuit stated: "'[A] judge is not disqualified merely because a litigant sues or threatens to sue him.' Such an easy method for obtaining disqualification should not be encouraged or allowed." Ronwin v. State Bar of Arizona, 686 F.2d at 701, quoting United States v. Grismore, 564 F.2d 929, 933 (10th Cir. 1977). . . . We agree; the mere fact that a judge has been sued by reason of his rulings in a case does not require recusal. Nor can the fact that all judges in the court have been sued require recusal. To honor such a technique would be to put the weapon of disqualification in the hands of the most unscrupulous . . . .

136 Ariz. 566, 575–576 (1983).

5. Former Chief Justice Rehnquist dissented in the principal case. Chief Justice Rehnquist's view on the subject of disqualification may well be tempered by his own controversial refusal to disqualify himself in Laird v. Tatum and his opinion justifying that refusal. 409 U.S. 824 (1972). The issue was the relation between testimony that he gave on behalf of the Justice Department before a Senate Committee on the general subject of the executive constitutional powers to gather information and the subject matter of the actual case in which he sat. In 1993, seven Justices of the Supreme Court, including Chief Justice Rehnquist, issued a statement with respect to the recusal policy they would follow when various lawyer-relatives of theirs were associates or partners in firms representing parties that were before the Court. 114 S. Ct. 52 (see first set of page numbers in that volume).

––––––––––

The following case presents the Supreme Court's most recent exploration of recusal and due process, in a case in which the judge at least generally knew that he had once played a role in the matter as a lawyer. In arguing that the judge's recusal was unnecessary, however, the state claimed that the judge's prior role was merely "administrative," and in any event, that the judge had played no role in the case for last thirty years. [In the interest of full disclosure, one of this book's authors, Prof. Swisher, drafted the ABA's amicus brief urging the Court to require recusal despite the state's arguments.] The judge's failure to recuse himself almost surely violated the Code of Judicial Conduct, but consider whether every such violation should also constitute a due process violation so as to require a reversal of the criminal conviction and a remand for a retrial.

Williams v. Pennsylvania
136 S.Ct. 1899 (2016)

Justice KENNEDY delivered the opinion of the Court.

In this case, the Supreme Court of Pennsylvania vacated the decision of a post-conviction court, which had granted relief to a prisoner convicted of first-degree murder and sentenced to death. One of the justices on the State Supreme Court had been the district attorney who gave his official approval to seek the death penalty in the prisoner's case. The justice in question denied the prisoner's motion for recusal and participated in the decision to deny relief. The question presented is whether the justice's denial of the recusal motion and his subsequent judicial participation violated the Due Process Clause of the Fourteenth Amendment.

This Court's precedents set forth an objective standard that requires recusal when the likelihood of bias on the part of the judge " 'is too high to be constitutionally tolerable.' " Caperton v. A.T. Massey Coal Co., 556 U.S. 868, 872 (2009) (quoting Withrow v. Larkin, 421 U.S. 35, 47 (1975)). Applying this standard, the Court concludes that due process compelled the justice's recusal.

I

Petitioner is Terrance Williams. In 1984, soon after Williams turned 18, he murdered 56-year-old Amos Norwood in Philadelphia. At trial, the Commonwealth presented evidence that Williams and a friend, Marc Draper, had been standing on a street corner when Norwood drove by. Williams and Draper requested a ride home from Norwood, who agreed. Draper then gave Norwood false directions that led him to drive toward a cemetery. Williams and Draper ordered Norwood out of the car and into the cemetery. There, the two men tied Norwood in his own clothes and beat him to death. Testifying for the Commonwealth, Draper suggested that robbery was the motive for the crime. Williams took the stand in his own defense, stating that he was not involved in the crime and did not know the victim.

During the trial, the prosecutor requested permission from her supervisors in the district attorney's office to seek the death penalty against Williams. To support the request, she prepared a memorandum setting forth the details of the crime, information supporting two statutory aggravating factors, and facts in mitigation. After reviewing the memorandum, the then–district attorney of Philadelphia, Ronald Castille, wrote this note at the bottom of the document: "Approved to proceed on the death penalty."

During the penalty phase of the trial, the prosecutor argued that Williams deserved a death sentence because he killed Norwood " 'for no other reason but that a kind man offered him a ride home.' " The jurors found two aggravating circumstances: that the murder was committed during the course of a robbery and that Williams had a significant history of violent felony convictions. That criminal history included a previous conviction for a murder he had committed at age 17. The jury found no mitigating circumstances and sentenced Williams to death. Over a period of 26 years, Williams's conviction and sentence were upheld on direct appeal, state postconviction review, and federal habeas review.

In 2012, Williams filed a successive petition . . . based on new information from Draper, who until then had refused to speak with Williams's attorneys. Draper told Williams's counsel that he had informed the Commonwealth before trial that Williams had been in a sexual relationship with Norwood and that the relationship was the real motive for Norwood's murder. According to Draper, the Commonwealth had instructed him to give false testimony that Williams killed Norwood to rob him. Draper also admitted he had received an undisclosed benefit in exchange for his testimony: the trial prosecutor had promised to write a letter to the state parole board on his behalf. At trial, the prosecutor had elicited testimony from Draper indicating that his only agreement with the prosecution was to plead guilty in exchange for truthful testimony. No mention was made of the additional promise to write the parole board.

The Philadelphia Court of Common Pleas, identified in the proceedings below as the PCRA court, held an evidentiary hearing on Williams's claims. Williams alleged in his petition that the prosecutor had procured false testimony from Draper and suppressed evidence regarding Norwood's sexual relationship with Williams. At the hearing, both Draper and the trial prosecutor testified regarding these allegations. The PCRA court ordered the district attorney's office to produce the previously undisclosed files of the prosecutor and police. These documents included the trial prosecutor's sentencing memorandum, bearing then–District Attorney Castille's authorization to pursue the death penalty. Based on the Commonwealth's files and the evidentiary hearing, the PCRA court found that the trial prosecutor had suppressed material, exculpatory evidence in violation of Brady v. Maryland, 373 U.S. 83 (1963), and engaged in "prosecutorial gamesmanship." The court stayed Williams's execution and ordered a new sentencing hearing.

Seeking to vacate the stay of execution, the Commonwealth submitted an emergency application to the Pennsylvania Supreme Court. By this time, almost three decades had passed since Williams's prosecution. Castille had been elected to a seat on the State Supreme Court and was serving as its chief justice. Williams filed a response to the Commonwealth's application. The disclosure of the trial prosecutor's sentencing memorandum in the PCRA proceedings had alerted Williams to Chief Justice Castille's involvement in the decision to seek a death sentence in his case. For this reason, Williams also filed a motion asking Chief Justice Castille to recuse himself or, if he declined to do so, to refer the recusal motion to the full court for decision. The Commonwealth opposed Williams's recusal motion. Without explanation, Chief Justice Castille denied the motion for recusal and the request for its referral. Two days later, the Pennsylvania Supreme Court denied the application to vacate the stay and ordered full briefing on the issues raised in the appeal. The State

Supreme Court then vacated the PCRA court's order granting penalty-phase relief and reinstated Williams's death sentence. Chief Justice Castille and Justices Baer and Stevens joined the majority opinion written by Justice Eakin. Justices Saylor and Todd concurred in the result without issuing a separate opinion. See 629 Pa. 533 (2014).

Chief Justice Castille authored a concurrence. He lamented that the PCRA court had "lost sight of its role as a neutral judicial officer" and had stayed Williams's execution "for no valid reason." Id., at 552. "[B]efore condemning officers of the court," the chief justice stated, "the tribunal should be aware of the substantive status of *Brady* law," which he believed the PCRA court had misapplied. Ibid. In addition, Chief Justice Castille denounced what he perceived as the "obstructionist anti-death penalty agenda" of Williams's attorneys from the Federal Community Defender Office. Ibid. PCRA courts "throughout Pennsylvania need to be vigilant and circumspect when it comes to the activities of this particular advocacy group," he wrote, lest Defender Office lawyers turn postconviction proceedings "into a circus where [they] are the ringmasters, with their parrots and puppets as a sideshow." Id., at 554.

Two weeks after the Pennsylvania Supreme Court decided Williams's case, Chief Justice Castille retired from the bench. This Court granted Williams's petition for certiorari. . . .

II

A

Williams contends that Chief Justice Castille's decision as district attorney to seek a death sentence against him barred the chief justice from later adjudicating Williams's petition to overturn that sentence. Chief Justice Castille, Williams argues, violated the Due Process Clause of the Fourteenth Amendment by acting as both accuser and judge in his case.

The Court's due process precedents do not set forth a specific test governing recusal when, as here, a judge had prior involvement in a case as a prosecutor. For the reasons explained below, however, the principles on which these precedents rest dictate the rule that must control in the circumstances here. The Court now holds that under the Due Process Clause there is an impermissible risk of actual bias when a judge earlier had significant, personal involvement as a prosecutor in a critical decision regarding the defendant's case.

Due process guarantees "an absence of actual bias" on the part of a judge. In re Murchison, 349 U.S. 133, 136 (1955). Bias is easy to attribute to others and difficult to discern in oneself. To establish an enforceable and workable framework, the Court's precedents apply an objective standard that, in the usual case, avoids having to determine whether actual bias is present. The Court asks not whether a judge harbors an actual, subjective bias, but instead whether, as an objective matter, "the average judge in his position is 'likely' to be neutral, or whether there is an unconstitutional 'potential for bias.' " *Caperton*, 556 U.S., at 881. Of particular relevance to the instant case, the Court has determined that an unconstitutional potential for bias exists when the same person serves as both accuser and adjudicator in a case. See *Murchison*, 349 U.S., at 136–137. This objective risk of bias is reflected in the due process maxim that "no man can be a judge in his own case and no man is permitted to try cases where he has an interest in the outcome." Id., at 136.

The due process guarantee that "no man can be a judge in his own case" would have little substance if it did not disqualify a former prosecutor from sitting in judgment of a prosecution in which he or she had made a critical decision. This conclusion follows from the Court's analysis in In re Murchison. That case involved a "one-man judge–grand jury" proceeding, conducted pursuant to state law, in which the judge called witnesses to testify about suspected crimes. Id., at 134. During the course of the examinations, the judge became convinced that two witnesses were obstructing the proceeding. He charged one witness with perjury and then, a few weeks later, tried and convicted him in open court. The judge charged the other witness with contempt and, a few days later, tried and convicted him as well. This Court overturned the convictions on the ground that the judge's dual position as accuser and decisionmaker in the contempt trials violated due process: "Having been a part of [the accusatory] process a judge cannot be, in the very nature of things, wholly disinterested in the conviction or acquittal of those accused." Id., at 137.

No attorney is more integral to the accusatory process than a prosecutor who participates in a major adversary decision. When a judge has served as an advocate for the State in the very case the court is now asked to adjudicate, a serious question arises as to whether the judge, even with the most diligent effort, could set aside any personal interest in the outcome. There is, furthermore, a risk that the judge "would be so psychologically wedded" to his or her previous position as a prosecutor that the judge "would consciously or unconsciously avoid the appearance of having erred or changed position." Withrow, 421 U.S., at 57. In addition, the judge's "own personal knowledge and impression" of the case, acquired through his or her role in the prosecution, may carry far more weight with the judge than the parties' arguments to the court. Murchison, supra, at 138; see also Caperton, supra, at 881. . . .

. . . [F]actual differences notwithstanding, the constitutional principles explained in Murchison are fully applicable where a judge had a direct, personal role in the defendant's prosecution. The involvement of other actors and the passage of time are consequences of a complex criminal justice system, in which a single case may be litigated through multiple proceedings taking place over a period of years. This context only heightens the need for objective rules preventing the operation of bias that otherwise might be obscured. Within a large, impersonal system, an individual prosecutor might still have an influence that, while not so visible as the one-man grand jury in Murchison, is nevertheless significant. A prosecutor may bear responsibility for any number of critical decisions, including what charges to bring, whether to extend a plea bargain, and which witnesses to call. Even if decades intervene before the former prosecutor revisits the matter as a jurist, the case may implicate the effects and continuing force of his or her original decision. In these circumstances, there remains a serious risk that a judge would be influenced by an improper, if inadvertent, motive to validate and preserve the result obtained through the adversary process. The involvement of multiple actors and the passage of time do not relieve the former prosecutor of the duty to withdraw in order to ensure the neutrality of the judicial process in determining the consequences that his or her own earlier, critical decision may have set in motion.

B

This leads to the question whether Chief Justice Castille's authorization to seek the death penalty against Williams amounts to significant, personal involvement in a critical trial decision. The Court now concludes that it was a significant, personal involvement; and, as a result, Chief Justice Castille's failure to recuse from Williams's case presented an unconstitutional risk of bias.

As an initial matter, there can be no doubt that the decision to pursue the death penalty is a critical choice in the adversary process. . . .

Pennsylvania nonetheless contends that Chief Justice Castille in fact did not have significant involvement in the decision to seek a death sentence against Williams. The chief justice, the Commonwealth points out, was the head of a large district attorney's office in a city that saw many capital murder trials. According to Pennsylvania, his approval of the trial prosecutor's request to pursue capital punishment in Williams's case amounted to a brief administrative act limited to "the time it takes to read a one-and-a-half-page memo." In this Court's view, that characterization cannot be credited. The Court will not assume that then–District Attorney Castille treated so major a decision as a perfunctory task requiring little time, judgment, or reflection on his part.

Chief Justice Castille's own comments while running for judicial office refute the Commonwealth's claim that he played a mere ministerial role in capital sentencing decisions. During the chief justice's election campaign, multiple news outlets reported his statement that he "sent 45 people to death rows" as district attorney. . . . Chief Justice Castille's willingness to take personal responsibility for the death sentences obtained during his tenure as district attorney indicate that, in his own view, he played a meaningful role in those sentencing decisions and considered his involvement to be an important duty of his office. . . .

The potential conflict of interest posed by the PCRA court's findings illustrates the utility of statutes and professional codes of conduct that "provide more protection than due process requires." *Caperton*, 556 U.S., at 890. It is important to note that due process "demarks only the outer boundaries of judicial disqualifications." Aetna Life Ins. Co. v. Lavoie, 475 U.S. 813, 828 (1986). Most questions of recusal are addressed by more stringent and detailed ethical rules, which in many jurisdictions already require disqualification under the circumstances of this case. See Brief for American Bar Association as Amicus Curiae 5, 11–14; see also ABA Model Code of Judicial Conduct Rules 2.11(A)(1), (A)(6)(b) (2011) (no judge may participate "in any proceeding in which the judge's impartiality might reasonably be questioned," including where the judge "served in governmental employment, and in such capacity participated personally and substantially as a lawyer or public official concerning the proceeding") . . . .

III

Having determined that Chief Justice Castille's participation violated due process, the Court must resolve whether Williams is entitled to relief. In past cases, the Court has not had to decide the question whether a due process violation arising from a jurist's failure to recuse amounts to harmless error if the jurist is on a multimember court and the jurist's vote was not decisive. . . . For the reasons discussed below, the Court holds that an unconstitutional failure to recuse constitutes structural error even if the judge in question did not cast a deciding vote.

The Court has little trouble concluding that a due process violation arising from the participation of an interested judge is a defect "not amenable" to harmless-error review, regardless of whether the judge's vote was dispositive. . . . The deliberations of an appellate panel, as a general rule, are confidential. As a result, it is neither possible nor productive to inquire whether the jurist in question might have influenced the views of his or her colleagues during the decisionmaking process. Indeed, one purpose of judicial confidentiality is to assure jurists that they can reexamine old ideas and suggest new ones, while both seeking to persuade and being open to persuasion by their colleagues. As Justice Brennan wrote in his *Lavoie* concurrence,

> The description of an opinion as being "for the court" connotes more than merely that the opinion has been joined by a majority of the participating judges. It reflects the fact that these judges have exchanged ideas and arguments in deciding the case. It reflects the collective process of deliberation which shapes the court's perceptions of which issues must be addressed and, more importantly, how they must be addressed. And, while the influence of any single participant in this process can never be measured with precision, experience teaches us that each member's involvement plays a part in shaping the court's ultimate disposition.

475 U.S., at 831. . . .

A multimember court must not have its guarantee of neutrality undermined, for the appearance of bias demeans the reputation and integrity not just of one jurist, but of the larger institution of which he or she is a part. An insistence on the appearance of neutrality is not some artificial attempt to mask imperfection in the judicial process, but rather an essential means of ensuring the reality of a fair adjudication. . . .

. . . Allowing an appellate panel to reconsider a case without the participation of the interested member will permit judges to probe lines of analysis or engage in discussions they may have felt constrained to avoid in their first deliberations. . . .

The judgment of the Supreme Court of Pennsylvania is vacated, and the case is remanded for further proceedings not inconsistent with this opinion.

Chief Justice ROBERTS, with whom Justice ALITO joins, dissenting.

In 1986, Ronald Castille, then District Attorney of Philadelphia, authorized a prosecutor in his office to seek the death penalty against Terrance Williams. Almost 30 years later, as Chief Justice of the Pennsylvania Supreme Court, he participated in deciding whether Williams's fifth habeas petition—which raised a claim unconnected to the prosecution's decision to seek the death penalty—could be heard on the merits or was instead untimely. This Court now holds that because Chief Justice Castille made a "critical" decision as a prosecutor in Williams's case, there is a risk that he "would be so psychologically wedded" to his previous decision that it would violate the Due Process Clause for him to decide the distinct issues raised in the habeas petition. Ante, at 1905–1906 (internal quotation marks omitted). According to the Court, that conclusion follows from the maxim that "no man can be a judge in his own case."

The majority opinion rests on proverb rather than precedent. This Court has held that there is "a presumption of honesty and integrity in those serving as adjudicators." Withrow v. Larkin, 421 U.S. 35, 47 (1975). To overcome that presumption, the majority relies on In re Murchison, 349 U.S. 133 (1955). We concluded there that the Due Process Clause is violated when a judge adjudicates the same question—based on the same facts—that he had already considered as a grand juror in the same case. Here, however, Williams does not allege that Chief Justice Castille had *any* previous knowledge of the contested facts at issue in the habeas petition, or that he had previously made *any* decision on the questions raised by that petition. I would accordingly hold that the Due Process Clause did not require Chief Justice Castille's recusal. . . .

It is abundantly clear that, unlike in *Murchison*, Chief Justice Castille had *not* made up his mind about either the contested evidence or the legal issues under review in Williams's fifth habeas petition. How could he have? Neither the contested evidence nor the legal issues were ever before him as prosecutor. The one-and-a-half page memo prepared by Assistant District Attorney Foulkes in 1986 did not discuss the evidence that Williams claims was withheld by the prosecution at trial. It also did not discuss Williams's allegation that Norwood sexually abused young men. It certainly did not discuss whether Williams could have obtained that evidence of abuse earlier through the exercise of due diligence. . . .

The Due Process Clause did not prohibit Chief Justice Castille from hearing Williams's case. That does not mean, however, that it was appropriate for him to do so. Williams cites a number of state court decisions and ethics opinions that prohibit a prosecutor from later serving as judge in a case that he has prosecuted. Because the Due Process Clause does not mandate recusal in cases such as this, it is up to state authorities—not this Court—to determine whether recusal should be required.

I would affirm the judgment of the Pennsylvania Supreme Court, and respectfully dissent from the Court's contrary conclusion.

———————

Notes

1. The majority above gave little consideration to the fact that Chief Justice Castille had reviewed the memorandum almost thirty years ago. Is, or should there be, a time limit for bias? Is Chief Roberts correct in arguing, essentially, that a presumption of impartiality should be bestowed to the judiciary and even when that presumption has been rebutted in the past, it should be returned after a certain number of years? To put it more simply, should we treat judges' biases as a life-long affliction?

2. In campaigning for the bench, Chief Justice Castille bragged to the media that he had successfully sent to death row forty-five defendants (including Mr. Williams). Were these boasts evidence of bias against Mr. Williams or against a certain class of litigants (namely death-row inmates whom Castille's office had prosecuted while Castille was the DA)? See generally Keith Swisher, "Pro-Prosecution Judges: 'Tough on Crime,' Soft on Strategy, Ripe for Disqualification," 52 Ariz. L. Rev. 317 (2010) (arguing that judges who campaign as tough on crime or who attack their challengers as soft on crime should generally recuse themselves from criminal cases). Most reviewing courts will not disqualify a judge from a criminal case for previous tough-on-crime campaigning, unless the campaigning related to a specific case or essentially promised a particular result. Is that a fair and assuring result for future litigants, including criminal defendants? If, for example, a judge had said during the campaign (or told an appointing authority) that he or she will treat harshly any corporation that has violated environmental laws or regulations, should a corporation in a toxic tort suit be stuck with that judge?

3. Chief Justice Castille, in his concurring opinion, harshly criticized the trial court for its "frivolous *Brady* claim," for "losing sight . . . of its role as neutral arbiter," and for permitting discovery into "the government's files" (including files of the DA's office during the time that Chief Justice Castille headed that office). See Commonwealth v. Williams, Nos. 668-69 CAP (Pa. Sup. Ct. Dec. 15, 2014) (Castille, C.J., concurring). He even called the trial court's actions "lawless." From these statements, can it be inferred that Castille was biased in favor of the DA's office? Courts generally will not disqualify a judge for statements in judicial opinions, insisting instead that disqualifying bias must come from an "extrajudicial" source. Why must that be?

4. The Court had to wrestle with the fact that Chief Justice Castille was a member of a multimember panel (as most appellate courts are constituted), and the panel had unanimously denied relief to Mr. Williams. Why was the court hesitant to apply the harmless error doctrine in such circumstances? See generally Pauline Kim, "Deliberation and Strategy on the United States Courts of Appeals," 157 Penn. L. Rev. 1319, 1322 (2009) (noting that "federal appeals court judges do *not* vote the same way regardless of panel composition, but instead appear to be influenced by the preferences of the other judges with whom they sit when deciding a case" and citing several studies finding such so-called "panel effects").

C. Timeless and Timely Selected Problems in Judicial Ethics

As noted above, the topic of judicial ethics can warrant a book in itself, but the following works give some general sense of the significant or recurring problems facing judges and the lawyers who appear before them.

Andrew L. Kaufman
Judicial Ethics: The Less-Often Asked Questions
64 Wash. L. Rev. 851 (1989)

I have selected from the menu of questions concerning judicial ethics the ones that have not been much discussed but that seem to me to be highly relevant for federal appellate judges and, indeed, for all judges. I have therefore ignored much-discussed questions relating to disqualification and financial interests of judges.

My topics are the following: *ex parte* communication by judges with others about pending or impending matters; permissible activities of judges' spouses; the obligation of judges to report disciplinary violations by lawyers to the appropriate disciplinary authorities; and extrajudicial comments by judges about legal matters.

I. THE GROWING FIELD OF JUDICIAL ETHICS

When I first began teaching the subject of professional responsibility over 20 years ago, the subject of judicial ethics was of little concern, either to judges, academics, the profession generally, or even to those special critics, the newspapers. There were occasional episodes that produced comment—a public squabble between Justices Jackson and Black over the propriety of Justice Black sitting in a case argued by his former law partner, or Justice Roberts serving as a member of the Pearl Harbor Commission, or the charges of bribery against Judge Manton of the Second Circuit and Judge Davis of the Third Circuit—but they were noteworthy because they were so occasional. Most judges, like most lawyers, appeared to believe they had their ethics well in hand.

Things are quite different today. Questions of judicial ethics have followed questions of professional ethics generally in becoming a staple of professional life. There is, however, one major difference between lawyers' ethics and judges' ethics. There is a substantial amount of substantive law relating to the former, and the possibility of sanctions for violation of that law has become quite real. Not only are there motions to disqualify lawyers from the representation of clients but there is also an increasing possibility of professional discipline, malpractice suits by clients, or even suits by third parties. A lawyer's ethics also may come under scrutiny in the event of appointment to public office, especially judicial office.

The same extensive body of sanctions does not exist with respect to judicial conduct. Occasionally, judges are disqualified from sitting in particular cases; less frequently, judges are disciplined or even removed from the bench; and rarely, judicial behavior is questioned in a confirmation hearing when a judge is promoted. Nevertheless, in recent years, especially since the adoption of the Code of Conduct for United States Judges and the Code of Judicial Conduct for state judges, a body of case law and advisory opinions has developed sufficiently to delineate a body of substantive law of judicial ethics. One possible explanation for the development of this substantive law is that lawyers have begun to use motions to disqualify judges in the same way that they sometimes use motions to disqualify opposing counsel: as matters of strategy to disqualify someone perceived to be unsympathetic to the client's cause. While there may be some truth to that observation, I think that it is not a major reason for the growing importance of the subject of judicial ethics.

A more persuasive explanation sees development in the field of judicial ethics as part of the ever-increasing focus in our society upon the conduct of our public officials. Watergate certainly ushered in a new era, one that shows little sign of waning. To be in public life is to live under a microscope. Although judicial business is shielded in part by the confidentiality of court proceedings, that has not protected judges completely from the scrutiny that must be endured by other public officials. Indeed, the very confidentiality that judges enjoy has seemed to some to justify, even to require, greater scrutiny of their conduct to assure or to ascertain the purity of the process. . . .

II. *EX PARTE* COMMUNICATION

The issue with respect to *ex parte* communication involves the permissible range of consultation by judges on the merits, or on procedures affecting the merits, of pending matters with others: law teachers; judges of other courts, including state courts; and judges of one's own court. The Code of Conduct tells judges not to initiate or consider *ex parte* communication, except as authorized by law. The Commentary to the Canon is quite explicit that the prohibition includes law teachers and excludes other judges and court personnel whose function is to assist judges in their decisionmaking.

Eighteen years ago as a member of a committee designed to assess the ABA's Code of Judicial Conduct, I fought the prohibition against consultation with law teachers on the ground that, given the pressure on judges, they were entitled to whatever assistance they could get from academics. Since then, I have changed my mind about the desirability of permitting such consultation for three reasons. Quick, offhand advice from law teachers, who may appear to be more informed about a precise question than they really are, is much too casual. Moreover, it is given without the responsible frame of mind that comes from having to cast a vote. Furthermore, so many law teachers are now engaged in outside activities, either for profit or in a nonprofit but partisan fashion, that their advice may well be affected by quite specific interest in ways that will not be known to an inquiring judge. I would therefore leave the prohibition in place. Indeed, I would do more than that. I would make the prohibition even more explicit, because I am continuously surprised at how often it is violated by federal and state judges alike, either directly or via their law clerks.

Ex parte communication with other judges is another matter. The purpose of the prohibition is to make sure that parties who appear before a judge have access to the relevant materials on which a judge may rely. Despite the language in the Commentary to Canon 3(A)(4) that judges are not precluded from talking with other judges, I simply cannot believe that can be taken literally. In his published notes, Professor Thode, the Reporter for the ABA Code of Judicial Conduct, states that this exception was recognized as falling within the "authorized by law" language of the Code. But despite Professor Thode's comments, it can hardly be "authorized by law" for a federal judge to talk about a pending matter with a state court judge. There is a formal procedure for certification of questions when a federal judge needs advice about matters of state law. That procedure avoids the too-casual giving of an opinion that is one problem when talking with a judge of another jurisdiction. Moreover, is it "authorized by law" for judges to talk with judges on potential reviewing courts— for a federal district judge in California, for example, to talk with a Ninth Circuit judge? I would think not, even though we know that this was occasionally done even by Supreme Court justices in the nineteenth century. Such consultation has something of the flavor of obtaining an advisory opinion. Likewise, it seems difficult to conceive of a discussion between a district judge in California and a United States Court of Appeals judge in New York as coming within the notion of "authorized by law" when the jurisdiction of the two judges is not coextensive.

In my view, the hardest questions relate to federal judges consulting with other federal judges on the same court. A narrow view might well restrict judges to talking only with other judges who have some responsibility with respect to the pending matter, that is, members of the panel to whom the case is assigned. The only case I am aware of that has discussed the matter takes a different view. In People v. Hernandez, a sentencing judge in California to whom a particular case had been cited consulted with the sentencing judge in the cited case about the circumstances of that case and about that judge's understanding of the meaning of the reviewing court's opinion. The Court of Appeals treated this consultation as entirely proper. Interestingly, the court did not simply say that consultation between the judges of the same court, the Superior Court of California, was always permissible. Its grounds were narrower. It took note of the tremendous time and caseload pressure placed on trial judges and stated that the discussion that occurred was well within the bounds of public expectation of judicial conduct. While the appellate court did not explicitly equate its perception of public expectation with what is "authorized by law," it seemed to do so implicitly. The California court's resolution of the problem is a reasonable accommodation of the conflicting policies, but a more restrictive approach also would be a reasonable assurance that the judge with responsibility is the one deciding the matter. . . .

While I am on the topic of *ex parte* communication, I have found myself wondering lately about the practice of judges sitting on law school moot court cases involving matters that either are actually pending in their courts or are, to everyone's knowledge, wending their way through the judicial system toward their courts. Such cases are the staple of the higher moot court rounds that judges are often asked to judge. Is it enough that the judge refrain from announcing a decision on the merits? I think not. Canon 3(A)(4) is directed against "communications concerning a pending or impending proceeding." The ABA Committee on Ethics and Professional Responsibility has advised that this same Canon prohibits a judge from asking for research help from a criminal law research project of a law school unless the judge complies with the provisions of the rule requiring notice to the parties, a summary of the advice received, and an opportunity to respond. The briefs and arguments in a moot court case are rather similar and seem to come within the letter and spirit of the rule. The same problem also may occur when judges who are also law teachers invite class discussion of cases pending before them.

III. ACTIVITIES OF JUDGES' SPOUSES

Another matter about which I was asked relates to the obligations put on judges by reason of the activities of their spouses. A major question relates to political activity by a spouse. The federal Advisory Committee has struggled with the difficult question of trying to accommodate its advice to the judge with the legal rights of the spouse in an age where an active life by both spouses outside the home is becoming increasingly common. The shift in position on this point is an interesting sociological commentary on our times.

Canon 7 of the Code of Conduct prohibits a judge from engaging in political activity except for activities relating to improvement of the law, the legal system, and the administration of justice. The Canon, however, refers only to the conduct of judges, not their spouses. Nevertheless, the Advisory Committee in 1977 went beyond Canon 7's specific injunction to state more generally, without any discussion, that although spouses have the legal right to hold office in a political organization and take part in its activities, the judge has the duty to try to dissuade the spouse from doing so. The Advisory Committee went even further in the very same Opinion in the following extraordinary statement:

> The spouses of many judges have concluded that the provisions of the Code should apply to them the same as to the judge. Thus, they refrain not only from political activity but from solicitation of funds for charities and churches and from public comment about matters pending before the spouse, to mention but a few of the prohibitions on judges. Many spouses have regarded the applying to them of the ban on solicitation of funds as a "fringe benefit" which they welcomed. Each spouse has the right to reach his or her own conclusion as to such activity. . . .

. . . In 1983, it issued a revised opinion that simply states that the canons themselves adequately define the judge's obligation when the spouse engages in political activity and that the committee does not advise spouses. It added that judges should, as far as possible, disassociate themselves from their spouses' political activity, and it gave some examples of how that might be accomplished. It also pointed out that the judge should make the spouse aware that involvement in politics will increase the number of times when the judge will be obliged to recuse. While the Committee did not state the reasons for issuing a revised opinion or specifically disavow any statements in the earlier opinion, the most plausible explanation is that it came to view its indirect attempt to limit spouses' activities as inappropriate. I assume that the same approach would apply to any other, nonpolitical activities of a spouse. Spouses may do what they wish. Spouses' political activity may sometimes lead judges to disqualify themselves in particular matters, but that is a problem that should be left to the spouses to resolve between themselves.

IV. JUDICIAL OBLIGATION TO REPORT DISCIPLINARY VIOLATIONS

The next question is a very serious one for federal judges, although it does not arise so frequently for Courts of Appeals judges as it does for district and bankruptcy court judges. It concerns the obligation of judges to report violations of the Code of Conduct. That is one issue on which the Code gives explicit advice. Canon 3(B)(3) states that "a judge should take or initiate appropriate disciplinary measures against a judge or lawyer for unprofessional conduct of which the judge may become aware." There are no qualifications, except for the use of the word "should" instead of "shall." I confess that I do not quite understand the distinction in the judges' Code of Conduct. In the lawyers' disciplinary rules, the words are used to differentiate mandatory rules, whose violation may be sanctioned, from hortatory or aspirational rules, whose violation may not. But since there are no sanctions directly linked to the judges' Code of Conduct—although there is the possibility of disqualification or discipline—the difference between "should" canons and "shall" canons is not entirely clear. But it also is true that since the possibilities of anything that might be called sanctions are so small, that simply increases the obligation on judges to abide by their own self-made rules of conduct.

I start with an observation that I believe to be true but that I cannot prove: federal and state judges, appellate and trial, do not often take or initiate disciplinary measures against lawyers, although recently instances of reporting seem to be increasing. The question is to explain the reluctance of judges to do so. It must be that trial judges and, occasionally, appellate judges see conduct that constitutes a serious violation of the disciplinary rules: lawyers who knowingly conceal from the court precedents that are directly on point; lawyers who knowingly make a false statement of law or fact to the court or engage in conduct that involves dishonesty, misrepresentation, deceit or fraud; and lawyers who engage in illegal conduct involving moral turpitude before the court. . . .

. . . Judges are lawyers and they may succumb to the same anti-snitch sentiment that has largely nullified the similar obligation to report violations that exists for lawyers in most jurisdictions. There is, however, a big difference between lawyers and judges in this regard. In reporting disciplinary violations by lawyers, judges would be enforcing the rules for which they themselves are responsible. By and large, courts have been jealous of their power to regulate the conduct of lawyers in this country and have been unwilling to cede this responsibility to legislatures or to administrative bodies. Courts should not be able to have it both ways. If they are going to maintain responsibility for rules of conduct and their enforcement, then they should be taking the lead in enforcement with respect to violations that occur in front of them. Lawyers can shield themselves to a large extent by taking refuge in the comfort that they do not "know" that a violation has occurred in most cases. Judges should not draw the line so finely with respect to their own rules. They should forward matters for investigation when there is an apparent violation even if they are not absolutely certain and do not have the time or the resources to make a crucial finding of fact. . . .

V. EXTRAJUDICIAL COMMENTARY

Another question that was put in a variety of ways relates to the propriety of extrajudicial statements by judges on issues of general public interest. As a formal matter, the Code of Conduct tries to walk a fine line between, on the one hand, respecting the needs of judges to exercise their own freedom of speech and (not to put too fine a point on it) to earn additional money and, on the other hand, forbidding judges from engaging in the kind of speech that may lead to reasonable fears of partiality or, ultimately, to disqualification. Canon 4 of the Code of Conduct reflects that tension when it tells judges that, so long as they do not cast doubt on their capacity to decide any issue impartially, they may write and teach about the law, may appear at public hearings before legislative or executive bodies on matters concerning the law or the administration of justice, may consult with such bodies on the latter topic, and may serve on organizations devoted to the improvement of the legal system.

I should interject here that I have been surprised (to use a mild word) at the increasing numbers of articles and speeches by judges, especially Supreme Court Justices, in the past 20 years in which they discuss all sorts of issues that seem likely to come before them and discuss also the views and foibles of their colleagues. There is a difference between exhibiting greater willingness to discuss the business of courts by way of educating the public and engaging in public argument for positions they hold dear. I said above that there is a relation between the perceived power of judges and public scrutiny of the propriety of their activities. There also would seem to be a relation between the willingness of judges to enter into the public fray and the increasing tendency of some academics and some media figures to equate judges with legislators. . . .

Canon 4 therefore requires the exercise of prudential judgment in interpreting its injunction against engaging in such outside activities that might cause a litigant or the public reasonably to question the judge's impartiality. It certainly is not the development of views on matters that might come before judges that we fear. We want our judges to read, to think, to educate themselves about law in the largest sense. But there is a difference between a private thought and a public speech or published article. Going public requires much more care and responsibility and also may indicate such a desire to persuade others as to bring it within the range of Canon 4's prohibition of speech that casts doubt on the impartiality of the judge.

An early opinion of the federal Advisory Committee resolved the tension inherent in the language and policies of Canon 4 by stating that a judge should "circumscribe his comments so as to avoid a positive commitment on any legal issue which is likely to arise before him." More recently, however, the Committee has quoted with approval the statement in the Reporter's Notes to the ABA's Code of Judicial Conduct that a "judge may write or lecture on a legal issue, analyzing the present law and its history, its virtues, and its shortcomings; he may commend the present law or propose legal reform without compromising his capacity to decide impartially the very issue in which he has spoken or written."

The Reporter's statement is far too broad, for many such reform proposals may well cast doubt on a judge's impartiality. There is not always such a clear line between expressing willingness to follow present law and urging legislative change in the law. If present law is unclear, an expression of a desirable legislative solution may well appear to signal the judge's view of the desirable judicial solution. Moreover if, as the Committee suggested, a judge ought not urge legislative passage of the Equal Rights Amendment, or, to take another example, if a judge ought not appear before a legislature to urge repeal of capital punishment, then it should not be permissible for a judge to write an article or to give a public talk on the deficiencies of our law with respect to capital punishment. The judge will have sufficient opportunity to express a view when the issue arises, appropriately argued, in a litigated matter. The reasonable public fear regarding the judge's impartiality in reviewing a capital sentence seems equivalent whether the judge appears before a committee or produces a speech or article because in those two situations both the testimony before the committee and the speech or article bespeak a significant commitment to oppose capital punishment.[38] . . .

[Professor Kaufman then suggests that on balance, he would choose to impose a more restrictive speech rule on judges in the context of their law school teaching, public speeches, and articles.] One reason for that choice is that, except for egregious conduct, judges enjoy what lawyers often say they themselves enjoy but which lawyers really have less and less these days — a self-regulating profession. The critical thing about such a status is that it is regarded quite jealously by those who do not enjoy it. If judges are perceived as abusing that status, it will come under fire and they may lose it.

---

38. A closely divided Florida Supreme Court concluded that although a trial judge had come close to the line in writing an article for a church newsletter opposing capital punishment, he had saved himself by making clear that "he would do his duty as a judge and follow the law as written." In re Gridley, 417 So. 2d 950, 955 (Fla. 1982). Cf. In re Mandeville, 144 Vt. 608 (1984) (imposing discipline on a trial judge who stated in a public interview that defendants who pleaded guilty would be treated more leniently than those who went to trial). See generally Lubet, "Judicial Ethics and Private Lives," 79 Nw. U. L. Rev. 983, 996 (1985). . . .

The second reason for my restrictive attitude toward public speech by judges is that, notwithstanding the policymaking function of the judiciary, there is still a big difference between judges and legislators. Reflecting that difference, our tradition has been that most judges, most of the time, have waited for cases to present issues to them before speaking out. I hope that today's judges will pause before undertaking extrajudicial activities that narrow that difference. If the differences between judges and legislators are eliminated one by one, we may some day find that we have eroded the essential nature of the separation of powers between our legislative and judicial branches that has been such a distinctive feature of our society.

Among other recurring issues, Professor Kaufman asks (1) whether and when judges should report or call out lawyers' disciplinary violations and (2) to what extent should judges comment publicly about issues or cases.

On the first issue, consider United States v. Ofshe, 817 F.2d 1508 (11th Cir. 1987). There, a defendant in a federal trial in Florida claimed denial of due process by reason of prosecutorial misconduct. The now-famous author Scott Turow (*One L* and *Presumed Innocent*) was then an Assistant United States Attorney in Illinois. While he was investigating the defendant's lawyer in connection with "Operation Greylord," a federal investigation of corruption in the Cook County courts, the lawyer offered to provide information in relation to the drug trade. The result was that without informing the prosecutors in Florida or the court, Mr. Turow arranged to "wire up" the lawyer to record conversations with the defendant and instructed the lawyer not to violate the attorney-client privilege. At that precise moment, the indictment against the defendant had been dismissed, but criminal proceedings were reinstituted shortly thereafter. No notice of the monitoring was given to defendant and indeed the attorney did not move to withdraw until ten months later, and even then the withdrawal was sealed so that defendant did not discover the reason for nearly a year.

After conviction, the court refused to order dismissal of the indictment because it found that the defendant had not demonstrated any prejudice. It added a footnote that although the conduct of Mr. Turow and of defendant's counsel was not "sufficiently outrageous" to require reversal of the conviction, it was "reprehensible." It therefore assumed that the district judge would "refer this matter to the Illinois Attorney Registration and Discipline Commission . . . for appropriate action." Id. at 1516 n.6. It did not state why it was not, in view of this conclusion, imposing any discipline itself. Perhaps it thought that procedural fairness necessary to support the imposition of discipline required notice and an evidentiary hearing whose focus was the lawyer's conduct. Perhaps it thought that a trial that occurred in Florida and was reviewed in the Eleventh Circuit ought not to be the occasion for discipline of a government lawyer who worked in Illinois and had taken no part in the Florida trial, although defendant's counsel, whose conduct was also criticized as reprehensible, had participated in the trial.

After the opinion was filed, Mr. Turow moved to have the footnote removed from the opinion. The court responded in a 13-page opinion, still unpublished, that rejected the motion. It concluded that since the defendant had argued that his conviction should be reversed because the lawyers' conduct had violated his due process, the review process necessarily had focused on the lawyer's conduct. Going beyond its earlier footnote, the court then concluded that criminal conduct on the part of the government attorney might be involved, and therefore ordered the clerk to forward its order to the United States Attorney for the Southern District of Florida. Subsequently, the Department of Justice announced that there was no basis for criminal prosecution because Mr. Turow's behavior had been proper.

The Court was quite correct in taking so seriously its duty to initiate disciplinary investigations of lawyers' conduct. The issue is whether it should have done so publicly. The issue is a subcategory of the larger question of the stage at which disciplinary authorities should make public the fact that disciplinary proceedings are pending against lawyers or judges. (States vary significantly on when and how much information goes public about lawyer disciplinary proceedings.) The difference here is that the notice is from the court itself, a body that might at least in some cases be taking further action after the disciplinary authorities have acted. Might the court's impartiality be "reasonably questioned" because it prompted the disciplinary action in the place? Cf. In re Murchison, 349 U.S. 133 (1955) (disqualifying a judge who served in multiple roles, including the trier of fact, in a criminal case), discussed in *Williams* above.

In *Ofshe*, the notice given by the court had the beneficial effect of sending an educational message to lawyers concerning the court's view of appropriate lawyer conduct. It also had the beneficial effect of assuring the public that the court was doing its duty with respect to required reporting. Those are important considerations. On the other hand, it clearly did serious injury to a lawyer's reputation in a proceeding in which he never appeared as a party.

It is true that the court was required to focus on the lawyer's conduct in connection with the defendant's appeal and it is also probably true that the major damage to the lawyer's reputation came from the description of his conduct rather than the reference to the disciplinary authorities. It is nevertheless one thing to reach a judgment about the lawyer's conduct for the purpose of dealing with defendant's rights and quite another to link the lawyer so publicly with charges of disciplinary violation when the court was unwilling to undertake the task of disciplinary assessment itself.

The court could certainly have sent a sufficient message to lawyers without the specific reference to possible discipline of this lawyer. The further message regarding discipline would come later if the disciplinary authorities found that the lawyer had engaged in disciplinable conduct. If, however, the state disciplinary authorities find no violation, it is possible that there will be no public notice of that at all. The only item of record in such a situation would be the court's negative comment and not any exoneration. Thus it seems that a court that has the power but is unwilling to undertake the discipline process itself, either directly or through a master or other body appointed by it, ought to be very cautious about the specific comments it makes about discipline. Compare In re Beiny, p. 507, where the court gave public notice of the referral to disciplinary authorities not only of the law firm's conduct in improperly obtaining confidential information but also of the allegation in a newspaper report that a member of the law firm had assaulted another attorney in the Surrogate's Court at a conference in the proceeding. In cases involving conflicts of interest, courts rarely refer the conflicted attorneys for disciplinary investigation. (It is possible that some courts refer the attorneys for disciplinary investigation without making note of that fact in their opinions.) If in fact courts rarely make such referrals (or if they do, they make no public mention of them), are courts neglecting their obligations? What specifically are those obligations? A duty to supervise bar members appearing in their courts? A duty to ensure that litigants receive fair treatment? A duty to protect the public's confidence in the courts by deterring lawyers' unethical conduct? See generally Model Code of Judicial Conduct R. 2.15 (requiring that judges who know that a lawyer or judge has committed an ethical violation must report the violation to the appropriate disciplinary authority whenever the violation "raises a substantial question regarding a lawyer's [or judge's] honesty, trustworthiness, or fitness as a lawyer [or judge] in other respects"). Does that rule clearly answer why judges must report and what conduct they must report?

On the final issue raised by Prof. Kaufman's piece, earlier materials in this book cover the effect of lawyers' rules of conduct on lawyers' freedom of speech. See, e.g., pp. 533–551. There are similar problems with respect to the impact of judges' rules of conduct on their freedom of speech.

Consider, for example, Problem 11–7, which is based on an incident that occurred during the campaign of former Governor Romney of Massachusetts to be the Republican presidential nominee in 2008. Should the judge be permitted to defend herself publicly against criticism from the governor — or from the parties in the case? (On the latter, see generally Mark Harrison & Keith Swisher, "When Judges Should Be Seen, Not Heard: Extrajudicial Comments Concerning Pending Cases and the Controversial Self-Defense Exception in the New Code of Judicial Conduct," 64 N.Y.U. Ann. Surv. Am. L. 559 (2009).) As a result of the Romney incident, the Supreme Judicial Court of Massachusetts appointed a special committee to recommend possible changes in the state's Code of Judicial Conduct relating to the ability of judges to make public comment on their decisions, among other things. In relevant part the Committee recommended the following Rule:

> Except as otherwise provided in this section, a judge shall abstain from public comment about a pending or impending Massachusetts proceeding in any court . . . . A judge does not engage in public comment when he or she speaks during any judicial proceeding in a case or when he or she issues a written memorandum of decision or order entered on the docket of a case.

In its Commentary to the proposed Rule, the Committee explained its intent:

Accordingly, a judge, at any time, may supplement the court record by a written memorandum explaining his or her reasons for judicial action. . . . Canon 2 does not prevent a memorandum of decision from being issued, even in response to public criticism, when that memorandum is based solely on the facts in the record and reflects the judge's reasoning at the time of the original decision, whether or not that reasoning previously was articulated. . . .

Andrew Kaufman, a member of the Committee, dissenting in a lengthy memorandum, commented in part:

> An opinion issued to explain a decision rendered several months or even years before may well be regarded as unfair, especially if it surprises litigants who now assert that they had a basis for appeal that was unknown to them. Even if a method is found for appeal, it may be too late to undo, say, the effects of a bail application decision now believed to have been wrongly denied or granted. In other situations if the Court adopts the Committee's recommendations, presumably it legitimates the use of the second-chance opinion in later proceedings in the matter and as precedent in other cases.
>
> In my view, the Committee's conclusion that a subsequent written opinion, if appropriately rendered, is part of official duties and is not "public comment" is correct. The principal job of judges is deciding controversies between parties. They do so in the courtroom by issuing orders and writing opinions explaining their decisions. Statements of the reasons for their decisions are communicated through those opinions. Considerations of propriety, impartiality, and the appearance thereof of both, enshrined in Canon 2 of Rule 3:09, have long dictated that judges do not explain their own decisions by way of newspaper interviews. . . .
>
> It is very difficult to judge the effect of the Committee's interpretation of Canon 2 on the willingness of judges to write subsequent explanatory opinions. On the one hand, the provision that a judge may write a subsequent opinion "at any time," and even in response to public criticism, assuming that the case is still pending, seems to promise immunity from any assertion of a violation under Canon 2. On the other hand, the immunity is conditioned on the requirement that the subsequent opinion is based solely on the facts in the record and reflects the judge's reasoning at the time of the original decision, whether or not that reasoning previously was articulated. I do not know whether the Committee thinks that judges will be safe because disproving a judge's statement that the second-chance opinion reflects the original reasoning will be exceedingly difficult. But such a view would be misplaced. Canons 2 and 2A prohibit impropriety and require impartiality but also explicitly refer to the appearance of impropriety and the appearance of impartiality. A second-chance opinion written long after the

original decision will, in my view, very often, maybe even nearly always, fail the appearance test. . . .

The Committee's recommendation is that it is up to the judge to decide whether to write an opinion in response to public criticism. The safe harbor provision is designed to banish the public criticism from the judge's mind as he or she complies. "Don't think about the public criticism. Put yourself back in time to the original decision and write the opinion you would have written then." While the Committee would have us believe that the purpose of the second-chance opinion is to educate the public, the opinion in most cases would not be written if there had been no public criticism. The permission given to judges to write a later supplementary opinion when an original opinion was lengthy underlines the "response to public criticism" purpose of the recommendation. But judges are supposed to free themselves as much as possible from outside pressure, from political or media influence. This is indeed one of the arguments made so often in favor of a system of appointed as opposed to elected judges. It will be difficult to write an opinion, months or years after a case was heard, in response to political or media criticism without being defensive in the face of that criticism. . . .

In my view, the more time that has passed from the original ruling, the greater the threat to impartiality (and the appearance of impartiality) of the subsequent opinion. In addition, responding to public criticism of a decision by writing an opinion seems to conflict with the public comment prohibition in the Committee's recommendations. I agree with the Memorandum of Observations that a Letter to the Editor is "fundamentally different" from an opinion on the record. However, the Committee's recommendation virtually directs judges who want to respond to public criticism to do so in the form of a second-chance opinion to be filed on the record. With today's modern technology, that opinion may then be disseminated widely to the media and on the internet. A Letter to the Editor will be the purpose of most such second-chance opinions. No one will be fooled. . . .

The Memorandum of Observations makes the point that the recommended Rule is permissive; the judge does not have to respond. But the judge who does not remember the complete record, or does not want to take the time to write an opinion, or does not believe it appropriate to do so after the fact will be met by the argument that the Rule has been changed to increase public education and judicial accountability, and the judge's refusal to take advantage of the new Rule is further reason for criticism. A true catch-22. . . . I regard the recommendations as an invitation by the Committee, and by the Court if it adopts the recommendations, to enterprising newspaper reporters to follow the dockets and to call upon judges to explain any and all decisions that they find problematic, especially in sensitive areas where there is the possibility of some public or private harm. The Memorandum of Observations states the belief that the advantages of public education given by the second-chance opinion will outweigh the disadvantage of the pressure on judges to write such opinions. In my view, whatever education follows such opinions will be the wrong kind of education as to what judges do. It is precisely because I think judges ought not be writing second-chance opinions in response to public criticism that I regard the Committee's recommendations on this score as harmful, not helpful, to public education about the judicial role. . . .

. . . [M]y own inclination is to limit the ability of a judge to write a subsequent opinion to three situations: *sua sponte* (as opposed to a response to public criticism) within a specific number of days of the original decision unless the judge has specifically stated that a subsequent opinion will be forthcoming; in response to the request of a party pursuant to the rules of procedure; and at the direction of an appellate tribunal. . . . But having limited the permission to write a subsequent opinion in this fashion, I would not restrict the judge, as the Committee has done, to writing the opinion he or she would originally have written. The parties will be available to take any desired action if the judge relies on different facts or a different legal theory.

Notes

1. Which view of the judicial role do you prefer? Is your view driven by a sense of how much like other "political" actors judges are?

2. Under the Committee's proposed Rule, what would a subsequent opinion by Judge Judith in Problem 11–7 defending her release of the defendant look like? Could she refer to the murders the defendant was alleged to have committed?

3. In the actual Problem 11–7 case, the judge in charge of her court, other judicial officials, and members of the bar publicly supported her. But it took time for the system to marshal that support and the support, when it came, could not undo the damage caused by the original headlines and stories. If that scenario is typical, does that lend support to the majority view?

4. The Supreme Judicial Court of Massachusetts ultimately adopted a watered-down version of the proponents' amendment, which now permits judges to issue an "explanatory memorandum" "if issued within a reasonable time of the underlying order and if the judge clearly recalls the judge's reasons for the decision." Mass. Code of Judicial Conduct R. 2.10 cmt. 10. As more narrowly tailored, will the explanatory memoranda likely be acceptable in terms of the balance of judicial values and fairness to the parties? Or will the memoranda likely be defensive and present challenges for parties who wish to challenge those delayed memoranda?

5. As for judges commenting publicly on political issues (and in particular on presidential candidates), Justice Ruth Bader Ginsburg in 2016 criticized the Republican presidential nominee, Donald Trump, in several press interviews. She called him "a faker," who has "no consistency," and argued that he should release his tax returns

(like other candidates had done). Do you think Justice Ginsburg's comments set a beneficial or detrimental precedent for judges? If you see some benefits, did you consider that Mr. Trump (or the next presidential nominee) may come before the Court in a dispute over the election results (see Bush v. Gore)? Or more generally, if the criticized candidate is elected, did you consider that the candidate's administration will routinely appear before the Court in a variety of litigated matters? (Would Justice Ginsburg's comments have been appropriate if she had placed them as a footnote in an opinion?) Justice Ginsburg backed down, however, after criticism from a host of Republican politicians (including Trump), and after several commentators, who seemingly agreed with the merits of Justice Ginsburg's comments, nevertheless concluded that a sitting Justice should not comment publicly on presidential candidates. See, e.g., Editorial Board, "Donald Trump Is Right About Justice Ruth Bader Ginsburg," N.Y. Times, July 13, 2016. Justice Ginsburg issued the following statement (excerpted): "On reflection, my recent remarks in response to press inquiries were ill-advised and I regret making them. Judges should avoid commenting on a candidate for public office. In the future I will be more circumspect." See also David. G. Savage, "Justice Ruth Bader Ginsburg Apologizes for 'Ill-Advised' Criticism of Donald Trump," Los Angeles Times, July 14, 2016.

A sitting judge of the Ninth Circuit, who once served as its Chief Judge, wrote the concluding piece below. He insightfully flags several recurring ethical issues (some recurring daily or hourly) that the judicial ethics code largely fails to address. As with lawyers, the governing code leaves much to individual discretion. (As a potentially interesting aside, the authoring judge would later find himself in judicial ethics trouble for saving sexually explicit and offensive images on his computer and inadvertently permitting the images to be publicly accessible. See In re Complaint of Judicial Misconduct, 575 F.3d 279 (3d Cir. 2009) (admonishing the judge, who was then Chief Judge of the Ninth Circuit, for his conduct). As you will see below, he did not identify this controversial-images issue in advance as a "real" issue in judicial ethics.

Alex Kozinski
The *Real* Issues of Judicial Ethics
32 Hofstra L. Rev. 1095 (2004)

The Canons of Judicial Ethics remind me of the old joke about the drunk who's crawling around on all fours under a lamp-post one night. A policeman comes along and asks him his business and the drunk explains that he's looking for a lost quarter. So the policeman offers to help and pretty soon they're both crawling around looking for the coin. After about a half hour of this, the policeman gets fed up and asks: "Are you sure you lost the quarter around here?" "Oh, no," answers the drunk, "I dropped it over in the alley, but it's too dark to look there."

So, too, it is with the Canons of Judicial Ethics. The Canons focus on the tensions and potential conflicts that are most easily detected by an outside observer. For example, pretty much everyone agrees that a judge should not sit in judgment on a case on appeal if he participated in the decision below. Similarly, everyone agrees that a judge may not sit in judgment in a case where he participated as a party or a lawyer. Of course, those are just two of the most obvious examples; we have plenty of rules and precedents saying that a judge may not participate in a case where doing so would create the appearance of impropriety.

I should mention at the outset that I'm not a fan of this approach to judicial ethics, nor do I believe that it's necessary or inevitable. Take the two examples I've given. As you will recall, in the early days of the Republic the justices rode circuit, and some of the cases they heard in the lower courts would later come before the Supreme Court, so they occasionally reviewed their own decisions. No one thought this was much of a problem. As to the second example, consider Marbury v. Madison. The issue that led to the landmark opinion in that case arose because a commission signed by President Adams, and counter-signed by the Secretary of State, wasn't delivered before Adams left office and Jefferson became President. The Secretary of State later said that he was really sorry not to have delivered the commission, but he was much too busy. Small wonder he was busy: He was holding down two jobs—Secretary of State and Chief Justice. This was, of course, Marshall himself. So Marshall ruled in an important case where he was involved in the underlying dispute.

The approach to disqualification reflected in Marbury v. Madison and cases of that era was based on the common law notion that an integral part of the judge's job is to set aside whatever personal interests and biases he might have, and to decide cases impartially on the merits. If a judge felt that he could not set aside personal biases in a particular case, he would recuse himself. But the primary obligation was to summon the internal fortitude to rise above personal considerations and decide cases impartially on the merits.

I'm not going to argue here that we ought to go back to a regime where a judge's ethical obligation consists entirely of setting aside his personal biases and interests, no matter how serious a conflict he might appear to have. What I do want to point out is that the modern approach, with its focus on *appearance* of impropriety, overlooks the most frequent and important ethical issues judges face. Many of these issues are dull, so get ready to be bored. Nonetheless, they represent the bread and butter of judicial life.

The first ethical issue I want to examine has to do with work allocation—the amount of time and effort judges spend on cases, particularly small cases. Judicial caseloads have increased tremendously over the last few decades, and they continue to do so. When I graduated from law school in 1975 I clerked for the Ninth Circuit, and at that time each judge disposed on the merits of approximately 210 cases per year. In 2002, the number stood at 492 cases per active judge, and the Ninth Circuit is far from the busiest court of appeals in the country. That dubious honor goes to the Eleventh Circuit, which decided 843 cases per judge in 2002. Just imagine what that means: Every judge of the Eleventh Circuit signed off on the merits disposition of 2.3 cases a day, every day of the year—weekends and holidays included.

Add to this the fact that not all cases are created equal. Most judicial work is routine and dull, involving issues that are of no consequence to anyone other than the parties. Only a few cases raise difficult and interesting issues—the kind of issues that make for an important judicial opinion. When lawyers seek appointment to judicial office, they generally think of the interesting cases as the core of judicial work; none I know seeks judicial office so he can spend his days, nights, weekends and holidays slogging through an unending stack of routine, fact-intensive and largely (in the grand scheme of things) inconsequential cases.

Human nature being what it is, there is a strong tendency to devote a disproportionate amount of judicial time to the big cases and to give short shrift to the small ones. There's actually a lot to be said for this. Preparing a precedential opinion requires a significant amount of time because such an opinion not only decides the dispute between the parties, but also sets the course of the law for innumerable cases to come. So you are justified in spending most of your time on the big cases, because you really do have a serious responsibility: A rushed and sloppy opinion can cause major problems for a lot of people down the road. Yet, the small cases, too, have a legitimate claim to a fair share of judicial time and attention.

An important part of the judicial function thus consists of allocating one's time between the big and small cases—and this is a decision judges make almost implicitly and with no possibility of complaint by the parties affected. In fact, no one knows precisely *how* judges allocate their time among the cases assigned to them, but the risk that small and seemingly unimportant cases will be given insufficient attention is ever-present. . . .

Most of the time—nine times out of ten, maybe more—when you're done, you reach the obvious result. And so it seems almost pointless to go to the trouble again and again and again, only to come up with the result you could have guessed from the beginning. It's a bit like banging your head against a padded wall. But then, once in a while, it turns out that what looked like an easy case is actually quite difficult, because of a small fact buried in the record, or a footnote in a recent opinion. After more than two decades of judging I have found no way to separate the sheep from the goats, except by taking a close look. But how close a look any one judge takes in a particular case is strictly a matter of the judge's own conscience. It's one of the embedded ethical issues that no one ever talks about.

A closely related issue is the tendency to delegate essential aspects of the judicial function to staff. At the time I clerked, each federal circuit judge had one secretary and two law clerks. Then, in the early 1980s, the staff complement was increased to five, made up of two secretaries and three law clerks. Sometime in the 1990s, judges were allowed to substitute a law clerk for one of the secretarial positions; I believe most circuit judges take advantage of this option, so that now judges generally have four clerks. In the Eleventh Circuit, by special dispensation, judges have been allocated an additional clerk, apparently because they have not sought the increase in judicial positions that their caseload would justify.

During the same quarter-century, there has been a steep increase in the number of central staff attorneys. In 1975, our court had a skeletal central staff whose function was largely to process motions; all merits cases were handled in chambers by judges and their elbow clerks. Today we have something like seventy staff attorneys, all located in our headquarters in San Francisco, and they process approximately forty percent of the cases in which we issue a merits ruling. When I say process, I mean that they read the briefs, review the record, research the law and prepare a proposed disposition, which they then present to a panel of three judges during a process we call "oral screening"—oral, because the judges don't see the briefs in advance, and because they generally rely on the staff attorney's oral description of the case in deciding whether to sign on to the proposed disposition. An oral screening panel meets for two or three days each month and during that time disposes of a hundred and fifty cases, sometimes more.

The increase in caseload coupled with the proliferation of staff creates a constant temptation for judges to give away essential pieces of their job. The pressure is most severe in the small and seemingly routine cases, especially those handled through the screening process. After you dispose of a few dozen such cases on a screening calendar, your eyes glaze over, your mind wanders and the urge to say okay to whatever is put in front of you becomes almost irresistible. The temptation is heightened by the fact that the staff attorneys who present these cases are very experienced and usually get it right. It often takes a frantic act of will to continue questioning successive staff attorneys about each case, or to insist on reading key parts of the record or controlling precedent to ensure that the case is decided by the three judges whose names appear in the caption, not by a single staff attorney.

A similar temptation exists as to the bigger cases. Writing opinions is a difficult, time-consuming, exacting process. It is a reality of current judicial life that few judges draft their own opinions from scratch. Generally, the judge will give instructions about how a case is to be decided and what points the opinion should make, but the initial drafting is almost always left to a clerk. The draft opinion, when it lands on the judge's desk some weeks later, is generally pretty good—after all, we pick only the best law students as clerks. On reading the opinion, the judge may be able to detect any obvious flaws in reasoning, and he'll certainly be able to make some word edits. But this casual read is a far cry from the time and effort required to study the opinion closely, deconstruct its arguments, examine key portions of the record and carefully parse the precedents—all the things a judge must do before he can call the opinion his own. Nevertheless, if the judge chooses merely to fiddle a bit with an opinion drafted by his clerk and then circulate it, nobody is the wiser. And we do occasionally get opinions circulated that look like they were written by someone a year out of law school with no adult supervision. The only guarantee one can have that judges are not rubber-stamping their law clerks' work product is each judge's sense of personal responsibility.

Let me now turn to the issue [of] . . . cases where a dispassionate application of the law to the facts leads to a result that the judge doesn't like. I want to put aside the close case where the law is murky enough so the judge might find a principled way to reach a result he considers just. I also want to put aside the controversial case where the morally offended judge applies the correct law but then makes noise to spark political efforts to change the law. Rather, I pose the more mundane—but far more common—case where the law is fair, no one in particular has an axe to grind, but the judge believes that the result dictated by precedent is unjust.

Most people would say that the judge in that situation must put aside his personal feelings about the result and decide the case in accordance with the law. But I also think that most would agree that the judge faces a conflict of obligations—the obligation to apply the law impartially, and the obligation to do justice. We generally reconcile these obligations by saying that justice is served when judges apply the law impartially, regardless of the personal views of the decision-maker.

So far so good. But what if a judge comes across a case where a straight-forward application of the law leads not merely to a result he doesn't like, but to what he believes is a shocking injustice? May a judge bend the rule of law to avoid a truly monstrous result? Might he have an ethical obligation to do so?

In theory, it's easy enough to say that a judge may never bend the rules to avoid a particular result, no matter how bad. But consider this example: You are reviewing a criminal appeal where a young man has been convicted of murder and sentenced to life without the possibility of parole. You examine the record and find that the evidence linking the defendant to the crime is quite flimsy—witness identifications are tentative and contradictory, and there is no circumstantial evidence whatsoever. The only solid piece of evidence supporting the conviction is what is known as a jailhouse confession—the testimony of an inmate who shared a cell with the defendant while he was awaiting trial, and who swears that the defendant confessed to the murder (a confession the defendant denies making). You read this testimony closely and find it transparently unconvincing. It contains no authenticating information that the witness could only have obtained from the real killer. And, of course, the witness has been given a sweetheart plea bargain in exchange for his testimony.

Applying the rules of appellate review in an objective manner, you would have to affirm the conviction. After all, the jury is the trier of fact and it was entitled to return a guilty verdict based on the jailhouse confession alone. Yet, what if you believe, to a moral certainty, that the confession is a fabrication and that the defendant didn't do it? Must you affirm the conviction and let a young man you believe to be innocent spend the next eighty years, or whatever time is left to him on earth, locked up in a ten-foot by fifteen-foot cell?

Or, if you're not moved by this hypothetical, consider the case where the defendant is convicted of multiple brutal murders of small children—crimes of which he is doubtless guilty. And let's say you're convinced that, if the defendant is released, he will surely do it again and again. As it happens, however, this defendant has a slam-dunk argument that the prosecution's entire case against him rested on the product of a technical procedural violation. In such circumstances, do you have an obligation to set the defendant free and possibly condemn unknown children to death by torture, or may you put justice above the law and find a way to affirm the conviction?

I used to think that questions like these had an easy answer—you apply the law conscientiously and don't worry about the consequences. But I'm no longer sure. I now wonder whether this isn't false modesty, a kind of hubris: I will accept whatever result the law calls for, no matter how much it hurts somebody else. A troubled conscience is certainly not pleasant, but the real-life, brutal consequences of an unjust judicial decision are suffered by others—the innocent kid who wastes his life in a prison cell, or the future victims of the slasher released on a technicality.

I am reminded that among the most reviled participants in the Third Reich's persecution of Jews and other minorities were the German judges who enforced the Nuremberg laws. These judges claimed as justification that they were simply applying the law. Our collective assessment seems to be that the judges shirked their responsibility—that they should have used their power and authority to undermine unjust laws. Do American judges have a similar ethical obligation? I'm not going to suggest an answer here because it's a tough question. Instead, I'll simply point out that this is the kind of ethical question that matters, that makes a difference. It arises all the time and yet the Canons of Judicial Ethics have no answers.

Lots of ethical questions like these pop up every day in the course of judging but don't show up anywhere in the Canons. Here are a few more examples, briefly stated:

• Do you have an ethical obligation to dissent, even if you know it won't change anybody's mind and will probably anger your colleagues?

• If you've decided a case in favor of a criminal defendant who is incarcerated pending the outcome of his appeal, do you have a responsibility to move the case ahead of other work so he will be released more quickly? Or, if you're going to rule that the giant corporation can evict the old lady because she can't pay the rent, is it okay to put that case at the bottom of the work pile and not get to it until the snow melts?

• If you are writing an opinion and there are inconvenient facts in the record, may you simply leave them out (as lawyers sometimes do), or do you have an obligation to mention them?

• In finding against a party, may you caricature the party's argument (as lawyers sometimes do) to make it seem less persuasive?

• Is it okay to swap votes with another judge—say vote in favor of taking en banc a case he's interested in, in exchange for having him vote with you in a case you're interested in?

• There's a death penalty case, a second petition. The panel votes to let the execution go forward, the en banc vote is tied and you are the last to vote, so your vote is going to be decisive. You are convinced that the Supreme Court will never take the case, so voting "no" means the petitioner will be dead in forty-eight hours. In deciding how to vote, may you take into account the life-and-death consequences of your decision, or are you ethically bound to approach the case as if it were about arbitrability of employment contracts? . . .

• You are a federal district judge. Naturally, you hope to be elevated to the court of appeals, and some friends in high places have intervened with the White House on your behalf; it looks like you have a good chance of getting the promotion. As you're waiting for the political process to run its course, you preside over a high-profile criminal case where the defendant is convicted, and you have to impose the sentence. You review the presentence report and various other materials, and you conclude that the defendant is entitled to a substantial downward departure from the range calculated according to the Sentencing Guidelines. The Assistant United States Attorney, though, vehemently opposes any downward departure. In determining the defendant's sentence, may you take into account that the Attorney General of the United States has instituted a policy requiring all Assistant United States Attorneys to report downward departures by district judges?

Every magistrate judge is a district judge in waiting; every district judge is a circuit judge in waiting; every circuit judge is an associate justice in waiting; and every associate justice is a chief justice in waiting. Every state judge wants to be re-elected and, hopefully, promoted—perhaps within the state judicial hierarchy, perhaps into the federal judiciary. How does a judge reconcile his personal ambitions with the requirements of principled application of the law and sensitivity to individual justice? The Canons of Judicial Ethics don't begin to address this issue. Indeed, they don't recognize it as an ethical issue at all, yet the temptation to decide cases in a way that will please those in the political process who have the power to appoint, retain and promote judges is one of the most ubiquitous moral hazards facing members of the judiciary.

How serious are these issues? Let me explain it this way: I file a financial disclosure report every year, telling the world what assets I own, just so litigating parties can confirm that I did not—God forbid—sit in a case involving a corporation whose stock I hold. I find this requirement a nuisance and a bit dangerous and intrusive, because it discloses things about me and my family, and our assets, that I would prefer to keep private. But I file the report because it's considered an important safeguard of judicial integrity.

Yet I can't imagine that I could possibly be tempted to change my vote in a case because I own stock in one of the parties. I don't claim a special virtue in this, if virtue means resisting temptation. What I'm saying is, I wouldn't be tempted. If money were important to me, I'd be in private practice and, in a month or a week—maybe in an hour—I would make much more than my one hundred shares of AT&T could possibly change in value based on my vote in a case. The idea that I would give up my honest judgment in a case for a few dollars is beyond silly—it's ludicrous and insulting. So many of the things contained within the Canons, the ones most talked about, are wholly irrelevant in practice. They make no difference at all.

But the internal temptations that I described above are ones I confront every day. Giving short shrift to small cases, signing on to the work of staff and calling it my own, bending the law to reach a result I like—and the dozens of other ways in which I feel the pressure to do something unethical, yet wholly undetectable by anyone other than me—all these temptations I must fight off many times every single day.

My problem with the appearance of impropriety standard isn't so much that it's bad on its own terms, though I think it probably is. Rather, the standard promotes the wrong idea—that in order to keep judges from acting unethically, ethical rules must prevent judges from *appearing* to act unethically. It also seems to suggest the converse: that if judges appear to be acting ethically, they probably are. Nothing could be further from the truth. A judge can appear to act ethically and still betray his responsibility in essential respects, and in ways that no one will ever know about. Increasing the number of rules and prohibitions—making sure that judges don't attend conferences at swank resorts with plush golf courses—will do absolutely nothing to increase judicial responsibility where it counts. To the contrary, the more rules you have, the more hoops judges have to jump through to avoid the appearance of impropriety, the more likely they are to feel that the hoop-jumping is the alpha and omega of their ethical responsibilities, and the less likely they are to give careful thought to the job's real ethical pitfalls.

I know there is a growing tendency to distrust judges—to craft more elaborate ethical rules and restrictions; to expand the scope of what is encompassed within the appearance of impropriety standard; to adopt more and better methods of intruding into judges' private lives—all in a misguided effort to promote ethical judicial behavior. But the hard truth is that none of these things really matters. Judicial ethics, where it counts, is hidden from view, and no rule can possibly ensure ethical judicial conduct. Ultimately, there is no choice but to trust the judges. Maybe we need some external rules, maybe we don't. But, to my mind, we'd all be better off in a world with fewer rules and a more clear-cut understanding that impartiality and diligence are obligations that permeate every aspect of judicial life—obligations that each judge has the unflagging responsibility to police for himself.

Notes

1. In your preliminary but now generally informed opinion, did Judge Kozinski identify the "real" issues in judicial ethics? If not, what are the real issues in judicial ethics?

2. Should the judicial ethics code particularly address the issues that Judge Kozinski raises? How could these issues be fairly and efficiently regulated?

3. Finally, Judge Kozinski calls "elaborate ethical rules and restrictions . . . a misguided effort," claims that "we'd all be better off in a world with fewer rules," and implies that matters of impartiality and diligence should be left to each judge "to police for himself." Are these claims just another example of a judiciary that does not wish to be regulated in any fashion? Is Judge Kozinski really asking whether we need legal ethics rules at all? Should lawyers and judges be regulated only by their professional conscience, with sanctions if any left to other controls (e.g., market, agency)?

Chapter 12

Demographics, Institutions, and Professional Identity: The American Legal Profession in the Twenty-First Century

The American legal profession has changed dramatically since its modest origins in the original colonies. From a few hundred mostly untrained purveyors of legal services in the 1600s, the American bar has grown to approximately 1.3 million lawyers, each of whom has completed four years of college, three years of law school, and passed a bar examination and character and fitness review. Changes in the organization of legal practices have been equally dramatic. During the colonial period—and for most of the next three hundred years—the vast majority of lawyers were solo practitioners engaged in the private practice of law. Today, most lawyers work in some form of organizational setting (e.g., law firm, government legal office, corporate law department), some of which consist of several thousand lawyers. Finally, the demographics of the profession have also been radically transformed. For the better part of its history, the American legal profession was the exclusive province of white, Anglo-Saxon, Protestant men. Beginning in the late nineteenth century and accelerating dramatically after 1970, a substantial number of women, and smaller, but still significant numbers of racial, ethnic, and religious minorities have integrated the bar. Demographic trends in the country as a whole, as well as globalization in the legal services market, seem destined to accelerate these trends in the coming decades.

Developments in the years since the global financial crisis that began in 2008 have further accelerated these developments as well as destabilized many existing patterns. Applications to law schools have fallen by more than 40%, and in 2015 the percentage of law school graduates who obtained employment in a job for which a J.D. was required fell to approximately 60%. The large law firm sector was particularly hard hit, with many firms laying off associates and even partners between 2008 and 2012, and several prominent law firms closing their doors altogether. Whether these developments signal the "Death of Big Law"—or even more apocalyptically "The End of Lawyers"—as some have speculated, there can be little doubt that the legal profession in the U.S. and around the world is undergoing an important transformation. The explosion in the number of legal start-ups attempting to bring what the business school scholar Clayton Christiansen calls "disruptive innovation" to virtually every phase of the legal marketplace underscores that this transformation is only likely to accelerate in the coming decades.

In this Chapter, we provide a brief overview of these trends and suggest some of the ways that changes in the profession's size, structure, and demographics may affect legal ethics, the delivery and distribution of legal services, and lawyer career paths. We concentrate on the transformation of the private practice sector. (For information about lawyers employed in government, legal services, and public interest organizations, see Chapter 9). Notwithstanding the growth in the number of lawyers employed by government and other public sector employers, the overwhelming majority of lawyers are engaged in the private practice of law. Part A surveys the demographic and organizational changes in private practice since 1960 and examines how these changes have helped to solidify the division of the legal profession into two increasingly unequal hemispheres: those lawyers who represent corporations and other large organizational interests and those who represent individuals. Part B examines the "corporate" hemisphere, with a particular emphasis on large law firms and in-house legal departments. Part C then turns to the "individual" hemisphere, examining the challenges and practice arena of solo and small firm lawyers and their clients. Part D concludes by examining what effect, if any, the profession's changing demographics might have on traditional notions about what it means to be a professional.

A. An Overview of the Modern Legal Profession

1. The United States Lawyer Population

The United States lawyer population grew from just over 64,000 in 1878 to over 100,000 in 1900, 200,000 in 1945 and 300,000 in 1965. The 1970s and 1980s saw a dramatic rise in the number of lawyers: from just over 325,000 in 1970 to just shy of 500,000 in 1979, an impressive increase of approximately 50%; to over 750,000 in 1990, yet another 50% increase. The lawyer population topped 1,000,000 in 1999, and exceeded 1,300,000 in 2016. See ABA National Lawyer Population Survey, Historical Trend in Total National Lawyer Population, 1878–2016, available at<http://www.americanbar.org/content/dam/aba/administrative/market_research/total-national-lawyer-population-1878-2016.authcheckdam.pdf>.

Since 1951, the growth rate of the lawyer population has regularly exceeded that of the general U.S. population as reflected in declining population/lawyer ratios from 1 lawyer per 695 persons in 1951, to 1 per 264 in 2000, to 1 per 249 in 2016. Of course, these numbers should be taken with a grain of salt, as they do not necessarily reflect improved access to law and lawyers for all people. To begin with, the U.S. population is not an accurate measure of consumers of legal services served by U.S. attorneys. Many lawyers and law firms serve, sometimes predominantly, organizations and entities as opposed to people, and some serve non-U.S. clients. Moreover, the lawyer population is not evenly distributed: whereas densely populated urban areas tend to have lower population/lawyer ratios; rural areas, as we shall see in Part C, feature higher ratios.

An essential component of lawyer population growth in the period from 1960 to 2016 was the steady rise in law school enrollments and a consequent yearly increase in law degrees conferred. Law schools graduated fewer than 10,000 in the 1963–64 academic year; doubled that to over 20,000 in 1972–73, and doubled the number of graduates to over 40,000 in academic year 1993–94. The number of graduates peaked in 2012–2013, reaching 46,766. Notably, in 2013–14 law schools graduated 43,832, a 6.5% decline from the previous year, and graduated only 39,984 in 2014–15, yet another decline of nearly 9% compared with the class of 2014. See ABA Section of Legal Education and Admissions to the Bar Statistics, available at<http://www.amer icanbar.org/groups/legal_education/resources/statistics.html>.

2. The Changing Gender Composition of the Lawyer Population

A corresponding change in the lawyer population growth over the last five decades has been the rise in the number of women entering the profession. While no more than 3% of the lawyer population in the early 1970s were women, by the year 2000 women accounted for 28% of all U.S. lawyers, and by 2016 they accounted for 36% of all lawyers. See ABA Lawyer Demographics Year 2016, available at<http://www .americanbar.org/content/dam/aba/administrative/market_research/lawyer -demographics-tables-2016.authcheckdam.pdf>.

Recent statistics collected by the ABA Commission on Women in the Profession reveal the rising prominence of women lawyers. Women attorneys in private practice account for 21.5% of all partners (but only 18% of equity partners), 18% of managing partners at the 200 largest law firms, 44.7% of all associates and 47.8% of all summer associates. In corporations, women attorneys account for 24% of Fortune 500 General Counsel. In legal academia, women account for 31.1% of all law deans, and women law students accounted for 47.3% of all J.D. degrees awarded. In the judiciary, women accounted for 27.1% of federal and state judges. See A Current Glance at Women in the Law May 2016, available at<http://www.americanbar.org/con tent/dam/aba/marketing/women/current_glance_statistics_may2016.authcheck dam.pdf>.

3. The Changing Age Composition of the Lawyer Population

The age composition of lawyer populations has varied over time. The median age of the lawyer population in 1960 was 46 years. By 1980, the median had declined to 39 years as the upsurge in new admissions during the 1970s swelled the ranks of young lawyers. The median age began to climb thereafter as the yearly rate of increase in the number of new admissions moderated, and veteran lawyers continued to practice past historically traditional retirement age. In 1991, the median age had risen to

41, in 2000 it reached 45, and in 2005 the median age was 49. See ABA Lawyer Demographics Year 2016.

4. Lawyers' Practice Settings

A majority and growing percentage of U.S. lawyers engage in private practice. Whereas in 1980 private practice accounted for 68% of all lawyers, that percentage has steadily risen to 73% in 1991, 74% in 2000 and 75% in 2005. In contrast, other practice settings have remained relatively stable over time, with government lawyers accounting for 8%, private industry for 8%, retired and inactive lawyers for 4%, the judiciary for 3% and law professors, legal aid and public defenders and private association lawyers each accounting for approximately 1% of all lawyers.

Within private practice, solo practitioners constitute a stable majority, accounting for 49% of lawyers in 1980 and again in 2005. Notably, law firms of 2–5 lawyers have been in steady decline, from 22% in 1980, to 15% in 1991 and 2000, and to 14% in 2005. Law firms of 6–10 and 11–20 lawyers have also declined somewhat over time from 9% and 7% respectively in 1980 to 6% in 2005, and were joined by law firms of 51–100 lawyers, which declined from 7% in 1980 to 4% in 2005. In contrast, law firms of 101+ lawyers have consistently grown, accounting for 13% in 1991, 14% in 2000 and 16% in 2005. See ABA Lawyer Demographics Year 2016.

The numbers suggest that the growth of the large law firms has come at the expense of their mid-size competitors, and that as large law firms continued to grow and redefine the meaning of "large," the allure of small law firms of 2–5 lawyers declined, perhaps as their lawyers realized that if solo practice was unappealing to them, they were better off finding relative shelter in law firms of at least 6–10 lawyers.

5. Lawyers' Pay

The National Association for Law Placement's salary distribution curves for the classes of 2006 to 2014 reveal a pattern of unequal income distribution. Whereas the median income of new lawyers rose from $62,000 in 2006 to $72,000 in 2008, and the adjusted mean was approximately $77,000 in both 2010 and 2014, these numbers hide a stark income inequality. While the majority of newcomers into the profession feature a more or less normal distribution peaking at $45,000–65,000 annually, entry-level associates at large law firm earn on average $135,000 in 2006 and $165,000 in 2014. See <http://www.nalp.org/salarydistrib>.

Other data supports this finding among more experienced lawyers. For example, based on IRS tax return numbers for solo practitioners and law firm partners, Ben Barton has argued that the middle class of American lawyers is hollowing out. Barton has found that adjusted for inflation, in 1967 law firm partners earned roughly $173,000 and solo practitioners earned $74,580. Both of these amounts were above the median income, and while partners were wealthier, there was not an unimaginable gap between the two groups. By 2012, however, solo practitioners had seen

Figure 12.1 Distribution of Reported Full-Time Salaries—Class of 2014

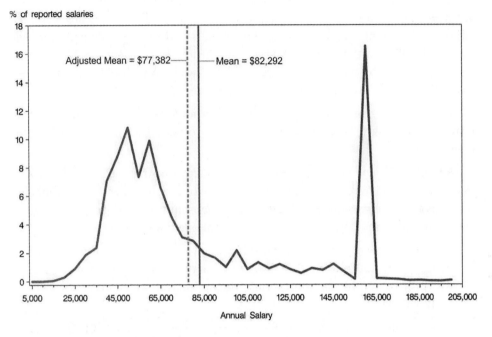

© NALP, 2015
www.nalp.org

their incomes fall to $49,130, a 34% decrease, while partners earned $349,000, a 100% increase. ($49,130, to be sure, was not the starting salary for solo practitioners. Rather, it is the average income of all 354,000 lawyers who filed as solo practitioners in 2012, including those who have practiced law their whole lives.) Thus, in 2012 partners in law firms earned more than seven times what a solo practitioner earned. American lawyers, asserts Barton, used to be able to count on a middle class existence. Now law school is much more of a high stakes gamble. See Benjamin H. Barton, *Glass Half Full: The Decline and Rebirth of the Legal Profession* (2015).

––––––––––

One obvious question raised by the tremendous growth in the number of lawyers in the postwar years—and particularly during the next thirty years, when the profession doubled in size from 1970 to 1985, and nearly doubled again in the last fifteen years is: Why are there so many lawyers? Consider the following explanation offered by then-Dean Robert Clark, of Harvard Law School.

Robert C. Clark
Why So Many Lawyers? Are They Good or Bad?
61 Fordham L. Rev. 275 (1992)

In 1960, there was one lawyer for every 627 people in the United States. In 1988, there was one lawyer for every 339 people. During the last half of this twenty-eight year period, the number of lawyers in the United States increased at a rate that was more than five times faster than the rate of growth for the general population. We are now moving toward the landmark figure of one million U.S. lawyers. And although the recent recession was accompanied by a drop in the demand for legal services, in 1991, for the fifth consecutive year, the total enrollment at ABA-approved law schools actually increased. I calculate that if we keep going in this way, by the year 2023 there will be more lawyers than people.

Is this trend bad or good? Do we really understand why it has occurred? I intend to return to the latter question, but I first want to establish the magnitude of the phenomenon.

Not only has there been an extraordinary increase during the last three decades in the number of lawyers, both absolutely and relative to the general population, but there has also been great measurable growth in the amount of legal services consumed and in the amount of law. This growth is evident in a few facts . . . :

— In the twenty-five year period after 1960, the population of the United States grew by 30%. Keep this 30% growth figure in mind as a benchmark for comparison. In the same period, the number of lawyers increased by almost 130%.

— In the same twenty-five year period, the percentage of GNP devoted to outside legal services more than doubled.

— In the same period, the amount of law increased exponentially, as suggested by these tidbits:

  • pages added annually to the Federal Register increased by 270%;

  • pages added annually to the West regional reporters grew by 149%;

  • pages added annually to the federal reporters grew by 336% (about 93,588 pages of federal cases added in 1985 alone, for example);

  • the full-time staff of the fifty-five major federal regulatory agencies grew 176%, and their budgets increased by 237%.

The point to note about these figures is that they are all *much* greater than the growth of the population and the economy, and that this difference has prevailed for a long time—since World War II, actually—not just for the last few years, or during the booming 1980s. Furthermore, other evidence suggests that many other countries are becoming more, not less, like the United States in their reliance on law and lawyers. In Europe, for example, the continued growth and complexification of the institutions of the European Community have been accompanied by an upsurge in legal activity. Brussels has become like Washington, D.C., where everyone is presumed to be a lawyer until proven otherwise. In South Korea, Taiwan, and Japan the legal profession acts like a monopoly to hold down pass rates on the bar exam, but inexorable pressures have built up to increase the yield of formally denominated lawyers. In Eastern Europe and in the former Soviet Union, the demand for legal experts to help devise an infrastructure for democratically oriented market economies is almost insatiable. In sum, law and lawyers have become more important in our society and, in fact, throughout much of the world. . . .

How should we regard these trends? To many observers and commentators, it has seemed clear that something rotten and unhealthy has been going on. Vice President Quayle caused a stir in the national media by suggesting that there are too many lawyers and too much litigation, and that something should be done about it. Commentator Walter Olson published a book entitled *The Litigation Explosion*, and many others have used the phrase, typically with an indignant tone. Derek Bok, the former president of Harvard University, has written and spoken of the regrettable situation that has resulted from the luring of the best and brightest young minds away from science, engineering, education, and public service and into the legal profession and business.

My view, however, is that it is premature to denounce the growth of law and lawyers. We should first seek to *understand* the causes and consequences of this growth far better than we currently do. . . .

[After looking at a variety of evidence, Dean Clark reaches the following conclusions:]

• The growth of law and lawyers in the last generation is real, dramatic, and pervasive.

• To understand the growth of law, it is important to develop a comprehensive notion of what lawyers do: they are specialists in normative ordering.

• Some explanations of the growth of law make it out to be a cancerous and essentially unhealthy process. Though some of these accounts contain a significant core of truth, they appear to be unsatisfactory if put forward as full (or even leading) explanations of the phenomenon of law's explosive growth.

• The theory of moral decline would appear to explain legal growth only in a few areas such as criminal and family law.

• Claims of lawyer-created demand seem implausible if meant to be major explanations of growth in law, for they do not seem to account satisfactorily for the creation of major legislative and regulatory schemes and they tend to ignore the reasons why individuals and organizations are willing to seek out and pay for lawyers' services.

• The theory of market imperfections does suggest that there may be significant fat and inflation in the market for legal services, as in the markets for all other professional services, but these flaws hardly seem capable of explaining the bulk of growth in the law, or its distribution across subject matters and types of practice.

• Some explanations for the growth of law suggest that it is essentially a benign process. My approach was to suggest that certain long term trends have increased the demand for normative ordering, and thus, the demand for law and lawyers. I concentrated on four such trends; I don't claim to have presented a full list. The four are:

- greater internationalization and other forms of interaction;
- greater diversity in the population;
- changes in wealth levels; and
- greater involvement of the workforce in formal organizations.

In each case, I presented preliminary evidence to indicate that the trend is real and serious, and I explained why there is a connection between the trend and demonstrable growth in specific areas of law and law practice that one would expect to be affected by that trend. It is a hidden leitmotif of these explanations that the normative ordering generated by these trends is in principle a value-increasing service, not a parasitic or pointless activity.

Obviously, much more work is needed to develop and test hypotheses of the sort I have put forth. I claim only to have made them plausible enough to warrant and stimulate further refinement and testing. Nevertheless, they do generate a certain sort of cautious hope about our profession. To the extent that they or similar accounts are valid, they hardly justify complacency about the legal system, but they do appear to rule out deep cynicism. No doubt there is much about the legal profession that ought to be changed. But the profession appears already to be a useful one, for the whole modern world is demanding its services. And it can properly aspire to be noble, for at its best its members' services can augment the sum of human welfare.

Notes

1. What are the implications for legal ethics of Dean Clark's contention that lawyers are specialists in "normative ordering"? For example, how might defining normative ordering as the "essence" of the lawyer's role affect the debate among Professors Pepper, Luban, and Kaufman regarding the ethical defense of an "amoral" role in which lawyers are required to zealously pursue their clients' objectives so long as they are within the "bounds of the law"? Similarly, does Clark's hypothesis suggest a greater or lesser role for public actors in the debate over who should regulate lawyers?

2. How convincing do you find Dean Clark's explanation for the growth in the number of lawyers — including both his rejection of the "cancerous" explanations and the four "benign" explanations that he offers in the alternative? Even if you agree that internationalization, diversity, increasing wealth levels, and larger organizations have spurred demand for "normative ordering," is it clear that society is better off when *lawyers* are hired to fill this need as opposed to other potential service providers? Does Dean Clark's — or your — answer to this last set of questions depend upon the scope and content of the unauthorized practice rules or the rules regarding multidisciplinary practice?

3. Are you surprised that Dean Clark takes a positive view about the growth in the legal profession?

4. Dean Clark identifies diversity, both in society and in the profession, as one of the causes for the growth in the number of lawyers. We will return to this issue below.

———————

The change has been even more dramatic, however, with respect to lawyers who have entered the bar in recent years. Consider the following excerpt from the third wave of data collection of a ten-year longitudinal study of over 5000 lawyers who entered the bar in 2000.

Ronit Dinovitzer, et al.
After the JD III: Third Results of a National Study
of Legal Careers (2014)

pp. 26–30

Where lawyers work varies substantially depending on their career stages. When we first surveyed AJD lawyers in 2003, they were just beginning their careers. At that time, about 70% of respondents were working in private law firms, just less than one quarter were working in the public sector, and the small remainder were in business (either practicing law or not). Wave 2, which provided a snapshot of lawyers seven years into their careers, showed a significant contraction in the private law firm sector, countered by strong growth in the business sector. The tremendous sectoral shifts experienced by respondents by Wave 2 appear to have persisted, with a continued contraction in the private sector and a growth in the business sector. At Wave 3, which is the 12-year career milestone, we found 48.5% of respondents working in the private law firm sector, 28% working in the public sector, and 20% working in business (with another 3.5% indicating working in "other" settings).

From the perspective of Wave 3, it now appears that the Wave 2 survey indicated another important milestone regarding respondents' employment patterns. While, at Wave 1, the proportion of respondents working full time was at a high of 94%, this number shrank to 87% at Wave 2, and Wave 3 shows the proportion had remained fairly stable since Wave 2, with 86% of AJD3 respondents working full time. As before, most of those working part time or not working in the paid labor force continue to be women.

Private Law Firm Practice

The overall proportion of lawyers working in private law firms has declined since Wave 2. As might be expected given both the economic context and respondents' career stages (with most respondents in law firms facing the partnership decision after the AJD2 survey), the proportion of AJD lawyers in large law firms (>250) showed the greatest decline since AJD respondents had begun their careers, from a high of about 18 percent at Wave 1 to 8.3% at Wave 3. Overall, the representation of lawyers in law firms of over 21 lawyers declined between Wave 2 and Wave 3, though in some cases the reduction was very small, while the proportion working in solo

Figure 12.2

TABLE 3.1a. Practice Settings by Firm Size and Waves 1-3

Practice Setting	Wave 1			Wave 2			Wave 3		
	N	% np	Total%	N	% np	Total%	N	% np	Total%
Solo	185	2.3	5.4	303	3.0	9.6	232	2.8	10.0
Firm of 2-20 lawyers	900	0.5	25.1	616	0.9	18.3	419	1.0	18.0
Firm of 21-100 lawyers	459	0.2	12.3	306	0.5	8.1	180	0.6	7.7
Firm of 101-250 lawyers	279	0.5	7.0	165	2.2	4.7	80	0.0	3.4
Firm of 251+ lawyers	726	0.5	18.2	433	5.4	11.1	192	4.2	8.3
Firm size unknown	21	1.7	0.5	101	0.0	3.2	26	4.1	1.1
Government—federal	173	20.4	4.5	188	25.9	5.2	129	28.2	5.5
Government – state	395	14.6	12.0	354	14.7	11.7	288	17.1	12.4
Legal services or public defender	103	1.4	3.0	66	10.9	1.7	68	19.9	2.9
Public Interest	41	14.4	1.1	35	31.3	1.1	22	13.1	1.0
Nonprofit or education and other	76	63.1	2.1	173	67.7	5.1	145	76.2	6.2
Business – inside counsel	160	0.0	4.2	360	0.0	11.0	293	0.0	12.6
Business—not practicing	157	100.0	4.2	256	100.0	7.9	171	100.0	7.4
Other	9	47.6	0.3	35	25.9	3.5	82	51.4	3.5
Total	**3,684**	**9.0**	**100.0**	**3,391**	**16.5**	**100.0**	**2,329**	**19.2**	**100.0**

Note: Using national sample. Not Practicing (np) = % within category not practicing law.

and small firms of 2–20 lawyers remained virtually the same between Waves 2 and 3 of the study.

Most private firm lawyers responding to AJD3 worked at smaller firms of 2–20 lawyers, with the next largest group in solo practice. It is also worth noting that the proportion of AJD lawyers working as solo practitioners remained fairly low when compared to the full population of lawyers: the ABF's *Lawyer Statistical Report for 2005* shows that, of lawyers working in private law firms, almost half were working as solo practitioners.

Government

As the private sector has been shrinking, the proportion of AJD respondents working in government has grown slightly, from 16.5% in Wave 1 to 17.9% at Wave 3. State and local government continue to employ a greater proportion of government lawyers, with the remainder working in the federal government. As noted above, a substantial proportion of government lawyers report they are not practicing law (28.2% in federal government and 17.1% in state or local government).

Legal Services, Public Interest and Nonprofit/Education

The legal services, public interest, and nonprofit sector also experienced minor growth since Wave 2 of the study. With 10.1% of AJD3 respondents working in these settings, compared to 7.9% in Wave 2, the growth since Wave 2 might be, in part, because of the current economic climate. Most of the growth has been among those holding positions in legal services or as public defenders, accompanied by a small increase in the nonprofit/education category. As noted, these are diverse positions, with many respondents reporting that they are not practicing law in their jobs; indeed, three quarters of those working in nonprofit/education (including law professors) reported they were not practicing law.

Business

The path to business appears well travelled among this cohort of lawyers, as this sector continues to represent a substantial segment of AJD respondents. While only 8% of AJD respondents began their careers in business, by Wave 2, those working in this sector grew to 19% and, in Wave 3, to 20%.

Working in business means different things for different respondents. Of AJD respondents working in the business sector, just over one third were not practicing law. Of those who were in business but not practicing law, about one quarter were working in Fortune 1000 firms, one third were working in a professional service firm, and 40% were working in some other business or industry. Of those who were in business but practicing law, about half were working in Fortune 1000 firms, 38% were in other businesses or industries, and 10% were in professional service firms.

Although the majority of lawyers continue to work in private practice, that should not be taken to mean that the careers of all lawyers in this sector are substantially the same. While it remains common to speak about "the" legal profession, a growing body of research has emphasized the important differences among lawyers who work in various sectors of the practicing bar. The following three excerpts explore one of the most important fault lines identified in this research—the difference between lawyers who represent "corporate clients" and those who represent "individuals—and explores the ramifications of this division, as well as its continuing significance as the legal profession has evolved in the first two decades of the twenty-first century.

John P. Heinz and Edward O. Laumann
Chicago Lawyers: The Social Structure of the Bar (1982)
pp. 319–321, 327–332

... As the analysis presented in this book has unfolded, we have advanced the thesis that much of the differentiation within the legal profession is secondary to one fundamental distinction—the distinction between lawyers who represent large organizations (corporations, labor unions, or government) and those who represent individuals. The two kinds of law practice are the two hemispheres of the profession. Most lawyers reside entirely in one hemisphere or the other and seldom, if ever, cross the equator.

Lawyers who serve major corporations and other large organizations differ systematically from those who work for individuals and small business whether we look at the social origins of the lawyers, the prestige of the law schools they attended, their career histories and mobility, their social or political values, their networks of friends and professional associates, or several other social variables. Though there certainly are distinctions among lawyers that cut across the line between the two broad classes of clients, this fundamental difference in the nature of the client served appears to be the principal factor that structures the social differentiation of the profession. . . .

. . . Like other persons, lawyers have private causes. They may act as "moral entrepreneurs," and this may bring them into conflict with other lawyers who have opposing moral principles. But their principles may also be influenced by their areas of practice. The corporate lawyers who dominate the Association of the Bar of the City of New York advocate "no fault" systems of automobile accident compensation. They never touch a personal injury case. And they are vigorously opposed by the personal injury plaintiffs' lawyers, whose voice is the American Trial Lawyers Association. The personal injury lawyers complain that the corporate lawyers "don't understand our problems." It is certainly true that one of the consequences of specialization is that the different roles may come to exist in separate social worlds and that, as they lose contact with one another, the lawyers may also lose some of their sensitivity to one another's problems, thus diminishing consensus on the profession's goals. . . .

. . . [T]he types of clients represented, the mechanism by which lawyers obtain business, the sorts of tasks performed, the organizational setting of the practice, the type of law school attended, and the religion of the practitioners appear to create an overall structure that is strongly associated with the extent to which Chicago lawyers perceive that each of the fields has a claim to deference within the profession. Further analysis persuaded us that the nature of prestige within the profession largely reflected the types of clients served by the fields. . . . Because there will be fewer [opportunities for the display of valued characteristics such as intelligence, creativity, professional skill in legal research] in the sort of law practice that processes a large volume of cases for relatively impecunious clients than in the practice of law for clients who are able to pay for the hours consumed in creativity and introspection, prestige accorded to creative, intellectually satisfying work will ipso facto be accorded to work done for clients with deep pockets. The wealth and intellectual challenge variables are, thus, closely interrelated, and it is therefore difficult to determine whether the prestige of the fields is to be attributed more to client type or to the differential opportunities that the fields present for the exercise of intellectual skills. But comparison of the prestige of the two sides of doctrinal areas of the law that the adversary system divides into opposing fields — criminal prosecution versus criminal defense, labor law work for unions versus labor work for management, personal injury plaintiffs' work versus personal injury defense, environmental plaintiffs versus environmental defense, antitrust plaintiffs versus antitrust defense, and consumer law work for debtors versus consumer work for creditors — discloses that the side of the case that characteristically represents corporate clients is consistently assigned higher prestige than is the side that more often represents individuals. . . . It may be that the greater wealth of the corporate clients means that their lawyers are regularly able to devote greater resources to the issues and thus that the opportunities for creativity are consistently higher in the corporate fields even when the general doctrinal area of the law is held constant. We believe, however, that our findings provide strong support for the inference that the prestige accorded by the legal profession to the fields of law, constituting a set of distinct lawyers' roles, is determined in large measure by the types of clients served by the fields. Fields that serve corporate, wealthier, more "establishment" clients are accorded more deference within the profession than are those that serve individual, poorer clients. This suggests the thesis that prestige within law is acquired by association, that it is "reflected glory" derived from the power possessed by the lawyers' clients.

We also found a strong relationship between the types of work that lawyers do and their social background characteristics, including ethno-religious origins. Lawyers from less prestigious social origins were overrepresented among those practicing in less prestigious fields. A Catholic respondent was three times more likely than either a Protestant or a Jew to be working as a prosecutor. A respondent who was affiliated with a high status Protestant denomination (that is, Type I Protestant—Episcopalian, Presbyterian, Congregationalist, etc.) was five times more likely than either a Catholic or a Jewish respondent to be found doing securities or antitrust defense work. Jews were more than twice as likely as were Catholics to do divorce work, and they were incalculably more likely to do so than were Type I Protestants—in our sample, we found no one of high status Protestant origin who did a substantial amount of divorce work. Other fields with particularly high concentrations of Type I Protestants were banking, patents, municipal, and personal tax; Jews were disproportionately represented in labor law, both on the union and on the management side, in business tax, commercial work, criminal defense, and personal injury plaintiffs' work; and Catholics were greatly overrepresented in personal injury work, on both the plaintiffs' and the defendants' sides, and in both business litigation and general litigation. Generally, WASPs were more likely to be found in the corporate hemisphere, Jews in the personal client hemisphere, and Catholics in the litigation fields. Thus, the kinds of tasks that a lawyer performs and the kinds of clients for whom he does those tasks are strongly associated with the lawyer's social origins.

John P. Heinz, Edward O. Laumann,
Robert L. Nelson & Ethan Michelson
The Changing Character of Lawyers' Work:
Chicago in 1975 and 1995

32 Law & Soc'y Rev. 751 (1998)

. . . Following the publication of *Chicago Lawyers*, the two-hemispheres hypothesis became a frequent point of reference in the scholarly literature, but the survey on which that book was based was conducted in 1975. There have since been important changes in the legal profession—women entered the bar in large numbers, the overall size of the profession almost doubled . . . , the management practices of those organizations became more formal and intrusive . . . . Many of these changes may well have . . . altered the degree of separation (or lack thereof) of the two hemispheres of law practice. . . .

. . . [Nevertheless,] the division between the two classes of clients—between large organizations, on the one hand, and individuals and small businesses, on the other—endures. . . .

Lawyers employed by large law firms do, of course, handle legal work for individuals—often for individuals who are officers of corporate clients. . . . To the extent that this occurs, the corporate and the personal client sectors of the bar are drawn closer. But there is a division of labor within these law firms . . . . If lawyers' work has become increasingly specialized—if lawyers who do securities work are now less likely to do probate or commercial work as well—this will tend to separate the two sectors of the bar. Fewer lawyers will cross the boundary.

Is the legal profession still divided into hemispheres? Well, "hemi" means "half," and it is now hard to argue that the two parts are of approximately equal size, at least in Chicago (and probably in other large cities). Work for corporate clients is a much larger part of the profession than is work for individuals or small businesses. The amount of Chicago lawyers' time devoted to corporate fields and to fields serving other large organizations is more than twice that devoted to personal client fields. [In 1975, 53% of lawyers' time was allocated to the corporate fields, while 40% was devoted to the personal client fields and another 7% was not clearly assignable. By 1995, 64% was devoted to the corporate sector and only 29% to individuals. The "large corporate cluster" of fields increased the most, expanding from 18% to 32% of lawyer time during the period.] But the relative size of the two parts is probably not a very important part of the thesis . . . and we have not assessed in this article the degree of socioeconomic, ethnoreligious, educational, and political separation of practitioners in the two sectors. Within each of these broad parts, the fields are now more distinct, more clearly separated than they were 20 years ago. In this respect, there is greater disaggregation of work and workgroups within the profession today. On the other hand, the increase in scale of law firms and other practice organizations may mean that the specialties are to some extent reintegrated within overarching structures. The departmentalization of the firms, however, appears to result in workgroups that are more narrowly defined than was previously the case. Our finding that specialization has increased markedly in most fields, especially in the corporate sector, suggests this. We think it unlikely that the present organizational structures provide enough interchange among the specialties to produce a bar that functions as a community of shared fate and common purpose.

Notes

1. Do you find the claim that client identity explains all of the other variation in the bar convincing? Are there reasons to suspect that lawyers in other areas of the

country may be different from those in Chicago? Is the answer to this last question likely to be the same for 1995 as it may have been for 1975?

2. What effect have the changes since 1995 had on the composition and division of the two "hemispheres" of the bar? How might these changes affect the efforts by some scholars and policymakers to use this division to create a "context-specific" approach to regulation that creates distinct rules for lawyers in different practice settings? Consider the following excerpt from Professor Wilkins both explaining this approach and recognizing how many of the changes documented in this and other Chapters—including the increasing mobility of lawyers across practice settings, the growing use of technology to allow lawyers in smaller firms to serve big clients while simultaneously allowing small claims to be bundled together to be handled efficiently and profitably by large companies, the growing ties between public interest organizations and law firm pro bono, and the effects of globalization on practices from complex mergers to family law—are complicating any attempt to create a simple set of context-specific rules based on the hemispheres model.

David B. Wilkins
Some Realism About Legal Realism for Lawyers
in *Lawyers in Practice: Ethical Decisionmaking in Context*
(Leslie Levin and Lynn Mather eds. 2012)

Over the years, scholars like me built on the "hemispheres" framework to move from the descriptive to the prescriptive or regulatory level of analysis. Thus, in *Legal Realism for Lawyers*, I argued that the clustering effect around certain areas of practice—for example, tax law or securities—meant that it was possible to develop effective middle-level rules for practitioners in these areas without worry about the complexities that might be caused by differences among the arguably relevant contextual factors. Similarly, two years later, in *Who Should Regulate Lawyers?* I argued that understanding the differences between the two hemispheres was central to constructing a plausible enforcement system that would encourage lawyers to fulfill both their duties to clients and to the public regulatory framework. The next year, I combined these perspectives to argue in favor of context-specific rules and enforcement practices for law firms like Kaye Scholer that represent federally insured depository institutions such as Lincoln Savings and Loan. Other scholars followed a similar path. . . .

. . . Although this scholarship continues to document such trends as specialization and the accelerated growth of large law firms that reinforce the hemispheres thesis, recent studies also document six trends that complicate the goal of creating a rich context-specific descriptive or normative account of the contemporary legal profession. . . .

Collectively these six trends—mobility, technology, unbundling and repackaging, new organizational forms for delivering legal services, the institutionalization of pro bono, and the connected set of changes falling under the general heading of globalization—complicate both the descriptive and the normative task faced by those of us who seek to analyze the legal profession "in context." Descriptively, each of these developments makes it more difficult to identify which contextual factors are relevant and for which purposes. Are large publicly traded plaintiffs' firms more like large defense firms or like traditional plaintiffs' firms? Are organizations that use technology and global supply chains to aggregate and process individual claims part of the corporate or individual hemisphere? Will deferred associates who spend time in a legal services or public interest organization think or practice differently when they return to their corporate law firms? These and the many other complexities introduced by the large-scale trends . . . are likely to destabilize many of our traditional ways of thinking about context.

The regulatory and normative implications are even more perplexing. [How will we train lawyers for careers that are both increasingly specialized and increasingly fluid? Or what rules should govern a field like family law which now includes traditional solo practitioners and lawyers in large law firms who do high end divorces on the side?] In *Legal Realism for Lawyers*, I argued that the traditional model's preference for general, universally applicable rules addressed to all lawyers in all contexts created a significant risk that these commands would acquire unintended, perhaps even perverse meanings once they were interpreted by real lawyers operating in the real and distinct contexts in which they worked. While I believe that this remains true, the growing complexity and fluidity resulting from the six trends . . . creates a parallel risk that regulation that is too narrowly tailored to fit a single context will produce similarly unforeseen consequences as lawyers, clients, and legal norms increasingly cross established contextual boundaries. My point, therefore, is not that we should abandon our attempt to craft context-specific rules. Instead, we need to temper our efforts to create appropriate middle-level rules with an equally vigilant search for the ways in which the increasingly blurred and porous boundaries that now characterize a significant amount of legal practice should also be incorporated into the regulatory process.

Notes

1. Given the changes that Professor Wilkins alludes to, how useful is it to continue to view the type of client that a lawyer represents as the central defining feature of the legal profession? Even if the core division between lawyers who represent corporate interests and those who serve individuals remains—and nothing in Professor Wilkins' analysis disputes that corporate clients consume a vastly disproportionate share of all legal resources—do these changes make it impossible to create a workable set of professional rules that apply to particular lawyers in specific practice settings?

2. More generally, to what extent are these complications to the hemispheres thesis a part of a more general blurring of the boundaries of the traditional categories that we have used to define our world? As Professor Wilkins has argued in another context:

[W]e are seeing an increasing "blurring together" of the traditional categories of knowledge and organization that we have used to understand our world. It was not so long ago that we confidently believed there was a sharp distinction between categories such as "public" and "private," or "global" and "local"—or more relevant for our purposes—"law" and "business." It is not that these categories are no longer important, but today no one believes that they are as sharply distinguished and hermetically sealed as we once did. Thus . . . is General Motors a "private" or a "public" corporation after the U.S. government pumped billions of dollars of taxpayer money to rescue it from bankruptcy? Or, once again closer to home, are large law firms engaged in a "profession" or a "business" as they seek to serve clients and the public interest across an increasingly competitive and deregulated environment? The answer in both cases is that these entities are both—or more accurately, that they exist at the intersection of these traditional categories—in large part because those categories no longer adequately define the complex world in which we live.

David B. Wilkins, "Making Global Lawyers: Legal Practice, Legal Education, and the Paradox of Professional Distinctiveness," in *Tribuna Plural La Revista Científica: Acto Internacional: Global Decisionmaking* (2014).

What are the implications of this broader boundary blurring for the project of creating any distinct set of rules for the legal profession—or for the independence of lawyers generally? We return to these questions below.

3. One area where there has been substantial change between 1975 and 1995 is exemplified by the ethnoreligious composition of the Chicago bar. In 1975, Jews, Catholics, and the children of recent immigrants from southern and eastern Europe were concentrated in the low-status and low-paying sectors of the profession, generally in the "personal" hemisphere. This concentration reflected the overt discrimination directed against ethnic and religious minorities by leaders of the bar dating back to the beginning of the twentieth century. These prejudices played an important role in shaping the structure—and perhaps even the ethics—of the modern bar. For example, some scholars argue that the bar's drive for mandatory legal education and more rigorous bar examinations was motivated in part by the desire to keep religious and ethnic minorities out of the profession. See Richard L. Abel, *American Lawyers* (1989). When Jews and Catholics nevertheless managed to gain admission to the growing number of law schools that opened in response to these new requirements in the first decades of the twentieth century, prominent lawyers in both the organized bar and in legal education responded by enacting accreditation requirements that forced many inexpensive part-time law schools to shut their doors and by imposing implicit (and often explicit) quotas on the number of Jews admitted to those schools that remained. Id. Similarly, there is evidence that many of the bar's traditional rules prohibiting lawyers from engaging in commercial practices to generate business (i.e., advertising, solicitation, and providing clients with financial support or help with paying court costs and other similar expenses) were enacted primarily

to stop the growing number of Jewish and Catholic lawyers who relied on these practices to provide services to clients in the ethnic enclaves in which they worked. See
Jerold Auerbach, *Unequal Justice* (1976). By the mid-1990s, however, the remnants
of this history appear to have substantially dissipated, as Heinz, Nelson, and Laumann describe in another article reporting the findings of their 1995 study:

> In the 1995 survey, ethnoreligious differentiation across fields and practice
> settings is greatly diminished. In 1975, the percentage of lawyers in any given
> field of practice who were Jewish was significantly correlated with the per-
> centage of all practitioners in that field who were in large firms, the percent-
> age in solo practice, the percentage who served clients who were blue collar
> workers, and the volume of clients served. Thus, the overall characteristics
> of the fields, including client type, were correlated with the percentages of
> Jewish lawyers in the fields. In 1995, none of these correlations was signifi-
> cant. Similarly, the overrepresentation of high-status Protestant denomina-
> tions among securities lawyers, for example, had disappeared by 1995.

John P. Heinz, Robert L. Nelson, and Edward O. Laumann, "The Scales of Justice:
Observations on the Transformation of Urban Law Practice," 27 Ann. Rev. Soc. 337,
350 (2001).

What are the implications of the apparent decline in significance of ethnoreligious
status among Chicago lawyers? Does this transformation suggest anything about the
future prospects for achieving gender and racial integration in the bar? Will the presence of significant numbers of Jewish and Catholic lawyers in high-status positions
affect the structure or the ethics of the bar? We will return to these questions later
in this Chapter.

4. The changes in the bar's ethnoreligious makeup have been spurred in part by
changes in legal education. Consider the following description of the changes in
"urban law schools"—law schools located in major metropolitan areas but not ranked
in the top tier—that have occurred since these law schools were first created in the
early years of the twentieth century:

> The urban law school was created largely as a place to provide education to
> immigrant groups who could not gain a place in the establishment law
> schools. . . . [G]raduates went into careers in government, litigation, and the
> judiciary. Catholics and Jews were especially well represented among the
> early urban law schools. . . .
>
> This pattern has changed in some striking ways. There are currently more
> children of immigrants in the elite law schools than in urban schools. The
> more elite schools, with more resources for financial aid to go with their high
> prestige, also have more diverse student bodies than other law schools. How-
> ever, the elite law schools are less diverse in the age of the students, the
> percentage of women who attend the schools, the number of students with
> children, and more generally, the social class background of the students.
> Jews and Catholics are now well-represented in the most elite law schools. . . .

The graduates of urban law schools are still more likely to serve individuals in personal injury practice, although litigation is now common among the graduates of many of the law schools. . . .

One notable change from the past is that the students who attend urban law schools do have an advantage being located in major legal markets. In particular, urban law students have greater access to the once unavailable corporate law firms than do comparable graduates [not from elite schools] from outside those urban areas.

Joyce Sterling, Ronit Dinovitzer, and Bryant Garth, "The Changing Social Role of Urban Law Schools," 36 Sw. U. L. Rev. 389 (2007). We will return to the data about urban law school graduates in large law firms below. Although, as we will see, there have been important changes in the last decade, it is still the case that law school status remains a key—and arguably *the* key—determinant for where a lawyer is likely to work as a lawyer. See David B. Wilkins, Ronit Dinovitzer, and Rishi Batra, "Urban Law School Graduates in Large Law Firms," 36 Sw. U. L. Rev, 433, 450 (2007) (finding that "it is clear that law school status continues to play a pivotal role in shaping the careers of today's law school graduates").

5. What difference might it make that the bar may no longer function "as a community of shared fate and common purpose"? Are some of the bar's traditional functions—for example, the bar's role in law reform or the commitment to make legal services "widely available"—threatened by a bar that is divided along client lines? Should a bar divided into hemispheres be regulated by a unitary system of professional rules and disciplinary procedures? Should it be trusted with drafting the rules at all? Does your answer depend upon whether lawyers from one hemisphere or the other dominate the rule-making process? For an argument that client-related concerns played an important role in the American Law Institute's drafting of the Restatement of the Law Governing Lawyers, see Monroe H. Freedman, "Caveat Lector: Conflicts of Interest of ALI Members in Drafting the Restatements," 26 Hofstra L. Rev. 1 (1998).

6. What are the implications of the tremendous growth in the percentage of lawyer time devoted to organizational clients during the last twenty years? The following excerpt suggests one possible answer to this question.

Gillian K. Hadfield
The Price of Law: How the Market for Lawyers
Distorts the Justice System
98 Mich. L. Rev. 953 (2000)

Q. How many lawyers does it take to screw in a light bulb?
A. How many can you afford?

. . .

Why *do* lawyers cost so much? Surprisingly, we have few insights into this basic question. Conventional popular culture has one suggestion: lawyers are an avaricious lot who will bleed you dry. Conventional economics has another: legal training is expensive. And conventional professional wisdom has another: lawyers enjoy a state-granted monopoly over which they control entry for the purposes of protecting the public. None of these is particularly compelling. While each seems to hold some grain of truth, each also raises more questions than it answers. How is it that the profession has come to be dominated by vice? Why is law so complicated that legal training is so expensive? Is the public better off with inexpensive low quality legal advice or high quality legal advice it cannot afford? ...

... [I]t is possible to identify three fundamental features of the market for lawyers as the source of the market power lawyers possess: the complexity of legal reasoning and process, the monopoly the profession holds over coercive dispute resolution, and the unified nature of the profession.

Complexity. The complexity of legal reasoning and process is fundamental to the entire market. It is the source of direct cost, as we have seen. But more importantly it plays a central role in a host of indirect distortions. It is responsible for the credence nature of legal services: the complexity of law is so extensive that even the expert providing the service has difficulty assessing the quality and necessity of services provided. This makes price and quantity in the market predominantly the result of beliefs and wealth, rather than of cost. Complexity and unpredictability are also responsible for the winner-take-all dynamics that structure successive tournaments among lawyers, tournaments in which winning may reflect only negligible quality differences in fact. Winning nonetheless establishes a public signal that drives clients to bid for the winner's services. Complexity also gives rise to the sunk costs associated with establishing a lawyer-client relationship, sunk costs that grant a lawyer power to extract wealth with only muted competition. Complexity is responsible for the incremental nature of legal billing, which results in sunk cost auction dynamics that leave clients vulnerable to being in a position where they face no rational choice but to expend legal fees beyond the value of the case and up to the amount of wealth available. And complexity places a practical limit on the supply of individuals who have the capacity to engage in legal reasoning. ...

Monopoly. But rather than controlling the consequences of complexity, monopoly forms the second leg on which the market power of the legal profession rests. The monopoly that is essential is not the monopoly the profession has over the provision of legal services. This monopoly is only of importance because it transfers into the hands of lawyers a much more fundamental monopoly: the state's monopoly over the democratically legitimate exercise of force. ...

The Unified Profession. The driving role that complexity and monopoly give to wealth takes on special significance in the market for lawyers because of the third leg on which the market power of lawyers rests: the unified nature of the legal profession. Although there are systematic differences among lawyers, and plenty of specialization and socioeconomic barriers affecting the distribution of lawyers across the corporate and personal spheres, we nonetheless have a single "legal system." We train all our lawyers in essentially the same way, and they receive the same license to practice. . . .

Seen from a market perspective, this means that all these interests, all the individuals and entities who represent and pursue these interests, are pitted against one another in competition for access to legal resources. If we divide the world into personal and business clients, personal and business legal matters (as empirical research confirms we confidently can), it is immediately evident that these client groups fundamentally differ in terms of their command of wealth. It is the wealth of the business client group that ultimately determines pricing in the market(s) for lawyers. Driven by corporate demand, backed by corporate wealth, the legal system prices itself out of the reach of all individuals except those with a claim on corporate wealth. . . .

A market that puts individual clients in a bidding competition with corporate clients therefore necessarily ends up serving predominantly corporate clients at a price determined by corporate pre-tax wealth. This is a price that is systematically out of the reach of individuals. The only exceptions are individuals who have claims on aggregated wealth which can be accessed to pay lawyers, such as the victims of torts committed by corporate or insured tortfeasors, or shareholders with the right to maintain a derivative action against corporate managers. These exceptions are the rule: the market for lawyers—lawyers who can provide services to individuals and corporations alike—overwhelmingly allocates legal resources to clients with interests backed by corporate aggregations of wealth. . . .

The wealth-based allocation of lawyers, and hence of access to the legal system, is of categorically different normative significance from the wealth-based allocation of ordinary goods and services across individuals. The market for lawyers allocates access to law not merely among individuals but, more importantly, between individuals as a group and corporations as a group. . . .

. . . [W]hen our legal system relies on the market allocation of lawyers under conditions of complexity, monopoly, and unification, it chooses the management of the economy over the justice of social and political relationships as its central preoccupation. It establishes the governance of the economy as the principal role of the justice system. . . .

Notes

1. Contrast Professor Hadfield's view about complexity in the legal system with Dean Clark's. Which do you find more persuasive? What are the implications of Professor Hadfield's characterization of legal complexity and the demand for legal services for the question of whether there are "too many" lawyers?

2. Assuming that Professor Hadfield is correct in her diagnosis of the causes of the increasing dominance of the "corporate" hemisphere, is there anything that society can or should do to reverse these trends? What would it mean to make our legal system "less complex"? Would you favor a proposal to "simplify" entire areas of law, for

example, by adopting a "flat tax" to reduce complexity in the internal revenue code or adopting strong presumptions about the existence of discrimination when minorities or women are terminated in employment cases? If we did, would that solve the problem? What about the state's monopoly on coercive force? Should we encourage the use of "private" forms of dispute resolution, such as arbitration, mediation, or "rent-a-judge" programs by backing the decisions of these alternative tribunals with the full coercive power of the state? Once again, is this likely to increase access to the justice system for individuals? Finally, what should be done about the "unified profession"? Would you favor formally dividing the profession into a branch dealing with the "justice system" and one devoted to the "legal governance of the economy"? How would we accomplish this division? Would we have to create separate law schools, licensing schemes, and professional organizations? If so, what effect do you think such a system would have on which students would choose to attend "justice" school or "governance of the economy" school? What decision would you have made before going to law school? Is it the same one you would make today—or that you anticipate that you might make after five or ten years of practice?

3. To what extent is our legal system *already* functionally divided along the lines that Professor Hadfield proposes? Consider, for example, family courts, juvenile courts, small claims courts, and other specialized tribunals. Isn't the purpose of such courts to provide an alternative route for individuals seeking access to the justice system? Are there reasons to prefer creating additional courts of this kind to encouraging greater use of private methods of dispute resolution as a means of addressing the problems Professor Hadfield claims flow from the state's monopoly over coercive force?

4. Are there other ways in which we might try to equalize access to lawyers for individual and corporate clients? Is increased funding for legal services or mandatory pro bono programs a promising way to combat the problems Professor Hadfield identifies? What about limiting the amount of money that corporations can spend on legal services in the same way that individuals and corporations have been limited in the amount that they can contribute to political candidates?

Is there any way in which the increasing demands of corporate clients for better, faster, and cheaper legal services might actually reduce the gap between the two hemispheres? Consider the following article by Professor Marc Galanter.

Marc Galanter
"Old and In the Way": The Coming Demographic Transformation of the Legal Profession and its Implications for the Provision of Legal Services
1999 Wis. L. Rev. 1081

Lawyers are growing older! For each of us, this is confirmed by the mirror each morning. But lawyers are getting older in another, collective sense. The legal profession is launched on a massive demographic transformation that will have dramatic but unknown effects on the way law is practiced and the way legal services are distributed in American society. . . .

To appreciate the effects of the dramatic change in the absolute number of lawyers, we have to consider the relative number of lawyers of different ages. Let us take lawyers in their fifties to represent senior lawyers who occupy the top positions in the various segments of the profession, and lawyers in their thirties to represent young aspirants making their way. In 1970, for every 100 lawyers in their fifties there were 127 lawyers in their thirties. The ratio of younger lawyers rose abruptly to 174 just five years later in 1975, to 233 in 1980, to 284 in 1985. Thus, when the profession was at its youngest, in the mid-1980s, there were almost three times as many younger lawyers as older ones. After 1985, members of those large cohorts of 1960s entrants began to fill the ranks of older lawyers. The ratio of younger to older lawyers fell to 270 in 1990 and to 199 in 1995. Barring another massive surge of law school enrollments, the ratio of younger to older lawyers will continue to fall. If the number of entrants remains steady, by 2005 the ratio will be only 126 lawyers in their thirties for each hundred lawyers in their fifties — virtually identical to the ratio in 1970 — and by 2020 it will fall to 104 lawyers in their thirties for each 100 lawyers in their fifties. That is, the broad-based age pyramid of the past quarter-century would be transformed into a steep wall with roughly equal numbers of lawyers at every age level. . . .

[Coinciding with this demographic shift from 1970 to the present has been the] dissolution of the world of assured tenure, infrequent lateral movement, and enduring retainer relationships with loyal, long-term clients. In its place rose a world of rapid growth, mergers and breakups, overt competition, aggressive marketing, attorney movement from firm to firm, fears of defection, and pervasive insecurity. . . .

. . . Partners are under mounting pressure to maintain a high level of performance that fits the business strategy of the firm. . . . Many new features of the law-firm world (mergers, lateral movement) amplify the power of dominant lawyers within a firm to sanction their errant colleagues, and the prevalent culture endorses such sanctions. . . .

Firms concerned about an excess of highly paid older lawyers and the need to create space for newly promoted partners have enacted new retirement policies that provide for mandatory retirement at lower ages and for earlier voluntary retirement. . . .

Increasingly, large-firm practice has become a young person's game. A 1999 survey of 34 Chicago firms, ranging in size from 21 to 371 lawyers, found only 17.1% were over fifty years of age (compared to over 30% of the lawyer population of Illinois). . . . In firms of more than 50 lawyers, the median age of associates was thirty and the median age of partners was only forty-three. Only 13% of the partners in these firms were fifty-five or older and only 3% were over sixty-five. . . .

. . . [T]he pressure to curtail the size of the partnership will fall on those who are already partners—to leave gracefully, take early retirement, accept "of counsel" status, or hang on with diminished status and a reduced share. In consequence, the shape of a career in large law firm practice is changing from a life-long trajectory, culminating as respected elder, to a compressed period of twenty to thirty years of intense and lucrative involvement, followed by a long "retirement." Unlike the old country doctor or lawyer who died in harness, a career in corporate law is beginning to resemble one in investment banking, where careers phase out by one's late forties. . . .

It seems highly probable, then, that many of the much larger number of over-fifty lawyers that will soon populate the profession will be involuntary retirees, underemployed, or otherwise inclined to forsake their practices. . . .

. . . [T]he entire legal services for the poor/public interest law sector is vanishingly small. It is estimated to comprise about 6,000 full time equivalent lawyers—about seven-tenths of 1% of the whole body of American lawyers. . . .

. . . [B]y any measure [there are] vast unmet legal needs. On the other hand, there is the prospect of an abundance of experienced but underemployed older lawyers. Can these be joined in a way that would deliver desperately needed legal services and at the same time provide fulfilling work to lawyers? Imagine that among the hundreds of thousands of experienced lawyers in their fifties and sixties, there is some fraction who would, if a path were readily available, choose to proceed to a second career as lawyers for the poor or for the public interest. . . .

Notes

1. In the years since Galanter's article, several leading bar associations have taken up the call of encouraging "retiring partners" to contribute some of their time to serving the legal needs of the poor. See, e.g., Report of the Senior Lawyers Committee of the City Bar of New York, *Retirement and Pro Bono Activities*, available at <http://www.nycbar.org/member-and-career-services/career-development/senior-lawyers/personal-experiences/retirement-and-pro-bono-activities> (2006). Nevertheless, questions remain. Are these lawyers likely to be qualified to provide competent legal services to the poor? Are they likely to be interested in or well suited for such work? Does the growing specialization of all forms of legal practice affect your assessment of Professor Galanter's proposal? Some pro bono organizations are attempting to provide training to address these issues. See Pro Bono Institute, Second Acts, available at <http://www.probonoinst.org/projects/second-acts/> (describing the program as an "innovative initiative to support transitioning and retired lawyers who are interested in a second, volunteer career in public interest law").

2. What are some of the other implications of the aging of the lawyer population? Consider the following findings from the consulting firm Deloitte from their 2016 Millennial Survey:

Millennials express little loyalty to their current employers and many are planning near-term exits. This "loyalty challenge" is driven by a variety of factors. Millennials feel underutilized and believe they're not being developed as leaders. They continue to express positive views of businesses' role in society; they have softened their negative perceptions of corporate motivation and ethics, and cite a strong alignment of values. However, Millennials feel that most businesses have no ambition beyond profit, and there are distinct differences in what they believe the purpose of business should be and what they perceive it to currently be. Millennials often put their personal values ahead of organizational goals, and several have shunned assignments (and potential employers) that conflict with their beliefs.

Deloitte, *The 2016 Millennial Survey: Winning Over the Next Generation of Leaders* (2016). What are the implications of these findings for law firms and other legal organizations, and for the legal profession generally? Are the Survey's findings relevant to the decline in law school applications since 2009? Regardless of cause and effect, does the fact that fewer millennials are choosing to go to law school make it even more critical that law schools, law firms, and other legal organizations address the challenge of recruiting, developing, and retaining this next generation of leaders? See Scott Westfahl and David B. Wilkins, "The Leadership Imperative: Preparing Lawyers to Lead, Adapt, and Thrive in the Global Age of More for Less," Stan. L. Rev. (forthcoming 2017)

3. In addition to figuring out what millennials want, the demographic shift Galanter documents also highlights the challenge that legal organizations face in transitioning the baby boomers who have dominated these institutions for the last twenty years. As the increase in the number of age discrimination law suits against law firms and other similar organizations attests, most legal organizations are struggling with this issue. See David B. Wilkins, "Partner Shmartner! EEOC vs. Sidley Austin Brown & Wood," 120 Harv. L. Rev. 1264 (2007). We return to these issues in the context of large law firms in the next section.

———————

Professor Galanter makes reference to a number of changes in the organization and practices of large law firms over the last thirty years. These changes are the subject of the next section.

B. The Transformation of Corporate Legal Practice

In this Part, we take an in-depth look at the "corporate hemisphere" and how this sector of the bar has evolved. We do so by looking at three imperfectly defined but nevertheless important periods in the history of this sector: the so-called "golden age" of the large law firm, from the turn of the 20th century through the 1970s; the "neo-Cravathist" period, from the 1980s through the years leading up to 2008; and a potential "age of disruption" that began in the years following the global financial crisis and which continues to produce important changes in the corporate legal sector as this book goes to press—changes (as indicated in Professor Wilkins's article "Some Realism About Legal Realism for Lawyers," excerpted above (p. 957) that problematize the very idea of a distinct corporate hemisphere. Needless to say, this history of the evolution of the corporate sector during these three periods is both long and complex and we can only present the barest outline here. Those interested in a more complete account should consult the following sources from which we drew much of what is presented below: David B. Wilkins, "Law Firms," *International Encyclopedia of the Social and Behavioral Sciences*, 2nd ed., Vol. 13, pp. 578–584 (James D. Wright, ed.); John P. Heinz, Robert L. Nelson, Rebecca L. Sandefur, and Edward O. Laumann, *Urban Lawyers: The New Social Structure of the Bar* (2005); Milton Regan, *Eat What You Kill: The Fall of a Wall Street Lawyer* (2004); Carole Silver, "Globalization and the U.S. Market in Legal Services—Shifting Identities," 31 Law & Pol'y Bus. 1093 (2000); Marc Galanter and Thomas Palay, *Tournament of Lawyers: The Transformation of the Big Law Firm* (1991); Richard Abel, *American Lawyers* (1989); Richard Abel and Philip Lewis, *Lawyers in Society* (4 volumes) (1988–1995); Robert L. Nelson, *Partners with Power: Social Transformation of the Large Law Firm* (1988); Erwin O. Smigel, *The Wall Street Lawyer: Professional Organization Man?* (1969); and Bernard A. Burk & David McGowan, "Big but Brittle: Economic Perspectives on the Future of the Law Firm in the New Economy," 2011 Colum. Bus. L. Rev. 1.

Before proceeding, however, a word of caution is in order. As we indicated at the beginning of this Chapter, although the majority of lawyers work in private practice, most do not work in the large law firms and in-house legal departments that we will spend the majority of this section exploring. Nevertheless, we believe that the kind of institutional history and analysis that we present here is relevant even to those who do not think that they will work in these institutions. Although we continue to talk about lawyers as "independent professionals," the majority of lawyers in the United States now work in some form of organization—law firms, government law offices, in-house legal departments, NGO or public interest organizations—and these organizations have grown in size and complexity in almost every sector. Understanding how organizations work and their effect on legal practice and legal careers is therefore critical to all lawyers regardless of where they practice. The fact that many small firms and even government law offices pattern many of their practices on what they perceive to be the practices of large law firms underscores the outsized influence—no doubt for better *and* for worse—that these institutions and the corporate sector generally continued to have on institutions throughout the legal profession. Moreover, the growing mobility of lawyers across jobs and even sectors of the profession means that many lawyers who do not currently anticipate working in the corporate sector may end up doing so at some point in their careers—or at least find themselves considering the option. This is particularly true given the escalating share of total lawyer effort as is documented in the *Urban Lawyers* study, cited above. And as the boundaries blur between the two hemispheres, even those who never work in large law firms, in-house legal departments, or the other institutions we discuss below will find themselves interacting with those who do work in this sector with increasing frequency. We discuss some of these interactions, as well as the contours of the individual hemisphere, in the next section.

1. The "Golden Age" (circa 1900–1980)

The New York law firm of Cravath Swaine & Moore is frequently credited with pioneering the model for the large law firm in the first decades of the twentieth century. (See especially Mark Galanter and Thomas Palay, *Tournament of Lawyers: The Transformation of the Big Law Firm* (1991); Robert Swaine, *The Cravath Firm and Its Predecessors* (1946).) Four features of the "Cravath Model" distinguished this firm and its progeny from its nineteenth-century American predecessors. First, the *work* of Cravath Model firms consisted of providing a full range of services to corporate clients—as opposed to individuals—with a particular emphasis on transactional and commercial matters, as opposed to courtroom litigation. Second, the *lawyers* in these firms were hired directly out of the country's newly emerging law schools; they were expected to stay with the firm for 6–10 years receiving training from senior lawyers on how to do the work of the firm's corporate clients. Third, at the conclusion of this probationary period, the best of these lawyers were *promoted to partnership* in an up-or-out system in which those not promoted were asked to leave the firm— and, in all likelihood, the large law firm sector altogether, since Cravath Model firms hired virtually no lateral partners or associates. Fourth, Cravath Model firms were *governed* as true partnerships, in which all partners shared equally in the firm's profits and losses (through a "lock-step" compensation system), and were entitled to equal participation in firm decision-making.

The Cravath Model proved to be particularly well aligned to the market conditions of the developing corporate legal sector in the United States during the first half of the twentieth century. That market was characterized by a rapidly expanding economy (particularly after World War II) and a growing pool of law school graduates as legal education spread throughout the country. Moreover, during this period very few U.S. companies had sophisticated in-house legal counsel, leading to significant information asymmetry between even the largest corporations and their law firm providers. Ronald J. Gilson, "The Devolution of the Legal Profession: A Demand Side Perspective," 49 Md. L. Rev. 869 (1990). As a result, corporate clients established long-term and near-exclusive relationships with their principal outside law firms, which in turn provided these organizations with significant freedom to maintain the internal training, promotion, and governance practices of the Cravath Model. Regulatory restrictions and informal norms that prevented or discouraged market behavior, such as advertising or recruiting lawyers away from other firms, further reinforced a protected environment in which Cravath firms faced little competition in their home markets for either clients or talent. Mark Galanter and Thomas Palay,

Tournament of Lawyers: The Transformation of the Big Law Firm (1991). By the "golden age" of the large law firm in the 1960s and 1970s—in quotation marks since the benefits of these organizations extended only to those with the "right" gender, race, religion, and social class—law firms organized on the Cravath Model (with some important regional variations which we will discuss below) had clearly become the industry standard in the United States, hiring the best law school graduates and occupying the most prestigious and lucrative positions in the American legal market. Id.; Erwin Smigel, *The Wall Street Lawyer: Professional Organization Man?* (1969).

2. Neo-Cravathism (circa 1980–2007)

With two notable exceptions discussed below, between 1980 and 2008 demand for corporate legal services in the United States continued to grow at an exponential rate. This growth, in turn, produced an exponential growth in the size, geographic scope, and profitability of large U.S. law firms. See William D. Henderson, "From Big Law to Lean Law," 38 Int'l Rev. Law & Econ. 5 (2014). This period of unprecedented growth, however, was also accompanied by significant changes in each of the four core elements of the Cravath Model. First, the *work* of many U.S. law firms became both broader and more specialized than the work typically performed by Golden Age law firms. It was broader in that previously excluded work—such as litigation, criminal defense (particularly with respect to white collar and corporate crime), and even plaintiffs' work (often for corporate clients who were increasingly willing to file suit)—became an important part of the work of many large law firms. At the same time, many law firms abandoned the full-service model that typified their Golden Age counterparts to concentrate on increasingly specialized areas of law. This trend was even more pronounced for partners—and even many associates—who spent virtually their entire careers concentrating on increasingly narrow subsections of transactional practice or litigation.

Moreover, as U.S. law firms grew in both size and geographic scope, many abandoned the Cravath Model's traditional *hiring* and *promotion* practices. With respect to hiring, virtually all U.S. law firms hired associates and even partners "laterally" from other law firms (and to a lesser extent, government agencies and in-house legal departments), with several firms sourcing the majority of their lawyers in this way. William D. Henderson and Luke Bierman, "An Empirical Analysis of Lateral Lawyer Trends from 2000–2007: The Emerging Equilibrium for Corporate Law Firms," 22 Geo. J. Legal Ethics 1395 (2009). Similarly, many U.S. law firms abandoned their traditional up-or-out promotion policy, creating new categories of professionals such as "permanent associates" and "non-equity partners." William D. Henderson, "An Empirical Analysis of Single Tier vs. Two Tier Partnerships in the Am. Law 200," 84 N.C. L. Rev. 1691 (2006).

Finally, the *governance* model of the prototypical U.S. law firm also changed significantly during this period. Although all U.S. firms were still formally organized as partnerships (a model, as discussed below, that is increasingly under pressure in many places around the world, most notably in the UK), few of these institutions retained the egalitarian decision-making structure and lock-step compensation system that formed the heart of the "partnership model" of Golden Age large law firms. Instead, with the exception of a handful of top-performing New York law firms (including Cravath itself), most U.S. law firms were organized bureaucratically, with an increasing amount of decision-making authority concentrated in the hands of formal managers—many of whom were not lawyers—and employed an "eat what you kill" compensation system that rewarded partners on the basis of their individual contribution to firm profits. David B. Wilkins, "Partner Schmartner!: EEOC v. Sidley Austin Brown & Wood," 120 Harv. L. Rev. 1264 (2007).

Although there is considerable debate about what caused the changes in the Cravath Model—which we label "neo-Cravathist" since many firms during this period continued to pledge their allegiance to the substance of the Cravath System even as they consistently deviated from many of the System's original premises and practices—there was widespread consensus that a key factor was the growth in the size and sophistication of in-house counsel in large U.S. companies. Beginning in the 1970s, many corporate clients began developing substantial in-house legal departments, allowing them to purchase most routine services "wholesale" rather than "retail." In addition, these new in-house lawyers, many of whom were former law firm partners, began to act as sophisticated purchasing agents, conducting so-called "beauty pageants" to choose the best lawyers to handle large cases or transactions at the best possible price, as well as acting as "chief diagnosticians" of the company's legal needs. See Mary C. Daly, "The Cultural, Ethical, and Legal Challenges in Lawyering for a Global Organization: The Role of the General Counsel," 46 Emory L.J. 1057 (1997); Ronald J. Gilson, "The Devolution of the Legal Profession," 49 Md. L. Rev. 869 (1990). This "in-house counsel movement," as the American legal scholar Robert Eli Rosen aptly labeled this transformation, significantly changed both the relationship between law firms and their corporate clients as well as the career paths of young lawyers; "going in-house" became an increasingly attractive employment option for lawyers, particularly for women. See Robert Eli Rosen, "The In-House Counsel Movement," 64 Ind. L. Rev. 479 (1989) (documenting the growth of in-house legal departments and the role that general counsels played in enhancing their own power and status); David B. Wilkins, "Is the In-House Counsel Movement Going Global?," 2012 Wis. L. Rev. 251 (documenting the increasing popularity of in-house positions—again, particularly for women).

This growth in the size and sophistication of in-house counsel in large companies in turn helped to spur the growth of neo-Cravathist law firms around the world. The United Kingdom is a case in point. In the 1940s, even the largest English solicitor firms had fewer than a dozen partners. By 2008, four of the UK's so-called "magic circle" law firms—Freshfields, Linklaters, Allen & Overy, and Clifford Chance—ranked among the largest, most profitable, and most globalized law firms in the world, with several other prominent UK firms arguably pursuing an even more ambitious global expansion strategy. John Flood, "Institutional Bridging: How Large Law Firms Engage in Globalization," 54 B.C. L. Rev. 1297 (2013). As UK firms grew, many were quick to adopt the major modifications to the Cravath Model that had already transformed U.S. law firms in the 1980s and 1990s. Indeed, spurred in part by the spread of the in-house counsel movement across the Atlantic by the first decade of the twenty-first century, many of the top English firms were even more specialized, more active in lateral hiring, and more bureaucratic than their U.S. counterparts. Id. However, unlike most American firms, the majority of large UK law firms still retained lock-step compensation as a core element of their structure. This variation in compensation systems became a key element in the competition between U.S. and UK law firms, even as the overall Anglo-American mode of production of law became increasingly dominant around the world. Id.

Similar developments occurred in other parts of the world. Spurred by rapid economic growth and the prospect of European integration, large and increasingly sophisticated law firms began to emerge in many Western European countries during the 1980s. These law firms were initially organized as hybrids between the Anglo-American model and the traditional European model, consisting of smaller and more hierarchical firms with strong ties to the academy and the state. David M. Trubek and Yves Dezelay, "Global Restructuring and the Law: Studies of the Internationalization of Legal Fields and the Creation of Transnational Arenas," 44 Case West. Res. 407 (1994). By the mid-1990s several of these hybrid European firms had grown to more than 100 lawyers, with the largest attempting to compete with the U.S. and UK firms that were rapidly expanding into the European market. This competition, however, proved to be short-lived. Once again spurred by the spread of the in-house counsel movement across the Channel, within a decade many of the top European firms had merged with—or more accurately, been acquired by—Anglo-American firms (primarily from the UK), and those that remained independent increasingly adopted the core features of the Anglo-American model to better represent clients whose internal legal advisors had similarly adopted the Anglo-American model of the sophisticated general counsel. Yves Dezelay and Bryant Garth, "Elite European Lawyers? The Common Market as Golden Age or Missed Opportunity," in *Transnational Power Elites: The European Complex in the Transnational Field of Power* (N. Kapuii and M.R. Madsen, eds. 2013).

A similar transformation occurred in Japan and the "Asian Tigers" of Hong Kong, Singapore, Taiwan, and South Korea—although regulatory barriers meant that the Anglo-American model of the large law firm spread more rapidly in these jurisdictions than did the presence of Anglo-American law firms. See Suzuki, "The Protectionist Bar Against Foreign Lawyers in Japan, China, and Korea: Domestic Control in the Face of Internationalization," 16 Colum. J. Asian L. 385 (2003). As in Western Europe, in the last decades of the twentieth century a handful of law firms grew rapidly in these jurisdictions to service the needs of multinational companies investing in these markets, as well as in the expanding domestic corporate sector. Like their

European counterparts, these Asian large law firms adopted many of the core elements of the Anglo-American model, often at the urging of their clients. Id.

Since 2000, the same pattern has emerged in the BRICS (Brazil, Russia, India, China, and South Africa) and other rising powers. In each of these jurisdictions, one can now find a growing number of large "corporate" law firms, some with hundreds—and in the case of China, thousands—of lawyers. David B. Wilkins and Mihaela Papa, "The Rise of the Corporate Legal Elite in the BRICS: Implications for Global Governance," 54 Boston College L. Rev. 1149 (2013). The best of these law firms now compete aggressively with Anglo-American and European large law firms for both clients and talent in their home jurisdictions. A few have even opened branch offices in major Western commercial centers such as New York and London. See Li and Liu, "The Learning Process of Globalization: How Chinese Firms Survived the Financial Crisis," 80 Fordham L. Rev. 2847 (2012). There continue to be many differences among these new entrants to the large law firm field and their more established Western peers. For example, many emerging-market large law firms are still controlled by founding families or partners, whereas most Anglo-American firms transitioned away from family or founder control several decades ago. Eli Wald, "The Other Legal Profession and the Orthodox View of the Bar: The Rise of Colorado's Elite Law Firms," 80 U. Col. L. Rev. 605 (2009). Notwithstanding these differences, however, most emerging-market large law firms continued to use the Anglo-American model as their organizational template.

Whether these new global players will continue to follow the neo-Cravathist root, however, depends upon whether the global financial crisis has brought about a true paradigm shift in the world's corporate legal services market or something more akin to the kind of market correction that we have seen from past recessions.

3. The Age of Disruption? (2008–?)

The global financial crisis had an immediate and dramatic effect on the market for corporate legal services. Demand for the kind of M&A and securitization work that had fueled so much of the growth in the global corporate legal services market declined significantly. William D. Henderson, "From Big Law to Lean Law," 38 Int'l Rev. Law & Econ. 5 (2014). Law firms that relied heavily on these transactions were especially hard hit, with several going out of business. Moreover, unlike previous downturns in the legal market in 1991 and 2001, this decline in transactional work was not counterbalanced by an increase in the demand for litigation, as companies sought out less expensive ways to resolve disputes arising from the global financial crisis. The net result was that by the end of 2009 many large U.S. law firms laid off significant numbers of associates and support personnel, with several also de-equitizing and/or laying off partners. By 2010, law firms in the UK and Western Europe were following suit. And while the BRICS and other important emerging markets initially fared better than the U.S. and other developed economies, growth in these countries has now slowed considerably, as has the foreign investment from the West that was fueling so much of the corporate legal market in these jurisdictions. Although economic growth has begun to rebound in the U.S. and most other major economies around the world, the legal market has grown more slowly, with hiring (particularly at the entry level), growth, and profitability all either flat or below pre-recession levels.

Both the size and duration of these changes have led some academics and more than a few professionals to conclude that we are now in the midst of a paradigm shift that will result in "The Death of Big Law" — or even more apocalyptically "The End of Lawyers." Larry Ribstein, "The Death of Big Law," 2010 Wis. L. Rev. 749; Richard Susskind, *The End of Lawyers? Rethinking the Nature of Legal Services* (2008). It is still far too early to tell whether anything this dramatic will take place — and most reasonable observers think it is unlikely that large law firms based on the Anglo-American model will soon disappear from the legal scene. After all, projections about the death of the big law firm model have been made since the 1991 recession, and pundits have been predicting the demise of the billable hour for decades. Nevertheless, there are good reasons to believe that a set of fundamental changes that have been accelerated and sharpened by the global financial crisis are likely to have an important effect on the future of the large law firm.

Three such changes are especially important. First, throughout the economy — and increasingly in the market for corporate legal services — there has been a dramatic reduction in information asymmetry between buyers and sellers. This gap began closing when corporations started to hire sophisticated in-house legal departments in the 1980s, a trend that is now spreading around the world (Benjamin W. Heineman, *The Inside Counsel Revolution: Resolving the Partner–Guardian Tension* (2016)). In recent years, however, in addition to their own knowledge of the legal marketplace, these in-house lawyers can now access a significant amount of data about the price and performance of law firms (and the individual lawyers who work in these organizations) from a range of public sources, and, more importantly, a new industry of private consultants dedicated to helping companies reduce their expenditure on outside law firms. As a result, sophisticated general counsel have the ability to take legal work that law firms traditionally sold as an integrated whole — e.g., "class action litigation," or "a $500 million acquisition" — and "unbundle" it into its component parts — e.g., "discovery," "pre-trial motions," and "trial," or "due diligence," "asset pricing," "negotiation," and "document drafting" — and then spread those different aspects of the work across an increasingly global supply chain of legal producers.

Second, this trend toward disaggregation has in turn spurred the development of a host of new producers that now aggressively compete for a portion of the work on this increasingly global legal supply chain. Thus, when sourcing "legal work," general counsels can now choose among legal process outsourcing organizations located in India and other low-cost jurisdictions; electronic discovery companies; contract lawyers and other temporary staffing solutions; the Big Four accountancy firms, which now offer advice on litigation management and deal pricing; and, of course, a growing number of increasingly sophisticated law firms around the world. Many of these new competitors are organized as corporations, giving them easier access to capital and managerial resources than law firms. As a result, these newcomers are increasingly developing new products and services that further challenge the large law firms' business model. See Gillian Hadfield, "The Cost of Law: Promoting Access to Justice Through the (Un) Corporate Practice of Law," 38 Int'l J. Law & Econ. 48 (2014). Traditionally, law firms have relied on a steady increase in the hourly rates that they charge corporate clients, and an equally steady increase in leverage (the percentage of associates, who do not share profits, to partners who do) to drive profitability. But as corporate consumers become more sophisticated about their legal needs, and have greater access to a global network of providers willing and able to provide these services, law firms have had a more difficult time utilizing either of these strategies. Instead, companies are demanding greater transparency and accountability from law firms about how they are doing the company's legal work—and requiring that the law firms price these services by their "output," as measured by the value to the company, as opposed to the traditional "input" model based on the number of associate and partner hours it took to produce the work.

Finally, this pressure on the law firm's traditional business model is in turn exposing problems in their human capital model. Notwithstanding the current downturn in entry level hiring, large law firms face increasing pressure to attract and retain the "best" associates and partners. Demographic changes in the pool of entrants to the profession are making this competition even more intense. Law is increasingly a "feminized" profession, where the majority—and in many countries, the overwhelming majority—of entrants are female. Yet the career path in large law firms is not only designed for a man, but a man who has a wife who does not work—a rarity in many societies. Indeed, the fact that law firms have had a poor record of integrating lawyers from all non-traditional backgrounds poses an important challenge to these organizations in a world where the talent pool is more diverse in every way—including a new generation of lawyers, many of whom have a different orientation toward work and family than their Baby Boom and Generation X predecessors. Furi-Perry, *The Millennial Lawyer: Making the Most of Generational Differences in the Firm* (2013). The steep decline in U.S. law school applications and enrollment since 2010 will only sharpen the challenge that law firms will face in recruiting and retaining top talent in the coming years. Brian Tamanaha, *Failing Law Schools* (2012). (See Chapter 13, p. 1109.)

Thus, as we approach the end of the second decade of the twenty-first century, the profits of Anglo-American model law firms around the world are being squeezed in three directions: vertically, by increasingly sophisticated corporate clients demanding "more for less"; horizontally, by competition from other law firms and from a range of new competitors seeking to "hollow out" the work done by law firms, either by removing routine work from the bottom through technology and process engineering, or by capturing strategic work at the top by employing multidisciplinary expertise; and internally, by a "war for talent" which, in a human capital–intensive business, talent will inevitably win. How law firms respond to this triple squeeze will determine the future viability of the Anglo-American model of the large law firm.

In the rest of this Chapter, we will explore some of the preliminary evidence of both continuity and change in the current environment. Before doing so, however, it is important to ask why law firms have grown so rapidly over the last quarter century and why these institutions, notwithstanding the changes outlined in the preceding paragraphs, continue to organize themselves around the Cravath System's basic partnership structure. In the excerpt below, Professors Marc Galanter and Thomas Palay posit a single answer to both questions.

Marc Galanter & Thomas M. Palay
Why the Big Get Bigger: The Promotion-to-Partner Tournament and the Growth of Large Law Firms

76 Va. L. Rev. 747 (1990)

An attorney, like any other producer, combines labor with the capital she has accumulated over time. Unlike an automobile manufacturer, most of a lawyer's capital consists of human assets. Her human capital combines four types of assets. First, she possesses her pre-law-school endowment of intelligence, skills, general education, and the like. Second, she invests in her legal education and experience-dependent skills. She attends law school, perhaps goes on to a clerkship, and participates in continuing legal education programs in order to acquire the basic skills of the profession. She also may acquire significant information and skills from more senior practitioners. Eventually, she acquires the experience-dependent skills that distinguish a practicing attorney from a "kid" just out of law school. These skills include, for example, the knowledge necessary to understand and evaluate a law or regulation, to decide which rules a regulator likely will enforce, or to anticipate where a client most likely will run into trouble. She does not acquire practical knowledge of this nature in a classroom. Acquiring experience-dependent skills requires significant hands-on experience—as well as somebody willing to invest in the time and resources needed to provide such experience.

Third, and perhaps more important, an attorney invests in her professional reputation. Through her reputation an attorney disseminates information to clients and other attorneys about her qualifications, skills, temperament, legal philosophy, honesty, and integrity. Reputation also acts as an ex ante indicator of the quality of service a client can expect from an attorney. To the extent that an attorney values her reputation, it will act to bond her future conduct. For if she behaves contrary to her reputation, she risks tarnishing it.

Finally, an attorney makes human-capital investments in developing relationships with her clients. A lawyer must familiarize herself with the personnel, procedures, history, finances, and goals of the client. She also must develop a cooperative working relationship and a degree of trust to enable her better to service the client. The process of eliciting client cooperation and trust often consumes significant time and energy. Such attorney-client relationships also help to attract new clients, retain old ones, and perpetuate the lawyer's reputation.

We assume that at least some attorneys will have surplus human capital—that is, more capital assets than they can productively use by themselves. . . .

Imagine, for instance, a sole practitioner, P, who has shareable surplus human capital. She would like to lend or rent these assets to A, an attorney with little human capital of his own, but a full complement of labor. For convenience, one can think of P as a "partner" and A as an "associate." P might contract with A to produce an output, using his labor and her capital, which one of them then would sell to a client. . . .

"Contracting" with anyone, even an attorney, while conceptually straightforward, often presents difficulties in practice. Assume for convenience that P, the lawyer with surplus capital, retains control over the output. The contract requires enforcement, monitoring, or adaptation as conditions change. . . . [Or] P could organize the sharing of her capital as a firm. She could hire A, the lawyer with extra labor, combine his labor with her assets, sell the additional output to her client, pay A a wage derived from the proceeds of this sale, and retain the remainder as compensation for her capital. . . .

In a world without transaction costs, there is no a priori reason a law firm—large or otherwise—must result from contracting among attorneys. Any form of coordination—a large law firm, an association of smaller practices, or a network of individual practitioners tied together by spot contracts—would yield an identical result. . . .

We interact, however, in an economy replete with transaction costs. . . .

To begin with, long-term agreements render the parties vulnerable to the opportunistic conduct of their trading opposites. P, as the lender of human capital, has three potential concerns. First, A might "grab" assets P lends to him. For instance, A might depart with a client in tow. Second, the prospect of A's prematurely "leaving," or at least threatening to leave, with firm-specific skills and information for which P has paid, but not amortized fully, may trouble P. While the investments are generally worthless to A if he leaves, P's inability to recover the unamortized portion of her investments in A makes her vulnerable to his departure. Third, A might "shirk," that is, either fail to make the expected (and already paid-for) human-capital investments that A must make to further P's interests, or fail to employ borrowed assets to their full potential, thereby depriving P of her expected returns. . . .

A, too, has concerns about potential opportunistic conduct. He needs assurance that P will fairly compensate him for his labor and for any human capital he brings to or develops on P's behalf. Where part of A's compensation involves a possibility of promotion to an ownership interest in P's business, A also seeks assurance that if he meets implicit conditions, P actually will promote him. In theory, P should be able to devise a contract specifying that A will receive rewards based on his productivity.

For the contract to be effective, however, both parties must be able to obtain inexpensive and reliable indicators of A's effort or output, or at a minimum, both parties must have identical information about A's productivity. Otherwise, both parties cannot verify compliance with the contract terms. But monitoring output in the provision of legal services to clients is difficult and costly. While P can measure the number of hours A puts in, she has a more difficult time assessing how many "quality" hours A has worked. Ultimately, the assessment of A's output comes down to a subjective evaluation of performance by those charged with observing him. Because of the inherent subjectivity of the assessment, A cannot verify it. He cannot, for instance, look up his performance and say, "Hey, you miscalculated my contribution." In addition, neither P nor A can easily separate one individual's contribution to the production of legal services from that of other participants. This problem especially arises where P, the supervisor, is one of the contributors (as she generally is) and therefore has an incentive to understate A's contribution. Thus, no monitoring system can assure the honest reporting of A's contribution—an assurance essential to accurate compensation under an output-based or piece-rate compensation scheme—because A cannot independently verify (or prove) his precise contribution.

When monitoring is costly or information is asymmetric, A has the opportunity to produce less-than-promised effort or output because detection is unlikely. P has the opportunity to reduce her compensation costs by purposely undervaluing A's effort. A cannot independently verify whether P has evaluated him correctly, but he recognizes P's incentive to cheat. Consequently, he will hesitate to produce a maximum effort for fear that P will not reward him adequately. Under these circumstances, P most likely will not extract more than minimal effort from A....

First, to assure the partners that they will receive the proper return on the investments they make—whether those investments are in client relationships, reputation, or the skills they impart to associates—the firm must induce associates not to grab or leave prematurely. The partner worries that the associate might walk off with the firm's clients or, often more realistically, depart with skills—or clients of his own—that the firm has paid the associate to develop. The firm wants to ensure that the associate has an incentive to remain with the firm until it fully amortizes those investments. Deferring payment of some percentage of the associate's salary creates part of that incentive. The firm fires those who act opportunistically and those let go lose this deferred income. Those who do not steal or leave prematurely receive the deferred salary in varying forms of promotion and bonuses....

...The rules are simple. For a fixed period of time (six to ten years), the firm pays salaries to associates who neither grab nor leave. At each successive stage in the hierarchy part of the associate's salary increase includes a deferred bonus for nonopportunistic behavior in the earlier years. In addition, during this period the firm implicitly tells its associates that it constantly evaluates them for a "super-bonus," paid in the form of promotion to partner. In effect, the firm holds a tournament in which all the associates in a particular entering class compete and the firm awards the prize of partnership to the top alpha (α) percent of the contestants. The firm evaluates associates on their production of two goods important to the firm's future welfare: high quality legal work and their own human capital. An associate's final standing in the tournament, measured subjectively not mechanistically, therefore will depend upon the size and quality of his "bundle" of both goods. In most instances a winner essentially must accumulate significant amounts of both high quality legal work and human capital, though amassing extremely high levels of one or the other might prove sufficient. After the fixed period of time has expired, the firm ranks the players in a particular class and declares the top α percent the winners. . . .

The tournament provides the assurances and incentives required by both the associates and the partners. Associates now have an incentive to produce the maximum combination of legal work and human capital. By declaring up front that, on average, it will promote a fixed percentage of associates after a period of time, the firm obligates itself to distribute a fixed amount of compensation to the winners of the tournament. Regardless of who wins the tournament the firm must pay out the same prizes. This point is essential to the firm's compensation scheme because it communicates to associates that it is in the firm's own interest to award the prize of partnership to those who have produced the largest combined bundle of output, quality, and capital. To award the prize on other grounds would saddle the firm with less productive attorneys at no savings in prize money. Moreover, the associate easily can verify that the firm pays out the agreed-to prizes by observing how the present and preceding classes fare and whether the firm continues to recruit new classes of associates. If the firm intends to continue recruiting new associates, current associates may safely assume that the firm will continue to adhere to the implicit contract rather than risk the adverse reputational and motivational effects associated with breaching. By promoting more than none but less than all of the associates, the firm communicates to them that it will reward productivity but not shirking; therefore, the associates will exert a maximum effort to win the contest. . . .

The promotion-to-partner tournament, originally instituted as a mutual monitoring device, contains an internal dynamic that explains why law firms must grow. Growth occurs because, at the end of the tournament, the firm must replace not only the losing associates who depart, but also all those who win and are promoted. If the firm did not hire associates to replace its newly promoted partners, then the pre-tournament partners would share their surplus human capital with fewer associates and, therefore, make less money. To maintain at least a constant ratio of pre-tournament associates to pre-tournament partners, the firm must hire new associates to take the place of those who won the tournament. By replacing promoted attorneys the firm grows by the number of promotions. . . .

. . . [O]nce established, the firm will find the promotion percentage costly to change. The integrity of the firm's compensation package depends upon the associates' ability to observe the promotion percentage. By its actions toward preceding classes, the firm implicitly tells the associates what percentage can expect to win promotion. Each year, the associates can observe who actually wins and determine whether this corresponds to the promotion percentage they have come to expect. If associates see the promotion percentage decline, they likely will not develop strong expectations about its ultimate level as their tournament draws to a close. Moreover, a firm that (implicitly) advertises one promotion percentage, but then unpredictably lowers it at the end of the tournament, will have difficulty recruiting in the future. Associates will not trust the firm to award as many prizes as it initially promises. Consequently, assuming adequate information and holding all other variables constant, prospective employees will downgrade the value of the firm's compensation package. This downgrading will place the firm in an inferior competitive position vis-à-vis other recruiters. This phenomenon does not require a firm to adhere strictly to a given promotion percentage, but rather suggests that on average the promotion percentage cannot decline.

If the promotion percentage is constant and the associate-to-partner ratio is not decreasing, a firm will grow exponentially.

Notes

1. How persuasive do you find "tournament theory" as an explanation for the growth of large law firms during the last thirty years? What factors appear to be left out of Galanter and Palay's explanation? What must be true about the way that law firms make new partners for the theory to explain all—or even the majority—of law firm growth? Are there other ways in which law firms grow that would undermine the explanatory value of tournament theory? For critique of Galanter and Palay's account of law firm growth, see Frederick W. Lambert, "An Academic Visit to the Modern Law Firm: Considering a Theory of Promotion-Driven Growth," 90 Mich. L. Rev. 1719 (1992); Robert L. Nelson, "Of Tournaments and Transformations: Explaining the Growth of Large Law Firms," 1992 Wis. L. Rev. 733; and Richard H. Sander & E. Douglass Williams, "A Little Theorizing About the Big Law Firm: Galanter, Palay, and the Economics of Growth," 17 L. & Soc. Inquiry 391 (1992).

2. Even if tournament theory persuasively explains the growth of *some* large law firms, is it persuasive as an explanation for the growth of *all* large firms, even during the "golden age"? Some commentators have argued that this account of law firm growth best describes a subset of traditional elite law firms but fails to capture a more diverse universe of growth models common among other large law firms. See, e.g., Eli Wald, "Smart Growth: The Large Law Firm in the 21st Century," 80 Fordham L. Rev. 2867 (2012).

3. Can large law firms continue to grow exponentially forever? Will corporate law firms one day reach the size of large accounting firms? Is such growth good for clients? For a dissenting view on growth by a former top general counsel, see Benjamin W. Heineman, Jr., "Bigger Isn't Always Better: One Stop Shopping at Giant Global Firms Has its Limits, Says GE's Former Top Lawyer," Corporate Counsel Magazine, Nov. 2008, at 71.

4. Galanter and Palay claim that growth in large law firms is inevitable and portray partners as having little ability to control or prevent their firms from expanding. This characterization conforms to a common lament among senior partners in

major firms that they preferred life when their firms were smaller, friendlier, and less competitive, but they are powerless to resist the economic logic of growth. Do you buy this characterization? In what ways has the current generation of law firm partners actively contributed to the growth in large law firms other than by honoring their promise to promote a fixed percentage of every entering class of associates?

Although Galanter and Palay employ tournament theory as a means of explaining law firm growth, the theory itself has a more general applicability. Specifically, many theorists who are skeptical that tournament theory explains the growth of large law firms nevertheless continue to use the tournament model to describe the internal labor markets of these institutions. Law firms, these theorists claim, are organized like a sporting event in which associates compete against each other in a fair competition at the end of which the "best" are selected for partnership.

Not surprisingly, law firms find this image of their work and promotion practices appealing. The question is whether it is accurate. Consider the following critique:

David B. Wilkins & G. Mitu Gulati
Reconceiving the Tournament of Lawyers: Tracking, Seeding, and Information Control in the Internal Labor Markets of Elite Law Firms
84 Va. L. Rev. 1581 (1998)

... Our critique of tournament theory proceeds along two seemingly paradoxical lines. First, we argue that a theory of law firm internal labor markets must take account of the ways in which the promotion-to-partnership tournament differs from a standard rank-order ... tournament. ...

[Second, such a theory must also acknowledge that] law firms employ a multiple incentive system that ... incorporates practices typically found in the kind of "real" tournaments upon which tournament theory is loosely based but that are not included in the standard economic model. ...

Galanter and Palay's model of the promotion-to-partner tournament rests on a number of interconnected assumptions about the internal labor practices of elite firms, and the motivations and actions of those who participate in and help to shape these practices. ...

These assumptions do not accurately describe the internal practices of contemporary elite law firms. ...

Not Everyone Is Competing

... [A]necdotal evidence ... strongly suggests that a large number of associates have opted out of—or more accurately, never opted into—the tournament.

The fact that a significant percentage of entering associates do not see themselves as participating in the tournament creates two important problems for firms. First, firms must find other ways to motivate those associates who do not intend to compete in the race to make partner. . . .

Second, firms must develop ways of identifying those associates who *are* interested in winning the tournament.

The Playing Field is Not Level

. . . Large law firms produce two categories of work that must be done by associates. The first category consists of work that provides valuable training in the skills and dispositions of lawyering. . . .

Training work encompasses a wide variety of tasks. Examples include writing a draft motion or brief and then going over the draft with the partner, watching a partner negotiate a contract or conduct a strategy session with a client, and writing a comprehensive report of a new regulatory development that will be distributed to clients. . . . [T]raining work also enables an associate to develop strong relationships with particular partners. . . .

. . . [Law firms also] produce a substantial amount of "paperwork." Examples of paperwork range from writing, answering, and supervising discovery requests, to proofreading and making slight modifications to pre-existing corporate documents, to writing legal memos to the file or for review by senior associates, to faxing important documents to the client. . . . Paperwork is unlikely, however, to develop the kind of higher order skills and judgment that partners look for when evaluating associates for partnership. Nor does this work typically result in an associate developing relational capital, since partners rarely have much contact with those who are only doing paperwork and tend to notice these unlucky associates only when something goes wrong. Given this division of labor, every associate who wants to have a chance of winning the promotion-to-partner tournament needs to gain access to training work.

Unfortunately [training work] is in short supply [for three reasons]. First, because of the sheer volume of paperwork generated by many areas of legal practice, firms must deploy a substantial number of associates to satisfy this demand. . . . More important, training work requires the firm to commit a substantial amount of uncompensated (or, at best, undercompensated) partner time . . . . Finally [because paperwork only requires minimal training] firms do not need to provide . . . all of their associates with firm-specific training. . . .

. . . [T]he importance and scarcity of training work undermines the effectiveness of the promotion-to-partner tournament as a method for resolving the mutual monitoring problems of partners and associates. Two problems are significant.

First, those not receiving training work have strong incentives to shirk or leave. . . .

. . . [Second,] if associates recognize that their chances for succeeding at the firm are directly tied to their ability to gain access to training work, then those who want to win the tournament are likely to engage in fierce struggles to obtain this scarce good. . . .

Individual Umpires Have a Stake in Who Wins the Tournament

. . . Partners are players with vested interests, as opposed to neutral decisionmakers, because partnership no longer means tenure. . . . It is a reality of today's competitive environment that if new partners find that they are generating the lion's share of the partnership's profits, they may well decide to terminate some of their older, less productive colleagues. Further, in addition to fighting to retain their hard-earned partnership positions, partners also compete to move up within the hierarchy of partners. . . .

. . . As a result [of the opportunity cost of training associates], partners have an incentive to ration time spent on training and invest only in those associates who are most likely to provide direct benefit to their practices (i.e., the one or two associates for whom an individual partner can provide a steady stream of billable assignments). . . .

. . . [When it comes time to make partnership decisions], [i]ndividual partners . . . have strong incentives to favor their own protégés over the arguably better qualified protégés of others. . . . [S]enior partners need junior partners who will do their work (without trying to steal their clients) while the senior lawyers go out to look for additional business. In later years, senior partners depend on their protégés to support them (perhaps by referring clients in the other direction) when the senior lawyers are no longer able to protect their own interests in the partnership. Given these realities, we should expect tournament winners to be selected as much on the basis of politics as on firm efficiency. . . .

Choosing the Best Representatives, Not the Best Performers

. . . [A]lthough the inclination and willingness to work hard as an associate may signal the same willingness as a partner, it is the acquisition of human capital that is crucial for the partner. If a partner does not acquire a sufficiently high amount of human capital, there will not be enough to rent out to the associates. As a result, as we indicated [in a prior section], partners do not rank "hours worked" highly on the list of criteria that are important to the partnership decision.

Moreover, partners need a substantively different kind of human capital than good associates need—even associates who do primarily training work. The most important work done by today's large law firm partners is bringing in business. Associates do virtually no rainmaking. Although accumulating the kind of general and firm-specific human capital that comes from being a good associate undoubtedly plays a role in whether a given lawyer is likely to become a rainmaker, even the best associate may not have the different mix of personal and professional qualities that enable someone to attract significant corporate business.

Finally . . . partnership decisions are beholden to the business cycle. Even if firms feel substantial pressure to make the same *number* of partners every year (regardless of swings in demand), the *location* of these partners (i.e., corporate, litigation, tax, etc.) will depend upon the amount of business that the firm believes each of these departments is likely to produce in the future. Thus, the fundamental issue with respect to both the individual candidate and the firm's needs is one of prediction, not reward.

Who's on First?

. . . If firms were structured as simple economic tournaments, . . . the firm would do everything possible to make the partnership process an open book, [including] permit[ting] associates to sit in on partnership meetings . . . or hir[ing] external verifiers, such as accounting firms, to make sure that the process involved a fair and accurate evaluation and ranking of [associates]. . . .

Needless to say, these standard tournament theory predictions never fail to draw laughter from associates and partners at elite firms. Why? Because the partnership decisions at these firms are explicitly structured to be a black box, i.e., to provide as little internal visibility as possible. Associates have little or no information about what goes on at partnership or committee meetings, and the partnerships at these firms do not see disclosing the details of these meetings as a way to increase efficiency. . . .

The Tournament Reconceived: Why This Is Not Your Father's Partnership Tournament

[Law firms employ a multiple incentive system to ensure that all associates work hard while concentrating scarce training and mentoring resources in the hands of those associates most likely to stay and compete for partner. This system has four main parts.]

. . .

High Wages

High [or efficiency] wages offer incentives for employees to exert high levels of effort where the wage paid is significantly higher than that paid at an alternative job. . . . [W]orkers fear losing these scarce high-wage jobs . . . [and] know that employers can easily find replacement workers who will gladly take their [place]. . . .

The contemporary market for lawyers matches what one would expect to find in a sector where the elite firms pay efficiency wages. Indeed, the difference in relative wages between the salaries paid by large law firms and those paid by other legal employers is one of the most striking features of contemporary legal practice. . . .

. . . [M]any students state that the high salaries paid by corporate firms are the primary reason why they choose jobs in this sector over what they consider to be more rewarding work in government or public interest practice. . . .

More important, once an associate joins a corporate firm, the wages paid by these employers create a substantial inducement to stay and to continue to work hard. . . .

Training [and Tracking]

Law students know that they need to develop their general human capital if they are to become successful lawyers. Law school offers little instruction in how to be a lawyer. Students, therefore, have good reason to seek out jobs that they believe will train them in the skills and dispositions that they need to become competent practitioners. Firms, in turn, have strong incentives to cater to this need by promising these aspiring professionals that in addition to their high salaries, associates will receive significant training that will be of value to them wherever they work. . . .

. . . [H]owever, it is inefficient for a firm to invest in training *all* of its associates. Given the confluence of high leverage ratios and low levels of commitment by many associates to winning the tournament, the majority of associates who join a given large firm will leave, most before reaching the rank of senior associate. Moreover . . . firms generate an enormous quantity of paperwork which can be done by associates with little or no training. Taken together, these two factors . . . give firms strong incentives to separate associates into two informal, but nevertheless quite real groups: training-work associates and paperwork associates.

Tracking is the norm in many sporting competitions [such as tennis tournaments]. . . . Tournaments in the workplace can also benefit from tracking. . . . The model of elite firms we describe fits this pattern. . . . Associates who do well on their initial training assignments are given preferential access to additional training opportunities. Those junior associates who successfully complete a number of such assignments move up to become senior associates, giving them even greater access to training opportunities, and, equally important, helping them build strong relationships with partners. . . . Finally, once associates are firmly on the training track, they are likely to be further protected in the evaluation process. . . .

Tracking . . . helps firms solve the dilemma created by the fact that many entering associates have only a weak commitment to winning the tournament. . . . Through tracking, firms strengthen the commitments of associates whom they want to stay while simultaneously giving those not receiving training reason to seek rewards other than winning the tournament. Associates who continue to get good work are more likely to be happy and stay at the firm. . . . [T]hose associates who consistently receive only paperwork are likely to realize that their partnership chances are limited and leave voluntarily . . . .

Seeding

. . . [S]ome associates are "seeded" directly onto the training track. These favored associates immediately get assigned projects with the potential for creating high levels of firm-specific and relational capital, e.g., assignments with lots of client and partner contact. . . .

In sporting tournaments . . . tournament officials commonly "seed" competitors and assign them to a track before the tournament begins. . . . [Law firms have an incentive to do the same thing.] Many—perhaps most—associates obtain their initial assignments on the basis of some combination of expressed preferences and random selection. . . . If initial assignments are left [entirely] to chance [, however], a highly prized associate—for example, a former Supreme Court law clerk—might get discouraged and leave the firm (or stop investing in winning the tournament) because he receives a bad initial assignment . . . . One way to prevent this from happening is to . . . [give such a valuable associate] immediate access to the training track. . . .

. . . [Firms] base their initial rankings largely on . . . law school [ranking], clerkships, law review membership, and law school performance. . . . By virtue of first, being admitted to a rigorous academic environment, and second, succeeding in that environment, these academic "superstars" have demonstrated their ability to win tournaments. Firms, however, have incentives for seeding academic superstars that go beyond whatever predictive judgments can be made about their potential quality from their previous academic success. Regardless of whether they have a high correlation with job skills, signals such as law school status and grades are both "visible" and "rankable" to two communities that are of pivotal importance to law firms: clients and students.

. . . [L]isting the pedigrees of their attorneys has always been considered an acceptable way for a firm to signal its quality to clients. . . . In addition to clients, firms also need a visible and rankable signal to send to the community of law students. . . . Given that many firms, particularly those in the same market, tend to have similar structures and policies . . . a firm's reputation among law students is substantially determined by its ability to be selective in recruiting law students. . . .

Because firms get additional signaling values by hiring lawyers with prestigious academic credentials (in addition to whatever productivity gains they may receive), these institutions have strong incentives to recruit heavily graduates with these credentials and to protect those that join the firm by immediately placing them on the training track. . . .

Information Management

[Contrary to tournament theory's assumptions about transparency,] firms have strong incentives to manage the flow of information to associates and law students in order to maximize the system's overall incentive effects. . . .

Information management systems . . . exist in some tournaments [as a means of maximizing participant effort]. For example, in certain debate tournaments, teams are not told whether they have won or lost their preliminary rounds until after all of these rounds have been completed. . . . Similarly, until recently, in soccer only the referee knew exactly how much time was left in the game. . . .

Elite firms utilize a similar information control policy. . . . [F]irms pursue a "black box" approach in which associates are provided only a vague idea about the criteria for making partner and almost no information about how these criteria are applied in particular cases. . . .

Indeed, the kind of information management in which the large elite law firms engage exceeds even what one finds in sports. In [sports,] participants know what the rules and criteria for victory are even if they are unaware at any given moment of exactly how these rules are being applied. Law firms . . . seek to conceal—or more often, to reveal selectively—both the rules and the criteria themselves. . . .

[Information management] maximizes the "end-of-game" effort by senior associates. . . . Having no more than a minimal amount of information about how they rank against their competitors and what weights are going to be given to different aspects of their performance/capital acquisition, these lawyers have strong incentives to work hard at everything possible. . . .

[For junior associates not on the training track] the less [they] know about the opportunities afforded those on the training track (or, to put the point somewhat differently, the harder it is for a paperwork associate to evaluate the difference between the work he is doing and training work) the more likely it is that he will be motivated to work hard . . . . This is one reason, we suspect, why firms keep the evaluations of associates in their first few years vague and generally upbeat.

Notes

1. Professors Wilkins and Gulati argue that associates are subtly, but nevertheless powerfully, "tracked" into a training track and a flatlining track. In a prior article (p. 994), they describe how this process occurs:

> [E]ven if the firm as a whole has an interest in ensuring that every associate gets some minimal level of training, individual partners do not. Associate training is both a public good for the firm and a private good for individual partners. The firm as a whole arguably benefits when all associates receive some credible level of training. Individual partners, however, have sub-optimal incentives to contribute to the production of this firm-wide benefit. Training is costly to individual partners; time spent training is time that the partner cannot spend either producing revenue or consuming leisure. The benefits of training, on the other hand, are diffuse. To be sure, every partner needs a certain number of well-trained associates to do his or her work. Time spent training these associates produces private gains for the partner—if that associate continues to work for the training partner. Given that associates typically work for more than one partner, however, no individual partner will be able to capture the full value of time invested in training. As a result, partners have strong incentives to ration time spent on training and to invest only in those associates who are likely to benefit them and their practices directly.

> Given these incentives, we expect partners to make decisions about how to staff projects according to the following criteria:

> First, partners will have a preference for associates who need little or no training. Monitoring the work of other lawyers is both difficult and expensive. Partners want to staff their projects with associates who will be able to do the work with relatively little supervision. Finding lawyers who can perform tasks competently and quickly is therefore the preeminent selection criterion.

> Second, if the partner can secure the services of such an associate, the partner will invest in further training that lawyer. Although this seems paradoxical (since the lawyer was selected because he or she only needed

minimal training to do the job), training superstar associates is nevertheless an important part of the implicit bargain that partners strike with these new entrants and their colleagues.

Third, to the extent possible, partners will leave training and supervisory functions to senior associates. These lawyers, however, have little incentive to invest in training, as opposed to supervising, their charges. As an initial matter, there is a limit to what any particular senior associate knows. More importantly, since senior associates are also competing for scarce training opportunities and attempting to signal partners that they are well trained, these associates have an incentive to keep good work assignments (e.g., those involving client contact, court appearances, or plum writing assignments) for themselves instead of passing them down the line. The fact that only a few of these lawyers will become partners further increases their incentive to take credit for good work done by their juniors and to blame their charges for their own mistakes.

As a result, associates will gradually be divided into two broad categories: those who have received training (or are considered worthy of receiving training) and those who have not (and who are not considered good training prospects). Although the boundaries between these two groups are fluid, they nevertheless will tend to be self-perpetuating. Trained associates can lose their privileged status by making mistakes that cause partners to doubt that their training investment will be recouped (or to suspect that the reputational costs of being seen as pushing a relatively weak associate outweigh the benefits of providing training). Similarly, previously untrained associates can come to the attention of partners by doing exemplary work on routine assignments. More often, however, once an associate has been trained, other partners have an incentive to use her and to provide additional training. Those who do not get trained, on the other hand, are less likely to receive the kind of work that will give them the opportunity to become trained (or otherwise to demonstrate their talent).

Those who have not been trained face diminishing opportunities for success. Although we have seen that firms generate a substantial amount of relatively routine work, clients will not pay for this work to be done by senior associates when it can be handled just as effectively by lower-cost junior associates. As a result, an associate who has not been trained will gradually find that she has less and less work assigned to her as the firm becomes unable to bill her increasingly expensive time to clients.

Figure [12.3] portrays this divergence. The curved line denoting associates receiving training represents the standard story told to law students by every hiring partner during recruiting season: "Our firm loses money on associates during the first several years because we invest heavily in training these young women and men to become excellent lawyers. Even if you only stay at our firm a few years, you will develop the skills and dispositions that will help you succeed at any legal job you choose to take on." The flat line denoting associates who are not receiving training, however, portrays the reality that many enthusiastic recruits find when they join elite law firms: an initial period of grinding but undemanding work, followed by a gradual slow down until they are gently but firmly told that their services are no longer needed.

Figure 12.3

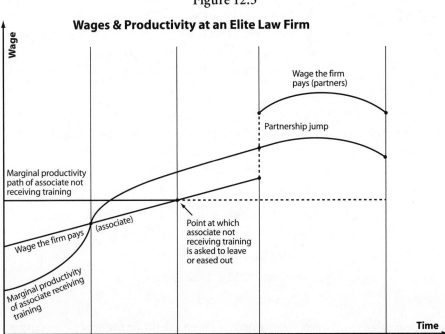

How persuasive do you find this claim? Many partners in large law firms — and most managing partners — vehemently deny that there is any formal or informal tracking of associates. Is there another way to account for the differences in work assignments and training opportunities that Professors Wilkins and Gulati describe, other than tracking?

2. In recent years, some law firms have taken steps to move away from the the ambiguity and unfairness of the informal work assignment system described by Professors Wilkins and Gulati by instituting a "competency based" model where associates must meet certain benchmarks before progressing from "junior," to "mid-level" to "senior" levels, often under the supervision of special work assignment coordinators (in many cases who are specifically hired for this purpose) to ensure that work assignments are distributed equitably. See Scott Westfahl, *You Get What You Measure: Lawyer Development Frameworks and Effective Performance Evaluation* (NALP 2008); Neil W. Hamilton, "Law-Firm Competency Models and Student Professional Success: Building on a Foundation of Professional Formation/Professionalism," 11 U. St. Thomas L.J. 6 (2013).

3. Is the "reconceived" model Professors Wilkins and Gulati describe sustainable over time? Can firms continue to keep information from associates and law students, given the burgeoning legal press and the availability of internet sites such as Above the Law? See also David B. Wilkins and G. Mitu Gulati, "What Law Students *Think* They Know About Elite Law Firms: Preliminary Results of a Survey of Third Year Law Students," 69 U. Cin. L. Rev. 1213 (2001) (reporting on a survey of third-year law students that demonstrates a growing awareness of how law firms work). Whereas the rise of legal websites like Above the Law gives law students access to new information into how law firms operate, some have argued that many newcomers to the profession continue to find law firms' policies, procedures and culture opaque and inaccessible. See Eli Wald, "BigLaw Identity Capital: Pink and Blue, Black and White," 83 Fordham L. Rev. 2509 (2015).

In 2008, Professor Galanter, this time writing with Professor William Henderson, revisited the tournament of lawyers to model its essential structure in light of the changes that have occurred since 1991. The following excerpt sets forth his new understanding.

Marc Galanter and William Henderson
The Elastic Tournament: A Second Transformation
of the Big Law Firm
60 Stan. L. Rev. 1867 (2008)

. . .

The promotion-to-partner tournament has been a defining feature of large corporate law firms since their emergence on the legal scene in the late nineteenth century. . . .

With minor variations, this was the shape of virtually all large American law firms providing legal services for organizational clients over the course of the last century. . . .

Developments in the past decade suggest a second and equally dramatic transformation in the character of the tournament and in the shape of the firm that it produces and that surrounds it. This transformation is the most drastic and significant metamorphosis in the large law firm since the invention and spread of the tournament firm in the closing years of the nineteenth century—a transformation that portends major shifts in the way that legal services are produced and delivered. It includes a number of discrete changes of considerable importance:

- Liberalization of the traditional up-or-out principle (by retention of "permanent associates" and appointment of non-equity partners who do not graduate to equity partnership);

- A growing share of non-tournament lawyers, such as of counsel, staff lawyers, staff associates, contract lawyers, and lawyers at outsourced locations, collaborating in the production of corporate legal services;

- Abandoning the equation of seniority with ownership and acceptance of permanent employee status for lawyers. Previously, power and standing were correlated with age; now they are not—a firm may have a thirty-five-year-old equity partner and a sixty-year-old associate, non-equity partner, or of counsel;
- Softening the commitment of partnership as a permanent achieved status—i.e., tenured—through de-equitization, outplacement, and mandatory retirement;
- Acceptance of lateral inward movement (which depends on client loyalty to lawyers rather than firms). But firms still fear the departure of rainmakers and stars;
- Acceptance of differentials in compensation and control that are not based on seniority or election;
- Management becoming a separate function performed by specialists; there are non-lawyer management auxiliaries like marketing director, public relations, technology, etc.

With these changes we see the inverted-funnel shape [Figure 12.4] of the classic early tournament firm replaced by what we might call the core-mantle model of the firm—a firm in which a core of owner-partners is surrounded by a much larger mantle of employed lawyers that includes not only aspiring associates, but also non-equity partners, permanent associates, of-counsel and de-equitized former partners. We visualize this model two-dimensionally in [Figure 12.5].

Figure 12.4 Inverted Funnel model

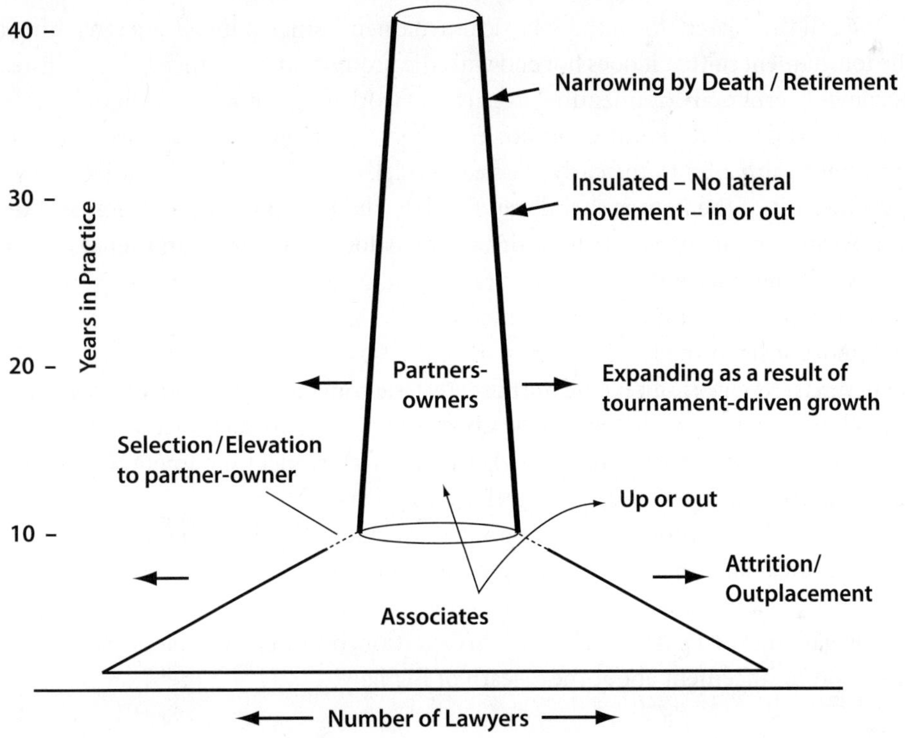

Figure 12.5 "Core & Mantle" model

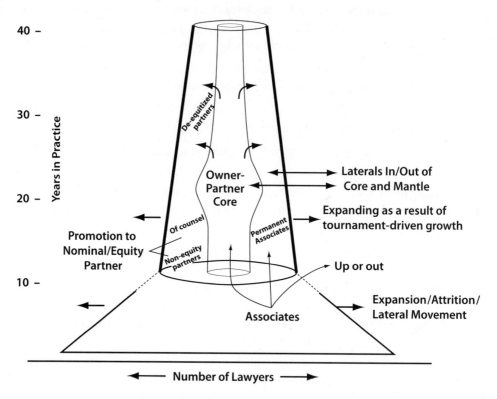

We call this "later" form the "elastic tournament" since it involves a stretching of the tournament so that it does not end with the promotion to partnership, but instead becomes "perpetual" or unending as partners work longer hours, accept differential rewards, and fear de-equitization or early forced retirement. The core of owners is thinner compared to the early classical model, and, arguably, its relative size vis-à-vis the rest of the firm is shrinking. Further, there is more competition and tension within the firm. Since the tournament is longer, thinner, and tenser, elastic seems a fitting image.

Notes

1. What do you think of the authors' "elastic tournament" model? Does it capture all of the changes that were described in the previous section about the transformation of corporate law practice? Is the "elastic" model fundamentally different from the "reconceived" tournament that Professors Wilkins and Gulati described? If so, is the "elastic" model likely to be any more stable than the "reconceived" one — or the traditional tournament Galanter and Palay described in 1991? If not, what do you believe law firms will look like in another twenty years? In 2013, Professor Henderson gave his own partial answer to this question, building on Professor Larry Ribstein's pronouncement about the "Death of Big Law":

The purpose of this Essay was to re-evaluate Larry Ribstein's seminal 2009 article, The Death of Big Law, with the benefit of three years of additional market data. The evidence suggests that the Big Law model is no longer viable. That is, there is insufficient client demand to support the perennial organic growth of large law firms. In search of growth, law firm managers are wading deeper into the lateral market and enriching lawyers whom they believe have large, portable books of business. Likewise, to preserve profitability, law firm managers are also axing lawyers who are unable to build and maintain their own client base, either internally within the firm (by being a highly skilled specialist) or externally (by being a rainmaker). Profitability is also being pursued through ever-higher amounts of leverage, albeit staff attorneys and non-equity partners appear to be supplanting traditional law firm associates.

None of these strategies make a law firm more attractive in the eyes of the clients—or, in Larry Ribstein's terminology, these strategies do not build a firm's reputational capital. Rather, most large law firms seem to be managed for the short-term benefit of individual rainmaking partners. To shield the firm against the defection of a large group of lateral lawyers, law firm managers are gravitating toward rapid lateral expansion and mergers—so, ironically, Big Law continues to grow. The resulting collection of lawyers may produce little or no synergistic value for clients, but it may create internal perceptions of firm vitality and growth and buy managers more time to deal with the vicissitudes of the lateral market. In this sense, Big Law is creating its own peculiar version of "Too Big to Fail." In the short term, the maintenance of relatively high profitability within these firms will convince stakeholders to stay the course—that is, to continue to pay out large profits and not invest too heavily in efforts to retool the underlying business model. These are the seeds of destruction.

Meanwhile . . . a new generation of legal entrepreneurs is beginning to occupy a portion of legal work traditionally performed by large law firms. Many of these companies are owned and controlled by nonlawyers. Further, they are establishing their own relationships with large corporate clients, thus positioning themselves for ascension up the value curve. Larry Ribstein was a strong proponent of market forces and private ordering to simulate innovation. He thus favored the reform of ethics rules that would permit nonlawyer investment and the enforcement of noncompete agreements among lawyers. Yet, in the year 2012 and without the benefit of regulatory reform, he might have been surprised by the rapid rate of growth of legal vendors owned and controlled by nonlawyer investors. Attracted by the large profit margins of a profession strongly wedded to its artisan modes of production, these new legal entrepreneurs are likely to compete for every portion of the legal supply chain that does not involve either direct client counseling or representation before a tribunal.

In the long run, I suspect that many Big Law brand names will survive, but a large number will also perish. Yet, even if a firm survives, its internal operations are destined to change. The owners may still make a handsome living, but the owners themselves will be either (a) fewer in number but more financially invested, akin to a closely held corporation with many employees, or (b) an employee-owned company in which each lawyer is carefully vetted at hiring and is expected to think and behave like an owner. With the emergence of more stable organizational forms that foster longer time horizons, we will witness a new era in which reputational capital—based on some variation of better, faster, cheaper—is built up rather than spent down.

William Henderson, "From Big Law to Lean Law," 38 Int'l Rev. Law & Econ. 5 (2014).

2. What are the implications of the changes in law firms identified above for the traditional claim that law firms are "pure" meritocracies in which the "best" associates are the ones who will be promoted to partnership? If making partner depends upon getting access to the "training track," how will this affect opportunities for women and minorities? Even if there is less "tracking" going on in large firms than Professors Wilkins and Gulati assert (pp. 984–985), what will happen if women or minorities *believe* that they will have more difficulty getting access to good work and mentoring opportunities?

––––––––––

In a prior article, Professors Wilkins and Gulati examined the implications of the organizational structure of large law firms on the career prospects of black lawyers.

David B. Wilkins and G. Mitu Gulati
Why Are There So Few Black Lawyers
in Corporate Law Firms?
An Institutional Analysis
84 Cal. L. Rev. 493 (1996)

. . .

Forty years after the Supreme Court's landmark decision in Brown v. Board of Education, society has made substantial progress toward eradicating the kind of overtly racist policies that excluded blacks from virtually every desirable sector of the economy. For many blacks, these changes have produced a dramatic growth in income and opportunity. In recent years, however, it has become painfully clear that simply dismantling America's version of apartheid has not produced economic parity between blacks and whites. Although poor blacks have benefited the least from the civil rights revolution, "high level" jobs in business and the professions have also proved surprisingly resistant to change. The fact that blacks have made so little progress in breaking into the corporate law firm elite—particularly at the partnership level—fits this larger pattern.

Commentators generally offer one of two explanations for this "glass ceiling" effect. The first, generally proffered by firms, posits a shortage of black applicants with both the qualifications and the interest necessary to succeed in the demanding world of elite corporate practice. The second, most often articulated by blacks, blames the slow progress on continued racism both inside corporate firms and among the clients upon whom these entities depend for their livelihood.

. . . [B]oth the "pool problem" and continuing racism against blacks play important roles in determining the employment opportunities available to African American lawyers. Standing alone, however, each explanation begs important questions. The "pool problem" explanation begs the question of whether the existing hiring and promotion criteria utilized by elite law firms to determine who is in the pool fairly and accurately predict future productivity. The racism story, on the other hand, fails to explain why firms that discriminate by refusing to hire or promote qualified black lawyers do not suffer a competitive disadvantage when those workers are employed by their competitors.

. . . [W]e present a stylized model of the contemporary elite corporate law firm. The model is premised on two related features of professional work: the inherent subjectivity of quality assessments and the difficulty and expense of monitoring. In response to these realities, we posit that it is efficient for firms to adopt the following tripartite strategy: high wages to create a large pool of available workers and to motivate those lawyers who are hired to work with relatively little supervision; a high associate-to-partner ratio, thus further encouraging associates to work hard in the hopes of becoming partners while at the same time allowing the firm to spread legal work among many lawyers with varying levels of knowledge and skill at the lowest possible cost; and a tracking system whereby the pool of associates is divided into those who will receive scarce training resources and those who will work on relatively undemanding assignments.

These . . . features [which make it harder for all associates to succeed] disproportionately disadvantage black lawyers. Two tendencies contribute to this result. First, because firms hire a large number of associates from a pool that has been artificially inflated by high salaries and ask many of them to do relatively undemanding work, these institutions have little incentive to invest in obtaining detailed information about the quality of potential employees. Hence, individuals within the firm can use race as a factor in their decisionmaking without hurting the firm's bottom line. The same goes for retention and promotion. Decisions to invest scarce training resources in average whites as opposed to average blacks will not hurt the firm's chances of producing the small number of high quality partners that it needs to guarantee its productivity in future years. As a result, firms have little incentive to root out employment decisions that, either consciously or unconsciously, prejudice blacks or favor whites.

Second, because firms have no incentive to stop these practices, black lawyers in firms (as well as those contemplating joining firms) are more likely to choose human capital strategies that, paradoxically, decrease their overall chances of success in these environments. Since blacks reasonably believe that they face an increased risk that their abilities will be unfairly devalued or overlooked, they have an incentive to over-invest either in avoiding visible negative signals or in obtaining easily observable positive signals that clearly identify them as superstars. Both of these strategies, however, are potentially counterproductive to the extent that they diminish a black lawyer's opportunity or incentive to obtain the skills upon which success at the corporate law firm ultimately depends. . . .

We divide our review of the data into two parts: recruiting and retention. As those concerned with law firm integration consistently report, simply hiring more black lawyers is unlikely to change the racial composition of these institutions in light of the fact that virtually all of these new entrants leave before making partner. Retention, not recruitment, is therefore the key to increasing the number of black lawyers. Retention, however, is affected by the dynamics of the recruiting process. Obviously, before a black lawyer can successfully move herself on to the "training track," she must first be hired. . . . [T]he fewer blacks that a firm already has among its associates and partners, the more difficult it will be to recruit black students. . . .

A. Recruitment

. . . Firms now expend enormous resources (in dollars and time) on interviewing second, third, and even some first year students for summer and full time positions. [Paradoxically, however,] they collect little information about a law student's actual substantive legal knowledge or skills, and the information that they do acquire on these issues is generally ignored. . . .

. . . The [on-campus] interview consists of a brief twenty-minute discussion with a single lawyer . . . taken up almost entirely by a discussion of the applicant's general interests, background and experience, and whatever questions the applicant has about the firm. . . .

Firms . . . make call-back decisions based on the information that appears on an applicant's resume and transcript and a single lawyer's assessment of the candidate's general promise and personality. . . . Rather than ranking candidates by academic standing, firms tend to use loose grade cutoffs pegged to the academic standing of the applicant's school. . . .

More often than not, call-back interviews merely repeat this pattern. . . .

. . . Although firms collect information about their summer associates, this information rarely influences hiring decisions. . . . Many of the country's most prestigious firms grant offers to all of their summer associates. . . .

The fact that firms rely on a few objective signals to identify qualified applicants at the visible stage and reserve the right to go behind these credentials to make judgments about personality and fit at the invisible stage doubly disadvantages black applicants. . . . [B]y relying on sorting devices such as law school status, grades, and law review membership, firms systematically exclude the majority of black applicants, who do not have these standard signals. Thus, although blacks may be more likely to attend higher status law schools than whites, the schools with the largest black populations are not ones from which large firms typically recruit. Even black students with superstar credentials from lower status schools have little or no chance of being hired by a large firm. Those blacks who do attend elite schools face recognized barriers (e.g., poor primary and secondary school education, diminished expectations, hostile environments, and part-time work) to performing well in the classroom or in extra-curricular activities such as law review. Given these added pressures, it is plausible, as both conservative critics of affirmative action in elite schools and supporters of historically black schools frequently assert, that some black students who are currently admitted to elite schools would be more successful . . . if they did not attend these academic institutions. However, given the nearly dispositive role that the status of an applicant's law school plays in the recruiting process, black students who want to have the option of working at an elite firm have little incentive to choose this option. . . .

. . . [T]o the extent that firms make hiring decisions based on signals such as grade point averages, as opposed to the substantive content of the courses a student has taken or other indicia of the skills that the candidate has acquired in law school, black applicants have an incentive to structure their education so as to maximize the former at the expense of the latter. . . .

At the same time, the emphasis on personality and fit at the invisible stage can disadvantage black applicants with traditional signals. . . . [A] consistent line of empirical research demonstrates that when whites evaluate blacks, they frequently attribute negative acts "to personal disposition, while positive acts are discounted as the product of luck or special circumstances." Empirical and anecdotal accounts of the experiences of black and white applicants in the interviewing process confirm that this phenomenon negatively affects employment opportunities for black lawyers. Pervasive myths about black intellectual inferiority combined with lower average levels of achievement in areas such as grades and test scores tend to make white interviewers question the credentials of blacks more than those of whites. In addition, interviewers generally expect to feel less comfortable when interviewing blacks. Similarly, as we note above, interviewers frequently tend to believe that blacks are "uninterested" in corporate practice. . . .

. . . Since race is costless to observe, it provides a convenient mechanism, much like "personality" and "fit," for sorting applicants. . . . [B]lacks on average have less access to influential contacts and other informal networks that allow some other candidates to bypass the formal screening requirements. . . .

B. Retention, Promotion, and Survival

. . .

An associate's perception about which track she is on will have a substantial impact on how long she decides to stay with the firm. . . .

Black associates face three significant barriers to getting on the training track. First, they are less likely than whites to find mentors who will give them challenging work and provide them with advice and counseling about how to succeed at the firm. Second, they face higher costs from making mistakes than their white peers. Third, their future employment prospects with other elite firms diminish more rapidly than those of similarly situated associates. . . .

. . . Blacks consistently report that they have difficulty in forming these supportive relationships. For example, in our survey of black Harvard Law School graduates, less than 40% of those surveyed, and only 24% of the pre-1986 graduates, stated that a partner had taken interest in their work or their career. Sixty-eight percent of those who did not find a mentor, including 79% of the post-1986 graduates, stated that this was a significant factor in their decision to leave the firm. . . .

. . . Chief among [the factors that contribute to this problem] is the bias that potential mentors have for protégés who remind them of themselves. . . . [B]lacks may also suffer from a general perception that they are "less interested" in corporate work than other lawyers. This sentiment may be reinforced by the fact that black associates appear to be more likely than their white peers to do more than the average amount of pro bono work, to hold skeptical views about the social utility of some of the goals of their corporate clients, and to leave corporate practice for jobs in the public sector. . . .

Finally, black associates will have difficulty getting onto the training track precisely because the generation of black associates before them did not. Partners have less incentive to invest scarce training resources in associates who they think are unlikely to be at the firm long enough for them to recoup their investment. Not only are black associates less likely to make partner, but their average tenure may also be shorter than that of their white peers. As a result, black associates are doubly penalized for the firm's failure to retain and promote black lawyers. . . .

Rational Strategies in the Face of Reasonable Fear

Black associates find themselves in a double bind. On one hand, they understand that they are less likely to get on the firm's training track. On the other, they face diminishing opportunities in the lateral job market the longer they stay at the firm. This combination produces a level of fear and anxiety about the future that is, even from the firm's perspective, sub-optimally high. . . . As a result, they have strong incentives to choose career strategies that either minimize the danger of sending a negative signal or, conversely, maximize their opportunity for being regarded as superstars. Both strategies, however, can end up diminishing a black associate's long term chances for success at the firm.

An associate wishing to reduce the chance of making mistakes can either steer clear of demanding assignments (because of either the difficulty of the work or the level or intensity of the scrutiny likely to be given by the partner) or take fewer risks in completing the work. There is some evidence to suggest that black associates disproportionately pursue both of these strategies. . . .

From a black associate's perspective, both of these risk-averse strategies are rational responses to his environment. Given the inherent subjectivity of "good judgment," a risky action can be interpreted as either a sign of innovativeness and independence or a mark of stupidity and an inability to follow instructions. Since black associates have reason to fear that they are more likely to be branded with the negative description and that this characterization will be more difficult to shake, it is not surprising that they tend to be overly cautious in their choices.

Nevertheless, both of these risk-averse strategies reduce the gains (in terms of retention and promotion) that black associates can expect to receive from their work. Successfully completing "difficult" work assignments is the best way for an associate to signal her quality and therefore to demonstrate that she is worthy of training. Since partners are looking for associates who can work effectively with relatively little supervision, traits such as initiative, creativity, speed, and confidence are highly valued. The more risk-averse one is, however, the more difficult it is to signal that one has these qualities.

At the opposite extreme, a black associate may seek out demanding assignments in order to overcome the presumption that she is "only" average—or worse. For example, a black lawyer might volunteer to work with a particularly demanding partner or take on a large number of assignments. To the extent that a black associate successfully completes these projects, she has a better chance of signaling that she is a superstar and therefore worthy of training. The risks, however, are also high. If the project is particularly difficult or the partner especially demanding, the black associate who is in fact "average" has a greater chance of failing—and failing big. Similarly, the high effort strategy of taking on a large number of assignments can also fail if the projects suddenly become due at once.

Notes

1. In the more than two decades since Professors Wilkins and Gulati published this piece, there have been many notable changes, not the least of which is the election of the first black president of the United States. As Professor Wilkins argues in another article, the new generation of black corporate lawyers who came of age after Brown v. Board of Education and the civil rights movement have played an important role in bringing these changes about. See David B. Wilkins, "The New Social Engineers in the Age of Obama: Black Corporate Lawyers and the Making of the First Black President," 53 How. L.J. 557 (2010). Yet notwithstanding these changes, after climbing slowly until the mid-2000s, the percentage of all associates in the nation's top law firms who are black has fallen from 4.6% to 3.9% between 2009 and 2015, and the percentage of black partners stands at a paltry 1.7%. See "2015 Diversity Scorecard: Minorities Gain Little Ground," American Lawyer, May 28, 2015, available at <http://www.americanlawyer.com/id=1202495217057/2015-Diversity-Scorecard-Minorities-Gain-Little-Ground>. Yet diversity efforts at law firms have never been higher.

What explains this lack of progress? In a lecture to commemorate the 20th anniversary of the publication of his and Professor Gulati's article, Professor Wilkins argued that three institutional features of the neo-Cravathist model that have become even more prevalent since the article was published have exacerbated the challenges black lawyers face in law firms:

- The shift from entry level to lateral recruiting. Lateral hiring contains less formal process than entry level hiring (there are no NALP disclosure requirements for recruiting laterals). It therefore places a greater emphasis on personal relationships, while increasing the perceived stakes since laterals are typically brought in to solve a specific and important need;

- The shift from apprenticeship to performance-based measures of associate advancement. Although designed to be more meritocratic, when not done well (which it often is not) the switch can lead to a shorter time horizon, and more pressure to demonstrate competency without necessarily giving all associates the opportunity and coaching to meet these metrics;

- The shift from partnership as (at least quasi-) tenure to increasingly tenuous roles. As law firms have resorted to "de-equitizing"—or even dismissing—partners in an attempt to boost profitability, there has been an increased emphasis on short term, top line individual revenue generation as the sole measure of partner contribution.

As Professor Wilkins argues, "all of these shifts disproportionately disadvantage blacks and other traditional outsiders, including white women." David B. Wilkins, "Why Are There *Still* So Few Black Lawyers in Corporate Law Firms: Lessons for Achieving Diversity and Inclusion in the New Global Age of More for Less," Vashon Lecture, May 20, 2016 (unpublished manuscript on file with the author). Recent empirical studies support Professor Wilkins's conclusion that blacks and other traditional outsiders have been disproportionately disadvantaged by these and other similar changes in the legal market since 1996. See Louise Ashley and Laura Empson, "Explaining Social Exclusion and the 'War for Talent' in the U.K.'s Elite Professional Service Firms," in *Diversity in Practice: Race, Gender, and Class in Legal and Professional Careers* (S. Headworth, R. Nelson, R. Dinovitzer, and D. Wilkins, eds. 2016) (arguing that the emphasis on "the War for Talent" falsely implies that there is a "scarcity" of qualified professionals in a way that privileges a certain "ideal type" that impedes diversity); Forest Briscoe and Andrew von Nordenflycht, "The Effectiveness of Inheritance vs. Rainmaking Strategies in Building Books of Business for Female and Minority Partners," id. (women and minorities are much less likely to "inherit" important client relationships which makes them much more vulnerable to economic shifts affecting the client relationships they can build on their own); Chris Rider, Adina D. Sterling, and David Tan, "Career Mobility and Racial Diversity in Law Firms," id. (minorities are the least likely to have the kind of relationships that protect them from institutional failure).

2. Professors Wilkins and Gulati confine their analysis to the experience of black lawyers in corporate law firms. To what extent do you think their analysis is applicable outside of this context? As we indicated at the beginning of this section, Hispanics, Asians, and Native Americans are also underrepresented in large law firms, particularly at the partnership level. Moreover, each of these groups has also been the subject of stereotyping and other forms of discrimination that might put them at a competitive disadvantage in a system that places a premium on tracking, relationships, and subjective decisionmaking. See, e.g., Linda E. Davila, "The Underrepresentation of Hispanic Attorneys in Corporate Law Firms," 39 Stan. L. Rev. 1403 (1987); Kiyoko Kamio Knapp, "Disdain of Alien Lawyers: History of Exclusion," 7 Seton Hall Const. L.J. 103 (1996) (describing discrimination against alien Asian lawyers).

Nevertheless, it is important not to assume that all minorities face identical obstacles. Although every minority lawyer confronts racial stereotypes, the *content* of these characterizations arguably differs for particular groups. Blacks, more than any other group in American society, face persistent and deeply held stereotypes about intellectual inferiority. See Andrew Hacker, *Two Nations: Black and White, Separate, Hostile, Unequal* 5–28 (1992). Asians, on the other hand, are often stereotyped as "foreign," "quiet," and "untrustworthy." Knapp, supra. These stereotypes — both pernicious — plausibly produce a different set of obstacles for black and Asian lawyers. The few empirical studies that disaggregate data by racial group support this intuition. See Elizabeth Chambliss, "Organizational Determinants of Law Firm Integration," 46 Am. U. L. Rev. 669 (1997) (finding important differences in the correlation between various structural characteristics of large law firms such as size, partnership track, and client base, with the number of black, Hispanic, and Asian associates and partners).

3. In the 1990s, a small but determined number of minority law firms attempted to escape both the limitations of traditional black law firms and the large law firms within which they did not feel fully included by creating a new breed of black — or minority — corporate firms. See David B. Wilkins, "If You Can't Join 'Em, Beat 'Em! The Rise and Fall of the Black Corporate Law Firm," 60 Stan. L. Rev. 1733 (2008). Propelled by the rise of powerful black mayors in a position to dispense lucrative legal work and growing pressure on companies to direct some of their business to minority lawyers, the founders of these institutions dreamed of establishing firms that might one day rival traditional firms in size and scope and which could compete with these institutions for both clients and talent. Although rarely articulated, their implicit model was the Jewish law firms founded half a century before out of a similar exclusion and which had grown sufficiently prosperous that they forced mainstream firms to abandon their anti-Semitic practices. For a time, the strategy appeared to work, and the scrappy entrepreneurs who had abandoned or transformed traditional black law firms to do corporate business, or who had dropped out of the traditional large firms that they felt neither wanted nor appreciated them, carved out a small, but successful, niche by representing public clients, publicly motivated companies, and

black capitalists. But by the early years of the twenty-first century, virtually all of these firms, some of which had grown as large as 100 lawyers, either shrank significantly or shuttered their doors altogether. Five interrelated factors contributed to this demise: the increasing difficulty of translating public power into private advantage due to growing constraints on black elected officials and legal restrictions against "pay to play" in awarding city business; the inherent limitation of affirmative action strategies that depend upon enlisting bar organizations to pressure corporate clients to change their purchasing decisions; the growing concentration and competition among traditional large firms for even the low end business these black corporate firms were getting; the widening gap between the world views and expectations of the black lawyers who founded these firms and the new generation of blacks who viewed going to a black law firm as a "lifestyle" choice as opposed to a "mission" to create a lasting black institution; and, paradoxically, their own success, as large firms recruited away successful partners and associates. Id., at 1737.

What—if any—difference does it make that the attempt to build black corporate law firms failed? Specifically, should we mourn the passing of these firms or celebrate them? Compare Eli Wald's assessment of the decline of the "Jewish" law firm with Professor Wilkins's evaluation of the decline of black corporate firms:

> There was never a compelling normative reason for the creation of the Jewish firm. It was created by discriminatory default, as a reaction and response to discriminatory hiring and promotion practices at WASP firms. Jewish firms never embraced a thick religious identity and presumably would be delighted to be rid of any such identity imposed upon them. . . . [Although] [t]he Jewish firm represented a safe haven . . . [r]elying on the existence of Jewish firms as professional havens in the event of renewed religious discrimination against Jewish lawyers comes at a cost—it keeps the fear of discrimination alive. Letting go of the idea of the Jewish firm is part of letting go of the fear of discrimination.

Eli Wald, "The Rise and Fall of the WASP and Jewish Law Firms," 60 Stan. L. Rev. 1803, 1865–66 (2008).

> Many of those who sought to build black corporate firms were interested in more than economic success. They also had a mission to create lasting black institutions that would reflect the sensibilities of the black community and help to serve its needs. In this respect, black corporate firms were very different from their Jewish predecessors which were, as Eli Wald documents, largely Jewish by default as a result of anti-Semitism in the mainstream corporate bar. The corporate law firms started by black lawyers beginning in the 1960s, on the other hand, were black by *design*. . . . Like those who continue to support the nation's historically black colleges and universities (HBCUs), these founders believed that even in a world without formal barriers to integration there was still an important place for black institutions dedicated to training young black lawyers and instilling in them a sense of pride, and to providing a range of services and support to the black

community with whom these founders felt a deep spiritual connection. . . . Moreover, like HBCUs, black corporate firms also provided the black lawyers who created and managed these organizations with an opportunity that even the most successful blacks in traditional elite firms almost never enjoy: the ability to be in charge of an institution that could pursue an approach to corporate law practice premised on the fact that blacks *as a group* hold decision-making authority. . . . Just as significantly, few *white* lawyers will learn what it means to participate in decisionmaking within institutions to which people like them are not ultimately in control.

David Wilkins, "If You Can't Join 'Em, Beat 'Em," 60 Stan. L. Rev. 1733, 1737–38 (2008). See also Heather K. Gerken, "Dissenting by Deciding," 57 Stan. L. Rev. 1745 (2005) (discussing the difference between minorities having the opportunity to participate in making a decision and their having the authority to make that same decision—and make it in a context where they are no longer in the minority).

4. What might convince law firms to change the rules of the tournament of lawyers to counteract the disadvantages that blacks and other minorities face? For example, should the ethics rules specifically address the issue of discrimination? In the 1980s, several jurisdictions, including New York, enacted ethics rules prohibiting lawyers from making employment decisions on the basis of race and other categories. As noted in Chapter 7, in 2016, the ABA amended Rule 8.4 to provide similar (and additional) protection. The new Section (g) makes it unprofessional conduct to:

> (g) engage in conduct that the lawyer knows or reasonably should know is harassment or discrimination on the basis of race, sex, religion, national origin, ethnicity, disability, age, sexual orientation, gender identity, marital status or socioeconomic status in conduct related to the practice of law. This paragraph does not limit the ability of a lawyer to accept, decline or withdraw from a representation in accordance with Rule 1.16. This paragraph does not preclude legitimate advice or advocacy consistent with these Rules.

What difference do you think a rule such as this might make? Is it likely to alter the dynamics of the tournament of lawyers that Professors Wilkins and Gulati describe? Might it have some other beneficial effects, perhaps by influencing the conduct or perceptions of clients, other lawyers, or the general public? Other than constitutional issues, are there any disadvantages to adopting such a rule? What are the implications of the new ABA rule for a lawyer's discretion about which clients or causes to represent? Recall the case of Anthony Griffin, the black lawyer who represented the Ku Klux Klan and was subsequently fired by the NAACP, discussed in Chapter 7. What if Griffin had *not* wanted to represent the Klan because of its racist views about blacks? Would the new ABA rule limit his discretion to do so? We will return to this question at the end of the Chapter.

5. Regardless of whether the ethics rules prohibit discrimination, lawyers, like other citizens, are subject to the limitations imposed by Title VII and other similar

statues. Is anti-discrimination law a good way to address the issues Professors Wilkins and Gulati describe? The evidence to date is not very promising. Many commentators have documented the difficulty of applying Title VII and other similar anti-discrimination laws to high-level jobs in which quality judgments are inherently subjective. See, e.g., Barbara J. Flagg, "Fashioning a Title VII Remedy for Transparently White Subjective Decisionmaking," 104 Yale L.J. 2009 (1995); Elizabeth Bartholet, "Application of Title VII to Jobs in High Places," 95 Harv. L. Rev. 945 (1982). Neither disparate treatment nor disparate impact analysis is well suited to rooting out the kind of adverse employment practices we describe. For the most part, the lawyers who prefer average whites to average blacks have no discriminatory animus as that term has been traditionally defined. Indeed, other things being equal, they would probably prefer to hire and/or promote (and indeed probably have hired and promoted) superstar blacks over average whites. (Some firms claim to go further, preferring average blacks over equally or better qualified whites. We return to the issue of affirmative action in Note 6.) Nor are the institutional practices that tend to keep blacks off the training track likely to be condemned under a disparate impact analysis, given that changing these practices would involve a fundamental restructuring of the way corporate firms do business. Not surprisingly, when they have been presented with claims of this type, courts have generally refused to second-guess the law firm's subjective decision. See Mungin v. Katten, Muchin & Zavis, 116 F.3d 1549 (D.C. Cir. 1997) (overturning a verdict for a black associate who alleged that he was turned down for partnership and terminated because of his race). For an informative discussion of the Mungin case, see Paul M. Barrett, *The Good Black: A True Story of Race in America* (1999). For a critique of Barrett's interpretation, see David B. Wilkins, "On Being Good *and* Black," 112 Harv. L. Rev. 1924 (1999).

6. The question of whether law firms have engaged, do engage or should engage in "affirmative action" to increase the number of minority lawyers they hire and/or promote has, like the question of affirmative action in the rest of American life, become increasingly controversial in recent years. Virtually every large law firm claims to be making special efforts to recruit and promote blacks and other minority lawyers. The scope and efficacy of these programs, however, are subject to dispute. Although few would deny that most law firms have made some effort in the last thirty years to hire and retain minorities, it is unclear how far these efforts extend beyond competing for minority lawyers who already meet a firm's established hiring credentials (or who have credentials similar to white lawyers hired by the firm under circumstances that are not characterized as affirmative action).

Professor Richard Sander, however, argues that law firms engage in extensive affirmative action for black applicants and that these actions paradoxically end up hurting their intended beneficiaries. See Richard H. Sander, "The Racial Paradox of the Corporate Law Firm," 84 N.C. L. Rev. 1755 (2006). Relying on data from the first wave of the *After the JD* study, Professor Sander argues:

Corporate law firms generally use aggressive racial preferences in hiring and recruiting blacks, and use preferences for Hispanics to a measureable, but somewhat smaller and less consistent degree. . . .

Once inside the firm, blacks and Hispanics report treatment that, on many dimensions, is very similar to the experiences of whites. However, in some critical areas—mentoring, training, and responsibility—blacks and (to a somewhat lesser degree) Hispanics fare much worse. In these same areas, white women in corporate law firms report treatment that is indistinguishable from the treatment reported by white men.

Black and Hispanic attrition at corporate firms is devastatingly high, with blacks from their first year onwards leaving firms at two to three times the rate of whites. By the time partnership decisions roll around, black and Hispanic pools at corporate firms are tiny.

These findings suggest an apparent paradox: . . . Although minority candidates are beneficiaries of large preferences on the job market, their opportunities to learn and perform once inside the firm are, in some ways, distinctly inferior.

I think the most plausible explanation of this paradox is that the use of large preferences by firms leads to disparities in expectations and performance that ultimately hurt the intended beneficiaries of those preferences.

Id., at 1758–59. How plausible do you find Professor Sander's thesis? Isn't the data he presents also consistent with the theory put forward by Professors Wilkins and Gulati that blacks are underrepresented in large law firms precisely because they are not given access to crucial developmental opportunities as a result of the complex interplay between stereotypes and implicit bias on the part of many white partners, on the one hand, and rational strategies that lead black lawyers to discount their chances for success in firms and look for opportunities elsewhere, on the other? See id., at 1759 (conceding that the data he presents is "consistent with more than one story about the behavior of corporate law firms," particularly the one Professors Wilkins and Gulati present). See also James E. Coleman & G. Mitu Gulati, "A Response to Professor Sander: Is it Really All About the Grades?," 84 N.C. L. Rev. 1823 (2006) (making a similar argument about Sander's data). For an argument that Sander has misinterpreted the AJD data in ways that fundamentally undermine his conclusions, see Monique R. Payne-Pikus, John Hagan, and Robert Nelson, "Experiencing Discrimination: Race and Retention in America's Largest Law Firms," 44 L. & Soc. Rev. 553 (2010). We will return to Professor Sander's broader argument that blacks are harmed by affirmative action in legal education, and that whatever remedial measures are appropriate should be done through programs that address class, not race, in Chapter 13.

7. Unfortunately, the problems faced by black lawyers do not disappear for those lucky few who do manage to become partners. Most diversity advocates tend to treat partnership as both the goal and the end of the inquiry. This orientation,

however, ignores the substantial obstacles to becoming a partner with power in today's competitive large law firms—obstacles that, like the rules of the revised promotion-to-partner tournament, disproportionately disadvantage blacks. See David B. Wilkins, "Partners without Power? A Preliminary Look at Black Partners in Corporate Law Firms," 2 J. Inst. Stud. Legal Ethics 15 (1999) (arguing that minority partners have a more difficult time succeeding than their white peers in the three markets in which partners must compete: the external market for new clients, the internal market for referrals from existing clients, and the labor market for talented associates).

8. Since 2000, there has been an increasing awareness of diversity issues in the legal profession outside of the United States. This is particularly true in the UK, where both major professional organizations and the government have issued reports calling on solicitors and barristers to increase the number of women and ethnic and racial minorities in their ranks. See Department of Constitutional Affairs, *Increasing Diversity in the Legal Profession* (2005); Law Society of England and Wales, *Delivering Equality and Diversity: A Handbook for Solicitors* (2004); Bar Council, *Equality and Diversity Code for the Bar* (2004). Indeed, the UK has gone further than the U.S. in addressing how issues of social class continue to frame opportunities in the legal profession, with some top law firms moving to "résumé blind" admissions to mitigate the strong bias in favor of students who have attended "elite" institutions such as Oxford and Cambridge. See Richard Garner, "Exclusive: Law Firm Clifford Chance Adopts 'CV Blind' Recruitment to Break Oxbridge Recruitment Bias," Independent, Jan. 9, 2014, available at <http://www.independent.co.uk/student/news/exclusive-law-firm-clifford-chance-adopts-cv-blind-policy-to-break-oxbridge-recruitment-bias-9050227.html>. See also Louise Ashley and Laura Empson, "Differentiation and Discrimination: Understanding Social and Class Exclusion in the UK's Leading Law Firms," 66 Human Relations 219 (2013). Notwithstanding these efforts, however, the percentage of racial and ethnic minorities in the UK is well below comparable percentages in the U.S., particularly with regard to lawyers in large law firms. See Black Solicitors Network, *Diversity League Tables: Ethnicity and Gender in the Legal Profession* (2006) (reporting that ethnic minorities constitute fewer than 9% of the lawyers in major UK law firms). For an example of the growing interest in diversity issues outside the English-speaking world, see Iyiola Solanke, "Where Are the Black Lawyers in Germany," in *Mythen, Masken und Subjekte* (Maureen Maisha et al., eds 2005).

The diversity issue that has by far received the most attention both outside and inside the U.S. is the paucity of women who have advanced to senior levels in large law firms notwithstanding the fact that they represent the majority—and in many countries around the world, the overwhelming majority—of entrants into the profession. The following section examines this critical issue in depth.

———————

In the mid-1970s, when women began entering the profession in significant numbers, they experienced explicit discrimination. Gradually, overt discrimination has declined and women lawyers have achieved parity with their male counterparts in entry-level positions out of law school. Positions of power and influence—for example, equity partners in large law firms—have proven, however, to be more elusive, with many women lawyers running into a glass ceiling, a phenomenon explored in the excerpt below.

Cynthia Fuchs Epstein, et al.
Glass Ceilings and Open Doors:
Women's Advancement in the Legal Profession
64 Fordham L. Rev. 291 (1995)

The profession in general and large firms in particular had undergone radical change with regard to the inclusion of women. Women had been an insignificant proportion of lawyers in the profession until the late 1960s (when they were about 3%) and constituted only a handful in the large firms. In the mid-1970s they started entering law schools in significant numbers and moving into all sectors of the law. This was probably in response to a number of legal cases against the law schools which maintained quotas that limited the number of women and minorities admitted. After law schools changed their policies in response to these suits and activism on the part of women in the profession and outside it, firms also faced sex discrimination law suits and changed their hiring policies.

Many partners within the firms had mixed feelings about bringing in women and minority lawyers: on the one hand, they believed it was probably the right thing to do legally and morally, and, on the other hand, they thought that women would not or could not measure up to the men whose backgrounds were familiar to them. A reference to the lingering presence of the traditional practices was made by Samuel Butler, then presiding partner at the Cravath firm, who stated, "[We do not make] partners of people who are very good lawyers and absolutely first-class people but are not what we think of as partners in our historical sense." But most law firms began to form committees to explore the special problems of people in the categories unfamiliar to them. One result was adoption of maternity leave policies and some provisions for part-time schedules. Other responses included the adoption of formal mentoring programs and various kinds of sensitivity training programs. And, of course, many men merely accepted women into their firms and treated them fairly.

By 1992 women made up 26.2% (up from 20.9% in 1989) of all the lawyers at the top 250 law firms in the country and 11.2% of their partners (up from 9.2% in 1989 and 3.5% in 1981). They were 37% of all associates (up from 33% in 1989 and 20% in 1981). They were 40% to 50% of the firms' new recruits in 1992. In 1992 all large firms had at least one woman partner, only six had only one, and a number had twenty or more. However, minorities were only a tiny percentage of the pool of recruits and of partners.

Of the many young people attracted to these firms, a subset hoped and expected to become partners but were aware of the poor odds they faced. In New York, for example, it was well known that chances for an associate to become partner could be as low as one in ten at the firm they entered as a young associate. And, of course, many did not attempt to predict the future and merely worked hard, adopting a come-what-may attitude.

The economic downturns of the early 1990s also created an atmosphere of pessimism as young and older lawyers alike experienced a turn in fortune for some firms, which was a clear reversal of the booming 1980's when growth offered opportunities to all. A number of firms found themselves in debt, because of expansion into real estate that lost value, as well as a general downturn in business. For the first time large firms laid off young lawyers. Firms became ever more entrepreneurial, and clients became less loyal, placing work with a number of firms instead of using only the one that had historically done their work. Firms had to compete for business in processes known as "beauty contests," in which they made presentations to clients regarding their competence and the economies of their legal work.

Traditional practices and criteria for partnership, too, have been challenged in recent times. In the past, the brotherhoods of partnership were served by cultural bonds reinforced through rituals and traditions, such as the use of segregated clubs for social events and stag parties, that excluded women and members of other outsider groups. Today there is far more sensitivity to such practices (although residues remain . . .), and, far from excluding women and minorities, some effort is made to include them. Yet many traditional prejudices remain at the same time.

It is in this atmosphere of changed conditions, practices, and rituals that we undertook this study of women's advancement and integration in large corporate law firms in New York City, exploring differences and similarities in the careers of women and men lawyers. . . .

*. * *

Executive Summary

This is a study exploring women's integration into large corporate law practices and their mobility within firms. . . .

Findings

1. There has been a steady upward trend in the proportion of women associates hired (now nearing equity with men). There has also been a steady but slight upward trend in the proportion of women partners in all firms, although there is variation between the firms. About half of women partners have moved upward through non-traditional tracks (e.g., laterally). Differences in firm cultures ("Midtown" vs. "Downtown") do not seem to explain receptivity to women partners. One Midtown firm and one Downtown firm had the best records of the eight.

2. Women can now be found working in all specialties instead of clustering in a few. Almost no women head a practice group or have a management role in a firm (the few exceptions thus far are a product of rotation of partners for one slot on the management team). Some attribute this to women's lack of seniority; others to their lower record of business development (which may be related to seniority). There were a number of women interested in holding these positions.

3. Men in our sample work more billable hours than women on average, but women's average is brought down by a subset who work part-time. Respondents report increased expectations regarding billable hours at all levels of the firm. There is dissatisfaction on the part of men and women regarding work loads at all levels, although women suffer disproportionately because they bear the greatest burden of family responsibilities. Most lawyers agree that long hours are tied to client expectations.

4. Men and women also experience greater pressures to become "rainmakers" in their firms, although the firms vary in their expectations that (a) associates bring in business and that (b) service partners bring in business.

Both women and men believe that women are disadvantaged in their ability to bring in business because they possess fewer contacts than men, have less time to devote to client development, and are not part of the networks in which business is generated. Women also believe that men do not create the same opportunities for women with regard to the inheritance of clients, or credit for business.

Women try to develop business through making their expertise visible (by lecturing and writing); keeping clients satisfied; and exploring new channels of contacts with women in the business world.

Women "junior" partners experience the most stress because they wish to bring in business but have, or are given, fewer resources with which to find it.

However, although most lawyers expressed the belief that client development skills or contact were necessary to attain partnership, many recently named partners (men as well as women) reported that they were not particularly accomplished at this task.

5. There did not appear to be a relationship between type of compensation arrangement and the proportion of women partners in a firm. Only one firm compensated lawyers according to a "lock-step" arrangement (where all partners share equally), while others used a point system in which an array of qualities were evaluated such as business, hours, and so on. The firm with the lock-step arrangement had a poorer record on the whole than other firms which compensated their members according to a point system.

6. Women's aspirations, like men's, are dependent on their assessment of opportunity in the firm, the current state of the economy, their assessment of the firm's needs for another partner in their practice group, and the feedback they get. Women who have done well report that when they got pregnant and had children, they were encouraged to come back and given good work to do. Many, however, report being passed over for good work at this time, and find that there is an expectation they

will drop out altogether or get off the partnership track. Some women do, independently, lower their aspirations when they have children finding the pressure of work too difficult to reconcile with their family responsibilities.

Women also face more ambivalence on the part of senior partners with regard to becoming their mentors (as advocates and teachers). Some women find having one advocate may backfire because there are suspicions that personal feelings rather than professional criteria motivate the mentor. Formal mentoring systems do not replace informal (and more effective) mentoring relationships. Women partners face problems in taking on mentoring relationships because they have less power and less time to perform this role.

7. Sexual harassment and sex discrimination contribute to glass ceilings. The most typical kind of sexual harassment is the use of coarse and vulgar joking and behavior; unwanted sexual overtures are rarely cited. More frequent discrimination occurs by differentiating women as "outsiders" and regarding them as less committed to the firm and less able to answer its needs for client satisfaction and development. The perception of difference, sex stereotyping, and treating women as a category rather than individually, provide serious obstacles to mobility. Women often share the stereotypes and use them in interpreting their own behavior. Not only do men stereotype women, but women stereotype men.

8. Women face prejudices that emanate from stereotypes regarding women's personality characteristics and the attribution of prejudice to clients, which may result in selective use of women on certain cases. Although this selectivity is denied by a majority of senior lawyers, a subset admit to it.

Women also face double-binds when they do not exhibit behavior based on male models (leading them to be branded as not tough enough) but are regarded as impaired women for acting "like men." Such "damned if you do; damned if you don't" situations act as a ceiling on their acceptance as a partner and a leader.

9. Although motherhood is usually considered a deterrent to career mobility, most women partners (three-quarters of them) in large firms are married and have children, although a somewhat higher percentage of men are married and have children. At the associate level a higher proportion of men are married. Overall, about half of the women attorneys in the firms had children. Most women partners successfully combine careers and child-rearing, employing a variety of coping strategies, although they do so under pressure. Because women lawyers (especially partners) are, on average, younger than the men, their children require more attention. Women have greater family obligations than male lawyers, many of whose wives do not work for pay. Women tend to assume conventional roles in the family, assuming major responsibility for children (although all use child care providers). Therefore, women, more than men, desire part-time work, although male lawyers also desire more time to spend with families.

10. Firm policies or informal practices that are "family friendly" may contribute to glass ceilings if women are penalized for taking advantage of them. The best

policies seem to be flexible and fitted to the needs of the lawyer and to the practice group in which she works. There are a number of models of flexible work time; some prove more successful than others.

11. Different perspectives regarding advancement are exhibited by many women in different cohorts. Many younger women feel that senior women have made excessive sacrifices as they have combined careers with families, while older women feel that the expectations of younger women are unrealistic. However, many senior women do feel that efforts should be made in the firms to accommodate the needs of younger lawyers and many have made efforts to accomplish this.

The study reveals that, although there has been steady progress in women's climb to partnership, it is slow. Stereotyping, traditional attitudes, and behaviors toward women, often focused around women's roles as mothers, discourage women's full participation and commitment, and accommodations to their family obligations often place them off-track. We have found that the integration of women depends on providing them with the support and rewards that men expect and on which they depend.

———————

Epstein and her co-authors explain that the glass ceiling effect results from gender stereotypes and biases, traditional attitudes, subpar training and mentoring, reduced business development opportunities and harassment. In the following article, Deborah Rhode examines the meaning and impact of gender stereotypes and biases.

Deborah L. Rhode
Gender and Professional Roles
63 Fordham L. Rev. 39 (1994)

Gender Stereotypes and Unconscious Bias

1. Defining the Problem

The insensitivity to work/family conflicts is symptomatic of broader patterns of gender bias within the legal profession. Virtually every bar commission and serious scholar in the field has documented persistent forms of discrimination, as well as substantial disparities in men's and women's perceptions of such behavior. In nearly all studies, between two-thirds and three-fourths of the women surveyed indicate that they have experienced some form of discrimination or bias, while only one-fourth to one-third of the men report observing such conduct. As one male lawyer responding to the Ninth Circuit Survey put it, "I have never witnessed nor heard of a single incident of gender bias." Moreover, men who do perceive such bias often discount its significance. As a Texas practitioner noted, "of all the problems we have as lawyers, gender discrimination is low on the list of important ones." Other men's responses to bias studies were less restrained: "'a complete waste of time and money!'; 'a pile of garbage'; 'much ado about nothing.'"

These differing perceptions in part reflect men's privileged status and the resiliency of unconscious bias. A major problem involves lingering skepticism about female competence, a problem compounded for women of color. Although such doubts are rarely aired in mixed company, their influence is still apparent in studies of unconscious bias. So, for example, surveys involving various professions find that the same work or the same resume is rated lower if it is attributed to a woman rather than a man. Female lawyers, particularly racial and ethnic minorities, frequently report that they lack the same presumption of competence that their white male colleagues enjoy. The persistence of adverse stereotypes is also apparent from minority lawyers' common experience of being mistaken for low-income clients, or for clerical and janitorial staff. In one recent report by the ABA's Multicultural Women Attorneys Network, a black woman partner from a major Chicago firm noted that she had been taken for a court reporter at every deposition she had ever attended.

Such biases also are reflected and reinforced through various forms of demeaning and harassing treatment. Women's contributions are often dismissed, devalued, or attributed to men. Individuals who have complained about sexual harassment have been dismissed as "irrational" or "bounty hunters," even when the harasser has a history of abusive conduct. The overwhelming majority of female lawyers report experiencing discriminatory practices that convey a lack of respect. Women attorneys have had to cope with labels such as "little lady," "young girl," "lawyerette," "pretty eyes," "baby doll," "sweetie," "sweetheart," and "attorney generalette." Litigators have encountered comments such as "Ladies and gentlemen, can you believe this pretty little thing is an Assistant Attorney General?" or "Do you really understand all the economics involved in this [antitrust] case?" Women of color face biases on two fronts. Racial slurs have ranged from the obviously invidious, such as "tarbaby," to the ostensibly benign, such as congratulations for being a "credit to your race."

Except for overt racism, such comments rarely prompt any remedial response. Women who object are frequently ridiculed as humorless or oversensitive. A representative case in point involved a male attorney who questioned prospective jurors on voir dire whether their decision would be influenced by the fact that his female opposing counsel was "younger and prettier." When she objected, the judge responded with a chuckle that she *was* "younger and prettier," although not apparently a very good sport.

Yet women who attempt to invoke humor themselves run other risks. One California attorney, whose opposing counsel repeatedly addressed her as "young lady," earned the judge's irritation when she referred to her adversary as "old man." "I could hold you in contempt," the judge pointed out. And he was not amused by her response that she "wasn't the one who brought up age and sex." Such reactions both compound women's injury and discourage protests that might prevent it. Even well-intentioned gallantry or seemingly trivial asides can undercut female lawyers' status and credibility.

The mismatch between characteristics traditionally associated with women and those typically associated with professional success also leaves female lawyers in a long standing double bind. They remain vulnerable to criticism for being "too feminine" or "not feminine enough." What is assertive in a man is abrasive in a woman. A wide array of experiential and clinical evidence indicates that profiles of successful professionals conflict with profiles of normal or ideal women. The aggressiveness, competitiveness, and emotional detachment traditionally presumed necessary for advancement in the most prestigious and well-paid occupations are incompatible with traits commonly viewed as attractive in women: cooperativeness, deference, sensitivity, and self-sacrifice. From most feminists' perspective, what needs to change are workplaces, not women.

Under current norms, female lawyers face continuing problems of "fitting in" and forming the client and collegial relationships necessary for advancement. In one representative survey, virtually all women partners reported losing business because of gender. Female professionals still do not have access to the same informal networks of advice, collaboration, and contacts on which successful careers depend.

To be sure, in many practice settings, the entrance of a critical mass has brought significant improvements. Few female attorneys today confront the situation that leaders of the bar can still recall, when large institutions had only one or two women. Sol Linowitz, in recently recounting such a description of his law school class, recalls that his male colleagues were "somewhat uncomfortable when [their two female classmates] were around." And, he acknowledges, "it never occurred to us to wonder whether *they* felt uncomfortable."

Yet insensitivity to women's isolation and underrepresentation remains a problem, particularly for lesbians and women of color. They face unconscious discrimination on two fronts and their small numbers amplify problems such as the absence of mentors and role models. Racial and ethnic minorities often have additional recruitment and committee responsibilities, while many lesbians are denied benefits or social acceptance for their domestic partners.

Given all of these biases, women must work harder than men to succeed. Those who do not advance under such circumstances or who become frustrated and opt for different employment confirm the adverse stereotypes that worked against their advancement in the first instance. The perception remains that women cannot succeed by conventional standards, or are less committed to doing so than men. In either event, female professionals do not warrant the same investment in training, assistance, and other opportunities as their male counterparts. Women disproportionately drift off the occupational fast track, leaving the most powerful sectors of the professions insulated from alternative values. Again, the result is a subtle but self-perpetuating cycle in which individual choices are constrained by gender biases.

Some commentators had hoped that the glass ceiling effect was a self-correcting problem, an approach Deborah Rhode has elsewhere called the "no-problem" problem perspective, see Deborah L. Rhode, "The 'No-Problem' Problem: Feminist Challenges and Cultural Change," 100 Yale L. J. 1731 (1991). "No-problem" problem proponents argued that over time, law firms would come to realize that failing to retain and promote women partners was inefficient. Just as the market had taught law firms to hire women lawyers, it would teach them to retain and promote them and sanction them for failure to do so. Old habits, stereotypes and biases may die hard, asserted the commentators, but they will die out. Experience, however, has proven otherwise, as women (and minority) lawyers continue to struggle with the effects of the glass ceiling. Below, Eli Wald and then Russell Pearce and his co-authors explain the lasting power of glass ceilings and biases. Wald argues that evolving and dynamic professional ideologies have emerged to sustain gender hierarchies and the status quo. Pearce and his co-authors study implicit biases that in turn explain implicit gender discrimination.

Eli Wald
Glass Ceilings and Dead Ends:
Professional Ideologies, Gender Stereotypes
and the Future of Women Lawyers at Large Law Firms
78 Fordham L. Rev. 2245 (2010)

From Glass Ceilings to Dead Ends: The Shift from Competitive Meritocracy to Hypercompetitive Meritocracy and Its Impact on Women Lawyers

Women lawyers first began to enter the legal profession, and in particular large law firms, in significant numbers in the early 1970s. The barriers to entry faced by first-generation women lawyers at large law firms were significant. Women lawyers faced daunting explicit and implicit discrimination coupled with [various] stereotyping: women lawyers did not belong in the practice of law, were incompetent, and lacked the sufficient professional drive to succeed as lawyers because of their inherently competing loyalties as wives and mothers.

First-generation women lawyers, however, entered large law firm practice during the ascendancy of the competitive meritocratic ideology, which played a positive role in opening the doors of large law firms to women lawyers and helped combat some of the negative consequences of the prevailing stereotypes, especially in contrast to the old WASP "meritocracy." Women lawyers were nearly unimaginable under WASP "meritocracy," and the few who ventured to enter faced significant . . . stereotyping. Women were supposed to stay home, look pretty, and support their lawyer-husbands' careers by hosting cocktail parties and doing charity work, not by invading the workplace. Women lawyers were incompetent and lacked the sophisticated business understanding required at the meritocratic law offices handling the affairs of large corporate clients. Finally, the kind of loyalty demanded by the large firm was understood to be strongly inconsistent with the role and commitment of women as women. Tales of associates' endless hours in the office are as old as the large firms themselves. Large, elite law firms have earned their reputation as sweatshops under the WASP "meritocracy," which demanded loyalty to the firm as a secular calling.

Moreover, while loyalty and intense commitment were essential, even a condition for success, they did not constitute the entire WASP ideology. Loyalty was necessary, but it was not sufficient. Indeed, many associates spent years logging endless hours without being promoted, a commitment and a practice reality hardly imaginable today. Notably, WASP "meritocracy" demanded more than loyalty. Its meritocratic aspect required demonstrated excellence, and its WASP component necessitated Protestant values, white-shoe culture, and socioeconomic indicia of elite status. Correspondingly, the WASP "meritocratic" ideology offered a lot more than mere financial rewards in return. It promised elite professional status, social and cultural standing, political power, intellectual challenge, and networking with society's power brokers. Women, and women lawyers in particular, were thought to be, relying on gender stereotypes, irrelevant and inconsistent given this ideology, which mixed professional values, business interests, ethnoreligious identity, and conservative socioeconomic and cultural sensitivities.

Against this background, opening the doors of large law firms was made somewhat easier by the rise of competitive ideology. Under the influence of competitive meritocracy, large law firms were, to a growing extent, both claiming to hire (and subsequently promote) the best and actually doing so, irrespective of ethnoreligious background and even gender. Women lawyers who met the merit criteria set by the large law firms were more likely to be hired under competitive meritocracy than they were under WASP "meritocracy." When elite law schools dropped their discriminatory admissions policies, women law students rose to the top of their classes and met the merit standards required by the large firms. Importantly, while WASP "meritocracy" restricted entry to women lawyers, competitive meritocracy eased it. As large law firms began to experience increased competition in the 1970s and 1980s, and as their new competitive ideology put a growing emphasis on competition to get the best associates and lessened the pressure to honor old WASP traditions, women lawyers gained entry to the large firms.

Women lawyers could have expected and in fact did fare better under competitive meritocracy. However, unlike its impact on male Jewish lawyers, competitive meritocracy did not create a "flip-side-of-bias" effect for women lawyers because the negative stereotypes impeding women lawyers' progress at large law firms — women belong at home, are incompetent, and are undercommitted — still imposed a disadvantage. . . . For women lawyers, the new emphasis on competition opened the door, but only so far. The new competitive spirit meant that it was harder to consistently and systematically overlook the most qualified women lawyers, but the familiar stereotypes still held women back. . . .

Imperfect as it certainly was, competitive meritocracy did help change the world of large law firms and open their doors to women lawyers. Had competitive meritocracy continued to prevail, perhaps it would have helped erode, over time, [most gender] stereotypes. Arguably, the stereotypical myth of being incompetent and incapable of understanding complex business affairs was bound to be disproven over time as more women lawyers entered the profession and demonstrated their competence. The stereotype of being insufficiently committed to the firm and its clients would still be a hurdle, yet competitive meritocracy could have allowed women lawyers to prove their loyalty and commitment and eventually disprove the stereotype.

The opportunity inherent in competitive meritocracy, arguably explaining the cautiously optimistic tone of the glass ceiling literature, has been severely limited given the rise of hypercompetitive ideology. While meritocracy is still an inherent feature of the ideology women lawyers can easily meet, the hypercompetitive aspect of the ideology celebrates over-the-top commitment and loyalty to clients and the firm above all else, even above meritocracy. The new ideology highlights and amplifies with new vigor [certain] stereotypes regarding women's lack of commitment and disloyalty to clients and the firm, and the negative consequences are devastating.

To be clear, scholars of the legal profession have long noted that legal careers are largely shaped by and designed for men with families who were "family-free," with models that expect utmost commitment to the workplace and a willingness to sacrifice family life. Hypercompetitive meritocracy is different from old, familiar models not in orientation but in scope and tone. It defines excellence in terms of total commitment, around-the-clock client service, and instant responsiveness. Thus, it forecloses, by its very nature, the possibility of reduced or flexible schedules and reliance on technology to allow for work-from-home alternatives. Objectively, laptops, wireless technology, blackberries, PDF attachments, video conferencing, etc., should have allowed lawyers to work from home, but the hypercompetitive ideology prevents that. What the ideology requires is not only physical attendance in the office, which objectively is somewhat obsolete given technological advancements, but physical attendance as a symbolic measure of loyalty, 24/7 commitment, and near-instant responsiveness. This means that even if one could work from home, one would actually work 24/7, thus frustrating the reasons for staying at home.

The hypercompetitive ideology accentuates and aggravates the negative consequences of [existing gender stereotypes]. The more emphasis put by the hypercompetitive ideology on around-the-clock commitment to the firm and clients, the more the disloyal and undercommitted stereotypes harm women lawyers at large law firms. . . .

This new powerful clash between the demands of the hypercompetitive ideology and [prevailing] gender stereotypes helps explain why, even as [certain] stereotypes are in decline, women lawyers at large law firms are still facing innumerable hurdles on the road to equality, and arguably are facing a more difficult challenge than they did under competitive meritocracy because the particular stereotypes that inhibit their progress—lack of commitment and sufficient loyalty to the firm and its clients and prioritizing family over work—have harsh consequences given the new prevailing ideology of hypercompetitiveness.

Unlike the case of WASP "meritocracy" in which loyalty played an important but not an all-consuming role, under hypercompetitive ideology total devotion to the firm and its clients has become the core of the ideology and its sole measure of excellence. Elite professional credentials are but a necessary condition to entry, and 24/7 loyalty is the measure of commitment and success. The dilution of the professional ideology and its reduction to firm and client-centered loyalty has been mirrored by the dilution of the rewards offered by the hypercompetitive ideology — mere financial rewards. And the reward aspect of the ideology reinforces its demand of total loyalty: one is only deserving of sharing in the riches if one is willing to sacrifice his or her personal life.

In a misleading sense, hypercompetitive ideology is gender blind. To the extent that women lawyers are willing to sacrifice their personal life and demonstrate total devotion and loyalty to the firm and its clients, the path to equity partnership appears to be open to them. Yet this is exactly where . . . stereotypes kick in to block the career advancement of women lawyers. Pursuant to the stereotypes, women lawyers are assumed to lack the necessary commitment and devotion to the firm because of their assumed desire to get married, start a family, become mothers, and care for their children. All women lawyers of all racial, ethnoreligious, socioeconomic, and cultural backgrounds are assumed similarly to lack what it takes to succeed as lawyers at large firms, and the desire to become a mother is imputed to them. Indeed, in today's cultural and legal environment, which appropriately recognizes the rights of same-sex families to have and adopt children, even gay women are labeled the same way.

Pursuant to the hypercompetitive ideology, motherhood and the practice as an elite lawyer at a large law firm are inherently and irreversibly incompatible. Presumably, a wife and a mother could simply not work 24/7, technological advancements notwithstanding. The only women lawyers who might escape the consequences of the stereotype are childless women lawyers, but they are assumed to want to have children and ironically lack the capacity to prove otherwise, even if they are committed to significantly delay or even altogether forgo having children in order to attain professional success. Moreover, arguably the "generation me" phenomenon further compounds the powerful interplay of [gender] stereotypes and hypercompetitive ideology. Women lawyers in the twenty-first century are presumed to lack the resolve and willingness to sacrifice that characterized the first-generation women lawyers of the 1970s.

Glass ceiling scholars have voiced cautious optimism regarding gender equality, hoping that part-time arrangements and parental leave policies will more commonly be implemented by large law firms. Rhode has correctly pointed out that "[r]estructuring both work and domestic roles is essential to achieving equal opportunity in fact as well as theory," that "[m]uch may depend on the size and profit margins of the institution and the predictability of work in part-time employees' areas of specialization," and finally, that "[g]ender hierarchies will persist until concerns about the quality of life become more central professional priorities."

Unfortunately, the conditions for gender equality identified by Rhode are less likely to hold under the hypercompetitive ideology. Large law firms are highly hierarchal, conservative, and, in the aftermath of the economic downturn, experiencing shrinking and increasingly unpredictable profit margins, all rendering it less likely that they will restructure to accommodate work-life arrangements. Further, pursuant to the hypercompetitive professional ideology, not only are concerns about the quality of life less central, but they are in fact in stark conflict with total devotion and utmost loyalty to the firm and its clients. Part-time arrangements and parental leaves are less likely under the hypercompetitive ideology because, irrespective of increased technological feasibility and formal institutional acceptance, they contradict the values of the ideology by their very nature. Taking advantage of such arrangements is thus discouraged and renders those who might do so not only less committed, but also worse, as those who either "do not get what it takes to succeed" or "get it but are unwilling or unable to do what it takes." Therefore, while it is true that "in many practice settings, the entrance of a critical mass [of women lawyers] has brought significant improvements," and that in many settings and arenas women lawyers are changing, even redefining, the practice of law, large law firms appear to be a practice setting in which gender equality is likely to be less attainable in the foreseeable future given their dominant inhospitable professional ideology.

Russell G. Pearce, Eli Wald & Swethaa Ballakrishnen
Difference Blindness vs. Bias Awareness: Why Law Firms with the Best of Intentions Have Failed to Create Diverse Partnerships
83 Fordham L. Rev. 2407 (2015)

Implicit biases are unintentional but fundamental biases that are pervasive across a range of institutions and environments. Recent research has shown that most instances of discrimination and stereotypes extend from not so much obvious discrimination or rejection of minorities, but, instead, as a function of these implicit cognitive biases in favor of people from the "in-group." The notion of an implicit bias extends more generally from a psychological theory called schema theory. It holds that we maintain unconscious models of reality to categorize the many bits of information we perceive at any given point in time. These categorical faculties mainly serve to allow us conscious decision and free will in what we do, because otherwise we would be overwhelmed with having to maintain what we wanted to do while actively perceiving everything going on around us. The schemas and biases we develop at early stages of development are used to categorize and simplify all the information we may encounter in our experience, including people. The colloquial term we use to refer to schemas that we attach to people around us is "stereotype." Often, we unconsciously perpetuate stereotypes about ourselves and other people by either agreeing with them or acting in ways that make them true. But stereotypes are not always conscious — most of the time we do not even remember, perceive, or act on the information that counters those beliefs. At these times, we can only consciously counter the implicit biases we have of other people by directly challenging them.

Implicit biases tend to reflect the existing power relations in society and manifest themselves in more micro interactions — and this is nowhere clearer than it is in the workplace. And the pervasiveness of implicit bias does not depend on just white men thinking they are superior. They take shape and become reality when *everyone* begins to believe, however subconsciously, that white men are deserving of this power. For example, given that white men disproportionately hold more powerful positions in elite organizations and in society more generally, people are more likely to perceive white men as being smarter and more competent than they are and therefore worthy of their positions and status atop elite organizations. In doing so, society as a whole perpetuates these dominant scripts by legitimizing the status quo. In turn, these implicit biases result in persistent institutional hurdles. They lead to a universal buy-in from both the dominant actors through the mechanisms of non-consciousness and privilege (here, white male partners) and the nondominant ones through mechanisms of low confidence, lack of self-esteem, and institutional socialization such as diversity initiatives to believe they are less deserving (here, women and minority lawyers).

In one popular test of implicit bias developed by Harvard researchers, test takers are told that the next picture they will see is of a person who is smart, competent, or reliable, and that they should press a button as soon as they see that picture. If the picture is of a white man, test takers press the button significantly faster than when the picture is of a black person or a woman. One lesson of this test is that most people assume that white men are smarter, more competent, and more reliable, and therefore take a longer time to acknowledge the intelligence, competence, and reliability of women and people of color. An illustration of how this micro phenomenon influences macro experiences is found in the work of David Thomas and John J. Gabarro, who concluded that women and people of color have a significantly longer path to becoming executives than their white male colleagues because it takes women and people of color more time to persuade colleagues of their competence and to gain access to networks of mentoring and sponsorship.

Indeed, implicit bias has been found to be pervasive across a range of workplace settings. In one study, for example, employers received resumes that were substantially identical except for the names of the applicants which were "stereotypically African-American" or "stereotypically white." Although the resumes were essentially identical, whites received 50 percent more job interviews. When applicants had "identical resumes and similar interview training . . . African-American applicants with no criminal record were offered jobs at a rate as low as white applicants who had criminal records."

Similarly, "[e]ven in experimental situations where male and female performance is objectively equal, women are held to higher standards, and their competence is rated lower." In elite institutions, when women speak, men often ignore or interrupt them, and when they offer good ideas, men take credit for their ideas without even acknowledging that a woman actually made the contribution. In turn, this results in settings where women are more tentative overall—and this tentativeness can be expensive, especially because we know that women negotiate differently from men, and all else kept equal, are judged on their social skills in ways that their male peers are not.

But it is not just that men and women are held to different standards. When women *meet* the standards that are created for men, institutions typically reject these women as "bossy" or "bitchy," exhibiting what gender theorists have most recently dubbed the "tightrope" between the competing poles of masculinity and femininity. For instance, in a classic experiment that parsed this difference in reception, male and female leaders were tested against audiences of different genders and their assertiveness was compared to tentative speech (e.g., "I'm no expert," "kind of," "sort of"), men were equally influential in both conditions whereas women were perceived to be more competent and exerted greater influence over female audiences, but were found to be less likeable by the male audiences who found them "too aggressive." In a similar vein, the leadership qualities of women are also evaluated differently, with strong women labeled "strident" and the "[s]elf-promotion that is acceptable in men is viewed as unattractive in women." When women succeed, their achievements are generally "attributed to . . . external factors," while the success of men is generally "attributed to internal capabilities."

Commentators have identified numerous implicit biases in the law firm workplace. Lawyers who are not white men are assumed to be less able "to connect with and generate business from . . . 'clients,' the preponderance of which are led by majority populations . . . . [U]nderrepresented minorities fall victim to the misperception of being less able to bring in business with majority populations." Without regular training and constant vigilance, these implicit biases on the basis of race and gender would permeate the legal workplace just as they permeate other workplaces. And, indeed, law firms do not universally require regular training and evaluations for these purposes, and neither do they have in place specific mechanisms to monitor interpersonal interactions.

Of course, not all groups face the same sorts of biases and the ways in which they differ are worth reflection. As noted above, women face the double bind that their achievements are disregarded and their leadership tends to be discounted. Other widespread biases are that blacks and Latinos "are less intelligent, less industrious, and generally less qualified; even if they graduated from an elite law school, they are assumed to be beneficiaries of affirmative action rather than meritocratic selection." Another common view among law firms is that "[b]lacks, especially women, . . . [are] angry or hostile." Asian Americans face a different constellation of biases—all of which impact their identity within firms differently. For example, they "are thought to be smart and hardworking, but not sufficiently assertive to command the confidence of clients and legal teams." They are "underrepresented at top management levels in [knowledge-intensive firms], despite being the largest minority group represented at junior levels." Modupe N. Akinola and David Thomas observed widespread "[p]ersonality and behavioral stereotypes asserting that Asians are 'submissive,' 'humble,' 'passive,' 'quiet,' 'compliant,' and 'obedient' mak[ing] Asian Americans vulnerable to being viewed as lacking key leadership traits, placing them at a disadvantage when being considered for management positions." . . .

. . . [I]t is not surprising who comes out ahead. In one of the few implicit bias studies that examined law firm conduct, researchers found that the evaluations central to the partnership tournament were biased toward white men. In that study, sixty law firm partners (thirty-nine white, twenty-one racial/ethnic minorities) were asked to evaluate the same memo written by a third year associate. Half of the partners were told that the author was black and half that the author was white. The name and law school background were the same. On a 1-to-5 scale, the partners awarded an average 3.2 rating when they thought the author was black and 4.1 when they thought the author was white. They identified far more spelling and grammar errors when they thought the author was black—an average score of 5.8 versus 2.9. The qualitative evaluations also differed significantly. The white author was described as a "generally good writer" who "has potential" and "good analytic skills," while the black associate received comments such as "needs lots of work," "can't believe he went to NYU," and "average at best."

Not only does this study call into question the accuracy and reliability of the partnership tournament, but it tracks the perceptions associates have of their own evaluations. Women and people of color believe (accurately as it turns out) that they are held to a different and higher standard than white men and that law firms do nothing significant to address implicit bias in the workplace. Specifically, "only 1% of white men, compared with 31% of women of color, 25% of white women, and 21% of men of color, reported unfair evaluations." This disparate perception extends to opportunities to develop business and skills. In one survey, "44% of women of color, 39% of white women, and 25% of minority men reported being passed over for desirable work assignments whereas only 2% of white men noted similar experiences." Similarly, with regard to business development, "women and minorities [report being] often left out of pitches for client business." In fact, data on "conventional client development possibilities" shows that "43% of surveyed women of color, 55% of white women, and 24% of men of color report having limited access to such opportunities, compared with only 3% of white men."

Similar perceptions explain why law firm mentoring programs are largely unsuccessful. For instance, the survey above "found that 62% of women of color and 60% of white women, but only 4% of white men, reported being left out of formal and informal networking opportunities." In turn, these results track the social science research on mentoring.

In significant part, the problem with mentoring results from an effect that researchers describe as homophily, the effect that people feel most comfortable with people like them and, absent significant intervention, will gravitate toward assisting those most like them. Akinola and Thomas explain that "[i]t is well-known that the relationships that are the easiest to develop, maintain, and gain comfort from are those in which the members share common identity characteristics and similar backgrounds." In law firms dominated by white male partners, the effect of homophily is to privilege white male associates.

As a result of homophily, the evaluation, mentoring, and networking that matters—the day-to-day business outside of the formal and occasional programs for people who are not white men—favors white men in the partnership tournament. White men who dominate partnerships are not comfortable evaluating, mentoring, or networking with people outside of their white male identity group. Akinola and Thomas explain that "researchers have found that cross-race interactions can engender feelings of anxiety and discomfort." They note that "[a] variety of explanations have been proposed that highlight the sources of anxiety in cross-race relationships, among which include: the desire to avoid appearing prejudiced, . . . the threat of rejection in intergroup encounters . . . , and minimal experience interacting with individuals of different races."

These effects occur in law firms and influence evaluations, networking, and mentoring. In law, white men express difficulty in conversations and relationships across race and gender. They often report discomfort or inadequacy in discussing "'women's issues,' and minorities express reluctance to raise diversity-related concerns with those who lack personal experience or empathy." As a result, "[u]nderrepresented minorities not only have fewer mentoring relationships but also have an increased likelihood of failed cross-race mentoring relationships which can have negative repercussions for career development." As G. Mitu Gulati and David B. Wilkins observe, "Studies of cross-racial and cross-gender mentoring relationships in the workplace repeatedly demonstrate that white men feel more comfortable in working relationships with white men."

Notes

1. Making partner is only just the beginning of a woman's quest for equality and legitimacy in a law firm. Consider the following findings from a study of female and male graduates from Harvard Law School about their relative likelihood of obtaining an important leadership position in a large law firm:

> Research on the legal profession makes clear that in today's law firms making partner is just the beginning of a new competition to become a "partner with power" in the organization. One measure of whether a given partner has achieved this status is whether he or she holds an important leadership position within the firm. In examining this question, we found that there are clear and significant gender disparities between the management positions held by women and men in our sample. As Figure 7.1 [of this CLP study; figures are not reproduced here] depicts, male respondents were considerably more likely than female respondents to hold leadership positions within their law firms. Of respondents who ever held the title "managing partner," 82 percent were men. Similarly, 75 percent of those reporting that they had ever held the position of head of a practice group/area head were men. Although the percentages of women holding these positions in our sample is larger than studies of women's representation in these positions typically report, it remains low given the relatively higher percentage of HLS women

who have become equity partners in the sample. The fact that women are less likely to hold these leadership positions has important consequences both for their own careers and for the governance, growth, and culture of the law firms in which they work.

A similar pattern emerges when we examine the committees that women and men serve on at the law firms in which they work. Although nearly all of the lawyers working in law firms in our sample reported serving on committees, there was a significant difference in the type of committee on which female and male respondents served. As any observer of law firms knows, not all committees are created equal, particularly with respect to prestige and influence. As Figure 7.2 makes clear, men traditionally have dominated what might be considered the "power" committees—committees dealing with things such as recruiting, promotions, compensation, and management. On the other hand, women were more likely to have served on the diversity and quality of life committee. These committees undoubtedly serve an important function—one that arguably has become even more important in the years since 2010 when our data was collected, given the significant emphasis that many law firms are now placing on these issues. Nevertheless, it is also commonly believed that membership on the diversity or quality of life committee does not carry nearly the institutional power and prestige as service on the committees where men have tended to serve. Indeed, to the extent that service on the diversity or quality of life committee is important to a firm, it is likely that the partner who will get the most benefit from this importance is the one who serves as chair. Yet as Figure 7.3 underscores, even in these committees where women tend to be more highly represented, relatively few women have been selected as chairperson compared to their male peers.

The lack of women in law firm leadership positions has important consequences for law firms as institutions, but also for the aspirations of women lawyers. Figure 7.4 examines law firm management aspirations by gender. Across all categories of potential leadership, men were significantly more likely than women to want to be involved in firm management. One might interpret this finding as an indication that HLS female graduates in fact do not want to hold leadership positions in firms, thereby explaining in part their historically low rates in holding these positions. However, as discrimination scholars have long argued, it is dangerous to attribute women's lack of participation in important positions to a "lack of interest"—particularly with respect to a group of women, such as those in our sample, who have consistently demonstrated their willingness and ability to succeed at the highest levels. It therefore may be more likely that the absence of women in leadership positions in law firms has conditioned what women view as realistic career opportunities in these organizations. Whichever is the case, the fact that so few women in our sample claim to aspire to leadership positions has troubling implications for the future leadership of law firms in a world in which women constitute an increasingly large percentage of the talent pool.

David B. Wilkins, Bryon Fong, and Ronit Dinovitzer, *The Women and Men of Harvard Law School: Preliminary Results from the Harvard Law School Career Study* (2015), available at <https://clp.law.harvard.edu/assets/HLS-Career-Study-FINAL-1.pdf>.

2. Lurking underneath all of these studies is the question of what role having children (and assumptions about wanting to have children) made by the hypercompetitive professionals described by Eli Wald plays in the differing career paths of women and men. Once again, the Harvard Law School study is instructive:

> Studies of legal careers consistently underscore that the most difficult work-life integration issues arise in the context of caring for children. These issues are reputed to be especially difficult for lawyers working in law firms. We therefore pay particular attention to the consequences associated with having children for lawyers working in this sector.

> As a preliminary matter, across all cohorts and job sectors, men are likely to have slightly more children (2.3) than women (2.1). However, when we look specifically at lawyers with no children, the difference between women and men is far more dramatic. As Table 10.7 [of the CLP study, not reproduced here] illustrates, across all employment sectors, women are far more likely than men to have no children (31 percent to 19 percent respectively). Although the gap is significant for lawyers working in law firms (7 percent), it is significantly higher for lawyers working in the public sector and in business (practicing law) — 15 percent and 13 percent respectively.

> Although Table 10.7 might make law firms appear to be relatively family-friendly compared to other employment sectors, when we look more specifically at the correlation between partnership and children, we see a far different story. Thus, as Table 10.8 underscores, the percentage of female partners who have no children (24 percent) is twice as large as the 12 percent of male partners with no children. Second, while most partners — almost three-fourths — have two or more children, men are significantly more likely than women to be in this category (77.5 percent to 64.1 percent).

> Although there are undoubtedly many factors that have contributed to the differential rates at which the women and men in our sample have decided to have children, many will believe that the time required to care for children may conflict with the "long and continuous" hours required to succeed as a lawyer. . . . [A] powerfully pernicious assumption experienced by women far more frequently than men that lawyers with children are "less committed" to their careers than their childless peers (72 percent to 28 percent). When combined with the fact that women with children are far more likely than their male counterparts to lobby their employers for more family-friendly policies, it is painfully evident that female lawyers still bear the overwhelming burden of the legal

profession's continuing struggles to integrate work and family. Notwithstanding all of their many advantages, HLS female graduates have not
been able to escape this burden.

Id.

3. There have been several efforts to bring women who have left the workforce to
have children back into the workforce. See, e.g., Sylvia Ann Hewlett, *Off Ramps and
On Ramps: Keeping Talented Women on the Road to Success* (2007). These efforts have
met with mixed success. Fiona M. Kay, Stacey Alarie, and Jones Adjei, *Leaving Law
and Barriers to Reentry: A Study of Departures From and Reentries to Private Practice,*
Law School Admissions Council (2013), available at<http://www.lsac.org/docs/
default-source/research-(lsac-resources)/gr-13-02.pdf>. More recent programs are
geared to get talented women to stay, in part by creating "institutional nudges" to
correct for seemingly neutral policies that unfairly disadvantage women, including around maternity leave and other family issues. See Paola Cecchi-Dimeglio,
"Nudges to Increase Diversity," The Practice, January 2017, available at<https://
thepractice.law.harvard.edu/article/nudging-to-increase-diversity/>.

4. Diversity discussions frequently confuse the relationship between gender and
race. Although women and minorities are both underrepresented in large firms and
undoubtedly face many similar problems, the common tendency to treat them as a
single undifferentiated group is misguided. In a comprehensive study of the relationship between certain structural features of large law firms and the integration of
women and minorities, Professor Elizabeth Chambliss found important differences
between the two groups:

> [E]ven controlling for labor supply and demand, law firm characteristics
> significantly affect the level of law firm integration. The most important
> determinants of gender integration are the structural characteristics of
> the firm such as the length of the internal promotion hierarchy and the
> degree to which the firm is geographically diversified. The most impor-
> tant determinant of racial integration is the racial composition of the firm's
> client base.
>
> These findings have important implications for employment stratification
> theory and research, as well as for the future of gender and race integration
> within law firms. First, my findings support recent empirical work, which
> indicates that organizations play a critical role in the perpetuation and alle-
> viation of gender- and race-based employment inequality. The firms in my
> sample vary significantly in their levels of gender and race integration, and
> much of that variation is the result of firm-level—versus market—condi-
> tions. These findings suggest that individual law firms (and firm leaders)
> bear a substantial responsibility for determining the level of law firm
> integration . . . .
>
> In particular, my findings suggest that, at least within elite law firms,
> structural conditions such as the length of the partnership track are a

critical determinant of gender, but not racial, integration. Structural conditions are especially important determinants of gender integration at the partnership level. Similarly, the nature of the firm's client base is a critical determinant of racial, but not gender, integration. The nature of the firm's client base is even more important than labor market conditions for determining racial integration at the partnership level.

Elizabeth Chambliss, "Organizational Determinants of Law Firm Integration," 46 Am. U. L. Rev. 669, 739–40 (1997).

5. Even the category "women" elides important complications. Although all women face important obstacles in the workplace, women of color have had particular difficulty in winning the modern tournament of lawyers. In 2006, for example, a joint report from the ABA's Commission on Women and Commission on Racial and Ethnic Diversity concluded:

> Nearly half of women of color but only 3% of white men experienced demeaning comments or harassment. Unlike white men, many women of color felt that they had to disprove negative preconceived notions about their legal abilities and their commitment to their careers. . . .

> Nearly two-thirds of women of color but only 4% of white men were excluded from informal and formal networking opportunities . . . . Women of color had mentors, but their mentors did not ensure that they were well integrated into the firm's internal networks, received desirable assignments (especially those that helped them meet their billable hours) or had substantive contacts with clients. Sixty-seven percent of women of color wanted more and/or better mentoring by senior attorneys and partners, whereas only 32% of white men expressed a similar need. . . .

> The careers of white women attorneys and men attorneys of color were neither as disadvantaged as those of women attorneys of color nor as privileged as those of white men. Fewer men attorneys of color indicated that discrimination had hobbled their careers compared to white women. However, white women, on average, had higher salaries than men of color (but the differences were not statistically significant). Men attorneys of color and white women had similar perceptions of how they felt others judged their competencies, their desire for more and better mentors, their rates of being selected as protégés by white men, and their desire to become partners in law firms. However, their retention rates were very different: 67% of white men but only 52% of men of color chose to remain in law firms.

ABA Commission on Women in the Profession, *Visible Invisibility: Women of Color in Law Firms, Executive Summary*, 10–11 (2006). See also NALP Press Release, "Law Firm Diversity Demographics Slow to Change: Minority Women Remain Particularly Scarce in Law Firm Partnership Ranks," Oct. 10, 2008 (reporting that minority women make up less than 2% of law firm partners, significantly less than the 4.2% of partners who are minority men); D.M. Osborne, "Why are Minority Female

Associates Leaving Law Firms," Minority L.J., Nov. 11, 2007 (finding that "minority female midlevel [associates] . . . were least likely to recommend their firms to a job-seeking friend and least inclined to identify with partners, and rated their firms more harshly overall" even when compared to minority men).

6. In light of robust evidence regarding the under-representation of women and minority lawyers in positions of power and influence in the profession, such as equity partnership positions at large law firms, as well as emerging insights about the prevalence of implicit biases and their impact in sustaining these realities, Pearce and his co-authors called on law firms to abandon their traditional commitment to difference blindness in hiring, evaluating, promoting and compensating their lawyers and embracing instead bias awareness policies. Pearce et al. argue that, whereas explicit discrimination requires difference blindness, implicit bias and implicit discrimination necessitates bias awareness. What are some of the risks inherent in trying to implement bias awareness policies?

7. In recent years, many diversity advocates have turned away from traditional civil rights approaches such as Title VII to argue that law firms and other legal employers should hire and promote more minority lawyers because it is "good for business." Trends in business in general—and in in-house counsel departments in particular—appear to support this claim. Responding to a series of reports proclaiming that the United States is rapidly becoming "majority minority" and to the growing purchasing power of minority consumers, companies have devoted increasing attention to diversity. See, e.g., Diversity Inc., *The Business Case for Diversity* (4th ed. 2003). At the same time, many of the women and minority lawyers who have left large law firms have found their way into in-house legal departments, often rising to senior levels. See L. Lum, "Women and Minorities as General Counsels," Diversity & the Bar, December 2014, <www.diversityandthebardigital.com/datb/november_december_2014#article_id=529114> (reporting that in 2014, 113 of the general counsels of Fortune 500 companies were women, and that 54 were racial minorities). Taken together, these trends have helped to spur a number of efforts by corporate general counsel to pressure the law firms they work with about increasing their hiring, retention, and utilization of women and minority lawyers. See David B. Wilkins and Young Kyu Kim, "The Action After the Call: What General Counsels Say About the Importance of Diversity in Legal Purchasing Decisions in the Years following 'The Call to Action,'" in *Diversity in Practice: Race, Class, and Gender in the Legal Profession and Legal Careers* (S. Headworth, R. Nelson, R. Dinovitzer, and D. Wilkins, eds. 2016). (See Note 9 below.)

8. What do you see as likely consequences of attempting to justify programs to hire and retain minority lawyers on the ground that doing so is "good for business"? What are some of the potential disadvantages of such programs—for minority lawyers, for firms, and/or for lawyers who are not covered by such initiatives? For an extensive analysis of the costs and benefits of moving from a "civil rights" to a "market" paradigm for thinking about diversity, see David B. Wilkins, "From 'Separate is Inherently Unequal' to 'Diversity is Good for Business': The

Rise of Market-Based Diversity Arguments and the Fate of the Black Corporate Bar," 117 Harv. L. Rev. 1548 (2004).

9. How effective are such initiatives in getting general counsels to value diversity, particularly when hiring law firms for important work? A study of the legal purchasing decisions of large U.S. companies for "very significant" work conducted by Professors Wilkins and Kim suggests that the results are mixed:

> Our survey reveals that diversity is a solidly second order consideration for the average GC of a large company when hiring law firms for very significant work. Once again, the impact of this finding should not be underestimated. In close cases where firms are similar in terms of "results in similar cases," "reputation," and "prior relationship," a secondary factor such as commitment to diversity could very well tip the balance, even if GCs tend to view this consideration as only "somewhat important" in the abstract. Indeed, many law firms have a difficult time distinguishing themselves on the primary factors identified in our survey—as one typical GC we interviewed succinctly put it: "Law firms spend too much time telling you how good they are. But if you weren't good I wouldn't be talking to you!" Second order considerations can thus potentially provide "visible rankable signals" of quality that can sometimes prove to be decisive. As another GC put it: "I think there was a firm or two that was on the bubble that made it on to the list of eight because of strengths in diversity and pro bono and civil justice reform. They really stood out on these issues."

> Nevertheless, these results also confirm the frustration that many minority and female lawyers have expressed about initiatives like the Call to Action ever since GM's Harry Smith wrote the first letter seeking to improve law firm diversity through demand-side pressure. Summing up this frustration, a black GC in a major company who had recently left a large law firm put the point bluntly: "I think people are lying when they tell you that [diversity] is at the very heart of outside counsel selection process . . . I never got selected because [a company] was trying to increase the diversity of their pool of providers."

> Even companies that claimed to value diversity often were candid about the fact that they were unlikely to terminate a relationship on this basis. As the GC of an investment bank put it "I don't think we have ever terminated a relationship exclusively because they have not been able to achieve the right kind of diversity mix." Instead, the GC went on to say, "we hope that by asking [about diversity] that we at least continue to keep the pressure on firms in general to develop their diversity programs."

> In the end, our data confirm what many have long argued. When the stakes are high, diversity considerations will frequently be swamped by other factors that decision makers consider more important.

David B. Wilkins and Young Kyu Kim, "The Action After the Call: What General Counsels Say About the Importance of Diversity in Legal Purchasing Decisions in the Years Following 'The Call to Action,'" in *Diversity in Practice: Race, Class, and Gender in the Legal Profession and Legal Careers* (S. Headworth, R. Nelson, R. Dinovitzer, and D. Wilkins, eds. 2016), at 53–54.

———————

The excerpt from Professors Wilkins and Kim underscores the increasingly important role that general counsels are playing in discussions about diversity in the profession. This, however, is only one of many areas where general counsels are asserting their influence in the legal profession. The following section explores this growing influence.

David B. Wilkins
Is the In-House Counsel Movement Going Global?
A Preliminary Assessment of the Role of Internal Counsel
in Emerging Economies
2012 Wis. L. Rev. 251

In 1989, the American legal scholar Robert Eli Rosen wrote an important article chronicling the dramatic growth in the size, prestige, and influence of internal legal counsel in large U.S. corporations. In fewer than twenty years, these lawyers had gone from a position of marginality and subservience—think "house counsel," as in "house pet"—to being "General Counsel," playing a pivotal role in both defining and serving the legal needs of their powerful corporate clients. . . .

In the more than two decades since Rosen's article, the apparent power and prestige of in-house lawyers in the United States has only continued to grow. Internal legal departments routinely employ dozens of lawyers, many large U.S. companies having general counsel offices that rival the size of large outside law firms. These lawyers now regularly perform legal work traditionally done by outside counsel. Specifically, today's general counsel (GC) routinely act as both "diagnosticians" of their company's legal needs, and as the primary "purchasing agents" deciding whether those needs will be served by an inside lawyer or by an outside firm—and if the work is sent outside, which firm will receive the business. As a result, the number of lawyers employed by in-house legal departments in the United States has expanded dramatically.

In-house legal departments in the United States now also rival large law firms as a destination of choice for talented lawyers. Although most GC offices do not recruit directly from law school, they now have their pick of talented mid-level associates and junior partners from the best law firms, with senior in-house lawyers frequently recruited from the top ranks of the partnerships of outside firms. Indeed, in a move that would have been unthinkable just a few years ago, outside law firms have begun to recruit partners laterally from in-house legal departments in order to acquire their experience and connections, strengthen relationships with existing clients, and to recruit new ones. All of this has profoundly restructured traditional mobility patterns and prestige hierarchies within the U.S. legal profession.

This restructuring is also evident in the increasingly important role that internal counsel now play in policy debates, both within the bar and in broader discussions about law and legal institutions. In the 1990s, for example, the Association of Corporate Counsel (ACC) was a driving force behind the effort to get the American Bar Association (ABA) to change its rules regarding multidisciplinary practice. Although that effort ultimately proved unsuccessful, ACC has emerged as a force to be reckoned with within the bar and is currently flexing its muscles in a variety of debates over the structure and ownership of law firms, professional regulation, and legal education. Similarly, both individually and collectively general counsels now routinely weigh in on important public policy debates on everything from free trade to human rights to corruption.

This heightened public profile has, in turn, helped to cement the general counsel's standing as a member of the company's senior leadership team. Indeed, many top in-house lawyers have traded in the legal sounding title of "general counsel" for the more corporate sobriquet Chief Legal Officer (CLO) in order to clearly signal that they are a part of the "C" suite of top executive officers in the company. In addition to their responsibilities as legal diagnosticians and purchasing agents, many CLOs now oversee a variety of related functions, including government relations, public relations, human resources, compliance, and corporate social responsibility. Many also participate either formally or informally in high-level discussions about general corporate strategy and policy. The fact that several CLOs have ascended to the CEO seat in recent years has only served to cement the image of these former low-status line functionaries as powerful members of the corporate elite.

Notes

1. General counsels have made three interlocking claims to support this impressive increase in their power and status: an *economic* argument that taking work inside saves costs; a *substantive* justification that, because of their proximity to the business, the advice inside counsel give corporate managers is likely to be better than the advice given by outside counsel; and a *professional* argument that because they are the guardians of the company's long-term interests and reputation, GCs are better able to fulfill the gatekeeping role of ensuring that companies comply with both the letter and the spirit of the law than their counterparts in large law firms, who (so the argument goes) have largely abandoned this role in the pursuit of short-term profits per partner. How persuasive do you find these arguments? Is it always clear that hiring full-time lawyers is cheaper than engaging outside lawyers for specific tasks? Is it always true that lawyers who are "close to the business" will give the best *legal* advice—particularly when the lawyer's role as a "partner" to the business leaders' pursuit of short term profits conflicts with the need to be a "guardian" not only for the company's long-term interests but the interests of the public as well? For a robust debate over these and other issues associated with the expanding role of GCs in U.S.

companies, compare Benjamin W. Heineman, *The Inside Counsel Revolution: Resolving the Partner–Guardian Tension* (2016) (offering an extensive defense of the ability of in-house lawyer to fulfill these roles) with John C. Coffee, Jr., *Gatekeepers: The Professions and Corporate Governance* (2006) (arguing that GCs will not be effective gatekeepers).

2. Are there other risks involved with the integration of legal, business, and strategic advice within the general counsel's function? For example, do clients risk compromising the attorney-client privilege or confidentiality more generally when in-house lawyers give both "legal" and "business" advice? To the extent that everything the general counsel does is treated as "legal advice," is there a danger that corporate actors will seek to cover up wrongdoing by "routing" everything through the general counsel's office? Will general counsel who are compensated in part through stock options or other measures tied to the company's performance have an incentive to look the other way (or at a minimum, not to investigate too closely) when the company wants to engage in questionable but profitable conduct? Or will tying lawyers' fortunes directly to the bottom line encourage them to look out for the company's long-term interests? For a review of the many ethical issues raised by the expanding responsibilities of in-house counsel, see Michele Destefano Beardslee, "The Corporate Attorney-Client Privilege: Third Rate Doctrine for Third Party Consultants," 72 SMU L. Rev. 727 (2009); Tanina Rostain, "General Counsel in the Age of Compliance: Preliminary Findings and New Research Questions," 21 Geo. J. Legal Ethics 485 (2008); Robert Eli Rosen, " 'We're All Consultants Now': How Change in Client Organizational Strategies Influences Change in the Organization of Corporate Legal Services," 44 Ariz. L. Rev. 637 (2002); Robert L. Nelson and Laura Beth Nielsen, "Cops, Counsel, and Entrepreneurs: Constructing the Role of Inside Counsel in Large Corporations," 34 Law & Soc'y Rev. 457 (2000); Nancy J. Moore, "Conflicts of Interest for In-House Counsel: Issues Emerging from the Expanding Role of the Attorney-Employee," 39 S. Tex. L. Rev. 497 (1998); Geoffrey C. Hazard, Jr., "Ethical Dilemmas of Corporate Counsel," 46 Emory L.J. 1011 (1997).

3. Is the U.S. model of the general counsel described by Professor Wilkins "going global" to new emerging economies such as India, China, and Brazil (as the title to his article suggests)? For evidence of the model's spread to India—along with important local complexities—see David B. Wilkins and Vikramaditya Khanna, "Globalization and the Rise of the In-House Counsel Movement in India," in *The Indian Legal Profession in the Age of Globalization: The Rise of the Corporate Legal Sector and Its Impact on Lawyers and Society* (D. Wilkins, V. Khanna, and D. Trubek, eds. 2017).

4. Professor Wilkins notes that in-house legal departments now have their pick of talented associates and even partners from top law firms. This is particularly true with respect to women, and to a lesser extent racial minorities, whose representation even at the top ranks of internal legal departments is far greater than in similar positions in outside firms. Why are minorities and women more likely to succeed in-house than in a corporate law firm? Are there structural features on the in-house environment—working for only one client, a relatively flat structural hierarchy with no inexperienced lawyers, the integration of business and legal advice, professional

management — that mitigate some of the disadvantages faced by women and minorities in corporate firms? See Zack Martin, "Women and Minorities Discover the Welcome Mat In-House," Chicago Lawyer, May 1999, at 68. Is there anything that law firms can learn from the success of women and minority lawyers in-house? On the other hand, are there factors that cut in the opposite direction? Consider the following observations by Professor Wald:

> Prevailing myths hold that in-house legal departments offer an attractive work-life balance and equality in their promotion policies, if only in contrast to the hypercompetitive and glass ceiling practice realities at large law firms. [These beliefs, however, are myths.] While in-house departments do offer greater flexibility, they increasingly impose on the personal lives of their lawyers, sometimes in less than obvious ways, [for example, replacing the familiar expectation of long billable hours with the expectation of long soft hours, proving that the in-house lawyer is a team player who understands the business and is not a naysayer]. And while in-house departments have a better gender record than large law firms in terms of promotion to senior positions of power and influence, they nonetheless feature similar patterns of implicit gender [bias and] discrimination. In-house myths obscure implicit discrimination by suggesting that one can opt out of the problem and that it may not afflict all segments of the profession. Disproving these myths [may] refocus attention on the complex problem and subtle manifestations of implicit discrimination in (and outside) the house.

Eli Wald, "In-House Myths," 2012 Wis. L. Rev. 407.

What effect are the changes in the "corporate hemisphere" documented above likely to have on the core ideals of lawyer professionalism that we have been discussing throughout this book? In recent years, the answers to this question given by many scholars and practitioners have been bleak. See, e.g., Anthony T. Kronman, *The Lost Lawyer: Failing Ideals of the Legal Profession* (1993); Mary Ann Glendon, *A Nation Under Lawyers: How the Crisis in the Legal Profession is Transforming American Society* (1996); Sol M. Linowitz, *The Betrayed Profession: Lawyering at the End of the Twentieth Century* (1994). Indeed, according to a widely read 1999 article published by Dean (now Judge) Patrick Schiltz, "it is hard to practice law ethically" in the new world of corporate legal practice. Patrick Schiltz, "On Being a Happy, Healthy, Ethical Member of an Unhappy, Unhealthy, Unethical Profession," 52 Vand. L. Rev. 871 (1999).

Sadly, there is evidence of some of the ethical issues Schiltz suggests. In a 1999 study, for example, Professor Lisa Lerman confirms Dean Schiltz's pessimistic predictions about the prevalence of billing fraud among lawyers in large law firms. See Lisa G. Lerman, "Blue-Chip Bilking: Regulation of Billing and Expense Fraud by Lawyers," 12 Geo. J. Legal Ethics 205 (1999):

In recent years, a disturbing number of well-respected lawyers in large established firms have been caught stealing large amounts of money from their clients and their partners by padding, manipulating and fabricating time sheets and expense vouchers. Some have gone to prison, been disbarred, and/ or been fired. Others have escaped prosecution or discipline. It used to be that lawyers inclined to steal from their clients wrote checks to themselves from their client trust accounts without client authorization and without having earned the money. Trust account fraud still occurs, but in recent years, theft from clients and from partners through billing and expense fraud has become more common and more pervasive.

In addition to discussing the ethical dangers of practicing in a large law firm, Dean Schiltz also pointed to several studies suggesting that many—if not most—of the lawyers who work in these institutions are unhappy as well. See Schiltz (reporting a Boston study concluding that "associates in big firms were the least happy of the eight categories of lawyers studied and another that reported "low morale" among partners). How credible do you find this claim? Are there reasons to suspect that, notwithstanding what the surveys say, lawyers in large law firms may be more satisfied with their careers (although perhaps disappointed that various aspects of their current jobs aren't what they hoped or expected them to be) than the many solo and small firm practitioners (described in the next section) who are finding it increasingly difficult to earn a living in the law? For a critique of the career satisfaction studies upon which Dean Schiltz relies, as well as the conclusions he draws from the available data, see Kathleen E. Hull, "Cross-Examining the Myth of Lawyers' Misery," 52 Vand. L. Rev. 971 (1999). Indeed, contrary to the prevailing wisdom, most systematic studies have concluded that the overwhelming majority of lawyers are satisfied with their careers. See, e.g., Ronit Dinovitzer, *After the JD: First Results of a National Study of Legal Careers* at 47 (reporting that 80% of lawyers who entered the bar in 2000 report being either "moderately" or "extremely" satisfied with their decision to become a lawyer); John Heinz, et al., *Urban Lawyers* (2005) (reporting an 83% satisfaction rate among all Chicago lawyers).

Satisfaction with one's decision to become a lawyer, however, is a blunt measurement. Compared to what?! In order to discover whether there are any important differences in whether lawyers in different practice areas are satisfied with different aspects of their lives as lawyers, the *After the JD* study asked lawyers to rate their satisfaction with a broad range of particular issues, ranging from the substance of their work, to their relationship with colleagues, to their compensation. The researchers then divided the respondents answers into four categories: "Job Setting Satisfaction," consisting of factors such as recognition received at work, relationships with colleagues, and job security; "Work Substance Satisfaction," reflecting the intrinsic interest of the work; "Social Value Satisfaction," which includes satisfaction with issues such as diversity, pro bono opportunities, and the social value of the job; and "Power Track Satisfaction," comprised of compensation and opportunities for advancement.

The researchers than tracked satisfaction with each of these four factors across the various settings in which lawyers work. The results are presented in Figure 12.6:

Figure 12.6

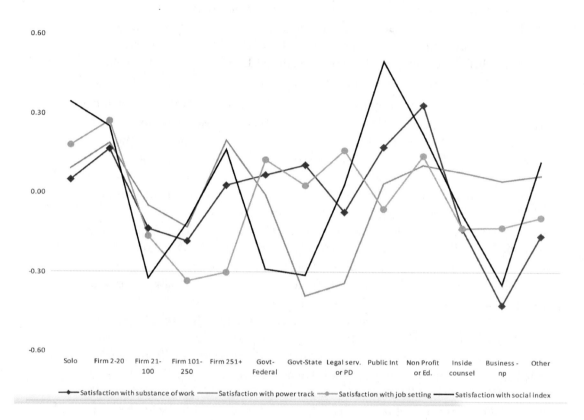

As the researchers underscore, there are important differences among these different measures across various legal jobs:

> The first three dimensions of satisfaction tend to correlate highly with one another—people happy with the substance of their work also tend to like their work environment and its social value. But "power track" satisfaction is often inversely related to the others. For example, attorneys in large firms tend to report the highest levels of satisfaction on the power track measure, but they tend to express much less satisfaction with other dimensions of their jobs. . . .

> These different patterns help provide a context for the literature that purports to find high levels of dissatisfaction among associates in large law firms. The relative dissatisfaction reported by associates suggests that high salaries and a perception of strong prospects for the future are counterbalanced by the less desirable aspects of their current work environment.

See id., at 48. See also Kenneth G. Dau-Schmidt and Kaushik Mukhopadhaya, "The Fruits of Our Labors: An Empirical Study of the Distribution of Income and Job Satisfaction Across the Legal Profession," 49 J. Legal Educ. 342 (1999) (finding that the dissatisfaction of lawyers in law firms is more than offset by their high levels of satisfaction with their income). Interestingly, Schmidt and Mukhopadhaya did not find job satisfaction to be highly correlated with either gender or race. Id., at 362. For an in-depth analysis of the AJD's data on satisfaction and how it relates to the broader literature on this issue, see Ronit Dinovitzer and Bryant G. Garth, "Lawyer Satisfaction in the Process of Structuring Legal Careers," 41 Law & Soc'y Rev. 1 (2007).

Are there ways that law firms, companies, and law schools can work together to define a new professionalism for the new realities of corporate law practice in the 21st century? Consider the following argument by the former general counsel of a leading company, the former managing partner of a large law firm, and a professor in a leading law school:

Benjamin W. Heineman, Jr., William F. Lee, and David B. Wilkins
Lawyers as Professionals and as Citizens:
Roles and Responsibilities for the 21st Century

Harvard Law School Center on the Legal Profession, Professionalism Project*
pp. 5–8

This essay presents a practical vision of the responsibilities of lawyers as both professionals and as citizens at the beginning of the 21st century. Specifically, we seek to define and give content to four ethical responsibilities that we believe are of signal importance to lawyers in their fundamental roles as expert technicians, wise counselors, and effective leaders: responsibilities to their clients and stakeholders; responsibilities to the legal system; responsibilities to their institutions; and responsibilities to society at large. Our fundamental point is that the ethical dimensions of lawyering for this era must be given equal attention to—and must be highlighted and integrated with—the significant economic, political, and cultural changes affecting major legal institutions and the people and institutions lawyers serve.

We have chosen to write this essay as a joint statement from a former general counsel of a global corporation, a former managing partner of an international law firm, and a professor of the legal profession at a major law school. We therefore focus our discussion on the four ethical duties in the institutions we know best—corporate legal departments, large law firms, and leading law schools—and on the important connections among them. But we also hope that both the ethical framework we propose and our commitment to a shared responsibility for giving it practical effect will have resonance in the many other important settings in which lawyers work. The four duties are, we believe, central to what it means to be a lawyer, even as the practical expression of these responsibilities will undoubtedly vary by context and

---

* Available at: <https://clp.law.harvard.edu/assets/Professionalism-Project-Essay_11.20.14.pdf>

will require new and greater collaboration that reaches across many of the profession's traditional divides.

. . . [W]e are mindful of the dramatic changes in both the legal profession and in society that make the realization of our — or any other — ethical vision of lawyering especially difficult today. *There is widespread agreement that the legal profession is in a period of stress and transition; its economic models are under duress; the concepts of its professional uniqueness are narrow and outdated; and, as a result, its ethical imperatives are weakened and their sources ill-defined.* We are also mindful that some will resist the invitation to review and address the broad array of ethical issues we raise in a time in which so many of the profession's traditional economic assumptions are in question. Nevertheless, we reject the idea that there is an inherent and irresolvable conflict between "business" and "service." To the contrary, we believe that, while tradeoffs about resource allocation will certainly be required, the proper recognition of each of the four ethical duties we explore is ultimately essential to the sustainability of "business" — whether that is the "business" of companies, law firms, or law schools, or more broadly, the health of our economic and political system as a whole. We therefore hope that this essay will stimulate an integrated discussion among the broad range of actors with a stake in the future of the legal profession not just about the pressing economic issues in major legal institutions but also about the equally pressing concerns relating to ethical responsibilities.

The rest of this essay proceeds in six parts.

Part II sets out our basic framework. It explicates lawyers' three fundamental roles as expert technicians, wise counselors, and effective leaders. It describes the sources and broad definitions of lawyers' four responsibilities: duties to clients and stakeholders; duties to the legal system; duties to one's own institution; and duties to the broader society. To effectively discharge these responsibilities, it argues that lawyers must not only have "core" legal competencies but also "complementary" competencies involving broad vision, knowledge, and organizational skills that, while not unique to lawyers, are essential to the counseling and leadership roles. This Part thus describes how our framework goes beyond the limits of the bar's formal ethical rules and challenges lawyers as both professionals and as citizens.

Part III describes the context for our analysis. While recognizing the profound importance of other entities, we explain that we have chosen leading companies, law firms, and law schools as the focus of our analysis because of their influence in setting norms for lawyers, their role in providing counselors and leaders across society, and their standing in public perception of the law. It outlines our assumptions about the large-scale forces transforming the economics of these institutions. These include accelerating competition, costs, technology development and transparency — and, in the case of companies and firms, undue focus on short-term profit maximization and profits per partner. All these factors gain greater force from globalization. A final contextual dimension is the cost and paradox of regulation of the legal profession: increasing the cost of becoming a lawyer while reducing the competition from other more effective and efficient providers of legal or legally related services. And, while noting that efforts to discharge the four responsibilities will entail allocation of resources and trade-offs, we maintain that forging a new, contemporary partnership between "service" and "business" is essential to the success, sustainability, and durability of these institutions.

Part IV discusses corporate law departments. Due to major trends in recent decades—the General Counsel becoming the senior counselor to boards and CEOs and the shift of power over money and matters from outside law firms to inside law departments—the General Counsel and inside lawyers have a special obligation to give practical meaning to the four responsibilities in leading corporations. The overarching theme of this Part is that the purpose of corporations, especially transnational ones, is the fusion of high performance with high integrity. Integrity is defined as ensuring robust adherence to formal rules, establishing binding ethical standards, advocating balanced public policy and fair political processes, and instilling the values of honesty, candor, fairness, reliability, and trustworthiness in employees. The General Counsel should also have a broad scope beyond law to include ethics, reputation, and geopolitical risk and should function as expert, counselor, and leader to assist the board and the business leaders in establishing an integrity culture in the institution. The General Counsel and all inside lawyers should aspire to be "lawyer-statespersons" who ask first "is it legal" but ask last "is it right," and who can resolve the central tension of being both a partner to the business leader and the ultimate guardian of the corporation's integrity. Inside lawyers have a special calling to surface, analyze, and recommend actions relating both to the corporation's employees and to other stakeholders that go beyond what the formal legal and accounting rules require and that address the many ethical issues facing global business in challenging environments. Finally, inside lawyers must recognize that they have a shared responsibility—and the obligation to share costs—with firms to provide challenging experiences and training for young lawyers. They must also use their influence (through, for example, new supplier guidelines) to encourage law firms to join with companies in addressing vital issues like provision of pro bono services, diversity, and needed reforms in the legal system both at home and abroad by making these issues important considerations in firm retention.

Part V addresses law firms and the imbalance between "service" and "business" that has resulted from a myopic focus on short-term economics. To be sure, there have been benefits to the profession from increased transparency concerning operation of firms and the resulting increased competition among firms. But the relentless focus on short-term economic success has adversely affected the culture and institutional integrity of firms; the training, mentoring, and development of young lawyers; the ability of firms and their lawyers to service the poor and underprivileged; and the ability of firms and their lawyers to devote time to the profession and the broader needs of society. We urge a rebalancing of the sometimes competing goals of "economic" and "professional" success. This rebalancing will require leadership and vision which will (1) affirm the priority of excellence and quality over mere hours generation; (2) articulate a vision for and create a culture which revives and restores the institutional fabric of firms; (3) affirm the commitment to meaningful mentoring and development of young lawyers; (4) affirm the commitment to the profession, including pro bono services and the "Rule of Law"; and (5) affirm the role of lawyers as the architects of a well-functioning constitutional democracy. This rebalancing will not be easy and will require commitment to long-term goals and values, even at the expense of short-term economics.

In Part VI, we turn our attention to the implications of our framework for "leading" law schools. We begin from the premise that law schools play a critical—but not exclusive—role both in teaching students to become expert technicians, wise counselors, and astute leaders, and in generating knowledge about law and legal institutions (including about the legal profession itself), and about the relationship between these institutions and the health and welfare of the broader society. To achieve these twin goals—and to find a proper balance between the two—law schools should reexamine how they are preparing students for the challenges that they will face throughout their increasingly diverse careers, and how faculty members understand their obligations to the legal framework and society, and to the law school as an institution. With respect to educating students, we urge law schools to create courses that focus directly on teaching lawyering roles and responsibilities in specific contexts and that explore key complementary competencies. We also advocate breaking down the artificial barriers that currently exist between "theory" and "practice," and between "law" and other disciplines, by developing new teaching materials (for example "business school" style case studies), new faculty (for example, Professors of Practice with significant experience outside of the academy, and team teaching with faculty from other disciplines), and a new integration between the placement function and the core educational objectives of the school. To achieve these goals, we put forward a number of specific reforms designed to restructure and refocus the third year of law school, while rejecting calls to eliminate it altogether. Finally, we underscore the critical need for deans and faculty to rededicate themselves to articulating a broad but nevertheless common understanding of the purposes of legal education and legal scholarship that gives appropriate recognition to the role that law schools—and law professors—play as part of the legal profession in addition to their role as an important part of the academy. Faculty and administrators should then use this purpose to guide the difficult tradeoffs around hiring, promotion, curricula, research, funding, and the allocation of other scarce resources that will inevitably be required to begin to achieve these common goals.

Part VII briefly discusses ways in which leading corporate law departments, law firms, and law schools can collaborate jointly to address the needs of young lawyers, to act on the needs of the legal system and society, to bridge the divide between the profession and the professoriate, and to develop better information on lawyers and the legal profession both here and abroad. . . .

Notes

1. Do you find this vision of the lawyer's role attractive? Do you find it plausible that companies, law firms, and law schools can work together to achieve this vision, given all of the changes to these institutions discussed above?

2. Who are the "lawyers" that society would need to produce to implement this vision? Consider what the authors say about the "complimentary competencies" that their ideal lawyers should possess:

> Most generally, we need lawyers who have a creative and constructive, not just a critical, cast of mind. Lawyers should be trained and encouraged to build an argument in a brief, a regulation, a complex piece of legislation, or a business plan that paints a persuasive vision about what "ought" to be, as opposed to simply delineating what already "is."

> We need lawyers who, in asking "ought" questions, base that inquiry on a relentless and fair-minded empirical quest for a broad set of facts which, to the greatest extent possible, reflect the complex reality of the world they would seek to change—cultural, systemic, and structural—by drawing on a diverse set of empirical disciplines outside of law.

> We need lawyers who, in asking these "ought" questions, can articulate a set of systematic and constructive options that expose and explore the value tensions inherent in most decisions. In the context of business decisionmaking, for example, when issues often come clothed in shades of gray, what are the alternatives for accomplishing a legitimate business goal with different degrees of legal, ethical, and reputational risk and with varying direct and indirect costs?

> We need lawyers who, in addition to exposing value tensions, can find a fair balance, in the ultimate course taken, between legitimate competing values. This may entail a balance between the policy or cost-benefit choices just mentioned, or, on a grander scale, a balance between the values that underlie so much of American history, legal and otherwise; for example, between freedom and equality or order and liberty, individualism and community.

> We need lawyers who think about the ethical, reputational, and enlightened self-interest of their client or the institution they are leading, not just about what is strictly legal or advantageous in the short-term. Exposing and analyzing these extra-legal issues is a critical function for lawyers.

> We need lawyers who, in making recommendations or decisions, are capable of assessing all dimensions of risk but who are not risk-averse. Taking well-considered chances is not a quality of mind customarily associated with lawyers but is often vital to innovation and change in the public and private sectors.

We need lawyers who have the ability to get things done, to understand how to make rules realities, particularly in the hurly-burly world of politics, media, and power. This includes not just the ability to understand and work within large institutions to achieve meaningful progress in implementing high-level rules, but also the role of lawyer as "facilitator"—to drive a transaction or negotiation to successful conclusion, often characterized as "getting to yes." It involves, on public issues in a democratic society, skill at fusing policy and politics.

We need lawyers who are not just strong individual contributors but who have the ability to work cooperatively and constructively in groups or on teams that are increasingly diverse and multidisciplinary—and who can lead these teams effectively. Teams are ubiquitous in the working lives of lawyers. Yet very little attention has been focused on what makes individuals effective team players. Moreover, working on teams and leading them are increasingly interconnected: much of leadership today is not command and control of the troops but persuasion, motivation, and empowerment of teams around a shared vision. All of these skills must now be practiced on teams that are increasingly diverse in every way, and where lawyers must work collaboratively with professionals from a broad range of other disciplines to get the job done.

We need lawyers who, when working on teams or developing arguments or positions, have the ability to understand the validity, value, and limits of related disciplines. This is particularly true with respect to the closely related disciplines of business and public policy, which are inseparable from law, particularly in the world of large companies and law firms that is our primary focus. But lawyers must also be familiar with the basic tenets of a broad array of other disciplines. Needless to say, lawyers cannot all have joint degrees, and choosing which disciplines to teach—and where and how—is a complex task. But lawyers must nevertheless have the aptitude and capacity to envision the relevance of a broad range of disciplines, and then, through the expertise of others, mine these other fields of knowledge to understand their strengths and the limitations inherent in their assumptions and their methods, and to separate what is established from what is hotly contested.

We need lawyers who can define problems properly in all of their increasingly complex global dimensions, and who can recognize the critical role of private ordering in addressing these problems. Particularly as they advance in their careers, lawyers will need to develop the vision, breadth, and inclination to be outstanding generalist-leaders. We recognize that there is a tension between the demands of super-specialization early in a career and the demands of a great generalist later in a career as one assumes broader types of responsibility and accountability. Nevertheless, it is critical that we develop lawyers who have the quintessential quality of the great generalist of envisioning and understanding the multiple dimensions of issues and the ability to comprehensively integrate those dimensions into the decision.

And, finally, with respect to all competencies, core and complementary, we need lawyers who can communicate effectively and concisely in a wide variety of formats and venues. Lawyers have always prided themselves on their ability to communicate. But as the range of problems they confront as experts, counselors, and leaders expands — and the modes of communication multiply — lawyers must explicitly work on developing competency in the full range of mediums and disciplines required to communicate effectively in today's information society.

Heineman, Lee, and Wilkins, "Lawyers as Professionals and as Citizens," at pp. 14–16.

Is this asking too much from lawyers? Is legal education designed to produce lawyers who have this kind of broad reach? Should it? We will return to these issues in Chapter 13. But before doing so, we first examine changes in the "individual hemisphere" of legal practice.

C. The Individual Hemisphere

In Chapter 9, we discussed four ways in which individuals receive legal services: legal services for the poor, public interest organizations, prepaid legal services, and legal clinics. Although these delivery systems are significant, most individuals — including most poor people — get their legal services from private practitioners working alone or in small firms. Although the number of solo practitioners has declined dramatically during the last several decades, more than half of all lawyers practice in firms of less than ten lawyers.

Perhaps because lawyers in this setting are rarely involved in big cases and do not recruit at law schools, we know much less about solo and small firm practice than we do about the much smaller number of lawyers working in the country's largest firms. Two notable exceptions are the following studies of solo and small firm lawyers, which provide a window into the rewards — and the pitfalls — of this form of practice.

Carroll Seron
The Business of Practicing Law:
The Work Lives of Solo and Small-Firm Attorneys
in Richard Abel, ed., *Lawyers: A Critical Reader* (1997)
pp. 35–44

Getting Started

There were three fairly typical career trajectories. One group began by working for the government. An equally notable group began as associates or employees of solo or small-firm practitioners; they often switched jobs any number of times and

③

then moved on to set up their own practices. Less typical was the small group of those who began their careers in major Wall Street firms.

Attorneys described three fairly distinct though not mutually exclusive strategies of coping with the initiation rights of professionalization. Some cultivated an informal network of attorneys and court officials on whom they could call to ask questions, copy legal forms, or clarify court procedures. Some learned by watching other lawyers and then trying out what they saw. . . . [One interviewee], Maisie Streep, "made the point of casually running into [attorneys] before [trial] and just sat down for an hour, talking about their cases." A minority of lawyers learned through mentors. Mark Velasquez of the Bronx and Daniel Friedman of Queens are the protégés of powerful, local political bosses who served them as mentors. These attorneys reported that "getting started" took five years.

lack of mentors

Expectations

The entrepreneurial lawyers began their careers with a crystal-clear sense of what they wanted — and eventually got. Many reported having worked as investigators for insurance companies, where they realized that this was one area where a "poor boy" could make a living. . . . [Most] knew they would be successful because they were excellent salespeople. . . .

Getting Clients

referrals from former clients (+)

. . . Most of [the] attorneys overwhelmingly agree that, with time, the single most important source of new clients is referrals from former clients. Most pointed out that referrals from professional colleagues — other lawyers, real estate agents, accountants or bankers — though neither as typical nor as important a source as client referrals, are another important source of business. . . .

The typical experimenter is a practitioner who begins with a core of referrals and builds a client base through professional networks and local activities, coupled with various forays into advertising or solicitation. Whether these attorneys place ads in local or citywide newspapers, develop brochures, or advertise on television, their efforts tend to be reluctant and haphazard. Typically, these attorneys have a modest listing in the Yellow Pages. Some join prepaid plans but rarely get any business that way. All try advertising at some point in their careers but tend to approach the decision with a professional's eye . . . to the bottom line. Most agreed that community-based Yellow Pages are the preferred place to advertise. The clients who come in through the Yellow Pages may be less desirable prospects, but the ads do tend to pay for themselves.

Mail (−)

Offering prepaid plans through direct mail advertising is neither very effective nor profitable. The promoters of prepaid plans, such as Hyatt Legal Services, market a networking device between consumers and lawyers. On the consumer side, they sell plans through direct mail to potential clients; in turn, they develop groups by state of participating attorneys who are paid a very small retainer and agree to take cases from these plan members at a "reduced" or, in some instances, a flat fee. Most who had joined such a plan reported that they never heard anything from it and, indeed, usually could not remember its name. . . .

Organizing Practices

... For partners in small, traditional law firms, friendship—if not the family—is the concept that captures the essential dynamic of their organization. The majority of these partnerships are between men of approximately the same age, many of whom met at other firms or in school, or shared office space and decided to start a firm together. Typically, partners explain, their agreement is verbal. By contrast, an associate in a small firm is an employee—somewhat marginal, isolated, or cut off from the partners. A partnership "track"—the essential building block of the corporate law firm—does not exist in most small firm practices. Although associates *may* become partners, there are no cues, no time frames, no ground rules, no clear expectations. Associates also reported that they are not quite sure how or if they are formally evaluated. The question of evaluation returns to an image of family, of fitting in, of being the right kind of person.

The process of hiring associates reveals the embeddedness of small firms in a local community. Most typically, partners responded, they look for attorneys with some work experience; they try to avoid hiring a recent law school graduate unless the individual worked for them while in school. They also prefer someone from the immediate area; the rationale is that they have watched the person function in court or in the legal district attorney's office; they "know" his or her reputation. ...

Some attorneys, opting for even more independence than collegiality allows, work on their own. Seymour Kaplowitz of Manhattan summed it up for most: "The advantages are easy enough. You're your own boss. You make your own hours; you take *flex* the time that you need to devote to the projects that you want. You're not harassed in the sense that someone is looking over your shoulder, and you don't have to report to anyone." ...

For many in full-time solo practice, however, the major disadvantage is that the work includes running a small business, a demand that many assumed they were sidestepping when they opted for *professional* careers. ...

Leslie C. Levin
The Ethical World of Solo and Small Law Firm Practitioners
41 Hous. L. Rev. 309 (2004)

More than forty percent of all practicing lawyers work in solo or small firms of five or fewer lawyers. These lawyers face many challenges. At a time when lawyers are increasingly employed within large organizations, solo and small firm practitioners often find themselves struggling for business, for control over their workload, and for respect. These lawyers tend to represent more individuals with personal plight problems than other lawyers, and they typically make less money than big firm attorneys. They report constant pressure to bring in clients and they confront frequent cash flow problems. ...

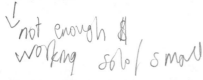
not enough $
working solo/small

Although the lawyers practiced in a variety of physical settings, had significantly different types of clientele, and very different areas of expertise, many of them agreed that the tremendous pressure to bring in clients, along with cash flow, are the biggest challenges of working in a solo or small firm practice. Some of the lawyers I interviewed explained these challenges:

Issues having clients ←

> The biggest challenge is continuing to have clients who come to see you. It's a never-ending battle of bringing in sources of business. Luckily again I haven't had to do much self-promotion, but I don't know from day-to-day from month-to-month from year-to-year where my business is coming from. In my particular area of law, as I said before, most of my work is one-time things. Client comes in, I do their estate planning, and they're gone.

> Definitely development, definitely getting out and getting my own clients no matter what's going on; . . . it's very hard to be seen, it's very hard for anybody to even know that you're practicing, and that is the biggest challenge, the hardest thing to do. And starting now, three years, starting now I'm supposed to start to get my own clients, by five years I'm supposed to have a fifth to a quarter of my practice be my own clients, which is coming up soon and I'm not doing well.

Not getting paid by clients ←

> Well, you know, making, making surviving, making a go of it is of course — the bottom line, the balance sheet, you know it's, that's, that can be very tough. I'm going through a very bad cash flow now where I'm not getting the checks in from the government. They owe me four or five checks that are back due. And I was just on the phone today trying to shake it loose — so . . . the cash flow is [always] a big problem . . . .

> Well, it is always generating business. You have got to get enough business in to meet your monthly — that is always a challenge. Every time the phone rings it's a challenge. But — preparing for trials is always a challenge, that sort of thing. But you know, when you own your own business, you have to pay the bills. You have to — it's your show. So you always have to be on guard for that.

As Carroll Seron has reported, there is a financial insecurity that permeates this form of practice and many practitioners feel close to the financial edge. This reality inevitably affects some of the ethical decision-making in which the lawyers engage, both on a conscious and a subconscious level.

Efforts to Provide Competent Representation

Tech. → easy to be up to speed

Forty years ago most lawyers practiced in solo and small firm practices, and it was not unusual for those lawyers to maintain general practices in which they did real estate closings, personal injury cases, wills, and small corporate transactions. As the practice of law has become more complex and technology has increased the speed at which law is practiced, it has become both easier and harder for solo and small firm practitioners to keep up with changes in the law and to perform their work in a competent fashion. As a threshold matter, the ability of these lawyers to provide competent representation is affected by decisions they make about the number of areas in which they practice law, the number and types of clients they take on, their willingness to reach out to colleagues for assistance, and their diligence in staying abreast of changes in the law. Many of the lawyers I interviewed reported that they made conscious decisions concerning these issues that had the effect of increasing their ability to provide competent representation. Some of these strategies are described below.

A. Specialization

While some lawyers reported that when they started out in practice they did "everything," a number of them eventually made decisions about how many substantive areas of law they could handle competently, and most decided to limit their practices to a few substantive areas. Six [out of forty-one] of the lawyers I interviewed devoted virtually all of their time to a single area of practice, and another thirteen of the forty-one lawyers I interviewed devoted seventy percent or more of their time to a single area of practice. The areas of specialization included areas traditionally associated with solo and small firm practice such as bankruptcy, family law, personal injury, residential real estate, and wills and estates, as well as areas more commonly associated with larger firm practice such as corporate securities, mortgage banking, complex commercial litigation, and education. The lawyers who specialized often worked in larger firm settings earlier in their careers. A slightly higher proportion of women specialized than men. In addition to the lawyers who specialized, some of the lawyers I interviewed limited their practices to two or three areas of the law and viewed themselves as "specialists" in at least one of those practice areas.

However, one third of the solo and small firm lawyers I interviewed were true general practitioners who regularly practiced in four or more areas. Most of them were male and worked outside of Manhattan. One important motivation for not limiting their work to a single practice area appears to be economic. Even in small firms that appeared financially successful, lawyers were tempted to take on matters beyond their areas of expertise. As one lawyer explained, "You're in a small firm, you have cash flow issues, you believe that you have the ability to reach out to resources or maybe you hope you do and you would take that case on." . . .

Lawyers who specialized were sometimes quite critical of those who did not, observing that the general practitioner often commits "naked malpractice," and that "most people don't know what they don't know." As one solo attorney observed, "I don't think that there's enough hours in the day to gain the knowledge that you need to do that." Yet those who specialized were also aware of the difficulties that specializing created for the small firm practitioner, particularly in the face of competition from larger law firms. . . .

B. Advice Networks

For lawyers in solo and small firm practices, part of the key to performing competently is their ability to draw on the knowledge and judgment of other lawyers. Many of the lawyers I interviewed reported that they routinely reached out with questions that arose in practice, not only to other attorneys with whom they were formally affiliated, but also to suite mates and to attorneys outside their offices. Many lawyers reported having a group of attorneys — ranging in size from three to twelve lawyers — to whom they would reach out with questions. The group of attorneys to whom a lawyer reaches out when the lawyer has a question in practice is referred to here as the lawyer's advice network.

These lawyers rely on advice networks early in their careers to learn how to practice law, and they typically look first to lawyers with whom they are formally affiliated, to suite mates and to lawyer friends. As they become more experienced, many of them still rely on those networks for questions of judgment, when they want to learn about a judge or an adversary, or when they face legal questions they have not previously confronted. . . .

The use of these networks by solo and small firm practitioners is significant not only because they can help improve the competence of individual lawyers, but also because in many cases, they are an important part of the communities of practice in which these lawyers operate and from which they learn professional norms. Of course, not all of the lessons taught are good ones, and not all of the advice is consistent. . . .

C. Staying Up-To-Date on the Law

Most of the solo and small firm lawyers I interviewed believed that they were able to stay up-to-date on the law in the areas in which they practiced. More than half of them reported reading the New York Law Journal, the local daily legal newspaper, on a regular basis. The lawyers who specialized also often read a variety of trade and specialized legal materials because they felt it was essential to their representation of their clients. A few of the lawyers who worked in partnerships mentioned that colleagues in their firms helped them stay up-to-date on the law.

General practitioners relied heavily on written materials distributed by bar associations and on CLE courses, which are mandatory in New York, to stay current on the law in the areas in which they practiced. Indeed, most of the lawyers I interviewed found continuing legal education to be at least somewhat useful. For these lawyers, CLE written materials, in particular, provided them with a way to stay up-to-date or to test whether they were staying up-to-date in their specialties. As one lawyer explained in a very common response, "There's a CLE course that's given every year by one of the associations called Statutory Updates where basically I just get the materials [laughs], but the outline's wonderful also because it tells you what's going on."

The local and specialized bar associations also play an important role in the efforts of these lawyers to stay up-to-date on changes in the law. All but four of the lawyers interviewed belonged to one or more state, local, or specialized bar association. Most of the lawyers reported that they read bar publications with regularity, although many of the lawyers noted with some regret that they did not have the time to attend many bar-sponsored functions other than those that provided CLE credit.

Technology also assists some lawyers in their efforts to stay up-to-date on developments in the law. For example, some use computer services that provide daily, weekly, or monthly updates on the law. Two attorneys described receiving CD-ROMs with updates of new developments in the law. Another one read the New York Law Journal online. Some lawyers pointed to the research that they performed through computer services such as Westlaw as their way of keeping up-to-date with the law. But a few older lawyers were not technologically competent and could not electronically check on developments in the law.

For solo and small firm lawyers, the cost and time commitment required to stay up-to-date on the law are substantial, and some lawyers are forced to balance those factors against other considerations. Women and solo practitioners were more likely to express doubts that they were able to stay up-to-date on legal developments than the other lawyers I interviewed. As one lawyer explained when asked whether he felt he was able to stay current on the law in the areas in which he practiced, "For the most part, yes. To some degree no, because you're just dealing with, you know, the daily every day things, so that it's hard to always stay abreast of what's going on in the law. The law's so expansive." . . .

Common Types of Ethical Challenges

My interviews with the New York lawyers revealed that they face a variety of ethical issues in their daily lives, which range from issues that present serious moral challenges to more mundane problems that constitute violations of formal bar rules. In this section I identify some of the more common ethical challenges. In some instances these issues may arise precisely because the lawyers are in solo or small firm practices or because they tend to represent individuals in personal plight matters. In other instances their manner of dealing with an ethical problem may also reflect the small practice settings in which they operate.

1. *The "Bad" Client.* The lawyers identified a wide array of ethical issues they encountered, but one of the most common ethical challenges encountered by solo and small firm practitioners was the problem of a client who wished to engage in some form of fraud. One attorney stated, "I've had clients ask me to change documents, change dates, change amounts, and I have had people ask me to do that. And you gotta be like, whoa, I have had [that] lots of times, many, many times." As another lawyer explained, "It's definitely clients who want to do stuff."

Some lawyers who frequently encountered clients who wished to engage in unethical conduct attributed this phenomenon to the nature of their practice specialty rather than to the size of their practice. For example, a lawyer who specialized in estate planning noted that many of his clients were in cash businesses and therefore "I'm constantly confronted with what my client is going to report." He observed, "Basically, my clients are hiring me to do things that are unethical." For this reason,

"If you want to be a lawyer and you want to practice [tax] law, sometimes you have to bend the law." . . .

A few of the lawyers I interviewed described conscious decisions to avoid certain clients in an attempt to limit ethical problems. The decision to refuse to take certain clients or certain types of matters is, however, a difficult one because of the challenges of making a living. . . .

2. *Office Management Problems.* One common view of solo and small firm lawyers is that they often face problems arising from poor law office management, ranging from taking on too many matters, to poor filing and calendaring systems, to an inadequate understanding of the economics of law practice. These problems can directly contribute to neglect of client matters and failure to communicate with clients, which are among the most common reasons for lawyer discipline. Contrary to the conventional view, however, most of the lawyers I spoke with reported that they had control over their caseloads and calendaring and filing systems. Only a small number indicated that these were recurrent problems in their practices. Of course, the lawyers I interviewed may have been uncomfortable sharing information that suggested that their office management was inadequate. Moreover, even if the lawyers I interviewed were being completely truthful, office management problems may be a more pervasive problem among solo and small firm practitioners than my small study indicates. . . .

Most of the lawyers I spoke with seemed to feel that their workloads were manageable. This is not to say that most of the lawyers I interviewed did not work hard, and indeed, some of them reported working on average at least seventy hours a week. Moreover, there was a small number, mostly composed of male solo practitioners and sole proprietors, who felt that their practices controlled them to the point that their work interfered significantly with their personal lives.

Work-Life Balance ←

The lawyers I interviewed reported that they were able to keep track of their client matters, appointments, and filing dates. Only a few of the lawyers I interviewed kept track of their caseloads with sophisticated computer programs designed specifically for their own practices or with case management software by Saga or Time Matters, which are designed for legal practices. A significant minority relied on simple calendaring software, such as Microsoft Outlook, to keep track of appointments. The majority of lawyers—including some with volume practices—relied on paper calendars or PDAs to keep track of their meetings and court appearances. . . .

Calendar Systems ←

3. *Problems Created by Office Sharing and Office Affiliations.* The ways in which solo and small firm lawyers share offices and form affiliations with other lawyers also present some ethical challenges not normally present in larger firm practices. Many solo and small firm practitioners practice in office suites with other lawyers, and the use of common secretaries, common telefax machines, and shared conference and file rooms poses risks to client confidentiality when lawyers are not formally affiliated. Casual conversations with suite mates and the use of speaker phones present similar kinds of risks. Indeed, several of the common office practices of the lawyers

who were interviewed ran counter to bar ethics opinions which counsel great caution in office-sharing arrangements. . . .

One of the other ethical problems that arose in office-sharing arrangements was that the lawyers often formed affiliations with other lawyers that they termed "of counsel" relationships, when they were often such loose relationships that they could not properly be described in that way. The principal characteristic of the "of counsel" relationship is "a close, regular, personal relationship," but not one of a partner or associate. Office sharing in itself, however, does not suffice to permit the representation that a lawyer is "of counsel," and it must mean more than an occasional collaborative effort among otherwise unrelated lawyers or firms. Nevertheless, many of the lawyers I interviewed held themselves out as having "of counsel" relationships with a variety of lawyers both in their offices and outside their offices, even though they consulted only infrequently and did not have a close, regular relationship. . . .

4. *Conflicts of Interest.* The office arrangements and affiliations described by the lawyers I interviewed presented potential—yet mostly unrecognized—conflict of interest problems. Most of the lawyers I interviewed had no formal system for checking conflicts of interest among their clients, relying on an "in your head" method when new clients sought representation. . . . [M]ost of the lawyers I interviewed employed erratic and informal conflicts-checking procedures even when they worked in law firms with other lawyers. These lawyers felt that they knew what their partners or associates were working on or informally canvassed their colleagues as new matters came in. . . .

5. *Escrow.* Escrow account violations are potentially a sensitive subject for lawyers because the mishandling or improper taking of client money from those accounts runs counter to public notions of morality and violates one of the most well known of the bar rules. I doubted whether any lawyers would admit they had improperly maintained client funds, and I therefore did not seek to determine whether the lawyers had, in fact, ever violated those rules. Nevertheless, any effort to understand the ethical world of solo and small firm practitioners cannot ignore this topic because much public discipline is imposed due to these violations. In this study, I therefore attempted to explore what these lawyers knew about the rules governing the maintenance of client escrow accounts as a first step toward understanding their compliance with these rules.

Before describing the responses of these lawyers, it is important to note that the rules for maintaining clients' funds are detailed and not all self-evident. New York lawyers are required to maintain funds that they receive in a fiduciary capacity from a client or third party in a segregated account or in an Interest on Lawyer Account (IOLA). IOLA accounts are to be used when the funds are too small or are expected to be held for too short of a time to generate sufficient interest income to justify the expense of administering a segregated account for the benefit of the client or beneficial owner. There are specific notification and record-keeping requirements concerning these accounts, which include, inter alia, the requirement that the lawyer promptly notify the client or third party of the receipt of funds in which the client or third party has an interest and the requirement that the records be maintained for seven years.

The lawyers I interviewed all professed to be aware of the need to safeguard clients' money, but not surprisingly, the younger attorneys who did not have responsibility for maintaining client escrow accounts knew little about the specifics of the rules. Some of the lawyers who had responsibility for maintaining the accounts said they learned what to do by asking mentors, suite mates, or relatives, or by going to their banks and seeking assistance in setting up the accounts. Relatively few said that they learned the rules in law school or through bar-sponsored activities.

While virtually all of the lawyers noted that they kept their bank records for the prescribed seven years or "forever," it was unclear whether they understood all of the rules governing escrow accounts. . . .

Although escrow account violations are not the largest source of complaints against lawyers, they are viewed as the most egregious violations of client trust, and therefore result in the most severe discipline. Because the discipline imposed for failure to properly maintain escrow accounts is often public in New York, the lawyers I interviewed perceived, incorrectly, that escrow account violations were the most common reason for the imposition of lawyer discipline. Although this perception might—theoretically—cause lawyers to fully familiarize themselves with all of the relevant rules, the reality seems otherwise. The reported cases suggest that client money is often deposited in segregated accounts but that discipline is imposed, at least in part, for violations of rules about which lawyers may be unaware, such as the client's right to receive interest on funds in an escrow account, the prohibition against depositing a lawyer's funds in an escrow account, and the need to provide a client with a formal accounting before taking legal fees and costs from an escrow account.

Of course, ignorance is not the only reason for violations of the rules governing the maintenance of escrow accounts. Pure venality accounts for some violations. In other cases, lawyers may not have the time or support staff to comply with the rules. In addition, the economic precariousness of some solo and small firm practices tempts some lawyers to "borrow" from escrow accounts to pay firm operating costs or other expenses. If this occurs, then these lawyers are likely to be discovered because New York banks are required to report to the Central Registry at the Lawyers' Fund for Client Protection when an overdraft in a client escrow account occurs.

Notes

1. Seron develops a typology of entrepreneurs, experimenters and traditionalists and argues that these groups of attorneys are distinguished by the degree of professional or business orientation exhibited in their practices. Entrepreneurs are business people first, making use of technology and new legal freedoms (advertising) to build large franchise practices. Experimenters dabble in the use of new technology and advertising but largely rely on traditional means of getting clients,

notably family and friendship networks. Traditionalists evidence a "professional ideology" and eschew advertising. Seron argues that most solo practitioners are experimenters and traditionalists and she concludes that solo firm practice has not changed drastically compared to other areas of the legal profession. Do you believe this conclusion is as valid today as it was in 1997? Will the rapidly expanding power and availability of information technology change what solo practitioners can do? Does your answer to this question depend upon the kind of lawyers who are becoming solo practitioners in the twenty-first century? Are these lawyers likely to conform to the models Seron observed, or are they more likely to create new ones? What impact might these new entrants have on more traditional solo practitioners?

2. Seron argues that the solo practitioners in her sample have not benefited significantly from pre-paid legal services. What are the implications of this finding for the ambitious plans of the pre-paid service providers discussed in Chapter 9?

3. The other major innovation we discussed in Chapter 9 for improving access to legal services among low and moderate income individuals was the "legal clinic" movement exemplified by franchise law firms such as Jacoby and Meyers. Does Seron's finding about the importance that many solo practitioners place on their professional independence help to explain why legal clinics have had such a mixed record over the last decade? For an insightful discussion of how the legal clinic movement has implicated solo practitioners, see Jerry Van Hoy, *Franchise Law Firms and the Transformation of Personal Legal Services* (1997).

4. To what extent do Seron's and Levin's descriptions of solo and small firm practice support the implication of the "hemispheres" thesis that the individual client sphere of the profession is fundamentally different from the corporate sphere? In what ways are the concerns of the young lawyers working in small firms similar to those of the lawyers described by Galanter and Palay (p. 976)?

5. What do you think about the employment policies of small law firms? According to at least one empirical study, minorities are the most underrepresented in small and medium sized firms. See Lewis A. Kornhauser & Richard L. Revesz, "Legal Education and Entry into the Legal Profession: The Role of Race, Gender, and Educational Debt," 70 N.Y.U. L. Rev. 829 (1995). The New York State Bar Association, however, in a report titled *Preserving the Core Values of the American Legal Profession: The Place of Multidisciplinary Practice in the Law Governing Lawyers* (Apr. 2000), offers a contrasting view of small and medium sized firms' practice:

> In 1995, more than 89,000 lawyers worked in one of the approximately 4,200 medium size law firms (11 to 50 lawyers). . . . In one sense, the middle-sized firm stands at the center of the profession today. Many have resisted the institutionalization of practice and the bureaucratic model. While now acknowledging the importance of effective law office management, they have continued to lend emphasis to the idea that law is first a profession, and only secondarily a business. As a consequence, lawyers from this segment of practice have

frequently been the backbone of activities within the organized bar, stressing "professionalism" and providing leadership for professional organizations. In some ways, the medium-sized firm appears to have mitigated the effects upon the profession as a whole of the transformation of the large firm. . . . [L]arge law firms have been the "critical catalyst" of recent changes in the legal profession.

Why do you think the New York State Bar made a point of identifying medium size firms as guardians of "professionalism" and large firms as the "critical catalyst" for recent changes in the profession? Does this characterization ring true to you, and if so why? Do the findings of Professors Kornhauser and Revesz affect your assessment of the claim put forward by the New York State Bar Association that small and medium sized firms are the "guardians of professionalism"?

6. What knowledge and skills do the lawyers Seron and Levin describe need to survive? Does law school teach these skills? Are they tested on the bar exam? Does your answer to this question affect your views about the unauthorized practice of law issues discussed in Chapter 8?

7. Consider the ways that solo and small firm practitioners find clients. Does this suggest something about the kinds of lawyers who are likely to engage in bar association and civic activities? Is the commingling of public and private motivations relevant to debates about pro bono activity among lawyers and professional self-regulation? Will the demands for solo and small firm practitioners to participate in community and bar association activities make it more difficult for women to succeed in this sector of the bar? Will this in turn affect the outlook of the organized bar of the general public toward women lawyers?

8. Describing the efforts of solo and small firm practitioners to stay up-to-date in representing their clients, Levin details reliance on traditional means such as print sources and attending CLE presentations, as well as on technology and virtual sources. Would you expect emerging technological innovations to allow solo and small firm lawyers to more cheaply and effectively stay up to date, and that over time these innovations might blur the lines separating the corporate and individual hemispheres?

9. How typical are the "typical" ethical challenges experienced by solo and small firm practitioners? Are they unique to these lawyers or common to all attorneys? Consider, for example, "bad clients." Do large law firm lawyers encounter bad clients? Are these bad clients likely to share some characteristics? Are lawyers' means of dealing with bad clients likely to differ across hemispheres?

Seron and Levin explain that a common challenge confronting solo and small firm practitioners is the constant need to bring in new clients and expand books of business, while continuing to offer clients competent representation and avoiding neglecting their matters. The following excerpt explores the perils of neglect and attempts to address it.

Richard L. Abel
Practicing Immigration Law in Filene's Basement
84 N.C. L. Rev. 1449 (2006)

A Case Study of Neglect

Joseph F. Muto was admitted to the New York bar in January 1987. Although he worked in Syracuse for a real estate firm, for the District Attorney, and twice as a solo practitioner, he never established a successful practice. After ten years he moved to New York City. In response to an advertisement, he began doing immigration cases for attorney David Rodkin. After a few months, having seen how much money could be made in immigration law, he left with another employee, Karen Jaffe, both of whom opened individual practices in Chinatown in space rented from Michael Lee. In February 2001, upon receiving a complaint from the Immigration Court's Judge Ferris, the Departmental Disciplinary Committee ("DDC") charged Muto with neglecting clients, assisting the unauthorized practice of law, mismanaging his escrow account, and failing to report his address, among other charges.

Prosecutor Sherry Cohen opened the June 4, 2001 disciplinary hearing by accusing Muto of being hired and paid by a "travel agency" to represent Chinese immigrants facing deportation. They did not choose him, rarely met him outside of court, and were unable to contact him. Four immigration judges complained about his failure to appear at hearings. Although he charged as little as $150 (compared with the $3,000 to $8,000 fees of competitors), even that was excessive for this quality of service.

Competence Issues

Muto responded to these accusations by displaying a photo of his office. "There's a contention that it's not a bona fide law office. Your Honor will note, my name is on the front of the building . . . . I'm not a dishonest attorney, [although] . . . I may be a little bit disorganized . . . ." He offered "poor people" "quality legal services" at an "affordable price." He was hard working. "[V]irtually every one of my clients is overjoyed and happy with my services . . . . I'm the only low budget lawyer in Chinatown." "[H]igh priced lawyers" were behind these complaints, "Lord and Taylor trying to put Filene's [B]asement out of business." Muto claimed the travel agencies also resented his refusal to solicit clients by doing the "Chinatown crawl." If agencies sent him business he "didn't know about it." Clients were complaining only in order to reopen their cases. He blamed defaulting clients for his own non-appearance at hearings. . . .

He didn't violate laws

[Following exhaustive disciplinary proceedings, Muto was disbarred.]

What to Do About Neglect?

. . . Unfortunately, Muto is not unique. The EOIR [Executive Office for Immigration Review] Bar Counsel deplored that "[t]here are many immigration lawyers out there who really don't know the immigration laws." A survey of 100 legal representatives practicing at 26 Federal Plaza concluded that "most lawyers in immigration proceedings are barely adequate and that small numbers are very good and very bad . . . . The high-volume private practice lawyers were usually considered among the very bad." Entry barriers to practice are high. Muto "graduated at the top of his class" (if at a low-ranked law school). He passed the two-day New York Bar Examination the first time he took it (in 1986). (In 1984, 74% did so, compared with 78% nationwide.) But neither hurdle tests for the fatal flaws Muto later exhibited, and it is not clear how they could be exposed prior to practice. His first decade in Syracuse offered telltale warning signals: four different jobs; resignation followed by the bizarre claim that his wife had submitted it without his authorization; suspension for misappropriating client funds; multiple complaints about failing to perform services; taking on work for which he was unqualified. Professions, including law, make aspirants surmount significant hurdles—to protect those inside—but are reluctant to punish practitioners—again to protect those inside.

Some of the problems in this case were peculiar to or aggravated by immigration practice. Clients are unusually vulnerable: poor, deeply in debt, uneducated, ignorant of language and culture, and threatened with losing everything they have so painfully won. Most, especially those from China, are totally dependent on non-lawyer intermediaries. The EOIR Bar Counsel warned against "immigration consultants," "visa consultants," and "notarios." The 26 Federal Plaza study found that "some asylum seekers are directed to lawyers by the travel agents who helped arrange their journeys." As Muto's case showed, these intermediaries dominate many practitioners: charging clients; choosing, switching, and paying lawyers; collecting and translating documents; maintaining the file; "preparing" clients for hearings; interpreting; and even choosing litigation strategies . . . . They are indispensable; regulation will just drive them underground and increase the vice tax they charge.

But I chose this case to illustrate neglect, not immigration practice. How does Muto's behavior illuminate it? Some of his disorganization may have been characterological. Lawyers have invoked the Americans with Disabilities Act to claim Attention Deficit Disorder as a defense to discipline for neglect. Courts have responded—I believe rightly—that the ADA does not prevent them from disciplining lawyers for injuring clients.

Solo practitioners—more than a third of all lawyers, and almost half of private practitioners in 2000—confront their own unique problems. "You can't be in the office and circulating at the same time. And you have to circulate to get known. But then office work takes a lot of time, a great deal of clerical work." Muto "solved" this problem by letting Blue Eagle deal with his clients. Organizations grant compassionate leave to employees coping with personal problems. But sole practitioners have difficulty getting someone to cover for them, as Muto did when his mother was dying. As I mentioned at the beginning of this Article, *all* service providers ration their time—their only market commodity. Producers prefer to have a queue of consumers waiting for their services. (The only antidote, discussed below, is competitors wooing dissatisfied customers.) More than forty years ago divorce lawyers complained:

> A lawyer to live must have volume. I have volume but it is killing me . . . .
> One week you're as busy as you can be, and then you sit around for weeks or
> months until another busy spell sets in . . . . To tell you the truth, I'm in no
> position to refuse any kind of client.

An Oregon State Bar survey found that 27% of lawyers had more work than they could handle and another 42% were at the limit of their workloads. "Franchise law firms" cram the maximum number of client interviews into the day. "I'm not interested in their life stories," said a lawyer, "When you have people scheduled only 15 minutes apart, I don't have time for it and it's not necessary." The 26 Federal Plaza study identified eight lawyers representing twenty-three to seventy-six cases a month; Muto bragged about doing three masters in five minutes each and four individual hearings in a day; he had 450 open cases. Solo and small firm lawyers like Muto can mistreat clients because they are "expendable": one-shot consumers who have been rendered a marginal source of new business by the advent of mass marketing and intermediaries like the "travel agencies." Carlin's classic study of lawyers' ethics found that violations were more common when the clientele was unstable and low status. Peer groups encouraged unethical behavior; although Carlin focused on law offices, for Muto the significant reference group was the 26 Federal Plaza regulars.

In light of this provisional diagnosis, do any remedies seem promising? We could limit solo practice. The English Law Society considered doing so when it found that sole practitioners were disproportionately responsible for defaults, which were driving up contributions to the compulsory Indemnity Fund. Solicitors already must apprentice for two years and be employed for three more before venturing out alone. But the half of American private practitioners who are on their own would fiercely resist and might claim class and race discrimination (as did English solicitors). Should immigration practice, whose substantive law is very complex, be restricted to specialists? For several decades most lawyers have claimed to be specialists; but the profession has refused to make specialization an additional entry barrier.

Can the market correct its own imperfections? The problem is not a shortage of lawyers. The 26 Federal Plaza study reported "a higher density of lawyers in New York City than anywhere else in the United States" and "many lawyers in private practice who offer services at a range of prices to meet meager budgets." Legal representation rates were high: 86% at master hearings, 95% at individual hearings. Carlin found, however, that competition *increased* the likelihood of ethical violation. Laissez-faire lets consumers trade quality for price. But professions emerge because information asymmetries make this risky. A shopper who chooses Filene's Basement over Lord & Taylor can see the goods *before* buying and adequately evaluate aesthetics. Consumers of legal services can do neither. For "most clients," said a small firm practitioner, "it's a toss-up whether it's fast and cheap or cheap and fast!" Muto boasted that he offered "poor people . . . quality legal services" at an "affordable price." But as an IC judge at 26 Federal Plaza said: "These are lawyers you'd rather not see . . . . They show up five minutes before trial. I think a person would be better off pro se than with a lawyer who's asked them thirty seconds' worth of questions, done no research, gets no background documents, and has told them nothing." Individual clients are extremely passive in monitoring their lawyers. Chinese immigrants facing deportation are likely to be even less assertive.

If there are unavoidable imperfections in the market for private practitioners, what about alternatives? Everyone acknowledges the importance of representation in immigration proceedings (even if courts refuse to extend Sixth Amendment rights beyond criminal trials). The EOIR permits representation by law students, non-lawyer employees of accredited representatives, and "reputable individuals" (friends of the alien). Fourteen organizations offer free legal services in New York City. The Board of Immigration Appeals has a pro bono project (though that does not help at trial). But though law students and accredited representatives offer higher quality services than most private practitioners, they cannot begin to represent all needy clients. Should the "travel agencies" and other for-profit entities that illicitly dominate lawyers like Muto be allowed to do so openly but made responsible for the quality of those services? That would violate the ban against lay intermediaries. Should they be allowed to appear in court for clients *without* lawyers? That would necessitate regulation, the creation of a paraprofession, with the attendant problems of quality control and rent-seeking behavior.

What, then, of post-hoc regulation? We saw that IC judges were atypically proactive. The creation of an EOIR disciplinary process—which suspended or expelled 195 lawyers in its first five years—may have reduced that motivation. If so, the system depends on client complaints. . . . [C]lients do complain about neglect. And [the] requirement of a grievance in order to reopen a deportation order encouraged Muto's clients to complain (although he then tried to discredit them on grounds of self-interest). But most neglected clients are deported or disappear to avoid deportation. For the same reason malpractice liability is not a meaningful threat. As Muto's case shows, a great deal of damage can precede any corrective action, a problem compounded by the reluctance of disciplinary bodies to act without a pattern of neglect, and even then to disbar. Solo and small firm lawyers tend to see the entire framework of ethical rules and discipline as illegitimate: "Lord and Taylor trying to put Filene's [B]asement out of business." Sole practitioners felt that the Chicago Bar Association "represent[s] the layman against the lawyer, rather than the lawyer's view . . . ." "We feel they're dominated by a small group of blue-blood lawyers. Their interests are not compatible with ours. They are the lawyers that represent the railroads and insurance companies." "The big difference between the large firm lawyer and the average practitioner is that the big firms give out more bullshit, superfluity, and unnecessary research." There is reason for skepticism about the efficacy of discipline as a means of ensuring competence.

Which brings me back to where I began. Unless we know the background and environmental variables that produce neglect and the self-understandings of the lawyers who engage in it, we cannot devise effective remedies. . . .

Notes

1. What ought the profession do about neglect of clients' cases? Should solo and small firm practice be limited to protect clients from abuse? How so? Are Abel's concerns about the class and race consequences of such limitations justified? If so, should regulations instead target specific practice areas that involve vulnerable clients and impose specialization requirements?

2. Exploring various market-based solutions to the problem of neglect, Abel suggests allowing non-lawyers to offer legal services to clients. Consider the "travel agencies" described by Abel and their interactions with immigration clients. Would such market-based deregulation of the market for legal services be likely to effectively address neglect and abuse concerns?

3. As Abel points out, neglect does not result from a shortage of lawyers. Yet as the following excerpt regarding rural lawyers reveals, shortage of lawyers is a serious problem that often afflicts clients served by solo and small firm practitioners.

Lisa R. Pruitt, J. Cliff McKinney II & Bart Calhoun
Justice in the Hinterlands: Arkansas as a Case Study of the Rural Lawyer Shortage and Evidence-Based Solutions to Alleviate It
37 U. Ark. Little Rock L. Rev. 573 (2015)

1. Attorneys per Capita

According to the A.B.A., 5,970 attorneys were "resident and active" in Arkansas as of fall 2014. Arkansas's population in 2014 was 2,966,369, so 2.01 attorneys per 1,000 residents practice in the state. This compares poorly with the national average of 4.08 active attorneys per 1,000 residents. Among states in the mid-South region, Arkansas has the lowest number of attorneys per capita serving its population. In 2014, Missouri had 4.18 attorneys per 1,000 residents; Tennessee, 2.74; Mississippi, 2.36; Louisiana, 4.04; Texas, 3.21; and Oklahoma, 3.47. Thus, the regional average is 3.33 attorneys per 1,000 residents.

While Arkansas appears underserved by attorneys generally, the per capita number of attorneys in the Rural Counties is far below the state average. The average 2014 population of the Rural Counties was 10,208 residents, and their total population was 255,212. The Arkansas Judiciary database ("AJD") showed a total of 197 attorneys in the Rural Counties in July 2015, and the IOLTA database listed ninety five as of December 2014. Among the Rural Counties, the highest per capita number of attorneys in a county is 1.42 per 1,000 residents (Lee County) according to the AJD, while the highest per capita attorney count according to the Interest on Lawyer Trust Accounts ("IOLTA") database is 0.79 per 1,000 residents (Monroe County). The lowest per capita number according to the AJD is Cleveland County with no attorneys; Scott County is the second lowest at 0.37 per 1,000 residents. With just one attorney who has an IOLTA account, Scott County is also second to Cleveland

County in terms of attorneys with IOLTA accounts per capita, at 0.09 per 1,000 residents. . . .

2. Attorney Age

Another disturbing trend among the attorney populations of the Rural Counties is that they tend to be older than the state average. The July 2015 look at the AJD reveals that the average year of first licensure of attorneys in the Rural Counties is 1987; the December 2014 IOLTA data also indicate 1987 as the average year of first licensure of private practice attorneys in the Rural Counties. Of course, older attorneys are typically closer to retirement, which means the attorney shortage will soon worsen unless younger attorneys are enticed to serve these areas.

The AJD shows only seven Rural Counties whose attorney(s) have an average bar number in the 1990s. The Rural County with the youngest bar admission year average is Pike County (1997), meaning the presumptive average attorney age there is forty-three. The county with the oldest average is Bradley (1978.2), with a presumptive average attorney age of sixty-two. . . .

Of particular concern is that very few lawyers recently admitted to the bar are locating in the Rural Counties. According to the AJD, thirty-two attorneys with addresses in the Rural Counties (16.2% of all attorneys in the Rural Counties) have been admitted in the last decade. Just fourteen attorneys who have been admitted in the last five and a half years have located to a Rural County (7.11% of all attorneys in the Rural Counties), and they comprise only 1.3% of the 1,067 attorneys admitted during the January 2010 thru July 2015 period. Twelve Rural Counties have no attorney licensed in the last decade, and sixteen Rural Counties have no attorney licensed in the last five years. Six of twenty-five Rural Counties have no attorney with a bar number dated in this millennium. These are Lafayette (most recent bar licensure 1995), Dallas (1997), Woodruff (1998), Bradley (1998), Fulton (1999), and Cleveland County, which has no attorneys according to the AJD. . . .

5. Where the Attorneys Are and Looming Shortages in Other Counties

. . .

The data also reveal that Arkansas's lawyers are heavily concentrated in central Arkansas, with a particularly high concentration in Pulaski County. While some concentration of lawyers in a state's capital city is to be expected, the extent of the Pulaski County concentration is somewhat surprising. Although the county has just 13.2% of the state's population, 42.9% of the state's lawyers (3,244) practice there. Further, 38.6% (1,130) of lawyers with IOLTA accounts list a Pulaski County address. Thus, 8.26 lawyers per 1,000 residents have an address in Pulaski County, and 2.88 IOLTA account lawyers per 1,000 residents do. The average year of admission of a Pulaski County lawyer is 1993. . . .

Conclusion

The disparity between rural and urban Arkansas in per capita attorney population is striking, and the consequences of that disparity for access to justice in the
state's rural reaches are alarming. Nearly half of the state's lawyers practice in Pulaski
County and neighboring Saline and Faulkner Counties, though just more than a fifth
of the state's population lives in that cluster of central Arkansas counties. Meanwhile,
the state's twenty-five least populous counties are home to more than 250,000 residents, but fewer than 200 lawyers serve them. Indeed, the situation is even more dire
when we consider the paltry number of attorneys—just ninety-five—accepting private representation in the Rural Counties. Further, many of these least populous
and underserved counties are clustered together in certain regions of the state,
suggesting that some geographic segments of Arkansas are, in their entirety, without a sufficient lawyer population.

Rural Arkansas has a lot to offer entrepreneurial lawyers, including low cost of
living, short commutes, easy access to civic leadership, variety of practice, and little
local competition for clients. But these attractions are perhaps not apparent to Generation X and the Millennials now entering the legal profession. Alternatively, young
lawyers may be aware of these benefits but nevertheless believe they are outweighed
by downsides like those enumerated by many of the law students who responded to
our survey.

Yet, even as many students articulated negative views of rural places, significant
numbers of students also expressed openness to rural practice, particularly if they
had adequate fiscal support, e.g., loan repayment assistance, and training in skills
and practice management. Indeed, the survey data strongly indicate that financial
incentives will be necessary to attract sufficient attorneys to Arkansas's underserved
rural areas. Detailed salary data like that recently gathered in Texas might also prove
useful, especially if it served to establish the economic viability—perhaps even the
entrepreneurial potential—of rural practice in Arkansas.

Our data suggest that providing incentives and resources for those interested in
practicing law in Arkansas's rural reaches—or at least open to doing so—would be
effective at getting more lawyers to where their services are needed. We hope that
the data we have gathered to substantiate in detail the nature of this problem, as well
as our exploration of the likely success of possible interventions, will inform policy-
maker action in Arkansas. We make no claim to offering an exhaustive list of possible interventions, but we hope we have helped raise awareness among attorneys and
the public at large regarding the looming access-to-justice crisis in rural Arkansas.
It is within the power of Arkansas's governing institutions—with strategic partnerships and investments in new institutions and programs—to close the rural-urban
justice gap. Doing so, in turn, can level the justice playing field and profoundly
improve the quality of life for rural Arkansans.

Apart from the import of our findings for the access-to-justice landscape in
Arkansas, we hope that our empirical work may also inform other states with

concerns about their own rural lawyer shortages. Most states do not keep systematic records that permit them easily to see where and how great their rural lawyer shortages are. This data deficit makes it difficult to convince stakeholder institutions that government intervention is necessary. We therefore encourage other states to do what we have done for and in Arkansas—map where the lawyers are and seek to identify trends that may shed light on the causes of shortages in particular places.

Second, states need data about why recent law graduates and other lawyers are generally reluctant to practice in rural places. If we do not know why graduates are rejecting rural practice, we will not know if those wishing to ameliorate the rural lawyer shortage are able to respond to their concerns. No state can lower or eliminate all structural roadblocks to rural practice, e.g., the relative shortage of potential life partners. Institutional stakeholders can respond, however, to the sort of economic and practical concerns that loom large for many young attorneys who are otherwise open to rural practice. In this regard, Arkansas may face fewer challenges than many other states because Arkansas's two public law schools are among the best legal education bargains in the nation.

It is harder to say what role Arkansas's slow pace of urbanization plays in the rural lawyer shortage. At first blush, the existence of significant pockets of rurality in each region of the state suggests that a high percentage of Arkansans have experienced some significant brush with rurality—if only visiting grandparents in the countryside or enjoying ecotourism in the "Natural State." But these typically limited experiences with rurality will not necessarily cause young lawyers to want to live in rural places and take up rural legal practice. It is possible that the old adage—familiarity breeds contempt—holds true in this context, as the comments of some student respondents suggest. On the other hand, law students who had grown up in Rural Counties seemed more open overall to practicing in such sparsely populated places. We will have a greater understanding of the impact of Arkansas's significant rural population on the state's rural lawyer shortage only after more urbanized states have explored the issues we have examined here.

Notes

1. Pruitt and her co-authors paint a grim picture. Rural clients experience a significant and growing shortage of lawyers, and the shrinking lawyer population that serves them is getting older. What policies might incentivize solo and small firm practitioners, and, in particular, younger attorneys to serve rural clients? Would loan repayment assistance or loan forgiveness programs be likely to induce younger lawyers to serve rural clients? State income tax breaks? Giving CLE credits to lawyers providing pro bono legal services to rural clients?

2. Is technology likely to play a significant role in addressing the shortage of lawyers in rural communities? Can urban-based lawyers, using technology such as video-conferencing or even smart-phone video interface, effectively represent clients remotely?

3. What role, if any, can corporate hemisphere attorneys (for example, large law firm lawyers) play in addressing the needs of rural clients?

4. Earlier in this Chapter we discussed some of the reasons that explain why the corporate hemisphere and its large law firm lawyers are relatively well studied whereas the individual hemisphere and its lawyers are what Pruitt and her co-authors describe as data-deficient. Who should bear the primary responsibility to address this deficit? Law professors interested in the legal profession? Law schools? The organized bar? Taxpayers?

———————

One of the most important sources of business for many solo practitioners, urban and rural alike, is plaintiffs' personal injury work. Although many lawyers in this sector work exclusively in areas such as divorce, real estate, and trusts and estates, the relative expansiveness of American law with respect to an injured person's ability to recover damages—comprehensive substantive protections against injury or deceit, liberal pleading requirements, broad discovery, the right to a trial by jury or to have a jury determine compensatory and (where appropriate) punitive damages, and, most important, the contingent fee—has lured many lawyers in this "hemisphere" into plaintiffs' work. We conclude this section with a short excerpt examining the work of the "bread and butter" lawyers who continue to constitute the majority of the plaintiffs' bar.

Stephen Daniels & Joanne Martin
"The Impact That It Has Had Is Between People's Ears": Tort Reform, Mass Culture, and Plaintiffs' Lawyers
50 DePaul L. Rev. 453 (2000)

[The following is an excerpt from the research of Professors Daniels and Martin on the effect of tort reform on plaintiffs' attorneys in Texas. In fall 1999 and winter 2000, Professors Daniels and Martin surveyed 552 attorneys spread throughout the state of Texas; this survey was supplemented by interviews of ninety-six attorneys, conducted over several years, and drawn mostly from the cities of Dallas, Houston, and San Antonio. In the sample, Daniels and Martin selected for attorneys who currently, or in the past years, have devoted at least twenty-five percent of their practice to plaintiffs' work based on a contingency fee. While the study was designed primarily to evaluate the effect of tort reform, the piece is illustrative of the lives of that segment of the plaintiffs' bar engaged in more routine—as opposed to class action or mass tort—cases.]

We define "bread and butter" lawyers as those respondents to our survey who have at least five years experience as a plaintiffs' lawyer, and for whom the average value of the contingency fee cases they handled over the twelve months prior to the survey is at or below the median value for all respondents who have at least five years experience as a plaintiffs' lawyer. That median value is a modest $32,750; the twenty-fifth percentile is $12,000; the seventy-fifth percentile is $250,000; and only 10 percent of the respondents reported an average value for their cases of one million dollars or more. Of the 220 lawyers who fit into this "bread and butter" category, 76.3 percent described the geographic scope of their practice as local, covering the county in which their principal office is located and adjacent counties. Another 21.5 percent of lawyers within this category described their practice as regional, and only 2.3 percent described their practice as statewide. . . .

"Bread and butter" practices tend to be built upon the frequently occurring, lower-value car wreck cases. In the survey, the median percentage of caseload for these lawyers comprised of car wreck cases is 50 percent. Such lawyers depend on a reasonable return on these cases, including non-economic damages, for cash flow and for survival. In the words of an Austin lawyer: "the kinds of cases I have, the 'bread and butter,' so to speak, day-in and day-out cases are auto accidents. They pay the bills and carry me between big cases . . . [which] tend to be death cases." Many lawyers say they are not getting a good return on these cases, especially when it comes to non-economic damages. "The cases . . . don't settle for what they used to," said one lawyer in a frequently heard complaint. With this sentiment in mind, we asked lawyers in our survey what the current (1999) multiplier used by insurance companies to settle cases is, and what the multiplier was five years ago. The median multiplier in 1999 given by respondents was 1.5 times specials (economic damages like medical expenses, auto repairs, etc.), and the median figure for five years ago was 3.0 times. A smaller multiplier means, of course, lower settlements and less income. This can quickly put a lawyer's practice in financial jeopardy. A Fort Worth lawyer whose practice relies heavily on car wreck cases summarized the situation bluntly: "Without cash flow coming in you can't pay your bills and you can't fund your cases . . . we are in a brutal process of some [lawyers] being weeded out—and I may be one of them."

Non-economic damages . . . are of vital importance to the "bread and butter" lawyers because they can make the difference between earning a profit on a typical case or failing to realize any gain. Without some amount of non-economic damages on these low-value cases, the lawyer may not be able to recover enough to pay the client's bills, collect all or even most of the fee, and recoup his or her out-of-pocket expenses (the lawyers almost always front the case's costs). Short-changing the client is not something most lawyers want to do in what is a very competitive market for clients, a market in which the primary way of attracting new business is still through word-of-mouth client referrals. In fact, a number of lawyers said that they would, and have, cut their fee in order to not short-change the client. . . .

What have "bread and butter" lawyers done in reaction to what they see as an altered, harsher environment [as a result of tort law reform in Texas]? There appear to be at least five general reactions: leaving the practice area, downsizing, more careful screening of cases and clients, changing the way in which cases are handled, and diversifying the mix of business. Together these reactions suggest changes in the nature of the plaintiffs' practice. The changes may, in turn, give some indication for the future of civil litigation. . . .

. . . Tort reform may reduce the number of plaintiffs' lawyers able to survive handling cases of low to modest value. However, those who do survive are likely to be very good at succeeding in the altered environment. This scenario suggests a smaller, but more proficient plaintiffs' bar.

Notes

1. Recall the proposals to modify or eliminate "standard contingent fees" discussed in Chapter 8. Are the consequences for bread and butter plaintiffs' lawyers what the advocates of such reform measures intended? Will these measures lessen or exacerbate the imbalance between the corporate and individual hemispheres?

2. Given the risks Professors Daniels and Martin discuss, why don't plaintiffs' lawyers pool their risks by joining together into large law firms? In 1986, Professor John Coffee argued that "monitoring problems" made it difficult for plaintiffs' lawyers to collectively pool their risk by forming large firms. See John C. Coffee, Jr., "Understanding the Plaintiff's Attorney: The Implications of Economic Theory on Private Enforcement of Law Through Class and Derivative Actions," 86 Colum. L. Rev. 669 (1986). Since Coffee's article was published, however, a number of plaintiff-oriented law firms have grown significantly in size and scope. Ness, Motley, Loadhold, Richardson & Poole in South Carolina, for example, was a firm of over 70 lawyers (plus a sizable support staff) with a national practice which included playing a leading role in bringing both asbestos and tobacco cases. It split apart in 2002 and each half has grown since then. In addition, there are now a number of "mixed" firms such as Boies Schiller & Flexner and Robins, Kaplan, Miller & Ciresi that combine a substantial plaintiffs' practice with traditional business litigation (both plaintiffs' and defendants' work) and other areas of corporate practice. See Michael D. Goldhaber, "Boies Schiller's Big Year," Natl. L. J., Feb. 12, 2001, at A1, A17.

3. Are the lawyers in the large plaintiff firms discussed above likely to be the "bread and butter" lawyers described by Professors Martin and Daniels? For an argument that the plaintiff bar has itself largely fractured into two hemispheres, one consisting of "bread and butter" plaintiffs' lawyers and the other consisting of lawyers who litigate "high risk, high return" speculative litigation such as products liability and mass torts, see Herbert M. Kritzer, "From Litigators of Ordinary Cases to Litigators of Extraordinary Cases: Stratification of the Plaintiffs' Bar in the Twenty-First Century," 51 DePaul L. Rev. 219 (2001).

4. What has happened to the insurance defense lawyers who typically oppose "bread and butter" plaintiff lawyers? Consider the following assessment:

> Insurance defense has never been the most lucrative field of practice for American lawyers. However, the absence of high fees and the resultant high income was offset by stability and predictability. Lawyers and law firms established relationships with specific insurance companies, and barring major changes (mergers of insurance companies or droppings of lines of insurance by the companies), lawyers and firms could rely upon a steady

stream of business over a period of many years. Unlike contingency fee practitioners who always had to worry about where the next client would come from, insurance defense lawyers knew that more files would be arriving next week.

The working environment for insurance defense practice has changed radically over the last two decades. Insurers are much more conscious of costs and are constantly looking for ways to reduce their expenditures on defense counsel. That may mean moving work in-house, it may mean seeking alternatives to hourly fees, it may mean putting work out to bid, and it may mean changing firms if a better price can be obtained. Today, insurance defense practitioners live in a highly competitive world where they must be prepared to lose a major source of work at any time. They also must be prepared to live with being "nickel and dimed" again and again and again by the insurers who send work to them.

Herbert M. Kritzer, "The Commodification of Insurance Defense Practice," 59 Vand. L. Rev. 2053, 2093–94 (2004).

Note: New Directions?

In 2016, the ABA House of Delegates approved the following new "regulatory objectives" governing the provision of legal services:

ABA Model Regulatory Objectives for the Provision of Legal Services

A. Protection of the public

B. Advancement of the administration of justice and the rule of law

C. Meaningful access to justice and information about the law, legal issues, and the civil and criminal justice systems

D. Transparency regarding the nature and scope of legal services to be provided, the credentials of those who provide them, and the availability of regulatory protections

E. Delivery of affordable and accessible legal services

F. Efficient, competent, and ethical delivery of legal services

G. Protection of privileged and confidential information

H. Independence of professional judgment

I. Accessible civil remedies for negligence and breach of other duties owed, disciplinary sanctions for misconduct, and advancement of appropriate preventive or wellness programs

J. Diversity and inclusion among legal services providers and freedom from discrimination for those receiving legal services and in the justice system

See Lorelei Laird, "ABA Approves Model Regulatory Objectives for Nontraditional Legal Services," ABAJ, Feb. 8, 2016, available at <http://www.abajournal.com/news/article/house_approves_proposed_model_regulatory_objectives_for_nontraditional_lega>. As then–ABA President William Hubbard (whose Commission on the Future of the Legal Services proposed the measure) said, the goal of the guidance is to help state and local bar organizations close the "justice gap" by developing effective regulation of the growing number of nontraditional legal service providers, including on-line startups and paraprofessionals, such as the Limited Licensed Legal Technicians currently operating in Washington state (see p. 693, Note 7). Only time will tell whether the Objectives will have this effect.

D. What Difference Will Difference Make?

In the preceding sections we have examined some of the important changes in the demographics and organizations of legal practice during the last half century and some of the challenges that these changes pose to traditional legal ethics discourse. In this Part we examine a broader question: how might the changing demographics, institutions and markets of legal practice affect the professional identity of lawyers? Consider the following Problems, each of which illustrates a different aspect of the issue.

Problem 12–1

Anthony Griffin, a black lawyer affiliated with the ACLU, agrees to defend the Grand Dragon of the Ku Klux Klan. The case involves the state of Texas' attempt to subpoena the Klan's membership list in order to assist a probe into Klan violence against black residents in a newly integrated housing project. The African-American head of the Port Arthur branch of the NAACP subsequently fires Griffin from his position as the unpaid general counsel for that organization when Griffin refuses to withdraw from representing the Klan. See Sam H. Verhovek, "A Klansman's Black Lawyer, and a Principle," New York Times, Sept. 10, 1993, at B9.

We have discussed this fascinating case on two prior occasions. In Chapter 7, we examined why the rules do not compel lawyers to represent clients the lawyer finds morally abhorrent. In Chapter 9, we considered whether Griffin's status as the general counsel of a public interest organization created a different standard for conflicts of interest than would have applied if he were operating outside of this context. Underlying these questions, however, is another inquiry: Should Griffin's race have had any bearing on the case at all? Should Griffin have taken his own racial identity into account when deciding whether to exercise the discretion given him under the rules to represent the Klan? Should the NAACP have considered Griffin's race in deciding whether his decision to represent the Klan rendered him "unfit" for leadership in the organization? If you were a black resident of Vidor, Texas, would you feel any differently because the Klan is being represented by a black lawyer as opposed to one who is white? What about your view if you were a member of the nonblack general public? Does the fact that a black lawyer is willing to represent the Klan convey any information about the nature of the Klan or the seriousness with which one should consider its claims? Should the answers to these factual questions have any bearing on the normative determination of whether Griffin should have represented the Klan and how the NAACP and the public should have reacted to his decision?

Problem 12–2

Judith Nathanson, a Massachusetts divorce lawyer, is approached by Joseph Stropnicky to review a draft settlement agreement between him and his wife. Nathanson is well known for winning large settlements on behalf of women who have sacrificed their own careers in order to put their husbands through school and to take care of children and household responsibilities. Stropnicky is in this situation, having put his former wife through medical school and delaying his own education for seven years while he stayed home as the primary homemaker and caregiver for the couple's children. Despite these similarities, Nathanson categorically refused to represent Stropnicky on the ground that "she does not represent men." The Massachusetts Commission Against Discrimination subsequently concluded that Nathanson's "women only" policy violates her obligations as a "public accommodation" by discriminating in her selection of clients on the basis of gender. See Stropnicky v. Nathanson, No. 91-BPA-0061 (Mass. Comm'n Against Discrim.) (Feb. 25, 1997) (Charles E. Walker, Hearing Commissioner).

Does the MCAD decision conflict with the principle of professional independence that underlies the Model Code of Professional Conduct? See Rule 1.16(b). Does it violate the principle of moral autonomy that underlies a lawyer's right not to represent a client that he or she finds morally abhorrent? Do you think that Nathanson finds Stropnicky—or all men—morally abhorrent? If your answer is yes, are there grounds for treating a lawyer's moral aversion to a class of individuals such as "men" or "whites" differently from lawyers who disagree with a client's views, positions, or actions? If your answer is no, what justifies Nathanson's "women only" policy and how should the rules of professional conduct or the law generally regard justifications of this kind? Should administrative agencies or courts be involved in making these decisions at all?

Problem 12–3

A devout Catholic lawyer petitioned the Tennessee Board of Professional Responsibility to determine whether he was ethically obligated to accept an appointment from a state court judge to represent a minor seeking a judicial waiver of the state's requirement that minors must have parental consent before obtaining an abortion. The lawyer argued, inter alia, that he should be relieved of the appointment on the basis of his deeply held religious opposition to abortion. The Board concluded that the question of whether the lawyer could withdraw on this basis was ultimately for the judge in the underlying proceeding to decide. The Board went on to state, however, that decisions by the Tennessee Supreme Court and other authorities "cast serious doubt on whether such an argument would prevail," notwithstanding the fact that the lawyer's duty to represent the minor zealously might preclude him (if the minor is sufficiently mature to know her own mind) from informing her about alternatives to abortion or urging her to consult her parents. See Tenn. Bd. of Professional Responsibility Formal Op. 96-F-140 (1996). Why should the Board have thought that the lawyer would be precluded from informing the minor about abortion alternatives or from urging parental consultation?

Do you agree with the Board's decision? Should religious objections to accepting a court appointment be treated differently from non-religiously based moral objections, for example, that a lawyer does not want to represent a person accused of child molestation? Should religious identity be treated differently from race or gender for the purpose of defining a lawyer's professional obligations or discretion? Should lawyers have less discretion to decline court appointed cases than those that come to the lawyer by some other means? Should the client have anything to say about this? What, if anything, should the lawyer in the Tennessee case say to his minor client about his religious views?

Problem 12–4

Gil Garcetti assigns a black prosecutor, Christopher Darden, to be one of the lead prosecutors in the racially charged prosecution of O.J. Simpson. During the course of the trial, Darden seeks to bar the defense from questioning Mark Fuhrman, a white police officer who found a damaging piece of evidence on Simpson's property, about whether Fuhrman used racial epithets in the past. In arguing that the court should exclude Fuhrman's racist remarks, Darden expressly relied on his own racial identity by telling the judge that allowing Fuhrman's statements to come before the jury will turn the case into "a race case" to be decided on the basis of who is "the blackest man up here." Subsequently, Johnnie Cochran, the black lead defense lawyer, argued to the predominantly black jury that they should acquit his client in part as a means of "sending a message" that police racism and misconduct will not be tolerated. See Margaret M. Russell, "Beyond 'Sellouts' and 'Race Cards': Black Attorneys and the Straitjacket of Legal Practice," 95 Mich. L. Rev. 766 (1997).

Once a lawyer accepts a given representation, should identity considerations influence the actions that he or she takes on the client's behalf? Should Garcetti have considered Darden's race in deciding whether to assign him to the Simpson prosecution? Should Darden have considered the LAPD's long history of questionable treatment of the black citizens of L.A. (exemplified by the infamous beating of Rodney King) when deciding whether to shield Fuhrman's racist statements from the Simpson jury? Assuming that he was justified in trying to exclude Fuhrman's statement, was Darden also justified in referring explicitly to his own racial identity in his argument to the court? Was it unethical for Cochran to call on his and the jury's common racial identity in asking jurors to "send a message" with their verdict?

Problem 12–5

Robert Johnson, the elected black district attorney representing the Bronx, announced that he would refuse to seek New York's newly enacted death penalty in part because he believed it would inevitably be applied in a racially discriminatory manner. Subsequently, Governor Pataki removed Johnson from considering whether to seek the death penalty in a highly publicized case involving three minority youths accused of shooting a white police officer. Pataki replaced the black D.A. with a white lawyer who was a committed death penalty hawk. See John M. Goshko, "Police Killing Sparks Debate on Death Penalty in New York," Washington Post, March 24, 1996, at A24.

Should the fact that a prosecutor is both a lawyer and an elected official affect the degree to which those who occupy this role are entitled to take identity-related considerations (for example, the fact that black and Hispanic constituents believe that the death penalty is administered in a racially biased manner) into account when exercising his or her professional discretion about whom to prosecute and which penalties to seek? Should politicians with the authority to hire and fire prosecutors consider these same race-conscious views by constituents when deciding whether to replace a prosecutor with whom the politician disagrees and when selecting the prosecutor's replacement?

Problem 12–6

While representing Monica Lewinsky in connection with her possible appearance before the grand jury investigating President Clinton, William Ginsburg made the following statement to an Israeli newspaper: "We are fans of President Clinton and admire his positions and policies concerning Israel. Clinton is very positive towards Israel and the Jews. Monica and I are Jews. I'm torn because I fear for the fate of the presidency in our democracy, and I don't want the president to resign. Who knows who will come after Clinton and how he will deal with Israel." When subsequently questioned about the propriety of this statement, Mr. Ginsburg responded: "I made the statement, I mean the statement, and I'm sincere about the statement. But my personal opinion has nothing to do with the Lewinsky matter. That's the point. The point is that the case is not about me. It's about our democracy. And so that particular statement, while it happens to be my opinion, has nothing to do with this case. As a lawyer, I could represent either or any side of this cases. And my contention is that we have to play by the rules." NBC News Transcripts, "William Ginsburg, Attorney for Monica Lewinsky, Discusses the Progress of the Investigation," Meet the Press, Feb. 22, 1998 (available in Lexis/Nexis Library, Script File).

Which of Ginsburg's two statements about his (and his client's) role in the Clinton investigation do you find more persuasive? Do you agree with Ginsburg that the two statements are consistent? Is either statement consistent with your understanding of the Model Rules? Is either consistent with your views about the nature of the lawyer's role? Do you agree with Ginsburg's claim that the Clinton investigation was about "our democracy"? Should lawyers involved in publicly significant cases have different obligations from those that would apply in "ordinary" cases? How would Professor Pepper (p. 123) answer this question? Does it matter whether the case is one in which identity-related considerations are especially salient? Was the Clinton investigation such a case? Does your answer depend upon whether you are considering religious identity, national identity, or political identity?

Problem 12–7

In the 1980s, several American law firms attempted to open branch offices in Tokyo, Japan. The Japanese bar strenuously resisted these efforts on the ground that American lawyers were not competent to practice law in Japan, and did not understand, nor have any allegiance to, Japanese understandings of lawyer professionalism or the public purposes of Japanese law. Eventually a compromise was worked out in which U.S. lawyers were entitled to establish offices in Japan on the condition that they place themselves under the jurisdiction of the Japanese bar, refrain from entering into partnerships with Japanese lawyers, and practice only "home country" (meaning U.S.) law. Mark Ramseyer, "Lawyers, Foreign Lawyers, and Lawyer Substitutes: The Market for Regulation in Japan," 27 Harv. Int'l L.J. 499 (1986).

What role should national identity play in defining a lawyer's professional responsibilities? To the extent that American lawyers practicing abroad remain "officers of the court," to which legal system do they owe their allegiance: the United States? the country in which they practice? all countries affected by their clients' actions? all of the above? Should countries have the right to set ethical standards for all lawyers who practice within their borders regardless of the lawyer's nationality? What happens when there is a conflict between the ethical rules of the jurisdiction in which the lawyer is practicing and the lawyer's home jurisdiction?

What defines whether a lawyer is "practicing" in a given jurisdiction? Is a New York lawyer who negotiates a takeover of a Japanese company on behalf of a syndicate which includes American, Japanese, and German investors and is financed through a bank in Hong Kong "practicing law" in Japan? Does it matter whether the lawyer negotiates the deal in Japan or simply conducts the transaction from his office in New York via email, video-conferencing, and faxes? Is the answer to where the lawyer is practicing any clearer if we imagine a purely domestic transaction, for example, by assuming that the target corporation is chartered and headquartered in California and asking whether the New York lawyer is "practicing law" in California? See Birbrower v. Superior Court, discussed in Chapter 8, p. 692.

Finally, should countries be entitled to protect their legal systems — or legal professions — by limiting the ability of foreign lawyers to practice law in their country? Would your answer be different if the question were a country's right to prohibit foreign citizens from becoming judges? In a global economy, does the advice lawyers give their clients — particularly in the corporate hemisphere — have as much influence on the practical content of legal rules (for example, labor standards, antitrust enforcement, environmental policy) as the decisions of a state's courts? Does your answer to this question have consequences for how U.S. corporate lawyers should be regulated when they are acting in a purely domestic context?

––––––––––

Each of these problems raises questions about the relationship between various aspects of a lawyer's identity—race, gender, religion, nationality—and his or her professional role. Should lawyers take these aspects of their non-professional identity into account when deciding how to act as a lawyer? Should the rules of professional responsibility or the legal system in general set standards for governing these issues? Does your answer to either question depend upon the kind of identity we are considering or the context in which the lawyer is acting? Whatever lawyers ought to do, is it possible to "check one's identity at the door" when performing any task? Similarly, even if lawyers can detach themselves from all non-professional group affiliations and commitments, is it likely that clients, state officials, or the public at large will be able to do the same? Should it matter if a lawyer is perceived by others, for example, as a "black" lawyer or a "Muslim" lawyer even if the lawyer does not view him- or herself as such?

The following excerpts discuss how various aspects of a lawyer's identity might affect his or her professional role as a lawyer.

David B. Wilkins
Beyond "Bleached Out" Professionalism:
Defining Professional Responsibility for Real Professionals
in *Ethics in Practice: Lawyers' Roles, Responsibilities, and Regulation*
(Deborah Rhode, ed., 2000)
pp. 212, 219, 222–225, 230–234

The claim that lawyers who interject identity issues into professional practice "pollute the legal profession" implicitly rests on the assumption that in the absence of this kind of intervention, identity-related considerations would *in fact* be irrelevant. This implicit factual assumption, however, is at best misleading, and at worst counterproductive, to creating appropriate ways for lawyers to respond to America's continuing failure to make good on its promise of providing equal justice under law. . . . First, contrary to the "bleaching" metaphor, current understandings of lawyer professionalism continue to reflect the identities of those who founded the modern American legal profession. This historical legacy both undermines the normative claim that identity is "irrelevant" and poses important challenges for the careers of certain lawyers who do not share these identity characteristics. Second, what is true for lawyers is even more true for litigants. Although the American legal system promises that justice will be "blind" to identity, the reality is that certain groups continue to encounter substantial impediments to gaining access to the public goods encoded in law as a result of their identity. By obscuring this fact, bleached out professionalism fails to help lawyers determine how to respond to this reality. Finally, bleached out professionalism ignores the extent to which a lawyer's own identity affects that lawyer's ability to perform his or her job. Once we understand that lawyers will often not be able to "check" their identities at the door, it is not at all clear that instructing them to act as though their identities do not matter is the appropriate ethical response. . . .

[Moreover,] contrary to the standard assumption of those who argue that lawyers should never allow their non-professional identities to influence their professional roles, sometimes it is precisely these identity-related commitments that provide the impetus for a lawyer to fulfill his or her most difficult role-specific obligations. . . . As Professor Alan Dershowitz eloquently argues in a related context: "I know I chose to become a criminal defense lawyer at least in part because I am Jewish. I was taught from the earliest age that Jews must always remember that they were persecuted, and that we must stand up for those who now face persecution. . . . I always wanted to be a Jewish lawyer, and, though many Jews disapprove of some of my clients, I believe I am a lawyer in the Jewish tradition." . . .

We are left, therefore, with a quandary: How can we preserve the values underlying bleached out professionalism while at the same time recognizing that this ideology neither can nor should be as "greedy" as traditionally understood. . . . [T]wo related issues [frame this inquiry]: the *moral justification* for considering any specific identity-related issue and the *social purposes* of the specific lawyering role into which the identity-related consideration is to be incorporated. . . .

Proponents of bleached out professionalism assume that "blindness"—color-blindness, gender blindness, religion blindness—is a fundamental principle of justice. Although intuitively appealing, this argument conflates ideal theory with the morality that should govern us in the real world. As Amy Gutmann argues, although "blindness" may be the just policy in an ideal society, it is not the correct moral stance in a nonideal society such as ours where benefits and burdens continue to be distributed on the basis of identity characteristics such as race and gender.[*] Identity-blind policies treat individuals fairly when racism, sexism, and other forms of disadvantage based on identity no longer affect the lives of citizens. But when identity continues to exert a major influence on the ability of citizens to participate equally in public and private life, as it surely does in the United States, identity-conscious policies may be the only way to accord individuals the fair treatment that is their moral due. Fairness, not colorblindness, is the fundamental principle of justice in a nonideal world such as ours.

Not all forms of identity consciousness, however, are likely to promote fairness. . . .

. . . One can group the forms of identity consciousness most relevant to bleached out professionalism into three broad categories. At the most basic level, identity consciousness can help individuals "notice" the extent to which identity—both their

---

[*] Amy Gutman, "Responding to Racial Injustice," in *Color Conscious: The Political Morality of Race* (A. Gutman, K. Appiah, eds. 1996).

own and others'—continues to affect their own lives and the life chances of other citizens. Second, identity consciousness can be an essential attribute of self-understanding and self-worth. Finally, identity consciousness gives individuals special reasons for caring about others who share their identity and to work together to advance the interests of their group. . . .

One can see the benefits of [noticing identity] by comparing Gil Garcetti's actions in the Simpson case with Governor Pataki's in the Johnson case. Garcetti took concerted steps to ensure that Simpson would be prosecuted in a jurisdiction where there were likely to be black jurors, by a prosecution team that included at least one prominent black attorney. . . . [T]hese race-conscious actions supported, rather than undermined the social purposes of Garcetti's role as district attorney. . . . [T]he simple fact that a black man was accused of murdering his white ex-wife and her handsome white friend ensured that race was likely to play an important role in how many participants in the process viewed the case. By coming to terms with this reality, Garcetti helped to produce a proceeding that would protect Simpson from unfair inferences based on the color of his skin.

Pataki's decision to replace Robert Johnson [the black district attorney from the Bronx] with a white attorney who was a committed death penalty hawk had the opposite effect. [Even though the social purposes for the role of district attorney supported Johnson's removal] by not "noticing" how race affects capital punishment cases, Pataki's actions arguably further entrenched existing racial divisions about the administration of capital punishment. . . . There is substantial evidence that race does play an important role in whether prosecutors seek the death penalty and whether juries are likely to impose this punishment. Replacing a black district attorney who has expressly attempted to take this reality into account with a white lawyer who is a known death penalty hawk sends a powerful message to the black constituents of this district that their concerns about the discriminatory nature of capital punishment will not be heard. . . .

Diversity within the lawyer's role poses a challenge to bleached out professionalism. Simply demonstrating that identity-related considerations tend to undermine *some* aspects of what lawyers do does not prove that these same considerations cannot play a legitimate role in *any* professional practice. . . .

The concept of social purpose begins to provide a way out of this dilemma. By social purpose, I mean those aspects of a particular lawyering role or take that disinterested social actors would consider to be essential to the proper performance of the job in question. The prosecution's strategy in the Simpson case illustrates how we can apply the concept of social purpose to distinguish those orally justified uses of identity that are *professionally* acceptable from those that are not. . . . Garcetti's statement denying that race would play any role in the Simpson prosecution [although false] . . . captured an important aspirational norm fundamental to our justice system: that race *ought not to* affect the determination of the accused's guilt or innocence. [As I argued above, t]o honor this norm, however, prosecutors are sometimes justified in engaging in race-conscious lawyering strategies. . . .

The argument that . . . race-conscious lawyering strategies support rather than undermine the legitimate social purposes of the criminal justice system presumes that the blacks who are brought into the process will honor their legitimate role obligations and will not simply become racial patriots. This does not require bleached out professionalism. Thus, black jurors in the Simpson case were entitled to bring their experience with and understanding of racism and official corruption into the jury room. At the end of the day, however, they were obliged to acquit or convict Simpson on the basis of the evidence and arguments presented during the trial. . . .

Ginsburg's attempt to introduce identity into the Clinton investigation cannot be justified on these terms. . . . Ginsburg had two charges in [his] role [as Lewinsky's attorney]. First and foremost, [his obligation was to] protect Lewinsky's interests. To the extent that Lewinsky did not in fact share Ginsburg's concerns, his statement to the Israeli press both failed to serve any purpose that Lewinsky may have had for the representation and posed a great risk of substantially prejudicing her case, since many in the United States (including many Jews) do not look favorably on a person who appears to be willing to subvert her own duties as a citizen to assist a foreign power. But even assuming that Lewinsky shared Ginsburg's views, a witness is not permitted to shade or distort her testimony before a grand jury simply because she does not want the target of the investigation to be convicted. Facilitating her doing so, therefore, would have been a violation of Ginsburg's duties to the legal system. . . .

Finally, the concept of social purpose helps us determine what to do when lawyers feel that their identities preclude them from performing their professional roles. . . .

. . . One can see [this point] by contrasting [Robert] Johnson's actions with those of Robert Morganthau, the respected district attorney for the Borough of Manhattan. Johnson publicly announced his intention not to seek the death penalty and carefully explained his reasons for not doing so. By all accounts, Morganthau shares Johnson's view that the death penalty is administratively inefficient and morally reprehensible. Unlike Johnson, however, Morganthau has consistently taken the position that "he would enforce the will of the people but privately has done as little as possible to actually prepare a death case." Although Morganthau has largely escaped criticism by covertly submerging his opposition to the death penalty into case-by-case decisionmaking, it is Johnson, not Morganthau, who has demonstrated the appropriate respect for the social purposes of his role as a prosecutor.

In June 2003, during the off-season, the National Basketball Association's Los Angeles Lakers' superstar player Kobe Bryant traveled to Colorado to have a medical procedure. Following an interaction with a front-desk employee at the hotel where Mr. Bryant was staying, he was charged with sexually assaulting the employee. The case, capturing the attention of millions in and outside of the United States, was subsequently dismissed. In the excerpt below, using the Bryant case for illustrative purposes, Eli Wald explores the impact of lawyers' racial and gender identity on the representation of clients and the outcomes of cases. In particular, the case featured the commodification of lawyers' personal identity by clients and lawyers alike—that is, the use and value clients and lawyers derive from the personal identity of lawyers. Note that the defense counsel in the case, Ms. Pamela Mackey, was a physically slender female Caucasian, whereas the defendant, Mr. Bryant, was an affluent, tall, African-American man.

Eli Wald
Lawyers' Identity Capital

University of Denver Sturm College of Law Legal Research
Working Paper No. 16–27*
pp. 3–4, 7, 8–14, 15–16, 20–23

The Bryant case triggers several intriguing questions relating to the operation of the criminal justice system and the role of lawyers in it. Was the alleged victim telling the truth? Why did she decline to participate in the criminal prosecution? Was her decision impacted by the aggressive representation of defense counsel and her related fears that she—the purported victim—and her sexual conduct and privacy interests would stand trial alongside the alleged perpetrator? Was her decision motivated by a desire to secure a settlement in the simultaneously pending civil action against her alleged abuser? The case thus illustrates the complex interplay of truth and justice considerations with financial incentives in rape cases, of the balancing of the rights of the victim with the rights of the accused, of zealous advocacy with rape shield law protections, of the impact of the identities of the victim and the accused on the disposition of allegations, of the impact of money and resources for both the victim and the accused on the outcome of the case, and of trying cases in the court of public opinion with trying them in a court of law. . . .

Moreover, the case reveals the impact of lawyers' racial and gender identity on the representation of clients and outcomes of cases. In particular, the case features the commodification of lawyers' personal identity by clients. In light of prevailing racial stereotypes in American society and the justice system, the black defendant in the case may have been legitimately concerned with the possible impact of disquieting stereotypes such as "black men are dangerous and violent" on the outcome of the case. Retaining a white female counsel may have allowed the defendant to combat disturbing stereotypes with opposing racial and gender stereotypes: "if a white female attorney agreed to represent the defendant and is not afraid of him, he must not be dangerous or violent," and "if a female attorney agreed to represent defendant suspected of raping a woman, he must not be guilty." By virtue of intentionally

* <https://papers.ssrn.com/sol3/papers.cfm?abstract_id=2809924>; published in a revised version in 23 Int'l J. Legal Prof. 109 (2016).

retaining a white female defense counsel for the purpose of obtaining benefits from the lawyer's personal identity, the defendant was commodifying the attorney's racial and gender identity. How should lawyers react to attempts by clients, colleagues and law firms to commodify their personal identity? . . .

Inevitable and Avoidable Uses of Identity Capital

Ms. Mackey's use of identity capital in the Kobe Bryant case was to a significant extent inevitable. When approached regarding the representation of Mr. Bryant, Ms. Mackey had but two choices. She could have accepted the representation, with the commodification of her racial, gender and physical identity immediately to follow (in the court of public opinion, before a judge and jury have ever been assigned), or she could have turned down the representation. But note that declining the representation would not have prevented the commodification of Ms. Mackey's personal identity. . . . Declining representation, that is, refusing to trade on her identity capital, would have . . . allowed racial and gender considerations to interfere with the exercise of her professional judgment. . . .

A general insight to be drawn from the Bryant case is that inevitability and avoidability ought not be thought of as binary choices but rather as two ends of a continuum: the commodification of lawyers' personal identity is never either inevitable or avoidable. Rather, it is either more or less inevitable, depending on the circumstances of the representation and of all the parties involved. The significance of this insight cannot be overstated: if commodification of personal identity is often inevitable, lawyers, let alone women and minority lawyers, can hardly be faulted for taking advantage of facets of their personal identity.

The Bryant case reveals a second insight regarding the inevitability of lawyers' personal identity commodification. While the commodification of Ms. Mackey's personal identity was inevitable as soon as she was approached regarding the representation, Mr. Bryant's choice was somewhat avoidable, or, more accurately, he had a choice in the matter of commodification in a sense in which Ms. Mackey did not. To be clear, because his case was to an extent about race and gender, any lawyer Mr. Bryant would have selected would have been commodified. But Mr. Bryant, an affluent defendant, had a choice of counsel. That is, while Mr. Bryant could not have chosen a race-free genderless attorney, he explicitly chose a white female attorney as opposed to a white male, a black male, or a black female and in that sense his identity capital decision was more intentional and more avoidable. Incidentally, it is important to bear in mind that while Mr. Bryant had a choice in the matter of deploying identity capital to his benefit, many if not most defendants do not. Indeed, in the context of the American justice system, often a poor black defendant will be assigned a white male (or female) attorney without a say in the matter. In such circumstances, a poor defendant would be passively commodifying the personal identity of his lawyer, but his conduct, unlike Mr. Bryant's, would be inevitable.

The general takeaway here is that lawyers do not exercise exclusive domain over the inevitability–avoidability continuum. Rather, consistent with Goffman's finding that identity performance is shaped by both environment and audience,[34] decisions and conduct by other actors, clients included, influence the extent to which a case entails the commodification of a lawyer's personal identity. The use of identity capital is often inevitable both in the sense that lawyers cannot prevent, even if they wanted to, facets of their personal identity from playing a role in professional decision-making regarding cases and clients, and in the sense that lawyers do not have exclusive control over whether and how their personal identity may be commodified by clients, judges and employers. As a result, the profession must avoid a hasty judgment that lawyers who consciously deploy identity capital in the representation of their clients are intentionally violating objective universal professional standards.

The Desirability of Using Identity Capital

Conceding that the commodification of lawyers' personal identity is often inevitable, is it nonetheless desirable? Critics of identity commodification argue that trading in identity capital is undesirable for at least three related reasons. First, identity capital exchanges risk essentializing lawyers, reducing them from complex individuals to a handful of traits and worse, treating each trait "as the equivalent of a particular viewpoint and set of experiences, even though the group trait, such as race or gender, is at best a rough proxy for those views and experiences."[35] Here, even if she had little choice in the matter, Ms. Mackey may be treated as a white, female lawyer, rather than as a competent, high-profile defense counsel, and her conduct may be judged through racial and gender lenses, rather than through a so-called objective professional lens.

Second, identity commodification rends to neglect and negate the relevance of intersectionality.[36] Here, emphasis on Ms. Mackey's race and gender neglects other possibly constitutive aspects of her identity, not just as a lawyer (she is a defense counsel, not merely a white, female defense counsel), but as a person, a significant other, a mother, a feminist, member of various communities, etc. Moreover, the focus on one group identity, for example, being a female, tends to negate other important facts of identity in the case. For example, treating Ms. Mackey and the alleged victim in this case reductively as women obscures a fundamentally important aspect of the victim's identity—her being an alleged rape victim. Similarly, treating Mr. Bryant reductively as a black man obscures a fundamentally important aspect of this case: power and money. That is, the Bryant case was as much about power and money as it was about race and gender, facts that may be lost in the focus on Mr. Bryant's race and gender.

Third, the use of identity capital risks perpetuating the status quo and the subjection of women and minority lawyers to the ideal of the white male lawyer. Building on historian David Hollinger's observation that "Racism is real, but races are

---

34. Erwin Goffman, *The Presentation of Self in Everyday Life* (1959).

35. Martha Minow, "Not Only For Myself: Identity, Politics, and Law," 75 Or. L. Rev. 647, 643 (1996).

36. Id. at 655.

not," Martha Minow explains that "[t]he power to create groups and oppress them is real," even as "the rationale for those groups or for the assignment of members is not."[37] Here, referring to Ms. Mackey's race and gender as constitutive aspects of the Kobe Bryant case help diminish her status as a first-rate defense counsel. That is, rather than being discussed as the top defense counsel in Colorado and the United States, identity commodification risks legitimizing description of Ms. Mackey as "a top female defense attorney."

These valid concerns exposing the significant risks inherent in identity commodification lead some commentators to call for banning identity markets or reducing trade in identity capital. Other commentators, however, argue that lawyers' use of personal identity is not only inevitable but may also be desirable. Sanford Levinson has cautioned that discouraging lawyers from turning to facets of their personal identity to help inform the exercise of professional judgment constitutes "bleaching out,"[38] which deems "irrelevant what might be seen as central aspects of one's self-identity."[39] Such bleaching out is disadvantageous, asserts Martha Minow, because lawyers' self-identity can meaningfully inform and enrich their exercise of professional judgment. While a lawyer's personal identity should not be allowed to lead to an "actual practice of bias against members of other groups in the way deals are negotiated or suits are litigated,"[40] and cannot solely justify an attorney's exercise of professional judgment,[41] it can and should constitute a "springboard for action," serving as a critical check on lawyers' practice as professionals.[42] David Wilkins similarly concludes that "the profession could make clear in its ethos and values that identity does play a legitimate role in defining what constitutes responsible advocacy, at least in some circumstances."[43]

The use of identity capital to inform, criticize and shape—but never to usurp or dominate—decision-making can enrich and improve lawyers' exercise of professional judgment. Thus, when the commodification of lawyers' personal identity counters professional bleaching out, empowers individual lawyers to practice law consistent with central facets of their self-identity, and improves the profession's exercise of judgment, the use of identity capital is desirable.

Here, to the extent that Ms. Mackey's racial and gender identity informed her exercise of professional judgment as defense counsel for Mr. Bryant, such use of identity

---

37. Id., at 662.

38. Sanford Levinson, "Identifying the Jewish Lawyer: Reflections on the Construction of Professional Identity," 14 Cardozo L. Rev. 1557, 1578 (1993); Russell G. Pearce, "Learning from the Unpleasant Truths of Interfaith Conversation: William Stringfellow's Lessons for the Jewish Lawyer," 38 Cath. Law. 255 (1998).

39. Levinson, "Identifying the Jewish Lawyer," supra note 38 at 1601.

40. Martha Minow, "On Being a Religious Professional: The Religious Turn in Professional Ethics," 150 U. Pa. L. Rev. 661, 680 (2001).

41. Id. at 686.

42. Id. at 675–76.

43. [David] Wilkins, "Race, Ethics, and the First Amendment: [Should a Black Lawyer Represent the Ku Klux Klan?," 63 Geo. Wash. L. Rev. 1030 (1995),] at 1070.

capital may have been desirable. For example, during the trial, Bryant's defense team sought discovery of the notes of a rape crisis center worker who sat in on a police interview with the accuser. A lawyer for the crisis center objected, arguing that revealing details about Bryant's accuser would lead to fewer women reporting rapes, pointing out that rape reports dropped elsewhere after a case in which an accuser's medical background was targeted by defense attorneys. Ms. Mackey countered by asking the judge to focus on the case at hand guarding against the "political agenda of the rape crisis center," and added that "[t]here is lots of history about black men being falsely accused of this crime by white women," and concluded that "I don't think we want to get dragged down into this history any more than we want to get into the history brought up by the rape crisis center."[44] Of course, exactly because race and gender were very much a part of the case, any defense lawyer could have made these statements, yet there is no discounting the possibility that Ms. Mackey's personal identity informed, if only unconsciously, her sensitivity to the importance of race and gender to the case and her decision to raise the issues in open court. Moreover, there is also no discounting the possibility that the comments had a particular impact on the judge and media exactly because they were made by a white female attorney.

At the same time, there is no denying that Ms. Mackey's use of identity capital benefited her client by combating prevalent social stereotypes he likely faced as a black defendant accused of raping a white female, and benefited her own self-interest in obtaining a favorable outcome for Mr. Bryant in a high profile case and solidifying her reputation as a leading defense counsel. Ultimately, assessing whether the use of lawyers' identity capital is appropriate and desirable in particular circumstances is a function not only of the extent of inevitability and benefit to the lawyer and client in question, but also, following Bourdieu, of the extent to which identity capital is deployed, the impact on third parties and the profession, and the terms on which capital identity is exchanged[45] . . . .

Active and Passive Uses of Identity Capital

While the use of identity capital may be inevitable, the scope of it — whether a lawyer commodifies her identity actively or passively — is often within a lawyer's control. Consider a Latina attorney who is hired by a large law firm. The mere hiring passively commodifies Attorney's personal identity; that is, without any additional action or conduct by either Attorney or the law firm, the hiring commodifies identity, because other lawyers and clients might take note and draw positive inferences about, for example, the firm's stance on diversity and equality. Yet the firm and Attorney may commodify Attorney's personal identity more actively: the firm and Attorney may agree to feature Attorney's image in hard print publications and on the

---

44. Lauren Johnston, "Kobe Lawyer Plays Race Card," CBS News (February 2, 2004), <http://www.cbsnews.com/news/kobe-lawyer-plays-race-card/>.

45. Pierre Bourdieu, "The Forms of Capital," in *Handbook of Theory and Research for the Sociology of Education* 241 (John G. Richardson, ed., 1986) . . . .

firm's website, may assign Attorney to certain cases and clients, may have Attorney serve on the firm's recruitment and diversity committee, etc. All of these actions would constitute additional, more active, forms of commodification , above and beyond the hiring of Attorney by the firm.

Many have studied the consequences and scope of identity construction by various professionals. For lawyers, a key distinction in terms of the scope of use of identity capital is between, on the one hand, agreeing to represent a client (or accept an employment offer from a law firm), and, on the other hand, invoking or allowing one's personal identity to impact the representation itself. Sanford Levinson eloquently made this point examining the identity of Sandy Koufax as a Jewish baseball pitcher, observing that it was one thing for Koufax to refuse to pitch for his team at the World Series because the game was to be played on Yom Kippur (akin to a lawyer's accepting a client's engagement), and another altogether to suggest that Koufax had a Jewish style of pitching or that he may have pitched more softly (or harder) against Jewish batters.[49] Deciding not to pitch on Yom Kippur was a relatively passive form of utilizing identity capital, whereas pitching differently to Jewish batters would have constituted an active, and a more controversial, use of identity capital.

David Wilkins' examination of the case of Anthony Griffin, a black lawyer who represented the Ku Klux Klan, is illuminating on the issue of the scope of use of a lawyer's identity capital. As to the passive decision whether to represent a client when the representation commodifies a lawyer's personal identity, Griffin, acknowledging that his "presence at counsel improves the Klan's chances of successfully resisting the State's disclosure order,"[50] maintained that while his decision to represent the Klan was legitimate and reasonable, he would not have agreed to defend the Klan against criminal charges involving threats to blacks."[51] That is, the decision to even passively commodify one's identity has to do with the circumstances of the case: just as Koufax regularly pitched on Saturdays but would not pitch on Yom Kippur, so did Griffin represent the Klan when the First Amendment, a fundamental component of American constitutional law to which he dedicated his professional life, was at issue but would not represent the client if mere criminal charges were involved.[52] The point here, to be clear, is not whether one finds Griffin's reasoning compelling on the facts of the case . . . . Rather, the point is that the impact of even passive commodification, and thus, its appropriateness, depends on the circumstances of the case. . . .

The Griffin case is further revealing because Mr. Griffin did invoke his identity capital more actively throughout his representation of the Klan, not to the benefit of

---

49. Levinson, "Identifying the Jewish Lawyer," supra note 38, at 1579–83.

50. Wilkins, "Race, Ethics, and the First Amendment," supra note [43], at 1042.

51. Id. at 1044.

52. Wilkins notes that "[u]ndoubtedly, Griffin believes that the Klan is entitled to a criminal defense lawyer. . . . He simply asserts that he feels no obligation to be that lawyer." Id. at 1050.

his client but rather to its determent. "From the outset of this case, Griffin has insisted on being both the Klan's staunchest advocate and its toughest critic."[53] Importantly, notes Wilkins, "[h]is initial warning to [the client] that the 'two need not talk about politics [or] race' . . . has not stopped Griffin from sharing his views about these issues—and about his client—with the public."[54] Once again, the point here is not to debate the wisdom of Griffin's conduct, though his actions to give rise to complex legal ethics questions.[55] Rather, it is to demonstrate that lawyers may deploy identity capital in active ways, above and beyond agreeing to represent clients in particular cases, usually to benefit their clients' interests but is sometimes inconsistent with the clients' objectives. . . .

All in all, passive commodification of lawyers' personal identity—agreeing to represent a client in one's area of professional expertise—is usually unobjectionable. More actively deploying identity capital following an obligation thesis to better the interests of certain groups, even if consistent with a client's interests in a particular case, seems more controversial. In the Bryant case, instances of more active commodification of personal identity would have included, for example, embracing Mr. Bryant, either in the courtroom or in front of the media, sending an implied message that Ms. Mackey personally liked the defendant, was not afraid of him and believed he was innocent. Applying an obligation thesis here would suggest that Ms. Mackey, as a female attorney, owes a duty to better the interests of women, and it is hard to see how embracing Mr. Bryant would have advanced that obligation. Accordingly, those subscribing to an obligation thesis would have found such active commodification of personal identity objectionable, especially in a rape case. . . .

The Appropriate Terms of Identity Capital Exchanges

May a lawyer charge higher fees when the commodification of facets of his or her personal identity benefits a client in a representation? Could Ms. Mackey have charged Mr. Bryant for commodifying her racial and gender identity? Irrespective of what the black-letter law answer in construing the pertinent rule of professional conduct is, some commentators may intuitively express normative discomfort with the notion of lawyers charging clients for the use of identity capital.

Such discomfort must be resisted. If clients and law firms routinely engage in capital exchanges in which they take advantage of, benefit from and commodify the identity capital of lawyers, it seems disingenuous to deny commodified lawyers the ability to reap the benefits of these very exchanges. Indeed, as I argue elsewhere, a troubling and inherently unfair aspect of capital exchanges is that they are often implicit and opaque.[79] A constitutive element of fair capital transactions must be their transparency: if we were to acknowledge the prevalence of capital transactions in the practice of law, insist that they become transparent and allow parties to these

---

53. Id., at 1053.
54. Id.
55. Id. at 1053–54.
79. Wald, "BigLaw Identity Capital," [83 Fordham L. Rev. 2509 (2015)].

exchanges to act on an informed basis, lawyers may demand and receive fair value for their commodified identity and all of us may come to terms with the exchanges we allow and the discomfort they cause.

The point is not merely that identity capital is a twice commodified loaded term of art, at both the capital and the identity levels. Rather, it is that the two interlocking levels of commodification render the process complex and its consequences hard to quantify. For example, counter-intuitively, even if lawyers were allowed to charge clients higher fees for the use of their identity capital, it is less than clear that such fees, a form of short-term economic capital, would constitute a fair compensation for the commodification of personal identity. As detailed above, identity capital exchanges may entail significant harms to exchanging lawyers (for example, in the form of essentializing and a loss of dignity resulting from performance of identity work)[80] and the community (for example, from the continued subjection of out-groups), injuries that may not be appropriately compensated by means of short-term economic capital (higher fees). Fairness may require instead that identity commodification be rewarded with long-term economic capital, as well as the buildup of social and cultural capital endowments.

Large law firms that commodify the identity capital of their lawyers, for example, ought to extend their attorneys opportunities to cultivate their capital infrastructure — their social and cultural capital endowments — such that they receive an equal opportunity to compete for positions of power and influence within the firms.[81] Paying women and minority lawyers a bonus for their service on diversity and recruitment committees may appear at first to constitute fair compensation for the commodification of their identity capital, but in the long run such bonuses may backfire. Disproportionate service on committees disadvantages women and lawyers of color and undermines their chances of making partner. Enhanced training (cultural capital) and mentoring (social capital) instead of bonuses (short term economic capital) thus constitute an appropriate compensation for the use of the lawyers' identity capital.

Similarly, allowing lawyers to charge clients higher fees for the use of the lawyers' personal identity may be short-changing the lawyers in the long run. Individual lawyers should be encouraged and aided instead to leverage their identity commodification to build up their social and cultural capital and secure long term economic capital. Defense counsel, for example, should take advantage of the notoriety of high-profile cases — the very cases in which their identity capital is most likely to be commodified — to secure mentors, build referral networks, and enhance their professional reputation.

Thus, while the possibility of permitting the exchange of lawyers' identity capital for explicit short-term economic capital (fees charged) may seem radical to some, it

---

80. Devon W. Carbado & Mitu Gulati, "Working Identity," 85 Cornell L. Rev. 1249, 1263 (2000).
81. Wald, "BigLaw Identity Capital," supra note [79].

actually risks obscuring an important aspect of capital transactions more generally: sometimes short-term economic capital gains do not constitute a fair and appropriate consideration for trading one's identity capital. Rather, the appropriate terms of capital exchanges may entail commodifying a lawyer's personal identity in return for other forms of capital, including long-term economic capital, as well as social, cultural and identity capital. A lesson to be learned from Ms. Mackey's representation of Mr. Bryant, regardless of the fees she charged her client, is her ability to build on the case and become a nationally known defense counsel with a robust national client base, arguably a fair compensation for the identity capital she exchanged in the representation.[82]

Next, analysis of the appropriate terms of identity capital exchanges reveals the incomplete nature of individualistic, rather than collectivist, approaches to capital. Mr. Griffin, importantly, represented the Klan on a pro bono basis, receiving no short-term economic capital at all for his efforts.[83] From an individualistic capital viewpoint, foregoing his compensation is significant: because in exchange for the commodification of his personal identity Mr. Griffin received no short term economic capital, the exchange between the Klan and Mr. Griffin may be characterized as unfair, unless Mr. Griffin was able to use the representation of the Klan to build his social and cultural capital and benefit from long term economic capital. If he did not, Mr. Griffin's experience can at least serve as a reminder that those endowed with identity capital do not fully control the terms on which their identity is commodified and do not always derive benefits from capital exchanges, even when others, such as clients and employers, do.[84]

But of course Mr. Griffin may have considered the exchange fair because his identity capital was used for the benefit of the black community, and for the vindication of fundamental constitutional principles and therefore for the greater good of the legal profession and the integrity of the legal system. Indeed, Mr. Griffin did explicitly identify such a collectivist consideration, namely the benefit to the black community from the assertion of First Amendment principles, as a significant justification for his decision to represent the Klan, suggesting that in some circumstances mere tallying of the individualistic capital benefits of an exchange — economic, social, cultural and identity — may be insufficient in assessing the fairness of it.

Conclusion

Every day, facets of lawyers' personal identities are commodified by clients, lawyers and law firms, and the legal profession. Most of the time, these identity capital exchanges are implicit and opaque, and sometimes they are unfair to the commodifying and commodified lawyers. Worse, because identity capital exchanges are not transparent, they often deprive lawyers of the opportunity to carefully consider

---

82. Sandy Graham, "Clearing Kobe: Pamela Mackey Reflects on Court Victory that Riveted Millions," ColoradoBiz, May 2005, at 18.
83. Wilkins, "Race, Ethics, and the First Amendment," supra note [43] at 1044, fn. 72.
84. Wald, "BigLaw Identity Capital," supra note [79].

important aspects of the commodification of their personal identity: whether the use of identity capital is inevitable or avoidable, the desirability of commodification of personal identity in particular cases, active and passive uses of identity capital, the impact of identity capital exchanges on third parties, the interplay of merit and identity capital, and the appropriate terms of identity capital transactions. Transparent capital exchanges, in contrast, will render them fair by allowing commodifying and commodified lawyers to decide on an informed basis whether and to what extent to commodify aspects of their personal identity and to reap the benefits of the commodification when it takes place. Greater transparency will also allow the profession to accurately assess the desirability of identity commodification by its members as well as its impact on merit and professionalism.

Joseph Allegretti
Lawyers, Clients, and Covenant:
A Religious Perspective on Legal Practice and Ethics
66 Fordham L. Rev. 1101 (1998)

The divorce of legal ethics from religion has had substantial costs. Let me mention just four . . . .

1. The Loss of Religious Wisdom

An exaggerated secularization deprives us of the accumulated wisdom of the religious traditions, which have wrestled for thousands of years with the perennial questions of the moral life. For example, Christianity is concerned with the meaning of human life, its purpose and its destiny. While Christianity insists upon the goodness of human beings, it also speaks honestly about their brokenness and estrangement. It places a high value on self-sacrifice and reconciliation, exhorting believers to "turn the other cheek" and even to lay down their lives for each other. Christianity has something to say about the purposes of law and its limits, the duties owed to the secular state, and the relationship between justice and love.

Most importantly, in the life, death, and resurrection of Jesus Christ, Christianity finds the central revelation about God's purposes for human beings. It entreats those who are followers of Jesus to model their lives in discipleship upon his. Christians are to love one another as Jesus has loved us.

Can anyone deny that this tradition, this way of thinking about life, has something to contribute to our debates about law, ethics, justice, and the role of lawyers? Can anyone deny that Judaism, Islam, and the other religious traditions have something to contribute as well? . . .

2. Law Fills the Void

When religion and the deep wellsprings of the human spirit are excluded from legal ethics, law fills the void. As [Daniel] Callahan notes, the removal of religion "leaves us . . . too heavily dependent upon the law as the working source of morality. The language of the courts and legislatures becomes our only shared means of discourse." Codes and court decisions become the fundamental arbiter of what is right and wrong.[28]

This development can be seen in the evolution—or, as some suggest, the devolution—of legal ethics codes. The earliest American Bar Association code of professional conduct for lawyers, dating from the early 1900s, was largely aspirational in nature, more like a gentlemanly code of character than a principled guide to decisionmaking. The 1969 Code of Professional Responsibility included bottom-line rules of conduct for lawyers, called the Disciplinary Rules, but maintained a link to earlier times by including a number of aspirational goals for lawyers, which were not enforceable, called Ethical Considerations. In the most recent American Bar Association draft rules for lawyers, the Model Rules of Professional Conduct, the Ethical Considerations are conspicuous by their absence. All that remains are the bottom-line rules and the accompanying comments that serve as aids to their interpretation.

In the shift from *canons of professional ethics*, to a *code of professional responsibility*, to *rules of professional conduct*, we can trace what Luban and Millemann call the "de-moralization" of legal ethics.[36] Reading or teaching the Model Rules, it is easy to embrace the illusion that rules constitute the whole of the moral life, with the result that legality and morality are conflated, and anything legal is assumed to be moral. When this happens, legal ethics is approached not as a subspecies of moral philosophy or professional ethics, but as a course in substantive law akin to torts or corporations. It is no surprise that the leading treatise on legal ethics is entitled simply *The Law of Lawyering*.[39]

Rules are important, of course, for a variety of reasons. Rules reinforce what lawyers already know but may be tempted to forget—they warn lawyers not to lie or to falsify evidence. . . .

Rules, however, are only part of the moral life. Many of the rules implicitly recognize this limitation by vesting discretion in lawyers to decide whether and how to act. Thus, the rules themselves envision that lawyers will exercise personal judgment. Furthermore, while rules can establish legal minimums, they ignore many of the interesting and important issues in legal practice. Rules cannot tell a lawyer whom her clients should be. Rules cannot empower a lawyer to be caring or courageous. They cannot teach a lawyer how to balance a client's lawful interests against the harm that will be done to opponents and third parties. They cannot tell a lawyer whether a tactic or strategy that *can* be employed *should* be employed. Moreover, rules provide no guidance for the lawyer who is grappling with questions that the rules themselves ignore—questions such as the ends of lawyering or the lawyer's moral

---

28. [Daniel Callahan, "Religion and the Secularization of Bioethics," 20 Hastings Center Report Special Supp. 2 (July/Aug 1990)] at 4.

36. [David Luban & Michael Millemann, "Good Judgment: Ethics Teaching in Dark Times," 9 Geo. J. Legal Ethics 31 (1995)] at 45.

39. Geoffrey C. Hazard, Jr. & W. William Hodes, *The Law of Lawyering: A Handbook on the Model Rules of Professional Conduct* (2d ed. 1985 with annual supplements).

accountability for her actions. No rule can tell a lawyer if the rule itself should be obeyed. If we are to deal with these profound and fundamental questions, we need a more-encompassing approach to legal ethics and legal practice. This leads to my third point.

3. The Avoidance of Particularity

When we exclude religion from legal ethics, we are tempted to delude ourselves into thinking that we are not members of particular communities but only one "sprawling, inchoate general community." We are encouraged to keep our private values to ourselves or to hide them beneath a veneer of detached and impartial rationality. As Callahan notes, "[t]ime and again I have been told by religious believers at a conference or symposium that they feared revealing their deepest convictions. They felt that the price of acceptance was to talk the common language, and they were probably right." The result is the trivialization and marginalization of religion—it is reduced to the status of a mere "hobby," as Stephen Carter observes in his book *The Culture of Disbelief.*

We thereby risk excluding questions of character and virtue from our moral reflections. We are tempted to ignore the most important things about ourselves—who we are and want to be, what particular communities and traditions have shaped us into the persons we are, how we see our lives lived against the backdrop of eternity. None of this seems relevant; instead, we feel obligated to speak what Jeffrey Stout calls the "moral esperanto" of autonomy and rights.[53]

But if we are unwilling to ask "who am I?" and "who do I want to be?," how can we hope to answer the question "what should I do?" As Stanley Hauerwas observes, "the kind of quandaries we confront depend on the kind of people we are and the way we have learned to construe the world through our language, habits, and feelings . . . . The question of what I ought to *do* is actually about what I am or ought to be."[54] For example, my thinking about the duties I owe to my client, or to a third party who may be injured by my actions, cannot be divorced from my understanding of myself as a disciple of Christ called to live out the Gospel message of love and reconciliation. . . .

A professional ethic that envisions the human person as an autonomous rational agent without ties to particular communities and traditions is an ethic that ignores these foundations of the moral life. It is also an ethic that tends to perpetuate the status quo. As Callahan notes, the culturally-free rationalism that dominates bioethics often leads to a "reluctance to question the conventional ends and goals of medicine, thereby running a constant risk of simply legitimating . . . the way things are." Religious thinking provides a challenge to the status quo by addressing the ends and purposes of medicine, law, and the human person. Christianity, for

---

53. Jeffrey Stout, *Ethics After Babel: The Languages of Morals and Their Discontents* 74–76 (1988).
54. Stanley Hauerwas, *The Peaceable Kingdom: A Primer in Christian Ethics* 117 (1983). . . .

example, affirms that the Gospel stands in judgment over *all* human institutions, including the legal profession and the justice system.

4. The Needs of Religious Believers

Finally, the exclusion of religion from legal ethics ignores the personal needs of many lawyers. Many lawyers are religious believers in the conventional sense (and if we adopt [Paul] Tillich's definition, all are religious). These lawyers want not only to abide by their professional codes of conduct, but to act in accord with their deepest values. They want to live a life of purpose and meaning. For such lawyers, rules and codes are a thin gruel that cannot furnish them with the sustenance they need. As Alley Verhey and Stephen Lammers observe, "Members of religious communities— or many of them, at any rate—want to make [the] choices they face with religious integrity, not just impartial rationality."[61] . . .

Catherine A. Rogers
Ethics in International Arbitration (2014)
pp. 1–3

International arbitration practices today present unique challenges that did not exist even a few years ago. The number of disputes has expanded dramatically. The increase in disputes has brought in new attorneys, parties, and arbitrators from diverse legal and cultural backgrounds. With this increasingly eclectic range of participants, the shared sense of what constitutes proper conduct has broken down. Resulting ethical conflicts and quandaries are escalating both in frequency and impact in arbitral proceedings.

These conflicts are surprising given that many attorneys are not even certain what rules might apply to their conduct. A survey conducted by the International Bar Association (IBA) Task Force on Counsel Conduct found a rather astonishing lack of certainty among counsel about which rules govern attorney conduct in international arbitral proceedings. . . . [Only] 63% . . . believed that they were subject to their home jurisdiction's rules . . . [and] a total of 87% of respondents indicated that they are either never or only sometimes sure what ethical norms govern the conduct of their opposing counsel. . . .

. . . The absence of clear regulation for counsel (and similarly for experts and third-party funders) has meant that those actors rely primarily on their own personal, nationally-derived assumptions about what constitutes proper conduct. This approach, however, raises a second common problem.

Nationally-derived assumptions about what constitutes proper conduct can and do often clash with the ethical assumptions of other participants from other jurisdictions, and sometimes with prevailing practices in international arbitral proceedings. These conflicts in professional standards can produce an unfair playing field at

---

61. [Allen Verhey & Stephen E. Lammers, *Theological Voices in Medical Ethics* (1993)] at 5.

multiple levels. Most obviously, if counsel are subject to different rules, differing standards of conduct may affect the fair conduct of arbitral proceedings. This potential imbalance is aggravated by the possibility that arbitrators may evaluate the propriety of the conduct of counsel and others appearing before them based on their own personal, nationally derived ethical assumptions. These implicit cultural assumptions, and tribunal decision-making based on their cultural assumptions, may not always be known to those whose conduct is being assessed.

The impact of these uncertainties is augmented by the fact that international arbitration is no longer primarily confined to the resolution of commercial disputes among commercial parties. It is increasingly called on to resolve more complex disputes involving a wider range of parties, important national regulatory interests, and public policies. . . .

Notes

1. How persuasive are the critiques by Wilkins, Wald, Allegretti, and Rogers of the current understanding of lawyer professionalism? Does taking account of how the manner in which race, gender, religion, or nationality affect the lawyer's role — or the operation of the justice system — require abandoning the goal of a universal set of professional ideals applicable to every lawyer regardless of his or her identity? Is the goal to abandon "bleached out" professionalism or to make professional norms more responsive to identity-related considerations for *all* lawyers? What might be the consequences of recognizing too great a role for a lawyer's non-professional identity in professional ethics? Is there a risk that the profession will be balkanized into separate identity-camps in which only lawyers from similar backgrounds or ideological commitments will represent certain clients? Are some forms of identity more dangerous for the profession to recognize than others? In light of the increasing heterogeneity within the profession at all levels, are there important dangers in not acknowledging the role that identity already plays in professional practice? For additional arguments about the role of various kinds of identity in professional practice, see Symposium, "Rediscovering the Role of Religion in the Lives of Lawyers and Those They Represent," 26 Fordham Urb. L.J. 821 (1999); David B. Wilkins, "Identities and Roles: Race, Recognition, and Professional Responsibility," 57 Md. L. Rev. 1502 (1998); Symposium, "Representing Race," 95 Mich. L. Rev. 723 (1997); Symposium, "The Relevance of Religion to a Lawyer's Work: An Interfaith Conference," 66 Fordham L. Rev. 1075 (1996); "Faith and the Law: A Symposium," 27 Tex. Tech L. Rev. 911 (1996); William B. Rubenstein, "In Communities Begin Responsibilities: Obligations at the Gay Bar," 48 Hastings L.J. 1101 (1997). See also Janet Halley, "Like-Race Arguments," in Judith Butler, John Guillory and Kendall Thomas, eds., *What's Left of Theory?* (2001) (Proceedings of the English Institute). For the classic article that first raised these questions, see Sanford Levinson, "Identifying the Jewish Lawyer: Reflections on the Construction of Professional Identity," 14 Cardozo L. Rev. 1577 (1993).

2. Can any lawyer ever "escape" his or her identity? Doesn't every lawyer use *something* about their identity — looks, connections, personality — to help him or her

succeed at work? At the same time, don't we all take on a personality at work that is, at best, a constructed approximation of who we think we "really are"? Isn't this dialectical process of getting the most out of our innate or acquired attributes, while at the same time forging a working persona that we think will help us get ahead, a form of "work" that we are all engaged in? For an insightful account of the inherent—and inherently interactive—connection between identity at work, see Devon W. Carbado and Mitu Gulati, "Working Identity," 85 Cornell L. Rev. 1259 (2000); Devon W. Carbado and Mitu Gulati, "Conversations at Work," 79 Or. L. Rev. 103 (2000).

3. Once we move to the international context, does it even make sense to talk about a "bleached out" understanding of the lawyer's role? We will return to this issue in Chapter 13.

Chapter 13

Some Final Thoughts

This concluding Chapter contains materials that relate to a number of the major themes of the course: the practice of law; the role of lawyers as representatives of clients, officers of the legal system and as public citizens; who should regulate lawyers (and other legal service providers); what lawyers do and what new lawyers need to know about what lawyers do; the exercise of professional judgment and the interplay of the rules of professional conduct and other forms of regulation, such as market forces. The first excerpt considers the subject of the appropriate drafters of the rules of professional conduct in the context of the ongoing debate over the rules of professional conduct that ought to apply in the federal district courts.

Andrew L. Kaufman
Who Should Make the Rules Governing
Professional Conduct in Federal Matters
(slightly amended and updated)
75 Tul. L. Rev. 149 (2000)

. . .

Some who have considered the confusion regarding the rules of attorney conduct believe that the federal system itself is the problem and that the appropriate solution would have Congress enact a single set of rules of attorney conduct to *all* courts, both state and federal.[29] Others, perhaps thinking that the Commerce Clause might not sustain such a thoroughgoing solution, believe that if uniform federal rules of attorney conduct were enacted, they would rather quickly supersede state rules at the demand of lawyers who would not wish to be subject to both state and federal attorney conduct rules. Such a solution might well please some national law firms, some national accounting firms who want to sweep away obstacles to their practice of law, perhaps the Department of Justice, and also theorists who like neat solutions.

I do not have the time here to do much more than state that I do not like the solution of Congress enacting a single set of rules for both state and federal courts. I happen to like our federal system for its diffusion of power. Of course there are many problems in our society today that demand national solutions at the hands of

---

29. See Linda Mullenix, "Multiform Federal Practice: Ethics and Erie," 9 Geo. J. Legal Ethics 89, 126–127 (1995) . . . ; Fred Zacharias, "Federalizing Legal Ethics," 73 Tex. L. Rev. 335, 379–80 (1994) . . . .

Congress. I do not think that the conduct of attorneys all over the country is one of them. I do not think that legislators are the preferred regulators of lawyers' conduct. Another branch of government, the judiciary, has more experience with the problems of lawyer conduct, and has traditionally been the ultimate regulator through the adoption and enforcement of the rules. Without pushing the issue of where, as a matter of the law of federal and state division and separation of power, the final authority ought to be constitutionally located, historically legislatures and judiciaries have avoided confrontation and, by and large, legislatures have left attorney conduct to the judiciary. Admittedly, when the judiciary fails to solve a major problem itself, and important interests are affected, then the temptation arises for the legislature to step in. The result can be disastrous, particularly if the legislation is ill-considered, as was the case with the McDade Amendment. [See p. 20.]

There is yet another aspect to the problem. As I have mentioned, for the last several years the American Bar Association has been engaged in its Ethics 2000 Project, revising its Model Rules of Professional Conduct for recommendation to the states. In my view, that very process is in need of revision. During the twentieth century, the ABA several times performed the very useful task of revising the professional rules for consideration by the various state and federal rulemaking authorities. There was a vacuum of power. We should be grateful that the ABA stepped in to do the job, for otherwise it might not have been done at all. The state courts, which have been the principal legislators of the professional rules, have not had the apparatus, or perhaps even the will, to undertake the arduous task of revision. They have been content to let the ABA do it.

This is not the occasion to analyze all the reasons why the ABA chose to involve itself in revising the professional rules of conduct. It is enough to say that it did so. But each successive revision has become more and more contentious. Lawyers and some of their clients have come to realize that, as with some of the major projects of the American Law Institute, a good deal is at stake for both lawyers and clients in the formulation of ethics rules, and that a great deal of law can be put in near final form out of the public eye in a forum where many affected interests are not even formally represented. While it is true that the ABA only recommends rules — it does not make them — and does not enact, the ABA knows, what every good lawyer knows, that the one who does the first draft of a document usually sets the parameters of the discussion. Whether the work of the ABA in drafting professional rules used to be more nonpartisan, more impartial or not, the fact is that in the American Bar Association, as in the American Law Institute, it does not seem that lawyers . . . can be counted on today to leave their clients behind them at the door. Their clients' interests tend to be in the room with them.

What does that say for the process of rulemaking for lawyers in both the federal and state systems? Change is in the air, and more change is called for. When the ABA recommended the Model Code of Professional Conduct to the states in 1969, state courts tended to adopt those proposals unchanged in most respects. When the ABA recommended the Model Rules of Professional Responsibility in 1980, the state courts scrutinized the proposals more closely. Few, if any, states adopted the 1980 proposals unchanged, and a majority of states rejected the critical proposals on confidentiality. Indeed, the longer particular states waited, the more changes they made. My own state, Massachusetts, changed a majority of the provisions, and then rewrote the Comments substantially. [I should disclose that I was a member of the committee appointed by the Supreme Judicial Court to make recommendations regarding adoption of the Model Rules.] The downside of this heightened scrutiny by individual state courts is that the hoped-for uniformity among the states has not been accomplished. The upside, however, is that this history demonstrates that many state courts have begun to take seriously their legislative responsibility regarding the governing rules of attorney conduct. The state courts' realization of what is at stake and, perhaps, their growing awareness that interest group battles within the ABA have helped shape the outcomes of its debates have led them to reclaim, to some extent, their lawmaking power from the ABA.

I suggest that they do more. Indeed, the very fact that the current major revision of the governing rules of attorney conduct is being performed once again by the ABA demonstrates the need for judges to consider their role in the process. It is true that the ABA is aware of its volunteer status in the rulemaking process. It sought to be more inclusive of the judiciary by having a state court judge (E. Norman Veasey, Chief Justice of the Delaware Supreme Court) as chair and a federal court judge (Patrick Higginbotham of the United States Court of Appeals for the Fifth Circuit) as a member of its Ethics 2000 project. But the ABA is still running the show, and nothing will be recommended without the approval of the ABA House of Delegates. I think that the time has come for the judiciary to run the show, just as the Judicial Conference controls the process of federal court rulemaking, with the ABA and other groups playing an important role as consultants.

The state courts now have their own administrative structure. The Conference of Chief Justices has been established, and it has begun to be heard on a variety of important issues involving the country's judiciary. It has its own administrative support in the Center for State Courts. At the moment, however, those organizations do not have the funding or the administrative capacity to play the role in the life of the state judiciaries that the Federal Judicial Center and the Judicial Conference of the United States play in the life of the federal judiciary. Those latter two institutions have grown in recent years to make the federal judiciary an effective force, not just in managing judicial affairs, but also in dealing with the other two branches of the federal government. The state judiciaries must find a way to function in a similar fashion, not only to enable them to deal effectively at home and vis-à-vis their federal counterparts, but also to help reclaim primary lawmaking authority from those private entities like the ABA that have moved into an existing vacuum of power and sought, in important ways, to exercise state judicial authority.

Indeed, in my view, much of the confusion that currently exists with respect to the governing rules of attorney conduct in federal courts is an outgrowth of the current system of lawmaking regarding attorney conduct. There is an ongoing struggle for lawmaking power, and the failure of the lawmakers themselves to take charge of the process has invited others—both private parties like the ABA and other branches of government, like Congress—to intervene.

A key to the solution of the process problem is the will of the respective state judiciaries to organize themselves, to create the necessary structure, and then to energize it, in order to take greater control of the lawmaking process with regard to attorney conduct. If such a mechanism had been developed, state judiciaries could have run the Ethics 2000 Project, perhaps with the ABA and other interested parties in an advisory capacity. In the twenty-first century it should become clear that a project like that is the judiciary's project, not the private bar's project.

Mobilization of the state judiciaries, however, is only a piece of the solution. The other piece of the solution relates to the issue with which I began—the rules of attorney professional conduct that govern in the federal courts. That there is an issue of horizontal versus vertical uniformity is one of the prices we pay for our federal system. Where the conduct of attorneys who practice in many different settings in tens of thousands of communities all across the country is at stake, I for one am willing to pay the price of vertical uniformity, at least as a starting point.

Those who want a national solution, imposed either by Congress, the Judicial Conference, or federal courts themselves through a process of common law adjudication, argue forcefully that the growing nationalization and internationalization of legal practice is hampered by the multiplicity of different rules governing attorney conduct in different states. But the great bulk of lawyers do not practice all over the country. Clients, with the advice of lawyers, deal with the differences in substantive law throughout the country all the time. And so do ordinary people, as we all do when, for example, we drive our cars from one state to another, and indeed from one community to another.

Local control and decentralization have their virtues too. Local control over lawyers has been the tradition; it is ingrained in every aspect of the profession. We lawyers organize ourselves locally, by community and by state, because we think we can exert some influence in the operation of the profession when organized in that fashion. To take just one example, the discipline of lawyers is carried on locally, through a large administrative apparatus that interprets and enforces the state law of professional responsibility. I doubt that that apparatus would be ready, willing, and able to enforce a federal law of professional responsibility. For myself, I think someone would have to demonstrate empirically that the present system, which tolerates some substantive differences among the state professional responsibility laws, has created so many serious problems that it needs to be altered in favor of a national solution.

If we can tolerate, at least for the time being, the current diversity in state professional responsibility law, then why not some diversity among the federal district courts? There is some virtue in a national solution that attempts to remedy the current state of confusion in the local rules of those courts. One hears anecdotally that district courts sometimes deal with the confusion by ignoring their own rules when they prove troublesome. That does not seem like a wonderful solution. Even if the number of instances when problems actually arise is small, the confusion is nevertheless troublesome because it means that lawyers who are trying to avoid trouble have no sure place even to begin looking for guidance. This may be one of those problems that isn't much of a problem when it is largely unnoticed, but becomes one just by reason of its discovery.

For me, the long-term solution begins with my instinct, which has no empirically proven basis, that there are many more private lawyers who practice in both the federal and state systems in their states than who practice in the federal system in many different states. If that is the case, then it seems that the better solution to the local federal rule problem starts with vertical uniformity between the federal and state courts in a given jurisdiction under the principle of dynamic conformity [i.e., a federal district court's rules of professional responsibility follows those of the state in which it sits, including, at least presumptively, changes in those rules]. In that fashion, most lawyers will not be faced with abiding by two sets of professional rules, which will occasionally be conflicting, and will therefore cause problems for lawyers in those litigation and transaction matters that have both state and federal aspects.

Even the most ardent advocate of dynamic conformity recognizes that such a solution does not mean that federal courts surrender control of the operation of their courtrooms. Nor does it threaten the well-established rule that matters of procedure remain matters of federal law. Lawyers and especially academics may worry about the possibility of a lawyer being disciplined for conduct that was permitted or even required as a matter of federal procedural law. The line between matters of procedure and matters of professional responsibility may not be easy to draw and perhaps a common law development would be the preferable solution. Let me give one example by way of illustration. A lawyer undertakes a matter in apparent violation of the ethics rules governing conflicts of interest. In the midst of a federal trial, the violation is noticed and is the subject of a motion to disqualify. The court decides that the trial itself would not be tainted by any conflict, that the trial has proceeded very far, and that it would be a waste of judicial resources to interrupt it by disqualifying one of the participating lawyers. Motion denied. Should a state disciplinary agency be precluded or preempted from disciplining the lawyer if the conflict was egregious? I think not. The federal court did not adjudicate whether the lawyer committed a serious violation, or even *any* violation of the conflict of interest rules. It only decided that, as a matter of procedure, it would not disqualify the lawyer. Some courts reaching that result even say that the question of ethical violation, if any, should be adjudicated elsewhere. The result should be different if the federal court had adjudicated the question whether there was an ethical violation and concluded that there was none.

I have thus far not discussed the concerns of the Justice Department about the effect of certain interpretations of the anti-contact rule on their law enforcement responsibilities. I believe that those concerns are reasonable. I also understand the belief of the Justice Department that a national solution—achieved by its own rules, by congressional action, or by national federal judicial rules—is the most efficient way to alleviate its concerns. However, the Justice Department's solution of making its own rules by Memorandum or Regulation has thus far failed in the courts . . . . The solution of congressional action has been turned against it in the McDade Amendment. Even if the Justice Department succeeds in getting the McDade Amendment repealed, and even if it persuades Congress to adopt its preferred solution, the lesson of the McDade Amendment is that one can lose everything with a national federal solution that is the product of hasty and ill-considered action. I think a congressional solution is the worst idea I have heard. Congress simply does not have time to deal thoughtfully with all the nuances that need to be dealt with in adjusting the interests of clients, lawyers, and the system of justice and to keep adjusting them as problems appear. The danger with a congressional solution is that these delicate issues will be left to committee staffs and the lobbyists for the best financed or best organized interests.

That leaves the possibility of national federal judicial rules, and those are still a real possibility, especially for some special situations that have strong federal concerns—such as some of the rules for government lawyers and perhaps also some of the rules for bankruptcy practice. One problem with crafting rules for federal government lawyers, however, is that the work of federal government lawyers very often is performed in a context where there is a private lawyer adversary. To avoid the problem of having different professional rules applying to lawyers in a single transaction or litigation, federal professional rules would have to govern those private lawyers too, thus imposing on private lawyers the potential of having two different sets of professional rules applying simultaneously in matters that had state and federal ramifications.

A further question is whether the problems of Justice Department lawyers, or federal lawyers generally, are unique or whether state government lawyers face similar problems. The claim is sometimes made that at least Justice Department lawyers are unique because, compared to state attorney general offices, they work much more closely with investigating officers and their work involves large complex litigation with nationwide implications. But local prosecutors often work just as closely with the police and face similar problems with interpretations of the anticontact rule. As far as nationwide activity is concerned, private law firms currently cope with issues similar to those faced by Justice Department lawyers.

A good deal of the furor surrounding the remedy for diverse rules of the federal district courts derives from the Justice Department's concern with Rule 4.2. The cry ought to be taken up by state and local prosecutors as well because they are potentially affected in quite similar ways. There is no doubt that the matter of Rule 4.2 needs to be solved, but it needs to be solved at both the state and the federal level.

That brings me around to the circle. I have urged that in the matter of the diverse local federal rules, the solution ought to be one of dynamic conformity, with an explicit acknowledgement that of course federal courts control their own procedure.

But federal courts also need to be involved in another way. It is appropriate to recognize the historical lodging of control of attorney behavior in the state systems, but reciprocity should follow such a recognition. State courts need to recognize that dynamic conformity means that federal courts have an interest in the professional conduct of lawyers practicing in federal courts in a given jurisdiction. That interest should be accommodated by bringing federal judges in each jurisdiction into the process of formulating those standards of conduct. State courts ought to take the lead in figuring out how, consistent with the respective operation of their courts, to include the federal courts in their jurisdiction in the process of making the rules that will govern the conduct of lawyers in both state and federal courts.

I also believe that there should be more global cooperation between the state and federal judiciaries. The Conference of State Court Chief Justices, in cooperation with the relevant committees of the federal Judicial Conference, ought to figure out how to superintend, or even to operate, the process of rewriting the rules of professional conduct — a task that the ABA has taken on for itself. That joint venture could then propose model rules of professional conduct that would be applicable in both the federal and state systems. Such model rules would, in my view, be more likely to command nationwide respect and thus lead to greater nationwide uniformity than rules recommended by the ABA.

Current experience with Rule 4.2 is a good example of what happens when the judiciary does not operate with a unified structure. ABA interposition thwarted the efforts of the Conference of Chief Justices and the Justice Department to agree on a proposal to recommend to the states. But the appropriate group to control this process is not the ABA, the political organization of private lawyers. The Conference of Chief Justices and the appropriate Judicial Conference Committee, representing the combined judiciaries, are the primary law-makers in this area. They should be working together to control the process of deliberation, which should include both federal and state prosecutors as well as the ABA and other interested groups. While this did not occur with respect to Rule 4.2 . . . I believe that for the future, the path to successful rulemaking in the area of attorney conduct lies in cooperative effective action of the federal and state judiciaries. Effective cooperation would make congressional action unnecessary and would reduce the power of the ABA from something that approaches lawmaking to something that more resembles true advising. If the judiciary is to be the effective ruler with respect to attorney conduct, as I think it should be, then the state and federal courts will have to combine their wisdom and their power to fend off those in the profession and in the legislative branch who would like to be the judiciary's senior partner. . . .

The next two excerpts from Professor Llewellyn, a prominent legal scholar and principal drafter of the Uniform Commercial Code, offer an overview of what law is, what lawyers do, and how best to prepare for the practice of law.

N. K. Llewellyn
The Bramble Bush (1930)
pp. 1, 2–3, 138–39

You have come to this school to embark upon the study of the law. Most of you have in the back of your heads an idea that as a result of that study you will become lawyers. Some of you have some notion of what it is that a lawyer does. You think of a man who tries cases before courts. Or do you think particularly of a man to whom to turn in case, for any reason, you happen to get arrested? But what a court does, what a lawyer does in court, and what he does outside, what relationship either court or lawyer has to the law, what relation the law school has to any of these things— around these things, I take it, there floats a pleasant haze. . . .

What, then, is this law business about? It is about the fact that our society is honeycombed with disputes. Disputes actual and potential; disputes to be settled and disputes to be prevented; both appealing to law, both making up the business of the law. But obviously those which most violently call for attention are the actual disputes, and to these our first attention must be directed. Actual disputes call for somebody to do something about them. First, so that there may be peace, for the disputants; for other persons whose ears and toes disputants are disturbing. And secondly, so that the dispute may really be put at rest, which means, so that a solution may be achieved which, at least in the main, is bearable to the parties and not disgusting to the lookers-on. This doing of something about disputes, this doing of it reasonably, is the business of law. And the people who have the doing in charge, whether they be judges or sheriffs or clerks or jailers or lawyers, are officials of the law. *What these officials do about disputes is, to my mind, the law itself.* . . .

What, then, do you need that we do not offer you, and how can you set about getting it? It is hard to answer that question. It is hard, first, because my own eyes are still muffled in tradition. On case teaching I was raised, and by it I have earned my living these twelve years. It is hard, second, because we still know so little of what constitutes the practice of law today. How much of the old-time practice has been taken over by trust and title companies, and how many lawyers do they use? How much of their "law" is in the cases, on the statute books, how much is based upon their own practices and understandings? How much of law practice lies in trial of cases, and with what differences between New York and Wichita and Cedar Forks? How does trial practice in the city court differ from trial practice before the federal courts or the Supreme? How much of practice lies in interviews with the dock commissioner or the tax commissioner, or the claim agent for the New York Central? Is there a special workman's compensation bar? How much of law practice lies in drafting contracts, how much in closing titles, how much lies in dispossessing tenants? How much in business strategy? How much in journeying to Albany or Washington to lobby; how much of the lobbying occurs when the committee has adjourned? How much of practice lies in getting business, and whose business, and how is it got? How much of practice lies in marrying the senior partner's niece, and which of them—and again, how? To these and to some hundred other questions we can answer: for some . . . more or wholly; for some, less or not at all; for how many, or how much for any, we can only guess. And which of these questions is later to concern particular ones of you, that is not worth guessing at.

So that it is hard to answer the question: what do you need? Still harder, because different ones of you have different needs, even if you were all to come out at the same place. The best I can do is to put before you some of the things that every lawyer, or almost every lawyer, is sure to need, but which case study does not offer. . . .

N. K. Llewellyn
On What Is Wrong With So-Called Legal Education
35 Colum. L. Rev. 651 (1935)[*]

. . . [L]et me avoid misconception. I hold that a lawyer's first job is to be a *lawyer*. I hold that we must teach him, first of all, to make a legal table or chair that will stand up without a wobble. Ideals without technique are a mess.

But technique without ideals is a menace. The boy must be hardheaded, with trained hands and brain. He must . . . be able to fight wolves. But is that all? I say, as well, that he must want to take wolves' pelts. The encouragement of that desire is a law school job. And if the man—as so many will—goes into legislation or administration, then it is the law school's job to give him, first, a decent fact-foundation from which to work; and second, understanding of the need of facts; and, third, a driving interest in their acquisition; and fourth, the first beginnings of the wherewithal to weigh them and their implications for a People. Techniques and interests, not merely as to "law," but as to "fact," and "policy." Peculiarly as to those *socially* vital facts which practice as such, in civil cases, so quietly and insidiously drops beneath the table.

Neither does the job stop with this. Above I spoke of the student's whole self. That whole self needs attention. From the angle of a lawyer's dealings with clients, witnesses, jury, judge, and bench of five or seven. No less from the angle of a lawyer's living with self or children, after forty. Till forty—sometimes even till fifty—he can make out, after a fashion, on hard work, and (if he achieves it) on success.

But as in so many things, our law schools presuppose here some sort of ectogenic Culture, sprouted at home or in college, and somehow to be automatically reintroduced into the system in harmonious combination with whatever it is we teach. Now first, this Culture mostly has not sprouted. And second, our methods are such as to kill it if we can. "Make him think like a lawyer!" Park Culture at the door! This would be fine, if, *after* making the boy think like a lawyer, we really did reintroduce the Culture. Do we?

Indeed, the more "progressive" the school, the less time is left the student for anything but reading cases and chasing references—all with an eye as good as

---

[*] While the gender use in this excerpt is dated, the content is not.—Eds.

single to The Law. I think (and hope) that the Columbia level for a C+ man has now risen to over fifty hours a week of work. As a measure of a full time job, fine. But how of the work itself? Rules, always rules—or decisions—in the forefront of attention. . . .

The need is, in some fashion, for an integration of the human and the artistic with the legal. Not an addition merely; an integration. Attempt at such integration finds response. . . .

Methods: Background of Social Fact

This matter of new economy comes to bear directly on the introduction of the background of social fact and policy. Unfortunate and often violent misconceptions fare abroad:

(1) There is the notion that introducing fact background means introducing it raw; e.g., as extracts, reprints, or references that swallow social science studies whole. In rare cases, this may pay.

In very rare cases. For social scientists have not gathered their data to our use, but to their own; their data are focused on the problem for which they have been gathered, and on the angle of that problem which interests the gatherer. However good, sound, thorough, illuminating, such a line of work, it intersects our lawyers' line at but a single point. Reading lines, to gather points, breaks the back. It is therefore normally the job of the instructor, and trebly the job of one who puts out a Materials book, to gather the strayed mass of materials together, and to extract from the intersections, in brief form, his *own* line of information. This costs editor's time; it means editor's education. *It overloads neither the student nor the curriculum.*

(2) There is the notion that adding social facts to The Law as law-course material makes the job harder, or longer, *for the student.*

This is sheer nonsense. The fact is that legal rules mean, of themselves, next to nothing. They are verbal formulae, partly conveying a wished-for direction and ideal. But they are, to law students, empty. . . .

Whereas to set rules into their social context, into the context of how men do things, and of what difference the rule makes to those men—this is to give body to a rule for any student. It has graphic value, it has movement value, it has memory value. Rules thus seen are not only more meaningful. *They are also easier to learn.* You *save* time, when you teach them thus. You also make *critique* of the rule take on its human content. You make critique inevitable, because the human content, once introduced, will never be denied. . . .

(3) The third notion abroad is that displacement of study-book space by "nonlegal" material depletes the room for "necessary" "legal" material. I hold this idea fallacious; but I recognize its power. Judgments as to balance of convenience will differ. . . .

Method: Social Background: Conclusion

The upshot seems to be that, within our time-limitation, we either integrate the background of social and economic fact and policy, course by course, or fail of our job. The early urge, say about 1910, was to pile on such courses as Legal History, Legal Philosophy, Jurisprudence, Comparative Law, in a fourth year. I, for one, am glad the students refused to follow the suggestion. Merely added on behind, such matters are well-nigh as ectogenic as Economics from college, frozen into harmlessness in the law school refrigerator. The students' sabotage of the Fourth Year has had as its function to wake faculty-members up to the job of *integrating* background—social or philosophical—into *every* course. And I shall be greatly surprised if the new four-year curriculum projected by the Yale Law and Harvard Business Schools does not, after a few years of experience, reconcentrate into a new and better Three Years.

Notes

1. Writing in the 1930s, Llewellyn foresaw that modern law practice would require of lawyers a lot more than knowledge of the law, narrowly constructed, and "thinking like a lawyer," in the sense of knowing how to read cases, statutes and regulations, extracting their holdings, understanding their meaning, arguing about them, and crafting legal arguments based on the law. Mastering the "law" in the sense of complying with Rule 1.1 on competence and thinking like a lawyer are necessary yet insufficient conditions for the practice of law in the twenty-first century. Llewellyn argued that modern lawyers must understand the culture, social conditions and context in which law is practiced. They must marshal immense interdisciplinary bodies of law, such as history, economics, psychology, philosophy, and sociology, as well as proficiencies such as ever-evolving technologies, not in an abstract way but instead as integrated in and integral to the law, to allow them to exercise professional judgment in context to the benefit of clients. Is the task of commanding these skills and bodies of knowledge a Herculean one? Do law schools provide a solid foundation for this undertaking? Does learning to think like a modern lawyer entail learning the "law" primarily in the first year of law school and then taking interdisciplinary courses subsequently, or is it more a question of approach to the study and practice of law?

2. If the practice of law requires mastery of a legal core supplemented by many bodies of knowledge, or, more accurately, mastery of law broadly defined which incorporates and internalizes many traditionally non-legal bodies of knowledge, are lawyers best positioned to practice law? To offer legal services to clients? Did Professor Llewellyn foresee the rise of legal service providers and the gradual decline of the central role that lawyers play in the market for legal services?

3. How does practicing law in context—appreciating and integrating the relevant culture and social facts—interact with increased specialization? Does specialization allow lawyers to zoom in on increasingly narrow areas of "law" while mastering relevant bodies of knowledge? If so, can a modern lawyer practice as a generalist? Is there some tension between the push, on the one hand, toward specialization and the call for greater interdisciplinary education, on the other? If what constitutes "law" in any specific practice area—cases, statutes, regulations—has increased so

significantly in the last half-century as to require more and more specialization of lawyers as a matter of avoiding malpractice and of acquiring expertness, what are we to make of the calls that at the same time hard-pressed lawyers must become knowledgeable in several other related disciplines—economics, sociology, psychology? Or does becoming "interdisciplinary" mean learning just enough to be able to talk to, and understand, the "experts" in those fields?

4. A central theme of the Carnegie Foundation's *Educating Lawyers*—*Preparation for the Profession of Law* (2007) was the need to offer law students integrated legal studies. Rather than relegating the teaching of legal ethics to the legal ethics class, law schools ought to infuse legal ethics throughout the curriculum in every class; rather than introducing law students to critical insights from fields of study such as history, economics and sociology, law schools should integrate these insights into bread-and-butter classes such as contracts, property and criminal law. How well have law schools done over the past 80 years heeding Llewellyn's and the Carnegie Foundation's call for such integration? Or in fact would teaching legal ethics by the so-called pervasive method tend to result in focusing on little pieces of the subject matter for an hour or so at best in each course during the course of the term?

Llewellyn chastises law schools for failing to provide lawyers with useful advice about the practical problems lawyers encounter in their daily professional lives. Where *should* lawyers learn about the practical realities of legal practice? Do law schools provide this kind of education? Do most law professors even *know* about the practical realities facing lawyers in this fast-changing environment, let alone how these realities are shaping how lawyers in different professional contexts understand and deal with ethical and moral questions? We have spent considerable attention in this book on the ethical obligations of lawyers. It is perhaps fitting that we close by examining the ethical obligations of those who purport to train them.

David B. Wilkins
Professional Ethics for Lawyers and Law Schools: Interdisciplinary Education and the Law School's Ethical Obligation to Study and Teach about the Profession*
12 Legal Educ. Rev. 47 (2001) (Australia)

What does it mean to be a "professional"? The question lies at the heart of any attempt to teach professional ethics. Yet, despite its undeniable centrality, there is remarkably little consensus among the current generation of legal ethics teachers about what this term actually means beyond its obvious historical and descriptive

---

* Parts of this essay were published previously in David B. Wilkins, "The Professional Responsibility of Professional Schools to Study and Teach About the Profession," 49 J. Legal Educ. 76 (1999) and David B. Wilkins, "Redefining the 'Professional' in Professional Ethics: An Interdisciplinary Approach to Teaching Professionalism," 58 Law & Contemp. Probs. 241 (1995).

connotations. Few would deny, of course, that lawyers have traditionally been considered "professionals" or that, in the minds of many, this designation carries with it certain normative implications about the relationship between lawyers and society that links the "legal profession" to the small number of other occupational groups (for example, doctors) that are also considered professionals. What has become quite controversial, however, is whether these normative claims are either true or, if true, socially desirable. Moreover, even among those who believe that the concept has some independent normative value worth preserving, the claim that "professionalism" can be taught remains deeply controversial.

In this essay, I argue that the lack of consensus over the meaning and normative value of professionalism is symptomatic of a profound ethical failing in American legal education . . . : the law school's persistent failure to make the norms, structures, and conditions of legal practice the subject of serious teaching or scholarship. This failure, I suggest, is deeper than the usual criticism that there is an increasing separation—or "disjunction" in the words of one influential account—between the legal academy and the profession that it is suppose to serve.[3] Instead, it is nothing less than an ethical failure by the legal academy to meet the legitimate needs of its three principal constituencies: students, the bar, and society. This is a time of tremendous upheaval and change for lawyers in the United States and around the world. If individual lawyers, the bar, and the public we serve are to emerge from this time of change with a legal profession capable of meeting the enormous challenges it now faces, then the legal academy must become an active participant in developing and transmitting the empirical and theoretical knowledge about legal practice that will allow us to construct a vision of legal professionalism fit for the twenty-first century instead of for the nineteenth. . . .

II. Theoretical Background and the State of the Field

The term "professional ethics" can be given at least three distinct, although admittedly interconnected, meanings. The most general understanding of the term refers to the ethics of "that entire family of vocations that we call 'the professions.'" Those who subscribe to this meaning assume that it is possible to identify a stable set of criteria for classifying which occupations are entitled to be called professions

---

3. This critique typically comes in two forms. The first, exemplified by the American Bar Association's MacCrate Report argues that law schools are not teaching students the skills they need to be competent and ethical practitioners. See American Bar Association, Committee on Legal Education, "Legal Education and Professional Development: An Educational Continuum: Report of the Task Force on Law Schools and the Profession—Narrowing the Gap" (1992) (the "MacCrate Report") [Chicago, Illinois: American Bar Association, Section of Legal Education and Admissions to the Bar]. The second, most often associated with Judge Harry Edwards and Dean Anthony Kronman, complains that legal scholarship is too theoretical and pays insufficient attention to the doctrinal questions faced by real lawyers and judges. See [Harry T.] Edwards, ["The Growing Disjunction Between Legal Education and the Legal Profession," 91 Mich. L. Rev. 34 (1992)]; Anthony Kronman, *The Lost Lawyer: Failing Ideals of the Legal Profession* (1993). See also Mary Ann Glendon, *A Nation Under Lawyers: How the Crisis in the Legal Profession Transformed American Society* (1994).

and that all those who properly fall under this designation will share important normative commitments.

The second meaning focuses on a particular profession, such as law, and attempts to identify those normative characteristics that are uniquely "professional." Unlike those who subscribe to the more general usage, persons interested in "legal ethics" need not claim that they can justify lawyers' professional status by some set of objective criteria or that the "professional" norms they identify will necessarily be shared by other professionals. Instead, these theorists tend to take professional status as a given and ask which ethical values lawyers ought to uphold in light of the legal profession's unique position in society.

Finally, the last usage takes a descriptive and instrumental view of professional ethics. Rather than asking what norms professionals (either in general or in a particular profession) ought to share, those using the term in this third sense ask what ethics professionals actually display. This investigation into the meaning of professional ethics can be conducted at the level of both group ideology and individual behavior. At the collective level, scholars examine the official justifications offered by professionals for their ethical standards and ask whether these norms actually serve their stated purposes or instead are better understood as a convenient cover for actions that do little more than promote professional self-interest. With respect to individuals, the question asked is whether practitioners actually conform their conduct to the profession's articulated norms, values, and standards.

Notwithstanding the fact that most scholars interested in professional ethics acknowledge the importance of all three understandings, one or the other of these approaches has tended to dominate each of the arenas in which professional ethics is generally taught. This segmentation has, in turn, nurtured and reinforced a growing cynicism among academics, practitioners, and the general public about whether the concept of professionalism has any independent normative content worth preserving.

Undergraduate and graduate level liberal arts courses that discuss professional ethics tend to embrace the first meaning. The question most frequently posed in these settings is whether there is something sufficiently distinctive about being a professional that justifies holding those occupying these social roles to normative standards that are different from the rules of common morality. For the most part, the academics who teach these courses tend to be skeptical about such claims. This skepticism comes from two quarters. First, many sociologists contend that it is impossible to identify a stable and objective set of criteria for separating existing professions from other occupations that, although desiring the social and economic benefits that flow from professional status, have had less success than doctors and lawyers in achieving their objectives. Second, philosophers are frequently critical of arguments that are premised on the existence of a "role differentiated morality," particularly where the argument asserts that people who occupy a given position in society are exempt from moral obligations that would govern the conduct of ordinary citizens.

Collectively, these skepticisms cast doubt on the claim that professionalism per se has any independent moral content. Thus, to the extent that sociologists can convincingly demonstrate that lawyers and doctors achieved their current status as a result of concerted political struggle, the traditional structural/functionalist account that links professional status — and therefore, professional ethics — to the unique functions that professionals perform for society is undermined. As a result, sociologists tend to view these normative claims as simply another tool that professionals use to pursue their objective of freeing themselves from state control and the constraints of the market. Consequently, although they begin by asking the question posed by the first understanding of professional ethics — what are the ethical claims that unite all professions? — the answers that these scholars give tend to devolve into the third approach that identifies self-interest as the common thread that unites all efforts to articulate a distinctive normative understanding of professional ethics. Similarly, once philosophers reject the idea that any group should be exempt from the demands of ordinary morality simply because they occupy a particular social role, there is no longer any reason to treat "professional ethics" as a separate and distinct area of moral inquiry. Once again, the overall effect is to shift the focus away from the norms and practices of particular professionals in favor of a more general examination of moral duties.

Not surprisingly, professional schools have tended to take a different tack. Required ethics courses in law schools are generally premised on the second model of professional ethics. Traditionally, these courses have started with the assumption that lawyers are "professionals" with their own unique ideals and practices. The task these courses set for themselves, therefore, is to identify which of these norms and practices are legitimate in light of the positions that lawyers occupy in society. In recent years, however, this standard orientation has increasingly come under attack. Taking as their inspiration many of the criticisms of the first model of professionalism outlined above, a growing number of legal ethics courses now include substantial criticism of both the self-interested nature of many traditional professional ideals and of the standard claim that lawyers are not governed by the rules of ordinary morality.

Both of these approaches to formal ethics instruction in law schools undermine the claim that professionalism per se has independent moral content. The insularity of the standard orientation strongly implies that lawyers have nothing to learn from social scientists, or indeed from other professionals, about the normative content of the lawyer's role. Although the critical approach adopted by many contemporary ethics teachers substantially reduces this insularity, it also paradoxically reinforces the view that professionalism is either irrelevant or pernicious. In these courses, professionalism is largely identified with the standard version of legal ethics as articulated in the Code of Professional Responsibility, the Model Rules of Professional Conduct, and other official sources. The question, therefore, is whether lawyers should follow these professional rules or the dictates of their personal conscience when deciding difficult ethical problems. However one resolves this question in any particular case, this way of framing ethical issues deflects attention from investigating whether lawyers *as professionals* ought to reject both the traditional model of legal ethics and the assertion that they should simply follow the dictates of their personal morality. By omitting this third choice, legal ethics courses have left themselves vulnerable to the criticism that they either reify the narrow and often self-interested view of lawyer professionalism articulated in the current ethics rules or that they attempt to teach a personal moral code that bears little or no relationship to the competence or the mission of legal education. Collectively, these criticisms reinforce a skeptical attitude about the meaning of professionalism.

The implicit and sometimes explicit messages about lawyers' professionalism conveyed by the rest of the law school curriculum only serve to deepen this skeptical attitude. While formal ethics courses tend to portray the legal profession's traditional ideals as both legitimate and important (even when they are being critical), when "ethics" is mentioned in the rest of the curriculum the focus is on the third model's descriptive claim that ethical rules are either ignored in practice or simply a cover for lawyer self-interest. In cases, hypothetical examples, and off-hand remarks, lawyers are frequently portrayed as ruthless economic actors unconcerned with the "niceties" of the profession's traditional ethics. This skeptical attitude is reinforced by powerful intellectual movements in legal education that focus attention on the indeterminacy of rules (including ethical rules), the need for functional as opposed to normative justifications for public policies, and the numerous ways in which law and lawyers entrench existing inequalities of wealth and power. At the same time, students who raise general ethical objections in traditional law school courses are often told that these concerns are irrelevant to the "legal" issues being discussed. When one puts all of these developments together, the clear message to law students is that lawyer professionalism, and indeed ethics in general, is either irrelevant to their lives or something to be deployed instrumentally to further their . . . self-interest.

Indeed, the fact that philosophers, legal ethics teachers, and the rest of the law school faculty have largely failed to generate a meaningful account of the normative value of professionalism has had important consequences beyond the academy. As I have argued, many commentators have complained of a growing separation between law schools and the legal profession itself. Each of the three approaches to professional ethics outlined above exacerbate this separation. By isolating the concept of "professionalism" from the actual practices of any group of professionals, the first definition leads many lawyers to believe that philosophers and other social scientists do not know (and probably do not care) enough about the realities of legal practice to render judgments that practitioners ought to heed.

The second account embraced by most traditional legal ethics courses also tends to have the same effect. Although these courses purport to speak directly to practicing lawyers, they often present a stylized account of lawyering that bears little relationship to the realities of contemporary legal practice. As a result, practicing lawyers often complain that law students are not being given the skills they need to cope with the massive changes that have transformed many areas of legal practice from the "gentlemanly" world of individual decisionmaking, apprenticeship, and noblesse oblige portrayed in most traditional ethics courses.

Not surprisingly, the practicing bar resents the third account as well. To many practitioners, most legal academics know almost as little about the bar's actual ethical practices as the philosopher proponents of the first model. They therefore tend to dismiss these critics, as they have tended to dismiss most of what is taught in law school, as being irrelevant to the contemporary realities of legal practice.

Ironically, when the bar formally attempted to define professionalism, it paid no more attention to the contemporary realities of legal practice than most traditional ethics courses. This failure further exacerbates the split between the bar and the academy by reinforcing the critical dimension of many contemporary legal ethics courses that portray the bar's understanding of professionalism as simply a cover for self-interest. At the same time, this critical attitude, as well as the even more openly cynical view of lawyers articulated in the mainstream legal curriculum, discourages practitioners from either acknowledging or confronting the difficult ethical problems caused by the growing bureaucratization and competitiveness of the market for legal services. This, in turn, simply fuels the claims by academics in both law schools and other parts of the university that the profession consistently fails to come to terms with academic criticism of its practices and its ideals.

The net result of this dynamic, as with the segmentation of the three models of professionalism in general, has been to reinforce the cynicism by both academics and practitioners about the normative value of professionalism. But matters are even worse than this bleak portrait suggests. The legal academy's failure to study the profession has created a knowledge vacuum of enormous proportions concerning the changes in law practice sweeping across the legal landscape. As with any vacuum, the academy's silence has attracted a host of other purveyors of information and ideas about legal practice who are all too willing to fill the void. Thus, the "New Information Order"* about law and legal practice is primarily the result of the increasingly cacophonous voices of legal recruiters, public relations specialists, trade associations, and legal journalists. Many of these sources, however, are more interested in furthering their own agenda than in providing disinterested information. Those who are not self-dealing often know little more about legal practice than those whom they purport to educate. By leaving students, practitioners, and citizens to fend for themselves among these self-interested and inaccurate information merchants, law schools have doubly failed each of these core constituents.

Let me briefly illustrate this unhealthy dynamic with respect to each of the three groups that the law school is designed to serve.

---

* See Marc Galanter & Thomas Palay, *Tournament of Lawyers: The Transformation of the Big Law Firm* 68–76 (1991) (describing the emergence of a new legal press consisting of publications such as the American Lawyer and the National Law Journal).

The Student Experience: The Fox and the Chicken Coop

Students are hungry about information about their future careers. The regular curriculum, however, offers them almost nothing to satisfy this hunger. As a result, students typically learn about potential careers from three sources: legal recruiters, the legal press, and each other. It should go without saying that each of these sources of information is seriously flawed. . . .

The Bar's Experience: The Blind Leading the Blind

Law schools have done no better in fulfilling their ethical duty to the profession. Indeed, a good argument can be made that they have done worse. Given that they depend upon tuition dollars for their survival, law schools must at least pay lip service to the goal of preparing their graduates to build successful and ethical careers. With few exceptions, however, the academy has not even given this much attention to the large-scale economic, social, and cultural forces that are reshaping the profession that their students are about to enter. . . .

The Public Experience: Whose Law is it Anyway?

Finally, the law school's failure to study and teach about the profession is an affront to the academy's ethical obligation to the public. The main ethical responsibility of law schools, of course, is neither to students nor to the profession. It is to the citizens who depend upon law, and therefore derivatively upon lawyers, to provide a fair, coherent, and efficient framework within which to live their lives. The recent changes in legal institutions and practices have their most important impact not on lawyers, but on the public as a whole. By failing to study these changes in any systematic way, we have deprived policy makers of the information that they need to determine how these developments might affect specific public values, and how those that are important might be regulated or controlled. . . .

. . . If the concept of professionalism is to have a coherent meaning to today's practitioners, it can neither be divorced from nor subsumed by the realities of contemporary practice. Critics of the attempt to give some transcendental meaning to professional ethics are correct insofar as they point out that it is impossible either to generate a set of historical criteria for determining which occupations qualify as "professions" or to provide a meaningful account of the attitudes, dispositions, or normative commitments that any given professional ought to hold on the basis of the abstract relationships between professionals and those they serve. Whatever may be said of ethics in general, professional ethics must be designed to serve specific societal needs. As such, it cannot be separated from the social, economic, and political contexts in which these needs arise and through which they must be met.

This does not mean, however, that we ought to confine our understanding of professional ethics to those norms and practices that have traditionally been the province of a single profession such as law. As David Luban and others persuasively argue, professional norms must always be justified in terms of some more general set of moral criteria.* One important element of this inquiry is how the normative claims of the legal profession compare with those of other actors in society who are confronted with similar problems. Those who occupy social roles that have traditionally been thought of as professions provide one obvious source (though by no means the only source) for such comparisons. Moreover, given the complexity of modern social interactions and the breakdown of many traditional barriers to inter-professional cooperation and competition, members of different professions are increasingly likely to interact with each other in a variety of contexts. It is therefore critically important that these actors learn to understand one another and not to make demands that subvert one another's legitimate ethical practices.

This comparative approach, however, must not conflate professional ethics with personal ethics. Although common morality stands as the ultimate check on any assertion of professional ethics (and on the value of any cross-professional comparisons), it does not define the normative stance of professionals. Lawyers are more than ordinary citizens; they have been given a monopoly by the state to occupy a position of trust both with respect to the interests of their clients and the public purposes of the legal framework. These unique responsibilities must be taken into account in defining a lawyer's professional obligations, even as we recognize that these obligations must account for the fact that lawyers are also individuals who are morally responsible for their own actions.

Finally, no attempt to provide a meaningful account of professional ethics can ignore the actual conduct of professionals. Without some attention to practice, professional ideals can easily degenerate into legitimation. Nor is it always appropriate to label the misdeeds of particular lawyers as individual deviance rather than as failings of the general ideals or practices. Certain officially sanctioned ideals or institutional arrangements make it more likely that individuals will transgress stated norms. More importantly, the substantive content that an individual practitioner gives to any ethical norm will inevitably be shaped by the institutional context in which the norm is developed and applied. Failure to pay attention to how these institutional structures shape lawyer conduct can both produce undesirable ethical norms as well as frustrate attempts to increase compliance with desirable ones.

These observations have both theoretical and pedagogical significance for any attempt to create a new understanding of professional ethics. At the theoretical level, the new model must embrace the prevalent, but nevertheless often neglected, truth that law is a practice that takes place in varying discrete institutional contexts. As a result, the goal of professional ethics instruction is to help students develop the skills, dispositions, and commitments that will allow them to navigate these complex arrangements in a manner that best promotes society's interest in the social goods produced by lawyers. While formal codes of conduct can sometimes be a useful guide,

---

* See David Luban, *Lawyers and Justice: An Ethical Study* 128–133 (1988).

developing those traits of character that are particularly suited to the lawyer's role is at the core of what we ought to mean by professional ethics.

Given these theoretical commitments, the pedagogy of a course designed to explore the contemporary meaning of professionalism must offer students both a window on actual professional practice and a vantage point to discuss and evaluate these practices from a critical distance. As David Luban and Michael Millemann argue, the kind of ethical judgment lawyers most need to cultivate is best taught through "trial and error and by imitation."* Observing others, although not a perfect substitute for individual effort, can provide valuable insight and encourage the development of both empathy and critical judgment.

Cross-professional exchanges further these goals. When students observe professionals in other fields coping with issues that are present in the students' own discipline, they often see these problems in a new light. Not only must they consider, for example, the doctor's justification for her approach to informed consent or patient confidentiality, but they must also ask whether these justifications are persuasive in their own disciplines. Even this level of comparison, however, may fall short of fully addressing the problem of professional insularity. The very features that make the two groups similar may obscure the degree to which each subscribes to norms that unduly protect their respective professional prerogatives. Therefore, a course in professionalism must ultimately infuse the study of particular professional practices with normative perspectives from disciplines such as philosophy, sociology, psychology, and political science that stand outside the traditional discourse of professionalism. . . .

A full proposal for [studying and teaching about] the profession would take me far beyond the confines of this essay. Moreover, the more [complete] the plan, the more schools are likely to claim that they don't have the resources to implement such an ambitious agenda. I therefore offer three very simple proposals, each of which could be adopted by any school committed to making progress on the issues I have addressed. . . .

By hiring faculty members committed to studying [and teaching about] the profession, creating in-depth case studies of legal organizations and practices, and beginning to study our own graduates, law schools could go a long way toward answering some of the fundamental questions about legal practice that currently bedevil students, practitioners, and citizens alike. . . . [I]f we expect our students to value "professional ethics," we must begin to provide them with an account of lawyer professionalism that neither reifies existing practices nor devolves into their own personal moral commitments. Teaching professional ethics through an empirically grounded interdisciplinary approach provides our best opportunity to forge this new understanding.

---

* David Luban & Michael Millemann, "Can Judgment Be Taught? Ethics Teaching in Dark Times," 9 Geo. J. Legal Ethics 31 (1995).

A Note on Legal Education

Professor Wilkins's critique of legal education is part of a growing chorus that has become much more pointed in the years following the 2008 financial crisis as law school applications have plummeted and the number of graduates obtaining jobs for which a J.D. is required has fallen to just over 50%. The following excerpt from a widely read book by Professor Brian Tamanaha is among the most stinging.

Brian Z. Tamanaha
Failing Law Schools (2012)
pp. x, xi, xii, xiii

Proud and dignified institutions that have long held themselves out as the conscience of the legal profession, law schools across the country have been engaging in disreputable practices. When called to account for these actions, law schools protest that they are just following the rules. They suggest that unhappy graduates should take responsibility for their poor decisions to incur such high debt. They universally place the blame for inflated employment numbers on the *U.S. News* rankings, as if a magazine were responsible for their conduct. Elite law schools distance themselves from the worst offenders, conveniently ignoring that they too engage in questionable actions, merely to a lesser extent. Law schools at every level have been failing their ethical responsibilities, while pointing the finger at others.

. . . I explore how law schools have arrived at this sorry state and the implications of this sad condition for the present and future. At the root of these problems is the way that law schools are chasing after prestige and revenue without attention to the consequences. The enviable resources that law schools enjoy relative to . . . economics and English departments are the riches obtained in the chase.

The economic model of law schools is broken. The cost of legal education today is substantially out of proportion to the economic opportunities obtained by the majority of graduates. There are a few winners—graduates who secure well-paying jobs in corporate law firms—while a significant number end up with mountainous debt that they will suffer under for decades with little to show for it. . . .

. . . Several dozen individual law schools are failing in the specific sense that a substantial [number] of their graduates suffer financial hardship. . . . If normal economic signals were operating, schools that fail to meet the interests of most of their students would not survive because people would stop enrolling. These law schools, however, are kept afloat by students making poor judgments to attend (encouraged by misleading job information from schools), while the federal government obligingly supplies funds to support their folly. . . .

What I write in these pages will affront many of my fellow legal educators. I reveal the ways in which we have repeatedly worked our self-interest into accreditation standards, from unnecessarily requiring three years of law school to writing special provisions to boost our compensation. We teach less and get paid more than other professors, and we earn more than most lawyers, yet we still complain about being underpaid relative to lawyers. I question the amount of money that goes into academic research. I challenge the efforts of clinicians to use accreditation standards to get job protection, and I question the academic efficacy of clinical programs. I identify schools that have dismal rates of success among graduates in landing jobs as lawyers, and I identify schools that publish highly unreliable salary numbers. I specify a set of characteristics of law schools that prospective students should be wary of attending. I argue that law schools extract as much money as [possible] by hiking tuition and enrollment, while leaving students to bear the risk, in the first instance, and taxpayers thereafter. And I propose changes to accreditation standards and the federal loan system that, if enacted, would drastically alter the situation of law schools.

Law schools, finally, are failing society. While raising tuition to astronomical heights, law schools have slashed need-based financial aid, thereby erecting a huge financial barrier to the legal profession. Increasing numbers of middle class and poor will be dissuaded from pursuing a legal career by the frighteningly large price tag. The future complexion and legitimacy of our legal profession is at stake.

Notes

1. Not surprisingly, Professor Tamanaha's critique has proved quite controversial and attracted many criticisms of its own. For a small sampling see, e.g., Nancy Rapoport's Book Review, 47 Law & Soc'y Rev. 229 (2013); Paul Horwitz, "What Ails Law Schools," 111 Mich. L. Rev. 955 (2013); Philip Schrag, "Misguided Missile," 26 Geo. J. Legal Ethics 400 (2013); Lucy Jewell, "Tales of a Fourth Tier Nothing," 38 J. Legal Prof. 125 (2013).

2. One of Professor Tamanaha's strongest claims is that "[t]he cost of legal education today is substantially out of proportion to the economic opportunities obtained by the majority of graduates." A recent study by a law professor and a labor economist strongly disputes this claim. See Michael Simkovic and Frank McIntyre, "The Economic Value of a Law Degree," 43 J. Legal Stud. 249 (2014). According to the authors:

> [F]or most law school graduates, the present value of a law degree typically exceeds its cost by hundreds of thousands of dollars. The median and 25th percentile earnings premiums justify enrollment. . . . Previous studies focused on starting salaries, generic professional degree holders, or the subset of law degree holders who practice law. We incorporate unemployment and disability risk and measure earnings premiums separately for men and women. After controlling for observable ability and sorting, we find that a law degree is associated with median increases of 73 percent in earnings and 60 percent in hourly wages. The mean annual earnings premium is approximately $57,200 in 2013 dollars. Values in recent years are within historical

norms. The mean pretax lifetime value of a law degree is approximately $1 million.

Also not surprisingly, this study has generated its own share of controversy. See, e.g., Elie Mystal, "Another Garbage Study Offering Misleading Statistics on the Economic Value of a Law Degree," Above the Law, July 17, 2013, available at <http://abovethelaw.com/2013/07/another-garbage-study-offering-misleading-statistics-on-the-value-of-a-law-degree/> (critiquing the study for overemphasizing "average" earnings, which can be inflated by the presence of a few very high earners, and for predicting future earnings on the basis of historical averages which don't take into account recent changes in the job market). Simkovic and McIntyre have responded by publishing a new paper using simulations and data from the After the JD Study to argue that downturns in the labor market for new law school graduates, while having a significant impact on employment and earnings in the short term, only have a moderate effect on long-term earnings as economic conditions rebound and lawyers develop new skills. See Frank McIntyre and Michael Simkovic, "Timing Law School," J. Emp. Legal Stud. (forthcoming) available at <https://papers.ssrn.com/sol3/papers.cfm?abstract_id=2574587>. As the authors concede, however, "future expansions and recessions may well be different" from those that have occurred in the past, and that "[c]ommenters should exercise considerable restraint in making strong claims about future outcomes based on current conditions." Id., at 28.

Given the changes described in Chapter 12, is there a strong argument that the "future expansions and recessions" in the market for legal services are likely to be very different from those in the past? Consider the following predictions from Professor Richard Susskind in his widely discussed—and alarmingly titled—book, *The End of Lawyers?*:

> I predict that there will be five types of lawyers in the future.
>
> The first will be the "expert trusted advisor." This is the purveyor of bespoke legal service. . . . My second category of lawyer for the future will be the "enhanced practitioner." . . . This lawyer will be supporting the delivery of standardized, systematized, and (when in-house) packaged legal service. The crucial point here, though, is that the market will only tolerate this lawyer's involvement where legal experience is genuinely needed. Otherwise, less costly sources of support will be favored, such as paralegals, legal executives, and legal process outsourcing service providers. . . . In contrast, there will be a much greater need for my third category of lawyer—the "legal knowledge engineer." If I am right and legal service will increasingly be standardized and (in various ways) computerized, then people with great talent are going to be needed, in droves, to organize the large quantities of complex legal content and processes that will need to be analyzed, distilled, and then embodied in standard working practices and computer systems. . . . Fourth will be the "legal risk manager." . . . Urgent demand from the

market will lead lawyers (perhaps bolstered and emboldened by external funding) to offer a wide range of proactive legal services whose focus will be on anticipating and pre-empting legal problems. . . . My final category of future lawyer is the "legal hybrid." . . . [L]egal hybrids of the future will be superbly schooled and genuinely expert in . . . related disciplines [such as project management, strategic consulting, market expertise, etc.] and will be able to extend the services they provide in a way that adds value for their clients.

Taking these five categories together, it is clear that there will be work for lawyers to do in the future. What is much less obvious is whether today's lawyers will be equipped to take on the jobs I envisage. . . .

I do not therefore anticipate (in the next twenty or thirty years at least) that there will be no lawyers. I expect instead that there will be significantly fewer lawyers providing traditional consultative advisory service; and I predict the emergency of new legal professionals with quite different roles in society. We will witness the end of many lawyers as we know and recognize them today and the birth of a new streamlined and technology-based generation of practicing lawyers who are fit for purpose in the twenty-first century.

Richard Susskind, *The End of Lawyers?* (2009) at 272–73. Professor Susskind has since written two more books elaborating these ideas, one aimed at law students, and one that applies his ideas to all professions. See Richard Susskind, *Tomorrow's Lawyers: An Introduction to Your Future* (2d ed. 2013); Richard Susskind and Daniel Susskind, *The Future of Professions: How Technology Will Transform the Work of Human Experts* (2015).

3. Professor Tamanaha claims that the third year of law school is unnecessary and should be eliminated. In so doing, he joins a long line of critics who question the value of the third year—including former President of the United States Barack Obama. See Dylan Matthews, "Obama Thinks Law School Should be Two Years. The British Think it Should be One." Washington Post, August 27, 2013, available at <https://www .washingtonpost.com/news/wonk/wp/2013/08/27/obama-thinks-law-school -should-be-two-years-the-british-think-it-should-be-one/?utm_term=.b700d3d 2061b>. See also Christopher T. Cunniffe, "The Case for the Alternative Third-Year Program," 61 Alb. L. Rev. 85 (1997) (noting that a 1971 report sharply criticized the requirement that candidates for the bar must attend a full three years of law school); Richard A. Posner, *The Moral Problematics of Legal Theory* 286–295 (1999) (proposing the elimination of the third year). In a related critique, other theorists suggest that whatever the theoretical value of a three-year legal education might be, as a practical matter so many students have "dropped out" of their third year classes that the year should either be eliminated or drastically reformed. See Mitu Gulati, Richard Sander, and Robert Sockloskie, "The Happy Charade: An Empirical Examination of the Third Year of Law School," 52 J. Legal Educ. 235 (2001) (reporting the results of a nationwide survey of third-year law students that found third-year students are doing almost no

work in their courses but are actually more satisfied and less depressed than they were as first-year students). See also Richard Kahlenberg, *Broken Contract* 159 (1999 ed.) (characterizing his reaction to the third year of law school as "bore[d] ... to death").

Do you agree with this critique? Do you believe that it is equally true for all law schools? Are there any important costs to eliminating the third year of law school? Consider the following argument by a former general counsel of a multinational company, the former managing partner of a leading law firm, and a professor at a highly ranked law school about the importance of the third year of law school in "leading" law schools:

> Arguably no aspect of the current debate over the future of legal education has been more heatedly discussed than the question of what to do with the third year of law school. ... We applaud this debate, and add our voices to the growing consensus calling for a serious reevaluation of the third year. ...

> Our commitment to preparing students for the complex challenges that they will face in their roles as expert technicians, wise counselors, and astute leaders, however, leads us to reject proposals that law schools such as those we are considering should eliminate the third year altogether. We are acutely aware of why many have made such proposals. The cost of legal education has skyrocketed, leaving far too many students mired in debt. Many hope that if these costs can be reduced, that more graduates might be able to pursue careers in public service, or delivering legal assistance to individuals of low or moderate means, who notwithstanding claims of "too many lawyers" remain chronically underserved. But unless the regulatory barriers ... are dramatically altered, even reducing law school to two years would not significantly improve access to justice, and would only create a partial, albeit important, reduction (one-seventh of the combined college and law school debt) in the cost of legal education — assuming that law schools actually reduced tuition by one-third if the third year is dropped, which has not necessarily been the case to date. More importantly, even if the United States were to significantly reduce the boundaries of the unauthorized practice of law to allow practitioners with various levels of legal training (including two, or even one, year of post-graduate legal education — or new paraprofessional certification programs at the college or junior college level), large law firms, corporate legal departments, and other similar employers are likely to continue to hire a significant number of lawyers who have gone through more traditional legal training. The question that the law schools that seek to supply this talent will have to answer, therefore, is whether the value to students of [pursuing] what will inevitably be an expensive educational credential is worth the cost.

> For all of the reasons set out above, we believe that introducing students to the fundamentals of their roles as expert technicians, wise counselors,

and astute leaders (and giving them the complementary competencies that they will need to operate in these roles) will make graduates more marketable to those entry level employers who need lawyers who are capable of functioning in today's increasingly complex, globalized and multidisciplinary world, and will make these graduates better able to succeed throughout their careers. Yet these are precisely the kind of learning experiences that are likely to be cut (or at least dramatically reduced) in a two year legal education, where both educators and students would inevitably feel great pressure to concentrate on the "core" legal courses and competencies. A third year focused specifically on providing this kind of education is, therefore, a reasonable requirement to impose for those schools that seek to prepare their students for these kind of demanding—and rewarding—careers.

The current debate over eliminating the fourth year of medical school reinforces this conclusion. As reported in a recent article in the New York Times, about 30 percent of medical schools are considering granting three-year medical degrees, with several, including NYU, already offering such a program. The reasons given by proponents—reducing student debt, replacing classroom learning with practical experience, and getting doctors out into the field more quickly—mirror those that are made for eliminating the third year of law school. But proponents of three-year medical degrees are also candid about the tradeoffs that eliminating the fourth year of medical school would entail—and the corresponding structures that would be required for this initiative to succeed. At NYU, for example, students applying to the three-year program must already know what kind of medicine that they want to practice (since they will not have sufficient time in three years to explore alternatives while gaining appropriate depth in their chosen field), and are also guaranteed places in NYU's own internship program, thus eliminating the need for interviewing for internships, while providing continuity between what these students have—and have not—learned during medical school and their post-graduate education.

Neither this front-end commitment nor the back-end support structure is applicable in the law school context. By the time students apply to medical school, they have been through a comprehensive "pre-med" curriculum specifically designed to give them at least a preliminary introduction to what they might want to do as doctors. There is no comparable "pre-law" process. Therefore most law school applicants have little knowledge about legal careers—and much of what they think they know is probably wrong. Nor, as indicated above, is there currently any systematic post-graduate education in law to pick up the slack for what students do not learn in law school. Indeed, this is precisely why we need greater collaboration among law schools, law firms, and companies to ensure that young lawyers receive the training that they need throughout their careers.

Finally, in medicine as in law, those seeking to engage with the most difficult problems recognize that they need more education, not less. Even at NYU, fifteen percent of graduates actually stay on for a fifth year to obtain a master's degree in public health or business administration—a percentage fifty percent greater than those seeking to graduate in three years. And the best medical schools are moving to expand opportunities for students to learn key complementary competencies like collaboration and cross-cultural fluency through experiential learning and international exchange. Law schools seeking to train students for the complex, global careers we have been describing need to do the same.

Once again, we recognize that our support for retaining—and restructuring—the third year of law school will be controversial. Individual schools—and regulators—will, and should, continue to debate whether other models of professional education, ranging from the undergraduate model prevalent in many European countries, to the certification model used in public accounting, should be incorporated in whole or in part to the system of training United States lawyers and other legal service providers. Our goal is only to insist that these debates take into account the need to ensure that those who will enter into the kind of complex institutions and careers that we have been describing will have sufficient exposure during their education to the broad core and complementary competencies that they will need to exercise their roles as expert technicians, wise counselors, and astute leaders.

Benjamin W. Heineman, William F. Lee, and David B. Wilkins, "Lawyers as Professionals and as Citizens: Roles and Responsibilities for the 21st Century," pp. 55–59, available at: <https://clp.law.harvard.edu/assets/Professionalism-Project-Essay_11.20.14.pdf>. In a footnote to this section, Benjamin Heineman states that "if law schools of all types are not willing or able to restructure the third year, then the option of graduation after two years, combined with enhanced continuing or executive education later in careers, deserves the most serious consideration."

4. In addition to the criticisms leveled by Professors Tamanaha and Wilkins, a number of other scholars claim that law school no longer adequately prepares students for contemporary law practice (assuming that it ever did so, which many critics deny), or is otherwise unnecessary, abusive or counterproductive. In the words of one recent commentator, contemporary law teaching is "impractical, frequently boring, fragmented if not incoherent, ideologically and morally confused, and ultimately damaging in important emotional and even intellectual terms." Ronald H. Silverman, "Weak Law Teaching," 9 Cornell J. L. & Pub. Pol'y 267 (2000). This criticism comes in several—not entirely consistent—forms:

• As Professor Wilkins notes, two important strains emphasize, respectively, the lack of "skills training" in law school and the abstract and theoretical character of scholarship and teaching that, in the eyes of critics, pays insufficient attention to legal doctrine.

- In addition, several commentators argue that law school alienates students from their own ideals, transforming them from a group bright with the hope of changing the world into demoralized and cynical careerists willing to do anything for a buck. See, e.g., James R. P. Ogloff, et al., "More Than 'Learning to Think Like a Lawyer': The Empirical Research on Legal Education," 34 Creighton L. Rev. 73 (2000); Patrick J. Schiltz, "Legal Education in Decline: The Elite Law Firm, the Elite Law School, and the Moral Foundation of the Novice Lawyer," 82 Minn. L. Rev. 705 (1998); David R. Culp, "Law School: A Mortuary for Poets and Moral Reason," 16 Campbell L. Rev. 61 (1994). For two different versions of this theme, compare Robert Granfield, *Making Elite Lawyers: Visions of Law at Harvard and Beyond* (1992) (arguing that Harvard Law School teaches its students a sense of "collective eminence" that encourages them to abandon their initial ideals and to value working for a corporate law firm) with Note, "Making Docile Lawyers: An Essay on the Pacification of Law Students," 111 Harv. L. Rev. 2027 (1998) (rejecting Granfield's thesis and arguing that Harvard encourages "collective pacification" that strips students of their self-confidence and leads them to accept law firm jobs as the alternative of least resistance).

- In a related criticism, some have argued that law schools instill a very particular brand of professional identity, forming students into individualistic self-interested lawyers. Such attorneys understand their professional role to be the aggressive pursuit of their clients' interests with little regard to the interests of others, the law itself, or the public; perceive their role as a representative of clients to dominate and supersede their roles as an officer of the legal system and as a public citizen; and believe that their duties to the public interest and to public service are fulfilled by their representation of private client interests such that they have no other responsibility to further the rule of law and access to justice. See Roger C. Cramton, "The Ordinary Religion of the Law School Classroom," 29 J. Legal Educ. 247 (1978); Roger C. Cramton, "Beyond the Ordinary Religion," 37 J. Legal Educ. 509 (1987); Susan Sturm & Lani Guinier, "The Law School Matrix: Reforming Legal Education in a Culture of Competition and Conformity," 60 Vand. L. Rev. 515 (2007); Eli Wald & Russell G. Pearce, "Making Good Lawyers," 9 U. St. Thomas L.J. 403 (2011).

- A number of writers working from different perspectives suggest that the real purpose served by law school is not education at all, but rather the sorting of law students into hierarchical categories for the benefit of future employers. Building on Michael Spence's classic work on the use of education as a "signal" to employers of an applicant's underlying qualities (for example hard work, competitiveness, etc.) that have little connection with the substantive knowledge conveyed by the curriculum, these critics argue that the primary purpose of legal education is to sort students — by school ranking, grades, and law review membership — into easily visible and rankable categories that allow employers to choose among applicants at relatively low cost. See, e.g., Russell Korobkin, "In Praise of Law School Rankings: Solutions to Coordination and Collective Actions Problems," 77 Tex. L. Rev. 403 (1998). For Spence's classic work on signaling theory, see Michael Spence, *Market Signaling* (1974). As noted in Chapter 12, one of us has applied this reasoning to the hiring practices of large law firms. See David B. Wilkins & G. Mitu Gulati, "Reconceiving the Tournament of Lawyers: Tracking, Seeding, and Information Control in the Internal Labor Markets of Large Law Firms," 84 Va. L. Rev. 1581 (1998), discussed supra at p. 981.

- Another group of critics argue that the Socratic method that pervades law school teaching obscures important substantive questions and intimidates and humiliates students. See, e.g., Maria Ciampi, "A New Dialogue for the Law," 58 U. Cin. L. Rev. 881 (1990). As a result, law students are abnormally alienated and depressed, leading to rates of alcoholism and drug abuse that are significantly higher than in comparable populations. See, e.g., Lila C. Coleburn & Julia C. Spring, "Socrates Unbound," 24 Law & Psych. Rev. 5 (2000); Matthew M. Dammeyer & Narina Nunex, "Anxiety and Depression Among Law Students: Current Knowledge and Future Directions," 23 Law & Hum. Behav. 55 (1999); G. Andrew Benjamin et al., "The Role of Legal Education in Producing Psychological Distress Among Law Students and Lawyers," 1986 Am. B. Found. Res. J. 225.

- Based in part on several of the above critiques, yet another group of scholars contend that the burdens of law school fall disproportionately on women and minorities. Students in these groups, critics assert, are especially prone to isolation and alienation and are most likely to be disadvantaged by the emphasis by employers on "signals" (such as grades and law review membership) rather than "skills" learned in law school. See, e.g., Lani Guinier, Michelle Fine & Jane Balin, *Becoming Gentlemen: Women, Law School and Institutional Change* (1997); Daria Roithmayr, "Barriers to Entry: A Market Lock-in Model of Discrimination," 86 Va. L. Rev. 727 (2000); Morrison Torrey et al., "What Every First Year Female Law Student Should Know," 7 Colum. J. Gender & L. 267 (1998). See also David B. Wilkins & G. Mitu Gulati, "Why Are There So Few Black Lawyers in Corporate Law Firms?: An Institutional Analysis," 84 Cal. L. Rev. 493 (1996), discussed in Chapter 12 at p. 994.

Examining the strengths and weaknesses of each of these critiques — let alone sorting through their competing implications — is beyond the scope of this book. Nevertheless, it is worth asking yourself whether some or all of these criticisms resonate with your own experience in law school, and if so, what (if anything) should be done to address the problems you see. Should we eliminate the third year or turn it into an intensive clinical experience that better prepares students for law practice? Should we abandon the Socratic method in favor of a curriculum based on "problem solving"? Should law schools attempt to better prepare students to enter the existing job market or help them to resist market pressures and pursue their view of the "public interest"?

5. Finally, whatever one thinks about legal education in general, students enrolled in a course in professional responsibility should think especially hard about how best to teach law students about ethics and the profession. Should a course in legal ethics be mandatory, or does requiring ethics instruction contribute to student apathy and resentment that undermines the value of what is being taught? Should there be a separate course at all or should ethics be taught "pervasively" throughout the curriculum? If there is a separate course, should it be targeted at first-year students (in order to shape or inform their thinking before they have worked in a legal job) or third-year students (in order to allow them to bring their own experiences to the course)? For a variety of perspectives on these questions, see, e.g., Ann Southworth, Catherine Fisk, and Bryant Garth, "Some Realism about Realism in Teaching About the Legal Profession," in *The New Legal Realism: Translating Law-and-Society for Today's Legal Practice, Vol. 1 Putting Law in its Place: The New Legal Realism Project* (McCauley, Mertz, and Mitchell, eds. 2016); Elizabeth Chambliss, "Professional Responsibility: Lawyers, A Case Study," 69 Fordham L. Rev. 817 (2000) (describing a comparative sociological approach to teaching about lawyers and professional ethics); Carrie Menkel-Meadow, "Telling Stories in Law School: Using Case Studies and Stories to Teach Legal Ethics," 69 Fordham L. Rev. 787 (2000) (endorsing use of case studies and stories); Deborah L. Rhode, "Ethics by the Pervasive Method," 42 J. Legal Educ. 31 (1992) (arguing that ethics should be taught "pervasively" throughout the curriculum). See also Symposium, "Teaching Ethics," 58 Law & Contemp. Probs. 1 (1995) and Symposium, "Case Studies in Legal Ethics," 69 Fordham L. Rev. 787 et seq. (2000).

As one would expect, we as teachers and scholars of legal ethics and of the profession generally have views on many of these questions—some of which are reflected in the organization and content of this book.

———

As this book is going to print, the legal profession appears to be in the midst of turmoil. As we have documented, many recent graduates struggle to find jobs as lawyers, law firms big and small struggle in the age of disruption and restructuring, non-lawyers are knocking on the doors of the market for legal services, regulators are exploring new methods of regulating lawyers and other legal services providers, and law schools are not keeping up with the ever-evolving practice realities and needs of lawyers. Not to belittle the many challenges facing today's lawyers, we selected excerpts from Professor Llewellyn's work to demonstrate that many of these challenges are not new and that lawyers have managed to cope with uncertainty and instability before, while retaining their elevated standing and status. Consider yet another century-old sage, Justice Louis Brandeis. In a classic, and timeless, address, Brandeis offers attorneys and law students a silver lining—a meaningful and exciting way to understand their law practice and role as lawyers while acknowledging the many challenges they face.

Louis D. Brandeis
The Opportunity in the Law

39 Am. Law Rev. 555 (1905)

I assume that in asking me to talk to you on the Ethics of the Legal Profession, you do not wish me to enter upon a discussion of the relation of law to morals, nor to attempt to acquaint you with those detailed rules of ethics which lawyers have occasion to apply from day to day in their practice. What you want is this: Standing not far from the threshold of active life, feeling the generous impulse for service which the University fosters, you wish to know whether the legal profession would afford you special opportunities for usefulness to your fellow men, and if so, what the obligations and limitations are which it imposes. I say special opportunities, because every legitimate occupation, be it profession or business or trade furnishes abundant opportunities for usefulness, if pursued in what Matthew Arnold called "the grand manner." It is, as a rule, far more important *how* men pursue their occupation than *what* the occupation is which they select.

But the legal profession does afford in America unusual opportunities for usefulness. That this has been so in the past, no one acquainted with the history of our institutions can for a moment doubt. The great achievement of the English speaking people is the attainment of liberty through law. It is natural, therefore, that those who have been trained in the law should have borne an important part in that struggle for liberty and in the government which resulted. Accordingly, we find that, in America, the lawyer was in the earlier period omnipresent almost in the State. Nearly every great lawyer was then a statesman; and nearly every statesman great or small was a lawyer. De Tocqueville, the first great foreign observer of American political institutions, said of the United States of seventy-five years ago: "In America there are no nobles or literary men, and the people are apt to mistrust the wealthy; lawyers, consequently, form the highest political class. . . . As the lawyers form the only enlightened class whom the people do not mistrust, they are naturally called upon to occupy most of the public stations. They fill the legislative assemblies and are at the head of the administration; they consequently exercise a powerful influence upon the formation of the law and upon its execution." . . .

The whole training of the lawyer leads to the development of judgment. His early training—I mean his work with books, in the study of legal rules—teaches him patient research and develops both the memory and the reasoning faculties. He becomes practised in logic; and yet the use of the reasoning faculties in the study of law is very different from their use, say, in metaphysics. The lawyer's processes of reasoning, his logical conclusions are being constantly tested by experience. The facts are running up against him at every point. Indeed it is a maxim of the law: Out of the facts grows the law: that is, propositions are not considered abstractly, but always with reference to facts. . . .

. . . [T]he practice of law tends to make the lawyer judicial in attitude and extremely tolerant. His profession rests upon the postulate that no contested question can be properly decided until both sides are heard. His experience teaches him that nearly every question has two sides and very often he finds—after decision of judge or jury—that both he and his opponent were in the wrong.

The practice of law creates thus a habit of mind, and leads to attainments which are distinctly different from those developed in most professions or outside of the professions. By reason of that fact the lawyer has acquired a position materially different from that of other men. It is the position of the adviser of men.

Your chairman said: "People have the impression today that the lawyer has become mercenary." It is true that the lawyer has become largely a part of the business world. Mr. Bryce said twenty years ago when he compared the America of 1885 with the America of De Tocqueville: "Taking a general survey of the facts of today, as compared with the facts of sixty years ago, it is clear that the bar counts for less as a guiding and restraining power, tempering the crudity or haste of democracy by its attachment to rule and precedent, than it did."

And in reviewing American conditions after his recent visit Mr. Bryce said: "Lawyers are now to a greater extent than formerly business men, a part of the great organized system of industrial and financial enterprise. They are less than formerly the students of a particular kind of learning, the practitioners of a particular art. And they do not seem to be so much of a distinct professional class."

This is a statement of a very sympathetic observer of American institutions; but it would seem from this that Mr. Bryce coincided in the view commonly expressed, that the bar had become commercialized in becoming a part of business. I am inclined to think that this view is not altogether correct. Probably business has become professionalized even more than the bar has become commercialized. Is it not this which has made the lawyer so important a part of the business world?

The ordinary man thinks of the bar as a body of men who are trying cases, perhaps even trying criminal cases.

Of course there is an immense amount of litigation going on and a great deal of the time of many lawyers is devoted to litigation. But by far the greater part of the work done by lawyers is not done in court at all, but in advising men in important matters, and mainly in business affairs. In the guiding of great affairs industrially and financially the lawyers have played an ever-increasing part; have played it mainly, because the particular mental attributes and attainments which the legal profession develops are demanded in the proper handling of these great affairs, be they financial, industrial, or commercial. The magnitude and scope of these operations remove them almost wholly from the realm of "petty trafficking" which people formerly used to associate with trade. The questions which arise are more nearly questions of statesmanship. The relations created call in many instances for the exercise of the highest diplomacy. The magnitude, difficulty, and importance of the questions involved are often as great as in the matters of State with which lawyers were formerly frequently associated. The questions appear in a different guise but they are similar. . . .

So, some of the ablest American lawyers of this generation after acting as professional advisers of great corporations have become finally their managers. . . .

It is true that at the present time the lawyer does not hold that position with the people that he held seventy-five or indeed fifty years ago; but the reason is not lack of opportunity. It is this: Instead of holding a position of independence, between the wealthy and the people, prepared to curb the excesses of either, able lawyers have, to a large extent, allowed themselves to become adjuncts of great corporations and have neglected their obligation to use their powers for the protection of the people. We hear much of the "corporation lawyer," and far too little of the "people's lawyer." The great opportunity of the American bar is and will be to stand again as it did in the past, ready to protect also the interests of the people. . . .

The leading lawyers of the United States have been engaged mainly in supporting the claims of the corporations; often in endeavoring to evade or nullify the extremely crude laws by which legislators sought to regulate the power or curb the excesses of corporations. . . .

. . . Up to the present time the legal ability of a high order which has been expended on those questions has been almost wholly in opposition to the contentions of the people. The leaders of the bar, without any preconceived intent on their part, and rather as an incident to their professional standing, have, with rare exceptions, been ranged on the side of the corporations, and the people have been represented in the main by men of very meager legal ability.

If these problems are to be settled right, this condition cannot continue. Our country is, after all, not a country of dollars, but of ballots. The immense corporate wealth will necessarily develop a hostility from which much trouble will come to us unless the excesses of capital are curbed, through the respect for law, as the excesses of democracy were curbed seventy-five years ago. . . .

The ethical question which laymen most frequently ask about the legal profession is this: How can a lawyer take a case which he does not believe in? The profession is regarded as necessarily somewhat immoral, because its members are supposed to be habitually taking cases they do not believe in. As a practical matter, I think the lawyer is not often harassed by this problem, partly because he is apt to believe at the time in most of the cases that he actually tries, and partly because he either abandons or settles a large number of those he does not believe in. In any event, the lawyer recognises that in trying a case his prime duty is to present his side to the tribunal fairly and as well as he can, relying upon his adversary to present his case fairly and as well as he can. As the lawyers on the two sides are usually reasonably well matched, the judge or jury may ordinarily be trusted to make such a decision as justice demands.

But when lawyers act upon the same principle in supporting the attempts of their private clients to secure or to oppose legislation, a very different condition is presented. In the first place, the counsel selected to represent important private interests possesses usually ability of a high order, while the public is often inadequately represented or wholly unrepresented. That presents a condition of great unfairness to the public. As a result many bills pass in our legislatures which would not have become law if the public interest had been fairly represented; and many good bills are defeated which if supported by able lawyers would have been enacted. Lawyers have, as a rule, failed to consider this distinction between practice in the court involving only private interests and practice before the legislature or city council where public interests are involved. . . .

Here, consequently, is the great, opportunity of the bar. The next generation must witness a continuing and ever-increasing contest between those who have and those who have not. The industrial world is in a state of ferment. The ferment is in the main peaceful, and, to a considerable extent, silent; but there is felt today very widely the inconsistency in this condition of political democracy and industrial absolutism. The people are beginning to doubt whether in the long run democracy and absolutism can co-exist in the same community; beginning to doubt whether there is a justification for the great inequalities in the distribution of wealth, for the rapid creation of fortunes, more mysterious than the deeds of Aladdin's lamp. The people have begun to think; and they show evidences on all sides of a tendency to act. . . .

. . . [T]he people's thought will take shape in action, and it lies with us, with you to whom in part the future belongs, to say on what lines the action is to be expressed; whether it is to be expressed wisely and temperately, or wildly and intemperately: whether it is to be expressed on lines of evolution or on lines of revolution. Nothing can better fit you for taking part in the solution of these problems, then the study and pre-eminently the practice of law. Those of you who feel drawn to that profession may rest assured that you will find in it an opportunity for usefulness which is probably unequalled. There is a call upon the legal profession to do a great work for this country.

We close by offering a few current thoughts on the role of lawyers in a changing society.

A Final Note on the Lawyer's Role

Philosophers who write about law approach the field from their own perspective, which involves thinking about systems of, or individual approaches to, right and wrong. The lawyer's theoretical concern, justice, may be different from "right and wrong" because of the law's concern with procedural matters. Even more important, the perspective of practicing lawyers is shaped by the daily necessity of speaking and acting for others. That difference in perspective may make it difficult for one not a lawyer to appreciate fully all the conflicts that practicing lawyers face. It is often (but not always) difficult for a lawyer to pass moral judgment on a client's proposed actions when the lawyer sees only a slice of the context and can only be privy to a portion of the inner motivation that goes into the client's decisions. But having said that, we do not mean to suggest that that difficulty necessarily clinches the argument for more "role differentiation." That answer lies in an assessment whether the one role or the other suits our individual perspective of the kind of lawyer we want to be — to the extent that we are (or should be) permitted to make an individual choice. To the extent that we are not, then the issue for us is to decide whether, in today's political, social, and economic context, the choice for the profession of one role or the other is likely to be more helpful in promoting our vision of social good.

We realize that that formulation and the materials discussed in Chapters 7 and 12 up the ante. But it is apparent that one must have a vision of social good, of the kind of fair and just society that seems realizable in a world of imperfect human beings, to which to connect one's view of the legal profession. An important question to ask, if one concludes that great changes are needed in the profession, is whether that conclusion is related to a more utopian view of the possibilities for improving the whole society. If one does not believe that great changes are needed in the profession, if one is a tinkerer, it is useful to ask whether that conclusion is connected to a less utopian view of the possibilities for improving our society, or to put the point somewhat differently, a belief in the fundamental fairness of the status quo.

As this book goes to press in the wake of one of the most divisive elections in American history, these questions about the overall fairness of our society have become even more salient. Moreover, whatever one's views about politics in general, it is important to ask whether there is a difference between what is best for society and how lawyers might best contribute to that goal. Once again, these issues are only likely to become more important in our present climate as both public and private lawyers find themselves increasingly engaged in hotly disputed questions ranging from the legality of President Trump's proposal to ban travel to the United States from certain countries, to whether the President's ownership of hotel properties around the world violates the Emoluments Clause of the Constitution. See Michael D. Shear, Mark Landler, Matt Apuzzo, and Eric Lichtblau, "Trump Fires Acting Attorney General Who Defied Him," New York Times, Jan. 30, 2017, available at <https://www.nytimes.com/2017/01/30/us/politics/trump-immigration-ban-memo.html> (reporting that the President fired Sally Q. Yates for instructing Justice Department lawyers not to enforce the President's travel ban order on the ground that she was "not convinced" that enforcing the order was consistent with her responsibilities to uphold the Constitution and laws of the United States); Eric Lipton and Adam Liptak, "Foreign Payments to Trump Firms Violate Constitution, Suit

Will Claim," New York Times, Jan. 22, 2017, available at <https://www.nytimes.com /2017/01/22/us/politics/trump-foreign-payments-constitution-lawsuit .html> (reporting on a lawsuit filed by four prominent law professors alleging that the President is violating the Emoluments Clause by allowing his hotels and other properties to accept payments from foreign governments).

In wrestling with these difficult issues, you will also have to consider whether some or all of these matters should be left to the conscience of individual lawyers or whether the profession as a whole (or some of its constituent parts) should take collective action or impose a common response. In resolving this ultimate question, it is important to remember that the profession's diversity—in terms of backgrounds, experiences, views, and commitments—is both a reality that must be taken into account and a potential source of strength. This diversity should make us hesitate before assuming that there are universal solutions to complex issues such as accommodating civil liberties with security that will apply to all questions and in all contexts. As former Solicitor General Walter Dellinger argued in the context of how to balance these issues following the attacks of September 11, 2001, "I am more willing to entertain restrictions that affect all of us—like identity cards and more intrusive X-ray procedures at airports—and somewhat more skeptical of restrictions that only affect some of us, like those that focus on immigrants or single out people by nationality." Matthew Purdy, "Bush's New Rules to Fight Terror Transform the Legal Landscape," New York Times, November 25, 2001. Needless to say, recent events have made former Solicitor General Dellinger's concerns even more important. At the same time, the bar's increasing diversity arguably provides the best protection against the all-too-common tendency, exemplified by the Japanese internment during World War II, for the profession to allow the government to base its security decisions on blanket stereotypes based on race, religion, or national origin.

This last comment highlights a point that we have made throughout these materials. As with the issue of civil rights and security, many of the issues we have addressed have been cast in terms of "more" or "less." That is the way we tend to look at the clash between the moral absolutists and the moral relativists (and the regulators and the deregulators), at least in this field. To be sure, there are some bright lines that should never be crossed. Lawyers should never violate fundamental laws or moral values—and they should be willing to stand up to those who seek to do so either in the name of profit or principle. But as we have seen throughout this book, many difficult decisions involve accommodation of conflicting principles (professional principles with moral elements or moral principles with professional elements). It is in these situations where calm but critical reflection and judgment are especially needed.

The same critical reflection is needed with respect to issues of professionalism that relate to lawyers as a group. Should lawyers maintain their monopoly over "the practice of law"—and if so, what kinds of regulation should come with this privilege and what institutions and mechanisms should we look to in order to ensure that whatever regulation we deem appropriate is being enforced? Conversely, should the

U.S. follow the UK and deregulate the legal profession? If so, should the deregulation be total or partial? Should the "new" occupations and organizations that spring up in the wake of deregulation be regulated as well, and if so by whom? What model seems to provide the greatest quality and quantity of service to clients and society? (Or does one sacrifice quality while the other sacrifices quantity?) Collectively, the answers to these questions, along with the changes in the institutions of legal practice and the market for legal services will tell us whether and to what extent lawyers will remain "professionals" in the middle decades of the twenty-first century.

Index